MW01006912

The New York Philharmonic Guide to the Symphony

Esterháza: Where Haydn Conducted His Symphonies.

The palace music room designed by Prince Miklos (Nicholas) Esterházy for concerts by his private orchestra under the direction of his resident composer-conductor-impresario, Joseph Haydn. (*Courtesy, Erich Lessing/Magnum*)

The New York Philharmonic Guide to the Symphony

by
Edward Downes

Walker and Company
New York

ACKNOWLEDGMENTS FOR MUSICAL EXAMPLES

Grateful acknowledgment is made to the following publishers for permission to use copyrighted musical examples in this book.

AMERICAN COMPOSERS ALLIANCE: Weber *Piano Concerto.*

BELWIN MILLS PUBLISHING CORPORATION: Creston *Janus;* Lutoslawski *Concerto for Orchestra* and *Funeral Music;* Rachmaninoff *Piano Concerto No. 3, Rhapsody on a Theme by Paganini, Symphony No. 2;* Resphigi *The Fountains of Rome* and *The Pines of Rome;* Stravinsky *Card Game, Violin Concerto in D major, Symphony in C, Symphony in Three Movements.*

CARL FISHER, INCORPORATED: Dello Joio *Variations, Chaconne, and Finale;* copyright MCML by Carl Fischer, Inc., New York; international copyright secured; all rights reserved; used by permission of the publisher.

HARGAIL MUSIC COMPANY: Mennin *Symphony No. 3.*

INTERNATIONAL MUSIC COMPANY: Schoenberg *Verklärte Nacht.*

MCA MUSIC, INCORPORATED: Kabalevsky *Overture to Colas Breugnon;* Prokofieff *Piano Concerto No. 3* and *Symphony No. 5;* Shostakovich *Symphonies Nos. 1, 5, 6,* and *9.*

PEER-SOUTHERN PUBLICATIONS: Diamond *Symphony No. 8;* Ives *Decoration Day, Symphony No. 2,* and *Unanswered Question.*

EDITIONS SALABERT, INCORPORATED: Honegger *Pacific 231* and *Symphony No. 2;* Milhaud *Suite provençale;* Poulenc *Concerto for Two Pianos.*

G. SCHIRMER, INCORPORATED: Barber *Piano Concerto, Violin Concerto, First* and *Second Essays, Overture to The School for Scandal;* Bernstein *Serenade;* Bloch *Schelomo;* Harris *Symphony No. 3;* Menotti *Apocalypse;* Prokofieff *Romeo and Juliet;* Schuman *American Festival Overture, Symphonies Nos. 3* and *5;* Thomson *The Seine at Night.*

STEINER AND BELL, LIMITED: Vaughan Williams *London Symphony.*

UNIVERSAL EDITION, A.G.: Berg *Violin Concerto, Lulu Suite, Three Orchestral Pieces, Symphonic Fragments from Wozzeck;* Bruckner *Symphonies Nos. 3* and *8;* Janáček *Sinfonietta;* Mahler *Das Lied von der Erde, Symphonies Nos. 1, 2, 3, 4, 8* and *9;* Webern *Symphony Opus 21* and *Variations Opus 30.*

Copyright © 1976 by The Philharmonic-Symphony Society of New York, Inc., and Edward O. D. Downes

All rights reserved. No part of this book may be reproduced or transmitted in any form or by any means, electric or mechanical, including photocopying, recording, or by any information storage and retrieval system, without permission in writing from the Publisher.

First published in the United States of America in 1976 by the Walker Publishing Company, Inc.

Published simultaneously in Canada by Fitzhenry & Whiteside, Limited, Toronto

ISBN: 0-8027-0540-5

Library of Congress Catalog Card Number: 76-13813

Printed in the United States of America

10 9 8 7 6 5 4 3

TO MARA AND MARION
WITH GRATITUDE AND AFFECTION

ACKNOWLEDGMENTS

My thanks go first of all to Carlos Moseley and the Philharmonic-Symphony Society of New York for asking me to write the Philharmonic Program Notes and for their cooperation in publishing this collection. I am particularly grateful to Leonard Bernstein, Music Director and later Conductor Laureate of the Philharmonic, for his active interest in the program notes, for his helpful suggestions, including the proposal to use musical examples, and for his continuing encouragement; to Ben Weber for his artistry in autographing the musical examples and to Martha Lattimore for taking over the delicate task of autographing with such skill when creative pressures obliged Mr. Weber to stop.

I owe much to Frank Campbell and the staffs of the Music, Dance, and Theater Research Divisions and Circulation Departments of the New York Public Library and Museum for The Performing Arts; and to Barbara Greener, Music Librarian of Queens College, and her staff. Over the years no question has been too great or too small for the benign, scholarly attention of Edward Waters, chief of the Music Division of the Library of Congress, to whom I emphasize my heartfelt thanks. For specialized help providing photocopies and in checking manuscripts and rare editions I am indebted to the William A Speck Collection of Goetheana in Yale University Library; to the Houghton Library of Harvard University; to Victor Bator, executor of the estate of Béla Bartók and keeper of the Bartók Archives of New York; to the (London) library of the British Broadcasting Corporation; and to the Music Librarians of the New York Philharmonic: Howard Keresey, Louis Robbins, and Robert De Celle, who were endlessly helpful in checking minutiae of scores, parts, and variant editions.

I owe warm thanks to Betty Snap of G. Schirmer, to Eugene Moon of Theodore Presser, and especially to Kurt G. Michaelis of C. F. Peters' offices in New York, who repeatedly took time and pains to give me the benefit of their expertise; to my colleagues, Professors George Perle, Felix Salzer, and Boris Schwarz of Queens College in the City University of New York, for help in their special fields.

Sydney Cowell and Louise Varèse were generous of their time and thought in clarifying points in the careers of Henry Cowell and Edgard Varèse; Mrs. Varèse graciously lent me one of her husband's letters to reproduce with the essay on his *Arcana*.

It would be impossible to list all the individual scholars and other specialists to whom I am indebted, but I should like at least to name Joseph Braunstein, Ellis Freedman, H. C. Robbins Landon (for information on many points besides the works of Haydn), Hans Moldenhauer, Claire McGlinchee, Samuel Orlinick, Isaac Stern, and John Vinton. Eric Werner gave unstintingly of his encyclopedic knowledge and skills, ranging from Biblical studies through interpretation of the medieval Latin hymn "Veni creator spiritus" to Felix Mendelssohn and Igor Stravinsky; my debt to him is unpayable. But neither he nor any of the other benefactors mentioned above can be held responsible for the errors I must inevitably have made.

I have been fortunate in my publisher and in my editor. From my first conversations with Samuel Walker, I was delighted to discover that we had much the same idea of what a collection of this kind should attempt. This was so true that when he offered suggestions I sometimes had the feeling that he had been reading my mind. I cannot remember our having disagreed, and our relationship could hardly have been a happier one. My editor, Wilson R. Gathings, has handled the many editorial aspects of this complex volume with great insight, sensitivity, and flexibility, yet with constant awareness of the harsh realities of time and space. For such skill and devotion he has my gratitude. I also want to thank Mary A. C. Fiske for her always-gracious organizational assistance; Fran Palminteri, director of manufacturing, for bringing this book into physical reality in a graceful and swift fashion; and Judith H. McQuown for her copy-editing skills.

I could not have written fourteen seasons of program notes for a repertory as adventurous of that of the New York Philharmonic without the support of three virtuoso collaborators: Judith Sullivan and her successors, Alice Smith Victor and Dwyla Donohue. All three bore patiently with my erratic work habits while functioning as research assistants, executive secretaries, and diplomats dealing with performers, composers, music publishers, program printers, copyreaders, and whole bevies of editors. Miss Donohue, with the added advantage of professional musicianship, had the added task of helping me select, check, organize, and revise the materials of this volume. I have relied upon her skill at every turn with increasing admiration and gratitude.

Contents

TO THE READER ... *xxv*

BACH, CARL PHILIPP EMANUEL
Symphony for Orchestra with Twelve Obbligato Instruments, D major ... *1*

BACH, JOHANN CHRISTIAN
Symphony, G minor, Opus 6, No. 6 ... *4*
Symphony, D major, Opus 18, No. 4 ... *6*

BACH, JOHANN SEBASTIAN
"Brandenburg" Concertos (introduction) ... *7*
"Brandenburg" Concerto No. 1, F major, BWV 1046 ... *9*
"Brandenburg" Concerto No. 2, F major BWV 1047 ... *10*
"Brandenburg" Concerto No. 3, G major, BWV 1048 ... *12*
"Brandenburg" Concerto No. 4, G major, BWV 1049 ... *13*
"Brandenburg" Concerto No. 5, D major, BWV 1050 ... *14*
"Brandenburg" Concerto No. 6, B-flat major, BWV 1051 ... *16*
Concertos for Violin and Orchestra (introduction) ... *17*
Concerto for Violin and Orchestra, A minor, BWV 1041 ... *18*
Concerto for Violin and Orchestra, E major, BWV 1042 ... *18*
Concerto for Two Violins and Orchestra, D minor, BWV 1043 ... *19*
Concerto for Violin, Oboe, and Orchestra, C minor, BWV 1060 ... *21*
Orchestral Suites [Overtures] (introduction) ... *23*

Orchestral Suite No. 1, C major, BWV 1066 ... *24*
Orchestral Suite No. 2, B minor, BWV 1067 ... *25*
Orchestral Suite No. 3, D major, BWV 1068 ... *26*
Orchestral Suite No. 4, D major, BWV 1069 ... *27*

BARBER, SAMUEL
Concerto for Piano and Orchestra, Opus 38 ... *28*
Concerto for Violin and Orchestra, Opus 14 ... *30*
First Essay for Orchestra, Opus 12 ... *32*
Second Essay for Orchestra, Opus 17 ... *33*
Overture to The School for Scandal ... *34*

BARTÓK, BÉLA
Concerto for Orchestra ... *35*
Concerto for Piano and Orchestra, No. 1 ... *37*
Concerto for Piano and Orchestra, No. 2 ... *39*
Concerto for Piano and Orchestra, No. 3 ... *41*
Concerto for Violin and Orchestra, No. 2 ... *43*
Dance Suite ... *46*
Divertimento for Strings ... *48*
The Miraculous Mandarin ... *50*
Music for Strings, Percussion, and Celesta ... *52*

BEETHOVEN, LUDWIG VAN
Concerto for Piano and Orchestra, No. 1, C major, Opus 15 ... *54*
Concerto for Piano and Orchestra, No. 2, B-flat major, Opus 19 ... *56*
Concerto for Piano and Orchestra, No. 3, C minor, Opus 37 ... *58*
Concerto for Piano and Orchestra, No. 4, G major, Opus 58 ... *60*
Concerto for Piano and Orchestra, No. 5, E-flat major, Opus 73, "Emperor" ... *62*
Concerto for Violin and Orchestra, D major, Opus 61 ... *64*
Missa solemnis, D major, Opus 123 ... *67*
Overture, The Consecration of the House, Opus 124 ... *74*
Overture to Coriolan, Opus 62 ... *75*
Overture to The Creatures of Prometheus, Opus 43 ... *77*
Overture to Egmont, Opus 84 ... *78*
Overture to Fidelio ... *80*
Overture, "Leonore," No. 1, Opus 138 ... *81*
Overture, "Leonore," No. 2 ... *82*
Overture, "Leonore," No. 3 ... *84*
Symphony No. 1, C major, Opus 21 ... *86*
Symphony No. 2, D major, Opus 36 ... *88*
Symphony No. 3, E-flat major, Opus 55, "Eroica" ... *91*
Symphony No. 4, B-flat major, Opus 60 ... *95*
Symphony No. 5, C minor, Opus 67 ... *99*

Symphony No. 6, F major, Opus 68, "Pastoral" *102*
Symphony No. 7, A major, Opus 92 .... *104*
Symphony No. 8, F major, Opus 93 .... *106*
Symphony No. 9, D minor, Opus 125, "Choral" *108*

BERG, ALBAN
Concerto for Violin and Orchestra *113*
Lulu Suite *115*
Lyric Suite *119*
Three Orchestra Pieces, Opus 6 .... *120*
Wozzeck, Symphonic Fragments, Opus 7 .... *124*

BERLIOZ, HECTOR
Damnation of Faust (three excerpts) *127*
Fantastic Symphony *147*
Harold in Italy *130*
Overture to Beatrice and Benedict *133*
Overture to Benvenuto Cellini *134*
Overture, The Corsair *135*
Overture to King Lear *136*
Overture, The Roman Carnival, Opus 9 .... *138*
Romeo and Juliet, Opus 17 (excerpts) *140*
Royal Hunt and Storm, from The Trojans *145*
Symphonie funèbre et triomphale *156*

BERNSTEIN, LEONARD
Age of Anxiety *158*
Serenade for Solo Violin and Orchestra (after Plato's Symposium) *162*
Symphonic Dances from West Side Story *164*

BIZET, GEORGES
Symphony in C major *165*

BLOCH, ERNEST
Schelomo, Hebrew Rhapsody for Cello and Orchestra *167*

BOULEZ, PIERRE
Pli selon pli (Fold by Fold) *168*

BRAHMS, JOHANNES
Concerto for Piano and Orchestra, No. 1, D minor, Opus 15 .... *174*
Concerto for Piano and Orchestra, No. 2, B-flat major, Opus 83 .... *177*
Concerto for Violin and Orchestra, A major, Opus 77 .... *179*
Concerto for Violin, Violoncello, and Orchestra, A minor, Opus 102 .... *181*

Overture, Academic Festival, Opus 80 .... *184*
Overture, Tragic, Opus 81 .... *186*
Serenade No. 1, D major, Opus 11 .... *187*
Serenade No. 2, A major, Opus 16 .... *189*
Symphony No. 1, C minor, Opus 68 .... *192*
Symphony No. 2, D major, Opus 73 .... *195*
Symphony No. 3, F major, Opus 90 .... *196*
Symphony No. 4, E minor, Opus 98 .... *199*
Variations on a Theme by Haydn, Opus 56a *202*

BRITTEN, BENJAMIN
Sea Interludes and Passacaglia from Peter Grimes *204*
Sinfonia da Requiem, Opus 20 .... *207*
Variations on a Theme by Frank Bridge, Opus 10 .... *209*

BROWN, EARLE
Available Forms II, for Orchestra Four Hands *211*

BRUCH, MAX
Concerto for Violin and Orchestra, No. 1, G minor, Opus 26 .... *214*
Scottish Fantasy, Opus 46 .... *215*

BRUCKNER, ANTON
Symphony No. 1, C minor, Linz Version *217*
Symphony No. 2, C minor *220*
Symphony No. 3, D minor *222*
Symphony No. 4, E-flat major, "Romantic" *227*
Symphony No. 5, E-flat major *230*
Symphony No. 6, A major *233*
Symphony No. 7, E major *235*
Symphony No. 8, C minor *238*
Symphony No. 9, D minor *241*

CAGE, JOHN
Atlas Eclipticalis *244*

CARTER, ELLIOTT
Concerto for Orchestra *246*
Holiday Overture *248*
Variations for Orchestra *250*

CASELLA, ALFREDO
La giara (Suite sinfonica) *252*

CHABRIER, EMMANUEL
España, Rhapsody for Orchestra *254*

CHAUSSON, ERNEST
Poème, for Violin and Orchestra, Opus 25 ..... *255*
Symphony in B-flat major, Opus 20 ..... *256*

CHOPIN, FRÉDÉRIC
Concerto for Piano and Orchestra, No. 1, E minor, Opus 11 ..... *257*
Concerto for Piano and Orchestra, No. 2, F minor, Opus 21 ..... *260*

COPLAND, AARON
Appalachian Spring (suite from the ballet) *262*
Billy the Kid *266*
Connotations for Orchestra *268*
Lincoln Portrait *271*
Music for the Theatre *274*
El Salón México *275*
Statements for Orchestra *278*
Short Symphony [No. 2] *279*
Symphony No. 3 ..... *281*

CORELLI, ARCANGELO
"Christmas" Concerto, Opus 6, No. 8, G minor *284*

COWELL, HENRY
Hymn and Fuguing Tune, No. 16 ..... *287*

CRESTON, PAUL
Janus, Opus 77 ..... *289*

CRUMB, GEORGE
Ancient Voices of Children *291*

DALLAPICCOLA, LUIGI
Variations for Orchestra *295*

DEBUSSY, CLAUDE
Images *298*
La Mer, Three Symphonic Sketches *302*
Nocturnes *304*
Prelude to "The Afternoon of a Faun" *305*

DELLO JOIO, NORMAN
Variations, Chaconne, and Finale *310*

DIAMOND, DAVID
Symphony No. 8 ..... *314*

DRUCKMAN, JACOB
Windows ... 316

DUKAS, PAUL
The Sorcerer's Apprentice, Scherzo after a Ballad of Goethe ... 317

DVOŘÁK, ANTONIN
Carnival Overture, Opus 92 ... 319
Concerto for Cello and Orchestra, B minor, Opus 104 ... 320
Concerto for Violin and Orchestra, A minor, Opus 53 ... 322
Symphony No. 7 (formerly No. 2), D minor, Opus 70 ... 324
Symphony No. 8 (formerly No. 4), G major, Opus 88 ... 326
Symphony No. 9 (formerly No. 5), E minor, Opus 95 "From the New World" ... 327

ELGAR, EDWARD
Cockaigne (In London Town) Concert Overture, Opus 40 ... 330
Variations on an Original Theme, "Enigma," Opus 36 ... 331

DE FALLA, MANUEL
El amor brujo ... 333
Nights in the Gardens of Spain (for piano and orchestra) ... 337
Three Dances from the Three-Cornered Hat ... 339

FOSS, LUKAS
Variations ... 340

FRANCK, CÉSAR
Symphony in D minor ... 344
Symphonic Variations for Piano and Orchestra ... 343

GERSHWIN, GEORGE
An American in Paris ... 346
Concerto in F ... 350
Rhapsody in Blue ... 352

GINASTERA, ALBERTO
Concerto for Piano and Orchestra ... 356
Concerto for Violin and Orchestra ... 359

GLINKA, MIKHAIL
Overture to Russlan and Ludmilla ... 360

GLUCK, CHRISTOPH WILLIBALD
Overture to Alceste ... 326
Overture to Iphigénia in Aulis ... 363

GRIEG, EDVARD
Concerto for Piano and Orchestra, A minor, Opus 16 .... *364*

HANDEL, GEORGE FRIDERIC
Concerto grosso, Opus 3, No. 1, B-flat major *366*
Grand Concertos, Opus 6 (introduction) *367*
Grand Concerto, Opus 6, No. 5, D major *368*
Grand Concerto, Opus 6, No. 6, G minor *369*
Grand Concerto, Opus 6, No. 10, D minor *370*
Grand Concerto, Opus 6, No. 12, B minor *371*
Royal Fireworks Music *372*
Water Music *375*

HARRIS, ROY
Symphony No. 3 .... *379*

HAYDN, JOSEPH
Concerto for Cello and Orchestra, C major *381*
Concerto for Cello and Orchestra, D major, Opus 101 .... *383*
Concerto for Clavier and Orchestra, D major *385*
Concerto for Trumpet and Orchestra, E-flat major *388*
Sinfonia concertante, B-flat major *389*
Symphony No. 22, E-flat major, "The Philosopher" *392*
Symphony No. 26, D minor, "Lamentatione" *394*
Symphony No. 31, D major, "Horn Signal" or "On the Lookout" *396*
Symphony No. 45, F-sharp minor, "Farewell" *398*
Symphony No. 48, C major, "Maria Theresia" *400*
Symphony No. 60, C major, "Il distratto" *404*
Symphony No. 82, C major, "L'Ours" *407*
Symphony No. 83, G minor, "La Poule" *409*
Symphony No. 84, E-flat major *411*
Symphony No. 85, B-flat major, "La Reine" *413*
Symphony No. 86, D major *414*
Symphony No. 88, G major *416*
Symphony No. 92, G major, "Oxford" *418*
Symphony No. 93, D major *420*
Symphony No. 94, G major, "Surprise" *423*
Symphony No. 95, C minor *425*
Symphony No. 96, D major, "The Miracle" *427*
Symphony No. 97, C major *431*
Symphony No. 98, B-flat major *434*
Symphony No. 99, E-flat major *436*
Symphony No. 100, G major, "Military" *438*
Symphony No. 101, D major, "The Clock" *441*
Symphony No. 102, B-flat major *444*
Symphony No. 103, E-flat major, "Drumroll" *446*

Symphony No. 104, D major ... *450*

HINDEMITH, PAUL
Concerto Music for Strings and Brass, Opus 50 ... *452*
Concerto for Violin and Orchestra ... *453*
Mathis der Maler, Symphony ... *455*
Nobilissima visione, Orchestra Suite ... *457*
Symphonic Metamorphoses of Themes by Carl Maria von Weber ... *460*

HONEGGER, ARTHUR
Pacific 231 ... *462*
Symphony No. 2 (for string orchestra and trumpet) ... *463*

D'INDY, VINCENT
Symphony on a French Mountain Air, Opus 25 ... *466*

IVES, CHARLES
Central Park in the Dark ... *468*
Symphony No. 2 ... *470*
Symphony No. 3, The Camp Meeting ... *472*
Symphony No. 4 ... *474*
A Symphony: Holidays ... *478*
Three Places in New England ... *483*
The Unanswered Question ... *486*

JANÁČEK, LEOŠ
Sinfonietta ... *487*

KABALEVSKY, DMITRI
Overture to Colas Breugnon ... *489*

KIRCHNER, LEON
Music for Orchestra ... *490*

LALO, EDOUARD
Symphonie espagnole, for Violin and Orchestra, Opus 21 ... *493*

LIGETI, GYÖRGY
Atmosphères ... *495*

LISZT, FRANZ
Concerto for Piano and Orchestra, No. 1, E-flat major ... *496*
Concerto for Piano and Orchestra, No. 2, A major ... *499*
A Faust Symphony ... *500*

Mazeppa 504
Les Préludes 506
Tasso: Lamento e trionfo 507

LUTOSLAWSKI, WITOLD
Concerto for Orchestra 510
Funeral Music 512

MACDOWELL, EDWARD
Concerto for Piano and Orchestra, No. 2, D minor, Opus 23 514

MAHLER, GUSTAV
Das Lied von der Erde (The Song of the Earth) 516
Symphony No. 1, D major 522
Symphony No. 2, C minor, "Resurrection" 528
Symphony No. 3, D minor 535
Symphony No. 4, G major (with soprano solo) 540
Symphony No. 5 544
Symphony No. 6, A minor 548
Symphony No. 7 552
Symphony No. 8, E-flat major, "Symphony of a Thousand" 555
Symphony No. 9, D major 564
Symphony No. 10, F-sharp minor 567

MENDELSSOHN, FELIX
Concerto for Piano and Orchestra, No. 1, G minor, Opus 25 571
Concerto for Violin and Orchestra, E minor, Opus 64 573
A Midsummer Night's Dream: Incidental Music 575
Overture, The Hebrides (Fingal's Cave), Opus 26 579
Overture, Ruy Blas, Opus 95 582
Symphony No. 3, A minor, Opus 56, "Scotch" 583
Symphony No. 4, A major, Opus 90, "Italian" 585
Symphony No. 5, D minor, Opus 107, "Reformation" 588

MENNIN, PETER
Symphony No. 3 590

MENOTTI, GIAN CARLO
Apocalypse 592

MESSIAEN, OLIVIER
Les Offrandes oubliées (Forgotten Offerings) 594

MILHAUD, DARIUS
Suite provençale 596

MOUSSORGSKY, MODEST
A Night on Bald Mountain *598*
Pictures at an Exhibition *602*
Prelude to Khovanshchina *606*

MOZART, WOLFGANG AMADEUS
Concerto for Clarinet and Orchestra, A major, K. 622 .... *607*
Concerto for Flute and Orchestra, G major, K. 313 .... *609*
Concerto for Flute and Orchestra, D major, K. 314 .... *611*
Concerto for Horn and Orchestra, E-flat major, K. 417 .... *613*
Concerto for Piano and Orchestra, E-flat major, K. 271 .... *614*
Concerto for Piano and Orchestra, B-flat major, K. 450 .... *617*
Concerto for Piano and Orchestra, G major, K. 453 .... *618*
Concerto for Piano and Orchestra, F major, K. 459 .... *620*
Concerto for Piano and Orchestra, D minor, K. 466 .... *622*
Concerto for Piano and Orchestra, C major, K. 467 .... *626*
Concerto for Piano and Orchestra, E-flat major, K. 482 .... *628*
Concerto for Piano and Orchestra, A major, K. 488 .... *630*
Concerto for Piano and Orchestra, C minor, K. 491 .... *632*
Concerto for Piano and Orchestra, C major, K. 503 .... *634*
Concerto for Piano and Orchestra, D major, K. 537, "Coronation" *636*
Concerto for Piano and Orchestra, B-flat major, K. 595 .... *639*
Concerto for Two Pianos and Orchestra, E-flat major, K. 365 .... *641*
Five Concertos for Violin and Orchestra (introduction) *644*
Concerto for Violin and Orchestra, B-flat major, K. 207, [No. 1] *645*
Concerto for Violin and Orchestra, D major, K. 211, [No. 2] *646*
Concerto for Violin and Orchestra, G major, K. 216 [No. 3] *647*
Concerto for Violin and Orchestra, D major, K. 218 [No. 4] *648*
Concerto for Violin and Orchestra, A major, K. 219 [No. 5] *649*
Masonic Funeral Music, K. 477 .... *651*
A Musical Joke (Ein musikalischer Spass) K. 522 .... *652*
Overture to The Abduction from the Seraglio *654*
Overture to Don Giovanni *655*
Overture to The Magic Flute *657*
Overture to The Marriage of Figaro *658*
Eine kleine Nachtmusik, K. 525 .... *659*
Serenade, D major, K. 320, "Posthorn" *660*
Serenade, B-flat major, K. 361, "Gran Partita" *663*
Sinfonia concertante, E-flat major, K. 297b *665*
Sinfonia concertante, E-flat major, K. 364 .... *668*
Symphony, No. 25, G minor, K. 183, "Little G minor" *671*
Symphony, No. 29, A major, K. 201 .... *673*
Symphony, No. 31, D major, K. 297, "Paris" *675*
Symphony, No. 34, C major, K. 338 .... *677*
Symphony, No. 35, D major, K. 385, "Haffner" *679*
Symphony, No. 36, C major, K. 424, "Linz" *682*

Symphony, No. 38, D major, K. 504, "Prague" ... *683*
Symphony, No. 39, E-flat major, K. 543 ... *685*
Symphony, No. 40, G minor, K. 550 ... *686*
Symphony, No. 41, C major, K. 551, "Jupiter" ... *688*

NICOLAI, OTTO
Overture to The Merry Wives of Windsor ... *690*

NIELSEN, CARL
Symphony No. 5, Opus 50 ... *691*

PAGANINI, NICCOLÒ
Concerto for Violin and Orchestra, No. 1, Opus 6 ... *693*

PISTON, WALTER
Symphony No. 4 ... *698*

POULENC, FRANCIS
Concerto for Two Pianos and Orchestra, D minor ... *700*

PROKOFIEFF, SERGEI
Concerto for Piano and Orchestra, No. 2, G minor, Opus 16 ... *702*
Concerto for Piano and Orchestra, No. 3, C major, Opus 26 ... *704*
Concerto for Violin and Orchestra, No. 1, D major, Opus 19 ... *706*
Concerto for Violin and Orchestra, No. 2, G minor, Opus 63 ... *709*
Lieutenant Kijé, Symphonic Suite, Opus 60 ... *710*
Romeo and Juliet ... *712*
Scythian Suite (Ala and Lolli), Opus 20 ... *717*
Symphony No. 1, D major, Opus 25, "Classical" ... *719*
Symphony No. 5, B-flat major, Opus 100 ... *721*

RACHMANINOFF, SERGEI
Concerto for Piano and Orchestra, No. 2, C minor, Opus 18 ... *723*
Concerto for Piano and Orchestra, No. 3, D minor, Opus 30 ... *726*
Rhapsody on a Theme by Paganini (for piano and orchestra), Opus 43 ... *729*
Symphony No. 2, E minor, Opus 27 ... *730*

RAVEL, MAURICE
Alborada del gracioso ... *733*
Bolero ... *734*
Concerto for Piano and Orchestra, G major ... *735*
Concerto for Left hand for Piano and Orchestra ... *737*
Daphnis and Chloé ... *739*
Mother Goose (Ma Mère l'oye) ... *742*
Rapsodie espagnole ... *744*

Le Tombeau de Couperin 746
La Valse (choreographic poem for orchestra) 747

REGER, MAX
Variations and Fugue for Orchestra on a Theme by Mozart, Opus 132 750

RESPIGHI, OTTORINO
The Fountains of Rome 752
The Pines of Rome 754

RIEGGER, WALLINGFORD
Study in Sonority, Opus 7 755

RIMSKY-KORSAKOFF, NICOLAI
Capriccio espagnol, Opus 34 757
Overture, "The Great Russian Easter," Opus 36 759
Scheherazade, Symphonic Suite, Opus 35 760

ROCHBERG, GEORGE
Symphony No. 2 764

ROSSINI, GIOACCHINO
Overture to The Barber of Seville 766
Overture to La gazza ladra 767
Overture to L'Italiana in Algeri 769
Overture to La scala di seta 770
Overture to Semiramide 770
Overture to William Tell 771

ROUSSEL, ALBERT
Bacchus et Ariane, Suite No. 2 772
Symphony No. 3, G minor, Opus 42 774

RUGGLES, CARL
Men and Mountains 775
Portals 777

SAINT-SAËNS, CAMILLE
Concerto for Cello and Orchestra, A minor, Opus 33 778
Concerto for Piano and Orchestra, No. 2, G minor, Opus 22 781
Concerto for Piano and Orchestra, No. 4, C minor, Opus 44 782
Introduction and Rondo Capriccioso, Opus 28 783
Omphale's Spinning Wheel 784
Symphony No. 3, C minor, Opus 78 785

SCHOENBERG, ARNOLD
Concerto for Piano and Orchestra, Opus 42 .... *787*
Five Pieces for Orchestra, Opus 16 .... *790*
Pelleas and Melisande, Symphonic Poem, Opus 5 .... *793*
A Survivor from Warsaw, Opus 46 .... *798*
Variations for Orchestra, Opus 31 .... *801*
Verklärte Nacht (Transfigured Night) Opus 4 .... *804*

SCHUBERT, FRANZ
Rosamunde Overture and Ballet Music *807*
Symphony No. 4, C minor, "Tragic" *808*
Symphony No. 5, B-flat major *810*
Symphony No. 6, C major, Opus 140, "The Little C Major" *812*
Symphony No. 7, C major [see No. 9 below] *816*
Symphony No. 8, B minor, "Unfinished" *814*
Symphony No. 9, C major *816*

SCHUMAN, WILLIAM
American Festival Overture *819*
Fantasy for Cello and Orchestra: A Song of Orpheus *820*
New England Tryptych: Three Pieces for Orchestra after William Billings *822*
Symphony No. 3 .... *823*
Symphony for Strings [No. 5] *826*

SCHUMANN, ROBERT
Concerto for Cello and Orchestra, A minor, Opus 129 .... *828*
Concerto for Piano and Orchestra, A minor, Opus 54 .... *829*
Overture to Manfred, Opus 115 .... *833*
Symphony No. 1, B-flat major, Opus 38, "Spring" *834*
Symphony No. 2, C major, Opus 61 .... *838*
Symphony No. 3, E-flat major, Opus 97, "Rhenish" *840*
Symphony No. 4, D minor, Opus 120 .... *843*

SCRIABIN, ALEXANDER
Poem of Ecstasy, Opus 54 .... *846*
Prometheus, the Poem of Fire, Opus 60 .... *847*

SESSIONS, ROGER
Symphony No. 8 .... *850*

SHOSTAKOVICH, DMITRI
Symphony No. 1, Opus 10 .... *852*
Symphony No. 5, Opus 47 .... *854*
Symphony No. 6, Opus 53 .... *857*
Symphony No. 9, Opus 70 .... *859*

SIBELIUS, JAN
Concerto for Violin and Orchestra, D minor, Opus 47 .... *861*
The Swan of Tuonela, Opus 22, No. 3 .... *862*
Symphony No. 1, E minor, Opus 39 .... *863*
Symphony No. 2, D major, Opus 43 .... *865*
Symphony No. 3, C major, Opus 52 .... *868*
Symphony No. 4, A minor, Opus 63 .... *870*
Symphony No. 5, E-flat major, Opus 82 .... *872*
Symphony No. 6, Opus 104 .... *874*
Symphony No. 7, C major, Opus 105 .... *876*

SMETANA, BEDRICH
The Moldau *878*
Overture to The Bartered Bride *881*

STOCKHAUSEN, KARLHEINZ
Hymnen *882*
Kontrapunkte *885*

STRAUSS, RICHARD
Don Juan, Opus 20 .... *887*
Don Quixote, Opus 35 .... *890*
Ein Heldenleben (A Hero's Life), Opus 40 .... *893*
Metamorphoses *896*
Salome: Dance of the Seven Veils *899*
Till Eulenspiegel, Opus 28 .... *901*
Thus Spake Zarathustra (Also sprach Zarathustra), Opus 30 .... *903*
Tod und Verklärung (Death and Transfiguration), Opus 24 .... *906*

STRAVINSKY, IGOR
Agon, A Ballet for Twelve Dancers *909*
Capriccio for Piano and Orchestra *913*
Card Game (Jeu de cartes), A Ballet in Three Acts *914*
Concerto for Violin and Orchestra, D major *917*
The Firebird (L'Oiseau de feu) *919*
History of a Soldier, Concert Suite *924*
Petrushka *927*
Pulcinella *934*
The Rite of Spring (Le Sacre du printemps) *936*
The Song of the Nightingale *940*
Symphony in C *943*
Symphony in Three Movements *944*
Symphony of Psalms *947*

TCHAIKOVSKY, PETER ILYITCH
Capriccio italien, Opus 45 .... *950*

Concerto for Piano and Orchestra, No. 1, B-flat minor, Opus 23 .... *951*
Concerto for Violin and Orchestra, D major, Opus 35 .... *957*
Francesca da Rimini, Opus 32 .... *959*
The Nutcracker, Opus 71 .... *961*
Romeo and Juliet Fantasy Overture *964*
Serenade for String Orchestra, Opus 48 .... *966*
Symphony No. 2, C minor, Opus 17, "Little Russian" *967*
Symphony No. 4, F minor, Opus 36 .... *969*
Symphony No. 5, E minor, Opus 64 .... *973*
Symphony No. 6, B minor, Opus 74, "Pathétique" *975*

TELEMANN, GEORG PHILIPP
Suite, A minor, for Flute and String Orchestra *978*

THOMSON, VIRGIL
The Seine at Night *979*

VARÈSE, EDGARD
Arcana *981*
Ecuatorial *985*
Intégrales *986*
Ionisation *988*

VAUGHAN WILLIAMS, RALPH
Fantasia on a Theme by Thomas Tallis *989*
Symphony No. 2, G major, "London" *992*
Symphony No. 4, F minor *995*

VIVALDI, ANTONIO
"The Seasons" [four *Concerti grossi*], Opus 8 (introduction) *998*
Concerto grosso, Opus 8, No. 1, E major, "Spring" *1002*
Concerto grosso, Opus 8, No. 2, G minor, "Summer" *1003*
Concerto grosso, Opus 8, No. 3, F major, "Autumn" *1004*
Concerto grosso, Opus 8, No. 4, F minor, "Winter" *1005*

WAGNER, RICHARD
The Flying Dutchman Overture *1006*
Götterdämmerung (Twilight of the Gods): Siegfried's Funeral Music ... *1008*
Götterdämmerung (Twilight of the Gods): Siegfried's Rhine Journey .. *1009*
Lohengrin: Prelude *1011*
Die Meistersinger von Nürnberg: Prelude *1013*
Parsifal: Prelude and Good Friday Music *1014*
A Siegfried Idyll *1018*
Tannhäuser: Overture *1020*
Tristan and Isolde: Prelude and Love Death *1021*

WALTON, WILLIAM
Symphony No. 1 .... *1024*

WEBER, BEN
Concerto for Piano and Orchestra, Opus 52 .... *1026*

WEBER, CARL MARIA VON
Konzertstück, Opus 79 .... *1028*
Overture to Euryanthe *1029*
Overture to Der Freischütz *1030*
Overture to Oberon *1032*

WEBERN, ANTON
Five Movements, Opus 5 (version for string orchestra) *1033*
Five Pieces for Orchestra, Opus 10 .... *1034*
Six Pieces for Orchestra, Opus 6 .... *1036*
Symphony, Opus 21 .... *1037*
Variations, Opus 30 .... *1039*

ZIMMERMANN, BERND ALOIS
Photoptósis, Prelude for Large Orchestra *1041*

INDEX *1043*

To the Reader

The purpose of this book is to add to your enjoyment of symphonic pieces you may be hearing, for the first, the fifth, or possibly the twenty-fifth time. Most of the essays collected here were written as program notes for concerts of the New York Philharmonic. A few have been added in order to round out the basic orchestral repertory. The collection is intended for the average listener to symphony concerts, records, and radio—not for professionals, although professionals may find it handy as a quick source of basic information on works of the symphonic repertory.

Beside the standard repertory the reader will find a number of works by standard composers such as Mozart, Haydn, and Mahler—works performed less often in the past, but which show signs of fast-growing popularity today. In response to this current growth, the book includes twenty-five Haydn symphonies, ten Mozart symphonies, twenty-one Mozart concertos, and all the Mahler symphonies, including his unfinished Tenth and *Das Lied von der Erde.*

Innovative twentieth-century works are represented not only by such established masters as Stravinsky, Bartók, and Prokofieff, or the American Ives, but also a substantial sampling of living composers such as Pierre Boulez and Karlheinz Stockhausen, with a slight emphasis on leading Americans from Leonard Bernstein to Ben Weber.

Since composers' comments on their own music offer unique and irreplaceable insights, I have used many, such as Berlioz's extravagant comments on his own extravagant works; Tchaikovsky's famous explanation of his Fourth Symphony; and Wagner's explications of the Preludes to his *Tannhäuser, Lohengrin,* and *Tristan and Isolde.* Living composers were invited to comment on new works of their own and many responded generously.

Broadly speaking each essay is divided into background (historical, biographical, or both) and description of the music itself, often including brief examples of one or more principal themes. (Readers unfamiliar with notation may confidently skip these examples, without interrupting the flow of the narrative or missing any essential point.) It is sometimes surprising what odd bits of information or peripheral facts will throw light on a piece of music or its historical context. Where I have thought anecdotes would help, I have not hesitated to use them.

One thing the reader will not find is negative criticism of the works included. Not all musical masterpieces are perfect. But their flaws, real or imagined, may safely be left for the listener to decide for himself. Any work important enough to be included repeatedly on programs of major symphony orchestras has attractions which will be the listener's first interest. And, as Donald Tovey remarked many years ago, the duty of the writer of program notes is that of counsel for the defense.

If the annotator's duty is defense, his pleasure is the indulgence of his enthusiasms. The following pages are one man's attempt to share a pleasure, a delight, a passion that has enriched his life from as far back as memory goes. The earliest of my memories is a vivid one of sharing—specifically of sitting (with lots of headroom to spare) under the enormous instrument at which my father, then a young pianist, was practicing. I sat for hours, enthralled, bewitched by the magical noises that engulfed me. Eventually, it dawned on me that those noises made patterns, which I now call tunes. Then I realized that the tunes had an added dimension, which I now call harmony. I am still discovering more new dimensions. But to this day I am stirred first by those magical noises—whether they come from a piano, a human voice, or the hundred instrumental voices of a symphony orchestra.

Only after that first physical impact, come (for me, at least) the seductions of sensuous beauty, then the sharper emotional reactions, and finally those rarer moments of blinding intensity when I suddenly feel as if the composer were speaking directly to me. I may know the composer died fifty, one hundred, two hundred years ago. No matter: there are no barriers of time or space. At that instant I believe that I know, that I feel exactly what he felt, what he meant, when he put those musical notes on paper. It is a foolish fancy (or perhaps not so foolish), when you feel that Bach, or Schubert, or Beethoven—not just the "spirit" of Beethoven, but the man himself—is speaking directly to you. Aside from passionate love, I know no more electric kind of human intimacy. Call it sharing, call it communication, call it identifying, call it a momentary loss of self in communion with another person. Whatever one calls it, I doubt there is any drug as mind-expanding or consciousness-raising as this. The experience is, of course, addictive. But it will not shatter your nervous system, destroy your liver, or damage your brain. On the contrary, it may do them all good. And even one such musical experience bears dividends for a lifetime.

I stumbled into such experiences early because my father (unknowingly at first) shared his piano with me, as he later knowingly shared the excitements of symphony concerts and other forms of music. And equally important: as soon as I knew words enough to ask and argue with him, he shared his thoughts and feelings about music. It never occurred to me that words could explain the *essence* of music, or its "meaning"—whatever that may be. But it was soon clear that words (even printed words) were one means of sharing feelings *about* music, ideas, opinions, intuitions, facts, and even certain kinds of musical understanding which—surprisingly enough—could not be communicated by any performance, however eloquent. Since then I have not stopped asking, arguing, and debating the works that stir me.

So, many years later, when the New York Philharmonic (The Philharmonic-Symphony Society of New York, to cite its full title) invited me to write program notes for its concerts, I felt that this was not merely an honor, but a pleasure I could not deny myself. And if now the following collection of notes add anywhere near as much to other listeners' pleasures as they have to mine, that will be the greatest possible reward.

The New York Philharmonic Guide to the Symphony

Carl Philipp Emanuel Bach

Born March 8, 1714, Weimar—died December 14, 1788, Hamburg

SYMPHONY FOR ORCHESTRA WITH TWELVE OBBLIGATO INSTRUMENTS, D MAJOR, WOTQUENNE 183, NO. 1

Of C. P. E. Bach, Mozart once said: "He is the father, we are the kids [*die Buben*]. Those of us who know a thing or two, have it from him." The only other composer Mozart acknowledged as an artistic parent was his beloved "Papa" Haydn. But Haydn, too, at the height of his fame, insisted: "Anyone who knows me well must realize that I owe a great deal to Emanuel Bach, that I studied him industriously, and understood him." Even Beethoven, much as he differed from both Mozart and Haydn, admired, studied, and was influenced by Carl Philipp Emanuel.

What was the fascination that this composer, so little known to present-day symphony audiences, exercised over three such different composers and three entire generations of Classical and Romantic artists—a fascination which is again becoming apparent to twentieth-century listeners?

Emanuel, or Carl Philipp Emanuel Bach, to give him his full identity, was a member of that incredible dynasty of musicians which spanned two centuries from the late sixteenth to the late eighteenth century—a dynasty so numerous and widespread that in more than one German town of the Baroque age, the town pipers became known colloquially as Bachs, even when the last local member of the Bach clan had ceased to work as a piper. C. P. E. Bach had the added advantage of studying with the greatest of them all, his father Johann Sebastian. "In composing and in keyboard playing I never had any other teacher than my father," wrote Philipp Emanuel in his autobiography.

His nonmusical education was broad for an eighteenth-century musician. He studied law at the universities of Leipzig and Frankfurt-an-der-Oder, and developed into one of the most intellectual members of the Bach clan. He was only twenty-four when he was called to the service of the Prussian Crown Prince Frederick, who two years later became Frederick II, known historically as "the Great." Frederick was a monarch of broad intellectual and artistic interests. When he came to the throne in 1740, Berlin became the residence of Philipp Emanuel Bach, and there he was able to indulge his own interests in literature, drama, and philosophy. The great German dramatist Lessing was only the *most* famous among Emanuel's nonmusical friends in Berlin and, later, in Hamburg.

With the advent of the Seven Years War (1756–63), however, court music languished. After the war Frederick's interest in music never completely recovered. But Emanuel's fame had spread. Hamburg needed a successor to Telemann, who had died in 1767; Emanuel was selected above a number of other distinguished candidates.

In the wealthy metropolis of Hamburg, Emanuel assumed a position both socially and financially far above what he had known in Berlin. He was music director at the five principal churches of the city. Hamburg also possessed a new concert hall, one of the first in Germany. Here Emanuel organized public concerts in which he appeared as soloist, and as director of chamber music and symphonies as well as oratorios by Telemann, Handel, Haydn, and others.

In Hamburg, as in Berlin, Emanuel's home became a meeting place for musicians, dramatists, philosophers, and poets, including Klopstock, the founder of German "Irrationalism" and the most influential leader of contemporary German literature. Emanuel was often given the complimentary nickname of the "Klopstock of music," so similar did the two men appear in their contemporaries' eyes. Like Klopstock, Philipp Emanuel became famous for having discarded what was now regarded as the plodding rationalism of an earlier age as well as the playful superficiality of a fashionable Rococo, replacing both by a new depth of feeling and spontaneous personal expression. This is not yet the stormy passion of Beethoven, or Beethoven's democratic appeal to all mankind. Emanuel's appeal is still to connoisseurs and amateurs and their new *Empfindsamkeit,* "sensibility," to use the term made fashionable by Lawrence Sterne's *Sentimental Journey* of 1768.

It was Klopstock who prepared an epitaph originally intended for a Bach memorial: "Carl Philipp Emanuel Bach, the profound harmonist, combined innovation with beauty, was great in the world of vocal music and greater still in the bold art of music unconfined by speech."

So great was Philipp Emanuel's fame that when the distinguished English historian and critic Charles Burney toured Europe gathering material for his epochal *History of Music,* he made a special trip to Hamburg only to visit Philipp Emanuel Bach, with whom he spent two days. Burney was deeply impressed by him both as a composer and a performer.

Shortly after Burney's visit Philipp Emanuel composed his four last and greatest symphonies (1775–76). A letter dated August 17, 1776, from Klopstock to an absent friend may refer to their first performance: "How often we have wished you were with us . . . for example yesterday, when we heard four new symphonies by Bach performed by forty instruments, and then spent the evening at the Büsch's [Professor Johann Georg Büsch's home was the liveliest intellectual center in Hamburg] and at the Lessings'."

Philipp Emanuel, who was not unaware of his own stature, subsequently wrote to the publisher Breitkopf: "I have recently completed four big orchestral symphonies with twelve *obbligato* instruments. They are the finest of my achievements in this field. Modesty forbids me to say more." The first of this set of four is in D major and was given the number 183 in the standard Wotquenne Catalogue of C. P. E. Bach's works.

I. *Allegro di molto.* Emanuel begins with a deceptive mildness. First violins sustain a single tone under which the remaining strings mark a sturdy rhythm, but no clear-cut theme. The sustained D of the first violins repeats, throbs in a pattern of more and more rapid syncopations until the entire ensemble breaks off abruptly. After a moment's silence the violins again initiate a sustained tone, higher in pitch and in volume, with the ensemble again supplying a nonthematic rhythmic momentum. Part of the essence of the new *Empfindsamkeit* was such rapid shifts: from soft to loud, to interruptions of complete silence, from the thinnest texture of a single tone to a raging *tutti.*

A moment's pause precedes the abrupt contrast of Emanuel's second theme, a duet for two solo oboes with a stalking bassoon in the background.

The oboe duet is followed by one for flutes, by a brief modulatory rough-and-tumble serving as a development section, and by a free recapitulation.

One more surprise awaits us at the end: a totally unexpected jump into the distant key of E-flat major, leading directly into the second movement.

II. *Largo.* The middle movement is a brief idyll, a songful interlude in which Emanuel again surprises, this time by the originality of his orchestral color. The chief melody is given to a solo viola:

Two octaves above the viola its melody is doubled by a solitary flute. Three instruments supply the background for this singular sound: a solo cello (similarly shadowed by a solo flute) and an independently striding string bass. Between phrases we hear the delicate punctuation of *pizzicato* violins.

At the conclusion of this lyric interlude Philipp Emanuel's orchestra modulates abruptly back to the tonic key of D major for the finale, which follows without interruption.

III. *Presto.* The lighthearted finale is closer to the current tradition of Philipp Emanuel's day. In a rollicking 3/8 meter the entire orchestra bursts into a rondo-like rejoicing:

The harmonies are of the simplest, the rhythms continuous in their flow, the orchestral texture bright and transparent.

The 12 *obbligato* instruments mentioned in Philipp Emanuel's letter to Breitkopf are 2 flutes, 2 oboes, bassoon, 2 horns, 2 violins, viola, cello, and double bass. Then, as now, the string parts were normally reinforced (hence the 40 instruments of Klopstock's description). The customary harpsichord was omitted only in the middle movement.

Johann Christian Bach

Born September 5, 1735, Leipzig—died January 1, 1782, London

SYMPHONY IN G MINOR, OPUS 6, NO. 6

Johann Christian Bach was the youngest (and apparently favorite) son of Johann Sebastian Bach. He was known in his day as the "London" Bach or, more often, simply as Bach. For his international fame far overshadowed the essentially local renown of his father.

Two portraits of Johann Christian by his friend Gainsborough show us a comfortably sophisticated man of the world, casual but assured and elegant in the white periwig, lace cuffs, and jabot of fashion. The cool, if good-natured, skepticism of his eyes, is balanced by sensuous lips, which seem about to break into a smile. Thus Gainsborough portrayed him, and thus he portrayed himself in his music—for the most part, that is. And thus he must have appeared only a few weeks after the portrait was painted in 1778, when he celebrated a reunion with another old friend, Wolfgang Amadeus Mozart, in Paris. Mozart's affection for Johann Christian and admiration for his music were warmer than for any contemporary except Joseph Haydn.

The friendship and mutual admiration of the two composers dated from 1764, when Mozart, as an eight-year-old prodigy, visited London with his father and sister. As music master to the Queen, Johann Christian was responsible for arranging the Mozarts' appearances at court. And the Mozarts, as a matter of course, must often have visited the popular Bach-Abel subscription concerts, which had been founded only a few weeks before they arrived in London.

Johann Christian's Symphony in G minor must have been written close to this time. It is possible that Mozart may have heard this Symphony performed during his fifteen-month stay in the English capitol. If so, it could not have failed to make a profound impression.

How wild this little Symphony must have sounded to that first audience! The choice of a minor key—any minor key—for a symphony was daring. How daring, we may measure from the fact that up to this time Haydn, the great experimenter, with some twenty-five symphonies to his credit, had not composed one of them in a minor key. G minor was particularly identified with the violent shocks of Storm and Stress, of powerful, dark emotions, revolt and tragedy, which stirred the European theater, literature, and music of the 1760s and 1770s.

Coming from the normally urbane and charming Johann Christian Bach, this agitated, pessimistic G-minor Symphony—his only symphony composed entirely in the minor mode—is particularly revealing. In spirit and style, it is closer to the bitter, rebellious "Little" G-minor Symphony Mozart composed in his teens, than to Mozart's riper masterpiece in the same key, K. 550.

I. *Allegro.* The first movement is based on a powerful figure, which relies more on its agitated rhythm than on melody for its effect:

It continues with brusque shifts of mood, from loud to soft, from sharp dissonance to the relatively restrained poignance of little lyric interludes for the oboes. The movement is rounded off with a stark insistence on the agitated opening rhythm.

II. *Andante più tosto Adagio.* Most Classical symphonies composed in a minor key turned to the more conciliatory major mode for the slow movement. Johann Christian not only keeps to the minor mode but purposely avoids the merely melancholy elegiac mood, which would have been more normal for an *adagio* of this period. The solemnity and almost portentous power of some phrases in this movement look far forward to some of the most imaginative scenes in Mozart's *Magic Flute.* The movement closes with the sort of poignant whisper we also associate with Mozart.

III. *Allegro molto.* Although this fiery finale is composed in a fast 12/8 meter associated with the *gigue,* its mood is far removed from even the most stylized of dances. As in the first movement, we are swept along by the driving rhythms relieved only by the briefest of lyric phrases for oboe duet. Even Mozart who so loved a quiet closing, rarely went so far as to conclude an entire major work with such a delicate *pianissimo* as we hear in this Symphony's final bar.

The score of this impressive little work calls for only 2 oboes, 2 horns, and the usual strings, to which a harpsichord or piano would probably have been added in eighteenth-century performances.

SYMPHONY IN D MAJOR, OPUS 18, NO. 4

For no other contemporary composer (except, of course, his beloved "Papa" Haydn) did Mozart have words of such warmth and praise as for Christian Bach. From their first meeting in London in 1764, when Bach was twenty-eight and Mozart an eight-year-old prodigy, they felt immediate admiration and affection for each other. Fourteen years later, Mozart, again on tour, wrote his father from fashionable Saint-Germain near Paris: "Mr. Bach of London has already been here for fourteen days; he is going to write a French opera. He is here only to listen to the singers; he will go back to London to compose the opera and then return to stage it [in Paris]. You can easily imagine his joy and mine at our meeting again,—perhaps his joy is not quite so great—but one may say that he is a thoroughly honorable man and deals fairly with people. I love him (as you well know) with all my heart—and really respect him. And he, I know this for certain, praises me not only to my face but to others, and not exaggeratedly, as some do, but seriously and sincerely."

Four years later, this time from Vienna, Mozart wrote his father: "No doubt you heard that the English Bach has died?—a sad day for the world of music!" Mozart's attraction to Christian Bach was shared by his contemporaries, and in our own century we find ourselves agreeing more and more with Mozart.

To most of the numerous Bach family in Germany, Christian must have seemed something of a renegade. For he went to Italy at an early age, turned Roman Catholic, wrote opera, and married an Italian prima donna—four things which no Bach had ever done in the two centuries of that stupendous dynasty. But during his lifetime, Johann Christian became the most famous of them all; from top to bottom of Italy he was applauded as the operatic maestro Don Giovanni Christiano Bach; in France he was the symphonist Jean Chrétian Bach; and in his adopted homeland it was John Christian Bach.

If it was Christian's operas which established his international fame, his instrumental works, chiefly his symphonies, are what we know best today.

The D-major Symphony is a festive work, rather like the Italian opera overtures, or *sinfonie* as they were called, which were so popular in the opera house long before it occurred to anyone to play them separately in an orchestral concert. As a matter of fact, the middle movement of this Symphony *was* the slow movement of the Overture to Christian Bach's opera, *Temistocle*, which he composed in 1772 for the court opera of the Elector Palatine in Mannheim, where the famous Mannheim Orchestra (like the Vienna Philharmonic today) did double duty for symphony concerts and opera. As befitted the rich instrumental resources of Mannheim, the orchestration of the opera overture was richer (including 3 *clarinetti d'amore*) than that of the more standard symphonic ensemble in London, which normally included 2 flutes,

2 oboes (or 2 clarinets), 2 bassoons, 2 horns, 2 trumpets, kettledrums, and a relatively small string choir.

The first and last movements of the Symphony may well have been composed after *Temistocle* and the premiere of the Symphony probably took place in the elegant Hanover Square Rooms in London, which were remodeled for the popular Bach-Abel concert series run by John Christian and his German colleague and friend Carl Friedrich Abel.

I. *Allegro con spirito.* This miniature sonata-form movement opens with a fanfare-like principal theme of a kind traditional in the opera house and in the early symphonies of Haydn, Mozart, and many a contemporary. Only after the Rococo grace of the delicate second theme has intervened does the principal theme develop into a more personal expression. The central development section is brief but ingenious as is the imaginative recall of the two themes in the recapitulation.

II. *Andante.* The languorous charm of the slow movement is voiced in almost chamber music terms. The orchestra is reduced to 2 flutes, bassoon, and strings.

III. *Rondo: Presto.* The high spirits of the recurrent rondo refrain are close to the quicksilver mood often shared by Mozart and Haydn:

In its first return the refrain is reduced from sixteen measures to only eight. Two intervening episodes give capricious contrast and the tiny *codetta* is an all-too-brief farewell.

The Symphony is scored for traditional pairs of oboes, bassoons, French horns, trumpets, kettledrums, and the usual string choir, to which a continuo harpsichord or piano might be added, according to local custom. Nowadays the keyboard instrument is sometimes omitted.

Johann Sebastian Bach

Born March 21, 1685, Eisenach—died July 28, 1750, Leipzig

BRANDENBURG CONCERTOS BWV 1046–1051

The world has long marveled that Bach's "Brandenburg" Concertos should have been wasted on the Margrave of Brandenburg. The Margrave Christian Ludwig, as brother of the reigning King Friedrich Wilhelm I of Prussia, resided in the Royal Palace in Berlin and was also styled "Royal Highness." The fulsome flattery of Baroque dedications may be familiar to many. But we still cringe to read the groveling phrases of such a giant as Bach, deprecating the products of his "little talents" and imploring the mighty Margrave (in provincial-courtly eighteenth-century French) to take a tolerant view of their imperfections:

> My Lord,
> As I had the good fortune a few years ago to be heard by Your Royal Highness, at Your Highness's commands, & as I noticed then that Your Highness took some pleasure in the little talents which Heaven has given me for Music, and as in taking Leave of Your Royal Highness, Your Highness deigned to honor me with the command to send Your Highness some pieces of my Composition: I have in accordance with Your Highness's most gracious orders taken the liberty of rendering my most humble duty to Your Royal Highness with the present Concertos, which I have adapted to several instruments; begging Your Highness most humbly not to judge their imperfection with the rigor of that discriminating and sensitive taste, which everyone knows Him to have for musical works, but rather to take into benign Consideration the profound respect & the most humble obedience which I thus attempt to show Him. For the rest, My Lord, I humbly beg Your Royal Highness to have the goodness to continue Your Highness's gracious favor toward me, and to be assured that nothing is so close to my heart as the wish that I may be employed on occasions more worthy of Your Royal Highness and of Your Highness's service—I, who with unparalleled zeal am,
> My Lord,
> Your Royal Highness's
> Most humble and most obedient servant
> Jean Sebastien Bach
> Coethen, March 24th, 1721

We wince again at the true tale that these Concertos, in one of the most painstakingly beautiful manuscripts Bach ever penned, lay apparently unused for thirteen years in the Margrave's library until his death, whereupon the inventory of His Royal Highness's music did not even include the "Brandenburg" Concertos among the works important enough to be listed by their composers' names. They were lumped together with a miscellaneous job lot of "concertos by various masters" valued at four groschen apiece. Such a price—pennies for six immortal masterpieces—seems to confirm the traditional Romantic view of misunderstood genius.

But the truth is more reassuring. To begin with, the Concertos were not composed for the Margrave of Brandenburg although they were copied into a special presentation manuscript for him. Nor did his estate ever put them up for sale. The now notorious inventory-appraisal was made only to facilitate the division of his estate among his five heirs. And if the Margrave did neglect the Concertos it must have been, in part at least, for the excellent reason that his musical staff (which averaged only six players) was neither large enough nor skilled enough to play them. Even the simplest of the set, No. 6 in B-flat major, would have required the help of at least one outside musician. And the other five "Brandenburg" Concertos demand many more.

For whom, then, *were* these Concertos written and how did Bach come to give copies to the Margrave? Recent musicological sleuthing summarized and interpreted by Heinrich Besseler in the new, scholarly edition of Bach's works demonstrates, beyond reasonable doubt, that the "Brandenburg" Concertos were composed for the young Prince Leopold of Anhalt-Köthen during the wonderfully fruitful years starting in 1717, when Bach was employed at the Court of Köthen. Prince Leopold was far more than the average aristocratic dabbler in music. He played not only the *viola da gamba,* but violin and harpsichord as well, and he sang with a pleasing bass voice. These accomplishments point to a music lover, an amateur in the best eighteenth-century sense of the word: a connoisseur and practitioner of music on a modest scale. "He loved music, he was well acquainted with it, he understood it." This was Bach's comment on his master in later years.

During a visit from Köthen to Berlin in the winter of 1718–19, Bach performed for the Margrave, who asked Bach to send him some of his compositions. Rather tardily—two and a half years later—Bach responded by choosing six concertos from a large supply he had accumulated in Köthen (apparently during the years 1718–21). He copied them out in his best hand with a florid French dedication and sent them to the Margrave. These six were not originally intended to form a unified set; each concerto calls for a different combination of instruments. Their requirements vary from seven to thirteen instruments, although performance practice in Bach's day was flexible enough so that some of the instruments could have been doubled, trebled, or multiplied to form a small chamber orchestra. The varied styles of the six Concertos suggest that they were composed over a span of three to four years. Bach called the set simply *Six Concerts Avec plusieurs Instruments* ("Six Concertos with Various Instruments"). The nickname "Brandenburg" was bestowed on them in the nineteenth century when the handsome manuscript was rediscovered in the Brandenburg archives.

BRANDENBURG CONCERTO NO. 1, F MAJOR, BWV 1046

The First "Brandenburg" Concerto in F major, one of the most brilliant and attractive of the set, is the least frequently performed today, probably because its most prominent solo part is composed for an obsolete instrument. The *violino piccolo* was a small-sized violin tuned a fourth or (as in this case) a major third higher than the standard violin. It bore some resemblance to the so-called half- or three-quarter-sized violins given to small children nowadays before they have the reach to cope with violins of standard size. But the quality of sound was entirely different because of the different tuning. Few musicians today play the *violino piccolo.* We cannot even be certain of exactly how the instrument *did* sound, though it cannot have been as feeble as some modern musicians have imagined—for Bach's *violino piccolo* obviously could hold its own against an oboe solo, a lusty horn, and finally two horns although none of these wind instruments had the overbearing tone of modern winds. In most modern performances the *violino piccolo* is replaced by a standard-size violin.

The First "Brandenburg" Concerto is the only one of the set which exists in two different versions, the earlier one (dating from around 1718) having no solo violin part. In its final form, the small ensemble is grouped into three sharply contrasting colors: (1) a pair of horns (which play in the florid style associated with Baroque trumpets), (2) three oboes, bassoon, and (3) six strings: *violino piccolo,* first and second violins, viola, cello, and double bass. A harpsichord would have been used to round out the ensemble in Bach's day.

I. [*Allegro*]. In Bach's manuscript, the first movement has no tempo mark. But its style and late Baroque tradition tell us that it is a vivacious *Allegro.* It is built around recurrences of the opening refrain:

II. *Adagio.* The melancholy song of this movement passes from solo oboe to *violino piccolo* to the bass line (cello, double bass, bassoon and harpsichord).

III. *Allegro.* A vigorous, jiglike rhythm builds up momentum while playful solos, duets and trios alternate with the brilliance of the full ensemble. Like the opening movement, this one is based on the recurring pattern of its opening refrain:

IV. *Menuet.* A graceful minuet refrain alternates (rondo fashion) with three successive trios dominated in turn by oboes, strings, and French horns.

BRANDENBURG NO. 2, F MAJOR, BWV 1047

Although this Second "Brandenburg" Concerto (like most of the set) was far too demanding for the modest musical staff of the Margrave of Brandenburg, it was perfectly suited for the larger and more sophisticated chamber group maintained by Bach's employer, the Prince of Anhalt-Köthen. The Prince's virtuoso trumpeter (whose name, Johann Ludwig Schreiber, has come down to us in the Köthen archives) must have gloried in his part, which determined so much of the style of the first and last movements. The finale in particular must have sounded extraordinarily brilliant on his instrument, the high Baroque trumpet or *clarino,* as it was called. (This was a "natural" trumpet, without the valves which facilitate the playing of florid scale passages for the modern trumpeter.) Because the *clarino* trumpeter performed chiefly in the highest range of a large-sized instrument, it had a powerful, dazzling tone impossible to duplicate on a standard twentieth-century trumpet.

I. [*Allegro*]. Like two-thirds of the "Brandenburg" Concertos' opening movements, this one bears no tempo mark in Bach's manuscript. But the dominant tradition of Bach's day and the character of the music tell us clearly that it was intended as a brisk *Allegro.* Its fanfare-like refrain seems ideally suited to the trumpet:

Yet Bach gives this refrain first to all the other solo instruments (recorder-flute, oboe, and violin) and the accompanying ensemble before it is finally taken up by the trumpet, almost halfway through the movement. In between the returns of the refrain come light-textured episodes: brief sparkling solos, duets, and trios, all related to each other and to the principal refrain.

II. *Andante.* The slow middle movement is an intimate, introspective piece of chamber music. The trumpet is silent. Only solo violin, oboe, and recorder over a minimum accompaniment of harpsichord and cello take up, one after the other, a pensive, convoluted melody:

III. *Allegro assai.* An exuberant fugue-finale launches the following subject, first in glittering tones of the high *clarino* trumpet:

As one instrument after the other dances upward with the theme, Bach seems a master juggler, exulting in the virtuosity with which he keeps four objects—or rather four solo instruments—flying through the air, each in its own astonishing orbit, each orbit similar, but never quite duplicating any other, and all combining in an effortless, harmonious whole. From a casual listening to this joyous fugue one might never notice that Bach was juggling with what was then considered one of the more difficult, learned contrapuntal procedures of his Baroque age.

The Second "Brandenburg" Concerto is scored for 4 solo instruments: trumpet (*clarino*), flute (recorder), oboe, and violin, with an accompanying group (or *ripieno*) of 2 violins, violas, cello, string bass, and harpsichord.

BRANDENBURG CONCERTO NO. 3, G MAJOR, BWV 1048

The "Brandenburg" Concerto No. 3 in G major, is one of the more conservative of the set, which means, according to Besseler, that it was probably composed early in the Köthen years, about 1718. It is conservative in the sense that this is a true ensemble concerto with no one instrument, or group of instruments, standing out above the others. It is scored for 3 violins, 3 violas, 3 cellos, with the continuo (or thoroughbass) allotted to a harpsichord and string bass. Since Bach's preferred instrument, when he was leading a chamber ensemble, was the viola, it is virtually certain that he played the first viola part in the first performances of this work at Köthen. Since *viola da gamba* players often took over the parts written for the cello, it seems more than likely that Prince Leopold himself played cello in this concerto.

In Bach's day the most modern concerto form was in three movements: fast, slow, fast. But the fast movements seem to have been the most popular, as they were the most exciting and brilliant. In this Third "Brandenburg" Concerto there is no slow middle movement, but only two slow chords providing for a cadenza, where Bach probably expected one or more of his players to improvise.

I. [*Allegro*]. What a pulse, what a stream of vitality flows through the apparently mechanical rhythmic figurations of this opening!

This is not only the start of a far-arching phrase; it is also the thematic root from which springs the luxuriant growth of the entire movement. From time to time we recognize the entire phrase, smaller portions of it, and very often the tiniest rhythmic unit, consisting of only the three-note combination: two eighths and a sixteenth. Sometimes we hear all ten instrumental parts together, sometimes we hear the groups of three each played all against each other. Only very rarely do we hear one or another of the individual parts play a brief solo. A striking device, taken over from Antonio Vivaldi, whom Bach greatly admired, is the massing of the entire group in octaves on a single phrase to mark the conclusion of a major division. The single measure of *Adagio* at the conclusion of the first movement leads without pause into the finale.

II. *Allegro.* For his final movement Bach chose the stylized dance with which Baroque composers loved to conclude their instrumental works. This was the jig, more professionally and fashionably known in the Baroque era as the *gigue.* Such gigues were frequently contrapuntal, even fugal, the beginning of the principal sections clearly imitative. This finale opens with a first violin figure shown below quickly imitated by second violin, third violin, violas and cellos with thoroughbass:

In this movement we have, if possible, an even more mechanical-seeming rhythm: a steady stream of sixteenth notes scarcely interrupted from start to finish of the movement. Yet Bach's robust harmonies and the great swirling melodic lines of his gigue are so powerful that the listener is swept along, as if by a torrent.

BRANDENBURG CONCERTO NO. 4, G MAJOR, BWV 1049

The lightest of the "Brandenburg" Concertos, both in spirit and in physical sound, is the Fourth in G major. To twentieth-century ears, this little masterpiece irresistibly recalls the decorative grace and sparkle of early eighteenth-century architecture, painting, dress, and manners which we call Rococo.

Bach was a towering giant of the late Baroque age, too powerful and too inventive to be bothered much with the fashionable fripperies of his time. Yet when he wished—and in this Concerto he did wish—he could be as urbane, as charming, and witty as the most worldy musician of a Parisian salon. With a mastery that amounted to sleight of hand, he simply took over whatever dazzling new devices appealed to him and combined them with his rich store of traditional techniques and forms.

An old-fashioned instrument used for new-fashioned purposes in this Concerto is the recorder, or *flauto dolce* (soft flute), as it was sometimes called. For his high-pitched solo group (*concertino*) Bach used 2 recorders and a single virtuoso violin. His background (*ripieno*) group was a string quintet with harpsichord.

I. *Allegro.* Instead of starting with the traditional, solid sound of the full ensemble, Bach launches his Concerto with an airy duet for 2 recorders. Their fluttering arpeggios and dipping parallel thirds supply the thematic foundation for this entire movement:

The middle part of the movement is dominated by breathtaking flights of the solo violin.

II. *Andante.* Even the pensive middle movement preserves some of the decorative grace which is so important in this Concerto. In Bach's day *andante* had not yet acquired its later connotation of "slow" (sometimes very slow), but was closer to its original meaning of "going" or "walking"—which means that the tempo of the movement should never drag, nor should the thoughtful mood ever become lugubrious.

III. *Presto.* The glittering final fugue is developed from the following theme:

To interweave and even combine virtuoso violin acrobatics with the structural strength of a master fugue seems a sort of impossibility. Bach makes it sound not only easy but exhilarating.

BRANDENBURG CONCERTO NO. 5, D MAJOR, BWV 1050

In the chamber music sessions at the Court of Köthen Bach himself habitually played the viola. But in this D-major "Brandenburg" Concerto, Bach apparently made an exception and took instead the unusually brilliant and prominent harpsichord part.

So prominent is the harpsichord, so far does it overshadow the two other solo instruments (solo flute and solo violin) that this Concerto actually counts as the earliest known concerto for solo harpsichord, and thus as the earliest known ancestor of the piano concerto. The solo flute called for in this Concerto is specifically a transverse flute, that is to say essentially our modern flute, as opposed to the old recorder, which Bach had used predominately in his earlier works. This and many other "modern" traits have led scholars to conclude that the Fifth "Brandenburg" Concerto was the last composed, presumably during the winter of 1720–21. It is cast in the "modern" three-movement form which Bach preferred.

I. *Allegro.* The brilliant, impassioned first movement opens with the following vigorous theme:

The theme is spun out for eight vigorous measures of orchestral *tutti.* These eight measures serve as a broad refrain, which returns again to round off the movement at its conclusion and to punctuate its middle point. Often the first two measures alone return as lesser punctuation points in the brilliant interplay which now ensues between the *tutti* and the three solo instruments; violin, flute, and harpsichord. Various lighter, often tiny, graceful ideas are introduced in the course of this interplay, as in the following sequence for violin and flute:

Yet, it is the harpsichord which dominates more and more, emerging at last into its gigantic, sixty-five-measure written-out cadenza. The concluding refrain is identical with the opening of the movement.

II. *Affettuoso.* It is interesting, and typical of the time, that Bach's earlier version of this movement is marked simply *Largo.* The final marking—*Affettuoso*—shows the trend of the day toward more sentiment, sensibility or *Empfindsamkeit.* The melancholy theme is announced by the solo violin and immediately imitated by the flute as follows:

Although the movement is performed by the three solo instruments alone, Bach has written the harpsichord part in such a manner that the right and left hands often function like separate instruments, and the texture of the movement is that of a quartet rather than a trio.

III. *Allegro.* The third movement is a marvelous example of Bach's love of amalgamating old and new. Its overall form is the three-part (ABA) form of the fashionable *da capo* operatic aria. The first and last sections are written in the older, more "learned" style of a fugue. The fugue subject is announced by the solo violin and immediately imitated by the solo flute, by the harpsichord left hand, then right hand, and finally by the orchestral *tutti.* The texture is often light, airy, even frivolous for a fugue. In the middle section it grows even lighter, and almost begins to resemble the later Classical development-section style. The whole movement has an exuberant mastery which reminds us that Bach, conservative as he was, could write as brilliantly and as modernly as anyone.

The "Brandenburg" Concerto No. 5 is scored for solo flute, solo violin, harpsichord *concertato,* and a string ensemble consisting of 1 violin part, 1 viola part, 1 cello part and 1 double bass part. At Köthen only one instrument would have played each part of this four-part ensemble. But where a large complement of strings was available it would also have been possible to double, triple or otherwise enlarge the basic string group. Thus, a concerto of this kind might be performed either as solo chamber music or as a work for small orchestra.

BRANDENBURG CONCERTO, NO. 6, B-FLAT MAJOR, BWV 1051

At least five of the six "Brandenburg" Concertos fit the (recently discovered) records of the musical resources at the Court of Köthen so precisely that the Concertos must have been written for that smaller, but more musical court. Indeed, No. 6 in B flat seems to have been composed with two particularly important local performers in mind: Bach himself and Prince Leopold of Anhalt-Köthen.

The Prince, whom Bach served from 1717 to 1723 as Kapellmeister, was a very active music patron. He sang, he played harpsichord and violin, but his principal instrument was the *viola da gamba.* The *gamba,* approximately the size of a cello, but with a thinner body with frets across the fingerboard and a delicate tone, was growing obsolete, although it had been a favorite of the aristocracy since Shakespeare's day. Good Bardolaters will recall Sir Toby Belch's puff for Sir Andrew Aguecheek in *Twelfth Night*: "he plays o' th' viol-de-gamboys and speaks three or four languages word for word without book, and hath all the good gifts of nature."

The "Brandenburg" Concerto Number 6, may have been written to give Prince Leopold a not too demanding part on his *viola da gamba.* Nowadays the Concerto is most often performed by orchestral ensembles with the *gamba* parts given to cellos. But its original scoring is for 7 instruments: 2 violas, 2 *gambas,* cello, and continuo (double bass and harpsichord). A professional gambist was available on Leopold's staff for the second gamba part. Bach himself preferred, in ensembles, to play the viola and he did so in this Concerto. The second viola, cello and continuo parts would not have been hard to fill from the twelve remaining instrumentalists of the Köthen court staff.

Besseler sets the date of this Concerto—the earliest of the six—around 1718 and points out that it is virtually a concerto for two solo violas. It is related in many ways to Bach's D-minor Concerto for Two Violins, BWV 1043, which was composed close to this time, perhaps a year or two later.

I. [*Allegro*]. The Concerto opens with a spirited chase, a canon, in which the first viola (or first viola section) is pursued by the second, playing the identical melody—except that the pursuing voice, having started a fraction of a beat later, is syncopated throughout. The pursuit continues through a full fifteen measures of exuberant, driving melody which climbs and tumbles over half a dozen musical hills and dales before pausing for breath. The opening:

later becomes a refrain, returning three times in changing keys, and concluding in the home key of B flat with a complete restatement of the opening canon. In between there are lighter passages in which fragments of the canon, especially the first three notes, are tossed about among the instruments.

II. *Adagio ma non tanto.* The songful, slow movement, a wonderful combination of poignance and repose, is a duet for the first and second violas. As the melody unfolds and develops, we hear more of the little three-note dip which opened the first movement, but now slowed down to suit its new environment.

III. *Allegro.* Lively as the first movement, the finale has the added impetus of rhythms derived from the jig or *gigue,* as it was called on the Continent. In conformance with an almost archaic Baroque tradition, its refrain is a varied version of the first-movement opening:

Like the first movement, this finale is built around its recurrent refrain interspersed with sprightlier conversational episodes and running comment for the first and second violas.

TWO CONCERTOS FOR VIOLIN AND ORCHESTRA, BWV 1041 AND BWV 1042

Johann Sebastian Bach's two surviving concertos for violin solo are among the greatest treasures of the literature. Beethoven, Mendelssohn, Brahms, Tchaikovsky—each has left us only one great violin concerto. Although Mozart left us a group of six early violin concertos, these, for all their undying youth and grace, do not rival the cosmic range of his own piano concertos.

Bach's two concertos were fashioned for the eighteenth-century court of Anhalt-Köthen with its appreciative private audience. Bach was stationed here during the years 1717–23. These were happy years, for the Prince appreciated Kapellmeister Bach and the music he wrote for his eighteen-piece orchestra. There was little religious music at court, but in the chamber and orchestral works the Prince preferred, Bach showed he could be as worldly and joyful as the next man, and that he could both move his listeners and entertain them as well.

These two violin concertos were conceived for an ensemble so small that to us today it would seem a chamber group, rather than a full-fledged symphony orchestra. The solo is almost totally lacking in the bravura display which became such an important and popular part of the Romantic violin concerto. Bach does not even try to rival the brilliance of Antonio Vivaldi's violin concertos, which served him as his models. Instead he writes for such music lovers as his understanding Prince. Externally the music is sober, as chamber music often is. But its rhythms dance, its melodic line soars, its harmonies branch and blossom with a richness and a sense of inevitable growth in which Bach has no equal.

CONCERTO FOR VIOLIN AND ORCHESTRA, A MINOR, BWV 1041

The A-minor Concerto is cast in the popular late Baroque three-movement form.

I. [*Allegro*]. Although the manuscript bears no first-movement tempo mark, none was needed in Bach's day, for tradition and the character of this opening movement call for *allegro*. Its *ritornello* form is based on an opening refrain, which returns thrice to punctuate the movement and a last time to round off the close. Contrasting episodes separate the five refrains. The melody of each section seems to flow on with uninterrupted drive.

II. *Andante*. Over a repetitive figure in the bass, a *semi-ostinato*, an elaborately ornamented solo line unfolds. Characteristic of the middle section are long, drawn-out solo notes followed by great dipping curves like the following:

III. *Allegro assai*. A sort of exalted orchestral jig, the finale is even more driving than the opening movement. With a melody that never seems to pause for breath, it drives on in familiar *ritornello* pattern.

CONCERTO FOR VIOLIN AND ORCHESTRA, E MAJOR, BWV 1042

I. *Allegro*. Three heavy "hammer strokes," with which the principal theme begins, were a striking device—almost a trick—which Bach took over from Italians like Vivaldi. Such "hammer strokes" served, among other things, to call attention to the many returns of the movement's vigorous refrain:

In broad structure the movement is a balanced, three-part ABA form, like the popular operatic *da capa aria.* The contrasting middle (B) section develops fragments of the refrain, especially of its opening "hammer strokes."

II. *Adagio.* The slow movement presents the solo violin in a delicately embellished, expressive melody over a recurrent rhythmic figure in the low strings.

III. *Allegro.* The finale is built on the following exuberant refrain, bounding upward over an octave and a half:

Easier to follow than even the *ritornello* form, the rondo form of this finale keeps its refrain identical, always the same sixteen measures in the same key of E major throughout its five appearances. The contrasting episodes also are sixteen measures apiece, excepting the last, which is thirty-two. Yet despite this almost mechanically balanced form, the feeling is one of irresistible forward drive.

The E major Violin Concerto is scored for four-part string ensemble with harpsichord and solo violin.

CONCERTO FOR TWO VIOLINS AND ORCHESTRA, D MINOR, BWV 1043

Although this glorious Concerto in D minor is traditionally known as a "double concerto," it is in fact one of the most beautiful examples we know of the much more familiar, standard, and enormously popular eighteenth-century form: the concerto grosso. In this form a small group of solo instruments, frequently two solo violins, supported by a continuo group (usually a harpsichord, cello, and double bass) is played off against the larger orchestral group, or *tutti.* The small group was called, logically enough, the *concertino,* while the larger ensemble was known as the concerto grosso, and it was the latter term which came to be applied to the composition type as a whole. The title on Bach's manuscript makes it unmistakably clear that this was the category of work to which he considered his D-minor Concerto to belong: *Concerto à 6, 2 violini concertini, 2 violini e 1 viola di ripieno, violoncello e continuo di J. S. Bach.* Bach's famous ensembles, which have come down to us under the title of "Brandenburg" Concertos, belong to this same category of concerto grosso, the chief difference being that those of the "Brandenburg" set call for slightly larger and more varied solo groups.

All of these, the D-minor "Double Concerto," the "Brandenburg" Concertos, Bach's two solo Violin Concertos in A minor and E major as well as a number of other chamber works, were composed for the court of Prince Leopold of Anhalt-Köthen, where Bach was stationed during the years 1717–23.

The Concerto is cast in the popular late Baroque three-movement form: fast, slow, fast.

I. *Vivace.* The dynamic opening of the movement is cast in a popular form beautifully adapted to building up the rhythmic momentum so dear to Baroque composers and listeners, a *ritornello* form in which the *ritornello,* or refrain, established at the very opening by the full orchestra returns (in part or in whole) at intervals throughout the movement. In between these main pillars of the form the soloists of the *concertino* intervene with episodes of lighter texture and often of contrasting thematic material. The principal phrase on which this entire opening movement is based is proclaimed at the outset by the second violins in unison with the second violin soloist:

The same figure is taken up almost immediately at a higher pitch by the first violins and the first soloist. After some twenty measures of full orchestral introduction, the large ensemble falls quiet to throw the two soloists into sharper relief. The remainder of the movement consists principally of similar alternations between the *concertino* and concerto grosso, and it is rounded off with one final emphatic citation of the Concerto's opening measures.

II. *Largo ma non tanto.* The slow movement, which in the opinion of many music lovers is the crown of the work, is dominated by the two soloists. Once again it is the second soloist who leads with the principal melody:

III. *Allegro.* The lively finale is dominated by a more complex refrain, which starts with a cascade of imitative counterpoint, led off this time by the first soloist:

Both style and form of the finale are considerably freer than those of the first movement although the basic *ritornello* structure is the same in both. In this movement the contrasts between the solo group of the *concertino* and the larger orchestral *tutti* are not quite so drastic, there are subtler transitions and a greater thematic variety, but no slackening of the dynamic rhythmic drive. The Concerto ranks high even among the works of such a giant as J. S. Bach, and its popularity seems to grow with the years.

CONCERTO FOR VIOLIN, OBOE, AND ORCHESTRA, C MINOR, BWV 1060
The immense riches of Bach's concertos were late in entering the international concert repertory. There was one very good reason for this: during Bach's lifetime there was no such thing as an international concert repertory.

It seems likely that Bach composed the first version of this Concerto for a coffeehouse concert—at Zimmermann's Coffeehouse, to be exact, in the Catherinenstrasse of Leipzig—on a Friday evening between eight and ten o'clock. Or, if the premiere took place during the celebrated Leipzig Fair (even today, the Leipzig Fair is still the most important annual business exposition in East Germany), it could have been a Tuesday. During Fair times (in Bach's day there were several: Easter, September, and others) the Collegium Musicum performed *twice* a week at the coffeehouse. The year would have been close to 1730, soon after Bach was appointed conductor of the Collegium. This group consisted largely of students, but included good musicians, many of whom later became virtuosos. Their concerts were predecessors of the regular professional concerts, which later developed into such famous subscription series as the Leipzig Gewandhaus concerts.

No matter how grand the coffeehouse, the audiences could hardly have been large. And the performing group was closer to what we think of as a chamber ensemble than to a symphony orchestra. Bach probably conducted from the harpsichord, which would enable him to reassure a faltering player and keep a firm grip on the rhythm of the ensemble.

To keep his Collegium supplied with new music for weekly concerts must have been a taxing job in itself. Many of Bach's works, originals as well as arrangements of his own and other composers' works, probably were produced for these modest weekly gatherings.

This Concerto for Violin and Oboe is a reconstruction of a lost Bach original. What survives is Bach's *arrangement* (for 2 harpsichords and orchestra) of his earlier concerto composed for either 2 violins or violin and oboe. Modern research leans toward the latter combination, and it is for these two instruments that the best reconstructions have been made. The process of reconstruction was fairly simple. The right hands of both harpsichord parts were transferred to the solo violin and oboe. The orchestral accompaniment remained virtually unchanged.

In its three-movement, fast-slow-fast, structure, this Concerto follows the model of the Vivaldi concertos, which were enormously popular in Bach's day and which he admired.

I. *Allegro.* The first movement is cast in the traditional late Baroque form of a recurrent main theme for the orchestral *tutti,* alternating with lighter episodes for the solo instruments. This main theme is a vigorous figure given out in the opening measures:

Sometimes the intervening episodes are spun out of a fragment of the main theme, sometimes they seem to be playfully fresh inventions. In the last analysis, the degree of connection between the episodes and the principal theme depends on the listener's imagination. The *tutti* refrain is heard in several closely related keys and returns to round off the movement with a final and complete restatement of its original form.

II. *Adagio.* The slow middle movement is a duet for the two solo instruments, a melancholy outpouring in which the two instruments almost seem to sing. The style of the beautiful melodic arch is vocal, certainly, yet with a certain instrumental touch, characteristic of Bach, even when writing for the human voice. The accompaniment by the full string orchestra is kept so discreetly in the background that one never thinks of it as an orchestral *tutti.* The movement concludes on a dominant harmony, producing a feeling of mild suspense resolved by the last movement which follows immediately.

III. *Allegro.* The finale is a fiery piece cast in the same basic form as the opening movement, that is to say: alternating *tutti* and solo passages. The recurrent *tutti* theme, which is given out immediately at the beginning, is a bold, assertive figure:

This finale has even more brilliance and drive than the opening movement did. Twice during the finale, the solo violin is given fast, triplet figurations over sustained chords in the orchestra, building considerable tension that is released in the final triumphant statement of the powerful opening theme.

Aside from the two solo instruments, the Concerto is scored for string orchestra only. It was understood in Bach's time that the ensemble would be completed by a keyboard instrument—in this case, presumably the harpsichord.

ORCHESTRAL SUITES (OVERTURES) BWV 1066–1069

The four masterworks we know today as Bach's "orchestral suites" were not originally called suites at all, but "overtures." The term "orchestral suites" is an invention, an "improvement" on Bach by nineteenth-century scholars and publishers who collaborated in the idealistic task of exhuming the enormous body of his surviving works from the archives and libraries where the (mostly manuscript) copies had lain largely forgotten for the better part of a century. During that time an appalling number of Bach's works, possibly a quarter of the total output, was lost or destroyed out of indifference or neglect, and probably will never be recovered. We may never know, for example, how many orchestral suites or overtures Bach may have written in addition to the four that survived.

Bach and his contemporaries who wrote such works all called them overtures simply because they were modeled after the operatic overtures which were originally composed for the pace-setting court of Louis XIV and had become one of the most popular forms of independent orchestral music. Because of their association with the court of Versailles, they had a connotation of royal majesty. They became firmly identified with the power and brilliance first of the "Sun King" and then of royalty in general. A century later, when Mozart invoked God as "King of tremendous majesty" *("Rex tremendae maiestatis")* in his Requiem Mass,he used the traditional pompous French overture style.

But from Lully to Mozart, no one ever surpassed Bach in the depiction of majesty and the four overtures which open and dominate each of his four orchestral suites are among his most majestic achievements. The custom of rounding off the grandiose Baroque overtures with a string of dances and other light pieces was perhaps suggested by popular Rococo collections (suites) of dances for chamber or keyboard instruments.

We do not know just when Bach composed his orchestral suites; the original manuscripts have all disappeared and only later copies have survived. Probably three of the four were composed for the worldly little court of Köthen shortly before he moved to Leipzig in 1723, and the fourth shortly thereafter. But these orchestral suites were too good to be simply laid aside after one or two performances. Bach continued to use them, sometimes in revised form. The earliest surviving copies suggest that Bach conducted all four suites at concerts of the Telemann Musical Society or Collegium Musicum which he directed for several years, starting in 1729.

While the Collegium was essentially a group of skilled amateurs their affairs were controlled by the court in Dresden, and their concerts were public. They must have been modest gatherings, since they were held in a coffeehouse: Zimmermann's Coffeehouse on a corner of Leipzig's Catharinenstrasse, Friday evenings from eight to ten during the winter. During the famous Leipzig Fair, when many people came from out of town, there were two concerts a week, on Tuesdays and Fridays. During the summer season the Collegium concerts moved out of doors to Zimmermann's coffee-garden just outside the old town walls by the Grimma Gate, not far from the present-day Leipzig Opera House. The summer concerts were held Wednesday afternoons from four to six. These coffeehouse (and coffee-garden) concerts were predecessors of the regular professional series which developed later in the century into such famous institutions as the Leipzig Gewandhaus concerts.

Each of Bach's orchestral suites was written for a different combination of instruments.

ORCHESTRAL SUITE NO. 1, C MAJOR, BWV 1066

Although we cannot be absolutely certain, the evidence of the music itself suggests that the Suite No. 1 is in fact the oldest of the four. The relatively old-fashioned fugue theme of the Overture, and other details, recall several of Bach's works dating from Köthen around the year 1718. It is composed for 2 oboes, bassoon and string ensemble with harpsichord.

I. *Ouverture.* [*Grave; Allegro*]. This opening is Bach at his most vigorous. The wonderful, striding bass, in particular, never lets us lose the almost physical feeling of dynamic forward motion—no matter how grandly deliberate the ceremonial tempo of French overture tradition may be.

Two oboes announce the sudden shift to this fast-moving athletic theme, which is developed in fugal style:

II. *Courante.* This is a lively triple-rhythm dance with subtly shifting accents, which leads off with the following characteristic pattern:

III. *Gavotte.* Originally a very straightforward peasant dance, then a ballroom dance, this *gavotte* assumes an added spice with Bach's sophisticated rhythms. There is a florid middle section, sometimes called a second *gavotte,* after which the first returns.

IV. *Forlane.* A lilting Italian dance, the *forlane* had come, by Bach's time, to be associated with French depictions of the carnival of Venice.

V. *Menuet.* Bach's use of the French names for the dances shows that here —as well as in his overture—he is taking his cue from French traditions.

VI. *Bourrée.* Originally a French peasant dance, the *bourrée* is imaginatively expanded here and made to sound like a subtle variation on the theme of the preceding *menuet* and on the concluding *passepied.*

VII. *Passepied.* A popular dance at the court of Versailles, the *passepied* provides a brilliant finale to this first orchestral suite.

ORCHESTRAL SUITE NO. 2, B MINOR, BWV 1067

Bach's Second Orchestral Suite is his only work that has survived for solo flute and orchestra. It is his closest approximation to a flute concerto. (The instrument in this case is the modern "transverse" flute, basically the same instrument still in use today, not the older recorder flute, which still plays such a charming role in Bach's Fourth "Brandenburg" Concerto in G major.) To Bach experts, including Heinrich Besseler, the editor of the Orchestral Overtures in the New Complete Edition of Bach, the style of the music suggests that it was written at the Court of Köthen about 1721.

I. *Ouverture.* The many jagged ("dotted") rhythms and the profusion of the trills give a sharply characteristic profile to the slow introduction. The high-spirited fugue that follows is beautifully suited to the light instrumentation with its graceful curves and almost butterfly lightness of the passages for solo flute. The concluding page returns briefly to the material of the slow introduction.

II. *Rondeau.* The special attraction of this movement is its beguiling refrain which launches the *Rondeau* and seems to sound better with each of its four subsequent returns.

III. *Sarabande.* The *sarabande* was the stateliest of the dance rhythms popular in arias, concertos, and in suites.

IV. *Bourrée.* This is the only dance movement of the Second Orchestral Suite to use the older three-part form, with a contrasting *bourrée* section in the middle, followed by a return of the opening section.

V. *Polonaise: Lentement.* The ceremonial reserve of this "Polonaise" (or "Polish Dance") no longer sounds particularly Polish, even to Poles themselves, but it has an insinuating grace which sticks in the memory and defies analysis. Here is its opening phrase:

After we have savored the melody as melody on the top of the ensemble, Bach shifts it to the bottom of the group and decorates it above with the capricious embroidery of a solo flute variation, or *double*:

The movement concludes with a recall of the original tune, unembellished.

VI. *Menuet.* The leisurely minuet is a variation on the preceding variation (i.e.: on the solo flute *double* of the "Polonaise").

VII. *Badinerie.* With the art that conceals art Bach allows a frisky "Badinerie" ("Bantering") to crown his masterpiece with laughter—or is it a chuckle? —for the solo flute:

But the curious-minded may discover, even in Bach's laughter, a scarcely disguised continuity: a variation of the "Polonaise" melody, which in turn was a subtler variation on preceding dances in this suite, the entire principle of which takes us back to the varied dance-pairs of the Middle Ages.

ORCHESTRAL SUITE NO. 3, D MAJOR, BWV 1068

"The opening [of the Suite No. 3] is so pompous and dignified," said Goethe when Mendelssohn played it to him on the piano in 1830, "that one can really envision an assemblage of important people descending a grand flight of steps." For once Goethe's musical intuition was right. Or perhaps Mendelssohn's performance was overwhelming. In any case, the French overture form, which Bach used to open the Suite, still conveyed the impression of royal pomp and majesty stemming from opera and other musical and dramatic acts of homage to Louis XIV at the court of Versailles.

I. *Ouverture.* The traditional French overture form opens with a powerful and imposing slow introduction characterized by heavy, dotted rhythms. This leads to an energetic orchestral fugue built on the following subject:

The Overture is rounded off with a return of the pompous dotted rhythms of the opening.

II. *Air.* The slow second movement is probably better known to music lovers the world over than almost any other Bach composition. Under the title "Air for The G String," an arrangement made by the German violinist Wilhelmj, it is beloved by many people who have never heard of the D-major Suite. Here is Bach's opening phrase, unedited:

III. *Gavotte.* The *gavotte* was originally a French folk dance which made its way via the ballroom to the dance movements of Baroque instrumental works. This movement is a sturdy rhythmic piece with a contrasting middle section, after which the opening is brought back.

IV. *Bourrée.* The *bourrée* too was originally an old French folk dance. The fact that its name comes from the word *bourrir* (meaning to flap the wings) suggests that it may go back to very primitive dances, possibly even of totem origin, in which the dancers imitated the movements of ritual beasts and birds.

V. *Gigue.* The jig, with its exuberant, driving triple rhythm, was a great favorite for the final movements of Baroque suites, sonatas and concertos.

The Third Suite is scored for 2 oboes, 3 trumpets, kettledrums, and the usual strings with continuo, which normally would have meant the inclusion of a harpsichord.

ORCHESTRAL SUITE NO. 4, D MAJOR, BWV 1069

Bach's C-major Orchestral Suite is the most "modern" of the four and the only one which is believed to have been composed in Leipzig—at least in the form that has come down to us. Fragments of an earlier version (without trumpets and drums) *may* date back to Bach's Köthen years, but this has never been proved. And since the fragments are small, we may never know. It does seem certain that the very festive final version of the Suite, with the addition of three trumpets and drums, must have been composed for some special occasion, probably in 1725 at the latest. Like the three earlier Suites, it probably regaled the audiences of Bach's Collegium Musicum at Zimmermann's Coffeehouse.

I. *Ouverture: Grave—Allegro—Grave.* The Overture opens with a sedate but vigorous section in the characteristically dotted rhythm associated with royal majesty and pomp. The texture of this opening is strongly contrapuntal, and tension is built up for the final cadence by a long, sustained note (or pedal-point) in the bass. A lively, fugue-like section in a lilting 9/8 meter is the main part of this movement. At the end, the form is rounded off by a return of the pompous dotted rhythms.

II. *Bourrée.* The *bourrée* of this Overture opens with the following lively phrase:

Bach follows a baroque usage of long standing by basing the opening phrases of successive dance movements on the identical figure, as in a set of variations. This movement has a middle section (*bourrée* 2) in the relative minor key, after which the first section (*bourrée* 1) is repeated.

III. *Gavotte.* The *gavotte,* too, was originally a French folk-dance, which made its way via the ballroom to the dance movements of baroque instrumental compositions. This movement is a sturdy rhythmic piece in two sections, each of which is repeated.

IV. *Menuetto.* This minuet, like those of many baroque composers, is a more straightforward, vigorous piece than the rather delicate aristocratic type that we associate with Mozart. This one is scored for strings and woodwinds, without the trumpets and kettledrums that lend such brilliance to the other movements of the Overture.

V. *Réjouissance.* Although it is not a dance form, this sparkling, little finale derives from the same phrase as the *bourrée,* which now takes the following shape:

In addition to the 3 trumpets and kettledrums mentioned above, the Fourth Suite enlists 3 oboes, a bassoon, harpsichord, and the traditional string instruments.

Samuel Barber

Born March 9, 1910, West Chester, Pennsylvania

CONCERTO FOR PIANO AND ORCHESTRA, OPUS 38

Although Samuel Barber had achieved fame and popularity by the time he was twenty, and although he continued to compose, with growing reputation, for most of the traditional orchestra, choral, solo, and chamber music combinations, he was past fifty before he composed a piano concerto. It was commissioned by the music publishing firm of G. Schirmer on the occasion of its 100th anniversary in 1961, and completed on September 9, 1962, at the composer's home, "Capricorn," near Mount Kisco, New York. The first performance was presented by the Boston Symphony Orchestra under the direction of Erich Leinsdorf on September 24, 1962 in Philharmonic Hall as part of the festivities of the opening week of the Lincoln Center for the Performing Arts in New York.

Almost immediately it became one of Barber's most highly regarded and widely performed works. In less than a year it had been heard in Boston, London, Brussels, the festivals of Spoleto and Tanglewood, and was scheduled for forty further performances in the British Isles, on the European continent, and in North and South America.

I. *Allegro appassionato.* The first movement opens with a short unaccompanied cadenza for the solo piano, introducing in bare, brilliant octaves, what eventually becomes the most prominent theme of the movement. Some of the rhythmic developments of the movement are also hinted before the orchestra joins the soloist, leading to a broad orchestral exposition of a fresh, lyric phrase:

This latter turns out to be the opening theme of a traditional first-movement sonata-allegro form. The orchestral statement of the phrase is echoed by the piano solo. An emphatic rhythmic figure marked "arrogant" leads to an expressive soft solo for flute, a gentle lyric statement of the theme announced so boldly by the piano solo at the very opening of its initial cadenza. This is the phrase which is most frequently recalled in the rich development that follows.

A virtuosic cadenza for the solo instrument, built on both principal themes, leads to the reprise of the basic thematic material and a poetic coda.

II. *Canzone: Moderato.* The songful middle movement, which has an almost chamber music lightness of texture, is in a simple two-part form. Muted strings often played *tremolando,* supply a gossamer background for discreet woodwind solos and the solo piano.

III. *Allegro molto.* The fiercely energetic finale resembles a free rondo with two main recurring musical thoughts. The first is the aggressive five-note figure proclaimed twice in succession at the very outset by the full orchestra. The second is an incisive *ostinato* figure with which the piano solo makes its entry:

The asymmetrical 5/8 beat, which continues throughout, accounts for some of the rhythmic drive of this movement. There is a slight relaxation of pace for some of the contrasting episodes, one of which begins with a solo clarinet accompanied by xylophone, and another of which has an almost scherzo-like lightness and humor. The brilliant conclusion recalls the opening motive.

The score, which is dedicated to Manfred Ibel, calls for piccolo, 2 flutes, 2 oboes, English horn, 2 clarinets, bass clarinet, 2 bassoons, 4 horns in F, 3 trumpets, 3 trombones, timpani, snare drum, bass drum, cymbals, suspended cymbal, antique cymbals, tom-tom, tam-tam (low), triangle, xylophone, whip, harp, and the customary strings.

CONCERTO FOR VIOLIN AND ORCHESTRA, OPUS 14

Looking nostalgically to the past and impatiently forward to the future, this Concerto is a pivotal work. Its two contrasting musical styles reflect a crisis in Samuel Barber's development which coincided with a crisis in world history: the outbreak of World War II. It would be hard to show a direct, one-to-one relationship between the German-Soviet invasion of Poland in September 1939 and the change in Barber's musical style; but one does not have to be a mystic to feel that a connection does exist, no matter how ripe Barber may have been for the change.

The first two movements of the Concerto are conservative and warmly romantic. They echo the lyric style of such early works as his *Essay for Orchestra* (1937), his First Symphony (1936), or even his Overture to *The School for Scandal* (1932), which won him prompt recognition, prizes, fellowships, and widespread popularity. The finale of the Concerto is more aggressive, with stronger dissonances and irregular driving rhythms, foreshadowing the more contemporary style of his Second Symphony (1944), *Capricorn Concerto* (1944), and his music for Martha Graham's ballet *The Serpent Heart* (1946), from which his orchestral suite *Medea* is drawn.

The songfulness which dominated Barber's early works and which returns, transmuted, in such mature works as his Cello Concerto (1945), may be related to his particular background. A nephew of the great American contralto Louise Homer, he was precocious musically. Barber started composing when he was seven years old (his musical training had started one year earlier), and he was only thirteen when he entered the Curtis Institute of Music in Philadelphia. Before graduating he won a $1,200 prize for his Overture to *The School for Scandal.*

His extensive European travels, which had begun when he was eighteen, now became extended periods of residence abroad for study and composition. In this he was helped by a number of further prizes and awards, including a Pulitzer Traveling Scholarship and the American Prix de Rome.

The Violin Concerto was a commission for the protégé of a wealthy American businessman. In the summer of 1939, after a visit to England and Scotland, Barber settled in the small Swiss village of Sils Maria to write the Concerto. The score developed slowly. Before the end of the summer, Barber went to Paris, where he hoped to complete his work in the fall. But hardly had he arrived in the French capital when all Americans were warned to leave. While he was crossing the Atlantic, news came that the Nazis had invaded Poland. Back in the United States, Barber joined the faculty of his alma mater, the Curtis Institute, to teach orchestration.

When he showed the finished first two movements of his Concerto to the violinist, the young virtuoso complained that they were too simple and lacking in the brilliance a concerto should have. In his otherwise illuminating biography of the composer, Nathan Broder tactfully withholds the name of the young virtuoso. But he does tell us that Barber promised to give the young man ample opportunity to display his technical brilliance in the finale. Alas, when the finale was completed, the violinist declared it was too difficult.

On this ground the sponsor demanded his money back. Unfortunately the money had already been spent in Europe. But Barber persuaded a different violinist, Oscar Shumsky, to play the finale in private, thus proving it was not unperformable. The upshot of the affair was that the composer returned half of his fee, and the violinist for whom it had been commissioned relinquished his right to the first performance. It was Albert Spalding, instead, who was the soloist for the premiere on February 7, 1941, with the Philadelphia Orchestra under the direction of Eugene Ormandy. The Concerto is in the traditional three movements.

I. *Allegro.* The first movement begins quietly, its graceful main theme sung by the violin solo:

The long, lyric arch of this theme is too long to quote. Indeed, the entire opening section is a single uninterrupted phrase of twenty-seven bars for violin solo up to the point where a fresh theme makes its appearance. This is a perky, syncopated little figure, using a rhythm known as the "Scotch snap," although it is also typical of American jazz. It is presented first by a solo clarinet and then developed by orchestra and soloist with great warmth and lyricism in traditional first-movement form.

II. *Andante.* The slow movement is, if possible, even more songful than the first. The mood is hushed. Over muted strings a single oboe intones a melody of great simplicity and melancholy. Like the opening theme of the first movement, the melody here has a strong rhythmic profile, with characteristic shifts among rhythmic groupings of two, three, and four notes. There is a contrasting middle section and a return to the opening melody, which rises to a climax of great intensity and concludes with a sudden return to the hushed mood of the beginning.

III. *Presto in moto perpetuo.* The fiery finale begins with a flurry of suppressed excitement. The brief opening solo of muffled kettledrums sets the perpetual motion pattern, which is then taken over by the solo violin. This triplet rhythm with occasional syncopated counter-rhythms dominates the entire movement until the sudden vertiginous change of pace in the brilliant concluding measures of the Concerto.

The Concerto is scored for 2 flutes, 2 oboes, 2 clarinets, 2 bassoons, 2 horns, 2 trumpets, kettledrums, military drum, piano, string choir, and the solo violin.

FIRST ESSAY FOR ORCHESTRA, OPUS 12

During the summer of 1937, Arturo Toscanini was preparing his programs for the first season of the NBC Symphony Orchestra; Artur Rodzinski was supervising the organization of the new orchestra. When Toscanini asked Rodzinski about some American work to perform, Rodzinski advised him to play a work of Samuel Barber. Toscanini replied that he would like to see a short *new* piece by Barber. On the strength of this news, Barber set to work. By October he had finished the *Essay for Orchestra,* which he submitted to Toscanini. He waited for Toscanini's verdict. At the end of his season, Toscanini sailed for Europe and returned the score to Barber without comment. The disappointed composer began to look for other conductors who might perform his new score.

That summer (1938) Barber decided not to accompany his friend Gian-Carlo Menotti when Menotti visited the Toscaninis at their summer home on Lake Maggiore, although Barber had visited them there earlier. When Toscanini asked why Barber had not come, Menotti claimed that Barber was ill. "Oh," said Toscanini, "he's perfectly well; he's just angry with me. But he has no reason to be—I'm going to do *both* of his pieces." (The second piece was Barber's *Adagio for Strings.*) But Toscanini did not ask for the scores again until one day before the first rehearsal; he had already memorized them. The premier took place as promised on November 5, 1938, and the *Essay for Orchestra* became one of Barber's most popular works.

It begins with a simple lyric theme in a quiet melancholy mood:

Heard first in the sober tone of violas, the theme is taken up by the violins, then by horns, develops to a brief but powerful climax. There is a delicate scherzo-like middle section, which grows more and more agitated. The opening theme is heard in the background sung broadly by a French horn. The agitation increases, and at its height the theme surges back into the foreground in a passionate outburst. Then, instead of a conventional reprise of the opening section, the orchestra suddenly subsides. The music fades on a slow echo of the opening, a phrase of brevity and poignance, and the tale is told.

The *Essay for Orchestra,* later renamed *First Essay for Orchestra,* is scored for 2 flutes, 2 oboes, 2 clarinets, 2 bassoons, 4 horns, 3 trumpets, 3 trombones, tuba, kettledrums, piano, and the traditional strings.

SECOND ESSAY FOR ORCHESTRA

Samuel Barber's *Second Essay for Orchestra* was given its world premiere by the New York Philharmonic on April 16, 1942. It was composed for Bruno Walter, who had expressed a wish for a new American work to play on his New York programs. Completed during World War II, Barber's *Second Essay* came at a turning point in the evolution of his style toward works of no less spontaneity than his *First Essay for Orchestra* or his earlier Overture to *The School for Scandal* but of greater harmonic tension and more probing spirit.

Like many of Barber's earlier works, the *Second Essay* is based on an extended melody as its principal theme. This we hear at the very outset, outlined by a solo flute against a barely audible background: a softly muttering bass drum blended with an even softer deep tone of the tuba:

The flute is echoed by a bass clarinet, which is soon joined by the somber voice of the English horn, then by oboe and other woodwinds, and finally by the swelling brightness of the entire violin section. As this development approaches its climax, we hear in the background a strongly rhythmic kettledrum figure, which is derived from the main melody and which will, in turn, launch the vigorous fugue that crowns the work.

A second, sinuous melody is sung by dark-voiced violas and a solo oboe before being taken over by the first violins to launch an agitated development. A new mood of tremendous excitement begins with the fugue. Announced by a single clarinet, the fugal subject, derived from the opening melody (via the kettledrum figure) races forward at such a dizzy speed that our principal impression is one of headlong drive.

Suddenly the texture lightens. A scherzo-like section of staccato winds and strings leads to a poetic transformation of the fugue subject chanted softly by a solo horn against quiet sustained harmonies of the strings, with only a fluttering clarinet to recall the previous tempo. As the fugue broadens toward its climax, it incorporates the two principal melodies of the work; the first in a broadly swelling version for all the violins and violas in unison, the other in a canonic trio for exuberantly clashing voices of trumpets, trombone and tuba. The *Second Essay* concludes with a stately hymn-like section marked *Più tranquillo, ma sempre muovendo.* This section, too, derives from the opening pages, thus emphasizing the close-knit structure of this strong score. It ends with an archaic-sounding modal cadence in a blaze of triumph.

The *Second Essay* is scored for piccolo, 2 flutes, 2 oboes, English horn, 2 clarinets, 2 bassoons, 4 horns, 3 trumpets, 3 trombones, tuba, kettledrums, cymbals, side drum of low pitch without snare, bass drum, tam-tam, and the traditional strings.

OVERTURE TO THE SCHOOL FOR SCANDAL

How fresh and spontaneous this Overture sounds. Despite its exuberant virtuosity it is in a sense a student work, for it was written when Barber was twenty-one and still studying composition with Rosario Scalero of the Curtis Institute in Philadelphia. It was first performed by the Philadelphia Orchestra in the Robin Hood Dell, under the direction of Alexander Smallens on August 30, 1933.

Its music does not follow any story line. Nor was it composed for any specific production of Sheridan's comedy. It was simply suggested by the wit and laughter of that nimble masterpiece. The music is Classical in spirit, in its transparent clarity of form, and the luminous texture of its orchestral sound.

The Overture begins with a dazzling fanfare sound. A quick descending figure of two notes, B flat and A, repeats itself with increasing speed until it grows into a raucous trill, like a derisive burst of orchestral laughter. The principal theme follows almost immediately in the violins: a light, lilting, jig-like melody, which seems to grow out of the two notes of the introductory laughter:

Beginning very softly (the composer directs the violins to play at the tip of the bow) it seems almost a stream of gossip, a whispering *venticello,* an echo of the airy, Rossinian slanders of *The Barber of Seville.* But this is an echo of the spirit, not of the overworked formula. As the whisper gains body and brilliance it is backed by chattering rhythms of the woodwinds.

A return to the laughter of the opening ushers in a second melody of charming sentiment sung by a solo oboe. A jocular clarinet chuckles softly over *pizzicato* strings. A frisky flute adds its comment and another burst of laughter leads to a short development section. In their return, which seems to fall spontaneously into the pattern of a Classical reprise, the basic themes seem more brilliant than ever. The Overture is rounded off with a scherzo-like *fugato* derived from the gossipy principal theme. The laughter which introduced and punctuated the story also concludes it.

The Overture to *The School for Scandal* is scored for piccolo, 2 flutes, 2 oboes, English horn, 2 clarinets, bass clarinet, 2 bassoons, 4 horns, 3 trumpets, 3 trombones, tuba, kettle drums, triangle, bass drum, cymbals, bells, celeste, harp, and the traditional string section.

Béla Bartók

Born March 25, 1881, Nagyszentmiklós, Transylvania, Hungary (now Sint Micolau Mare, Romania)—died September 26, 1945, New York City

CONCERTO FOR ORCHESTRA

One of his most popular scores, Bartók's Concerto for Orchestra was composed two years before his death. Indeed, there is good reason to believe that the psychological stimulus of the commission for this work postponed his tragic end.

Early in 1943, Bartók's frail health had taken a sudden turn for the worse; he grew so weak that he could hardly walk from one room to another. He was able to deliver only three of a series of lectures which Harvard University had invited him to give during the spring semester of 1943. These three exhausted him; he was unable to continue, although he had counted on the series to support himself and his wife until the fall. The Harvard authorities sponsored a complete medical examination and, on his return to New York, the American Society of Composers, Authors and Publishers (although Bartók was not a member) sponsored another complete hospital examination and diagnosis. But in vain. The diagnoses were conflicting and uncertain. Bartók's strength ebbed; his weight sank to eighty-seven pounds. By the end of June 1943, he felt there was no hope of recovery; it was out of the question for him to take a job, and he had no foreseeable income.

At this point Serge Koussevitzky, acting on a suggestion of Joseph Szigeti and Fritz Reiner, came to Bartók's hospital room to offer him a commission of $1,000 from the Koussevitzky Foundation to write a work in memory of the late Mrs. Natalie Koussevitzky. Knowing that Bartók would resist any proposal that smacked of charity, Koussevitzky told Bartók flatly that the commission had been decided by his board of trustees and was irrevocable. Acting on their instructions, Koussevitzky declared, he had brought with him a check for $500, which he was obliged to leave with the composer, whether or not Bartók felt he could execute the commission or was even willing to attempt it. The remaining $500 was to be paid on completion of the score.

Koussevitzky later described the interview to Bartók's friend H. W. Heinsheimer. At first Bartók made no reply. Then suddenly he began to talk of other things. He grew animated, seemed more confident, and kept Koussevitzky for almost an hour more, their talk ranging over a wide variety of topics. Bartók's health took a sudden turn for the better. The hospital released him and, with the financial assistance of the American Society of Composers, Authors and Publishers, the Bartóks were able to spend the summer at Saranac Lake, New York. On August 15, 1943, he began composing his Concerto for Orchestra, and when he returned to New York in October he brought the completed score.

The first performance of the Concerto was given by the Boston Symphony Orchestra under Koussevitzky's direction on December 1, 1944, in Symphony Hall, Boston (not in Carnegie Hall, as is stated in the printed score of the Concerto). Bartók's doctor allowed him to go to Boston for the rehearsals and the performance, which was a triumphant success. Further elated by Koussevitzky's enthusiasm, Bartók wrote a friend that the conductor "says it is 'the best orchestral piece of the last twenty-five years' (including the works of his idol Shostakovich!)." The New York premiere in Carnegie Hall on January 10, 1945, by the same forces, was equally successful.

By now a number of commissions were coming Bartók's way, and his publishers, Boosey and Hawkes, had signed an agreement which guaranteed him what Bartók called a "modest living" for the next three years. But it was too late. He grew steadily weaker, and although an attack of pneumonia was quickly conquered by antibiotics, he apparently contracted leukemia. On September 26, less than a year after the premiere of the Concerto for Orchestra, he died in the West Side Hospital in New York City.

Bartók himself, in a brief note written for the Boston Symphony premiere, declared that the "general mood" of the Concerto "represents, apart from the jesting second movement, a gradual transition from the sternness of the first movement and the lugubrious death-song of the third, to the life-assertion of the last one." And he added: "The title of this symphony-like orchestral work is explained by its tendency to treat the single orchestral instruments in a *concertant* or soloistic manner." In addition to its musical allure, the score offers brilliant opportunities for the display of a virtuoso orchestra.

I. *Introduction: Andante non troppo—Allegro vivace.* The eerie instrumental coloring of the slow preliminary section, with dark double basses and cellos contrasting to the tremolos of the high muted strings, recalls the Romantic opening of the young Stravinsky's *Firebird.* As new instrumental groups are added, each comes with the shock of a new primary color. The faster main body of the movement, according to Bartók's notes, is in "more or less regular sonata form." But this is a very free twentieth-century version of the form. The principal theme with its irregular meter and vigorous rhythm is launched by all the violins together:*

A certain family resemblance seems to link the above to another important theme announced soon after by a solo trombone:

* *This and the following musical example from this composition Copyright 1946 by Hawkes & Son (London) Ltd. Renewed 1973. Reprinted by permission of Boosey & Hawkes, Inc.*

In the development of these themes, the first measure of the first theme plays a prominent part. The second theme is played off against itself, *fugato* style, in its original form and in its upside-down, mirror form, in what Bartók himself called " 'virtuoso' treatment."

II. *Game of the Pairs: Allegretto scherzando.* This lighthearted movement is also a play of orchestral colors. A pair of bassoons is succeeded by a pair of oboes, then a pair of clarinets, and pairs of flutes and finally muted trumpets. A contrasting, hymn-like section for soft brass instruments leads to a return of the opening material with three bassoons now, instead of only two. Other woodwind instruments are succeeded by fresh color effects with great splashes of harp against whispering strings.

III. *Elegy: Andante, non troppo.* This is the movement Bartók described as a "lugubrious death-song." Its opening theme in the low strings is related to the opening of the first movement. There follows a "misty texture of rudimentary motifs," little arabesques of the flutes and clarinets against harp glissandos and softly trembling, trilling strings. The middle section is melodic, after which the misty texture returns.

IV. *Intermezzo interrotto: Allegretto.* Folklike melodies take up most of this movement except for an interruption in the middle. According to the composer's son, Péter Bartók, while his father was working on the Concerto for Orchestra he heard a broadcast of Shostakovich's Seventh Symphony and he found one of its themes so ludicrous and vapid that he decided to burlesque it here. The vulgarity and raucousness of the interruption are intentional.

V. *Finale: Presto.* Like the first movement, this one is a very free sonata form. It opens with a fiery sort of *perpetuum mobile* figure which is succeeded by dancelike rhythms. The development includes a tremendously complicated fugal passage. The conclusion is extraordinarily brilliant, even for Bartók.

The Concerto is scored for 3 flutes, 3 oboes, 3 clarinets, 3 bassoons, 4 horns in F, 3 trumpets in C, 2 tenor trombones, bass trombone, tuba, kettledrum, snare drum, bass drum, tam-tam, cymbals, triangle, 2 harps, and the customary strings.

CONCERTO FOR PIANO AND ORCHESTRA, NO. 1

Like Beethoven and many a great composer before him, Béla Bartók was a concert virtuoso. Like Beethoven, he established himself in the public mind first as a pianist and only much later as a major composer. This may account in part for the large proportion of his piano works composed during his early career, many of them as vehicles for his own concert appearances. It was from his mother, a professional piano teacher, that he had his first instruction. He made his first public appearance at the age of ten in the double role of pianist and composer, performing the first movement of Beethoven's "Waldstein" Sonata and a work of his own, *The Danube,* which described the river from its source all the way to the Black Sea.

As Bartók matured, his piano music responded vividly to his growing enthusiasm for Hungarian folk music. It was this enthusiasm which led him far beyond the radical innovations of even so advanced a composer as Debussy. Bartók's famous *Allegro barbaro* of 1911 appeared as a turning point. The sharp, percussive dissonances and the hammering, *martellato* rhythms were perhaps the most arresting traits of what was sometimes called Bartók's *martellato* style. This was especially characteristic of his middle period, which reached approximately from the *Allegro barbaro* to his First Piano Concerto of 1926.

In an article on the influence of peasant music on modern music, Bartók once described three principal ways in which a composer may use folk material. One was to take over a peasant melody unchanged or only slightly varied. Another was to imitate the character of folk melodies. The third, which was Bartók's own mature practice, he described as follows: "Neither peasant melodies nor imitations of peasant melodies can be found in his music, but it is pervaded by the atmosphere of peasant music. In this case we may say [the composer] has completely absorbed the idiom of peasant music which has become his mother tongue. He masters it completely as a poet masters his mother tongue."

Bartók himself was the soloist in the world premiere of his First Piano Concerto, which was presented on July 1, 1927, at the Festival of the International Society for Contemporary Music at Frankfurt under the direction of Wilhelm Furtwängler.

I. *Allegro moderato; Allegro.* In the almost inaudible opening bars of the introduction, with deep, percussive rumblings of kettledrum, solo piano, and brasses in their lowest range, we hear an anticipation of the furiously hammering *(martellato)* repeated notes of the principal themes that lie ahead. As the tempo increases, we are also given hints of the powerful syncopations that characterize the rest of the movement.

The main body of the movement begins with an insistent, fourteenfold hammering on one note, but with all the pianistic might of octave doublings against a syncopated orchestral background. Soon the soloist combines his obsessive note-repetitions with melodic counterpoint:*

* *This and the following musical examples from this composition are copyright and renewal assigned to Boosey & Hawkes, Inc., for U.S.A. Reprinted by permission.*

II. *Andante.* Against a quiet, rhythmic *ostinato* of drums and cymbals, the piano introduces the principal theme of the *Andante.* Here again, rhythm plays the principal role:

The special color of this movement is determined in part by the fact that the string choir is omitted entirely. The solo pianist is accompanied by woodwinds, brass, and percussion only. The movement, which is in three-part form, rises to an impressive climax built over a strongly dissonant *ostinato* figure of the solo pianist.

III. *Allegro molto.* The finale (which follows without interruption) opens with another, even more striking *ostinato,* this time allotted to the strings:

As in the first movement, the form is loosely related to the traditional sonata-allegro. Heavy repeated octaves in the piano characterize the principal theme. In the working out of this movement, Bartók uses a contrapuntal technique *(fugato)* which harks back to Baroque tradition.

The score calls for 2 flutes (one interchangeable with piccolo), 2 oboes, (one interchangeable with English horn), 2 clarinets (one interchangeable with bass clarinet), 2 bassoons, 4 horns, 2 trumpets, 3 trombones, kettledrums, bass drum, tam-tam, triangle, 4 cymbals, small snare drum, and small drum without snares, plus the traditional string choir.

CONCERTO FOR PIANO AND ORCHESTRA, NO. 2

By the time Béla Bartók completed his Second Piano Concerto, he was fifty years old. Fame was on its way, but slowly. Neither conductors nor pianists raced for the first performance rights to the new Concerto, which waited fifteen months for a public hearing. Completed on October 9, 1931, it was first presented by the Frankfurt Radio Orchestra, conducted by Hans Rosbaud, on January 23, 1933, with Bartók himself as soloist. Now the Concerto took hold quickly, and within a few months (according to Halsey Stevens) Bartók had performed the solo part with orchestras in Frankfurt, London, Vienna, Strasbourg, Stockholm, Winterthur, and Zurich. It did not reach the United States until 1938 however and was not widely performed there until the 1960s.

It is a colorful virtuoso piece. It even includes a few of the familiar externals of piano virtuosity: cadenzas, difficult passages in double thirds, sixths, octaves, and more. The melodic and rhythmic styles are clearly influenced by the folk music Bartók adored and collected with such pride and passion. But the piano style is far from traditional and the harmonies are often stringently dissonant.

I. *Allegro.* Bartók was too much his own man to be dominated even by so powerful a personality as Stravinsky. Yet Bartók's driving, almost mechanical rhythms, the intentionally harsh brilliance of his orchestra (he omits the strings altogether in this movement), the traces of folk music and even some of the piano writing are closer to Stravinsky's *Petrouchka* than the twenty years which separate the two scores might lead one to expect. *Petrouchka,* we are reminded, was first conceived as a virtuoso piano concerto or *Konzertstück.*

Two of the most important ideas of Bartók's Concerto, both of which return in the finale, splash across the opening page, launching a whole group of related themes. The first is announced by a solo trumpet over a loud trill of the piano:*

It is answered immediately by a swift stream of percussive chords in the solo piano part:

There is a briefly contrasting group and a series of developments, largely contrapuntal, sounding extraordinarily like Bach. The free reprise leads to an impressive cadenza, written out by the composer, and a brilliant surprise ending.

II. *Adagio; Presto; Adagio.* The second movement presents as violent a contrast as possible to the first. Where the first movement was loud, fast, brilliant, percussive, and contrapuntal, the opening of the second movement is soft, slow, subdued, and sustained. Where the first movement omitted the

* *This and the following musical example from this composition are copyright and renewal assigned to Boosey & Hawkes, Inc., for U.S.A. Reprinted by permission.*

string choir altogether, the second movement begins with muted strings alone. Their hymn-like phrases alternate with freely declamatory piano solos accompanied only by kettledrums. A ghostly *Presto* middle section culminates in long-sustained trills by the entire string body, while the piano soloist plays "trills" between two tone-clusters; one cluster being made of all the white notes within an octave, and the second cluster all the black notes.

III. *Allegro molto.* The finale is a tumultuous rondo. The recurrent refrain which opens and closes the rondo is a heavily syncopated barbaric-sounding figure for piano solo over an even more primitive sounding two-note *ostinato* of the kettledrums. Between appearances of the refrain, the contrasting episodes are built of themes from the first movement, especially those from the very first page.

The score calls for 3 flutes, 2 oboes, 2 clarinets, 3 bassoons, 4 F horns, 3 C trumpets, 3 trombones, tuba, kettledrums, bass drum, military drum, cymbals, triangle, and the usual strings.

CONCERTO FOR PIANO AND ORCHESTRA, NO. 3

Bartók's Third Piano Concerto was virtually his last complete work. On the evening of the last day he spent in his small New York apartment at 309 West 57th Street, Bartók's friend and compatriot Tibor Serly found him feverishly scoring the finale. Only seventeen or eighteen measures were left to be filled in when he left the next day for West Side Hospital. Four days later he was dead.

Since the myth of Bartók's death from starvation and neglect in these stonyhearted United States has been discredited, it has become possible to see Bartók's last months here a little more realistically. What we see will not make us proud, but we need not shoulder quite the burden of shame that many American music-lovers felt when first they learned of Bartók's tragic end during his self-imposed exile in this city. Bartók died not of starvation but of an ailment, or combination of ailments, which long defied diagnosis by leading medical authorities, including the finest that Harvard University could summon (and *did* summon, free of charge) and the best available medical advice in New York (also furnished gratis).

Other factors contributed. Like Mozart in his last illness, Bartók seems to have worked far more intensely and relentlessly than he should have, with the purpose of completing a final work which might contribute to his widow's support. When his friend and helper Victor Bator complained that as soon as Bartók was not sick he worked too much all the time, Bartók replied: "You have insulted me, Victor, I do work all the time also while I am invalided." He was in financial need. Mr. Bator, the executor of Bartók's will and trustee of his estate, tells us that at no time did his income in the United States fall below $4,000. But even allowing for the vastly greater purchasing power such a sum would have today, this was inadequate for a sixty-year-old chronic invalid with a wife and young child.

The greater tragedy was the lack of any wide public following which was a blow to the artist's self-esteem. Not until the last year of his life did enough commissions come in to begin to assure him a modest financial competency. And by then it was too late. Twenty years later, Mr. Bator reports, the annual income from Bartók's works was close to $100,000.

Although it proved unnecessary, Bartók evidently hoped, by completing his uncommissioned Third Piano Concerto ahead of other commissioned works, to make some provision for his wife, Ditta Pásztory, who could use the work as a vehicle for her appearances as piano soloist with orchestras.

Tibor Serly, who knew Bartók's musical shorthand, completed the few missing measures and the Concerto was first performed on February 8, 1946, by György Sándor as soloist with the Philadelphia Orchestra under the direction of Eugene Ormandy. The score has neither the percussive power of Bartók's First Piano Concerto nor the *bravura* drive of the Second. It seems, quite appropriately, a more gentle, graceful, almost feminine work. It is in three movements, the second of which leads directly into the third without pause.

I. *Allegretto.* Over pulsating violas and second violins, the piano spins out a single melodic line capriciously ornamented with syncopations suggestive of a folk dance tune:*

The first violins strike up a similar strain against trills of the piano, leading to a complex group of subordinate themes. These, in turn, die away as the piano and a solo clarinet echo back and forth the tiny figure of a falling third.

The development begins over deep, pounding arpeggios of the piano, with a melodic expansion of the opening. The reprise of the basic themes begins after a series of descending trills in the violins. The conclusion fades away on the return of the falling third figure which echoes among clarinet, flute, oboe, and piano solo.

II. *Adagio religioso.* There seems to be no religious intention behind the adjective *religioso,* but simply an indication of the musical character of the opening section in which the strings imitate each other melodically in a manner somewhat reminiscent of the Renaissance motet, alternating with a chorale or hymn-like phrases for the solo piano:

---

* *This and the following musical examples from this composition are copyright 1947 by Boosey & Hawkes, Ltd. Reprinted by permission of Boosey & Hawkes, Inc.*

The contrasting middle section suggests an exotic array of bird-calls with tiny, repetitious motives for woodwinds and piano against a background of murmuring violins in clusters of soft, dissonant trills. With the return of the opening material, the chorale-like phrases are sung by the woodwind choir. The finale follows without pause.

III. *Allegro vivace.* Although Bartók's manuscript bore no tempo mark for the finale the *Allegro vivace* supplied by the editors seems convincing. In the pointed rhythms of the principal (opening) theme there is again a suggestion of folk dance which turns into a rondo refrain. The contrasting episodes introduced by a kettledrum solo are elaborately and learnedly contrapuntal, being built on various combinations and transformations of the following subject:

Yet the working out is so light in spirit and texture, so sparkling and spontaneous in manner that the technical virtuosity often passes unnoticed. The dance rhythms are brought back for a brilliant, flashing conclusion.

The Third Piano Concerto is scored for piccolo, 2 flutes, 2 oboes, 2 clarinets, 2 bassoons, 4 horns, 2 trumpets, 3 trombones, tuba, kettledrums, xylophone, tamburo, piccolo, cymbals, bass drum, tam-tam, and the traditional strings.

CONCERTO FOR VIOLIN AND ORCHESTRA, NO. 2

Listening to the exuberant flood of music that is Bartók's Second Violin Concerto, one would never guess that it was penned when Bartók was passing through the greatest agony of soul. For all about him he saw the cancer of Nazism corrupting and destroying the civilization of Central Europe. In one despairing letter of April 13, 1938, some five months before the Violin Concerto, he wrote to a friend in Switzerland that the most terrible thing of all was "the imminent danger that Hungary, too, will surrender to this system of robbers and murderers. . . . Hungary, where unfortunately the 'educated' Christian people are almost exclusively devoted to the Nazi System: I am really ashamed that I come from this class."

Indeed, Bartók says, he almost feels it is his duty to emigrate, while that is still possible. But even in the most favorable case, to earn his daily bread in some foreign country would be so enormously difficult for him and cause him such spiritual discomfort—now in his fifty-eighth year to begin all over again to give lessons somewhere and be wholly dependent on them—that he can hardly even think of such a thing. On the other hand he cannot imagine that it would be possible for him either to live or to continue working in Hungary if the Nazis do take over. And his letters continue, full of the horrors and stupidities he sees developing all around him.

Composing must have been a solace, perhaps even momentary escape. It was sometime in 1937 that Bartók's old friend Zoltán Székely came to him with a commission for a violin concerto. Bartók, who was enamored of the variation technique, suggested making the entire work one vast set of variations. But Székely objected, insisting that he wanted a real violin concerto. Bartók agreed, although in the end he was able to accomplish both his own desire and that of Székely, with a very sophisticated development of the traditional three-movement concerto form.

Bartók began the composition in August 1937, and completed it in September 1938, in Budapest, according to a letter of October 9, 1938, to his friend Mrs. Müller-Widmann, at Davos, Switzerland. When he showed the manuscript to Székely, the violinist was unhappy about the conclusion of the last movement, which Bartók had made entirely orchestral, omitting the solo violin for the last twenty-two measures. Again Székely insisted that he wanted a real violin concerto, one which would end with the traditional brilliant solo flight for the violin in the concluding pages. Bartók, after reconsidering the great nineteenth-century violin concertos, agreed with Székely and composed a new conclusion according to his wishes. Yet, though he conceded the rightness of Székely's request, Bartók may still in his heart of hearts have preferred his own original version, and when the score was published, it appeared with both endings, the original one appended as an alternative. The score was completed, new ending and all, on the last day of 1938.

Bartók was prevented from hearing the premiere of his Violin Concerto, which Székely performed on April 23, 1939, with the Amsterdam Concertgebouw Orchestra under the direction of Willem Mengelberg. The United States premiere was given on January 21, 1943, by The Cleveland Orchestra under the direction of Artur Rodzinski with Tossy Spivakovsky as soloist.

Bartók achieved his aim of making the entire Violin Concerto one vast variation form by writing a final movement which was a variant in structure, and in themes of the opening movement. The middle movement he made a traditional theme-and-variations form.

I. *Allegro non troppo.* After six measures of soft preluding by the harp, the solo instrument enters with a rhapsodic theme, which forms the basis not only of the first movement, but in varied form furnishes the foundation of the finale: *

* *This and the following musical example from this composition are copyright 1946 by Hawkes & Son (London) Ltd; renewed 1973. Reprinted by permission of Boosey & Hawkes, Inc.*

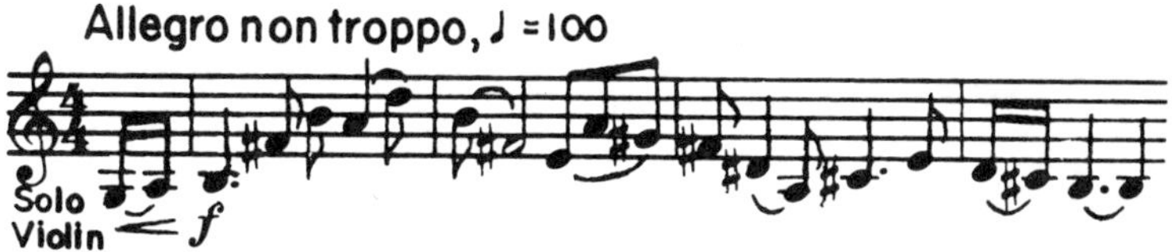

Although this theme is obviously no folk tune, its strong emphasis on the intervals of fourths, fifths, and seconds gives it a characteristically Hungarian flavor. It is one example of many that could be cited in this Concerto showing how Bartók's long years' study of Hungarian folk music had enabled him to absorb something of the character of that music into his own sophisticated style.

The brief preliminary development of this opening theme, interspersed with virtuoso spurts for the solo instrument, leads to the principal contrasting theme which (strangely for Bartók) is a complete twelve-tone row. Bartók was not given here or elsewhere in his works to orthodox twelve-tone procedures, or to the alleged atonality so often associated with them. The central development of the movement is based chiefly on the principal theme, which is varied melodically, rhythmically, and contrapuntally, one of the most beautiful passages being an upside-down, or mirror inversion of the principal theme played as a soaring cantilena for the solo violin against a delicate background of harp, celesta, muted violins and high shimmering tremolos. The return of the basic thematic material begins with the solo violin singing the principal theme softly, tranquilly, an octave above its original position. The recapitulation is full of striking harmonies and new color devices, including the almost shocking effect of the entire string section plucking *pizzicato* chords so violently that the strings slap back with a sharp report against the fingerboard. There is a richly varied cadenza by Bartók himself and a fiery orchestral closing page.

II. *Andante tranquillo.* The melody on which the variations of this movement are built has a distinctly folk quality with an appealingly melancholy tinge. It is presented by the solo violin. In the first variation, the embellished melodic version of the theme is accompanied at first by soft kettledrums and string basses alone. Prominent in the second variation is the florid melody for harp which bridges the pauses between phrases of the principal melody. In the third variation, the solo part is thickened by a continuous series of double stops. In the fourth variation, the solo instrument weaves fantastic garlands of coloratura about the principal theme. The fifth variation glitters with high flute and piccolo tone and prominent passages for the harp. After a featherlight, virtuoso beginning, the sixth variation subsides to a slower pace, closer to that of the original theme, which returns at last, an octave higher than originally. The movement concludes with high, muted violins echoing fragments of the theme.

III. *Allegro molto.* While its rhythm is different, the principal theme of the finale is clearly derived from that of the first movement:

Most listeners would not be aware, and probably Bartók did not intend them to be aware, of the often minute resemblances of the theme, subordinate themes and even overall structure between the finale and first movement. What does strike the listener is a feeling of organic integration, a general feeling that the last movement grows out of what has gone before, although its character is much more vivacious.

The Bartók Second Violin Concerto is scored for piccolo, 2 flutes, 2 oboes, English horn, 2 clarinets in A, bass clarinet, 2 bassoons, contrabassoon, 4 horns in F, 2 trumpets in C, 2 tenor trombones, bass trombone, kettledrums, 2 side drums, bass drum, 2 cymbals, triangle, tam-tam, celesta, harp, and the traditional strings.

DANCE SUITE

Perhaps the greatest love of this most lovable composer was the folk music of his own and neighboring lands. So strong was Bartók's passion for this ancient traditional music that he developed into one of the most skillful pioneer collectors in the first half of our century, spending many months of his career visiting remote peasant villages to record what remained of musical treasures threatened by the progress of modern industrial civilization. Bartók's enthusiasm was contagious and so it was probably no accident that his first really big popular success as a composer came with this orchestral *Dance Suite* based on folk tunes. In 1923, the fiftieth anniversary of the merging of the cities of Pest, Buda, and Óbuda into the Hungarian capital of Budapest was celebrated with commissions to the three leading Hungarian composers: Kodály, Dohnányi, and Bartók. Bartók's contribution, the *Dance Suite,* was given its first performance by the Budapest Philharmonic Society under the direction of Dohnányi on November 19, 1923. It was popular from the start and was quickly scheduled by orchestras all over Europe, with fifty performances in Germany alone in a single year.

By the time of his success Bartók already had an impressive list of major works behind him, including his first two sonatas for violin and piano, his first two string quartets, his opera *Bluebeard's Castle,* and his ballet *The Miraculous Mandarin,* a striking number of Hungarian, Slovak, Romanian, Transylvanian folk-song arrangements, and piano pieces including his famous *Allegro barbaro.* The very title of the latter emphasized Bartók's interest in the primitive aspects of folk art. Not only was Bartók one of the great pioneers in the collecting of folk music; as a composer he was inspired by the variety and vitality of the melodies he discovered. He was proud too of the geographical and cultural scope of his investigations, and used to point out that the *Dance Suite* was testimony of this breadth of interest.

Although the word "suite" normally suggests a series of separate movements, Bartók's *Dance Suite* is so close-knit—so effectively bound together by the *ritornello,* which returns in refrain fashion between almost all of the movements, and is so strongly summarized in the finale, which integrates almost every theme in the entire composition—that the total impression is of a continuous symphonic whole. The movements are played without pause.

I. *Moderato.* The opening movement, which Bartók felt showed a certain Arabic influence, begins in moderate tempo and with dark coloring. The primitive syncopated melody is presented first in the low register of two bassoons. The orchestral colors warm, the rhythms grow livelier, and the movement builds to a sharp climax before fading away to the tranquil *ritornello.* The melody of this connecting link which returns often in the course of the Suite, is led by four muted violins: *

Bartók felt that the melody of his *ritornello* had a certain Magyar quality which carries over into the second movement.

II. *Allegro molto.* This vigorous dance theme (presented by the first violins) consists of only two notes which alternate. Later the range is extended, but it remains narrow, seldom overstepping the limit of a fourth; this gives the melody part of its primitive quality. Only as the movement approaches its climax does the range briefly expand still further. The clarinet recalls the melody of the *ritornello* which links this to the following movement.

III. *Allegro vivace.* This movement, also strongly Magyar in quality, is brightly colored. Among the more striking passages is one introduced by sweeping arpeggios of the celesta and harp with high trills of the flute. The principal theme itself is then heard played by the flute and bassoon separated by a distance of four octaves.

IV. *Molto tranquillo.* Soft syncopated chords of the orchestra alternate with bare unaccompanied melodic phrases sung by woodwinds in unison and in octaves. A brief reminiscence of the *ritornello* leads without pause to the next movement.

V. *Comodo.* The striking rhythms of this section, with their punched-out triplet accents, and heavily syncopated repeated chords are influenced by Rumanian folk music.

VI. *Finale: Allegro.* The pounding rhythms of the opening bars lead to a rich development of all the preceding themes of the suite (except that of the fourth movement) combined with the *ritornello* melody.

---

* *Musical example copyright 1924, 1925, by Universal Edition; renewed 1951, 1952. Copyright and renewal assigned to Boosey & Hawkes, Inc. for U.S.A. Reprinted by permission.*

The *Dance Suite* is scored for 2 piccolos, 2 flutes, 2 oboes, English horn, 2 clarinets, bass clarinet, 2 bassoons, contrabassoon, 4 horns in F, 2 trumpets in Bb, 2 trombones, tuba, kettledrums, tenor drum, side drum, bass drum, triangle, bells, cymbals, tam-tam, celesta, 2 pianos (one for 4 hands), and the customary string choir.

DIVERTIMENTO FOR STRINGS

As World War II approached, the anguish Bartók felt at the future he foresaw for his country was matched by his fury at those fellow Hungarians he saw rushing to align themselves with Hitler and the increasingly pro-Hitler government of his native Hungary.

This had a devastating effect on Bartók's creative faculty. There were moments when his inspiration seemed to have run completely dry. Then, early in the summer of 1939, a friendly gesture from a professional admirer made things momentarily easier for Bartók and his wife. Paul Sacher, the director of the Basel Chamber Orchestra, offered to the Bartóks the use of his chalet at Saanen in the *massif* of la Gruyère near Fribourg in Switzerland. The Bartóks accepted happily and the chalet provided a kind of enchanted isolation where the sterile period of Bartók's creativity was suddenly broken. For two blessed weeks the music poured forth from him with tremendous spontaneity, and the result was this small masterpiece.

It was not that Bartók forgot reality—he was still well aware of the war—but at a distance, as he explained in a letter of August 18, 1939, to his son: "The poor peace-loving loyal Swiss are forced to glow with war fever. Their daily papers are full of articles on protection of the country; in the more important passes are defense measures, military preparations. On the Julierpass I myself saw, for example, groups of rocks set into the earth against tanks, and similar nice things. In Holland the situation is the same—even in Scheveningen. . . . I don't like your wanting to go to Romania; in such uncertain times one should not travel to such an uncertain place. Also the thought constantly disquiets me whether I can travel home from here, should this or that happen. Luckily I can banish these anxiety-provoked thoughts, if necessary—while I am at work it doesn't disturb me. . . . For two weeks I have read no papers; yesterday one fell into my hands. The lack was not at all noticeable —it was as if I had seen an already two-week old issue. Nothing had happened in the meantime, thank God!"

Was it the feeling of professional obligation which unlocked the floodgates of Bartók's inspiration? We shall probably never know for sure. In any case, Sacher had had the wisdom to commission a new work from Bartók and it was this which became his Divertimento. Bartók tried to explain to his son, still in the letter of August 18, 1939: "Somehow I feel like an old-time musician summoned as the guest of a Maecenas. As you know, I am the guest of the Sachers here, who look after everything—from a distance. . . . As to excursions, I can of course not start anything, in spite of the friendliness of the weather: I must work. And specially for Sacher: commission—something for string orchestra; even this makes my situation like that of the musician of yore. Luckily the work has gone well; in 15 days I have already turned out a work about 25 minutes long; just yesterday I finished it. . . ."

It was, of course, Paul Sacher who had the honor of presenting the world premiere of the new Divertimento with his Basel Chamber Orchestra on June 11, 1940. Many Bartók authorities have pointed out resemblances between the Divertimento and Bartók's string quartets. Such connections seem logical, since the Divertimento was composed immediately before the Sixth String Quartet, and because the Divertimento is written for strings alone, albeit for a string orchestra. This listener feels, however, that the Divertimento stands rather to one side of the string quartets, being, except possibly in the middle movement, of much lighter, gayer texture and emotional content than one associates with the intensely concentrated music of the great quartets.

In response to a request from Paul Sacher, Bartók characterized the form of the Divertimento briefly as follows: "First movement sonata form, second movement approximately ABA, third movement rondo-like."

I. *Allegro non troppo.* Over the strumming accompaniment of strings, the first violins alone introduce the folk song-like principal theme:*

Almost immediately Bartók breaks up his string ensemble into a small group of solo instruments versus the string *tutti,* somewhat in the manner of the late Baroque concerto grosso. In the central development section of this sonata form, Bartók uses some very sophisticated contrapuntal devices, yet the overall impression is one of simplicity. The traditional reprise of the opening themes is disguised to a certain extent as a continuation of the development section.

II. *Molto adagio.* The traditionally songful second movement is darkly introspective. It opens with the entire orchestra of strings playing with mutes. Over a softly murmuring background of lower strings, the second violins have the following melancholy, sighing motive, in which chromatic half-steps play a decisive role:

* *This and the following musical examples from this composition are copyright 1940 by Hawkes & Son (London) Ltd. Renewed 1967. Reprinted by permission of Boosey & Hawkes, Inc.*

The contrasting middle section, introduced by the whispering solo for the first violin section, begins with a wild, almost agonized outcry of unison violins and violas, *fortissimo.* The ensuing agitation is more closely related to the string quartets, especially, perhaps, the Sixth Quartet. The latter part of this middle section turns to a lament-like *ostinato,* using the little three-note motive of the opening, preparing us for the return to the opening thematic material of this movement.

III. *Allegro assai.* A few measures of seemingly improvised introduction brings us quickly to a folk song-type of melody sung by the first violin solo against a strumming background of other solo strings, recalling the overall impression of the first movement. Again, as in the first movement, the mood is lively, almost abandoned. Again the overall impression is one of simplicity although Bartók has used fugal procedures and other sophisticated devices, mixed freely with gypsy-like melismas and a cadenza—all of which sounds in reading like an incongruous potpourri of elements, but which, in fact, makes a triumphant finale.

THE MIRACULOUS MANDARIN

It may be true that, as some commentators claim, *The Miraculous Mandarin* depicts the unconquerable power of human aspiration—even beyond death itself. This would be entirely in harmony with Bartók's idealism, which was deep and true. His own tragic life bears witness to his unflinching aspiration in the face of frail health, misunderstanding, neglect, poverty, exile, disease, and the death he faced in a New York hospital, far from his native land which meant so much to him.

And yet—one wonders what deeper motive led such a man to choose for one of his major works a story so certain to repel or frighten his contemporaries that he could scarcely expect it ever to be performed in its original form. What led this deeply innocent, sensitive, idealistic man to place his ballet in a brothel room, where men are lured to be robbed by thugs? It can hardly have been youthful experimentation, for *The Miraculous Mandarin* was composed in 1918 and 1919 when Bartók was thirty-seven, with several major works behind him: his opera *Bluebeard's Castle;* his ballet *The Wooden Prince;* and two of his great string quartets.

The story of *The Miraculous Mandarin* seems a gruesome distortion of the love-death theme which runs through so much nineteenth-century Romantic literature and music, reaching its climax in Wagner's *Tristan und Isolde.* Richard Strauss had already given audiences a thrill of horror with Salome's love-death: her ecstatic song to the severed head of John the Baptist. *Salome* caused much righteous indignation. But *The Mandarin* was simply refused everywhere as a ballet. Even as late as 1925 it was banned after one performance in Cologne. Not until after World War II was *The Miraculous Mandarin* widely performed on European stages, and not until 1951 did New York see it performed as a ballet.

A Suite from the ballet, arranged by the composer in 1928, is heard more often on symphony programs than the ballet itself. It consists roughly of the first two-thirds of the ballet, plus a concert ending.

The Suite, like the ballet, opens with a wild orchestral fracas, the pre-curtain music depicting the hectic city traffic outside the girl's room. Sudden quiet and a roll of the timpani announce the rise of the curtain. Three thugs go through their pockets and discover they have no money. They force the girl to the window to lure victims whom they can rob.

At first she refuses, but finally she begins a decoy dance (clarinet solo). The first to respond is a pathetic, elderly gentleman who has no money. He courts the girl with exaggerated, lovelorn gestures (*glissandos* of muted trombones). The three thugs pounce on him, throw him out and force the girl to resume her post at the window.

The second arrival is a timid young man who trembles with confusion. The girl dances with him, but as he has no money either, he is speedily thrown out by the thugs.

Back at her post, the girl is frightened by a sinister figure, a Mandarin, whose approach is described in the orchestra by a pseudo-Oriental theme for the trombones:*

Suddenly the Mandarin appears in the doorway. (This Suite omits forty-three measures during which the girl, repressing her dread, invites him to come in and take a chair.) She dances for him, shyly at first, then with increasing abandon. During her long dance the Mandarin is motionless, only his eyes betraying his rising passion. When at last she throws herself on his knees, he tries to embrace her, but she is so terrified that she struggles free again. There is a wild chase depicted by scurrying string figures over a pounding *ostinato* of the low instruments of the orchestra. The Mandarin catches the girl and they fight. The Suite concludes with a brief concert ending.

In the ballet, at this point, the three thugs rescue the girl and rob the Mandarin of his jewels and money. Then they decide to murder him. But the Mandarin is kept alive by the intensity of his longing. The thugs try smothering him and running an old rusty sword through his body. Nothing works. Finally they hang him from the chandelier. The light goes out and his body begins to glow a greenish blue, but his eyes, filled with longing, still follow the girl. At last, when he is cut down and resumes his pursuit of the girl, she no longer resists. With his longing appeased, the Mandarin's wounds begin to bleed and he is able to die.

* *Musical example copyright 1925 by Universal Edition; renewed 1952. Copyright and renewal assigned to Boosey & Hawkes, Inc. for the U.S.A. Reprinted by permission.*

The score of *The Miraculous Mandarin Suite* calls for piccolo, 3 flutes, 3 oboes, English horn, 3 clarinets and bass clarinet, 3 bassoons, 2 contrabassoons, 4 horns, 3 trumpets, 3 trombones, bass tuba, timpani, bass drum, large drum, small drum, cymbals, triangle, gong, xylophone, harp, piano, organ, and the usual strings.

MUSIC FOR STRINGS, PERCUSSION, AND CELESTA

Among the many tragedies of Bartók's career, and consequent tragedies for us, was the fact that he composed so little music for large symphony orchestra, especially in his middle years. This was not for lack of interest or desire. But as Bartók's musical style matured, his artistic profile grew more pronounced, his harmonies harsher, his rhythms more irregular, and his melodies reflected more and more the primitive aspect of folk music. His early popularity dimmed. Bartók grew more and more reluctant to compose large scores without reasonable assurance that they would be performed.

Fortunately he was also drawn to chamber music, which was less expensive to perform. Chamber players could afford to be more adventurous in their repertory, and the result was that Bartók wrote six of the greatest string quartets of this century. And two of his greatest orchestral works were composed for chamber orchestra, specifically for the Basel Chamber Orchestra, which was founded, financed, and conducted by Bartók's admirer Paul Sacher.

Bartók's Divertimento of 1939 is dedicated to the Basel Chamber Orchestra. His *Music for Strings, Percussion and Celesta,* commissioned for the tenth anniversary of the Basel Chamber Orchestra and completed on September 7, 1936, was first performed by that organization at Basel on January 21, 1937, under the direction of Sacher. Nine months later the new score was introduced to the United States by the New York Philharmonic under the direction of Sir John Barbirolli. Today the *Music for Strings, Percussion and Celesta* has become a popular work. It is in four movements: slow, fast, slow, fast.

Bartók did not call his score either a suite or a symphony, although it is related to both forms. It is related to the early Baroque variation suite, in that all four movements are based on variants of the same theme. It is related to the symphonic form in its use of four movements, including one movement in free sonata-allegro form and a finale of a brilliant dance-like quality.

I. *Andante tranquillo.* The first is a wild and passionate movement of elemental drive, despite its slow tempo. The nonprofessional music lover can safely ignore the fact that it is also a tightly knit fugue. The turning, twisting, writhing effect of its half-tone tensions gives Bartók's whole movement its basic character:*

* *This and the following musical examples from this composition are copyright 1937 by Universal Edition; renewed 1964. Copyright and renewal assigned to Boosey & Hawkes, Inc. for U.S.A. Reprinted by permission.*

After the mournful strain has been sung by violas alone, it is taken up by third and fourth violins, by first and second cellos, by second violins, first and second double basses and finally by the first violins—all muted. As the movement mounts toward its climax, each instrument takes up the melody in full voice, the tensions growing as the instruments rise in pitch and intensity, the cymbals and finally kettledrums softly, subtly adding resonance to the climax: a bare, *fortissimo* E flat, the note farthest removed, harmonically speaking, from the opening note (A natural) of the movement.

The climax subsides quickly. Individual voices, again muted, take up the opening melancholy strain but now in upside down or "mirror" form. As the melody grows softer, an exquisite touch of color is added by the celesta in a rapid, repeated figure, or *ostinato,* derived from the fugue subject itself. At the end, fragments of the opening strain pass from one instrument to another like pathetic little sighs, and the movement ends at last on the single note A with which it began.

II. *Allegro.* In the second movement one immediately becomes more aware that Bartók's strings are divided into two opposing choirs. The very opening theme is divided in half: the first half taken by the first string choir and the second by the opposing group. Both halves are related to the opening theme of the first movement. This movement, although it sounds impulsive in the extreme, is a traditional, Classical form: the sonata-allegro.

III. *Adagio.* The nocturne-like slow movement opens with a monotone solo for the xylophone. The violins add exotic, apparently wayward phrases, which are, however, derived from the opening fugal melody. The movement develops in a sort of pyramid form: A-B-C-B-A, its middle section being an almost Impressionistic shimmering web of *tremolo* strings with delicate *glissandos* of harp, piano and celesta.

IV. *Allegro molto.* A violent, guitar-like strumming of the string section opens the finale, subsiding quickly into an accompaniment for the wild, syncopated violin melody, which is related in feeling to the opening melody of the first movement, but now completely transformed by a Bulgarian dance rhythm:

The *Music for Strings, Percussion, and Celesta* is scored for two separate string sections, the first made up of first and second violins, violas, cellos and double basses; the second group comprising third and fourth violins, second violas, second cellos and second double basses. The harp and piano, although technically string instruments, are frequently used in percussion style. The percussion group proper includes side drum without snares, side drum with snares, cymbals, tam-tam, bass drum, kettledrums, and xylophone.

Ludwig van Beethoven

Born December 16, 1770, Bonn—died March 26, 1827, Vienna

CONCERTO FOR PIANO AND ORCHESTRA, NO. 1, C MAJOR, OPUS 15

When the twenty-two-year-old Beethoven came to settle in Vienna, which became his home for the rest of his life, he brought a whole sheaf of his own compositions: chamber music, piano solos, a concerto, even cantatas. But there was no money for him in composition, as yet. On the other hand, he was a stirring pianist and soon he was much in demand as a performer; indeed, he made his first big successes in Vienna as a performer of his own works. Beethoven wrote most of his piano concertos to be played by himself; he even delayed the publication of his early piano concertos in order to assure himself of their exclusive use, there being then no copyrights to give him legal protection.

This Concerto, although published first and therefore called "No. 1," was actually second in the order of composition. It was completed in 1798, when Beethoven was twenty-eight years old, and he seems to have played the first performance of it that same year at a concert in Prague.

A fair picture of the overwhelming impression Beethoven's playing made on his contemporaries is left us by the Czech composer Václav Tomášek, who was present at that performance: "It was in 1798, when I was studying law, that Beethoven, that giant among players, came to Prague. At a crowded concert in the Seminary hall he played his Concerto in C (Op. 15), the *Adagio* and *Rondo grazioso* from the Sonata in A (Op. 2,) and extemporized on a theme from Mozart's *Clemenza di Tito*, "Ah tu fosti il primo oggetto." His grand style of playing, and especially his bold improvisation, had an extraordinary effect upon me. I felt so shaken that for several days I could not bring myself to touch the piano."

Beethoven did wisely to present himself first as a performer, for there were things in these early works which even admirers found wild and disturbing. After hearing Beethoven twice more Tomášek wrote: "This time I was able to listen with greater calmness, and although I admired the power and brilliance of his playing as much as ever, his frequent daring deviations from one theme to another, which destroyed the continuity and gradual development of his ideas, did not escape me. Evils of this nature, springing from a too exuberant fancy, often mar his greatest compositions. It is not seldom that the unbiased listener is awakened from his transport. The singular and original seem to be his chief aim in composition. . . ."

I. *Allegro con brio.* It takes an effort of the imagination today to hear the "daring deviations" and the effort to be "singular and original" in this well-behaved Concerto. The *pianissimo* opening presents the main theme as delicately as you please. It seems a model of Rococo decorum:

Yet a few measures later, when the full orchestral *tutti* proclaims it with trumpets and drums, the theme has an assertive stride which its eighteenth-century manners cannot conceal. The orchestra then introduces the remaining thematic material of the movement, including the following graceful melody:

It works up to a little climax on the rhythm of the opening measure, takes a formal bow, with an emphatic cadence and clears the stage for the arrival of the piano.

The soloist makes a lyrical entrance with what seems to be a new theme but which develops more and more into graceful embellishment of themes already established by the orchestra. The movement continues, quite according to the Classical rules of the game, with grace and power. Before the exuberant closing measures, there is a solo cadenza for the pianist.

II. *Largo.* The songful second movement, despite its Rococo embellishments, has a depth and poignance that ally it to the great slow movements in which, according to reliable reports, Beethoven sometimes left his listeners speechless, in tears. It begins with the following beautiful melody:

III. *Rondo. Allegro scherzando.* The finale is a lively rondo, bordering on the boisterous humor for which Beethoven later became notorious. Its cunningly calculated irregularities give a special vitality to the recurring rondo refrain, which is announced first by the piano solo:

The intervening episodes enrich the rondo with touches of sonata style. And there are two more brief, but brilliant splashes—tiny cadenzas—for the solo piano before the orchestra rounds off this happy work.

The Concerto is scored for 1 flute, 2 oboes, 2 clarinets, 2 bassoons, 2 horns, 2 trumpets, kettledrums, and the traditional string choir.

CONCERTO FOR PIANO AND ORCHESTRA, NO. 2 B-FLAT MAJOR, OPUS 19

Beethoven's B-flat Piano Concerto bears the number "two" only because it was second in order of publication. But in order of composition it came first. Indeed this was the earliest of Beethoven's orchestral works that he saw fit to publish. When he began the Concerto in 1794, he was only twenty-three. He may have performed the first version (of which only a tiny fragment survives) the following year in Vienna; the exact date of the first performance has eluded scholars. But we do know that Beethoven himself was the soloist in the premiere of the revised version (which has come down to us) in Prague in 1798. On that occasion the Czech composer-pianist Václav Tomášek heard him and was so shaken by the experience that he did not touch the piano for several days after.

Paradoxically, the very qualities that overwhelmed Tomášek and many early Beethoven admirers, seem also to have disturbed them. The disciplined storms of emotion and the powerful contrasts we admire so today appeared to Tomášek and his contemporaries as "daring deviations" cultivated deliberately for the sake of being different. On second thought, after repeated hearings, Tomášek decided that "the singular, the original" seemed to be his chief aim in composition.

The truth is that Beethoven *did* want to be different. And heaven knows he succeeded. So, if our twentieth-century ears tell us that his B-flat Concerto is a puzzlingly traditional work for Beethoven, we are as wrong as the Tomášeks, who felt that the Concerto verged on the chaotic.

In order to keep the B-flat Concerto for his personal use as a pianist, Beethoven delayed its publication until 1801. Not until it was needed for the engraver, did Beethoven write out the solo part in full. "According to my habit," wrote Beethoven to the publisher, "the piano part was not written in the orchestral score and I have only just written it out; so, because of the hurry you will receive it in my own not-very-legible handwriting."

I. *Allegro con brio.* In this concerto, Beethoven is still following earlier models, particularly Mozart, the unsurpassed master of this form. The movement opens with an orchestral statement of the principal theme:

This orchestral exposition ends with a full cadence and the orchestra bows off the stage, so to speak, to give place to the solo piano.

The piano enters, as sometimes in the Mozart concertos, with its own variation of a subordinate theme; not until the orchestra has intervened once more does the soloist launch into the vigorous principal theme with which the orchestra had begun. A more flowing lyric theme enters in the violins and the solo piano rounds off the exposition with a passage of traditionally brilliant scale figures and virtuoso display. The dialogue between piano and orchestra grows livelier as thematic fragments are tossed back and forth. The return of the opening themes follows the familiar Classical pattern of the day, including the usual pause for the cadenza display of the solo instrument just before the end.

II. *Adagio.* The slow movement is a pensive, broadly flowing melody:

It is elaborated and embellished as the movement progresses, until at the very end it returns *pianissimo* in its original form.

III. *Rondo: Molto allegro.* The bouncing little rondo which concludes this Concerto is built around a refrain with characteristically Beethovenish syncopation:

Announced first by the piano solo, then echoed by full orchestra, this refrain returns three times again in the course of the movement. The imaginatively contrasting episodes are related to each other in a way that turns the whole movement into a marriage of rondo and sonata form.

The orchestra for Beethoven's Second Piano Concerto employs only 1 flute, 2 oboes, 2 bassoons, 2 horns, and the traditional string sections.

CONCERTO FOR PIANO AND ORCHESTRA, NO. 3, C MINOR, OPUS 37

The key of this Concerto had an especial significance for Beethoven: C minor was his key of "Storm and Stress." Although the literary and musical movements known as the "Storm and Stress" *(Sturm und Drang)* belong to the years of Beethoven's earliest boyhood (the 1770s), the same revolutionary attitudes and stormy emotions broke out again and again in the nineteenth century—and nowhere more forcefully than in Beethoven's heroic works in C minor. The most famous example is his Fifth Symphony. The earliest of his stormy, heroic string quartets, Opus 18, No. 4, is in C minor. His early Piano Sonata, Opus 13, the "Pathétique," is a popular embodiment of the same mood. But his last Piano Sonata, Opus 111 in C minor, shows the same emotional tensions magnified to almost inconceivable intensity.

In date as well as in character, this C-minor Piano Concerto stands on the borderline between Beethoven's first style period, when he had built on Mozart and Haydn, and his middle period of complete individuality. The manuscript bears the inscription: "Concerto 1800 da L. v. Beethoven." But the sketches for the Concerto preserved in the British Museum go back some three years earlier, and the finishing touches were not put on the work until at least 1802, possibly later, for the solo part was not yet written out for the first performance on April 3, 1803, in Vienna.

That program, at the Theater an der Wien, included not only his new Concerto, but two additional premieres: his Second Symphony and his oratorio *Christus am Oelberg*. The only familiar work was his First Symphony. Other works had been planned, but were dropped before the concert because of the excessive length of the program.

The final rehearsal began at eight o'clock in the morning of the day of the concert. "It was a terrible rehearsal," Ferdinand Ries recalled: "and at half past two everybody was exhausted and more or less dissatisfied. Prince Karl Lichnowsky, who had attended the rehearsal from the beginning, sent out for large baskets of buttered bread, cold meat and wine. He warmly invited everyone to help himself, which was done with both hands, with the result that a warm atmosphere was restored."

Beethoven himself was the soloist that evening. As it was customary for the soloist to play from the music at that time, Beethoven invited one of his pupils, Ignatz von Seyfried, to turn pages for him. "But—Heaven help me!" wrote Seyfried thirty years later, "That was easier said than done. I saw almost nothing but empty leaves, at the most here and there a few Egyptian hieroglyphs, wholly unintelligible to me, scribbled down to serve as clues for him. He played nearly all the solo part from memory, since, as was often the case, he had not had the time to put it all on paper. So whenever he reached the end of such an invisible passage, he gave me a secret nod. My obvious anxiety not to miss the decisive moment amused him greatly and at our convivial dinner afterwards it still sent him into gales of laughter."

I. *Allegro con brio.* Beethoven follows the tradition of presenting his thematic material in a long orchestral exposition before the solo piano is heard. The principal theme, a bold figure built about the C-minor triad, opens the movement in an ominous whisper:

This is echoed in the woodwinds then taken up by a full orchestral *tutti* with shifting harmonies. A gracefully flowing second theme, hovering between major and minor, supplies the traditional contrast:

The piano enters alone with three furious C-minor scales leading to the principal theme. The last two notes of that theme and their sharp rhythm play a vital part in the development section and again in the coda. There is a reprise of the opening themes, a cadenza for the piano solo and an imaginative coda, full of harmonic surprises.

II. *Largo.* The broad flow of melody is introduced by the soloist and taken up by muted strings. Later the piano weaves garlands of arpeggios around the melody, which is carried by the strings and woodwinds. The movement concludes with a return of the opening melody and an expressive cadenza for the piano.

III. *Rondo: Allegro.* The lively finale is among Beethoven's many ingenious combinations of rondo and sonata forms. The framework is a regular rondo, built upon the following perky refrain:

In between the tantalizing recurrences of this refrain, the first contrasting episode presents a cascading melody (which also serves as the lyric second theme of a traditional sonata form):

The second episode starts innocuously enough, with an even more gracefully flowing melodic contrast. But this is interrupted by a little *fugato:* the beginning of a fugue, on the rondo refrain. This in turn is interrupted by a startling harmonic wrench in which the piano momentarily escapes into the distant key of E natural, the key of the slow movement. The return of the rondo refrain is swift and dramatic; the third episode brings back the theme of the first, but now in the tonic key of C. A tiny cadenza, or *Eingang,* leads into a delirious *presto* conclusion in 6/8 meter with further joyous transformations of familiar themes.

The Concerto is scored for 2 flutes, 2 oboes, 2 clarinets, 2 bassoons, 2 horns, 2 trumpets, kettledrums, and strings.

CONCERTO FOR PIANO AND ORCHESTRA, NO. 4, G MAJOR, OPUS 58

Beethoven wrote four of his five piano concertos for himself as a performing virtuoso. They were his stock in trade, especially during the early years when he was far more popular as a performer than as a composer. And since there were no copyrights, he took the precaution of withholding his concertos from publication until he himself had made good use of them. Thus the Fourth Concerto, which he composed in 1805 and 1806, was not published in the orchestral parts until August 1808. The first performance of the Fourth Concerto was given in private, on one of two subscription concerts, both all-Beethoven programs, given at the palace of Prince Lobkowitz in March of 1807. The first public performance of the Concerto, again with Beethoven as the soloist, was presented at the incredible concert of December 22, 1808, in the Theater an der Wien, which included the world premieres of four major masterpieces: his Fifth and Sixth Symphonies, his Fourth Piano Concerto and his Choral Fantasia, to say nothing of four movements from his Mass in C and the soprano aria, "Ah! Perfido."

The theater was freezing cold. The audience struggled through more than four hours of modern music, most of it never before heard in public. The performances were so rough that at one point the orchestra broke down entirely and had to begin over again. Nevertheless, Beethoven's performance of his own Concerto seems to have been overwhelming. J. F. Reichardt, who heard Beethoven on this occasion, wrote: "He played . . . with astounding cleverness and in the fastest possible tempi. The *Adagio,* a masterly movement of beautifully developed song, he sang on this instrument with a profund melancholy that thrilled me."

I. *Allegro moderato.* From Beethoven's sketchbooks we know that the serene motive at the beginning of this Concerto grew out of the same thought which supplied the tempestuous opening of his Fifth Symphony—the imperious motive of which Beethoven is said to have declared, "Thus Fate knocks on the door":

But how gentle and ingratiating it sounds here, and how it can sing:

We hear it first in the hushed voice of the piano, unaccompanied. The orchestral strings answer softly, as if from a far distant key—a Romantic color effect which still sounds as fresh as if it had not been imitated through the hundred years that followed.

By way of gentle contrast, the first violins, followed by a solo oboe, sing a more lyric, lilting phrase.

The piano solo returns, with an almost pensive cadenza-like passage, to join the orchestra in a restatement and development of the basic themes. One graceful phrase chases another across these melodious opening pages, and in spite of the stormy grandeur with which they are all developed, the sweeping *arpeggios,* the brilliant scales and sudden dynamic contrasts, this is supremely lyrical music from beginning to end.

II. *Andante con moto.* The striking dialogue between orchestra and piano in this movement was once compared by Franz Liszt to Orpheus taming the wild beasts. Beethoven's orchestra is not exactly a wild beast—not in this movement, anyway—but the peremptory octaves in which it speaks, and the gentle, pleading phrases with which the piano replies, do seem a conversation between two totally different musical temperaments, which, quite astoundingly, reach agreement. The stern voice of the orchestra relents, the octaves melt into harmony, and at the very end, orchestra unites with solo in a little sigh of acquiescence.

III. *Rondo: Vivace.* The melancholy spell of the *Andante* is broken by whispering strings in the following vivacious theme, the refrain of the rondo finale:

The piano answers with graceful variants of the string phrases. But after this discreet beginning, the orchestra *tutti* bursts in with a boisterous repetition of the refrain, and the rondo turns out to be full of surprises. The violence of its gaiety, following the deep shadows of the slow movement, recalls the stories of Beethoven's sudden fluctuations of mood when improvising for his friends. Sometimes, when he had finished and turned around to find his listeners shattered, overwhelmed with emotion, he would burst into a roar of laughter. "We artists don't want tears," he would mock, "we want applause."

The finale is rich in sudden contrasts. It charms, it blusters, it crackles, and after the great flourish of the cadenza and some humorous afterthoughts, it launches into a triumphant *presto,* with the obstinate refrain still dominating the grand orchestral frenzy.

The Fourth Piano Concerto is scored for 1 flute, 2 oboes, 2 clarinets, 2 bassoons, 2 horns, 2 trumpets, kettledrums, and the standard string choir.

CONCERTO FOR PIANO AND ORCHESTRA, NO. 5, E-FLAT MAJOR, OPUS 73

Beethoven himself had taken the solo part in the earliest performances of all his first four piano concertos. His earliest triumphs in Vienna had been as a virtuoso performer of his own works. But by 1809, when he finished his Fifth, or "Emperor," Concerto, he had grown too deaf to perform. This could be one reason why his Fifth Concerto was his last.

He finished it in 1809, the year of the Austrian defeat at Wagram, the year of Napoleon's siege and occupation of Vienna. When the bombardment of the city grew too loud, Beethoven would take refuge in the cellar of his brother Carl's house and cover his head with pillows—not out of cowardice, but to protect his ears and what little hearing he had left. Napoleon took the Austrian capital. Beethoven was defiant and furious. A friend found him in a café, shaking his fist at the back of a French officer. "If I were a general," he said, "and knew as much about strategy as I do about counterpoint, I'd give you fellows something to think about."

Perhaps because of the war, the Concerto had to wait two years for its premiere. This seems to have taken place in Leipzig on November 28, 1811, with one Friedrich Schneider as soloist, and an orchestra conducted by Johann Philipp Christian Schulz. Its reception was enthusiastic. The *Allgemeine Musik Zeitung* of January 1812 was rapturous: "It is without doubt one of the most original, imaginative, most effective but also one of the most difficult of all existing concertos."

For the first Viennese performance three months later, on February 12, 1812, Beethoven entrusted the solo part to his brilliant pupil Carl Czerny. Yet this performance was unsuccessful. The periodical *Thalia* attributed the failure to the refusal of the "proud and overconfident" Beethoven to write down to his audience. "He can be understood and appreciated only by connoisseurs," the editor claimed.

Nevertheless, there is a story—perhaps apocryphal—that one member of that first Viennese audience, a French army officer, was so carried away by the music that he acclaimed it as "an emperor among concertos." Whether this was the source of the now-familiar designation "Emperor," or whether the nickname was bestowed by an early publisher or pianist, we may never know.

I. *Allegro.* The first movement begins with a decisive chord for the full orchestra, whereupon the piano enters unconventionally with a sweeping cadenza—the kind of thing customarily reserved for the close of a movement. There are two more such chords, the piano continuing its rhapsodic outbursts after each. These outbursts are written out in careful detail by Beethoven, rather than being left to the discretion of the soloist, as was customary with cadenzas. Only after this impulsive opening is the orchestra permitted to announce, in traditional style, the principal theme:

This principal theme branches out into a rich variety of subordinate musical thoughts, the chief of which, a gently rocking figure, is presented first by soft *pizzicato* strings (in the tonic minor) and immediately taken up by two golden-voiced horns in the mellow tonic major:

Both themes are presented by the orchestra and developed at some length before the piano returns to present its own version of the same material. There is a stormy development and dialogue between piano and orchestra before the themes are restated in approximately their original form. At the point where one traditionally expects a cadenza, Beethoven has written for the pianist "Do not play a cadenza but attack immediately the following." The following material, however, is really Beethoven's own (brief) cadenza on the two main themes of the movement, with the orchestra joining in for a triumphant coda.

II. *Adagio un poco mosso.* The slow movement is a nocturne-like, songful piece, in which the melody is sung first by muted violins followed by pianistic garlands of variations. As the final harmony of the third and last variation dies away, the bassoons very softly sustain the key note of the movement, a B natural. Then, without any transition, the whole orchestra seems to sink a half tone, down to B flat. Above this soft, sustained tone, we hear hints of the rondo finale, which follows without break.

III. *Rondo: Allegro.* This main theme now bounds upward in excited, powerful syncopations. It is the refrain of a vast rondo:

Much of the dynamism and exhilaration of this finale is achieved through Beethoven's almost miraculous mastery and creative use of form. This is no place for a searching formal analysis, fascinating as that can be. Broadly speaking, the movement is a new and original marriage of rondo and sonata form, in which the returns of the refrain quoted above serve as a framework, while the episodes enclose the major sections of a complete sonata form. The first episode, for example, presents a tiny sonata-form exposition, the principal theme of which is:

The second episode is a tiny development section, which, in turn, is a minuscule rondo. Yet for all the formal virtuosity of boxes within boxes, this finale seems totally spontaneous, unfettered, and impulsive.

The score of the "Emperor" Concerto calls for 2 flutes, 2 oboes, 2 clarinets, 2 bassoons, 4 horns, 2 trumpets, kettledrums, and the standard strings.

CONCERTO FOR VIOLIN AND ORCHESTRA, D MAJOR, OPUS 61

Composed in a tremendous rush for a specific concert on December 23, 1806, Beethoven's Opus 61 is generally acknowledged to be the greatest of all violin concertos. It has been surrounded with a certain amount of mystery almost since its world premiere in Vienna on December 23, 1806. Beethoven composed it with a specific virtuoso in mind: the twenty-six-year-old Franz Clement, a former child prodigy, sensational concert performer, and already (at that early age) first violinist and conductor at the famous Theater an der Wien. The occasion was a concert for the benefit of Clement himself.

It was logical that the performer's style should influence the music Beethoven wrote for him. He probably even sought the young man's advice on technical matters. Yet all the evidence suggests that Beethoven was far from decided on how much of Clement's advice to take, for he left two strikingly different versions of the solo part. One appears to be his original inspiration, uninfluenced by advice; the second version is a more idiomatic, more violinistic version, and technically less difficult. Beethoven's only surviving autograph makes no final decision between the two versions, and neither version agrees with the printed version which appeared (in two separate editions, one in Vienna, the other in London) during Beethoven's lifetime.

We know that Beethoven worked on the Concerto until the last feasible moment before the performance. Since he habitually made endless revisions in his works, his manuscript left ample extra staves for revisions of the solo part. In some places all four staves are filled with his changes. The story which has come down to us from Beethoven's friend and pupil Carl Czerny, according to which the score was finished barely two days before the concert, may, of course, be true. On the other hand, the often-repeated assertion that it was finished so late that Clement had to play the first performance at sight from the manuscript—corrections and all—has an obviously apocryphal sound, all the more so since Clement must have watched and discussed the growth of the Concerto with Beethoven.

What were the characteristics of this violinist who almost certainly influenced the music we know? For one thing, Clement was not above a certain amount of circus sensationalism. On the same program with this Concerto he played a composition of his own on one string with the violin upside-down. But when he wished, Clement had great distinction, purity, and nobility of style. "His performance is magnificent," said one contemporary, "in its way probably unique. It is not the bold, robust, powerful playing of the school of Viotti, but it is indescribably graceful, dainty, elegant." Another adds that "gracefulness and tenderness were its main characteristics."

These qualities are reflected in Beethoven's music. He gave Clement plenty of technical bravura, but he also paid him the compliment of writing music which placed Clement's highest artistic gifts in the foreground. He dedicated the manuscript with a dubious bilingual pun: "Concerto par Clemenza pour Clement primo Violino / e direttore al theatro a Vienna / Dal L v. Bthvn 1806."

But the premiere was no great success—and perhaps no wonder, when one recalls how hastily it was prepared.

It was only two years later that the Concerto was published—in a version of the solo part for which no Beethoven manuscript exists. However, we do have the manuscript of the professional copyist, which was used for the printed edition, and this copyist's manuscript contains markings in Beethoven's hand, showing that he examined it carefully before it went to the printer. In addition, the English musicologist Alan Tyson has demonstrated that Beethoven must also have corrected the proofs for that edition. Thus he obviously gave his approval to the solo part as it was printed and as it is still usually performed. In essence this version is a compromise between his own original and his more violinistic second version, although some bars of the published version are new.

Although we may never know with 100 percent certainty that Beethoven himself composed every note of the final printed version of the solo part, it seems highly unlikely that he would have entrusted the formulation of the version to anyone else. But the tantalizing question remains, as it does in the case of the various versions of Beethoven's opera *Fidelio.* How much did he restore from his original version (because he considered it artistically superior) and how much of the simpler, more violinistic version did he retain out of purely practical considerations (which would scarcely be necessary for the vastly greater techniques of twentieth-century violinists)? Most astounding of all, perhaps, is the question of why the world had to wait until 141 years after his death for Beethoven's two manuscript versions to be published for all to see and, possibly, one day, to hear. (The preparation of this belated edition of Beethoven's manuscript published by Breitkopf and Härtel of Wiesbaden is chiefly the work of two devoted musicologists: Fritz Kaiser and Willy Hess, whose years of idealistic labors have given us all an opportunity to see more deeply into one of the greatest masterpieces of the symphonic literature.)

Whatever new understandings may await us, the traditional familiar version of the Violin Concerto remains a rejuvenating experience.

I. *Allegro ma non troppo.* The fundamental serenity of the music comes interestingly closer to the spirit of Mozart than Beethoven had been able to do in his early works, when he was actually imitating Mozart. The first movement opens with five soft beats on the kettledrums, introducing the wonderfully calm principal theme:

When the opening five beats of the kettledrum are taken up by the violins and repeated on D sharp, the effect is startling. It all resolves in the most natural way in the world, however, and the rhythm of those five beats haunts the development.

II. *Larghetto.* The slow movement opens with a deceptively simple theme in the muted violins. Next, two horns and a clarinet take up the theme very tenderly as the solo violin weaves garlands of simple embellishment. A series of beautiful variations follows. A pensive coda and a cadenza for the solo violin lead without pause into the brilliant rondo finale.

III. *Rondo: Allegro.* This is a vivacious virtuoso piece with a dance-like refrain starting on the deep G-string of the solo violin and later leaping far above the staff in sparkling runs, trills and arpeggios:

The exuberant spontaneity of the movement is enhanced by the form in which Beethoven cast it: a marriage of rondo and sonata-allegro, in which the Rondo refrain quoted above serves as the principal sonata theme, while the subordinate-theme group and development section appear as the episodes of the rondo. After the cadenza for the solo violin, the whole structure is rounded off with a brilliant coda for soloist and orchestra.

The orchestra for this Concerto calls for flute, 2 oboes, 2 clarinets, 2 bassoons, 2 trumpets, 2 horns, kettledrums, and the usual strings.

MISSA SOLEMNIS, D MAJOR, OPUS 123

"From the heart, may it go to the heart!" was Beethoven's inscription on the manuscript score of his *Missa solemnis ("Von Herzen–Möge es wieder—zu Herzen gehen!")*.

These words alone suggest that Beethoven's "Solemn Mass" is far from a traditional prayer, and further yet from any abstract liturgical sacrifice. Like the Ninth Symphony on which he worked at the same time, the *Missa* is an intensely personal work, which nevertheless is addressed to humanity at large—or rather to each individual within the human brotherhood. The dramatic manner, the almost volcanic fervor of the *Missa solemnis* has convinced many that, while the music is overwhelming, or perhaps *because* it is overwhelming, it is not suited for church service. But some Roman Catholic authorities have taken a more liberal point of view, and have expressly approved its performance on great religious occasions.

It was conceived for a great religious occasion: the installation of Beethoven's pupil and patron, the Archduke Rudolph (the youngest son of Emperor Leopold II), as Archbishop of Olmütz. The young Archduke had been a pupil of Beethoven in piano and composition for fifteen years. In April 1819 he was elected a Cardinal and two months later he was appointed to the Archbishopric; his enthronement was scheduled for March 20, 1820. Beethoven decided to compose a grand Mass for the ceremony.

"The day when a solemn mass by myself is performed as part of the ceremonies for Your Imperial Highness will be the happiest day of my life," he wrote to Rudolph in June 1819, "and God will inspire me so that my poor gifts may contribute to the glorification of this solemn day." Although Beethoven was neither a faithful churchgoer, nor even a believer in any narrow doctrinal way, he seems to have been deeply religious in a broader sense. He took the composition of the Mass very seriously. Amid his personal notations for the year 1818, when he began to sketch the Mass, we find the following memorandum to himself:

"In order to write true church music look through all the liturgical chorales of the monks, etc., to find out the best translations of the verses as well as the most perfect prosody of all Christian Catholic psalms and chants in general." A bit later in his notes, but still in 1818, we find: "God above everything! For an eternal, all-knowing Providence guides the fortune and misfortune of mortal men."

Begun as an occasional work (in the most exalted sense), the *Missa solemnis* soon began to grow and expand beyond its original purpose, until it became what Beethoven described more than once as his greatest work. (At the time he made these statements, he had already composed eight of his nine symphonies, all the piano concertos, all the piano sonatas and string quartets, except the last five "late quartets.")

Beethoven's struggles with the Mass seem to have been as monumental as the work itself. To his intimates, especially Anton Schindler, they appeared apocalytpic. One of these battles was overheard—involuntarily—by Schindler and a friend toward the end of August 1819. Beethoven was writing the fugue of the "Credo" (or possibly the fugue of the "Gloria," for it is not certain that Schindler had the fugue correctly identified). It was four o'clock in the afternoon when Schindler arrived at Beethoven's summer quarters in Mödling, just south of Vienna (today a suburb of the city).

> As soon as we entered, we learned that in the morning both maidservants had left, and that there had been a quarrel after midnight which had disturbed all the neighbors, because both of them had waited so long that they fell asleep and the food they had prepared [for Beethoven] had become unpalatable. In one of the rooms, behind a locked door, we heard the master singing parts of the fugue in the "Credo"—singing, howling, stamping. After we had been listening a long time to this almost terrifying scene, and were about to go away, the door opened and Beethoven stood before us with distorted features, fearful to behold. He looked as if he had been in mortal combat with the whole host of contrapuntists, his everlasting enemies. His first utterances were confused, as if he had been disagreeably surprised at our having overheard him.

The enthronement of Rudolph came and passed while the Mass remained unfinished. In part this was due to the fact that each section of the Mass was expanding into a giant structure that even Beethoven could scarcely have foreseen. In part, it was due also to personal problems, especially Beethoven's passionate struggle to "save" his nephew from what he regarded as the evil influence of the boy's mother.

By the beginning of 1822, Beethoven had finished the composition sketch for the Mass. But between the composition sketch and the completed autograph score many changes were made, and the full score manuscript was not delivered to the Archduke until March 19, 1823. In the working copy, which Beethoven retained, he continued to make changes and additions up to the middle of 1823.

With all due allowance for the fact that Beethoven at fifty-two had become eccentric (to put it mildly), difficult and morbidly suspicious of even his most devoted admirers and supporters, it is still surprising to realize that no performance of the complete *Missa solemnis* was heard in Vienna during his lifetime. The Philharmonic Society of faraway St. Petersburg had the honor of presenting the world premiere. Prince Nicholas Galitzin, a passionate admirer of Beethoven, to whose initiative we owe three of Beethoven's last and greatest works (his String Quartets, Op. 127, 130 and 132) took the initiative (and most of the financial responsibility) for the first performance of the *Missa solemnis,* which was presented in St. Petersburg on April 7, 1824 (March 26 Old Style Russian calendar) at a Philharmonic concert for the benefit of widows and orphans of musicians. Galitzin's enthusiastic account must have warmed Beethoven's heart.

> Monsieur, I am eager to give you an account of the performance of your sublime masterpiece which we presented here to the public the night before last. For several months I have been extremely impatient to hear this music performed, the great beauties of which I glimpsed in the score. The effect of this music on the public cannot be described, and I have no fear of exaggerating when I say that for my part I have never heard anything so sublime; I don't even except the masterpieces of Mozart which with their eternal beauties have not wakened in me the same sensations that you have given me, Monsieur, by the "Kyrie" and "Gloria" of your Mass. The masterly harmony and the moving melody of the "Benedictus" transport the heart to a realm of true happiness. This whole work, in fact, is a treasure of beauties; it can be said that your genius has anticipated the centuries and that there are no listeners enlightened enough to savor all the beauty of this music; but it is posterity that will pay homage and will bless your memory much better than your contemporaries can. Prince Radziwill, who you know is a great amateur of music, arrived just a few days ago from Berlin and was present at the performance of your Mass, which he had not known before; like myself and all those present he was enraptured with it.—I hope that your health is restored and that you will give us many more products of your sublime genius.—Excuse the nuisance that I often am to you with my letters, but it is a sincere tribute from one of your greatest admirers.
>
> P. NICHOLAS GALITZIN

On May 7, 1824, one month after St. Petersburg, Vienna heard three movements from the *Missa* ("Kyrie," "Credo," and "Agnus Dei"). Beethoven had intended to present the Viennese premiere of the entire *Missa solemnis* in one single concert which was also to include the world premiere of the entire Ninth Symphony plus his new Overture "The Consecration of the House." But even the impractical composer soon realized that this would make the program uncomfortably long, and he therefore decided to omit the "Gloria" of the Mass. After rehearsals had begun he decided to also omit the "Sanctus." Then there were difficulties with the Imperial Censor because Church authorities were opposed to the performance—even of excerpts from a Mass—in a theater. Finally, with the help of Count Lichnowsky, permission was obtained to perform the excerpts in German translation under the title of "Three Grand Hymns with Solo and Chorus." For the performance on May 7, the Kärntnertortheater was crowded and the applause overwhelming.

The rarity of opportunities to hear the *Missa solemnis* in Beethoven's day as well as ours must be put down largely to the difficulty of the choral as well as solo vocal parts.

I. *Kyrie.* The massive, monumental choral invocations of the Lord are contrasted, from the very opening, to the personal, individual voice of a single soloist: tenor, then soprano, then alto. Through most of the Mass, the most subjective emotions are entrusted to the solo voices, whereas the chorus seems to speak for all mankind.

(Assai sostenuto)
Kyrie eleison — Lord, have mercy

(Andante assai ben marcato)
Christe eleison — Christ, have mercy

(Assai sostenuto)
Kyrie eleison — Lord, have mercy

II. *Gloria.* The opening phrase, *"Gloria in excelsis,"* (the words of the angels as they appeared to the shepherds in the night of the Nativity) is set to triumphant rising lines, wave after wave soaring upward. At the words, "Peace on earth," which to Beethoven embodied one of the most important ideas of the entire Mass, a sudden hush comes over the music. At the phrase, "God, the Father Almighty" (*"omnipotens"*), Beethoven unleashes the thunder of the trombones which he has held in reserve up to this point. Half a dozen measures later, at the mention of the "only-begotten Son," the music suddenly grows tender. The repetitions of the prayer, *"Miserere nobis,"* become a more and more anguished appeal. And in order to intensify the language, Beethoven does not scruple to add an emotional exclamation to the sacred text, so that the line becomes *"O, miserere nobis."*

The climax of the *Gloria* is the tremendous fugue on the closing words, *"in Gloria Dei Patris. Amen."* This is the theme out of which Beethoven builds this towering structure:

When the fugue is concluded and one would think that nothing more could be added to the tremendous affirmation of its final *"Amen,"* the orchestra and chorus burst into a *presto* coda. Both the words and the soaring theme of the opening return and, as the chorus repeats the words *"in excelsis,"* the voices climb higher and higher until they reach a top B natural. The close comes with the exuberant threefold *"Gloria, gloria, gloria."*

(Allegro vivace)

Gloria in excelsis Deo.	Glory be to God in the highest.
Et in terra pax hominibus bonae voluntatis.	And on earth, peace to men of good will.
Laudamus te. Benedicimus te.	We praise Thee. We bless Thee.
Adoramus te. Glorificamus te.	We adore Thee. We glorify Thee.

(Meno allegro)

Gratias agimus tibi propter magnam gloriam tuam.	We give Thee thanks for Thy great glory.

(Allegro vivace)

Domine Deus, Rex coelestis!	Lord God, heavenly King!
Deus Pater omnipotens!	God, the Father Almighty!
Domine, Fili unigenite, Jesu Christe!	Lord Jesus Christ, the only-begotten Son!
Domine Deus! Agnus Dei! Filius Patris!	Lord God! Lamb of God! Son of the Father!

(Larghetto)

Qui tollis peccata mundi, miserere nobis.	Who takest away the sins of the world, have mercy upon us.
Qui tollis peccata mundi, suscipe deprecationem nostram.	Who takest away the sins of the world, receive our prayer.
Qui sedes ad dexteram Patris, miserere nobis.	Who sittest at the right hand of the Father, have mercy upon us.

(Allegro maestoso)

Quoniam tu solus sanctus.	For Thou alone are holy.
Tu solus Dominus. Tu solus altissimus, Jesu Christe!	Thou alone art Lord. Thou alone, O Jesus Christ, art most high!
Cum Sancto Spiritu in gloria Dei Patri. Amen.	Together with the Holy Ghost, in the glory of God the Father. Amen.

(Allegro ma non troppo e ben marcato)

In gloria Dei Patris. Amen.	In the glory of God the Father. Amen.

(Presto)

Gloria in excelsis Deo.	Glory be to God in the highest.

III. *Credo.* At the very start of his gigantic "Credo," the orchestra hurls forth a theme characteristically Beethovenian in its brevity and striking power —a theme which is immediately taken up by the chorus, starting with the basses:

The extraordinarily vivid word-painting and word-expression we meet throughout the "Credo" springs from Beethoven's intensive study of each detail of the ritual text. Famous examples are the vocal plunge at *"descendit de coelis"* ("descended from heaven"), the flying scales at *"Et ascendit in coelum"* ("and ascended to heaven"), the mystical beginning of the incarnation *"Et incarnatus est"* ("and was made flesh") with its hesitant, awe-struck repetition of the first word: *"Et,"* and the (quite unecclesiastical) return of the opening affirmation, *"Credo, credo,"* in the latter part of the movement.

The climax of the Mass thus far comes with the conclusion of the "Credo" on the all-important words, *"Et vitam venturi saeculi"* ("And the life of the world to come"). Here tradition called for a fugue, and Beethoven's optimistic spirit responded with a fugue of irresistible fervor. Part of its power stems from the insistent repeated notes of the opening words:

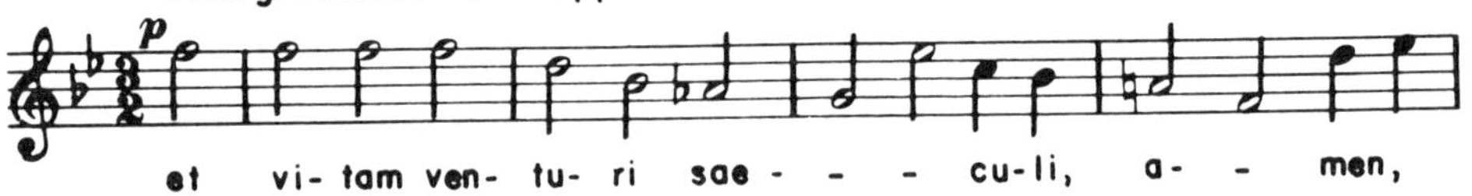

(Allegro ma non troppo)

Credo in unum Deum, Patrem omnipotentem, factorem coeli et terrae, visibilium omnium, et invisibilium.	I believe in one God, the Father Almighty, Maker of heaven and earth, and of all things visible and invisible.
Et in unum Dominum Jesum Christum, Filium Dei unigenitum.	And in one Lord, Jesus Christ, the only-begotten son of God.
Et ex Patre natum ante omnia saecula.	Born of the Father before all ages.
Deum de Deo, lumen de lumine, Deum vero de Deo vero.	God of God, light of light, true God of true God.
Genitum, non factum, consubstantialem Patri: per quem omnia facta sunt.	Begotten, not made; being of one substance with the Father: by whom all things were made.
Qui propter nos homines, et propter nostram salutem descendit de coelis.	Who for us men, and for our salvation came down from heaven.

(Adagio)

Et incarnatus est de Spiritu Sancto ex Maria Virgine:	And was made flesh by the Holy Ghost of the Virgin Mary:

(Andante)

Et homo factus est.	And was made man.

(Adagio espressivo)

Crucifixus etiam pro nobis: sub Pontio Pilato passus, et sepultus est.	He was also crucified for us, suffered under Pontius Pilate, and was buried.

(Allegro; Allegro molto)

Et resurrexit tertia die, secundum Scripturas.	And on the third day He arose again, according to the Scriptures.
Et ascendit in coelum: sedet ad dexteram Patris. Et iterum venturus est cum gloria judicare vivos et mortuos: cuius regni non erit finis.	And ascended into heaven; He sitteth at the right hand of the Father. And shall come again with glory to judge the living and the dead: and of His kingdom there shall be no end.

(Allegro ma non troppo)

Et in Spiritum Sanctum, Dominum, et vivificantem: qui ex Patre, Filioque procedit.	And in the Holy Ghost, the Lord and Giver of life, who proceedeth from the Father and the Son.
Qui cum Patre, et Filio simul adoratur, et con glorificatur: qui locutus est per Prophetas.	Who together with the Father and the Son is no less glorified: who spoke through the Prophets.
Et unam, sanctam, catholicam et apostolicam Ecclesiam.	And in one, holy, catholic and apostolic Church.
Confiteor unum baptisma in remissionem peccatorum.	I confess one baptism for the remission of sins.
Et expecto resurrectionem mortuorum.	And I await the resurrection of the dead.
Et vitam venturi saeculi. Amen.	And the life of the world to come. Amen.

(Allegretto ma non troppo; Allegro con moto; grave)

Et vitam venturi saeculi. Amen.	And the life of the world to come. Amen.

IV. *Sanctus.* Instead of the customary pomp of the opening "Holy, holy, holy, Lord God of hosts," Beethoven speaks at first through hushed single, solo voices—as if overcome by wonder. Brilliant rejoicing bursts forth at the *"Pleni sunt coeli"* ("Heaven and earth are filled with Thy Glory"), and in the fugal *"Osanna."* One of the tenderest moments of the entire Mass is the orchestral interlude which accompanies the miracle of the transformation of the Host. From here a seraphic violin solo continues into the peaceful "Benedictus."

(Adagio)

Sanctus, Sanctus, Sanctus, Dominus Deus, Sabaoth.	Holy, holy, holy, Lord God of Hosts.

(Allegro pesante)

Pleni sunt coeli et terra gloria tua.	Heaven and earth are filled with Thy Glory.

(Presto)

Osanna in excelsis.	Hosanna in the highest.

(Sostenuto ma non troppo)

Benedictus qui venit in nomine Domini. Osanna in excelsis.	Blessed is he that comes in the name of the Lord. Hosanna in the highest.

V. *Agnus dei.* Beethoven himself called this "a prayer for inward and outward peace." The most dramatic of the pleas for outward peace occurs in the final *"dona nobis pacem"* ("grant us peace"), when the martial trumpet fanfares, heard first as if in the distance, draw nearer and nearer until each soloist breaks out in successive, in terrified appeals to the Lamb of God. In Beethoven's mind, and in his feelings, the prayer is granted, and the Mass ends in confidence and serenity.

(Adagio; Allegretto vivace; Allegro assai; Presto)

Agnus Dei, qui tollis peccata mundi: miserere nobis.	Lamb of God, Who takest away the sins of the world, have mercy on us.
Agnus Dei, qui tollis peccata mundi: miserere nobis.	Lamb of God, Who takest away the sins of the world, have mercy on us.
Agnus Dei, qui tollis peccata mundi: dona nobis pacem.	Lamb of God, Who takest away the sins of the world, grant us peace.

The score of the *Missa solemnis* calls for soprano, alto, tenor and bass solos, 4-part chorus, an organ, 2 flutes, 2 oboes, 2 clarinets, 2 bassoons, contrabassoon, 4 horns, 2 trumpets, 3 trombones, kettledrums, and the traditional string choir.

OVERTURE, THE CONSECRATION OF THE HOUSE, OPUS 124

One can scarcely imagine a more appropriate work to open a symphonic series in a new concert hall than Beethoven's festive Overture, *Consecration of the House. Die Weihe des Hauses,* to use its German title, was composed for the inauguration of the remodeled Theater in der Josefstadt in Vienna, on October 3, 1822.

This charming little theater had been famous from Mozart's time as a suburban home of traditional Austrian folk comedy. In Beethoven's day the entire suburb of Josefstadt was still separated from Vienna proper by the massive ancient city wall. In our century, its fame revived by Max Reinhardt's brilliant productions, the Theater in der Josefstadt stands almost in the center of Vienna, where it is still in daily use.

When Beethoven was called upon late in the summer of 1822 to help celebrate its reopening, it was too late for a major new drama to be written for the occasion. Instead, Kotzebue's play, *The Ruins of Athens,* which, with incidental music by Beethoven, had opened the Budapest Theater eleven years earlier, was to be adapted. Rebaptized *Die Weihe des Hauses,* the text was refurbished by the Josefstadt poet Carl Meisl, and Beethoven added a new chorus and the Overture. Before completing the score, Beethoven confided to his young friend and later biographer, Anton Schindler, that two possible themes had occurred to him: one in free style and the other in strict Handelian style. As a great admirer of Handel, he chose the latter theme. He also chose a form which had been favored by Baroque composers from Lully through Bach and Handel: the so-called French overture, consisting of a slow ceremonious introduction, followed by a lively orchestral fugue.

Beethoven consciously imitated Handel's Baroque style, using ceremonial "dotted" rhythms in his introduction, and his "Handelian" theme for the fugue:

But Beethoven's own style is unmistakable in the massive harmonic blocks of his introduction, in the way he leads up to his fugue theme, the way he develops it, and builds to his incisive climax and conclusion. The score calls for a Classical orchestra of 2 flutes, 2 oboes, 2 clarinets, 2 bassoons, 4 horns, 2 trumpets, 3 trombones, kettledrums, and the usual strings.

CORIOLANUS OVERTURE, OPUS 62

Imperious, passionate, and iron-willed as Beethoven himself, the character of the Roman general Coriolanus must have appealed to Beethoven through bonds that penetrated deeply into his own character. Even Coriolanus's self-righteous vindictiveness when he felt himself the victim of ingratitude and injustice was more characteristic of Beethoven than he might have cared to think. The romantically minded Johann Friedrich Reichardt, composer and critic of Beethoven's day, thought that Beethoven's Overture was intended as a self-portrait rather than a portrait of Coriolanus.

The immediate stimulus for the composition seems to have been the tragedy of the same name by the Viennese dramatic poet Heinrich Joseph von Collin, whom Beethoven admired so much that he had planned to compose an opera, *Macbeth*, on a libretto which Collin was to adapt from Shakespeare's tragedy. The liberetto never got beyond the middle of the second act, but

Beethoven, stirred by Collin's treatment of another Shakespearean subject, Coriolanus (which Shakespeare in turn had taken from Plutarch), determined to write an overture to it.

Collin's *Coriolan* was first performed on November 24, 1802, in the Vienna Hofburg Theater and enjoyed considerable popularity for over two years, largely because of the success of Mozart's brother-in-law, Joseph Lange, in the title role. By the time Beethoven composed his Overture in 1807, Collin's tragedy was scarcely performed anymore. Indeed, it was given only once during the years 1805 to 1809. The Overture seems to have had its first performance at a private concert in the palace of Prince Lobkowitz in March 1807. It is more than likely that the one performance of Collin's *Coriolan* on the twenty-fourth of the following April used the new Overture; indeed the revival may have been arranged expressly for the purpose of using Beethoven's music.

The Overture seems to center upon the psychological conflict, which is the climax of both Shakespeare's and Collin's tragedies and the crisis of Coriolanus's career as related by Plutarch. According to Plutarch, Coriolanus was a general of the most reckless bravery who led the Romans to victory against the neighboring Volscians. Subsequently, his scorn for the Roman plebeians and his insults so roused the populace against him that the Senate sent him into permanent exile. In his fury at such injustice, Coriolanus went over to the Volscians and led their forces against his native Rome. The city lay at his mercy and Coriolanus scorned every emissary sent to implore mercy for the city, until they sent his mother, his wife, and his small son. At last his hard resolution cracked. He gave up his revenge and with it his life. In Shakespeare's version, the Volscians murder him for betraying his command; in Collin's, he commits suicide. In both versions Coriolanus sacrifices his righteous revenge for something greater than himself.

The Overture begins with a commanding gesture—a gesture of triumph, perhaps. Or one might take the opening phrase to be the contemptuous conqueror himself. But the agitation, the angry defiance, are interrupted by a gently flowing theme, the Classical contrast of traditional sonata-allegro form, which in this case is often taken to express the gentle pleas of Coriolanus's wife:

In the musical development, one may choose to hear the rising tide of indecision in the hero's mind, the inner turmoil, then the collapse of pride and the stoical self-destroying victory as the last murmurs of the orchestra drop away into silence.

The Overture is scored for 2 flutes, 2 oboes, 2 clarinets, 2 bassoons, 2 trumpets, 2 horns, kettledrums, and strings.

OVERTURE TO THE CREATURES OF PROMETHEUS, OPUS 43

We may never know just when Beethoven's fertile imagination began to associate Napoleon Bonaparte with the figure of the Greek demigod Prometheus. Possibly the association was not even original with Beethoven. The titan Prometheus, who defied the gods of Mount Olympus, stealing fire from heaven to bring warmth, light and enlightenment to mankind—such a hero would appeal not only to the idealist and rebel in Beethoven but also to many another admirer of the young Bonaparte, the general of the French Revolution. For at that time, Napoleon was still the defender of "liberty, equality, and fraternity," and First Consul of the French Republic. Whether the association of Napoleon with Prometheus was original or not, it eventually bore fruit in what many people consider the greatest symphony ever written: Beethoven's *Sinfonia eroica* of 1804.

In 1800 Beethoven, who had never before written a major work for the theater and was very anxious to do so, must have been pleased to be invited to compose music for a new "heroic and allegorical ballet," *The Creatures of Prometheus (Die Geschöpfe des Prometheus).* The production was choreographed by the distinguished dancer Salvatore Vigano. The premiere took place on March 28, 1801 (not March 26, the date given by some authorities), in the Hofburg Theater, Vienna, with Signor Vigano and his wife, who was a noted beauty and an exceptionally brilliant dancer, in the leading roles of two statues created by Prometheus.

The subject of the ballet was outlined in the program as follows: "The Greek philosophers . . . describe [Prometheus] as a lofty soul, who found the people of his time in ignorance, refined them by means of science and the arts and gave them manners, customs and morals. As a result of that conception, two statues which have been brought to life are introduced into this ballet, and these, through the power of harmony, are made receptive to all the passions of human existence. Prometheus leads them to Parnassus, in order that Apollo, the god of the arts, may enlighten them. Apollo gives them as teachers Amphion, Orion, and Orpheus to instruct them in music; Melpomene to teach them tragedy; Terpsichore and Pan, the Shepherds' dance; and Bacchus, the heroic dance, of which he was the originator."

Beethoven felt that Vigano did not take full advantage of the opportunities offered by the Prometheus subject. It is easy to guess from the summary in the program of the premiere and from the more detailed scenario of the ballet, which survives in a contemporary book on Vigano, what Beethoven felt the lack to be. The ballet puts no emphasis on Prometheus's traditionally rebellious, heroic character, nor on the suffering inflicted on him as the price of his benefactions for mankind.

The score for the ballet is divided into sixteen numbers, the finale of which is a set of variations on the theme which reappears three years later in the finale of the *Eroica*.

The Overture to *The Creatures of Prometheus* begins with a solemn *Adagio* introduction, brief, but richly scored and an effective contrast to the vivacious main section of the Overture. The main section, *Allegro molto con brio,* is based on a dashing little theme given out *pianissimo* by the first violins:

and echoed almost immediately by the full sonority of the orchestral *tutti.* The second thematic idea, a lilting figure for the woodwinds, is rounded off by a more lyric closing theme and a *codetta* so richly developed that it is almost like a tiny development section in itself. Beethoven bypasses any real development section, however, and recapitulates the entire *Allegro* section up to this point, with simple changes of key as they would occur in a normal recapitulation of the standard symphonic sonata form. The conclusion is a brilliant coda, which maintains the lightness, brightness and verve appropriate for a Classical ballet.

The score calls for 2 flutes, 2 oboes, 2 clarinets, 2 bassoons, 2 horns, 2 trumpets, kettledrums, and strings.

OVERTURE TO EGMONT, OPUS 84

Defiance of tyranny was a principle of supreme importance to Beethoven. And it is a subject that gives explosive power to Goethe's tragedy *Egmont.* Beethoven's admiration for Goethe bordered on worship. So it is no wonder that when the Vienna Burgtheater invited Beethoven (in 1809) to contribute the incidental music for a revival of *Egmont,* he responded with one of his most eloquent scores. It includes nine numbers, of which the Overture is the most stirring.

Like Beethoven's three "Leonore" Overtures, his *Egmont* Overture forecasts the essence of the action to come. And to feel the *full* impact of the Overture it is almost essential to have seen or, at least, read the drama it introduces. Goethe's *Egmont* plays during the sixteenth-century military subjugation of the Netherlands by the Spanish Duke of Alva; it shows their betrayal, their agony, the seeds of their growing defiance, a dream of victory, and it ends with a call to revolution.

Beethoven's Overture opens with heavily accented chords in an ominous F minor. Is it only coincidence that their rhythm is that of an ancient Spanish dance, the saraband, slowed down to a threatening pace? If Beethoven intended such an association, the chords might refer to the vindictive Duke of Alva. But one need not be so literal.

More lyric phrases follow. An innocent little melodic offshoot grows in importance by sheer repetition until suddenly, as we plunge into the main section of the Overture, our innocent little offshoot has become a sweeping, plunging phrase in the cellos—a thematic leader and herald of revolt:

This theme builds to a great climax for full orchestra. Its forward drive culminates in a commanding, quick version of the chords which open the Overture. There is the briefest sort of symphonic development before the return, or reprise, of the main themes.

Suddenly the headlong pace of the orchestra is arrested. There is a tiny pause of terror. The orchestra, drained of color and motion, fades almost to silence. Then, out of the depths of—defeat? of weakness? of despair?—no matter: out of the depth of the orchestra, almost inaudibly at first, we hear a fresh excitement spread among the instruments, swelling irresistibly, with mounting confidence and power, to unmistakable fanfares of victory, to paeans of rejoicing.

But why joy? How can such tumultuous triumph prepare us for tragedy. Goethe and Beethoven withhold the answer until the final seconds of the drama:

The Duke of Alva has had the champion of Netherlands freedom, Count Egmont, lured into a trap, thrown into prison and condemned to death. The night before his execution, Egmont's love, Clärchen, comes to him in a dream as the Goddess of Freedom. She prophesies that his death will be the spark which fires the Netherlands to rebellion and the recapture of their lost liberty. She proclaims Egmont the true victor and crowns him with a laurel wreath. Dawn shows gray through the prison bars; the reality of a drumroll disperses the dream. Involuntarily, Egmont feels for the laurel wreath.

"The wreath has vanished," he says. "Fair vision, the light of day has taken you away. Yes, the two deepest joys of my heart were one: divine freedom borrowed the form of my love. . . . She came to me with bloodstained feet, the swaying hem of her gown stained with blood. It was my blood and the blood of many a noble man. No, it has not been shed in vain. Stride forth, brave people! The goddess of victory leads you on. Like the sea bursting through your dikes, you must burst and overwhelm the ramparts of tyranny, drown it, and sweep it from the land it has usurped. [Drums approach . . . the background is filled with Alva's soldiers.] Yes, bring them on! Close your ranks! I do not fear you. . . . My enemies surround me on every side; swords flash. Friends, take heart! Behind you are your parents, your wives, your children! . . . Guard your sacred heritage! And to defend all you hold most dear, fall joyfully, as I do before you now!"

After Egmont has said all that words can say—all that Goethe's poetry, with its untranslatable fire can say—then Goethe himself calls for something beyond words, for music, for "a symphony of victory" which envelopes Egmont and ourselves as he marches off to his death. Beethoven concludes

Goethe's drama with a climax of such exaltation that it almost ceases to be tragedy at all. Now we understand the triumphant conclusion of Beethoven's Overture. It consists of the final, transfiguring moments with which Beethoven concludes the drama.

Beethoven labored on the incidental music for *Egmont* from October 1809 into June 1810. The Overture was the last number he completed (just before the middle of June), far too late for the revival of *Egmont*, which had taken place on May 24, 1810. Beethoven's music was first heard at the fourth repetition of the play on June 15. The score calls for piccolo, 2 flutes, 2 oboes, 2 clarinets, 2 bassoons, 4 horns, 2 trumpets, kettledrums, and the string choir.

OVERTURE TO FIDELIO

In giving shape to his only opera, *Fidelio,* Beethoven had been goaded not only by his own habitual and almost obsessive reworking and re-reworking of his musical thought, but he had been under heavy pressure from his friends to revise his opera for greater theatrical effect. He did, in fact, undertake not only two radical revisions of *Fidelio,* but at least four separate versions of the Overture.

The first three are known as the "Leonore" Overtures Nos. 1, 2, and 3. Only the fourth is known as the *Fidelio* Overture. The "Leonore" Overture No. 1 was composed for the first version of the opera, but performed only once during Beethoven's lifetime, at a private tryout, after which Beethoven decided that this Overture was too slight to do justice to the overwhelming opera. The boldest and most experimental of the Overtures, No. 2, was the one performed at the world premiere of the opera in 1805. The "Leonore" Overture No. 3, composed for the revision of 1806, has, for most listeners, a more powerful emotional impact—so powerful that Beethoven realized it threatened to dwarf the entire opera.

With this in mind, he composed the completely different fourth, or *Fidelio* Overture, for the 1814 revision of the opera. It is this Overture which normally precedes the opera today.

In the *Fidelio* Overture, Beethoven avoided any anticipation or artistic summary of the overwhelming drama to come. Instead he composed a joyous, festive score, one of his sunniest works, in the warm key of E major, with a richly colored orchestra giving especial prominence to the glowing tone of the French horn. In terms of the musical theater, this proved by far the most effective preparation for his opera. In terms of the concert hall, it has proved one of the most rewarding short symphonic works of the entire repertory.

The Overture's opening pages are built around a characteristically abrupt, Beethovenian contrast between a commanding fanfare-like figure for the entire orchestra and the pensive, romantic mood evoked by a duet of solitary French horns followed by pairs of clarinets and other woodwinds.

The main body of the Overture is built on a lively French horn theme which incorporates and extends the fanfare figure of the opening:

A sprightly skipping figure of the strings offers a moment's distraction, but the orchestra keeps returning to the opening figure, which is developed with easy symphonic sleight of hand, recapitulated and, at last, apotheosized in an exultant *presto* coda.

Although it was composed for the second revision of *Fidelio* (first performed at the Vienna Kärtnertor-Theater on May 23, 1814), the Overture was not completed in time. The last-minute substitute was Beethoven's Overture to *The Ruins of Athens.* At the second performance on May 26, 1814, the program bore the note: "The new Overture, omitted by force of circumstances at the previous performance of this opera, will be performed for the first time today." It is scored for 2 flutes, 2 oboes, 2 clarinets, 2 bassoons, 4 horns, 2 trumpets, 2 trombones, kettledrums, and the Classical string choir.

LEONORE OVERTURE NO. 1

Beethoven's first overture to his first and only opera suffered a harsh fate. The opera, which he always wished to have called *Leonore* and which has always been called *Fidelio,* was first performed in Vienna in 1805. During the preparations for the premiere Beethoven grew dissatisfied with his Overture. His feeling was reinforced by the reaction of friends and patrons and confirmed by a private performance of the Overture at the palace of his patron Prince Lichnowsky. According to Beethoven's friend, helper, and subsequent biographer Anton Schindler (who, however, did not actually meet Beethoven until much later), it was generally agreed that the first Overture was too light and inconsequential for a drama of the importance of *Leonore.* Hence, it was discarded, and Beethoven composed a new Overture (which we know today as "Leonore" Overture No. 2). This was the Overture performed at the world premiere. For the 1806 revision of the opera, Beethoven wrote a third Overture ("Leonore" No. 3) and for the 1814 revision a fourth. This last is the one we know today as the Overture to *Fidelio.* By a curious irony the fourth and last version (the one always used today) represents a return to the lighter character of the discarded "Leonore" Overture No. 1.

The reason for this was simple. In his "Leonore" Overtures 2 and 3 Beethoven had composed symphonic masterpieces of such concentrated might that they overwhelmed the entire first act of the opera. The lighter "Fidelio" Overture was immediately, and is still, admired as being exactly right for its function.

Meanwhile the "Leonore" Overture No. 1 lay neglected and unperformed, and it was not until eleven years after Beethoven's death that it was published with the opus number 138. For many years there was great confusion as to when it had actually been composed. When all the musicological dust had settled and Joseph Braunstein clarified the entire situation in a famous essay, it turned out that the "Leonore" Overtures had in fact been written in the sequence of their numbers, as outlined above.

The "Leonore" Overture No. 1 opens with a leisurely introduction of graceful, decorative character, merging finally into a vivacious *Allegro con brio,* which constitutes the main body of the score. The principal theme, fiery rather than heroic, is characterized by swiftly fluctuating moods. The most famous theme (the only theme common to all three "Leonore" Overtures) is an echo of Florestan's Second Act lament as he lies in the Stygian darkness of his prison: *"In des Lebens Frühlingstagen"* ("In the Springtime of Life"):

After this melancholy interlude, the Overture brings back the basic *Allegro* themes, as if in an outburst of rejoicing.

Beethoven's orchestra for the "Leonore" Overture No. 1 is slightly smaller than the ensemble required for the two subsequent Overtures to the opera. The latter two call for 3 trombones, whereas the first, omitting trombones altogether, requires only 2 flutes, 2 oboes, 2 clarinets, 2 bassoons, 4 horns, 2 trumpets, kettledrums, and the Classical string choir.

LEONORE OVERTURE NO. 2

"Of all my children," said Beethoven during his last illness as he presented the manuscript of *Fidelio* to his friend, Anton Schindler, "this is the one that caused me the worst birth-pangs, the one that brought me the most sorrow; and for that reason, it is the one most dear to me." Beethoven's work on his opera spread over more than a decade of his most productive years: 1803–14. His reworking and re-reworking of his own musical inspiration, until it approached the perfection he sought, was almost obsessive.

He was goaded, not only by his own perfectionism, but by his friends, who pressed him to revise his opera from a purely theatrical point of view. Beethoven undertook two painful revisions of the opera (which he originally wished to have titled *Leonore*) and at least four separate versions of the Overture.

The "Leonore" Overture No. 1, written for the first version of the opera, was discarded even before the premiere as too simple. The "Leonore" Overture No. 2, which sacrificed traditional sonata form in favor of a more faithful résumé of the dramatic action, was used for the premiere of 1805. The "Leonore" Overture No. 3, used for the revision of 1806, has, for some listeners, a more stunning emotional impact, so stunning in fact that Beethoven, realizing that it tended to dwarf the entire opera, wrote a fourth overture, known today as the *Fidelio* Overture. This version was performed with the 1814 revision of *Fidelio* and is the one that generally precedes the opera today.

Fidelio, or rather the borrowed plot of *Fidelio,* was said to be based on historical fact, on the hair-raising last-minute rescue of an innocent man during the French Revolution's Reign of Terror. (Bouilly, the author of the French libretto of Gaveaux's opera *Léonore, ou l'amour conjugale,* claimed to have had personal knowledge of the events and to have shifted the scene to Madrid to shield the people involved.) For Beethoven the essence of the plot was the triumph of liberty over tyranny, of heroism and love over corruption and hate.

Florestan, the innocent idealist, has been unjustly imprisoned by a powerful enemy in a secret subterranean dungeon. When the enemy, Pizzaro, learns that the prison is about to be inspected, he decides that Florestan must be murdered and buried before the inspecting minister arrives. But Florestan is saved by the heroism of his wife, Leonore, who disguises herself as a man and assists the jailor in the gruesome task of digging a grave for the intended victim. At the very last moment she shields her husband's body with her own. They are saved by the trumpet call announcing the arrival of the minister-inspector.

The Overture begins with a solemn passage of descending octaves, which could suggest the descent into Florestan's dungeon. It leads to the melody of Florestan's second-act dungeon lament, "In des Lebens Frühlingstagen" ("In the springtime of my life"):

In the fast main section of the Overture this melody, sung by horns and woodwinds, becomes the lyric second theme, suggesting a traditional sonata-form overture. The development climbs to a tremendous climax capped by the trumpet call announcing Florestan's liberation. At this point, traditional sonata form would have dictated a recapitulation of much basic thematic material. But Beethoven discarded this whole traditional recapitulation, which would have held up the headlong dramatic sequence of his music. Instead, there is a brief reminiscence of Florestan's lament in its original form, and then the music launches into the *presto* finale in which the lament is transformed into a song of triumph:

The score of Beethoven's "Leonore" Overture No. 2 calls for 2 flutes, 2 oboes, 2 clarinets, 2 bassoons, 4 horns, 2 trumpets, 3 trombones, kettledrums, and the traditional orchestral strings.

LEONORE OVERTURE NO. 3, C MAJOR

If Beethoven were alive today he would almost certainly be regarded as a dangerous radical—or at best, as a naïve political crackpot, to be tolerated because of his genius as a composer. Liberty, Equality, Fraternity was a subversive slogan which had sparked the greatest political explosion of modern history. To Beethoven and to many another idealist of his age, these words were more than slogan, more even than ideals, they were passions which could help shape the fate of mankind. They also helped shape some of Beethoven's greatest music, the two most obvious examples being his "Eroica" Symphony and his opera, *Fidelio.*

The passions also met defeats. There were leaders who persisted in viewing the French Revolution as an overgrown riot. Order was restored with a "whiff of grapeshot." Liberty, Equality, and Fraternity came to seem little more than the emptiest sort of Fourth of July (or Fourteenth of July) oratory. Yet the ideas smoldered and from time to time they exploded. Those eighteenth-century passions have become passions again in our time; and the impact of Beethoven's music should warn us, if our intelligence does not, that we ignore these passions at our peril.

The stature of this Overture grows. Or so it seems today. Of course we cannot really know how it affected the first audience when it burst from the pit of the little Viennese Theater an der Wien on the night of March 29, 1806. At that first hearing it introduced Beethoven's revision (his first revision) of the opera he always wished to have called *Leonore* and which always has been known as *Fidelio.*

Fidelio is a "rescue opera" with a plot of a kind which first became popular in France during the Revolution of 1789. It glorifies defiance of tyranny and the heroic devotion of married lovers. And in its final triumph of virtue and freedom Beethoven celebrated something greater than the deliverance of one individual victim of injustice.

Florestan, a champion of truth, has been imprisoned by his powerful enemy, Pizarro, in the lowest dungeon of a fortress near Seville. Word is given out that he has died. When Pizarro hears the fortress is to be inspected by a minister from Seville, he decides that Florestan must perish before his presence is discovered. Meanwhile Florestan's wife Leonore has disguised herself as a boy and entered the service of old Rocco, the jailer. Rocco takes her with him down into the dungeon to help dig the grave. There she recognizes her own husband and at the crucial moment she throws herself between him and his would-be murderer. The desperate Pizarro resolves to kill both husband and wife, but Leonore draws a pistol. At that moment a trumpet call is heard from the ramparts of the castle announcing the arrival of the minister from Seville, and Florestan is saved.

It was characteristic of Beethoven that he wrote four overtures for *Fidelio* before he was satisfied. The "Leonore" Overture No. 1 was composed for the first version of the opera, but was discarded, even before the premiere, as too simple for such a powerful work. In the "Leonore" No. 2, performed at the premiere on November 20, 1805, in the Theater an der Wien, Beethoven sacrificed traditional sonata form to gain a more faithful resume of the drama. But this music proved too difficult technically for the orchestra of Beethoven's day. There were woodwind passages, some thirty-odd bars, which the players never got right. Thus when Beethoven was persuaded to revise his opera for a revival the following March, he revised the Overture once more.

Once caught up in his revision, he ended by writing a virtually new overture on the same themes: the "Leonore" No. 3. Its predecessor, the "Leonore" No. 2, was a masterpiece in its own right. It is fascinating to see how a master outdoes his own masterpiece. One of his most powerful devices for heightening the tension of his newest overture, was a return to traditional sonata form. There are many eloquent changes of detail. To most listeners the "Leonore" No. 3 has the more stunning emotional effect. So stunning in fact that Beethoven later realized that it tended to dwarf his entire opera. The result was that he eventually wrote a fourth overture, a lighter piece, better adapted to its function in the theater, and known today as the *Fidelio* Overture. This fourth overture was performed for the 1814 revision of *Fidelio* and is the one that generally precedes the opera today.

The "Leonore" Overture No. 3 begins with a solemn passage of descending octaves, which may suggest the descent into Florestan's subterranean dungeon. This leads to the melody of Florestan's second act dungeon lament: *"In des Lebens Frühlingstagen"* ("In the Springtime of Life"):

When the slow introduction gives way to the fast main section of the Overture, Florestan's lament returns as the broadly lyric second theme of the sonata form. The dramatic development section builds to a tremendous climax, cut short by the trumpet call announcing Florestan's liberation. There are few more stirring moments in opera than the soft hesitant measures which follow that trumpet call—the seconds after the danger is past, when Florestan's mind gropes out of the horror of darkness, almost afraid to believe that he is still alive and that his savior is his beloved wife, Leonore. Once more the trumpet sounds, more loudly, the door to the dungeon is thrown open. The light of liberation streams into the dungeon cell. The enemy Pizarro disappears like a shadow, and the couple is left alone.

It is at this point that Beethoven's genius most clearly outdoes itself. Instead of following the opera plot, as he had done in the preceding overture, to end here with a coda of rejoicing, Beethoven drops the story line to follow the more powerful line of sheer emotion. This it is that brings him back to the sonata tradition. For in his reprise, the basic themes of the Overture pass in review, but now in a blaze of triumph. And now, when Beethoven passes from *this* to the peak of the *presto* finale, his coda expands into a cosmic jubilation transcending the joy of Florestan and Leonore. Florestan's lament for lost liberty is transformed into a fanfare of victory:

But the voice is that of Beethoven himself singing his paean to the liberation and freedom of all mankind: his vision of liberty, equality, and fraternity.

The score of the "Leonore" Overture No. 3 calls for 2 flutes, 2 oboes, 2 clarinets, 2 bassoons, 4 horns, 2 trumpets, 3 trombones, kettledrums, and the standard string choir.

SYMPHONY NO. 1, C MAJOR, OPUS 21

At age twenty-nine Beethoven himself was very like the First Symphony he presented in its world premiere at an *Akademie* (as concerts were then called) for his own benefit at the Hofburg Theater of Vienna on April 2, 1800. Beethoven already had the self-assurance which characterized him the rest of his life, but he was still far from the Beethoven of Romantic tradition: the beetle-browed uncouth titan, whose slovenly dress, unshaven face, eccentric manners, and domineering conduct were tolerated because of his genius. The Beethoven of 1800 was still rather a man of the world, a man with aspirations to elegance, to the world of high society, which of course meant aristocratic, wealthy society. His popularity as a piano soloist was at its height and his circle of aristocratic friends, patrons and pupils opened wide to him the doors of the most influential houses in Vienna. He was financially secure since one of the great Austrian aristocrats, Prince Lichnowsky, had assured him support as long as he was without an official position worthy of his talents. He had more commissions than he could fill and an excellent income from his compositions.

Just as Beethoven himself was still conforming in large part to the social patterns of his surroundings, so his First Symphony followed established eighteenth-century symphonic patterns. It is in the customary four movements, scored for 2 flutes, 2 oboes, 2 clarinets, 2 bassoons, 2 horns, 2 trumpets, kettledrums, and the usual strings. Not only is the Symphony rather light in mood, it shows deference to Mozart and Haydn in form and style.

Yet in a way this is almost a masquerade. It wears an eighteenth-century periwig; it speaks the courtly language and behaves with the restraint expected of a well-bred symphony. Only under the surface does one sense the untamed power and virility, the breadth and sweep that distinguished it from its predecessors. But Beethoven's contemporaries were not deceived. The conservatives smelled a revolutionist. They were rightly alarmed.

The beginnings of the First Symphony lay some years back. The theme for the last movement (quoted below) was sketched as early as 1796 and the greatest of Beethoven biographers, Alexander Wheelock Thayer, thought Beethoven must have begun the sketches by the winter of 1794–95, perhaps at the suggestion of Baron van Swieten, the patron of Mozart and Haydn, to whom Beethoven dedicated the first movement. And the theme of the third movement is identical with the second of a dozen German dances that Beethoven wrote as ballroom music for the famous Vienna Redoutensaal. But the date of those dances is uncertain.

I. *Adagio molto; Allegro con brio.* There is a slow introduction following the example of Haydn, but with shifting, ambiguous harmonies, before the first movement settles down to its clear and Classical-sounding first theme:

The contrasting subordinate theme is a graceful little fragment which passes in quick succession from oboe to flute to violins. The brief development section is built almost entirely on the first theme. The reprise of the opening material is more powerful and more varied.

II. *Andante cantabile con moto.* The lyric slow movement is built around a very simple theme heard in the opening measures, which is developed and expanded in sonata-allegro form, with added embellishments of the main theme when it returns for the reprise at the end of the movement.

III. *Menuetto: Allegro molto e vivace.* Beethoven calls this movement by the older conventional name of a minuet. But as the impatient rush of the principal phrase shows, this is no traditional minuet. It is an irrepressible nineteenth-century scherzo:

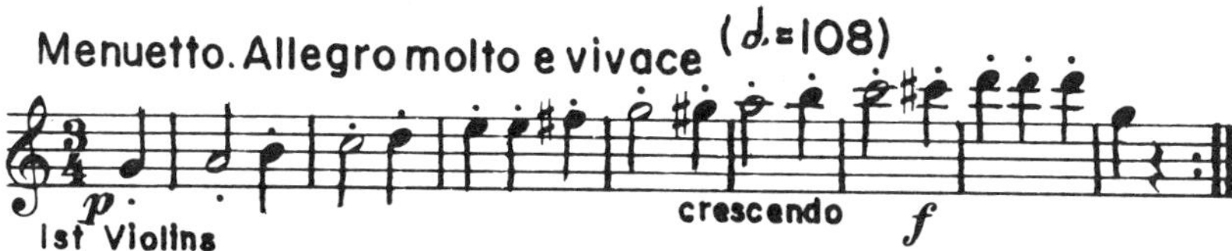

IV. *Adagio; Allegro molto e vivace.* The finale begins with an amusing trick. A simple scale creeps slowly upward through the violins, reaching one note further with each repetition, until in a sudden flurry of impatience it rushes into the dance-like theme of the finale:

The wit and laughter that follow are as infectious as anything Haydn ever wrote. The form is the simplest possible version of the sonata-rondo form Haydn seems to have invented and which he practiced with such inexhaustible imaginative resource. Beethoven is not yet nearly as bold and experimental as Haydn had been in his late symphonies. But something in Beethoven's manner confused, frightened and infuriated the conservatives of his day.

Why conservative listeners through the ages should have reacted to unfamiliar music as if it were a personal affront, a sort of insult to their intelligence planned by the composer with malice aforethought, is a puzzle. But they have so reacted.

One German critic wrote after the premiere of Beethoven's First Symphony that it was "the confused explosions of the outrageous effrontery of a young man." And ten years later a Parisian musician could still write that the "astonishing success" of this Symphony was "a danger to the musical art." "It is believed," he added, "that a prodigal use of the most barbarous dissonances and a noisy use of all the instruments will make an effect. Alas, the ear is only stabbed; there is no appeal to the heart."

SYMPHONY NO. 2, D MAJOR, OPUS 36

Beethoven's Second Symphony is scarcely a heroic work. Yet it has been called "a heroic lie" because Beethoven was able to write such graceful, witty, exuberant music while he himself was passing through agony. Begun in 1801, but composed chiefly during the summer and early fall of 1802, at the little village of Heiligenstadt outside Vienna, the Symphony was probably finished there in October, shortly after he wrote that secret, tragic letter to his brothers, which we know as his "Heiligenstadt Testament."

Beethoven was growing deaf. The symptoms had begun a few years earlier with a roaring in his ears, but not until the summer of 1802 did he really face the thought that he might lose his hearing altogether. Deafness is hard enough for anyone to bear. But it seemed to Beethoven that for a musician deafness was a ridiculous and shameful malady. For a while he did his best to hide it. "I shall, as far as possible, defy my fate," he wrote, "although there will be moments when I shall be the most miserable of God's creatures."

Beethoven's doctor had advised him to protect his ears by spending the summer of 1802 outside noisy Vienna. One of his favorite country haunts for composing was Heiligenstadt. So he took rooms in a solitary peasant house which stood in high fields outside the village where his windows looked out far over the plain, across the Danube and beyond to the Carpathian Mountains that lined the horizon.

In these idyllic surroundings, in the midst of composing the gracious music of his Second Symphony, Beethoven realized with crushing certainty what was in store for him: total deafness. To be merely hard of hearing was a bearable misfortune. But it could be passed off—or so he thought—as absentmindedness. But now a total silence was closing in upon him, cutting him off from the world, from his friends, from the sound of music.

Beethoven loved to take long walks into the woods about Heiligenstadt. "On one of these wanderings," says his pupil, Ferdinand Ries, "I called his attention to a shepherd who was piping very prettily in the woods on a flute made of elder wood. For half an hour Beethoven could hear nothing, and though I repeatedly assured him that I no longer heard him either (which was not true), he became extremely quiet and morose.—And when he occasionally appeared to be merry, it was mostly exaggerated to the point of boisterousness; but even that seldom happened."

It may have been this very incident which suddenly confronted Beethoven with the trials that lay ahead and which inspired the "Heiligenstadt Testament."

> You men who think or declare that I am hostile, stubborn, or misanthropic [he wrote], how greatly do you wrong me, you do not know the secret causes of my seeming so . . . I was compelled early to keep apart, to live in loneliness; when at times I tried to surmount all this, O how harshly was I defeated by the doubly tragic experience of my bad hearing, and yet I could not bring myself to say to people, "Speak louder, shout, for I am deaf." Ah, how could I possibly admit an infirmity in the *one sense* which should have been more acute in me than in others . . . Oh, I cannot do it, so forgive me when you see me draw back when I would gladly mingle with you, my misfortune is doubly painful because it must lead to my being misunderstood, for me there can be no refreshment from association with my fellows, no subtle conversation, no exchange of confidences, only the barest needs of communication; if I venture into society, I must live like an exile. If I come near people a hot terror seizes me, a fear that something may happen that will reveal my condition—this is the way it has been during the half year I have been spending in the country, as ordered by my intelligent physician that my hearing might be spared as much as possible. This was in accord with my inclinations, although sometimes, in my longing for society, I allowed myself to be drawn into it. But what a humiliation when someone stood beside me and heard a flute in the distance, and I heard *nothing,* or someone *heard a shepherd singing,* and again I heard nothing, such incidents brought me to the verge of despair, I was near to putting an end to my life—only art, only that held me back, ah, it seemed impossible to leave the world until I had brought forth all that I felt called upon to produce, and I endured this wretched existence. . . .

Still he dined and joked and played music with his friends. Not until after his death did the record of the "Heiligenstadt Testament" reveal what he had gone through during that apparently serene summer.

The first performance of the Symphony took place on the following April 5 at the Theater an der Wien. This was the famous *Akademie,* as concerts were then called, the gargantuan program for which offered *three* world premieres: his C minor Piano Concerto (with Beethoven as soloist), his oratorio *Christus am Oelberge (Christ on the Mount of Olives),* and his new Second Symphony, in addition to his familiar First Symphony, and a group of lesser works, which were omitted because the concert had already lasted so long without them. Despite the length of the program, it was the resounding success that Beethoven had confidently expected. Indeed, he had been so sure of himself that he had doubled the ordinary concert price of some seats and tripled others, and the concert is said to have netted him a very substantial sum (1800 florins).

The Symphony, which is in four movements, is scored for 2 flutes, 2 clarinets, 2 bassoons, 2 horns, 2 trumpets, kettledrums, and the usual strings.

I. *Adagio molto; Allegro con brio.* A slow introduction, which sounded even more romantic and mysterious in Beethoven's day than it does now, leads to the lively first movement. This is based chiefly on an energetic, bustling little theme:

A more songful subordinate theme is chanted by the woodwinds. Beethoven chops up both themes into handy little rhythmic fragments, out of which he builds the whole middle section of this movement. After the traditional return or reprise of the opening themes, there is a perky little coda based on the main theme quoted above.

II. *Larghetto.* The traditionally songful second movement begins with a broadly flowing melody for strings, echoed at once by woodwinds. The whole movement overflows with melodies, many with an infectious lilt and a lighter grace than the opening strain.

III. *Scherzo: Allegro.* The delicate Scherzo is full of sudden dynamic and rhythmic surprises, which were to become more and more characteristic of Beethoven as he developed. The middle section, or trio, starts out like a dainty well-behaved little eighteenth-century trio for winds, only to explode in wild, unpredictable blasts of the full orchestra, or to fade as suddenly into silence.

IV. *Allegro molto.* The finale, which puzzled so many of Beethoven's contemporaries, begins with a startling orchestral somersault:

The somersault comes back again and again, refrain-fashion, in this boisterous rondo-sonata movement. The first two notes and the last two notes of the somersault also serve as magnificent thematic fragments to toss back and forth among the instruments of the orchestra with an exuberance and momentum that grow right up to the final bar.

How disturbing all this energy and drive could be to conservatives of the day was emphasized by a Leipzig critic, who described the Second Symphony as "a gross monster, a pierced dragon, which will not die, and even in losing its blood [in the last movement], wild with rage, still deals furious blows with its tail, stiffened in the last agony."

SYMPHONY NO. 3, E-FLAT MAJOR, OPUS 55 (EROICA)

Over a fish dinner at the little tavern Zur Rose, Beethoven's poet friend Christoff Kuffner asked him which of his eight symphonies was his favorite. (The Ninth had not yet been composed.)

"Ah, ha!" exclaimed Beethoven, "the 'Eroica.' "

"I should have guessed the C-minor [the Fifth]," said the poet.

"No," insisted Beethoven, "the 'Eroica.' "

Posterity has agreed with Beethoven. Some even place the "Eroica" at the very top of the list, above his Ninth. But there were more than musical reasons for Beethoven's special feelings about this "Eroica."

The Finale of the "Eroica" is built on a theme which Beethoven used in four different compositions. The first was in a set of little "country" dances or *Kontretänze.* The second was his ballet, *The Creatures of Prometheus.* The heroic figure of Greek mythology who defied the gods and stole fire from heaven to bring warmth, light, and enlightenment to mankind was the central figure of Beethoven's ballet, in which he used this theme for his Finale. He used it again as the basis of his so-called "Eroica" Piano Variations. We meet the theme for the fourth time in the variations which are the crowning glory of the "Eroica" Symphony.

At the time he was composing his Third Symphony in 1803 and early 1804, Beethoven had in mind one of his great heroes—a man who must have seemed to him a modern Prometheus: Napoleon Bonaparte. For, up to that time, Napoleon still seemed to be the daring young genius whose meteoric career had made him the chief military and political defender of the French Revolution, with its message of "Liberty, Equality, Fraternity"—not just for France but for all men. When he led the revolutionary armies against France's foreign enemies (who hoped to crush the Revolution) Napoleon was still widely worshiped as the great liberator, the smasher of ancient tyrannies and cramping conventions. It is obvious that this idealistic picture played a role in Beethoven's imagination as he shaped his own revolutionary score.

In the spring of 1804 the epoch-making work was complete. Arrangements had been made through the French Embassy in Vienna to forward the Symphony to Paris. The fair copy of the score lay ready, with the name "Bonaparte" at the very top of the title page and at the very bottom: "Luigi van Beethoven"—these two names and nothing else. But then one late spring day Beethoven's friend Ferdinand Ries brought him the news that Napoleon had had himself crowned Emperor. Beethoven flew into a rage and cried, "Is he then, too, nothing more than an ordinary human being? Now he, too, will trample on all the rights of man and indulge only his ambition. He will exalt himself above all others, become a tyrant!" In the presence of Ries and a second friend and reliable witness, Beethoven went to the table, seized the title page by the top, ripped it in two, and threw it to the floor.

The Symphony received a new name: *Sinfonia Eroica, Composed to Celebrate the Memory of a Great Man.* For the Napoleon Beethoven had admired was dead. Beethoven had seen him as a symbol of freedom. Now the Symphony was rededicated to the spirit beyond any symbol.

The autograph copy of the Symphony has disappeared. But Beethoven's personal copy (a copyist's manuscript, which Beethoven used for conducting and which contains many corrections and additions in Beethoven's hand) has survived. Its Italian-language title page originally read:

Sinfonia grande	*Grand Symphony*
intitolata Bonaparte	*entitled Bonaparte*
del Sigr	*by Mr*
Louis van Beethoven	*Louis van Beethoven*

Below the elegant Italian calligraphy of the title, Beethoven penciled in large: GESCHRIEBEN AUF BONAPART [COMPOSED ON BONAPART]. Beethoven's words are still faintly legible, although they were erased. But the second line of the copyist's title with the name *"Bonaparte"* was scratched out so vigorously, apparently with such passion, that a gaping hole was ripped in the page. This eloquently mutilated title page and the well-thumbed, marked-up score it covers may still be consulted in the library of the Viennese Gesellschaft der Musikfreunde, and it is reproduced here with their kind cooperation. The lines at the very top and bottom of the page are technical elucidations in Beethoven's hand. (The German date-line inserted in a later hand, with heavier ink, in the middle of the Italian title, cannot refer to the completion of the Symphony or of this specific copy, but conceivably to the first private performance.)

There were several private performances at the Viennese palace of Prince Lobkowitz. At least one of these was conducted by Beethoven himself in December, 1804. The first public performance, also conducted by Beethoven, was delayed until April 7, 1805, at the Theater an der Wien. The most frequently quoted early criticisms of the "Eroica" are those which complain of its great length and of Beethoven's willfully chaotic style and form. But there were enthusiastic reviews as well in important publications, and the notion that the greatness of the "Eroica" went unrecognized at first does not hold up under investigation.

I. *Allegro con brio.* The Symphony has no introduction. There are two sharp *staccato* chords and the orchestra sails ahead with its energy-packed swinging theme. Beethoven's sketches for this Symphony suggest that this theme may have been derived from the "Prometheus" theme of the finale. It starts the first movement so simply, so primitively, that it could easily recall

BEETHOVEN'S "EROICA" SYMPHONY.

Scars of Beethoven's rage at Napoleon on the title page of the composer's personal conducting copy: Beethoven's erasure of the words *intitolata Bonaparte* ("entitled Bonaparte") was so violent that he tore a hole in the paper. (*Courtesy, Gesellschaft der Musikfreunde, Vienna*)

a military trumpet signal and so, possibly, a reference to Napoleon's battles. But this theme ends—if it has any real end at all—on a note of powerful unresolved tension, a long-held C sharp. If there were any doubt as to Beethoven's intention, look (or rather listen) to the swelling volume (the *crescendo*) of that low C sharp:

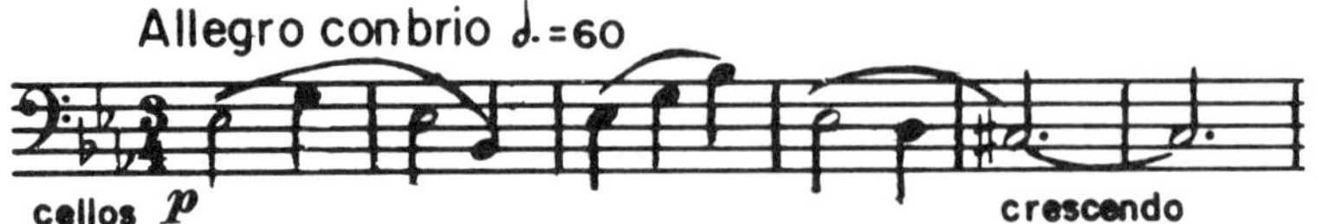

This tension then pervades the entire movement. In what immediately follows and even more in the central development of this movement, the famous theme seems to take on a life of its own, as if it were struggling to find some solution to its own built-in tension. To take only the first of many examples: in the rising sequence that follows, each "attempt" of the theme to find a resolution, takes an upward twist which, far from reducing the tension, drives it higher and higher with each repetition:

Each subsequent "attempt" to find a new solution adds to the volcanic pressures until, at the peak of the development, we reach an explosion of harmonic dissonance and syncopated rhythms that seem a cataclysm of nature. Nothing like this had ever been heard in music before.

Almost more startling, although the dynamics have diminished to a whisper, is the conclusion of this famous development. In the suspenseful bars when the orchestra is preparing the return to the basic thematic material of the movement, Beethoven upset all the pedants of his day and all the rule-of-thumb musicians for decades to come. A faint *tremolo* of the violins hovers on a harmony obviously meant to lead back into the main theme. Suddenly one timid-sounding horn plays the theme we are all expecting, but before the harmony has changed to fit the theme. This creates a peculiar impression—as if the horn player had jumped his cue and come in four measures too soon.

II. *Marcia funèbre: Adagio assai.* The great Funeral March of the "Eroica" puzzled some literal-minded people who thought that a funeral march should come at the end. But Beethoven wasn't writing a biography. He was portraying heroism, or rather, heroic grief. There is no pessimistic whining, no luxury of self-pity. The march step seems to falter as the shuddering rhythm starts, but its tread becomes firmer. It is an epic lamentation over heroes slain in the defense of everyone's freedom. They could be Leonidas and his Spartans at Thermopylae. But even that thought is too confining.

III. *Scherzo: Allegro vivace.* Neither death nor sorrow could have the last word in Beethoven's faith. The Scherzo which follows is full of life: of delicate, shifting light and shadow, of laughter and outbursts of raucous humor.

IV. *Finale: Allegro molto.* As if to symbolize the creative vitality of the heroic spirit, Beethoven uses his "Prometheus" theme for the finale. The movement opens with a brilliant rushing passage for the strings and some emphatic chords. Then the *pizzicato* strings give out, very softly, an enigmatic, angular theme that seems to make no particular musical sense (at first):

The theme continues and Beethoven even gives us two variations upon it before introducing his "Prometheus" melody with which it combines very simply as follows:

In the tremendous series of eleven variations and a *presto* coda (which is really a twelfth variation), Beethoven sometimes uses the "Prometheus" melody without the bass, sometimes the bass without its melody. Each variation is a little cosmos in itself and the sum of them is overwhelming. Indeed, this listener has never been able to avoid the impression that even the famous opening theme of the first movement is one more variant of the "Prometheus" melody, thus suggesting a powerful structural link between first and last movements—the kind of link Beethoven used much more obviously and explicitly to bind together the movements of his Fifth Symphony. Whether he intended it or was even aware of it is questionable, but the connection is too close to be entirely accidental. One feels that Beethoven himself must have been startled at the depth and power of his own creation.

The Symphony is scored for 2 flutes, 2 oboes, 2 clarinets, 2 bassoons, 2 horns, 2 trumpets, kettledrums, and the customary strings.

SYMPHONY NO. 4, B-FLAT MAJOR, OPUS 60

Beethoven's gentle Fourth Symphony was born in an explosive year—explosive in the composer's inner world and in the brutal reality that surrounded him. In occupied Vienna, 1806 began with the withdrawal of Napoleon's occupation troops. Beethoven's imperial and aristocratic patrons returned to their town palaces. But the reprieve was only local: from Naples to Hanover the thunderbolts of Napoleon, his allies, and his puppets continued to strike while the "Corsican upstart" toppled old thrones, set up new ones, redrew old boundaries, created new states. This was not mere onslaught: it was an earthquake. The thousand-year-old Holy Roman Empire simply disintegrated. A shrunken, impoverished Austro-Hungarian monarchy was all that remained.

For Beethoven, 1806 began with emotional and physical turmoil, with the anguish of a series of operations on his problem child: the cutting and remodeling of his beloved opera *Fidelio* (which had failed during the Napoleonic occupation). There followed the strain of supervising inadequate rehearsals and the faltering first performances, culminating in Beethoven's explosion of fury at the theater manager (whom he suspected of cheating him) and his enraged withdrawal of his score.

This turmoil would have unstrung a lesser man. In Beethoven it stimulated a burst of incredible creativity. Eight major masterpieces were taking shape almost simultaneously: his Sonata "Appassionata," the three epochal "Razumovsky" String Quartets, his Fourth Piano Concerto, his Fourth and Fifth Symphonies, his Violin Concerto. And most of these were finished before the end of the year! In this season of jostling masterpieces, the gentle Fourth Symphony thrust itself ahead of more heroic works. Beethoven's sketchbooks show clearly how the beginnings of what eventually became the Fifth Symphony were crowded aside by the sketches for our B-flat Symphony, which was begun later but finished earlier and therefore given the number four.

Most of the work on the Fourth was done during September and October of 1806, while Beethoven was visiting at Prince Lichnowsky's summer castle of Grätz near Troppau (the modern city of Opava, just south of the Polish-Czechoslovak border). There Beethoven met another great music lover, Count Franz von Oppersdorf, who maintained his own private orchestra at his castle in nearby Ober-Glogau (some forty miles to the north, in present-day Poland). Oppersdorf is said to have been so determined to have a complete symphony orchestra that he was unwilling to hire any domestic servant who did not play an orchestral instrument. He was also a great admirer of Beethoven. When Beethoven and Prince Lichnowsky visited Ober-Glogau, the Count had Beethoven's Second Symphony performed for his guests. He also commissioned the Fourth Symphony. Beethoven's receipt for the 500 florin fee (roughly $3,000 in purchasing power today) is dated February 3, 1807.

Beethoven's fruitful stay at Lichnowsky's came to an abrupt end with another characteristic explosion. (The story has come down to us in four independent accounts differing in details but agreeing in essentials.) Among his guests at Grätz, the Prince entertained a French general, "a fine gentleman and a great music lover." There may have been several French officers. The Prince led his guests to expect they would hear the great composer perform some of his latest works at a *soirée*. (Beethoven had just completed the "Appassionata.") Despite Lichnowsky's earnest and repeated requests, Beethoven refused to play. When Lichnowsky jokingly threatened him with house arrest, Beethoven took offense. There was "an unpleasant, even vulgar scene," after which Beethoven stormed out of the castle and trudged through pouring rain to Troppau, where he spent the night at the house of a Dr. Weiser, Lichnowsky's physician. The next day, before leaving for Vienna, Beethoven (according to a tradition treasured in the Weiser family) sent Lichnowsky the following note:

> Prince!
>
> What you are, you are by accident of birth. What I am, I am through myself. There have been and will be thousands of princes. There is only one Beethoven.

Upon arriving at his apartment in Vienna, Beethoven seized a bust of Prince Lichnowsky and smashed it in a hundred pieces.

Whether the Fourth Symphony was performed by Count Oppersdorf's domestic orchestra at Ober-Glogau we do not know. One would assume they at least tried. According to custom, Oppersdorf's exclusive right to the Symphony he had commissioned lasted six months. Thus he must have had a hand in the earliest documented performance, a private subscription concert in mid-March for "a very select circle" which, according to the Leipzig *Allgemeine Musikalische Zeitung*, "contributed a very considerable sum for the benefit of the composer." This was reported to have taken place at the Vienna palace of "Prince L." Although Beethoven was on good terms again with the patient Lichnowsky, the weight of evidence suggests that the host for this concert was another of Beethoven's more generous patrons, Prince Lobkowitz.

The Symphony is in the traditional four movements.

I. *Adagio—Allegro vivace*. The slow introduction is thoughtful, rather than brooding or portentous. Its pensive mood is interrupted by six sharply rhythmic repetitions of the same chord, which launch one of the most carefree, buoyant allegros in all Beethoven:

A group of contrasting ideas begins with a little three-way melodic conversation among a solo bassoon, oboe, and flute. As the movement develops, these little scraps of melody and the skipping first theme are all churned up together with enchanting symphonic sleight of hand. Beethoven prepares the traditional return of his opening theme with a dramatic stroke of genius. Berlioz described the passage a hundred years ago with characteristic vividness:

> This astonishing *crescendo* is one of the most skillfully contrived things we know of in music: You will hardly find its equal except in that which ends the famous Scherzo of [Beethoven's Fifth] Symphony in C minor. And this latter, in spite of its immense effectiveness, is conceived on a less vast scale, for it sets out from *piano* to arrive at the final explosion without departing from the principal key, while the [*crescendo* of the Fourth Symphony] starts from *mezzo forte,* is lost for a moment in a *pianissimo* beneath which are harmonies with vague and undecided coloring, then reappears with chords of a more determined tonality, and bursts out only at the moment when the cloud that veiled this modulation is completely dissipated. You might compare it to a river whose calm waters suddenly disappear and only leave the subterranean bed to plunge with a roar in a foaming waterfall.

The movement ends with an exuberant coda, built on the opening theme.

II. *Adagio.* The theme of the nocturne-like slow movement consists of little more than the slow descending E-flat-major scale, falling just over an octave and then rising again to the halfway point:

This wonderful placid flow is enhanced by a gently rocking accompaniment figure, which we hear first very softly in the second violins, later building volume in a variety of instruments and finally dying to a *pianissimo* whisper for kettledrum solo.

In all, this melody occurs four times. These, with the three intervening episodes and their deliciously contrasting phrases for woodwinds, achieve a perfect marriage of what we call rondo and sonata form. Yet, to quote Berlioz again, "its melodic expression [is] so angelic and of such irresistible tenderness that the prodigious art of workmanship completely disappears."

III. *Allegro vivace.* The *scherzo* bursts upon us with a bewildering kaleidoscopic variety of moods, beginning with a sort of roughhouse, upside-down reminiscence of the Symphony's opening theme:

Mysterious whisperings among strings and woodwinds alternate with loud gusts of orchestral laughter. In the lyric trio sections, *Un poco meno allegro,* woodwinds take the lead.

IV. *Allegro ma non troppo.* The finale opens with whirling violin figures, almost a "perpetual-motion" rhythm rather than a clear-cut theme:

In one of its many rondo-like returns, this figure is given to a comically scurrying bassoon solo. In between, little wisps of melody, tiny thematic fragments, glints of woodwind tone emerge briefly and are as quickly submerged again in the symphonic swirl. The movement is one of Beethoven's merriest conclusions.

The score calls for pairs of flutes, oboes, clarinets, horns, trumpets, kettledrums, and the traditional string choir.

SYMPHONY NO. 5, C MINOR, OPUS 67

Like Beethoven himself, this Fifth Symphony is music of concentrated energy, struggle, and triumph. In its emotional high voltage it is an intensely forward-looking work, embodying one of the most powerful musical trends of the following hundred years. In the central importance it gives to rhythm, it reaches beyond the century span, past Stravinsky's *Rite of Spring,* and who can say how much farther?

Beethoven labored some four years, 1804–08, on his Fifth Symphony. He interrupted himself to compose another symphony, which was completed earlier and hence numbered Fourth, and also to compose his Violin Concerto and his Fourth Piano Concerto. The Fifth Symphony was first performed on December 22, 1808, in Vienna at that incredible concert in the Theater an der Wien which consisted entirely of new Beethoven works: the Fifth Symphony, the Sixth Symphony, the Fourth Piano Concerto with Beethoven as soloist, the aria "Ah! perfido," three numbers from his Mass in C major, Opus 86, and the Fantasy in C minor for Piano, Chorus and Orchestra, Opus 80!

I. *Allegro con brio.* The first movement is one savage onslaught of rhythm. It opens with an imperious gesture: a commanding, motto-like figure of just four notes. More rhythm than melody, it is one of the briefest, the most powerful, and certainly most famous symphonic themes ever penned. It is repeated instantly, not quite literally, but with even more savage insistence:

That added insistence, the prolongation of the final D, was an afterthought. (In Beethoven's manuscript and in the first hundred copies of the first printed edition, the D had been one measure long, like the preceding E flat.) Notice too that the slight change in the motto's repetition makes an open-ended effect, almost like an unanswered question.

Beethoven is reported (by a friend, Anton Schindler, who knew him well) to have pointed to this theme in his score and declared: "Thus fate knocks at the door!" (*"So pocht das Schicksal an die Pforte!"*) The report has been questioned, even ridiculed by some, on the grounds that Schindler's memory sometimes played him false, or that Beethoven would never have made such a childishly portentous remark. But the truth is that people of Beethoven's day, including even serious, professional musicians *did* talk and write in just such extravagant metaphors and rhetorical flourishes, in their attempts to suggest the intensity of music that stirred them deeply. In an age of stripped-down prose, such writing makes men uneasy. "Roaring cataracts of nonsense" is a phrase often repeated to ridicule the style of such composer-critics as E. T. A. Hoffmann (whom Beethoven admired), and his Romantic successors, Berlioz and Schumann, who used equally extravagant language. But such ridicule is too easy and more than a little superficial. We cannot simply dismiss the possibility that Schumann, Berlioz, Hoffmann, and Beethoven did mean what they said, despite language that can sound extravagant or improbable to us.

In any case, Beethoven's motto theme permeates his entire first movement. It dominates—sometimes in a roar, sometimes in a whisper, sometimes as a barely audible throbbing in the depths of the orchestra. Even the relatively lyric second theme is built on it, and it brings the movement to a close with implacable rhythmic drive. This is one of the most powerfully integrated movements in all symphonic literature.

II. *Andante con moto.* The second movement is a series of variations on a double theme, one might almost say, on two alternating, contrasting themes. The first, sung by violas and cellos in A-flat major, is a smooth-flowing melody of feminine grace and charm:

The second, obviously related to the first, but square-shouldered and aggressive, asserts itself in a blazing C major. The first two double variations follow the model of the theme quite closely, dissolving the opening melody first into flowing sixteenth-notes and then into more swiftly undulating thirty-seconds. But by the time we come to the third double variation, Beethoven treats his themes with the utmost freedom and fantasy.

III. *Allegro.* The beginning of the *scherzo* is shadowy and haunted. Suddenly two horns blaze out a menacing theme based on the rhythm of the first-movement theme quoted above:

Except for the rather elephantine gambols of the double basses in its middle section (the so-called trio), this movement has little of the traditional dance character of minuets and scherzos. At the end the rhythmic motto returns, answered by whispering, plucking sounds of the string instruments, and the whole orchestra seems to collapse, as if exhausted, onto a softly sustained chord of uncertain tonality. The music seems in a state of suspended animation except for one muffled drum that throbs like a slow heartbeat—beating in the rhythm of the first movement. The suspense grows, fragments of the *scherzo* theme weave through the orchestra, the uncertain harmonies shift more and more toward the C major you feel is waiting, like the sun, to burst out of the clouds. Just at the moment when the suspense seems unbearable, the orchestra pulls itself together with a sudden *crescendo* and strides into the magnificently heroic theme of the last movement.

IV. *Allegro.* The principal theme is like a trumpet fanfare:

It is like a fanfare except that the harmony is filled out by a grand orchestral *tutti,* including, for the first time in Beethoven's symphonies, 3 trombones, a contrabassoon, and a piccolo. In contrast to the stark unity of the opening movement, the thematic riches of his finale pour forth in a torrent. There is a second fanfare-like theme in the opening group, a bridge theme which leads to a second cluster of themes dominated by a driving triplet rhythm.

In the midst of the turbulent development of these themes the orchestra slows down to a majestic halt. The rhythm, tempo, and, finally, the rasping trumpet theme from the *scherzo,* are recalled here in ghostly pizzicatos of the strings echoed by woodwinds. This passing reminder of the *scherzo* barely suffices to recall the terrors that are vanquished and to lead back, through a transition of a swelling suspense to the tremendous fanfare-like principal theme of the finale. All the riches of this movement are now recalled, this time all in C major, leading to a coda and a concluding *presto* of overwhelming excitement, power, and brilliance.

Beethoven's Fifth Symphony is scored for piccolo, 2 flutes, 2 oboes, 2 clarinets, 2 bassoons, contrabassoon, 2 horns, 2 trumpets, 3 trombones, kettledrums, and the traditional string choir.

SYMPHONY NO. 6, F MAJOR, OPUS 68 (PASTORAL)

Beethoven had his conflicts, and wild ones, too, with everyone from his princely patrons to his housekeepers and his rebellious nephew. But with nature he felt at ease. He liked best to compose during long walks through the countryside near Vienna. His feeling for the familiar fields and forest was close to pantheistic worship. Yet the "Pastoral" Symphony suggests that his worship had more of love than awe. In the utter simplicity and peace of the "Pastoral" Symphony there is something beatific. The way he dwells with tireless, repetitious wonder over the simplest of his lovely phrases suggests the moments when time stands still for us too, while we watch a single autumn leaf, sunlight on the water, or smell the scent of warm grass.

From Beethoven's sketches we know that he originally planned a more detailed explanation of the Symphony's meaning than was finally published in the score: "Anyone who has an idea of country life," he finally noted in his sketches, "can make out for himself the intentions of the author, without a lot of titles."

In contrast to the Fifth Symphony, the "Pastoral" was written relatively fast, between the summers of 1807 and of the following year. It was completed about June 1808 in Heiligenstadt on the outskirts of Vienna.

The program for the first performance, on December 22, 1808, in Vienna, listed the work as "A Symphony entitled: Recollection of Country Life, in F major," and specifically warned the audience that it was "more an expression of feeling than painting."

I. *Awakening of cheerful feeling on arriving in the country: Allegro ma non troppo.* The first movement opens in a sunny F major with the lively melodic phrase:

It is hard to believe that almost the whole long movement is nourished on that simple phrase. There are no elaborate thematic developments, but little melodic fragments of the opening theme keep repeating themselves in a sort of naïve joy at their own beauty and charm, with subtle variations of tonality and instrumental color, like the play of light and shade in nature itself. One tiny five-note figure (the second measure of the example above) is repeated some eighty times almost without interruption, and yet the whole movement makes an impression of inexhaustibly fertile imagination.

II. *Scene by the brook: Andante molto mosso.* The second movement is filled with soft murmuring sounds. Little trills of the violins could be the chirpings of insects. Toward the end we hear the unmistakable call of the cuckoo preceded by a quail and a nightingale. But the delicious melody of the violins can depict nothing—nothing that is, but feeling at its happiest and most relaxed.

III. *Merry gathering of country-folk: Allegro.* This is the scherzo of the "Pastoral" Symphony, and here Beethoven rang in passages recalling rustic bands he sometimes heard at such places as the Tavern of the Three Ravens in the country outside Vienna. There are suggestions of dance music: some heavy-footed stomping and some phrases of beguiling grace as in the following oboe solo:

But most of the scherzo seems too light-footed for peasant dancing or even for the daintiest ballerina. This leads without pause into the fourth movement.

IV. *Thunderstorm; Tempest: Allegro.* The tavern music is interrupted by a realistic storm. Notice how wonderfully Beethoven has caught the atmosphere of suspense of the last few seconds before a storm breaks. You can almost see the ominous quiet broken by the first scurries of wind and the first big drops of rain. Then the tempest roars. The growling of the lowest strings is a masterstroke of Impressionistic technique ninety years before Debussy. We hear the thunder and the lightning too, and the wind screams in the high-pitched piccolo. It is violent but not frightening and it vanishes almost as quickly as it came, leading directly into the finale.

V. *Shepherd's song; Happy, thankful feelings after the storm: Allegretto.* The receding thunder is answered by the piping of the shepherd's song of thanksgiving which opens the last movement with a solo clarinet, then with a solo horn. In Beethoven's day, shepherds did actually herd their flocks on the outskirts of Vienna. They sang and played their pipes. To Beethoven this was all a part of the nature he loved and worshipped. But by the time he composed the "Pastoral" Symphony he was too deaf to hear them. It had been a bitter day for Beethoven when he realized that a friend standing beside him could hear a shepherd singing and piping when he, the composer, the musician heard nothing. The humiliation, the despair of such experiences brought him to thoughts of suicide. (For Beethoven's own description of these feelings in a famous letter to his brothers known as Beethoven's "Heiligenstadt Testament," see the lengthy quotation on page 56.)

But when Beethoven's orchestra, led by the violins, takes up the shepherd's tune as the principal theme of this finale, his tragedy ceases to exist. It is as if the whole world were exulting in the miracle of the fresh-washed sky and air and the return of the sun:

The entire finale seems an ecstatic hymn of thanks to some pantheistic god, to Nature with a capital "N," to the sun, to whatever beneficent power one can perceive in a universe that seemed as dark and terrifyingly irrational in Beethoven's day as it can in ours. That a man of sorrows and self-erected miseries like Beethoven could glimpse such glory and, by the incomprehensible alchemy of his art, lift us to share his vision—even if only for a few moments—is a miracle that remains as fresh as tomorrow's sunrise.

The Symphony is scored for piccolo, 2 flutes, 2 oboes, 2 clarinets, 2 bassoons, 2 horns, 2 trumpets, kettledrums, and the usual strings.

SYMPHONY NO. 7, A MAJOR, OPUS 92

A bloody reshaping of the map of Europe gripped men's attention at the time Beethoven was composing his Seventh Symphony: the fall, winter, and spring of 1811–12. By the time it was finished in June, the final *crescendo* of the Napoleonic Wars had been launched: the catastrophic invasion of Russia. History moved fast. By the time the score was given its first performance, Napoleon's empire was in the last stages of disintegration. The Symphony was to outlast all the empires involved in that spectacular cataclysm: the French Empire, the Holy Roman Empire, the Empire of All the Russias, and the British Empire.

Beethoven himself conducted the premiere of his Symphony on December 8, 1813, in the Hall of the University of Vienna as a benefit for wounded Austrian and Bavarian soldiers. The first performance in New York City was presented by the New York Philharmonic on November 18, 1843, under the direction of Urelli Corelli Hill.

I. *Poco sostenuto; Vivace.* The slow introduction is long and richly developed. A theme of majestic simplicity strides boldly downward through the orchestra, unadorned except for an occasional punctuating chord of the full orchestra. There is a magnificent development of this material together with a more graceful, feminine second theme before we come to the fast main part of the movement, based on a lightly skipping figure which inspired Berlioz to call the movement a peasant round:

But it soon swells beyond the bounds of any merely human dance. Its tremendous power never gets out of hand, though it confused some of Beethoven's contemporaries. A famous passage toward the end, for example, made Weber exclaim that Beethoven was now "quite ripe for the madhouse." This is the place in the coda where the violas, cellos and double basses take hold of a powerful five-note phrase down at the bottom of the orchestra and keep obstinately repeating this short figure (derived from the skipping principal theme) while the orchestra above swells to its magnificent final climax:

II. *Allegretto.* In spite of the marking, *Allegretto,* there is nothing light about this movement. We know that Beethoven hesitated whether to call it an *andante.* It begins with a soft sustained chord of the wind instruments, then there is the quiet rhythmic pulse of the lower strings—less a melody than a persistent heartbeat—pervading the entire theme and the set of variations that follow:

Around it weave the voices of violas and cellos. Later there is a switch from the melancholy A minor to the sunnier major mode and new and more flowing melodies in another rhythm for clarinets and bassoons. But even here, if you listen carefully, the old rhythmic pulse sounds softly at the bottom of the orchestra. As the climax dies down, fragments of the theme are whispered from one part of the orchestra to the other and the movement ends with an echoing sigh of the violins.

Even at the first performance of the Symphony, this *Allegretto* was encored, a compliment rarely accorded to slow movements, and it soon became so universally loved that some conductors used to insert it into the less popular Eighth to help put that Symphony over!

III. *Presto; Assai meno presto.* The scherzo, with its explosive, dynamic contrasts, is amazing, not only for its buoyant rhythms, its kaleidoscopic shifts of orchestral color and its rough-and-tumble wit, but for its ingenious thematic relations and its formal perfection. The two burly opening bars are balanced by a dainty rain of *staccato* notes:

This abrupt contrast is magnified when the opening bar (now shortened to its first four notes) bounces upward from the bottom to the top of the string section, and is thereupon answered by a saucy trio of high woodwinds which balance back and forth on a tiny two-note figure.

The trio, itself rich in contrast, stands out abruptly from the main scherzo sections. It returns once again in its entirety and, at the very end of the movement, it seems about to resume for a third time when it is abruptly dismissed—by five sharp chords of the entire orchestra—as if with a sudden gesture of humorous impatience.

IV. *Allegro con brio.* With the whirlwind finale, we meet in even more powerful form the same dynamic drive and energy of the dance. Indeed, Richard Wagner, in his worship of Beethoven, called it the "apotheosis of the dance." The opening theme might conceivably suggest a sort of vast Virginia reel, but it soon develops into such a cosmic commotion as to leave any dance patterns far behind:

This restless, whirling power sweeps on with a sort of bacchantic fury to climax after climax, which, marvelous to say, are all enclosed within a Classical sonata form, concluding in a coda of a grandeur past description.

The Symphony is scored for 2 flutes, 2 oboes, 2 clarinets, 2 bassoons, 2 horns, 2 trumpets, 2 kettledrums, and the usual strings.

SYMPHONY NO. 8, F MAJOR, OPUS 93

Beethoven was a many-sided man, at once gentle and violent, a man of powerful inner conflicts—which may account, in part, for the tensions, the titanic sense of battle, which have always struck listeners in his more heroic works. The many sides of his character were also reflected in the striking contrasts among his compositions.

He was typically apt to work simultaneously on two scores of opposing character. Thus his Seventh and Eighth Symphonies were both begun in 1811. Hardly had Beethoven finished the explosive *Scherzo* and the whirlwind *Finale* of the Seventh (in late May or early June 1812) when he turned his full attention to its gentler companion. His manuscript of the Eighth is dated "October 1812, in Linz on the Danube."

The Seventh was an instant success at its premiere in Vienna in December 1813. Such was the enthusiasm that the entire concert was repeated a few days later, and on both occasions the *Allegretto* movement was encored.

The Eighth made its way more slowly. At its first performance on February 27, 1814, in the Redoutensaal of Vienna, the Eighth Symphony was sandwiched between another repetition of the Seventh and Beethoven's thunderously popular *Wellington's Victory, or the Battle at Victoria.* When a friend pointed out that the new Eighth had received less applause than the other works, Beethoven growled: "That's because it's so much better!" And although the Seventh is still the more popular of the two works, there is reason to believe that Beethoven meant what he said. For the whole texture of the Eighth Symphony is incomparably more finespun, more sophisticated—and in certain ways it is even more adventurous, despite its seeming restraint. It is in the traditional four movements.

I. *Allegro vivace e con brio.* The Symphony begins with an agreeably well-mannered, well-balanced little theme which sounds at first as if it might have come out of the workshop of a dozen delectable symphonists of the latter eighteenth century:

For the moment Beethoven seems to put on the Rococo elegance of the past. But hardly has he made his first decorous bow when he seems to forget the masquerade and goes surging ahead in his accustomed giant stride. This leads him quickly to his second theme, where he pauses as if to juggle again with the old Classical formulae. And so he continues, savoring each change of pace, each shift of musical gears, which he manages with dexterity and wit.

Now he develops his principal theme by chopping it in half and tossing it from one instrument of the orchestra to another in a miniature symphonic storm. His reprise of the opening material and an exuberant coda are rounded off with a quietly humorous surprise.

II. *Allegretto scherzando.* In place of the traditional slow movement, Beethoven gives us a delicious little *Allegretto scherzando,* with the theme on which he later improvised a famous joking round: "Ta, ta, ta, . . . my dear Mälzel, fare thee well, very well. . . ." The "Ta, ta, ta," which we hear in the measured tick-tock of the woodwind chords, referred to the metronome, or rather to its predecessor, the "musical chronometer," which Mälzel had perfected:

III. *Tempo di menuetto.* In keeping with the lightness of the rest of this Symphony, Beethoven returns here to the eighteenth-century minuet tempo, though not entirely to the old style. Closest to the traditional minuet is the conventional yet ravishingly beautiful duet for two French horns which opens the middle, trio section:

IV. *Allegro vivace.* The glittering dancing finale is a sort of cross between a rondo and traditional symphonic sonata form. The rondo refrain starts in a breathless whisper:

It is full of formal surprises, violent harmonic twists that must once have seemed outrageous and still sound fresh and unhackneyed. On and on the music goes as if unable to stop for sheer delight in its own inventive zest.

Beethoven's orchestra, as restrained in size as the style of the Symphony, calls for 2 flutes, 2 oboes, 2 clarinets, 2 bassoons, 2 horns, 2 trumpets, kettledrums, and strings.

SYMPHONY NO. 9, D MINOR, WITH FINAL CHORUS ON SCHILLER'S ODE TO JOY, OPUS 125

Both Beethoven and Schiller, whose words he used in the Ninth Symphony, belonged roughly to the same generation. In their youth, both felt the impact of the French Revolution, which erupted across borders into Germany and Austria. The brotherhood of man, which is hymned in the finale of the Ninth Symphony, was a goal for which both Schiller and Beethoven fought, each in his own way, as long as he lived. Schiller's death came in the midst of that epic struggle, barely a week before Napoleon—perverting the French Revolution into an instrument of absolutism—had himself proclaimed Emperor of France. Beethoven lived to see the fall of Napoleon, the restoration of order in Europe—albeit a reactionary order—and the close of one chapter in the fight for freedom.

In the Ninth Symphony he was able to look back on the battles, the victories and defeats, with a long perspective, to draw their sum and crown his nine symphonies with the prophetic vision and optimism of the great choral finale.

Schiller's ode "To Joy" had long attracted Beethoven. He was only twenty-two when he first planned to set the poem to music. He was forty-two when he planned to use the ode in an overture with chorus! The earliest surviving sketches for the Ninth Symphony date from 1817. But it was another seven years before Beethoven completed the Symphony, in a year and a half of concentrated labor. He put the finishing touches on his score in February 1824.

At the first performance of the Ninth Symphony in Vienna on May 7, 1824, Beethoven was far too deaf to think of conducting. He sat in the middle of the orchestra, trying to follow the performance with his score. But he seemed to have lost his place. At the conclusion there was tremendous applause, which Beethoven could not hear. The incident was described by George Grove, who heard about it from Fräulein Unger, the alto of that first performance, long after Beethoven's death: "The master, though placed in the midst of this confluence of music, heard nothing of it at all, and was not even sensible to the applause of the audience at the end of his great work, but continued standing with his back to the audience and beating the time, until Fräulein Unger turned him, or induced him to turn and face the people, who were still clapping their hands and giving way to the greatest demonstrations of pleasure. His turning about, and the sudden conviction thereby forced on everybody that he had not done so before because *he could not hear what was going on* acted like an electric shock on all present, and a volcanic explosion of sympathy and admiration followed."

The first performance in the United States was presented by the New York Philharmonic on May 20, 1846, under the direction of George Loder.

I. *Allegro ma non troppo, un poco maestoso.* The mysterious open fifths of the introduction are like the darkness and void before creation. They suggest the vastness of the design that lies ahead. Gradually, fragments of the main theme emerge from the darkness until suddenly the theme itself blazes out like a flash of orchestral lightning:

The main theme is followed by a wealth of subordinate ideas, mostly lyric. There is a great climax, after which the orchestra suddenly subsides into the tremulous empty fifths of the opening. A highly concentrated development of the opening material follows, then a recapitulation of the whole opening section. The coda, with its ominous *ostinato* in the depths of the orchestra, seems an apocalyptic vision.

II. *Molto Vivace—Presto—Molto vivace.* The hammer-blow octaves which introduce the second movement, a scherzo, are said to have struck Beethoven once as he stepped from darkness into sudden light. Although Beethoven may never have intended it so, this listener cannot shake off the impression that his hammer blow, with its falling motion and dotted rhythm, is related to the principal theme of the first movement, as a reduction of that theme to its most basic, irreducible essence.

A puckish, gossamer-light theme grows out of those first three notes, starting in the second violins:

It is taken up in rapid succession by violas, cellos, first violins and basses in the style of a tiny fugal exposition. But the hammer blows return, more and more insistently, until the entire string section is rocking to their rhythm, while the wind instruments have melodies of their own. There is a contrasting "trio" or middle section, serene and playful, after which the opening section repeats.

III. *Adagio molto e cantabile—Andante moderato.* The songful slow movement makes an impression all the more profound because of the boisterous drive and the drama of the movements that surround it. It is in Beethoven's beloved variation form, actually double variations, for there are two basic themes, of which the second has an unmistakably Romantic yearning quality:

For warmth and depth of feeling this movement is unsurpassed, even by Beethoven.

IV. *Allegro assai.* The lengthy introduction to the finale is really a bridge linking the themes of the first three movements with the finale, where Beethoven is among the stars. After a fierce, almost warlike clamor of the entire orchestra, Beethoven recalls briefly, like a passing memory, the principal theme of each preceding movement. Then comes the hint of a new theme on which the finale itself is built.

The main body of this precedent-shattering finale is a gigantic set of variations on the simplest melody imaginable. This is the melody which Beethoven gives to the first stanza of Schiller's ode, "*Freude, schöner Gòtterfunken*" (see below). We hear this melody first *without* words, a bare melody sung by cellos and basses without even any accompaniment. The first three variations are entirely instrumental, the only changes being addition of harmonic accompaniments; the melody is repeated unchanged.

An even wilder warlike outburst of the orchestra precedes the voices. In an introductory recitative with words by Beethoven himself, the baritone cries out: "Oh friends, no more of such sounds" (or, more freely: "Away with such painful, clashing dissonances!") and, calling for more joyous tones, leads the way himself with the first stanza of Schiller's ode "To Joy":

The chorus joins in to repeat the last four lines as a sort of refrain. The next two stanzas (each a new variation of the basic melody) are sung by the quartet of soloists, with the chorus joining each time for its repetition of the final bars.

Next the theme is transformed into a lilting orchestral march in the "Turkish music" *(alla turca)* style so popular in Mozart's and Beethoven's day, with the characteristic "Turkish" sound of triangle, cymbals and bass drum:

The variations which follow include a vivacious orchestral fugue, a tremendous double fugue for chorus and an exultant coda. Altogether, the finale is a structure of emotional depth and intensity, and musical splendor past description. The Symphony ranks as one of the greatest achievements of the human spirit.

CHORAL FINALE

The words for the baritone recitative that opens the choral section of the fourth movement are by Beethoven. The remainder of the text is from Friedrich Schiller's ode "To Joy."

(Baritone Solo, Quartet and Chorus)

O Freunde, nicht diese Töne! Sondern lasst uns angenehmere anstimmen, und freudenvollere!	O Friends, no more of these sad tones! Let us rather raise our voices together in more pleasant and joyful tones!
Freude, schöner Götterfunken, *Tochter aus Elysium,* *Wir betreten feuertrunken,* *Himmlische, dein Heiligtum!* *Deine Zauber binden wieder,* *Was die Mode streng geteilt;* *Alle Menschen werden Brüder,* *Wo dein sanfter Flügel weilt.*	Joy, thou shining spark of God, Daughter of Elysium! With fiery rapture, Goddess, We approach thy shrine. Your magic reunites those Whom stern custom has parted, All men will become brothers Under your protective wing.

Wem der grosse Wurf gelungen,
Eines Freundes Freund zu sein,
Wer ein holdes Weib errungen,
Mische seinen Jubel ein!
Ja, wer auch nur eine Seele
Sein nennt auf dem Erdenrund!
Und wer's nie gekonnt, der stehle
Weinend sich aus diesem Bund!

Let the man who has had the fortune
To be a helper to his friend,
And the man who has won a noble woman,
Join in our chorus of jubilation!
Yes, even if he holds but one soul
As his own in all the world!
But let the man who knows nothing of this
Steal away alone and in sorrow.

Freude trinken alle Wesen
An den Brüsten der Natur;
Alle Guten, alle Bösen
Folgen ihrer Rosenspur.
Küsse gab sie uns und Reben,
Einen Freund, geprüft im Tod;
Wollust ward dem Wurm gegeben,
Und der Cherub steht vor Gott!

All the world's creatures draw
Draughts of joy from Nature's breast;
Both the just and the unjust
Follow in her gentle footsteps.
She gave us kisses and wine
And a friend loyal unto death;
She gave the joy of life to the lowliest,
And to the angels who dwell with God.

(Tenor Solo and Chorus)

Froh, wie seine Sonnen fliegen
Durch des Himmels prächt'gen Plan,
Laufet, Brüder, eure Bahn,
Freudig wie ein Held zum Siegen.

Joyous, as His suns speed
Through the glorious order of Heaven,
Hasten, Brothers, on your way
Of joyous deeds to victory.

(The first stanza is repeated.)

(Chorus)

Seid umschlungen Millionen!
Diesen Kuss der ganzen Welt!
Brüder! Über'm Sternenzelt
Muss ein lieber Vater wohnen.
Ihr stürzt nieder Millionen?
Ahnest du den Schöpfer, Welt?
Such' ihn über'm Sternenzelt!
Über Sternen muss er wohnen.

Be embraced, all ye Millions!
With a kiss for all the world!
Brothers, beyond the stars
Surely dwells a loving Father.
Do you kneel before him, O Millions?
Do you feel the Creator's presence?
Seek him beyond the stars!
He must dwell beyond the stars.

The remainder of the movement repeats various verses from the above text.

The Ninth Symphony is scored for piccolo, 2 flutes, 2 oboes, 2 clarinets, 2 bassoons, contrabassoon, 4 horns, 2 trumpets, 3 trombones, kettledrums, triangle, cymbals, bass drum, and strings.

Alban Berg

Born February 9, 1885, Vienna—died December 24, 1935, Vienna

CONCERTO FOR VIOLIN AND ORCHESTRA

"To the memory of an Angel," is the inscription of the manuscript score of Berg's Violin Concerto. The angelic girl, in whose memory the Violin Concerto was composed as a sort of Requiem Mass, was the eighteen-year-old Manon Gropius, daughter of the famous architect and Alma Maria Mahler.

In February 1935 Berg was approached by the Boston violinist Louis Krasner, with the suggestion that he compose a concerto to which Mr. Krasner would have sole performing rights for a certain period of time. Berg, however, was engaged in completing the composition of his last opera, *Lulu,* and showed no inclination to interrupt it for the Violin Concerto. But in May of the same year, he received the news that the beautiful Manon Gropius, to whom he had been a devoted friend, had died of infantile paralysis after a tragic battle with the disease, which she had fought with heroism as well as with sweetness and calm. Berg was deeply moved and decided to make the Violin Concerto a memorial. He began work upon it at once, interrupting the final act of *Lulu,* working with an almost feverish haste and a speed which for him was most unusual. On the 15th of July, 1935, he wrote to his composer-friend Anton Webern: ". . . and then I was so dead tired after an almost thirteen-hour work day, that I was incapable of absorbing any more music, so I went to bed. For on that day [12 July] I had practically completed the *composition* of the Violin Concerto, [i.e., the composition sketch, not the complete orchestration] and I had been sitting at the piano or at my desk from seven o'clock that morning until nine o'clock that night almost without interruption. I hope to complete the orchestration during the next six or seven weeks so that then I can go to Karlsbad, to resume work on the score of *Lulu.*"

The same feverish pace is reflected in another letter, again to Webern, dated August 7: ". . . I hope to be able to write you more next week. At the moment I am working like a madman at my full score [of the Violin Concerto] in the hopes of finishing it by the middle of August and therefore I have put everything else aside."

According to Willi Reich, who visited Berg in mid-August, the score was completed on the 11th of the month. Thus Berg, who normally had taken one to two years of concentrated work for a major instrumental score, completed his first and only concerto in approximately four months.

His Violin Concerto uses so-called serial or twelve-tone techniques, but in Berg's personal way, which allowed him not only to retain a sense of traditional tonality when this suited his purpose, but to integrate into his score symbolic quotations from traditional music. The most important of these symbolic phrases is the melody of a Lutheran chorale, "*Es ist genug!*" ("It Is

Enough!"). Berg uses this traditional melody in virtually the same harmonization as that of Johann Sebastian Bach in his Cantata No. 60, *O Ewigkeit, du Donnerwort (O Eternity, Thou Thunderous Word).* Bach's Cantata bears the subtitle *Dialogue between Fear and Hope.* It seems likely, although this cannot be documented, that the struggle between fear and hope in the face of impending death was also one of the ideas embodied in the Concerto.

The first phrase of the chorale *"Es ist genug! Herr wenn es Dir gefällt,"* ("It is enough, Lord if it be Thy will"), is striking not only for its words, but for its use of the (traditionally avoided) melodic succession of three whole steps (the medieval "Devil in Music" or *Diabolus in Musica*) which Berg incorporated into the end of his basic tone row:

The Concerto is in two movements, of two parts each, which the composer characterized in a letter to Schoenberg of August 28, 1935, as "I (a) *Andante* (Preludium), (b) *Allegretto* (Scherzo); II (a) *Allegro* (Cadenza), (b) *Adagio* (Chorale Variations)," Hans Redlich, the Berg scholar, suggests that the first movement was intended as a musical portrait of Manon Gropius, while the second represents "the catastrophe of death and the transfiguration in heaven."

I. *Andante—Allegretto.* There is a quiet introduction with a theme built on the perfect fifths which sound naturally on the four unstopped strings of the violin. These four notes are the odd-numbered notes (the first, third, fifth, and seventh notes) of the basic tone row shown below. The top four notes of the row are the ones that correspond to the chorale words *"Es ist genug."* Contrary to much customary procedure, Berg uses his basic tone row as an identifiable theme. It is presented (after the brief introduction by the solo violin) as follows:

During the most of the tender reverie which constitutes the first part of this movement, the violin solo moves rhapsodically, almost as if improvising, although the music is actually a highly disciplined construction.

The second half of the movement [I (b) *Allegretto*] with its scherzo character is said to recall Manon's natural cheer and gaiety. At one point in the score a solo horn introduces a Carinthian folk melody, which starts as follows:

This merry tune is also related to the basic tone row, but its gaiety is overcast with melancholy and there is little to remind one of its peasant *Ländler* origin.

II. *Allegro—Adagio.* The vigorous first half of the finale is directed to be played *sempre rubato, frei wie eine Kadenz,* that is to say, with frequent fluctuations of rhythm, freely as in a cadenza. It is easy to imagine in this music the growing struggle with death which Redlich suggests. At the climax (which Berg has specifically marked *"Höhepunkt"*) we hear a sharply syncopated rhythm similar to that which Berg used as a death motive in both of his operas, *Wozzeck* and *Lulu.*

This climax leads to the complete melody of the chorale *"Es ist genug!"* and two variations upon it. In these the violin solo seems an elegy for the loss of Manon. At the end the violin ascends, perhaps symbolically, in a final tranquil statement of the basic tone row, ending serenely on a soft high G, while the other strings of the orchestra descend into the depths, sounding in reverse the perfect fifths of the opening. The cycle is complete. The final chord suggests reconciliation and peace.

The first performance of Berg's Violin Concerto took place after his death. The honor fell to the Barcelona Festival of the International Society of Contemporary Music on April 19, 1936. The soloist was Louis Krasner; Hermann Scherchen conducted.

The Concerto is scored for 2 piccolos, 2 flutes, 2 oboes, English horn, 1 clarinet in A, 2 clarinets in B flat, bass clarinet in B flat, alto saxophone in E flat, 2 bassoons, 1 contrabassoon, 4 horns, 2 trumpets, 2 trombones, bass tuba, 4 kettledrums, bass drum, snare drum, cymbals, low-pitched tam-tam, high-pitched gong, triangle, harp, and the usual strings.

LULU SUITE

"Femme fatale" is far more than a humorous phrase. The fatal woman is an ancient, perhaps very primitive dream. Lulu's venerable ancestry includes the sirens of Classical mythology, who lured sailors to their doom; and the coldly beautiful Sphinx, who devoured men unable to read her riddle. She was the Lorelei of the ancient Teutons. And in the eighteenth century, beginning with Manon Lescaut, she spawned a grand line of Romantic temptresses, each more lethal than the last, culminating in Carmen, Delilah, Nana, Kundry, Salome, and Lulu.

Alban Berg's opera *Lulu* is founded on two extraordinary plays by Frank

Wedekind, a German Expressionist at the turn of the nineteenth to twentieth centuries, an idealist who shocked his Victorian-Edwardian world with the subject matter of his highly moral (though far from moralistic) masterpieces: *Erdgeist (Earth Spirit)* and *Die Büchse der Pandora (The Box of Pandora).*

By skillful cutting (changing virtually nothing of Wedekind's text) Berg shaped a libretto which, like the late Wagner librettos, was governed by musical forms. The opera is in three acts. During the first half (up to the middle of Act II) as Lulu climbs the social ladder, we see her destroy three husbands in quick succession. During the second half the pattern is reversed: Lulu herself is destroyed by three men (three nemesis figures, corresponding to her three husbands) as she falls back into the depths from which she came.

Lulu's first husband, a physician, dies of a heart attack when he discovers her with a portrait painter. The painter, who becomes her second husband, shoots himself when he discovers she is the mistress of Dr. Schön. When Dr. Schön, her third husband, discovers that she has seduced his son Alwa, he tries to make Lulu commit suicide. But Lulu shoots Schön, is arrested for murder, and serves a prison term. Rescued after a year by a trio of her admirers including the tragic, grotesque Countess Geschwitz, Lulu flees with them, first to Paris and then, as her fortunes ebb, to London. She falls lower and lower in the social scale, finally becoming a common prostitute. In the last scene Lulu meets her nightmare end at the hands of a customer, Jack the Ripper.

Berg died before he could complete the orchestration of his last act. But in 1934, he put togehter a five-movement suite of passages from the opera and orchestrated them in full. He thought of calling the whole a *Lulu* Symphony, but the movements were published after his death under the title of *Lulu Suite.* Its five movements are: I. *Rondo,* II. *Ostinato,* III. *Lied der Lulu,* IV. *Variationen,* V. *Adagio.* But, with the exception of the second and third movements, these are not merely excerpts taken unchanged from the opera score; the first and last movements show substantial elisions in the original material, and even new connective tissue.

I. *Rondo* (*Andante* and Hymn). Introduced by two musical motives associated with Lulu herself, this rondo is a combination of the two scenes between Lulu and Alwa in Act II, during which it becomes apparent that Alwa is to be his father's successor in Lulu's favors.

II. *Ostinato (Allegro).* This symphonic interlude links the two halves of Act II. Thus it falls in the middle (of the middle act) of Berg's opera, which is the turning point in Lulu's career: her arrest and imprisonment for the murder of Dr. Schön. Berg makes this a turning point in a formal musico-dramatic sense as well, that is to say the second half of this opera mirrors, in many subtle ways, the first half. This mirror form is given its most obvious emphasis in our *ostinato* interlude, which is itself cast in two halves, the second of which exactly repeats the first half, but backwards. The entire interlude is built over the following *ostinato* theme:

In his libretto for the opera, Berg specifies that the mirror form of this musical interlude is to be accompanied by a silent film sketching Lulu's fate during this time. This film sequence should correspond to the symmetrical structure of the music by being practically symmetrical (that is to say moving forward and then backwards). For this purpose corresponding events and their accompanying phenomena are to be given, as far as possible, a parallel sequence.* This produces the following succession of pictures (following the direction of the arrows):

↓	Read up ↑
Lulu's arrest	Lulu on her way to complete freedom
The three participants in her arrest	The three participants in her escape
Lulu handcuffed	Lulu without chains (disguised as the Countess Geschwitz)
In detention for arraignment	In the hospital quarantine ward
Nervous expectation and dwindling hope	Nervous expectation and rising hope
The trial	The medical consultation
Her guilt	Her sickness
Judge and jury	Physicians and students
The three witnesses to her deed	The three confederates in her escape
The sentencing	Release
Transfer by prison automobile	Transfer by ambulance
The prison	The prison
The prison door closes	The prison door opens
Initial resignation	Returning zest for life
Lulu's likeness: her shadow on the prison wall	Lulu's likeness: her reflection on a shovel

→ One year of prison →

* *[Composer's footnote:] "In addition to the above correspondence of the principal events in parallel columns such as 'The Trial—The medical consultation,' etc., there should also be small, even minute correspondences such as: revolver-stethoscope, bullets-vials, law-medicine, paragraph symbols-cholera bacillae, handcuffs-bandages, prison uniforms-hospital uniforms, prison corridors-hospital corridors, etc. Similarly there should be correspondences of persons as for example: judge and jury—physicians and students, policemen—nurses, etc., etc."*

III. *Lied der Lulu (Lulu's Song).* "Lulu's Song" is her self-defense, her self-justification, in response to Schön's attempt to make her commit suicide. She sings her first words, appropriately enough to the basic series or row of twelve tones, which is associated with her throughout the opera (and from which many lesser themes are derived):

Wenn sich die Menschen um meinetwillen umgebracht haben, so setzt das meinen Wert nicht herab.	If human beings have killed themselves because of me, that does not detract from my worth.
Du hast so gut gewusst, weswegen Du mich zu Frau nahmst, wie ich gewusst habe, weswegen ich Dich zum Mann nahm.	You knew why you took me to be your wife just as well as I knew why I took you for my husband.
Du hattest Deine besten Freunde mit mir betrogen, Du konntest nicht gut auch noch Dich selber mit mir betrügen.	You had betrayed your best friends with me; you could not very well betray yourself with me.
Wenn Du mir Deinen Lebensabend zum Opfer bringst, so hast Du meine Ganze Jugend dafür gehabt.—	If you have sacrificed the evening of your life to me, you have had in exchange all of my youth.
Ich habe nie in der Welt etwas anderes scheinen wollen, als wofür man mich genommen hat.	Never in the world did I wish to appear to be anything other than what I was taken to be.
Und man hat mich nie in der Welt für etwas anderes genommen als was ich bin.	And never in the world was I taken to be anything other *than what I am.*

IV. *Variationen* (Variations). This instrumental interlude links the two scenes of Act III, and prepares the spectator for the hopelessness of the final scene in the London garret where Lulu plies her trade as a streetwalker. The theme is a Berlin streetwalkers' song taken from a volume of songs collected by Wedekind. The four variations are marked 1. *Grandioso,* 2. *Grazioso,* 3. *Funèbre* and 4. *Affettuoso.*

V. *Adagio.* This is a symphonic condensation of the final scene in the London garret. The Countess Geschwitz, who has followed Lulu with hopeless, helpless devotion through the entire drama, sees Lulu go into her room with her last customer, Jack the Ripper. We hear Lulu's death screams. The Countess rushes to her rescue and struggles in vain to open the door. Suddenly it is thrust violently open and the Ripper emerges with a knife, on which he impales the Countess. In her death throes the Countess murmurs, to music of astonishing tenderness, a kind of nightmarish *Liebestod:* "Lulu my angel—let me see you once more!—I am near to you. I will always be near to you, in eternity. . . ."

The *Lulu Suite* is scored for 3 flutes, 3 piccolos, 3 oboes, 2 E-flat clarinets, bass clarinet, 3 bassoons, contrabassoon, 4 horns, 3 trumpets, 3 trombones, 2 contrabass tuba, 4 kettledrums, bass drum, cymbals, side drum, big tam-tam, small tam-tam (gong), triangle, vibraphone, piano, harp, and the traditional strings.

The *Lulu Suite* was first heard in Berlin on November 30, 1934, under the direction of Erich Kleiber. The first performance of the (incomplete) opera was given by the Stadttheater of Zürich on June 2, 1937. The opera is dedicated to Berg's teacher, Arnold Schoenberg. ("Lulu's Song" is separately dedicated to Anton von Webern for his fiftieth birthday.)

THREE MOVEMENTS FROM THE LYRIC SUITE

Alban Berg's popular *Lyric Suite*, composed in 1925–26 as a string quartet, was a turning point in his development. As the title suggests, it is a melodious work. It recalls the Romantic style of Berg's youth at the same time that it foreshadows his last and ripest works.

The *Lyric Suite* shares its basic musical material (its twelve-tone row, or series) with a song on which he worked simultaneously: his second setting of Theodor Storm's poem *"Schliesse mir die Augen beide"* ("Close, O Close my Eyes"). Berg had composed his first song on the Storm poem in 1900. As a tribute to the silver jubilee of his publishers, the progressive Universal Edition (who had also strongly supported Schönberg and Webern), Berg planned to publish simultaneously his two songs on the Storm poem: the 1900 song and that of 1925. The contrast between the two songs was intended to emphasize the change in Berg's style over the quarter of a century.

In a letter to Anton Webern on October 12, 1925, Berg linked his song to the future *Lyric Suite*: "I, too, sent a (love) song, the words of which have no connection whatsoever with the jubilee; or rather, I sent *two* songs on the same poem: a very old song, and a brand-new one. The latter I composed up here [i.e.: at the summer resort Trahütten]—my first attempt at really strict twelve-note [tone-row] composition. Unfortunately I am not as far advanced in this art as you are; hence for the time being I do not have much news for you about my work on the string quartet. (By the way, this is to be a suite for string quartet: six rather short movements of a more lyric than symphonic character.)"

When completed, late in 1926, this quartet was given the title *Lyric Suite*. It was first performed on January 8, 1927, in Vienna by the Kolisch Quartet and quickly became popular. By August, 1927, the director of Universal Edition, Emil Hertzka, suggested that Berg arrange excerpts from the *Lyric Suite* for string orchestra. Berg sought Webern's advice: "I'm considering doing the second, third and fourth movements," he wrote. "Do you think that would be feasible? Possibly with small changes in the instrumentation? (For example in passages where the cello goes up too high.) I *need* your advice badly!! Please write me *now!* Later we can discuss it. Please!"

The project proved better than feasible; Berg's arrangement of the three movements became one of his most attractive and successful orchestral works. It was first performed in Berlin under the direction of Jascha Horenstein on January 21, 1929. The New York Philharmonic presented the United States premiere of the three movements in their orchestral form on October 22, 1931, under the direction of Erich Kleiber.

The *Lyric Suite* is intensely emotional music. Even if we had no other evidence, Berg's intention would be clear enough from the markings of the six original movements: 1. *Allegretto gioviale;* 2. *Andante amoroso;* 3. *Allegro misterioso; Trio estatico;* 4. *Adagio appassionato;* 5. *Presto delirando; Tenebroso;* and 6. *Largo desolato.* But we have the additional evidence that the basic tone row of the *Lyric Suite* is identical with that of the song *"Schliesse mir die Augen beide"* in its second version mentioned above. Furthermore, the emotional climate of the song as expressed both in its words and music seems very close to the *Lyric Suite*. The subject of the poem is the traditional Romantic association of love with death. And if any added evidence is needed, we find it in the final movement of the *Lyric Suite* where Berg quotes the opening theme of Wagner's *Tristan und Isolde*. The three orchestral movements are:

Andante amoroso. This extremely subjective movement is a free rondo. The refrain announced at the outset by the first violins is easy to recognize in its three principal recurrences. Between refrains we hear brief, contrasting sections of slightly livelier tempo and of contrasting, chordal texture. Toward the end the hitherto clear outline of the rondo form is intentionally blurred.

Allegro misterioso; Trio estatico. The ghostly sonorities result in part from special bowing techniques: bowing close to the bridge, over the fingerboard, playing harmonics and using the wooden back of the bow to stroke or occasionally even to strike the strings. These effects are greatly intensified by the use of a full string orchestra, yet Berg chose to enhance the effect still further by extensive rewriting of the instrumental parts, often dividing his string choir into as many as nine separate sections.

Adagio appassionato. As its title suggests, this movement is the emotional climax of the *Lyric Suite*. From the opening theme, with its characteristic wavering half-step taken up by each of the instrumental choirs, the entire movement seems to be a tissue of thematic reminiscences. The stormy intensity of the final climax is succeeded by a lofty contemplative calm.

THREE ORCHESTRAL PIECES, OPUS 6

"To my teacher and friend Arnold Schoenberg, in immeasurable gratitude and love," is the dedication of Alban Berg's Romantic early work: his Three Orchestral Pieces, Opus 6.

This fascinating opus was the product of a crisis in Berg's development, provoked by a stern heart-to-heart discussion with the older composer, and followed by considerable self-searching on the part of the younger man:

> You will, of course, understand, dear Mr. Schönberg [wrote Berg to his master on June 14, 1913], that among the most wonderful memories of unclouded joy, there also obtrudes the memory of that last afternoon, with its depressing home-truths. However, I must thank you as much for your reproof, as for everything else you have given me, well knowing that it was for my own good. . . .
>
> I hope to show you soon by deeds what I am scarcely able to express now in words. As soon as I am out in the country, I want to begin that suite. Perhaps someday I shall be able to compose something joyful. . . .

Berg's hopes for a suite developed into the draft for his Three Orchestral Pieces, now planned as a birthday tribute to Schoenberg for his fortieth birthday on September 13, 1914. But Berg worked slowly, with infinite care and relentless self-criticism. "I keep asking myself, again and again," he wrote Schoenberg, "whether what I express [in the Three Orchestral Pieces], often brooding over certain bars for days on end, is any better than my last things. . . ." The result was that only the first and last of the Three Pieces were finished in time for Schoenberg's birthday. In the letter which accompanied them Berg wrote:

> For years it has been my secret but strong wish and will to dedicate something to you. The works written under your supervision, Mr. Schönberg: the Sonata, Lieder and Quartet, were automatically eliminated, having been received from you. My hope to write something more independent and yet as good as these first compositions, something I could dedicate to you without incurring your displeasure, has been repeatedly disappointed for several years. . . .
>
> I cannot tell today whether I have succeeded or failed. Should the latter be the case, then in your fatherly benevolence, Mr. Schönberg, you must take the goodwill for the deed.

I. *Präludium: Langsam.* The first movement begins with an almost inaudible throbbing of eight percussion instruments. This misty sound is soon enriched with murmurs of the other instrumental choirs. But it is not until the fifteenth measure that we hear a distinct melodic line, the principal theme of the movement, played by violins and bassoons in unison:

ALBAN BERG WITH HIS PORTRAIT.

Berg's close relation to Schoenberg is suggested by this photo of Berg with his portrait in oil by Schoenberg about 1910. (*Courtesy, The Bettman Archive*)

The bold arch of the third full measure plays a prominent role in the brief, but intensive thematic development. At the end, the movement fades back to the same hazy sonority with which it began.

II. *Reigen: Anfangs etwas zögernd; Leicht beschwingt; Langsames Waltzer-tempo.* This movement is close in spirit and technique to the peasant *Ländler* and waltz-inspired movements in Mahler. But it also looks forward in its grotesque melodic jumps and occasional pounding accompaniment to the beer-garden scene of Berg's opera *Wozzeck* (Act II, Scene 4).

III. *Marsch: Mässiges Marschtempo; Viel langsamer; Allegro energico; Sehr langsam.* This finale, which lasts as long as the first two movements combined, is based quite freely on traditional sonata-allegro form. The feeling of the movement, however, is almost more dramatic than symphonic. It rises to a series of catastrophic climaxes. At the most striking of these the whole orchestra breaks off suddenly and the kettledrums crash out a cataclysmic syncopated rhythm:

This stark climax has been compared to the doom-laden "hammerblows" in the finale of Mahler's Sixth Symphony and the "death rhythm," the syncopated heartbeat, in the first movement of Mahler's Ninth. Actually, such suggestive syncopations can be traced back through the realistic, irregular heartbeats in Strauss's *Death and Transfiguration* to Tristan's collapse in the last act of Wagner's *Tristan und Isolde*, when Kurvenal sings: *"Bist du nun tot?"* But Berg's brutal explosion also looks forward to his opera *Wozzeck:* the entr'acte following the murder of Marie, where a tremendous orchestral *crescendo* breaks off with just such nerve-racking series of crashes. There are many other anticipations of *Wozzeck* and endless fascinating links to both past and future in this highly imaginative score.

The score of Berg's Opus 6 calls for piccolo, 4 flutes, 4 oboes, English horn, 4 clarinets, E-flat clarinet, bass clarinet, 3 bassoons, contrabassoon, 6 horns, 4 trumpets, 4 trombones (including one bass trombone), contrabass tuba, bass drum, small drum, cymbals (one hanging free, another attached to the bass drum), large tam-tam, small tam-tam, 2 pairs of kettledrums, side drum, triangle, large hammer (with nonmetallic sound), glockenspiel, xylophone, celesta, 2 harps, and a strong string choir divided into five sections.

WOZZECK, SYMPHONIC FRAGMENTS, OPUS 7

Alban Berg's *Wozzeck* ranks with Debussy's *Pelléas et Mélisande* among the most influential operas of our century. It is, moreover, the only Expressionist opera to have been accepted into the standard repertory. Its text is taken from the tragedy, *Woyzek,* which Georg Büchner left unfinished at his death in 1837. Büchner's *Woyzek* was a burning social indictment not only of the reactionary Germany of Metternich's day before the revolutions of 1848 and 1849, but also of the brutality and cruelty which Büchner saw as part of the human lot.

In Berg's opera, Wozzeck, a simpleminded soldier, is shown to us as a helpless victim of his environment: his captain who ridicules him; the garrison doctor who uses him as a guinea pig for scientific experiments; the drum major who beats him; and his mistress, Marie, who betrays him. In despair, Wozzeck murders Marie, and then drowns as he tries to wash her blood from his hands in a pond.

Begun in 1914, the opera was finished in 1921. At first no editor would publish and no opera house would touch the difficult work. So on the advice of Hermann Scherchen, Berg chose three excerpts for presentation in concert form. These excerpts were first heard under Scherchen's direction at Frankfurt in June, 1924. Their success was so remarkable that *Wozzeck* was accepted for production at the Berlin State Opera, where it had its premiere on December 14, 1925, under the direction of Erich Kleiber.

I. The first excerpt begins with the entr'acte music linking the Second and Third Scenes of Act I, and continues through the first half of Scene 3 in Marie's room. It is evening. Marie is standing with her child on her arm at the window. A military band approaches. Marie admires the strapping Drum Major who struts at the head of the parade. A spoken dialogue over the music brings Marie's neighbor, Margaret, to taunt Marie for her infatuation with the Drum Major. Marie, enraged, insults Margaret and slams the window, whereupon the sound of the band is shut out. Marie turns to her child. Her endearments are mixed with her thoughts of guilt that the child is born out of wedlock. She sings the child to sleep with a fantastic lullaby.

ACT I, SCENE 3

Marie

Tschin Bum, Tschin Bum, Bum, Bum,	Chin boom, Chin boom, boom, boom,
Bum! Hörst Bub? Da kommen sie!	Boom! D'ya hear, boy? There they come!

(The band, headed by the Drum Major, passes before Marie's window.)

Soldaten, Soldaten sind schöne Burschen!	Soldiers, Soldiers are handsome fellows!

[In Berg's concert version, the *spoken* dialogue between Marie and her neighbor Margaret is omitted.]

(Marie slams the window, the band is no longer heard. She is alone with her child.)

Komm, mein Bub! Was die Leute wollen! Bist nur ein arm'Hurenkind und machst Deiner Mutter doch so viel Freud' mit Deinem unehrlichen Gesicht!	Come, my child! Pay no attention! You're only a poor whore's child, and yet you give your mother such joy with your sweet bastard's face!

(she rocks the child)

Eia popeia . . .	Rock-a-bye baby . . .
Mädel, was fangst Du jetzt an?	Girl, what can you do now?
Hast ein klein Kind und kein Mann!	You have a child but no husband!
Ei, was frag' ich darnach,	What's the good of asking!
Sing' ich die ganze Nacht:	If I sing the whole night through
Eia popeia, mein süsser Bu',	Rock-a-bye baby, my sweet boy,
Gibt mir kein Mensch nix dazu!	Nobody will care at all!
Hansel, spann' Deine sechs Schimmel an,	Hansel, harness your six white steeds,
Gib sie zu fressen auf's neu,	Give them more to eat,
Kein Haber fresse sie,	They shall eat no fodder,
Kein Wasser saufe sie,	They shall drink no water,
Lauter kühle Wein muss es sein!	They shall have only cool wine!

(she notices that the child is asleep)

Lauter kühle Wein muss es sein!	They shall have only cool wine!

II. The second excerpt begins with Act III, Scene 1, set in Marie's room at night by candlelight. It is composed in the form of a theme with seven variations and a concluding fugue. The theme is in two contrasting parts: the first, a contrapuntal passage led off by a single muted viola.

This accompanies the first line Marie reads from the Bible. The second half of the theme is her violent outburst *"Herr-Gott! Sieh' mich nicht an!"* The variations tend to preserve this violent alternation of moods of hope and despair, which characterize Marie's monologue.

ACT III, SCENE 1

Marie

"Und ist kein Betrug in seinem Munde erfunden worden . . ."	"And there is no guile found in his mouth . . ."
Herr-Gott! Herr-Gott! Sieh' mich nicht an!	Lord, Lord! Look not upon me!

(she turns the pages)

"Aber die Pharisäer brachten ein Weib zu ihm, so im Ehebruch lebte. Jesus aber sprach: 'So verdamme ich dich auch nicht, geh' hin, und sündige hinfort nicht mehr'." Herrgott!	"But the Pharisees brought unto him a woman that lived in adultery. Jesus said: I condemn thee not; go and sin no more!" Lord God!

(Covers her face with her hands. The child presses up to Marie.)

Der Bub' gibt mir einen Stich in's Herz. Fort!	The boy stabs me to the heart! Get away!

(pushes the child away)

Das brüst' sich in der Sonne!	The shameless thing!

(suddenly more gentle)

Nein, komm, komm her!	No, come, come here!

(draws him closer)

Komm zu mir!	Come here!
"Es war einmal ein armes Kind und hatt' keinen Vater und keine Mutter . . . war Alles tot und war Niemand auf der Welt, und es hat gehungert und geweint Tag and Nacht. Und weil es Niemand mehr hatt' auf der Welt . . ." Der Franz ist nit kommen, gestern nit, heut' nit . . .	"Once upon a time was a poor child that had neither father or mother . . . they were both dead and the child had no one in the world, and it went hungry and wept day and night, because it had no one more in the world . . ." Franz didn't come, not yesterday, not today . . .

(She hastily turns the leaves of the Bible.)

Wie steht es geschrieben von der Magdalena? . . . "Und kniete hin zu seinen Füssen und weinte und küsste seine Füsse und netzte sie mit Tränen und salbte sie mit Salben."	What does it say about the Magdalen? . . . "And she knelt and kissed his feet and wept, moistening them with her tears, and anointed them with ointment."

(Beats her breast)

Heiland! Ich möchte Dir die Füsse salben! Heiland! Du hast Dich ihrer erbarmt, erbarme Dich auch meiner!	Savior! I wish I might anoint thy feet! Savior! Thou hadst pity on her, have pity on me, too!

III. The final excerpt starts at the exact moment when Wozzeck drowns near the end of Act III, Scene 4. The horror of the night scene is enhanced by slowly rising chromatic scales for divided strings and woodwinds, like tiny bubbles rising slowly from the corpse. As the curtain falls, the longest and most eloquent interlude of the opera opens with the following melody:

This expands into an overpowering orchestral lament for all the downtrodden Wozzecks of this world. In its dramatic function, this interlude has been compared to Siegfried's funeral music, which links the last two scenes in Wagner's *Götterdämmerung.*

As the lament dies away, the curtain rises on the street in front of Marie's house. It is a sunny morning. Children are playing ring-around-a-rosy. Marie's and Wozzeck's child is riding a hobbyhorse. Other children come rushing in; they whisper excitedly together. Then one goes up to Marie's child and says: "Hey you! Your mother's dead!" All rush off to have a look at the body. Only Marie's boy, too young to understand, is left alone singing "Hop, hop!" as he rides his toy horse. At last he too trots off. The curtain falls on an empty stage.

The *Wozzeck* excerpts call for a very large and colorful orchestra including 4 flutes, 4 piccolos, 4 oboes, English horn, 4 clarinets in A, B flat, and E flat, bass clarinet, 3 bassoons, contrabassoon, 4 horns, 4 trumpets, alto trombone, 2 tenor trombones, bass trombone, contrabass tuba, 2 pairs of kettledrums, cymbals, bass drum, snare drum, whip, large and small tam-tams, triangle, xylophone, celesta, harp, and "at least 50 to 60" strings (often subdivided into as many as 12 parts).

Hector Berlioz

Born December 11, 1803, Côte-Saint-André, Isère—died March 8, 1869, Paris.

DAMNATION OF FAUST (3 EXCERPTS)

Berlioz had not yet recovered from the artistic convulsion of his introduction to Shakespeare in the fall of 1827, when he was swept up in another tremendous literary experience. Only a few weeks after the visit of the English actors in *Hamlet* and *Romeo and Juliet*, Goethe's *Faust* was published in a translation by the twenty-year-old Gérard de Nerval. The translation was so good that even Goethe, who had grown tired of reading *Faust* in German, enjoyed reading it in French. "This marvelous book fascinated me from the very first moment," wrote Berlioz. "I could not put it down. I read it incessantly, at meals, in the theater, in the street, everywhere."

It was a fruitful encounter for Berlioz. It inspired his Eight Scenes from *Faust*, his *Dramatic Legend, The Damnation of Faust,* and many of the ideas for his *Fantastic Symphony*. Berlioz was unable to resist setting eight episodes from *Faust* to music; "and having completed this rash deed I was foolish enough without having heard a note of my music, to have my score engraved . . . at my own expense." In later years Berlioz decided that his Eight Scenes was an immature work. He even went so far as to round up as many copies of the score as he could and destroyed them. Yet he still felt his original ideas were good. "Indeed," he wrote, "I used them again, very differently developed in my *Dramatic Legend, The Damnation of Faust*."

Berlioz completed his oratorio-like *Damnation of Faust* which he gave the unconventional subtitle of *Dramatic Legend* in 1846. It was so coldly received at its premiere on December 6 of that year that Berlioz was ruined financially —not for the first time in his life. "Nothing in my career as an artist has wounded me more deeply than this unexpected indifference," he wrote in his *Memoirs*. Only seven years after Berlioz's death, the Parisian public changed its mind; the first revival of the *Damnation* in 1876 was such an overwhelming success that it had to be repeated for six successive Sundays and for the next quarter of a century the prestigious Colonne Orchestra played Berlioz's score an average of half a dozen times each year.

Among Berlioz's most popular pieces in the concert hall are three orchestral excerpts from *The Damnation:* "Hungarian March," "Ballet of Sylphs," and "Minuet of the Will-o'-the-Wisps." Although the March occurs first in the score, it is usually played last. It is so brilliant that almost any following work comes as an anticlimax. None of the three excerpts corresponds to any scene of Goethe's *Faust* and, as Berlioz pointed out, there is no reason that they should. The Faust legend is ancient and Berlioz felt free, as others had done, to invent his own episodes.

I. *Dance of the Sylphs*. Revolted by the coarse company of the tipplers in Auerbach's Cellar, Faust asks if Mephisto has nothing better to offer him. Mephisto spreads out his mantle, and a few measures of Berlioz's magic orchestra transport Faust to the banks of the River Elbe, where Mephisto lulls him to sleep with a sort of lullaby, "*Voici des roses*" ("Here are sweet roses"). Faust dreams. The melody of Mephisto's lullaby is transformed, first into a chorus of gnomes and sylphs (during which Marguérite appears to Faust for the first time in a vision) and finally into a waltz for the sylphs:

Above a single, sustained note, a D which is held *pianissimo* through the entire piece by muted cellos and basses, the waltz floats, like a disembodied wraith of violins and violas, with an occasional glint of the piccolo, flute, clarinet, or harp.

II. *Minuet of the Will-o'-the-Wisps.* Scarcely has Berlioz introduced Marguérite to us (a scene we are to imagine taking place in her bedroom), when Mephisto summons the Will-o'-the-Wisps to bewilder the spirit of the innocent girl and lull her to sleep. The Will-o'-the-Wisps are soft, gleaming woodwind harmonies which seem to float weightlessly through the orchestral fabric.

III. *Hungarian March* was not originally written for the *Damnation of Faust* at all, although it finds its place magnificently in the finished work. Berlioz wrote his old friend the poet Humbert Ferrand, describing the genesis of this movement which he wrote while on a concert tour. It was 1846 and the passionate longings for national independence were coming to a boiling point in Hungary as well as in many other European countries. A few days before Berlioz left Vienna for Budapest "a Viennese amateur," as Berlioz cautiously called him in his *Memoirs,* brought him a collection of old Hungarian melodies. In fact, "the Viennese amateur" may have been the Hungarian director of the National Theater in Budapest, where Berlioz was to conduct a concert. "If you want the Hungarians to like you," he advised, "compose a piece on one of their national melodies. They will be overjoyed, and when you return you must tell me what you thought of their cheers and applause." Berlioz took his visitor's advice and chose the traditional Hungarian Rákóczy theme, which he describes in his score as the "Hungarian hymn of war." Berlioz was a bit nervous about the outcome:

> On the day of the concert [February 15, 1846] a certain anxiety gripped my throat when the moment came to produce this devil of a piece. After a trumpet fanfare based on the rhythm of its opening bars, the theme, you may remember, is announced *piano* by flutes and clarinets accompanied by *pizzicato* strings:

> The audience remained calm and silent during this unexpected exposition. But when a long *crescendo* ensued, with fragments of the theme introduced fugally, broken by dull thuds of the bass drum, like the boom of distant cannon, the whole hall began to hum with an indescribable sound; and when the orchestra unleashed, in a furious melee, the long-delayed *fortissimo,* the theater was shaken by a tumult of shouting and stamping; the accumulative

> pressure of that seething mass of emotion exploded with a violence that sent a thrill of fear right through me; I felt as though my hair were standing on end. From that moment on I had to give up all thoughts of the peroration of my piece; the thunders of the orchestra were powerless against the eruption of such a volcano; nothing could stop it. As you can imagine, we had to repeat the piece. The second time, the audience could scarcely contain itself a few seconds longer to hear a bar or two of the coda. . . . It was a good thing that I had put the *Rákóczy-induló* (the Hungarian title of the piece) at the end of the program, for anything we had tried to play after it would have been lost. . . I was mopping my face in a little room behind the stage [after the performance] when a shabbily dressed man came in without warning; his face was shining and working strangely. On seeing me he fell on my neck and embraced me passionately, his eyes filling with tears, and he barely managed to stammer:
>
> "Ah, Monsieur—me Hungarian—sorry fellow—no speak French—*un poco l'italiano*—forgive—my rapture—ah! understand your cannon . . . know how to make music of revolution!" I cannot attempt to describe the man's alarming exaltation. He wept and gnashed his teeth. It was sublime.

A piece which produced such a sublime effect obviously deserves a place in the score of the *Damnation of Faust.* Berlioz straightforwardly and disarmingly gives this explanation for leading his Faust at the beginning of the score, to a Hungarian plain, where an army passes by. Although the tune is ancient the temperament, the dramatic cunning, and the fiery orchestral imagination are Berlioz's. The combination is still electrifying.

The "Three Excerpts" from *The Damnation of Faust* call for 2 piccolos, 2 flutes, 2 oboes, 2 clarinets, bass clarinet, 4 bassoons, 4 horns, 2 trumpets, 2 cornets (or chromatic trumpets), 3 trombones, tuba, ophicleide, 2 harps, kettledrums, cymbals, bass drum, tambourine, triangle, and the customary strings.

HAROLD IN ITALY, SYMPHONY IN FOUR MOVEMENTS FOR VIOLA AND ORCHESTRA, OPUS 16

It was after a triumphant performance of his *Fantastic Symphony* that Berlioz met the great violin virtuoso Niccolò Paganini, who spurred him on to compose two of his greatest works: *Harold in Italy* and *Romeo and Juliet.* Berlioz recalled the scene in the fervid, romantic language of his *Memoirs:*

> . . . My happiness was crowned when the public had all gone, and a man with long hair, piercing eyes, and strange, haggard face, a genius, a Titan among the giants, a man whom I had never seen before, and at first sight of whom I was deeply moved, waited for me alone in the concert hall and stopped me in the corridor to press my hand; he overwhelmed me with burning eulogies that set both my heart and brain on fire. It was *Paganini!!* (December 22, 1833).
>
> From that day dates my relations with the great artist, who exercised such a happy influence upon my destiny, and whose noble generosity to me, as will be seen later, has given birth to such absurd and malicious comments.

The hostile comments have continued into our century. More than one biographer has doubted not only Berlioz's recollection of the *date* of his meeting with Paganini (which he apparently *did* confuse), but Berlioz's whole story of the commissioning of the work which eventually became *Harold in Italy*. However, two distinguished Berlioz authorities, Jacques Barzun and David Cairns, both agree in accepting Berlioz's own version of the commission, which follows:

> Some weeks after the triumphant concert which I have just described, Paganini came to see me.
>
> "I have a wonderful viola," he said, "an admirable Stradivari, and should greatly like to play it in public. But I have no music for it. Would you write a viola solo? I have no confidence in anyone but you for such work."
>
> "Certainly," I answered. "I am more flattered than I can say. But in order to fulfill your expectation, in order to write a composition which would display the qualities of a virtuoso like yourself, one must play the viola oneself; and I do not. It seems to me that you alone can solve the problem."
>
> "No, no, I insist," said Paganini, "you will succeed. As for me, I am too unwell at present to compose. I could not think of such a thing."
>
> In order to please the illustrious virtuoso, then, I endeavored to write a solo for the viola, but so combined with the orchestra as not to diminish the importance of the latter, feeling sure that the incomparable power of Paganini's playing would always keep the viola in first place. The proposition seemed new, and soon a happy plan came to my mind; I was on fire to realize it.
>
> No sooner was the first movement written than Paganini wished to see it. At the sight of all the rests in the viola part of the *Allegro,* he exclaimed: "That's not it at all! I am silent too long in that; I must be playing the whole time."
>
> "That is exactly what I told you," I replied. "What you really want is a Viola Concerto and this being the case, only you can write for yourself." Paganini did not reply but he seemed disappointed, and left me without any further comment on my symphonic sketch. A few days afterwards, already suffering from a throat affliction which was ultimately to prove fatal, he left for Nice and did not return until three years later.
>
> Realizing that my plan of composition could not fit his need, I applied myself to carrying it out in another way, without troubling myself any further about how to make the viola shine. I conceived the idea of writing a series of scenes for the orchestra, in which the viola should find itself involved, like a person more or less in action, always preserving his own individuality. By fitting the viola into my poetical memories of my peregrinations in the Abruzzi [section of the Apennines northwest of Rome]. I wanted to make the instrument into a sort of melancholy dreamer, in the style of Byron's *Childe Harold*. Hence the title of the symphony, *Harold in Italy*. As in the *Symphonie fantastique*, one principal theme (the first melody of the viola) is reproduced throughout the work, but with this difference, that the theme of the *Symphonie fantastique*—the *idée fixe*—intrudes itself obstinately, like a passionate, episodic idea, into scenes wholly foreign to it, disrupting them, whilst Har-

old's strain is added to the other orchestral strains, with which it contrasts, both in movement and character, without hindering their development.

As Berlioz implies, there is very little connection between his symphony and Byron's poem, except, perhaps, a general romantic melancholy, a characteristic rhetorical vividness.

I. *Adagio—Allegro. Harold in the Mountains: Scenes of Sadness, of Happiness, and of Joy.* The melancholy opening section anticipates the principal melody, which is to represent Harold himself. It is presented first in a minor key by the woodwinds. Then the solo viola sings Harold's broadly flowing melody:

Immediately the viola repeats the melody, "as softly as possible." The delicate accompaniment is given chiefly to the harp. The lively main section of the movement includes a symphonic development of fragments of the *idée fixe.*

II. *Allegretto. March of the Pilgrims Singing Their Evening Prayer.* A hymn-like melody is chanted by the strings, softly at first, then growing louder, as if the pilgrims were approaching, then dying away again. Harold's melody, the *idée fixe* appears in almost its original form as well as in transformation.

III. *Allegro assai—Allegretto. Serenade of an Abruzzi Mountaineer to His Mistress.* After a fast introduction, the serenade melody, related to the *idée fixe* is introduced by a solo English horn:

IV. *Allegro frenetico. Brigands' Orgy; Memories of Past Scenes.* In between the episodes of a wild and brilliant tarantella-like dance, the orchestra recalls episodes from the first three movements of the Symphony.

This colorful score uses a relatively modest orchestra of piccolo, 2 flutes, 2 oboes, English horn, 2 clarinets, 4 bassoons, 4 horns, 2 cornets, 2 trumpets, 3 trombones, ophicleide or tuba, triangle, kettledrums, cymbals, harp, the viola solo part originally conceived for Paganini, and a substantial string section: Berlioz specifies "at least 15 first violins, 15 second violins, 10 violas, 12 cellos, and 9 double basses."

OVERTURE TO BEATRICE AND BENEDICT

Berlioz's love of Shakespeare was more than a love; it was a passion, it was worship, a transfiguration. The Shakespeare performances he saw in Paris as a young man of twenty-four, the *Hamlet* and *Romeo and Juliet*, changed his entire life. Not only did he fall in love with and eventually marry the Ophelia and Juliet of those performances, Henrietta Smithson, but his whole vision of what music and all the arts could aspire to was transfigured by the passion and poetry of Shakespeare.

Berlioz appears to have conceived the idea of making an opera of Shakespeare's comedy, *Much Ado About Nothing,* during a trip to Italy in 1831. Within two years, he had sketched the musical situations suggested to him by Shakespeare's masterpiece.

Twenty-seven years later, when he finally turned in earnest to the completion of the *Béatrice et Bénédict,* as he called it, his sketches served him well. His inspiration took wing. "I can scarcely keep up with the music of my little opera," he wrote, "so rapidly do the pieces come to me. Each wants precedence and sometimes I begin a fresh one before the previous one is finished." Berlioz used the form of *opéra-comique,* with *spoken* dialogue connecting the musical numbers. "The thing is a caprice written with the point of a needle, and it requires an extremely delicate performance," Berlioz wrote during his rehearsals for the premiere, which took place on August 9, 1862 at Baden-Baden. As his title suggests, Berlioz's adaptation of the Shakespeare comedy concentrated on his two title characters, their comic conflicts, and their final reconciliation and love.

The Overture shares the qualities of the opera. It is lively, capricious, of needlepoint brilliance. Its bubbling chief theme comes from the accompaniment of a lighthearted love duet in the last act: "Love is a torch" *("L'amour est un flambeau"):*

The lyric contrast is taken from Béatrice's aria, "I recall the day" *("Il m'en souvient le jour").* The contrast of these two themes and their imaginative transformations are the heart of the Overture.

The Overture to *Béatrice et Bénédict* is scored for piccolo, flute, 2 oboes, 2 clarinets, 4 horns, 2 bassoons, 2 trumpets, cornet, 3 trombones, kettledrums, and the customary strings.

OVERTURE TO BENVENUTO CELLINI

No wonder Berlioz felt drawn to Benvenuto Cellini! He read the extravagant *Memoirs* of the Florentine sculptor, goldsmith, musician, military hero, murderer and spinner of incredible yarns—and the centuries that separated the two men were as nothing. Berlioz had found a dramatic figure with whom he could identify himself, with whom he could commiserate and exult: a man who had lived as an artist-hero, a "genius" (to use the Romantic term of Berlioz's day), a superhuman human being who, Prometheus-like, conferred the fiery gift of his art on a dazzled and only partly comprehending mankind —in short, a kindred spirit.

In Cellini, Berlioz found his own feverish intensity of feeling, his own hyper-excitable imagination. See, for example, the passage in Cellini's *Memoirs* where he describes in all seriousness how he and a Sicilian priest-turned-necromancer met by night in the Roman Colosseum, where they conjured up several legions of devils. Although Cellini's courage on this terrifying occasion seems to have been exemplary, he admits that when the ordeal was over, he went home and *dreamt* of devils for the rest of the night. A skillful flutist and a musician of the Papal Court in Rome, Cellini must have seemed to Berlioz the perfect hero for a Romantic opera.

For his libretto Berlioz appealed to the pioneer poet and dramatist Alfred de Vigny. But Vigny was too busy with his own work to contribute anything more than criticism and occasional retouching to an unfortunate libretto perpetrated by two respected mediocrities of the Académie Française.

The premiere at the Opéra on September 10, 1838, was hissed, as Berlioz stoically reports, "with admirable energy and unanimity." But the Overture proved a tremendous success and was greeted with what Berlioz himself called "exaggerated applause." Its electric effect has hardly diminished with the years. It does not so much begin as it explodes, with a syncopated principal theme suggesting the fiery temperament of Cellini:

This impetuous opening is interrupted by a hushed slow section presenting the first of several melodies taken from the opera. The first, plucked out by the low strings, as if it were a mere accompaniment figure, is taken from the solemn melody with which the Cardinal first offers and finally grants Cellini absolution from his sins in return for Cellini's casting of his famous statue of Perseus. The Cardinal's melody is joined by a harlequin's arietta sung in the Roman Carnival scene of Act II. Almost halfway through, the woodwinds introduce a love theme,

which is adapted and varied from the duet of Cellini and his beloved Teresa, whom he finally wins as his wife, and for whom he stabs his rival, Pompeo. For a climax and conclusion the melody of the Cardinal's absolution is brought back with the brilliance of pealing trumpets, supported by full brass and surrounded by swirling arabesques of the strings.

Berlioz's orchestra calls for 2 flutes (1 alternating with piccolo), 2 oboes, 2 clarinets, 4 bassoons, 4 horns, 4 trumpets, 2 cornets, 3 trombones, ophicleide (usually replaced by tuba in modern performances), kettledrums, bass drum, cymbals, triangle, and the traditional strings.

OVERTURE, THE CORSAIR, OPUS 21

How Berlioz loved a contrast! "I followed the 'Corsair' [Byron's *Corsair,* that is] in his desperate adventures; I adored that inexorable yet tender nature—pitiless, yet generous—a strange combination, apparently contradictory feelings: love of woman, and hatred of his kind." And where was Berlioz reading the desperate tale? In St. Peter's Cathedral in Rome. "During the fierce summer heat I used to spend whole days there, comfortably established in a confessional, with Byron as my companion. I sat enjoying the coolness and stillness, unbroken by any sound save the splashing of the fountains in the square outside, . . . and there, at my leisure, I sat drinking in that burning poetry."

It would be tempting to think that "that burning poetry" was the entire inspiration for Berlioz's *Corsair* Overture. But the story, as befits Berlioz's ramified life and mind, is more complex. The prime source of the Overture seems to have been a firsthand experience. On his way to Rome in February, 1831, Berlioz had a dangerously stormy voyage from Marseille to Livorno. During a gale which nearly wrecked their small vessel, he made the acquaintance of a Venetian corsair. Later, while the ship lay becalmed, an old sea dog recalled his command of Lord Byron's corvette during the poet's adventures in the Adriatic and the Greek archipelago.

Having escaped death at sea, Berlioz almost found it at his own hand. It was mid-April in Florence when Berlioz learned that his fiancée, Camille Moke, had broken faith and married Ignatz Pleyel. Berlioz immediately planned murder and suicide, plans which evaporated after an undignified dousing in the Mediterranean from which he was "yanked out like a fish." He spent three weeks convalescing in the neighborhood of Nice. Later he recalled these days of spring sunshine as "the twenty happiest days of my existence." These days included the composition of, or at least the full sketch for, an overture which eventually was to be known as *Le Corsaire.*

The first title of the Overture was "The Tower of Nice," after the picturesque ruin on which Berlioz had gazed and in which he occasionally sat while composing the Overture. The premiere of the Overture in Paris on January 19, 1845, under Berlioz's direction was enough to convince him that his score needed revision. He set it aside until a visit to London in 1851–52, when he did revise it and changed the title to "Le Corsaire rouge." Alas for the theory that the Overture sprang wholly from Berlioz's passionate reading of Byron: *Le Corsaire rouge* turns out to have been the *Red Rover* of James Fenimore Cooper, another of Berlioz's passionately admired authors. Cooper died in 1851 just as Berlioz was revising his Overture. In Cooper's tale of the *Red Rover,* a prominent landmark is a tower or mill on a rocky coast, which Berlioz may well have associated with his tower at Nice.

As Jacques Barzun points out, in his colorful and informative *Berlioz and the Romantic Century,* many ingredients must have gone into the ultimate Overture: the stormy voyage to Livorno; perhaps a touch of the Venetian adventurer, corsair-type, whom Berlioz met on that trip; some of the spirit of Byron's "Corsair"; perhaps a touch too of the redoubtable *Red Rover,* unless of course the reference to Cooper's novel was merely a sentimental gesture of commemoration. In any case, Berlioz obviously was afraid listeners would think he had intended the title too literally, and therefore struck out the word "red."

After the sharp crack of the two opening chords, fiery flourishes of the strings alternate with agitated wind chords. A momentary soft *adagio* recalls the contrasts Berlioz so relished in Byron's tale, and then the orchestra is off again in the same fiery tempo for an extended symphonic movement. The lyric second theme, a gracefully curving phrase, is presented and developed by the violins before it is woven into the more complex orchestral fabric. It would be futile and probably would violate Berlioz's own intentions if one were to search this exhilarating score for any kind of specific tone painting. The spirit of storm and adventure and Berlioz's romantic fantasy are not to be pinned down.

In its final version, the work is scored for 2 flutes, 2 oboes, 2 clarinets, 2 bassoons, 4 horns, 2 trumpets, 2 cornets, 2 trombones, tuba, timpani, and "at least" 15 first violins, 15 second violins, 10 violas, 10 cellos, and 9 double basses.

OVERTURE TO KING LEAR, OPUS 4

Berlioz shouted aloud when he made the acquaintance of Shakespeare's *King Lear* in April 1831. He rolled on the grass of the laurel grove on the banks of the Arno where he was reading. He felt as if he were going to burst with emotion as he savored the storms of Lear's rage, his grief, and perhaps most of all, the old king's madness. Madness was a favorite topic of the Romantic imagination from Goya to Géricault, from Bellini to Donizetti and Verdi, whose great unfulfilled dream was to write an operatic Lear. The examples could be multiplied.

Yet the otherwise perceptive Donald Francis Tovey assures us in three pages of brilliant paradoxing, that Berlioz's *King Lear* Overture is not about Lear at all. "No," says Tovey, "let us frankly call this overture the Tragedy of the Speaking Basses, of the Plea of the Oboe, and of the Fury of the Orchestra . . ."

One can only plead that Berlioz *thought* he was writing about Lear. Can it be only a coincidence that Berlioz completed his Overture some four weeks after he read *King Lear* for the first time? The actual composing followed upon a wild sentimental crisis culminating in Berlioz's attempt at suicide by drowning. Then suddenly the skies cleared, Berlioz was cured of his rage and frustration, his rashness was forgiven, and for a moment all was well. He found himself on the Riviera.

By May 6, 1831, Berlioz wrote to a group of his friends: "I have almost finished the Overture to *King Lear;* I have only the instrumentation to do." And by the "tenth or eleventh of May," he reported: "My repertory is enlarged by a new overture. I completed yesterday an Overture to Shakespeare's *King Lear.*"

The date of the premiere is uncertain. We know that there was a performance of the Overture at a Paris Conservatoire concert organized by Berlioz who, however, did not yet fully trust himself as conductor. The concert, on April 9, 1834, was led therefore by Narcisse Girard. It has been claimed that an earlier performance was given in Paris on December 9, 1832, on a program with Berlioz's *Fantastic Symphony* and *Lélio,* but this performance of the Overture seems hard to authenticate.

Evidently the music was close to Berlioz's heart. Thirty years later during a tour of Germany, where he was now an established popular composer, Berlioz was invited to conduct this Overture—for the first time in ten or twelve years, according to his *Memoirs.* The orchestra must have been superb. Berlioz appeared for rehearsal. "On the conductor's desk," he tells us in his *Memoirs,* "was the score of *King Lear.* I lift my arm, I commence; all start together with *verve* and precision; the wildest rhythmical eccentricities in the *Allegro* are attacked without the slightest hesitation." As he conducted, he was amazed by his own inspiration. "Why, it is overwhelming," he said to himself. "Did I really write that?" He wrote friends at home that he found himself "unable to hold back a tear . . . I was thinking that perhaps Father Shakespeare would not curse me for having made his old British King and his sweet Cordelia speak in such strains."

Lear himself is probably represented by the commanding figure for the low strings in octaves which stands at the opening of the slow introduction:

Cordelia is commonly thought to be alluded to by a plaintive oboe solo marked *dolce assai* in a barely audible *ppp*.

A few pages later, this Cordelia melody is given out in the warm harmonies of four French horns and soft trombones. It is a temptation to read dramatic meaning into the sudden interruption of this melody by barking brass and the Lear theme, backed now by furious thunder of the kettledrums.

The main section of the Overture, *Allegro disperato ed agitato assai,* is a traditional sonata-allegro movement. Its violent principal theme (recalling the opening Lear motive) is accompanied by a sweetly lyric phrase for first violins *espressivo.* The central development of these themes, suggesting Lear's wild storm scenes on the heath, brings, as might be expected, ever more violent outbursts culminating in a raging reprise of the principal theme. This recapitulation, in reality an expansion and intensification of the exposition, is enriched by a return of the figure of Lear from the introduction, now in the majesty of the full orchestra. The music grows wilder as it approaches its climax and end.

The Overture to *King Lear* is scored for 2 flutes, 2 oboes, 2 clarinets, 2 bassoons, 4 horns, 2 trumpets, 3 trombones, ophicleide (nowadays normally replaced by tuba), kettledrums, "at least" 30 violins, 10 violas, 12 cellos, and 9 stringed basses.

OVERTURE, THE ROMAN CARNIVAL, OPUS 9

Berlioz's Overture, "The Roman Carnival," was composed as an afterthought to serve as an introduction to the second act of his opera, *Benvenuto Cellini.* It was completed in Paris in 1843 and was performed for the first time under the direction of the composer at a concert in the Salle Herz, Paris, on February 3, 1844.

The Overture is based on a reminiscence of *Benvenuto Cellini's* first act aria *"O Teresa, vous que j'aime"* ("O Teresa, whom I adore") and an anticipation of the lively *saltarello* which is danced on the Piazza Colonna in Rome during the second act. This is the *saltarello* which caused Berlioz and the dancers such agonies during the rehearsals of the opera in September 1838. François Antoine Habeneck, the conductor, was hostile to Berlioz, in part, perhaps, because Berlioz could not restrain his indignation at Habeneck's sluggishness. Whether Habeneck's understandable irritation at Berlioz influenced his conducting, we may never know, but the opera was a resounding fiasco. Only the Overture, as Berlioz assures us: "received exaggerated applause, but the rest was hissed with admirable energy and unanimity."

Years later, when Berlioz wrote his memoirs, he still boiled. Habeneck, he declared:

> . . . never could catch the lively turn of the saltarello danced and sung on the Piazza Colonna in the middle of the second act. The dancers, not being able to adapt themselves to his dragging time, complained to me, and I kept on repeating, "Faster, faster! Put more life into it!" Habeneck struck the desk in irritation, and broke one violin bow after another. Having witnessed four or five of such outbursts, I ended at last by saying, with a coolness that exasperated him:
>
> "Good heavens! if you were to break fifty bows, that would not prevent your time from being too slow by half. It is a *saltarello* that you are conducting!"
>
> At that Habeneck stopped, and, turning to the orchestra, said:
>
> "Since I am not fortunate enough to please M. Berlioz, we will leave off for today. You can go."
>
> And there the rehearsal ended.
>
> Some years afterwards, when I had written the *Carnival Romain* overture, in which the theme of the allegro is this same *saltarello,* Habeneck happened to be in the green-room of the Hertz concert-hall the evening that this overture was to be played for the first time. He had heard that we had rehearsed it in the morning without the wind instruments, part of the band having been called off for the National Guard. "Good!" said he to himself. "There will certainly be a catastrophe at his concert this evening. I must be there." On my arrival, indeed, I was surrounded in the orchestra by all the wind players, who were in terror at the idea of having to play an overture of which they did not know a note.
>
> "Don't be afraid," I said. "The parts are correct; you all know your jobs; watch my baton as often as you can, count your bars correctly, and it will be all right."
>
> Not a single mistake occurred. I launched the allegro in the whirlwind time of the Trasteverine dancers. The public cried "Bis!" We played the overture over again; it was even better done the second time. And as I passed back through the green-room, where Habeneck stood looking a little disappointed, I just flung these few words at him: "That is how it *ought* to go!" to which he took care to make no reply.
>
> Never did I feel more keenly the delight of being able to direct the performance of my music myself; and the thought of what Habeneck had made me endure only enhanced my pleasure. Unhappy composers! learn how to conduct, and how to conduct yourselves well (with or without a pun), for do not forget that the most dangerous of your interpreters is the conductor himself.

The Overture to the second act, which Berlioz describes with the title "Roman Carnival," opens with a wild flourish from the *Tarantella.* Benvenuto's aria is chanted by a mournful English horn. The tempo of the *saltarello* returns, first in a light, scherzo-like passage, but soon bursting out *fortissimo* with the main *saltarello* theme:

This dominates the rest of the Overture. Toward the end, the *saltarello* seems to fade away in the distance, only its rhythm remains faintly throbbing in the second violins. But this is a mere feint: what Berlioz's countrymen call *"reculer pour mieux sauter."* The dance returns, wilder than ever in a glorious melee of canonic entrances, shifting meters, and dazzling orchestral color.

The Overture is scored for 2 flutes, 2 oboes, English horn, 2 clarinets, 4 bassoons, 4 horns, 2 trumpets, 2 cornets, 3 trombones, cymbals, 2 side drums, triangle, kettledrums, "at least" 15 first violins, "at least" 15 second violins, "at least" 10 violas, "at least" 12 cellos, and "at least" 9 double basses.

ROMEO AND JULIET, EXCERPTS FROM THE DRAMATIC SYMPHONY, OPUS 17

The discovery of Shakespeare, of *Romeo and Juliet,* and of the actress Harriet Smithson, whom he loved so desperately and who later became his wife, all happened to the twenty-three-year-old Berlioz on two fateful evenings of September 11 and 15, 1827. "The most important drama of my life," Berlioz called these events, when he came to describe them in his *Memoirs.*

> The impact of her prodigious talent, or rather her dramatic genius, on my imagination and on my heart can be compared only to the overwhelming impact of the poet whom she was worthy to interpret. I can say no more.
>
> Shakespeare, bursting upon me so unexpectedly, was like a thunderbolt. His lightning flash, opened the entire heavens of art for me with a sublime tumult, illuminating its most distant depths. I recognized, I grasped true grandeur, true beauty, true dramatic truth.

Romeo and Juliet was almost more than his volcanic temperament could take, with its "love swift as thought, burning as lava, imperious, irresistible, immense, pure and beautiful as the smile of an angel; the furious scenes of vengeance, the delirious embraces, the desperate struggles between love and death were too much for me. And so, from the Third Act on, barely breathing, suffering as if an iron fist had seized my heart, I said to myself with complete conviction: 'Ah! I am lost!' "

Six years later, in 1838, Berlioz married his Juliet, who turned into a jealous, untamable shrew, and eventually took to the bottle. Yet after five years of married life when Berlioz embarked on his masterpiece *Roméo et Juliette,* his early Romantic frenzies fired him again.

For the existence of this score the world owes a debt of thanks to another great Romantic musician, the fantastic violin virtuoso Paganini. In December 1838, at the conclusion of a concert of Berlioz's works conducted by Berlioz himself, Paganini dragged the composer out onto the stage, knelt before him and kissed his hand in homage. Two days later he sent Berlioz the following letter:

> My dear friend,
>
> Since the death of Beethoven, none but Berlioz has been able to make him live again; and I, who have savored your divine compositions, worthy of the genius that you are, feel it my duty to beg you to accept, as a token of my homage, twenty thousand francs, which will be remitted to you by the Baron Rothschild on presentation of the enclosed. Believe me your most affectionate friend.
>
> Paris, 18 December, 1838. NICCOLO PAGANINI

Paris was incredulous and Berlioz was overwhelmed. For once he could find no adequate words for his feelings. He visited Paganini. Speechless with emotion, they embraced. Then Berlioz stammered some words of thanks. But Paganini cut him off: "Don't speak of that. No, not another word. It is the greatest satisfaction I have ever felt in my life. You will never know how your music affected me; it is many years since I had felt anything like it. . . . "

With Paganini's gift, Berlioz paid off his debts and still had left what he describes as "a very handsome sum." He decided that he should "leave off all other work, and write a masterpiece, on a vast new plan, a grandiose, passionate work, full of imagination, and worthy to be dedicated to the illustrious artist to whom I owe so much."

He wrote Paganini about subjects for the work. But Paganini replied: "I can give you no advice. You know what will suit you better than anyone else." When at last Berlioz hit on the subject of *Romeo and Juliet,* it must have seemed to him predestined.

"Paganini had given me money that I might write music [says Berlioz in his *Memoirs*], and write it I did. I worked for seven months at my symphony, without interrupting myself more than three or four days out of every thirty for anything whatsoever.

"And during all that time how ardently did I live! How vigorously I struck out in that grand sea of poetry, caressed by the playful breeze of fancy, beneath the hot rays of that sun of love which Shakespeare kindled, always confident of my power to reach the marvelous island where stands the temple of true art. Whether I succeeded or not it is not for me to decide."

But when, after three highly successful performances under Berlioz's own baton (November 24 and December 1 and 15, 1839), one critic wrote that

Berlioz had not understood Shakespeare, it was more than he could stand. "Toad, swollen with imbecility!" he roared in his *Memoirs.* "If you could prove that to me!" Berlioz's music was no more temperate than his words.

Although *Roméo et Juliette* uses chorus and vocal solos as well as a symphony orchestra, it is neither an opera in concert form, an opera-oratorio, nor a symphonic summary of Shakespeare's tragedy. It is a series of discontinuous episodes from the drama, high points, which seized Berlioz's imagination. Some of these moments, like Romeo's sadness [at the beginning of the third movement] are not in Shakespeare at all, but were created by David Garrick, whose Shakespeare adaptation was the basis of the production offered by the English players Berlioz saw. The most passionate moments of all: the scenes between Romeo and Juliet, are entrusted to the orchestra alone. Berlioz explains in the Preface to his score that there are several easily understandable reasons for this: "First of all (and this reason alone would justify the composer) this is a symphony and not an opera. In addition, since duets of this kind have been treated vocally a thousand times and by the greatest masters, it was both prudent and interesting to try another means of expression. It is also because the very sublimity of this love made it so dangerous for the musician to depict, that he needed more latitude for his imagination than the definite meanings of a text would have allowed, and therefore he had recourse to the language of instruments which, in this case, is richer, more varied, less precise and, in its very vagueness, incomparably more powerful."

The three most popular excerpts from *Romeo and Juliet* for concert performance are:

I. *Love Scene.* This movement, which at one time was Berlioz's favorite among all his works, is of course, the very passage where, as he tells us, he would have felt hampered by words, even Shakespeare's words, and preferred the freedom of instrumental music.

Since it was freedom that Berlioz sought, it would be folly to try as some have tried, to pin down this phrase or that to the lark or nightingale, much less the nurse's knock on the door: This entire musical scene, a tender *adagio,* swelling to a passionate song of violas and cellos in unison, reaching a climax of agitation with almost disjointed phrases, pausing suddenly for a speaking cello passage (marked *col carattere di recitativo*), subsiding once more to a tender *adagio,* finally trembling into silence—all of this is no mere description, interpretation, or even parallel to any specific Shakespeare scene. It is Berlioz's embodiment of the consuming love—possibly too, a reflection of the feelings he himself experienced when he fell in love with his first Juliet: Henrietta Smithson, who later became Madame Berlioz.

II. *Queen Mab or The Dream Sprite.* Here is a scene where Berlioz was intoxicated by words, words which he first heard, of course, in Shakespeare's English and which he loved more and more as he deepened his knowledge of the original language. And yet, for the supreme embodiment of this very speech, he had once more to free himself of words. Here is the speech which sparked his imagination. The music needs no other explanation.

O, then, I see Queen Mab hath been with you.
She is the fairies' midwife, and she comes
In shape no bigger than an agate-stone
On the forefinger of an alderman,
Drawn with a team of little atomies
Over men's noses as they lie asleep.
Her waggon-spokes made of long spinners' legs;
The cover, of the wings of grasshoppers;
Her traces, of the smallest spider web;
Her collars, of the moonshine's wat'ry beams;
Her whip, of cricket's bone; the lash, of film;
Her waggoner, a small grey-coated gnat,
Not half so big as a round little worm
Pricked from the lazy finger of a maid.
Her chariot is an empty hazel-nut,
Made by the joiner squirrel or old grub,
Time out o' mind the fairies' coachmakers.
And in this state, she gallops night by night
Through lovers' brains, and then they dream of love;
O'er courtiers' knees, that dream on curtsies straight;
O'er lawyers' fingers, who straight dream on fees;
O'er ladies' lips, who straight on kisses dream
Which oft the angry Mab with blisters plagues,
Because their breaths with sweetmeats tainted are.
Sometime she gallops o'er a courtier's nose,
And then dreams he of smelling out a suit;
And sometimes comes she with a tithe-pig's tail
Tickling a parson's nose as 'a lies asleep,
Then dreams he of another benefice.
Sometimes she driveth o'er a soldier's neck,
And then dreams he of cutting foreign throats,
Of breaches, ambuscadoes, Spanish blades,
Of healths five fathom deep; and then anon
Drums in his ear, at which he starts and wakes,
And being thus frighted swears a prayer or two,
And sleeps again. This is that very Mab
That plaits the manes of horses in the night,
And bakes the elf-locks in foul sluttish hairs,
Which once untangled much misfortune bodes.
This the hag, when maids lie on their backs,
That presses them and learns them first to bear,
Making them women of good carriage.

III. *Romeo Alone—His Sadness—Concert and Ball—Festivities in the Capulet's Palace.* The solitary lover is introduced in a sighing *pianissimo* by the first violins—*andante malinconico e sostenuto.* Even when they are joined by other instruments, it is the violins whose yearning, soaring line seems to impersonate Romeo. His melancholy is interrupted by sounds as of distant festivities, dance rhythms faintly heard, and a lively melody associated with the giddy whirl of guests. A hush passes through the orchestra as Juliet appears at the ball. Like the Beloved in Berlioz's *Symphonie fantastique,* Juliet is a melody, a graceful, almost reticent phrase for oboe alone:

She appears, or rather, her melody appears against a magical background of soft cello arpeggios, *pizziccato,* the merest whisper of trembling muted violins and an almost inaudible touch of the tambourine. This is Romeo's first sight of Juliet. During this first moment the ball music scarcely exists, for everything pales beside her beauty that teaches "the torches to burn bright!"

Did my heart love till now? Forswear it, sight!
For I ne'er saw true beauty till this night.

Romeo's ecstasy is interrupted by a sudden burst of brilliant dance music, measures of incomparable verve and brilliance. At the climax, Juliet appears again. Her melody, now in long gleaming notes of the brass, combines with the giddy theme of the festivities:

"Which of the two powers, Love or Music, can elevate man to the sublimest heights? . . . It is a great problem, and yet it seems to me that this is the answer: 'Love can give no idea of music; music can give an idea of love.' . . . Why separate them? They are the two wings of the soul." So wrote Berlioz on the last page of his *Memoirs,* a quarter of a century after the premiere of his *Roméo et Juliette, Symphonie Dramatique.* As he concluded this story of his life, Berlioz characteristically recalled not only his first love, Estelle, but also the artists he had loved: Virgil, Gluck, Beethoven, and "Shakespeare, who might have loved me."

The "Romeo and Juliet" Symphony enlists a large orchestra of 2 flutes, 2 oboes, 2 clarinets, 4 bassoons, 4 horns, 2 trumpets, 2 cornets, 3 trombones, ophicleide (usually replaced in modern orchestras by a tuba), kettledrums, "at least 15 first violins, at least 15 second violins, at least 10 violas, at least 11 cellos, and at least 7 double basses."

ROYAL HUNT AND STORM, DESCRIPTIVE SYMPHONY FROM THE TROJANS

Passion was Berlioz's specialty. In its multiple meanings of consuming emotion, of rage, suffering, and love, it was his life-style and the recurring *Leitmotif* of his art. Nowhere is his Romantic preoccupation with passion more obvious than in the allegedly Classical masterpiece of his maturity, *The Trojans.*

The myth of Berlioz's late conversion to a sober Classicism is founded in part on the subject matter of *The Trojans* which was Virgil's *Aeneid.* From his twelfth year on, Berlioz had been devoted heart and soul to the *Aeneid.* In his middle fifties (while composing *The Trojans*) Berlioz wrote to a friend that the musical expression of the feeling in the *Aeneid* was from the outset, "the easiest part of my task. I have spent my whole life with that tribe of demigods," he added, "and I have known them so long that I have come to feel they know me." But like any great artist, Berlioz transformed his subject matter to reflect his own feelings, which in this opera were as explosively, as passionately romantic as they had been in his early *Symphonie fantastique.*

For years he hesitated on the brink of composing "a vast opera" on the *Aeneid.* For years he resisted the temptation. "My blood boils," he wrote in his autobiography, "at the bare notion of encountering again those senseless obstacles to the mounting of such a work, which I myself have endured, and daily see endured by other composers writing for our grand Opéra." It seems to have been Liszt's love, the Princess Sayn-Wittgenstein, who gave Berlioz the final push to the undertaking he dreaded and desired. In 1856, having learned of his dream and his misgivings during Berlioz's visit to Weimar, the Princess cunningly spurred his competitive sense by praising Wagner's courage in embarking on *his* quixotic design for a four-evening work on the Nibelungen myth. (Wagner had begun the music of his *Rheingold* less than three years earlier.) Berlioz, she declared, would be untrue to himself if he did not undertake his own grand project, at whatever cost in suffering and strain. She ended by declaring that if he refused his own manifest destiny she never wanted to see him again.

The following May (1856) Berlioz began his own libretto. By the end of July he was able to send the Princess the completed libretto. The musical score was completed on April 7, 1858.

As Berlioz had foreseen, he was unable to obtain a performance of his masterpiece at the Paris Opéra. Finally, in 1863 the Parisian Théâtre Lyrique undertook to present the second half only under the title *The Trojans at Carthage.* Even this second half was too long for the taste of the director Carvalho, who insisted on cut after cut, driving Berlioz almost to despair. What was almost worse was Carvalho's request that his depredations be carried over into the printed vocal score. "To see a work of such a kind laid out for sale," lamented Berlioz, "with the cuts and trimmings of the publisher! Is there any such torture as that? A score lying dismembered in the musicsellers' windows, like a carcass of veal on a butcher's stall, with small cuts offered for sale like tidbits for the concierge's cat!"

Among the most striking scenes of *The Trojans at Carthage* is the almost entirely orchestral *Royal Hunt and Storm.* This was published as Act III of the truncated opera. In the preceding action the audience has seen Queen Dido's growing interest in Aeneas who, with his remaining troops and navy, has found refuge at Carthage after the fall of his native Troy. During a royal hunt near Carthage, Dido and Aeneas are overtaken by a storm and separated from their retinue. They take refuge in a grotto where, during the height of the storm, their love is consummated. Here Berlioz's cue for passion was a fragment of three lines from the *Aeneid,* Book IV:

Speluncam Dido dux et Trojanus eamdem	(To that very cave came Dido and the Trojan chief . . .
Devenient . . .	This was their nuptial hour.)
Hic Hymenaeus erit.	

A "virgin African forest in the morning," is Berlioz's description of the opening scene. Even before the curtain rises, the sylvan cool is suggested by the cool colors of flute, oboe, clarinet, and high violins. At the beginning naiads are glimpsed through distant reeds as they bathe in a pool. Distant thunder is suggested by a trio of kettledrums (two of them to be played offstage.) The sport of the naiads is disturbed by faraway hunting calls (played offstage by lightweight saxhorns, though Berlioz allows for possible performance by standard orchestral French horns):

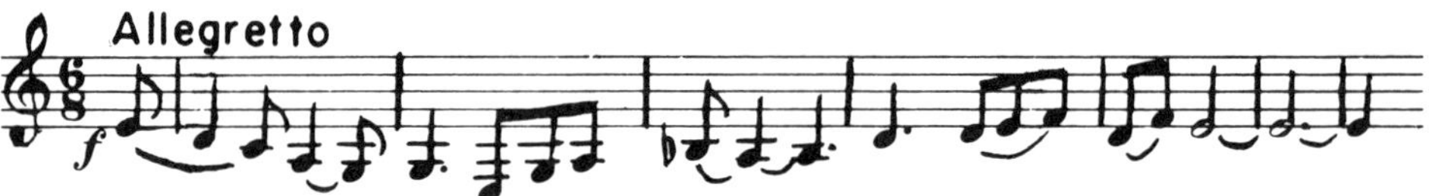

This is a figure which Berlioz varies ingeniously in later pages to bind the scene together. It consists largely of pantomime, ballet, and spectacle, with only a few choral cries (of nymphs and satyrs) at the height of the storm.

As the horn-calls swell the naiads take flight and disappear among the reeds. Several hunters cross the stage. The thunder draws nearer, the orchestra takes up a vigorous stylization of the hunting-call, the sun darkens, rain begins to fall, other hunters appear and then disperse. Dido and Aeneas appear, braving the storm. They take shelter in a grotto, just as the full fury of the storm bursts in the orchestra. Berlioz's stage directions continue: "Wood-nymphs with disheveled hair appear on the rocks above. They run about, crying and gesturing. Enter dancing fauns. The brook that trickles among the rocks swells to a noisy cascade. Several other waterfalls form about the rock and mingle their noise with the tumult of the tempest. . . . Satyrs and sylphs do a grotesque dance with the fauns in the darkness. Lightning strikes a tree, which bursts into flame. Burning fragments of the tree fall to the ground. . . .

The fauns and sylphs gather the flaming branches and dance, holding them in their hands. . . . The nymphs, fauns, sylphs and satyrs disperse, running. . . ."

The climax of the storm subsides quickly. Calm is restored and with it the caroling woodwinds. The naiads returning to their pool seem reassured as the scene lightens and the hunting-calls fade into the distance.

The "Royal Hunt and Storm" is scored for piccolo, 2 flutes, 2 oboes, 2 clarinets in E flat, 4 bassoons, 4 horns, 2 cornets, 2 trumpets, 3 trombones, ophicleide (now obsolete, usually replaced by a tuba), kettledrums, bass drum, and the standard string choir plus an offstage group of 4 tenor saxhorns (may be replaced by French horns), 3 trombones, and 2 kettledrums.

FANTASTIC SYMPHONY: EPISODE IN THE LIFE OF AN ARTIST

The battles over Berlioz's *Fantastic Symphony* began even before a note of it had been heard. And they have continued with unabated vigor (and an occasional flash of wit) through a century and a half. "Boiling oil," wrote Donald Tovey in 1939, "awaits me for my irreverent treatment of Berlioz." And as late as 1950 a wise and equally witty crusader for Berlioz, Jacques Barzun, could make the astounding suggestion (in his two-volume *Berlioz and the Romantic Century*) that we dismiss Berlioz's entire program for the *Fantastic Symphony* as a sort of "promotional aid" designed to snare the interest of less thoughtful concertgoers.

When it was new, Berlioz's program, which was an autobiographical masterpiece of exhibitionism and self-pity, drew passionate denunciations. In fact, the virulence of the attacks, counterattacks, and counter-counterattacks, which followed, suggest that the real issue lay far deeper than the ancient question of the descriptive powers of music. Far more volcanic was the revolutionary temper of the age.

In 1830, the year when Berlioz's *Fantastic Symphony* burst on an astonished Parisian audience, there were three related revolutions. It was the year of the political revolution that swept Louis-Philippe, the bourgeois "Citizen King," onto the throne of France. It was the year of the literary and theatrical revolution which swept Victor Hugo onto the spiritual throne of France with the triumphant performance of his Romantic drama *Hernani.* And finally it was the year of the musical revolution which established Berlioz as the father of a great line of radical Romantic orchestral composers that was to continue not only through Liszt, Wagner, Mahler, and Strauss, but the Russians, Tchaikovsky and Rimsky-Korsakoff, and even through French composers from Saint-Saëns to Ravel.

The "father" of these fantastic developments and of the *Fantastic Symphony* itself was a twenty-six-year-old student at the Paris Conservatory. The immediate inspiration for his Symphony was his unhappy love for the Irish actress Harriet Smithson, but the Symphony had other, deeper roots as we shall see.

Berlioz was twenty-three when he first saw Harriet (or Henriette, as she was called in France) in the roles of Ophelia and Juliet with an English company visiting Paris. The year was 1827 and the moment was ripe for the French Romantics to take Shakespeare to their hearts. The English company caused a furor. Berlioz, too, was ripe, not only for Shakespeare, but for the love at first sight, which struck him like a thunderbolt. There were moments in the theater when he felt physically choked by emotion. The first performance of *Hamlet*, which took place on September 11, was almost too strong a shock, Berlioz later recalled, "and it was long before I recovered. A feeling of intense, overpowering sadness overwhelmed me and I fell into a nervous condition, like a sickness of which only a great writer on physiology could give any adequate idea." He could not sleep; he could not work; he could not study. He wandered aimlessly about the Paris streets and through the fields outside the city.

Nevertheless when Berlioz saw the announcement of the premiere of *Romeo and Juliet,* only four days later (September 15), he rushed to the box office and bought himself a seat in the orchestra. "It was too much. By the third Act, hardly able to breathe—as though an iron hand gripped me by the heart—I knew that I was lost." It was reported that after this performance Berlioz declared, "I shall marry that woman [Henriette Smithson, the Juliet] and on that drama I will write my greatest Symphony." Berlioz later denied having made such a statement, but added: "I did both." At the time Berlioz was "too overwhelmed even to dream of such things." He even avoided any more performances by the English company. "I dreaded it as one dreads acute physical pain."

His anguish was a mighty spur to artistic activity. Contrasting Henriette's dazzling reputation with his own "miserable obscurity," he decided to make a supreme effort to bring himself to her attention. "I would dare what no composer in France had ever attempted before: I would present a concert exclusively of my own works, . . . *I would show her that I too was a dramatic artist.*" Miraculously, he managed: he did give the concert. It was poorly attended, but an artistic success and was flatteringly reviewed by the leading music critics. Alas, Henriette never heard of the concert.

Finally, early in 1829, Berlioz managed to get a letter to her. But when she left Paris later that year, they still had not met. Berlioz seems to have drawn the conclusion that she wished to test his constancy. While she was gone he heard malicious (and totally unfounded) rumors of loose sexual behavior on her part, in London and elsewhere. Again he was in despair, and again his despair was fruitful. Early in 1830 he wrote to his sister Nanci and to his bosom friend, the poet Humbert Ferrand, that he had conceived a project for a grand symphonic work that would surely draw attention to him. By February 6, 1830, he wrote that the work was "all in his head." On April 16 he announced triumphantly that he had completed the score and he proceeded to outline its contents.

Imagine, wrote Berlioz, that an artist gifted with vivid imagination first glimpses a woman who embodies the ideal he has long carried in his heart. He falls desperately in love, but by a strange quirk whenever his beloved

HARRIET SMITHSON AS OPHELIA.

Berlioz's future wife as he first saw her, September 11, 1827, on the opening night of the English players' visit to Paris. Her mad scene (*Hamlet,* Act IV, Scene 5) moved the audience to audible sobs.

appears before his mind's eye she is accompanied by a melody which seems to embody his beloved. He is pursued by this double obsession, which Berlioz called an *idée fixe.* [*Idée fixe* was not a musical term, but a medical expression, an invention of the then new psychology.]

Berlioz called his revolutionary work *Episode in the Life of an Artist (Grand Fantastic Symphony in Five Parts).* The First Part describes the restlessness, the artist's intimations of passion (*vague des passions*) before meeting his beloved, his frenzied passion after he finds her, his tenderness, jealousy, fury, fears, etc. Part Two takes place in the country where he hears two shepherds piping to their flocks; his reverie is interrupted by the beloved melody. In Part Three he goes to a ball but the *idée fixe* pursues him, making his heart pound during a brilliant waltz.

In a fit of despair the artist poisons himself with opium. But instead of killing him, the dose induces horrible nightmares. He believes that he has killed his beloved and has been condemned to death. Part Four of the Symphony is the march to the scaffold. At the very last moment the beloved melody returns but is cut off by the fatal blow. In the final movement the artist watches "a foul assembly of sorcerers and devils" gathered for the sabbath to celebrate the artist's funeral. They are joined by the beloved melody which appears in caricature as a vulgar trivial tune. For she is "now only a prostitute, fit to take part in such an orgy." Bells toll. The assembly join in a burlesque of the plainchant for the dead, the *Dies irae,* followed by a round dance which reaches its climax in combination with the *Dies irae.*

Autobiographical as it was in the emotional sense, the program of the symphony obviously included much else beside Berlioz's unhappy love for Henriette, his rage and anguish over her alleged loose behavior. As an enthusiastic admirer of Victor Hugo, Berlioz had read that poet's verses, "Sabbath Round," describing a sacrilegious round dance of witches and sorcerers with Satan to a parody of ancient church chant. Berlioz had also just read Goethe's *Faust* in the French translation, which was so vivid that it earned even Goethe's praise. The theme of opium poisoning, too, was modern: French readers had recently been presented with a translation of DeQuincy's *Confessions of an English Opium Eater.*

Berlioz hoped to produce his Symphony a bare six weeks after completing the score, with an orchestra of 220 players. He did not quite reach his aim; it was December 5 when the performance took place and the musicians numbered only 130.

Meanwhile, having a lively sense of publicity value, he had sent the program of his Symphony (in a considerably milder version) to the newspapers. It was duly printed in the *Figaro* and in the *Revue Musicale,* the latter of which was edited almost single-handedly by the authoritative critic François-Joseph Fétis. While expressing his determination not to prejudge the Symphony, Fétis observed that Berlioz was attempting the impossible by trying to describe in music both physical objects and moral quality.

This put Berlioz on the defensive even before a note of his music had been heard. At his concert two different sets of leaflets were distributed; one with the program as planned and the other with a carefully reasoned refutation of Fétis's attack. Berlioz prefaced his program with the following note: "The composer's intention has been to develop, insofar as they contain musical possibilities, various situations in the life of an artist. The outline of the instrumental drama, which lacks the help of words, needs to be explained in advance. The following program should thus be considered as the spoken text of an opera, serving to introduce the musical movements, whose character and expression it motivates."

To this introduction Berlioz added, without naming Fétis, his refutation of the critic's attack in words worth rereading since they apply not only to the *Fantastic Symphony* but to many another piece of what is loosely called "program music."

> There is absolutely no question of the program reproducing (as some people seem to have thought) what the composer is trying to communicate through the orchestra. On the contrary, it is precisely in order to fill in the gaps which the language of music necessarily leaves in the development of the dramatic thought, that the composer has had recourse to the written word to explain and justify the *Symphony*. He knows perfectly well that music cannot substitute for either words or pictures. He never made the absurd claim to express abstractions or moral qualities, but rather passions and sentiments; nor has he made the still stranger claim to depict mountains; he tried only to reproduce *the style and melodic forms* characteristic of the songs of the peoples who inhabit the mountains, or the *emotion* stirred in the soul by the sight of these impressive masses under given circumstances. If the few lines furnished in the program had been suited to recitation or singing between the movements of the *Symphony*, like the choruses of ancient [Greek] tragedy, there would presumably have been no such misunderstanding of their meaning. But instead of being listened to, they must be read. And those who make the strange accusation, against which the composer is forced to defend himself, do not stop to think that if he really had such an exaggerated, silly idea of the expressive power of his art, then the program would have seemed to him a completely useless duplication [of the music].
>
> As to the imitation of the sounds of nature, Beethoven, Gluck, Meyerbeer, Rossini, and Weber have all proved, with illustrious examples, that it has its place in the realm of music. But since the composer of this *Symphony* is convinced that the abuse of imitation is a great danger, that it should be very sparingly used, and that its most successful effects are always close to caricature, he has never considered that branch of the art as an end but as a means. And when, for example in the "Scene in the Fields" he tries to portray a distant thunder roll in the midst of peaceful surroundings, it is not at all for the puerile satisfaction of imitating this majestic sound, but on the contrary to emphasize the silence, and by this means to emphasize the impression of unquiet melancholy and of painful isolation that he wishes to induce in his audience in the concluding section of this movement.

The performance as Berlioz recalled in his *Memoirs*, "was by no means perfect—it hardly could be, with works of such difficulty and after only two rehearsals. But it was good enough to give a reasonable idea of the music. Three of the movements, the 'Waltz,' the 'March to the Scaffold,' and the 'Witches' Sabbath,' created a sensation; the 'March' especially took the audience by storm." The "Scene in the Country," on the other hand, made no impression at all. For this reason Berlioz revised it almost at once. Later he returned to other movements, retouching and extending the close of the opening movement, enriching the "Waltz" movement, reversing the order of the second and third movements, and revising the program itself, still further toning down the uncomplimentary references to the beloved and making the *entire* story an opium dream instead of only the final two movements.

The *Symphony* was first published in a piano version by Franz Liszt who was an enthusiastic member of that first-night audience. On the basis of Liszt's score, Fétis returned to the attack, formulating what has remained until today the traditional conservative view of Berlioz as a wild genius incompetently trained, lacking melodic invention and harmonic skill, but having an inventive mastery of orchestral effects, ingenious devices which better composers could put to better use. What a dramatic contrast to the thoughtful review of Robert Schumann. Schumann printed Fétis's review complete in German translation as a preface to his own, which was a model of imaginative insight combined with analytical acumen.

In our own time Berlioz's program has been widely attacked on the grounds that it is inaccurate as autobiography. It has been solemnly pointed out that Berlioz never took Henriette to a ball, that he did not poison himself with opium, and that by the time the *Symphony* reached performance he was wooing another woman. Musicologists found no difficulty in unearthing the fact that parts of the *Fantastic Symphony* were lifted or adapted from earlier works. The "March to the Scaffold," for example, was taken almost entire from Berlioz's unperformed opera *Les Francs-juges,* and therefore could not possibly embody a nightmare related to Henriette. The *idée fixe* had already been used in Berlioz's cantata *Herminie* of 1828, etc., etc.

The truth is, as Berlioz himself pointed out, that the germ of his *idée fixe* was much older yet. It dated back to his twelfth year and to his first love which, like his passion for Henriette, had struck him like a thunderbolt. Indeed, the *idée fixe* was in fact the obsession of Berlioz's entire life. Tragic, hopeless love was a theme that he shared with his contemporaries and which we meet from Walter Scott's Mad Lucy o'Lammermoor to Wagner's *Tristan and Isolde.*

Berlioz was only twelve when he met his fate. Estelle Duboeuf, at eighteen, was a beauty who dazzled family, friends, and the small countryside not far from Berlioz's home. To her young Hector was a child and she treated him as such. But he was more than a child and he never forgot that first vision of Estelle:

> . . . her tall, elegant figure with large eyes poised for attack, though they were always smiling, and the feet, I won't say of an Andalusian, but of a

> pure-bred Parisienne. And . . . little pink boots! . . . I had never seen such before . . . You laugh!! . . . Well, I have forgot the color of her hair (though I think it was black), but I cannot think of her without seeing the glow of those great eyes and of her tiny pink boots.
>
> The instant I saw her I felt an electric shock. I loved her. That says everything.

Berlioz was in a daze. He hoped for nothing. He knew nothing, but he was filled with an immense sorrow. He passed nights of sleepless misery. He hid by day like a wounded animal. Everyone in the house—the whole neighborhood—laughed at the sad twelve-year-old, broken by a love beyond his strength. At a party game when he had to choose a partner he did not dare. "My heart was beating too hard; I lowered my eyes, tongue-tied. They all began to tease me. . . . Alas, the cruel girl was laughing too as she looked down from the height of her beauty."

"No," wrote Berlioz looking back over the years, "time is powerless, it does not help a bit." He was thirteen when he stopped seeing Estelle. He was thirty when he saw her again for a blinding moment and learned she was married. He was over forty when, hearing she was widowed, he wrote her a passionate letter she did not answer. He was past sixty and she was nearly seventy when she permitted him to call on her. She was kindly, but formal, and puzzled by the unreasonable obsession of the elderly man, famous, a member of the French Academy. Almost bitterly, Berlioz reflected: "She thinks that what is in the imagination is unreal." He seems to have loved her to the day he died; in his will he left her an annuity.

One of Berlioz's earliest childhood works was a song of his despair at leaving the countryside of his Estelle. He destroyed the song with its sentimental text before moving to Paris. But the melody came back to him six years later and he developed it for an entire aria expressing the unhappy love of the heroine in his prizewinning cantata *Herminie.* And again, when he attacked the composition of his *Fantastic Symphony,* the tune of the original came back to him. "It seemed to me just right to express the overwhelming sadness of a young heart first experiencing the torture of unhappy love, and I welcomed it. It is the theme played by the first violins at the beginning of the *Largo* introduction to the first movement entitled: 'Reveries; Passion.' I used it unchanged."

Here is the beginning of the melody as it opens the *Fantastic Symphony,* the melody Berlioz chose again, near the end of his life, to inscribe on his portrait published in his *Memoirs:*

In the final published form, Berlioz reversed the title to read *Fantastic Symphony, Episode in the Life of an Artist.* He no longer insisted, as he did in earlier versions, that it is indespensable for a complete understanding of the work to have the detailed program distributed to the audience; he added: "One can even, if necessary *(à la rigueur)* do without distributing the program, keeping only the titles of the five movements. The *Symphony* can (the composer hopes) offer musical interest independent of any dramatic purpose."

The following is the program as Berlioz hoped it would be placed in his listener's hands:

A young musician of morbidly sensitive temperament and fiery imagination poisons himself with opium in a fit of lovesick despair. The dose of the narcotic, too weak to kill him, plunges him into a deep slumber accompanied by the strangest visions, during which his sensations, his emotions, his memories are transformed in his sick mind into musical thoughts and images. The loved one herself has become a melody to him, an *idée fixe* as it were, that he encounters and hears everywhere.

I. *Reveries, Passions* [*Largo; Allegro agitato e appassionato assai*]. He recalls first that soul-sickness, those *intimations of passion,* those seemingly groundless depressions and elations that he experienced before he first saw the woman he loves; then the volcanic love that she suddenly inspired in him, his frenzied anguish, his jealous furies, his returns to tenderness, his religious consolations.

[After the introductory "Reveries," the main body of the first movement (an agitated *Allegro*) begins the full statement of the melody of the beloved (the *idée fixe*) as follows:

It continues with more passionate phrases from the Estelle melody that opened the slow introduction, developed now with increasing urgency:]

II. *A Ball* [*Valse: Allegro non troppo*]. He meets his beloved again during the tumult of a brilliant fete. [Here the *idée fixe* is transformed into a graceful waltz melody, combining with the ballroom dances.]

III. *Scene in the Country* [*Adagio*]. On a summer evening in the country, he hears two shepherds piping back and forth to each other a *ranz des vaches* (traditional tune played by Swiss shepherds to call their flocks); this pastoral duet, the scenery, the quiet rustling of the trees gently stirred by the wind, some prospects of hope he has recently found—all combine to sooth his heart with unaccustomed calm, and lend a more smiling color to his thoughts. But *she* appears again, he feels a tightening in his heart, painful presentiments disturb him—what if she were to deceive him?—One of the shepherds takes up his simple tune again; the other no longer answers. The sun sets—distant roll of thunder—solitude—silence.

IV. *March to the Execution* [*Allegretto non troppo*]. He dreams that he *has* killed his beloved, that he is condemned to death and is being led to execution. The procession moves forward to the sounds of a march that is now somber and wild, now brilliant and solemn, in which the muffled sound of heavy steps gives way without transition to the noisiest clamor. At the end, the *idée fixe* returns for a moment, like one last thought of love interrupted by the death blow.

V. *Dream of a Witches' Sabbath* [*Larghetto; Allegro*]. He sees himself at the sabbath, in the midst of a frightful troop of ghosts, sorcerers, monsters of every kind, come together for his funeral. Strange noises, groans, bursts of laughter, distant cries which other cries seem to answer. The beloved melody appears again, but it has lost its character of nobility and shyness; it is no more than a dance tune, base, trivial, and grotesque: it is she, coming to join the sabbath.—A roar of joy at her arrival.—She takes part in the devilish orgy.—Funeral knell, burlesque parody of the *Dies irae*:

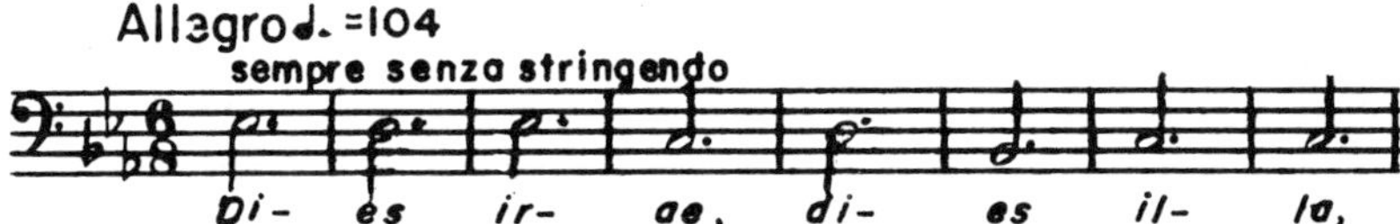

sabbath round-dance:

The sabbath round and the *Dies irae* combined.

Although Berlioz originally hoped for an orchestra of over 200 for the premiere, he seems never to have had more than 130 players. And even this large number was achieved by copious doubling of parts. The amazing variety of orchestral colors in the *Fantastic Symphony* is normally achieved with the relatively modest list specified in the printed score: piccolo, 2 flutes, 2 oboes, E-flat clarinet, 2 B-flat clarinets, 2 bassoons, 4 horns, 2 cornets, 2 trumpets, 3 trombones, 2 tubas, kettledrums, bass drum, bells, and the customary strings.

SYMPHONIE FUNÈBRE ET TRIOMPHALE

Berlioz was no friend of the July Monarchy of Louis Philippe. But he seems to have been eager to help celebrate the heroes of the July (1830) Revolution, despite the bourgeois regime that had followed their futile sacrifice. As July 1840 approached, the government of Louis Philippe decided to celebrate the tenth anniversary of the July Revolution with a grand ceremony transferring the bodies of what Berlioz called "the more or less heroic victims of the Three Days" to a monument constructed in their memory on the Place Bastille. Fortunately for Berlioz, a new French cabinet headed by Adolphe Thiers included a Minister of the Interior who liked music.

> It was his idea [writes Berlioz in his *Memoirs*] to have me write, for the ceremony of transferral of the bodies, a symphony—the form and means of performance being left entirely to my own choice. For this work the sum of 10,000 francs was guaranteed me, out of which I was to pay the expenses of copying and performance.
>
> I thought that the simplest plan would be best for such a work, and that a large body of wind instruments would alone be suitable for a symphony which was—at least on the first occasion—to be heard in the open air. I wished in the first place to recall the famous Three Days' conflict amid the mourning accents of an awesome, grief-stricken march accompanying the procession; to follow this by a sort of funeral oration, or farewell address to the illustrious dead, while the bodies were being lowered into the tomb; and finally to sing a hymn of praise as an apotheosis, when, after the sealing of the tomb, the public would see before it only the column surmounted by the figure of Liberty, with her wings outstretched, soaring toward heaven, like the souls of those who had died for her. . . .
>
> When I had finished the march and the funeral oration, and found a theme for the apotheosis, I was delayed for some time by the fanfare, which I wished to bring up by degrees from the depths of the orchestra to the high note where the apotheosis breaks in. I don't know how many I wrote, but I liked none of them. Either they were too common, or too narrow in form, or not sufficiently solemn, or wanting in sonority, or badly graded. What I imagined was a sound like the trump of archangels, simple but noble, chivalrous, militant, ascending radiantly, triumphantly, resoundingly, grandly, announcing to earth and heaven the opening of the Empyrean gates. Finally I decided, not without trepidation, on the one now in the score . . .

The first performance, on July 28, 1840, was a problem. It began upon the open boulevard amid the shouts of the populace. Berlioz, marching ahead in his uniform of the National Guard, could be seen only by the nearest members of his huge marching band. At one point there was a near panic when the vast structure bearing the fifty coffins of the July heroes in the procession nearly toppled into the crowd.

There was an elaborate burial service before the monument of the Place Bastille. The second movement of Berlioz's Symphony, the "Funeral Oration," was duly conducted by the composer, but before he finished, the National

Guard, which had stood about as long as it could under arms in the blazing sun, began to march off to the sound of their own fifty drums which,according to Berlioz,"continued to beat brutally throughout the whole of the Apotheosis, so that not one note could be heard." And he continues wryly: "Music is always thus respected in France at all celebrations or public rejoicings, where they think it ought to be prominent . . . to the eye."

Fortunately Berlioz had realized long before the official premiere, that acoustical conditions would be poor. Accordingly he held a "dress rehearsal" of the "Military Symphony," as he called it on the invitation cards, before a select audience of friends, critics, and celebrities in the Salle Vivienne two days before the public ceremony. The rehearsal was such a stupendous success that the manager of the Concerts Vivienne immediately engaged Berlioz for four repetitions of the Symphony. Two were actually held on August 7 and August 14. An attempted *coup d'état* by Louis-Napoleon, the future Napoleon III, dislocated the plans for the last two performances.

I. *Funeral March: Moderato un poco lento.* The first movement opens with the heavy thud of covered side drums while brasses mark the basic rhythm of the funeral march. The march melody is announced by flutes and clarinets:

Flutes and clarinets

There is a slow impressive buildup of sonorities and a series of episodes derived from the opening tune. A more peaceful, trio-like interlude for the woodwind choir, with discreet support from the French horns, is in the consoling major mode. The remainder of the march, including a return of the trio episode, is an imaginative but appropriately simple development of what has gone before.

II. *Funeral Oration: Adagio non tanto; andantino poco lento e sostenuto.* The slow middle movement is divided into three parts. The first is an alternation of pompous chords for the full orchestra with speech-like passages for a solo trombone in free rhythm marked *quasi recitativo.* In the succeeding sections the trombone solo grows more melodious and the orchestral parts more rhythmic, until by the end the texture of the whole has become thoroughly symphonic. The final movement follows without pause.

III. *Apotheosis.* A roll of the side drums, now no longer covered, leads to the fanfare intended to suggest "the opening of the Empyrean gates." This in turn leads to the chief melody of the "Apotheosis." It is stirring, simple enough to be whistled on the way home, and yet characteristically Berlioz.

For the first (processional) performance of this *Military Symphony* (as it was first called) Berlioz conducted a marching band of some 200 players; no precise count seems to survive. Five months later (November 1, 1840) Berlioz conducted an indoor performance at the Paris Opéra with 450 musicians (according to a surviving copy of the program) or 600 (according to Berlioz's *Memoirs*). Early in 1842 Berlioz revised his score with the addition of what he described (to his sister Nanci) as a "second orchestra (of strings)." Later in the same year he also added a chorus to the "Apotheosis" and gave the score its final title of *Funeral and Triumphal Symphony*. During Berlioz's lifetime this extravagant work was performed with forces that varied anywhere from 130 (at the Paris Conservatory in 1843) to 1,800 in the open-air Hippodrome of Paris in July, 1846. After the latter performance, which Berlioz did not conduct, he wrote in his column in the *Journal des Débats:* "Open-air music is a chimera: 150 musicians in a closed building produce more effect than 1,800 in the Hippodrome scattering their harmonies to the winds."

Leonard Bernstein

Born August 25, 1918, Lawrence, Massachusetts

THE AGE OF ANXIETY, SYMPHONY NO. 2 FOR PIANO AND ORCHESTRA (AFTER W. H. AUDEN)

Bernstein's meteoric career has been particularly associated with the New York Philharmonic. He was only twenty-four when he was appointed Assistant Conductor of the Philharmonic. He was only twenty-five when he won acclaim and almost instant fame by taking over, on the briefest notice and without rehearsal, a Philharmonic concert, replacing Bruno Walter, who had suddenly been taken ill. That was in 1943. In 1944 Bernstein conducted the world premiere of his First or "Jeremiah" Symphony with the Pittsburgh Symphony Orchestra, his popular ballet *Fancy Free* was produced by the American Ballet Theater, his hit musical *On the Town* opened on Broadway, and his "Jeremiah" Symphony won the New York Music Critics Circle award. It was a good year for the new Assistant Conductor. Bernstein also appeared as guest conductor with the Philharmonic for six seasons before he became a principal conductor with Dimitri Mitropoulos in the fall of 1958. The following season he inaugurated an eleven-year tenure as Music Director of the Philharmonic. Since retiring from that post at the end of the 1968–69 season he has held the title of Philharmonic Conductor Laureate and has continued to appear frequently with the orchestra.

Meanwhile he has continued to compose. In his role as composer-conductor, Bernstein has illustrious precedents, including Gustav Mahler, a pre-World War I conductor of the Philharmonic. Indeed, a heavy proportion of the greatest composers represented in this book, from J. S. Bach to Richard Strauss, were professional conductors—that is, they earned their livings at first as conductors of other men's music. And their conducting experience seems to have enriched their composing. Bernstein had produced his First

Leonard Bernstein Conducting The New York Philharmonic.

(Courtesy, Paul de Hueck)

Symphony during his first season as Assistant Conductor. He completed his Second Symphony, *The Age of Anxiety,* during his third season as guest conductor with the Philharmonic. Bernstein was the piano soloist at the world premiere on April 8, 1949, with the Boston Symphony under the direction of Serge Koussevitzky. Bernstein describes the genesis and content of the Symphony best himself in a note appended to his score.

> W. H. Auden's fascinating and hair-raising poem *The Age of Anxiety; a Baroque Eclogue* began immediately to affect me lyrically when I first read it in the summer of 1947. From that moment the composition of a symphony based on *The Age of Anxiety* acquired an almost compulsive quality; and I worked on it steadily in Taos, in Philadelphia, in Richmond, Mass., in Tel-Aviv, in planes, in hotel lobbies, and finally (the week preceding the premiere) in Boston. The orchestration was started during a month-long tour with the Pittsburgh Symphony, and was completed on March 20, 1948 in New York City.
>
> I imagine that the conception of a symphony with piano solo emerges from the extremely personal identification of myself with the poem. In this sense, the pianist provides an almost autobiographical protagonist, set against an orchestral mirror in which he sees himself, analytically, in the modern ambience. The work is therefore no "concerto" in the virtuosic sense, although I regard Auden's poem as one of the most shattering examples of pure virtuosity in the history of English poetry.
>
> The essential line of the poem (and of the music) is the record of our difficult and problematical search for faith. In the end, two of the characters enunciate the recognition of this faith—even a passive submission to it—at the same time revealing an inability to relate to it personally in their daily lives, except through blind acceptance.
>
> No one could be more astonished than I at the extent to which the programmaticism of this work has been carried. I had not planned a "meaningful" work, at least not in the sense of a piece whose meaning relied on details of programmatic implication. I was merely writing a symphony inspired by a poem and following the general form of that poem. Yet, when each section was finished I discovered, upon rereading, detail after detail of programmatic relation to the poem—details that had "written themselves," wholly unplanned and unconscious. Since I trust the unconscious implicitly, finding it a source of wisdom and the dictator of the condign in artistic matters, I am content to leave these details in the score.
>
> If the charge of "theatricality" in a symphonic work is a valid one, I am willing to plead guilty. I have a deep suspicion that every work I write, for whatever medium, is really theater music in some way, and nothing has convinced me more than these new discoveries of the unconscious hand that has been at work all along in *The Age of Anxiety.*
>
> I have divided Auden's six sections into two large parts, each containing three sections played without pause. A brief outline follows:
>
> PART ONE:
>
> (a) *The Prologue* finds four lonely characters, a girl and three men, in a Third Avenue bar, all of them insecure and trying, through drink, to detach

themselves from their conflicts, or, at best, to resolve them. They are drawn together by this common urge and begin a kind of symposium on the state of man. Musically the *Prologue* is a very short section consisting of a lonely improvisation by two clarinets, echo-tone, and followed by a long descending scale which acts as a bridge into the realm of the unconscious, where most of the poem takes place.

(b) *The Seven Ages.* The life of man is reviewed from the four personal points of view. This is a series of variations which differ from conventional variations in that they do not vary any one common theme. Each variation seizes upon some feature of the preceding one and develops it, introducing, in the course of the development, some counter-feature upon which the next variation seizes. It is a kind of musical fission, which corresponds to the reasonableness and almost didactic quality of the fourfold discussion.

(c) *The Seven Stages.* The variation form continues for another set of seven, in which the characters go on an inner and highly symbolic journey according to a geographical plan leading back to a point of comfort and security. The four try every means, going singly and in pairs, exchanging partners, and always missing the objective. When they awaken from this dream-odyssey, they are closely united through a common experience (and through alcohol), and begin to function as one organism. This set of variations begins to show activity and drive and leads to a hectic, though indecisive, close.

PART TWO:

(a) *The Dirge* is sung by the four as they sit in a cab en route to the girl's apartment for a nightcap. They mourn the loss of the "colossal Dad," the great leader who can always give the right orders, find the right solution, shoulder the mass responsibility, and satisfy the universal need for a father-symbol. This section employs, in a harmonic way, a twelve-tone row out of which the main theme evolves. There is a contrasting middle section of almost Brahmsian romanticism, in which can be felt the self-indulgent, or negative, aspect of this strangely pompous lamentation.

(b) *The Masque* finds the group in the girl's apartment, weary, guilty, determined to have a party, each one afraid of spoiling the others' fun by admitting that he should be home in bed. This is a scherzo for piano and percussion alone (including harp, celesta, glockenspiel, and xylophone) in which a kind of fantastic piano-jazz is employed, by turns nervous, sentimental, self-satisfied, vociferous. The party ends in anticlimax and the dispersal of the actors; in the music the piano-protagonist is traumatized by the intervention of the orchestra for four bars of hectic jazz. When the orchestra stops, as abruptly as it began, a pianino in the orchestra is continuing the *Masque,* repetitiously and with waning energy, as the *Epilogue* begins. Thus a kind of separation of the self from the guilt of escapist living has been effected, and the protagonist is free again to examine what is left beneath the emptiness.

(c) *The Epilogue.* What is left, it turns out, is faith. The trumpet intrudes its statement of "something pure" upon the dying pianino: the strings answer in a melancholy reminiscent of the *Prologue:* again and again the winds reiterate "something pure" against the mounting tension of the strings' loneliness. All at once the strings accept the situation, in a sudden radiant *pianis-*

> *simo,* and begin to build, with the rest of the orchestra, to a positive statement of the newly recognized faith.
>
> Throughout the *Epilogue* the piano-protagonist has taken no part, but has observed it, as one observes such development on a movie screen, or in another human personality. At the very end he seizes upon it with one eager chord of confirmation, although he has not himself participated in the anxiety-experience leading to this fulfilment. The way is open; but, at the conclusion, is still stretching long before him.
>
> LEONARD BERNSTEIN

(The above description was written on completion of *The Age of Anxiety.* Six years later Bernstein revised the finale of his Symphony and added the following note.)

> In the years that have passed since 1949, I have reevaluated my attempt to mirror Auden's literary images in so literal a way. It seems to me to have succeeded least well in the finale, where the nonparticipating of the solo piano did not so much convey the intended "detachment" as rob the soloist of his *concertante* function. With this in mind, I have revised the finale so as to include the solo pianist, even providing him with a final burst of cadenza before the coda. I am now satisfied that the work is in its final form.

The *Age of Anxiety* is scored for solo piano, piccolo, 2 flutes, 2 oboes, English horn, 2 clarinets, bass clarinet, 2 bassoons, contrabassoon, 4 horns, 3 trumpets, 3 trombones, tuba, kettledrums, snare drum, bass drum, tenor drum, tam-tam, cymbal, temple blocks, triangle, glockenspiel, xylophone, celeste, harp, upright piano (in the orchestra), and the traditional strings.

SERENADE (AFTER PLATO'S SYMPOSIUM)

Dedicated "to the beloved memory of Serge and Natalie Koussevitzky," Bernstein's Serenade was completed on August 8, 1954. On the following day Bernstein wrote a description of the stimulus that led to his music:

> There is no literal program for this *Serenade* despite the fact that it resulted from a rereading of Plato's charming dialogue, "The Symposium." The music, like the dialogue, is a series of related statements in praise of love, and generally follows the Platonic form through the succession of speakers at the banquet. The "relatedness" of the movements does not depend on common thematic material, but rather on a system whereby each movement evolves out of elements in the preceding one.
>
> For the benefit of those interested in literary allusion, I might suggest the following points as guideposts:
>
> I. *Phaedrus; Pausanias (Lento; Allegro).* Phaedrus opens the symposium with a lyrical oration in praise of Eros, the god of love. (*Fugato,* begun by the solo violin). Pausanias continues by describing the duality of lover and beloved. This is expressed in a classical sonata-allegro, based on the material of the opening fugato.

II. *Aristophanes (Allegretto).* Aristophanes does not play the role of clown in this dialogue, but instead that of the bedtime storyteller, invoking the fairy-tale mythology of love.

III. *Erixymachus (Presto).* The physician speaks of bodily harmony as a scientific model for the workings of love-patterns. This is an extremely short *fugato* scherzo, born of a blend of mystery and humor.

IV. *Agathon (Adagio).* Perhaps the most moving speech of the dialogue. Agathon's panegyric embraces all aspects of love's powers, charms and functions. This movement is a simple three-part song.

V. *Socrates; Alcibiades (Molto tenuto; Allegro molto vivace).* Socrates describes his visit to the seer Diotima, quoting her speech on the demonology of love. This is a slow introduction of greater weight than any of the preceding movements, and serves as a highly developed reprise of the middle section of the *Agathon* movement, thus suggesting a hidden sonata-form. The famous interruption by Alcibiades and his band of drunken revelers ushers in the Allegro, which is an extended rondo ranging in spirit from agitation through jig-like dance music to joyful celebration. If there is a hint of jazz in the celebration, I hope it will not be taken as anachronistic Greek party-music, but rather the natural expression of a contemporary American composer imbued with the spirit of that timeless dinner-party.

LEONARD BERNSTEIN

Conventionally speaking, Bernstein's Serenade could be called a one-movement violin concerto, or perhaps a concerto in five connected movements. It opens peacefully with a long lyric line for the unaccompanied solo violin. Seemingly simple, but ingeniously constructed, it embodies the most prominent thematic material of the Serenade, starting as follows:

While the solo violin continues, the entire first violin section, all muted, then the violas, also muted, take up the opening melody (quite literally, that is, in strict canon, at intervals of the lower minor third). In this development, the tiny opening motive (also a minor third, rising and falling) seems to grow in importance. A final canonic entrance of all the remaining strings leads, with quickening tempo, to the main *Allegro* part of the movement, the speech of Pausanias. Pausanias's main theme is a bouncing, strongly rhythmic transformation of the Serenade's opening melody. The crown of the whole is the fourth movement, an *Adagio* of the most moving simplicity and lyricism. Its main melody, for muted solo violin and the murmuring accompaniment for strings, both stem from the chief theme of the work. A passionate middle section culminates in a strong cadenza for the solo instrument and then subsides, with touching laconicism, into the exalted calm of the opening.

Commissioned by the Koussevitzky Foundation, Bernstein's Serenade was first performed on September 12, 1954, at the Teatro La Fenice, Venice, with Isaac Stern as soloist and the composer conducting. It is scored for string orchestra with harp and a rich percussion section, including kettledrums.

SYMPHONIC DANCES FROM WEST SIDE STORY

Among his many enthusiasms, Bernstein seems to have had a running love affair with New York City. It has not been a blind love: he has expressed tragedy and squalor of the city as well as its manic high spirits, its relentless pressures, its glitter and gloom, its rarer moments of poetry and even of human warmth. But the number of Bernstein's dramatic works reflecting the kaleidoscope of New York can be no accident: the ballet staple *Fancy Free* (1944), the related musical *On the Town* (1944), the film score for Elia Kazan's *On the Waterfront* (from which Bernstein drew his *Waterfront Suite*), the musical *Wonderful Town* (1952), and *West Side Story,* which landed on Broadway on September 26, 1957.

When asked point-blank by an interviewer whether it was the fascination of his adopted city that inspired *West Side Story,* Bernstein replied that, on the contrary, he had not initiated the project at all. Others had suggested the subject to him and he had taken to it largely because he wanted to see whether it would be possible to write a serious musical. (Bernstein, who is well aware of the history of his art, may have had in mind the development of German opera from eighteenth-century operetta-like, comic plays with songs, or *Singspiele,* which led later to serious operas with spoken dialogue, such as *Fidelio* and *Der Freischütz.*)

In any case, Bernstein demonstrated beyond any shadow of doubt that a serious musical was not only possible but could be a popular hit—both in its original stage version, which ran for 973 performances on Broadway alone, and as a film.

On the surface, *West Side Story* depicts the tragic lives of ordinary people in one small, grubby section of a cruelly indifferent-seeming city: New York. Below the surface, however, the sympathies of *West Side Story* are deeper, its stylistic references far wider. Two of its themes—urban violence and youthful delinquence—are not confined to any quarter of any city but range the continent, perhaps the world. A third theme, young love destroyed by clan hatred, is as universal as Shakespearean tragedy. Some basic ideas of *West Side Story* come from Shakespeare's *Romeo and Juliet.* However, Bernstein's star-crossed lovers are Tony and Maria, and in place of warring Montagues and Capulets, *West Side Story* has rival teen-age gangs: the Jets and the Sharks.

The excerpts which Bernstein has merged in his concert score are called "symphonic" not because they are arranged for a symphony orchestra, but because of the way the dances of *West Side Story* were originally conceived: most of them, indeed, most of the score of the entire musical, grew out of a few basic themes, transformed and combined to express a variety of moods, action, songs and dances. The Symphonic Dances are performed continuously, without pause:

1. *Prologue: Allegro moderato.* The opening music suggests the growing rivalry between the two gangs: the Jets and the Sharks.

2. *Somewhere: Adagio.* In a dream-dance sequence the two gangs are united in comradeship.

3. *Scherzo: Vivace leggiero.* The teen-age boys break through the city confines and find themselves in a spacious world of sunshine and good air.

4. *Mambo: Presto.* The reality of violence returns with a competitive dance between the Jets and the Sharks.

5. *Cha-Cha: Andantino con grazia.* The lovers Tony and Maria dance together.

6. *Meeting Scene: Meno mosso.* This music accompanies the first exchange of words between the lovers.

7. *Cool, Fugue: Allegretto.* The hostility of the Jets explodes in a contrapuntal dance.

8. *Rumble: Molto allegro.* This is the climax of violence, in which the leaders of both Jets and Sharks are killed.

9. *Finale: Adagio.* At the end, after Tony has died in Maria's arms, a victim of the reality of gang violence, the dream of "Somewhere" is brought back with tragic irony in his funeral procession.

Bernstein's orchestra for the Symphonic Dances calls for piccolo, 2 flutes, 2 oboes, English horn, E-flat clarinet, 2 B-flat clarinets, bass clarinet, alto saxophone, 2 bassoons, contrabassoon, 4 horns, 3 trumpets, tuba, kettledrums, 4 pitched drums, bongos, tom-toms, tenor drum, 3 snare drums (one with snares off), concert bass drum, jazz drums (traps), conga drum, cymbals, suspended cymbals, finger cymbals, tambourine, gourds, maracas, 3 cowbells, woodblock, triangle, tam-tam, police whistle, xylophone, vibraphone, glockenspiel, chime, harp, piano, celesta, and the usual strings.

Georges Bizet

Born October 25, 1838, Paris—died June 3, 1875, Bougival

SYMPHONY IN C MAJOR

"You were the beginning of my life as an artist," wrote Bizet late in his career to his older friend and colleague, Charles Gounod. "I can now admit that I was afraid of being absorbed." Probably it was this fear of being absorbed by Gounod, or perhaps a fear that he had *been* temporarily absorbed that made Bizet put aside this attractive youthful Symphony in C major, composed while he was still a student at the Paris Conservatory. The score was neither published nor, as far as we know, performed during his lifetime.

It is easy to see why Bizet was afraid of being absorbed. From his twelfth year, when he first heart Gounod's opera *Sappho,* he had fallen under the spell of the older master. He was sixteen when he made a four-hand piano arrangement of Gounod's opera *La Nonne sanglante.* A few weeks later he made the piano arrangement of Gounod's First Symphony. (Before the day of the phonograph such piano arrangements were the most popular means of performing orchestral and operatic music in the home and even in concert when orchestral forces were not available.)

In the fall of the same year, only four days after his seventeenth birthday, Bizet started composing his own C-major Symphony which does show striking resemblances to that of Gounod. He finished by the end of November, which means that the whole took him barely a month. Its spontaneousness and verve are astonishing. The resemblance to Gounod, which seems to have concerned Bizet and which might have piqued a Parisian audience of the 1850s, is of little more than historical, anecdotal interest to us.

The Symphony lay long unnoticed among a pile of Bizet's manuscripts which his widow bequeathed to Reynaldo Hahn and which Hahn in turn gave to the Paris Conservatory in 1933. Later that year the first English biographer of Bizet, D. C. Parker, came across the manuscript in the library of the Conservatory and called it to the attention of Felix von Weingartner, who conducted the world premiere of the Symphony in Basel on February 26, 1935. The United States premiere was given by the New York Philharmonic, under the direction of John Barbirolli on October 17, 1940.

I. *Allegro vivo.* The lighthearted *Allegro vivo* is cast in traditional first movement form. But although the form is traditional, the music does not plod. The perky opening has an almost Rossinian verve. And there is a graceful contrasting theme, a lyric phrase played by the solo oboe. Both themes are tossed about from one group of instruments to another in a dexterous little development section, and the movement is rounded off by a reprise of the basic themes.

II. *Adagio.* After a few measures' introduction, the oboe solo sings a serenade-like melody over an accompaniment of pizzicato strings. The melody has an exotic turn recalling Pedrillo's serenade in Mozart's *Abduction from the Seraglio.* A second, very beautiful cantilena for the violins flows with a fervor that anticipates *L'Arlésienne* and *Carmen.* After a brief, contrasting middle section the movement is rounded off by a reprise of the basic themes.

III. *Allegro vivace.* The third movement has the lightness and grace of the old-fashioned minuet and the sprightly tempo of the more modern scherzo. In the trio section a drone accompaniment of open fifths suggests a stylized folk dance.

IV. *Allegro vivace.* The fluttering first violins and lilting wood winds of these opening measures almost recall Mendelssohn's *Midsummer Night's Dream* music. The dapper little second theme has an infectious lilt which cannot be explained simply as a clever conservatory student's imitation of Gounod:

The entire finale is concocted out of these two simple but beguiling musical ideas.

The symphony is scored for 2 flutes, 2 oboes, 2 clarinets, 2 bassoons, 4 horns, 2 trumpets, kettledrums, and the usual strings.

Ernest Bloch

Born July 24, 1880, Geneva—died July 15, 1959, Portland, Oregon

SCHELOMO, HEBREW RHAPSODY FOR CELLO AND ORCHESTRA

During World War I, just before Ernest Bloch emigrated to the United States, he visited the cellist Alexander Barjansky in Switzerland. In Barjansky's home Bloch saw a statue of King Solomon by Madame Barjansky. This was the inspiration for Bloch's *Hebrew Rhapsody,* which he composed in January and February 1916, in Geneva.

In 1917, soon after his arrival in the United States, Bloch wrote to Philip Hale, the program annotator for the Boston Symphony Orchestra, explaining his aims in *Schelomo* and his other works of Jewish inspiration.

"It is not my purpose, not my desire, to attempt a 'reconstitution' of Jewish music [Bloch wrote] or to base my works on melodies more or less authentic. I am not an archaeologist. I hold it of first importance to write good, genuine music, my music. It is the Jewish soul that interests me, the complex, glowing, agitated soul, that I feel vibrating throughout the Bible; the freshness and naiveté of the Patriarchs; the violence that is evident in the prophetic books; the Jew's savage love of justice; the despair of the Preacher of Jerusalem; the sorrow and the immensity of the Book of Job; the sensuality of the Song of Songs. All this is in us; all this is in me, and it is the better part of me. It is all this that I endeavor to hear in myself and to transcribe in my music; the venerable emotion of the race that slumbers way down in our soul."

In his *Hebrew Rhapsody,* Bloch not only used his rich orchestra to suggest the richness and the pomp of King Solomon, or *Schelomo,* he personified the philosopher-king with the reedy tones of a solo cello. The *Rhapsody* is a free-form cello concerto in one movement.

During a cadenza-like introduction, the cello anticipates the poignant chief theme in a passage of characteristically uneven dotted rhythms, so rich in half-steps that it sounds almost Oriental:

This is the voice of the Preacher of Jerusalem, the noble Hebrew long believed to have been identical with King Solomon, the ruler who, having known all the power and pleasures of man, meditated and found that all was vanity: "Vanity of vanities, saith the Preacher, *Hebel habalim, hacol hebel* . . . all is vanity. What profit hath a man of all his labor which he taketh under the sun? . . . I the Preacher was king over Israel in Jerusalem. And I gave my heart to seek and search out by wisdom concerning all things that are done under heaven . . . I have seen all the works that are done under the sun; and, behold, all is vanity and vexation of spirit. . . . And I gave my heart to know wisdom, and to know madness and folly: I perceived that this also is vexation of spirit. For in much wisdom is much grief: and he that increaseth knowledge increaseth sorrow." (From the first book of Ecclesiastes.)

In its basic form, the principal theme is introduced by the entire viola section of the orchestra:

This is the foundation of a series of symphonic developments. Between these moments of jubiliation and barbaric bursts of orchestral splendor, we hear the pessimistic voice of the cello, skeptical, despairing, descending finally to the lowest range of the instrument, and ending on a deep unanswered question.

The colorful score of *Schelomo* calls for piccolo, 3 flutes, 2 oboes, English horn, 2 clarinets, bass clarinet, 2 bassoons, contrabassoon, 4 horns, 3 trumpets, 3 trombones, tuba, kettledrums, side drum, tambourine, bass drum, cymbals, tam-tam, celesta, two harps, solo cello, and the traditional strings.

Pierre Boulez

Born March 26, 1925, Montbrison (Loire), France

PLI SELON PLI (FOLD BY FOLD)

Boulez's *Pli selon pli* was inspired—or perhaps one should not use such a Romantic term for a truly contemporary composer—so let us say instead that

Pierre Boulez Conducting The New York Philharmonic.

(Courtesy, Don Hunstein/CBS)

the *core* from which Boulez's masterpiece grew, the structure which his music parallels, is the verse of Stéphane Mallarmé (1842–98).

The fountainhead of modern French poetry—one could almost say the fountainhead of most innovative poetry and much prose of the Western world during the early years of our century—was Mallarmé. In any case, much of Mallarmé and, by implication, much of the music he stimulated, from Debussy to Boulez, is illuminated by that part of Mallarmé's credo which said: *"Nommer un objet, c'est supprimer les trois quarts de la jouissance du poème qui est fait du bonheur de deviner peu à peu; le suggerer, violà le rêve."* ("To name a thing is to eliminate three-quarters of the pleasure of poetry, which consists of the joy of gradual discovery; to suggest—that is ideal.")

The very title *Pli selon pli,* which Boulez takes from Mallarmé, implies a gradual unfolding, the slow revelation, as if through lifting veils of mist, of something which must not be named too quickly, in too heavy-handed or flat-footed fashion.

Another attraction which Boulez's score shares with the verse of Mallarmé is sheer sensuous sound. Obviously there is much more to Boulez's *Pli selon pli* than pretty noises. The final hoarse whisper, *"(la) mort"* ("death"), which ends the last movement, can make your blood run cold. But at the risk of irritating the composer with what might be (wrongly) interpreted as a back-handed compliment, this listener would say without hesitation that pure sound—curious and ravishingly beautiful sound—is a very prominent and important *part* of *Pli selon pli.* I must confess that at my first hearing of its earliest-composed movements ("Improvisations on Mallarmé" I and II) at the 1959 Festival of the International Society for Contemporary Music in Rome, all I could remember from the experience was a mysteriously beguiling series of shifting iridescent sonorities held together by a strongly poetic mood. And although the vocal texts (Mallarmé's sonnets: *"Le vierge, le vivace et le bel aujourd'hui"* and *"Une dentelle s'abolit"*) were printed in the program, this listener was far from grasping the multiple relationships of those exquisitely chiseled verses to their sensitive musical settings.

As might have been expected, the explanatory note that accompanied that early performance of such allusive (and elusive) music, hinted more than it revealed:

"Two sonnets, two *states* of improvisation; from total predetermination to total indetermination:
—different possible versions, according to a pre-established choice
—definitive version, the improvisation grafted onto the unchanging text
—polyvalent versions, with probable declensions. At first the musical structures envelop the text; little by little the procedure produces the contrary: the acoustic structures of the text evoke the music. Homage to Mallarmé, *'l'ombre qui devînt'* ["the shadow that became" (or "materialized")]."

Since then Boulez has composed three additional movements of *Pli selon pli* and commented more concretely on the completed work which occupied him over a span of five years (1957–62):

Pli selon pli suggests several solutions to the problems of marrying a poetic text to music: these solutions vary from the inscription to the amalgam. They give a meaning to each piece and a significance to its position in the complete cycle.

The work comprises five pieces, of which the first, "*Don*," and the last, "*Tombeau*," are instrumental, calling for the largest grouping. The voice part is sporadically interpolated to present the Mallarmé poem from which the piece originates. The other three pieces, forming the central portion of the work, require more modest instrumental forces: they are centered around the voice part that enunciates, in part or whole, the poem that brings them together.

The two outer pieces, then, have a form completely independent of the poem, which only intervenes as a quotation.

Don: the poem is registered at the beginning of the piece, the only direct vocal participation; for the other places where the voice intervenes are the quotations in the central cycle, a kind of pre-echo of what is to be heard later. The musical quotations are engendered by the title of Mallarmé's "*Don du poème*," which becomes here a "*don de l'oeuvre*." They are not literal, but abstracted from their context, displaced; they are like glimpses into the future. The enunciation of the initial poem is, on the contrary, extremely simple, clear, direct, and syllabic.

Je t'apporte l'enfant d'une nuit d'Idumée!
I bring you the child of an Idumaean night!

Tombeau: the poem is registered at the end of the piece. The enunciation of the poem is in conflict with a very ornate vocal style and an extended *tessitura;* only the two final spoken words are clearly comprehensible.

Un peu profond ruisseau calomnié la mort.
A so shallow rivulet, much maligned death.

This opposition between direct and indirect understanding will be found throughout the three sonnets that constitute the central cycle: *Le vierge, le vivace et le bel adjourd'hui—Une dentelle s'abolit—A la nue accablante tu.* Before tackling this question, which is fundamental to music based on a poetic text, it must first be said that the form of these pieces is strictly the form of the sonnet itself; that the marriage of the poem and music here certainly bears the stamp of emotional significance, but seeks to go deeper than the invention, to its very structure. It cannot be forgotten that Mallarmé was obsessed by formal purity and by his single-minded quest for it: his language and his prosody bear witness to this. He completely rethought French syntax in order to make it an *original* instrument, in the literal sense of this term. As to the organization of the poem itself, if it has recourse to accepted values—the alexandrine, the octosyllabic—it is dominated by the strictness of the number, by the rhythm of the sonorous values implied in an extreme concentration of language. The esoterism nearly always linked with the name of Mallarmé, is nothing more than this perfect adequation of language with thought that admits no waste of energy.

So, the musical form may be found already determined if the finished, perfect structure that is the sonnet is taken into consideration. The necessary transposition demands the invention of equivalences; equivalences that may be applied both to the exterior form of the musical invention and to its quality or inner structure. The field of possible transpositions is vast; their diversity is compensated by strictness in their use.

As to the actual understanding of the poem in its musical transposition, how far can one cling to this? To what point must this be considered? My idea is not to be restricted to immediate understanding, which is only *one* of the forms (the least rich, perhaps?) of the transmutation of the poem. It strikes me as too restrictive to limit oneself to a kind of "reading in/with music;" from the point of view of simple understanding, this will never replace a reading *without* music, which remains the best way of being informed as to the contents of a poem. Then again, a concert piece, based mainly on poetic thought, cannot be confused with a stage work: this demands a maximum of direct understanding in order to follow the *action,* the *events,* onto which, if necessary, poetic thought may be grafted.

In my transposition, or transmutation, of Mallarmé, I take for granted that the direct sense of the poem has been acquired by reading it; I take it that the data communicated to the music by the poem have already been assimilated. I can therefore play on a variable degree of immediate understanding. This play, moreover, is not to be left to chance, but tends to give prominence sometimes to the musical and sometimes to the poetic text.

The instrumental sonority varies from one piece to another. The percussion has a much wider range of activity than is normal. Nevertheless, it includes many more instruments of defined pitch, like xylophones, vibraphones, and several kinds of bells, than instruments of indefinite pitch bordering on noise (these are more easily integrated with "classical" instrumental groupings). The two outer pieces call for a relatively large ensemble producing an orchestral sound; the three central pieces more nearly approach chamber music both in writing and sonority, particularly the second sonnet: *"Une dentelle s'abolit."*

The title *Pli selon pli* is taken from a Mallarmé poem not used in my musical transposition; it indicated the meaning and direction of the work. In this poem, the author describes the way in which the dissolving mist gradually reveals the stones of the city of Bruges. In the same way, as the five pieces unfold, they reveal, fold by fold, a portrait of Mallarmé.

PIERRE BOULEZ (translated by Felix Aprahamian)

IMPROVISATION I

Le vierge, le vivace et le bel aujourd'hui	Will the virginal, strong and handsome today
Va-t-il nous déchirer avec un coup d'aile ivre	Tear for us with a drunken flap of the wing
Ce lac dur oublié que hante sous le givre	This hard forgotten lake which the transparent glacier
Le transparent glacier des vols qui n'ont pas fui!	Of flights unflown haunts under the frost!

Un cygne d'autrefois se souvient que c'est lui
Magnifique, mais qui sans espoir se délivre
Pour n'avoir pas chanté la région où vivre
Quand du stérile hiver a resplendi l'ennui.

A swan of former times remembers it is he
Magnificent but who without hope gives himself up
For not having sung of the region where he should have been
When the boredom of sterile winter was resplendent.

Tout son col secouera cette blanche agonie
Par l'espace infligée à l'oiseau qui le nie,

All his neck will shake off this white death-agony
Inflicted by space on the bird which denies space,

Mais non l'horreur du sol où le plumage est pris.

But not the horror of the earth where his wings are caught.

Fantôme qu'à ce lieu son pur éclat assigne,
Il s'immobilise au songe froid de mépris

Phantom whom his pure brilliance assigns to this place,
He becomes immobile in the cold dream of scorn

Que vêt parmi l'exil inutile le Cygne.

Which the Swan puts on in his useless exile.

IMPROVISATION II

Une dentelle s'abolit
Dans le doute du Jeu supréme
A n'entr'ouvrir comme un blasphème
Qu'absence éternelle de lit.

A lace is effaced
In the doubt of the supreme Game
By revealing as a blasphemy
The eternal absence of a bed.

Cet unamine blanc conflit
D'une guirlande avec la même,
Enfui contre la vitre blême
Flotte plus qu'il n'ensevelit.

This one white combat
Of a garland with itself
Pressed against the pale glass
Waves more than it enshrouds,

Mais chez qui du rêve se dore
Tristement dort une mandore
Au creux néant musicien

But in him who is gilded with the dream
Sadly sleeps a mandolin
With its empty hollowness of sound

Telle que vers quelque fenêtre
Selon nul ventre que le sien,
Filial on aurait pu naître.

Such as toward some window
From no womb but one's own
As a son one might be born.

IMPROVISATION III

À la nue accablante tu	Under the massive cloud silenced
Basse de basalte et de laves	Base of basalt and lava
A même les échos esclaves	Even with the slavish echoes
Par une trompe sans vertu	By a powerless trumpet
Quel sépulcral naufrage (tu	What sepulchral shipwreck (you
Le sais, écume, mais y baves)	Know, foam, but drool there)
Suprême une entre les épaves	Supreme among the debris
Abolit le mât dévêtu	Abolishes the stripped mast
Ou cela que furibond faute	Or perhaps, furious for lack
De quelque perdition haute	Of some high perdition
Tout l'abîme vain éployé	The entire vain ocean spread out
Dans le si blanc cheveu qui traîne	In the very white hair which lingers
Avarement aura noyé	May have drowned avariciously
Le flanc enfant d'une sirène.	The child torso of a siren.

Pli selon pli was first performed in its entirety by the Südwest Funkorchester at the Holland festival of 1962 under the direction of Pierre Boulez. The score calls for 3 piccolos, 3 flutes, alto flute, oboe, English horn, A-flat clarinet, bassoon, contrabassoon, 4 horns, 3 trumpets, tenor trombone, bass trombone, contrabass trombone, kettledrums, cymbals, 30 other percussion (sic) requiring 7 players, mandolin, guitar, 4 violins, 8 violas, 5 cellos, and 6 contrabasses.

Johannes Brahms

Born May 7, 1833, Hamburg—died April 3, 1897, Vienna

CONCERTO FOR PIANO AND ORCHESTRA, NO. 1, D MINOR, OPUS 15

Brahms was a pianist from his earliest child-prodigy years. Yet with all his early facility, his approach to the piano had something orchestral about it, and this shows in his compositions. Robert Schumann spotted this quality when the obscure twenty-year-old first ventured to visit him. In the privacy of the Schumann home, with only the master and his wife Clara as audience, Brahms played his own music.

"Sitting at the piano, he began to disclose wonderful realms to us," wrote Schumann barely a fortnight later in a famous article of October 28, 1853, entitled "New Paths" *("Neue Bahnen").* Schumann's tribute continued: "We were drawn into more and more magical regions. Besides, he proved to be a player of genius, transforming the piano into an orchestra of lamenting and loudly jubilant voices. There were sonatas or rather veiled symphonies; songs, the poetry of which would be understood even without words, . . . string quartets, and every work so different from the others that it seemed to stream from its own individual source. And then he seemed to unite them all into one surging stream, its vast waves plunging down a great waterfall, overarched by a peaceful rainbow and accompanied by voices of nightingales as butterflies played about the banks."

It was generous, heartfelt praise, intended to smooth the way for a man whose genius was every bit as great as Schumann believed. But Brahms seems to have had less confidence in his own powers than Schumann. It was nearly a quarter of a century before he produced his first symphony. What was to have been his first symphony turned into the D-minor Piano Concerto. It first took shape as a sonata for two pianos, which Brahms brought to show to Schumann's pianist wife, Clara. Together, they played the sonata through several times. Clara wrote in her diary: "It struck me as quite powerful, quite original, conceived with great breadth and more clarity than his earlier things."

Obviously, Brahms's thought was orchestral, symphonic in scope. In the following months, he set about making a symphony of the sonata, but he had technical difficulties with the orchestration, despite the help of a scholarly friend, Julius Grimm. Finally, Grimm suggested a solution to this conflict between pianistic and orchestral concepts, namely a piano concerto.

Brahms agreed. The first two movements of the sonata became the *Maestoso* and the *Adagio* of the D-minor Piano Concerto. (The third movement of the sonata, set aside for many years, eventually became the chorus, "Behold all Flesh," in Brahms's *A German Requiem.*) After many revisions of the first two movements and the addition of a new finale, the Concerto was completed in its first version early in 1858.

It was first performed on January 22, 1859, with Brahms himself at the piano and Joachim conducting. Five days later, Brahms again played the Concerto at a Gewandhaus concert in Leipzig. After further revisions, the piano part was published in 1861, and the orchestral parts the following year.

I. *Maestoso.* What an opening theme for a timid young man starting his first orchestral score! Brahms hurls his heavy theme like a thunderbolt:

The kettledrums roar in the background as the stormy second half of the theme repeats and develops, culminating in a burst of heavy trills that cascade through the orchestra like a shower of fiery sparks.

The storm breaks off as dramatically as it began. A long wave-like strand of melody, a gently rocking figure, leads to a chain of lyric episodes. And it is with one of these that the piano makes its unobtrusive entrance, before seizing upon the great trills and vaulting intervals of the main theme.

The serenity of a marvelous contrasting melody, given out first by the piano alone:

provides the opposite pole of feeling in the first movement, which is a grandiose Romantic expansion of the Classical sonata-allegro pattern.

II. *Adagio.* The manuscript of the gentle slow movement originally bore the inscription: *Benedictus qui venit in nomine Domini.* Aside from its religious connotation, the words suggest a double dedication to the deceased Schumann and his widow, whom Brahms had come to worship. Since Brahms had used to refer to Schumann as master, or "Dominus," the "blessed one who comes in the name of the master" must have been the gentle Clara. This theory is strengthened by a letter of Brahms to Clara on December 30, 1856, in connection with this Concerto, saying: "I am also painting a lovely portrait of you. It is to be the *Adagio.*"

III. *Rondo: Allegro non troppo.* This colossal finale combines the brilliance of a traditional nineteenth-century showpiece with a symphonic weight which almost balances the first movement. The rondo refrain:

serves also as the principal theme of an exuberant conclusion to this powerfully original work.

The Concerto is scored for 2 flutes, 2 oboes, 2 clarinets, 2 bassoons, 4 horns, 2 trumpets, 2 kettledrums, and string choir.

CONCERTO FOR PIANO AND ORCHESTRA, NO. 2, B-FLAT MAJOR, OPUS 83

"I wish I were sending you something different and better than this hasty line, but there's no help for it right now; what I wanted to tell you is that I have written a tiny little piano concerto with a tiny little wisp of a scherzo." This was Brahms's playful way of disclosing to his close friend Elisabeth von Herzogenberg the completion of one of the most gigantic piano concertos ever written.

Brahms's confidential announcement of the new work went to two of the most understanding women in his life: Elisabeth von Herzogenberg and his beloved Clara Schumann, the widow of Robert Schumann. The score, with Brahms's description of it as "a couple of little piano pieces," went to a man on whose artistic understanding Brahms relied more and more: the Viennese surgeon Theodor Billroth.

Elisabeth and Clara replied in humorous kind. Elisabeth was enchanted and thankful at the prospect of the "tiny, tiny piano *Konzerterl* with the tiny, tiny *Scherzerl.*" Clara was overjoyed. "But I don't really trust your word 'little,' " she added. "However I wouldn't mind a bit [if it were little] because in that case I might even be able to play it myself."

Billroth responded with a six-page letter congratulating Brahms on the grandeur of his achievement. This second Piano Concerto, wrote Billroth, compared to Brahms's First as one might compare a mature man to a youth.

It is from Dr. Billroth that we learn much of the background of this Concerto. Like many a German artist from Dürer to Goethe and Richard Wagner, Brahms was mellowed by Italy. He was forty-four when he made his first trip under the friendly guidance of Dr. Billroth. It was spring, and their journey took them as far south as Rome, Naples and, finally, Sicily. On his return to Austria, Brahms sketched the themes of this Concerto on the evening before his birthday, in the little resort town of Pörtschach. It is far from an Italian work, but it does reflect the age-old German nostalgia and affection for the sunlit grace of Italy.

Brahms seems to have put aside his sketches until three years later. Again it was spring. Again he visited Italy. This time as his own guide, he visited Venice, Florence, Siena, Orvieto, and, again, Rome, Naples and Sicily. On his forty-eighth birthday he was back in Vienna and, with the Italian spring once more in his veins, he resumed work on the Concerto. Two months later, on July 7, 1881, the score was finished.

Brahms himself was the soloist at the world premiere in the Redoutensaal of Budapest on November 9, 1881. On the twenty-seventh of the same month, he repeated the Concerto at Meiningen with Hans von Bülow conducting.

During his Italian trip, Brahms had written enthusiastically to a German friend of "the Italian spring turning to summer." A full measure of this vernal strength and warmth seems to have found its way into the score of the B-flat Concerto.

I. *Allegro non troppo.* The beautiful horn call which opens the score is like a magical summons to the other instruments:

As the horns continue the piano responds between their phrases with garlands of *arpeggios.* The woodwinds add a lyric comment and the piano plunges into a solo cadenza. All this has been mere introduction to the main body of the movement. The overall form of the movement is a grandiose expansion of traditional first-movement form, or sonata-allegro form. The exposition presents such a profusion of thematic beauties that they might, in another composer's hands, have been an embarrassment of riches. But Brahms's powerful sense of structure is never overwhelmed by detail.

The central section is a stormy development of these ideas, but still with the chief emphasis on the opening horn call. This same call, in a mellow orchestral harmony, ushers in the return of the opening material. The close is brilliant, with flashing octave trills for the solo piano against fanfare-like reiterations of the horn call theme.

II. *Allegro appassionato.* It is rare for a concerto to include a scherzo, and this one is of symphonic proportions and richness. The principal theme boils upward in a crashing pianistic wave:

while the bass instruments in the depths of the orchestra tug away in the opposite direction. This excitement is succeeded by a plaintive melody for the violins, which is taken up by the piano and developed in a typically Brahmsian rocking, seesaw movement. The rich development of both themes culminates in a heroic D-major "trio" section, after which the opening scherzo material is brought back for a stormy close.

III. *Andante.* The nocturne-like mood of this slow movement is based on the song of a solo cello, a simple eight-measure phrase which begins:

Coming immediately after the stormy scherzo, it brings a serenity that is often close to tears. So poignant is the melody that Brahms returned to it years later for his bittersweet song *"Immer leiser wird mein Schlummer."* So ambiguous the melody, it could have been conceived to illustrate Shelley's words: "Our sweetest songs are those that tell of saddest thought." The melody passes from solo cello to violins to solo piano in a delicately embellished variation.

There is an agitated middle section with shuddering tremolos for the orchestra, and fierce trills and plunging arpeggios for the solo instrument (still another dramatic variation of the opening cello phrase)! Then a hush falls upon the orchestra for a brief but magical dialogue of two clarinets with accompaniment by the piano solo. In conclusion the song of the cello returns, embellished with delicate trills of the piano, rising higher and higher as they fade into silence.

IV. *Allegretto grazioso*. The finale is an unorthodox rondo, a fusion of rondo form with sonata-allegro techniques. Such combinations had, of course, been practiced since Haydn's day, but never with quite the ingenious surprises that greet us here. The principal rondo refrain, a bright, skipping figure for the piano, opens the movement:

This refrain serves to punctuate the middle of the movement and to round it off at the end. It also is a thematic seed which sprouts many fascinating branches as the movement develops. There are two contrasting episodes which share each other's melodies and are richly developed in themselves. The piano part is of the utmost brilliance, particularly in the final return of the rondo refrain where the tempo grows even faster. The conclusion comes with more glittering arpeggios for the piano and a sudden, powerful *crescendo* for the full orchestra.

The orchestra includes 2 flutes, 2 oboes, 2 clarinets, 2 bassoons, 4 horns, 2 trumpets, kettledrums, and the traditional strings.

CONCERTO FOR VIOLIN AND ORCHESTRA, D MAJOR, OPUS 77

Brahms's Violin Concerto has taken its place alongside that of Beethoven as one of the two greatest violin concertos ever written.

Like Beethoven and Mendelssohn before him, Brahms wrote his Violin Concerto with a specific virtuoso performer in mind. And, like them, he asked his virtuoso's criticism in technical matters. Brahms's virtuoso was his old friend Joseph Joachim. On August 22, 1878, Brahms wrote him with characteristic humility: "Now that I have copied it out for you, I hardly remember what I expected you to do with the solo part alone [i.e., without the orchestral score].

"Naturally, I wanted you to correct it—and I didn't want you to have any excuse of any kind: either that the music is too good [to be changed] or that the whole score isn't worth the trouble. But I shall be satisfied if you just write me a word or two, and perhaps write a word here and there in the music, like 'difficult,' 'awkward,' 'impossible,' etc."

Joachim took great pains going over the solo part, pointing out chiefly technical details which he felt should be changed. Brahms listened solemnly and then changed almost nothing but bow markings and fingerings.

Brahms had originally conceived his Violin Concerto in four movements, as he did his Second Piano Concerto. But he finally deleted the Scherzo he had planned and revised his original slow movement. "The middle movements have gone," wrote Brahms, "and of course they were the best! But I have written a poor *adagio* for it." This was Brahms's customary self-deprecating way of describing one of his warmest and most thoughtful slow movements.

The Romantic concerto tradition included a strong component of show. Like the Schumanns (both Robert and Clara), from whom he learned so much, Brahms frowned on mere virtuoso display. He never hesitated to write music that was difficult to play, either in his piano concertos or in this Violin Concerto. But he never indulged in fireworks for their own sake.

The Concerto was completed during the summer and fall of 1878 at a charming little out-of-the-way Austrian village, Pörtschach, on Lake Wörth. It was dedicated to Joachim, who was the soloist in the first performance at a Gewandhaus concert in Leipzig on New Year's Day of 1879. Brahms conducted. After the premiere, but before the Concerto was published the following October, Joachim persuaded Brahms to make some further changes in the score.

I. *Allegro non troppo.* A sober warmth pervades the opening, in which Brahms harks back to Classical models by writing a long orchestral introduction, almost a first exposition. The very first measures present the main theme of the movement in the low strings and bassoons to which the horns soon add a touch of warmth:

The solo violin makes its entrance with a flourish and a splash of bravura, over forty measures of it, before settling down to the solo exposition. Of the second group of lyric themes, the following is particularly beguiling, the very essence of Romantic yearning:

II. *Adagio.* The serene opening theme for oboe is related to the opening theme of the first movement. This movement is remarkable for the profusion of delicate tracery for the solo violin and its imaginative embellishment of the main melodic material.

III. *Allegro giocoso, ma non troppo vivace.* The finale is an exuberant rondo with a Hungarian-tinged refrain:

In this refrain some musicians believe they hear an added homage to the Hungarian-born Joachim. It abounds in double stops and other brilliant effects, but none of them for mere show.

Brahms's Violin Concerto is scored for 2 flutes, 2 oboes, 2 clarinets, 2 bassoons, 4 horns, 2 trumpets, kettledrums, and the traditional string choir.

CONCERTO FOR VIOLIN, VIOLONCELLO, AND ORCHESTRA, A MINOR, OPUS 102

This grave and beautiful score, Brahms's last orchestral work, seems to have been composed in part with the intention of bringing about a reconciliation between Brahms himself and his old friend, the Hungarian violinist Joseph Joachim.

When the two men first met, Brahms was a little-known twenty-year-old and Joachim a twenty-two-year-old virtuoso of international renown. An instant artistic sympathy between the two soon developed into a strong personal bond. The friendship with Joachim had grown and deepened over a period of nearly thrity years, only to come to a painful end at the time of Joachim's divorce. Brahms believed Joachim's wife to be innocent of the infidelity with which she was charged and said so in a letter which, to Brahms's surprise, was used as evidence at the trial. Joachim considered that Brahms had betrayed their friendship and broke off all relations. Brahms suffered from the break, especially because, as he grew older, he found it harder and harder to make and keep simple, warm personal relationships.

In 1887 Brahms sent a postcard to Joachim, to whom he had not spoken for years, with the characteristically shy, almost timid query: "I should like to send you some news of an artistic nature which I heartily hope might more or less interest you." Joachim replied by return mail saying that he was anxiously awaiting the news, adding: "I hope you are going to tell me about a new work, for I have read and played your latest works with real delight."

With evident relief Brahms replied on July 24:

Your friendly message makes my confession all the more pleasant!

But be prepared for a little shock. I have been unable to resist the ideas that have been occurring to me for a concerto for *violin and cello*, much as I have tried to talk myself out of it.

Now, the only thing that really interests me about this is the question of what your attitude toward it may be. Above all, I beg you, with heartfelt friendliness not to be embarrassed about your opinion. If you send me a card which simply says: "Not interested [*Ich verzichte*]," that will be quite sufficient for me, and I shall know what to do.

If not, I shall start asking questions: "Would you care to see a sample of it?" I am in the middle of copying the solo parts; would you and Hausmann [Robert Hausmann, a well-known cellist and member of the Joachim String Quartet] take the trouble to see if they are playable? Would you consider trying the work over somewhere with Hausmann and with me at the piano, and later, in whatever town you prefer, with an orchestra and ourselves?

Please send me a line and I repeat that I—but perhaps you will send me the above-mentioned card after you have seen the sample!

I will not say out loud and in detail what I hope in secret.

But give my kindest regards to Hausmann . . .

The increasingly cordial exchange of letters was followed by exchanges of music. By the end of the month Joachim and Hausmann had gone over their parts; Joachim returned the music to Brahms and wrote:

I have just mailed the parts back to you with a few suggestions for unimportant changes; I hope they may prove acceptable. On the whole it seems extremely playable. Now what do we do? Both Hausmann and I . . . are most anxious to go on with it and await your suggestions. Where do you think we should have a rehearsal, first of all with piano? . . . Be assured that Hausmann and I are always ready to fulfill any wish of yours with the greatest pleasure.

Although Joachim spoke only of unimportant changes, his suggestions were far from unimportant in the aggregate. The manuscript shows many alterations. In certain cases, Brahms agreed with Joachim's criticism, but not with his solution, adopting instead a third version of his own. In one case, it was a fourth version which finally reached print. Alterations continued during the early rehearsals. In view of early criticisms of the work as "unplayable," it is interesting to see that the revisions during rehearsal made the solo parts more difficult, not easier.

The first performance of the Double Concerto took place soon after it was completed, at a private concert in Baden-Baden under the direction of Brahms with Joachim and Hausmann as soloists. The public premiere with the same three men was presented at Cologne on October 18, 1887. The score was published the following year with the dedication "To him for whom it was written: Joseph Joachim."

This Double Concerto took longer to achieve popularity and it still is more rarely played than the other Brahms concertos—partly perhaps because two soloists must share the limelight. And there is little limelight to share, for by the time he wrote this last of his orchestral works, Brahms was bored by external glitter. He sought a more inward, deeper beauty tinged with exaltation in the slow movement and with resignation even in the gay finale.

I. *Allegro.* It is the darker tone of the cello, rather than the brilliant violin, which responds to the opening phrase of the orchestra. The cello continues alone in a rhapsodic cadenza-like passage. Eventually it is joined by the solo violin and their double cadenza leads, with increasing exuberance, to a full orchestral statement of the principal theme: an assertive figure with a characteristically Brahmsian mixture of dotted rhythms and triplets. The second important theme, a gently rocking melody, is introduced *dolce* by the cello and echoed by the solo violin.

It is often said that this Double Concerto recalls the practice of the older Baroque *concerto grosso,* in which a small group of solo instruments alternated and contrasted with the full orchestra. In fact, there is almost no connection with the style, form, technique or emotional expression of the *concerto grosso.* Brahms's Double Concerto is much closer to the standard Romantic solo concerto of the nineteenth century, except that the solo has become a duet. The first movement is a richly developed traditional sonata-allegro form in true symphonic style.

II. *Andante.* One of Brahms's greatest and most laconic slow movements opens with a melody of melancholy, almost somber cast. The first four notes are announced very slowly by the orchestral winds as a sort of motto, which opens and closes the movement. The melody proper is sung by the solo violin and cello together but at a distance of an octave from each other, much as if a male and female voice were joined:

The mixed resonance has a striking color of its own, particularly when reinforced later on by all the orchestral violins and cellos. Other melodies, some more gentle and plaintive, also play a role, but the first theme dominates the movement with its individual and unforgettable beauty.

III. *Vivace non troppo.* The mood of subdued gaiety with which this finale begins is set by the solo cello with a lilting dance-like figure:

The entire melody is repeated by the solo violin and soon after by a thundering *tutti*. The Hungarian rondo-refrain character of the melody suggests rondo form. But this finale, like the first movement, is cast in clear, traditional sonata-allegro form. The development of the dance-like theme quoted above has almost the manner of an airy scherzo. The return of the chief themes is altered with many a subtle and delightful touch.

The Concerto is scored for pairs of flutes, oboes, clarinets, bassoons; 4 horns, two trumpets, kettledrums, and the usual strings.

ACADEMIC FESTIVAL OVERTURE

"A jolly potpourri of student songs à la Suppe" was Brahms's own description of his "Academic Festival" Overture. His friend and biographer Max Kalbeck asked ironically whether Brahms had also included the boisterous "Freshman Ride," or "*Fuchsenritt.*" Brahms answered, "Yes, indeed!" Kalbeck was shocked, and added that he could hardly imagine using such a tune for an academic homage to the stiffly formal *Rector magnificus* of the University of Breslau. "And that" retorted the composer, "would be entirely superfluous!"

Brahms did not feel especially reverential when the University conferred the honorary doctoral degree upon him in March, 1879. In fact, he thought a postcard sufficient acknowledgment—that is, until his friend, Bernhard Scholz, the conductor of the subscription concerts in Breslau, indicated that the University would expect him to express his gratitude in musical form: a "*Doktor-Symphonie*" perhaps, or "at least a solemn song."

Brahms was willing enough. He had not been a university man himself, but he could draw on his memories of the convival student life he had shared with his violinist friend Joseph Joachim and others during his stay many years earlier in the university town of Göttingen. He centered his Overture on four traditional German student songs, integrating them with subtly related themes of his own.

"Jolly potpourri" does describe the spirit of this music. But, as so often with Brahms, the simple manner conceals masterly cunning. In shape the Overture is a perfectly orthodox, traditional (not to say, academic) first-movement sonata-allegro with imaginative introduction and a very grand coda. Brahms was much given to humorous belittling of his own masterpieces and this may have been one reason for his word, "potpourri." Another was that he disliked the title "Academic Festival" Overture—at least enough to ask his friend Scholz if he couldn't think up a better one. Scholz couldn't either.

Composed during 1880, the Overture was first performed at Breslau on January 4, 1881, in the presence of the University Rector, Senate, and the Faculty of Philosophy, under the direction of Brahms himself.

The introduction begins softly, with premonitory mutterings in the strings: thematic fragments anticipating the principal theme of the Overture as well as the first student song which forms the climax and crown of the introduction. "*Wir hatten gebauet ein staatliches Haus*" ("We Had Built a Stately House") was a nostalgic lament for the glorious days of the student associations *(Burschenschaften)*, which played a glamorous role in the early nineteenth-century Wars of Liberation; only to be banned by the reactionary German governments of the Metternich era. This hymn-like tune wells up softly in solemn horn and trumpet tone, swelling gradually as it merges into the vigorous main section of the Overture:

The principal theme, marked *Un poco maestoso*, is a quickened rhythmic fragment from the "Stately House," but so sharply profiled here that it seems entirely new. The next two student songs, both said to date from the eighteenth century, are the *"Hochfeierlicher Landesvater"* ("Most Solemn Song to the Father of the Country") and *"Fuchsenritt,"* a freshman initiation ditty beginning, *"Was kommt dort von der Höh'?"* ("What Comes There from on High?"). The first song appears as a flowing melody for second violins, the second as a jocular duet for two bassoons echoed by a smashing orchestral *tutti*. Together these two songs form the contrast section of traditional first-movement form.

A brief development leads to a reprise of the principal themes, merging at last into an exhilarating coda built on the joyous *"Gaudeamus igitur,"* the first stanza of which says, to the tune printed below:

Gaudeamus igitur,	Let us now enjoy ourselves,
Juvenes dum sumus;	While we are still young;
Gaudeamus igitur,	Let us now enjoy ourselves,
Juvenes dum sumus;	While we are still young;
Post jucundem juventutem,	For when golden youth has fled,
Post molestam senectutem,	And in age our joys are dead,
Nos habebit humus,	Then the dust doth claim us,
Nos habebit humus.	Then the dust doth claim us.

The combined splendor of brass and woodwind choirs, decked out with flashing scales of the violins brings Brahms's "potpourri" to a conclusion of considerable majesty.

The orchestra, unusually large for Brahms, calls for piccolo, 2 flutes, 2 oboes, 2 clarinets, 2 bassoons, contrabassoon, 4 horns, 3 trumpets, 3 trombones, bass tuba, kettledrums, bass drum, cymbals, triangle, and the traditional strings.

TRAGIC OVERTURE, OPUS 81

While Brahms was composing his carefree "Academic Festival" Overture at the summer resort of Bad Ischl, he felt impelled—for no clear reason—to write a serious companion piece. "I could not refuse my melancholy nature the satisfaction of composing an overture for a tragedy," he wrote to his friend, the publisher Simrock. To another friend, Carl Reinecke, he wrote: "One of them weeps, the other laughs."

The one that "weeps" is the "Tragic" Overture. The question whether it is really tragic or not, needn't bother us any longer than it did the composer. Brahms himself did not much like the title and he settled upon it only because neither he nor his friends, whom he asked for suggestions, could think of a better one. We have Brahms's word for it that when he composed the Overture, during the summer of 1880, he had no stage work in mind, nor was he inspired by any tragedy of a personal or impersonal nature. In fact some seventy or eighty measures of the exposition, had been sketched way back in the late 1860s, for what project we do not know.

The Overture opens *Allegro non troppo* with two sharp chords which later play a thematic role. This launches a rather stark, unaccompanied melodic arch which is the Overture's principal subject:

The Overture is cast in very free sonata form. The stern opening is spun out at length, intensifying the melancholy of which Brahms himself spoke. Not until rather late does he introduce a more flowing, lyrical second theme. The vigorous conclusion of this exposition is the section which Brahms had composed over a decade earlier. A short but poignant development section starts with the slackening of tempo: *Molto più moderato.* Two oboes take up a prominent dotted rhythm from the exposition, transforming it into a sad little march tune of almost Schubertian pathos. The reprise of the basic thematic material is very free.

After the world premiere of the "Tragic" Overture, which was presented by the Vienna Philharmonic on December 26, 1880, under the direction of Hans Richter, Brahms revised the score at Bad Ischl in the summer of 1881. The final version is scored for piccolo, 2 flutes, 2 oboes, 2 clarinets, 2 bassoons, 4 horns, 2 trumpets, 3 trombones, bass tuba, kettledrums, and the usual strings.

SERENADE NO. 1, D MAJOR, OPUS 11

Compared to the D-minor storms of Brahms's Piano Concerto, his First Serenade seems a simple pastorale, an innocent country idyll. And in part it was just that. Brahms began it as a three-movement octet, inspired by his love of Mozart's and Haydn's serenades and by his delight in their performances by the orchestra of the city where he held his first official position. This was the little city of Detmold, residence of the Prince of Detmold and his music-loving wife, Princess Fredericke. For the last four months of each year (1856 to 1859) Brahms was Detmold Court Pianist, conductor of the local choral society, and piano teacher to the Princess. His salary as court musician supported him modestly for the whole year. Better still: his Detmold functions left him time for composing.

An added attraction and a source of spiritual strength for the nature-loving Brahms was the neighboring Teutoburger forest. After the emotional stress of the crisis years of Schumann's insanity and death, long walks in these woods helped Brahms to regain his calm. Each year he returned to the woods with increasing affection. Returning to Detmold in the fall of 1859, where the premiere of the Serenade was scheduled for late in the year, Brahms wrote his Aunt Auguste:

> I felt odd when I saw these beautiful wooded heights again and walked into the marvelous forest. I have not seen such beautiful nature for a whole year, and in that time much has changed. But I was quite ecstatic: I thought only music.
>
> I am in love with music, I love music, I think of nothing but music and of other things only when they make music more beautiful to me. You just watch: I'm going to write love songs again, and not to A—— Z——, but to music itself.

The original octet version of the Serenade was composed with members of that Orchestra in mind and was completed in 1858 in time for a late-summer tryout before a group of friends, including Clara Schumann, who were vacationing in the university town of Göttingen. Brahms, at twenty-five, was not yet fully master of instrumentation; Clara is said to have declared prophetically that only a rearrangement for full orchestra could do justice to the wealth of attractive ideas in the Serenade. Before the summer was over, Brahms's friend, the great violinist Joachim, arrived in Göttingen. When Joachim suggested that a modest chamber orchestra expansion of the score would be appropriate, Brahms took his advice, and for good measure, added three shorter movements, bringing the total to six.

The first performance of this revision was conducted by Joachim himself at a gala concert in Hamburg on March 28, 1859. The citizens of Brahms's native city had not hitherto distinguished themselves by their enthusiasm for his works, but on this occasion they unbent, in part, perhaps, because of their enthusiasm for Joachim. In any case, Brahms was happy. The Serenade, he wrote to Clara Schumann, "really seemed to reach the audience yesterday. The applause continued until I showed myself on the platform. You would scarcely have known the Hamburgers."

But Brahms was soon dissatisfied with what he dubbed this "halfbreed" version, *(Zwittergestalt)* and finally came around to Clara's point of view. His final rearrangement of the Serenade, now for large orchestra, was performed for the first time anywhere at the command of King George of Hanover at a Hanover subscription concert on March 3, 1860, again under the direction of Joachim.

I. *Allegro molto.* The first and most elaborate movement of the Serenade is based on a theme which frankly and charmingly proclaims Brahms's affection for the genius of Haydn. Over a peasant-style drone bass (open fifths of violas and cellos) a solo horn chants a tune recalling the finale of Haydn's D-major Symphony, No. 104:

A jaunty clarinet takes up the strain, in light, divertimento style, as does a solo oboe. A brilliant *tutti* dominated by horns, trumpets and kettledrums proclaims the theme again before Brahms permits a gracefully arching second theme and a vigorous triplet closing figure to round off his exposition.

An adventurous development section in symphonic style leads to a traditional recapitulation of the principal themes and an unconventional coda, full of Haydnish surprises.

II. *Scherzo: Allegro non troppo.* The first of the Serenade's two scherzos is delicate, subtle, complex in its rhythms and harmonies—typical of Brahms when he refuses to woo the listener with facile tunes, as if he were too shy to display his riches openly. After a vigorously contrasting trio, *Poco più moto,* there follows a traditional repeat of the opening section.

III. *Adagio non troppo.* For many lovers of this Serenade the *Adagio* is the crown of the work. True to the traditional character of many an eighteenth-century open-air serenade, or *Nachtmusik,* this movement is rich in the woodwind colors: solos for clarinet, flute, French horn (a courtesy member of the woodwind choir), oboe and even bassoon, as well as the most imaginative combinations. For the most part the strings serve as framework and background for the winds, although one of the high points of the movement is an impassioned duet between the first violin and cello sections.

IV. *Menuetto 1; Menuetto 2.* The transparency of this minuet movement brings us close to the Mozartean grace Brahms so admired, yet without losing its basically Romantic character. It is like a bit of eighteenth-century Rococo heard with the nostaglic ears of a later age. At the first performance in Vienna, it beguiled the much-feared critic of the *Freie Presse,* Eduard Hanslick, who wrote: "The first minuet seems to us the pearl of the work and perhaps the prettiest movement as yet written by Brahms. The instrumental coloring and the grace of the melody give it the characteristic of night music, and it is full of moonlight and the scent of lilac."

V. *Scherzo: Allegro.* The burly second scherzo opens with a duet for solo horn and cello section which Brahms seems to have intended as a double homage to Haydn *and* Beethoven:

In the following four measures the horn echoes a catchy phrase from the scherzo (trio section) of Beethoven's Second Symphony:

Conscious or not, the affinity with the spirit of the late Haydn and early Beethoven is clear enough. The marvel is that Brahms can be drawn so close to them without for an instant losing his own individuality.

VI. *Rondo: Allegro.* The finale is a rondo incorporating traits of the traditional sonata-allegro form, a combination which Haydn particularly loved and which he may well have invented. But the opening refrain has a heavy bearish quality which is very Brahmsian and remote from the elegance and clarity of Haydn. Two lyric episodes are framed by the rhythms of the refrain, after which a Romantic hush precedes the brilliant concluding page.

The D-major Serenade is scored for 2 flutes, 2 oboes, 2 clarinets, 2 bassoons, 4 horns, 2 trumpets, kettledrums, and the traditional string choir.

SERENADE NO. 2, A MAJOR, OPUS 16

New York, of all unlikely cities, seems to have pioneered in performing the music of Brahms when he was very young and still little known outside of his native city of Hamburg. Brahms was only twenty-two when the world premiere of his chamber work, his B-major Trio, Opus 8, was presented in New York on November 27, 1855, at the first of William Mason's renowned chamber music concerts. The first performance of any Brahms orchestral work outside of Hamburg, Hanover or Leipzig, was presented by the New York Philharmonic on February 1, 1862. The work was Brahms's Second Serenade which he had completed in 1859 and published late in 1860.

Brahms composed both of his serenades in the little city of Detmold, the residence city of the Princes of Detmold, where he held his first official position. Both are gentle scores, so modest in physical volume of sound, so tender, idyllic in mood, that they suggested a conscious reaction against the cyclopean drama of his preceding masterpiece, the D-minor Piano Concerto, which took shape during the crisis years of Schumann's insanity and death and Brahms's frustrated love for Clara Schumann.

For September 13, 1859, Clara's birthday, Brahms sent her the second and third movements of the A-major Serenade, writing: "I am looking forward to hearing from you at last about the Adagio for the new Serenade, I hope you will write without the slightest constraint and give full vent to your opinions." Eight days later Clara replied: "What shall I say about the Adagio? . . . I can find no words to express the joy it has given me and yet you want me to write at length! It is difficult for me to analyze what I feel; I have to try to think of something extremely beautiful, something which gives me the greatest pleasure, perhaps as if I were looking at the stamens of a beautiful flower one by one. It is incredibly beautiful! . . . The whole piece has something churchly about it, it could almost be a *[Kyrie] eleison*. My dear Johannes, I'm sure you know that I can feel this better than I can express it in words. The Minuet is very charming (a bit Haydnish), and the oboe in the Trio—I look forward so much to hearing it, it must sound very special with its soaring melody; I could almost have guessed what was coming."

Brahms, who so often had torturing doubts as to the value of his new works, seems to have enjoyed the Second Serenade almost as much as Clara. Later that spring, he wrote to his friend, the violinst Joachim: "I have just been arranging my Second Serenade for four hands. Don't laugh! I had the greatest joy in it. I have seldom written musical notes with such extreme pleasure. The tones permeated my being so gently and so lovingly that I was delighted through and through."

The first performance was given by the Hamburg Philharmonic under the composer's direction on February 10, 1860. Three years later, after Brahms had moved to Vienna, the Second Serenade helped establish him in public favor there. But not without a struggle. At rehearsals the players of the Vienna Philharmonic complained of the exorbitant difficulty of many of the passages and at the final rehearsal there was open mutiny. The first clarinetist suddenly stood up and in the name of the other players announced their refusal to perform the score. The conductor, Otto Dessoff, white with anger, replied by laying down his baton and declaring his resignation. The concert master, one of the most celebrated musicians in Vienna, and the almost equally illustrious first flutist followed the conductor and this decided the conflict. The rebels gave way, the performance took place as announced on March 8, 1863 (one year later than the New York performance) and was a tremendous success. The influential critic Eduard Hanslick wrote: ". . . [Brahms] has showed himself

. . . an independent, original individual, a finely organized, true, musical nature, an artist ripening toward mastery by means of unwearied, conscious endeavor. His A major Serenade is the younger, tender sister of the one in D lately produced by the *Gesellschaft [der Musikfreunde]* and is conceived in the same peaceful, dreamy garden mood. . . . The work had an extremely favorable reception. The hearty applause became proportionately greater at the close as the modest composer made himself even smaller in his seat in the gallery."

Perhaps the most striking quality of the Second Serenade is its tone color, which is due chiefly to the omission of violins. The violas, as the highest string instruments, plus cellos and double basses, give a strikingly rich but sober hue to the orchestra, which is of chamber proportions. ("Eight or more violas, six violoncellos, four double basses or something like that, seem good to me," wrote Brahms to a later conductor. "And of course it depends on how they play.") In 1875 Brahms revised some details of the orchestration. Karl Geiringer who examined Brahms's own copy preserved in the library of the Gesellschaft der Musikfreunde, reports that the original version, in which Brahms entered his revisions, used the same instruments; 2 flutes, 2 oboes, 2 clarinets, 2 bassoons, 2 horns, violas, cellos, and string basses. The Serenade is in five movements.

I. *Allegro moderato.* A typically Brahmsian seesawing melody, alternately rising and falling, launches the first movement with softly glowing clarinet tone. The winds are rounded out with bassoons, more mellow horns, and the silvery gleaming tone of flutes. When the strings join in with the principal theme we hear first only violas and cellos, the double basses being held in reserve. The second principal theme, a gently rocking figure for the two clarinets in parallel thirds lingers in the memory. The rocking motion of the two principal themes is taken up and developed, with rhythmic changes in the central section, to which the basic thematic material returns, fading at last into silence.

II. *Scherzo: Vivace.* The bouncing principal scherzo theme is enlivened by a characteristic Brahmsian cross-play of two beats against three. Woodwind tones dominate the contrasting trio section after which the opening returns and the whole is rounded off by a brief coda built on the principal theme.

III. *Adagio non troppo.* The slow movement, which is not only the center, but the crown of the work, is permeated by an obstinately recurring, or *ostinato* theme heard first at the bottom of the orchestra in bare octaves of the entire string body:

In the contrasting middle section of this movement the sensuous song of the woodwinds is enriched with the glow of two French horns:

In the concluding section, when the opening *ostinato* figure returns in the violas it is answered by a delicate contrapuntal web of melodies, each derived from the *ostinato,* upside-down or right side up, sometimes in flowing legato, sometimes in detached notes.

IV. *Quasi Menuetto.* Almost, but not quite a minuet, the fourth movement supplies a symmetrical balance to the scherzo. Again a gently rocking principal melody is suddenly altered in the central section after which the opening material returns.

V. *Rondo: Allegro.* Two lightfooted clarinets execute the dance-like principal theme, which serves not only as the refrain of the Rondo, but also as the principal theme of a sonata-allegro form:

The small rondo-sonata combination is filled with high spirits and delicate humor. The more lyric second theme is sung by a solo oboe. This leads to an almost symphonic development of all the themes heard so far, the whole being dominated by the rondo refrain, sometimes heard at half speed as a sentimental duet for clarinets, sometimes with its original speed heightened by little embellishments. A brief coda ends the movement in a rush of brilliance.

SYMPHONY NO. 1, C MINOR, OPUS 68

Brahms's early friends and admirers (like his admirers today) felt that he was a born symphonist. Brahms was only twenty-one when Robert Schumann wrote to their mutual friend Joachim: "But where is Johannes? Is he flying high or only under the flowers? Is he not yet ready to let drums and trumpets sound? He should always keep in mind the beginning of the Beethoven symphonies; he should try to make something like them. The beginning is the main thing; if only one makes the beginning, then the end comes of itself."

But Brahms held back. "I shall never write a symphony," he said to his conductor-friend Hermann Levi. "You have no idea how the likes of us feel when we hear the tramp of a giant like *him* behind us." By "him" Brahms meant Beethoven. To a composer as reverent as Brahms, the works of Beethoven could be a crushing heritage.

Brahms was twenty-one when he heard Beethoven's Ninth Symphony for the first time. It moved him so deeply that he decided to attempt a symphony himself in the same key of D minor. He struggled long with the sketches. But it was not to be. The first two movements of the intended symphony were finally incorporated into his D-minor Piano Concerto, and the third movement was incorporated into his "German" Requiem.

We do not know exactly when Brahms began the sketches for the C minor Symphony. As a young man he had been in the habit of jotting down musical thoughts whenever they occurred to him and often he worked on several compositions at the same time. Sometimes a composition grew and changed for many years before taking its final form. Max Kalbeck, the famous Brahms biographer, believed that the germ of the First Symphony dated from 1855.

By 1862, two of Brahms's friends saw an early version of the first movement. One of them was his beloved Clara Schumann. Karl Geiringer believes that the storm mood of the opening movement reflected the conflict in Brahms's emotions between his love and admiration for Robert Schumann and his unadmitted love for Schumann's wife Clara. Whatever the reasons, it was fourteen years more before the First Symphony was completed (1876). The first performance was given at Karlsruhe on November 4 of that year. Brahms was in the audience, and a few days later he himself conducted the Symphony at Mannheim.

I. *Un poco sostenuto; Allegro.* Curiously enough, the tremendous surging introduction, one of the most impressive parts of the Symphony, was an afterthought. Over the deep insistent pounding of the kettledrum there rises a gigantic procession of indistinct figures which crystallize later into the chief themes of the first movement. The main part of the movement, the *Allegro,* begins stormily with a typical Brahmsian theme that bounds upward, surpassing the octave range, then hesitating like a breaking wave before plunging downward again:

II. *Andante sostenuto.* The placid, melancholy opening of the second movement has a long melodic line. It rises to an impassioned climax with the violins soaring at the top of the orchestra while strong double basses tug away in the depths. After brief, plaintive interludes in the woodwinds, and several dramatic surprises, the orchestra returns to the meditative pathos with which the movement began.

III. *Un poco allegretto e grazioso.* Instead of the traditional scherzo, Brahms wrote a gracefully flowing, song-like movement. With its emphasis on the soft woodwind colors, especially clarinet and flute, this movement often recalls the Classical serenades and divertimentos which Brahms knew and loved so well.

IV. *Adagio; allegro non troppo, ma con brio.* The finale has a rich and poetic introduction. It opens with a deeply melancholy, minor transformation of what is to become the main theme of this movement:

This is followed by ominous *pizzicato* pluckings of the string instruments at the bottom of the orchestra. They move slowly at first, and then faster, until, as in a rush of panic, they infect the whole orchestra with their agitation. The excitement comes to an abrupt end with a crashing roll of drums followed by one of the most colorful contrasts in all Brahms: through the rainbow shimmering of high string instruments, we hear the peaceful melody of a solo horn, the echo of a shepherd's horn that Brahms had heard in the alpine country, where he loved to spend his summers. Then the horn melody reappears in the silvery tones of the flute in the upper reaches of the orchestra. Then still another contrast: a soft, majestic chorale for the brass instruments alone. All this has been introduction.

The main body of the finale begins with a bold, swinging theme that recalls the finale of Beethoven's Ninth Symphony:

When a friend pointed this out to Brahms, he answered: "Any fool can see that!" The resemblance is beside the point. Brahms was using one word from Beethoven's vocabulary to say something very different. This and several subsidiary themes are developed in traditional symphonic form, but without the usual development section. It is as if the development had all taken place in the great introduction and now the tension of the symphonic drama were too great for any digression. The gathering momentum finds its outlet in a headlong *presto.* This is interrupted to bring back the great chorale of the introduction with the full splendor of *fortissimo* brass. And then the Symphony sweeps on to its exultant close.

The First Symphony is scored for 2 flutes, 2 clarinets, 2 bassoons, 1 contrabassoon, 4 horns, 2 trumpets, kettledrums, and the customary strings.

SYMPHONY NO. 2, D MAJOR, OPUS 73

Brahms's sunlit Second Symphony is as warmly lyric as his First had been stormy and dramatic. There was more than one reason for this. Having taken some fifteen to twenty years to complete his First Symphony, he may have felt that he had agonized enough for several symphonies. But to his friends he attributed the new ease and grace of the melodies to the charms of the Austrian summer resort he had chosen.

"Pörtschach is an exquisite spot," wrote Brahms from the little village on Lake Wörth, where he was composing, "and I have found a lovely, and apparently, pleasant abode in the Castle! You may tell everybody just this; it will impress them. But I may add in parentheses that I have only two rooms in the housekeeper's quarters. They could not get my piano up the stairs, it would have burst the walls."

The longer Brahms stayed, the more he loved the tiny town and the countryside of Lake Wörth. As the work progressed, Brahms enjoyed teasing his friends about the character of the new score. "I do not know whether I have a pretty symphony; I must inquire of clever persons," he wrote to his friend Dr. Billroth, the famous Viennese surgeon and music patron. To his dear friend Elisabeth von Herzogenberg he wrote that the new work was not really a full-fledged symphony but only a little *sinfonia,* adding that there would therefore be no need to play it for her beforehand. "You have only to sit down at the piano," he added with his usual self-deprecating humor, "and with your little feet on both pedals alternatingly, strike the chord of F minor several times in succession, first in the treble, then in the bass, *fortissimo* and *pianissimo,* and you will gradually get a vivid impression of my 'latest.' " The day before the premiere of the Symphony in Vienna, he wrote Frau von Herzogenberg that the orchestra would perform the score with crape bands on their sleeves, "because of its dirgelike effect." When published, he added, the music would have a black border.

Completed in the fall of 1877, the Symphony was first performed by the Vienna Philharmonic, under the direction of Hans Richter, on December 30 of the same year. The second performance was conducted by Brahms himself on the following January 10 at the Gewandhaus of Leipzig.

I. *Allegro non troppo.* In contrast to the heroic opening of Brahms's First Symphony, the Second begins in a quiet, lyric vein, with just the profusion of melody that Brahms had reported finding at Pörtschach. In the very opening bars we hear a brief motive or motto, a sort of melodic kernel, from the first three notes of which many later melodies derive:

Here, for example, is the flowing second theme which Brahms introduces some fifty bars later, a lyric expansion of the opening motto:

Many other rhythmic and melodic transformations of this figure occur in the course of this movement, and we will hear it echoed in later movements, especially in the third and the finale.

II. *Adagio non troppo.* The basically melodic character of the whole Symphony is emphasized in this profound slow movement. It is a simple three-part A-B-A structure, although the return of the A is slightly disguised as a variation.

III. *Allegretto grazioso, quasi andantino.* Instead of the traditionally fast and vigorous scherzo, Brahms often preferred a more relaxed tempo for his third movement. In this Symphony, he keeps the scherzo form, with three refrains separated by two contrasting episodes. But the tempo has an easy lilt, close to the old-fashioned minuet. The two episodes, which almost recall the gossamer scherzo of Mendelssohn's *Midsummer Night's Dream,* are fanciful variations of the principal melody.

IV. *Allegro con spirito.* As Beethoven had so often done, Brahms makes his finale the climax of the Symphony. The opening theme, with its reference to the motto of the first movement, reinforces the strong structural interrelationships of his score:

This is only one of the more obvious examples of the thematic threads that run from one movement to another, strengthening and enriching the score with an art that conceals art. This finale is the most nearly heroic of the four movements, but for all its power and dynamism it preserves the basically lyrical character of the Symphony.

The Second Symphony is scored for 2 flutes, 2 oboes, 2 clarinets, 2 bassoons, 4 horns, 2 trumpets, 3 trombones, bass tuba, kettledrums, and the customary strings.

SYMPHONY NO. 3, F MAJOR, OPUS 90

An especially genial warmth pervades the whole of Brahms's F-major Symphony, rising in the first and final movements to climaxes of real passion. The Symphony was completed during the summer of 1883 when Brahms had just turned fifty. Many of the songs which Brahms wrote at this time express such ardent feelings that Brahms's old friend Dr. Billroth wrote him: "If these are really new, you must be in the grip of such a strong and wholesome midsummer passion as is in keeping with your indestructible, healthy nature. I believe there is something behind this. So much the better; one doesn't choose such words and write such songs out of the mere habit of composing. All the more wonderful for you! And for us!"

Was Brahms's old friend deceiving himself? It is easy to reject the whole idea as Romantic nonsense. But before we dismiss it entirely, it is well to remember that the fifty-year-old Brahms apparently *had* fallen in love with a much younger woman whom he had met in January 1883.

Hermine Spiess, although twenty-six years old, is said to have had a contralto voice equal in beauty to any of her time. Already she surpassed most of her contemporaries in her interpretation of *Lieder*. Her power of emotional projection was so intense that experienced impresarios tried to persuade her to go into opera. But her only interest was in the world of the art song, and for her Brahms was already a figure of worship. How far the mutual attraction may have gone we may never know although Hermine never concealed her *"Johannes Passion."* Brahms, on the other hand, who normally chose to spend his summers in a rural retreat among the Austrian mountains or lakes, decided to spend the summer of 1883 in Wiesbaden, where Hermine lived. It was here that he did the bulk of the work on his Third Symphony.

Like most of his symphonies, the Third is permeated by a melodic motto almost too brief to be called a theme. In this case it consists of three notes which not only open the Symphony but are frequently woven unobtrusively into its texture and return with dramatic emphasis at crucial moments in the later movements:

I. *Allegro con brio.* The motto (in the guise of the three stern chords of the brass and woodwinds) introduces the sweeping principal theme of the first movement:

While the above theme is sung *passionato* by the violins, the motto supplies the harmonic foundation deep in the double basses. An intimate second theme, an engaging series of melodic curlicues, is played *grazioso* by a solo clarinet. There is a brief development. The return of the original thematic material is heralded by the appearance of the motto, transformed into a warmly nostalgic melody in the soft tones of a solo French horn.

II. *Andante.* The almost Olympian melodic grace and poise of the second movement recall the spirit if not the letter of Mozart. The motto, in lyric form, is subtly woven into the fabric of this serene movement from its fourth measure onward.

III. *Poco allegretto.* This is the relaxed tempo which Brahms preferred to the more traditional scherzo in three of his four symphonies. The tempo is complemented by a delicate chamber music texture in the orchestra. There is a German proverb, "Restraint is the mark of a master" (*"In der Beschränkung zeigt sich der Meister").* Brahms would have agreed with that. This modest movement is in simple three part form: ABA. Brahms varies the return of the first A section by the simple device of reorchestrating it. For example, the opening phrase of the movement, originally announced by the cellos, is given at its return to the French horn.

IV. *Allegro.* The finale is the most dramatic of the four movements and the climax of the entire Symphony. This shift of emphasis from the first to the last movement is a device which Brahms took over from his model, Beethoven. The movement begins *sotto voce,* with barely restrained excitement:

Later it rises to a passion of agitation and rhythmic complexity. But first it is opposed by a broadly lyric theme chanted by the entire cello section, reinforced by the mellow tone of a solo horn:

Peace is not restored until we reach the wonderful coda in which the motto returns, purged now of the earlier stress. Its final appearances are again melodic: in the oboe, then the French horn and at the very last, floating above the orchestral *tutti,* in the soft tones of the flute. As the flute reaches the last and highest tone of the motto, the first theme of the first movement shimmers softly in the first violins, and the Symphony ends *pianissimo.*

The Third Symphony, completed during the summer of 1883, was first performed by the Vienna Philharmonic on December 2, 1883, under the direction of Hans Richter. It is scored for 2 flutes, 2 oboes, 2 clarinets, 2 bassoons, contrabassoon, 4 horns, 2 trumpets, 3 trombones, kettledrums, and the traditional strings.

SYMPHONY NO. 4, E MINOR, OPUS 98

A wonderful autumnal warmth and strength pervade this Fourth and last Symphony of Johannes Brahms. Yet he was only fifty-two when he completed it—an age at which Haydn had not even *begun* to write his twenty-nine last and greatest symphonies. Brahms's autumnal qualities developed relatively early: a characteristic sobriety, almost severity, and a melancholy which is no romantic *Weltschmerz,* but that rare state in which sorrow and understanding seem one—an exalted mood which found its apotheosis in his *Four Serious Songs.*

The Fourth Symphony was written during the summers of 1884 and 1885 in the tiny Alpine town of Mürzzuschlag, which lay so high that its spring was late, autumn early and local fruit hardly had time to ripen before winter set in again. From this chilly realm Brahms sent the completed first movement to one of his dearest and most musical friends, Elisabeth von Herzogenberg.

"Might I venture to send you a piece of a piece of mine," he asked, "and would you have time to take a look at it and write me a word? On the whole, unfortunately, my pieces are pleasanter than I am and need less setting to rights! But the cherries never get ripe for eating in these parts, so don't be afraid if you don't like the taste of the thing. I'm not at all eager to write a bad No. 4."

Always severely self-critical, Brahms worried. When Elisabeth's answer did not come as quickly as he had hoped, he wrote her husband a typically gruff attempt at humor: "My latest attack was evidently a complete failure—and a symphony too! But I do beg that your dear lady will not abuse her pretty talent for pretty letter-writing by inventing any friendly pretense for my benefit." Later a four-hand piano performance from the manuscript score of the entire Symphony for half a dozen of Brahms's most trusted musician friends roused little enthusiasm. The composer's worry deepened.

Fortunately Hans von Bülow, to whom Brahms offered the first performance, was enthralled. After the first rehearsal, which he held before Brahms's arrival in Meiningen, Bülow wrote: "Number Four is stupendous, quite original, individual and rocklike. Incomparable strength from start to finish." Apparently Bülow prepared his orchestra so well that the first performance, which took place under Brahms's direction on October 25, 1885, was superb. Accounts of the audience's reaction vary. In any case the new Symphony became the chief feature of the orchestra's ensuing tour, with Brahms conducting it in nine of the cities visited.

Among American orchestras there was considerable competition for the honor of presenting the first American performances of Brahms's symphonies.

The first performance of Brahms's Fourth in this country was announced by the Boston Symphony for November 26, 1886, only thirteen months after the world premiere under the composer's direction. At the Friday afternoon "public rehearsal" of the Boston Symphony on November 25, the Symphony was duly performed. But the conductor, Wilhelm Gericke, was dissatisfied with the orchestra's performance and withdrew the score for further preparation, and the honor of the official first U.S. performance went to the Symphony Society of New York on December 11 with Walter Damrosch conducting.

The score calls for 2 flutes, piccolo, 2 oboes, 2 clarinets, 2 bassoons, contrabassoon, 4 horns, 2 trumpets, 3 trombones, kettledrums, triangle, and strings.

I. *Allegro non troppo.* The first movement opens with a vast, undulating flow of melody in a vein of subdued melancholy. Its rocking seesaw motion is typical of Brahms, and his biographer, Karl Geiringer, points out that the construction of the whole theme from a single motive of two notes is especially characteristic of Brahms's late style:

The whole opening is a succession of beguiling melodies with one vigorous fanfare-like theme for contrast. Yet the first theme dominates the movement in various transformations. Perhaps its most surprising disguise is the pensively elongated form with which it ushers in the reprise of the basic opening themes:

II. *Andante moderato.* A bare, unaccompanied melodic motto in the Phrygian mode stands sternly at the outset of this slow movement:

But after three measures the sternness melts and the melody is harmonized in a soft E major with clarinets and *pizzicato* strings in mellifluous thirds and sixths. It goes through a series of ingenious transformations of great warmth and sensuous appeal.

III. *Allegro giocoso.* This boisterous movement, with its delicate, sometimes humorous episodes, comes nearer the Beethoven tradition of the scherzo than the more relaxed *allegretto* movements Brahms had preferred for the third movements of his earlier symphonies.

IV. *Allegro energico e passionato.* This finale is a grandiose procession of variations. The eight chords at the start of the movement supply the basic harmonic structure. The eight-note melody which they support persists through most of the thirty variations:

But the melody often is found in the bass or in a middle voice, and frequently disguised. The whole is rounded off with a great coda, which is in itself a set of four additional variations. The dispute, which once loomed so large, as to whether these variations constitute a chaconne or a passacaglia, is useless, since musical scholars and composers differ with each other and among themselves as to which name belongs to which form. The important thing is the relentless power of this vast musical structure, the richness of Brahms's thought and feeling.

Of all cities, Brahms's adopted home, Vienna, seems to have been the slowest to warm to his Fourth Symphony. Yet gradually it took hold. And at the last orchestral concert Brahms heard on March 7, 1897, it caused a storm of enthusiasm. At the close of the first movement the applause persisted until Brahms came to the front of the box where he sat. He was a tragically different Brahms from the hearty, stocky figure they had known. He had suffered a terrible blow the year before, when his dearest friend and early champion, Clara Schumann, died. He never recovered from that shock. And a chill he caught at her burial aggravated a long-standing cancer of the liver which killed him.

The demonstrations were repeated after each movement of the Fourth Symphony and at the end there was an extraordinary scene. The applauding, shouting house stared at the figure standing in the box and seemed unable to let him go. "Tears ran down his cheeks," his biographer, Florence May, tells us, "as he stood there, shrunken in form, with lined countenance, strained expression, white hair hanging lank, and through the audience there was a feeling as of a stifled sob, for each knew that he was saying farewell. Another outburst of applause and yet another; one more acknowledgment from the master; and Brahms and his Vienna had parted forever."

VARIATIONS ON A THEME BY HAYDN, OPUS 56A

When he composed this magnificent set of Variations Brahms was forty years old. "The Brahms-Haydn Variations," as they are familiarly known, proved a turning point in his career. Up to this point he had not dared to complete a symphony, though he had tried often enough, and writing in any form for orchestra alone had filled him with inhibitions.

Robert Schumann's enthusiastic trumpeting of Brahms's genius when Brahms was only twenty had proved almost as much of a handicap as a help. "New Paths," Schumann's famous article, proclaimed the beginner a musician "called to give the highest expression to his time in ideal fashion . . . a young man over whose cradle Graces and Heroes have stood watch. . . . His fellow musicians hail him on his first step through a world where wounds perhaps await him, but also palms and laurels."

There were raised eyebrows and skeptical smiles. Brahms himself seemed skeptical and fearful of entering a field of music where he knew he would be measured by the symphonies of Beethoven. "You have no idea," Brahms said to a conductor friend, "how the likes of us feel when we hear the tramp of a giant like *him* behind us."

For some reason these Variations seem to have unlocked the door; the next fifteen years were rich in orchestral works. The Variations were composed in two versions at almost the same time: one for orchestra, another for two pianos. It is not certain which was completed first. In any case, so much of the writing (even in the piano version) is clearly orchestral in concept and grows so idiomatically out of the style and color of the instruments that Brahms must have had the orchestra in mind as he conceived it.

The Variations have a curious background. In 1870 Brahms's friend, the great Haydn biographer Karl Ferdinand Pohl, showed Brahms a B-flat *Feldpartita* (an open-air suite for wind instruments) believed to have been composed by Haydn. Brahms was much attracted to the theme of the second movement, apparently a traditional tune, marked "Choral St. Antoni." He copied it down and three years later used it as the basis of "The Brahms-Haydn Variations." Until recently the *Feldpartita* seems generally to have been accepted as authentic Haydn. But in 1951 the Haydn expert, H. C. Robbins Landon, wrote in the *Saturday Review of Literature* ("The True and False Haydn," August 25, 1951) that the whole series of works in the manuscript containing this *Feldpartita* "is spurious and . . . not one note was by Haydn. One of his students, perhaps Pleyel, was probably the real author."

Whoever wrote the *Feldpartita,* Brahms's liking for the "Choral" is easy to understand. Its irregular five-bar phrases must have particularly appealed to his unconventional rhythmic imagination. His score consists of the theme, eight variations and a passacaglia finale.

Choral St. Antoni: Andante. Brahms presents the opening phrase of the "Choral":

in virtually the same instrumental color as the original *Feldpartita:* 2 oboes, 2 bassoons, contrabassoon and 2 horns. The contrabassoon replaces the serpent, a picturesque but already obsolete wind instrument. Brahms adds only a light reinforcement of the bass line by *pizzicato* cellos and double basses. The following variations keep very closely to the phrase lengths and harmonic structure of the "Choral."

I. *Poco più animato.* The repeated chords with which the "Choral" ends are echoed softly by horns and woodwinds, while the strings weave graceful arabesques in a complex two-against-three rhythm.

II. *Più vivace.* Built on the simple dotted rhythm of the first two notes of the "Choral," this variation is dominated by woodwind color.

III. *Con moto.* The long melodic line is an even-flowing rhythmic variant of the original melody.

IV. *Andante con moto.* A languorous 3/8 transformation of the "Choral" glows in the warm tone of a solo French horn with added tints of woodwind color.

V. *Vivace.* Its sprightly 6/8 rhythms give this delicate variation almost the buoyancy of a Mendelssohn scherzo.

VI. *Vivace.* Traditional fanfares associated with the hunting ancestor of the orchestral horn inspired this vigorous variation.

VII. *Grazioso.* A graceful, lilting melody in traditional siciliano rhythm is another example of Brahms's sensitive feeling for orchestral color, here a subtle interplay of woodwind and string tone. In this variation the first great biographer of Brahms, Max Kalbeck, believed the composer pictured one of St. Anthony's temptations—clearly a feminine temptation and "the most atrocious because it is the sweetest!"

VIII. *Presto non troppo.* Muted strings and whispering woodwinds give a phantom-like quality to the last variation.

Finale: Andante. The Finale is built on the ancient passacaglia form, which Brahms so loved and which he was to use again so memorably for the finale of his Fourth Symphony. The passacaglia, of course, is itself a variation form. As its basis Brahms uses a five-bar phrase adapted from the "Choral St. Antoni." Beginning in a quiet hymn-like statement, it builds to a climax of majestic momentum when the "Choral" returns, decked out with flashing scales, first for the woodwinds and finally for the entire string section.

The rich variety of sonorities in this score draws on a relatively modest orchestra of 1 piccolo, 2 flutes, 2 oboes, 2 clarinets, 2 bassoons, contrabassoon, 4 horns, 2 trumpets, kettledrums, triangle, and string choir.

Benjamin Britten

Born November 22, 1913, Lowestoft, Suffolk, England
—died December 4, 1976, Aldeburgh, Suffolk, England

PASSACAGLIA (OPUS 33B) AND SEA INTERLUDES (OPUS 33A) FROM PETER GRIMES

Britten's first full-scale opera turned out to be a masterpiece. Like Wagner's first masterpiece, *The Flying Dutchman,* Britten's *Peter Grimes* is both a drama of the sea and the tragedy of an outcast who longs for acceptance by his fellows and for the redeeming love of a woman. Both dramas were born in part of personal experience. Of the two composers, Britten has had the longer, more intimate association with the sea.

"For most of my life," Britten has written, "I have lived closely in touch with the sea. My parents' house in Lowestoft directly faced the sea, and my life as a child was colored by the fierce storms that sometimes drove ships on our coast and ate away whole stretches of neighboring cliffs. In writing *Peter Grimes,* I wanted to express my awareness of the perpetual struggle of men and women whose livelihood depends on the sea—difficult though it is to treat such a universal subject in theatrical form."

Peter Grimes's struggle with the sea is also the struggle of an outsider with the community to which he yearns to belong but which he despises with a passionate love-hate. Many an artist has experienced a similar ambivalence: scorn for shallow values of the average John Doe—and a conflicting desire to be admired and loved by the many.

In 1939 Britten, deeply depressed by the long European appeasement of fascist predators, and by the mentality which expected this path to lead to "peace in our time," left England for the United States. He may also have been swayed by the slow acceptance of his music in England and by the example of his friend and mentor, W. H. Auden. Auden had emigrated to the United States, where he eventually became a naturalized U. S. citizen. In any case Britten's visit was surprisingly fruitful; during some two years he produced in quick succession such major works as his Violin Concerto, *Les Illuminations,* his First String Quartet, the operetta *Paul Bunyan,* his *Seven Sonnets of Michelangelo,* and the *Sinfonia da Requiem.* Meanwhile, an important seed was planted in his mind. An article by E. M. Forster on the eighteenth-century poet George Crabbe who, like Britten, was a native of Suffolk, led him to Crabbe's poem "The Borough," with its tragic nonhero Peter Grimes.

On his way back to England Britten stopped in Boston for a performance of his *Sinfonia da requiem* by the Boston Symphony under the direction of

Serge Koussevitzky. Koussevitzky asked whether Britten had plans to compose a full-scale opera. The composer pointed out that the expense of commissioning a libretto, and the large span of time necessary to compose, score, and guide preparations for a performance far exceeded his financial means. Koussevitzky offered to have the expenses met by the Koussevitzky Music Foundation and asked that the opera be dedicated to the memory of Mme. Koussevitzky, who had recently died.

The composition of *Peter Grimes* occupied Britten from January 1944 to February 1945. The world premiere followed in London at Sadler's Wells on June 7, 1945. In the United States *Peter Grimes* was presented for the first time in a student production at the Berkshire Music Center, Tanglewood, during the summer of 1946 under the direction of Leonard Bernstein. The Metropolitan Opera premiere came in February 1948.

Although Britten follows the tradition of pre-Wagnerian opera in giving primary importance to his voices, it is the orchestra which provides the setting of the sea in its many moods. This is accomplished largely during the orchestral Interludes which introduce each act and link the separate scenes.

Passacaglia. The *Passacaglia* stands at the focal point of the opera structurally, dramatically and emotionally. Structurally it is the Interlude which links the two scenes of Act Two, which places it at dead center of the three-act opera. The theme or ground bass of the *Passacaglia* embodies the tragic cry of Peter Grimes at the turning point of the drama, when he strikes the woman he loves, the gentle Ellen, who has been trying to help him. It is an eruption of despair: Peter's sudden realization that he cannot be helped, that he cannot accept the love he so desperately needs and longs for. In his anguish at the blow he has dealt to Ellen and to himself he crys: "So be it. . . . And God have mercy upon me!" The foundation of the *Passacaglia-Interlude* is the insistent repetition of the ground bass:*

This orchestral echo of Peter's cry, heard twice by itself before the variations begin, always strikes this listener as a kind of horrified whisper, as if the enormity of the thought only slowly dawned on Peter himself. (It will be noticed that the theme uses only eleven of the twelve beats in a three-measure span. Thus each repetition of the theme shifts in relation to the strong beats of the measure.) There are eleven variations during which the theme swells in volume like an unshakable obsession. The upper voices of the variations begin with a desolate solo viola, moving on to more agitated patterns of wood-

---

* *This and the following musical examples from this composition are copyright 1945 by Boosey & Hawkes, Ltd.; renewed 1972. Reprinted by permission of Boosey & Hawkes, Inc.*

winds, then of woodwinds with high strings punctuated by sharp interjections of the brass. The progress of the variations also reflects the mounting dramatic tension of the approach of a village posse to Peter's hut. The fact that the villagers in the preceding scene had sung a variant of the notes of Peter's cry in their hostile shout ("Grimes is at his exercise!") adds a second threatening meaning to the ground theme. In the opera the *Passacaglia* breaks off at the moment of the rising curtain which reveals the interior of Peter's hut. The concert version is rounded off by the concluding bars of the scene, which are a quieter orchestral commentary on the inexorable progress of Peter's downfall.

Sea Interlude I: "Dawn." This *interlude* linking the Prologue to Act I depicts the mood and scene of early morning by the seashore. The high flutes and violins of the opening may suggest cries of seagulls or the vast loneliness of a deserted beach. A sudden swirl of harp, clarinets and violas evokes the swift sliding motion of an encroaching wave. Soft sustained brass chords suggest the slow massive cadence of the sea itself.

Sea Interlude II: "Sunday Morning." The clangor of church bells is used to suggest the visual clamor of bright sunshine as well as a festive Sabbath mood. Four horns, in overlapping, clashing pairs, could be the larger, lower-pitched bells:

Soon brighter, livelier bells (high woodwinds) combine with the slower *ostinato* of the horns. By way of contrast the violas and cellos sing, *sotto voce,* the melody of Peter's beloved Ellen as the curtain rises on her words: "Glitter of waves and glitter of sunlight. . . . " The alternation of the bells with Ellen's Sunday song makes up the entire *interlude,* the concert version of which continues far into the Sunday scene.

Sea Interlude III: "Moonlight." This *interlude* which precedes the night scene with offstage village dancing and drinking suggests anything but a glamorous moonlight scene. The mood is lonely, brooding and dark, as if the moon could only emphasize the surrounding blackness.

Sea Interlude IV: "Storm." This twofold storm embraces the roaring wind and sea and the storm in Peter's heart and brain. It opens with a storm theme derived from the preceding scene in which the physical approach of the storm is announced:

As turmoil reaches its climax, Peter's thought seems to veer to his hopeless quest for peace of soul and the consolation of Ellen's love. His longing takes shape in the wide arching phrase already sung by Peter in the preceding scene on his words: "What harbour shelters peace? . . . What harbour can embrace terrors and tragedies? . . . " But his question is snuffed out by the renewed fury of the storm.

The *Passacaglia* and *Sea interludes* are scored for piccolo, 2 flutes, 2 oboes, 2 clarinets, 2 bassoons, contrabassoon, 4 horns, 3 trumpets, 3 trombones, tuba kettledrums, side drum, tenor drum, bass drum, tam-tam, gong, cymbals, tambourine, celeste, xylophone, harp, and the traditional strings.

SINFONIA DA REQUIEM, OPUS 20

Benjamin Britten found several of his most poignant inspirations in his Roman Catholic faith. This early *Sinfonia da Requiem* is one of many examples. As we might expect from a man whose Christianity leads him to abhor war and fascism, the young Britten was deeply depressed by the trend of European politics leading to World War II; by the long appeasement of Hitler, Mussolini, and even Generalissimo Franco; by the abandonment of Ethiopia, Austria, Czechoslovakia, and Spain to the Fascist predators; and by the mentality which expected this path to lead to "peace in our time." By early 1939, when Britten left England to live in the United States, Europe looked black indeed. His last work, composed in England before going to the United States, was *Ballad of Heroes,* completed on March 4, 1939, and was dedicated to the men of the British Battalion of the International Brigade who had fallen in Spain.

In his decision to go to America, Britten (then twenty-five years old) may also have been swayed by the slow acceptance of his music in his native country and by a feeling among his friends that he was restricted in England. Certainly he was influenced by the decision of his friend and mentor, the poet W. H. Auden, who emigrated to the United States where he eventually became a naturalized citizen. Apparently Britten, too, came to America with serious thoughts of settling.

What he expected to find here we do not know. What he did find was himself, or, more specifically, his own maturity as an artist. And logically, that meant that he rediscovered and reaffirmed his own Englishness. So true was this that after some two and one-half years, at a point when England's fortunes were at low-ebb, he decided to return to his own country. The difficulty of obtaining passage home delayed his return until April 1942. In the meantime, his visit here had been extraordinarily fruitful.

His American sojourn produced, in quick succession, such major works as his Violin Concerto, *Les Illuminations,* his First String Quartet, his *Seven Sonnets of Michelangelo* and the *Sinfonia da Requiem.*

The *Sinfonia* had a curious origin. Early in 1940 Britten was approached in the United States through a high cultural official of the British Council with an inquiry. Would he be willing to compose a symphony for a celebration in honor of a foreign dynasty? Britten saw no objection so long as no nationalistic propaganda was expected of him. After undertaking the work, he learned that his new symphony was to be part of the festivities for the 2,600th anniversary of the founding of the Japanese dynasty. This must have put Britten in an odd position. Japan had already been long involved in her war against China. Britten, a lifelong and passionate pacifist, seems to have hoped his choice of the Mass for the Dead as the subject of his music would not only express his own feelings about war but arouse similar feelings in his listeners. His first outline of the symphony and its subject was (rather surprisingly) accepted by the Japanese authorities. But soon after sending the finished manuscript, Britten received indirect word that something was wrong. At last, late in 1940, the Japanese government sent an indignant protest to England through the Japanese Embassy in London, claiming that the young Englishman had insulted the Emperor of Japan by submitting a work based upon Christian doctrine and liturgy.

Since the Japanese commission was cancelled, there was no reason to withhold the *Sinfonia* which, accordingly, was given its world premiere the following March 29 by the New York Philharmonic, under the direction of John Barbirolli.

Although the composer's comment printed below is formal and objective, the subject is one of the most emotional it is possible to imagine. Many listeners may remember the words of the service. Others may like to be reminded of the texts in Britten's mind.

The *"Lacrymosa"* concerns "that day of fear and mourning when guilty man shall rise from the dust to face eternal judgment." The *"Dies irae"* describes the Last Judgment: that day of wrath and doom when the world shall be dissolved in ashes and man will tremble at the approach of the eternal Judge. "The *"Requiem aeternam"* is a gentler prayer: "Give them eternal rest, oh Lord, and let eternal light shine upon them. . . ."

The following is Mr. Britten's analysis:

I. *Lacrymosa.* A slow marching lament in a persistent 6/8 rhythm with a strong tonal center on D. There are three main motives: 1) a syncopated, sequential theme announced by the cellos and answered by a solo bassoon;*

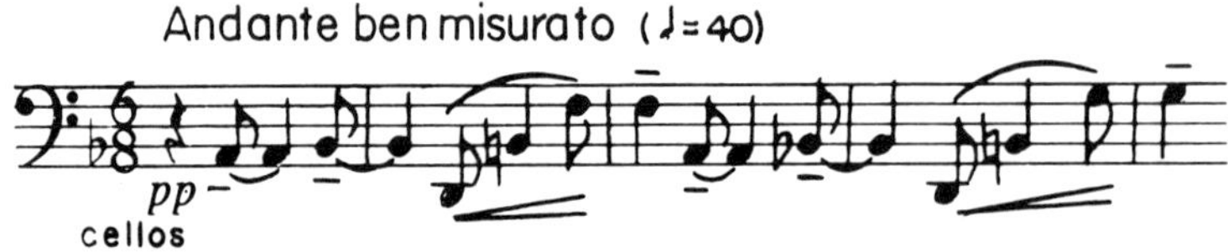

2) a broad theme, based on the interval of a major seventh; 3) alternating chords on flute and trombones, outlined by the piano and harps. The first

* *Musical example copyright 1942 by Hawkes & Son (London) Ltd.; renewed 1969. Reprinted by permission.*

section of the movement is quietly pulsating; the second is a long crescendo leading to a climax based on the first cello theme. There is no pause before:

II. *Dies irae.* A form of Dance of Death, with occasional moments of quiet marching rhythm. The dominating motif of this movement is announced at the start by the flutes and includes an important *tremolando* figure. Other motives are a triplet repeated-note figure in the trumpets, a slow, smooth tune on the saxophone, and a livelier syncopated one in the brass. The scheme of the movement is a series of climaxes of which the last is the most powerful, causing the music to disintegrate and to lead directly to:

III. *Requiem aeternam.* Very quietly, over a background of solo strings and harps, the flutes announce the quiet D-major tune, the principal motive of the movement. There is a middle section in which the strings play a flowing melody. This grows to a short climax, but the opening tune is soon resumed, and the work ends quietly in a long, sustained clarinet note.

The *Sinfonia da Requiem* is scored for 3 flutes, piccolo, bass flute, 2 oboes, English horn, 2 B-flat clarinets (the second alternating with E-flat clarinet), bass clarinet (alternating with B-flat clarinet), 2 bassoons, contrabassoon, E-flat alto saxophone, 6 horns, 3 trumpets, 3 trombones, tuba, kettledrums, bass drum, side drum, tambourine, cymbals, xylophone, whip, 2 harps, piano, and the customary strings.

VARIATIONS ON A THEME BY FRANK BRIDGE, OPUS 10

One of Benjamin Britten's most brilliant scores and the first to win him world-wide attention was his popular set of Variations on a Theme of Frank Bridge. Britten was only twenty-three when he was invited to write a new work for the Boyd Neel String Orchestra to perform at the Salzburg Festival of 1937. Neel himself recalled that within ten days time of the invitation, Britten appeared "with the complete work sketched out. In another four weeks it was fully scored for strings as it stands today, but for the addition of one bar."

Britten chose his theme from the second of the *Three Idylls* for string orchestra by Frank Bridge, his first and most influential teacher. A distinguished composer himself, Frank Bridge (1879–1944) was also prominent in English musical life as conductor of the Chapman Orchestra, the London Philharmonic, the London Symphony, and the Covent Garden Opera.

The speed and facility with which Britten composed his Variations were characteristic. Characteristic, too, was his choice of the string orchestra. Britten declared in an interview published in *Tempo* in February, 1944: "I am attracted by the many features of the strings. For instance, the possibilities of elaborate *divisi*—the effect of many voices of the same kind. There is also the infinite variety of color—the use of mutes; *pizzicato,* harmonics and so forth. Then again, there is the great dexterity in technique of string players. Generally speaking, I like to think of the smaller combinations of players, and I deplore the tendency of present-day audiences to expect only the luscious *tutti* effect from an orchestra."

The first performance of the *Theme and Variations* on August 27, 1937, at the Salzburg Festival by the Boyd Neel Orchestra was a decisive success; within less than two years the new score had been heard more than fifty times in various parts of Europe and America. It consists of an introduction, theme, ten variations, and a finale.

Introduction and Theme. Lento maestoso. Brilliant flourishes for the upper strings, punctuated by sharp *pizzicato* chords, make up the brief introduction. The strongly lyric theme is characterized by the falling fifth and falling fourth of the opening, which form the basis of several variations:*

1. *Adagio.* Soft sustained chords echo the falling fifth of the theme and alternate with recitative-like interruptions of the violins. Toward the end, the violins grow softer and tenderer, merging at last into a long, sustained C-major chord with the remaining strings.

2. *March. Presto alla marcia.* The vivacious march variation with its perky dotted rhythm takes off from the falling fourth of the theme. Triplet rhythms mobile as quicksilver are played off against the basic rhythm of this variation. The close comes with a sudden hush as all rhythm evaporates into silence.

3. *Romance. Allegretto grazioso.* Over the airiest of *staccato* and *pizzicato* accompaniments an elegant melodic line soars and shimmers in the violins.

4. *Aria italiana. Allegro brilliante.* One of the most attractive of Britten's tongue-in-cheek, affectionate, enthusiastic parodies, this is an early nineteenth-century *cabaletta,* replete with trills, staccatos, runs, and great swooping jumps all performed, of course, by the soprano section of the orchestra, the first violins. The *pizzicato* accompaniment is marked to be played *quasi chitarra,* a reference to the familiar denigrations of the early nineteenth-century Italian opera orchestra as just "a big guitar."

5. *Bourrée Classique. Allegro e pesante.* Still starting with the falling fifth of Bridge's theme, this variation recalls the Baroque bourrées of Bach and his contemporaries, with many an ingenious rhythmic surprise.

6. *Wiener Walzer. Lento, vivace.* A parody of Viennese waltz clichés: the languishing *rubatos,* the fiery runs, the triplet twists. The falling fifth appears in the motto-like opening measures and again in a cascade of falling fifths, plunging and rising and falling again in wave formation.

7. *Moto perpetuo. Allegro molto.* The plunging, soaring wave-like motion is carried over from the previous variation, extended and developed with dazzling virtuosity.

---

* *This and the following musical example from this composition are copyright 1938 by Hawkes & Son (London) Ltd.; renewed 1965 by Boosey & Hawkes, Inc. Reprinted by permission.*

8. *Funeral March. Andante ritmico.* Here the falling fifth of the theme appears as a persistent *ostinato* rhythm in the basses and celli, while the violins sing an intensely expressive elegiac melody.

9. *Chant. Lento.* The eerie combination of high sustained harmonics with deep double bass tone, punctuated by heavy *pizzicati* of the cello form one of the most evocative pages of this ingenious score.

10. *Fugue and Finale. Allegro molto vivace.* The fugue subject is a play on the falling fourth and fifth of Bridge's theme:

The cumulative momentum of the fugue owes much to its jig-like rhythmic pattern suggested to Britten by the *gigue* finales of many Baroque composers. As it approaches its climax, the strings subdivide into fifteen parts. Over this diaphonous texture, the solo leaders of the violin, viola, and cello sections unite in a broadly songful version of the original theme.

The conclusion, *Lento e solenne,* is another songful variant of the original theme played by all the violins on the G string. The final bar is dated July 12, 1937, Peasen Hall, Suffolk.

Earle Brown

Born December 26, 1926, Lunenburg, Massachusetts

AVAILABLE FORMS II, FOR ORCHESTRA FOUR HANDS

Like many of the most fruitful composers of our time, Earle Brown is intensely aware of, and stimulated by other arts besides music. It is no mere imitation or mechanical transference of techniques that interests him, but more basic approaches to expression and structure. Alexander Calder and Jackson Pollock, for example, are the two most important stimuli Brown pointed out to New York Philharmonic listeners on the occasion of the first United States performance in Philharmonic Hall on February 9, 1964:

> Spontaneous decisions in the performance of a work and the possibility of the composed elements being "mobile" have been of primary interest to me for some time. The former, to an extreme degree, in *Folio* (1952) and the latter, most explicitly, in *Twenty-Five Pages* (1953). The mobility of the elements was inspired by the mobiles of Alexander Calder, in which, similar to

> his work, there are basic units subject to innumerable different relationships or forms. The insistence that the work be conducted and formed spontaneously in performance was to a large extent inspired by the working process and works of Jackson Pollock, in which the immediacy and directness of "contact" with the material is of such importance and produces an intensity in the working and in the result. The performance conditions of this work are similar to a painter working spontaneously with a given palette. These comparisons are extremely dangerous and I emphasize that it is to the nature of the working process and formal possibilities that I refer, not the quality of the results.
>
> I have felt that the conditions of spontaneity and mobility of elements which I have been working with create a more urgent and intense "communication" throughout the entire process, from composing to the final realization of a work. I prefer that each "final form," which each performance necessarily produces, be a collaborative adventure and that the work and its conditions of human involvement remain a "living" potential of engagement.

Available Forms II was commissioned by the Rome Radio orchestra for its concert at the Venice Biennale in April 1962. The composition was begun in New York in the fall of 1961 and completed in Paris in February 1962. At the first performance at the Venice Biennale and at subsequent performances in Cologne and Munich, the work was conducted by Bruno Maderna and the composer. Two conductors are necessary for each performance, one for each half of the divided orchestra. The following specific comments on *Available Forms II* are by the composer:

> There are two separate and independent but compositionally related scores of four pages each, one score for each conductor. Each page contains either four or five composed orchestral events (in a sense, brief musical units) which differ from each other in their basic sound characteristics, such as: articulation, density, contour, timbre, registration and potential rhythmic energy. In the work as a whole there are thirty-eight different sound events which function as the basic structural material of the work. Of the thirty-eight events, only three are in any way "improvisational" as far as the musicians are concerned. The other thirty-five events are fully composed, orchestrated and balanced as notationally self-sufficient structural units whose basic sound configurations and characteristics are always maintained but whose ensemble tempo and loudness may be modified by the conductors. The following example shows the notation of the cello line from one of the explicitly notated events:*

* *Musical example copyright 1962 by Associated Music Publishers, Inc. Used by permission.*

> The three "improvisational" events function as textural density units. The particular textures and densities are predetermined, but the specific sound is obtainable only by improvisation within the predetermined framework. Obviously, the structure is not dependent upon improvisation, rather it is a matter of utilizing it as one element in a continuum of compositional controls from explicit, finitely controlled elements to elements whose interior characteristics can only be implied and arrived at through the use of generalized notations. The details of these three events are secondary to their use as sound masses of different timbral qualities. Given these thirty-eight structural units, the conductors may call for them in any combinations, sequences, or any juxtapositions of two or more events at any moment. The title of the work refers to the availability of many possible forms which these composed elements may assume, spontaneously directed by the conductors in the process of performing the work. The individual musical events are rehearsed, the performances are not. The conductors work independently of one another but are of course dependent and related by their mutual knowledge of the combinatorial sound possibilities and by their intuitive and aural responses to the materials (events) and to each other's sound-forms as they develop in the process of performing.
>
> No two performances will arrive at the same formal result but the work will retain its identity from performance to performance through the unchanging basic character of the events.
>
> Apart from the composing of the basic materials of this work (the events), the aspect of the work which interests me most is the attempt to provoke a performance situation in which there is an intensification of the working process in the performance itself. I do not believe in a final best form for these materials and they were composed "in the abstract," so to speak, which is to say, as basic structural possibilities having more than one conceivable function within their implied context. There is obviously a "best form" for a work which is based upon thematic development or upon a programmatic continuity. However, I prefer to base the work and its formal future on the immediate and spontaneous responses which occur to the conductors in relation to the composed basic material and to the unique qualities of the conductors and the conditions of each performance. With the exception of the basic materials these are all variables and my intention is that they become creative correlatives between the composer, the materials, the conductors, the musicians, and the audiences; as one constantly changing and continuing "process" in the nature of the work.

In addition to his involvement with the visual arts a further concern Brown shares with many contemporary composers is mathematics. At Northeastern University in Boston he majored in mathematics and engineering. He studied music privately and became intensely interested in the techniques of Joseph Schillinger, which he subsequently modified for his own purposes. He has been a prolific composer, pioneering in contemporary techniques, forms, media, and notation. He has also been, more briefly, a recording engineer, literary editor, and a frequent lecturer on musical topics.

Max Bruch

Born January 6, 1838, Cologne—died October 2, 1920, Friedenau, near Berlin

CONCERTO FOR VIOLIN AND ORCHESTRA, NO. 1, G MINOR, OPUS 26

Max Bruch is remembered today chiefly as the composer of this G-minor Violin Concerto. Yet he was also a brilliant conductor, a famous pedagogue, and a well-known composer with three symphonies, three operas, over a dozen choral works, chamber music, songs and a variety of works for solo instrument with orchestra including two violin concertos, the *Scottish Fantasy* for violin and orchestra, and his *Kol Nidre* for cello and orchestra.

Bruch started his career as a child prodigy and was only nineteen when he began jotting down ideas for the G-minor Violin Concerto. However, it was several years before he seriously went about welding these ideas into a unified composition. On April 24, 1866, he conducted the first performance of the Concerto at a concert of the Music Institute of Koblenz on the Rhine. The soloist was Otto von Königslöw, the concertmaster of the Gürzenich Orchestra of Cologne.

Immediately after the premiere, Bruch set about revising his Concerto, and that very summer, he sent the score to Joseph Joachim for advice and criticism. He told the great violinist he felt that because of the free form of the first movement he ought to call the whole work a fantasy, rather than a concerto. Joachim disagreed. "For a fantasy," he argued, "the last two movements are too completely and symmetrically developed. The different sections are brought together in a beautiful relationship, yet—and this is the principal thing—there is sufficient contrast."

After further changes, the version of the Concerto we know today was dedicated to Joachim, who was the soloist at its first performance in 1868 with Bruch conducting. Even when new, the Concerto was not considered revolutionary, and it had no difficulty in establishing itself as the popular work it remains.

I. *Prelude: Allegro moderato.* For all its brilliance, the first movement has a melancholy strain. Its deliberate avoidance of monumental form, which made Bruch hesitate to call his work a concerto, gives us the impression that we are hearing merely an elaborate introduction to the slow movement, which follows appropriately without pause.

II. *Adagio.* There are three chief themes, langorous melodies all, which alternate and intertwine freely. The second of these has an especially yearning, romantic quality:

The movement works gradually to a passionate climax, with great sweeping arpeggios and graceful *fioriture* for the solo instrument. The conclusion brings back the second theme, quoted above, in a last ecstatic climax which then suddenly fades into silence.

III. *Finale: Allegro energico.* The principal theme of this finale is a temperamental dance-like figure with copious double and quadruple stops which Brahms may have remembered when he came to write the finale of his own Violin Concerto. In form, it is rather like a very free amalgamation of rondo and sonata. There are passages of passionate declamation for both violin and orchestra, but the dominating mood is one of brilliance and fire.

The G-minor Concerto is scored for 2 flutes, 2 oboes, 2 clarinets, 2 bassoons, 4 horns, 2 trumpets, kettledrums, and the customary strings.

SCOTTISH FANTASY, OPUS 46

"Bruch's *Scottish Fantasy* is much better than his concertos," wrote Bernard Shaw in a burst of irritation at the "standardness of standard repertory." But one need not downgrade Bruch's melodious G-minor Violin Concerto in order to praise the melodic appeal of his *Scottish Fantasy.*

Bruch, like so many Romantic composers, was deeply attracted to folk song—not merely to the folk song of his native Germany, but also to Scottish, Welsh, and Hebrew traditional melodies. Indeed, for many years he was most popularly known for his arrangement for cello solo and orchestra of the famous Hebrew ritual chant *Kol Nidre.* Although he is best known today for his works for solo violin or cello with orchestra, Bruch was a many-sided musician: a brilliant conductor, pedagogue, an eminent and prolific composer. He began his career as a child prodigy, was trained in piano and theory by his mother first, later by (largely conservative) professionals in Bonn and Cologne. His strong melodic gift showed early and determined much of the character of his music, which was closer to the Mendelssohn tradition than to the spirit of Richard Wagner. With time Bruch became a more and more bitter anti-Wagnerite, which estranged him more and more from the innovators of later years.

The full title of the *Fantasy* is *Fantasia (Introduction—Adagio—Scherzo—Andante—Finale) for Violin with Orchestra and Harp, with the Free Use of Scottish Melodies.* It was composed in Berlin during the winter of 1879 and 1880, and dedicated to the great Spanish violin virtuoso, Sarasate. The world premiere, with Sarasate as soloist, was presented in late September of 1880 at a Bach festival in Hamburg. The critics did not receive it favorably, but, according to a friend of Sarasate who was present, the public was enthusiastic.

Introduction: Grave. Solemn brass and harp chords, dark and somber, alternate with freely rhapsodic solo violin phrases accompanied by a soft choir of the strings. The contrasting colors are gradually blended until a short phrase for the soloist leads without break to the first movement proper.

I. *Adagio cantabile.* After some muted preparatory measures for the entire orchestra, the solo violin sings, *molto espressivo,* the nostalgic Scottish melody,

"Auld Robin Morris," embellishing it with parallel thirds in double stops and with rhapsodic interludes.

II. *Scherzo: Allegro; Dance.* The opening measures for full orchestra anticipate the principal strains of "Hey, the Dusty Miller," in double stops. The strain is varied with flying staccatos, swooping arpeggios, trills and runs, soaring into the melodic stratosphere and cascading down to the unstopped G string. After the conclusion of this *Scherzo,* a bridge, recalling the theme of the first movement leads directly into the following *Andante.*

III. *Andante sostenuto.* Another nostalgic Scottish air, "I'm a-Doun for Lack o' Johnnie," is the basis of this slow movement, which gives the soloist scope for some delicate flights of fancy, ending with an expressive dying fall.

IV. *Finale: Allegro guerriero.* An old Scottish war song, "Scots wha hae," also known as "Hey tutti taitie," sets the vigorous mood of the finale. It is spurred on by elaborate acrobatics of the solo violin. Once more the theme of the first movement is recalled in hushed tones of the soloist before the fiery strain of the *Finale* returns to round off the *Fantasia.*

The *Fantasia* is scored for 2 flutes, 2 oboes, 2 clarinets, 2 bassoons, 4 horns, 2 trumpets, 3 trombones, tuba, kettledrums, bass drum, cymbals, harp, and the customary string choir.

Anton Bruckner

Born September 4, 1824, Ansfelden—died October 11, 1896, Vienna

SYMPHONY NO. 1, C MINOR (LINZ VERSION)

"The impudent urchin" *("das kecke Beserl")* was Bruckner's designation for his First Symphony, when he looked back on it from the majestic achievements of his later years. But lest we be tempted to think that Bruckner was a boy when he wrote this youthful-sounding Symphony, it is well to remember that he was forty years old when he began it, almost forty-one when he finished and forty-three when his First Symphony was given its premiere under Bruckner's own direction on May 9, 1868, in the Redoutensaal of Linz.

Why such a late start? No one has ever known precisely, least of all Bruckner himself. But there is general agreement that the turning point in Bruckner's development came when he made the acquaintance of Richard Wagner's music.

Bruckner was a man of simple Austrian peasant origins and simple education, although his grandfather and father had been village schoolmasters and Bruckner himself was trained for the same fine profession. His early professional years were divided between the classroom and the choir loft of various village churches, and he reached his thirtieth year before he decided to become a full-time musician. Bruckner continued to study counterpoint and fugue even after he was appointed organist of the cathedral of Linz two years later. He also studied symphonic form and orchestration with the local conductor. Bruckner had been composing since he was thirteen years old—quantities of competent but not very distinguished or interesting music.

Then came the miracle. Bruckner's conductor-friend and instructor introduced him to the scores of Richard Wagner. In February 1863 Bruckner heard his first performance of a complete Wagner opera. His teacher conducted two performances of *Tannhäuser* at the local Linz opera. Three months earlier he had shown Bruckner the score and now he presented his pupil with tickets to the performances. Very likely he had invited him to rehearsals as well. Bruckner was transfixed. Almost at once he started composing his first true masterpiece: the Mass in D minor, and immediately thereafter he embarked on his Symphony No. 1. In a matter of weeks rather than months Bruckner was set on the path that was to transform him from a plodding provincial church organist-choirmaster-composer into an artist of international stature, a figure of passionate controversy, who lived to see his own symphonies ranked by many of the most competent judges of his day as the greatest since Beethoven's Ninth.

The Trio to his Scherzo was the first portion of the score to be completed. The manuscript bears the mark 23 January, 1865, 1:30 A.M. The first movement was completed on the following May 14 and the Scherzo on May 25. A preliminary version of the slow movement seems to have been completed in 1865, then revised between January 27 and April 14, 1866. By July 26, 1866, the imposing Finale and with it the entire score was completed. This is known as the "Linz" version as opposed to the "Vienna" version, which was largely a reorchestration completed in 1891.

During the composition of the First Symphony, Bruckner had one of the most stimulating experiences of his life: he was invited to the world premiere of Wagner's *Tristan und Isolde* at the Court Opera of Munich in June 1865. Bruckner took the unfinished manuscript of his First Symphony with him. He was able to show it to Anton Rubinstein, a fellow guest at his hotel, and to Hans von Bülow, the conductor of the *Tristan* production. But Bruckner did not dare to show his score to Wagner himself.

There seem to be no traces whatsoever of *Tristan* in the Bruckner Symphony, and precious few even of *Tannhäuser*. Bruckner's creative reaction to the overwhelming stimulus of Wagner's music did not consist of mere imitation. It was a considerable time before Bruckner digested the Wagnerian idiom sufficiently for parts of it (very limited parts) to become a natural part of his own personal language.

The premiere of the First Symphony at Linz took place under conditions which might well have been depressing to the composer. The orchestra was pieced together from the theater orchestra, members of two regimental bands stationed in Linz and dilettantes. In all, we are told, there were 12 violins, 3 violas, 3 cellos, and 3 double basses to make do for the weighty string choir Bruckner's score requires.

The audience was tiny, in part because of a local catastrophe: one day earlier, the bridge across the Danube had collapsed and the citizens of Linz were still much too wrought up by the disaster to flock to Bruckner's program. "It cost me a lot of money to cover the deficit," the composer remembered ruefully.

I. *Allegro.* There is no introduction. The principal theme of the movement is announced at once, rather softly by the first violins in what, for Bruckner, seems a comfortable jog-trot:*

This rhythm permeates the entire opening section, rising to a brief climax and subsiding again before the songful second theme is introduced by the first violins:

After a brief interruption by woodwinds, the theme is repeated by solo cello. The last theme of this rich exposition, a climactic passage for trombones in octaves, is one of the few moments of the Symphony which might recall Bruckner's recent impressions of *Tannhäuser,* particularly the climax of the *Tannhäuser* Overture, where the decorative figure of the violins may have suggested a similar brilliant, repeated figure of Bruckner's violins.

The development section begins very softly with strings alone, echoed by woodwinds and solo horn. But the music is soon dominated by a return of the heroic trombone theme and its accompanying violin embellishments. This, in turn, gives way to a development of the Symphony's opening rhythm.

The recapitulation of the opening themes is very free, and toward the end completely changed to make room for an expansive coda with yet another heroic climax.

II. *Adagio.* Instead of the broadly melodic type of theme which opens most Bruckner slow movements, this one begins in a darkly brooding mood of great

* *This and the following musical examples from this composition are reprinted by permission of C.F. Peters Corporation; sole agents Musikwissenschaftlicher Verlag.*

originality. Soon this is relieved by a contrasting melody for first violins in a gracefully flowing style, leading to a contrasting middle section, warmer in feeling and slightly livelier in tempo. The first section is brought back again, not quite literally but clearly enough to give the impression of a free ABA form. A majestic climax at the end is rounded off by an ethereal coda fading into silence.

III. *Scherzo: Schnell.* A few boisterous measures of introduction lead quickly to the vigorous Scherzo theme announced by violins in octaves:

The trio is brief, delicately orchestrated, almost in chamber music style, with an especially poetic solo for French horn.

IV. *Finale: Bewegt, feurig.* Like the first movement, the Finale begins without introduction, the principal theme being thundered out at once by heavy brass and woodwinds:

In later years Bruckner came to consider such an abrupt, unannounced presentation of the principal theme to be amusingly brash, as if his "impudent urchin" came bursting through the door unannounced, shouting: "It's me!" *("Da bin i!").* This finale has the most elaborate structure of the four movements. Toward the end, the key changes to a triumphant C major in preparation for the overpowering brilliance of the climactic coda.

The "Linz" version of the Symphony No. 1 is scored for 3 flutes, 2 oboes, 2 clarinets, 2 bassoons, 4 horns, 2 trumpets, 3 trombones, kettledrums, and the traditional string choir. Almost a quarter of a century later, when Bruckner revised the orchestration extensively, he toned down much of what seemed to him too brash. Many Bruckner admirers today feel that the vitality of the Symphony suffered in this so-called "Vienna version" (Wiener Fassung) of 1890–91. Even as Bruckner undertook the revision there were many who hoped he would not change it too much. Among them was the great Wagner conductor Hermann Levi, who wired to Bruckner: "First Symphony wonderful! It must be published and performed. But please, please do not alter it too much; everything is just perfect, the instrumentation too. Not too much touching up, please."

SYMPHONY NO. 2, C MINOR

Although Bruckner composed music in a heroic mold, he was a timid man wracked by self-doubt, humiliated by failure of some of his finest works and tortured by his critical enemies in the Vienna press. He was a naïve provincial who happened to be a musical genius, when (in 1867) he took a giant step: from the post of cathedral organist at Linz to that of Imperial Court Organist in the capitol of the Austro-Hungarian Empire. The year after moving to Vienna Bruckner had returned to Linz to conduct the premiere of his First Symphony on May 9, 1868. The Symphony was a failure, for the audience was quite simply puzzled. Fortunately, soon after the fiasco of his First Symphony, Bruckner's Viennese friend and protector, the conductor Johann Herbeck, lifted the composer's spirits by arranging for his appointment as professor of counterpoint, thoroughbass and organ at the Conservatory of the Gesellschaft der Musikfreunde in Vienna. He also was able to arrange organ recitals for Bruckner at Nancy, Paris (the Cathedral of Notre Dame) and London. The tremendous success which Bruckner won, particularly at the international competition for organists, playing the recently constructed giant organ of the Royal Albert Hall in London, gave Bruckner some badly needed self-confidence and with it a desire to resume composing. On his return to Vienna in 1871 Bruckner began sketches for his Second Symphony, which he completed in October, 1872.

While he was working on his Second Symphony Bruckner received another great psychological lift from the successful premiere of his F-minor Mass, which was almost universally praised, even by the music critic Eduard Hanslick, who later became one of Bruckner's bitterest opponents. Soon after he had completed his Second Symphony Bruckner persuaded the Vienna Philharmonic to run through the score at a rehearsal. The conductor was Otto Dessoff, who declared according to Bruckner's later recollection, that:

> . . . the Symphony was nonsensical and impossible to perform. The flutist Doppler retorted: "Anyone who writes a Mass like the F-minor cannot write nonsense."
>
> Thereupon I begged Dessoff to allow me to conduct. "That is not our custom," he replied. "But come close to me and give me the *tempi.*"
>
> I did so and all of a sudden the whole orchestra was all eyes and ears. Every movement was loudly applauded. The cellist Popper, in particular, was beside himself with delight.
>
> The Symphony would have been accepted then—but it was too long.
>
> I was supposed to make cuts. And I did. But twenty to forty measures were not nearly enough for them.

A year later, however, Bruckner was able to hire the Vienna Philharmonic for a performance. In the violin section sat a young student from the Vienna Conservatory who was often called upon to substitute. It was Artur Nikisch, who later became a celebrated champion of Bruckner's works. Nearly half a century later Nikisch recalled the occasion with emotion:

> Bruckner's admirers persuaded Prince Liechtenstein to make available the funds for a special concert at which the Court Opera Orchestra [which was identical with the Vienna Philharmonic] was to perform under Bruckner's direction his Second Symphony—the first of his symphonies to be performed in Vienna. I can still hear Bruckner's voice as he stepped up to the podium and said: "Now then, gentlemen, we can rehearse as long as we like; I have someone who will pay for it." *("I' hab an der's 'zahlt.")* Playing the Symphony aroused in me instantly the same enthusiasm that I still feel forty-six years later for this and all its sister symphonies.

The enthusiasm of the entire orchestra was such that they took pay for only two rehearsals, playing a third rehearsal and the performance free. The premiere took place October 26, 1873, under Bruckner's direction. The enthusiasm of the players is said to have contributed greatly to the success of the Symphony. In gratitude Bruckner wished to dedicate the Symphony to the Vienna Philharmonic, but his proposal, extended in a touchingly humble letter, was never answered.

Despite the success of the premiere Herbeck persuaded Bruckner to make changes in the score. Bruckner complied and the new version was given a second successful performance, again under Bruckner's direction, on February 20, 1876. A year later the score was again revised, once more on Herbeck's advice. The final revision of 1877 was the basis of the first edition of the Second Symphony published by Doblinger in Vienna in 1892. During the thirties and early forties, Robert Haas edited most of the Bruckner symphonies, restoring what he considered to represent Bruckner's real wishes. In 1965 the Bruckner Society in Vienna published a scholarly edition of the final 1877 version, edited by Leopold Nowak.

I. *Ziemlich Schnell.* The gently melancholy principal theme of Bruckner's first movement is announced at once by the cellos against a background of shimmering strings.*

Bruckner took extra care to make his Second Symphony easily understandable; one of the devices he used for this was to introduce a pause marking the boundary between the major sections of the movement. Hence the pregnant silence, punctuated only by soft taps of the kettledrum, which introduces the broadly flowing second theme, also entrusted to the cellos:

---

* *This and the following musical example from this composition are reprinted by permission of C.F. Peters Corporation; sole agents Musikwissenschaftlicher Verlag.*

There is a third vigorous theme of outstanding importance, to say nothing of the profusion of lesser melodies and striking rhythms with which the score abounds.

II. *Adagio: Feierlich, etwas bewegt.* As was Bruckner's habit he made his slow movement a majestic, rather solemn type of melody which is sometimes referred to as "hymnic." In the coda Bruckner quotes a passage from his own F-minor Mass which, as we have seen, was so warmly received while Bruckner was composing this Symphony. The passage is taken from the *"Benedictus,"* where it is sung to the words *"In nomine Domini."*

III. *Scherzo: Schnell.* This is a typically burly scherzo movement, such as Bruckner tended to write throughout the rest of his symphonic career, with sudden dramatic contrasts of loud and soft and delicate bits of orchestral color in a near chamber music style. The central trio section switches from the Symphony's tonic key of C minor to a joyous C major and a theme which will recall to some the transformation of the principal theme in the first movement recapitulation of Beethoven's "Eroica" Symphony.

IV. *Finale: Mehr schnell.* The grandiose finale starts delicately enough in the violins alone but soon works up to a stormy bridge section leading to a gentle, almost lullaby-like contrasting theme. A sudden silence ushers in the prayerful closing measures of Bruckner's exposition: measures quoted, this time, from the *"Kyrie"* of his F-minor Mass, *"Eleison, eleison . . . ."* After a brief but concentrated development section, Bruckner brings back the principal theme of his finale, cites once more the *"Kyrie"* from his Mass and rounds off the Symphony with a sudden shift from C minor to a blazing triumph in C major.

The Symphony is scored for 2 flutes, 2 oboes, 2 clarinets, 2 bassoons, 4 horns, 2 trumpets, 3 trombones, kettledrums, and the standard string choir.

SYMPHONY NO. 3, D MINOR

When Bruckner left Wagner's luxurious Villa Wahnfried one September evening of 1873, he was in a state of supreme confusion. Exultation over the fulfillment of a cherished dream (Wagner had just accepted the dedication of Bruckner's Third Symphony) mingled with the elation produced by generous draughts of Bayreuth beer. "Weihen-Stephan—a wonderful drink," said Wagner, as he toasted the Symphony and urged the timid composer on to drink. Bruckner could hardly believe his own happiness as Wagner himself waited on him.

ANTON BRUCKNER.

From a set of caricature-silhouettes by Otto Böhler: Bruckner being welcomed to Bayreuth by Richard Wagner. In actual life Bruckner was of rather imposing stature, considerably taller than Richard Wagner.

"But Master!—What a waiter!" protested Bruckner, as Wagner kept refilling his glass: "For heaven's sake, Master! I can't! It'll be the death of me! I've just come from Marienbad!"

"Oh, come on!" urged Wagner. "It's good for your health! Drink!" Despite his protests Bruckner drank and drank, while Wagner's wife Cosima smiled benignly and observed that Bruckner was a real child of Vienna (*"ein echtes Wiener Kind"*).

Naturally absentminded, Bruckner was so excited that when he got back to his hotel room he could not remember which one of the two symphonies he had brought to Wagner had been chosen by "The Master" for the honor of dedication to him. In his embarrassment and despair, Bruckner finally sent a messenger to Wagner, with a note: "Symphony in D minor—the one where the trumpet starts the theme? A. Bruckner." Soon the note came back with the added words: "Yes! Yes! Hearty Greetings! Richard Wagner." Bruckner preserved the slip of paper as a sacred relic.

Bruckner's description of the incident, preserved for us in his picturesque Austrian peasant dialect, is confirmed by the account of the sculptor G.A. Kietz, who happened to be working on a bust of Cosima Wagner when Bruckner paid his visit to Wahnfried.

Was there ever a stranger artistic relationship than Bruckner's adoration of Wagner? Despite Wagner's pleasure in allowing himself to be worshiped by the humble Bruckner, there is no sign that Wagner had any lasting enthusiasm or understanding for Bruckner's music or that Bruckner played any role in Wagner's life or art. Two more dissimilar natures can hardly be imagined: Bruckner, the simpleminded, provincial son of a long line of peasants and village schoolmasters, and Wagner, the sophisticated cosmopolite, son of a theatrical family; Bruckner the devout Catholic, whose greatest works were religious music or symphonies often tinged with religion, and Wagner, the skeptic, "the old magician" of Bayreuth.

Bruckner, for his part, basically misunderstood Wagner. He seems to have been indifferent to both the dramatic and intellectual content of Wagner's works. It is amazing to think that Bruckner studied the score of *Tristan und Isolde,* which he so worshiped, in a piano reduction *without* text. And according to one report transmitted by Friedrich Blume, Bruckner asked a friend with whom he left the opera house after a performance of *Die Walküre* why they burn up Brünnhilde at the end.

Yet despite Bruckner's limited grasp of Wagner's art this experience was the great turning point in his development. This it was which seems to have transformed Bruckner from a village organist of high contrapuntal skill and with orchestral ambitions to a symphonic master of world stature, the center of a controversy not yet settled even in our day, when Central European musicians tend to rank Bruckner far above Brahms as the greatest symphonist since Beethoven and Schubert.

Of all Bruckner's symphonies, the Third has the most complicated history. It exists in three versions (some students even count four) each of which in turn has its own variants. The first, composed in 1872–75, was the version Bruckner showed to Wagner even before he had completely finished the Finale. Bruckner authorities are agreed that this first version is the weakest of the three, the longest and the least cohesive. It contains many direct quotations from Wagner's *Tristan* and the *Ring of the Nibelung*. It was never published and seems never to have been performed.

Bruckner began work on what he called a "completely new revised version" of his Third Symphony in the summer of 1876 (soon after finishing his Fifth). He conducted the premiere of this second version on December 16, 1877, in Vienna. It was a resounding failure with public and press alike. Despite his discouragement Bruckner made further slight changes after the premiere, and Theodor Rättig undertook to publish the full score, the instrumental parts and a piano (four-hand) reduction of the score by Gustav Mahler and R. Krzyzanowsky. This second version, was republished in 1950 in a scholarly edition which eliminated numerous minor mechanical errors.

A third version of the Third Symphony was undertaken with the assistance and advice of Bruckner's friend and ardent admirer, the conductor Franz Schalk, early in March 1889. Bruckner himself felt the weight of his initial failure and was amenable to most, though not all, of Schalk's suggestions. The changes, far too numerous to catalog here, involved the development of a richer orchestral sound, closely related to that of Bruckner's Eighth Symphony and, above all, important cuts in the *Adagio* and Finale. The most striking cuts were those in the Finale where the entire beginning of the recapitulation (some fifty-four measures) was omitted. This and a further cut of forty-nine measures in the Finale served the purpose of brevity. Though authorities are by no means agreed today as to how willingly Bruckner's consent was given, the fact remains that he did consent and even wrote in a letter of 1889 that he had "fundamentally improved" his Third Symphony and did not want to hear anything more about the "old version." First performed by the Vienna Philharmonic on December 21, 1890, under the direction of Hans Richter, this third version proved as great a success as the second had been a failure. A few weeks before the premiere, the revised full score third version was published, again by Rättig, and the very considerable costs of republication were underwritten by Emperor Franz Joseph I. Each conductor's choice of which version and which variants to use depends on his personal taste, habits, and insight into Bruckner's musical mind. In view of the multiple differences, the following description gives only the broadest outline of the Symphony. The musical examples are taken from the second (1878) version, as are the tempo marks.

I. *Gemässigt, mehr bewegt; Misterioso.* This movement is an imposing structure. The opening, like some other Bruckner openings, recalls the beginning of Beethoven's Ninth. Not only is the key the same, but the first measures consist of softly weaving string tone, outlining the tonic chord of D minor. A solo trumpet, as if from afar, sounds the principal theme of the Symphony: a fanfare-like figure which Bruckner particularly loved, and which struck Wagner's imagination at his first examination of the score:

This and several related phrases build to a great climax and die away almost to silence.

A contrasting thematic group begins with a flowing figure for the second violins:

The great development makes extensive use of Bruckner's famous contrapuntal skill, one of the more obvious devices being the mirror-inversion of the Symphony's opening theme in various combinations, with the original form of this and other themes.

II. *Adagio bewegt, quasi andante.* The lyrical *Adagio,* like many Bruckner slow movements, seems to have religious overtones. It is cast in a free three-part form, with a slightly faster middle section. The return of the opening strain is embellished with elaborate accompaniment figures and freely developed to a powerful climax.

III. *Scherzo: Ziemlich schnell.* Whispering strings establish the swift pace of the scherzo before the pounding rhythm of the main theme crashes out in the full orchestra. A lyric contrast intervenes in the form of a quiet melody for the first violins. There is also a delicate waltz-like trio section before the return of the principal scherzo themes.

IV. *Finale: Allegro.* Like the opening movement, the finale, a giant sonata-allegro form, begins with the soft suggestion of a harmony out of which there grows the heroic, fanfare-like principal theme. The more lyric group of contrasting themes encloses a further contrast in the combination of two melodies which Bruckner himself is said to have described as embodying the two sides of life: a lilting dance-like figure for the first violin which combines with a serious chorale-like melody sung by two horns in unison:

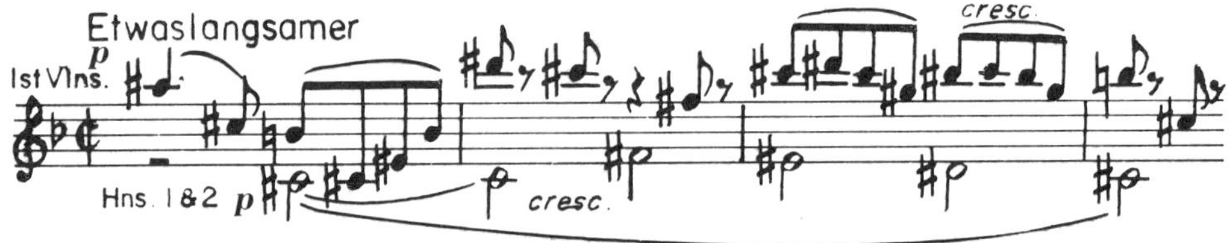

After a rich development of all the foregoing basic themes, a hush descends on the orchestra in preparation for the return of the principal theme. (This return is cut in the third [1890] version, one of several amputations which, to this listener, seriously lessen the power of the finale.) In the concluding pages Bruckner brings back the opening theme of the first movement in a triumphant D major.

The Third Symphony is scored for a relatively modest orchestra of 2 flutes, 2 oboes, 2 clarinets, 2 bassoons, 4 horns, 3 trumpets, 3 trombones, kettledrums, and the standard strings.

SYMPHONY NO. 4, E-FLAT MAJOR (ROMANTIC)

The title "Romantic" was given to the Fourth Symphony by Bruckner himself —but as an afterthought. Indeed, Bruckner's entire symphonic career was an incredible mass of afterthoughts, of deletions, of additions, of simplifications, amplifications, reorchestrations, revisions and new versions: some reluctantly permitted on the pressing advice of well-meaning conductors and friends, some undertaken out of discouragement and fear lest his music prove too difficult to perform or to understand, and some spontaneously as the result of later and finer inspiration.

Such long-drawn-out, often torturing uncertainty suggests some deep inner insecurity in Bruckner, which may have been aggravated by his humble provincial background, his long struggle for artistic maturity and his even longer battle for professional status and public recognition. The orphan son of a village schoolmaster, Bruckner was trained for his father's profession and at first studied music only on the side. Not until his thirtieth year did he decide to become a full-time musician. Two years later he won a position as Cathedral organist in the small city of Linz. He was forty-three years old before he achieved a position in Vienna as court organist, and forty-four when his First Symphony was first performed (under his own direction in Linz).

The overwhelming artistic experience of Bruckner's life was Richard Wagner, whose music he began to study in his late thirties. But profound as Wagner's influence was, it may have been exaggerated in the reorchestration of Bruckner's scores by his well-meaning Wagnerian friends and conductors who anonymously edited many of his symphonies (including his "Romantic") for their first publication. It is these "edited" first prints of Bruckner's symphonies which have caused the bitter controversies that still flare up today.

The crux of the controversy is: which versions did Bruckner wish to be final, definitive? It was long believed that the now-controversial first printings were authentic. Then in 1932, a scholarly edition of the Bruckner symphonies was begun, based on Bruckner's own final manuscript versions, which were found to differ astoundingly from the first printed editions. The editor of the first eight volumes of this edition, including the "restored," undoctored version of the Fourth Symphony (published in 1936) was Robert Haas. There was a great reaction among conductors and German and Austrian audiences in favor of the scholarly *Originalfassungen,* which are not Bruckner's original (in the sense of first) versions, but his *final* manuscript versions. Nevertheless, there have been distinguished conductors who have felt that the doctored first prints, most of which (except the unfinished Ninth Symphony) were issued during Bruckner's lifetime and with his official approval, represent Bruckner's final wishes and are, therefore, *more* authentic than his own manuscripts.

After World War II, a whole new scholarly edition, based in large part on Haas but incorporating more recent research, was published in Vienna by Leopold Nowak.

The tortuous history of the "Romantic" Symphony may be summarized as follows: first version (1874); multiple revisions, including a completely new Scherzo and an almost completely new Finale (1878–80); last autograph score, with further minor changes, made by Bruckner for Anton Seidl to take to the United States, where he hoped to find a publisher (1886–87, this manuscript now in Columbia University Library); revisions (1887–89, presumably by Löwe) for first *publication* of the score in 1889.

The argument in favor of the last (1889) revision as Bruckner's final choice is that the score sent to the printer, although not in Bruckner's hand, bears many annotations in his hand, indicating that he went over it very carefully. The argument against the 1889 edition is Bruckner's own demand. On the first page of the manuscript, in his handwriting, he asks that the score be printed *entire,* without cuts. Instead, this edition appeared with huge slices of the music cut, the most crippling of which was the entire beginning of the recapitulation of the Finale, which Bruckner had designed to begin with the return of the movement's principal theme. It is thus perfectly clear that the first edition of the Symphony violated Bruckner's expressed wishes in a way that he himself felt damaging to the entire structure.

The first performance of the Symphony anywhere was given on February 20, 1881, by the Vienna Philharmonic under the direction of Hans Richter. At rehearsal Bruckner seemed pathetically anxious to please. When Richter came to a puzzling passage he stopped the orchestra and, turning to the composer, asked: "What note is this?" Bruckner replied: "Any note you please. Just as you like." When the rehearsal was over Bruckner, naïve and still pathetically anxious to please, slipped the conductor a tip! It was a Thaler (about 75 cents). Richter kept the Thaler and had it attached to his watch chain. Years later, he recalled: "The Thaler is the memento of a day when I wept. For the first time I conducted a Bruckner symphony, at rehearsal. Bruckner was an old man then. His works were hardly performed anywhere. When the Symphony was over Bruckner came to me. He was radiant with enthusiasm and happiness. I felt him put something in my hand. 'Take it' he said, 'and drink a mug of beer to my health.' "

The premiere of the Fourth was a success. The applause was so enthusiastic that Bruckner had to come to the stage for bows after each movement. The first performance in the United States was given in New York by Anton Seidl's Orchestra under Seidl's direction on March 16, 1888.

I. *Bewegt, nicht zu schnell.* Over a soft tremolo of the strings, the solo horn calls very softly, as if it were a magic incantation, the opening notes of the main theme. It is built around the open fifth:*

Soon the horn is echoed by high woodwinds. A more flowing figure for violins and flutes rises and then falls in the rhythm Bruckner particularly loved, two quarters and a triplet:

This builds to a brief climax, which breaks off suddenly. A delicate contrapuntal passage serves as second theme of a free sonata-form movement. A soft kettledrum roll introduces the development section, which swells to a big climax and then dies away almost to silence for the return of the basic thematic material.

II. *Andante quasi allegretto.* The melancholy, almost tragic slow movement opens with a suggestion of a funeral march in the muted strings and a cello melody built about the open fifth which was so important in the first movement:

At the climax of the movement the melody is transformed into a chant of triumph.

III. *Scherzo: Bewegt.* The distant horn-calls with which the Scherzo opens were intended to suggest a hunting scene in the forest. In the contrasting middle section (the trio) a flute and clarinet have a flowing *Ländler*-like theme which Bruckner marked in his manuscript: "Dance tune during the hunters' meal."

IV. *Finale: Bewegt, doch nicht zu schnell.* The introduction consists basically of one long buildup of harmonic tension over a dominant pedal and a crescendo that seems finally to explode into the heroic main theme of the movement:

---

* *This and the following musical examples from this composition are reprinted by permission of C.F. Peters Corporation; © Copyright 1953; sole agents Musikwissenschaftlicher Verlag.*

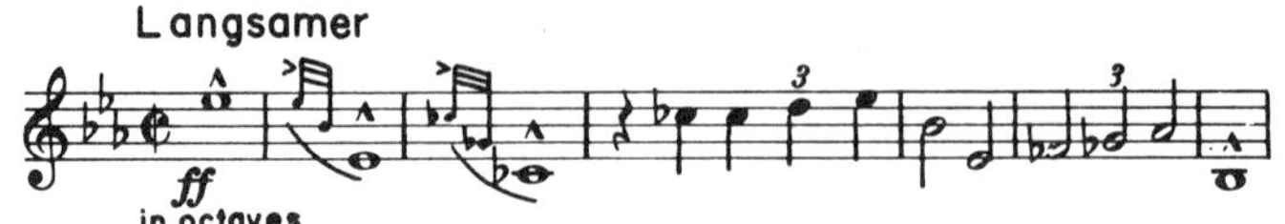

There are reminiscences of the scherzo as the movement develops to another powerful climax. The coda is radiant and majestic.

The "Romantic" Symphony is scored for 3 flutes, piccolo, 2 oboes, 2 clarinets, 2 bassoons, 4 horns, 3 trumpets, 3 trombones, tuba, 3 kettledrums, cymbals (used only in the Finale), and strings.

SYMPHONY NO. 5, B-FLAT MAJOR (ORIGINAL VERSION)

Bruckner never heard his Fifth Symphony performed. The Fifth, probably the most individual of all his symphonies, was born under an unlucky star. When he undertook the Symphony, Bruckner was in the depths of personal depression, artistic discouragement and financial need. After it was finished, the Symphony had to wait sixteen years for a performance. When the premiere came, Bruckner was too sick and too old to attend. When the Symphony was published (April 1896), it was a garbled version: hardly a single measure was left untouched and crippling cuts distorted the form. Before it was published and performed as Bruckner wrote it, another forty years had passed.

To this day one can still find musicians (usually of an older generation) who defend the first, garbled editions of some Bruckner works, on the grounds that the composer consented, or *would have* consented to the changes. The Fifth Symphony, however, shows no evidence that Bruckner ever approved or even knew the extent of the changes incorporated in the first publication. The version usually performed today is based on Bruckner's own final manuscript score.

Although Bruckner was timid, unaggressive and humble to a fault, he appeared to conservative Viennese music lovers a dangerously subversive wild-eyed radical. His worship of Richard Wagner made Bruckner especially objectionable to dominant Viennese musical opinion led by Eduard Hanslick, the brilliant and popular critic of the *Neue Freie Presse*. The powerful opposition of Hanslick and Bruckner's ineptitude in advancing his own affairs combined to make the years of Bruckner's writing and revising of his Fifth Symphony particularly bleak.

The day before he began the score of his Fifth Symphony (February 13, 1875) Bruckner wrote in despair to his friend Moritz von Mayfeld: "My ultimate fate may be to incur debts upon debts and reap the fruits of my diligence in debtors' prison where I can repent at leisure the folly of my having moved to Vienna. One thousand florins a year have been taken away from me, and this year I have no compensation—not even a fellowship. I cannot afford to have my Fourth Symphony copied."

After completing the original version of his Fifth Symphony in 1876, Bruckner made his second pilgrimage to Bayreuth for the world premiere of Wagner's *Ring*. The following year, 1877, he revised his Fifth Symphony, and he added the finishing touches on January 4, 1878.

In 1893, Bruckner's former student and favorite disciple, Franz Schalk, who had become conductor of the Graz Opera, determined to give the Bruckner Fifth, which had never yet been performed, a hearing in Graz. Schalk, who enjoyed the traditional privilege of conducting a performance for his own benefit, made the bold decision to conduct not an opera, but an orchestral concert of modern works. (The other two modern works on the program were Liszt's E-flat-major Piano Concerto and the Overture to Wagner's *Meistersinger*.) But during the rehearsals for the Bruckner Fifth, Schalk ran into difficulties. The parts for the brass instruments were so strenuous that the players were unable to hold out for the entire work. This gave Schalk the idea of having the climactic chorale of the Finale performed by twelve fresh brass players, whom he proposed to place apart on a raised platform at the back of the orchestra. Schalk obtained Bruckner's permission for this procedure and he wrote out the new brass parts himself.

Bruckner unfortunately was ill and unable to attend the world premiere of his Symphony on April 9, 1894. But the performance was a triumph. Schalk wrote from Graz:

> You must surely have had advance oral reports of the tremendous effect achieved by your great, wonderful Fifth.
>
> I can only add that for me the evening will remain one of the most glorious memories of my entire life. Profoundly moved, I felt myself to be a happy wanderer in the fields of eternal greatness. Nobody who has not heard it can imagine the overwhelming power of the Finale.
>
> I lay at your feet, my most deeply and dearly beloved master, all my admiration and sincerest enthusiasm, and I send my homage to the man who has given me these feelings.
>
> Your profoundly thankful, eternally faithful
>
> Francisce

"Francisce" was Bruckner's affectionate nickname for Schalk. Schalk's deep devotion to Bruckner and his music remains unquestioned. It is important to keep this in mind because Schalk has often been blamed for the drastic changes in Bruckner's score when it was first published.

For many years it was assumed that this first printing of the Fifth Symphony was faithful to Bruckner's intentions. Not until 1932 and 1936, when Bruckner's Fifth and Ninth Symphonies were first performed in the version of Bruckner's own manuscript, was it generally realized how very different and much more characteristic of Bruckner the original versions were. The first complete edition of the Bruckner Symphonies based on Bruckner's manuscripts, as far as they were still available, was initiated by Robert Haas. After World War II, a second complete edition of Bruckner with further corrections was undertaken by Dr. Leopold Nowak for the International Bruckner Society in Vienna. Nowak's edition of the Fifth Symphony was published in 1951.

I. *Adagio; Allegro.* This is the only one of Bruckner's symphonies to begin with a slow introduction. In the course of some fifty measures it introduces half a dozen fragments of themes which are important throughout the first movement. It builds to an impressive climax for the entire orchestra and then suddenly falls back to a soft *tremolo* of the violins. Beneath shimmering violins, the cellos and violas in unison proclaim the principal theme of the movement:

A second, contrasting group begins with soft *pizzicato* notes of the strings over which the first violins sing a yearning melody on the G string. This exposition of the basic themes concludes with a vigorous climax for the entire orchestra, dying away to another soft *tremolo* of the string instruments.

The central development section begins with the leisurely tempo and the thematic fragments of the slow introduction. It continues with an elaborate fantasia on all the themes heard so far building to a fresh climax, at the peak of which the principal theme returns in a triumphant proclamation by the trombones and other bass instruments of the orchestra.

II. *Adagio: Sehr langsam.* The melancholy song of the solo oboe, with which the slow movement begins, was the first melody Bruckner put down when he began composing the Fifth Symphony in February of 1875. It appears first in D minor:*

A contrasting melody in the warm key of C major is given to the string choir alone. The entire slow movement consists of the alternation and embellishment of these two principal melodies.

III. *Scherzo: Molto vivace.* A lively opening theme for the woodwinds is followed by a more leisurely, characteristically Austrian *Ländler*—a waltz-like passage. These two groups of melodies are developed in symphonic style. A more delicate so-called "trio section" supplies a striking contrast, after which the main scherzo section is repeated.

---

* *This and the following musical examples from this composition are reprinted by permission of C.F. Peters Corporation; sole agents Musikwissenschaftlicher Verlag.*

IV. *Finale: Adagio; Allegro moderato.* The slow intruduction to the finale recalls the introduction to the first movement. This is followed by a recall of the principal theme of the first movement, quoted above, and by the principal melody of the slow movement, also quoted above. The main body of the finale, a lively *Allegro moderato,* begins with the following principal theme:

The same theme is taken up in succession by the violas, the second violins and finally by the first violins: an exposition in the style of a fugue. But the fugue is interrupted by two lyric contrasting themes, by a heroic fanfare-like theme for the brass and woodwinds and finally by a majestic "chorale" for the entire brass choir:

After echoes of the chorale have died away to silence, the opening phrase of the chorale becomes the subject of another fugal development. As this fugue progresses, the chorale theme is combined with the principal theme of the finale as quoted above. Later, the fugue incorporates more and more familiar thematic fragments, reaching its final climax with the return of the chorale in the blazing colors of trumpets and trombones in slow motion against the livelier figurations of the woodwinds and strings.

The Fifth Symphony is scored for 2 flutes, 2 oboes, 2 clarinets, 2 bassoons, 4 horns, 3 trumpets, 3 trombones, bass tuba, kettledrums, and the traditional strings.

SYMPHONY NO. 6, A MAJOR

The long, often acrimonious debates over which of Bruckner's own versions of his own symphonies represent his final artistic will, do not arise in the case of his Sixth Symphony. Bruckner's Sixth is the only symphony he never revised. But this did not prevent his well-meaning disciples from revising it—radically. Cyrill Hynais, to whom Bruckner entrusted the preparation of his score for the printer, meant well by the master. The famous conductors, Franz Schalk and Ferdinand Löwe, wanted only to help their revered friend. Yet Schalk and Löwe both appear to have urged Hynais on to extensive "improvements" in Bruckner's score—principally in the orchestration, which they made vastly more Wagnerian than it had originally been. It was some three years after Bruckner's death when the printed score of the Sixth Symphony finally appeared. It had been so extensively reorchestrated that Bruckner scholars today consider the composer's intentions had been grievously garbled.

The several editions of Bruckner's Sixth Symphony published in the ensuing years were all based on this first, faulty edition. Not until 1937 was Bruckner's own original version made available in a scholarly edition edited by Robert Haas and published by Breitkopf and Härtel. A more recent scholarly edition of Bruckner's original was published in Vienna in 1952 by Leopold Nowak.

We do not know how far back Bruckner's first inspiration for the Sixth Symphony may date. Nor do we know how long he worked on preliminary sketches. The only certain dates we possess are those of the manuscript full score, which appears to have been begun on September 24, 1879. It was completed on September 3, 1881.

Bruckner never heard a complete performance of his Sixth Symphony. Two movements, the *Adagio* and *Scherzo,* were given their first performance by the Vienna Philharmonic on February 11, 1883 under the direction of Wilhelm Jahn. On February 11, 1899, more than two years after Bruckner's death, Gustav Mahler conducted the first complete performance of the work, but with the score radically cut and reorchestrated. The first uncut performance was conducted by Karl Pohlig in Stuttgart on March 14, 1901. Later that year, on December 13, the first uncut performance of the work using Bruckner's orchestration was given by the Vienna Konzertverein under the direction of August Göllerich. This last was a notable success.

It is interesting that the one symphony which Bruckner never revised is also the least heroic in style. On the other hand the Sixth Symphony is like its fellows in that it is broad in structure, lasting approximately one hour in performance.

I. *Majestoso* [sic; Bruckner's term]. The Symphony has no introduction. The broad principal theme is announced by the cellos and double basses of the orchestra against a very soft but sharply articulated rhythm in the violins:*

A whole group of contrasting themes is introduced by a passionate melody in the violins. This exposition builds to a great climax, then dies away to a whisper. The development of the themes is somewhat shorter and less complex than we often find in Bruckner's first movements. It too builds to a great climax which in turn ushers in the reprise of the basic themes.

---

* *This and the following musical example from this composition are reprinted by permission of C.F. Peters Corporation; sole agents Musikwissenschaftlicher Verlag.*

II. *Adagio: Sehr feierlich.* This *Adagio* is one of the rare examples in Bruckner of a slow movement in fully worked out sonata form. The somewhat declamatory first theme is introduced by the violins. The contrasting, lyric theme has great romantic warmth and is interestingly contrapuntal in its texture. Its most prominent melodic strand, carried by the first violins, begins as follows:

III. *Scherzo: Nicht schnell.* The relaxed tempo of this movement is unusual in Bruckner's scherzos. It is in the simple three-part form: a lively scherzo proper in A minor, followed by a slow trio in which Bruckner enjoys contrasting three colors: the string choir, the French horns, and the woodwind choir. At the conclusion of the trio section the entire scherzo proper is repeated.

IV. *Finale: Bewegt, doch nicht zu schnell.* A whispering tremolo of the violas opens the final movement in typically Brucknerian fashion. The suppressed agitation of the opening page is emphasized by the A minor tonality. When the principal theme, a heroic fanfare-like figure, is proclaimed in A major by horns, trumpets and trombones, it comes with an effect of blazing triumph.

As usual in Bruckner's finales, there is a rich profusion of themes, several of them broadly lyric. After these have been developed and restated, the principal theme of the first movement is recalled by the trombones in a grandiose peroration.

The Sixth Symphony is scored for 2 flutes, 2 oboes, 2 clarinets, 2 bassoons, 4 horns, 3 trumpets, 3 trombones, bass tuba, kettledrums, and the traditional strings.

SYMPHONY NO. 7, E MAJOR

It is almost symbolic of Bruckner that the greatest page of his most popular work—the *Adagio* of his Seventh Symphony—should have been completed as a lament for Richard Wagner. When the news of Wagner's death reached Bruckner on February 14, 1883, he was overwhelmed. He had worshiped Wagner above any living artist. It was the inspiration of Wagner's music that had transformed Bruckner from a plodding provincial composer, church organist, and school master, into an artist of international stature.

Much ink has been spilt over the question of whether Bruckner really did compose this *Adagio* as a lament for Wagner. However, the manuscript score bears the date April 21, 1883, at the close of the *Adagio*. This was nine weeks after Wagner's death and it is hardly to be imagined that this tragedy was not in Bruckner's mind as he completed the movement. On the other hand, the *sketch* for the *Adagio* was begun the previous year and completed on January 22, over three weeks *before* Wagner's death.

Bruckner, himself, explained that he had the master's death in mind in the sketch, in fact, it was this thought which fathered the principal theme of the movement. In a letter to his pupil, Felix Mottl, Bruckner wrote: "One day I came home and felt very sad. It is impossible, I thought, that the Master should live much longer. And then the C-sharp minor *Adagio* came to me."

There seems no very cogent reason to doubt Bruckner's word. And the instrumentation of the *Adagio* with four so-called "Bayreuth" or "Wagner" tubas strengthens the case. The Bayreuth tubas, a sort of cross between the conventional tuba and French horn, had been devised by Wagner himself to obtain a special tone color he needed in the *Ring* operas—a color midway between the mellow sound of the horn and the solemn quality of the trombone. The Bayreuth tubas had never before been used in a symphony by Bruckner or anyone else, and it is hardly possible that Bruckner would have used them for the first time in this movement without intending a reference to Richard Wagner.

The Seventh Symphony, begun in 1881, was completed on September 5, 1883. The first performance, conducted by Artur Nikisch on December 30, 1884, in the Stadtheater of Leipzig, was a triumph as was the second in Munich on March 10, 1885.

In contrast to all Bruckner's earlier symphonies, the Seventh was rapidly acclaimed, and soon established him in the public eye as a major contemporary composer. By 1886 it was performed at Hamburg, Cologne, Graz, Vienna, and on July 29 of that year Theodore Thomas conducted the American premiere in Chicago. The following year it was acclaimed in London (under the direction of Hans Richter), Budapest, Dresden, and Berlin.

Because of its speedy success, the Seventh is the only one of Bruckner's symphonies which was published without major revisions by his well-meaning friends or by Bruckner himself. The first edition published in 1885 by Albert Gutmann in Vienna does differ but only in details from the scholarly *Originalfassung* edited by Robert Haas in Leipzig in 1944. The most famous difference concerns the cymbal crash at the climactic change of harmony in the *Adagio*. This was added by Bruckner between the first performance and publication of the first edition. Later he decided the addition had been a mistake and wrote in the margin beside it: "Invalid" *(Gilt nicht)*. But since the editions of the Seventh differ in details only, the controversies which have raged around other Bruckner symphonies as to which of the several *versions* is authentic do not have the same urgency.

I. *Allegro moderato.* The principal theme of this movement came to Bruckner in a dream, which he regarded as a good omen. His old friend, Kapellmeister Dorm, from his former home in Linz appeared to him in his sleep, whistled the theme, and prophesied: "With this theme you will make your fortune." Bruckner immediately woke, lit a candle, and wrote down the melody. In a sense the prophecy came true because it is the Seventh which brought Bruckner general recognition.

From the soft shimmer of its opening bars, to the mellow splendor of its concluding fanfares, this first movement is assured and serene. The principal theme, introduced against a scarcely audible tremolo of the violins, is a soaring melody sweeping upward over two octaves:*

The richly developed first movement presents other, contrasting themes, but it is dominated by the opening melody in the form shown above, in abbreviated form, in inverted or mirror form, and in the fanfare form with which it concludes.

II. *Adagio: sehr feierlich und langsam.* The principal theme of the second movement is the famous phrase for Wagner tubas which returns throughout the movement as a dirge-like refrain:

The above phrase for Wagner tubas is followed immediately by the contrasting warmth of the string choir alone in an emphatic three-note figure built on a rising major third. This rising third appears in the closing pages of the *Te Deum* as a symbol of triumph over death, and it seems at least probable that Bruckner intended it to have a similar meaning here. In fact, it is this theme which he selects to build the greatest climax of the movement on a triple *fortissimo* for the entire orchestra. We know that this climax was especially important to Bruckner. In another letter to Mottl, he writes: "Please take a very slow and solemn tempo. At the close, in the Dirge (in memory of the death of the Master) think of our Ideal! . . . Kindly do not forget the *fff* at the end of the Dirge." And speaking of the quiet epilogue which follows this climax Bruckner wrote: "At letter x in the Adagio—Funeral music for tubas and horns etc."

III. *Scherzo: sehr schnell.* The scherzo is as exuberant as if thoughts of death had never crossed Bruckner's mind. One feels, as so often in Bruckner, that Beethoven's *Ninth Symphony* is lurking in the back of his mind, an impression which is strengthened by the octave leap and the dotted rhythm of

---

* *This and the following musical example from this composition are reprinted by permission of C.F. Peters Corporation; sole agents Musikwissenschaftlicher Verlag.*

Bruckner's principal theme. There is a somewhat slower, more mournful trio section, after which the boisterous scherzo proper is repeated.

IV. *Finale: Bewegt, doch nicht schnell.* Like the first movement, the finale begins with a shimmering violin tremolo, and a lively theme which seems a scherzo-like transformation of the opening melody of the first movement. The contrasting theme is a soft chorale-like melody sung by the first violins accompanied by *pizzicati* of the cellos and double basses. The symphony ends in triumph with a climactic return of the chief melody of the opening movement.

The score of the Seventh Symphony calls for 2 flutes, 2 oboes, 2 clarinets, 2 bassoons, 4 horns, 3 trumpets, 3 trombones, 2 tenor tubas, 2 bass tubas, contrabass tuba, kettledrums, and the customary strings. The triangle and cymbals, which Bruckner added for the first edition of the Symphony and later marked "invalid" are still occasionally used by conductors loath to part with that extra touch of drama.

SYMPHONY NO. 8, C MINOR

Bruckner regarded his Eighth Symphony as the artistic high point of his career. He began work on it in 1884 in the wake of a series of triumphs of his Seventh Symphony, in a mood of optimism and self-confidence such as he had never known before. The humble son of a village schoolmaster, orphaned early in life and largely self-taught on the organ, Bruckner had begun his career as a provincial organist and was over forty when he finally came as Court Organist to Vienna. He was late to mature as a composer, and much later still in achieving recognition.

The virulence of the opposition to Bruckner, particularly in Vienna, was partly due to his identification with the radical "new-German" tendencies of Wagner and Liszt, which were anathema to conservative Viennese and especially to Eduard Hanslick, the powerful music critic of the Vienna *Neue freie Presse.*

There is no question of Bruckner's overwhelming admiration for Wagner, or the influence of Wagner's music on Bruckner's mature style. Yet the influence of Beethoven is just as great, and that of Schubert lay perhaps deeper.

I. *Allegro moderato.* Of all Beethoven's symphonies it is the apocalyptic Ninth which most possessed Bruckner's imagination. The influence shows here in the opening bars of the Symphony with the soft string *tremolo.* Even the rhythm of Bruckner's principal theme

is strikingly close to that of Beethoven's Ninth. In the course of fifty bars, this rhythm undergoes some alteration and from the new rhythmic pattern there emerges a second principal theme, a broadly melodic phrase sung by the violins. This in turn, after almost fifty measures more, develops into a third and concluding principal theme. The exposition now builds to a tremendous climax and then fades to a soft violin *tremolo* like the start of the movement, with dying echoes of the opening theme heard now in a solo horn and oboe.

The richly dramatic development section is built first of all upon the opening theme, although the second, lyric theme later plays an important role. In a mild alteration of Classical precedent, Bruckner allows the mood of strife to continue from the development section into the normally more straightforward recapitulation of the opening material.

II. *Scherzo: Allegro moderato—Langsam—Allegro moderato.* This typical, boisterous Brucknerian scherzo opens with the following vigorous theme proclaimed by violas and cellos:

Among the beauties of the slow trio section is the warm poetry of a horn solo. The movement concludes with a repetition of the vigorous opening.

III. *Adagio: Feierlich langsam doch nicht schleppend.* Many of Bruckner's admirers are agreed that if there was one type of symphonic movement in which he excelled, it was his adagios. Bruckner himself considered the *Adagio* of his Eighth the greatest movement in any of his symphonies. It begins with a soft murmuring in the strings, a syncopated figure clearly suggested by the similar background to the love duet of Wagner's *Tristan and Isolde: "O sink' hernieder, Nacht der Liebe."* Against this background, the first violins sing the brief principal theme:

IV. *Finale: Feierlich, nicht schnell.* Against a persistent hammering rhythm of the entire string body the heavy brass proclaims a heroic theme recalling the rhythmic character of the Symphony's opening. This is followed by brilliant fanfares of the trumpets.

The structure of this Finale is similar to that of the first movement. But its thematic richness is even greater. For in addition to the themes of this movement the principal themes of the three preceding movements are recalled and finally combined as follows in the resplendent C major of the Symphony's closing pages:

The Eighth Symphony has a curious and complicated history characteristic of much of Bruckner's work, of his long struggle for recognition and of his deep inner insecurity. Authorities differ as to whether Bruckner may be considered to have written one or two versions of his Eighth Symphony between 1884 and 1887 when he sent the score to the conductor, Hermann Levi. Levi, whom Bruckner regarded as his protector and "artistic father," had previously agreed to perform the Symphony, but when he saw the gargantuan score, he was forced to tell Bruckner that he was unable to understand it, much less perform it. When this message was brought to Bruckner, the composer almost suffered a nervous breakdown. All his earlier doubts of his own ability returned redoubled.

He undertook to revise the Symphony and worked on it for three more years, shortening it notably to what is now known as the 1890 version. When the Symphony was published simultaneously in Vienna and Berlin in 1892 (with a partial subvention from the Austrian emperor), slight further changes were made in the score. We do not know whether these changes were wholly arbitrary on the part of Bruckner's well-intentioned "helpers" or not.

In 1935, Robert Haas published in the framework of the new Bruckner Complete Edition, what purported to be the original version or *Urfassung* of the Eighth Symphony. Actually it was Haas's own compromise between the 1890 and the 1887 versions—Haas's educated guess as to what Bruckner's final choice would have been, if he had been free of external pressures.

After World War II the editorship of the scholarly complete edition of Bruckner was entrusted to Dr. Leopold Nowak. In 1955 Dr. Nowak published what he designates specifically as the 1890 version. This is now widely believed to represent Bruckner's final intentions. But we can never be absolutely sure. We may never know which version, or what compromise Bruckner would have wished to be the final version for posterity. In his own day, for the sake of reaching an audience, he made changes, some of which he doubtless approved, some of which were apparently made under pressure and in the hope that they would remain temporary. It is probably impossible for us ever to know how Bruckner would have shaped a definitive Eighth Symphony. Perhaps he would never have known himself. For he was tortured all his life by self-doubt and was much given to agonized revising of his own revisions.

The first performance of the Symphony was given by the Vienna Philharmonic on December 18, 1892, under the direction of Hans Richter in the Vienna Musikvereinsaal. Among the members of the first audience was Hugo Wolf, who wrote to a friend: "This Symphony is the creation of a giant and it towers above all the other symphonies of the master in its spiritual dimensions, in its fertility and grandeur. Despite the most Cassandra-like predictions of disaster, even among the initiated, the success was almost without parallel. It was a complete victory of the powers of light over darkness. As each of the individual movements ceased to sound, a storm of enthusiasm broke out with elemental violence. In short, no Roman emperor could have wished for a greater triumph."

Bruckner's Eighth Symphony is scored, in its 1890 version, for 3 flutes, 3 oboes, 3 clarinets, 3 bassoons, 8 horns, 3 trumpets, 3 trombones, bass tuba, kettledrums, and the traditional string body.

SYMPHONY NO. 9, D MINOR

"I have made dedications to two earthly majesties," said Bruckner to Dr. Richard Heller, who attended him in his last illness: "poor King Ludwig (of Bavaria), as the patron of the arts, and our illustrious dear Emperor, as the highest earthly majesty that I know, and I now dedicate to the Lord of lords, to my dear God, my last work, and hope that He will grant me enough time to complete it and will generously accept my gift." This was the Ninth Symphony.

In a sense, all of Bruckner's works were dedicated to God. He was one of the most pious of nineteenth-century composers and had begun his career as a dedicated church musician. But his intention, reported by Dr. Heller, to dedicate the Ninth to God had a more specific meaning. He regarded the Ninth as a summation of his life work, and we know that he felt the *Adagio* of the Ninth, or at least a certain passage of it, to be his farewell to life.

Bruckner began work on this Symphony in the summer of 1887, immediately after completing the scoring of his tremendous Eighth; but he interrupted his work to return to the Eighth and to revise his First and Third Symphonies. His health began to fail. In the spring of 1890, he suffered a chronic catarrh of the larynx and began to show symptoms of an abnormal nervous condition. In the fall of that year he was relieved of his duties as organ professor at the Vienna Conservatory, and in January of the following year he retired as professor emeritus of that school. In 1892 he retired from the service of the Court Chapel. In the fall of 1893 he fell gravely ill with dropsy and his condition caused such anxiety that he made his will before the end of the year.

"I have done my duty on earth," Bruckner declared to a caller shortly after his seventieth birthday. "I have accomplished what I could, and my only wish is to be allowed to finish my Ninth Symphony. Three movements are almost complete. The *Adagio* is nearly finished. There remains only the finale. I trust death will not deprive me of my pen."

He was exhausted by his labors of revision, which cost him spiritual as well as physical agonies. His friends were amazed that the ailing composer could find the energy and determination to continue with the Ninth Symphony. He gave his last lecture at the University of Vienna in November, 1894. The Emperor seems to have done what he could to help. In addition to a government subsidy, Bruckner received an outright donation of a substantial sum in 1895. The Emperor also gave him free lodging in the Imperial Palace of Belvedere, surrounded by a beautiful garden, with a commanding view of the city below.

The third of the four movements was completed on November 30, 1894. The struggle with the finale dominated the two remaining years of Bruckner's life. It was a heroic battle, but a tragic one. Six versions of the finale exist, all of them incomplete. The very last version lacked only the coda when Bruckner laid aside the score on the morning of October 11, 1896, to go for a walk in the Belvedere Park. On his return to the Palace that afternoon, he died. Perhaps he would never have shaped the keystone for the last symphonic arch, for he had already been failing mentally as well as physically. The funeral took place three days later in the great Baroque Karlskirche near the Grosse Musikvereinsaal, where so many of his symphonies had first been heard.

I. *Feierlich, misterioso.* Like Beethoven's Ninth, on which Bruckner so often built, Bruckner's Ninth opens with a mysterious string *tremolo* in D minor. An heroic theme for eight horns flashes out of the darkness and disappears. It is replaced by a yearning, melodious theme for the strings and a further great wealth of thematic ideas, culminating in the following bold figure proclaimed in triple-forte octaves by the entire orchestra, *feierlich, misterioso:* *

These are developed on a grand scale, each main section of the movement dying away to a *pianissimo* before the next starts its climb to a fresh climax.

II. *Scherzo: Bewegt, lebhaft; Trio: Schnell.* The relentless rhythmic drive of this scherzo refrain, once heard, is hard to forget. Although it makes its first appearance in the eerie tones of woodwinds and *pizzicato* violins, it returns often in a thunderous version for full orchestra, with kettledrums and heavy brass pounding out the basic rhythm:

---

* *This and the following musical examples from this composition are reprinted by permission of C.F. Peters Corporation; sole agents Musikwissenschaftlicher Verlag.*

This basic rhythm, whether it thunders or whispers, seems to generate the basic *Scherzo* theme: a cascading figure which plunges downward over two octaves and a half and whips upward again almost to its starting point. With his love of upside-down or mirror reflections of his themes, Bruckner also inverts the principal figure into a rapidly climbing theme, which then slashes downward almost to its starting point.

The contrasting middle *(Trio)* section is subtly related to the main body of the *Scherzo*, although its texture is considerably lighter.

III. *Adagio: Langsam, feierlich.* The principal melody of the slow movement starts with a broad, sweeping phrase of the first violins:

It continues in a solemn style suggesting the gestures of the theatrical Baroque saints depicted in the eighteenth-century Austrian churches Bruckner knew so well. There are many subordinate, contrasting themes including, toward the end, quotations from Bruckner's own Seventh and Eighth Symphonies and the "Gloria" from his D-minor Mass.

The Ninth Symphony is scored for 3 flutes, 3 oboes, 3 clarinets, 3 bassoons, 8 horns, 4 Wagner tubas, 3 trumpets, 3 trombones, contrabass tuba, kettledrums, and the customary strings.

The first performance of the unfinished Ninth Symphony was given in Vienna seven years after Bruckner's death, on February 11, 1903, with the Vienna Konzertverein Orchestra under the direction of Ferdinand Löwe. In this performance, and in the first printed edition of the Ninth Symphony which Löwe edited, he made a very large number of changes that substantially distorted Bruckner's clear intentions. This was done with the blameless aim of facilitating public understanding of Bruckner's work. The original version of the Ninth Symphony was not performed in public until nearly thirty years later, when Siegmund von Hausegger conducted the Munich Philharmonic Orchestra in a performance of two versions: the garbled Löwe version and Bruckner's original. These performances convinced most listeners and lovers of Bruckner's music that his original version should be restored for future performances and published. It was published first by Otto Haas and Alfred Orel, and subsequently by Leopold Nowak.

John Cage

Born September 5, 1912, Los Angeles

ATLAS ECLIPTICALIS

A Yankee tinkerer, whose tinkering set off an international revolution, John Cage is as American as Charles Ives and Walt Whitman and apple pie. It is a Yankee trait to rebel; at least, Yankees of both north and south like to think that this is so. And this may be one reason for the sneaking admiration Cage enjoys even among his severest native critics. For he has been a maverick on a grand scale, on such a gargantuan scale and with such conviction that he has become a prophet honored in his own country, even in his own house, supported by devoted and brilliant performing artists as well as foundation funds. At the same time he has been widely influential in European *avant garde* music.

Probably Cage's most important revolution has been his espousal of so-called "chance" or "aleatory" (or "aleatoric") music. This could be regarded as a massive rebellion against the powerful reign of the twelve-tone (serial) method of composing, or its midcentury extension regulating not only pitch, but also rhythm, tempo, instrumentation, dynamics—in short, almost every imaginable ingredient of a music—to a point where the art of composing had come to seem dangerously like a mechanical working out of a mathematical equation in which everything was predetermined.

Against such a background, the controlled chaos of chance music could seem a liberation. Cage's famous *Music of Changes* for piano (with the almost symbolic date of 1951) inaugurated the second half of our century with the earliest well-known example of aleatory music. In *Music of Changes* the pitches of the notes are carefully written out but the length (or duration) of the notes and frequency of occurrence are determined by the *I-Ching (Book of Changes)*, a venerable Chinese system of selecting random numbers by tossing coins or sticks.

It is known that dice were used as a sort of toy for composing music in the eighteenth century. Various chance methods have been ascribed to Mozart, Haydn, and other serious artists. But Cage initiated a more fruitful trend toward more sophisticated and picturesque methods of chance composition, which have been eagerly imitated and expanded the world over. The Greek composer and mathematician Yannis Xenakis, and the German Karlheinz Stockhausen are among the most renowned second-generation leaders of the aleatory revolution.

Cage's *Atlas Eclipticalis and Winter Music* was commissioned by the Montreal Festivals Society and performed under Cage's direction by the Festival Orchestra with David Tudor as piano soloist on August 3, 1961, during the International Week of Today's Music in Montreal, Canada. Originally *Atlas*

Eclipticalis and *Winter Music* were two separate compositions. Either work may be performed alone, or they may be combined with each other. In addition to the Chinese principles of chance employed in composing, the performance of both works leaves great latitude of choice to the executants.

Winter Music may be performed by from one to twenty pianists using all or part of the twenty pages of the score to provide a program of agreed-upon length. The composing of the score involved "both chance operations and observation of imperfections in the paper on which the music was written."

The score of *Atlas Eclipticalis* may be performed in whole or in part, for any duration, by any ensemble, chamber or orchestral, drawn from an eighty-six-part orchestra of conventional instruments with miscellaneous unspecified nonpitched percussion instruments.

The title, *Atlas Eclipticalis,* is taken from a book of astronomical maps Mr. Cage used in composing. This involved chance operations, including the placing of transparent templates on the pages of the atlas and inscribing the positions of the stars. There is no score in the conventional sense, Mr. Cage informs us, since the work is an example of "indeterminacy."

According to Cage:

> It is also an example of what may be called "live" electronic music. Most electronic music is dependent on magnetic tape for its performance and so becomes a recording. This music uses electronic circuits (mircophones, amplifiers, loudspeakers) in connection with musical instruments.
>
> I wrote *Winter Music* for piano(s) in the winter of 1956–57. This was accomplished quickly. *Atlas Elipticalis* required some nine months. I began it, being commissioned by the Montreal Festivals Society, in 1961, while I was a Fellow of the Center for Advanced Studies at Wesleyan University in Middletown, Connecticut. The writing of the 86 parts was completed early in 1962, but performances of ensembles of the already finished parts took place earlier. It has been choreographed by Merce Cunningham and then has the title *Aeon.*
>
> In 1954, while in Europe, I met the Japanese musicologist, Hidekazu Yoshida, who gave me his notion of the three lines of Haiku poetry, the first line referring, he said, to nirvana, the second to samsara, and the third to specific happening. I thought in writing *Atlas Elipticalis* of the first line and of the stars as nirvana. And I had the intention of writing two other works which would complete the trilogy. This I did in 1963 with *Variations IV* and *0'00"*.
>
> I am principally indebted in my work to my teachers, Richard Buhlig, Adolph Weiss, Henry Cowell and Arnold Schoenberg; to many composers with whom I have been closely associated, Lou Harrison, Alan Hovhaness, Virgil Thompson, Morton Feldman, Christian Wolff, Earle Brown; with two others whom I never knew except through their works, Anton Webern and Erik Satie. I am devoted to the works of Edgard Varèse. Without close association with David Tudor, the pianist, my recent work, that of the past fifteen years, would be unthinkable. And there are many people not actually in the field of music who have influenced me. This would be a long list but includes

> particularly the artists Robert Rauschenberg and Jasper Johns, the sculptor Richard Lippold, the philosopher Daisetz Suzuki, and the botanist Guy G. Nearing. And of course my father, the inventor John M. Cage. And Merce Cunningham, dancer and choreographer. And now the young composers, particularly Toshi Ichiyanagi who helped me in some of the manuscript work of *Atlas*, George Brecht and La Monte Young.

Atlas Eclipticalis is scored for piccolo, flute, alto flute, 3 oboes, English horn, saxophone, 3 clarinets, bass or contrabass clarinet, 3 bassoons, contrabassoon, 5 horns, 3 trumpets, 2 tenor trombones, bass trombone, 3 tubas, 4 to 12 kettledrums, 3 harps, 12 first violins, 12 second violins, 9 violas, 9 cellos, 3 doublebasses, and "miscellaneous unspecified nonpitched percussion instruments," [the] instrumental parts (86) to be played in whole or part, any duration, in any ensemble, chamber or orchestral, of the above performers; with or without *Winter Music* . . . ; an electronic version is made possible by use of contact microphones with associated amplifiers and loudspeakers operated by an assistant to the conductor.

Elliott Carter

Born December 11, 1908, New York City

CONCERTO FOR ORCHESTRA

Mr. Carter kindly furnished the following information about his Concerto for Orchestra on the occasion of its world premiere by the New York Philharmonic on February 5, 1970:

> The general character of my Concerto for Orchestra, which the New York Philharmonic Society commissioned for its 125th anniversary, was suggested by the Nobel Prize-winning poem *Vents* ("Winds") by the French poet who calls himself St. John Perse. The poem had attracted me by its expansive, almost Whitmanesque, descriptions of a United States constantly swept by forces like winds, forces that are always transforming, remolding, or obliterating the past and introducing the fresh and the new. In the course of the poem many such changes are described, as, for instance, winds that disintegrate and blow away the meaningless husks of past seasons—of *hommes de paille*—and scatter seeds and moisture for the next season. From time to time a shaman is invoked who magically encourages the works of the winds, and the poet himself speaks in a prophetic voice.
>
> But Perse's poem only served as a point of departure, for as I worked on this Concerto, the music naturally began to take precedence over the poem and I began to find Perse's poetic tone, especially his, to me, rather contrived primitivism, did not correspond to the tone of the work that was taking shape and so I took no further thought of the poem after a certain point and followed the musical conceptions the work seemed to impose on me.

In a piece that deals primarily with the poetry of change, transformation, reorientation of feelings and thoughts, and gradual shifts of emphases as do most of my works and in particular this one, the matter of succession of material becomes very important, since how the ideas are formed and how they are related and connected gives expression to the poetry they evoke. Thus the individual instant, the characterized sound or brief passage, like trees in a storm, gain an added meaning by their contexts. In this piece four movements interpenetrate each other throughout. Each movement comes into focus against a background of the other three. Each, of course, has its own character, sound, and development during the entire length of the piece.

Hence to call these four movements by number is somewhat misleading, since the largest statement of each, which comes in the order described, is counterpointed or interrupted by more or less extended fragments of the others. The first movement, which emerges from one of the layers of music heard at the beginning, features the cello section (sometimes divided into as many as seven different soloists, as are all the strings), piano, harp, marimba, xylophone, and wooden percussion. It centers around the lower middle register and is in a moderately fast speed throughout the work. The second movement features high strings, high winds, and metallic percussion, and starts very fast and lightly and bit by bit becomes slower over the whole work. The third features the double basses, tuba, horns, timpani, and other low-pitched instruments, and keeps to its recitative-like character. The fourth features the violas, oboes, trumpets, snare drums, and other medium high instruments and starts with slow fragments that become faster as the work progresses until it expands into a rapid conclusion. As with all my works, the primary intention is expressive and the entire musical vocabulary, instrumentation and form have been chosen to further this. I do not espouse any of the present aesthetic points of view consciously and this score is a continuation of the musical thinking that has always been present in my compositions and that characterizes all of them, especially from my Piano Sonata (1945) to my Piano Concerto (1965).

I am told, the line of continuity of my works is very definite, so much so that it would be hard to situate them in relation to the various musical trends that have come and gone during the past 20 years. For instance, the "serialism" prevalent here and in the late 20's and 30's was influenced by the Schoenberg school, Ives, Varèse, Ruggles, Crawford, Scriabin and Roslavetz, all of whom had certain tendencies in that direction.

In fact, I was very much interested in the avant-garde in the 20's and 30's with its random, its collages, its fun and games with audiences and its artistic paradoxes, and have felt that the cause was won then and did not need to be repeated again. The next step had to be taken and this is what I have tried to do in so far as my works can be said to adopt any aesthetic position, for I have been more concerned with the works than in the aesthetic they represent.

ELLIOTT CARTER

As an undergraduate student at Harvard, Carter majored in English literature, but studied and heard a great deal of music outside college. After taking his A.B. he remained to do graduate work in music at Harvard with Walter Piston, Archibald T. Davison, Edward Burlingame Hill and Gustav Holst, then a visiting professor in composition. Upon taking the M.A. degree in 1932, Carter went to Paris for three years of study with Nadia Boulanger.

The first public performances of Carter's music took place while he was still a student. The list of his works, which place him in the top rank of contemporary composers, is long and in any case would not be appropriate for a necessarily abbreviated program note. But it may be of interest to read Stravinsky's comments of 1962 as they appeared in *Musical America* for June of that year. The comment was elicited by Robert Craft's question, "What composition by an American-born composer has most attracted you to date?" Stravinsky replied, in part:

> Elliott Carter's Double Concerto, I think, but you would have to know what other music I have heard to evaluate the preference . . . I like the mood of Carter's Concerto, first of all. It is full of newfound good spirits, as his quartets were not . . . I like the shape and sense of proportion in the Concerto, the measure of time wholly absent from, say, Stockhausen's *Carré*. But I like the harpsichord and piano writing very much too. And the intended high point, the coda, is the real climax of the piece . . . I cannot comment upon or add to the composer's own analysis, but analysis as little explains a masterpiece or calls it into being as an ontological proof explains or causes the existence of God. There, the word is out. A masterpiece and by an American composer.

In addition to his activities as a composer, Mr. Carter has taught at the Peabody Conservatory of Music in Baltimore, Columbia University, at the Salzburg Seminars in Austria, at Yale University and at the Massachusetts Institute of Technology. In 1962 he was composer-in-residence at the American Academy in Rome, and in 1964 held a similar position in Berlin, having been invited by the Berlin Senat and the Ford Foundation. He was composer-in-residence at the Berkshire Music Center in 1965, and since 1966 he has been a member of the composition faculty of The Juilliard School.

HOLIDAY OVERTURE

Elliott Carter, one of the most individual and arresting figures in contemporary American music, was long in achieving the prominence and general admiration he enjoys today. In part this was due to the character of his own artistic evolution, which has been slow, unforced, and deeply serious. Carter's basically thoughtful personality did not prevent him, however, from writing exuberant, brilliant works, like the *Holiday Overture*. Nor does it preclude a beguiling wit, which sparks many of the lighter pages of the *Holiday Overture* and gives Rabelaisian zest to such an early score as *The Defense of Corinth*.

Mr. Carter was not an infant prodigy. His attraction to music did not become strong until his high school years, when he was encouraged by Charles Ives.

"Carter began serious work in music rather late," writes his able and perceptive commentator, Richard Franko Goldman in the *Musical Quarterly*, "and acquired what may be called professional status as a composer considerably later. As the son of a well-to-do New York family, he was not faced with the economic necessity of choosing a career, and was able to pursue an education in the leisurely fashion no longer common.

"He is one of the few musicians, indeed one of the few persons of our time, who may still, in Jacques Barzun's sense of the phrase, be called an educated man. Carter's mind is neat, precise, and well stocked; his interests cover a wide range, and his curiosity is restless. His formal education includes four years as an undergraduate at Harvard, where he majored originally in English."

During his last years at Harvard he began to study music professionally, taking courses with Walter Piston, Archibald T. Davison, and Gustav Holst. From 1932 to 1935 he studied in Paris with Nadia Boulanger and wrote the earliest compositions he still acknowledges. Several of his finest early works, including *The Defense of Corinth,* are choral music.

The *Holiday Overture* was written in 1944 during a holiday on Fire Island, New York. The score has a holiday exuberance, an expansive vigor and rhythmic vitality that make it inviting music even on first acquaintance. The main theme of the Overture, to which many subordinate themes are related and which returns in the climactic final pages, is announced by full orchestra in the opening bars:*

The Overture seems sectional in structure, each section being thematically related to a preceding section or to a principal theme quoted above. Yet each section has a strong rhythmic profile of its own, often with considerable syncopation. A large amount of elaborate counterpoint is so skillfully handled that the Overture sounds simpler than it is. The conclusion bears the note: "Saltaire, L. I., Aug., 1944."

Carter's orchestration consists of piccolo, 2 flutes, 2 oboes, English horn, 2 clarinets, bass clarinet, 2 bassoons, contrabassoon, 4 horns in F, 3 trumpets, 3 tenor trombones, bass trombone, tuba, kettledrum, snare drum, bass drum, triangle, suspended cymbal, 2 cymbals, tam-tam, slapstick, piano, and the usual strings.

---

* *Musical example copyright 1962 by Associated Music Publishers, Inc. Used by permission.*

VARIATIONS FOR ORCHESTRA

Elliott Carter is a contemporary composer in more than one sense of the phrase, not the least of which is the fact that he is an educated man. The phenomenon of the composer as an educated man or an "intellectual" is a relatively recent one, having taken root only in the Romantic era of the nineteenth century. Only in our century has it become almost a norm. The phenomenon was regarded with serious misgivings by those who felt that artists should be creatures primarily of inspiration and that it was dangerous for any artist to become "sicklied o'er by the pale cast of thought." This is a fear to which we are by no means immune today, as is demonstrated by the apprehension with which many a music lover learns that composer X of our time has worked seriously in the field of mathematics, sociology, or atomic physics as well as music.

Although Elliott Carter's interest in music became intense during his high school years when he was encouraged by Charles Ives, Carter went on to acquire that old-fashioned variety of training which used to be known as a liberal education. Carter's musical works have placed him in the top rank of American composers. He is a member of the American Academy of Arts and Letters and has taught at Columbia University, Harvard, Cornell, Yale, Princeton, Massachusetts Institute of Technology and The Juilliard School.

Carter's Variations for Orchestra is dedicated to Robert Whitney and the Louisville Orchestra, which gave the score its first performance on April 21, 1956. The following comment on the music was furnished by the composer:

> My Variations for Orchestra was written for the Louisville Orchestra during 1955 from sketches made in 1953 and 1954. The project of writing such a work has interested me for some time as I was eager to put into concrete musical terms a number of ideas I had about this old form. Traditionally, of course, this type of composition is based on one pattern of material, a theme or a succession of harmonies out of which are built many short contrasting pieces or sections of music. The theme and each little section form musical vignettes usually presenting one single, unchanging mood or character and often only one musical idea or technique. Viewed as a series of separate pieces of sharply defined character, a set of musical variations resembles certain old literary works such as the collection of brief, trenchant delineations of *Ethical Characters* by Theophrastus, held together by one common idea or purpose. Such a set implicitly gives expression to the classical attitude toward the problem of "unity in diversity."
>
> In this work I was interested in adopting a more dynamic and changeable approach. The general characteristics of the form are maintained—one pattern of material out of which a diversity of characters come, but the principle of variation is often applied even within the scope of each short piece. In some, great changes of character and theme occur; in others, contrasting themes and characters answer each other back and forth or are heard simultaneously. By these and other devices, I have tried to give musical expression to experiences anyone living today must have when confronted by so many remarkable examples of unexpected types of changes and relationships of

character uncovered in the human sphere by psychologists and novelists, in the life cycle of insects and certain marine animals by biologists, indeed in every domain of science and art. Thus the old notion of "unity in diversity" presents itself to us in an entirely different guise than it did to people living even a short while ago.

Musically, the work is based on three ideas. The first two, *ritornelli,* are repeated literally here and there throughout the work in various transpositions of pitch and speed, while the third is a theme that undergoes many transformations. Of the *ritornelli,* the first, rising rapidly shortly after the opening, becomes progressively slower at each restatement (Variations I, III, VIII and the Finale). The material of the main theme is used in many different ways, and its characteristic motive is frequently referred to.

The large plan consists in a presentation of degrees of contrast of character and their gradual neutralization during the first four variations. In the Fifth Variation, contrast is reduced to a minimum, and from there on there is increasing definition and conflict of character until, in the Finale, the restatement of the notes of the theme by the trombones reestablishes unity.

Each variation has its own shape, since shape, too, as a mode of musical behavior, helps to define character. For instance, the First Variation and the Finale are both rapid dialogues of many contrasting motives in contrasting rhythms. The Second Variation presents contrast of character by quoting the theme almost literally and confronting it with its own variants derived alternately by intervallic expansion and intervallic diminution. The Third contrasts textures of dense harmony and expressive lines with transparent fragmentary motives. The Fourth Variation is a continual *ritard,* and the Sixth an accelerating series of imitations. The Fifth obliterates contrast in a succession of chords using the notes of the theme. The Seventh is an antiphonal variation presenting three different ideas played in succession by the strings, brass and woodwinds, and representing three different rhythmic planes. The line the woodwinds play in Variation VII is continued and developed in Variation VIII, while ideas of a much lighter musical nature are presented against it. The same idea is carried over into Variation IX where it is rejoined by the other two ideas from Variation VII, now played simultaneously. The Finale is a rapid interplay of different characters, finally called to order by the trombones who restate the notes of the first half of the theme while the strings play those of the second half softly.

The orchestration in detail, and the orchestral style of the whole was conceived taking into account the exact size of the Louisville Orchestra with its limited string group, though of course the work can be played by a symphony orchestra of the customary size. The following are called for: 2 each of flutes (second doubling piccolo), oboes, clarinets, bassoons, 4 horns, 2 trumpets, 3 trombones, tuba, percussion (2 players), harp (2 harps ad lib), 9 first violins, 6 second violins, 6 violas, 4 cellos, and 4 basses.

ELLIOTT CARTER

Alfredo Casella

Born July 25, 1883, Turin—died March 5, 1947, Rome

LA GIARA (SUITE SINFONICA)

One of the most brilliant scores to come from the Italy of the turbulent twenties was Casella's ballet (or "choreographical comedy," as he called it), *La giara*. Based on a short story of the same name by Luigi Pirandello, *La giara* or "The Jar" was composed in 1924, the same year as Ottorino Respighi's tone poem, *The Pines of Rome*, and it had its world premiere within a month of the Respighi score. Yet the two works are worlds apart. The epicurean opulence of Respighi's *Pines of Rome* and its thunderous rhetoric look backward to the giant coloristic orchestras of the late Romantic age. Casella's ballet looked forward to the more economical Neoclassical style.

In his memoirs (*I segreti della giara*, translated into English as *Music in My Time*), Casella tells us that in the spring of 1924 he received a very roundabout inquiry from the French *avant-garde* composer Erik Satie, asking whether Casella would be willing to compose a ballet for the following season of the Swedish Ballet. Casella immediately went to Paris, where he learned that the director of the Swedish Ballet, Rolf de Maré wanted a typically Italian ballet, something which could compete with Falla's *Three-Cornered Hat*. He wished not only the music but the scenario and stage designs as well to be by Italian artists. Casella's proposal to take his plot from one of the short stories of Pirandello and to have the scenery designed by Giorgio de Chirico pleased Maré.

On his return to Rome, Casella consulted his composer friend, Mario Labroca, later the impresario of La Scala. Labroca had just given up a long-cherished project to compose an opera based on Pirandello's short story, "The Jar," and he urged Casella to use that subject for his ballet. Casella was delighted, Pirandello agreed to collaborate on the scenario, and the ballet was completed on October 7, 1924. The first performance took place on the 19th of the following month at the Théâtre de Champs-Elysées in Paris, with Casella himself conducting.

It was so successful that Casella arranged a symphonic suite, which was given its world premiere by the New York Philharmonic on October 29, 1925, under the direction of Willem Mengelberg. The Metropolitan Opera Ballet offered the United States premiere of the complete ballet on March 19, 1927, with choreography by Rosina Galli (Mrs. Giulio Gatti-Gasazza), who also danced the role of Nela. The Metropolitan Opera orchestra was conducted by Tullio Serafin.

The Symphonic Suite from *La giara* consists of the opening and closing scenes of the ballet. The action takes place before the Sicilian farmhouse of Don Lollò, on the crest of a hill.

I. A peaceful prelude is dominated by the pastoral sound of solo woodwinds and by the gently lilting rhythm of the traditional *siciliano*. One of the chief characters of the ballet, the hunchback village tinker, absentmindedly scurries across the stage in front of the curtain accompanied by a sudden spirit of comically spry *allegro,* which comes to an abrupt end as he becomes aware of the audience and ducks behind the curtain. The prelude is rounded off by another peaceful melody of folk character "sung" by a combination of solo oboe and solo clarinet two octaves apart from each other.

As the curtain rises Don Lollò's farm hands are returning from work. Being Sicilians they naturally dance the *chiovù,* a lively local folk dance, closely related to the Neapolitan tarantella. Although the sun is setting, the peasants' spirits rise in a series of ebullient, almost Rossinian crescendos.

(The middle section of the Ballet, which is omitted from the Suite, brings first a catastrophe: an enormous oil jar [*la giara*] on which Don Lollò puts great store has had a piece broken out of it. Don Lollò is enraged, but his daughter Nela succeeds momentarily in calming him. The peasants send for the hunchback tinker, Zi'Dima, who creeps inside the jar and repairs it. All is well, except that Zi'Dima cannot squeeze his way out of the repaired jar because of his hump. Perplexed and amused, the peasants consider breaking the jar again to liberate Zi'Dima. But Don Lollò, warns that the tinker must pay if the jar is broken again. In a fury of frustration Lollò disappears into his house.)

II. One of the peasants lights a pipe and passes it into the jar to Zi'Dima with gestures indicating that he should keep calm, for all will be well. The peasants leave and the deserted stage is flooded by moonlight. From time to time a peaceful puff of smoke arises from the mouth of the jar.

Against a murmuring orchestral background, a lovelorn, distant offstage tenor (sometimes replaced in symphonic performances by an instrumental part) sings a sentimental serenade, a Sicilian folk song, the "Story of the Maiden Abducted by Pirates." Nela comes skipping out of the house and dances for a few moments alone around the jar. Presently she gestures to the peasants, who have been watching her from a distance. They enter joyfully, drinks are brought, they drink to Zi'Dima's liberation and, as the peasants grow drunk, the general dance becomes an *Allego rude e selvaggio* ("crude and savage").

Don Lollò is wakened by the racket. Infuriated once again, he dashes out of the house and charges among the dancers like a maddened bull. In the confusion the jar is overturned and rolls over the edge of the hill. The terrified peasants dash after the jar to save the old tinker. Soon they return carrying Zi'Dima in triumph and now an even livelier dance of rejoicing ensues. Don Lollò in desperation has fled into his house and the concluding dance is led by his daughter Nela.

The orchestra for *La giara* consists of piccolo, 2 flutes (one alternating with piccolo), 2 oboes, 1 clarinet, 1 bass clarinet, 2 bassoons, 4 horns, 2 trumpets, 1 trombone, 3 kettledrums, snare drums, triangle, bass drum with attached cymbals, tambourine, cymbals (in addition to those on the drum), small bells, castanets, and the traditional string choir.

Emmanuel Chabrier

Born January 18, 1841, Puy-de-Dôme—died September 13, 1894, Paris

ESPANA, RHAPSODY FOR ORCHESTRA

Chabrier, like many a Frenchman before and after him, was intoxicated with Spain. When he visited that country, he studied the music, the dances, and the dancers, making elaborate notes and writing vivid letters about it. In November, 1882, he wrote to a friend from Granada:

> In a month I must leave adorable Spain and say good-bye to the Spaniards—because (I say this only to you) they are very nice, the little girls! I have not seen a really ugly woman since I have been in Andalusia. I do not speak of the feet, they are so small that I have never seen them; the hands are tiny and well-kept and the arms of an exquisite contour; I speak only of what one can see. Add the arabesques, the side-curls and other ingenuities of the coiffure, the inevitable fan, the flower and the comb in the hair, placed well behind, the shawl of Chinese crepe, with long fringe and embroidered in flowers, knotted around the figure, the arm bare, the eye protected by eyelashes which are long enough to curl, the skin of dull white or orange color, according to the race; all this smiling, gesticulating, dancing, drinking, and careless to the last degree—
>
> That *is* the Andalusian.
>
> Every evening we go to the café-concerts where the *Malaguenas,* the *Soledas,* the *Zapateados* and the *Peteneras* are sung. Then the dances, absolutely Arab, to speak truth. If you could see them wiggle, unjoint their hips, contort, I believe you would not try to get away! At Malaga the dancing became so intense that I was compelled to take my wife away; it wasn't even amusing any more. I can't write about it, but I remember it and will describe it to you. I have no need to tell you I have noted down many things; the Tango, a kind of dance in which the women imitate the pitching of a ship, is the only dance in two time; all the others are 3/4 (Seville) or in 3/8 (Malaga and Cadiz). In the North it is different, there is some music in 5/8, very curious. The 2/4 of the Tango is always like the Habanera. This is the picture: two women dance, two silly men play—it doesn't matter what—on their guitars, and five or six women howl, with excruciating voices and in triple figures; it is impossible to note down what, because they change the air—every instant, a new scrap of tune. They howl a series of figurations with syllables, words, rising voices, clapping hands which strike the six eighths, emphasizing the third and sixth, cries of *Andá! Andá La Salud! eso es la Maraquita! gracia nationidad! Baila, la chiquilla! Andá! Andá! Consuelo! Olé, la Lola, olé la Carmen! que gracia! que elegancia*—all that to excite the young dancers. It is vertiginous, it is unspeakable! . . . And the more cries, the more the dancer laughs with her mouth wide open, and turns her hips, and is mad with her body.

This is the color and excitement we hear in Chabrier's Rhapsody, *"España."* Written first for piano, it was later orchestrated by the composer. It consists chiefly of two Spanish dances: the *Malagueña,* a sultry, languishing dance, and the *Jota,* fiery, driving, impetuous, a kind of quick waltz, which is both sung and danced.

The first performance of the orchestral version of *"España"* was given by the Lamoureux Orchestra in 1883, with immediate, resounding success. The work is scored for piccolo, 2 flutes, 2 oboes, 2 clarinets, 4 bassoons, 4 horns, 2 trumpets, 2 cornets, 3 trombones, tuba, triangle, tambourine, keddledrums, bass drum, cymbals, 2 harps, and the usual strings.

Ernest Chausson

Born January 20, 1855, Paris—died June 10, 1899, Limay, near Mantes

POEME, FOR VIOLIN AND ORCHESTRA, OPUS 25

When Ernest Chausson was killed in a bicycle accident at the age of forty-four, France lost one of the most individual and distinguished composers of the day. As fastidious an artist as Debussy, as sensuously French as Massenet, with whom he studied, Chausson had a Romantic fervor of his own. A mystic, a profound admirer of César Franck, with whom he studied, Chausson was also a friend of Debussy. Perhaps for that reason he has been called the link between Franck and Debussy. But Chausson was more than a mere link.

Something of the character of the man, and his music, was caught in a sketch penned by his friend, the Parisian critic Camille Mauclair, only a few weeks after Chausson's death: "In fact, Chausson did not care for society, his affability masked a grave spirit, his good cheer was often mere consideration for other people, and his peaceful manner concealed a soul deeply pained by the sufferings of humanity."

Thus it was characteristic of Chausson that when he set out to write a solo vehicle for the great Belgian violinist, Eugène Ysaÿe, it was for the display of emotional intensity and poetic style rather than technical polish or fireworks. The *Poème* was composed in 1896, and Ysaÿe played the premiere performance in Paris on April 4, 1897.

A slow introduction with mysterious harmonies in the dark, low range of the orchestra, leads to an unaccompanied solo for the violinist: the languorous principal theme of the *Poème:*

The theme is echoed by the orchestra in full, warm harmony before the soloist launches into a rhapsodic cadenza-like passage which opens the main body of the work. There are several subsidiary themes in the course of this rich score. But it is the melody announced by the solo violinist, which reappears in different keys, to form the structural skeleton of this work, so improvisatory and impulsive in effect, but so neatly constructed in fact.

The orchestra for the *Poème* consists of woodwinds in pairs, 4 horns, 2 trumpets, tuba, kettledrums, harps, and strings.

SYMPHONY IN B-FLAT MAJOR, OPUS 20

The polished personal appearance of Ernest Chausson seemed to belie his music, which is charged with Late Romantic fervor, emotional ardor, and an almost hothouse warmth. According to the distinguished French critic, Camille Mauclair, Chausson "impressed one as the man of the world, wholly without ostentation, amiable, cheerful, serene." But in fact, Mauclair added, Chausson was by inclination an unworldy man of a melancholy turn of mind. "He was a Christian, a mystic, with the most exalted understanding of life, forever mindful of the debt which his happiness imposed. . . . His concern for spiritual beauty took precedence over all others. Rather than prodigies of form and style, he loved the intellectual emotion of Gluck, Bach, César Franck, and the mystics above the votaries of passion."

In this country Chausson's two best known works are his *Poème* for violin and orchestra, Opus 25, and his Symphony. The latter was completed in 1890 and first performed under Chausson's direction at a concert of the *Société Nationale de Musique* in Paris on April 18, 1891. Apparently the work did not really strike fire with French audiences until May, 1897, when Artur Nikisch conducted it in a Paris concert of the Berlin Philharmonic. It is in three movements.

I. *Lent; allegro vivo.* Like many other Romantic symphonies, this one begins with a brief motto-theme, which returns in the finale with powerfully unifying effect:

The dark orchestral color of this opening page brightens in the course of the introduction, rising to an impassioned climax. With a sudden quickening of tempo the main body of the movement launches a soaring phrase for horn against a soft *tremolo* of the strings:

As the music gathers intensity and momentum the tempo increases and the movement ends with a presto.

II. *Très lent.* The melancholy opening phrase, with its three ascending notes, derives from the motto of the first movement. The songful middle section gives especial prominence to the rich colors of solo English horn, French horn, violas.

III. *Animé; très animé.* The fiery introduction begins with whirling string figures, cut through by a sharp fanfare anticipating the dynamic main theme of the finale. Toward the end the golden tone of the brass choir alone stands out in a climax of quiet grandeur built on the motto with which the Symphony began. The motto is transfigured once more in the almost prayer-like concluding pages.

The Symphony is scored for 3 flutes, piccolo, 2 oboes, English horn, 2 clarinets, bass clarinet, 3 bassoons, 4 horns, 4 trumpets, 3 trombones, tuba, kettledrums, 2 harps, and strings. It is dedicated to Chausson's brother-in-law, the painter Henry Lerolle.

Frédéric Chopin

Born February 22, 1810, Zelazowska Wola, near Warsaw—died October 17, 1849, Paris

CONCERTO FOR PIANO AND ORCHESTRA, NO. 1, E MINOR, OPUS 11

While Chopin's later works have greater sophistication—perhaps even greater passion—his two early piano concertos have a special freshness, which, in the nature of things, could never be duplicated, even by Chopin himself. The E-minor Concerto, his *second* in sequence of composition, was the first to be *published* and therefore was designated as No. 1. Chopin was only twenty.

In a letter of March 1830, Chopin mentions that he is already at work on the first movement. By May he is busy with the Rondo: "It is not yet finished because the right inspired mood has kept eluding me. But if I just have the *allegro* and the *adagio* completely finished I shall have no anxiety about the finale." [The term *adagio* was a general designation for slow movements, in this case the middle movement of the E-minor Concerto, the tempo mark of which is actually *Larghetto.*]

On the morning of September 22, Chopin wrote his closest friend, Titus Woyciechowski, that the Concerto was finished. "And I feel like a novice," he added, "just as I felt before I knew anything of the keyboard. It is far too original and I shall end by being unable to learn it myself."

But any such doubts were swept away at the premiere, which Chopin played on October 11, 1830, in the Warsaw National Theater. The following day he wrote to Titus: "Yesterday's concert was a great big success, I hasten

CHOPIN PLAYING FOR GEORGE SAND.

This introspective portrait was originally part of a larger canvas showing Chopin's mistress, George Sand, spellbound by the composer, who was playing the piano. Painted in 1838 by the couple's close friend and frequent house guest, Eugène Delacroix. (*Louvre, Paris; photo Bulloz; courtesy, Art Reference Bureau*)

to let you know. I must inform Your Lordship that I was not a bit, not a bit nervous and I played the way I play when I am alone, and it went well. Full Hall: We started with Görner's Symphony, they My Highness played the *Allegro* of the E-minor Concerto, which I reeled off with ease . . . Deafening applause."

I. *Allegro maestoso.* The twenty-year-old composer follows Classical tradition with a long orchestral introduction, presenting all the principal themes of the movement. Traditional, too, is the rather vigorous, assertive character of his opening theme:

More lyric motifs follow, the most typically Chopinesque of them being a graceful *cantabile* phrase sung by the first violins in the warmer major mode. The solo piano makes its entrance with a boldly rhetorical version of the opening theme and proceeds to vary the other themes presented by the orchestra, particularly the *cantabile* theme:

After a florid development, consisting largely of brilliant pianistic display, the original themes return. This time the second, *cantabile* theme returns in the relative key of G major, rather than its original E major, thus reversing the traditional modulations of first-movement concerto form.

II. *Romance: Larghetto.* The soft, misty color of the muted violins provides the perfect introduction to the nocturne-like melody of the solo piano. Chopin described it to Titus as being "of a romantic, calm, and rather melancholy character. It is intended to convey the impression which one receives when the eye rests on a beloved landscape that calls up in one's soul beautiful memories, a kind of reverie in the moonlight on a beautiful spring night."

After an agitated middle section in C-sharp minor, the nocturnal melody returns, now in the violins, while the piano weaves airy garlands of embellishment. The finale follows without pause.

III. *Rondo. Vivace.* There is a touch of Polish national color in this finale, which is rhythmically related to the *Krakowiak,* or *Cracovienne,* a popular dance said to have originated near the city of Krakow. In form it is a rondo, for the opening refrain for piano solo makes several reappearances separated by a series of sometimes glittering, usually tuneful, and always graceful episodes.

The Concerto is scored for 2 flutes, 2 oboes, 2 clarinets, 2 bassoons, 4 horns, 2 trumpets, trombone, kettledrums, and the usual strings.

CONCERTO FOR PIANO AND ORCHESTRA, NO. 2, F MINOR, OPUS 21

Chopin was only nineteen when he wrote this F-minor Concerto. It was actually the first of his two piano concertos, but since it was the second to be published, it bears the number two. Chopin was still living in his native Poland and had not yet ventured far afield to conquer the sophisticated salons of music and fashion in Paris. He was nineteen, delicate, a poet in mind as well as appearance and, for the first time, desperately in love. Like a true Romantic, he poured his amorous dreams into his art, specifically (as he explained to his bosom friend Titus Woyciechowski) into the songful second movement of his Concerto:

> I have—perhaps to my own misfortune—already found my ideal, whom I worship faithfully and sincerely. Six months have elapsed, and I haven't yet exchanged a syllable with her of whom I dream every night—she who was in my mind when I composed the *Adagio* of my Concerto. [Chopin's slow movement is actually a *Larghetto,* but *"adagio"* was a customary casual designation for any slow movement.]

Almost as soon as he had finished his Concerto, Chopin announced it for a public concert, his Warsaw debut in fact, which took place on March 17, 1830. In those days, a concerto played straight through was considered rather too serious a strain for most audiences, so an operatic aria or a lighter piece was frequently interpolated between the movements. In this case, the first movement was followed by a *divertissement* for French horn. Even so, the audience apparently had its difficulties:

> The first Allegro of my concerto (unintelligible to most) received the reward of a "Bravo," [wrote Chopin to his friend, Titus] but I believe this was given because people wanted to show that they understand and know how to appreciate serious music. There are people enough in all countries who like to assume the air of connoisseurs! The *Adagio* and Rondo produced a very great effect; after these, the applause and the "Bravos" came really from the heart.

I. *Maestoso.* The first movement begins quite according to Classical tradition, with a substantial orchestral exposition of the principal themes. The first and most important theme of all is the following:

This theme is taken up again by the piano at its entrance, and serves as the principal material for the central development section of the movement.

From the moment the piano makes its appearance on the scene, the orchestra fades into the background. Chopin's instrument was the piano; with the orchestra he never felt particularly at home. It takes its place here, as in many an early Romantic concerto, as discreet support for the soloist.

II. *Larghetto.* This is the movement in which Chopin dreamed of his new ideal, Constantia Gladkowska. This wonderful nocturne-like movement seems to have been inspired by the Italian *bel canto* singing Chopin so admired in the opera and concert performances he described with such enthusiasm in his letters at the very time he was composing his two piano concertos. He makes the piano sing in an astounding range of vocal styles from such a simple *cantilena* as the following:

to the most delicate flights of coloratura. The middle of this movement is a stylized version of a fiery operatic recitative, complete with shuddering background of string tremolos. A return of the opening melodic material rises to a passionate climax. The pensive orchestral postlude is rounded off by a lingering piano *arpeggio,* as though the poet-composer were loath to take leave of his dream.

"Passages of surprising grandeur may be found in the *Adagio* of the Second Concerto," wrote Liszt, "for which he [Chopin] showed a decided preference, and which he liked to repeat frequently. . . . The whole of this piece is of a perfection almost ideal; its expression, now radiant with light, now full of tender pathos."

III. *Allegro vivace.* The finale, marked "simply and gracefully," is crystal-clear brilliance and melody, with a hint of the wayward Polish mazurka rhythm. It has little of the melodic or harmonic sophistication of the later Chopin, but the simplicity of its appeal is irresistible. It was Anton Rubinstein who later said of the composer of the F-minor Concerto: "The piano bard, the piano mind, the piano soul is Chopin."

The F-minor Concerto is scored for 2 flutes, 2 oboes, 2 clarinets, 2 bassoons, 2 horns, 2 trumpets, trombone, kettledrums, and the usual strings.

Aaron Copland

Born November 14, 1900, Brooklyn, New York

APPALACHIAN SPRING, SUITE FROM THE BALLET

October 30, 1944, was a fruitful evening for the dance theater, and for three distinguished contemporary composers, when Martha Graham produced, choreographed, and herself danced in three entirely new works created with three new scores, which had been commissioned by Elizabeth Sprague Coolidge. These were *Mirror Before Me* (Hindemith's *Hérodiade,* based on the famous poem of the same name, which occupied Mallarmé for most of his life), *Imagined Wing* (Milhaud's title: *Jeux du printemps*), and Aaron Copland's *Appalachian Spring*. It was a memorable evening for those, like this writer, fortunate enough to have been in the tiny Whittall Auditorium of the Library of Congress in Washington, D.C. Memory would have to search back as far as Serge Diaghilev to find a dance impresario whose impact on contemporary composers had been equally fruitful. For Graham was even then an impresaria as well as choreographer and a great dancer. However much she may have grown since, she seemed then at the very peak of her art.

The following spring Graham and her company presented *Appalachian Spring* in New York (May 14, 1945). That same year *Appalachian Spring* received both the Pulitzer Prize for music and the award of the Music Critics Circle of New York for the outstanding theatrical work of the season 1944–1945. Meanwhile Copland arranged an *Orchestral Suite* from his ballet which was given its first performance by the New York Philharmonic on October 4, 1945 in Carnegie Hall under the direction of Artur Rodzinski. In a program note for this occasion Copland described the genesis of his ballet:

> The music of the ballet takes as its point of departure the personality of Martha Graham. I have long been an admirer of Miss Graham's work. She, in turn, must have felt a certain affinity for my music because in 1931 she chose my Piano Variations as background for a dance composition entitled *Dithyramb*. I remember my astonishment, after playing the Variations for the first time at a concert of the League of Composers, when Miss Graham told me she intended to use the composition for dance treatment. Surely only an artist with a close affinity for my work could have visualized dance material in so rhythmically complex and esthetically abstruse a composition. I might add, as further testimony, that Miss Graham's *Dithyramb* was considered by public critics to be just as complex and abstruse as my music.
>
> Ever since then, at long intervals Miss Graham and I planned to collaborate on a stage work. Nothing might have come of our intentions if it were not for the lucky chance that brought Mrs. Elizabeth Sprague Coolidge to a

> Graham performance for the first time early in 1942. With typical energy, Mrs. Coolidge translated her enthusiasm into action. She invited Martha Graham to create three new ballets for the 1943 annual fall Festival of the Coolidge Foundation in Washington, and commissioned three composers—Paul Hindemith, Darius Milhaud and myself—to compose scores especially for the occasion.
>
> After considerable delay Miss Graham sent me an untitled script. I suggested certain changes to which she made no serious objections. I began work on the music of the ballet in Hollywood in June 1943, but didn't complete it until a year later in June 1944, at Cambridge, Mass.
>
> The premiere took place in Washington a year later than originally planned—in October 1944. The principal roles were danced by Miss Graham, Erick Hawkins, Merce Cunningham and May O'Donnell. Isamu Noguchi designed the architectural setting. Edith Guilfond supplied the costumes, Louis Horst conducted. Needless to say, Mrs. Coolidge sat in her customary seat in the front row, an unusually interested spectator. (She was celebrating her eightieth birthday that night.)
>
> The title *Appalachian Spring* was chosen by Miss Graham. She borrowed it from the heading of one of Hart Crane's poems, though the ballet seems to bear no relation to the text of the poem itself.

The preface to Copland's published score of his *Orchestral Suite from Appalachian Spring* summarizes the action of the ballet in the words of Eric Denby's *Herald Tribune* review (May 15) of the New York premiere of the ballet. The action, he wrote, concerns: ". . . a pioneer celebration in spring around a newly-built farmhouse in the Pennsylvania hills in the early part of the last century. The bride-to-be and the young farmer-husband enact the emotions, joyful and apprehensive, their new domestic partnership invites. An older neighbor suggests now and then the rocky confidence of experience. A revivalist and his followers remind the new householders of the strange and terrible aspects of human fate. At the end the couple are left quiet and strong in their new house."

Copland's original ballet score was for a tiny chamber orchestra consisting of flute, clarinet, bassoon, piano, 2 first violins, 2 second violins, 2 violas, 2 cellos, and one string bass. The sound of this ensemble seemed intentionally lean, clean, beautifully clear and suited to the musical and choreographic thought. The concert orchestral arrangement intended for larger halls is of necessity fuller, although it keeps a remarkably transparent sound and a freshness which is indeed suggestive of spring. (For although the title was chosen after the ballet score had been completed, the orchestral version came after the title *and* the extremely poetic choreography, and may not have been uninfluenced by them.)

Copland's program note for the concert premiere of the Suite listed the following sections of the ballet, which are linked in a continuous whole (the musical examples which have been added to Copland's note are from the *Orchestral Suite* which is usually performed, not from the rarely heard original for thirteen instruments):

THE FIRST "APPALACHIAN SPRING."

Martha Graham and Eric Hawkins as Bride and Groom in the original production of *Appalachian Spring,* with music by Aaron Copland and choreography by Graham. (*Photo, Arnold Eagle; courtesy, Martha Graham School of Contemporary Dance*)

1. Very slowly. Introduction of the characters, one by one, in a suffused light.
2. Fast. Sudden burst of unison strings in A-major *arpeggios* starts the action. A sentiment both exalted and religious gives the keynote to this scene. [The principal theme of this section, and indeed of the entire ballet, is hinted several times before it takes on this typical form in a gleaming trumpet sound]: *

3. Moderate. Duo for the Bride and her Intended—scene of tenderness and passion.
4. Quite fast. The revivalist and his flock. Folksy feelings—suggestions of square dances and country fiddlers.
5. Still faster. Solo dance of the Bride—presentiment of motherhood. Extremes of joy and fear and wonder.
6. Very slowly (as at first). Transition scenes reminiscent of the introduction.
7. Calm and flowing. Scenes of daily activity for the Bride and her Farmer-husband. There are five variations on a Shaker theme. The theme, sung by a solo clarinet, was taken from a collection of Shaker melodies compiled by Edward D. Andrews, and published later under the title *The Gift to be Simple.* The melody I borrowed and used almost literally is called "Simple Gifts." [This is the tune of the first four lines of the Shaker text which follows]:

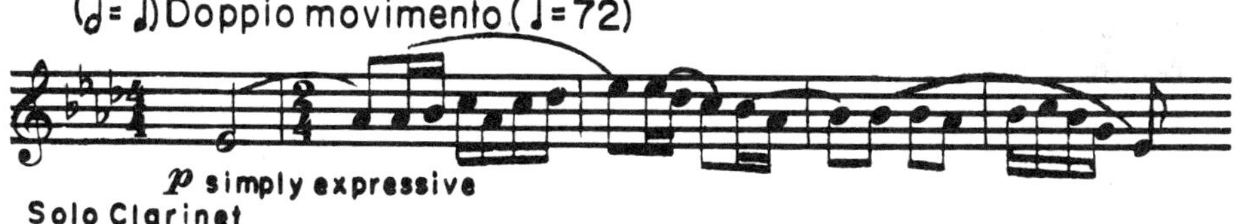

'Tis the gift to be simple,
'Tis the gift to be free,
'Tis the gift to come down
Where we ought to be.
And when we find ourselves
In the place just right
'Twill be in the valley
Of love and delight.

* *This and the following musical examples from this composition are copyright 1945 by Aaron Copland. Renewed 1972. Reprinted by permission of Aaron Copland copyright owner, and Boosey & Hawkes, Inc., sole licensees.*

When true simplicity is gain'd
To bow and to bend we shan't be asham'd
To turn, turn will be our delight,
'Till by turning, turning we come round right.

8. Moderate. Coda. The Bride takes her place among her neighbors. At the end the couple are left "quiet and strong in their new house." Muted strings intone a hushed, prayer-like passage. We hear a last echo of the principal theme sung by a flute and solo violin:

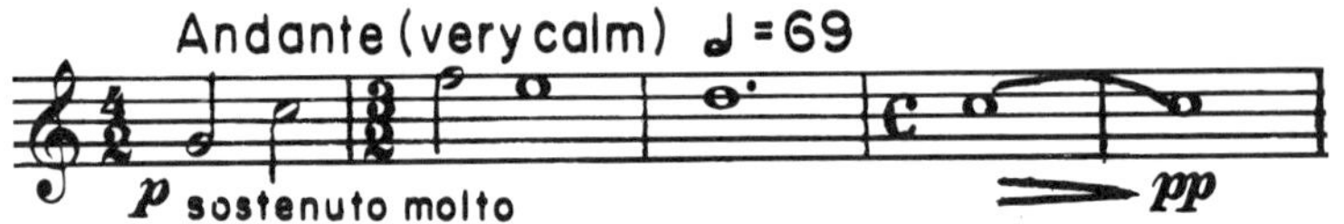

The close is reminiscent of the opening music.

The Suite from *Appalachian Spring* is scored for 2 flutes, 2 oboes, 2 clarinets, 2 bassoons, 2 horns, 2 trumpets, 2 trombones, kettledrums, xylophone, snare drum, bass drum, cymbals, tabor (long drum), claves, woodblock, glockenspiel, triangle, harp, piano, and the usual strings.

BILLY THE KID, BALLET SUITE

Hard on the heels of Copland's exploration of Mexican folk tunes in *El Salón México* (performed in 1938) came Copland's first ballet exploring folk tunes of the United States, specifically cowboy tunes for a cowboy ballet, *Billy the Kid.*

Billy the Kid of ballad fame—one of the badman heroes of American song and story—was a real person. His name was William Bonney; he was born in Brooklyn, New York, in 1859. But his family moved west in the wake of the Gold Rush and Billy grew up in the newly acquired New Mexico Territory, in Santa Fe and Silver City, where his mother ran a boardinghouse. By the time he was twelve, the Kid was frequenting saloons, gambling spots, and is said to have stabbed a man who insulted his mother.

The Kid quickly developed into a cold-blooded killer, the most famous outlaw, the terror and admiration of the Southwest, concentrating his maurading forays between Lincoln City and the Pecos River in the southwest corner of what is now the state of New Mexico. He was twenty-one when he was captured and condemned to hang. While shackled and handcuffed, he managed to escape by murdering two guards, bringing his total of killings to twenty-one for his twenty-one years. Before his next birthday he was trapped and shot by a sheriff who had been his friend. It is recorded that Billy was tall, slender, well proportioned and graceful, with a cheerful, carefree manner, even in moments of extreme danger. When he came to town he frequented balls, danced well, was a favorite with the ladies and had many loyal friends who tended to glamorize his career of crime.

According to one of the ballads he inspired (over a dozen different Billy the Kid ballads have been tracked down and recorded):

When Billy the Kid was a very young lad,
In Old Silver City, he went to the bad;
At twelve years of age the Kid killed his first man,
Then blazed a wide trail with a gun in each hand.

Fair Mexican maidens played soft on guitars
And sang of *Billito* their king 'neath the stars;
He was a brave lover, and proud of his fame,
And no man could stand 'gainst the Kid's deadly aim.

Now Billy ranged wide, and his killings were vile;
He shot fast, and first, when his blood got a-rile,
And, 'fore his young manhood did reach its sad end,
His six-guns held notches for twenty-one men.

In 1938, Lincoln Kirstein, director of the American Ballet Caravan, offered Copland a commission to write the music for a ballet depicting the adventures of Billy the Kid. Copland felt that such a score should include some cowboy music, but he is alleged to have had an active dislike of cowboy songs. Yet as he worked at the ballet in July and August in Paris, New Nork, and finally at the MacDowell Colony in Peterboro, New Hampshire, he found that his attitude changed. The finished score contains more or less recognizable bits of "The Old Chisholm Trail," "Git Along, Little Dogies," "Great Granddad," "Good-bye Old Paint," and "The Dying Cowboy" ("Oh, Bury Me Not on the Lone Prairie"). Copland did not include "Home on the Range" for, he said: "I had to draw the line somewhere."

The scenario of the ballet was by Lincoln Kirstein, choreography by Eugene Loring, who also danced the title role in the world premiere at the Chicago Civic Opera House on October 16, 1938.

In 1939 Copland arranged a "Billy the Kid" *Ballet Suite,* which includes about two-thirds of the ballet. The printed score bears Copland's outline of the action. (Some of the cowboy tunes of the score are added below in square brackets):

> The action begins and closes on the open prairie. The central portion of the ballet concerns itself with significant moments in the life of Billy the Kid. The first scene is in a frontier town. [It opens with a jaunty cowboy tune, "Great Granddad" whistled by the piccolo:]*

---

* *This and the following musical example from this composition are copyright 1946 by Aaron Copland. Renewed 1973. Reprinted by permission of Aaron Copland copyright owner, and Boosey & Hawkes, Inc., sole licensees.*

Familiar figures amble by. Cowboys saunter into town, some on horseback, others with their lassos. [Here trombones allude to another cowboy song, "Git Along, Little Dogies".] Some Mexican women do a *jarabe* which is interrupted by a fight between two drunks. Attracted by the gathering crowd, Billy is seen for the first time as a boy of twelve with his mother. The brawl turns ugly, guns are drawn, and in some unaccountable way, Billy's mother is killed. Without an instant's hesitation, in cold fury, Billy draws a knife from a cowhand's sheath and stabs his mother's slayers. His short but famous career has begun. In swift succession we see episodes in Billy's later life. At night, under the stars, in a quiet card game with his outlaw friends. [In this quiet section muted first violins transform the song of "The Dying Cowboy" beginning "Oh, bury me not on the lone prairie":]

Hunted by a posse led by his former friend Pat Garrett, Billy is pursued. A running battle ensues. Billy is captured. A drunken celebration takes place. Billy in prison is, of course, followed by one of Billy's legendary escapes. Tired and worn in the desert, Billy rests with his girl. *(pas de deux).* Starting from a deep sleep, he senses movement in the shadows. The posse has finally caught up with him. It is the end.

The orchestration of *Billy the Kid* calls for 2 flutes, 2 oboes, 2 clarinets, 2 bassoons, 4 horns, 3 trumpets, 3 trombones, tuba, timpani, percussion, harp, piano, and the customary strings.

CONNOTATIONS FOR ORCHESTRA

When plans were completed for the New York Philharmonic to move to a new home at Lincoln Center for the Performing Arts in 1962, composers of several countries, including the United States, were invited to contribute to the opening season. Both as conductor and as composer, Leonard Bernstein, the Philharmonic Director at that time, had a lively, lifelong interest in contemporary music. In addition the management and board of the Philharmonic took the festivities of the opening season as a welcome opportunity to demonstrate the

Orchestra's commitment to contemporary orchestral music by commissioning new works from composers of many origins and of a wide spectrum of styles.

While the United States does not enjoy the impressive number of government-supported radio orchestras and radio stations which seem to provide the backbone of support for contemporary orchestral music in most other countries, it is a matter of vital community pride in a surprisingly large number of American cities that our privately supported orchestras are not only increasingly hospitable to contemporary music but consider it a point of prestige to commission important works from prominent living composers. This change has been especially striking in the years since World War II.

Among the vanguard of conductors who have helped bring about this change have been three conductors of the New York Philharmonic: Dmitiri Mitropoulos, Leonard Bernstein, and Pierre Boulez. All three profited of course from the crusading decades of Serge Koussevitzky in Boston and Tanglewood, and Leopold Stokowski in Philadelphia and New York, to say nothing of the vigorous pioneering of Gustav Mahler during his two seasons at the head of the New York Philharmonic, just before World War I.

Thus the flowering of a considerable tradition lay behind the opening program of the New York Philharmonic in its new home. And it seemed especially appropriate that Brooklyn-born Aaron Copland, who himself had done so much to help his American colleagues, should contribute to the very first program.

For that occasion Copland wrote the following comment (to which only two musical examples have been added here):

> The offer of a commission from the New York Philharmonic to compose a work for performance at the opening concert in its new home, Philharmonic Hall in Lincoln Center, sparked the writing of my *Connotations for Orchestra.* I began sketches for the composition early in 1961 and completed it in September 1962. After some consideration, I concluded that the classical masters would undoubtedly provide the festive and dedicatory tone appropriate to such an occasion. For my own part, I decided to compose a work that would bring to the opening exercise a contemporary note, expressing something of the tensions, aspirations and drama inherent in the world of today.
>
> The *Connotations for Orchestra* is the first purely symphonic work I have composed since completing my *Third Symphony* in 1946. I have produced other works for orchestra since that time—the *Orchestral Suite* from my opera, *The Tender Land,* the revised version of my *Symphonic Ode,* the *Orchestral Variations* based on the *Piano Variations* of 1930, and the as yet unproduced *Ballet in Seven Movements* (1959). None of these (with the exception of the *Ode*) were composed in the first instance for orchestral performance.
>
> *Connotations* also represents the first orchestral work in which I made use of twelve-tone principles. My first venture along Schoenbergian lines may be found in my *Piano Quartet* of 1950. This was further developed seven years later in my *Piano Fantasy.* Some critics have discerned earlier traces of these methods in my *Piano Variations* and in an earlier Song on an e.e. cummings text, written in 1927. In the *Quartet* and the *Fantasy,* the row is first presented

as a theme. In the *Connotations,* the row is first heard vertically in terms of three-four-voiced chords with, needless to add, no common tones:*

When spelled out horizontally, these chords supply me with various versions of a more lyrical discourse. [One such example of the row spelled out horizontally for more lyrical discourse occurs very near the beginning when against an agitated background of leaping brass figures (themselves derived from the row) the violins in unison carry the following soaring *melodic* version of the row]:

The dictionary states that the verb *connote* means "to imply," to signify meanings "in addition to the primary meaning." In this case the skeletal frame of the row is the "primary meaning"; it denotes the area of exploration. The subsequent treatment seeks out other implications—connotations that come in a flash or connotations that the composer himself may only gradually uncover. The listener, on the other hand, is free to discover his or her own connotative meanings, including perhaps some not suspected by the author.

Structurally the composition comes closest to a free treatment of the Baroque form of the chaconne. A succession of variations, based on the opening chords and their implied melodic intervals, supplies the basic framework. The variations are sometimes recognizably separate, one from another, sometimes not. The problem, as in my *Orchestral Variations,* was to construct an overall line that had continuity, dramatic force and an inherent unity. As has been pointed out many times, the dodecaphonic method supplies the building blocks, but it does not create the edifice. The composer must do that.

On the title page, *Connotations for Orchestra* bears the inscription: Commissioned by the New York Philharmonic in Celebration of Its Opening Season in the Lincoln Center for the Performing Arts, and Dedicated to the Members of the Orchestra and Its Music Director, Leonard Bernstein.

---

* *This and the following musical example from this composition are copyright 1962 by Aaron Copland. Reprinted by permission of Aaron Copland copyright owner, and Boosey & Hawkes, Inc., sole licensees.*

The work is scored for large orchestra: three flutes, piccolo, two oboes, English horn, four clarinets (including E flat and bass clarinets), two bassoons, contrabassoon, four horns, four trumpets, four trombones, tuba, timpani, piano, celesta and a large percussion group of instruments (played by five performers [glockenspiel, xylophone, vibraphone, snare drum, tenor drum, cymbals, bass drum, conga drum, wood block, temple blocks (high and medium), timbales (pair), claves, triangle, metal sheet, tam-tam].

LINCOLN PORTRAIT

Soon after the United States was drawn into World War II, Andre Kostelanetz approached three American composers with the suggestion of composing three musical portraits of eminent Americans, to express the "magnificent spirit of our country." The proposal resulted in Virgil Thomson's *The Mayor LaGuardia Waltzes,* Jerome Kern's *Portrait for Orchestra of Mark Twain,* and Copland's *Lincoln Portrait.*

Copland has described his own reaction to the invitation:

It was January, 1942, that André Kostelanetz suggested the idea of my writing a musical portrait of a great American. He put teeth into the proposal by offering to commission such a piece and to play it extensively. My first thought was to do a portrait of Walt Whitman, the patron poet of all American composers. But when Mr. Kostelanetz explained that the series of portraits he was planning already included a literary figure, I was persuaded to change to a statesman. From that moment on the choice of Lincoln as my subject seemed inevitable.

On discussing my choice with Virgil Thomson, he amiably pointed out that no composer could possibly hope to match in musical terms the stature of so eminent a figure as that of Lincoln. Of course, he was quite right. But the sitter himself might speak. With the voice of Lincoln to help me I was ready to risk the impossible.

The letters and speeches of Lincoln supplied the text. It was a comparatively simple matter to choose a few excerpts that seemed particularly apposite to our own situation today. I avoided the temptation to use only well-known passages, permitting myself the luxury of quoting only once from a world-famous speech. The order and arrangement of the selections are my own.

The first sketches were made in February and the portrait finished on April 16th. The orchestration was completed a few weeks later. I worked with musical materials of my own, with the exception of two songs of the period: the famous "Camptown Races" and a ballad that was first published in 1840 under the title of "The Pesky Sarpent," but is better known today as "Springfield Mountain":*

---

* *This and the following musical examples from this composition are copyright 1943 by Aaron Copland. Renewed 1970. Reprinted by permission of Aaron Copland and Boosey & Hawkes, Inc., sole publishers.*

In neither case is the treatment a literal one. The tunes are used freely in the manner of my use of cowboy songs in *Billy the Kid.*

The composition is roughly divided into three main sections. In the opening section I wanted to suggest something of the mysterious sense of fatality that surrounds Lincoln's personality. Also, near the end of that section, something of his gentleness and simplicity of spirit. [This is suggested by the first of many subtle transformations of "Springfield Mountain" for solo clarinet:]

The quick middle section briefly sketches in the background of the times he lived. [Prominent in this section are fragments recognizably derived from Stephen Foster's "Camptown Races":]

This merges into the concluding section where my sole purpose was to draw a simple but impressive frame about the words of Lincoln himself. [By the simplest means, the originally comic ditty "Springfield Mountain," having gone through many transformations, as did the man Lincoln, returns in dimensions expanding and suggesting the almost mythic quality of the man we remember:]

The text of *A Lincoln Portrait* is as follows:

"Fellow citizens, we cannot escape history."

That is what he said:
That is what Abraham Lincoln said:

"Fellow citizens, we cannot escape history. We of this Congress and this administration will be remembered in spite of ourselves. No personal significance or insignificance can spare one or another of us. The fiery trial through which we pass will light us down, in honor or dishonor, to the latest generation. We—even we here—hold the power and bear the responsibility."

He was born in Kentucky, raised in Indiana, and lived in Illinois.

And this is what he said:
This is what Abe Lincoln said:

"The dogmas of the quiet past are inadequate to the stormy present. The occasion is piled high with difficulty, and we must rise with the occasion. As our case is new, so we must think anew and act anew. We must disenthrall ourselves and then we shall save our country."

When standing erect he was six feet four inches tall.
And this is what he said:
He said:

"It is the eternal struggle between two principles—right and wrong throughout the world. . . . It is the same spirit that says, 'You toil and work and earn bread and I'll eat it.' No matter in what shape it comes, whether from the mouth of a king who seeks to bestride the people of his own nation and live by the fruit of their labor, or from one race of men as an apology for enslaving another race, it is the same tyrannical principle."

Lincoln was a quiet man.
Abe Lincoln was a quiet and a melancholy man.
But when he spoke of democracy,
This is what he said:
He said:

"As I would not be a slave, so I would not be a master. This expresses my idea of democracy. Whatever differs from this, to the extent of the difference, is not democracy."

Abraham Lincoln, sixteenth President of these United States, is everlasting in the memory of his countrymen,
For on the battleground at Gettysburg, this is what he said:
This is what Abe Lincoln said:

". . . that from these honored dead we take increased devotion to that cause for which they gave the last full measure of devotion; that we here highly resolve that these dead shall not have died in vain; that this nation, under God, shall have a new birth of freedom; and that government of the people, by the people and for the people shall not perish from the earth."

The score is dedicated to Andre Kostelanetz, who conducted the first performance at a pension fund concert of the Cincinnati Symphony Orchestra in Cincinnati on May 14, 1942. The work entered the New York Philharmonic repertory under the direction of Artur Rodzinski on February 14, 1946. The score calls for 2 flutes, 2 piccolos, English horn, 2 clarinets, bass clarinet, 2 bassoons, contrabassoon, 4 horns, 3 trumpets, 3 trombones, tuba, kettledrums, bass drum, snare drum, cymbals, tam-tam, glockenspiel, sleigh bells, xylophone, celesta, harp, and strings.

MUSIC FOR THE THEATRE

One of Aaron Copland's earliest influential works was his immediately successful *Music for the Theatre,* which may have owed part of its popularity to his deliberate incorporation of various devices of American jazz. In the search for an indigenous American musical idiom, what could be more logical than to follow the example of European composers who had drawn inspiration from the folk music of their own peoples?

Although he was only in his mid-twenties, Copland had already attracted such attention by his early works that he was commissioned to compose a new score for the League of Composers. And even before the concert of the League of Composers, Serge Koussevitzky, who had already formed a high opinion of the young Copland, gave the world premiere of *Music for the Theatre* with the Boston Symphony in Symphony Hall, Boston, on November 20, 1925. Eight days later Koussevitzky and a small group of Boston Symphony musicians played the lively work at a concert of the League of Composers in New York's Town Hall where, according to the next day's *New York Times,* it was "wildly applauded."

It is a modest piece, essentially a suite in five short movements sparsely orchestrated for a small ensemble consisting of flute, piccolo, oboe, English horn, B-flat clarinet, E-flat clarinet, bassoon, 2 trumpets, trombone, xylophone, glockenspiel, snare drum, woodblock, bass drum with suspended cymbal, piano, 2 first violins, 2 second violins, 2 violas, 2 cellos, and double bass. (In large concert halls the strings may be increased at the discretion of the conductor.)

I. *Prologue: Molto moderato.* After a rather cocky, fanfare-like exchange between two trumpets, the mood grows quieter, giving way to a nostalgic solo for the oboe. A driving, jazzy section of *semi-ostinato* rhythms intervenes, after which the melancholy mood of the oboe solo returns.

II. *Dance: Allegro molto.* A catchy fragment of typical early jazz idiom, with its characteristic alternation of major and minor thirds, is announced motto-like by a bassoon solo with a snarling muted trombone accenting the first beat of each measure: *

---

* *Musical example copyright 1932 by Cos Cob Press, Inc. Renewed 1960 by Aaron Copland. Reprinted by permission of Aaron Copland, copyright owner, and Boosey & Hawkes, Inc., sole licensees.*

Soon an echo of the words "East side, west side" from Charles Lawlor's "The Sidewalks of New York" recalls Copland's birth in New York City. Again and again the jazzy opening phrase returns to set the mood of the "Dance"—most often in the brassy tones of trumpets and trombones.

III. *Interlude: Lento moderato.* The blues-like slow movement opens with a melancholy solo English horn. The melody is picked up by a clarinet set off against an imaginatively glinting background of soft piano and glockenspiel tones. At the end, the English horn recalls the fanfare opening of the first movement.

IV. *Burleske: Allegro vivo.* The brash humor of this scherzo-like movement borders on parody of commercial pop music of the twenties. Copland is said to have had in mind the antics of Fanny Brice, the creator of the burlesque character, Baby Snooks.

V. *Epilogue: Molto moderato.* The cocky trumpet fanfare of the opening movement echoes softly now in the clarinet, as if from a great distance. This brief and poetic conclusion is a dreamlike tissue of reminiscences. Perhaps, after all, the twenties were not so tough or so corny as we like to think.

EL SALON MEXICO

When Carlos Chavez conducted the Orquesta Sinfonica of Mexico City in the world premiere of Aaron Copland's *El Salón México* on August 27, 1937, the music critic of the *Excelsior,* G. Baqueiro Forster, reported that Copland's music had been a surprise. Copland, he said, had synthesized what is strongest and most characteristic of Mexican folk melody, rhythm, and harmony without taking away "one whit of the freshness and beauty of the Mexican song." He added that Copland had composed Mexican music as only Mexican composers ought to make it, "embodying the very elements of our folk song in the purest and most perfect form." (This was almost the precise compliment that the Spanish composer Falla had paid to the Spanishness of Debussy's *Ibéria.*) Not only the Mexican critic, but the Mexican audience, greeted Copland's new score with the same warmth as they received the best work of their own Revueltas. The following summer *El Salón México* was received with equal enthusiasm in its European premiere at the London Festival of the International Society for Contemporary Music.

Although Copland may not have been aware of it at the time, *El Salón México* was a harbinger of a number of his works of the following years (*Billy the Kid,* 1938; *Lincoln Portrait,* 1942; *Appalachian Spring,* 1944; see pp. 266, 271, and 262), which included folk tunes of his own country assimilated and adapted in a popular style, while nevertheless preserving the Copland touch. For this reason too, Copland's account of the genesis of *El Salón México* is of particular interest, although it is phrased in his typically modest, almost self-deprecating manner.

> If you have ever been in Mexico you probably know why a composer should want to write a piece of music about it. Nevertheless, I must admit that it came as something of a surprise when I left Mexico in 1932, after a first visit, to find myself with exactly that idea firmly implanted in my mind. It isn't as if I had never been away from home before. I had done my share of wandering about, and had even ventured as far as old Fez in Morocco without bringing back any musical souvenirs. But there must have been something different about Mexico. Or perhaps it wasn't just Mexico—perhaps my piece might never have been written if it hadn't been for the existence of the Salón México.
>
> I remember reading about it for the very first time in Anita Brenner's guide book. Under "Entertainment" she had this entry: "Harlem type night-club for the peepul [sic], grand Cuban orchestra, *Salón México*. Three halls: one for people dressed in your way, one for people dressed in overalls but shod, and one for the barefoot." Miss Brenner forgot to mention the sign on the wall which said: "Please don't throw lighted cigarette butts on the floor so the ladies don't burn their feet." The unsuspecting tourist should also have been warned that a guard stationed at the bottom of the steps leading to the "three halls" would nonchalantly frisk you as you started up the stairs just to be sure you had checked all your "artillery" at the door. One other curious custom, special to Salón México, might as well be mentioned here: when the dance hall closed its doors at five A.M. it hardly seemed worthwhile to the overalled patrons to travel all the way home, so they curled themselves up on the chairs around the walls for a quick two-hour snooze before getting to a seven o'clock job in the morning.
>
> Of course Mexico has other, and deeper, aspects than the Salón México, several of which suggested music during that first trip. . . . But I must instinctively have felt that to write a piece about those more profound manifestations of a strange land, a composer would have to be something more than a mere tourist. That is why my thoughts turned to the Salón México. It wasn't the music that I heard there, or the dances that attracted me, so much as the spirit of the place. In some inexplicable way, while milling about in those crowded halls, one felt a really live contact with the Mexican *people*—the electric sense one sometimes gets in far-off places, of suddenly knowing the essence of a people—their humanity, their separate shyness, their dignity and unique charm. I remember quite well that it was at just such a moment that I conceived the idea of composing a piece about Mexico and naming it *El Salón México*.
>
> To have an idea for a piece of music is not the same as to have the piece itself. Any composer will tell you that. Sooner or later you must begin to collect musical themes or tunes out of which a composition will eventually emerge. It was only natural that I should have thought of using popular Mexican melodies for my thematic material. Chabrier and Debussy didn't hesitate to help themselves to the melodic riches of Spain (in *España* and

Ibéria [See page 254 under Chabrier and page 300 under Debussy, *Images* no. 2]) so Americans like Robert McBride and myself have plenty of precedent for using the tunes of the Hispanic land on *our* southern doorstep. It's an easy method composers have for translating the flavor of a foreign people into musical terms. At any rate, I found myself looking about for suitable folk material as the basis for *El Salón México.*

There is nothing very remarkable about a Mexican popular melody. My purpose was not merely to quote them literally, but to heighten without in any way falsifying their natural simplicity. [Copland is too modest. His "heightening" of the Mexican melodies is often a quite sophisticated metric, rhythmic, melodic and even harmonic evolution, but only in ways which (to this listener's Yankee ears) seem only to emphasize their Latin-American traits.] Most of my tunes were taken from an unpretentious little collection [*Cancionero Mexicano*] gathered together and published by Frances Toor, resident American in the capital. Others I added later from the erudite book of Ruben M. Campos, *El Folk-lore y la Musica Mexicana.* To both authors I owe thanks. Probably the most direct quotation of a complete melody is that of *El Mosco* (No. 84 in the book by Campos):*

which is presented twice, immediately after the introductory measures (in which may be found fragments of *El Palo verde* and *La Jesusita*). The use of folk material in a symphonic composition always brings with it a formal problem. Composers have found that there is little that can be done with a folk tune except repeat it. Inevitably there is the danger of producing a mere string of unrelated "melodic gems." In the end I adopted a form which is a kind of modified potpourri, in which the Mexican themes and their extension are sometimes inextricably mixed for the sake of conciseness and coherence.

This composition celebrating Mexico was completed, strangely enough, in Bemidji, Minnesota, 250 miles north of Minneapolis, where I spent the summer of 1934. (You can see that my Mexican impressions were strong ones.) Because of other projects that intervened, the orchestration was not undertaken until two years later, when I was once again in Mexico. I was able to write "finis" to the whole work in July, 1936.

The orchestra for *El Salón México* enlists piccolo, 2 flutes, 2 oboes, English horn, 2 clarinets, bass clarinet, 2 bassoons, contrabassoon, 4 horns, 3 trumpets, 3 trombones, tuba, kettledrum, cymbals, military drum, tambourine, bass drum, Chinese brush, wood blocks, block, gourd, xylophone, piano, and the customary strings.

---

* *Musical example copyright 1939 by Aaron Copland. Renewed 1966. Reprinted by permission of Aaron Copland copyright owner, and Boosey & Hawkes, Inc., sole licensees.*

STATEMENTS FOR ORCHESTRA

Statements, commissioned by the League of Composers for performance by the Minneapolis Symphony Orchestra, is one of Copland's most serious works. It belongs to the period of a small group of scores including the marvelous *Vitebsk,* a study of a Jewish theme (for piano, violin, and cello); the Piano Variations, which are of a "density" or expressive concentration rare even in Copland's canon; and the "Short" Symphony, on which he worked simultaneously with *Statements.* Some of these scores seemed difficult to many a music lover when they were new. One had then the impression that Copland was not worrying too much about their "accessibility" but was writing under an artistic compulsion.

Statements was composed bewteen 1932 and the summer of 1935 at the artists' colony of Yaddo, at Mexico City; at Friends' Lake, New York; at Bemidji, Minnesota; Cambridge, Massachusetts; and at the MacDowell Colony at Peterborough, New Hampshire. The orchestration was completed in New York City in June 1935.

"The title of 'statement' was chosen," wrote Mr. Copland, "to indicate a short, terse orchestral movement of a well-defined character, lasting about three minutes. The separate movements were given suggestive titles as an aid to the public in understanding what the composer had in mind when writing these pieces."

I. *Militant:* The first statement is based on a single, bold theme, announced in an uncompromising unison of flutes, oboes, bassoon and strings:*

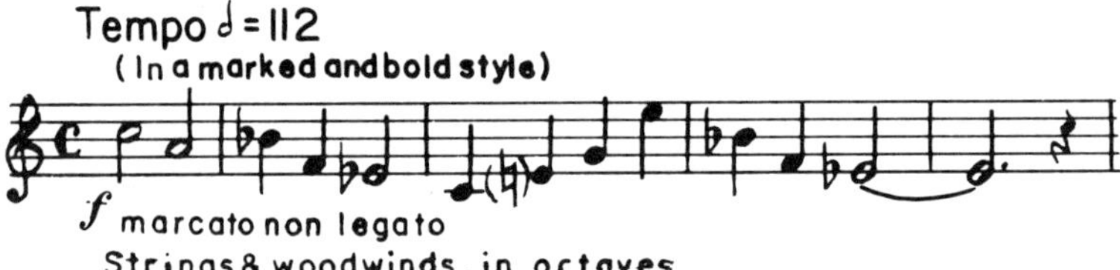

As the movement develops there is increasing use of a spare, harsh, but expressive counterpoint.

II. *Cryptic.* Tiny thematic fragments marked *dolce, misterioso* set the tone of this brief movement. The orchestral color is striking with its emphasis on solo flute and brass, to the total exclusion of strings.

III. *Dogmatic.* This assertive movement for full orchestra is in a three-part A-B-A form. The brief central section consists of the theme of Copland's Piano Variations in a forceful proclamation by solo horn alternating with solo trumpet.

IV. *Subjective: Calmo, expressivo.* In this context, the sound of strings alone, for which this movement is composed, has an especial freshness. Traditionally, of course, the strings have been ideally suited for the subtlest expression of fluctuating subjective moods.

---

* *This and the following musical example from this composition are copyright 1947 by Aaron Copland. Renewed 1974. Reprinted by permission of Aaron Copland and Boosey & Hawkes, Inc., sole publishers.*

V. *Jingo.* The title suggests a humorous, if not mocking, intent. So does the quotation of the popular ditty, "The Sidewalks of New York," in the casual whistling of a piccolo:

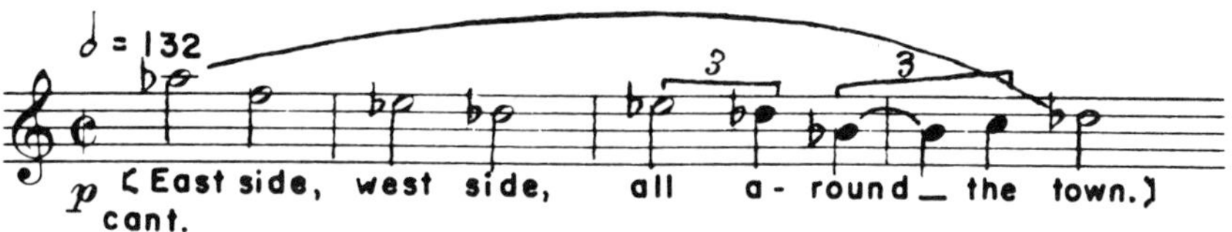

The rhythmically out-of-phase accompaniment with its suggestion of a hurdy-gurdy or merry-go-round gone awry (three clarinets with a touch of snare drum) adds to the caricature effect.

VI. *Prophetic.* The final movement seems to return to a strongly subjective mood, with a solemn melody for solo trumpet at its core. A majestic climax in fanfare style interrupts the trumpet melody which fades away at the end with delicate touches of the glockenspiel.

Statements is scored for 3 flutes, piccolo, 2 oboes, clarinet in E flat, 2 clarinets in B flat, bass clarinet, English horn, 2 bassoons, contrabassoon, 4 horns, 3 trumpets, 3 trombones, tuba, kettledrums, tam-tam, bass drum, cymbals, glockenspiel, triangle, side drum, slap stick, and the customary string choir frequently subdivided. The fifth and sixth sections of *Statements* were first performed by the Minneapolis Symphony under the direction of Eugene Ormandy on an NBC broadcast on January 9, 1936. The first complete performance was given by the New York Philharmonic, Dimitri Mitropolous conducting, in Carnegie Hall on January 7, 1942. The score is dedicated to Mary Senior Churchill.

SHORT SYMPHONY (NO. 2)

Aaron Copland's "Short" Symphony may last a brief fifteen minutes, but those minutes are concentrated in meaning as only the music of a master can be. Whether it strikes one's ears as intense expression, close logic, intricate design, or simply enthralling music, no one could possibly doubt that a great deal happens in this music—in a manner far removed from the carefree "happenings" of a later day. This does not mean that the "Short" Symphony sounds dated in any sense except the very positive one of belonging clearly to a period of Copland's development when he produced some of his most powerful and individual works. Begun in 1931 and completed in 1933, the "Short" Symphony was preceded by Copland's *Vitebsk* by his Piano Variations, and by his *Statements for Orchestra.* When these works were new they tended to sound austere, sometimes harsh, or downright esoteric to many music lovers. The "Short" Symphony, moreover, with its shifting meters and cross rhythms, was difficult to play. Thus, it happened that although the "Short" Symphony was performed in Mexico City under the direction of Carlos Chávez as early as November 23, 1934, it had to wait ten years for its first performance in the

United States, when Leopold Stokowski presented it with the NBC Symphony on January 9, 1944. It is still less often performed than Copland's really popular works, although one would think that most of its terrors had worn off for orchestral players as well as listeners.

It is cast in three movements which are played without pause:

I. *Tempo: quarter-note equals 144 (incisivo).* The opening movement bears a strong relation to traditional first-movement, or sonata-allegro, form. A boldly skipping *staccato* theme first heard in the woodwinds leaps from one orchestral choir to the other through an intensive development for some twelve pages of score:*

It breaks off suddenly at its peak, interrupted by a sustained tone of a soft, muted trumpet. Against this tone a solo clarinet in duet with an oboe sings the strongly contrasting, slightly jazzy second theme:

The central development section tosses about fragments of both principal and secondary themes. There is a strong impression of recapitulation or reprise of both themes in slightly modified and abbreviated form. A soft phrase for flute and oboe links the first movement to the second, which follows without pause.

II. *Tempo: half-note equals circa 44.* The first four notes of a slowly descending scale, one of the most ancient and yet freshest of melodic ideas, dominates the middle movement from the opening phrase of an alto flute to the final climax:

Tempo 𝅗𝅥 =circa 44

mp espressivo

Alto flute

---

* *This and the following musical examples from this composition are copyright 1955 by Boosey & Hawkes, Inc., sole publishers. Reprinted by permission.*

In between, the mildly contrasting melody of the middle section hovers between two adjacent notes in gently rocking rhythm. At the end there is again a brief thematic link to the next movement, which follows without pause.

III. *Tempo: quarter-note equals 144 (preciso e ritmico).* The scherzo-like finale, one of Copland's most dazzling movements, recalls and transforms thematic material from both the earlier movements, combining them with the jaunty thematic material of the finale proper. A lyric transformation of the Symphony's opening theme precedes the incisive brilliance of the final page.

The "Short" Symphony is scored for piccolo, 2 flutes, alto flute, 2 oboes, heckelphone, English horn, 2 clarinets, bass clarinet, 2 bassoons, contrabassoon, 4 horns, 2 trumpets, piano, and the customary string choir.

SYMPHONY NO. 3

Having consciously wooed and won a broad musical public by developing a simpler style and adapting traditional and folk tunes, starting with such works as *El Salón México* (1937), *Billy the Kid* (1938), and continuing through his *Lincoln Portrait* (1942), and *Appalachian Spring* (1944), Copland began to compose works with fewer popularly identifiable themes and more traditional (so-called "classical" or "abstract") such as his Piano Concerto, Piano Sonata, Clarinet Concerto, Piano Quartet, and his Symphony No. 3, which was commissioned by the Koussevitzky Foundation in 1943.

When Copland received this commission, he had, by his own account, been collecting themes over a period of years with the idea of someday putting them together in a symphony. He began working on the score in August, 1944, in a small Mexican village. The first movement was completed in April of the following year, the second in August, and the third in January of 1946. The orchestration of the fourth movement was completed on September 29, 1946, barely in time to have the instrumental parts copied for the first performance, which was presented by the Boston Symphony on October 18, 1946.

For that occasion Mr. Copland prepared the following comment:

> Inevitably the writing of a symphony brings with it the question of what it is meant to express. I suppose if I forced myself I could invent an ideological basis for my symphony. But if I did, I'd be bluffing—or at any rate adding something *ex post facto,* something that might or might not be true, but which played no role at the moment of creation. . . .
>
> One aspect of the symphony ought to be pointed out: it contains no folk or popular material. During the late twenties it was customary to pigeonhole me as a composer of symphonic jazz, with emphasis on the jazz. More recently I have been catalogued as a purveyor of Americana. Any reference to jazz or folk-material in this work was purely unconscious.
>
> For the sake of those who like a purely musical guide through unfamiliar terrain, I add a breakdown by movements of the technical outlines of the work:
>
> I. *Molto moderato.* The opening movement which is broad and expres-

sive in character, opens and closes in the key of E major. (Formally it bears no relation to the sonata-allegro with which symphonies usually begin.) The themes—three in number—are plainly stated: the first is in the strings, at the very start without introduction:*

the second in related mood in violas and oboes; the third, of a bolder nature, in the trombones and horns:

The general form is that of an arch, in which the central portion is more animated and the final section an extended coda, presenting a broadened version of the opening material. Both the first and third themes are referred to again in later movements of the Symphony.

II. *Allegro molto.* The form of this movement stays closer to normal symphonic procedure. It is the usual scherzo, with first part, trio and return. A brass introduction leads to the main theme, which is stated three times in Part I: at first in horns and violas, then in unison strings, and finally in augmentation in the lower brass:

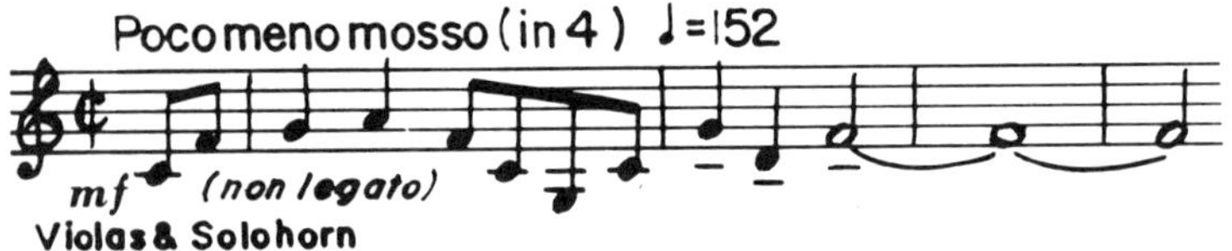

The three statements of the theme are separated by the usual episodes. After the climax is reached, the trio follows without pause. Solo woodwinds sing the new trio melody in lyrical and canonical style. The strings take it up and add a new section of their own. The recapitulation of Part I is not literal. The principal theme of the scherzo returns in a somewhat revised form in the piano solo, leading through previous episodic material to a full restatement in the *tutti* orchestra. This is climaxed by a return to the lyrical trio theme, this time sung in canon and in *fortissimo* by the entire orchestra.

III. *Andantino quasi allegretto.* The third movement is the freest of all in formal structure. Although it is built up sectionally, the various sections are intended to emerge one from the other in continuous flow, somewhat in the manner of a closely knit series of variations. The opening section, however, plays no role other than that of introducing the main body of the movement.

---

* *This and the following musical examples from this composition are copyright Boosey & Hawkes, Ltd. Copyright 1947. Renewed 1974. Reprinted by permission of Boosey & Hawkes, Inc.*

High up in the unaccompanied violins is heard a rhythmically transformed version of the third (trombone) theme of the first movement of the Symphony:

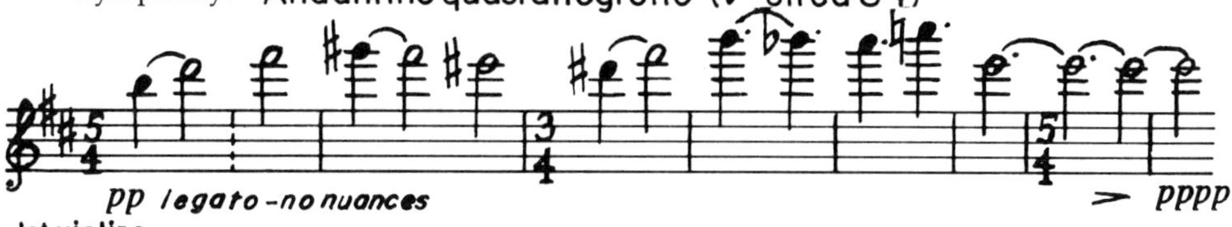

It is briefly developed in contrapuntal style, and comes to a full close, once again in the key of E major. A new and more tonal theme is introduced in the solo flute. This is the melody that supplies the thematic substance for the sectional metamorphoses that follow: at first with quiet singing nostalgia, then faster and heavier—almost dance-like; then more childlike and naïve, and finally more vigorous and forthright. Imperceptibly, the whole movement drifts off into the higher regions of the strings, out of which floats the single line of the beginning, sung by a solo violin and piccolo, accompanied this time by harps and celesta. The third movement calls for no brass, with the exception of a single horn and trumpet.

IV. *Molto deliberato* (Fanfare)—*Allegro risoluto.* The final movement follows without pause. It is the longest of the symphony, and closest in structure to the customary sonata-allegro form. The opening fanfare is based on "Fanfare for the Common Man" which I composed in 1942, at the invitation of Eugene Goossens for a series of wartime fanfares introduced under his direction by the Cincinnati Symphony. In the present version it is first played *pianissimo* by flutes and clarinets, and then suddenly given out by brass and percussion. The fanfare serves as an introduction to the main body of the movement which follows. The components of the usual form are there: a first theme in animated 16th-note motion; a second theme—broader and more song-like in character; a full-blown development and a refashioned return to the earlier material of the movement, leading to a peroration. One curious feature of the symphony consists in the fact that the second theme is to be found embedded in the development section instead of being in its customary place. The development as such concerns itself with the fanfare and first theme fragments. A shrill *tutti* chord, with flutter-tongued brass and piccolos, brings the development to a close. What follows is not a recapitulation in the ordinary sense. Instead a delicate interweaving of the first theme in the higher solo woodwinds is combined with a quiet version of the fanfare in the two bassoons. Combined with this, the opening theme of the first movement of the symphony is quoted, first in the violins and later in the solo trombone. Near the end a full-voice chanting of the song-like theme is heard in horns and trombones. The symphony concludes on a massive restatement of the opening phrase with which the entire work began.

The score of Copland's Third Symphony calls for 2 piccolos, 3 flutes, 2 oboes, English horn, E flat clarinet, 2 clarinets, bass clarinet in B flat, 2 bassoons, contrabassoon, 4 horns, 4 trumpets, 2 trombones, bass trombone, tuba, kettledrums, tenor drum, bass drum, snare drum, wood block, cymbals, suspended cymbal, anvil, tam tam, ratchet, slap stick, claves, celesta, xylophone, glockenspiel, tubular bells, piano, 2 harps, and the traditional strings.

Arcangelo Corelli

Born February 17, 1653, Fusignano, near Imola—died January 8, 1713, Rome

CHRISTMAS CONCERTO, OPUS 6, NO. 8, G MINOR (FATTO PER LA NOTTE DI NATALE)

In the glamour, power and prestige of his art, Arcangelo Corelli seemed an archangel of music—not only to his Roman contemporaries who were fortunate enough to hear him in the flesh, but to music lovers throughout his native Italy, across the continent of Europe and even in faraway London. At the peak of Italy's great Baroque age, he was hailed as the greatest living composer of instrumental music. This meant, in effect, the greatest who had *ever* lived. For prior to Corelli's day, mere instrumental music had—if one disregards such exceptional achievements as the shofars at the Battle of Jericho or the lyre of Orpheus in the Underworld—rarely rivaled the glorious traditions of vocal art.

Although Corelli came from the small town of Fusignano, his ancestors were no mere landed gentry but an ancient and illustrious clan, which included medical doctors, lawyers, mathematicians and poets. However, they were not musicians. Corelli had his chief musical training not at home but at the great musical center of Bologna.

In Rome, where he spent most of his professional life, he was honored as befitted his genius. His patrons were not only the high clergy, including two cardinals, but also Queen Christina of Sweden, who, since her abdication, lived in Rome as one of the most enlightened patrons of the arts. One of the youngest and richest cardinals in Rome, Pietro Ottoboni, the nephew of Pope Alexander VIII, engaged Corelli as his director of music and first violinist, lodging him in the magnificent Ottoboni Palace. The palace was famous for its library, museum, and salon, and after Corelli's appointment, Ottoboni's musical Mondays became the rendezvous of the best Roman society. The fame of these Monday concerts spread across Europe.

Corelli may have seemed angelic in the almost supernatural power of his music, but not in the sense of any pallid purity. Today, to the nonprofessional, Corelli's music may look "purer" (that is, simpler) on paper than it sounded in performance. For like many Baroque composers, Corelli often wrote only a melodic skeleton of his music, which he intended for embellishment by the performer. When Corelli himself was the performer, his manner was far from angelic. "Whilst he was playing on the violin," reports the eighteenth-century historian Hawkins, "it was usual for his countenance to be distorted, his eyes as red as fire, and his eyeballs to roll as in agony."

It was Corelli's violin sonatas and trios that established him as the greatest instrumental composer in Europe. But his orchestral concertos or *con-*

certi grossi, published the year after his death, and acknowledged to be his greatest works, maintained Corelli's popularity to the very end of the century. In London alone one concert society, the Concerts of Antient Vocal and Instrumental Music, performed Corelli's concertos ninety-seven times in less than twenty years (1776–1792), according to the records of the Society itself. And the English historian and critic Charles Burney declared in 1789: "The *Concertos* of Corelli seem to have withstood all the attacks of time and fashion with more firmness than any of his other works. The harmony is so pure, so rich, and so grateful; the parts are so clearly, judiciously, and ingeniously disposed; and the effect of the whole, from a large band, so majestic, solemn, and sublime, that they preclude all criticism, and make us forget that there is any other Music of the same kind existing."

The most famous of them all was and still is known as his "Christmas" Concerto, although "Christmas Eve" Concerto would correspond more accurately to the Italian subtitle "Fatto per la Notte di Natale." We do not know when it was composed—perhaps anytime during the thirty-year span from 1682 (when Corelli began conducting his own works for Cardinal Ottoboni) to 1711, the year when a contemporary reported Corelli was polishing the dozen *concerti* for publication as his Opus 6.

These concertos were composed for two collaborating groups: four soloists (normally 2 violins, cello, and harpsichord) known as the *small* group or *concertino* and an accompanying string orchestra known as the *big* group or *concerto grosso,* which also gave the form its name.

In addition to the bowed string instruments, this large group had its bass line (or *basso continuo*) reinforced by a second harpsichord, small organ, harp, bass lute, or some combination of these, plus string basses and even bassoons, according to the size of the auditorium and players available.

The "Christmas" Concerto is in six short movements:

I. *Vivace; Grave.* A dozen ceremonial chords for full orchestra open the Concerto like a grand Baroque gesture. The solemn *Grave* consists of intertwining melodic lines which Corelli specifically asked to have played in broadly flowing style "as its stands" *(come sta),* which is to say: as written, without any embellishment. The fact that Corelli felt it necessary to ask the performers *not* to embellish the music, tells us very clearly that embellishment was standard operational procedure—at least in slow movements like this.

II. *Allegro.* Here for the first time Corelli contrasts his solo *concertino* group with the accompanying *concerto grosso.* The two solo violins have a duet in which their voices intertwine almost as if they were braided, sometimes one voice being on top, sometimes the other, while the cello and harpsichord stalk along at a livelier pace. The soloists' song is punctuated at frequent intervals by the full *concerto grosso.*

III. *Adagio; Allegro.* This movement is the only one of the six which leaves the tonic key of G for the "warmer" tonality of E flat. It begins very peacefully with the two solo violins seeming to float above the more earthbound *concerto grosso,* in arpeggios that have been interpreted to suggest the hovering of angels over the manger. There is a more urgently dramatic middle section after which the "hovering" figures return.

IV. *Vivace.* This lively, dance-like movement, is lead off by the *concertino:*

It reflects the spirit of the popular French minuet as developed at the court of Louis XIV by Lully.

V. *Allegro.* This movement is a vigorous play of forces between the *concertino* and the *concerto grosso* in swift alternation and combination.

VI. *Pastorale: Largo.* This *Pastorale* does not refer to any nature description, but rather to the shepherds *(pastori)* who gathered at the manger. For hundreds of years it had been customary for Italian shepherds to go into town (especially into Rome) on Christmas Eve or Christmas Day to play their pipes before the manger scenes set up in churches and many other public places. Gradually a special type of tune, a gently lilting melody in triple meter, reminiscent of Sicilian shepherd music (and sometimes called *siciliano*), became traditional for these occasions and for art music which depicted them. Corelli may have been the first to embody the tradition in orchestral music. Here is the opening of his *Pastorale* in which the two solo violins imitate the ancient shepherds' pipes:

Here for the first time in this Concerto, Corelli moves from his basic G minor into a radiant G major. In the background we hear very simple, long-held notes intended to suggest the peasant accompaniments, or drones (which could most easily be played by bagpipes.)

But Corelli does not limit himself to imitation of shepherd music. He lets the little duet wander from one combination of instruments to another, from *continuo* to *concerto grosso* and back again. At the end the music seems to fade away in the distance, as if the shepherds were still playing their pipes on their homeward journey.

Although this was the most famous movement of Corelli's most famous Concerto, Corelli marked it to be played "ad libitum," or at will, meaning that this beautiful finale could be omitted, presumably if performed at other times than the Christmas season. Strangely enough, or perhaps because of the high value placed on this movement, this is one of only two brief pieces of Corelli's music manuscript that are known to have survived to the present day.

Henry Cowell

Born March 11, 1897, Menlo Park, California—died December 10, 1965, Shady, New York

HYMN AND FUGUING TUNE, NO. 16

When he died in 1965 at his country home in Shady, New York, gentle Henry Cowell, he of the sharp mind, the puckish humor, and the generous heart, had become one of the grand figures of contemporary American music. He was at work on his Symphony No. 20. He had been enormously prolific, imaginative, and influential in many other styles and forms, some of which, like the great series of his *Hymns and Fuguing Tunes,* were his own inventions inspired by the traditions of other ages and other cultures. Cowell also had been a prominent pedagogue, champion of younger composers, and propagandist for a dazzling spectrum of contemporary musical styles.

He was a major creative force in American music and, as Hugo Weisgall wrote of him, "His musical gifts and the range of his energy, the scope of his music, the breadth of his influence and the recognition he has achieved, combine to make of him a figure a little larger than life, a kind of Paul Bunyan in music."

"Henry Cowell's music [wrote Virgil Thomson] covers a wider range in both expression and technique than any other living composer. No other composer of our time has produced a body of work so radical and so normal so penetrating and so comprehensive. Add to this massive production his long and influential career as pedagogue, and Henry Cowell's achievement in music become impressive indeed. There is no other quite like it. To be both fecund and right is given to few."

Long before musical Americana became a fashion—not to say a fad—Cowell's acquisitive ear retained the echoes of old-time American hymns, which he heard as a child sung among Oklahoma country relations. In 1941 Mrs. Henry Cowell introduced her husband to music of the Southern Appalachian composer, William Walker, whose *Southern Harmony* (published in 1835) contained hymns, largely adaptations of older, modal ballad tunes to metrical psalm texts. This collection recalled to Cowell his childhood impressions of the Oklahoma country hymn singing, and provided the stimulus for his own series of "hymns and fuguing tunes," which are dedicated as a group to Mrs. Cowell.

According to Mrs. Cowell, "three-part hymns, with melody in the middle, and the simple polyphony of the fuguing tunes, were a feature of early sixteenth-century Scottish Presbyterianism and were inherited by a few Southern shaped-note hymnbook composers as well as by the New Englanders." She continues:

> The old "fuguing tune," cultivated also by the famous New England "primitive," William Billings (1744–1800), differed from simple hymn style by

introducing, after the beginning of the hymn, the more artful device of allowing one voice part to lead off alone, the others joining in succession in contrapuntal, often imitative (but rarely strictly fugal) style. At the close there was generally a return to simple block chords.

The early such Henry Cowell pieces transfer the singing-school music fairly literally, depending for their interest and vitality on the vigorous doubling of eights and fifths (men and women both sing on all the parts) and the consequent intense resonance. Later hymns and fuguing tunes, as in Symphony No. 6, have increased dissonance of various sorts and are of course extended. Cowell sometimes surrounded the plain lines of the style with the secundal harmonic texture that he used more and more elaborated in the course of his life—beginning in 1912 with the broad masses of adjacent tones, called tone clusters, used to produce sea-sounding music for a play. He later developed more than one logical system of harmony and counterpoint based on seconds instead of thirds, and they can be found in most of his chamber and orchestral music. . . .

One point H.C. always made is that (with one or two special exceptions) he never used actual traditional tunes—instead he wrote his own in the style of whatever tradition he was concerned with.

Stimulated by the freshness and spontaneity of Walker's art, Cowell developed his own two-movement form of hymn and fuguing tune, which he used not only for independent compositions but also as part of larger works such as his Violin Sonata, String Quartet No. 5, and his Symphonies Nos. 4, 5, 6, 7, 9, 10, and 12. His *Hymn and Fuguing Tune, No. 16* was completed at Shady, New York, shortly before his death. It is cast in simple form and in unpretentious, diatonic, somewhat modal style.

I. *Hymn (Moderato):* The opening chordal strain, given out by trumpets and trombones with a response of strings and winds (including horns) gives the framework of a traditional three-part (A-B-A) form.

II. *Fuguing Tune (Allegro):* The first violins lead off with a lively phrase imitated by solo horn and clarinet:*

and, more freely by other individual voices. In keeping with the manner of William Walker, the texture is kept generally light, often in three voice-parts. As in the Hymn, the opening section is recapitulated after a mildly contrasting middle section.

The orchestration calls for 2 flutes, 2 oboes, 2 clarinets, 2 bassoons, 2 horns (2 additional horns *ad lib.*), 3 trumpets, 3 trombones, tuba, and the traditional strings.

---

* *Musical example copyright 1966 by C. F. Peters Corporation. Reprinted by permission.*

Paul Creston

Born October 10, 1906, New York City

JANUS, OPUS 77

The title *Janus,* Creston informs us, is merely a means of identification and is not intended to be descriptive of this music. Any resemblance to the two-faced Italic deity is purely coincidental—although the two-part form of the work did suggest the title. Actually, this bipartite form is Creston's favorite. It has been familiar to music lovers from time immemorial in the form of prelude and fugue, fantasia and fugue, recitative and aria, and in symphonic works having a slow introduction to a fast movement. Creston's favorite combination is prelude and dance. He has used this many times, for it is a form which suggests to him many possibilities in character of the sections and their relationships.

This score was commissioned by the Association of Women's Committees for Symphony Orchestras and was completed in June 1959. Its first performance was by the Denver Symphony Orchestra under Saul Caston on July 17, 1959. The composer speaks of the two sections of *Janus* as a prelude and dance, although in the score itself the sections are designated merely as *Slow* and *Allegro moderato,* respectively.

The lyric first section opens with a quiet figure for muted strings over which the oboe immediately intones the principal theme of the entire work:

This is taken up in a variant but clearly related form first by the solo flute and then by various combinations. The theme is broken into small fragments, several of which are developed on their own. The development proceeds with great smoothness and logic, building to an impressive climax.

Although *Janus* is written in 3/4 meter throughout, the rhythmical organization of the work is complex. Rhythm dominates, not merely in the sense of strong beats and accents but in the most basic structural sense. Creston points out multimeters, polymeters, polyrhythms, and a large variety of rhythmic patterns. At the climax of the first section, the orchestra breaks off for a sudden silence, and the second section *(Allegro moderato)* begins very softly with fluttering woodwinds against the faint rasping of a snare drum. A triplet figure from the main theme appears very softly but distinctly in the depths of the orchestra and gradually a wild dance is built up: often violent—even marked *feroce* at one point—but rich in contrast.

Creston's score calls for 4 flutes, 3 oboes, 3 clarinets, 3 bassoons, 4 horns, 3 trumpets, 3 trombones, tuba, kettledrums, percussion (not specified), piano, and strings.

In a letter to Henry Cowell dated January 11, 1948, Creston expressed his feelings about composition:

> I look upon music, and more specifically the writing of it, as a spiritual practice. This may be a complete variance with the speculations of art theorists, but inasmuch as it pertains to my way of life, I have found it the most satisfactory justification of my pursuit of art. Not that this view may not equally apply to other persons. I believe that everyone should compose and that musical composition should be a definite course in our educational system, as much as history and mathematics, without deeming it a special privilege of the professional composer. To me, musical composition is as vital to my spiritual welfare as prayer and good deeds; just as food and exercise are necessities of physical health, and thought and study are requisites of mental well-being.
>
> My philosophic approach to composition is abstract. I am preoccupied with matters of melodic design, harmonic coloring, rhythmic pulse, and formal progression; not with imitations of nature, or narrations of fairy tales, or propounding of sociological ideologies. Not that the source of inspiration may not be a picture or a story. Only that regardless of the subject matter, regardless of the school of thought, a musical composition must bear judgment purely on musical criteria. Its intrinsic worth depends on the integration of musical elements toward a unified whole. . . .

Creston was born in New York City in 1906 and studied piano there with Randegger and Dethier, and theory and organ with Pietro Yon. What he considers his first "professional encouragement" came when Henry Cowell presented him in the premiere of his *Seven Theses for Piano* on a Composers Forum program at the New School for Social Research in 1934. Two years later Creston's string quartet was played at the Yaddo Festival. In 1943 his First Symphony won the award of the New York Music Critics Circle; the American Academy of Arts and Letters gave him a $1,000 grant for creative work; and the National Association of Composers and Conductors cited him as the outstanding American composer of serious music for the season 1942–43. Since then he has been prominent in the front rank of contemporary American composers.

George Crumb

Born October 24, 1929, Charleston, West Virginia

ANCIENT VOICES OF CHILDREN

One of the most widely discussed and admired American composers of the group that could be called the middle generation, George Crumb was made composer-in-residence at the University of Pennsylvania as of 1965. He grew up in a musical family. His father was a band conductor who played the clarinet and his brother was a flutist. He studied at the Mason College of Music in Charleston, received his Master's degree at the University of Illinois and his Doctor of Musical Arts from the University of Michigan, where he studied with Ross Lee Finney. He was also a pupil of Boris Blacher at the Hochschule für Musik in Berlin, in 1955 and 1956. He taught for six years at the University of Colorado before joining the faculty of the University of Pennsylvania. Crumb's *Ancient Voices of Children* was first performed in public on October 31, 1970 at the Fourteenth Festival of Chamber Music at the Library of Congress, Washington, D.C. Arthur Weisberg conducted the Contemporary Chamber Ensemble with Jan De Gaetani, soprano, and Michael Dash, boy soprano. The first New York Philharmonic performance was presented at a "Prospective Encounter" concert on February 18, 1972 at New York University under the direction of Pierre Boulez with Jan De Gaetani as soloist. It was so successful that it was repeated the following season in the regular Philharmonic concert series and has been widely performed elsewhere.

Mr. Crumb has commented on his score as follows:

> *Ancient Voices of Children* was composed during the summer of 1970 on commission from the Elizabeth Sprague Coolidge Foundation, while I was in residence at Tanglewood, Massachusetts. This work forms part of an extended cycle of vocal compositions based on the poetry of Federico García Lorca, which has absorbed much of my compositional energy over the past eight years. . . .
>
> In *Ancient Voices of Children,* as in my earlier Lorca settings, I have sought musical images that enhance and reinforce the powerful yet strangely haunting imagery of Lorca's poetry. I feel that the essential meaning of this poetry is concerned with the most primary things: life, death, love, the smell of the earth, the sounds of the wind and the sea. These "*ur*-concepts" are embodied in a language which is primitive and stark but which is capable of infinitely subtle nuance. . . .
>
> The texts of *Ancient Voices* are fragments of longer poems which I have grouped into a sequence that seemed to suggest a "larger rhythm" in terms of musical continuity. . . .
>
> The vocal style in the cycle ranges from the virtuosic to the intimately lyrical, and in my conception of the work I very much had in mind Jan

DeGaetani's enormous technical and timbral flexibility. Perhaps the most characteristic vocal effect in *Ancient Voices* is produced by the mezzo-soprano singing a kind of fantastic vocalise (based on purely phonetic sounds) into an amplified piano, thereby producing a shimmering aura of echoes. The inclusion of a part for boy soprano seemed the best solution for those passages in the text where Lorca clearly implies a child's voice. The boy soprano is heard offstage until the very last page of the work, at which point he joins the mezzo-soprano onstage for the closing vocalise.

The instruments employed in *Ancient Voices* were chosen for their particular timbral potentialities. The pianist also plays toy piano (in the 4th song), the mandolinist musical saw (2nd song)—although a separate player can be used for the saw—and the oboist harmonica (4th song). Certain special instrumental effects are used to heighten the "expressive intensity"—e.g., "bending" the pitch of the piano by application of a chisel to the strings (2nd song); use of a paper-threaded harp (in "Dances of the Ancient Earth"); the frequent "pitch-bending" of the oboe, harp and mandolin. The mandolin has one set of strings tuned a quarter-tone low in order to give a special pungency to its tone. The three percussionists command a wide range of instruments, including Tibetan prayer stones, Japanese temple bells and tuned tom-toms. The instrumentalists are frequently called upon to sing, shout and whisper.

In composing *Ancient Voices of Children* I was conscious of an urge to fuse various unrelated stylistic elements. I was intrigued with the idea of juxtaposing the seemingly incongruous: a suggestion of flamenco with a Baroque quotation (*"Bist du bei mir,"* from the *Notebook of Anna Magdalena Bach*), or a reminiscence of Mahler with a breath of the Orient. It later occurred to me that both Bach and Mahler drew upon many disparate sources in their own music without sacrificing "stylistic purity."

It is sometimes of interest to a composer to recall the original impulse—the "creative germ"—of a compositional project. In the case of *Ancient Voices* I felt this impulse to be the climactic final words of the last song: ". . . and I will go very far . . . to ask Christ the Lord to give me back my ancient soul of a child."

ANCIENT VOICES OF CHILDREN

[texts by Federico García Lorca*]

I. "El niño busca su voz" ("The Little Boy Was Looking for his Voice") from "El niño mudo" ("The Little Mute Boy"); translated by W.S. Merwin

El niño busca su voz.	The little boy was looking for his voice.
(La tenia el rey de los grillos.)	(The king of the crickets had it.)
En una gota de agua	In a drop of water
buscaba su voz el niño.	the little boy was looking for his voice.

* *Excerpts from* Selected Poems *by Federico García Lorca. Copyright 1955 by New Directions Publishing Corporation. All rights reserved. Reprinted by permission of New Directions Publishing Corporation, New York, N.Y.*

No la quiero para hablar;
me haré con ella un anillo
que llevará mi silencio
en su dedo pequeñito.

I do not want it for speaking with;
I will make a ring of it
so that he may wear my silence
on his little finger.

II. "Me he perdido muchas veces por el mar" ("I Have Lost Myself in the Sea Many Times") from "Gacela de la Huida" ("Gacela of the Flight"); translated by Stephen Spender and J.L. Gili

Me he perdido muchas veces por el mar
con el oído llena de flores recién cortadas,
con la lengua llena de amor y de agonía.
Muchas voces me he perdido por el mar,
como me pierdo en el corazón de algunos niños.

I have lost myself in the sea many times
with my ear full of freshly cut flowers,
with my tongue full of love and agony.
I have lost myself in the sea many times
as I lose myself in the heart of certain children.

III. "¿De dónde vienes, amor, mi niño?" ("From Where Do You Come, My Love, My Child?") from "Yerma"; translated by J.L. Gili

¿De dónde vienes, amor, mi niño?
De la cresta del duro frío.
¿Qué necesitas, amor, mi niño?
La tibia tela de tu vestido.
¡Que se agiten las ramas al sol
y salten las fuentes alrededor!
En el patio ladra el perro,
en los árboles canta el viento.
Los bueyes mugen al boyero
y la luna me riza los cabellos.
¿Qué pides, niño, desde tan lejos?
Los blancos montes que hay en tu pecho.
¡Que se agiten las ramas al sol
y salten las fuentes alrededor!
Te diré, niño mío, que sí,
tronchada y rota soy para ti.
¡Cómo me duele esta cintura
donde tendrás primera cuna!
¿Cuándo, mi niño, vas a venir?

From where do you come, my love, my child?
From the ridge of hard frost.
What do you need, my love, my child?
The warm cloth of your dress.
Let the branches ruffle in the sun
and the fountains leap all around!
In the courtyard a dog barks,
in the trees the wind sings.
The oxen low to the ox-herd
and the moon curls my hair.
What do you ask for, my child, from so far away?
The white mountains of your breast.
Let the branches ruffle in the sun
and the fountains leap all around!
I'll tell you, my child, yes.
I am torn and broken for you.
How painful is this waist
where you will have your first cradle!
When, my child, will you come?

Cuando tu carne huela a jazmín.	When your flesh smells of jasmine flowers.
¡Que se agiten las ramas al sol *y salten las fuentes alrededor!*	Let the branches ruffle in the sun and the fountains leap all around!

IV. "Todas las tardes en Granada, todas las tardes se muere un niño" ("Each Afternoon in Granada, a Child Dies Each Afternoon") from "Gacela del niño muerto" ("Gacela of the Dead Child"); translated by Edwin Honig

Todas las tardes en Granada, *todas las tardes se muere un niño.*	Each afternoon in Granada a child dies each afternoon.

V. "Se ha Ilenado de luces mi corazón de seda" ("My Heart of Silk Is Filled With Lights") from "Balada de la placeta" ("Ballad of the Little Square"), translated by J.L. Gili

Se ha llenado de luces *mi corazón de seda,* *de campanas perdidas,* *de lirios y de abejas.* *Y yo me iré muy lejos,* *más allá de esas sierras,* *más allá de los mares,* *cerca de las estrellas,* *para pedirle a Cristo* *Señor que me devuelva* *mi alma antiqua de niño.*	My heart of silk is filled with lights, with lost bells, with lilies, and with bees, and I will go very far, farther than those hills, farther than the seas, close to the stars, to ask Christ the Lord to give me back my ancient soul of a child.

The score of *Ancient Voice of Children* calls for soprano, boy soprano, oboe, mandolin, harp, paper-threaded harp, electric piano (a normal grand piano amplified by means of contact microphones [attached, by taping, to the sound-board], a stereo amplifier, and two speakers), a ⅝ inch chisel (for "chisel piano" effect), fine quality toy piano with two and a half octave range. Small harmonica (with chromatic lever), 1 fine quality musical saw with string-bass or cello bow, and three percussion groups, which perform both separately and occasionally overlapping with each other:

Percussion I: large tam-tam, pair of finger cymbals, 1 mounted antique cymbal (g′ sharp), tambourine, 1 single timbale (creole), marimba, 2 maracas, tubular bells, very small suspended triangle, and 1 large suspended cymbal.

Percussion II: medium size tam-tam, 4 tunable tom-toms, large suspended cymbal, tenor drum, 2 maracas, tubular bells, sleighbells.

Percussion III: small tam-tam, pair of Tibetan prayer stones, claves, vibraphone, large-pedal kettledrum, 2 mounted antique cymbals (e′ and f′), mounted glockenspiel plate tuned to f″-sharp, sleighbells, 2 maracas, large suspended cymbal, and 5 Japanese (bowl-shaped) temple bells of different sizes.

Luigi Dallapiccola

Born February 3, 1904, Pisino, Istria—died February 19, 1975, Florence

VARIATIONS FOR ORCHESTRA

"I am a man of the Middle Ages," said Dallapiccola to this writer some years ago, "but nobody will believe it." It *is* hard to believe at first. For a more modern man would be hard to find. Yet Dallapiccola is quick to point out that one cannot understand one's way in the present without the past in which it is rooted. "How can you expect to understand twelve-tone music without a thorough knowledge of Wagner?" he asks. Mr. Dallapiccola admits to having been a Wagnerite since he was twelve.

His metaphorical claim to be a man of the Middle Ages is strengthened by many aspects of his music, most prominently, perhaps, by his love of religious symbols. The twelve-tone system itself has many points of resemblance to the late Medieval isorhythmic motet with its highly involved, intellectual-mathematical structure, and its tense emotional expression.

"I have been interested in the twelve-tone system since 1937," he has written of himself. "In 1942, after long years of experiment, I began to apply it in very free fashion. Since 1952 I have used it strictly."

The Variations for Orchestra is an orchestration of his *Musical Notebook of Annalibera,* composed in 1952 during the course of a trip across Canada, the United States, and Mexico. The *Musical Notebook of Annalibera* was commissioned by the Pittsburgh International Contemporary Music Festival of 1952. This ultraserious piano work was dedicated to Dallapiccola's daughter Annalibera, who was born in the time of the liberation of Dallapiccola's chosen home, Florence, from German occupation. Her unusual name had a profound emotional meaning for the composer.

The subjects of liberty and prisons had played a tremendous role in Dallapiccola's thinking and composing for many years, even in his adolescence before he decided to become a composer. The experiences of World War II (both private and public) intensified these emotions. His *Songs of Imprisonment (Canti di prigionia)* occupied him during the early years of World War II. Among the best known of his works is the opera *The Prisoner (Il Prigioniero),* on which he worked from 1944 to 1948. On the tenth anniversary of the liberation of the city of Florence, Dallapiccola began the composition of his *Songs of Liberation (Canti di liberazione).* For a man of Dallapiccola's acute self-awareness, it is significant that the *Songs of Liberation* are based on the same tone-row as the *Notebook of Annalibera* and the Variations for Orchestra.

The Variations was commissioned by the Louisville Orchestra. When the composition was given its world premiere at Louisville on October 3, 1954, Dallapiccola wrote as follows: "In an essay published in the English review *Music Survey,* October 1951, I have explained my progress along the route of the 12-tone system: a rather strange and very long progress. Beyond [what I have learned from] the works of Schoenberg, Berg and Webern, I have received very extraordinary illuminations (precisely in the 12-tone domain) from the writings of Proust and James Joyce. Such a declaration, strange as it may seem, should lead us to the conclusion that the arts, at a specific moment of history, have a common problem. If I were competent in painting, I am sure that even in this art I could find very striking analogies with 12-tone music.

"The Variations for Orchestra are not at all variations in the traditional sense of the word. At the base of the whole composition there is the same 12-tone row that I use for my *Songs of Liberation,* a work for chorus and orchestra now in progress, and that I used for *Annalibera's Notebook,* for piano, and of which the Variations represent the orchestral interpretation. . . . In the *Notebook* I have tried to demonstrate the treatment of the 12-tone row applied to the different elements of music."

Often a tone-row is a sequence of twelve notes used so technically that most laymen and musicians cannot and should not try to follow, as they might follow a traditional symphonic theme. But Dallapiccola uses at least one part of his row as a clearly recognizable theme—a musical symbol, in fact. The name of Bach, spelled out in musical notation, has fascinated many musicians, starting with Bach himself. (In German, the letter "B" stands for our B flat, and the letter "H" stands for our B natural.) Thus, Bach may be symbolized in music by our notes B flat, A, C, B natural:

For Dallapiccola's special musical purpose, he uses this easily recognizable theme transposed down a fifth to start on E flat, as follows:

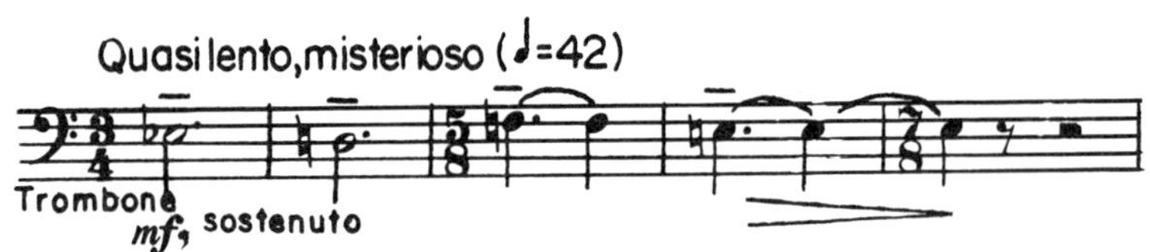

This is the musical "symbol" to which the title of Dallapiccola's first variation refers.

Variation I: [Symbol]. Quasi lento. The titles given in brackets are the original titles of each variation as they appear in the *Notebook of Annalibera,* although the composer did not keep these titles for his orchestral variations. First heard "mysteriously" in the trombone, as shown above, this Bach symbol dominates the first and weightiest of the Variations—sometimes slowly, as above, sometimes fast, sometimes varied in almost traditional symphonic style.

In the most ingenious way, the B-A-C-H theme is also embedded in a twelve-tone row (as the 3rd, 6th, 9th and 12th notes of the row) which serves as the basis for all eleven Variations:

In a piece of music which is romantically emotional and so imaginative in its orchestral colors, it would be too distracting to concentrate on technical devices. It is enough for our purposes to point out that Dallapiccola uses his vast technical virtuosity with complete intuitive abandon, or so it would seem.

Variation II. [*Accents*]. *Allegro, con fuoco.* Shrill, violent and dramatically brief, this Variation presents the utmost contrast to the flowing canon that follows.

Variation III. [*Contrapunctus primus*]. *Mosso; Scorrevole.* The delicate, chamber music style of this Variation is emphasized by its lean, exotic orchestral texture. The fact that this is a canon of considerable complexity based on four different versions of the row does not seem to inhibit the graceful flow of the music or its expressive power.

Variation IV. [*Lines*]. *Tranquillamente mosso.* The emphasis on woodwinds, particularly the oboe, gives a pastoral hue to this peaceful Variation.

Variation V. [*Contrapunctus secondus*]. *Poco allegretto; alla Serenata.* A canon in contrary motion, or mirror canon, this Variation has more of the capricious, outlandish melodic skips we associate with traditional twelve-tone style.

Variation VI. [*Friezes*]. *Molto lento; con espressione parlante.* The strong relief with which the melodic line stands out from its accompaniment may have suggested the title *Friezes.*

Variation VII. Andantino amoroso esitando. [*Contrapunctus tertius (canon-cancrizans)*]. This tightly organized Variation is a canon in which one group of instruments duplicates another, but plays the melody in reverse order starting from the end and going back to the beginning.

Variation VIII. [*Rhythms*]. *Allegro; con violenza.* This is a carefully, symmetrically constructed Variation, giving an impression of rhapsodic wildness.

Variation IX. [*Colors*]. *Affettuoso; cullante.* Even in the absence of the original title of this Variation, one could scarcely fail to notice the supersensitive use of orchestral color.

Variation X. [*Shadows*]. *Grave.* The gravity of this section is underscored by the heavy brass chords of the opening and the close. The central part, with its eerie, whispering, divided strings, is marked *misterioso.*

Variation XI. [*Quatrain*]. *Molto lento fantastico.* The four phrases of this poignant finale represent four variants of the row, the last being a return to its original version.

The Variations for Orchestra are scored for 2 flutes (alternating with 2 piccolos), 2 oboes (second oboe alternating with English horn), 2 clarinets, 2 bassoons, 4 horns, 2 trumpets, 3 trombones, tuba, kettledrums, bass drum, celesta, xylophone, vibraphone, cymbals, tam-tam, small drum, military drum, whip, tambourine, covered drum, and the usual strings.

Claude Debussy

Born August 22, 1862, Saint-Germain-en-Laye—died March 25, 1918, Paris

IMAGES (PICTURES) FOR ORCHESTRA
Gigues (Jigs)
Ibéria
Rondes de Printemps (Spring Rounds)

Debussy might have agreed that consistency is the hobgoblin of small minds. For he himself seems to have been interestingly inconsistent in his attitude toward the label "Impressionism," which began to be applied to his works early in his career. Debussy objected to what he considered the indiscriminate use of the term. In 1908, while working on two movements from his orchestral *Images (Ibéria* and *Rondes de printemps)* he wrote to his publisher, Jacques Durand: "I am attempting to something else, a kind of *reality*—what imbeciles call 'impressionism.' "

But in 1910 when Debussy himself conducted the first performance of *Spring Rounds* in Paris, the program contained a note signed by his friend, the composer and critic Charles Malherbe, but probably (or so Leon Vallas believes) inspired by Debussy himself. The note reads in part: ". . . the musician attempts to translate for the ear impressions received by the eye. . . . The melody, with its infinitely varied rhythms, corresponds to the multitudinous lines of the design; the orchestra is a vast palette where each instrument supplies its different color. Just as the painter takes pleasure in the contrasts of tonality, the play of light and shadow, so the musician plays with the shock of unexpected dissonances, with the fusion of rare musical *timbres*. . . . This is musical impressionism of particular nuance and rare quality."

It is curious that this last—and one of the most colorful of Debussy's major orchestral works—was begun as a piano duet. On September 29, 1905, he wrote to Durand, "I am now going to complete as quickly as possible the *Images* for two pianos." The following July he wrote Durand that he hoped to finish *Ibéria* "next week" and the other two pieces "in the course of the month." But *Ibéria* was not completed until February, 1910. *Rondes de printemps* was finished in March 1910. On October 11, 1911, Debussy wrote

Durand: "I can send you the arrangement for piano duet of 'Gigues' but the orchestral version is not yet completed." He never was to finish the orchestration. He trusted it to his friend André Caplet, who completed it in 1912 and conducted the first performance on January 26, 1913, at the Concerts Colonne. Exactly three months later, Debussy was able to hear a performance of all three works of *Images* at the Concerts Colonne.

Two of the three works comprising *Images* were introduced to the United States by the New York Philharmonic. The first was the "Rondes de printemps," performed by the New York Philharmonic on November 15, 1910, under the direction of Gustav Mahler, only eight months after the score was first heard in Paris. The second was the better-known *Ibéria,* which the New York Philharmonic presented on January 3, 1911, also under the direction of Mahler.

I. *Gigues.* Although it was the last to be completed, "Gigues was given first place in the sequence of scores comprising *Images.* Its original title was *Gigues tristes,* a typically Debussian paradox, for the *gigue* (French for the English-Scottish-Irish jig) was traditionally a high-spirited, often wild dance in triple meter. This is an untraditional, low-spirited, slow non-dance in duple meter. André Caplet, who knew the score better than anyone, having completed it under the composer's direction, wrote:

> *Gigues* . . . sad *Gigues* . . . tragic *Gigues* . . . A portrait of a soul in pain, a soul which borrows the shawm of an oboe d'amore to breathe out its indolent languorous plaint! A wounded soul, so reticent that it dreads and shuns all lyrical effusions and quickly hides its sob behind the mask and the angular gestures of a grotesque marionette. Or else it may cloak itself suddenly in a mantel of the most phlegmatic indifference. . . . The ever-changing moods, the rapidity with which they merge, clash and separate to unite once more, make the interpretation of this work very difficult. . . . Underneath the convulsive shudderings, the sudden efforts at restraint, the pitiful grimaces, which serve as a kind of disguise, we recognize . . . the spirit of sadness, infinite sadness. . . .

The thematic kernel of this entire elusive development is a lonely little figure for a solo flute heard in the opening bars:*

This sad jig was inspired in part by a bittersweet poem Verlaine wrote while he was in London and which he gave an English title: "Streets." In 1890

---

* *Musical example copyright 1913 by Durand et Cie. Used by permission of the publisher. Elkan-Vogel, Inc., sole representative, U.S.*

the poem had been set to a Scottish tune "The Keel Row" by Debussy's friend, Charles Boredes.

Dansons la gigue!	Let's dance a jig!
J'aimais surtout ses jolis yeux,	I loved above all her pretty eyes,
Plus clairs que l'étoile des cieux,	Brighter than the starry sky,
J'aimais ses yeux malicieux.	I loved her malicious eyes.
Dansons la gigue!	Let's dance a jig!
Elle avait des façons vraiment	She had a way about her
De désoler un pauvre amant,	To torture a poor lover,
Que c'en était vraiment charmant!	A really charming way!
Dansons la gigue!	Let's dance a jig!
Mais je trouve encore meilleur	But better still I find
Le baiser de sa bouche en fleur,	The kiss of her radiant lips
Depuis qu'elle est morte à mon cœur.	Since she has died to my heart.
Dansons la gigue!	Let's dance a jig!
Je me souviens, je me souviens	I remember, I remember
Des heures et des entretiens,	Those long hours of our leisure,
Et c'est le meilleur de mes biens.	They're the best of all my treasure.
Dansons la gigue!	Let's dance a jig!

II. *Ibéria.* For those of us who like Debussy may have crossed the Spanish border only for a few hours, to see a bullfight at San Sebastian, Spain is still a distant dreamland: a montage of bright sun, high-keyed colors, of fiery flamenco rhythms, clattering heels and castanets, and exotic Moorish laments. It is just such a dream of Spain—Spanish colors and Spanish rhythms—that Debussy lets us glimpse in his *Ibéria.* A dream, yet somehow an accurate dream. For that most Spanish of Spanish composers, Mañuel de Falla, has testified that Debussy's fleeting impressions catch the true color and rhythms of Spain better than any serious Spanish composer had yet done.

"The Andalusians," adds Falla, commenting on certain harmonic effects in *Ibéria,* "obtain these sounds from their guitars, needless to say, in a rudimentary form and quite unconsciously; and curiously enough, Spanish composers have neglected and even despised these effects which they looked upon as something barbaric. Or they might at most have sought to reduce them to old musical forms until the day when Debussy showed them how they could be used."

Ibéria was completed in 1908 and first performed February 20, 1910, at one of the Concerts Colonne in Paris under the direction of Gabriel Pierné. The first performance in the United States was given by the New York Philharmonic in January, 1911. It is in three movements, the second and third of which are continuous and are played without pause.

1. *Par les rues et par les chemins* ("On the Highways and the Byways"). The first movement opens with a burst of bright orchestral color and dance rhythms spiked by the sound of castanets and tambourine. Orchestral strings

imitate the strumming of guitars while woodwinds pipe bits and fragments of almost Oriental or Moorish-sounding melodies like the following recurrent figure: *

Halfway through, a sudden shadow—perhaps a particularly dark alley—seems to engulf the scene. But brassy horns and trumpets soon dispel this mood with a return to daytime brilliance.

2. *Les parfums de la nuit* ("Fragrances of the Night"). The opening spell of this nocturne movement is cast by high, shimmering violins. Again the woodwinds recall nostalgic Spanish or Ibero-Oriental airs. Soft velvety harmonies of the low strings suggest deep darkness. A sound as of distant bells heralds the finale which follows without pause.

3. *Le matin d'un jour de fête* ("A Holiday Morning"). Loud *pizzicato* strummings of the string choir clash with the holiday bells in a swelling procession of glittering sounds and rhythms.

III. *Rondes de printemps* ("Spring Rounds"). Debussy associated this music and perhaps wished his listeners to associate it with two lines of an ancient Italian May Day song, which he quoted (in French translation) at the head of his score. The song is one of a collection of *Canzoni a ballo* by the fifteenth-century poet Poliziano, entitled "La Maggiolata," which begins.

Benvenga maggio	Welcome to May
E'l gonfalon selvaggio!	With its sylvan banner!

"Sylvan banner" was an antique Italian phrase referring to wild laurel. Debussy found these lines in a book on Dante by Pierre Gauthiez describing a medieval May Day celebration, which perhaps helped to spark Debussy's imagination: "On the first of May the whole countryside wakens and rejoices. The women and girls, their heads circled with garlands of flowers, form processions and pair off with happy dancers or musicians. There are contests and games, and young men carrying the May banner [i.e., "the sylvan banner," the wild laurel], branches brought from the woods, deposit them at their sweethearts' doors and burst into the May song, 'La Maggiolata.' "

---

* *Musical example copyright 1910 by Durand et Cie. Used by permission of the publisher. Elkan-Vogel, Inc., sole representative, U.S.*

Early in the score, Debussy also refers to a French children's song, a round, "Nous n'irons plus au bois" ("No More to the Woods We'll Go"). The tune sung rather simply by an oboe, is taken up a moment later in a wild, impulsive transformation by the strings:*

The orchestra of *Images* enlists 2 piccolos, 3 flutes, 2 oboes, oboe d'amore English horn, 3 clarinets, bass clarinet, 3 bassoons, contrabassoon, 4 horns, 4 trumpets, 3 trombones, tuba, kettledrums, snare drum, tambourine, triangle, castanets, xylophone, celesta, cymbals, 3 bells, 2 harps and strings.

LA MER, THREE SYMPHONIC SKETCHES

"The sea has been very good to me," wrote Debussy to his publisher Jacques Durand shortly before he finished *La Mer.* "She has shown me all her moods." Debussy had begun the score at least as early as 1903. On September 12 of that year, he wrote André Messager (who had recently conducted the premiere of *Pelléas et Mélisande*) that he was working on "three symphonic sketches entitled: 1. *Mer belle aux îles sanguinaries,* 2. *Jeux de vagues,* 3. *Le vent fait danser la mer*—under the general title *La Mer.* You do not know, perhaps, that I was intended for the fine career of a sailor and that only the chances of life led me away from it. Nevertheless, I still have a sincere passion for it."

A rough draft of the orchestral score was finished (according to the notation on a manuscript at the Eastman School in Rochester) on Sunday, March 5, 1905, at 6 o'clock in the evening. Details of orchestration took some months longer, but the finishing touches were added during the summer of 1905 at the English seaside resort of Eastbourne.

La Mer was introduced at one of the Concerts Lamoureux in Paris on October 15, 1905, under the direction of Camille Chevillard. Debussy had kept only one of the original titles of the three movements.

Soon after the first performance, Debussy, again writing to Durand, said: "Here I am again with my old friend, the sea; it is always endless and beautiful. It is really the thing in nature which best puts you in your place. But people don't respect the sea sufficiently. To wet in it bodies deformed by daily life should not be allowed. Truly, these arms and legs which move in ridiculous rhythms—it is enough to make the fish weep. In the sea, there should be only sirens, and how do you suppose those estimable persons would consent to return to waters frequented by rather low company? [And again later he speaks of] the sea which is stirred up, wants to dash across the land, tear out the rocks, and has tantrums like a little girl, singular for one of her importance."

---

* *Musical example copyright 1910 by Durand et Cie. Used by permission of the publisher. Elkan-Vogel, Inc., sole representative, U.S.*

I. *From Dawn Until Noon on the Sea.* Low, sustained strings, including harps, give an impression of the immense resting power of the ocean at dawn. Gradually the waters seem to awaken: a lazy wisp of foam is cast aloft. A simple two-tone figure from *Sirènes* is the starting point of a development of astonishing imagination and mastery. An English horn and one muted trumpet announce, very softly, a theme which will return in the last movement in the approach to its great climax:

Debussy is less concerned with conventional melody than with the play of minute fragments of rhythm and harmony, with the ever-changing reflections of sky, clouds and sunlight on his flashing, tossing orchestral sea. Toward the end, the depths themselves are set in motion with a quiet but impressive chorale phrase, which will return to cap the climax of the last movement:

II. In *The Play of the Waves,* the ocean, from the most delicate beginnings, lashes itself into a sportive fury. Rainbow colorings appear and vanish in the fountains of spray. Debussy's instrumental palette is of the utmost delicacy and subtlety, fading at the end almost imperceptibly into silence.

III. A deep, threatening voice, as of approaching storm, opens the *Dialogue of the Wind and the Sea.* A shiver of anticipation runs through the orchestra; there is a swift gathering of forces and the tempest seems about to break. Instead, there is an abrupt silence; then suddenly, as from afar, we hear a nostalgic call, like the siren song of Debussy's imagination:

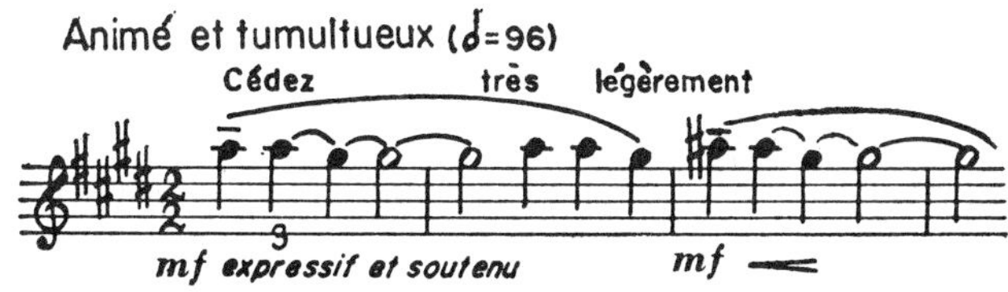

The call is repeated, more insistently, by oboe, English horn and bassoon. It is answered by Tritons' horns; the clamor grows and in the depths of the orchestra, cellos, double basses and bassoons take up the first theme quoted above. At last the first-movement chorale returns in an exultant climax and the sharply dissonant sound of trilling brass ends the never-ending tale of the sea.

La Mer is scored for piccolo, 2 flutes, 2 oboes, English horn, 2 clarinets, 3 bassoons, 4 horns, 3 trumpets, 2 cornets, 3 trombones, tuba, kettledrums, bass drum, cymbals, tam-tam, triangle, glockenspiel (or celesta), 2 harps, and the traditional strings.

NOCTURNES
Nuages (Clouds)
Fêtes (Festivals)
Sirènes (Sirens)

For most of his life Debussy was drawn to new artistic and literary currents. In the 1880s as a very young man he began frequenting the famous Tuesday evenings at the home of the symbolist poet Stéphane Mallarmé, where he met people with ideas and feelings sympathetic to his own.

"Impressionism, symbolism, poetic realism were all merged in a great current of enthusiasm, curiosity, and intellectual passion," wrote the composer-critic Dukas. "Painters, poets, sculptors were all bending questioningly over the material of their mediums, dissecting or recomposing them according to their desires—all trying to give to words, sounds, color and design, new nuances and significances."

Debussy's Impressionist painter friends had discarded the clear outlines of the preceding generation for misty visions, dissolved in light. His poet friends, headed by Mallarmé, were dissolving the logic of language into a musically suggestive succession of words. Verlaine sought in his poetry *de la musique avant toute chose.* There was a general preoccupation with the confusion of the perceptions, and of the arts themselves which had been anticipated by Baudelaire in his *Fleurs du mal.*

O métamorphose mystique	O mystical metamorphosis
De tous me sens fondus en un!	Of all my senses blended in one!
Son haleine fait de la musique	Her breath has become music
Comme sa voix fait le parfum.	And her voice is a perfume.

Debussy was caught up in these currents and his compositions of the ensuing years were influenced more deeply by the men of Mallarmé's salon than by purely musical factors. Camille Mauclair, who has written with special sympathy and understanding of this period of art, has spoken of the paintings of Monet and Degas as symphonies and suites of light, and the music of Debussy as sonorous impressionist painting.

In his *Nocturnes,* Debussy took nature—slow-moving clouds, dancing lights, the sea—as his subject. The title, he explained, does not have the traditional significance of a nocturne. It has, he says, "a more general and above all a more decorative meaning."

I. *Nuages* ("Clouds"), reflects in Debussy's words, "The unchanging aspect of the sky, with the slow and melancholy passage of clouds dissolving into a vague grayness tinged with white." The high woodwinds weave soft, fluctuating patterns, which repeat and yet change as imperceptibly as the clouds.

II. *Fêtes* ("Festivals") opens with a burst of light and excited rhythm and vivacious little scraps of melody miraculously derived from the first Nocturne. "It reflects," says the composer, "the movement, the restless dancing rhythms of the atmosphere, interspersed with brusque bursts of light. There is also the episode of a procession—a dazzling and wholly visionary pageant—passing through the festival and blended with it. But the background of uninterrupted festival persists with its mixture of music and luminous dust participating in the universal rhythm." Debussy's orchestration, spare and delicate, achieves its greatest effects by reticence. Perhaps the most marvelous moment of the "Festivals" comes about halfway through when, after a moment of sudden silence, we catch the almost inaudible rhythm of a distant march, and over it a fanfare of muted trumpets:

III. *Sirèns* ("Sirens"), calls for a chorus of eight women's voices, which may be why this one is more rarely heard than the other two. It describes "the sea and its endless rhythms. Then amid the billows silvered by the moon, the mysterious song of the sirens is heard; it laughs and passes."

The orchestra for *Nocturnes* calls for 3 flutes, 2 oboes, English horn, 2 clarinets, 3 bassoons, 4 horns, 3 trumpets, 3 trombones, tuba, kettledrums, 2 harps, cymbals, snare drum, and the customary strings.

PRELUDE TO THE AFTERNOON OF A FAUN

Debussy must be the gentlest revolutionary who ever attacked an ancient establishment structure, and brought it thundering down about the ears of his frightened contemporaries—while he acted the innocent bystander, claiming that he disliked loud noises. And Debussy was perfectly sincere. He did hate such Wagnerian cataclysms, all theatrical bombast and obvious emotions. His was a world of moonbeams, of reflections on the water, of muted passions, of suggestive symbols, hinted thoughts and words half-spoken, *des choses dites à demi.*

He set off his first orchestral time bomb, so to speak, in his dreamlike *Prelude to "The Afternoon of a Faun."* His music had been inspired, as the title suggests, by the famous poem of his friend, Stéphan Mallarmé, *The Afternoon of a Faun (L'Après-midi d'un faune).* Although this little tone-poem bewildered many listeners with its exotic melody and elusive harmonies, it proved, to everyone's surprise, a popular success. It remains his most famous and popular orchestral masterpiece.

Despite its strong appeal, or perhaps because of it, professionals puzzled over the tonal modulations of the *Faun.* With good reason. For half the point (and certainly half the charm) of this sensuous revolution lies in its tonal ambiguity, just as half the point of Mallarmé's *L'Après-midi d'un faune* lies in the poet's musical manipulation of verbal and syntactical ambiguities. Although Mallarmé was some twenty years older, the two men were in many ways kindred spirits. Each in his own way was engaged in destroying the conventional syntax of his art, exploring new sensibilities and new syntaxes to express them.

It is not certain when Debussy first read Mallarmé's *Faun,* but it was no later than 1887, the year when Debussy returned to Paris from Italy where he had gone as winner of the prestigious Prix de Rome. In that year a definitive edition of Mallarmé's much-revised *Faun* was published and Debussy admired it enough to buy a copy as a present for his composer friend Paul Dukas. Debussy also began to frequent the now legendary Tuesday evening gatherings at Mallarmé's small apartment in the unfashionable rue de Rome.

There was a special magic about these evenings where Debussy met a devoted group of (mostly young) poets, painters, critics, musicians, sculptors, novelists united by their admiration for Mallarmé and their thirst for the penetrating conversations he led. The regulars included Paul Verlaine, who came here often until his leg got so bad that he could not longer climb the four flights of stairs; Monet, Rodin, Pierre Loüys, Gustave Kahn; journalists of the period, novelists and critics of a future day; Paul Claudel, Camille Mauclaire, André Gide, Paul Valéry, Jules Laforgue, Édouard Dujardin, Félix Fénélon, and often a celebrated foreigner: Stuart Merrill, John Payne, Whistler, Maeterlinck, or Stefan Georg.

Many preserved vivid memories of climbing the four flights to the Mallarmé flat on winter evenings, leaving behind them the garish gas lamps and the clattering noises of the rue de Rome. They died away on the threshold of the apartment, and in the middle of a small, discreetly lighted dining room which served as the poet's salon, supporting himself against the warmth of a porcelain stove, would stand Mallarmé, in pantoufles, with a shawl drawn over his frail shoulders.

The room's few decorations (all of them gifts) were unusual for a bourgeois interior of that period. There was a Monet landscape; a Renoir head of Mallarmé; Whistler's fine lithograph of Mallarmé, which was later reproduced in his volume *Vers et Proses;* a painting of Hamlet and one of the young Mallarmé, both by Manet; a small Rodin cast and a wooden statue sent from Tahiti by Gauguin.

From his post in the center of the room, Mallarmé, with a soft voice would lead the conversation which often became a monologue. He fascinated his listeners, not alone with his thoughts, but with the musical cadence of his voice, his luminous eyes, and the subtlety of his gestures. Talk flowed easily and naturally, occasionally with long pauses of silence. Music, poetry, painting, sculpture, and their aesthetics were the topics on which the conversation centered.

To an American musician and writer, Francis Grierson, who was a regular visitor from 1889 to 1892, Mallarmé recalled Walt Whitman in his informality of dress and gentle charm. Grierson noted that Debussy's particular friend, the poet Henri de Régnier, "who on each occasion occupied the same seat in the corner at the host's right, was always silent. He seemed to be the guest of honor. Mallarmé frequently addressed his conversation to him, but M. de Régnier was not there to talk, but to listen; instead of replying he simply took a few extra puffs of his cigarette. Everyone understood."

It was in this atmosphere and from these associations with an intellectual and artistic elite that Debussy drew nourishment far greater than he had from his conventional musical studies and his dull months at the Villa Médicis, the official residence of those honored by the Prix de Rome.

Debussy began to compose his *Prelude* to Mallarmé's poem at the latest by 1892, the date inscribed on his orchestral draft. By this time he knew Mallarmé well enough for Debussy specialists including William Austin to assume that the two probably discussed the *Après-midi* from the point of view of the music in Mallarmé's words as well as the music they might evoke. The finished manuscript of the music is dated 1894, and the first performances were scheduled for December 22 and 23 by the pioneering Société Nationale de Musique under the direction of Gustave Doret. Two days before the premiere Debussy invited Mallarmé in a letter, the convoluted style of which suggests something of the young composer's attitude to his revered elder:

> Dear Master,
>
> Need I tell you what joy I shall have if you will be so kind as to indulge with your presence the arabesques which I have been led to believe, through a pride perhaps reprehensible, were inspired by the flute of your Faun?
>
> Yours very respectfully,
> Claude Debussy

The atmosphere as the evening of the premiere approached was understandably tense. As the conductor Doret himself recalled in later years:

> For try to understand what a revolution Debussy brought into the technique of instrumentation! What to any conductor today seems only a simple formula, in those times raised problems that had to be solved, so much so that Debussy had great misgivings, doubtful himself about certain effects that he hoped to obtain. I assured him that we would take all the time needed for this delicate preparation. . . . Constantly Debussy modified this or that sonority. We tried; we started over; then we compared. Everyone kept calm. . . . The players, having got used to this new style, understood that we would have to fight a serious battle. Of course Debussy was not unknown to the

> true connoisseurs, but the big public was still ignorant of him. Would it try to resist? . . .
>
> But the hour of the great test has arrived. Debussy hides his anxiety with a grin that I well knew. He presses my hands. The orchestra tunes up in the corridor. I ask for silence. "My friends," I say to the musicians, "you know that we are going to defend a great cause this evening. If you have some friendship for Debussy and for me, you will give yourselves completely." My good colleagues applauded: "Don't worry, maestro! We'll win."
>
> I ascend the podium with some emotion, but much reassured and full of confidence. I wait a long moment after having imposed silence on the last lingering conversations among the audience. The hall is packed. An impressive silence reigns, when our marvelous flutist Barrère unrolls his opening theme. . . .
>
> Suddenly I feel behind my back—it is a special ability of certain conductors—a completely captivated public! The triumph is complete, so much so that in spite of the rule forbidding encores I did not hesitate to break the rule. The orchestra, delighted, joyfully repeated the work that it had loved and had imposed on the conquered public.

It is impossible to imagine how misty, evanescent, and bewildering the beauty of this Prelude seemed when it was new—even to professional musicians like my father, Olin Downes, who told me that the first time he heard the *Prelude to "The Afternoon of a Faun"* around the year 1900, it was as if a rosy mist, or an invisible fragrance had passed and evaporated leaving nothing clear for memory to grasp.

Today we have no trouble at all in hearing the clearly etched line of the simple unaccompanied flute of the beginning. Obviously this recalls or, this being a Prelude, it anticipates the languid notes played by Mallarmé's faun.

Mallarmé's poem with its sensuous, symbolist language is far from clear. Indeed its ambiguities are part of the essence. The blurred impression of the drowsy faun's vision and the musical cadence of Mallarmé's words seem perhaps more closely akin to this early orchestral work of Debussy than does some later symbolist poetry. The general outline and mood of the poem are clear enough. The words are assumed to be the monologue of a faun, a simple-minded sensuous creature of the mythological imagination, who wakens in the sunlit forest and tries to recall an experience or dream, he cannot tell which, of an encounter with two beautiful nymphs, white and golden semigoddesses who shrank from his fiery wooing and resisted his impulsive embrace. But the forest grows warmer, the faun's mind drowses, perhaps after all they were a dream. As he falls asleep, he murmurs: "Farewell! Oh Nymphs, I go to see the shades that ye already be."

That clearly etched line of the flute, the languorous, capricious melody, probably played by the faun himself, is soon enveloped in the warmth of velvet horns, woodwinds and a splash of harp tone. Often again the flute's initial arabesque is repeated, but each time with different, shifting, ambiguous harmonies in the background and delicate orchestral color: softly shimmering *tremolos* of divided strings, sudden bursts, little clusters of woodwind tone—possibly the grapeskins puffed idly aloft by the faun or the "arid rain" of notes from his flute.

A hush falls over the orchestra and a new, more sensuous melody is sung by woodwinds, a more conventionally sensuous melody perhaps, which has been called Chopinesque, or more maliciously Massenettish.

If the listener does a double-take, however, he may hear in this sentimentally arching flow a subtle transformation of the flute's first-etched arabesque. Now that original arabesque returns accompanied by ever more iridescent orchestral tints. There is a suggestion of the glitter of water, of sunlight and warmth, the hush of a passing breeze, the drowsing forest, the blurring senses of the faun, and the dream fades into thin air.

Debussy's magic is accomplished with a small orchestra of 3 flutes, 2 oboes, English horn, 2 clarinets, 2 bassoons, 4 horns, 2 harps, tiny antique cymbals and the customary strings.

Mallarmé seems to have been moved, or at least impressed, for after the performance he sent Debussy a copy of his poem which he inscribed with the following quatrain:

Sylvain d'haleine première
Si ta flûte a réussi,
Ouïs toute la lumière
Qu'y soufflera Debussy.

This has been roughly translated as follows:

Oh forest god of breath primeval
If your flute be true,
Listen now to all the light
Debussy will breathe through you.

From the vantage point of the mid-twentieth century, the revolutionary importance of the Mallarmé-Debussy *Faun* has grown still clearer. No less a modernist than Pierre Boulez repeated, "The flute of the *Faun* brought new breath to the art of music; what was overthrown was not so much the art of development, as the very concept of form itself, . . . the reservoir of youth in that score defies depletion and exhaustion." As surely as modern poetry sprang from certain poems of Baudelaire's so surely it can be said modern music was awakened by *L'Après-midi d'un faune.*

Norman Dello Joio

Born January 24, 1913, New York

VARIATIONS, CHACONNE, AND FINALE

Is there anything wrong with a piece of music that can be understood and enjoyed at first hearing? The question is not as silly as it sounds, for there is scarcely a serious composer today who is not self-conscious about writing music that is called easily "accessible." And stranger yet, there are music lovers and professional musicians who are made positively uneasy by a serious new work that is easy to understand. One result of this attitude has been an increasing gulf between modern—serious modern composers and the bulk of our concert-going, opera-going, and record-buying audience. Another result of this attitude has been to threaten the spontaneity of certain composers whose artistic natures seem to require an uninhibited flow of musical thought—at least in the initial stages of composition. Among those so threatened at an early stage of development was Norman Dello Joio, who managed to escape that particular trap with the help of his teacher, Paul Hindemith.

Among established composers of serious music in this country, Dello Joio is outstanding for an outgoing directness of expression and a simplicity of manner, if not always of means, which have an intentionally broad appeal. A strong melodic vein, rhythmic vitality, a relatively restrained harmonic vocabulary, an infectious brio and freshness of invention, are among the earmarks of his style. Inseparable from this style is Dello Joio's feeling, almost an ethical conviction, that his music *should* communicate with a broad, contemporary public—not merely with an alert *avant-garde,* few fellow composers, or some hypothetical future public. The style in which this conviction is embodied sets Dello Joio somewhat apart from a majority of his peers.

No thoughtful musician—least of all Norman Dello Joio—cavils at any composer who knows that what he needs to communicate cannot be put simply. One obvious characteristic of much twentieth-century music has been that it is difficult to grasp at first hearing. No intelligent listener expects to be able to grasp *all* of a great work at first hearing, or at tenth or hundredth hearing. Nor is obscurity in itself an abuse: obscurity has long-recognized artistic uses. They have been confined neither to the twentieth century nor to the art of music. But they have been more often analyzed, attacked, and defended in the theory and criticism of other arts than music. "Certain poets," observed Paul Valéry long ago, "insist that the mind shall work for its pleasures. They propound riddles to us." Before Valéry, Mallarmé considered the solving of riddles essential to the enjoyment of poetry. "To name an object," he wrote, "is to spoil three-quarters of the pleasure of a poem, which consists in divining it bit by bit. It must be suggested. Poetry must always remain a riddle."

Three hundred years earlier, George Chapman, the chief theorist among the metaphysical poets in the time of John Donne, declared: "Obscurity in affection of words, and indigested conceits, is pedantical and childish, but where it shroudeth itself in the heart of his subject, uttered with fitness of figure, and expressive epithets; with that darkness will I still labour to be shadowed."

Many a great twentieth-century poet, painter, and composer has labored in deed, if not in conscious intent, to be shadowed in such a darkness. But it is quite another thing when some listeners come to *expect* obscurity, as an automatic concomitant of any vital creative work in the twentieth century. This expectation is, of course, rooted in nineteenth-century attitudes, or rather in our lopsided picture of a callow, mercantile nineteenth-century society, with its bitter resistance to new and difficult great art, its fatuous critics, its popular mediocrities, its rejected and misunderstood geniuses.

But that sick situation has not always prevailed. In the time of Haydn, Mozart, Bach, Handel and earlier, music lovers were avid for what was new. For example, the popular reception of Haydn's great "London" symphonies which are discussed elsewhere in this volume.) A symphony or opera that was ten, twenty, or thirty years old tended to sound old-fashioned. Audiences had scant interest in works older than a generation back, and earlier works were for the most part simply forgotten. Whether this was a healthier attitude than the Romantic conservatism of the nineteenth century, or the reverse (and often unconscious) snobbism of many twentieth-century connoisseurs may be an open question.

In any case, Dello Joio began to suspect early in his career that such self-consciousness had become a kind of cliché, a blight, which should not be allowed to dominate his feeling about his music. "I began to wonder," he said, "why I should feel guilty if a piece were accepted. We have inherited a Romantic notion of ourselves as composers, a picture of the artist battling against philistines. I began to realize that with my kind of gift it would be silly to play that kind of role."

Equally non-Romantic is the composer's declaration: "My concern is with the present, and in this I know I am in good company." Two members of this "good company" most influential in Dello Joio's development have been his last teacher, Paul Hindemith, and Giuseppe Verdi, who made a deep impression on Norman from his boyhood.

Another powerful influence was Roman Catholic liturgical chant. His oldest music memory is of hearing his father, Casimiro Dello Joio, practice organ accompaniments for the chants at the Church of Our Lady of Mt. Carmel on East 116th Street in New York City. This repertory of chant provided him with a rich musical experience echoed in the thematic material and mood of many of his mature scores.

To the two influences, plain chant and Italian opera, jazz was soon added as an important third. To Aaron Copland and a generation of American composers reaching their maturity in the decade of the 1920s, jazz at one time suggested itself as a strong basis for a truly American style of serious music. This hope, suggested in part by the Romantic theory that all great music has its roots in the soil of folk music, did not long outlast the 1920s.

For the following generation, including Dello Joio, jazz played an important but more indirect and far from decisive role. Dello Joio never seriously considered making jazz the basis of his own compositions, but he was strongly influenced by what he calls the spontaneousness of jazz, and several of his mature works have more than a touch of jazzy rhythms and syncopations.

The most powerful final influence in the clarification of Dello Joio's style, indeed his sense of artistic direction was Paul Hindemith, with whom Dello Joio studied in 1940 and 1941. A turning point came one day when Hindemith casually asked why Dello Joio didn't let his natural lyric bent assert itself spontaneously and fearlessly. At this point Dello Joio began to realize more forcefully how conventional the idea was that a serious contemporary style *must* be difficult, that a good composer must initially be misunderstood, and that audiences are automatically hostile or unsympathetic to innovation.

Among Dello Joio's most characteristic and widely performed symphonic works is his orchestral *Variations, Chaconne, and Finale* composed in Wilton, Connecticut, during the summer of 1947. Here even his choice of form is characteristic. For he had come to feel, like many of his contemporaries that the symphony (in the traditional sense of a four-movement work dominated by one or more movements in traditional sonata-allegro pattern) was simply not suited to the expression of mid-twentieth-century feelings. But the variation form, although one of the most ancient we know, still held infinite challenge to him and to many a contemporary.

For his subject Dello Joio reached back to his personal past, to a heritage centuries old, to a fragment of Roman Catholic plain chant, so-called Gregorian chant: a melody believed to have originated in the fifteenth or sixteenth century and still used to this day as part of the Mass: a prayer known as the Kyrie "De Angelis" ("Of the Angels"). The score is in three movements.

I. *Theme and Variations.* The basic theme of the entire work, changed only to give the ancient chant a definite rhythm, is sung "simply" by a solo oboe.

The phrase is taken up by a flute and clarinet with discreet orchestral background, and the entire *Theme* is less than twenty bars long. Six variations follow.

Variation 1: Semplice e grazioso. The melody, slightly modified, wanders from French horns to cellos and to higher strings, with delicately contrasting harmonic background.

Variation 2: Andante religioso. This is a hymn-like setting for eight-part strings, with brief commentaries for woodwind solos.

Variation 3: Vivacissimo. This jaunty, scherzo-like variation is spiced with charming syncopations.

Variation 4: Allegro pesante. Against a rapid-fire accompaniment of heavy brass, the theme appears in brilliant trumpet transformations.

Variation 5: Amabile. Lilting, dance-like fragments of the theme pass from low strings to high woodwinds.

Variation 6: Funebre. An effect of tolling bells, first among the horns, then passing to other instruments, accompanies a lament which rises to a passionate climax but fades into final silence.

II. Chaconne: Adagio serioso. The Chaconne is built on four chromatically rising notes derived from the opening measure of the Kyrie theme. This Chaconne is handled freely; the theme is often transposed, and sometimes so arranged that two statements together make seven consecutive rising chromatic steps to fill out a perfect fifth. This well-sustained movement rises to an exciting climax and subsides in a long diminuendo ending, a Romantic trait that recurs often in Dello Joio's music.

III. Finale: Allegro vivo, giocoso e ritmico. "In a highly rhythmic *Allegro vivo* that follows," writes the composer, "the character of the Gregorian theme is transformed into the purely contemporary and secular. [Vigorous fragments of the chant are tossed back and forth, first among trumpets and trombones:]

The concluding pages resolve into a chorale that is set against the prevailing rhythmic tension of the last movement." Here again we find slightly jazzy syncopations and a mounting motor drive that brings the finale to a particularly brilliant finish.

Dello Joio's score calls for piccolo, 2 flutes, 2 oboes, English horn, 2 clarinets, bass clarinet, 2 bassoons, contrabassoon, 4 horns, 3 trumpets, 3 trombones, tuba, kettledrum, cymbals, xylophone, bells, and the traditional string choir.

David Diamond

Born July 9, 1915, Rochester, New York

SYMPHONY NO. 8

Hearing David Diamond's Eighth Symphony, one would never guess that one of the earliest of his works is a *Homage to Erik Satie,* the composer of *Parade.* The gulf between Diamond's Symphony and Erik Satie's urbane spoof seems unbridgeable.

Yet Diamond's youthful admiration for the Gallic approach of Satie was more than a passing whim. The next object of his homage was Maurice Ravel, for whom he composed an *Elegy* upon hearing of Ravel's death in 1937. Twelve years later Diamond composed a song cycle, *L'Âme de Debussy,* based on Debussy's letters. It is significant that Diamond should have chosen these three composers—and only these three—as titular subjects of his own works.

If further evidence of his Francophile leanings be needed, we may recall that, like Virgil Thomson and other North American composers, Diamond made the pilgrimage to Paris and to Fontainebleau to study with Nadia Boulanger.

Bernard Shaw once said that the alpha and omega of style is force of assertion. Independence and force of assertion have marked Mr. Diamond's musical personality from his beginnings. He taught himself to play the violin, invented his own system of musical notation, and began to compose by the time he was seven years old. At eight he began music lessons. After his family moved from Rochester to Cleveland, young David was entered at the Cleveland Institute of Music, where he was a student from 1927 to 1929. On his return to Rochester, he studied for several years at the Eastman School of Music, where Bernard Rogers was among his teachers. In 1931, when he was only sixteen, his Symphony (now discarded) was performed at Eastman. For two years, 1934–1936, Mr. Diamond studied with Roger Sessions and Paul Boepple at the New Music School (Dalcroze Institute) in New York.

Diamond's Eighth Symphony is dedicated to Aaron Copland for his sixtieth birthday. The score was completed on November 15, 1960, one day before Copland's birthday. The actual composing of the Symphony covered a two-year period. It is in two movements related to each other through the use of a basic twelve-note row. Yet while Diamond uses serial techniques, his row is arranged to produce a strongly tonal feeling. And in addition to serial techniques, he uses more traditional procedures of thematic fragmentation, sequence and development which have been familiar since the Classical era of Mozart and Haydn.

I. *Moderato; Adagio; Allegro vivo.* The basic row is proclaimed in the very opening bars of the introduction. It is in two halves. The first, a forceful rhythmic theme of five notes, is thundered out by the orchestral *tutti.* The second, a more lyric theme of seven notes, is sung softly by a single clarinet:

Thematically, the second phrase is destined to be the more important of the two; in fact, the row is immediately rearranged and presented by a solo horn, which starts with this second phrase, in an even more lyric version, and concludes with a lyric transformation of the thunderous five-note opening.

The fast body of the movement, a free *sonata-allegro* structure, starts with a heavily syncopated version of the row as presented by the French horn in the introduction. This is the principal theme of the sonata form. There is a contrasting second theme presented at a more relaxed tempo and *ben cantando* by a solo clarinet over a soft counterpoint of the strings. Both themes are developed and return in very nearly their original form during the course of this long but highly concentrated movement. The conclusion is a stunning climax compounded of the essence of both themes.

II. *Theme (Adagio), Variations and Double Fugue.* After a two-measure introduction, which turns into a sequential accompaniment, the first violins begin a high, flowing melody which is the theme:

Soon the orchestral basses and cellos enter with the same melody, while the violins continue the forty-measure theme.

Variation No. 1 is a canon, in which the violins lead and the cellos follow with the same melody, always at a distance of one measure. There are seven Variations in all, the last of which repeats a long section from the first Variation and then leads, without pause, into the lively Double Fugue. The first and principal theme of the Double Fugue is derived from the principal theme of the first movement. Other themes from the first movement make their appearance, too, as the Symphony moves on to its climax and conclusion.

Diamond's Eighth Symphony is scored for piccolo, 2 flutes, 2 oboes, English horn, E-flat clarinet, 2 B-flat clarinets, bass clarinet, 2 bassoons, contrabassoon, 4 horns, piccolo trumpet in D, 3 trumpets, 3 trombones, tuba, kettledrums, snare drums, tenor drum, bass drum, xylophone, vibraphone, glockenspiel, triangle, large gong, large cymbals, harp, piano and strings.

David Diamond has been honored by many institutions, having held two Guggenheim Fellowships (1938, 1941), the 1941 award of the American Society for the Publication of American Music, the 1942 award of the American Academy in Rome, the 1943 Paderewski Prize for his Piano Quartet, a grant from the National Academy of Arts and Letters, and several commissions.

Jacob Druckman

Born June 26, 1928, Philadelphia, Pennsylvania

WINDOWS

Mr. Druckman, a resident, though not a native of New York City, belongs to no neatly definable school, clique, cult, or "ism." He is not a serial or twelve-tone composer, although serialism was an influence in his early development (chiefly in his Second String Quartet). He is not an aleatory man, although he does not hesitate to use aleatory (chance) elements or "controlled improvisation" within a larger framework, when it suits his purpose—as it does in *Windows*. He is not an electronic composer, for he has written only one completely electronic work (*Synapse*, for the Joffrey City Center Company's ballet, *Jackpot*). Yet he has used both abstract and *concrete* electronic tapes as important ingredients in his predominantly instrumental music for at least eight years, according to his own estimate.

Jacob Druckman's *Windows* was commissioned by the Koussevitzky Foundation in the Library of Congress in 1969. The commission was fulfilled in 1971 and 1972 and the score was first performed by the Chicago Symphony Orchestra on March 16, 1972, under the direction of Bruno Maderna. It won the 1972 Pulitzer Prize for Music.

Mr. Druckman feels that a broadly subjective description of his aims in *Windows* is apt to be more helpful to the listener than an analytical approach. He himself supplied the type of a description he prefers on the occasion of the world premiere in Chicago: "The *Windows* of the title are windows inward. They are points of light which appear as the thick orchestral textures part allowing us to hear, fleetingly, moments out of time—memories, not of any music that ever existed before, but memories of memories, shadows of ghosts. The imagery is as though having looked at an unpeopled wall of windows, one looks away and senses the after-image of a face."

The reaction of the *Chicago Tribune* critic Thomas Willis was in key with Druckman's description: "Any window must have an accompanying wall, and Mr. Druckman has built his out of the plastic musical materials in vogue today. Using an augmented orchestra and a wide range of playing techniques for the individual instruments, he has fashioned planes, layers and corners of sound. Calling upon the orchestra men to function with more than customary independence, he has found some fascinating, translucent textures of extraordinary vitality.

"As his roving sonic eye scans these walls, the openings of the title appear as needle-sharp images etched in surrounding silence. The suddenness of the transition is as startling as a shaft of sunlight appearing in a darkened room. But the figures behind the curtain are no amorphous beam of light. They are ghosts from the orchestra's past. . . . "

Much of the fascinating light and color effects of Druckman's music come from his manipulation of a huge battery of percussion instruments. And since he has been quoted as saying that a concert is for him also in part "a theater experience," it may not be unduly distracting to name the instruments which are normally more or less visible to the audience. Aside from the familiar, traditional choirs of strings, woodwinds (piccolo, 3 flutes, 2 oboes, English horn, 2 clarinets, bass clarinet, 2 bassoons, contrabassoon) and brass (4 horns, 3 trumpets, 3 trombones, tuba) the score calls for harp, electric organ, a piano with amplification, and the following percussion instruments, divided into three groups:

Percussion I: cymbals (small and large), 2 wood blocks, 3 temple blocks, conga, vibraphone, saw, bass drum and tam-tam.

Percussion II: triangle, sizzle cymbal (a suspended cymbal with loosely attached bolts or metal strips to provide the additional vibration or "sizzle" effect), bongos, timbales (South American drum pairs of 2 pitches, similar to bongos but open-ended), conga, chimes, snare drum, kettledrums, bass drum, gong and tam-tam.

Percussion III: cymbals (small and large), bongos, marimba, glockenspiel, spring coil with sizzles, gong and steel drum.

Mr. Druckman has been a member of the Julliard School faculty where he taught orchestration and the literature and materials of music from 1957 to 1972. He has also taught at the Electronic studio of the Yale University School of Music (1971–72) and the Electronic Music Studio of Brooklyn College of the City University of New York. In 1967 he became an associate of the Columbia-Princeton Electronic Music Center.

Paul Dukas

Born October 1, 1865, Paris—died May 17, 1935, Paris

THE SORCERER'S APPRENTICE, SCHERZO AFTER A BALLAD OF GOETHE

The story of the sorcerer's apprentice was old in ancient Egypt nineteen centuries ago. Retold in Greek by the Syrian satirist Lucianos of Samosata and told yet again as a German ballad *"Der Zauberlehrling"* by Goethe, it inspired Dukas's crackling orchestral joke or *scherzo,* to use that French composer's Italian term.

The malicious humor of Luciano's dialogues collected under the title *The Lie-Fancier or the Skeptic,* his virtuoso narrative technique and the devastating wit of his attacks on the most respected philosophers of his day, Platonists, Pythagoreans, Peripatetics, and Stoics, have dazzled and delighted readers ever since.

In one such dialogue the young Eucrates describes his apprenticeship to the philosopher Pancrates, who had spent twenty-three years in a cave, studying the magic of Isis. Despite all the lore Pancrates imparted to Eucrates, there was one secret he refused to divulge; the spell enabling him to take a broom or the pestle of a wooden mortar, put clothes on it, and transform it into a servant who drew water and waited upon both men as skillfully as the finest domestic. Then, one day Eucrates thought he had outwitted his master.

> I found an opportunity [said Eucrates, in the 1820 English translation of William Tooke] to hide me in an obscure corner, and overhear his charm, which I snapped up immediately, as it consisted of only three syllables. After giving his necessary orders to the pestle without observing me, he went out to the market. The following day when he was gone out about business, I took the pestle, clothed it, pronounced the three syllables, and bid it fetch me some water. He directly brought me a large pitcher full. "Good," said I, "I want no more water; be again a pestle." He did not, however, mind what I said; but went on fetching water and continued bringing it, till at length the room was overflowed. Not knowing what to do, for I was afraid lest Pancrates at his return should be angry, as indeed was the case, and having no alternative, I took an ax and split the pestle in two. But this made bad worse; for now each of the halves snatched up a pitcher and fetched water; so that for one water-carrier I now had two. Meantime, in came Pancrates; and understanding what had happened, turned them into their prime form; he, however privily took himself away, and I have never set eyes on him since.

Goethe's ballad substitutes a broom for the pestle and rollicking humor for satire. Dukas, as if to make sure that his interpreters got the point of his little masterpiece, prefaced his printed score with the entire fourteen stanzas of Goethe's ballad. And while he did not publish labels for his themes, his manuscript score has notations in Dukas's hand identifying three principal themes. The first, the mysterious opening bars of the introduction with the hocus-pocus of the violins and the rising phrase of the woodwinds are the magic spell, the first part of which, says Dukas, remains unchanged throughout. The second part develops into the principal theme quoted below.

A sudden flurry of scampering woodwinds represents the apprentice. The third theme, a fanfare of muted trumpets and stopped horns, Dukas calls Evocation. "This summons by the brass instruments," he continues, "mixes with different combinations of the two principal themes. When it appears magnified in the postlude, it expresses the idea of mastery, bringing back the calm tempo of the introduction."

The introduction ends with a sharp thwack of the kettledrum. A prolonged silence follows. Did the broom stir? A faint grunt from the bottom of the orchestra suggests that it did. The grunts multiply, acquire a rhythm, and turn into a bouncing accompaniment figure. Three bassoons suggest the awkward gait of the broom as it hobbles off to fetch water.

Woodwinds chatter and giggle as the apprentice's theme returns. A sharp climax suggests the hatchet blow, which succeeds only in doubling the apprentice's distress. The principal theme comes back, again in the bassoons. The instruments seem to burst into roars of laughter as the two themes tangle. At last the master reappears with great blasts of sustained trumpets and horns. Order is restored. Once more we hear the mysterious muted strings of the introduction. The theme of spells seems to evaporate into thin air, and the sudden close is like an explosion of comic relief.

The Sorcerer's Apprentice is scored for piccolo, 2 flutes, 2 oboes, 2 clarinets, bass clarinet, 3 bassoons, contrabassoon (or contrabass surrusophone), 4 horns, 2 trumpets, 2 cornets, 3 trombones, kettledrums, harp, glockenspiel, bass drum, cymbals, triangle, and the customary string choir. It was composed early in 1897 and first performed in Paris on May 18 of that year at a concert of the Société Nationale.

Antonin Dvořák

Born September 8, 1841, Mühlhausen, Bohemia (now Nelahozeves, Czechoslovakia)—died May 1, 1904, Prague

CARNIVAL OVERTURE, OPUS 92

The original title of Dvořák's exuberant "Carnival" Overture was "Life." It was the second in a trio of overtures entitled "Nature, Life and Love" *(Príroda, zivot a láska)* which Dvořák composed in his fiftieth year. The three Overtures were united by a recurrent musical theme of Nature and, according to the Czech scholar, Otakar Sourek, Dvořák intended each Overture to illuminate a different aspect of "Nature and her powers for good and evil." In his search for a title, Dvořák, like many a composer before and after, had difficulty finding the right words to express what had already been expressed more precisely in music. He finally settled on the titles: "In Nature's Realm," "Carnival," and "Othello."

The "Carnival" Overture was sketched between July 28 and August 14 and the orchestration completed by September 12, 1891, at Dvořák's country estate of Vysoká. It was first performed, together with the other two Overtures, under Dvořák's own direction at his farewell concert of April 28, 1892, before his departure for the United States. The orchestra was that of the National Theater in Prague. The first performance in the United States also was given in conjunction with the other two Overtures under the direction of the composer. This, the composer's first concert here, his greeting to the new world so to speak, was played on October 21, 1892, in New York's Music Hall, since renamed Carnegie Hall.

The Overture follows the traditional pattern (of symphonic first-movement form) except for a poetic slow section which Dvořák introduces before his central "development section." It opens with a brilliant orchestral tutti, a driving, whirling series of melodies, which could well suggest either a carnival scene or, more symbolically, the hurly-burly of life.

As the excitement dies down, the slow section is introduced by a blast on the French horn fading to a delicate *pianissimo*. A languorous melody for flute and oboe is interrupted by a solo clarinet, which recalls a caressing theme of Nature from the preceding Overture, against an accompaniment of murmuring, muted first violins. But this pensive mood soon gives way to a mercurial *Allegro* in which the earlier themes are developed, recapitulated, and rounded off with a dazzling coda.

The Overture is scored for piccolo, 2 flutes, 2 oboes, English horn, 2 clarinets, 2 bassoons, 4 horns, 2 trumpets, 3 trombones, tuba, kettledrums, cymbals, tambourine, triangle, harp, and strings.

CONCERTO FOR CELLO AND ORCHESTRA, B MINOR, OPUS 104

When Brahms first read the score of Dvořák's Cello Concerto he exclaimed: "Why on earth didn't I know it was possible to write a cello concerto like this? If I had only known, I would have written one long ago!" And Brahms was not alone in his admiration. Dvořák's Cello Concerto has become his most popular work after the "New World" Symphony.

It was written in the United States at the height of Dvořák's fame. He had arrived in this country in 1892 on leave from his position at the Prague Conservatory of Music. He remained in New York for three years, rousing the highest enthusiasm as teacher and as conductor of his own works, which he continued to produce in extraordinary profusion.

The Cello Concerto was the last work completed in the United States. It was begun in New York City (in Dvořák's East 17th Street apartment) on November 8, 1894, and completed three months later on February 9, 1895. Part of his inspiration is said to have come from hearing a performance by the New York Philharmonic of Victor Herbert's Second Cello Concerto with the composer as soloist. Herbert was best known at the time as a virtuoso cellist who had played in the Metropolitan Opera Orchestra and in concerts conducted by Theodore Thomas. His triumphs as a composer of operettas still lay in the future.

Two other cellists influenced the growth of Dvořák's Concerto. One was Alwin Schroeder, first cellist of the Boston Symphony. The other was the Bohemian cellist Hans Wihan. When Dvořák returned to Prague with his completed score in 1895, Wihan proved an industrious reviser—so industrious that Dvořák wrote his publishers: "The principal part with finger and bowing indications has been done by Professor Wihan." Apparently Wihan pressed a number of changes upon Dvořák which the composer finally rejected. Wihan must have been insistent, for Dvořák, on submitting his manuscript to the publisher, wrote: "I must insist on my work being printed as I have composed it . . . I will give you my work only if you promise not to allow anyone to make changes—friend Wihan not excepted—without my knowledge and consent—and also not the cadenza which Wihan has added to the last movement. . . . There is to be no cadenza in the last movement either in the orchestral score or in the piano arrangement. I told Wihan straight off when he showed it to me that it was impossible to stick on such a bit. The Finale closes gradually, *diminuendo*—like a sigh—with reminiscences of the first and second movements—the solo dies away to *pianissimo*—then swells again—the last bars are taken up again by the orchestra and the whole concludes in a stormy mood.—That was my idea and I cannot depart from it."

Dvořák had already revised the end of his Concerto once to take the form described, but he had made that change for sentimental reasons. Shortly after his return to Bohemia, Dvořák was shocked by the death of his sister-in-law Josephina Kaunic. Josephina not only had been a dear friend but many years earlier when he was still an unknown viola player and she a charming young actress, she had aroused in him a secret passion. He had voiced his unrequited love in a song entitled "The Cypresses," which he composed in 1865. Before her death Dvořák had included in the second movement of this Cello Concerto a phrase from another of his songs, a particular favorite of Josephina's: "*Kezduch muj sam*" ("Leave Me Alone"), the first of the four in his Opus 82. After the news of her death, Dvořák revised the coda of the Cello Concerto to incorporate one last reference to Josephina's favorite song.

Dvořák himself conducted the first performance of the Cello Concerto in London on March 19, 1896, with Leo Stern as soloist. It is in the standard three movements.

I. *Allegro*. The fiery orchestral introduction opens with the Concerto's principal subject, a strongly rhythmic, almost improvisatory sounding phrase announced by clarinets:

The second theme, a yearning, nostalgic melody, is chanted by a solo French horn against a background of soft string tone. This melody seems to have been one of Dvořák's favorites. Indeed, in a letter from America to one of his friends in Czechoslovakia, Dvořák wrote that whenever he played this theme his whole being was moved:

When the solo cello makes its entrance the principal theme is actually marked *Quasi improvisando.* It is developed in the distant key of A-flat (G-sharp) minor against whispering tremolos of the violins and violas. The return (or recapitulation) of the basic themes is reversed in sequence·so that the yearning melody comes first, now in a blazing B major, and the opening theme returns to conclude the movement in a brilliant climax marked *grandioso.*

II. *Adagio ma non troppo.* In the slow movement, Dvořák almost surpasses himself in emotional warmth and songfulness. The shape of the movement is a free, three-part (A-B-A) form. In the middle section the solo cello sings the melody adapted from Josephina's favorite song:

III. *Finale: Allegro moderato.* The Finale is a rousing dance-like movement infused, according to Dvořák's Czech biographer Otakar Sourek, "with the tone of happy anticipation of the composer's early return to his own country." There is a melodious middle section, and finally the Concerto reaches the key of B major in which the solo cello joins the first violins in a duet of passionate tenderness. The conclusion brings back the opening theme of the work, followed by a reminiscence of the song quoted in the slow movement and a fresh allusion to the principal theme of the Finale. A brilliant crescendo for full orchestra rounds off one of Dvořák's most ingratiating scores.

The Concerto is scored for piccolo, 2 flutes, 2 oboes, 2 clarinets, 2 bassoons, 3 horns, 2 trumpets, 2 trombones, bass trombone, tuba, kettledrums, triangle, and strings.

CONCERTO FOR VIOLIN AND ORCHESTRA, A MINOR, OPUS 53

Dvořák wrote his popular Violin Concerto in the summer of 1879, during the first, intoxicating years of his climb to international fame. He was thirty-eight years old. Prizes and honors of many kinds had begun to pour in. His *Slavonic Dances* of 1878 had won him quick acclaim beyond the Czech provincial borders, even beyond the borders of the Austro-Hungarian Empire. The respect and friendship of such a composer as Brahms, of a critic of Hanslick's standing, of conductors like Bülow and Richter, made the world a new and exciting place. It was not illogical for Dvořák to hope for further help from the great violinist, Joachim.

Joachim had helped both Brahms and Bruch by going over the solo parts of their respective Violin Concertos, by accepting the dedications of the Concertos and finally by performing them. Joachim played the first performance of Brahms's Violin Concerto in January 1879. Dvořák was spurred to work on his own Violin Concerto, and by mid-September of the same year it was finished. By May 1880 he had finished the first revision of his score and he sent the manuscript to Joachim.

Joachim kept the manuscript two years. By September 1882 Dvořák reported to his publisher, Simrock, that he had visited Joachim in Berlin and played over the Concerto with him twice and that Joachim liked it. "He was so kind as to make over the solo part," Dvořák added, "and I have to make a few alterations, only in the finale, and to lighten the instrumentation in several places." Dvořák hoped to have it all finished by November, and to hear Joachim hold a dress rehearsal. But one thing after another interfered, and in the end Joachim never did play a public performance of the Concerto. The first performance took place on October 14, 1883, with the Orchestra of the Czech National Theater and Frantisek Ondřicek as soloist, under the direction of Moric Anger.

The Concerto is in the usual three movements, but the first movement leads without break into the second.

I. *Allegro ma non troppo.* The main theme of the opening movement is in two parts: a fanfare-like theme for full orchestra, followed by a dancing figure for the solo violin:

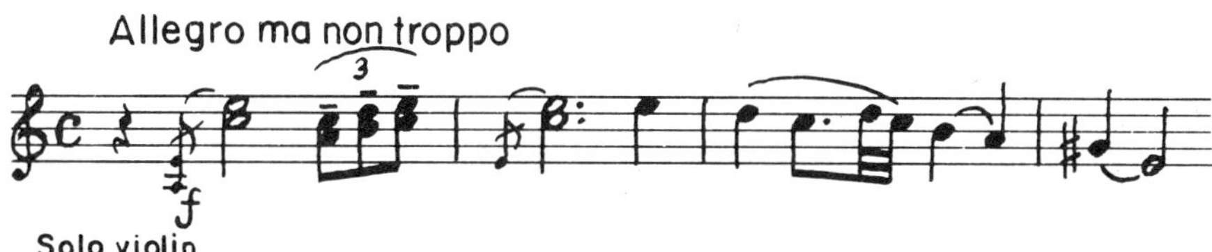

There are a number of striking phrases which are developed in familiar symphonic style, but instead of completing the movement with a traditional reprise of the opening material, Dvořák writes a cadenza-like passage for soloist and orchestra which serves as a bridge to the slow movement.

II. *Adagio ma non troppo.* The slow movement, which follows without break, develops from the serenely arching melody sung at the outset by the solo violin. An impassioned central section in F minor displays the soloist in bravura contrasts: sonorous octaves, sweeping arpeggios and graceful *fioriture.* The movement closes with a poetic return of the opening melody, now in the mellow voice of the French horn, above which the delicate sound of the solo violin soars slowly higher and higher.

III. *Allegro giocoso, ma non troppo.* The folk-vein of the finale is close to the spirit and style of Dvořák's popular *Slavonic Dances.* It opens with a ten-bar theme in the syncopated style of a Czech *furiant* announced by the solo violin:

This melody returns again and again with the persistence of a rondo refrain, changing its instrumental garb with each return.

The orchestra of the Dvořák Violin Concerto is composed of 2 flutes, 2 oboes, 2 clarinets, 2 bassoons, 4 horns, 2 trumpets, kettledrums, and strings.

SYMPHONY NO. 7 (NO. 2), D MINOR, OPUS 70

Although Dvořák's "New World" Symphony is his most famous symphonic score, many musicians, including his principal Czech biographer, Otakar Sourek, consider the D-minor Symphony, Opus 70 to be his greatest. This is often known as his Second Symphony simply because it was the second to be published. Actually it is his seventh. In all, Dvořák composed nine symphonies of which "New World" was the last.

In his Symphony No. 7 it was Dvořák's ambition to surpass everything he had hitherto achieved in the symphonic field. There were several reasons for this. One was that the London Philharmonic Society had nominated him an honorary member in June 1884, and invited him to compose a new symphony for the Society. The request emphasized his newly won international standing, and he wished to increase it with his new score.

Another factor which had fired Dvořák's ambition was the overwhelming impression which Brahms's Third Symphony made upon him at the premiere in December 1883. Dvořák believed Brahms's new score to be the greatest of all modern symphonies, and he was filled with the desire to produce a work of similar stature.

Finally as a Czech composer deeply involved in the revival of Czech culture and its future growth, Dvořák wished to enrich the Czech symphonic repertory with a work of international as well as national appeal.

In the months following the Philharmonic invitation the symphony absorbed him more and more. Late in December 1884, he wrote his lawyer friend, Antonín Rus: "Now I am occupied with my new symphony (for London), and wherever I go I have nothing else in mind but my work, which must be such as to make a stir in the world and God grant that it may!"

On the last day of 1884, he wrote another friend, Alois Göbl: "Today I have just finished the second movement . . . of my new Symphony, and am again as happy and contented in my work as I always have been and, God grant, may always be, for my slogan is and always shall be: God, Love, and Country! And that alone can lead to a happy goal . . ."

The composition sketch and the orchestration of the score were completed in Prague between January 13 and March 17, 1885. The first performance took place in London on April 22, 1885, with the composer conducting the London Philharmonic Society. Two years later the Symphony had its first hearing on the continent when Hans Richter conducted the Vienna Philharmonic. Not until October 27 and 28, 1889, however, did the Symphony enjoy a real triumph. These latter performances in Berlin under Hans von Bülow were so important to Dvořák that he pasted a picture of Bülow on the title page on the manuscript of his Symphony and wrote underneath: "Glory be to you! You brought this work to life!"

I. *Allegro maestoso.* The stormy first movement begins with muttering double basses, kettledrums and horns, in the depths of the orchestra. They sustain a low "D" tonic pedal, over which the main theme of the movement twists and turns its way:

Agitated figures follow and, by way of contrast, a graceful, lilting woodwind melody. These are developed to a climax, on the crest of which the opening themes return. The movement ends as it began with the principal theme dying away over a long sustained low D.

II. *Poco adagio.* A serenely flowing clarinet melody opens the slow movement, but a subdued agitation creeps into the music and bursts out into a stormy middle section recalling the mood of the first movement. In the concluding section, the first melodies return, the excitement ebbs and the instruments fade into silence.

III. *Scherzo: Vivace.* The Scherzo too seems infected by the stress of the opening movement. The contrasting middle section, the so-called trio, is lighter and fresher in mood and texture.

IV. *Finale: Allegro.* Like the opening movement, the Finale is a stormy piece cast in traditional sonata-allegro form. But where the tension of the first movement ebbed into silence, the conflict of the Finale concludes in triumph.

The yearning principal theme is announced in the warm romantic tones of cellos, horns, and clarinets:

A jubilant contrasting melody suggests the possibility of a happy outcome of the symphonic struggle:

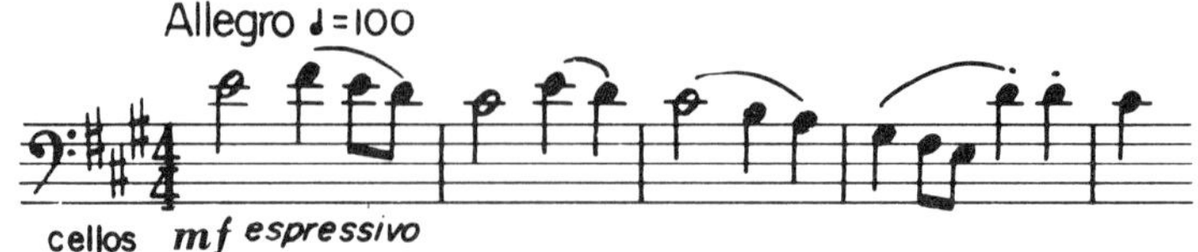

Dvořák's optimistic conclusion may have been inspired by the example of Beethoven's triumphant perorations rather than by the gentle end of the Brahms Third. Dvořák's final bars are a powerful affirmation of his principal theme in a blazing D-major *molto maestoso.*

The Symphony is scored for piccolo, 2 flutes, 2 oboes, 2 clarinets, 2 bassoons, 4 horns, 2 trumpets, 3 trombones, kettledrums, and strings.

SYMPHONY NO. 8, G MAJOR, OPUS 88

Dvořák's finest music is as spontaneous and unpretentious as the composer himself. His origins were simple. His father was the butcher of his tiny town of Nelahozeves on the Vltava (Moldau) River about ten miles north of Prague. Dvořák kept a lifelong preference for simple people, country surroundings, for the language, customs and folklore of his native landscape.

Dvořák composed his G-major Symphony in 1889 at home in his beloved Bohemian countryside amid a floodtide of inspiration so swift that his pen could hardly keep pace with it. On August 26 he started to jot down his ideas. Ten days later he began the formal composition which occupied him from September 6 to 23. He completed the instrumentation in Prague on November 8 and conducted the first performance with the Prague National Theater Orchestra on February 2, 1890. The score was published as his Fourth Symphony, although it was actually his eighth work in that form and is usually so numbered today.

I. *Allegro con brio.* The pensive melody which opens the first movement is brought back at crucial points of its structure, but as a framework rather than an integral part of the movement itself. Its long, flowing line is drawn in the typically Romantic, warm color mixture of cellos, horns, bassoons, and clarinets in unison.

The principal theme of the movement is an airy figure for solo flute, which to the bucolically minded has suggested bird-song:

The movement continues with a profusion of catchy melodies, many of them with dance-like rhythms akin to Dvořák's *Slavonic Dances.*

II. *Adagio.* The slow movement is built around several imaginative variants of its short opening phrase. One of the most appealing of these comes with another Schubertian effect of a shift from C minor to the sunnier C major. The new version of the melody soars upward in the flutes and oboes against a background of delicate descending scales in the violins.

III. *Allegretto grazioso.* The waltz-like third movement recalls some of Tchaikovsky's more graceful inspirations, yet at the same time it has a sturdy peasant lilt:

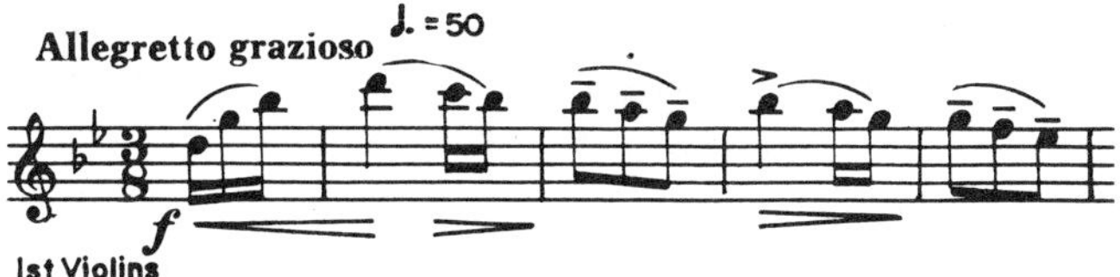

IV. *Allegro ma non troppo.* A festive solo trumpet call prefaces the last movement, like a summons to some celebration. The theme of this finale is one more demonstration of the infinite variety and charm of Dvořák's dance melodies, for this too might have been included in one of his collections of *Slavonic Dances.*

The Symphony is scored for 2 flutes, piccolo, 2 oboes, 2 clarinets, 2 bassoons, 4 horns, 2 trumpets, 2 trombones, bass trombone, tuba, kettledrums, and the usual strings.

SYMPHONY NO. 9 (FORMERLY NO. 5), E MINOR, OPUS 95, FROM THE NEW WORLD

From time immemorial, the Czechs—or the Bohemians as they used to be called—have been famous as musicians as far as European music was made. In dusty chronicles from the Middle Ages, we find their names inscribed as pipers and fiddlers to the great dukes and kings of France and Germany. In the eighteenth century, Bohemian composers settled in France, Italy, Austria and Germany, contributing richly to the new symphonic style, many years before Haydn was given his misleading title of "father of the symphony." Thus Dvořák was following a tradition more ancient than he perhaps knew, when he accepted an important musical position in a far-off land and came to teach at the National Conservatory of Music in New York. His "New World" Symphony became a hymn to the folk spirit of two countries: The United States and Czechoslovakia.

When Anton Seidl conducted the New York Philharmonic in the premiere of Dvořák's Symphony, there were hopes that this might prove the starting point of a style of national American composition. Before the premiere, which took place on December 16, 1893, in Carnegie Hall, Dvořák had made clear just what he felt the basis of an American school should be.

As a good Romantic, he was convinced that great art music must grow, plantlike, from the healthy soil of native folk music. This he had no difficulty in identifying for us as the Negro spiritual and the songs and dances of American Indians. Furthermore, having heard Henry T. Burleigh sing spirituals and having studied "a certain number of Indian melodies, which a friend gave me," Dvořák concluded, rather hastily perhaps, that the music of the Negroes and the music of the Indians were "practically identical."

His advice to future American composers was unequivocal. In an interview with the *New York Herald* he was quoted as saying: "I am convinced that the future music of this country must be founded on what are called Negro melodies. These can be the foundation of a serious and original school of composition to be developed in the United States. When first I came here, I was impressed with the idea, and it has developed into a settled conviction. These beautiful and varied themes are a product of the soil. They are American. They are the folk songs of America, and your composers must turn to them. . . . Only in this way can a musician express the true sentiment of a people. . . . In the Negro melodies of America, I discovered all that is needed for a great and noble school of music. They are pathetic, tender, passionate, melancholy, solemn, religious, bold, merry, gay, gracious, or what you will. . . . There is nothing in the whole range of composition that cannot find a thematic source here." Dvořák's belief in the near-identity of Negro and American Indian music is reflected in the famous English-horn melody of the second movement of the "New World" Symphony, which to most Americans seems steeped in the character of Negro spirituals, whereas Dvořák actually had been inspired, according to his own declaration, by the scene of the forest funeral of Minnehaha in Longfellow's epic poem, *The Song of Hiawatha.* The Scherzo, he explained, "was suggested by the scene at the feast in *Hiawatha* where the Indians dance, and is also an essay I made in the direction of imparting the local color of Indian character to music."

Four days before the premiere, Dvořák declared in another interview: "It is this spirit which I have tried to reproduce in my new symphony. I have not actually used any of the melodies. I have simply written original themes embodying the peculiarities of the Indian music and, using these themes as subjects, have developed them with all the resources of modern rhythm, harmony, counterpoint and orchestral color."

The Indian peculiarities Dvořák noted seem to be chiefly the tendency to a pentatonic (five-tone) scale, which is common to folk music around the globe, and a modal scale (usually in this case a minor scale with a lowered seventh step) common to most European folk music. Czech listeners, indeed, are prone to find the "New World" Symphony rich with inflections of their own folk music.

As far as *Hiawatha* is concerned, Dvořák had read it in a Czech translation some thirty years before his arrival in this country on September 27, 1892. He was attracted here by the very large salary offered him for teaching at the National Conservatory of Music in New York, sponsored by the idealistic Mrs. Jeanette Thurber. Anxious to have him compose an American opera, Mrs. Thurber arranged to have *Hiawatha* developed into a libretto. The Hiawatha opera never materialized, but Dvořák indicated that some of the sketches for it found their way into his Symphony. The earliest sketches date from December 1892. The full score of the Symphony was written out between February 9 and May 24, 1893. It was not given its title, *Z Nového sveta* ("From the New World"), until mid-November, just before it was delivered to Seidl. A public rehearsal aroused tremendous enthusiasm and the premiere on December 16th was a triumph. The score was published the following year as Dvořák's Symphony No. 5. Actually, it was the ninth symphony he had composed and it is often so designated on present-day programs.

I. *Adagio; Allegro molto.* A slow introduction foreshadows the main *Allegro* theme, a bold fanfare for two horns:

Flutes and oboes follow with a fetching little tune that twists and turns upon itself. The strongest contrast comes with the famous melody for solo flute irresistibly recalling "Swing Low, Sweet Chariot," one of Dvořák's favorite spirituals:

All three themes are developed separately and together, with increasing excitement. The reprise of the opening themes is followed by a triumphant coda.

II. *Largo.* A solemn procession of chords leads to the celebrated melody of the slow movement. The English horn chants a strain that has been adopted in this country almost as another spiritual:

III. *Scherzo: Molto vivace.* We need not be overly concerned whether the opening gaiety is of American Indians or Czech peasants. The beginning and end are fiery and excited. In between there are moments which could conceivably suggest a more relaxed village scene with dancing peasants, a tootling village band and laughing crowd.

IV. *Allegro con fuoco.* A finale of tremendous sweep and splendor is built around the sturdy, assertive theme proclaimed by horns and trombones.

Material from earlier movements, recalled and combined with the new, concludes this popular score in another burst of triumph.

The "New World" Symphony is scored for piccolo, 2 flutes, 2 oboes, English horn, 2 clarinets, 2 bassoons, 4 horns, trumpet, 3 trombones, tuba, kettledrums, triangle, cymbals, and the customary string choir.

Edward Elgar

Born June 2, 1857, Broadheath, near Worcester—
died February 23, 1934, Worcester

COCKAIGNE (IN LONDON TOWN), OPUS 40

As jaunty as its half-humorous, half-affectionate title, *Cockaigne (In London Town),* is the music Elgar wrote for his second most popular work. The first is, of course, his *Pomp and Circumstance March* in A minor. Both scores show a man who is not afraid to be obvious, when his aim calls for broad appeal.

As Elgar uses it, the word "Cockaigne" refers to London in the sense of Cockney land, the country of Cockneys, or Cockneydom. Elgar's score contains no other explanations, but this does not necessarily mean Elgar had none in mind. Sir George Grove, for example, felt it showed that side of the English capital "represented by its parks and open spaces, the bands marching from Knightsbridge to Buckingham Palace, Westminster with its dignified associations of Church and State, . . . mirrored in glowing orchestral colors."

It is written with an easy mastery of traditional sonata-allegro form, with a richness of orchestral texture that owes much to Wagner's Prelude to *Die Meistersinger,* and with a spontaneous eruption of melodies which are almost an embarrassment of riches. One of the most infectious of these is the lyric phrase that opens his second group of themes:*

Elgar's best is so fine that many of the most perceptive British critics have wondered whether he should not be classified among the "greats." Even the superconfident G. B. Shaw hesitated, for, as he observed: " . . . if you say that Elgar's Cockaigne Overture combines every classic quality of a concert overture with every lyric and dramatic quality of the overture to *Die Meistersinger,*

* *Musical example copyright 1901, 1924, by Boosey & Co., Ltd. Renewed 1929, 1951. Reprinted by permission of Boosey & Hawkes, Inc.*

you are either uttering a platitude as safe as a compliment to Handel on the majesty of the Hallelujah chorus, or else damning yourself to all critical posterity by a *gaffe* that will make your grandson blush for you. Personally, I am prepared to take the risk. What do I care about my grandson. Give me Cockaigne."

The *Cockaigne Overture* was completed, published and first performed in 1901 under the direction of the composer. It was an immediate and lasting success. The score calls for 2 flutes, piccolo, 2 oboes, 2 clarinets, 2 bassoons, contrabassoon, 4 horns, 2 trumpets, 2 cornets, 3 trombones, tuba, 3 kettledrums, bass drum, cymbals, triangle, side drum, bells, tambourine, organ, and strings.

VARIATIONS ON AN ORIGINAL THEME, ENIGMA, OPUS 36

When Sir Edward Elgar labeled the theme of his Opus 36 Variations "Enigma," he could scarcely have foreseen the frenzy of speculation and detective work his label would cause. But if he did not foresee, he nevertheless enjoyed the result. His friend and biographer, W. H. Reed, tells us that Elgar took particular pleasure in making casually mystifying or startling remarks for the pleasure of seeing how people would react.

Although Elgar's theme, as the title declares, was his own invention, he let it be known that the enigma of it was that there was another, larger theme, which combined with the written theme, but only in the composer's mind. This theme, which is never heard, was said to be a very well-known tune. But Elgar steadfastly refused to reveal its identity. The most prominent candidate advanced by Elgar fans during his lifetime and for a whole generation after his death has been "Auld Lang Syne." But logical and satisfying as this solution has seemed to many, there are concrete difficulties in combining this melody with Elgar's theme. The defenses of "Auld Lang Syne," the attacks, counterattacks, and counterdefenses grew so elaborate and sophisticated that they began to seem naïve, and the whole controversy began to resemble the ingenious proofs that Shakespeare's plays were written by Francis Bacon. The music itself is more worthy of our attention.

Elgar's score, generally conceded to be his masterpiece, is dedicated "To my friends pictured within." After Elgar's death their identities were published. The first Variation is a portrait of his wife. Twelve of the Variations, numbers 2 through 13, bear initials or a cryptic name for Elgar's friends. The fourteenth and last is a self-portrait. Elgar himself has described the genesis of his work: "One evening after a long and tiresome day's teaching, aided by a cigar, I musingly played on the piano the theme as it now stands. The voice of C.A.E. [Lady Elgar] asked with a sound of approval 'What was that?' I answered 'Nothing—but something might be made of it; Powell would have done this (Variation 2) or Nevinson would have looked at it like this (Variation 12),' Variation 4 was then played and the question asked, 'Who is that like?' The answer was, 'I cannot quite say, but it is exactly the way W.M.B. goes out of the room. You are doing something which I think has never been done before.' Thus the work grew into the shape it has now. Two Variations were discarded—Hubert Parry and Sullivan—as the suggestion of their musical styles seemed more obvious than the allusions to unmusical things in the rest of the work, and in another mood from these."

Elgar's score is dated Malvern, 1899. It caught the attention of the famous German conductor Hans Richter's London agent, who sent Richter the score in Vienna. Richter, who had something of the crusader's blood, was impressed by the score and conducted it on his English tour starting in London on June 19, 1899. After the first performance, Elgar, on Richter's advice, made various changes in his orchestration and added the *Presto* coda. This revised version, which is that known today, was first performed at the Worcester [England] festival on September 13, 1899, under the direction of the composer.

Theme: Andante. The curiously reticent, almost plaintive theme is characterized from the start by shifting accents, interlocking intervals of the third and two expressive drops of a minor seventh:

I. *(C.A.E.) L'istesso tempo.* A warmhearted, lyric variation, said by all who knew Lady Elgar to be an eloquent portrait.

II. *(H.D. S-P) Allegro.* H.D. Stuart-Powell, a pianist friend.

III. *(R.B.T.) Allegretto.* Richard Baxter Townshend, a amateur actor, remarkable for a trick of suddenly shifting from a deep voice to a falsetto, which apparently never failed to convulse his audience.

IV. *(W.M.B.) Allegro di molto.* William M. Baker, a vigorous English country squire.

V. *(R.P.A.) Moderato.* Richard P. Arnold, said to have mixed dreaminess and vivacity in his character.

VI. *(Ysobel) Andantino.* Isabel Fitton, an amateur viola player.

VII. *(Troyte) Presto.* Arthur Troyte Griffith, a stormy, argumentative friend.

VIII. *(W.N.) Allegretto.* Winifred Norbury, a gracious, elderly patrician.

IX. *(Nimrod) Adagio.* August Jaeger; a memory of "a long summer evening talk, when my friend grew nobly eloquent (as only he could) on the grandeur of Beethoven, and especially of his slow movements."

X. *(Dorabella) Intermezzo. Allegretto.* "Dorabella" (after the character in Mozart's *Così fan tutte*) was Elgar's affectionate nickname for Dora Penny, (later Mrs. Richard Powell), whose talk was marked by a fetching hesitation of speech.

XI. *(G.R.S.) Allegro di molto.* Dr. George Robinson Sinclair, organist of Hereford Cathedral. But the musical portrait is chiefly of the Doctor's bulldog, Dan.

XII. *(B.G.N.) Andante.* Basil Nevinson, a cellist who joined Elgar in chamber music sessions.

XIII. *(***) Romanza, Moderato.* Lady Mary Lygon, who, when the music was written, was aboard an ocean liner en route to Australia.

XIV. *(E.D.U.) Finale. Allegro; Presto.* "Edu" was Lady Elgar's name for Sir Edward. The Finale is said to portray the struggles and ideals of the composer, ending with a suggestion of triumph.

The "Enigma" Variations are scored for 2 flutes, piccolo, 2 oboes, 2 clarinets, 2 bassoons, contrabassoon, 4 horns, 3 trumpets, 3 trombones, bass tuba, kettledrums, snare drum, bass drum, triangle, cymbals, organ, and the traditional strings.

Manuel De Falla

Born November 23, 1876, Cádiz—died November 14, 1946, Alta Gracia, province of Córdova, Argentina

EL AMOR BRUJO (LOVE THE MAGICIAN)

It was a Spanish gypsy who inspired the songs and dances of Falla's *El amor brujo* and who played the principal role in the premiere of Falla's ballet at the Teatro Lara of Madrid on April 15, 1915. Pastora Imperio was one of the greatest gypsy dancers and singers of Spain, a descendant of a family famous for its devotion to Andalusian dance and song. The link between Falla and the great gypsy dancer was an even more famous figure: the Spanish poet, playwright, novelist and critic Gregorio Martinez Sierra (1881–1947), author of *The Cradle Song (Canción de cuna)* and other plays which were performed in the United States and influenced the development of drama in this country and in Europe. Pastora told the poet that she would like to interpret "a song and dance" to be written and composed by Martinez Sierra and Falla.

Falla, whose opera *La vida breve* had just been produced with brilliant success at the Opéra-comique in Paris and the Teatro de la Zarzuela in Madrid, was attracted to Pastora's proposal. After hearing her sing and making the acquaintance of her mother, Rosario de la Mejorana, who had also been a famous dancer, Falla was completely won over. He made careful notes of the traditional songs the two women sang for him, while Martinez Sierra listened attentively to the old gypsy's rich repertory of folk tales and legends, which gave him the material for a scenario. The "song and dance" grew into a chamber ballet. Originally scored for eight instruments (piano, flute, oboe, trumpet, horn, viola, cello and string bass) this first version of the ballet had only two characters: the beautiful young gypsy Candélas and her *novio,* or new love. The memory of a former, faithless lover haunts Candélas and dampens the ardor of her *novio.* Candélas exorcizes the malignant memory and is joyfully reunited with her *novio* as dawn breaks, and morning bells ring.

The 1915 premiere of this modest production aroused enthusiasm only among the gypsy members of the audience. But Falla and Martinez Sierra had faith in their work. They revised it, deleting some songs and recitatives, but expanding the action, introducing two new characters, including the ghost of the former lover, and enlarging the orchestra to include piccolo, 2 flutes, oboe, English horn, 2 clarinets, bassoon, 2 horns, 2 trumpets, kettledrums, piano, bells, and a full orchestral complement of strings.

This expanded version was produced in Paris on May 22, 1927, at the Trianon-Lyrique in a series of theatrical spectacles presented by Marguerite Bériza. With two of the greatest Spanish dancers of the age, Argentina and Escudero, in the leading roles, the revised ballet was a sensational success. Although those who witnessed the Argentina-Escudero presentation declare that no subsequent productions have touched its quality, *El amor brujo* has been staged many times and the score has become a popular staple of the symphonic repertory. Martinez Sierra's scenario has been paraphrased by Trend as follows:

Candélas, a beautiful and passionate gypsy, was once loved by another gypsy, a "tough" in every sense of the word, a man of evil reputation, jealous and dissolute, but one whom no woman could resist. She had been unhappy with him as long as he lived, but she mourned him and could not forget him. She is still afraid of him; she believes that the dead man is not quite dead, and that he may come back and continue to love her in his old savage and faithless fashion. Thoughts of the past prey upon her; she feels herself entirely in the power of the man's ghost. She is still young, however. Spring returns, and brings a new lover in the shape of Carmélo.

Carmélo is young too, *beau garçon,* attentive, very much in love. He presses his suit on Candélas, who is ready to be convinced, if it were not for the past, which is always there to hinder her present happiness; and whenever Carmélo draws near, in the hope that she may share his passion, the ghost returns and frightens Candélas away from her lover.

Having refused Carmélo, Candélas seems to pine away; she feels herself bewitched; memories of her past love flit about her "like malevolent and foreboding bats." (This elegant expression is taken from the "argument" printed in the score—a production which is almost as curious an example of French prose as the "synopsis" is odd as a piece of English.) Something must be done however, and Carmélo thinks that he has found the remedy. He had known the man whose ghost haunts Candélas—a typical Andaluz, jealous and unfaithful; and as, even after his death, women still seem to have an attraction for him, he must be attacked at his weakest point, if jealousy stronger than death is to be done away with.

So Carmélo persuades, Lucia, a young friend of Candélas, to allow the ghost to make love to her instead; and Lucia agrees, partly out of friendship for Candélas and partly out of feminine curiosity. She is on the lookout when Carmélo comes next day to see Candélas; the ghost comes as well, but is confronted with Lucia, whom he finds irresistible. While he is making love to her, Carmélo has time to convince Candélas of his love; nature prevails, life vindicates its rights over death and the past and the lovers fall into each other's arms, while the ghost is laid to rest for good and all.

The musical score of the ballet is in thirteen connected sections:

I. *Introduction and Scene.* The ballet opens with the savage, shrill cry of woodwinds, trumpet and piano, said to symbolize the fury of the jealous ghost:

This figure permeates Falla's scores in many transformations.

2. *In the Cave: Night time.* Eerie mutterings of Falla's colorful orchestra are interrupted by the plaint of a solo oboe which foreshadows Candélas' "Song of Sorrowing Love":

This is Falla's second fundamental strain, which returns in many transformations: doleful, tender and, at the end, exultant.

3. *Song of Sorrowing Love.*

Ay! Por querer o otra se orvía de mi!
ni sé qué me pasa
cuando éste mardito gitano me farta.

Ah! I know not what I feel
nor what happens to me
when I long for this accursed gypsy.

Candélas qué ardes,
más arde el infierno
que toita mi sangre
abrasa de celos!
Ay! Cuando el rio suena
qué querrá decir?
Ay! Por querer o otra se orvía de mi!

You burn, Candélas,
hell burns no hotter
than all my veins
afire with jealousy!
Ah! When the river murmurs,
what is it trying to say?
Ah! To love another girl, he has forgotten me!

Ay! Cuando el fuego abrasa,
cuando el rio suena,
si el agua no mata el fuego
a mí el penarme condena!
A mí el querer me envenena!
A mí me matan las penas! Ay! Ay!

Ah! When the fire flames,
when the river murmurs,
if the water does not extinguish the fire,
I am condemned to longing!
I am poisoned by love!
I am slain by sorrows! Ah! Ah!

4. *The Apparition.* A muted horn announces the frightening presence of the lover's ghost.

5. *Dance of Terror.* Candélas's fright is increased by the nervous, stabbing sound of the muted trumpet and the twisting, writhing solo-oboe figure associated with the spector.

6. *The Magic Circle: The Tale of the Fisherman.* This placid interlude was a song sung by Pastora in the original version of the ballet.

7. *Midnight: Witchcraft.* A distant bell (piano-sound spiced by subtle orchestral additions) strikes twelve. The orchestra shudders.

8. *Ritual Fire Dance to Drive Off Evil Spirits.* Candélas's danced exorcism is perhaps the most popular single number of the entire ballet. It is dominated by an obsessive wailing figure for solo oboe:

This recalls the theme of the ghostly lover and even harks back to the oboe lament of the second movement.

9. *The Scene.* Once more we hear the shrill cry of the jealous ghost.

10. *Song of the Will-o'-the Wisp.*

Lo mismo que er fuego fátuo, *lo mismito es er queré.* *Le juyes y te persigue* *le yamas y echa a corre.* *Lo mismo que er fuego fátuo,* *lo mismito es er queré.* *Malhaya los ojos negros* *que le alcanzeron a ver!* *Malhava er corazon triste* *que en su llama quiso ardé!*	Just like the will-o'-the-wisp, just so is love. You flee him and he pursues you; you call him and he starts to run. Just like the will-o'-the-wisp, just so is love. Cursed be the black eyes that followed him to watch. Cursed be the sorrowing heart that wished to be burned in his flame.
Lo mismo que er fuego fátuo *se desvanece er queré.*	Like the will-o'-the-wisp, love dissolves and vanishes.

11. *Pantomime.* The ghost's shrill theme is followed, this time, by a tender melody for cello solo suggesting the affectionate presence of Candélas's *novio,* Carmélo. His melody is remarkable for many reasons, among other qualities, its 7/8 meter.

12. *Dance of the Game of Love.* The flirtation between Candélas's friend, Lucia, and the philandering ghost is accompanied in part by the following words sung *in modo popolare:*

Tú eres aquel mal gitano	You are that evil gypsy
que una gitana quería;	whom a gypsy girl once loved;
El queré que ella te daba	The love that she once gave you
tú no te lo mercías!	you did not deserve!
Quién lo había de deci	Who would have said
que con otra la vendias!	you would betray her with another?
Soy la voz de tu destino!	I am the voice of your destiny!
Soy er fuego en que te abrasas!	I am the fire in which you burn!
Soy er viento en que suspiras!	I am the wind in which you sigh!.
Soy la mar en que naufragas!	I am the sea in which you are wrecked!

13. *Finale: the Bells of Morning.*

Ya está despuntando el día!	Now day begins to dawn!
Cantad, campanas, cantad!	Sing out, oh bells, sing out!
Que vuelve la gloria mia!	For now my bliss soars.

NIGHTS IN THE GARDENS OF SPAIN (FOR PIANO AND ORCHESTRA)
After Ravel's *Rhapsodie espagnole* of 1907 (with one movement called "Prelude to the Night") and Debussy's *Iberia* of 1908 (with a movement called "Fragrances of the Night"), it seems almost inevitable that Falla, who knew and admired both Ravel and Debussy, should have written his *Nights in the Gardens of Spain.* Falla's masterpiece would scarcely be what it is if Ravel's and Debussy's works had not preceded it, but Falla's individuality was strong enough to guarantee an original work.

His first concept dates, in fact, from 1909, when he planned a set of three nocturnes for piano. The score was not finished until six years later, during which more than one friend seems to have urged him to transform his piano nocturnes into an orchestral tone-poem. Perhaps the most important of these was the eminent Spanish composer Albéniz, to whom Falla played themes and excerpts from the planned nocturnes. Albeniz suggested an orchestral work with a prominent piano part. Falla took the suggestion and finished his score in 1915. Falla has been quoted (in English translation) as commenting:

> If these "symphonic impressions" have achieved their object, the mere enumeration of their titles should be a sufficient guide to the hearer. Although in this work—as in all which have a legitimate claim to be considered as music—the composer has followed a definite design, regarding tonal rhythmical, and thematic material . . . the end for which it was written is no other than to evoke places, sensations, and sentiments. The themes employed are based (as in much of the composer's earlier work) on the rhythms, modes, cadences, and ornamental figures which distinguish the popular music of Andalucía, though they are rarely used in their original forms; and the orches-

> tration frequently employs, and employs in a conventional manner, certain effects peculiar to the popular instruments used in those parts of Spain. The music has no pretentions to being descriptive; it is merely expressive. But something more than the sound of festivals and dances has inspired these "evocations in sound," for melancholy and mystery have their part also.

The three movements of Falla's score are called "At the Generalife," "Distant Dance," and "In the Gardens of the Mountains of Cordoba." The last two are played without pause.

I. "At the Generalife," *Allegretto tranquillo et misterioso.* The Palace of the Generalife (Moorish *Jennat al Arif,* meaning "Garden of Arif" or "Garden of the Architect") is a thirteenth-century villa, one of the outlying buildings of the complex of residences of the Moorish monarchs of Granada known as the Alhambra. Falla uses Spanish Andalusian themes, suggesting an Oriental background. A *canto* is heard from the very start in the hoarse voice of the violas played with a tremolo quaver close to the bridge. Like many primitive melodies, this one has a narrow range: only a minor third to start with, expanding gradually to a fourth and finally to a fifth but always returning, twisting and coiling on itself:*

The way Falla makes this primitive seed of a melody grow, expand, luxuriate, is a dazzling feat of virtuosity.

II. "Distant Dance," *Allegretto giusto.* Although the rhythmic fragments of this Distant Dance are too vague to identify, the whirring trills, the runs and the rhythmic strumming of the orchestra recall the versatile Spanish guitar. The piano seems to play an especially brilliant role and it leads with a brilliant upward sweep of octaves into the third movement, which follows without pause.

III. "In the Gardens of the Mountains of Cordoba," *Vivo.* This finale appears to depict a *zambra gitana,* that is, an evening party where a band of gypsy musicians have been engaged as a traditional entertainment. The *zambra,* both the word and the music, seem to derive from the ancient Moorish *sâmira* meaning night revelry or even a quiet meeting at night when friends pass the time telling stories like those of the *Thousand and One Nights.* Since no such meeting was complete without music, the word came to be used for a band of musicians. And when Philip the Second forbade the Moorish *zambras* and their instruments, the gypsies took over from the Moors some of their characteristic manner of playing.

---

* *This and the following musical example from this composition are copyright 1951 by Editions Max Eschig. Used by permission of Associated Music Publishers, Inc.*

The finale is built in the form of a *copla* with *estribillo* closely resembling the classical rondo with refrain. The refrain-like *estribillo* appears in dazzling octave unisons of the high woodwinds and strings:

At the end the dance rhythms seem to fade into the night.

The first performance of the *Nights in the Gardens of Spain* was given by the Orquesta Sinfonica of Madrid under the direction of Fernandez Arbós, with José Cubiles as soloist in the Teatro Real of Madrid on April 9, 1916. The score calls for piccolo, 2 flutes, 2 oboes, English horn, 2 clarinets, 2 bassoons, 4 horns, 2 trumpets, 3 trombones, tuba, harp, celesta, piano, kettledrums, triangle, cymbals, and the traditional strings.

THREE DANCES FROM THE THREE-CORNERED HAT

Manuel de Falla was one of the last brilliantly creative composers of the Romantic, nationalistic tradition, who based their styles on the traditional popular music of their lands. He was a pupil of Felipe Pedrell, the eminent Spanish musicologist, composer, teacher and proponent of the ancient traditions of Spanish popular and art music.

The second decisive ingredient of Falla's music was French. Saint-Saëns and other French composers were much admired in Spain during Falla's youth, and in 1907 he went to Paris, where he lived for seven years. There he won the friendship and support of Dukas, Debussy, and Ravel and was strongly influenced by his French contemporaries.

The original version of Falla's *The Three-Cornered Hat* was composed for a pantomime, *The Corregidor and the Miller's Wife,* adapted from a short story, *El Sombrero de tres picos,* by Pedro de Altarcon. This was produced with great success in Madrid at the Eslava Theater in April, 1917. Soon after, when Serge Diaghilev's Ballets Russes were touring Spain, Falla played some of the music to Diaghilev, who urged him to arrange it as a ballet. Falla not only revised his score but added two of the most popular numbers: "The Miller's Dance" and the "Final Dance." The first performance of the ballet version with choreography by Massine took place in July, 1919, at the Alhambra Theatre in London. The leading roles were danced by Karsavina, Massine and Woizikowsky.

The story of the ballet concerns a young miller, his pretty wife and an elderly corregidor (or governor) who unsuccessfully plays court to the miller's wife.

I. "The Neighbors' Dance" *(Seguidillas)* is part of a merrymaking scene of the villagers at the mill, which opens the second half of the ballet. "It is a fine

Andalusian night, perfumed, starlit and mysterious." The sinuous melodies, with their typical Andalusian triplet rhythms, are orchestrated with the utmost delicacy.

II. "The Miller's Dance" *(Farruca)* follows immediately. It opens with brilliant, cadenza-like phrases for solo horn and English horn. The dance proper begins with heavy, stamping, rhythmic figures, which alternate with melodic fragments in the winds and strings.

III. "Final Dance" *(Jota)*. The corregidor has had the miller arrested to get him out of the way and comes to the mill at night. However, he falls into the mill stream, awakening the miller's wife. He pursues her and she runs off in a fright. The corregidor, shivering with cold, takes off his wet clothes and goes to sleep in the miller's bed. The miller returns and, finding the corregidor's discarded clothes, fears his wife has betrayed him. In a jealous rage he goes off with the corregidor's clothes. In the scene of the Final Dance the miller, his wife, the police and the neighbors all return. The misunderstandings are cleared up, the miller and his wife are reconciled, while the neighbors mock the amorous corregidor. Through the final rejoicing there runs the following characteristic refrain:

The score calls for 2 flutes, piccolo, 2 oboes, English horn, 2 clarinets, 2 bassoons, 4 horns, 3 trumpets, 3 trombones, tuba, kettledrums, bass drum, triangle, cymbals, castanets, xylophone, tam-tam, celesta, harp, piano, and the traditional strings.

Lukas Foss

Born August 15, 1922, Berlin

VARIATIONS

Although the completion of Foss's Variations was commissioned by the Lincoln Center Fund for the 1967 Festival of Lincoln Center for the Performing Arts in New York City, the genesis of the score is considerably more interesting—and characteristic of one mainstream of Western music at the time it was composed. (I say *one* mainstream because obviously there were several, it being impossible, as yet, to detect any single, dominating, one embracing mainstream in the third quarter of our century.) When the completed work was given its world premiere by the New York Philharmonic, with Seiji Ozawa conducting, on July 5, 1967, it was the latest addition to a series of scores which placed the composer not merely in the experimental avant-garde but, in the eyes of the public and many musicians and critics, among the leaders of contemporary music. The erstwhile *Wunderkind,* the Lukas Foss of the 1930s, the brilliant young émigré to the United States, the youngest composer to win a Guggenheim Fellowship (1943), had continued a prodigy in many ways, notably as conductor, composer, pianist, teacher and musical catalyst-at-large.

In 1963, after ten years at the University of California at Los Angeles, where he succeeded Arnold Schoenberg as professor of composition, Foss accepted the position of conductor of the Buffalo Philharmonic, a position arranged to allow him time for other important activities including composition. Beginning with his *Time Cycle* for soprano and orchestra, which was given its world premiere by the New York Philharmonic in October, 1960, Foss's interests as a composer seem to have turned increasingly toward a variety of techniques which cannot be called exactly "chance" (or aleatory) music, but which usually involve elements of choice (or even improvisation) by conductor or performers in such ways that no two performances of the same work are likely to sound the same.

The genesis of Foss's Variations was *Phorion*, an independent work commissioned by the Association of Women's Committees for Symphony Orchestras. The idea for *Phorion* occurred to Foss in a dream which he utilized as a metaphor for a style or technique of composition. Foss points out that the title *Phorion* is the Greek word for stolen goods. In a program note for the first performance he wrote:

> . . . I had been working on my Cello Concerto for Rostropovich of which the last movement is based on a Bach Sarabande. In my dream I heard (or saw) torrents of Baroque 16th notes washed ashore by ocean waves, sucked in again, returning, *ad infinitum.* This rather basic dream-vision only began to interest me when, upon awakening, the technical realization of my dream suddenly became clear to me in terms of a composition.
>
> Groups of instruments play and keep playing, inaudibly, tonelessly. Only when called upon by the conductor do they emerge for a moment, submerge again into inaudibility on another conductorial sign. These signals are given at different moments to different instruments or groups of instruments and in varying order, so that even the conductor cannot keep track of the point at which a certain instrument will have arrived in its inaudible rendition when he calls upon it to emerge.
>
> I decided to use (borrow, steal) the Prelude from the solo violin Partita in E by Bach. I also decided to use normal strings, organ (preferably electronic since the fading in and out is characteristic of electronic instruments) an electronically amplified harpsichord or electric piano and an amplified harp or electric guitar.
>
> My score is made out of the Bach Prelude in every detail; the Bach piece is used as if no other notes were available. This purism of technique seemed to me essential lest the piece deteriorate into a melange or potpourri.

The first performance of *Phorion* as an independent work was given on April 28, 1967, during the regular season of the New York Philharmonic under Leonard Bernstein. Later that spring Foss incorporated *Phorion* into his three-movement Variations. For the program book of the Lincoln Center Festival premiere of the Variations, Foss wrote the following explanatory note:

> The three pieces on which the three variations are based are all in E major, which may have been an accident, but not an unwelcome one.
>
> *Variation I,* on Handel's *Concerto Grosso,* Opus 6, Number 12, slow movement [i.e., the third movement, entitled "Aria: Larghetto e piano" for the theme of this movement, see below, page 000]. Groups of instruments play the Handel unchanged, but keep submerging into inaudibility (rather than pausing) and emerging again, etc. In other words, Handel's notes are always present but often inaudible. The inaudible moments leave holes in Handel's music (I composed only the holes). The perforated Handel is played by different groups of the orchestra in an overlapping manner (I set up only the structure for the overlapping). The resulting juxtaposition and silences render the original unrecognizable. Something else is there in its place. It is like cutting many diversely shaped holes into two identical pictures, then laying them inaccurately, one on top of the other: the one on the bottom will shine through the holes of the top picture. Now shift the latter around (different performances) and always, new shapes, formations, will appear.
>
> *Variation II,* on Scarlatti's Sonata Number 23. The entire Sonata is heard in the distance (harpsichord) but is often obscured by the foreground (orchestral groups playing Scarlatti fragments, emerging, submerging). In this variation, the loveliness of the original wants to be preserved: a form of neo-Classicism: a piece of music in love with a piece of music, like setting a poem, complete in itself, (Scarlatti's Sonata does not need my setting) an unsolicited present, an abuse, an homage.
>
> *Variation III,* "Phorion," on Bach's Partita in E for solo violin, Prelude. The submerging into, and emerging out of inaudibility is rendered more hazardous for the players because it is executed at moments varying with each performance. Though the conductor cues the various instruments in and out, he himself cannot keep track of the point at which an instrument will have arrived in its inaudible rendition, when he calls upon it to emerge.
>
> As in Variation I where only Handel's notes were listed, Variation III is entirely made out of Bach's violin solo. Even the *glissandi* are Bach derived. What I wanted can perhaps best be described as "torrents of Baroque sixteenth notes, washed ashore by ocean waves, sucked in again, returning"—a Bach dream—abruptly changing situations: some humorous (2 flutes racing each other—the xylophone spelling out Johann Sebastian Bach in Morse code —etc.) some frightening (the organ-percussion duel at the end).
>
> Variations is scored for flutes, clarinets, oboes, bassoons, horns, trumpets, trombone, tuba, percussion, electric piano, guitar, organ, harpsichord, and strings.

César Franck

Born December 10, 1822, Liège—died November 8, 1890, Paris

SYMPHONIC VARIATIONS FOR PIANO AND ORCHESTRA

"Father" Franck, as they often called him, was worshipped as a sort of secular saint by a whole generation of his pupils and artistic disciples. This seraphic image still inhabits our music history and reference books, which are largely based on Vincent d'Indy's canonization of the master in his first authoratative biography. In 1930 the critical study by Maurice Emmanuel attempted in a number of ways to bring the image of the saint down to earth. And a quarter of a century later the French critic and historian Léon Vallas, in his *True Story of César Franck,* attempted to strike a balance between what he called hagiography and debunking. Yet even so objective an historian as Vallas admitted that he, for one, would not be sorry if the image of the saint survived.

It seems to be true that Franck was almost angelically unaggressive and slow to anger, even when anger over poor performances of his works, or neglect, would have been well justified. Yet in an age which no longer feels it necessary to worship everything about a man's character, or to attribute the tardy recognition of his greatness entirely to the stupidity, malice and jealousy of his colleagues, it is generally admitted that a chief reason for the belated recognition of Franck's genius was that it did not show until very late in his career. And even after his stature had become clear for any well-wisher to see, there were occasional lapses into an oversweet chromaticism which might give even the staunchest admirer pause.

Franck's *Symphonic Variations* belong to that last period of his career, which is rich in acknowledged masterpieces. In addition it is happily free of the occasional cloying chromaticisms which mar even some of his finest works. Composed in 1885, the *Symphonic Variations* were first performed by Louis Diémer at the Salle Pleyel in Paris on May 1, 1886. The much-reported disaster of the second Paris performance on June 30, 1887 at a Pasdeloup concert was partly due, according to Léon Vallas, to the widespread irritation against Franck caused by his overzealous disciples. Even today it seems difficult to be impartial about César Franck, and so serious a biographer as Norman Demuth, despite his efforts to be objective, can assert that in the *Symphonic Variations* he is "absolutely certain that we have a flawless work and as near perfection as human composer can hope to get in a work of this nature [i.e., a concerto]."

In effect a one-movement piano concerto, Franck's score is eloquent testimony of the Romantic love of integrating more than one form into a single movement. Franck might equally well have entitled his work "introduction, variations, and finale."

The introduction presents us at the outset with two strongly contrasting ideas: a vigorously dotted rhythm asserted by the orchestral strings and answered by a plaintive, pleading melody in the piano:

These two contrasting ideas are immediately varied, the second variation changing to three-quarter time and anticipating the central theme of the work which will be announced later in full by the piano solo.

The middle section of the work, constituting the more formal set of theme and variations, is based on an eighteen-measure theme presented first by the piano solo and beginning as follows:

The first five variations observe, by and large, the eighteen-measure structure of the piano theme, gradually reintroducing the vigorous dotted rhythms which open the score. In the sixth variation the melody is sung by the cellos, against undulating figurations for the piano solo. This in turn merges into a free interlude, in which the graceful piano figuration continues, with a diaphonous background of muted strings.

The third section, or finale, begins with a long trill for both hands of the pianist, introducing a tiny symphonic movement, or sonata-allegro form, the principal theme of which is derived from the pleading piano phrase quoted above from the first pages of the score. There is a properly contrasting, lyric theme, which sounds new, but is actually an ingenious adaptation of the principal piano theme. The tiniest of symphonic development sections and a traditional recapitulation lead to a brilliant coda, in which the seraphic "Father" Franck showed that he could write music of the most superb worldly elegance and glitter.

The *Symphonic Variations* are scored for 2 flutes, 2 oboes, 2 clarinets, 2 bassoons, 4 horns, 2 trumpets, kettledrums, and the standard string choir.

SYMPHONY IN D MINOR

It is hard to imagine that César Franck's only Symphony could have been a failure when it was first performed in Paris, a few months before the composer's death. But the failure was partly Franck's own fault, for he had never troubled to thrust himself or his music before the public. Either he did not know how to use his elbows or he did not want to. He had none of the commanding manner of Beethoven and none of the aggressive egotism of Wagner, though he learned much from Wagner's music.

Franck's Symphony was given its first performance by the orchestra of the Paris Conservatory on February 17, 1889. The famous account of the premiere by Franck's disciple Vincent d'Indy may have exaggerated the malignance of Franck's fellow composers. Gounod, for example, has long been credited with the foolish remark that the new work was "the affirmation of impotence carried to the point of dogma." Yet Franck's Symphony was destined to become almost as popular in the symphonic world as was Gounod's *Faust* in the opera house. One irritated pedant, a professor at the Conservatory, asked D'Indy contemptuously: "But my dear sir, who ever heard of writing for the English horn in a symphony? Just name me one symphony by Haydn or Beethoven that uses an English horn! There! So you see: your Franck's music may be whatever you please, but it will certainly never be a symphony!" The speaker's knowledge of Haydn was as scanty as his appreciation of Franck, for Haydn did indeed use the English horn, in fact, a pair of them in his Symphony No. 22, "The Philosopher."

I. *Lento; Allegro ma non troppo.* The opening theme of Franck's Symphony is a type of phrase that had fascinated composers for more than a century. Beethoven used it in one of his last quartets where he wrote over the notes: "Must it be?" Wagner used it in his *Ring of the Nibelung* as the questioning theme of Fate. And Franz Liszt used it again as the main theme of his symphonic poem, *Les Préludes.* César Franck does not give the theme any name, but he places it as a slow portentous question at the very opening of his Symphony:

Again and again, with rising insistence, the orchestra asks this question till we come to the main part of the first movement, an *Allegro.* Here the question is transformed into an energetic, aggressive principal theme. There is a turbulent development until suddenly all yearning and straining resolves into soaring melody:

The rest of the movement is taken up with the conflict between these two moods, and at the end the solemn question is answered in a blaze of affirmation.

II. *Allegretto.* The second movement begins with soft pluckings of the harp and other string instruments. And soon there rises above it the melancholy song of the English horn:

The middle part of this movement lets through a gleam of light, a gayer, more carefree atmosphere.

III. *Allegro non troppo.* The finale is festive music. There are great thematic riches, the most important being the opening theme:

There are reminiscences of the melancholy and the questioning themes of the past, but they give way to a mounting wave of assurance and strength. The sad song of the second movement is transformed into a song of joy and the answer to all the questionings is triumph.

The Symphony in D minor is scored for 2 flutes, 2 oboes, English horn, 2 clarinets, bass clarinet, 2 bassoons, 4 horns, 2 trumpets, 2 cornets, 3 trombones, tuba, kettledrums, harp, and the usual strings.

George Gershwin

Born September 28, 1898, Brooklyn, New York—died July 11, 1937, Beverly Hills, California

AN AMERICAN IN PARIS, FOR SYMPHONY ORCHESTRA

By the time George Gershwin received his second commission for an orchestral work to be performed by Walter Damrosch's New York Symphony Society (the first commission had been for his Concerto in F) he was far more than a dizzy success on the Broadway musical comedy scene. He was twenty-nine years old and with his *Rhapsody in Blue* (of 1924) and his Concerto (1925) behind him he was making waves in the symphonic world. There were still some critics (and composers) who patronized him for his ambitions as a "serious" composer, but attitudes were changing fast. The mixed feelings caused by Gershwin's meteoric rise were expressed in the widely repeated (but surely apocryphal) word that he had cabled Stravinsky in Paris asking whether Stravinsky would accept him as a pupil in composition and what his fee might be. Stravinsky asked the amount of Gershwin's annual income and on receiving Gershwin's impressive six-digit figure, Stravinsky was said to have replied: "How about my taking lessons from you?"

In March 1928 Gershwin set out for his fifth or sixth trip to Europe in company with his sister "Frankie," his brother Ira, and Ira's wife Leonore. In George's luggage were sketches for the new symphonic work commissioned by Damrosch. The family group stopped off for the final performance in the London run of George's and Ira's *Oh, Kay!*

Before the end of March they settled in Paris, where the Gershwins encountered the first of a string of performances of *Rhapsody in Blue,* of receptions, parties, interviews and meetings with important men and women from George's new domain of serious music, including Ravel (with whom George hoped to study), Milhaud, Stravinsky, Prokofieff, Poulenc, Stokowski, and Alexander Tansman, who accompanied George on an expedition to secure four French taxi horns. To Gershwin, as to most American tourists, the squeaky-high French taxi horns sounded irresistibly Parisian, exotic, irresponsible, and suggestive of the happy chaos of Parisian traffic. George felt that four such horns were needed in his new symphonic work, which he had decided to call *An American in Paris.*

By June the Gershwin party was back in New York, and on the first of August George finished the piano sketch of his score. He was obliged to divide the rest of his summer and fall between a new Broadway show, *Treasure Girl,* and the orchestration of *An American in Paris,* which he completed on November 18—less than a month before the scheduled premiere. He also issued his own informal description of what he had aimed to do in his new score:

> This new piece, really a rhapsodic ballet, is written very freely and is the most modern music I've yet attempted. The opening part will be developed in typical French style, in the manner of Debussy and the Six, though the themes are all original. My purpose here is to portray the impression of an American visitor in Paris, as he strolls about the city, and listens to various street noises and absorbs the French atmosphere.
>
> As in my other orchestral compositions, I've not endeavored to represent any definite scenes in this music. The rhapsody is programmatic only in a general impressionistic way, so that the individual listener can read into the music such as his imagination pictures for him.
>
> The opening gay section is followed by a rich blues with a strong rhythmic undercurrent. Our American friend perhaps after strolling into a café and having a couple of drinks, has succumbed to a spasm of homesickness. The harmony here is both more intense and simple than in the preceding pages. This blues rises to a climax followed by a coda in which the spirit of the music returns to the vivacity and bubbling exuberance of the opening part with its impressions of Paris. Apparently the homesick American, having left the café and reached the open air, has disowned his spell of the blues

and once again is an alert spectator of Parisian life. At the conclusion, the street noises and French atmosphere are triumphant.

In the interval between Dr. Damrosch's commissioning of the new work and the first performance, his Symphony Society had been amalgamated with the New York Philharmonic, so that the orchestra which played the premiere under his direction was the New York Philharmonic-Symphony Society, to use the full official title by which it is still known.

For the program book of the premiere Gershwin's friend and composer colleague, Deems Taylor, wrote (in collaboration with Gershwin) a more detailed program of the piece, which has the historical value of having been approved by the composer. It is also interesting because of the passages where it differs from Gershwin's first, untutored description, proving again (what we knew already anyhow) that the music came first and the explanations of what the music allegedly describes were afterthoughts. Since Gershwin wrote one explanation himself and approved the other, it seems clear that the composer may not have originally had anything so specific in mind. Yet the spirit of the music is in both and Taylor's jocose style suits the carefree music:

By its composer's own confession, *An American in Paris* is an attempted reconciliation between two opposing schools of musical thought—a *Pax Romana,* as it were, imposed upon two customarily warring camps. It is program music in that it engages to tell an emotional narrative; to convey, in terms of sound, the successive emotional reactions experienced by a Yankee tourist (perhaps from Broadway) adrift in the City of Light. It is absolute music as well, in that its structure is determined by considerations musical rather than literary or dramatic. The piece, while not in strict sonata form, resembles an extended symphonic movement in that it announces, develops, combines and recapitulates definite themes. . . .

While Mr. Gershwin has been heard to hope—and probably not in vain—that his new work can be absorbed and enjoyed purely as a piece of orchestral music, he admits that *An American in Paris* (which, oddly enough, was largely written in Paris) follows a fairly explicit story. What follows is based upon Mr. Gershwin's own version of the succession of events, augmented by a few details supplied by the helpful commentator and—as yet—unrepudiated by the composer.

You are to imagine, then, an American visiting Paris, swinging down the Champs-Elysées on a mild, sunny morning in May or June. Being what he is, he starts without preliminaries and is off at full speed at once to the tune of The First Walking Theme, a straightforward diatonic air designed to convey an impression of Gallic freedom and gaiety:*

* *This and the following musical example from this composition are copyright 1929, New World Music Corporation. Copyright renewed. All rights reserved. Used by permission of Warner Bros. Music.*

Our American's ears being open, as well as his eyes, he notes with pleasure the sounds of the city. French taxicabs seem to amuse him particularly, a fact that the orchestra points out in brief episodes introducing four real Paris taxi horns (imported at great expense for the occasion). These have a special theme allotted to them (the driver, possibly?), which is announced by the strings whenever they appear in the score.

Having safely eluded the taxis, our American apparently passes the open door of a café where, if one is to believe the trombones, *La Maxixe* is still popular. Exhilarated by this reminder of the gay nineteen-hundreds, he resumes his stroll through the medium of the Second Walking Theme, which is announced by the clarinet in French with a strong American accent.

Both themes are now discussed at some length by the instruments, until our tourist happens to pass—something. The composer thought it might be a church, while the commentator held out for the Grand Palais—where the *Salon* holds forth. At all events, our hero does not go in. Instead, as revealed by the English horn, he respectfully slackens his pace until he is safely past.

At this point, the American's itinerary becomes somewhat obscured. It may be that he continues down the Champs-Elysées; it may be that he has turned off—the composer retains an open mind on the subject. However, since what immediately ensues is technically known as a bridge passage, one is reasonably justified in assuming that the Gershwin pen, guided by an unseen hand, has perpetrated a musical pun, and that when the Third Walking Theme makes its eventual appearance our American has crossed the Seine and is somewhere on the Left Bank. Certainly it is distinctly less Gallic than its predecessors, speaking American with a French intonation as befits that region of the city where so many Americans foregather. "Walking" may be a misnomer for despite its vitality, the theme is slightly sedentary in character and becomes progressively more so. Indeed, the end of this section of the work is couched in terms so unmistakably, albeit, pleasantly blurred as to suggest that the American is on the *terrasse* of a café exploring the mysteries of an Anise de Lozo.

And now the orchestra introduces an unhallowed episode. Suffice it to say that a solo violin approaches our hero (in the soprano register) and addresses him in the most charming broken English; and his response being inaudible—or at least unintelligible—repeats the remark. This one-sided conversation continues for some little time.

Of course, one hastens to add, it is possible that a grave injustice is being done to both author and protagonist, and that the whole episode is simply a musical transition. The latter interpretation may well be true, for otherwise it is difficult to believe what ensues: our hero becomes homesick. He has the blues; and if the behavior of the orchestra be any criterion, he has them very thoroughly:

He realizes suddenly, overwhelmingly, that he does not belong to this place, that he is the most wretched creature in all the world, a foreigner. The cool, blue Paris sky, the distant upward sweep of the Eiffel Tower, the bookstalls on the quay, the pattern of horse-chestnut leaves on the white, sun-flecked street—what avails all this alien beauty? He is no Baudelaire, longing to be "anywhere out of the world." The world is just what he longs for, the world that he knows best; a world less lovely—sentimental and a little vulgar perhaps—but for all that, home.

However, nostalgia is not a fatal diesease—nor, in this instance, of overlong duration. Just in the nick of time the compassionate orchestra rushes another theme to the rescue, two trumpets performing the ceremony of introduction. It is apparent that our hero must have met a compatriot; for this last theme is a noisy, cheerful, self-confident Charleston, without a drop of Gallic blood in its veins.

For the moment, Paris is no more; and a voluble, gusty, wise-cracking orchestra proceeds to demonstrate at some length that it's always fair weather when two Americans get together, no matter where. Walking Theme number two enters soon thereafter, enthusiastically abetted by number three. Paris isn't such a bad place after all: as a matter of fact, it's a grand place! Nice weather, nothing to do till tomorrow, nice girls—and by the way, whatever became of that lad Volstead? The blues return but mitigated by the Second Walking Theme—a happy reminiscence rather than a homesick yearning—and the orchestra, in a riotous finale, decides to make a night of it. It will be great to get home; but meanwhile, this is Paris!

The score for *An American in Paris* requires 3 flutes, piccolo, 2 oboes, English horn, 2 clarinets, bass clarinet, 2 bassoons, contrabassoon, alto saxophone, tenor saxophone, baritone saxophone, 4 horns, 3 trumpets, 3 trombones, tuba, kettledrum, cymbals, celeste, glockenspiel, snare drum, bass drum, triangle, bells, xylophone, rattle, 2 tom-toms, 4 French taxi horns, wire brush, wood block, and the customary string choir.

CONCERTO IN F

One of the most dazzled listeners on the extraordinary occasion when George Gershwin first played his *Rhapsody in Blue* with Paul Whiteman and his Palais Royal Orchestra in New York's old Aeolian Hall, was the conductor of the New York Symphony: Walter Damrosch. The date was February 12, 1924. A short time later Dr. Damrosch inquired whether Mr. Gershwin would be willing to compose a piano concerto on commission for the New York Symphony and to appear with the Orchestra as soloist in New York and half a dozen other cities. The result was Gershwin's Concerto in F, which was given its world premiere by the New York Symphony on December 3, 1925, in Carnegie Hall, with Gershwin himself at the piano under the baton of Walter Damrosch.

The story is often told that after signing on the dotted line, Gershwin went out to buy a book to find out just what a concert was! The story sounds almost too pat to be true. For the picture of young genius out to storm Mt. Parnassus with a do-it-yourself manual in hand does have great appeal. Somewhat easier to believe is the story that he also invested in a copy of Forsyth's *Standard Manual of Orchestration.* For although Gershwin was already a famous composer with a string of musical comedies to his credit, from *La La Lucille* (1919) to *Lady Be Good* (1924), and *Oh, Kay* (1925), Broadway composers were and are discouraged from orchestrating their own works. Even the *Rhapsody in Blue* had been orchestrated for Gershwin by Ferde Grofé.

Gershwin appears to have begun jotting down ideas for the Concerto by May of 1925 while he was in London. By July, back in New York, he was already playing fragments of the Concerto to friends. And before the end of the month he had completed the first movement. His manuscript of the second movement is dated August-September, and the third movement is also dated September. During October and November of 1925 he completed the orchestration. Gershwin later said:

"Many persons had thought that the *Rhapsody* was only a happy accident. Well, I went out, for one thing, to show them that there was plenty more where that had come from. I made up my mind to do a piece of 'absolute' music. The *Rhapsody,* as its title implied, was a *blues* impression. The Concerto would be unrelated to any program. And that is exactly how I wrote it. I learned a great deal from that experience. Particularly in the handling of instruments in combination."

Gershwin had originally intended to call his new score *New York Concerto,* but eventually settled instead on the simple wording: Concerto in F. For the Sunday New York *Tribune* of November 29, 1925, just four days before the premiere, Gershwin prepared a short analytical description of his new score:

[I. *Allegro.*] The first movement employs the Charleston rhythm. It is quick and pulsating, representing the young, enthusiastic spirit of American life. It begins with a rhythmic motif given out by the kettledrums, supported by other percussion instruments and with a Charleston motif introduced by bassoon, horns, clarinets and violas. The principal theme is announced by the bassoon:*

Later, a second theme is introduced by the piano.

[II. *Adagio; Andante con moto.*] The second movement has a poetic nocturnal atmosphere which has come to be referred to as the American blues, but in a purer form than that in which they are usually treated.

---

* *Musical example © 1927, New World Music Corporation. Copyright renewed. All rights reserved. Used by permission of Warner Bros. Music.*

[III. *Allegro agitato.*] The final movement reverts to the style of the first. It is an orgy of rhythms, starting violently and keeping the same pace throughout.

The Concerto in F is scored for piccolo, 2 flutes, 2 oboes, English horn, 2 clarinets, bass clarinet, 2 bassoons, 4 horns, 3 trumpets, 3 trombones, tuba, kettledrums, bass drum, snare drum, cymbals, bells, xylophone, triangle, and the standard complement of strings.

RHAPSODY IN BLUE

George Gershwin almost failed to write his most famous work—the *Rhapsody in Blue*—because he didn't quite have the nerve. It took all the persuasive powers of Paul Whiteman, who had invited him to compose a serious "jazz concerto," to convince the twenty-five-year-old Gershwin that he was capable of composing such a work, and composing it in less than a month—in time to perform it himself at a concert already announced for February 12, 1924.

When Gershwin objected that he didn't even know how to orchestrate, Whiteman replied that all he need do was to sketch the orchestral part; Ferde Grofé would do the instrumentation for him. Gershwin's situation was complicated by the fact that he was busy with the final stages of preparing his songs for a musical comedy, *Sweet Little Devil,* which was about to begin its Boston tryout. But he liked the idea of a "jazz concerto." He had always wanted to write serious music which would incorporate jazz elements.

Themes for the "concerto" began to run through his head, but the first time the whole began to jell as a connected composition seems to have been during a trip to Boston for the premiere of *Sweet Little Devil.* Gershwin described it later: "It was on the train, with its steely rhythms, its rattlety-bang that is often so stimulating to a composer . . . I frequently hear music in the very heart of noise. And there I suddenly heard—and even saw on paper—the complete construction of the *Rhapsody,* from beginning to end. No new themes came to me, but I worked on the thematic material already in my mind and tried to conceive the composition as a whole. I heard it as a sort of musical kaleidoscope of America—of our vast melting pot, of our unduplicated national pep, of our blues, our metropolitan madness. By the time I reached Boston I had a definite *plot* of the piece, as distinguished from its actual substance."

A week after his return from Boston, Gershwin recalled, he completed the *Rhapsody in Blue,* except for a few of the solo piano figurations, which he simply left out. "I was so pressed for time," he wrote, "that I left them to be improvised at the first concert. I could do that as I was to be the pianist." On February 4 Ferde Grofé completed the orchestration.

On February 12 the concert took place as planned. Aeolian Hall was jammed with composers from Tin Pan Alley and from the world of "serious" music, with pop performers and concert virtuosos of the rank of Mischa Elman, Fritz Kreisler, Jasha Heifetz, Moritz Rosenthal, and Sergei Rachmaninoff, with conductors of the eminence of Walter Damrosch, Leopold Stokowski,

PAUL WHITEMAN AND HIS PALAIS ROYAL ORCHESTRA.

The orchestra augmented to twenty-two players for the premiere of *Rhapsody in Blue* on February 12, 1924. *(Courtesy, Edward Jablonski)*

Willem Mengelberg, with music critics from far and near, composers from John Philip Sousa to Igor Stravinsky, with literary figures including many, such as Fannie Hurst and Carl van Vechten, to whom Gershwin was already a genius of meteoric brilliance.

> The stage setting [reported *The New York Times*] was as unconventional as the program. Pianos in various stages of deshabillé stood about, amid a litter of every imaginable contraption of wind and percussion instruments. Two Chinese mandarins, surmounting pillars, looked down upon a scene that would have curdled the blood of a Stokowski or a Mengelberg. The golden sheen of brass instruments of lesser and greater dimensions was caught up by a gleaming gong and carried out by bright patches of an Oriental backdrop. There were also, lying or hanging about frying-pans, large tin utensils, and a speaking-trumpet, later stuck into the end of a trombone—and what a silky, silky tone came from that accommodating instrument! The singular assemblage of things was more than once, in some strange way, to combine to evoke uncommon and fascinating sonorities.

The early part of the program included examples of earlier popular music as historical background to the development of "modern" jazz. My father, Olin Downes, then music critic of *The New York Times* and an enthusiastic admirer of ragtime, jazz and of Gershwin's Broadway show tunes, relished the antics of the musicians:

> The man with the clarinet wore a battered top hat that had ostensibly seen better days. Sometimes he wore it, and sometimes played into it. The man with the trombone played it as is, but also, on occasion, picked up a bathtub or something of the kind from the floor and blew into that. The instruments made odd, unseemly, bushman sounds. The instrumentalists rocked about. . . .
>
> They did not play like an army going through ordered maneuvers, but like the melomaniacs they are, bitten by rhythms that would have twiddled the toes of St. Anthony. They beat time with their feet—*lèse-majesté* in a symphony orchestra. They fidgeted uncomfortably when for a moment they had to stop playing. And there were the incredible gyrations of that virtuoso and imp of the perverse, Ross Gorman [the clarinetist of the Whiteman band]. And then there was Mr. Whiteman. He does not conduct. He trembles, wabbles, quivers—a piece of jazz jelly, conducting the orchestra with the back of the trouser of the right leg, and the face of a mandarin the while. It was late in the evening when the hero of the occasion appeared.
>
> Then stepped upon the stage, sheepishly, a lank and dark young man—George Gershwin. He was to play the piano part in the first public performance of his *Rhapsody in Blue* for piano and orchestra. This composition shows extraordinary talent, just as it also shows a young composer with aims that go far beyond those of his ilk, struggling with a form of which he is far from being master. His first theme alone, with its caprice, humor, and exotic outline, would show a talent to be reckoned with. It starts with an outrageous cadenza of the clarinet. It has subsidiary phrases, logically growing out of it,

and integral to the thought. The original phrase and subsidiaries are often ingeniously metamorphosed by devices of rhythm and instrumentation.

That "outrageous" war-whoop—alias cadenza—that opens the *Rhapsody in Blue,* was a trick for which Ross Gorman was famous. Gershwin thought it would be just perfect to set the unconventional mood of the *Rhapsody.* And, of course, he was right. It starts with a slow trill near the bottom of the clarinet range, then ripples up the scale in orthodox fashion—until suddenly the individual notes merge into one siren-like wail: a sliding, scooping effect supposedly impossible on the clarinet, skyrocketing up and bursting into the jazzily syncopated opening theme:*

The outrageous clarinet has opened the floodgate and now one theme chases another so fast, and in such rhapsodic profusion that there is hardly time to grasp one before the next one jostles it aside, and the next and the next. Yet, in some mysterious, perhaps unplanned way, one rhythmic fragment seems to grow out of the other. A saxophone, first cousin to Gorman's clarinet, steals a little of his theme and dances off with it as follows:

The pianist enters with still another variant, leading to a brilliant solo commentary on everything that has gone before.

Out of this there grows a lively scherzo-like section of a jazz cliché that still sounds so fresh it is hard to believe it is over half a century old:

* *This and the following musical examples from this composition are © 1924, New World Music Corporation. Copyright renewed. All rights reserved. Used by permission of Warner Bros. Music.*

Halfway through the *Rhapsody* we meet a broadly flowing, warmly sentimental theme which could recall Tchaikovsky except for the jazzy little afterthought of the horns.

The *Rhapsody* concludes with an increasingly brilliant free-for-all of the entire thematic material and ends with a burst of virtuosity for soloist and orchestra, returning to the opening theme.

Ferde Grofé's concert orchestration of the *Rhapsody in Blue* (as opposed to the jazz-band version of the premiere) calls for 2 flutes, 2 oboes, 2 clarinets, bass clarinet, 2 bassoons, 3 horns, 3 trumpets, 3 trombones, tuba, 2 alto saxophones, tenor saxophone, kettledrums, cymbals, bass drum, snare drum, triangle, gong, piano solo, and the standard string choir.

Alberto Ginastera

Born April 11, 1916, Buenos Aires

CONCERTO FOR PIANO AND ORCHESTRA

When Alberto Ginastera's Piano Concerto had its world premiere in 1961, Ginastera was already one of the tiny band of contemporary composers who not only enjoyed wide popularity in the concert halls of North and South America, but also had won the respect and enthusiasm of professional musicians on both sides of the Atlantic. With dramatic speed, he has since become a major figure in the operatic world. His *Don Rodgrigo,* commissioned by the city of Buenos Aires and first performed there at the Teatro Cólon in 1964, was a striking success in the production with which the New York City Opera inaugurated its first season at the Lincoln Center for the Performing Arts in February 1966. Ginastera's *Bomarzo,* commissioned by the Opera Society of Washington, D.C., in May 1967, was scheduled for its South American premiere at Buenos Aires the following August. Two weeks before the date set, the opera was banned on the grounds that it is "obsessed with sex, violence, and hallucinations," an accusation which Ginastera calmly confirmed, adding that these are the overt or covert subjects of most serious opera and that contemporary opera is simply more frank in its evolvement of these topics. In September 1971 Ginastera's *Beatrix Cenci,* commissioned by the Washington Opera Society, inaugurated the new opera house of the Kennedy Center for the Performing Arts in Washington, D.C.

It was Ginastera's chamber music which established his reputation in Europe early in his career, and he has been productive in many other fields.

His Piano Concerto was commissioned by the Koussevitsky Foundation in the Library of Congress. Composed during the early months of 1961, it was first performed at the Second Inter-American Music Festival on April 22, 1961. Howard Mitchell conducted the National Symphony Orchestra of Washington, D.C. and the young Brazilian virtuoso João Carlos Martins was the soloist in the Crampon Auditorium of Howard University. The Buenos Aires premiere of the Piano Concerto followed some three years later on May 19, 1964.

For this occasion Ginastera was asked to write a program note. In complying, he voiced the ambivalence many composers feel when faced with the problem of helping listeners with words:

> Although I am always a little reluctant to write commentaries on my own compositions, I have decided to do it this time in order to say why I feel it is not essential to explain a work of art. I think that such a work must produce a feeling of comprehension, a flow of attraction between public and artist, independent of its structural implications. If this perceptible feeling of understanding and sympathy is not established, then no explanation will help the average public to fathom the inner meaning of the work. . . .
>
> . . . art is first perceived by our senses. It then affects our sentiments and in the end awakens our intelligence. Today too much is written and spoken on the subject of modern art and that is possibly because a great part of this art fails to impress the feelings of the public. . . . A work which speaks only to the intelligence of man will never reach his heart. Of course, the feelings of the XXth Century man are not impressed in the same way as the feelings of a man of the Romantic era, because neither art nor life are the same as they were. . . . Without sensibility the work of art is only a cold mathematical study, and without intelligence or technique it is only chaos. Thus the perfect formula would be sensitive beauty plus technical skill.
>
> I think then that commentaries are not essential for the general public. But, on the other hand, analyses are very useful for the learned public. Musicologists, critics, composers, performers and music students are always aware of the basic structure of a work and conscious of its implicit aesthetic, deep significant and mysterious meaning. The analysis of a new work is consequently an invaluable help for all those who wish to discover the secret planning of a work. I shall therefore transcribe, for the benefit of all those studious people, on separate pages, the brief analytical studies written on the occasion of the premieres of these two works in Buenos Aires.

On a separate page "for all these studious people" Ginastera wrote the following brief program note, to which musical examples from three key passages have been added, as explained by the words enclosed in square brackets:

[I. *Cadenza e varianti.*] Although the Concerto is divided into the four traditional movements, the composer has renewed the structure of each movement. The first one, *Cadenza e varianti,* begins with the presentation of a serial chord.

Then the piano begins the cadenza, giving a melodic transposition of the same row. On these basic elements is based the whole movement. In the cadenza, piano and orchestra alternate with violent contrasts. The "varianti" are 10 micro-structures in different moods. [The first of these "varianti" or variants is a tiny nocturne-like structure for piano solo based on the basic row given out in the opening cadenza. The first two measures, of rare poetic beauty, consist exclusively of the basic row: *

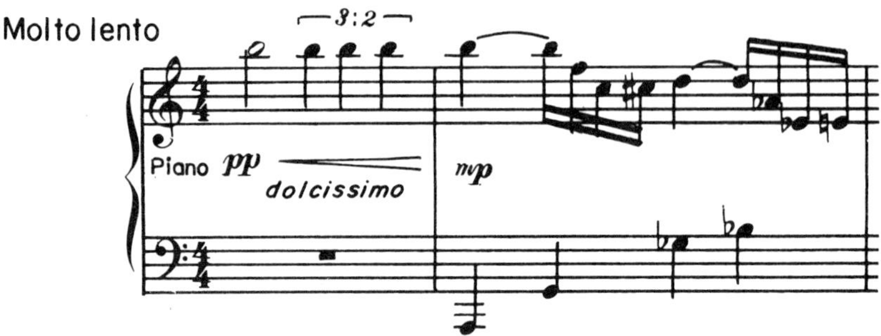

Most of the following "varianti" are even briefer.] The first movement ends with a coda which is a kind of amplified variation recalling the cadenza.

[II.] The second movement, *Scherzo allucinante,* is very fast and it is played throughout with the dynamics *pianissimo.* The composer uses a pointillist instrumentation and the arch form in five sections: three central symmetrical sections framed by an introduction and a coda.

[III.] The third movement, *Adagissimo,* is an intense lyrical interlude formed by three sections recalling the ternary form and reaching in the central part a very passionate climax. [The movement opens with a hesitant whisper of a lone viola, swelling to a sigh-like figure:

The two pairs of sigh-like falling notes grow into the passionate outpouring of the central section.] This movement ends with the whole sub-divided string section playing a dodecaphonic chord until it gradually vanishes. Some notes on the piano emphasize the feeling of distance.

IV. The fourth and last movement, *Toccata concertata,* with strong rhythms, is a real *bravura* piece in which there is a dialogue between piano and orchestra. The form recalls the rondo form of seven sections preceded by an introduction and finishing with a coda. [The recurrent rondo refrain is first presented by the pianist as a powerfully syncopated, pounding figure:]

---

* *This and the following musical examples from this composition are copyright 1964 by Barry Editorial Company, Inc., S.R.L. Reprinted by permission of Boosey & Hawkes, Inc., sole agents.*

Ginastera's Piano Concerto calls for an orchestra consisting of 1 piccolo, 2 flutes, 2 oboes, English horn, small E-flat clarinet, 2 B-flat clarinets, bass clarinet in B flat, 2 contrabassoons, 4 horns, 3 trumpets, 3 trombones, tuba, harp, kettledrum, 2 pair of crotales (tiny "antique" cymbals with very thick metal), triangle, tambourine, castanets, 3 tom-toms, tam-tam, side drum, 2 cymbals, 1 small cymbal, bass drum, xylophone, glockenspiel, celesta, and the traditional complement of strings.

CONCERTO FOR VIOLIN AND ORCHESTRA

Although Ginastera's colorful nationalism is perhaps his best-known trait, his musical horizon is not limited by the map, or by a folkloristic point of view. While much of his music has been a conscious reflection of the Argentine landscape, the people, and their culture, including Argentine folk music, Ginastera has also participated in the broader, international currents: the impressionism and radical harmonic experimentation of his earliest youth, Neoclassicism, and in recent years serial, twelve-tone techniques.

Ginastera's Violin Concerto was commissioned by the New York Philharmonic celebration of its opening season in Lincoln Center for the Performing Arts. The score, dedicated to Leonard Bernstein and the New York Philharmonic, was begun early in 1962 and completed in September 1963.

His Violin Concerto, which uses serial devices, is written in a virtuoso style intended to explore the sonorous capacities not only of the solo violin but of the individual instruments of the orchestra. The following notes are based on information supplied by the composer.

I. *Cadenza e Studi.* The first movement is divided into two sections. The opening cadenza, cast in a rhapsodic, virtuoso style, serves to introduce the basic musical materials of the entire Concerto. This leads without pause to a group of six studies and coda, each study "a kind of variation" of the basic series or tone-row: (1) for chords, with accompaniment of basses; (2) for intervals of the third with string *pizzicato* accompaniment; (3) for other intervals with woodwind accompaniment; (4) for arpeggios with accompaniment of violins and violas in unison; (5) for harmonies with accompaniment of glockenspiel, celesta, and harp; and (6) for twenty-four quarter-tones with accompaniment of the entire choir of muted strings.

II. *Adagio per 22 solisti.* The lyric slow movement is intended as an homage to the solo players of the New York Philharmonic.

III. *Scherzo pianissimo e Perpetuum mobile.* The finale, like the first movement falls into two sections. The opening scherzo section is directed to be played at a flying pace, in a mysterious, scarcely audible whisper. In the middle, themes from Paganini's *Capriccios* appear briefly, "as if the shadow of this great violinist were passing through the orchestra." The concluding "perpetual motion" section serves as an extended coda to the entire concerto.

Mikhail Glinka

Born June 1, 1804, Novopasskoye, District of Smolensk—died February 15, 1857, Berlin

OVERTURE TO RUSSŁAN AND LUDMILLA

"All music in Russia stems from him." Thus spoke Igor Stravinsky one hundred and one years after Glinka's death. And Stravinsky should know, if anyone did. He was speaking a bit elliptically, of course; he cannot have meant to exclude the rich heritage of Byzantine-Slavonic church chants and of Russian folk music. But in commenting on Russian art music in the Western tradition, Stravinsky only reflected the amazingly universal opinion of his Russian contemporaries and forebears. Yet Glinka himself was born of a much vaster movement than all of Russian music or all of Russian culture, for that matter. He sprang from the great wave of Romantic nationalism that swept the Western world in the nineteenth century.

Pushkin, the greatest of all Russian poets, was born only five years before Glinka. And both Pushkin and Glinka were influenced by the elder Romantic poet Vasily Zhukovsky, who suggested the subject of Glinka's first and enormously successful opera *A Life for the Tsar*.

It was the fairy-tale poem *Russlan and Ludmilla* that made the twenty-one-year-old Pushkin famous almost over night. His masterpiece, Russian to the core, stimulated by the Romantic rediscovery of the ancient Slav *byliny* or "old-time tales" (epics comparable to the Arthurian romances, the *Chanson de Roland*, or the *Niebelungenlied*, with origins in pre-Christian myth and magic), by the highly sophisticated epic art of Ariosto's *Rolando Furioso*, by the Romantic sensibility of Zhukovsky's verse, and spiced with an ironically modern, conversational tone, provoked instant controversy and final triumph.

Pushkin was attracted by Glinka's project for an opera on the subject. And only Pushkin's tragic death in a duel prevented him from helping Glinka make the operatic adaptation of *Russlan and Ludmilla*. Lacking his guidance, the whole crew of liberettists enlisted by Glinka made a confused spectacle of Pushkin's already fantastic tale. This misfortune may even have contributed to the oddly disconnected character, like a series of independent tableaux, of many later Russian operas. In any case, the awkward libretto contributed to the initially lukewarm reception of *Russlan and Ludmilla* at the Bolshoi Theater of St. Petersburg on December 9, 1842.

The plot, in brief, concerns Ludmilla, the beautiful daughter of Grand Duke Sviatoslav of Kiev, and the hero, Russlan, who is one of her three suitors. Ludmilla chooses Russlan, but during the betrothal festivities evil spirits whisk her away to the realm of the dwarf-wizard, Chernomor. Ludmilla's father promises her hand to whichever of the three suitors rescues her. After many fantastic adventures, Russlan defeats Chernomor, but not before the wizard has cast Ludmilla into a magic sleep. Unable to waken her, Russlan is carrying her back to Kiev, when she is abducted again, this time by a wicked fairy, who transports her to Kiev and makes it appear that she was rescued by one of Russlan's rivals. Fortunately the rival is also unable to waken her. At last Russlan arrives and, armed now with a magic ring, wakens Ludmilla himself. Amid general rejoicing the young couple are united.

The Overture opens with two vigorous themes, both from the final scene of rejoicing, and both consisting of brilliant *tutti* chords followed by even more brilliant, dashing scales. The bright colors and transparent texture of Glinka's orchestration established a Russian tradition, which echoes into the twentieth-century orchestra of Rimsky-Korsakoff, Stravinsky, and Prokofieff.

The contrasting lyric theme of the Overture is a fervent melody from Russlan's second-act aria, a battlefield scene, where his thoughts turn to Ludmilla. We hear it first in the warm tenor tones of cellos and violas with bassoon reinforcement:

The development of all three themes and reprise of all but the first, hew close to Classical sonata-allegro form. In the coda we hear the theme of the wicked Chernomor, its descending whole-tone scale proclaimed by trombones. But the threat of Chernomor is brief and the jubilation of the final bars recalls the fairy-tale formula: "They lived happily ever after."

The Overture to *Russlan and Ludmilla* is scored for 2 flutes, 2 oboes, 2 clarinets, 2 bassoons, contrabassoon, 4 horns, 2 trumpets, 3 trombones, kettledrums, and the customary strings.

Christoph Willibald Gluck

Born July 2, 1714, Erasbach near Nürmberg—died November 15, 1787, Vienna

OVERTURE TO ALCESTE

Gluck was one of the great revolutionists. Since he lived in an age of revolution, it was no wonder that he was ultimately attracted to Paris, the great focal point of social, artistic and political change. First produced in Vienna in 1767, Gluck's *Alceste* was radically revised for its Paris production of 1776.

Gluck's revolution was directed against the courtly tradition of *opera seria:* its high artifice, its polite conventions, which were part and parcel of the rigid social-political structure of the *ancien régime.* More specifically, his operas embodied the stormy emotions, the "Storm and Stress" which invaded the European arts during the seventeen-sixties and seventies. To his contemporaries, Gluck's *Orfeo, Alceste* and his two *Iphigénies* were overwhelmingly emotional experiences. If we today label them Classical, in the restricted meaning of cool, restrained, balanced, etc., we distort them, we bar ourselves from hearing the passion that was and is the vital center of his art. Gluck's operas were no more "coolly Classical" than were the so-called Neoclassical paintings of his contemporary, Jacques-Louis David. Both artists used ancient Greek subjects to communicate feelings of revolutionary violence.

Although Gluck's *Alceste* is based on Euripides, the opera is centered on a single idea: the power of love to conquer death. Admetus, King of Thessaly, is mortally ill and doomed to die unless before sundown another mortal can be found who is willing to sacrifice himself in Admetus's place. His most devoted subjects shrink in terror. Only his wife Alceste loves him so deeply that she embarks on the terrifying journey to the Underworld. The fact that Alceste is restored to her husband at the very end does not mitigate the anguish of her ordeal.

When Gluck first published his *Alceste* in 1769, he outlined his aims in a famous preface. "I resolved," he declared, "to divest *Alceste* entirely of all those abuses which have so long disfigured Italian opera and made of the most splendid and most beautiful of spectacles the most ridiculous and wearisome." In addition to radically simplifying the dramatic action and vocal style Gluck declared: "I felt that the Overture ought to apprise the spectators of the nature of the action that is to be represented and to form, so to speak, its argument."

The opening measures of the Overture to *Alceste* alternate loud outbursts of the full orchestra with soft, sighing phrases for the violins. It is as if the inexorable power of the Underworld were confronting the pathetic pleas of helpless humans. The key is D minor: a tonality normally avoided in the courtly *opera seria,* because of the association of minor keys in general with sadness, and of D minor with despair and tragedy. The trombones, so prominent in *Alceste,* were associated with religious music and the supernatural. None of the Overture is taken from the opera itself. It simply amplifies in varying forms the basic conflict of its opening bars.

Since the Overture leads directly into the opening scene of the opera without coming to a full close, concert performances necessarily are given a formal conclusion. Felix Weingartner, whose arrangement is often used, adds the orchestral background for the first chorus at the rise of the curtain, and concludes with twenty-nine additional bars adapted from the opening of the Overture. Weingartner's score calls for the same instruments as Gluck's 1776 Paris version of the Overture, but with certain balances changed (chiefly by deleting some of Gluck's instrumental doubling) in order to achieve greater variety of instrumental color. The instruments of Gluck's Paris version are 2 flutes, 2 oboes, 2 clarinets, 2 bassoons, 2 horns, 3 trombones, and the traditional body of strings.

OVERTURE TO IPHIGENIA IN AULIS

Fifteen years before the Bastille fell, an operatic French revolution took place in Paris under the auspices of Marie-Antoinette. Gluck's *Iphigénie en Aulide* took the Paris Opera by storm on the evening of April 19, 1774 and that night was the beginning of the end as far as the *ancien régime* of Baroque French opera was concerned. A great, indeed royal tradition, founded by Lully and crowned by the masterworks of Rameau, came crashing to ruin in the space of a few years.

The director of the Opera had foreseen this. When Gluck's *Iphigénie en Aulide* was first offered to him, he had made a surprising reply: if Gluck would contract to write *six* such operas for the Opera, he would be extremely interested; otherwise not, since *one* such opera would merely have the effect of killing all the old French repertory. Fortunately for Gluck, he had been music master to Marie-Antoinette before she left her home at the court of Vienna. Now that she inhabited Versailles as wife of the future Louis XVI, she was in a position to persuade the director of the Opera to reconsider his rejection. She did, and he did. Later, after Gluck had produced three operas in Paris, he did contract to write three more (for a total of six, as the director had suggested). And the old repertory did crumble away.

A prominent point in Gluck's revolution was the overture. Instead of the old-fashioned Italian opera overture, which had normally been a piece apart, a merely festive prelude to the evening's entertainment, Gluck decided that an overture "ought to apprise the spectators of the nature of the action that is to be represented and to form, so to speak, its argument." This idea was not entirely new. Critics of French opera had long since pushed this point of view and Rameau had made some attempts to put it into practice.

The action of *Iphigénie en Aulide* revolves about the goddess Diana's demand that King Agamemnon sacrifice his daughter Iphigenia in order to obtain the favorable wind which will enable the Greek fleet to sail forth to wage war against Troy. In the first scene we find Agamemnon protesting to Diana that he will never carry out the horrible sacrifice she demands. Agamemnon's opening phrase as he invokes "pitiless Diana" sets the pleading mood in which the Overture begins:

The sighs of the woodwinds and strings are interrupted by stern, stark octaves for the orchestra, which might suggest the imperious commands of the goddess. Further pleading phrases and a longer melody of charming simplicity alternate and contrast with the preceding material. The Overture leads without conclusion directly into the first scene of the opera.

The best-known concert conclusion is the characteristically Romantic one of Richard Wagner with its die-away *pianissimo* ending. Closer to the spirit of Gluck is an eighteenth-century conclusion long attributed to Mozart, and more recently to Johann Philipp Samuel Schmidt (1779–1853). Actually this ending, mentioned as early as 1795 in J. J. W. Heinse's famous musical novel, *Hildegarde von Hohental,* is probably by a third, now-forgotten composer. The Overture is scored for 2 flutes, 2 oboes, 2 bassoons, 2 trumpets, kettledrums, and strings.

Edvard Grieg

Born June 15, 1843, Bergen, Norway—died September 4, 1907, Bergen

CONCERTO FOR PIANO AND ORCHESTRA, A MINOR, OPUS 16

"The Chopin of the North" was one great pianist's name for Edvard Grieg. Certainly this Piano Concerto does recall Chopin, who was Grieg's favorite composer. Spiritually, as well as musically, the two had much in common. In Chopin's mazurkas and polonaises we hear the voice of Chopin's native Poland alternately lamenting and exulting over the tragedy and the heroism of the oppressed Polish people.

Although Grieg's Norway had no such tragic history, his country was not happy under the rule of the Swedish King. The longing for full independence gained a national bard, so to speak, in Grieg, whose music was the first to sing an unmistakable language of the North.

Grieg was only twenty-five and newly married when he composed this Concerto. In the summer of 1868 he went with his wife and baby daughter to a secluded country cottage in Denmark, where the A-minor Concerto was written. It was first performed in Copenhagen on April 3, 1869. Grieg may have benefited by the advice of Liszt whom he visited early in the following year. Liszt was enthusiastic, but suggested some changes which Grieg incorporated before publishing the score in 1872. Even after publication, Grieg made further changes and continued to touch up the score until late in life. Meanwhile it became, and long remained, one of the most popular of all piano concertos.

It is in the traditional three movements: fast, slow, fast, the brief middle movement functioning as a sort of slow introduction to the finale, which follows without pause.

I. *Allegro moderato.* The soloist begins with brilliant, crashing chords and octaves plunging from the top range of the piano down to its lowest depths and then sweeping upward in exhilarating waves of arpeggios. The tranquil main theme begins softly in the woodwinds:

It has a flowing continuation in the woodwinds and is soon taken up by the piano. A gracefully drooping second theme which Grieg (on Liszt's advice) gave to a trumpet in his first edition of 1872, is more appropriately begun, in the version we know, by the cello section. It is impetuously developed by the piano soloist before the orchestra takes over. Toward the end of the first movement, there is an extraordinarily exciting cadenza for the piano alone.

II. *Adagio.* The melodious slow movement opens with the tender sound of muted strings. The piano enters with its own theme. At the end, high trills for the piano and a languorous *arpeggio* lead to the corruscating brilliance of the finale, which follows without pause.

III. *Allegro moderato molto e marcato.* The finale is a whirlwind combination of rondo and sonata-allegro form, built around the following principal theme:

This theme, built on the rhythm of a popular Norwegian folk-dance, the *lalling,* serves as the rondo refrain. There is a songful middle section, after which the *lalling* refrain returns and is finally transformed from its original duple meter into another, triple-beat popular dance rhythm: a *springdans.* The conclusion is majestic without lapsing into pomposity.

The A-minor Concerto is scored for 2 flutes, 2 oboes, 2 clarinets, 2 bassoons, 4 horns, 2 trumpets, 3 trombones, kettledrums, and the traditional string choir.

George Frideric Handel

Born February 3, 1685, Halle—died April 14, 1759, London.

CONCERTO GROSSO, OPUS 3, NO. 1, B-FLAT MAJOR

The Baroque grandeur and vitality of this *Concerto grosso,* the exuberant flow of Handel's invention, his range of expression within three short movements —all these are miracles enough in themselves. But when you realize that this is only one masterpiece among a half-dozen in his Opus 3 alone, and that his thirty-odd surviving concertos are the merest fragment from an avalanche-like outpouring of operas, oratorios, and instrumental works on the highest level of inspiration and craftsmanship, you no longer wonder that Beethoven considered Handel to be the greatest composer who ever lived.

Although they were not published until 1734, probably on the occasion of the wedding of Anne, the Princess Royal, to the Prince of Orange, Handel's Opus 3 Concertos seem to have been written largely during the first decade of his years in England, roughly from 1710 to 1720. Their popularity must have been enormous. Twenty-nine printings were issued within a space of some thirty years, according to Frederick Hudson and other Handel scholars.

In contrast to the familiar modern type of solo concerto, which presents a single instrument, usually piano or violin, against orchestral accompaniment, the Baroque *concerto grosso* pitted a whole group of solo instruments against the orchestra. In this B-flat concerto the solo group consists of 2 oboes, 2 recorders, 2 violins, 2 bassoons, and a harpsichord.

The main orchestra of his Opus 3 includes 2 additional oboes (for a total of 4), 6 first and 6 second violins, 4 violas, 3 cellos, 2 string basses, and a second harpsichord.

Thus to modern ears the sound of this Concerto as Handel heard it might seem strangely lean; its grandeur is no mere matter of physical dimension or volume of sound. It is cast in the popular three-movement form (fast-slow-fast) of the Late Baroque *concerto grosso* as established by Vivaldi.

I. *Allegro.* The first movement begins with a vigorous, assertive octave-unison passage for the full orchestral *tutti,* minus the oboes. This is followed by an interlude of oboes alone. In between further *tutti* outbursts we hear the oboes again, and a solo violin with the lightest accompaniment of violins and violas only.

II. *Largo.* The second movement again contrasts the woodwinds (this time recorders, bassoons and a solo oboe) with the string ensemble. A third and very beautiful small combination consists of solo violin, solo bassoon, and solo oboe. It is the violin which leads the group with a graceful undulating melodic line.

III. *Allegro.* The finale is brilliant and vigorous again, somewhat in the manner of the first movement, but with still further variety in the small instrumental combinations (among these, a lively bassoon duet!) which alternate with the dynamic *tutti* sections.

GRAND CONCERTOS (CONCERTI GROSSI) OPUS 6

Handel's Twelve Grand Concertos, Opus 6, are the crowning orchestral achievement of one of the greatest composers who ever lived. Together with the "Brandenburg" Concertos of J. S. Bach, they represent the peak of Late-Baroque orchestral writing. Yet the two sets are as different as the vastly differing natures of the two masters. Both were considered conservative, old-fashioned for their time. Bach's carefully wrought, often "learned," music could nevertheless be dazzlingly brilliant, or playful, when he chose. When Handel wrote in fugal or other "learned" styles, they were often camouflaged by the improvisatory dash of the music, its unpredictable variety of form, which has baffled critics ever since and led some to the naïve conclusion that Handel was undisciplined or lacking in profundity.

It is true that the Twelve Grand Concertos, like so much of Handel's music, were composed at a dizzying speed. At least eleven and probably all twelve were written down between September 29 and October 30, 1739. But Handel was accustomed to operating on dizzying heights.

They are generally referred to as *concerti grossi* because they used the standard Late-Baroque technique of playing off a solo or *small* group (called *concertino*) against a *big* group (called *concerto grosso*) which gave the name to this entire class of composition. Often the *concertino* consisted of only two violins, a cello, and a harpsichord; the *concerto grosso* only a small string orchestra with a second keyboard instrument and perhaps a bassoon or two to reinforce the bass line. This bass part, to which Baroque composers and performers attached such importance, was called a "thoroughbass" (meaning continuous bass) or *basso continuo* or, more briefly, just *continuo.*

The addition of a reinforcing bassoon was automatic when a work included wind instruments, and several of Handel's Opus 6 Concertos did include two oboes—in his original manuscript. But oddly enough, the first edition of these Concertos (printed under Handel's supervision) left out the oboe parts for reasons that have never been satisfactorily explained. Stranger yet, the complete score of these Concertos with their original oboe parts was not published until 1961 (in the scholarly complete edition of Handel: the Hallische Händel-Ausgabe).

There was a time when much ado was made of Handel's generous borrowings—from himself and from other composers. They *were* generous—but they were beside the point. In Handel's day the tradition of borrowing was as old as the art of music. Composers had always borrowed other men's melodies, basses, tenor parts, harmonizations, whole chunks of compositions—even entire older works were incorporated into new ones. And the farther back we go, the rarer it was for a composer to build a new work on any *other* basis than borrowed material. The point then, as now, was not so much the borrowing as how well the composer chose and how creatively he transformed the borrowed material.

CONCERTO NO. 5, D MAJOR

For the first and last movements of this Fifth Grand Concerto, Handel transformed the two-movement Overture of his own *Ode for St. Cecilia's Day* (completed only two weeks earlier) which in turn had borrowed material from a set of delightful keyboard pieces *(Componimenti musicali)* published earlier that year by the Austrian Gottlieb Muffat. The fact that two of the Concerto movements were adaptations may account for the incredible speed, astounding even for Handel, with which he dashed off this score. Begun on October 8, 1739, it was completed on October 10, just two days later!

I. *Larghetto e staccato; Allegro.* One of the most sophisticated music lovers of the generation following Handel, Charles Burney considered this opening movement to be the greatest example of a French overture ever composed. The popular French overture form consisted of two contrasting sections: the first slow and grand, often with jagged, "dotted" rhythms; the second light and lively, often fugal. In this case the fugue is more than lively. It dances, it bounces, it surges ahead with a kind of inexhaustible freshness characteristic of Handel. It leads off with the first violins alone:

In rapid succession this theme is taken up by the second violins, then the violas, according to the rules of the fugal game, after which the theme and fragments of it, are tossed back and forth among the solo instruments of the *concertino* and finally through all sections of the accompanying orchestra as well. This is the only movement of the Concerto that does not include two oboes in the accompanying orchestra.

II. *Presto.* In contrast to the sturdy Overture, this Presto is so thinly orchestrated it seems almost transparent. Four brief chords launch a whirling, twirling, twisting, spiraling violin solo phrase echoed by a second solo violin, then taken up by the violins and finally by other sections of the accompanying orchestra. Before we reach the end, this movement too has accumulated a tremendous dynamic drive.

III. *Largo.* A solemn, sustained melody with a procession of rich harmonies unfolds among the soloists of the *concertino,* much in the style of Arcangelo Corelli, the elder Italian composer whose music Handel had heard and admired in Rome. The same melody and harmonies are then taken up by the full orchestra in alternation and combination with the *concertino.*

IV. *Allegro.* Handel seems to have borrowed the start of this movement from another contemporary even more illustrious than Muffat: namely the harpsichord virtuoso and composer Domenico Scarlatti. The opening phrase, with its profusion of trills, is a greatly altered, yet clearly recognizable version of the principal theme from a Scarlatti harpsichord sonata. But the mood and texture of the movement shift with bewildering speed, to a rising, erupting scale figure, then to a chain of harmonic figurations in which the massed violins play with a shimmering, trembling intensity, a measured *tremolo* of rapidly repeated notes, which we tend to associate with nineteenth-century music but which, in reality, had been cultivated over a century earlier in the stage music of Handel's great predecessor Monteverdi.

V. *Minuet: Un poco larghetto.* The graceful minuet-finale was an instant favorite. Actually, it is a minuet with two variations of increasing grandeur. Thus a movement that began with playful grace ends with the power and sweep characteristic of Handel.

CONCERTO NO. 6, G MINOR

With the borrowed, or rather adapted, material he used in his Concerto No. 5, Handel took only two days to finish that score. For his Concerto No. 6, which is almost entirely original, he took three days: October 12–15. In all five movements, two oboes, double the first and second violins of the accompanying orchestra most of the time.

I. *Largo affettuoso.* Handel's original marking for this opening movement was *Largo e Cantabile* or "slowly and songfully." The change from "songfully" to *affettuoso* ("emotionally" or "with feeling") was a turn toward more modern, subjective description. Yet while Handel asks his performers to play with a "modern" sensibility, his broadly flowing melody and rich harmonies recall his beloved Italian model from the preceding generation: Arcangelo Corelli.

II. *A tempo giusto.* There is no end to Handel's variety! While the fugue of Handel's preceding Concerto seemed to dance, this fugue is dark, complex, craggy. Its striking theme is announced by all the first violins (and, in Handel's manuscript, the first oboe as well):

Handel's fan Charles Burney, one of the greatest critics and connoisseurs of the century, was filled with admiration: "The fugue is remarkably curious in its subject; which is so unobvious and difficult to work, that no composer of ordinary abilities, in this learned species of writing, would have ventured to meddle with it, if such an unnatural series of sounds had occurred to him." The sounds did occur to Handel because he *could* work them, in fact, they opened an unparalleled opportunity.

III. *Musette: Larghetto.* The only reminiscence of the peasant origin of the *musette* (literally bagpipe) is the sustained, drone-like bass which Handel uses from time to time in the course of this remarkable movement. Handel has been accused of adapting his principal theme from his contemporary, Leonardo Leo. However this may be, he gave the opening phrase a particularly dark coloration by using the strings massed in their low register; the violins start together on their lowest note, the open G string, then divide into a duet:

The oboes, which cannot get down that low, duplicate the duet an octave above. The Musette movement, which Handel liked so much that he used it by itself for various concert occasions, is a simple A-B-A form with a powerfully contrasting middle section in C minor.

IV. *Allegro.* An athletically vigorous movement for full orchestra, this has a contrasting middle section in which the first violin soloist displays his agility, dominating the scene almost in the style of a solo violin concerto.

V. *Allegro.* The brief finale is a striding piece of concentrated energy, with the entire orchestra (*concertino* plus *concerto grosso*) fused into a trio-like texture of only three voices. On occasion, for greater emphasis, the ensemble is still further reduced to stark octaves bare of any harmony at all.

CONCERTO, NO. 10, D MINOR

The tenth Concerto in D minor is in five movements:

I. *Ouverture: [Maestoso], Allegro, Lentement.* Handel begins with a form he loved: the traditional French overture. Its slow, majestic introduction in pompous, "dotted" rhythms leads to a lively fugal section based on the following subject:

Six bars of majestic peroration in slow tempo bring the French overture to its powerful close.

II. *Air: Lentement.* This movement could scarcely have been written if it had not been for Handel's love of Italian song and specifically of Italian opera. Although the texture is rich this is primarily melody, *bel canto* for orchestra.

III. *Allegro.* A brief, almost playful movement forms a sort of bridge from the *Lentement* to the following movement.

IV. *Allegro.* This is the only movement of the Concerto in which the small *concertino* plays a major role. It launches the fiery principal theme given to the first violin alone then second violin for four bars before the main orchestra falls in. Again and again those opening bars for the *concertino* violins return first alone, later in combination with the orchestral *ripieno*, in a variety of keys.

V. *Allegro moderato.* The exuberant finale is the only one of the five movements composed in the sunny major mode as opposed to the D minor of the preceding movements.

The Concerto is composed for string orchestra with a harpsichord or other keyboard instrument for the *continuo*, plus a *concertino* for 2 solo violins, solo cello, and a second keyboard instrument.

CONCERTO NO. 12, B MINOR

Although the final Concerto of Handel's Opus 6 is in the key of B minor, the minor mode still retains its tremendous vigor and capacity for joyful expression, as we meet it so often in other Late-Baroque works. Handel's use of the minor mode was still far from having the exclusively melancholy or tragic meaning that it had begun to take on for most Classical and Romantic composers. Even Handel's then-famous contemporary, the composer, theorist, and critic Johann Mattheson (a more "modern" minded man) roundly declared the key of B minor to be "bizarre, disagreeable, and melancholy."

I. *Largo.* Handel's B minor here and throughout this Concerto is bursting with vitality, optimism and exuberance. This opening *Largo* has Handel's characteristic grandeur, which alternates with the delicate *concertino* group of soloists: two violins, a cello and keyboard instrument.

II. *Allegro.* Although the vigorous dotted rhythms of the opening movement suggested the beginning of that favorite Baroque curtain-raiser, the French overture, this *Allegro* dispenses entirely with any hint of the fugal style which normally characterized the second movement of the French overture. Instead we have an impetuous, almost improvised-sounding movement featuring the two solo violins so prominently that for the moment we might easily feel that we are hearing what we might call today a double violin concerto. Again we feel the enormously refreshing spontaneity, the seemingly inexhaustible flow of energy which was a Handelian specialty.

III. *Aria: Larghetto e piano.* Variety was another of Handel's strong points. Here in this beautiful "Air" Handel changes the texture of his entire orchestra and gives us in effect a string trio with a pensively flowing melodic line in the style of a *bel canto* aria:

A repetition of the "Air," officially marked *Variatio,* continues the majestic flow, merely allowing one or more rarely two of the instrumental parts to move in more rapid eighth-notes.

IV. *Largo.* This is a sudden change of mood: a mystery-laden, harmonically complex moment, only seven measures in duration. It serves as a contrast and link between the preceding Aria and the jiglike finale which follows without pause.

V. *Allegro.* Basically, this happy finale is our old friend the Baroque jig, or to use the more elegant spelling of that day, gigue. And like many a Handelian gigue-finale this one starts off as a bustling fugue. But ingenious and virtuosic as the fugue may be, it still has the dash and daring, the improvisational derring-do which are among Handel's most endearing qualities.

The whole minor miracle of this short Concerto is achieved with the simplest orchestral body: the traditional string orchestra plus bassoon and keyboard instrument, which in Handel's day could be either harpsichord or pipe organ, the latter especially if the Concerto was performed between the halves of an oratorio or other sacred work; the *concertino* of two violins, cello, and a second harpsichord or organ.

ROYAL FIREWORKS MUSIC

One of the last and greatest of Handel's orchestral works, his *Royal Fireworks Music,* was commissioned for a great English celebration of the peace (the Treaty of Aix-la-Chapelle) which ended the long and unpopular War of the Austrian Succession. Almost from the moment of the armistice (late in 1748), plans were laid for the festivities which were to include a tremendous display of fireworks and music of matching brilliance. The celebrated Italian architect, stage designer, and fireworks virtuoso Giovanni Niccolò Servandoni was brought over from Paris to stage-manage this spectacular glorification of the peace, which the government decided to hold in London's Green Park. Handel contributed an imposing score which combined the Baroque pomp of the French overture and the rhythmic drive of the Italian *concerto grosso.* Handel apparently wished to use string instruments as well as the warlike brass and winds. But the king declared emphatically that he wanted no "fiddles." And the king's taste is reflected on the first page of the original *Royal Fireworks* manuscript score, which calls for 24 oboes, 9 horns, 9 trumpets, 3 kettledrums, 12 bassoons, and a newly invented instrument, the contrabassoon. Even larger numbers of brasses and winds seem to have been used for various early

FIREWORKS OF APRIL 27, 1749.

The display for which Handel composed his Royal Fireworks Music: anonymous print entitled "The Grand Whim for Posterity to Laugh At." (*Courtesy, The Bettman Archive*)

open-air performances, and the effect was calculated to outdazzle the fireworks.

A preview, or public rehearsal of the *Royal Fireworks Music* was held (without fireworks) on April 21, 1749, in the spacious parklike Vauxhall Gardens. Twelve thousand persons paid half a crown each to attend the rehearsal and, according to the report of *The Gentlemen's Magazine,* the traffic jam on London Bridge was such that carriages took three hours to cross the river.

The official celebration on the evening of April 27 was an anticlimax—as far as the fireworks were concerned. Only a fraction of Servandoni's grand spectacle was ever realized: many fuses of the bombs and rockets would not light, and finally the huge scaffolding which had been errected for the fireworks caught fire itself. Servandoni, in a rage, is said to have drawn his sword upon the Duke of Montague, who was in charge of the festivities. Servandoni was promptly arrested and released on the following day only after appropriate apologies to the noble duke.

Fortunately, the grandest and most impressive movement of Handel's music, the *Ouverture,* had already been performed as a prelude to the fireworks.

In later revisions of the score Handel added strings to his orchestra. There are six movements in all:

I. *Ouverture.* This opening movement, in Handel's most vigorous style, avoids the fugal complexities of the traditional French overture. It is a monumental structure: slow-fast-slow-fast. The very first dozen bars demonstrate Handel's genius for seeming simple, while concealing an art which could seize and hold the attention of a crowd of 12,000. The simple, six-bar opening phrase is immediately repeated, but with a Baroque richness of harmony and melodic growth that grip even the most unmusical listener.

Then, instead of beginning his principal Allegro with a traditional *fugato,* Handel opens with a more dramatic effect. A Baroque device long associated with the *concerto grosso* was the contrasting of instrumental groups—in this case, trumpets, oboes (with strings), and finally French horns:

As these groups begin to overlap, their rhythms grow more dynamic and the texture more complex. But the basic simplicity is maintained by an insistence on such primitive, driving figures as the sweeping downward scales of oboes and violins:

II. *Bourrée.* This is a miniature interlude for small combinations in D minor.

III. *La Paix ("The Peace").* A serenely flowing *Largo alla Siciliana,* this central movement recalls the peaceful pastorales of Baroque Christmas music, but with the added golden sound of nine French horns.

IV. *La Réjouissance: Allegro.* The rejoicing of this brief movement is based on the exuberant Baroque trumpet theme:

V. *Menuet.* This is a subdued, contrasting movement in D minor.

VI. *Menuet.* Apparently, this festive finale in D major was originally performed by oboes and bassoons alone. Later, Handel doubled the wind parts with string instruments and automatically included a harpsichord.

WATER MUSIC

In the days before industrial pollution of water and air, evening pleasure trips on the River Thames were among the favorite warm-weather diversions of London society, including the court and royal family. In the early eighteenth century, these leisurely entertainments, aboard richly caparisoned barges, were surrounded by swarms of gaily bedecked sailboats and other barks, and often accompanied by the royal luxury of a floating orchestra—a whole bargeload of musicians playing "water concerts" or "water serenades." The inexhaustibly fertile Handel composed at least two, probably three or more suites of "water music" for such festive occasions.

It was in the reign of Good Queen Anne that Handel first visited London. Though he was only twenty-five, he had already made a brilliant name for himself in Italy. In England his music was acclaimed by the public and smiled upon by the court. Such was his success that on his second visit in the autumn of 1712 he composed a "Birthday Ode" for the queen as well as the official "Te Deum" celebrating, among other things, England's acquisition of the rock of Gibralter. These works won him a yearly stipend of 200 pounds from the queen and such prestige that he stayed on in fashionable, cosmopolitan London, instead of returning to the provincial German court of Hanover which still claimed his services.

The Elector of Hanover is said to have been annoyed with Handel not merely for overstaying his generous leave of absence, but for glorifying the birthday of Queen Anne and the Peace of Utrecht, which was disliked in Germany. Now the elector's feelings need not have bothered Handel, except for the fact that the elector was heir to the English throne. When Queen Anne died shortly after and the elector arrived in London as George I of England, Handel may have had good reason to worry.

One of the most diverting and hotly contested of musical anecdotes centers on Handel's earliest water music and his reported reconciliation with the king. According to Handel's first biographer, John Mainwaring, a ruse was divised by two influential courtiers: the English Lord Burlington and a German Baron Kilmansegge (or Kilmanseck), whom Handel may have known from Hanover. King George, who seems to have cared more for music than for politics, was persuaded to plan a river party. The date was August 22, 1715, the summer after George's ascent to the throne.

> Handel [writes Mainwaring] was appraised of the design, and advised to prepare some music for that occasion. It was performed and conducted by himself, unknown to His Majesty, whose pleasure on hearing it was equal to his surprise. He was impatient to know whose it was . . . The Baron then produced the delinquent, and asked leave to present him to His Majesty as one who was too conscious of his fault to attempt an excuse for it . . . This intercession was accepted without difficulty. Handel was restored to favor.

Another such royal fete held two summers later (on July 17, 1717) was described by a London newspaper the *Daily Courant*:

> . . . On Wednesday [the 17th] Evening, at about 8, the King took Water at Whitehall in an open Barge, wherein were also the Dutchess of Bolton, the Dutchess of Newcastle, and the Countess of Godolphin, Madam Kilmanseck, and the Earl of Orkney. And went up the River towards Chelsea. Many other Barges with Persons of Quality attended, and so great a Number of Boats, that the whole River in a manner was cover'd; a City Company's Barge was employ'd for the Musick, . . .

A Prussian diplomat in London, Frédéric Bonnet, reported to his government in even greater detail:

> . . . Next to the King's barge was that of the musicians, about 50 in number, who played on all kinds of instruments, to wit trumpets, horns, hautboys, bassoons, German flutes, French flutes, violins and basses; but there were no singers. The music had been composed specially by the famous Handel, native of Halle, and His Majesty's principal Court Composer. His Majesty approved of it so greatly that he caused it to be repeated three times in all, although each performance lasted an hour—namely twice before and once after supper. The [weather in the] evening was all that could be desired for the festivity, the number of barges and above all of boats filled with people desirous of hearing was beyond counting. In order to make this entertainment the more exquisite, Mad. de Kilmanseck had arranged a choice supper in the Late Lord Ranelagh's villa at Chelsea on the river, where the King went at one in the morning. He left at three o'clock and returned to St. James's about half past four.

The earliest (manuscript) scores of the original *Water Music* have disappeared. The most careful modern reconstruction (by Hans F. Redlich in Vol.IV/

13 of Bärenreiter's Hallische Händel-Ausgabe, 1962) includes three groups of *Water Music* pieces, which may well correspond to the three occasions described above (22 August 1715, 17 July 1717, and 26 April 1736).

[SUITE I]

The first group, often referred to as Suite No. I, consists of ten pieces all in F major (except two in the relative D minor). This group is scored for 2 oboes, bassoon, 2 horns, 2 solo violins and four-part string choir, and a *continuo* instrument (probably harpsichord or organ). However, Handel scholars are agreed that neither harpsichord nor organs were customary in open-air performances. The *continuo* parts were presumably added for later, indoor concert performances and almost certainly were not included on the river barges for which the music was originally designed.

Ouverture. This rather grand introductory movement in F major is cast in the popular Baroque form of the French overture, that is to say, it opens with a pompous *Largo* followed by a lively fugal section.

Adagio e staccato. A broadly flowing melody for the oboes is accompanied by slow-moving chords for the string choir.

[*Allegro*]. One of the most brilliant movements of the *Water Music* bears no tempo mark in early editions. It features two solo horns which are played off against the remainder of the orchestra.

Andante. In this contrasting slow movement in D minor, the woodwind group (two oboes and bassoon) alternate and combine with the strings. The end of the movement leads back to a repetition of the preceding [*Allegro*].

[*Allegro*]. Like the preceding section, this one bears no tempo mark in the earliest editions but seems designed for a lively performance, again featuring two solo horns.

Air. The majestic flow of this orchestral melody is among the best remembered from Handel's instrumental works. The entire movement is spun out on the opening rhythm:

Minuet. This stylized dance movement starts as a vigorous duet for two horns alone. The duet is then repeated with the added sonority of strings, oboes, bassoons, and harpsichord. A softly contrasting middle section in F minor omits the brilliant horns and oboes and the movement concludes with a return of the opening strain for full ensemble.

Bourrée. Part of the charm of this airy Bourrée comes from its piquant, shifting rhythms.

Hornpipe. The hornpipe was an ancient English dance performed, in the eighteenth century, as a solo dance for sailors, with folded arms and many characteristic steps and gestures. Handel's movement begins with superb vigor:

[*Allegro*]. A magnificently powerful, driving piece of Handelian counterpoint in D minor, this movement is rarely heard because it is hard to place in performance sequence with other *Water Music* excerpts. Since his manuscripts have not survived, we do not know where Handel himself placed it—possibly in conjunction with other *Water Music* movements now lost.

This entire first group of ten *Water Music* movements is scored for 2 oboes, 1 (or more) bassoons, 2 horns, 2 solo violins, and the standard orchestral string choir (to which a harpsichord would normally have been added for later, indoor performances). There were many such indoor, concert performances during Handel's lifetime and many differing editions of his *Water Music* which was extremely popular.

[SUITE II]

The second group—often called Suite II—includes five pieces in D major. This is the only group that is scored for trumpets *and* horns as well as oboes, bassoons, and strings.

[*Allegro*]. The overture, which has come down to us without title or tempo mark, is a festive, march-like movement in which pairs of trumpets and horns echo each other's increasingly florid fanfares.

Alla Hornpipe. Handel's superbly vigorous tune is one of his most famous, with catchy syncopations and, once more, echoing pairs of trumpets and horns.

Minuet. With its emphasis on trumpets and horns, this is a more vigorous dance than the delicate strains we associate with the minuet of Mozart's day.

Lentement. This is a more stately flowing measure with an almost vocal grace of line: an idiom in which Handel particularly excelled.

Bourrée. Part of the charm of this airy, stylized dance comes from its piquant shifting rhythm. In the earliest version that has come down to us the tune is marked "to be played three times over," presumably with varied instrumentation.

[SUITE III]

The third group of only four dance movements (in G major and minor) is much shorter than Suites I and II. Some movements may have been lost. Barely half of its brief, stylized dance movements have come down to us with any title or tempo mark. These have to be deduced from the character of the music; and even the sequence of the individual movements is somewhat conjectural. They are scored very modestly for one flute (not a recorder but a version of the modern transverse flute), piccolo, 2 oboes, and standard string group plus a keyboard instrument (probably harpsichord) for indoor performances.

[*?Sarabande*]. The popular *sarabande* rhythm, a stately three-quarter beat with accent on the second beat, inspired some of Handel's noblest melodies, both instrumental and vocal.

Rigaudon. One of the lightest and liveliest Baroque dance types, the *rigaudon,* is developed here with striking rhythmic sophistication, syncopations, elided phrases, and shifting phrase lengths. It is followed here by a second Rigaudon in G minor, probably intended to alternate with the first two for a simple A-B-A pattern.

Minuet. For this courtly movement, Handel goes into the key of G minor. A second Minuet in the relative key of B flat was probably intended as the centerpiece of an A-B-A form.

[*?Gigue*]. The burly Scotch-Irish jig was exported to France and returned to the British Isles as the elegant *gigue.* Its driving rhythms made it a favorite for finales of Late-Baroque suites. Here, a pair of *gigues* (one in G major, one in G minor) were probably to be linked in the traditional A-B-A pattern.

Roy Harris

Born February 12, 1898, Lincoln County, Oklahoma

SYMPHONY NO. 3

When Roy Harris's Third Symphony was first performed in 1939, many musicians, including Serge Koussevitzky, the conductor of the Boston Symphony, felt it was the most important symphonic work yet produced in the United States. There was widespread agreement that the Symphony reflected Harris's western American background, an Americanism that was not of the big cities or of Tin Pan Alley, but rather of the more expansive landscape of western prairies and mountains, of stronger and more fundamental emotions than were associated with the entertainments of American jazz. Among the first critics to hail Roy Harris's Third Symphony as a major American score was Leonard Bernstein, then a twenty-year-old Harvard undergraduate. Bernstein reviewed the first performance in February 1939 by the Boston Symphony Orchestra under the direction of Serge Koussevitzky. Writing in the columns of the crusading magazine *Modern Music,* Bernstein called the Harris Symphony "mature in every sense, beautifully proportioned, eloquent, restrained, and affecting." Time has confirmed his judgment.

Harris was born in a log cabin in Lincoln County, Oklahoma, of Scotch-Irish parents who had come to Oklahoma in an oxcart with only an ax, a gun and a few provisions. This was a time when newcomers staked out their claims. They cut down the trees and built their own cabins.

He was five years old when his family moved to California, where he had his schooling, attended the University of California, studied music and composed his first works. Then, in 1926 he had his first work performed, his first trip to New York, and a private fellowship that enabled him to go to Paris to study with Nadia Boulanger. Three years later he returned to the United States, where he has held a number of teaching positions. Serge Koussevitzky was perhaps the most influential conductor in furthering his early career.

The Third Symphony was completed late in 1938. In January 1939 Mr. Harris finished reading the final proofs of the score, and the following month Koussevitzky conducted the Boston Symphony premiere. Like Harris's own feelings about America and the mission of American music, his Symphony is deeply serious. It is straightforward to the point of occasionally seeming awkward. But this trait may one day stand out as a strength.

It is composed in one continuous movement. The total effect is one of strongly organic unity. From the slow-moving, boldly arched melody of the opening, it gathers momentum, the melodic line becomes more graceful, livelier; the spare colors grow in intensity. Despite many contrasts by the way, the line rises inexorably to its climax: a fugal section with violent clashes of the brass instruments. Finally a soaring, dirgelike melody in the violins seems to dominate the angry, rhythmic brass and timpani.

For the program notes of the Boston Symphony premiere Mr. Harris wrote the following structural outline of his Symphony:

Section I. Tragic—low string sonorities.

Section II. Lyric—strings, horns, woodwinds.

Section III. Pastoral—woodwinds with a polytonal string background.

Section IV. Fugue—Dramatic.

A. Brass and percussion predominating:

B. Canonic development of materials from Section II constituting background for further development of fugue.

C. Brass climax, rhythmic motive derived from fugue subject:

Section V. Dramatic—Tragic.

A. Restatement of violin theme of Section I; *tutti* strings in canon with *tutti* woodwinds against brass and percussion developing rhythmic motive from climax of Section IV.

B. Coda—Development of materials from Sections I and II over pedal timpani.

The Third Symphony is scored for 3 flutes, piccolo, 2 oboes, English horn, 2 clarinets, bass clarinet, 2 bassoons, 4 horns, 3 trumpets, 3 trombones, 2 tubas, kettledrums, bass drum, cymbals, triangle, xylophone, vibraphone, and the customary strings.

Joseph Haydn

Born March 31, 1732, Rohrau-on-the-Leitha—died May 31, 1809, Vienna

CONCERTO FOR CELLO AND ORCHESTRA, C MAJOR

This beguiling early Haydn Cello Concerto had been missing for some 200 years when it turned up in 1961 in the Czech National Library of Prague. There was understandable excitement. If it seems odd that a major work by Haydn should lie about unnoticed in a public library for so long, one explanation is that it spent most of the 200 years not in a public library but in the huge private library of one of the greatest noble families in the land. Possibly the family did not realize the importance of its own possessions. The post-World War II confiscation of great private libraries in Czechoslovakia transferred enormous riches to the National Library. Czech musicologists estimated that it would take fifteen to twenty years to catalogue this new wealth. An eighteenth-century manuscript of the long-lost Haydn Cello Concert in C major (H.Vii b:1) was discovered in the music collection formerly owned by the counts of Kolovrat-Krakovský and now a part of the National Library.

Although the manuscript is not in Haydn's hand, its authenticity is well established. Aside from musical traits which point to Haydn's style of the 1760s, we have Haydn's own catalogue of his own works in his own handwriting (the so-called *Entwurf-Katalog*), where he lists the opening measures of his major works, including the C-major Cello Concerto. Other circumstantial details of the manuscript paper, the handwriting, etc., all confirm the authenticity, which was quickly accepted by Haydn authorities.

The honor of presenting the twentieth-century premiere of the Concerto fell to the Prague Spring Festival. Miloš Sádlo was the soloist with the Czechoslovak Radio Symphony Orchestra under the direction of Charles Mackerras on May 19, 1962. Two years later Janos Starker performed the solo part in New York with the Festival Orchestra under the direction of Thomas Dunn.

Haydn must have composed the Concerto during the earliest years of his service with the Esterházy family. When he began this half-century association (1761–1809), the Esterházy princes maintained a private orchestra of a dozen men. In the month when Haydn joined the Esterházy service, two additional violinists were engaged. If we include Haydn himself, that made fifteen regular players. For Haydn was hired not merely as a composer, but in a multitude of capacities, including conducting. This he normally did from his seat at the harpsichord, improvising his own part as he went along, as was the standard practice of the day.

The fourteen regular members of the orchestra accounted for 5 violins (one or more of whom probably played viola), cello, string bass, flute, 2 oboes, 2 bassoons, and 2 horns. But in addition to his regular players, Haydn could borrow from other Esterházy sources: additional winds, trumpeters, and kettledrummers from the military staff, 2 or 3 extra strings from the chapel or church, and so on. In all (according to the Haydn authority H.C. Robbins Landon) Haydn soon was able to muster 14 or 15 string players, 2 flutes, 2 oboes, 2 bassoons, 2 trumpets and horns (occasionally up to the number of 4) for a stately total of 24 to 26 or conceivably even 28 men. But more important than their numbers was the high skill of the players. Haydn was so delighted that he wrote concertos for several of them: for violin, cello, string bass, flute, for 2 horns and, as early as 1761, a concerto for solo horn. His star cellist, for whom he probably wrote this C-major Concerto, seems to have been Joseph Franz Weigl, who served in the Esterházy orchestra from 1761 to 1769, and who was a fine enough musician to have composed himself a concerto, which survived in the archives alongside that of Haydn.

If Haydn's musicians were like latter-day instrumentalists, he must have won their hearts by writing concertos for them. He in turn learned from them more and more about the idiomatic capabilities of each instrument. The results showed fast, both in the freedom and brilliance of Haydn's solo concerto parts, but also in the growing flexibility and resourcefulness of his symphonic writing.

For all its early Classical graces, the C-major Cello Concerto retains traces of older Baroque orchestral practice. As in the old *concerto grosso,* the soloist is very lightly accompanied (often by only 4 string players with harpsichord), while the full orchestra (remaining strings, 2 oboes, 2 horns, and one or 2 bassoons on the bass part) tends to be reserved for introductions, interludes and the conclusions of movements. At the time when Haydn composed this Concerto, he may have had only one cello in his orchestra. For there is no part for any orchestra cello, and during the brief *tutti* sections, the soloist was expected to join the orchestra in a subordinate role. Nowadays the cello soloist is less likely to do this, since twentieth-century cello sections rarely need reinforcement from the soloist.

I. *Moderato.* The principal theme of the opening movement, a lilting, almost dancelike figure, is announced by the ensemble:

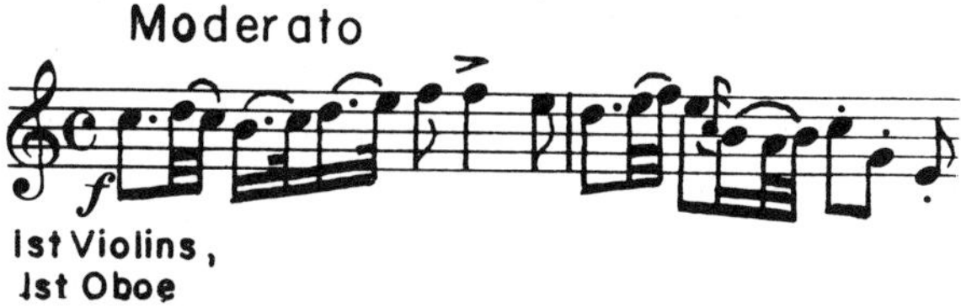

The soloist makes his entrance with the same theme. As is so often the case in Haydn's first movements, there is no strongly contrasting theme. Both the central development section and the concluding reprise are dominated by the principal theme quoted above. The lively solo part holds the center of the stage right up to the grand moment of display in his final cadenza.

II. *Adagio.* The slow middle movement is based on a refrain which combines Rococo graces with the newly fashionable "sensibility," or *Empfindsamkeit,* as the Germans call it. The soloist makes his poetic entrance with a long-held soft note while the orchestra repeats the initial refrain. There are two mildly contrasting sections and two further returns of the basic refrain. The movement concludes, as did the first, with a cadenza for the soloist.

III. *Allegro molto.* The breezy finale centers about a tiny thematic fragment given out in the opening bars by the violins and oboes:

Haydn must have enjoyed the way he introduced his soloist in the slow movement, with that long-held tone, for he did the same thing in this movement, though with an entirely different effect. The solo cello enters with a long sustained tone while the orchestra repeats the opening theme. But this time the breathless activity of the orchestra seems too exciting for the soloist to bear and he soon abandons the sustained tone and goes zipping up the scale to join the orchestra in its quicksilver play. Haydn uses the central section largely for a display of the soloist's virtuosity. There are a few harmonic surprises (notably excursions into the minor mode), but the soloist's virtuosity continues to dominate the scene up to the final exuberant bars of the Concerto.

CONCERTO FOR CELLO AND ORCHESTRA, D MAJOR

Haydn composed this, the finest of his cello concertos, in 1783 for Anton Kraft, the first cellist in the orchestra of their master, Prince Nikolaus Esterházy. We do not know the precise occasion for which it was composed, but the Viennese musicologist Leopold Nowak has suggested that it may have been for the wedding of Prince Nikolaus to the Princess Maria Josepha Hermengild Liechtenstein, which took place at the Liechtenstein Palace in Vienna on September 15, 1783. The prince would naturally have had his famous orchestra on hand for such an occasion.

A virtuoso of considerable reputation, Anton Kraft was born in 1752 near Pilsen. His father was a brewer, but a music lover too, and he encouraged his son to play the cello. Young Kraft went to Vienna, and before he was twenty-six years old Haydn persuaded him to come to Esterháza. He entered on his duties there on New Year's Day of 1778 and remained until the orchestra was disbanded in 1790. Haydn obviously continued his high regard for Kraft, for he taught him composition as well as composing this Concerto for him.

It was not published until 1810 (by Anton André in Offenbach with the notice on the title page, "Edition from the composer's manuscript"). Soon after, the manuscript disappeared, with the result that the authenticity of the Concerto began to be questioned as early as 1835 and again at intervals for over one hundred years. Among others, Anton Kraft himself was often suggested as the composer. But midway into our century Haydn's manuscript, which had been in private hands, was confided to the Austrian National Library in Vienna for safekeeping. The first page of the manuscript bears the inscription in Haydn's hand: "*Concerto per il violoncello . . . di me Giuseppe Haydn mp 1783* [by me, Joseph Haydn, in my handwriting, 1783]," and at the end, under the last bar of the music, Haydn's usual pious thanksgiving: "*Laus Deo.*"

I. *Allegro moderato.* The first movement is in Classical concerto form. The opening orchestral *tutti* presents the two principal themes, the more important being the first:

As so often in Haydn, the second theme has a strong family relation to the first.

The solo cello enters with a slightly embroidered version of the principal theme. The central development section consists more of virtuoso passage-work for the soloist than of thematic development in the style of Haydn's later works. The reprise of the opening themes is followed by an *ad libitum* cadenza for the cello.

II. *Adagio.* The slow movement is built around a recurring refrain announced by the cello solo:

The refrain is echoed by the orchestra and there follow contrasting episodes for *tutti* and solo. As in the first movement, there is a cadenza at the close.

III. *Allegro.* The finale, perhaps the most engaging of the three movements, is a bouncy little rondo with the following refrain:

In between the recurrences of the rondo refrain there are three contrasting episodes in a bravura style. The Concerto concludes with a fourth extended and varied statement of the refrain.

For many years before the rediscovery of Haydn's manuscript it was customary to play an "improved" version of the Concerto by the Belgian scholar Gevaert, who filled out the orchestra by adding 2 flutes, 2 clarinets and 2 bassoons. Most present-day performances use Haydn's orchestration, which calls for only 2 oboes, 2 horns, and the traditional body of strings. Contemporary custom also called for a bassoon and harpsichord (or piano) to round out the ensemble.

CONCERTO FOR CLAVIER AND ORCHESTRA, D MAJOR

The last, greatest and most popular of Haydn's clavier concertos is a flattering reflection of the world in which it was written: the fairy-tale world of Esterháza. Conjured out of a lonely eastern Hungarian plain, this dazzling domain of the Esterházy princes was modeled on the palace and gardens of Versailles. Like its model, Esterháza was a world apart—an aristocratic preserve of conscious glamor, grace, wit, learning and display based on seemingly limitless wealth.

In this world Haydn wore the livery (albeit very splendid livery) of a servant; his social status approached that of a highly prized kitchen chef. But there were enormous compensations.

First, Haydn was what we might call today a composer-in-residence to the autocratic Esterházy princes in a society in which music and musicians were an aristocratic status symbol. Quite aside from the personal pleasure Haydn's music gave them, it was a matter of princely Esterházian pride not only to have the most gorgeous palace and impressive gardens on their gigantic country estate, to wear the most glittering clothes, to savor the finest foods and wines, but also to entertain themselves and their constant swarm of guests with the most attractive music that good taste and money could buy. This called for, among other amenities, their private resident orchestra, solo and choral singers for regular concerts and operas in their palace and their private opera house on the palace grounds. Even in the heyday of eighteenth-century aristocratic patronage, few composers had such lavish forces at their disposal as did Haydn.

But more important than what Veblen would have called the conspicuous consumption aspect of his situation was the insatiable musical appetite of Haydn's employers and their guests. These included the cream of European aristocracy and royalty, a high proportion of whom were skilled amateur performers and even composers. They were sophisticated listeners. If Queen Marie-Antoinette of France did not visit Esterháza, her mother, the Empress of the Holy Roman Empire, did. And although the Empress had the not-inconsiderable forces of the Vienna Imperial-Royal Opera at her beck and call, she declared afterward that when she wanted to hear a good opera, she went to Esterháza.

In addition to composing, selecting, arranging and conducting opera at Esterháza, Haydn was expected to provide an unending stream of outdoor music, marches, serenades, chamber music of many kinds, cantatas, incidental music for dramatic productions, religious music for services in chapel and church, clavier music (which could mean either harpsichord or, in later years, piano), as well as symphonies and concertos.

Finally Haydn enjoyed another important compensation for his near-menial rank in the glittering, but still largely feudal world of Esterháza: a material security undreamed-of today. As a faithful family servant, "our worthy Haydn" became a permanent fixture on the Esterházy estate, with an increasingly generous salary, permanent living quarters for himself and his wife, a horse and carriage at his disposal, fuel for his stoves and a comfortably long list of perquisites which today would be called fringe benefits.

As a provider of, first, musical entertainment, then of immortal masterpieces and as a status symbol, Haydn was successful beyond the most ambitious imaginings of any Esterházy. For Haydn's fame soon outstripped that of his employers. While he was still resident at Esterháza, Haydn became an international celebrity wooed and pirated by publishers, managers, copyists, public institutions and amateur collectors from the University of Oxford to the King of Naples. And the powerful dynasty of Esterházys might have been dumbfounded to be told that they would be remembered two centuries later chiefly as the lucky employers of their "worthy Haydn."

We know that Haydn, among his other accomplishments, played the harpsichord as well as the somewhat newfangled fortepiano. So there seems little reason to doubt that he was the soloist (as well as conductor) in the first performance of this charming Concerto, which seems to have been written at Esterháza some time before 1782, more probably before 1780. Whether it was first performed on harpsichord or piano we may never know. The autograph manuscript is lost. Haydn's first and only mention of it in his correspondence calls it a concerto for clavier, which can mean either instrument, and the earliest surviving edition (of about 1784) says that it is for either "*clavicembalo o fortepiano*." A joyous piece of entertainment music, it has no more serious aim than to beguile us. It is in the traditional three movements of Classical concerto form.

I. *Vivace.* The irresistible gaiety and vitality of the first movement center about the pert little theme launched at once by the first violins:

As was often Haydn's preference, there is no real constrasting theme. The soloist makes his entrance with the principal theme, which is chopped into little bits and mixed with darting scales and brilliant harmonic figurations to build an excitingly dynamic whole.

II. *Un poco adagio.* In this slow movement the intricate Rococo graces of the solo part suit the silvery sustaining tone of the piano quite as well as the pinpoint glitter of the plucked harpsichord. The movement is in a simple A-B-A form, in which the return of the A section is decked out in ever more fanciful Rococo garlands of embellishments.

III. *Rondo all'ungherese: Allegro assai.* The rollicking exuberance of many a Hungarian folk dance echoes in the opening refrain of this "Rondo in Hungarian Style":

Originally a rondo was a piece characterized by mechanical returns of its opening refrain. But Haydn juggles his rondo form with breathtaking boldness and freedom. The very first episode wanders off into minor keys, transforming the opening refrain:

The skill of the master hand is concealed by the naturalness and spontaneity of the music, as it rushes from one episode to another, sometimes only hinting at the rondo refrain and ending in a whirl of sixteenth-notes derived from the opening measure.

Aside from the standard string choir, the score for this Concerto calls only for 2 oboes and 2 horns. Custom called for one or 2 bassoons to double the orchestral bass and the harpsichord (or piano) to join in the orchestral *tutti* as a thorough-bass instrument whenever it was not specifically featured as the solo instrument.

CONCERTO FOR TRUMPET AND ORCHESTRA, E-FLAT MAJOR

Haydn's last and finest Concerto was composed as an experiment—or at least to help with an experiment. The standard orchestral trumpet of Haydn's day was a very limited instrument, confined largely to a rigid pattern of few notes in its middle register. The virtuoso art of the old Baroque trumpeters with their dazzling acrobatics in the trumpet's highest register, had died out. The nineteenth-century valve trumpet, able to play all the notes of the scale (including the chromatic semitones), had not yet been invented. In an effort to break through the trumpet's cramping limitations, Haydn's friend Anton Weidinger, a trumpeter of the Court Orchestra in Vienna, devised a new kind of trumpet with keys (something like those on the modern saxophone) which made it possible to fill in the notes of the scale.

Haydn, who had been an avid experimenter for most of his career, could hardly fail to be interested now. Late in 1795 he returned to Vienna from London where he had just composed his last and greatest Symphony. The sixty-three-year-old master was looking for new musical worlds to conquer. The oratorio was on his mind for he had been overwhelmed in London, had burst into sudden tears, at a performance of Handel's *Messiah*. But the concerto too was a field Haydn had not cultivated in many years—not for ten years in fact. The impulse of friendship strengthened the lure of experimentation. In 1796 Haydn composed the exuberantly youthful, the richest and most brilliant of his Concertos for his friend Weidinger.

We do not know when Weidinger first performed this Concerto; we know only that the Concerto outlasted the instrument for which it was written. It seems that the keys of Weidinger's keyed trumpet sadly dulled the instrument's tone, but they could not dull Haydn's zest or his inventive mind. The Concerto is not only the best, but the most popular he ever wrote. It has three movements:

I. *Allegro.* Since an outstanding quality of this Concerto is brilliance, Haydn sagaciously begins his first movement very softly. The first violins announce the principal theme:

The basic themes of the entire movement are all presented by the brief opening orchestral *tutti*. The solo trumpet makes its entrance with exactly the same theme as the one mentioned above, but the continuation is considerably expanded as compared with the orchestral introduction and a mildly contrasting second theme is presented in the traditional dominant key.

II. *Andante.* The songful middle movement is pensive and purposely darker in mood than the two outer movements. It is in a very simple three-part A-B-A form with a middle section in which Haydn obviously delights to exploit the new capabilities of Weidinger's experimental instrument, especially its potential for playing consecutive chromatic tones in its middle register. This new capability not only allows Haydn to write a strikingly innovative melodic line but to delve suddenly into distant tonalities, which would have been inaccessible to the standard trumpet of the day. Passages like the following must have sounded startling indeed to the listeners who first heard them:

III. *Allegro.* Once more, since this is to be a dazzling finale, Haydn begins with a whisper. Only violins and violas combine in an diaphonous web of sound. The strand of melody in the first violins presents this simple refrain:

This finale is in one of Haydn's favorite forms, one he invented himself: a combination of rondo and sonata form. The violin melody given above serves as both the principal theme of the sonata form and as the recurrent refrain of the rondo. Having begun in a whisper, it is immediately repeated in a loud and joyous orchestral *tutti.* This is not the place to dissect a finale of such spontaneous brio. But the appreciative listener can hardly miss the dramatic surprises with which Haydn spices the coda of his entire work. Sudden outbursts of *tremolo* for the entire string body, are followed by equally sudden *pianissimo* passages of *tremolo.* And the harmonic twists are just as startling.

Just before the end there is a place for the trumpet soloist to show his mettle with a cadenza of his own invention. The orchestra then falls in, not in the usual clamorous *tutti,* but once more in a whisper tinged with a melancholy minor harmony which then gives way at the last moment to the familiar festive repeated cadences of Classical tradition.

The Concerto is scored for pairs of flutes, oboes, bassoons, horns, and trumpets, with kettledrums and the customary strings.

SINFONIA CONCERTANTE, B-FLAT MAJOR

The eighteen months of Haydn's first visit to London (January 1791 to the summer of 1792) were among the happiest in his life. They were months of intoxicating fulfillment for the modest composer, now recognized as one of the greatest artists of his century; and they were months of richness and excitement for the fortunate subscribers to Salomon's concerts, where Haydn's new works, including his *Sinfonia concertante* were performed under his own direction. And there is every sign the Londoners knew what they were getting and enjoyed it to the hilt.

A bit of their excitement glints through even the quaintly formal reports (one cannot really call them reviews) in the London press of the day. Three days after Salomon's fourth concert of the 1792 season on March 9, the *Morning Herald* reported the premiere of Haydn's *Sinfonia concertante*:

> The last performance at SALOMON'S Concert deserves to be mentioned as one of the richest musical treats which the present season has afforded. A new concertante from HAYDN combined with all the excellencies of music; it was profound, airy, affecting, and original, and the performance was in unison with the merit of the composition. SALOMON particularly exerted himself on this occasion, in doing justice to the music of his friend HAYDN.

According to the *Morning Chronicle,* Haydn shone with even "more than his usual luster," the new *Sinfonia concertante* being performed "with admirable effect."

> The *solo* parts were finely contrasted with the "full tide of harmony" of the other instruments, and they were very ably sustained by the respective performers.
>
> The new Overture of the former Friday [i.e., the Symphony in B flat, No. 98, which had had its world premiere one week earlier] was repeated: it is one of the grandest compositions we ever heard, and it was most loudly applauded; the first and last movements were encored.

Nowadays, of course, we have been trained to take our symphonic pleasures so solemnly that we hardly dare applaud between movements. Who among us would be so uncouth as to call for an encore? And, in the unlikely event of such a call, what conductor would be so naïve as to comply? Haydn, however, was delighted by encores. He reported them in his letters and he recorded them in his diary with obvious pride. Our churchlike silence would probably have hurt his feelings.

The enthusiasm of Haydn's London audience was so great that he put the *Sinfonia concertante* on the program of the concert for his own benefit two months later, and it was repeated again on February 24, 1794.

The eighteenth-century *Sinfonia concertante,* as the title suggests, was a sort of cross between a Classical symphony and a concerto, except that the soloists were two or more in number. In this case there were four soloists headed by Salomon himself, who was not only the resourceful impresario of his concert series, but an accomplished violinist and his own concertmaster. The other three soloists, who must have been virtuosos in their own rights, were a cellist, an oboist, and a bassoon player.

Haydn's manuscript, which appears to have been written in great haste, is no complex symphonic structure. It makes no attempt to plumb emotional depths or to scale any heights except the airy spaces above the staff, where the soloists could glitter and float with elegant ease, Salomon in particular beguiling his subscribers with the sweetness of his tone. There are three movements.

I. *Allegro.* The graceful opening measures set the tone for the entire *Concertante* and lay the foundation for the sonata-form first movement:

There is no formal orchestral exposition such as we find in most Classical solo concertos. As if he were impatient to let his soloists shine, Haydn has them pick up the thread of conversation almost at once from the orchestral *tutti.* And the conversation never flags. It is witty, charming, ingenious, with some startling harmonic shifts and sudden dramatic pauses. The orchestral *tutti* intervenes only rarely, chiefly to clarify the formal layout of the movement. Haydn himself supplied a lighthearted cadenza in which all four soloists take equal part just before the concluding bars.

II. *Andante.* The middle movement could scarcely be more lyric than the first, but its lyricism flows at a statelier pace set by the solo violin:

The soloists take turns embroidering the theme, or accompanying each other in fluttering thirty-second notes. The orchestra is kept discreetly in the background.

III. *Allegro con spirito.* The unconventional finale begins with an aggressive unison-octave version of the principal theme, serving here as introduction to a violin solo in the style of an operatic recitative. But just when things sound as if they might be getting serious, the solo violin proposes the following creampuff theme:

It is a delicious trifle which cannot be made to sound important even when it is echoed with the sonority of the full orchestra. But importance is the last thing on Haydn's mind. A second orchestral repetition of the theme serves merely to catapult the four soloists into an even livelier conversation. But lighthearted as their exchanges may be, they never become conventional.

The principal theme quoted above might well suggest a rondo finale, but Haydn's fancy is not to be tied down to any such standard form. Even when he leads us to think we have reached the moment for a traditional cadenza, he substitutes the mock-serious recitative from the introduction. One more dramatic harmonic wrench, one more breathtaking pause, and the end is upon us, complete with Haydn's habitual pious words: "Fine laus Deo."

In addition to the four solo instruments—oboe, bassoon, violin and cello—the accompanying orchestra calls for flute, 2 oboes, 2 bassoons, 2 horns, 2 trumpets, kettledrums, and the traditional string choir.

SYMPHONY NO. 22, E-FLAT MAJOR, THE PHILOSOPHER

How in the world did Haydn come to be thought a conventional composer? By what malicious irony could one of the boldest, most original experimental, most prophetic composers of his age have been represented as a custodian of convention, a periwigged "Papa" Haydn, whose shallow brain never penetrated below what Berlioz called "the innocent joys of the fireside and the *pot-au-feu*? But the misunderstanding grew. Eighty years after his death, Haydn's ghost was invoked to crush César Franck's new D-minor Symphony, with its beautiful English horn solo.

"That a symphony?" sneered a professor of the Paris Conservatory after the premiere of 1889. "But my dear sir, whoever heard of writing for the English horn in a symphony? Just mention a single symphony by Haydn or Beethoven introducing the English horn. There, well, you see—your Franck's music may be whatever you please, but it will certainly never be a symphony!"

The professor's familiarity with Haydn was as shaky as his logic. For one hundred and twenty-five years earlier, Haydn *had* composed a symphony not with one but two English horns: the Symphony in E-flat we know today as "The Philosopher."

The Symphony No. 22 was composed in 1764 for Haydn's new master, Prince Anton Esterházy, whose court was still at Eisenstadt. (The famous palace at Esterháza was not inhabited until 1766.) During his five years' service at Eisenstadt, Haydn composed some nineteen symphonies, of which three (Numbers 18, 21, and 22) are cast in the archaic, Late-Baroque church-sonata sequence: slow-fast-slow-fast.

I. *Adagio.* The fact that the first movement uses muted violins in addition to the striking combination of English and French horns must make its sheer physical sound almost unique in symphonic literature. Unusual too is the majestic pace of the chorale-like principal melody, carried alternately by the French and English horns:

The slow-moving melody standing out contrapuntally against the "walking" bass line recalls the Baroque concerto and organ chorale. H. C. Robbins Landon, in his monumental work *The Symphonies of Joseph Haydn,* suggests that this melody may in fact be an ancient chorale melody which so far has eluded identification.

II. *Presto.* Haydn continues to use his pair of English horns in this and subsequent movements of the Symphony, but since the violins play in their normal, unmuted tone, the color effect is not so striking. This lively little second movement is cast in familiar sonata-allegro form with the following principal theme:

The second theme is so unobstrusive that it barely makes itself felt, and Haydn emphasizes the dominance of the principal theme by bringing it back in the original key soon after the start of the development section with a characteristically playful device sometimes known as a "false recapitulation."

III. *Menuetto.* The simple minuet, with a mildly contrasting "trio" section halfway through, keeps to accepted form and style, with its politely symmetrical phrases and balanced repetitions.

IV. *Finale: Presto.* The Finale, built on a popular jig rhythm, uses themes which recall the fanfares of hunting horns. It begins softly with the following phrase in the violins:

It grows more exuberant as it progresses and ends in a burst of high spirits.

When we consider that the string choir for which Haydn composed this Symphony numbered at most sixteen: 9 violins, 2 violas, 2 cellos, 2 basses, and of course a harpsichord, we can imagine how the 2 English horns and the 2 French horns must have stood out. A bassoon was probably added to reinforce the orchestral bass, at least in the last three movements.

SYMPHONY NO. 26, D MINOR, LAMENTATIONE

This rebellious little Symphony does not fit our familiar inherited picture of Haydn. But what a prim little caricature that is. Periwigged "Papa" Haydn, the father of the symphony, who was content to be the liveried servant of a motheaten *ancien régime,* a corrupt Establishment embodied in the fairy-tale wealth of the Esterházy princes! In the eyes of the Romantic nineteenth century, Haydn was an all-too-willing prisoner of the Rococo social, artistic, and emotional patterns into which he was born; he was a stunted spirit who could see the French Revolution only as an overgrown riot, Napoleon as an ambitious bandit, and who referred sarcastically to bumptious young Beethoven as "the Grand Mogul." Today we know enough, we have *heard* enough, to realize how misleading that picture is.

Incredible as it may sound, a sampling in depth of Haydn's symphonies would not have been possible even one generation ago. Not until the late 1960s was the *first* complete edition of Haydn's Symphonies published: this giant undertaking by two major Viennese publishing houses, Universal Edition and Doblinger Verlag, was accomplished under the editorship of the eminent American scholar H. C. Robbins Landon, a century and a half after the composer's death.

The "Lamentatione" Symphony is a landmark of rebellion in Haydn's development. It is the first of a set of a half-dozen Haydn symphonies dating from 1768 through 1772, all composed in minor keys (which had been virtually taboo in polite entertainment music). All of these symphonies are deeply agitated, some even tragic in expression, all of them deliberately avoiding the surface charm, the merely sensuous appeal long considered essential to any music worth the name. And Haydn was not alone. While he was composing his "Lamentatione," Jean-Jacques Rousseau was writing his sensational *Confessions.* In England Horace Walpole had just published the first of the great "Gothic" horror novels, *The Castle of Otranto.* A deep groundswell of emotional revolt against Classical rules, reason and decorum was sweeping the European arts, literature, drama and music. A vogue for violent emotion, which the Germans dubbed *Sturm und Drang* or Storm and Stress, was approaching its peak in such theatrical works as Goethe's *Götz von Berlichingen* and Schiller's *Die Räuber* and *Kabale und Liebe.*

Measured against such heaven-storming cataclysms Haydn's may seem a modest revolt. But revolt it was and exploration, too, which enriched and deepened Haydn's art for the rest of his life and blazoned new paths for Mozart, Beethoven and many a lesser mind.

I. *Allegro assai con spirito.* The opening measures are a furious rhythmic onslaught rather than a theme, a persistent, almost obsessive syncopation over shifing D-minor harmonies: a prophecy of the opening of Mozart's great D-minor Piano Concerto. Heavy *appoggiatura* sighs interrupt the agitation, but only momentarily. Suddenly, without transition or modulation of any kind, the orchestra plunges into a contrasting section, which in a conventional symphony might be called the second theme. Here, in the heart of the orchestral texture, half-camouflaged by the lively motion of the first violins, Haydn introduces a stern little tune, which Landon was able to identify as a local Austrian variant of an ancient liturgical recitation tone for the reading of the Gospel Passions during the celebration of the Mass in Holy Week. This inner voice is carried by a solo oboe with the second violins:

Since Haydn's Catholic listeners were more faithful churchgoers than modern audiences, they presumably recognized the chant and its significance at once, particularly if, as seems likely, the Symphony was performed in Holy Week. After a brief development, the Symphony's opening burst of agitation is followed once more by the liturgical chant, now made more prominent by the addition of a French horn to the oboe and second violins.

II. *Adagio.* Even more than the first movement, the pensive *Adagio* is dominated by a liturgical chant, this one drawn from a local variant of the traditional recitation tone for the initial letters of the Lamentations of Jeremiah:

Again it is the solo oboe and the second violins which carry the plainchant in the heart of the symphonic texture, while a more gracefully moving melody is sung by the first violins. Tiny interludes between phrases of the chant recall the interludes which traditionally separated the phrases of Lutheran chorales in the organ chorale preludes of J. S. Bach and other great German composers. As in the first movement, the final recall of the chant is reinforced by the addition of a French horn. Haydn embellishes the closing page of the movement with some subtle harmonic surprises before allowing the music to die away to a Romantic *pianissimo.*

III. *Menuet.* Haydn concludes with a deliberate note of understatement. The lack of a conventionally lively fourth movement led for a while to speculation that such a finale had been composed and was lost. But Landon believes that the three-movement form was Haydn's original intention. The somber Minuet is far indeed from the atmosphere of the Rococo ballroom. Its melody is angular, its harmonic implications tense, and the Minuet proper culminates in a true canon in which the violins imitate at a lag of one measure the melody of the low strings. The central trio section brings us the most nearly playful measures of the entire Symphony, after which the Minuet section returns to round off the movement and the Symphony with a quiet lack of ostentation.

The score of Symphony No. 26, conspicuously lacking the gentle tone of flutes, calls only for 2 oboes, 2 horns, and the conventional string choir, to which a bassoon would have been added as well as a harpsichord to round out the ensemble according to the continuo practice of Haydn's time.

SYMPHONY NO. 31, D MAJOR, HORNSIGNAL / ON THE LOOKOUT

From the frieze of stags in the paleolithic cave of Lascaux to our own savage century, hunting, with its magic, its rituals and its more innocent joys, has left us a rich heritage of art. One of the liveliest and most sophisticated musical forms in the Middle Ages was the hunting scene: the *caccia* or *chace*. In the eighteenth century "hunting symphonies" were popular. The instrument we call French horn (descended from the hunting horn) had only recently been admitted to the orchestra. In Late-Baroque music these horns often put on virtuoso acrobatic displays rivaling those of the glamorous *clarino* trumpets. In the following Classical era, the horns tended to subside into the more modest role of harmonic "filler." For a few years, however, the old Baroque virtuoso performers were still available to early Classical composers. This suited perfectly the composers of hunting symphonies of whom Mozart's father Leopold was one and Haydn another. Haydn wrote two hunting symphonies, No. 31 and his less interesting No. 72.

Symphony No. 31 was composed only four years after Haydn had joined the domestic staff of the Hungarian Prince Esterházy, one of the wealthiest music patrons in Europe. The Symphony acquired two nicknames, both of them probably added during the nineteenth century. The more familiar nickname is the "Hornsignal," the second, *"Auf dem Anstand"* ("On the Lookout"). Both refer to traditional hunting-horn signals. Hunting was one of the favorite sports of the Esterházy princes and Haydn himself was an enthusiastic hunter. As a musician he had probably listened fully as carefully as his princely master to the many traditional horn-calls native to the region of the Esterházy estates. One of the most ancient of these he featured in his Symphony No. 31, composed and presumably first performed at the Esterházy castle of Eisenstadt in the year 1765. (Eisenstadt, the present-day capital of the Austrian province of Burgenland, lies close to the Austro-Hungarian border.)

Cast in the traditional four movements, this Symphony is relatively brief and light in style, being closely related to the popular entertainment forms of the divertimento and suite.

I. *Allegro*. The Symphony begins with two successive sets of hunting calls flung forth by four horns (rather than the single pair of horns customary in most symphonies of the day). The first, a triadic fanfare of repeated notes, is so simple that it could be derived from any of several dozen hunting signals. The second, on the other hand, with its characteristic octave leaps, is almost identical with one of the horn signals of ancient lineage which has been well documented for this specific area of Austria-Hungary:

The joyous peal of these horn-calls and their characteristic rhythms dominate the entire movement. Where tradition calls for a secondary theme, Haydn gives us a breezy little scale for solo flute which, however, is soon swallowed up in the varied returns of the two horn signals. The formal reprise omits the opening bars of the movement, starting at once with the octave-leap theme quoted above, and the movement is rounded oft by one more exuberant outburst of both signals in succession.

II. *Adagio.* The gracefully melodious slow movement is built around a phrase announced by the solo violin (concertmaster) and taken up by a pair of horns. The solo cello also joins with the solo violin in a duet of almost Rococo delicacy. Later four horns take over the theme in a passage which sends the first horn, in a passage of excruciating delicacy, up the scale to a high "D":

III. *Menuet.* The sturdy Minuet is built on a theme which begins, like the horn signal of the first movement, with an octave leap:

All four horns, the oboes and flutes are prominent in the engaging little trio section.

IV. *Finale: Moderato molto.* More than any other of the four movements, the *Finale* shows the lightness and coloristic solo appeal of the contemporary divertimento. It is in the popular variation form, the theme being announced by the violins in unison:

Variation 1. Two oboes and two horns are accompanied by the string section.

Variation 2. A solo cello accompanied by strings alone has the elaborate embellishment of the theme.

Variation 3. This light and frothy Variation is for solo flute with string accompaniment.

Variation 4. All four horns are displayed, the first horn rising to extraordinarily high pitches, demonstrating again, as did the slow movement, that Haydn must have had at his command some of the finest horn players in Europe.

Variation 5. The concertmaster is asked once more to display the grace and delicacy of his style in what was, for Haydn's day, a high and glittering region of violin tone.

Variation 6. The solo flute, supported by all four horns, gives the characteristic color.

Variation 7. The solo cello is called upon to exhibit the warmth of timbre of which his instrument is capable in its upper-middle register.

Coda. A brilliant closing flourish for the full orchestra brings this joyous Symphony to a close, emphasizing once more the brilliant sound of four horns, and concluding with the vigorous horn-signal rhythms which opened the first movement.

Haydn's Symphony No. 31 calls for solo flute, 2 oboes, bassoon (traditionally required for the continuo part in such a symphony, but not actually written out in the score), 4 horns, the traditional string choir, and harpsichord (likewise a traditional requirement not specifically noted in the score).

SYMPHONY NO. 45, F-SHARP MINOR, FAREWELL

To many music lovers this wonderful symphony, one of the most sensitive, passionate, and imaginative that Haydn ever wrote, is merely part of a rather sweet little anecdote. The standard version of the anecdote (which survives in more than one form) is that Haydn composed this masterpiece to persuade his employer, Prince Nikolaus Esterházy, to cut short his stay at Esterháza and return to Vienna. Prince Nikolaus loved his magnificent palace and gardens at Esterháza so much that he spent a longer and longer time there each year. The musicians of Esterházy's private orchestra were less delighted, however. For with the exception of Haydn, they were not allowed to take their families with them to Esterháza. Toward the end of the long season they grew restless in their gorgeous establishment built on a wild and remote Hungarian marsh.

In 1772 Prince Nikolaus stayed even later than usual. His musicians, growing desperate, asked Haydn to help. Haydn did so by composing the "Farewell" Symphony, so called because the traditionally fast tempo of its finale breaks off and is followed by a long Adagio. During this Adagio, in the first performance before Prince Nikolaus, one player after another finished his part, blew out the candle at his music stand, and left, until out of the whole orchestra only two violin players remained. As they too were about to leave the Prince is supposed to have said, "Well, if they all leave, we might as well leave too." And his whole court left the next day for Vienna.

It is possible that the story is true, although there are reasons to doubt it. But true or false, the "Farewell" Symphony is something more than a benign trick which "Papa" Haydn played on his good-natured prince to persuade him to release his players to go home to their families. It is part of a great upheaval in Haydn's art lasting almost a decade (1766–74), when he depicted passionate and even tragic feelings which had hiterto been taboo, when he experimented with form more boldly than he ever did again.

It may be tempting to ascribe this new freedom to Haydn's personal maturing—not only in years but in the command of his technical and artistic resources. Haydn's new assurance may also have been due to the fact that he was promoted in 1766 from the position of Prince Esterházy's Assistant Chapel Master to Chapel Master with greatly increased authority and responsibility. Yet such personal explanations tell at best only half the story. This emancipation of one whole side of Haydn's nature was part of a much vaster emancipation, a liberating wave of Storm and Stress which swept the arts in the sixties and seventies of the eighteenth century.

It ranged from the fashionable melancholy of the Ossian forgeries to the fatal despair of young Werther, from Fuseli's painted nightmares to the recitative nightmares in Gluck's *Iphigénie en Tauride* and beyond these to Franz Moor's vision of the Last Judgment and the overwhelming "Dies irae" of Mozart's unfinished *Requiem.* The works touched by the Storm and Stress have in common an almost Romantic desire to reach depths of the human heart, to get below the polished surface of courtly taste which had dominated the eighteenth-century arts for so long, to shatter, if need be, the artistocratic facade of grace, wit, and charm, which had so often served to hold all passionate or painful feelings at bay.

These outbursts of Storm and Stress were by no means always welcome. Mozart was well aware that such feelings were not popular among aristocratic patrons of music. Possibly, Haydn's Prince Nikolaus did not take kindly to them either—which may be one more reason to doubt the popular anecdote about the "Farewell" Symphony. In the 1770s the very key of the Symphony—F-sharp minor—was a challenge to conservative musical tastes. Any minor key was rare enough for a symphony, but F-sharp minor seemed so remote and wild that it was sure to be associated with what Charles Burney, describing Gluck, called "complicated misery and the tempestuous fury of unbridled passion."

I. *Allegro assai.* The relentless rhythmic drive of the opening and the stark simplicity of Haydn's main theme:

do recall Gluck—for example, the "Dance of the Furies" in the "Underworld" Scene from the Paris version of *Orpheus and Eurydice.*

Agitated syncopation and harmonic clashes lead to a climax of tension, which is suddenly relieved by a quiet lyric interlude.

II. *Adagio.* The dreamlike quality of this slow movement comes partly from the simple device of having the violins play throughout with mutes. The immaterial, disembodied character of this sound so fascinated Haydn that he used it in the slow movement of every symphony—fourteen in all—composed between 1771 and 1774. Other Romantic touches in this *Adagio* include tiny, but effective bits of French horn color and major-minor harmonic fluctuations we associate with as late a composer as Franz Schubert.

III. *Menuetto; Allegretto.* Some of the delicacy of the preceding *Adagio* seems to linger into this minuet. The middle trio section has a duet of French horns based on an ancient Gregorian recitation tone for the Lamentations of Jeremiah traditionally chanted at the office of Matins in Holy Week. We do not know what connotation the melody had for Haydn here, but it can hardly have been a merry one.

IV. *Finale: Presto—Adagio.* In its first half the finale is almost like a delicate *scherzo,* as vivacious as it is light and transparent in texture. The concluding Adagio grows more and more diaphonous. Although it deserts F-sharp minor for the more serene A major and F-sharp major, there is a veil of melancholy over it. The simpler the music grows as the orchestra thins out, the more poignant it becomes. As the movement nears its close, there is indeed an atmosphere of farewell, but this is a very different leavetaking from what the official anecdote leads one to expect. The instruments sound not eager but reluctant to go as they fade, one by one, into the final silence.

Haydn's score calls for 2 oboes, 2 horns, and the traditional strings, with a bassoon added to reinforce the bass.

SYMPHONY NO. 48, C MAJOR, MARIA THERESIA

Even in the heyday of eighteenth-century aristocratic patronage, few composers commanded such lavish forces as Haydn at the fabulous palace and estate of Esterháza. For a quarter of a century, from 1766 to 1790, Haydn was what we would call composer-in-residence to the reigning Esterházy princes. The Esterházys' dazzling Rococo domain, conjured out of a lonely West Hungarian plain, was modeled on the palace and gardens of Versailles. Like its model, Esterháza was a world apart: an aristocratic preserve of glamour, grace, wit, beauty and conspicuous consumption based on apparently limitless wealth. Both the lavish hospitality and the luxurious personal tastes of the Esterházy family demanded, among other delights, a private resident orchestra for the regular palace symphony and chamber music concerts, as well as singers, chorus and an entire operatic establishment to perform in their private opera house.

A contemporary description of Esterháza (possibly the anonymous work of Prince Nikolaus himself), after enumerating the exquisite palace furnishings, its one hundred and twenty-six richly gilded and paneled guest rooms, its art gallery, hothouses, orangeries, its immense park and game preserves, devotes particular attention to the performing arts:

> In an avenue of wild chestnut trees stands the magnificent opera house. The boxes on the sides [of the auditorium] open into charming rooms furnished most luxuriously with fireplaces, divans, mirrors and clocks. The theater easily holds four hundred people. Every day at six o'clock there is a performance of an Italian *opera seria* or *buffa* or of German comedy, always attended by the Prince. Words cannot describe how both eye and ear are delighted here. When the music begins, its touching delicacy, the strength and force of the instruments penetrate the soul, for the great composer, Herr Haydn himself, is conducting. But the audience is also overwhelmed by the admirable lighting and deceptively perfect stage settings. At first we see the cloud on which the Gods are seated sink slowly to earth. Then the Gods rise upwards and instantly vanish, and then again everything is transformed into a delightful garden, an enchanted wood, or, it may be, a glorious hall.
>
> Opposite the opera house is the marionette theater built in grotto style. All the walls, niches, and apertures are covered with variegated stones, shells, and snails that afford a very curious and striking sight when they are illuminated. The theater is rather large and the decorations are extremely artistic. The puppets are beautifully formed, and magnificently dressed; they play not only farces and comedies, but also *opera seria*. The performances in both theaters are open to everyone.

These were the everyday pleasures! For special guests there were special preparations, which often meant that Haydn was expected fo furnish a new symphony or opera in honor of the visitor. The most august guest to visit Esterháza was the Empress Maria Theresia herself, in 1773. Later, a special festival book *("Rélation des Fêtes Données à Sa Majesté l'Impératrice . . . le 1er et 2e 7bre 1773)* described the festivities in glamorous detail. Haydn's biographer Karl Geiringer has summarized part of the description:

> On her arrival, the Empress and her retinue were escorted in fifteen of the prince's magnificent carriages through the park, the wonders of which Maria Theresia could not sufficiently admire, though she was used to a beautiful park in the French style at her own residence of Schönbrunn. In the evening Haydn's burletta *L'infedeltà delusa* was performed, which so impressed the Imperial guest that she was overhead to say: "If I want to enjoy a good opera, I go to Esterháza."
>
> The performance was followed by a masked ball in the luxurious hall of the castle. Then the Empress was taken to the Chinese pavilion, whose mirror-covered walls reflected countless lanterns and chandeliers flooding the room with light. On a platform sat the princely orchestra in gala attire and played under Haydn's direction his new symphony "*Maria Theresia*," as well as other music. The Empress then retired to her magnificent suite, while her retinue continued to enjoy the masked ball until dawn. The next day a great banquet took place in the *sala terrena*, during which the virtuosos of the

PRINCE ESTERHÁZY'S "BAGATELLE."

The Chinese Pavilion on the Esterháza Palace grounds where Haydn conducted his "Maria Theresia" Symphony for the Empress. The architect's ground plan (*Grundt Riss*) shows the intimate scale of the main room (No. 1) measuring 16 x 32 Schuhe, or "shoes" (roughly equivalent to English feet). (*Courtesy, Oesterreichische Nationalbibliothek, Vienna*)

> orchestra demonstrated their skill. In the afternoon the Empress attended a performance of Haydn's *Philémon et Baucis* in the marionette theater and she was so fascinated by it that four years later she had the complete marionette theater brought to Vienna for some special festivities. [There followed a *souper,* a fireworks display, and folk singing and dancing by peasants in their Hungarian and Croatian costumes.]
>
> The next morning the Empress left after distributing costly presents. Haydn received a valuable gold snuff box filled with ducats. He was proud to have impressed Her Majesty not merely as a musician, for during her stay he succeeded in killing with one shot three grouse that were graciously accepted for the Empress's table. . . . Among the countless treasures amassed at Esterháza, the newly erected Chinese pavilion [where Haydn's *"Maria Theresia"* Symphony had been performed] particularly impressed the Empress. The Prince, however, waved aside her praise with the airy remark that this was merely a "bagatelle," a designation henceforth applied to that exquisite building.

Obviously, Haydn and his music were among the chief ornaments of Esterháza: a source of pride to the princely family and (as contemporary accounts assure us) to the Hungarian nation itself.

For his symphonies and operas, Haydn could draw on the players not only of the Esterházy palace orchestra, but the instrumentalists of the Esterházy chapel, as well as trumpeters and kettledrummers from the Prince's military forces. All in all, according to the distinguished Haydn scholar H. C. Robbins Landon, Haydn could summon an orchestra of approximately 8 or 9 violins, 2 violas, one or 2 cellos, 2 strings basses, 2 flutes, 2 oboes, 2 bassoons, 4 horns, 2 trumpets and percussion including kettledrummers. (Clarinets were not added to the orchestra until 1776). For the "Maria Theresia" Symphony, Haydn used pairs of oboes, horns, trumpets and kettledrums, in addition to the basic string choir. There are four movements.

I. *Allegro.* As befitted the occasion, this is festive music. The very key, C major, was one of the few which, for Haydn, had a well-defined character: it was a key of pomp, proper for princes, a vehicle for brilliance and festivity. This character is enhanced by Haydn's use of C horns in the high range.

There is no slow introduction. We plunge directly into the fanfare-like first theme proclaimed by brass, woodwinds and kettledrums:

A passing excursion into the shadowy realm of C minor only emphasizes the sunny character of the major key, when it returns for a second proclamation of the principal theme.

There is no modulation. Instead, the orchestra shifts abruptly to the contrasting key of G major, deploying a wealth of tiny melodic fragments, including this figure:

The brief development section touches G minor, with similar expressive results. The reprise of the principal themes is condensed.

II. *Adagio.* The thoughtful slow movement was an indirect compliment to the musical understanding of Maria Theresia. Although simple in form, the movement is subtle and complex in melodic style; it is permeated by the veiled tone of muted violins.

III. *Menuetto: Allegretto.* The sturdy minuet has a rolling rhythm closer to a waltz than to the aristocratic dance of tradition. Here Haydn ventures again into C minor, to which he devotes the entire central, so-called trio section.

IV. *Finale: Allegro.* The lightest of the four movements, the *Finale* is a breezy *moto perpetuo* in style. In form, it approaches one of Haydn's most famous inventions, the combination rondo and sonata form. The exuberant scales and arpeggios of the opening serve both as a rondo refrain, and as the principal theme of a sonata–allegro. There is scarcely any contrast, for the stream of gossamer eighth-notes is sustained from start to finish. Nor is there any learned development, but rather a brief transition to the reprise of the refrain. The end is festive again, with the full majesty of trumpets, horns, and kettledrums.

SYMPHONY NO. 60, C MAJOR, IL DISTRATTO

Haydn's Symphony No. 60 was not originally a symphony at all (in the present-day meaning of the term) but an overture plus incidental music for a French farce, *Le Distrait,* by Jean-François Regnard (1655–1709). In the eighteenth century the term *sinfonia* meant interchangeably a symphony, an overture, or simply a piece of orchestral music (often a piece from an opera, oratorio, or incidental music for a play). *Il distratto* (the Italian form of *Le Distrait*) is an abbreviation for the full title of Haydn's *Sinfonia per la commedia intitolata "Il distratto" (Symphony for the Comedy Entitled "The Absent-Minded Man.").*

The infinite variety of Haydn's symphonies was due, of course, to the infinite variety of his imagination. Yet circumstances played a powerful role. In the service of the Esterházy princes Haydn was obliged to compose not only dozens of symphonies but also a steady stream of dances, marches, cantatas, string quartets, masses, oratorios, operas, compositions for musical clocks and even incidental music for the vast repertory of spoken dramas which were played at Esterháza.

Haydn became an insatiable experimenter. No one had ever told him that symphonies should be "pure" or "abstract" music. So he was quite willing to include in them anything from medieval religious chant to Balkan folk song or contemporary French farce.

Regnard's farce *Le Distrait* had been knocking about the theaters of Europe for over three-quarters of a century, when it landed on the stage of the Esterházy private theater in 1774, in a German translation as *Der Zerstreute.* Regnard's hero Leandre is a man of farcical absentmindedness. When he gets up in the morning, instead of dressing himself, he starts to dress his valet. At meals, instead of his bread, he bites into his own finger. In leaving a party he gets into another man's coach, is driven to the wrong home, goes to bed in the wrong bed and is violently confronted by the "wronged" husband. In the last act Leandre almost forgets to go to his own wedding. Crude as it sounds, it worked. And it tickled Haydn's funny bone. He composed an elaborate overture, intermission pieces and a finale (which he later used for a six-movement symphony). In June 1774, the newspaper of nearby Pressburg, the *Pressburger Zeitung,* reported that Haydn had completed the incidental music for a production of *Der Zerstreute* at Esterháza: "Connoisseurs consider this music to be a masterpiece. It is full of the musical humour, the good spirits and the intelligence which characterize Haydn productions. The connoisseurs are amazed on the one hand, whilst the rest of the public is simply enchanted. For Haydn knows how to satisfy both. From the most affected pompousness he drops into doggerel, and thus Haydn and Regnard vie with each other to see who can produce the most whimsical absentminded entertainment [*wer am launischesten zerstreut*]. The play's value is thus much increased. The music describes the content better and better as the play progresses, and as the actors grow more and more absentminded."

The Esterháza premiere of *Der Zerstreute* with Haydn's music took place on St. Cecilia's Day (November 22), 1774. Again the *Pressburger Zeitung* reported that the music was "admirable, most admirable" and that:

". . . the finale, upon incessant applause of the audience, had to be repeated. In this number, which is most effective, allusion is made to the absentminded gentleman who, on his wedding day, forgets that he is a bridegroom and has to remind himself by tying a knot in his cravat. The musicians start the piece with great pomp, and it takes them some time to remember that their instruments are not tuned."

The following year the play was repeated at Esterháza with Haydn's music, and with the famous actor, Stephan Stephanie, the Elder, in the title role. In 1776 the play was performed with Haydn's music at the Kärntnerthor-Theater in Vienna and in 1778 there were two further revivals at Esterháza.

A quarter of a century later, we find Haydn writing to a friend still in active service with the Esterházy family: "Please be good enough to send to me, at the very first opportunity, the old Symphony entitled *[Der] Zerstreute,* for Her Majesty the Empress expressed a desire to hear the old chestnut *[den alten Schmarn].*" Haydn promises "not to harm it in any way."

He did not "harm" the manuscript, but he did change two tempos. The first movement became a *Presto* in place of the original *Allegro di molto* and the original Minuet became *Menuetto non troppo presto.* Whether Haydn's feeling about how the Symphony should be performed had changed in twenty-eight years or whether the term *presto* in 1803 meant what *allegro di molto* had meant in 1774 we have no present way of knowing. Most modern editions retain Haydn's original tempo marks.

I. *Adagio; Allegro di molto.* The first movement (the Overture to the play) begins with a slow introduction of the type that later became a standard feature of Haydn's symphonies. The main body of the movement is built around a mercurial little figure for the violins which is immediately echoed by the oboes:

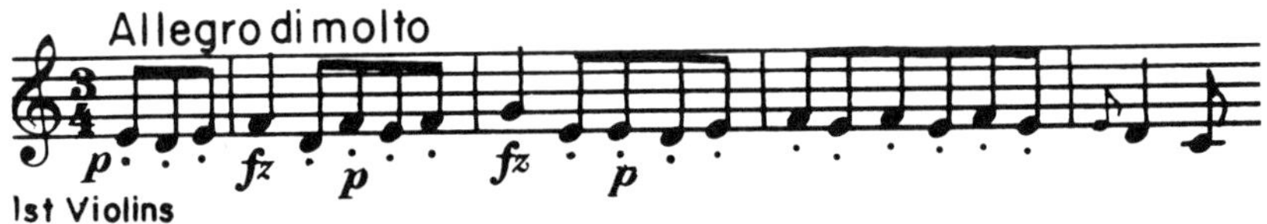

In the midst of this bubbly movement, the orchestra seems to trail off absentmindedly into near silence only to be shaken by a violent *fortissimo* and then continue merrily on its way. This way is a sonata-allegro form, customary for overtures as well as first movements of symphonies.

II. *Andante.* The surprises which plague the absentminded man with growing frequency in the play, multiply in this slow movement. It starts decorously enough with a quiet melody for the violins only to be interrupted by boisterous oboes and horns. Partway through the second half of the movement a perky little melody makes an unexpected appearance. In the French publication of the Symphony the tune is marked "Old French Song." We know neither the identity of the song, nor its function in the play, but it seems likely that it was the tune to which one of the characters sang some carefree verses beginning: "In the pub I find comfort and advice."

III. *Menuetto.* The *Minuet* begins in familiar, courtly style, reserving its surprises for the middle (trio) section, which brings in a number of Balkan folk melodies.

IV. *Presto.* The dizzy pace of this highly rhythmic movement begins with the following tune:

Halfway through, Haydn resumes his pell-mell quotation of Balkan folk tunes. A stamping peasant dance jumps awkwardly from F minor to E-flat major, producing what were considered comically uncouth parallel fifths and octaves in the harmony.

V. *Adagio.* This songful movement bears in one reliable manuscript the subtitle *di Lamentatione.* If Haydn used a fragment of traditional church plainchant here (as he did in his "Lamentatione" Symphony, No. 26), it has not as yet been identified. On the other hand the lamentation in question may refer simply to a moment of sadness in the play:

This pensive melody is suddenly interrupted by the martial din of horns, trumpets and drums. We cannot be sure which boisterous incident of Regnard's farce the interruption represents. What is clear is that we have another of Haydn's musical embodiments of the comic spirit so relished by his contemporaries.

VI. *Finale: Prestissimo.* This grand *Finale* begins with considerable pomp only to break down for one of Haydn's most obvious jokes. The entire violin section has "forgotten" to tune its instruments. The violin players test their strings, revealing that the lowest (properly G) strings have sagged down to F. All this is written in the score, as is the tuning up. There is a pause and the movement starts over again. But this piece of slapstick, which presumably brought roars of laughter from even the most unsophisticated listeners, does not spoil the artistic finish with which Haydn brings his popular spoof to a close.

The Symphony *"Il distratto"* is scored for 2 oboes, 2 horns, 2 trumpets, kettledrums and the standard string choir.

SYMPHONY NO. 82, C MAJOR, L'OURS (THE BEAR)

In the 1770s and 1780s, Marie Antoinette and ladies and gentlemen of the court of Versailles were frequent visitors to the Parisian Concerts de la Loge Olympique. In 1786 when Haydn completed the six symphonies commissioned by the fashionable Concerts (Nos. 82, 83, 84, 85, 86 and 87), the fall of the Bastille still lay three years in the distant future. The first Bastille Day was only eighteen months off when the Parisian publisher Imbault advertised the six Haydn symphonies for sale in January 1788. Yet Marie Antoinette was still popular enough to make it seem worthwhile for the publication to distinguish No. 85 in B-flat, believed to have been her favorite, with the subtitle *"La Reine de France,"* by which it is still known.

The *ancien régime* vanished and with it Marie Antoinette. But Haydn's popularity continued to grow. Around the turn of the century, French audiences' enthusiasm bestowed programmatic subtitles on two more symphonies of the set. No. 83 in G-minor became "The Hen" *("La Poule"),* and No. 82 in C-major, "The Bear" *("L'Ours").*

Whether Haydn's style in these symphonies was influenced by the large orchestra for which they were intended is hard to say. The Loge Olympique disposed of forty violins, ten double basses, and four of each woodwind. This far surpassed the small ensembles for which Haydn was accustomed to write at Esterháza and even exceeded Salomon's orchestra in London, for which Haydn was soon to compose his last twelve symphonies.

In any case, the style of the six Paris symphonies is often considered closer to the Classical ideal of clarity, simplicity, elegance and force, than Haydn's final dozen of "London" symphonies. The latter are often more dramatic, more dynamic, and closer to the Storm and Stress which had convulsed Haydn's style and Mozart's too in the 1770s. Although Symphony No. 82 in C Major is first of the Parisian six, according to the traditional numbering by Eusebius Mandyczewski, we now know that it was not composed first. And a letter from Haydn to his Viennese publisher, Artaria, in August 1787, clearly suggests that it was the last. The autograph score is marked only 1786 and, at the end: *Finis Laus Deo.*

I. *Vivace assai.* Haydn launches his energetic first movement with a theme characteristic of his rich inspiration and in three contrasting parts, first a boldly soaring figure, festive and brilliant, derived from the C-major triad. Then, with a sudden hush, the strings alone sing a pensive, intimate phrase:

This principal theme concludes with an outburst of the orchestral *tutti*: a brilliant, almost military-sounding, fanfare. In another sudden contrast, the blustering opening phrase, quoted above, is transformed into a delicate *pizzicato* figure for the violins, accompanied only by the cool, transparent tones of flutes and oboes. The entire movement is filled with delicious touches of instrumental color spiced with harmonic surprises, including some sharp dissonance. The form of this opening movement is traditional, but its content as fresh as the day it was written.

II. *Allegretto.* The second movement, a theme and variations, has more grace than depth, but is none the less fascinating. The theme itself is in two parts: the first, a simple tune in F major; the second, in the contrasting minor mode, is ingeniously constructed of fragments of the opening tune. Since the first half returns always in easily recognizable forms, with only its instrumentation changed, it gives somewhat the impression of a recurrent rondo refrain.

The more involved developments of the minor strain sound almost like the contrasting episodes of a rondo.

III. *Menuetto.* The opening of this minuet movement is festive and ceremonial in a way that recalls the courtly origins of the minuet, but Haydn quickly turns to more delicate, ingenious solo passages, in which the character and color of the woodwinds play a prominent role. Once again, the form is traditional, yet the actual music is highly original.

IV. *Finale: Vivace.* The finale, with its humorous drone of the low strings, later imitated by the violins, is what suggested the symphony's nickname, "The Bear."

The drone, of course, suggests bagpipes, and this suggestion is reinforced by the jaunty tune with which the finale begins. Dancing bears often performed at country fairs and elsewhere to the sound of bagpipes. Furthermore, the repeated *appoggiatura* which punctuates the low drone might well have suggested the growl of a bear. The bagpipe opening is answered by a light-footed, dance-like passage for woodwinds accompanied only by soft drum taps and discreet touches of the mellow French horn. Despite the simplicity of its basic material, the whole finale is richly imaginative and full of infectious high spirits.

The score of Haydn's "Bear" Symphony calls for flute, 2 oboes, 2 bassoons, 2 trumpets or 2 horns, kettledrums, and the usual strings.

SYMPHONY NO. 83, G MINOR, LA POULE (THE HEN)

Queen Marie Antoinette is said to have been one of Haydn's most fervent admirers in Paris and her favorite symphony was reputed to have been Haydn's No. 85 in B flat major, which for that reason was given the nickname, "The Queen of France" (*"La Reine de France"*). The Symphony "The Hen," like *"La Reine,"* was one of a set of six commissioned by the fashionable Parisian concert organization, *Les Concerts de la Loge Olympique,* and composed in 1785 and 1786.

Parisian enthusiasm for Haydn's symphonies is echoed by the *Mercure de France* in the spring of 1788 commenting on the preceding season of *Concerts Spirituels.* This latter series, a close rival of the *Concerts de la Loge Olympique,* seems happily to have pirated all six of the new Haydn scores and perhaps earlier ones as well. "At every concert symphonies by Haydn were played [writes the *Mercure de France*]. Every day one realizes better and consequently admires more the products of this great genius, who, in every one of his works, knows so well how to draw such rich and varied developments from a single theme; in contrast to those sterile composers, who constantly fly from one idea to another, for want of knowing how to present a single theme in varied forms, and who pile effect on effect without connection and without taste. Haydn's symphonies, always sure of their effect, would be even more effective if the auditorium were more sonorous. . . . Some symphonies of Mr. Guenin were also performed and it is high praise for them to say that they were applauded alongside those of this great Master. . . ."

The nickname of this Symphony, *La Poule* or "The Hen," is not original with Haydn but was added, like the title, *"La Reine,"* by the Parisians, who seem to have had an especial fondness for programmatic titles.

I. *Allegro spiritoso.* Without the formality of a slow introduction, Haydn launches his agitated principal theme:

In the serene, not to say elegant, company of the other five Paris symphonies, this opening may have sounded a little wild. But this G minor is far from the tragic Storm and Stress of Mozart's two G-minor Symphonies and it is relieved by a coquettish, almost kittenish secondary theme in the strings. The gently clucking sound of the oboe, which soon joins, is a humorous touch, which seems to have suggested the Symphony's nickname. The opening theme and its associated minor tonalities dominate the development, but the movement concludes in a more optimistic G major.

II. *Andante.* There is greater depth in the slow movement. The graceful opening phrase:

sets the almost Mozartean mood of mixed nostalgia and warmth. The *"Porgi amor"* of Mozart's Countess Almaviva is not far off.

III. *Menuetto: Allegretto.* One of Haydn's gentler minuets, this one is distinguished by the ingeniously shifting accents of its main theme. Its form is traditional and crystalline in its clarity.

IV. *Vivace.* This dancing finale in 12/8 time has an almost jig-like drive and energy. The humorous pauses just before the end are typical Haydn and the exuberant close is like a burst of laughter.

The score of "The Hen" Symphony calls for flute, 2 oboes, 2 bassoons, 2 horns, and the customary strings.

SYMPHONY NO. 84, E-FLAT MAJOR

Haydn may or may not have been aware of the unusually large size of the orchestra for which he was composing his "Paris" Symphonies. It was far larger than the modest ensembles at the glittering court of Esterháza in Hungary, for which Haydn had hitherto composed—larger even than the English orchestras for which Haydn was later to compose his last dozen "London" symphonies. With its forty violins, the orchestra of the Loge Olympique exceeded many twentieth century symphony orchestras; it had ten double basses and four each of the several woodwinds.

Whether or not Haydn was influenced by the dimensions of the Parisian orchestra, he seems to have been untouched by the growing tensions of the French capital which were to explode in 1789. The Symphony No. 84, as H. C. Robbins Landon remarks in his monumental volume on the Haydn symphonies, is "filled with the inner peace and tranquility which a quarter of a century of fruitful work in Eisenstadt and Esterháza had taught the composer."

The unclouded joy of this music, its unobtrusive vitality, are still so fresh, the voice of Haydn speaks to us with such spontaneity that for a moment it seems as if all the horrors of the interim—all the reigns of terror and gas ovens —were only the passing bad dreams of a humanity born for happiness. Haydn was aware of this quality of his music. The composer, who often expressed a hope that he would not "wholly die," was characteristically moved by a letter he received in 1802 from the members of a music club in the small city of Bergen on the island of Rügen in North Germany, expressing their enjoyment of his music. Haydn answered in part: "You give me the most touching assurance that I am often the enviable source from which you and many families derive their pleasure, their happiness. Often when contending with obstacles of every sort which interfered with my work, often when my powers of body and of mind were failing, and I felt it hard to persevere on the course I had entered, a secret feeling within me whispered: 'There are but few contented and happy men here below; grief and care prevail everywhere; perhaps my labors may one day be the source from which the weary and worn, or the man burdened with care, may derive a few moments' rest and refreshment.' This was a powerful motive for pressing onward, . . . And now I thank you in the fullness of my heart for your kindly thoughts of me, . . . a gradually dying veteran, who would feign even after his death survive in the charming circle of which you draw so wonderful a picture."

I. *Largo; Allegro.* The seeming simplicity of Haydn's slow introduction is deceptive. The casual majesty of these twenty opening bars, with the art that conceals art, hints, right and left, at the principal themes of the first and second movements, echoing, imitating, and developing as it goes. The broadest hint of what is to come, a reference to the principal theme of the second movement, is contained in the serene opening measures:

The main body of the movement, the *Allegro*, is built around a single melody, an irresistibly vivacious, graceful strain of a full twelve measures:

We do not need to listen far below the surface of this innocently bubbling melody to hear its inner complexity and the riches which will enable Haydn to build an entire movement of astonishing drama, subtle surprises, and sensuous appeal. At the point where many other composers, Mozart for example, habitually introduce a new and contrasting theme, Haydn gives us a variant of the principal theme quoted above, but in a contrasting key and a different orchestral color: the woodwind choir. In the more dramatic "development" section Haydn modulates suddenly into minor keys, developing considerable tension before he returns to his principal theme.

The first return however is a feint, a false return or *fausse reprise,* which merely tantalizes the listener and builds up still further tension before the real recapitulation of the entire melodic strain on which the movement is built. To describe even half the beguiling details, musical wit and innuendo of this movement would take longer than the music does!

II. *Andante.* The melody of the slow movement is an outgrowth of the slow introduction to the first movement. Here it takes the following form:

The continuation of this melody serves as a theme on which Haydn builds three leisurely variations plus an ingenious coda. The first variation is a vigorous minor version of the theme, for full orchestra. The second variation, for strings alone, begins like an eerie waltz, but is soon distorted rhythmically by syncopations and other rhythmic devices. The third variation engages once more the modest orchestral *tutti*, with sturdy, striding bass figure for cellos, double basses, and bassoons. This variation, instead of concluding with a harmonic full close, pauses, for all the world like a concerto, with the traditional harmonic preparation for an unaccompanied cadenza. Instead of a solo cadenza, the woodwind choir takes up the opening phrase in characteristic cadenza style. The string choir rounds off the movement with a tiny coda recalling the opening phrase.

III. *Menuet: Allegretto.* The graceful minuet, with its traditional repeats, and phrases that nod and bow to each other with balanced formality, is the least adventurous movement of the four.

IV. *Finale: Vivace.* The last movement, like the first, is cast in familiar symphonic sonata form, using Haydn's favorite device of deriving his second theme from the opening strain. The theme itself has charm and to spare, but it is in the bridges linking its various appearances that Haydn surprises us with Romantic shadows, with chromatic progressions and sudden hushes between the more familiar outbursts of gaiety. At the conclusion of this enamoring work we find Haydn's customary pious inscription: *Finis Laus Deo.*

The score of the E-flat Symphony calls for flute, 2 oboes, 2 bassoons, 2 horns, and the customary strings. However, it seems likely that the doubled woodwinds and the full stringed complement of the Loge Olympique were used for the first performances. The date of the premiere is not known precisely but it cannot have been much later than 1786, for by 1787 the rival Concerts Spirituels were giving pirated performances of all six "Paris" symphonies.

SYMPHONY NO. 85, B-FLAT MAJOR, LA REINE (THE QUEEN)

This is said to have been Marie Antoinette's favorite symphony and for this reason the first Paris edition of the Symphony in 1788 bore the label, *"La Reine de France,"* by which it is still known. It was commissioned as one of a set of six by the fashionable Parisian concert organization, the *Concert de La Loge Olympique,* where the queen and her ladies-in-waiting were frequent visitors. But the Symphony is regal in style as well as in historical association. As H. C. Robbins Landon points out in his monumental volume *The Symphonies of Joseph Haydn,* the Symphony No. 85 has a queenly grace and dignity, an elegance and formal perfection to match its musical strength.

The orchestra of the *Loge Olympique* was very large for its day and included 40 violins, 10 double basses, with woodwinds doubled to balance the large body of string tone. To suit the fashionable tone of these subscription concerts, the players were required to wear brocaded coats, lace ruffles, and swords.

"La Reine," composed in 1785 or 1786, is cast in the Classical four-movement form.

I. *Adagio—Vivace.* The slow introduction is short but pithy and dignified. It includes a thrice-repeated rising scale, which returns prominently in the principal fast part of the movement. This section, as is characteristic of Haydn, is based on one main theme, rather than two contrasting ideas. It consists of a sustained tone in the violins held over a quietly descending figure in the other strings. The development is rather dramatic and also includes the rising scale figure we met first in the introduction.

II. *Romanze: Allegretto.* This is a theme and variations on the French folk song *La gentille et juene Lisette,* chosen perhaps with an eye to the French audience. The simple melody is in two short sections, each of which is repeated. One of the four variations is in the minor variant of the key, a characteristic device of French variations. Despite its simplicity, this movement has much greater depth of expression than in most of Haydn's earlier *allegretto* variations.

III. *Menuetto: Allegretto.* We know that Haydn took great pains with the minuets of all six "Paris" Symphonies. This one still shows clearly the vigor of the Austrian peasant *Ländler* dance, but it also has a subtlety and sophistication which are new. A particularly charming example of this occurs in the middle (or trio) section of the *Menuetto,* where, over a softly sustained pedalpoint in the horns, a fragment of the trio theme is echoed dreamily by one solo oboe after another, by a solo flute, and finally by a single bassoon.

IV. *Finale: Presto.* True to Haydn's tendency to throw more emphasis on his final movements, he casts this finale in a new form he had devised only three or four years earlier: a mixture of sonata and rondo form. Once again the entire movement is based on a single theme, the rondo refrain:

This movement has all the traditional gaiety, lightness and brilliance of the rondo, complete with Haydn's trick of tantalizing his listeners before the return of the refrain. Yet one of the episodes of this rondo is a full-fledged, dramatically modulating development section in richly symphonic sonata style. This combination of grace and strength, of gaiety and seriousness help to make *"La Reine"* one of the most perfect and satisfying of Classical symphonies.

The score of *"La Reine"* calls for flute, 2 oboes, 2 bassoons, 2 horns, and the customary strings.

SYMPHONY NO. 86, D MAJOR

During the last two decades before the French Revolution swept them aside, Queen Marie Antionette and her aristocratic entourage of the court of Versailles were frequent visitors to the fashionable Parisian Concerts de la Loge Olympique, where the periwigged players wore brocade coats, lace ruffles at their wrists, gleaming swords at their sides and plumed hats which, however, they were permitted to take off while actually performing. Their conductor was the illustrious Belgian composer François Joseph Gossec, who had founded this concert series in 1770. In keeping with the exalted station and presumably demanding taste of its listeners, the Loge Olympique sought to present only the best. In symphonic music of the 1770s and early 1780s, the best meant Joseph Haydn, the most sought-after symphonic composer in Europe, whose fame extended from London to Naples and Madrid to Moscow, with many more commissions than he could hope to fulfill. Nevertheless, Haydn found time to compose a set of six symphonies for the Concerts de la Loge Olympique, a set still known as his "Paris" symphonies.

Number 86 in D major is the fifth and one of the finest of Haydn's superb "Paris" Symphonies. Its manuscript is dated 1786. Like the majority of this set, this one employs trumpets and kettledrums, which had been rare in Haydn's symphonies before this time.

I. *Adagio; Allegro spiritoso.* The slow introduction is one of the stateliest and most aristocratic of Haydn's symphonic output. Beginning with a graceful, falling phrase for violins and oboes, it swells slowly to a full, sonorous *tutti,* dying away again on a diaphanous dominant chord.

The fast main body of the movement begins rather strikingly on a harmony suggesting the key of E minor, but modulates quickly toward the tonic D. The principal theme falls into two contrasting halves, the first an ebullient phrase for first violins over light string staccatos:

The second half of the theme is a vigorous five-note figure in a persistent rhythm, which Haydn repeats and expands until it dominates the long transition passage leading to the lyric second subject.

The brief development section takes up the principal themes in the order of their initial appearance, leading each through a sequential development and expansion.

II. *Capriccio: Largo.* The slow movement is as fascinatingly unorthodox as the first was regular in form. It was probably for this reason that Haydn gave it the title of *Capriccio.* Whereas it is normally the first movement that is related to the slow introduction of Haydn's symphonies, in this case it is the second movement which builds on the opening theme of the Symphony's slow introduction. A contrasting theme in the dominant key leads us to expect a sonata-form movement, but instead, the principal theme returns in the tonic key in rondo fashion. The movement keeps wavering between the two forms and is full of surprises, including a minor-key return of the principal theme.

III. *Menuet: Allegretto.* As in most of the "Paris" symphonies, this *Minuet* belongs to the aristocratic type, possibly out of deference to the members of the French court, who were such an important part of the audiences of the Loge Olympique.

IV. *Finale: Allegro con spirito.* A sparkling little figure for the first violins provides the thematic basis of the entire rondo-sonata *Finale:*

For all of the lightness of texture, Haydn does not shy away from a canonic treatment of the principal theme in the development section.

The Symphony No. 86 is scored for flute, 2 oboes, 2 bassoons, 2 horns, 2 trumpets, kettledrums, and the traditional string choir.

SYMPHONY NO. 88, G MAJOR

Whatever induced Haydn to compose one of his most bewitching, indeed one of his greatest, symphonies for such a questionable character as Johann Peter Tost, is hard to say. But we have the evidence of Haydn's own letters that he did write his Eighty-eighth Symphony in G major for Tost, a sort of rapscallion violinist and a good enough musician to lead the second violins in Haydn's own orchestra at Esterháza. For five years, from March 1783 to March 1788, Tost was on the payroll of the famous concert and opera orchestra at Prince Esterházy's magnificent country palace.

In 1788 he voyaged to Paris, taking the manuscripts of two Haydn symphonies and six String Quartets, Op. 54 and Op. 55. Evidently, Haydn had given him the rights to these works and expected him to sell them in Paris. But Tost was better than his word. He apparently sold the Parisian publisher Sieber not two but at least three "Haydn" symphonies (the third being by the less famous Adalbert Gyrowetz) as well as six Haydn piano sonatas to which he had no right at all. "Thus Herr Tost," Haydn dryly wrote to Sieber, "has swindled you; you can claim your damages in Vienna."

It can hardly have been personal devotion that gave wing to Haydn's imagination in his No. 88. The second symphony of the pair he wrote for Tost is a relatively shallow piece. In fact, the Haydn authority H. C. Robbins Landon likens No. 89 to "a parody of Haydn made by a malicious and brilliant ill-wisher." No. 88, on the other hand, he calls: ". . . rightly one of Haydn's most beloved symphonies, . . . an inspired work from beginning to end, containing every contrapuntal, melodic and instrumental device Haydn knew. But this fantastic display of craftsmanship is only the vehicle for Haydn's inspiration: the canon in the last movement, in itself a *tour de force,* is the logical outcome of the foregoing material; the idea of keeping the trumpets and drums silent in the first movement, in order to reserve their entrance for the first crashing *tutti* of the *Largo* is in itself a stroke of genius, growing out of the music rather than being superimposed on it; the delightful drone bass in the trio, with its strange dynamic effects (bassoons' *forte assai* against the other instruments' *p*), is inherent in the music, and not an extraneous effect. Seldom did Haydn reach the pinnacle of perfection achieved in No. 88. . . ."

I. *Adagio; Allegro.* The serene little introduction attempts little more than to arouse an harmonic sense of expectancy for the *Allegro.* The bouncy principal theme is announced twice, at first softly by the strings alone:

Immediately it is echoed by full orchestra, with a vigorous new figure added in the bass. This swirling figure almost immediately develops great importance on its own, both with and without the theme for which it was originally a mere accompaniment. As so often happens in Haydn, the unobtrusive second theme is closely related to the first and is almost swallowed up in all the bustle and excitement.

In the development that follows, the contest between the principal theme and the accompaniment figure grows more dramatic, eventually leading back to a very free recapitulation of the opening. The return of the principal theme (quoted above) is even softer than on its first appearance and it is now combined with a graceful little flute solo. And this is only one of the dozens of imaginative changes in the original material.

II. *Largo* This is one of Haydn's most beautiful slow movements. The basic pattern of its theme:

is an eighteenth-century cliché used dozens of times by Gluck and Mozart, perhaps the most famous example being the opening of the Countess's aria, *"Porgi amor,"* in Mozart's *The Marriage of Figaro.* Yet Haydn not only makes the old formula as warm and spontaneous as Mozart did, he builds his whole second movement out of it in a series of very free variations. The variations *are* as artful and sophisticated as they *seem* to be simple, unpremeditated, even naïve. Their songful quality is emphasized by the use of the solo cello as the chief melody-carrying instrument.

III. *Menuetto: Allegretto.* The sturdy *Minuet* is full of rhythmic surprises. The country-dance atmosphere of its contrasting middle section, or trio, suggests the bagpipes not only in the sustained drone bass, but in the amusingly "wooden," pseudo-primitive charm of its melody.

IV. *Finale: Allegro con spirito.* As if the riches that have gone before were not enough, the Symphony is crowned by one of the most beguiling of all rondos. It is based on this refrain:

Haydn had just recently discovered how much more fascinating he could make his rondos by getting away from the traditional, mechanical alternation of rondo refrain and contrasting episodes, enriching the rondo with touches of sonata form and style. This Finale is one of the simpler examples, but a dazzlingly adroit and humorous one.

Among his humorous devices is the tantalizing, teasing preparation for each reappearance of the refrain, by anticipating its opening repeated notes. By contrast, halfway through the movement, a most sophisticated, "learned" contrapuntal device, the canon, appears, but disguised in a whirl of virtuosity.

The Symphony is scored for flute, 2 oboes, 2 bassoons, 2 horns in G, 2 trumpets in C, kettledrums, and the standard strings.

SYMPHONY NO. 92, G MAJOR, OXFORD

The "Oxford" Symphony takes its name from its ceremonial performance at Oxford University on July 7, 1791 as an expression of Haydn's gratitude for the doctor's degree *honoris causa.* In his diary Haydn noted soberly that he had to pay "1½ guineas for having the bells rung at Oxforth *[sic]* in connection with my doctor's degree, and ½ a guinea for the robe. The trip cost six guineas." In obedience to ceremonial regulations Haydn wore his doctoral robes of cherry and cream-colored silk for three days, although they made him feel silly. But if he felt awkward in the robes, Haydn for the rest of his life cherished the degree, more than any other distinction in his long and distinguished career.

To celebrate the conferring of the degree, three concerts, consisting chiefly of works of Handel and Haydn, were performed on July 6, 7, and 8 in the Sheldonian Theater of Oxford. The first concert was to have included "a New M. S. Overture by Haydn" ["overture" was the usual term at this time in England for a symphony]. But as Haydn did not arrive at Oxford in time for a rehearsal, an older symphony of his was substituted, and Haydn himself presided at the pipe organ, according to the *Morning Herald* of July 8. Next morning there was time for a rehearsal under Haydn's direction and thus it was possible to prepare, for the second concert, the "new" symphony Haydn had designed for the Oxford celebrations. This was his Symphony No. 92 in G major, which seems to have been new to England. According to the *Morning Herald*: "The new Overture of HAYDN, prepared for the occasion, and previously rehearsed in the morning, led on the second Act, and a more wonderful composition never was heard. The applause given to HAYDN, who conducted this admirable effort of his genius, was enthusiastic; but the merit of the work, in the opinion of all the Musicians present, exceeded all praise."

Actually the Symphony was two years old, having been composed in 1789, one of a set of three (numbers 90, 91, and 92) commissioned by Count d'Ogny, a French aristocrat in charge of the postal service between Paris and Marseilles. The very next year (1790) Haydn sold all three Symphonies, as new works, to the German Prince Oettingen-Wallerstein, who had been trying for years to commission symphonies from Haydn. The prince was displeased when he did not receive the original autograph manuscript, but only copies of the orchestral parts, and still more annoyed when he discovered that "his" three Symphonies were being played all over Europe. "But being a generous patron," writes H. C. Robbins Landon, "he forgave Haydn and received him with great friendliness when the composer passed through the Prince's territory in December, 1790, on the way to England."

Without defending Haydn's ethics on this occasion, Landon points out that "copyists and printers had been stealing his works for nearly forty years, and he must have justifiably resented the vast amounts of money (of which he never saw a penny) constantly being made from his pirated compositions. . . ."

The nickname "Oxford," was not given to this twice-sold Symphony No. 92 until the early years of the nineteenth century. The autograph manuscript, lost for many years and rediscovered in 1956, is now in the Bibliothèque Nationale in Paris. It calls for flute, 2 oboes, 2 bassoons, 2 horns, 2 trumpets, kettledrums, and strings.

I. *Adagio; Allegro spiritoso.* One of the subtlest of Haydn's slow introductions, and one of the gentlest, anticipates the principal theme of the *Allegro.* The questioning Allegro theme itself is given out almost in a whisper by the first violins:

The reply is a burst of full orchestral sonority with leaping string figures, rushing scales and vigorous harmonic rhythms. As the whispering theme repeats a solo flute adds a touch of silver. Whispers and tutti outbursts alternate with unbelievable richness and agility, leading to a little dancing figure, which might have stepped off the stage of an Italian *opera buffa.* Now, with exuberant symphonic sleight-of-hand, Haydn tosses about the fragments of his themes. When he comes to the traditional restatement, or recapitulation, Haydn is not content to bring the themes back in original form but embellishes them with fresh instrumentation, new counter-melodies, and surprising harmonic twists.

II. "The *Adagio cantabile,*" writes Landon, "is one of the most moving pieces in Haydn's entire output; it contains pages of indescribable beauty, tinged with an autumnal sadness and yet radiant with deep inward peace."

The opening strain has a Mozartean grace, which may have been nourished by the friendship and mutual admiration of the two great composers:

A stormier middle section leads to a beautifully embellished recall of the opening melody. Among the striking traits of this movement are the deliciously cool colors of the passages for woodwinds alone, and the romantically dying *pianissimo* close, which seems to fade into silence.

III. *Menuetto: Allegretto.* The vigorous *Minuet* is full of rhythmic and harmonic surprises: sudden syncopations, and unexpected excursions into minor keys.

IV. *Presto.* The quicksilver finale is cast in a traditional, but free sonata-allegro form. The opening strain, could serve as the refrain of a lighthearted rondo:

An equally airy second theme is embellished by little glittering phrases for the solo flute. A series of dramatic pauses for the full orchestra introduce a contrapuntal whirlwind in which the first and second themes are played off against each other with breathtaking virtuosity. The recall of the principal themes is artfully varied, and a witty coda rounds off one of Haydn's most inviting works.

SYMPHONY NO. 93, D MAJOR

Haydn was quietly at work in his apartment in Vienna one day in the fall of 1790 when a strange man came into the room quite unexpectedly and announced abruptly: "I am Salomon from London, and I have come to fetch you; we will make an agreement tomorrow."

Salomon had arrived at a crucial moment, and he knew it. A well-established concert impresario, he had tried, by letters from London, to interest Haydn in visiting the English capital, but Haydn had been too attached to his great patron, Nikolaus Prince Esterházy. When Salomon heard of the prince's death, he rushed to Vienna. And Haydn was in fact free. Prince Nikolaus's successor had disbanded the Esterházy orchestra; he had kept Haydn as titular chapel-master with a very comfortable salary but no duties. Haydn was much in demand but in no particular need of a new job. In fact he had turned up his nose at one offer from a princely relative of the Esterházy family and was at the moment considering a very flattering invitation from the King of Naples.

But Salomon's offer swept Haydn off his feet. Salomon, it turned out, was not only a fine violinist, concertmaster of his own orchestra in London, and impresario for his own popular subscription concerts, he also offered dazzling financial guarantees: twelve hundred pounds (a small fortune in those days) for one new opera, six new symphonies and twenty smaller new works, the performances of which Haydn agreed to supervise in London.

When Mozart heard that his beloved older friend Haydn had agreed to make the perilous trip to London, he was alarmed.

"Oh, papa, you have had no education for the wide world," he said, "and you speak so few languages." In fact, Haydn spoke no English at all. But he replied serenely, "My language is understood all over the world."

The chief terror of the trip was the crossing of the English Channel, which took him longer than a transatlantic flight does today, and was considerably rougher. Haydn sailed for his new life in England, appropriately enough, on New Year's Day, 1791.

> After attending early mass [he wrote to his dear friend, Frau von Genzinger in Vienna], I boarded the ship at 7:30 A.M. and at 5 in the afternoon I arrived, thank God! safe and sound in Dower [sic]. . . . I remained on deck during the whole passage, so as to gaze my fill at that mighty monster, the ocean. So long as it was calm, I wasn't afraid at all, but towards the end, when the wind grew stronger and stronger, and I saw the monstrous high waves rushing at us, I became a little frightened, and a little indisposed, too. But I overcame it all and arrived safely, without vomiting, on shore. Most of the passengers were ill, and looked like ghosts, but since I went on to London, I didn't feel the effects of the journey right away, but then I needed two days to recover. Now, however, I am fresh and well again, and occupied in looking at this endlessly huge city of London, whose various beauties and marvels quite astonished me.

Haydn's fame had preceded him and his arrival caused a sensation. "Everyone wants to know me," he wrote with naïve pride to Frau von Genzinger. "I had to dine out six times up to now, and if I wanted, I could dine out every day; but first I must consider my health, and second my work. Except for the nobility, I admit no callers till 2 o'clock in the afternoon; and 4 o'clock I dine at home with Mr. Salomon. I have nice and comfortable, but expensive, lodgings. My landlord is Italian, and also a cook, and serves me four very respectable meals; we each pay one florin 30 kreutzer a day excluding wine and beer, but everything is terribly expensive here."

Haydn's new symphonies and his appearances at the Salomon concerts, which started in March, were phenomenally successful. His visit lasted for two seasons. The symphonies were not composed in the order of their numbers.

The Symphony No. 93 in D major was composed in London, probably in the late spring of 1791, and first performed on February 17 at the opening concert of the 1792 season. Salomon led the orchestra as his own concertmaster, and Haydn presided at the harpsichord, as was still customary at that time. The audience was enthusiastic, and the London *Times* was ecstatic:

> A new Overture [meaning "symphony"] from the pen of the incomparable *Haydn*, formed one considerable branch of this stupendous musical tree.
>
> Such a combination of excellence was contained in every movement as inspired all the performers as well as the audience with enthusiastic ardour.
>
> Novelty of idea, agreeable caprice and whim, combined with all *Haydn's* sublime and wonted grandeur, gave additional consequence to the *soul* and feelings of every individual present.
>
> The Critic's eye brightened with additional lustre—then was the moment that the great Painter might have caught—that which cannot be thrown on the human frame, but on such rare and great occasions . . .
>
> The Orchestra, under the direction of SALOMAN [sic], produced an effect that may with propriety be said was A SOUL AND BODY OF HARMONY.

I. *Adagio; Allegro assai.* The first movement opens with Haydn's habitual slow introduction which presents, in pensive guise, what is later revealed as the most important theme of the movement:

There is a sudden, Romantic shift into a distant key before the main body of the movement begins. It starts in a fast whisper of strings alone and there is a lively outburst of full orchestra before a tripping little scale of the violins leads into the second, but most important theme, derived, as we have said, from the slow introduction:

The central development section is based entirely on this theme.

II. *Largo cantabile.* The theme of this set of free variations is announced, chamber-music style, by four solo strings. Only when the bassoon takes up the theme does the full string choir join in a normal orchestral texture. The prominence of the minor mode emphasizes the seriousness of this slow movement. But there is also humor, for example toward the end, when the faint dialogue of violins and flutes is interrupted by a booming bass note of the bassoons.

III. *Menuetto: Allegro.* As Haydn's symphonic style continued to ripen, his minuets tended to get faster and closer to the symphonic scherzo which eventually replaced the minuet. This *Minuet,* which hints at themes of both the first and second movements, is full of delightful rhythmic shifts and surprises.

IV. *Finale: Presto ma non troppo.* The mercurial *Finale* is another of Haydn's diverting combinations of the traditional light rondo conclusion with the richer and more dramatic symphonic sonata form. Haydn seems to have invented this combination, and no one ever quite equalled him in the imaginative zest and brilliance with which he varied each new combination of the traditional forms.

The Symphony is scored for 2 flutes, 2 oboes, 2 bassoons, 2 horns, 2 trumpets, kettledrums, and the standard string sections.

SYMPHONY NO. 94, G MAJOR (SURPRISE)

The surprise in Haydn's "Surprise" Symphony is so gentle that twentieth-century listeners have to be told when to be surprised or they are certain to miss it. Tradition tells us it is one loud chord in the otherwise quiet theme of the *Andante*—in the sixteenth measure of the second movement, to be precise. The chord, so the tale goes, was intended by Haydn as a sort of prank, to startle drowsy subscribers out of their sleep at his London concert series of 1791–92. But three different versions of this story have come down to us from contemporaries, all of whom knew Haydn and claimed to have the information from the composer himself. The butt of Haydn's joke, if a joke it was, is variously said to have been: (1) late arrivals at the London concerts who, having lingered over large dinners with an aftermath of port, dozed in the soft, slow movements, (2) the ladies, who nodded because the programs lasted past midnight, and (3) one lone old man, who always sat in the same seat and promptly fell asleep at the beginning of every program. In German-speaking cities, where the "Surprise" Symphony became known as the Symphony "with the Drum Stroke" *("mit dem Paukenschlag"),* these stories circulated quickly. But they were probably pure fantasy. As a matter of fact, Haydn's slow movements were often the very sections that aroused his audiences to the greatest enthusiasm. One of his more reliable biographers, Georg August Griesinger, once asked him whether it were true "that he had written the *Andante* with the kettledrum stroke in order to waken the English public, which had fallen asleep at his concert. 'No,' [Haydn] answered me. 'Rather it was my wish to surprise the public with something new, and to make a debut in a brilliant manner in order not to be outdone by my pupil [Ignatz] Pleyel, who at that time was engaged by an orchestra in London (in the year 1792) which had begun its concert series eight days before mine. The first *Allegro* of my Symphony was received with countless bravos, but the enthusiasm reached its highest point in the *Andante* with the kettledrum stroke. *Ancora, ancora!* sounded from every throat, and even Pleyel complimented me on my idea.' "

Haydn need not have worried about being outdone by his pupil, Pleyel. The sixty-year-old master was the established lion of London audiences. His arrival in January 1791 had been heralded by his own Continent-wide reputation. He had been launched in the musical world by his astute impresario, Johann Peter Salomon, in the social world by the Prince of Wales, the future George IV, and he soon became the darling of the ladies—which also did not hurt. His symphonies composed expressly for Salomon had been acclaimed at their true worth with tremendous enthusiasm, and his entire first season was a triumph.

Now halfway through his second season with Salomon, on March 23, 1792, he presented the fifth of his new "London," or "Salomon" Symphonies, which was later to become famous as the "Surprise" Symphony. The reviews the next morning, as quoted by H. C. R. Landon in his authoritative book on the Haydn symphonies, show clearly enough how it was received. "Critical applause," wrote the *Morning Herald,* "was fervid and abundant." *Woodfall's Register* described the music as "simple, profound and sublime. The *Andante* movement was particularly admired." The *Oracle* declared that the second movement was "equal to the happiest of this great Master's conceptions. The surprise might not unaptly be likened to the situation of a beautiful shepherdess who, lulled to slumber by the murmur of a distant waterfall, starts alarmed by the unexpected firing of a fowling-piece. The flute *obbligato* was delicious."

The score calls for 2 flutes, 2 oboes, 2 bassoons, 2 horns, 2 trumpets, kettledrums, and the usual strings. Salomon's orchestra, for which the Symphony was composed and which does not necessarily represent Haydn's ideal, included 12 to 16 violins, four violas, three cellos, and four string basses.

I. *Adagio; Vivace assai.* The sometimes chromatic, almost Romantically subdued introduction begins with a phrase which, by a little stretch of the imagination, might be derived from the lighthearted principal theme of the *Vivace assai:*

This lilting, dance-like figure is rather like some of the rondo refrains that were so popular for the finales of eighteenth-century symphonies. In keeping with its character, the first movement is more caressing and charming than profound. It is in traditional sonata-allegro form.

II. *Andante.* The theme of the famous slow movement is deliberately kept in the simplest folksong, almost nursery rhyme style, beginning as follows:

The surprise chord comes exactly halfway through the theme, at the end of the sixteenth measure. In form the movement is a theme with four variations and a surprisingly Romantic coda.

III. *Menuet: Allegro molto.* The high speed of this rollicking movement takes it far afield from the archly sedate dance of its courtly origin.

IV. *Finale: Allegro di molto.* Haydn's favorite mixture of rondo gaiety and sonata sophistication give wings to this Finale. The sparky theme:

serves both as rondo refrain and as the principal theme of the symphonic sonata form. But Haydn's formal mastery and imagination are the art that conceals art. The final effect is of an adroitly told anecdote, ending in a burst of laughter.

SYMPHONY NO. 95, C MINOR

Haydn's arrival in London on New Year's Day 1791 electrified the musical world of England and inaugurated a whole new era of his career.

> My arrival caused a great sensation throughout the whole city [wrote Haydn a week later] and I went the rounds of all the newspapers for 3 successive days. . . . I wished I could flee for a time to Vienna, to have more quiet in which to work, for the noise that the common people make as they sell their wares in the street is intolerable. At present I am working on symphonies [Numbers 96 and 95, and apparently in that order, according to H. C. R. Landon] because the libretto of the opera is not yet decided on [Haydn was also to write an opera which, as a result of musical intrigues, was not performed], but in order to have more quiet I shall have to rent a room far from the center of town.

Haydn became the darling of London society. Aristocratic and well-to-do middle-class music lovers (whose sophisticated taste was destined to play an important role in the final expansion of Haydn's symphonic genius) flocked to his concerts, lionized him socially, urged him to take up residence in England, confirmed his international fame in the most rewarding fashion and made him a rich man before he finally returned to spend his declining years in Vienna.

The C-minor Symphony, No. 95 in the standard (but somewhat inaccurate) numbering of Mandyczewski, appears to be the second symphony Haydn composed in London for the subscription concerts organized by Johann Peter Salomon. The first performance was given in April 1791 (on either the first or the twenty-ninth of the month) in the fashionable Hanover Square Rooms. As was the custom of the time there were two conductors: Salomon, the concertmaster, and Haydn himself, who presided at the harpsichord.

The C-minor Symphony was repeated in the same subscription series during both the first and second seasons, so it must have been well received. It is cast in the traditional four movements, although it is the only one of Haydn's twelve "London" or "Salomon" Symphonies that does not begin with a slow introduction.

I. *Allegro moderato.* The Symphony begins starkly with five hammer-blows, bare octaves of Beethovenian abruptness:

But the aggressive opening is answered by a gentle, arching phrase for first violins. The violence and the gentleness alternate and combine in an extended statement of this principal theme until, after a full-orchestral pause, the contrasting second theme—a lilting, dance-like figure—skips gracefully through the string section starting in the violins:

The three moods combine, sometimes in rather artful counterpoint, and then are brought back in almost their original form to close the movement.

II. *Andante cantabile.* The slow movement is a theme with free variations, in which the solo cello plays a prominent role. The movement concludes with a brief coda in which the nursery-rhyme simplicity of the theme takes on an almost sunset warmth from the subtle Romantic harmonic changes.

III. *Menuet.* Despite its name, this movement seems closer to a peasant merriment than to the graces of a Versailles ballroom. In the middle section a solo cello again takes the center of the stage, while the remaining strings provide a light *pizzicato* accompaniment.

IV. *Finale: Vivace.* This is one of the many movements in which the supposedly conventional "Papa" Haydn shows himself to be one of the most masterful innovators of his era. Outwardly a lighthearted sonata allegro, this brisk *Finale* incorporates techniques and style traits of the fugue. The movement opens with a simple, graceful theme:

As so often in Haydn, the "second theme" is really a development of the first. In this case it starts in the same key as the first theme:

It continues momentarily in the style of a fugue, moving quite naturally into the contrasting key area expected of a second theme in a Classical sonata allegro. The ensuing development, too, is somewhat contrapuntal, but the reprise of the opening themes is orthodox enough in its restoration of the opening tonality and texture minus fugal complications. The Finale contains other harmonic surprises, even in its rousing coda.

The Symphony is scored for 1 flute, 2 oboes, 2 bassoons, 2 horns, 2 trumpets, kettledrums, and the traditional string body.

SYMPHONY NO. 96, D MAJOR, THE MIRACLE

At the age of fifty-eight, Haydn began a new life. On September 28, 1790, his patron, the fabulously wealthy, fantastically hospitable Prince Nikolaus II of Esterházy, whom Haydn had served for twenty-eight years, died, leaving Haydn a pension of a thousand florins a year. Thereafter events moved fast. The new Prince Esterházy did not care for music. He immediately disbanded the famous Esterházy orchestra and to Haydn's pension he added a salary of four hundred florins a year to keep him nominally in the family service, but actually leaving him free to do whatever, wherever he wished.

Haydn moved from Esterháza to Vienna so fast that he left most of his belongings behind. Hardly had he settled in a new apartment in the capital, when a stranger appeared in his room one day, apparently quite prepared to take charge of Haydn. "I am Salomon from London," he announced (according to Haydn's early biographer Dies), "and have come to fetch you; we will make an agreement tomorrow." Dies claimed to have the incident from Haydn himself. But Griesinger, another biographer who also talked with Haydn, reports that Salomon's first words were even more abrupt: "Get ready to travel. In a fortnight we go together to London."

A fortnight was too little time. It took two months. But to everyone's amazement, on New Year's Day of 1791 Haydn, who spoke no English, who had never ventured far beyond the vicinity of Vienna, found himself crossing the English Channel—in the solicitous charge of Salomon.

For various reasons, Salomon was obliged repeatedly to postpone the opening of his concert series in the fashionable Hanover Square Rooms. But when the day arrived at last (March 11, 1791) it was a triumph for Haydn. "I created a furor with a new Symphony," wrote Haydn to his friend Luigia Polzelli in Vienna, "and they had to repeat the Adagio: this had never before occurred in London. Imagine what it means to hear such a thing from an Englishman's lips!" Haydn did not exaggerate. The famous critic and music historian Dr. Charles Burney, the father of Fanny Burney, was present at this concert and described its "electrical effect on all present," adding that it was "such a degree of enthusiasm as almost amounted to frenzy."

The brief report of the *Morning Chronicle* declared:

> The First Concert under the auspices of HAYDN was last night, and never, perhaps, was there a richer musical treat.
>
> It is not wonderful [sic] that to souls capable of being touched by music, HAYDN should be an object of homage, and even of idolatry; for like our own SHAKSPEARE [sic], he moves and governs the passions at his will.
>
> His new *Grand Overture* [overture was the term habitually used in London for works we now term symphonies] was pronounced by every scientific ear to be a most wonderful composition; but the first movement in particular rises in grandeur of subject, and in rich variety of *air* and passion, beyond any even of his own productions. The *Overture* has four movements—An Allegro—Andante—Minuet—and Rondo—They are all beautiful, but the first is pre-eminent in every charm, and the Band performed it with admirable correctness.

On the same day the *Diary; or, Woodfall's Register* reported:

> A musical treat, under the immediate direction of the great HAYDN, promised the connoisseurs an exquisite repast, and they were not disappointed. . . . A new grand overture by HAYDN, was received with the highest applause, and universally deemed a composition as pleasing as scientific. The audience was so enraptured, that by unanimous desire, the second movement was encored, and the third was vehemently demanded a second time also, but the modesty of the Composer prevailed too strongly to admit a repetition. . . .

In accordance with the practice of the day in performing major orchestral works, there were two conductors for Haydn's Symphony: Salomon as concertmaster (occasionally directing with his violin bow in lieu of the modern baton) and Haydn, who presided at the harpsichord, furnishing a traditional *continuo* part. This *continuo* practice has long since been abandoned in works composed with as full instrumentation as Haydn's "London" Symphonies.

One result of Haydn's personal appearances was the incident which gave this Symphony its nickname: "The Miracle." When Haydn came to take his place at the keyboard during one of Salomon's concerts, the audience, curious to observe the great man at close quarters, crowded forward toward the orchestra, leaving empty a large number of seats in the middle of the auditorium. While the seats were still empty a huge chandelier plunged down and smashed, terrifying the whole audience. When those whose lives had perhaps been saved by the accident of their curiosity realized what had happened, the cry went up: "Miracle! miracle!"

The odd thing about this incident, which was reported in the newspaper, is that it did not happen at the performance of the Symphony No. 96, which traditionally bears the nickname "The Miracle," but much later (in 1794) at the premiere of Haydn's Symphony No. 102. The reason for the confusing of the two Symphonies has never been entirely clarified, but the nickname has stuck to No. 96.

At the next concert, exactly one week after the premiere, the Symphony No. 96 was repeated. And again it was received with great enthusiasm. According to the *Morning Chronicle* the Prince of Wales came to the concert just in time [i.e., the beginning of the second half of the concert] to join in the triumph of Haydn. The Symphony, "which had so powerful an effect on the Company of the first night, was repeated; and its influence was equally felt. It is a sublime composition—as much from the rich variety of the subject as the grandeur with which it is managed. Every instrument is respected by his Muse, and he gives to each its due proportion of efficacy. He does not elevate one, and make all the rest contributary as a mere accompaniment; but the subject is taken up by turns, with masterly art, and every performer has the means of displaying his talent."

These were no empty compliments. The present-day listener can easily spot, in any of the four movements of this Symphony, examples of the solo writing for wind instruments (including French horns) mentioned by the *Morning Chronicle*. Indeed the English concert public seems to have been a particularly discriminating one, so discriminating that the Haydn scholar H. C. Robbins Landon believes that the sensitive audience reactions to Haydn's "London" Symphonies contributed to Haydn's growth. That is, they responded to superb slow movements like that of Symphony No. 96, but remained cooler to other movements of other symphonies when Haydn did not quite match his own high standard. Symphony No. 96 aroused such enthusiasm that it was performed four times in the course of Salomon's spring season, 1791, and was repeated at least once the following spring (March 5, 1792).

I. *Adagio; Allegro.* Like all but one of Haydn's so-called "London" or "Salomon" Symphonies, No. 96 has an impressive slow introduction. It lasts only seventeen measures, yet within this narrow space an almost Romantic shift of mood takes place from the D-major pomp of the opening bar to a D-minor echo, ending with a plaintive oboe solo lingering on a dominant harmony in preparation for the main body of the movement. The *Allegro* is built upon the following graceful phrase of the first violins:

As Haydn often loved to do, he hardly used any contrasting theme at all in the exposition. The development section is elaborate and sophisticated, yet simple on the surface. Halfway through the development Haydn plays a familiar and popular trick on his audience. There is a full two-measure pause of the entire orchestra, whereupon the violins take up the opening theme, for all the world as if it were beginning to recall the traditional thematic reprise structure of the opening. But the key is wrong and the music almost immediately veers off into other thematic and tonal areas before bringing us to the home key of D major and the true reprise. But even here, just when the conventional listener may imagine himself safely at home with repeating material, Haydn changes the entire conclusion from what is expected, concluding with an astounding D-minor outburst derived from the opening measures of the slow introduction.

II. *Andante.* The slow movement, which found such favor with its first London audiences, is built upon a graceful, Rococo curlicue:

The basic form of the movement is one of the simplest known to man: A-B-A. While the opening A section appeals by its grace and variety, the central B section plunges suddenly into minor keys with a rich contrapuntal development of the most serious kind. The return of the A section is varied—first in orchestration, later by melodic embellishment of the theme quoted above. As we arrive at the expected end of the simple form, the orchestra pauses on a harmony of the sort traditionally used in an operatic aria or concerto movement to introduce a cadenza. Instead of a solo cadenza, however, there follows an extraordinarily free and imaginative passage for full orchestra, with many of the sudden harmonic and thematic shifts so characteristic of solo concerto cadenzas. Toward the end of this orchestral "cadenza" the listener will notice the tiny duet and solo passages given to the wind instruments. Like most traditional cadenzas, this passage concludes with a long-held dominant trill, starting as a trill for the oboe solo, gradually growing to an ensemble trill and resolving to one last recall of the basic theme embellished.

III. *Menuetto: Allegretto.* The vigorous minuet is the only movement of the entire Symphony which follows established traditional form. There is an especial charm in the central trio section, when the solo oboe is heard in a melody recalling the Austrian peasant dance type known as the *Ländler.*

IV. *Finale: Vivace assai.* This *Finale* is one of Haydn's lightest, brightest and wittiest rondos: a cunningly constructed "teasing" rondo, using a humorous technique of which Haydn was now past master. It is also a movement of symphonic richness: a true marriage of rondo and sonata-allegro form and style built almost entirely on the whispering four-measure refrain which opens and closes the movement:

When Haydn sent a copy of this Symphony and his Symphony No. 95 to a friend and patron, Herr von Keess in Vienna, he clearly was worried by the frequent practice of performing symphonic works without any rehearsal at all! So he asked Keess "respectfully to have a rehearsal of both these Symphonies, because they are very delicate, especially the last movement of that in D major [i.e., the Finale of No. 96], for which I recommend the softest *piano* and a very quick tempo."

Haydn's Symphony No. 96 is scored for 2 flutes, 2 oboes, 2 bassoons, 2 horns, 2 trumpets, kettledrums, and the standard string choir, in addition to which, as noted above, Haydn himself played a *continuo* part on the harpsichord.

SYMPHONY NO. 97, C MAJOR

Haydn's Symphony No. 97, composed in London in 1792, is the last and greatest of a long rather dazzling series of trumpet symphonies in C major. Ordinarily Haydn did not associate specific keys such as D major, F major, B-flat major, and so on, with any particular mood or character, as nineteenth-century Romantic composers were apt to do. But C major was another story. All in all, Haydn composed twenty symphonies in C major, and fifteen of these have a special festive character, a pomp and brilliance traditionally associated with royalty, as for example Haydn's "Maria Theresia" Symphony No. 48 (see pages 400-4). This association was particularly strong when the trumpets were used in conjunction with kettledrums, for this was a combination of instruments which since the Middle Ages had been a special prerogative of royalty and the highest aristocracy. The ancient guilds of trumpeters and kettledrummers ranked far above their colleagues who were mere fiddlers or pipers. And this memory survives (quite subconsciously) today in the feeling of many a music lover that there is something inherently noble about the sound of the trumpet. Three more of the symphonies Haydn composed in this festive C-major tradition included in this volume are his No. 60 (pages 404-7), No. 82 (pages 407-9), and the present No. 97.

We do not know the exact dates of Haydn's composition of No. 97, except that he wrote it in the year 1792 and that it was the last of the six symphonies he composed for his first London visit. We do know, however, that it was first performed on either May 3 or 4 (probably the latter date), in which case it is the symphony which was repeated "by particular desire" one week later. These concerts, like the others of Haydn's London series, took place in the fashionable Hanover Square Rooms, with Salomon directing as concertmaster and Haydn presiding at either the harpsichord or the pianoforte; the newspaper announcements vary from concert to concert on this point.

I. *Adagio; Vivace.* The Symphony opens with Haydn's now-customary slow introduction, this one being of particular importance since its brooding first theme appears twice again in the first movement: once at the end of the exposition, and finally at the coda which rounds off the entire movement. This is the phrase which Haydn used in this movement with such unusual effect; we hear it in the opening measures of the Symphony in the first violins:

The principal *vivace* section of the movement bursts upon us with the full brilliant force of trumpets, horns, and timpani, reinforced by the entire ensemble. It is primitive in its fanfare shape and for Haydn it is furiously aggressive in the hammered repetitions of the two last notes: G-C, G-C, etc.

This forceful beginning comes to a sudden halt with the long pause before the gentle secondary theme, a soft, playful figure for first violins makes its appearance dancing, as it were, over the lightest of *pizzicato* accompaniments. It is followed by another graceful triplet melody before the orchestra grows suddenly pensive, and the meditative phrase from the slow introduction returns to round off this exposition.

The development section starts off with another furious onslaught of the principal theme, but this soon fades away to a more playful fragmentation of just two notes, the C to G motive we heard so insistently at the start but which now appears in the merest whisper, playing hide-and-seek, as it were, as it dodges from one instrumental group to another. Gradually the orchestra reassembles its forces for a reprise of the ferocious principal theme as well as its gentler playfellow, and the richly hued coda to the movement begins with a last recall of the pensive phrase from the slow introduction.

II. *Adagio ma non troppo.* The slow movement is made up of a songful theme for the violins, followed by a series of three decorative variations, the second of which takes us momentarily into a minor-key version of the melody. The last variation is remarkable for Haydn's unusually detailed direction for the violins to bow their instruments close to the bridge to produce an almost whispering sonority. The movement is rounded off by a surprisingly Romantic coda in which throbbing basses and cellos sustain the tonic fundamental while solo woodwinds and trembling strings shift through a series of exotic progressions before coming to rest with a reassuring home cadence.

III. *Menuetto: Allegretto.* Haydn, who was always looking for ways to give variety to his minuet, does so here by changing the orchestration every time he repeats a section, in the *Minuet,* as well as the central trio section. One charming personal note occurs at the very end of the trio where Haydn directs his concertmaster and impresario Salomon to play alone one octave higher than the rest of the violins, "but," say the directions, "softly."

IV. *Finale: Presto assai.* This lighthearted *Finale,* which goes as fast as the wind, is a rondo based on this little refrain presented first in the still, small voice of the first violins:

It is a rondo, but a rondo with a difference—that is to say, a rondo enriched with all kinds of tricks and expressive devices borrowed from first-movement sonata form. This is a combination which Haydn had practiced with increasing delight for over a decade, and with results which never failed to bewitch his delighted audience. This one has more than the usual quota of Haydnish surprises and seems to end in a final burst of laughter.

The Symphony is scored for pairs of flutes, oboes, bassoons, horns, trumpets, kettledrums, plus the traditional group of strings, with a harpsichord or piano to fill out the *continuo* part.

SYMPHONY NO. 98, B-FLAT MAJOR

A pleasant custom and one which Haydn's delighted audiences and the composer himself both enjoyed was that of applauding between the movements of a symphony and, when enthusiasm ran especially high, of encoring the movement on the spot. Not only Haydn, but Mozart and Beethoven, all noted with pride when a movement was encored. And sometimes a note of disappointment crept in; for example, when Haydn noted in his London diary after his first concert of the 1792 season presented by his impresario Salomon in the Hanover Square Rooms: "only the Adagio of the new Symphony was repeated."

But two weeks later on March 2, when the new B-flat Symphony we know as No. 98 was heard, Haydn noted happily: "In the 3rd concert, the new Symphony in B-flat was given, and the first and last Allegros encort [sic]." The enthusiasm was so great that the B-flat Symphony was promptly repeated the following week on a program which the London *Morning Herald* said was "one of the richest treats the present season has afforded." And the *Morning Chronicle* declared: "The new Overture [i.e.: Symphony] of the former Friday was repeated: it is one of the grandest compositions we ever heard, and it was most loudly applauded; the first and last movements were encored." The B-flat Symphony was performed for the third time on the same concert series on the seventh program of April 13.

Under the stimulus of such appreciation Haydn continued to grow, as he consciously pushed himself to find fresh and more imaginative symphonic forms and ideas.

I. *Adagio; Allegro.* For all its brevity and concision, the slow introduction is one of Haydn's starkest and most foreboding. The opening subject of the *Allegro* is anticipated almost literally except that it is cast in the darker minor mode:

Even when we come to the lighter, faster version with which the main *Allegro* section begins, we enter a more somber world than most of Haydn's opening allegros, and the central development section is a richly contrapuntal struggle, almost, as H. C. Robbins Landon suggests, an intellectual struggle, though Haydn always knows how to subordinate his virtuoso technical skill to the turbulent emotions. As the music delves farther and farther into the regions of the minor mode, we are increasingly reminded of the prophetic slow introduction.

II. *Adagio.* Even in the slow movement of this Symphony, which Haydn casts in a free form, a sort of hybrid with elements of both variations and sonata, a more serious note than usual creeps into its central episode. Again there is eloquent exploitation of the tensions of the minor mode.

III. *Menuet: Allegro.* In this vigorous *Minuet* movement Haydn went far toward fulfilling his own long-standing wish that someone would invent "a really new kind of minuet." Trumpets, drums, and horns emphasize the almost aggressive drive of the tempo, which takes us far indeed from the courtly dance from which the minuet evolved. This is not yet a scherzo in the Beethoven sense, nor should it be heard as a mere predecessor of the Beethoven scherzo type; it has a breadth and sweep of its own that need no historical or other justification.

IV. *Finale: Presto.* The *Finale* takes off with a light-footed theme, suggesting a mercurial rondo of the kind which Haydn so often enjoyed:

A frisky oboe echoes the theme. But we are in for surprises. Instead of a rondo, or even a rondo-sonata hybrid like many magnificent finales of the late Haydn symphonies, we are plunged into a full-fledged sonata-allegro movement which gives further scope for Haydn's serious thoughts, even where gaiety and brilliance are so often the order of the day.

One last beguiling and quite personal surprise awaits us just before the end. As the violins return to the playful theme of the opening, we hear a rippling, silvery sound in the background. This is the only place in Haydn's symphonies where he actually wrote down the continuo part (that is, the normally improvised *right-hand* part of the continuo), the part which he himself played in these London performances, showing that the convention of the piano or harpsichord participation in the orchestral ensemble was by no means the perfunctory—even superfluous—survival of ancient custom which we so often imagine it to be. Here are the first of these dozen airy measures which remind us once more of Haydn's inexhaustibly inventive imagination:

This B-flat Symphony is scored for flute, 2 oboes, 2 bassoons, 2 horns, 2 trumpets, kettledrums, and the customary body of strings including, of course, a harpsichord or pianoforte.

SYMPHONY NO. 99, E-FLAT MAJOR

One of the greatest miracles of the continually surprising Haydn was the way in which he continued to grow. Not only do his late symphonies grow in depth and imagination, but they seem almost to grow in youthfulness as well. After his prodigious output of symphonies through a long career, Haydn throws himself into the fast movements of his Symphony No. 99 in E-flat major with a temperament which suggests a man of thirty, rather than his true age of sixty-one years. Even the profoundly stirring *Adagio,* which the Haydn authority H. C. Robbins Landon believes a lament for the death of a dear friend, suggests none of the world-weary tragic vision one might expect, but rather the bursting heart of a younger man who bears the loss because he must, but bears it with strength unimpaired.

The E-flat Symphony was composed in Vienna, 1793, during the interval between Haydn's two visits to London. It was the first of Haydn's final set of six symphonies intended for Salomon's subscription concerts and it was first performed under the joint direction of Haydn and Salomon at the Hanover Square concert rooms on February 10, 1794. It was greeted ecstatically by both public and press. The *Morning Chronicle* on the following day declared: "The incomparable HAYDN, produced an Overture [the customary English term for a symphony at this time] of which it is impossible to speak in common terms. It is one of the grandest efforts of art that we ever witnessed. It abounds with ideas, as new in music as they are grand and impressive; it rouses and affects every emotion of the soul.—It was received with rapturous applause."

The new Symphony was promptly repeated at Salomon's second subscription concert the following week. That some of Haydn's listeners at any rate were well aware of the fresh developments in his style is shown by the report of the *Morning Chronicle* following the Symphony's repetition, praising in particular one of its most delightful attributes, the imaginative use of the woodwinds: "The overture, being performed with increasing accuracy and effect, was received with increasing rapture. The first movement was encored: the effect of the wind instruments in the second movement was enchanting; the hautboy and flute were finely in tune, but the bassoon was in every respect more perfect and delightful than we ever remember to have heard a wind instrument before. In the minuet, the trio was peculiarly charming; but indeed the pleasure the whole gave was continual; and the genius of Haydn, astonishing, inexhaustible and sublime, was the general theme."

I. *Adagio; Vivace assai.* Haydn opens his first movement with a slow introduction of romantically shifting moods. The main body of the movement, the *Vivace assai,* opens with a theme so carefree and mercurial that one could almost imagine it to be the subject of one of Haydn's lighter finales:

But Haydn plunges at once into a stormy *tutti* extension of the theme with sharply clashing minor ninths. The dramatic intensity that Haydn reaches so early in the movement could almost be compared to Beethoven were it not so vividly characteristic of Haydn himself. The stormy passage comes to an abrupt close and after a pause a gently sighing second theme is sung by the first violins and a solo clarinet. (This is, by the way, the first of Haydn's symphonies to use clarinets.)

In the development that follows, the gentle second theme spreads through the entire orchestra down to its very foundations in the cellos and the double basses. It is turned upside down, combined with itself and acquires an urgency which also infects the development of the principal theme. Even the reprise of the basic thematic material is full of surprises: melodic, harmonic and instrumental, the latter including a soft, sepulchral pedal tone, the lowest note obtainable on the E-flat horn.

II. *Adagio.* The slow movement begins innocently enough with a songful tune for the first violins. This is followed by the passage for four woodwinds alone, which so enchanted Haydn's early audiences and still has not lost its charm. From here on the movement grows in emotional tension and depth, reaching, in two successive climaxes, a startling intensity of grief—reflecting, according to Landon, Haydn's sense of bereavement at the death of his dearly beloved Marianne von Genzinger.

III. *Menuetto: Allegretto.* The *Minuet* is vigorous and original. It has lost everything but the form of the courtly dance which was its origin. The delicate trio section is introduced so quietly that one can easily miss the almost Schubertian Romantic shift of tonality from E-flat major to C major.

IV. *Finale: Vivace.* Another ingratiating, dance-like theme launches one of Haydn's most original and powerful rondo finales:

The mixture of rondo and sonata-allegro form and style, which Haydn so loved in his later years, takes fresh and surprising form. The innocent little theme surprises us not only with the grandeur and power of its development, with all its contrapuntal complexity, but with its teasing, mocking echoes, passing from one instrumental group to another, with a sudden wayward *adagio* in the middle of the movement and then with the whirlwind brilliance of the closing pages.

The Symphony is scored for 2 flutes, 2 oboes, 2 clarinets, 2 bassoons, 2 horns, 2 trumpets, kettledrums, and the traditional strings.

SYMPHONY NO. 100, G MAJOR, MILITARY

[The striking rebirth of public and professional enthusiasm for Haydn in our time is due in no small measure to the pioneering scholarship of H. C. Robbins Landon. In addition to his discovery of lost Haydn works, Landon has published hundreds of Haydn works in scholarly and practical performing editions: he has supervised an impressive corpus of Haydn recordings, has edited the first complete collection of the Haydn symphonies, and has written what may well remain the definitive book on *Symphonies of Joseph Haydn.* The following essay on Haydn's "Military" Symphony was commissioned especially for the New York Philharmonic.]

On the last day of March 1794, Haydn gave the first performance of a "New Grand Overture (M.S.)" in the Hanover Square Rooms in London. It was the eighth concert of the series organized by Johann Peter Salomon, who had brought Haydn to England the first time in 1791 and had persuaded him to return in 1794. The English loved Haydn the man and worshiped his music —indeed, not since Handel had a musician been so popular with the English. Salomon's concerts were patronized not only by the "nobility and gentry," including the Prince of Wales (later George IV), but also by London's wealthy society: wealthy because the tickets were very expensive; a subscription for the whole series of twelve concerts cost five guineas, while a single ticket to one of Haydn's benefit concerts cost half a guinea—the price of a big meal for four with wine in those days.

Haydn's previous symphonies had been popular, and some were already household favorites, such as the "Surprise" (No. 94, composed in 1791); but his new "Overture," as the contemporary newspapers like to call a symphony, became instantaneously Haydn's greatest public success. *Fin-de-siècle* London went mad over it. They could not hear it enough. Salomon, who had the publication rights for all Haydn's new symphonies, brought out an edition for home consumption: arranged as a piano trio, the violin parts "accompanying" (as, indeed, they did in Haydn's own late piano trios). The second movement, with the "military" percussion section (triangle, cymbals, bass drum), was invariably encored. What is perhaps hard for us to imagine is that audiences, *anno* 1794, found the music not only brilliant—we can hear that aspect of the music easily—but also horrifying. It summed up to men the horrors of war in general and the Napoleonic Wars, which had just begun, in particular.

Haydn's new Symphony struck a responsive chord in everyone who loved music; seldom has a composer so completely understood what the public needed; his "Salomon" Symphonies, as they are rightly called, in tribute to the great impresario who was responsible for their existence, entered the repertoire the very night they were first performed. Haydn's music was totally integrated in the society that first heard it; perhaps it is the last time in musical history that the public completely understood and appreciated great music at its first performance: from Beethoven to Stockhausen and from Schubert to Berio, the fatal gap has always existed.

There was, in late-eighteenth-century London, a flourishing press, which informed its readers regularly of the Salomon concerts and of the new symphonies by "Dr. Haydn" (who had received a doctor of music, *honoris causa,* from Oxford in 1791). The "Military" Symphony, as it came to be called within one month, was repeated at Salomon's ninth concert on April 7, 1794. Two famous singers, Madame Mara and Ludwig Fischer (for whom Mozart had written the role of Osmin in *Die Entführung aus dem Serail* a dozen years before), sang arias, and Viotti played a violin concerto. The *Morning Chronicle* —the principal newspaper of London in those days—reviewed the concert as follows:

> Though under the necessity of repeating the same names (for where are their equals?) and the same praises, which never sufficiently express the delicious sensations that these performers at some moments excite, yet to be silent would be flagrant injustice. What we have on former occasions so ardently spoken, particularly of those first of Performers Mara and Viotti, is again their due, and more if we had it to bestow. Some of the connoisseurs profess to like the playing of Viotti better than his Music.—Judgments differ; we will not pretend to affirm they are mistaken; we can only say, though his Compositions partake of the Old French School, there is yet a richness, unity and grandeur in them, that in our opinion place them far beyond the jigs, quirks and quackery, in which modern music is so apt to indulge. Not that we are enemies of modern music: it has many essential improvements, but it has no few radical vices. Another new Symphony, by Haydn, was performed for the second time; and the middle movement [*i.e.,* the second] was again received with absolute shouts of applause. Encore! encore! encore! resounding from every seat: the Ladies themselves could not forbear. It is the advancing to battle; and the march of men, the sounding of the charge, the thundering of the onset, the clash of arms, the groans of the wounded, and what may well be called the hellish roar of war increase to a climax of horrid sublimity! which, if others can conceive, he alone can execute; at least he alone hitherto has effected these wonders.

Haydn seems to have begun Symphony No. 100 in G major when he was still in Vienna; at least the Minuet of the autograph manuscript is written on Italian paper which Haydn used in Austria (which he had left in January 1794), while the first and last movements are on British paper and the beginning is signed and dated 1794; the autograph of the famous "Militaire Movement" has disappeared.

I. *Adagio; Allegro.* The stately slow introduction with which the work begins introduces a serious note: We shift with a sinister *crescendo* into G minor. The *Allegro* thus shines the more brilliantly; the scoring of the opening subject, for flute and two oboes only, looks far forward to the "toy" music of Rimsky-Korsakov.

The scoring, or rather the layout, of the ensuing *tutti* shows how much Salomon's fabulous orchestra had influenced Haydn the composer: solid middle parts in slow motion (horns, trumpets, viola), the second violins accompanying in nervous eight-notes, the cellos pounding out the bass line in bouncing eight-notes, the double basses providing an impetus to the first beat of each bar by dropping an octave. It is scoring which "works" immediately and shows on the one hand a lifetime of experience and on the other an almost quicksilverish ability to adapt to new circumstances. There is an extended second subject which dominates not only much of the very serious and weighty development section but also the coda:

When the development section occurs, we see the architectural bridge between that sinister *crescendo* in the introduction and the equally ominous ones that mark the early part of the development. The movement ends with the most brilliant coda of Haydn's career—fifty bars that startle with their sudden plunge into the flatted submediant (E flat) and then delight for the sheer joy of trumpeting, drumming and fiddling in an orgy of G major.

II. *Allegro.* Haydn lifted the entire "military" movement up to the entrance of the trumpet solo from an earlier work which had disappeared into the wilds of Caserta [summer residence of the kings of Naples]: a Concerto for two *lire organizzate* (a sophisticated variety of hurdy-gurdy), composed in 1786 for the King of Naples (Ferdinand IV). Haydn completely reorchestrated the movement. For the first time clarinets appear in the scoring [of this symphony], which is now very large: 2 flutes, 2 oboes, 2 clarinets, 2 bassoons, 2 horns, 2 trumpets, kettledrums, triangle, cymbals, bass drums, and strings with two viola parts. There is some beautiful writing for unaccompanied woodwind. When the music plunges into the tonic minor (C minor) the extra percussion appears for the first time; it must have created a tremendous effect. The coda—beginning with the ominous low trumpet call—is all new and, as we have read, it brought the house down.

III. *Minuet: Moderato.* The slow Minuet has a complicated middle section, and once again that serious note struck in the introduction reappears; it also appears, most ominously, in the Trio (in the dotted "French" overture rhythm: an accident? or an undercover reference to Britain's, and of course, Austria's, great enemy across the Channel?).

IV. *Presto.* The finale is a great example of the increased scope of Haydn's late-period final movements: On a huge scale (334 bars), it is as complex in form as it is many-channeled in its emotions. There is a timpani solo which is twice the size of the famous "Surprise" (in Symphony No. 94), and the extra percussion rejoin the orchestra at the end of the movement.

A great Symphony which was popular from its birth in March 1794 and has remained so ever since.

H.C. ROBBINS LANDON

SYMPHONY NO. 101, D MAJOR, THE CLOCK

At the age of sixty-two, with a hundred symphonies behind him, Haydn might have been forgiven for repeating himself a bit in his 101st. But no. He was still full of surprises. His symphonies grew more and more individual as their numbers rose and he himself advanced in years. Variety of imagination was one of the qualities for which he was most often praised as he presented his last half-dozen symphonies to delighted London audiences in 1794 and 1795.

"As usual [wrote the London *Morning Chronicle* after the concert of March 3, 1794, at which Haydn directed the premiere of his "Clock" Symphony] the most delicious part of the entertainment was a new grand Overture by HAYDN; the inexhaustible, the wonderful, the sublime HAYDN! The first two movements were encored; and the character that pervaded the whole composition was heartfelt joy. Every new Overture he writes, we fear, till it is heard, he can only repeat himself; and we are every time mistaken. Nothing can be more original than the subject of the first movement; and having found a happy subject, no man knows like HAYDN how to produce incessant variety, without once departing from it. The management of the accompaniments of the Andante, though perfectly simple, was masterly; and we never heard a more charming effect than was produced by the trio to the minuet.— It was HAYDN; what can we, what need we say more?"

Nowadays, of course, it would be very bad form to applaud between movements of a Haydn symphony and only peasants would think of suggesting an encore. But one suspects that there were few in Haydn's audience who felt that their mood had been shattered by the applause. And perhaps Haydn himself was not exactly angered by the double encore. After all, applause is a very direct form of communication. And one week later, on March 10, when Haydn repeated the same Symphony for the same audience, he probably did not complain when they again encored the *Andante,* the movement which eventually won this Symphony its nickname of "The Clock."

Although this nickname does not seem to have become traditional until the early nineteenth century, it was more appropriate than many. Aside from the familiar tick-tock rhythm of the *Andante,* which Haydn may or may not have intended to suggest the sound of a clock, there was another movement he most certainly did associate with a specific clock. For while Haydn was home in Vienna in 1793, he devised twelve short pieces for an elaborate musical clock which he presented before returning to London, as a gift to his great patron Prince Esterházy. This musical clock incorporated a minute pipe organ with flute pipes constructed by Prince Esterházy's librarian, Father Primitivius Niemecz. Father Niemecz seems to have enjoyed international fame as a builder of such tiny mechanical organs, or *Flötenuhren,* as they were called. One of Haydn's pieces for the 1793 mechanical clock is so close to the *Menuet* movement of the "Clock" Symphony that the movement has been considered simply an elaboration of the piece composed for the mechanical clock. However, the well-known Haydn authority, H. C. Robbins Landon, believes (on the basis of the manuscript paper Haydn used, and other evidence) that parts of this Symphony, too, were composed in Vienna in 1793, before Haydn returned to London, and that quite probably the version for the mechanical clock was an adaptation from the Symphony. Whichever came first, it is clear that Haydn had his own good reasons for associating this Symphony with a clock that played fairly elaborate tunes.

I. *Adagio: Presto.* The slow introduction to Haydn's first movement establishes a Romantic mood, partly by means of its chromatic harmonies. It opens with a slowly rising scale which anticipates the principal theme of the movement, a lively lilting figure in a 6/8 meter often associated with hunting music, and with symphony finales:

The gentle introduction of the above theme in the first violins is echoed by a brilliant *tutti* version of the same subject with woodwinds, brass and kettledrums.

Haydn introduces his subordinate theme with a similar lilt and a similar light touch, followed by a parallel *tutti* burst. Both themes are then developed in delicate, almost chamber music style. There is a brief climax, after which a playful flute solo leads back to a recapitulation of the two principal themes.

II. *Andante.* The slow movement, from which the Symphony takes its nickname, opens with a measure of clocklike tick-tock rhythm supplied by two bassoons and *pizzicato* strings:

Above this persistent rhythm the first violins have the following rather dainty melodic line, which could well be associated with a musical clock, music box or any number of the pretty, musical mechanisms which so delighted the eighteenth century:

Suddenly Haydn's orchestra plunges into an agitated G-minor section, which we soon recognize as a peculiarly forceful variation of the opening strain. The G-minor variation is followed by a second, imaginative variation, in which the tick-tock rhythm is taken up by two solo instruments: a flute and a bassoon, while the first violins embellish the original melody. A third variation seems to spirit us away to a distant harmonic region, only to return us to orthodoxy by leading the melody back to its original key with a splendiferous *tutti.*

III. *Menuet: Allegretto.* There is little here to remind the unsuspecting listener of a mechanical clock, but this is the tune that Haydn used for his *Flötenuhr* present to Prince Esterházy. It is a characteristically vigorous, late-Haydn minuet, more of a folk dance, stamping style than the older aristocratic tradition. The middle, or "trio" section, includes a delightfully stylized drone, or repeated harmony, which is maintained like the drone of the bagpipes, while a solo flute dances jauntily in the air above. The movement is rounded off by a return of the opening minuet section.

IV. *Finale: Vivace.* Playful though this Symphony may be, it is as rich in surprises and original in form as the discerning critic of the London *Morning Chronicle* declared. The finale begins with the following lively melody:

It continues in a way that leads us to expect a rondo, one of the most popular forms of the day and one especially favored for symphony finales. But hardly is this innocent refrain completed than we plunge into the kind of complex, stormy music associated with the development of a sonata-allegro movement. The little refrain is chopped up and tossed about, its first three notes being a most easily recognizable fragment.

For a moment the refrain returns as innocently as if nothing had happened. But not for long. Suddenly the full orchestra veers off into a churning maelstrom of D minor. Then, as if to cap the ambiguity with still another surprise, the surging D minor stops dead in its tracks. The dramatic pause is followed by a lively whispering passage for strings alone, which turns out, on close listening, to be one of the most "learned" styles of music at Haydn's command: a full exposition of a fugue (based on the rondo refrain). By this time, anyone expecting any kind of formal or stylistic orthodoxy is thoroughly baffled. This, of course, is the moment for Haydn to return to what would have been an orthodox and quite brilliant close for a lighthearted rondo. The final bar bears Haydn's customary pious exclamation: *"Laus Deo."*

The "Clock" Symphony is scored for 2 flutes, 2 oboes, 2 clarinets, 2 bassoons, 2 horns, 2 trumpets (which Haydn calls *clarini*), kettledrums, and the traditional string choir. Although the clarinets are not included in Haydn's manuscript score, the consensus of scholarly opinion is that they were probably added by Haydn himself before the Symphony was published.

SYMPHONY NO. 102, B-FLAT MAJOR

In his sixty-second year and midway in his second, highly profitable visit to London, Haydn stood at the peak of his fame, popularity, financial success and in a new flood tide of his creative power. He had already produced over a hundred symphonies and, if three early symphonies had not escaped Haydn's conscientious cataloguer Eusebius Mandyczewski, the B-flat Symphony (we know as No: 102) might well be known as Haydn's Hundred and Fifth! Yet far from repeating any tired formula, this new score is such an explosion of high spirits, so youthful in all but its craftsmanship that it almost suggests a new composer at the start of a great career. It not only *sounds* fresh, it strikes out new paths of emotion and form, which might have surprised even such an experimenter as Haydn.

The Symphony No. 102 was first performed at the King's Theatre in the Haymarket, London, on February 2, 1795, for the opening of the so-called "Opera Concerts" season. This was the tenth of Haydn's "London" symphonies, the preceding nine of which had been composed for Johann Peter Salomon's fashionable subscription concerts. Salomon had been obliged to suspend his series because the disorders in France (which we know as the Reign of Terror) prevented him from importing all the foreign talent he felt necessary to maintain his high musical standards. This in turn enabled the management of the "Opera Concerts," which habitually enlisted the finest artists available in London, to engage not only Haydn, but eventually Johann Peter Salomon himself as their concertmaster.

Haydn conducted the first performance from his seat at the keyboard (in this case a piano), an established orchestral practice, which persisted even into the nineteenth century. His new Symphony, billed in the language of the day as "A new Grand Overture composed on the Occasion by—Haydn," was a triumph. The finale was encored and not even the crash of a chandelier into the middle of the parterre seems to have dampened the enthusiasm. Fortunately, many listeners appear to have left their seats for the encore, crowding forward to watch the composer close at hand, and leaving the center of the house empty. Thus no one was seriously hurt and the encore, as the *Morning Chronicle* reported next day, "was performed with no less effect."

The triumph no more than confirmed the hold Haydn already exerted over London audiences. The new Symphony seems to have been repeated with equal success two weeks later at the very next Opera Concert. "What shall we say of HAYDN," asked the *Morning Chronicle* the following day, "and the sublime, the magical Overture, with which he began the second Act [i.e.: the second half of the program]? The rapture it gave cannot be communicated by words; to be known it must be heard." And the rapture held. On March 16 the Symphony had what appears to have been its third performance in six weeks at the same subscription series. "Of the Overture," the *Morning Chronicle* wrote, "what more can be said than that the best judges seem to doubt whether Haydn himself ever surpassed it. The last movement was encored; and the Adagio still more deservedly ought to have been."

I. *Largo—Allegro vivace.* The slow introduction opens with a theme from which are derived both the principal and the subordinate themes of the following *Allegro.* A solemn octave B-flat for the entire band leads to a delicately arching figure in the high strings:

The whirlwind start of the *Allegro vivace:*

grows recognizably out of the arch of the introduction, or rather bursts out of it in exuberant repetitions until it merges into a still more driving figure which makes the connections still more obvious:

After a sudden pause, a strong orchestral octave (recalling the introduction) launches the secondary theme on a gently rocking figure also derived from the Symphony's opening arch.

Thus far the exposition has been a relatively clear interplay of relatedness and contrast. In the development that follows, both the themes, and half a dozen figures derived from them are churned up in a symphonic maelstrom, a *crescendo* of planned chaos. The *tutti* now storms its way from C minor through a whole series of tonalities with inexorable harmonic pull toward the Symphony's key center of B flat. The urgency of this harmonic return is heightened by hints of the main theme tossed from the violins to oboe to flute and by a dramatic roll of the kettledrums, which make the suspense almost unbearable so that the return of the principal theme in its home key seems as powerful and inevitable as a force of nature. This was something new in Haydn, and the effect is still irresistibly exciting.

The return is anything but literal however, and even the most practiced listener will delight in the originality and surprise of Haydn's conclusion to one of his greatest movements.

II. *Adagio.* The sensitive, graceful slow movement has a characteristically free form, rather like a theme and variations, but with tonal relations based firmly on sonata form. The orchestral color is remarkable for the use of a solo cello with muted horns and muted trumpets. The music is identical with the slow movement of Haydn's F-sharp minor Piano Trio (Breitkopf and Härtel edition, No. 2), which was written about the same time. We do not know which version came first.

III. *Menuetto: Allegro.* The *Allegro* of this movement is considerably faster than the traditional minuet tempo. The vigorous stomping character of the music recalls Haydn's own expressed wish that someone would "invent a really new minuet."

IV. *Finale: Presto.* No wonder this *Finale* was encored! The mercurial little rondo refrain and its tantalizing returns, which Haydn devises with such zest and wit, are an invitation to laughter, to wonder, and to still further repetition. Repetition is, after all, the essence of the rondo spirit as well as its form. Haydn had long pioneered in new ways of combining rondo and sonata forms and this *Finale* is a mature fruit of that experimentation. Yet all that is needed to enjoy it is the ability to recognize a catchy tune.

The Symphony is scored for 2 flutes, 2 oboes, 2 bassoons, 2 horns, 2 trumpets, kettledrums, and the traditional string choir.

SYMPHONY NO. 103, E-FLAT MAJOR, THE DRUMROLL

It was said that King George III and Queen Charlotte were rather miffed at Haydn's refusal to stay in England. But to tell the truth, they had been rather late in inviting him. Haydn had not even been presented to Their Majesties until shortly before he conducted the premiere of his E-flat Symphony, No. 103, the next-to-last of the twelve he composed for London. He had already been world-famous when he came for his first English visit in 1791, and the first half-dozen of his "London" Symphonies were greeted with overwhelming enthusiasm. In 1794 and 1795, when Haydn returned for his second visit and his second set of London symphonies, audiences received him with affection as well as admiration. Moreover, they realized that they were hearing the latest and greatest works of the greatest living composer.

Only six months before his last departure from England, Haydn was presented to Their Majesties. The occasion was a private concert given by the Duke of York at York House in London attended by King George, Queen Charlotte, the Prince of Wales, and many other members of the Royal family and the higher nobility. The program consisted entirely of works by Haydn, with the violinist-impresario Salomon conducting and Haydn himself presiding at the piano. At the end of the first half of the program the Prince of Wales presented Haydn to King George III.

"At the end [Haydn later recalled] I had to sing too. The King, who up to now could or would hear only Handel's compositions, was attentive; he talked with me and introduced me to the Queen, who payed me many compliments. I sang my German song, *'Ich bin der verliebteste.'* On 3rd February I was invited to the Prince of Wales, also on the 15th, 17th, 19th April, 1795; on the 21st to the Queen in Buckingham Palace."

From that day, Haydn was a frequent guest at the queen's musicales. One evening, according to Haydn's early biographer Griesinger, after he had played to the Queen for some time on the piano, the King said that he knew Haydn had been a good singer, and he would like to hear him sing a few German songs. Haydn pointed to the joint of his little finger and said: "Your Majesty, my voice is only this big now." The King laughed and then Haydn sang his song again, *"Ich bin der verliebteste."*

The King and Queen wanted to keep Haydn in England. "I will give you rooms in the Windsor [Castle] for the summer," the Queen declared. But Haydn declined on the ground that he owed service to his lifetime patrons, the Esterházy family. Haydn was repeatedly pressed to stay, but he remained steadfast. Later Haydn came to the conclusion that this was the reason the king never gave him anything.

How different from symphony audiences of the twentieth century were the innovation-hungry London audiences at the end of the eighteenth century, when the management of the fashionable Opera Concerts lured their subscribers by promising them *at least two* new works on every program. The atmosphere in the King's Theatre, when one of the new works was by Haydn, is suggested by the following report of March 25 by the London correspondent of the Weimar *Journal des Luxus und der Moden.*

> . . . . But what would you say to his [Haydn's] new symphonies composed expressly for these concerts and directed by himself at the pianoforte? It is truly wonderful what sublime and august thoughts this master weaves into his works. Passages often occur which render it impossible to listen to them without becoming excited. We are altogether carried away by admiration and forced to applaud with hand and mouth. This is especially the case with Frenchmen, of whom we have so many here that all the public places are filled with them. [London was overflowing with Parisian refugees from the Reign of Terror.] You know that they have great sensibility and cannot restrain their transports, so that in the midst of the finest passages in soft *adagios* they clap their hands in loud applause and thus mar the effect. In

> every symphony of Haydn the *adagio* or *andante* is sure to be repeated each time, after the most vehement [calls for] "encore!" The worthy Haydn, whose personal acquaintance I highly value, conducts himself on these occasions in the most modest manner. He is indeed a good-hearted, candid, honest man, esteemed and beloved by all.

The E-flat Symphony was first performed on March 2, 1795, at the fourth of the Opera Concerts subscription series at the King's Theatre in the Haymarket. Haydn himself presided at the harpsichord or piano (the advertisements had announced it would be the harpsichord). The day after the concert, the (anonymous) critic of the *Morning Chronicle* reported:

> Another new Overture ["overture" was the current English term for a symphony], by the fertile and enchanting HAYDN, was performed; which as usual, had continual strokes of genius, both in air and in harmony. The Introduction excited the deepest attention, the Allegro charmed, the Andante was encored, the Minuets, especially the Trio, were playful and sweet, and the last movement was equal, if not superior to the preceding.

I. *Adagio; Allegro con spirito.* In Haydn's manuscript the drumroll which earned the Symphony its early-nineteenth-century nickname has no dynamic marking, thus forcing each conductor to decide for himself how long, how loud. The almost Tchaikovskian blackness of the ensuing bass line (an unusual unison of cellos with string basses and bassoon):

is so unlike anything we usually associate with Haydn that we rightly expect the theme to play a prominent part in what follows. No wonder it "excited the deepest attention."

The main body of the *Allegro con spirito* is built on the following phrase of the first violins:

After a brief climax (which includes a passing reference to the Introduction), Haydn introduces his contrasting subject: a lilting little waltz tune in the violins. The unpretentious development section tosses about tidbits of the basic *Allegro* theme, bits of the waltz and (unobtrusively in the bass) a bit of the Introduction:

Just when the movement seems about to conclude in familiar, lighthearted style, the orchestral landscape darkens, kettledrum thunder rolls, string tremolos descend into ominous regions of the subdominant minor, brass and woodwinds add a somber note, and the rhythmic pulse slows to a halt. The solo drumroll with which the Symphony began returns, and with it the threatening introductory phrase. But suddenly this dramatic suspense dissolves, as if in a gale of laughter, and the movement ends with a quick return of the basic *Allegro con spirito.*

II. *Andante più tosto allegretto.* For his slow movement Haydn used the popular old variation form—but with a modern twist: namely a double theme, or, rather, two themes. Both are folk songs of Slav—probably Croatian—origin, the first in minor, the other in major; yet they are so alike, that each seems a variation of the other. The first in C minor begins as follows:

Like the alternating themes, the variations alternate C minor and C major. One of the major variations includes a charming little solo for the concertmaster. The richly imaginative coda is full of harmonic surprises.

III. *Menuet.* The vigorous *Minuet* movement encloses a delicate trio section in chamber style with graceful clarinet solos.

IV. *Finale: Allegro con spirito.* The *Finale* opens with an almost overfamiliar traditional fanfare for a pair of horns:

But hardly has this thought occurred to the horns when the violins beg to differ, with the following lively commentary:

It is such a light little phrase, one would not exactly expect it to sustain an entire symphonic finale. Yet that is exactly what Haydn proceeds to do with it. At the points where we might expect contrasting ideas, Haydn recalls the old one, puts it in a new key, gives it to new instruments, extends, cuts, combines it with other fragments. The result, far from sounding thin, gives an impression of growing fertility and thematic plenty.

The E-flat Symphony, No. 103, is scored for 2 flutes, 2 oboes, 2 clarinets, 2 bassoons, 2 horns, 2 trumpets, kettledrums, and the standard complement of strings.

SYMPHONY NO. 104, D MAJOR

Haydn was sixty-three when he took leave of London with a farewell concert for his own benefit. The symphony he chose for this program was No. 104, in D major, the last of the London series and the last of his career. The performance took place on May 4, 1795. "The hall was filled with a picked audience," wrote Haydn in his diary. "The whole company was delighted and so was I. I took in this evening 4000 gulden. One can make as much as this only in England."

This may have been the first performance of Symphony No. 104, but it seems more likely that it had already been at the sixth concert of the season on April 13, 1795 at the King's Theatre. It is arguable that this was the greatest symphony that Haydn ever wrote, though such speculation seems idle in the face of Haydn's overwhelming productivity. And of this the public and press were well aware. After the concert of the thirteenth, the *Morning Chronicle* observed: "This wonderful man never fails; and the various powers of his inventive and impassioned mind have seldom been conceived with more accuracy by the Band, or listened to with greater rapture by the hearers, than they were on this evening."

I. *Adagio; Allegro.* Clearly Haydn felt no necessity to curry favor, to assure himself an easy triumph with light or catchy tunes for his final symphony. His slow introduction is probably the most profound of his entire series. It is in the dark, minor variant of his basic D major. The stark opening is awesome in its force. The sudden, almost terrified whispers and sighs that follow, the reiterations of the commanding first gesture, the sudden harmonic surprises, and the tension that leads to the main body of the movement remain unsurpassed.

The gentle tune of the *Allegro* comes as a dramatic release and relief:

Moreover, Haydn maintains this lyric mood with serene consistency, even returning to his older habit of building his entire first movement around one basic theme. Not until we come to the development do we realize what drama is inherent in the innocent lilt of Haydn's melody. As the tension of the movement mounts, Haydn concentrates with relentless insistence on the repeated-note fragment from the last two bars of his theme. First they seem mere echoes that pass from one orchestral group to another. But soon the entrances overlap and the pounding rhythm of the repeated notes gathers formidable force and momentum:

Then suddenly the reprise of the *Allegro* opening comes as a longed-for relaxation and completion.

II. *Andante.* What could be more peaceful than the melody of the slow movement?

One forgets the form (which is freely related to both rondo and variations) for the musical content is so filled with surprises. The middle section seems to wander off into a plaintive little woodwind lament, a minor variant of the opening phrase, but is almost immediately overwhelmed by a wild outburst of the full orchestral *tutti* in the unexpected tonality of the minor dominant. Not the least of this movement's surprises is a delicate, cadenza-like episode for a solo flute, a pensive, dreamlike recall of the movement's opening phrase, before the movement is rounded off with more orthodox variations on the theme.

III. *Menuet: Allegro.* This is another of Haydn's late-style, burly minuets, but with a tenderly contrasting trio section and many a detailed surprise by the way, including tiny solos for the bassoon and other winds.

IV. *Finale: Spiritoso.* For the principal subject of his finale, Haydn returns to one of his oldest and best loved sources of inspiration, which is to say folk music:

This theme has only fairly recently been tracked down and identified as a Croatian ballad ("Oj Jelena") which was sung not only by members of the Croation colony in Haydn's onetime residence of Eisenstadt, but with minor variations throughout Croatia, Serbia, and Carniola. But what is much more astonishing: it has also been identified with two different cries of street-hawkers in eighteenth-century London: one for "Hot cross buns" and the other for "Live cod." Of course, it is quite possible that the musical street cries Haydn heard all about him in London may have put him in mind of his far earlier musical impressions in Eisenstadt. In any case, Haydn builds one of his most imposing and one of his richest finales almost exclusively on this simple tune. It was a fitting and embracing finale to the greatest and most varied collection of symphonies in the entire tradition of a form that is one of the glories of Western culture.

This Symphony No. 104, sometimes nicknamed the "London" Symphony is scored for 2 flutes, 2 oboes, 2 clarinets, 2 bassoons, 2 horns, 2 trumpets, kettledrums, and the customary body of strings.

Paul Hindemith

Born November 16, 1895, Hanau, near Frankfurt—died December 28, 1963, Frankfurt

CONCERT MUSIC FOR STRINGS AND BRASS, OPUS 50

This is one of Hindemith's most brilliant works. From start to finish, the score is one exuberant flood of music in the spontaneous, uninhibited manner, which is one of Hindemith's most attractive traits. Commissioned for the fiftieth anniversary of the Boston Symphony Orchestra, it makes technical demands which only a virtuoso orchestra can fulfill: the precise execution of light staccatos in the brass, the intonation of complicated chords, and the requirements of expressive solo passages are beyond the capacity of a mediocre brass section.

In spirit, this *Konzertmusik* belongs very much to Hindemith's first creative period with its athletic rhythms, and sustained dynamic drive, inspired in part by the mechanical rhythms of the Baroque *concerto grosso.* Yet the fact that it was composed in 1930, on the threshold of Hindemith's more Romantic style, is reflected in its relatively consonant harmonic language.

Hindemith specifies that the orchestra should consist of the most numerous possible string section plus four horns, four trumpets, three trombones, and a bass tuba. The score is in two movements.

I. *Mässig schnell, mit Kraft; Sehr breit, aber stets fliessend.* Trumpets and trombones in octaves proclaim a broad lyric melody of bold intervals. The strings have a faster moving, powerfully rhythmic line, often in dotted rhythms. Brass and strings clash, eventually the faster rhythmic patterns are taken up by the brass and the style grows strongly contrapuntal. At the change of tempo, the roles of the two sections are reversed. The broad melody first pronounced by the brass is now given to the strings, with strongly syncopated rhythms in the brass.

II. *Lebhaft; Langsam; Lebhaft.* The second movement opens with three sharp chords, which launch an otherwise delicate, scherzo-like theme in the violins:

This is taken up successively by the violas and the cellos with double basses. The development is punctuated by returns of the three opening chords.

The middle section transforms the three chords into a leisurely five-chord figure, which contrasts with a flowing, lyric line carried largely by strings. The third section brings back the thematic material of the first and works it up to a brilliant climax.

The score was completed on December 27, 1930, and was given its first performance in Boston by the Boston Symphony under the direction of Serge Koussevitzky on April 3, 1931.

CONCERTO FOR VIOLIN AND ORCHESTRA

Hindemith's Violin Concerto was almost the last work he composed before moving to the United States in 1940. The strong stylistic unity of this Concerto, its serenity and inner assurance, may well be related to the fact that by 1939, despite the turmoil of world affairs, Hindemith had found his answers not only to artistic problems of style and technique, but to the political and ethical problems which tortured many an artist in those years. Like all Germans of that time, Hindemith had to face the problem of his attitude and actions toward Hitler's National Socialist regime, which was abhorrent to him. Finding himself totally powerless to modify the turn of events, even in the narrow sphere of music, Hindemith spent more and more time outside his native Germany until by 1939, the year of the completion of his Violin Concerto and of the outbreak of World War II, he had established residence in Switzerland.

The Concerto has three movements in the traditional sequence: fast, slow, fast.

I. *Mässig bewegte Halbe.* The first and most important theme is announced at the outset in a soaring solo violin passage:

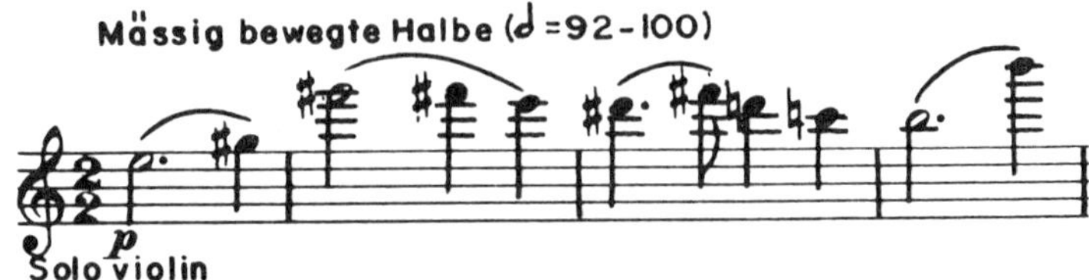

The opening solo flight is answered immediately by a melody for the woodwind choir, echoed by the strings. Two more important melodies are introduced by the solo violin: one a sustained, archlike figure, the other a brilliant figuration, which is taken up by the string choir in a lively *fugato* style.

The climax of the development comes when the heavy brass instruments take up the opening violin theme in a series of overlapping entrances of horns, then trumpets and finally trombones. Toward the end the traditional reprise of the opening themes is only hinted.

II. *Langsam.* The slow movement is one of Hindemith's most songful. A beguiling woodwind introduction leads to the long, lyric solo with elaborate and original embellishments. Among the most beautiful pages are the brief duet between the violin and a solo clarinet, with which the movement closes.

III. *Lebhaft.* After an opening flourish for full orchestra, the solo violin launches into the lighthearted rondo-like theme of the finale:

The much broader melody of the middle section is also announced by the soloist, against a background of string tremolo:

A substantial cadenza ushers in the reprise of the light opening theme and the Concerto concludes with a lively coda.

Hindemith's orchestra calls for 2 flutes, piccolo, 2 oboes, 2 clarinets, bass clarinet, 2 bassoons, 4 horns, 2 trumpets, 3 trombones, tuba, kettledrums, bass drum, snare drum, tambourine, cymbals, triangle, gong, and the traditional string choir.

SYMPHONY, MATHIS DER MALER

When the New York Philharmonic introduced Hindemith's symphony *Mathis der Maler* to this country in 1934, the connection between this music and the steadily deepening world crisis, a crisis precipitated largely by the growth of National Socialism in Germany, was perfectly obvious. In Germany, many a sensitive writer, artist and composer asked himself how he could continue to create mere art, while the entire civilization to which his art belonged was threatened. Was it not the duty of every perceptive, thinking person to drop his personal concerns and to take part in the national struggle, which was so soon to develop into a world catastrophe?

Hindemith found an answer, or at least a partial one, in the life of another great artist who had been confronted with the same problem. Matthias (or Mathis) Grünewald, the painter of the great Isenheim Altar at Colmar in Alsace, lived at the time of the Reformation, when the struggle between Catholic and Protestant forces rent Germany. Little is known of Grünewald's personal life, so Hindemith, building on the few biographical facts that have come down to us, was able to shape for an opera his libretto without violating history. He chose one of the darkest moments of the Reformation, the frightful Peasant War of 1524—that violent outburst of popular force which ended in scenes of appalling slaughter.

Mathis, his social conscience aroused by a leader of the peasant cause, his faith in his art momentarily shaken, gives up his painting and joins the battle to free the oppressed peasants. In the background of the scene where he takes leave of his past is the threatening glow of a bonfire of "heretical" books in the marketplace of Mainz. Was Hindemith thinking of Nazi book-burnings?

But Mathis finds he is powerless to prevent either the arrogance and injustice of the nobles or the plundering and slaughter by the peasants, many of whom forget the ideals for which they join battle. Confusion and doubt, and with them self-torture, grow in Mathis's mind. In an allegorical nightmare, he experiences the temptations of St. Anthony, which the real Mathis himself painted as a part of the triptych of the Isenheim Altar. Demons gather to plague him, calling him to account for the failure of his political action and the neglect of his God-given artistic gift. Finally, Mathis recognizes that artistic creation too is part of the good battle. Out of the struggle and torture come clarity and confidence in the mission of the artist, to which he returns.

The Symphony *Mathis der Maler,* based on excerpts from the opera, was first performed by the Berlin Philharmonic under the direction of Wilhelm Furtwängler on March 12, 1934. (The opera, completed *after* the Symphony, was scheduled by Furtwängler for production by the Berlin Staatsoper during the 1934–35 season, but was banned by the Nazi authorities. Furtwängler resigned briefly in protest, but to no avail. The world premiere took place four

THE TEMPTATION OF SAINT ANTHONY.

The panel from the tryptich of Matthias Grünewald's Isenheim Altar (1513–15), which may have suggested some of the agitated counterpoint in the finale of Hindemith's *Mathis der Maler.* (*Unterlinden Monastery Museum, Colmar, Alsace; photo Bruckman; courtesy, Art Reference Bureau*)

years later in Switzerland [Zürich Stadttheater, May 28, 1938] and the opera was not heard in Central Europe until after World War II.)

The Symphony is in three movements, each of which is named for one of the panels of the Isenheim Altar.

I. *Angelic Concert.* The first movement of the Symphony is the Prelude to Hindemith's opera. The slow introduction is built around an old German religious melody, *"Es sungen drei Engel"* ("Three angels sang"). After some serene preparatory measures this choral tune is intoned softly by the trombones, then taken up by horns and other instruments. The remainder of the orchestra weaves a gentle counterpoint against the main melody somewhat in the style of an organ chorale-prelude of the era of J. S. Bach. The three livelier themes that follow refer to the three angel-musicians who perform for the newborn Babe on the altarpiece.

II. *Entombment.* The second movement is an orchestral interlude bridging the two final scenes of the opera in which Mathis, near the end of his own life, bids a quiet farewell to the art which has sustained him and to the human beings he has loved. The movement is named for the predella of the altar showing the entombment of the Savior.

III. *Temptation of Saint Anthony.* A boldly sculptured unison melody with recitative-like freedom leads directly into the dream scene of the opera, where Mathis is surrounded by the demons that plague Saint Anthony on a panel of the Isenheim Altar. Against agitated brass and woodwind chords the strings have a passionate, striving melody, to which the demons sing: "Your greatest foe is within yourself" *("Dein ärgster Feind sitzt in dir selbst"):*

Fierce clashes of contrapuntal forces lead to a succession of harsh climaxes. Finally, over the orchestral commotion, there soars another ancient chorale melody, *"Lauda Sion Salvatorem"* ("Praise thy Savior, O Zion"). A final, triumphant Alleluia ends in a blaze of harmonic clarity suggesting spiritual illumination.

The Symphony *Mathis der Maler* is scored for 2 flutes, piccolo, 2 oboes, 2 clarinets, 2 bassoons, 4 horns, 2 trumpets, 3 trombones, bass tuba, kettledrum, bass drum, snare drum, glockenspiel, triangle, cymbals, small suspended cymbal, and the usual strings.

NOBILISSIMA VISIONE, ORCHESTRA SUITE

Gentle St. Francis of Assisi, who inspired generations of painters from Giotto on, and whose rhapsodic "Canticle of the Sun" echoes through six centuries of poetry from Dante to Walt Whitman, may not strike us as a likely subject for a ballet. Yet it was no accident that, when the great dancer and choreographer Leonide Massine approached Hindemith with a commission for the Ballets Russes de Monte Carlo, Hindemith chose St. Francis as his subject. Again and again in the course of his long and agitated career—particularly at major turning points of his development—Hindemith was drawn to religious subjects. His song cycle *Das Marienleben (The Life of The Virgin)* and his opera *Mathis der Mahler (Mathis* [Grünewald] *the Painter)* are only two of the most outstanding examples.

As early as 1929 Serge Diaghilev, the now-legendary impresario of the first Ballets Russes, had invited Hindemith to compose a ballet said to have been planned on a mystical subject. The project was halted by Diaghilev's sudden death in the summer of 1929. In 1937 (the year before Hindemith left his native Germany to take up residence, first in Switzerland, then in the United States) the composer spent considerable time in Italy. There he met Massine, who renewed Diaghilev's offer for the reassembled Ballets Russes. The two men agreed upon the subject of St. Francis and collaborated on the scenario. Just as Hindemith's *Mathis* had centered about a spiritual crisis and its resolution in a dream-vision, so the new ballet centered about the spiritual crisis of St. Francis and the mystical dream (or *nobilissima visione*) that converted him to a life of poverty and service to his fellow men.

The ballet scenario is in five scenes. The first shows Francis as a modishly dressed young man in the shop of his father, the rich draper Bernardone. Francis helps display rich fabrics to the cavaliers and their ladies who come to buy. A beggar in rags creeps in; Francis kicks him toward the door, but repents, runs after him and thrusts money into his hands. Lured into a mock duel with a knight, Francis is defeated. He resolves to seek experience with knightly arms, puts on chain mail, helmet and sword, and goes off to war. But he is revolted by what he finds. Scene 2 shows him in a roadside encampment of soldiers. The soldiers seize a traveling burgher, torture him, plunder his possessions and abduct his wife. The horrified Francis tries to intervene but is brutally beaten. Alone and in despair, he has a vision: three graceful female figures—Poverty, Obedience and Chastity—appear in a dance symbolic of the pious life.

In Scene 3 Francis returns to Assisi and finds his friends at a rich feast. They try to persuade him to join their revels, but Francis cannot forget the sight of poverty. His eye lights on a group of beggars cowering in a corner. He embraces them and gives them all the riches of the feast, including the dishes of silver and gold. His friends think he has gone mad and his father denounces him for his quixotic charity. Francis's reply is to take off his rich clothes and lay them at his father's feet. Dressed only in a plain white garment, he leaves home forever with the beggars. Scene 4 takes place in the mountains near Assisi. Francis wanders in deep meditation, praying for a sign from heaven. Suddenly his spirit is flooded with happiness. He picks up two sticks and mimes with them as if playing with a violin and bow, dancing his newfound spiritual joy. He meets a ferocious wolf, the terror of the countryside. He tames the wolf, which grows docile and friendly. Francis and his followers lie down to sleep on the bare ground. In a vision Mistress Poverty appears to them, and Francis confirms his mystical union with her by an exchange of rings. They celebrate their heavenly marriage with a frugal feast of bread and water.

The fifth and final scene of the ballet is a danced version of St. Francis's masterpiece, his "Hymn to the Sun" often known as *"Il cantico di frate sole"* or as *"Il cantico delle creature,"* in which he apostrophizes the creatures of God and all creation—including the sun, moon, water, fire, wind and earth—as his brothers and sisters in Christ. Mistress Poverty leads the symbolic dance, which is joined by men and women of the Franciscan order in their robes and hoods, and concludes with the transfiguration of St. Francis and his companions.

The world premiere of the ballet *Saint Francis* was given by the Ballets Russes de Monte Carlo in London at the Drury Lane Theatre on July 21, 1938. The United States premiere was given by the same company at the Metropolitan Opera House on October 14, 1938.

The Orchestra Suite *Nobilissima visione* is a regrouping of slightly less than half of the ballet numbers with orchestration slightly expanded. The ballet used a small orchestra: flute, oboe, 2 clarinets, bassoon, 2 horns, 2 trumpets, trombone, percussion and strings. The score of the Orchestra Suite calls for piccolo, 2 flutes, 2 oboes, 2 clarinets, 2 bassoons, 4 horns, 2 trumpets, 3 trombones, large cymbals, small cymbals, kettledrums, tenor drum, bass drum, snare drum, side drum without snares, triangle, glockenspiel, and string choir. Hindemith has described his Suite as follows:

> The suite, *Nobilissima visione,* consists of three movements: (1) Introduction and Rondo; (2) March and Pastorale; (3) Passacaglia.
>
> The Introduction consists of that part of the original music (for the ballet) during which the hero of the action, Francis, is sunk in deep meditation [No. 8 of the ballet score]. The Rondo corresponds to the music in the stage score for the mystic union of the Saint to Mistress Poverty [No. 10], the scene having been inspired by an old Tuscan legend. The music reflects the blessed peace and unworldly cheer with which the guests at the wedding participate in the wedding feast—dry bread and water only.
>
> The second movement pictures the March [No. 14] of a troop of medieval soldiers:

> First heard but distantly, their gradual approach is observed. The middle portion of this movement suggests the brutality with which these mercenaries set upon a traveling burgher and rob him. The pastoral section of the second movement pictures the sleeping St. Francis. In his inspired dream [No. 16] he visions the appearance of three inspired, symbolic female figures: Obedience, Chastity and Poverty. The short closing section of this movement

imitates a scene, often on paintings of Sassetta and other masters of the Florentine School. These artists picture the sleeping St. Francis. Poverty, her eyes fastened upon him, is his constant companion.

The third and closing movement, Passacaglia, corresponds to that portion of the ballet score representing the dance "Hymn to the Sun." Here, all the symbolic personifications of heavenly and earthly existence mingle in the course of the different variations through which the six-measure-long theme of the Passacaglia:

is transformed. In the ballet this closing piece bears a special title borrowed from a chapter heading in an old version of the *Cantique du soleil,* which reads: *"Incipiunt laudes creaturarum."*

SYMPHONIC METAMORPHOSES OF THEMES BY CARL MARIA VON WEBER

This is one of Hindemith's playful works. And Hindemith, in a playful mood, used to spout music. With the exuberance of a frisky Triton, trumpeting and splashing about in a Bernini fountain, he poured forth a flood of joyous sounds. This spirit of plenty, of irrepressible productiveness, was part of Hindemith's temperamental affinity for Baroque music. It was stimulated, of course, by the neo-Baroque wave, the "back-to-Bach" vogue, which was at its height during Hindemith's earliest creative years, the 1920s. But Hindemith's response to this Baroque vogue was vigorous and lasting, and it continued to color the entire range of his music, from the most serious to the lightest.

His *Symphonic Metamorphoses of Themes by Carl Maria von Weber* was written in 1943, when he was teaching at Yale University. Although Hindemith did not divulge the exact sources of his themes, they are all to be found in a single volume of Weber's works composed or arranged for piano duet. They are not very serious pieces, but surely no one owning the volume could resist the fun of persuading a friend to join in playing them through. One can easily imagine that the composer was "playing," in both senses of the word, when the idea for these four movements occurred to him.

The first performance of Hindemith's *Symphonic Metamorphoses* was given by the New York Philharmonic in Carnegie Hall on January 24, 1944, under the direction of Artur Rodzinski.

I. *Allegro.* The jaunty opening movement is based on the fourth of Weber's *Huit pièces,* Opus 60, for piano duet. Brightly orchestrated for a large modern orchestra, it tends to play off the woodwinds as a group against the massed brass on one hand and massed strings on the other.

II. *Turandot Scherzo: Moderato.* The distant ancestor of this exotic movement is an old Chinese melody which, in Hindemith's adaptation, starts as follows:

This is the basis of a theme on which Hindemith composed a set of eight variations building to a big climax. Finally, after a few soft transitional measures for violins alone, the trombones begin a fugue-like section with considerable contrapuntal elaboration.

The melody has a curious background. It is adapted from Weber's Overture to Schiller's adaptation of Carlo Gozzi's fantastic eighteenth-century drama, *Turandot*—the same *Turandot* that was adapted for Puccini's opera. Weber had found the melody in the eighteenth-century *Dictionnaire de musique* of Jean-Jacques Rousseau, who, in turn, had the melody from the famous traveling Sinologist, Father Jean Baptiste Duhalde. However, Rousseau disclaimed responsibility for the accuracy of this and his other examples of oriental melody. "In all these pieces," he remarks, "will be found a conformity to the Modulation of our Music, in which some may admire the rightness and universality of our [European] rules, but which may cause others to suspect the intelligence or fidelity of those who have transmitted these tunes."

III. *Andantino.* This charming lyric interlude in the style of a slow *Siciliano* is based on the second piece in Weber's six *Pièces faciles* for piano duet, Opus 3, Book 2.

IV. The march-finale follows very closely the model of the "Marcia," which is No. 7 of Weber's *Huit pièces,* Opus 60. Hindemith's fidelity to his model includes even the contrasting trio section of Weber's "Marcia." But, thereafter, Hindemith greatly extends the material and develops it to a powerful climax and a true metamorphosis.

Hindemith's *Symphonic Metamorphoses* calls for piccolo, 2 flutes, 2 oboes, English horn, 2 clarinets, bass clarinet, 2 bassoons, contrabassoon, 4 horns, 2 trumpets, 3 trombones, tuba, kettledrums, large drum, small drum, snare drum, tam-tam, tambourine, triangle, woodblock, small gong, cymbals, small cymbals, bells, glockenspiel, and the traditional strings.

Arthur Honegger

Born March 10, 1892, Le Havre—died November 27, 1955, Paris

PACIFIC 231

Honegger did not have to wait long for the premiere of his *Pacific 231.* He finished his score early in 1924, and in May 1924 it was given its first performance at one of the brilliant Concerts Koussevitzky in Paris. Honegger became famous almost overnight. His success was not slowed down by his gift for picturesque comment. "I have always had a passion for locomotives," he said in an interview soon after the premiere of *Pacific 231.* "To me they are living beings and I love them as others love women or horses. My aim in *Pacific 231* was not to imitate the noises of a locomotive, but to translate a visual impression and physical enjoyment into a musical construction. The point of departure is objective contemplation: the quiet breathing of the engine at rest, the effort of starting, the gradual acceleration until it reaches a lyric pace, and finally the drama of a 300-ton train hurtling through the dead of night at a mile a minute. As my 'subject' I chose a locomotive of the 'Pacific' type, number 231 for heavy trains of great speed."

Did Honegger regret his words and the authority conferred upon them when his publishers printed them in the score of *Pacific 231?* Did he change his mind about the meaning of his music? Be that as it may, when he was interviewed again for the series of little dialogues published in 1951 under the title, *Je suis compositeur,* he reversed his explanation. "In truth," he was now quoted as saying: "I was following a very abstract and ideal thought in *Pacific,* by giving the feeling of a mathematical acceleration of rhythm while the tempo itself slows down. Musically speaking, I composed a sort of great chorale variation, laced with counterpoint in the manner of J. S. Bach. . . .

"I had originally entitled the piece *Symphonic Movement.* On reflection this seemed to me a little drab. All at once a rather novel idea passed through my mind and I inscribed the finished work with the title, *Pacific 231,* after a class of locomotives for heavy trains of great speed. (Today this type is obsolete and has been sacrificed, alas, to electric traction.)"

This would not be the first time that a composer has contradicted himself on the subject of his own music. Whether the title was conceived before, during, or after the composition of the music, it is perfectly clear that Honegger intended his listeners to associate the music with a spectacular type of locomotive. However, according to railroad men, the title *Pacific 231* is, strictly speaking, redundant. For "231" and "Pacific" are two separate designations for the same engine: an extra-heavy locomotive type with six wheels on each side, grouped in the pattern 2 plus 3 plus 1. This is the European usage. The United States custom of counting the wheels on both sides of a locomotive results in the "231" type being designated in this country as "462."

The evocative opening page, with its suggestion of the faint hiss of escaping steam, and the immense resting weight of the locomotive, is a little masterpiece of orchestral color from the murky trill of the double basses at the bottom of the orchestra, through the dissonant tremolos of the remaining strings to the flutter-tonguing brass and flutes on top. After the heavy, chugging rhythms of the orchestra have got the train fairly under way, we hear one of the contrapuntal figures Honegger mentions, which could suggest the whirling wheels of the locomotive:

Surrounded by this and many other whirring figures we hear a more majestic melody which, for the composer, recalled the *cantus firmus* or slow-moving chorale melody in some of Bach's chorale variations:

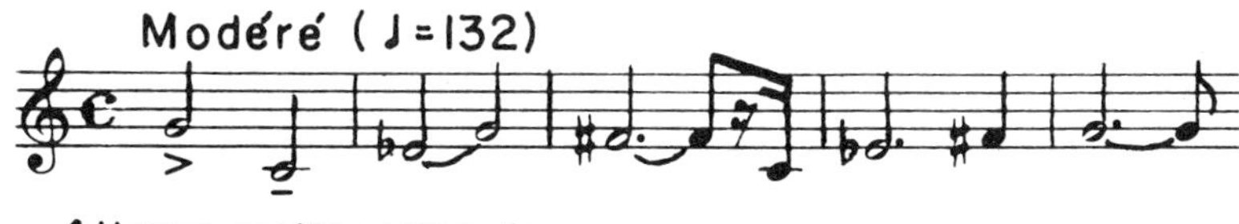

The score of *Pacific 231* calls for piccolo, 2 flutes, 2 oboes, English horn, 2 B-flat clarinets, bass clarinet, 2 bassoons, contrabassoon, 4 horns in F, 3 trumpets in C, 3 trombones, tuba, tenor drum without snare, bass drum, cymbals, tam-tam, and the usual strings.

SYMPHONY NO. 2 (FOR STRING ORCHESTRA AND TRUMPET)

Honegger, who reveled in dramatic music, in descriptive titles, programs and elucidations of his instrumental works, was surprisingly reticent concerning this score.

This Second Symphony began to take shape during the darkest hours of World War II. Paris fell on June 13, 1940. Americans—even those old enough to have felt the shock and to recall it today—cannot know what this meant to Frenchmen.

The odds for civilization looked poor. Hitler and Stalin were still official bedfellows. Against this terrifying alliance of German efficiency with seemingly inexhaustible Russian resources, one nation still stood: Britain, depleted, blockaded, bombarded, lashed from the air, and—alone. It was a moment in history when many an artist felt overwhelmed by doubt of his chosen profession, doubt even of his "right" to pursue creative work, while the new barbarism was taking over.

But Honegger was made of more resilient mettle. For five years preceding this crisis he had been trying sporadically to execute a commission from his friend Paul Sacher, who wanted an orchestral work for the tenth anniversary of his Basel Chamber Orchestra in 1936. Honegger had made several starts on a work for string orchestra and had discarded one after another.

But in the dark, cold months of early 1941 something began to stir in Honegger. Let us not read anything into his mind. Here is Honegger's own sober account:

> The string symphony goes back to a promise that I had given Paul Sacher several years earlier. Several beginnings, several sketches followed, with no result.
>
> During the winter of 1941, the *Adagio* gradually took form; for I always begin the composition of a symphonic work with this middle section of the triptych; indeed, it is hard for me to conceive a symphony in any other form than three movements. As I heard it, it impressed me as a rather gloomy piece, yes, in places, it even seemed to me a little desperate. I foresee already that the very slow tempo of this movement will not please all conductors; they will "improve" it, by taking it a little faster.
>
> I worked long on the first movement to give it a really concentrated, condensed form without weakening the inner violence with which I quite consciously endowed it. This violence is intended to contrast with the powerless, so to speak, exhausted opening theme.
>
> For the finale, I introduce an element of brilliance as a contrast to both the first two movements. In order to strengthen the chorale at the end of the finale I have indicated a trumpet *ad libitum*. This by no means indicates a coloristic intention; it is only a support for the melody in the long notes of the first violins which threaten otherwise to be swallowed up by the polyphony of other instruments of the same character. Under certain circumstances this trumpet may be replaced by an oboe or a clarinet. The timbre plays no decisive part. It is exactly the same as when one draws a new register on the organ.
>
> My principal aims in this symphony are the same as they have been in all my symphonies up to now. [These lines were written in 1943.]
>
> 1. Condensation of form, omission of the recapitulation as practiced in classical works, where it always leaves an impression of length.
>
> 2. Search for themes characteristic enough to seize the listener's attention and to allow him to follow the course of the entire "story."
>
> 3. I have sought no program, no literary or philosophical concept. If this work releases a certain emotion, the reason is that this forced itself upon me in a perfectly natural way. For I express my thoughts through music and perhaps without being entirely conscious of them.

I. *Molto moderato—Allegro.* The violent contrast which Honegger emphasized is embodied in the alternation of these two *tempi*. The opening slow section could be a lament, verging on despair. It is built around insistent repetitions of an almost moaning figure which appears first in a solo viola:

In this brief opening section the theme is repeated eleven times. The following *Allegro* takes off with a sharply rhythmic theme of central importance in this movement. Twice again the themes and tempo alternate from slow to fast with the same recurring contrasts of mood, except that in its final return the *Allegro* seems robbed of its violence. It is held down to a constant, tense *pianissimo* and finally fades off into silence.

II. *Adagio mesto.* The tragic central movement is based primarily on a tiny two-note figure which for centuries has served as both symbol and expression of a sigh. Although the composer does not specifically say so, the figure is also related to the Symphony's opening theme given above. Momentarily this figure functions as an accompaniment to a more flowing melody which the first violins carry to a climax. The connection to the first movement grows steadily clearer; it becomes explicit when the first movement theme returns in the agitated double basses with an accompaniment of shuddering violas and cellos. Like its predecessor, this movement fades slowly into silence, but before it does there is a brief hint of the chorale which is to conclude the last movement.

III. *Vivace, non troppo.* The finale begins delicately in the violins like a light-footed *scherzo.* Its basic rhythm is a jig-like triplet figure but soon a broader melody soars in the first violins and strongly syncopated rhythms of the lower strings clash with the persistent jig. The orchestra grows more polyphonic, the pace increases to a headlong *presto* until at last the long notes of the chorale melody rise in triumph over the orchestral turbulence:

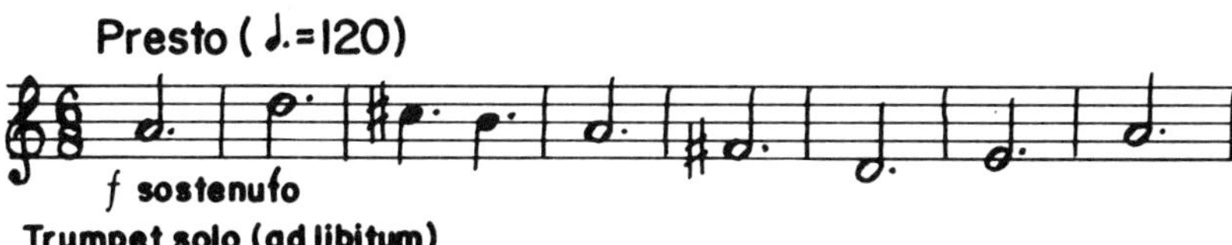

The final bar of the score is dated Paris, October 1941.

Vincent d'Indy

Born March 27, 1851, Paris—died December 2, 1931, Paris

SYMPHONY ON A FRENCH MOUNTAIN AIR, OPUS 25

Vincent d'Indy and his friend, Julien Tiersot (the great collector and scholar of French folk song), both felt that mountain melodies have an especial quality of their own, "something of the purity of their atmosphere," as Tiersot wrote, "something fluid, ethereal, a gentleness that is not found in folk songs of the plains."

Mountain lovers, anyone who has hiked in mountain country—from those hardy souls who conquer the great rocky peaks for an almost mystical experience, to those of us who relish the landscape below the timber line, the serene pastures, the silence sweetened by the sound of cowbells—all can share d'Indy's feeling for mountain music.

During a hike in the Cévennes Mountains (that part of the Massif Central overlooking the southern Rhone valley), d'Indy was so fascinated by the songs of the mountaineers that he formed the habit of jotting the melodies down in a notebook. The following summer (1886) in the same region of the Cévennes, a melody heard in the far distance seized his imagination. At first, he thought of a modest fantasy on the tune.

Working with extreme rapidity, d'Indy felt himself swept along by the innocent little tune, almost as if it had a life and will of its own. Before the summer vacation was through, d'Indy had completed the entire score, including its brilliantly evocative orchestration. He called it *Symphonie sur un chant montagnard français.*

Barely six months elapsed before the *Symphonie* was first performed at a Concert Lamoureux on March 20, 1887, with a repetition exactly one week later. This Symphony also came to be known as *Symphonie cévenole,* after the Cévennes homeland of the melody. The Symphony was a triumph at its first performance; it quickly spread beyond the borders of France, and is still considered d'Indy's masterpiece.

I. *Assez lent; Modérément anime; Un peu plus vite.* Here is the original mountain melody as d'Indy jotted it down:

From the folk tune to the theme of d'Indy's Symphony is a short step, but a magical one, a true transformation:

Compared to the rather conventional, foursquare folk tune, d'Indy's theme is all that the Romantic imagination felt true folk music to be: wayward, unsymmetrical, unconventional, with a hint of improvisation, and an echo of ancient, medieval modes. This English horn melody is caught up by a solo flute and by subtle combinations of other instruments against the barest whisper of muted strings, *tremolando*.

With a wonderful contrast of color, the solo piano enters in its dark low register reinforced by bassoon and other bass instruments; it rises in wavelike figures, lap after lap, until the highest wave breaks on its crest.

Another delicious color contrast comes when a charmingly sentimental melody is sung by two flutes with solo harp against a diaphanous background of high piano arpeggios and trembling violins. Even as the development builds to its climax, the orchestra retains its marvelous characteristically French transparency.

II. *Assez modéré, mais sans lenteur.* The solo piano announces a gentle variant of the mountain melody, which is taken up by strings and flute. Even in this predominantly lyric movement, much of the beauty lies in its imaginative orchestral color.

III. *Animé; Plus modéré; Un peu plus agité.* Over the pounding excitement of a piano *ostinato,* the woodwinds launch a jaunty, exultant version of the original mountain air. The movement consists of a kaleidoscopic series of changing color, rhythm and tempo in a *crescendo* of excitement. The piano part grows more and more brilliant as we approach the explosion of the final page.

The *Symphony on a French Mountain Air* is scored for 3 flutes, English horn, 2 oboes, 2 clarinets, bass clarinet, 3 bassoons, 4 horns, 2 trumpets, 2 cornets, 3 trombones, tuba, kettledrums, bass drum, cymbals, triangle, harp, piano, and the conventional string choir.

Charles Ives

Born October 20, 1874, Danbury, Connecticut—died May 19, 1954, New York City

CENTRAL PARK IN THE DARK

"There is a great Man living in this country [the United States]," wrote Arnold Schoenberg many years ago:

"—a Composer.
He has solved the problem how to preserve oneself and to learn.
He responds to neglect by contempt.
He is not forced to accept praise or blame.
His name is Ives."

These lines on an undated sheet were found among Schoenberg's papers after his death in 1951 by his widow, who mailed the sheet to Mr. and Mrs. Ives.

How many Americans, even today, would consider Ives "a great man" is impossible to say. Our national pride may be tickled by the reflection that Ives, who was born in the same year as Schoenberg, was at least ten years ahead of that master and of Igor Stravinsky, too, in experimenting with polyrhythms, polymeters, dissonant counterpoint, polychords, polytonality, so-called "atonality"—in short with techniques which have become integral parts of twentieth-century musical style. But we can take little pride in the fact that we not only considered Ives to be a freak, but enveloped him in such blankets of indifference as would have smothered a man of less character and determination.

Ives's interest and training in music went back to his childhood, having been imparted by his experimental-minded father, who had been a band leader in the Civil War. But the young composer decided at the outset of his career to make himself independent of any need to make money through his music. He went into insurance and, after serving an apprenticeship, founded his own firm which, by the time he retired in 1930, had become the largest single insurance agency in the United States. One can admire the fierce independence of the spirit that forged such a business career for the sake of composing. But who would not wish that the imagination and energy of that effort could have gone into his creative work?

As the First World War came and went, loud artistic battles were fought in Paris and Vienna over "innovations" of avant garde European composers, innovations that had slumbered for a decade or more in the unpublished and unperformed scores of Charles Ives. Even so conservative and Romantic a score as Ives's Second Symphony written between 1896 and 1902 waited almost half a century to be performed. (It was played for the first time anywhere on February 22, 1951 by the New York Philharmonic conducted by Leonard Bernstein.)

Central Park in the Dark, a considerably more experimental work, seems to have been composed between the years 1898 and 1907. It eventually became the finale of an orchestral trilogy, *Three Outdoor Scenes,* completed in 1911. The two additional movements are called "Hallowe'en" and "The Pond." When *Central Park in the Dark* was published, shortly before Ives's death, he added the words "Some Forty Years Ago" to the title.

The music describes a safer place than Central Park after dark in later years. It was suggested by a walk along a path that Ives knew very well, for his New York home was close to the park. According to his biographer Henry Cowell, Ives "could hear sounds of others walking without being able to see them; it is not the mystery of loneliness in the dark, but of the dark seething with unseen activity."

The mystery of the dark is suggested from the outset by the whispering string choir alone in slow moving, dissonant harmonies. This slow pace *(molto adagio)* of the string choir is maintained steadily throughout the score. A quiet melodic theme is alloted to a lone clarinet:*

Gradually a flute and an oboe add their voices and a syncopated theme played by a piano suggests a far-off strain of mechanical music.

Gradually the orchestra separates into two halves. The strings are directed to continue, their pace unchanged throughout. The woodwinds and piano, to which brass, percussion and a second piano are gradually added, move faster and faster. The path, according to Mr. Cowell, "runs close to a merry-go-round, and in the middle section there are superimposed fragments of an old ragtime song in jerky syncopation above the calm-flowing basic dissonances." The ragtime syncopations grow wilder and faster and louder to a triple and quadruple *fortissimo* climax *con fuoco.* At its peak the climax breaks off and the whispering strings continue their slow progress. They recall the opening twenty measures or so of the score. The lonely clarinet melody returns briefly and the music fades into silence. Ives intended that the two halves of the orchestra should be led by two conductors.

When the orchestra divides into two halves, the first half consists of the string choir, while the second half enlists piccolo, flute, oboe, B-flat clarinet, E-flat clarinet, 2 pianos, bassoon, trombone, trumpet, snare drum, and bass drum.

---

* *Musical example copyright 1963 by Boelke-Bomart, Inc. Used by permission of Associated Music Publishers, Inc.*

SYMPHONY NO. 2

(The following article is by Dr. Joseph Braunstein, the specialist charged with identifying and putting in order the manuscripts of Charles Ives for photoduplication and deposit of copies in the New York Public Library and the Library of Congress.)

Charles Edward Ives is a unique figure in the history of music. Recognized today as a forceful trail blazer, bold pioneer and artistic personality of great distinction, he is at the same time the only important American composer who was not a professional musician. He had a very successful career in the insurance field and demonstrated there not only a fine business acumen but also creative inventiveness. There have been other musicians of consequence who engaged in business and commercial activities, as for example Tallis, Byrd, Morley, Palestrina, Lully, Geminiani, Locatelli, Viotti and Clementi. Yet their mercantile occupations, in some instances profitable, in others disastrous, didn't mean much to the world at large. The Romans hardly cared for Giovanni Pierluigi, the fur dealer, but revered him as *maestro di Capella Giulia* (St. Peter's Cathedral) and creator of divine music. By the same token the contemporaries did not admire Muzio Clementi, the publisher and piano manufacturer, but the brilliant piano virtuoso and composer. The case of Charles Ives is different.

The son of a musician, Ives had studied composition with Horatio Parker during his college years at Yale. Realizing that the music he wanted to create was anything but "practical" and would never enable him to earn a living, he decided upon a career in the insurance field. After graduation in 1898, he went to work for The Mutual Life Insurance Company in New York and started with a weekly salary of $5. On January 1, 1907, he opened his own firm (Ives & Myric) which did an annual business of $48,000,000 when he retired in 1929. Ives was also *creative* in business. He initiated things that became basic in the field of life insurance and wrote a booklet which, reprinted many times, was considered a "Bible" for insurance agents.

In spite of this absorbing business activity, Ives continued incessantly to create music. When? After work, burning the midnight oil, on weekends and in the vacation period, which he limited to two or three weeks. The amount of music created under these pressing circumstances between 1896 and 1921 is astonishing, and our amazement grows if we take a close look at his working method by studying his sketches and manuscripts. The extant material is now reposing at Yale University, Ives's Alma Mater.

Ives was a great pioneer in harmony, a bold innovator in matters of rhythm and an imaginative experimenter in the field of orchestral sound. He created bold harmonic combinations, wrote polytonal passages and conceived rhythmical complexities that anticipated by ten years similar passages in the works of Schoenberg and Stravinsky and other avant gardists. Yet while these composers had a chance to hear their works and to test their creations by means of actual sound, Ives was in the main denied this opportunity, which is so vital to a creative musician. His works were rejected by America's leading musical organizations as impossible to perform and some of his scores, for example, that of his Second Symphony, submitted for consideration were not even returned to him. Thus, when the latter work was to be given its world premiere by the Philharmonic-Symphony Society of New York in 1951, the score had to be copied again from the pencil autograph at great expense.

According to a short prefatory note in the published score (1951), the Second Symphony was composed between 1897 and 1901. This information, signed "C.E.I.," is somewhat a variance with the composer's entries in his autograph. There we read: "The second and fourth movements originally written as overture for the Hyperion Theatre Orchestra, New Haven, 1896–98 [his college years] but revised for Symphony 1900/01." The third movement originated as an Organ Prelude in 1896 and was orchestrated in 1902. The score of the first movement also shows the entry: "See organ sonata." It may be noted parenthetically that the first movement as well as the finale of the Third Symphony also grew out of organ pieces (both composed in 1901).

The Second Symphony expresses in the words of the composer the "musical feelings of the Connecticut country around Redding and Danbury in the 1890s, the music of the country folk. It is full of tunes they sang and played then. . . ."

I. *Andante moderato.* The first movement in B minor is mainly for strings. The opening theme:

which is manipulated in imitation and contrapuntal manner is of structural importance and returns in the introduction to the Finale. A typical American note is struck in the middle of the *Andante moderato* when "Columbia, the Gem of the Ocean" is proclaimed by the horns.

A recitative passage of the oboe effects the transition to the following movement.

II. *Allegro.* The chief theme has a marchlike character which contrasts to the simple, folklike second theme in F major. The composer surprises the listener in the middle section with quotations from the first movement of Brahms's Third Symphony. Formally speaking, Ives clings here as well as in the finale to the time-honored sonata scheme with exposition, development, recapitulation and coda. Note also that the tranquil second theme is transformed into a marching tune in the coda to emphasize the basic quality of the piece.

III. The *Adagio cantabile,* which follows, reverts to the serene F-major tonality. Ives has described the movement as "a reflection of the organ and choir music of the *Long Green Organ Book*" to which he also referred in his sketches. This placid movement, which contains some thematic allusions to the opening *Andante moderato,* closes gently with a quotation from "America the Beautiful."

IV. The *Lento maestoso* though numbered as fourth movement is actually an introduction to the *Finale.* Reverting to both the key (B minor) and the main idea of the first movement:

this introduction not only provides the structural link between the first and last movements but, in addition, it creates a spiritual coherence. The reappearance of "Columbia, the Gem of the Ocean," which becomes an essential thematic element in the finale, underlines the organic and spiritual importance of the *Lento maestoso.* The movement closes with a transitional passage preparing the key of the *Finale.*

V. *Allegro molto vivace.* This is a spirited and merry piece studded with American folk tunes. We hear first "De Camptown Races" (horns) and "Turkey in the Straw," the minstrel song enormously popular in the time of Andrew Jackson (violins). The second theme (in the sonata sense) is, as Ives informs us, "partly from an early piece called 'The American Woods' (Brookfield). The part suggesting a Steve Foster tune, while over it the old farmers fiddled a barn dance with all its jigs, gallops and reels, was played in Danbury . . . in 1889."

"Columbia" reenters in the recapitulation which, of course, repeats the "American Woods" episode. The coda introduces still another folk tune, "Down in the Cornfield," but is dominated by "Columbia, the Gem of the Ocean," proclaimed by the trombones and combined with the barn dance of the old farmers. The conclusion is surprising. Ives denies the listener the expected ending on the F-major chord and bids farewell with a combination which includes D♭, D, D♯, E, F, G♭, G, G♯, A, B♭ but excludes C and B, the first and last notes of the chromatic scale. The conclusion conforms to one of the nicknames given to Ives at Yale, namely Sam, the punster and joker addicted to paradoxes.

The Symphony was played for the first time anywhere on February 22, 1951, by the New York Philharmonic Orchestra directed by Leonard Bernstein.

The Second Symphony calls for piccolo, 2 flutes, 2 oboes, 2 B-flat clarinets, 2 E-flat clarinets, 2 bassoons, contrabassoon, 4 horns, 2 B-flat trumpets, 2 A trumpets, 3 trombones, kettledrums, snare drum, bass drum, and strings.

SYMPHONY NO. 3, THE CAMP MEETING

When Charles Ives's Third Symphony was first performed in 1947 and promptly won the Pulitzer Prize, the score had waited forty-three years for a hearing.

The story of Ives's originality and daring as a musical pioneer, the hostility and neglect his works encountered, and the stubborn pride with which he followed his chosen path are too well known to need elaboration today. But it is worth recalling that over a thirty-year period, 1899–1929, only three conductors even *looked* at *any* of Ives's music. Of these only one planned to perform an entire work. The man was Gustav Mahler, then conductor of the New York Philharmonic, and the work was the Third Symphony. Mahler told Ives he would conduct the Symphony in Europe, but this plan was blocked by Mahler's death.

The Symphony bears the subtitle, "The Camp Meeting." Its origins go back at least to the year 1896 when Ives completed his First String Quartet, the original first movement of which was incorporated in the Third Symphony. Ives himself has described the other sources of the Symphony and its chronology: "The themes are mostly based around hymns and from organ pieces played in Central Presbyterian Church around 1901. Lead pencil score was finished about 1901. But the final ink score (now lost) had I think a few of less off-shadow parts in it, and also church bells, that are crossed out in the old score. . . . The middle movement was the *Children's Day Parade* (for string quartet and organ), played in Central Presbyterian Church, New York, for the organ alone, 1902. Scoring of this symphony was finished about 1904; copied out in full in 1911."

In one of the composer's lists of his own works, Ives notes that in 1911 the Symphony was recopied "with slight revision." The revised copy may have been made in anticipation of Mahler's planned performance. As it turned out the first performance was given in New York on May 5, 1947 by the New York Little Symphony under the direction of Lou Harrison.

I. *"Old Folks Gatherin':" Andante maestoso.* Despite its descriptive title, this follows recognizably traditional first movement symphonic form, which may account in part for the fact that the Third Symphony is often regarded by Europeans as one of Ives's most successful and accessible scores. The principal theme is announced at the outset by the first violins: *

A contrasting theme given out by the violas has been identified as "Coronation," one of the hymns referred to by Ives and known also as: "All hail the power of Jesus' name" and as "O for a thousand tongues" by Oliver Holden (1765–1834?):

---

* *This and the following musical examples from this composition are copyright 1964 by Associated Music Publishers, Inc. Used by permission.*

There is a rather intense contrapuntal development rising to a powerful climax, followed by a sort of recapitulation of the opening theme, now in counterpoint with another hymn, "What a friend we have in Jesus," sung by solo flute.

II. *"Children's Day:" Allegro.* Ives told the composer Bernard Herrmann, that he wished in this movement "to represent the games which little children played while their elders listened to the Lord's word." The principal theme with which the violins open the movement, bears a striking resemblance to Lowell Mason's hymn, "There is a fountain filled with blood." The movement grows livelier and concludes with a marchlike section on the Welsh battle song known in this country as "All through the night."

III. *"Communion:" Largo.* The free-form finale is based on two main themes, both of which are anticipated contrapuntally before they make their complete appearance. The first of these shows some relation to the opening theme of the Symphony, the second is based on the hymn tune, "Just as I am, without one plea:"

At the very end as the music dies away to silence Ives has suggested the faint sound of distant church bells.

The orchestra for the Third Symphony is small: flute, oboe, clarinet, bassoon, 2 horns, trombone, bells (optional), and strings.

SYMPHONY NO. 4

It is often said that a composer like Charles Ives is ahead of his time. This, of course, is nonsense. It is *we* who fall *behind* our time. And in the case of Charles Ives we had fallen forty-nine years behind our time when Leopold Stokowski reaped the glory of conducting the first complete performance of Ives' Symphony No. 4 in Carnegie Hall on April 26, 1965. The premiere, for which Mr. Stokowski conducted the American Symphony Orchestra, was a tremendous success with public and critics alike. Harold Schonberg of *The New York Times* called the Symphony "a masterpiece" with "tremendous personality and authentic stature." In the Symphony's wilder moments, he was reminded of our greatest and most American of poets: "It has wild polyrhythms, clumps of tonalities that clash like army against army; Whitmanesque yawps and—suddenly—the quiet of a New England church." Most of Mr. Schonberg's colleagues agreed with him, *Time* magazine agreed, and the audience agreed, as it showed with its bravos.

It was all very heartwarming, but no great occasion for self-congratulation. For as William Bender pointed out in the *New York Herald Tribune*, Ives, who had been dead for ten years, was by now regarded "both in the United States and Europe, as a giant of American music." But this widespread recognition was of fairly recent date. It dated specifically from January 20, 1939, when the American pianist and harpsichordist John Kirkpatrick gave what appears to have been, the first complete performance in New York City of Ives's gigantic "Concord" Sonata in Town Hall. The reaction, not only of critics but of the music-loving public generally, was sensational; Henry Cowell spoke of it as "a riot of enthusiasm." If any single event could be said to do such a thing, this recital established Ives as a great American composer.

But why the delay? There is no single answer. In part it was the incredible technical complexity of the music. In part the delay was due to the artistic conservatism of this country up to World War I. Partly it was our tendency to look for European models and standards in the arts. Part of the reason was Charles Ives's fierce independence, which led him to embark on a business career, making him financially independent of the music world. His unusual success in the field of life insurance made it possible for him to compose exactly as he pleased. He paid a high penalty in discouragement and even self-doubt. Today we are the beneficiaries of Ives's savage independence.

His Fourth Symphony, completed in 1916, was Ives's last major work. But since its roots extend back over a period of twenty years, indeed, into his student years, it epitomizes much of the character and development of the artist, who was so far ahead not only of his American colleagues, but Europeans as well.

In an autobiographical memorandum which Ives jotted down in 1932, he says: "Fourth Symphony. This was started with some of the Hawthorne movement of the second piano sonata around 1910–11 [Ives later changed this date to 1909–10]. . . . It was all finished around the end of 1916. . . . Some things in it were from other things that I had been working on before or at that time. . . . The second movement . . . is in some places an orchestration of the *Celestial Railroad* idea from the second movement of the "Concord" Sonata. . . . The last movement (which seems to me the best, compared with the other movements, or for that matter with any other thing that I've done) was finished in the summer of 1915 [date later changed to 1914]. The fugue was written before the entire thing was finished in 1916, but the last movement covers a good many years."

Ives's dating of the Fugue (i.e., the third movement of his Symphony) refers to the form it took in the Symphony. But the origins of this Fugue stretch back to at least 1896, when Ives was a student at Yale. One of the fugues he wrote for his professor, Horatio Parker, was on Lowell Mason's

"Missionary Hymn" ("From Greenland's Icy Mountains") and it had a counter subject taken from another hymn, Oliver Holden's "Coronation" ("All hail the power of Jesus' name.") The manuscript of this organ fugue was lost, but the fugue itself was adapted in Ives' First String Quartet in about 1898. Ten or eleven years later, Ives started to orchestrate the fugue from the First String Quartet. It was 1916 before he completed the orchestral form of the Fugue which appears as the third movement of his Symphony No. 4.

This is not the place to trace all the dozens of allusions Ives makes in this one Symphony to other earlier works of his own, to much Americana: hymn tunes, marches, popular ditties such as "Yankee Doodle," "Turkey in the Straw" and "Columbia, the Gem of the Ocean," which was one of his favorites. Ives also liked Mason's Epiphany Hymn, "Watchman, Tell Us of the Night." He used this as early as 1901 in a solo for a member of his church's quartet and again in the finale of his Violin Sonata, a good three years before he incorporated it into the opening movement of his Fourth Symphony.

Like many of Ives's works, his Fourth Symphony is related to his philosophical ideas. "The aesthetic program" he wrote, "is that of the searching questions of 'what?' and 'why?' which the spirit of man asks of life. This is particularly the sense of the Prelude. The three succeeding movements are the diverse answers in which existence replies."

I. *Prelude: Maestoso.* The essence of the brief Prelude is the hymn:

Watchman, tell us of the night,
What the signs of promise are;
Traveler, o'er yon mountain's height,
See that Glory-beaming star!
Watchman, aught of joy or hope?
Traveler, yes; it brings the day,
Promised day of Israel.
Dost thou see its beauteous ray?

The orchestra, for the first movement, is divided into two separate groups: the main orchestra and a high ethereal group consisting of flute, harp, violins and violas.

The Prelude begins with a massive proclamation of the main orchestra, (a "deep sigh" John Kirkpatrick calls it in his study of the Symphony) alternating with the celestial sound of flutes and harps. Thereupon, violins and a solo cello start what sounds like a cross between "My Bonnie Lies Over the Ocean" and "In the Sweet Bye and Bye." This leads to the principal melody of this movement, "Watchman, Tell Us of the Night" for choral voice or, optionally, for solo trumpet. At the same moment the violins and flutes embark upon "Nearer My God to Thee," so that we hear both melodies simultaneously.

II. *Allegretto.* Ives considered this movement to be the first answer to the "what?" and "why?" of the Prelude. "It is not," he said, "a scherzo in an accepted sense of the word, but rather a comedy—in which an exciting, easy and worldly progress through life is contrasted with the trials of the pilgrims in their journey through the swamps and rough country. The occasional slow episodes—pilgrims' hymns—are constantly crowded out and overwhelmed by the former. The dream, or fantasy, ends with an interruption of reality—the Fourth of July in Concord—brass bands, drum corps, etc."

The comedy consists in part of the combination in a fantastically rich and complex score of at least nine famous American traditional tunes, of which one, Ives's lasting favorite, is "Columbia the Gem of the Ocean":

At one point, a large section of the orchestra takes off on its own (sometimes led by an assistant conductor) in a wild independent foray ending in a crash of seeming disaster, while the main part of the orchestra continues serenely on its way.

III. *Fugue: Andante moderato.* Ives described this second answer to the questions of his opening Prelude as "an expression of the reaction of life into formalism and ritualism." As a college student, Ives may well have felt that the writing of an academic fugue for submission to his conservative professor, Horatio Parker, was indeed an act of "formalism and ritualism." When he adapted this Fugue for his First String Quartet he gave the Quartet the subtitle "A Revival Meeting." Here is the principal subject of the Fugue:

IV. *Very slowly—Largo maestoso.* "The last movement," Ives explained, "is an apotheosis of the preceding content, in terms that have something to do with the reality of existence and its religious experience."

From the purely sensuous point of view there are four main bodies of sound. The first, a percussion group (snare drum, small kettledrum or medium drum, bass drum, cymbals, and gong), opens the movement with a complex eight-bar rhythmic pattern. This begins very softly, continues virtually unchanged throughout (although it is often overwhelmed by the other instruments) and is the last sound heard as the tremendous movement dies away into silence.

The second body of sound is the main orchestra, which begins almost imperceptibly with the low string basses intoning a fragment of "Nearer My God to Thee," which becomes the central theme of the finale. The opening phrase of the Prelude (the "great sigh") returns briefly and is answered by the third body of sound.

This third body is a small, ethereal "distant choir," as Ives calls it, consisting of five violins and a harp (and doubtless meant to recall the similar, though not identical, group in the opening Prelude).

The fourth group, which is not heard until after the climax of the finale has been passed, is the mixed chorus (or brass choir replacement) in a wordless version of "Nearer My God to Thee."

As the movement gains momentum, one hymn tune after another joins the majestic progress until fragments of half a dozen surround the central melody. There is even a grotesque worldly note ("like a gargoyle up in the tower," to use John Kirkpatrick's happy phrase) which might well escape notice by non-Yale men: "As Freshmen First We Came to Yale."

The rhythmic complexity of the movement defies description in nontechnical terms, yet the overall impression is one of basic simplicity: the unhurried climb to a peak of intensity and the serenely ebbing coda crowned by the wordless hymn.

The Ives Fourth Symphony is scored for 4 flutes, piccolo, 2 oboes, 3 clarinets, 3 saxophones, 3 bassoons, 4 French horns, 6 trumpets, 4 trombones, tuba, ensemble piano (for 2 players, 4 hands), solo piano, a quarter-tone piano *ad lib* (if one is available), celesta, pipe organ, "ether organ" (an instrument as yet uninvented when the Symphony was composed, but when the theremin was invented eight years later, Ives declared this would do very nicely), kettledrums, snare drum, military drum, tom-tom ("Indian drum"), small kettledrum or medium drum, bass drum, triangle, cymbals, high bells, low bells, light gong, heavy gong, 2 harps, and the traditional string choir.

A SYMPHONY: HOLIDAYS

On Thanksgiving Day of 1897, the organist of New Haven's Centre Church on the Green (a twenty-three-year-old Yale undergraduate and student in Horatio Parker's composition class) startled his congregation, pleased his pastor, and baffled Mr. Parker with the stirring music that crowns this "Holiday" Symphony.

Young Charles Ives, first taught by his father, had got tired of always playing the same old hymns in the same old standard way. His ears kept hoping for a fresher sound. So his fingers sometimes wandered, as if by accident, with results as refreshing to us as they were disconcerting to his conservative parishioners. His staunch pastor, Ralph Griggs, stood by him.

"Never you mind what the ladies' committee says," he told Ives. "My opinion is that God must get awfully tired of hearing the same thing over and over again, and in His all-embracing wisdom He could certainly embrace a dissonance—might even positively enjoy one now and then."

But when Ives, who had been thoroughly grounded in Bach and in traditional harmony and counterpoint since he was a child, tried such experiments in composition class, Professor Parker was less encouraging than Pastor Griggs and the Deity.

"I did [wrote Ives, in an autobiographical sketch] sometimes, do things that got me in wrong: for instance, a couple of fugues, with the theme in four different keys: C, G, D and A; and in another: C, F, B-flat, and E-flat. . . .

When all four keys got going at once, it resulted, of course, in the most dissonant-sounding counterpoint. Parker took it as a joke; he was seldom mean, and I did not bother him much after the first few months—(but occasionally all the same). He would just look at a measure or so, hand it back with a smile, or joke about 'hogging all the keys at one meal,' and then talk about something else."

So with the approach of Thanksgiving in 1897, Ives composed an Organ Prelude and Postlude for the Thanksgiving service, which he later judged to be his first good "serious piece away from the rulebook." Six or eight years later, as closely as Ives could recall (i.e.: in 1903 or 1905), he orchestrated his Prelude and Postlude under the title *Thanksgiving and/or Forefathers' Day,* which eventually became the finale of his "Holidays" Symphony. The three additional movements of the "Holidays" Symphony are *Washington's Birthday,* completed in 1909 (also as an independent piece); *Decoration Day,* completed in 1912; and *Fourth of July,* completed in 1913. Finally in 1913 Ives reorchestrated *Washington's Birthday* and combined it with the other three symphonic pieces to make the four-movement Symphony, "Holidays," which he described as "recollections of a boy's holidays in a Connecticut country town." That country town was Danbury, Connecticut, where Ives grew up, and the recollections are of course his own. The fact that a boy's recollections should be so sophisticated harmonically should not surprise us. For Ives's father, a Civil War bandmaster, Danbury bandmaster, choirmaster, organist, pianist, and teacher of almost all musical instruments, was an experimenter of the most astounding, radical imagination.

Young Charles adored his father's experiments and wished to try some himself. But his father told Charles in no uncertain terms that before he could experiment he would have to learn the fundamentals of traditional music theory (especially harmony and counterpoint) and become a performer as well.

By the time Charles was thirteen he had a regular job as church organist in Danbury and was playing snare drum in his father's band. Among the musical impressions which captured the budding composer's imagination was that of hearing two brass bands approaching from opposite directions, playing different marches in different keys, passing each other in a blaze of glory, and disappearing in the distance. Thus polytonality was a conscious experience and a cherished recollection from boyhood days.

Soon after he completed *Washington's Birthday* in 1909, Ives felt the need to hear the physical sound of his music. But because the idiom Ives preferred seemed to most musicians outlandish, if not actually mad, he almost never had the opportunities that came more easily to more conforming composers. Nevertheless he was able to persuade a few theater orchestra men to come to a back room in Tam's Copying Bureau in New York to run through the score of *Washington's Birthday.* Twice again, in 1914 and 1915, the score was tried over, apparently at Ives's own expense. Although not all the instruments were present, Ives felt, according to Henry Cowell, that they got through it "fairly well." On one other occasion a personal friend, Reber Johnson, assistant concertmaster of the New York Symphony Orchestra, brought a group of players to Ives's apartment to try over the same score. As Ives recalled:

"These were supposed to be the best men in the orchestra and they were good musicians, but the Globe Theatre orchestra did as well, if not better. They made an awful fuss about playing it. . . . After six or eight rehearsals it was approximately well played, but only after some of the parts which seemed to me the strongest and the best were cut out. Harmisch, the viola player, was the only one who was not more or less mad at the trouble the music gave them. He suggested that the piece be played at one of their concerts, but Reber Johnson answered: 'No, we must think of the audience.' "

The first performance of the movements *Washington's Birthday* and *Fourth of July* were not given until February 21, 1932, when Nicholas Slonimsky conducted the Orchestre Symphonique de Paris in the French capital.

I. *Washington's Birthday. Very slowly; Allegro* (in *Quadrille and Lancer time); Andante.* The composer prefaces the score of this opening movement with the following:

> "Cold and Solitude," says Thoreau, "are friends of mine. Now is the time before the wind rises to go forth and see the snow on the trees."
>
> And there is at times, a bleakness, without stir but penetrating, in a New England mid-winter, which settles down grimly when the day closes over the broken-hills. In such a scene it is as though nature would but could not easily trace a certain beauty in the somber landscape!—in the quiet but restless monotony! Would nature reflect the sterness of the Puritan's fiber or the self-sacrificing part of his ideals?
>
> The older folks sit
> "The clean winged hearth about
> Shut in from all the world without
> Content to let the north-wind roar
> In baffled rage at pane and door"
> (Whittier)
>
> But to the younger generation, a winter holiday means action!—and down through "Swamp hollow" and over the hill-road they go, afoot or in sleighs, through the drifting snow, to the barn dance at the Center. The village band of fiddles, fife and horn keep up an unending "break-down" medley and the young folks "salute their partners and balance corners" till midnight;—as the party breaks up, the sentimental songs of those days are sung half in fun, half seriously and with the inevitable "adieu to the ladies" the "social" gives way to the grey bleakness of the February night.

The opening "cold and solitude" are suggested by muted string choir with small touches of flute and horn color. A gradual increase of sonority and tempo, suggesting "the clean winged hearth" where the older folk sit, is followed by an abrupt switch of mood. The young people's barn dance with its lively rhythms and quotations of musical Americana, includes some still popular favorites such as "Camptown Races," a phrase from which is flung up by a solo horn. The gaiety rises to a great climax followed by a sudden hush and an almost sentimental parting mood in the course of which we hear a wraithlike fragment of "Goodnight, Ladies"—a master stroke of simplicity accomplished by a sudden shift of key and instrumental color to solo flute and solo muted violin. There is no ritard, but a quick fading to the cold sonority of the opening bars and to silence.

II. *Decoration Day.* It is perhaps pure accident, yet it seems characteristic of Charles Ives that one of his earliest profoundly stirring boyhood memories should be of a Memorial Day morning when he sensed "an exultant something gleaming with the possibilities of this life, an assurance that nothing is impossible . . ."

Ives has left us a description of the background of this movement:

> In the early morning the gardens and woods about the village are the meeting places of those who, with tender memories and devoted hands, gather the flowers for the Day's Memorial. During the forenoon as the people join each other on the Green there is felt, at times, a fervency and intensity—a shadow, perhaps, of the fanatical harshness—reflecting old Abolitionist days. It is a day, as Thoreau suggests, when there is a pervading consciousness of "Nature's kinship with the lower order—man."
>
> After the Town Hall is filled with the Spring's harvest of lilacs, daisies and peonies, the parade is slowly formed on Main Street. First come the three Marshals on plough horses (going sideways); then the Warden and Burgesses *in carriages,* the Village Cornet Band, the G. A R., two by two, the Militia (Company G.), while the volunteer Fire Brigade, drawing the decorated hose-cart, with its jangling bells, brings up the rear—the inevitable swarm of small boys following. The march of Wooster Cemetery is a thing a boy never forgets. The roll of muffled drums and "Adeste Fideles" answer for the dirge. A little girl on the fencepost waves to her father and wonders if he looked like that at Gettysburg.
>
> After the last grave is decorated "Taps" sounds out through the pines and hickories, while a last hymn is sung. Then the ranks are formed again and "we all march back to Town" to a Yankee stimulant—Reeves' inspiring "Second Regiment, Quick-Step,"—though to many a soldier, the somber thoughts of the day underlie the tunes of the band. The march stops—and in the silence, the shadow of the early morning flower-song rises over the Town and the sunset behind West Mountain breathes its benediction upon the Day.

A fragment of the "early morning flower-song" is first heard in the English horn:

Later it is woven into the scene of the decoration of the graves and the closing "benediction upon the day."

III. *Fourth of July. Adagio molto; Andante; Allegretto; Geschwindmarsch; Allegro con spirito.* A sketch for the movement, begun on the Fourth of July, 1911, bears the subtitle: "a boy's 'Fourth of July' in these here you Knighted States." The preface to the published score is a touch more serious:

> It's a boy's "4th"—no historical orations—no patriotic grandiloquence by "grown-ups"—no programs in his yard! But he knows what he's celebrating —better than some of the county politicians. And he goes at it in his own way, with a patriotism nearer kin to nature than jingoism. His festivities start in the quiet of the midnight before and grow raucous with the sun. Everybody knows what it's like. The day ends with the rocket over the Church-steeple, just after the annual explosion sets the Town Hall on fire.

This musical Fourth starts as peacefully as the midnight hour Ives recalled. Against a dark background of muted violas, cellos, and double basses, one-quarter of the violins outline a phrase that is to return again and again. It is a slowed-down, slightly distorted version of Ives's favorite, "Columbia, the Gem of the Ocean." "Columbia" is echoed ever more softly, and further distorted, in other sections of the violins, and double basses. It could be misleading to call these opening pages "impressionist"; they have so little in common with the Impressionism of Debussy. The blurred harmonies and the subtle manipulation of instrumental colors do convey an almost misty, visual impression. Yet the broad structure of the music could scarcely be simpler or more clearly conveyed by the composer's words.

IV. *Thanksgiving and/or Forefather's Day.*

In later years Ives recalled that the organ Prelude and Postlude on which he based this final movement were "the first pieces that seems to me much or any good now."

> The Postlude [he wrote] starts with C minor and D minor together, and later major and minor chords together, a tone apart. This was to represent the sternness, strength and austerity of the Puritan character, and it seemed that any of the major, minor or diminished chords, used alone, gave a feeling of bodily ease to which the Puritan did not give in. There is also in this some free counterpoint in different keys and rhythms going together. There is a scythe, or reaping-harvest, theme which is a kind of off-beat, off-key counterpoint. Six or eight years later (sometime before we left 65 Central Park West in the fall of 1906), these two pieces were arranged as a single movement for orchestra.

In its final version the climax and conclusion is reinforced by a full chorus in the traditional Thanksgiving or Forefathers' Day hymn:

God! Beneath Thy guiding hand
Our exiled fathers crossed the sea;
And as they trod the wintry strand,
With prayer and praise they worshiped Thee.

Ives's Symphony, "Holidays" is scored for an elaborate and colorful orchestra including piccolo, 2 flutes, 2 oboes, English horn, 2 clarinets, E-flat clarinet, 3 bassoons, contrabassoon, 4 horns, 3 trumpets, 2 cornets, 3 trombones, tuba, piano, celeste, kettledrums, cymbals, high bells, middle bells, low bells, church chimes, low chimes, side drum, bass drum, xylophone, jew's-harp, and the customary strings.

THREE PLACES IN NEW ENGLAND

A generation ago, the music of Charles Ives was practically unknown, except to a small group of interested composers and crusading performers and critics. Ives's *Three Places in New England* was completed in 1914, but had to wait until 1930 for its first performance, which was presented in Boston by the Chamber Orchestra of that city, under the direction of Nicholas Slonimsky. In January 1931 Slonimsky conducted his chamber group in the first New York performance. In both cities, Ives is reported to have been heartily booed and hissed. Today, Charles Ives is a sort of patron saint, if not a founding father, of American serious music. We acclaim him today for the very boldness and imagination which condemned him to musical obscurity for most of his life.

Like many of Ives's works, *Three Places in New England* was composed over a large span of years: the score is dated 1903 to 1914.

I. *The "Saint Gaudens" in Boston Common (Col. Shaw and his Colored Regiment).* The first movement, inspired by Augustus St. Gaudens's sculptural memorial to Colonel Robert Gould Shaw and his black regiment, was completed in 1911. Colonel Shaw's Fifty-fourth Massachusetts Regiment of black soldiers had fought a famous battle at Fort Wagner, South Carolina, in the Civil War. What this meant to Ives, he suggested in the poem (presumably written by himself) with which he prefaced the score of this first movement:

Moving,—Marching—Faces of Souls!
Marked with generations of pain,
Part-freers of a Destiny,
Slowly, restlessly—swaying us on with you
Towards other Freedom! . . .

Far from militant, Ives's music is thoughtful, gentle, even melancholy. Tiny fragments, as of half-remembered tunes, glint briefly in woodwind solos with an occasional touch of French horn. The only suggestion of martial glory is a three-measure climax toward the end, which quickly lapses into the poignant, thoughtful mood of the beginning.

II. *Putnam's Camp, Redding, Connecticut.* Far better than any musical analysis, Ives's own words prefacing the second movement tell what was in his mind and heart as he composed this exhilarating movement:

> Near Redding Center, Conn., is a small park preserved as a Revolutionary Memorial; for here General Israel Putnam's soldiers had their winter quarters in 1778–1779. Long rows of stone campfire places still remain to stir a child's imagination. The hardships which the soldiers endured and the agitation of a few hot-heads to break camp and march to the Hartford Assembly for relief, is part of Redding history.
>
> Once upon a "4th of July," some time ago, so the story goes, a child went there on a picnic, held under the auspices of the First Church and the Village Cornet Band. Wandering away from the rest of the children past the camp ground into the woods, he hopes to catch a glimpse of some of the old soldiers. As he rests on the hillside of laurel and hickories, the tunes of the band and the songs of the children grow fainter and fainter—when—*mirabile dictu*—over the trees on the crest of the hill he sees a tall woman standing. She reminds him of a picture he has of the Goddess of Liberty—but the face is sorrowful—she is pleading with the soldiers not to forget their "cause" and the great sacrifices they have made for it. But they march out of camp with fife and drum to a popular tune of the day. Suddenly a new national note is heard. Putnam is coming over the hills from the center—the soldiers turn back and cheer. The little boy awakes, he hears the children's songs and runs down past the monument to "listen to the band" and join in the games and dances. . . .

The repertoire of national airs at that time was meager. Most of them were of English origin. It is a curious fact that a tune very popular with the American soldiers was "The British Grenadiers." A captain in one of Putnam's regiments put it to words, which were sung for the first time in 1779 at a patriotic meeting in the Congregational Church in Redding Center; the text is both ardent and interesting.

The tune of "The British Grenadiers," to which Ives refers, occurs about halfway through the movement, played by a jaunty flute:*

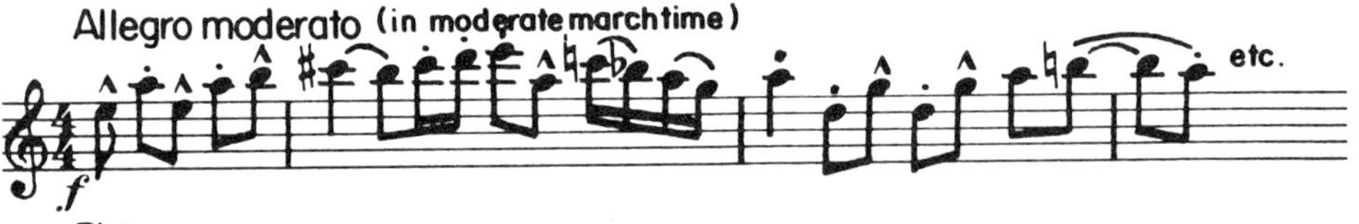

That frisky tune, which had long served to exalt British grenadiers far above Alexander, Hercules, "and such great names as these," was adapted, with equally "ardent and interesting" self-praise, to hurl defiance at the mother country. Two of the seven stanzas (by a Massachusetts volunteer officer, Joseph Warren, killed at Bunker Hill) declared:

---

* *This and the following musical example in this composition are copyright 1935, Mercury Music Inc. Used by permission.*

Proud Albion bowed to Caesar,
  And numerous lords before;
To Picts, to Danes, to Normans
  And many masters more;
But we can boast, Americans,
  We've never fallen prey.
Huzza, huzza, huzza, huzza
  For free America. . . .

Some future day shall crown us
  The masters of the main.
Our fleets shall speak in thunder
  To England, France and Spain.
And the nations o'er the oceans spread
  Shall tremble and obey
The sons, the sons, the sons, the sons
  Of free America.

In later years, skeptical critics suggested that this movement with its clashing harmonies and rhythms, its reckless counterpoint, had been influenced by Stravinsky and Hindemith. Ives pointed out with some asperity that this movement was composed long before Hindemith became a composer and at a time when he (Ives) had not seen or heard a note of Stravinsky's music.

III. *The Housatonic at Stockbridge.* Ives has left us his own account of the impressions which inspired this movement: "The last movement, 'The Housatonic at Stockbridge,' was suggested by a Sunday morning walk that Mrs. Ives and I took near Stockbridge the summer after we were married. We walked in the meadows along the river and heard the distant singing from the church across the river. The mist had not entirely left the riverbed, and the colors, the running water, the banks and trees were something that one would always remember." Ives prefaced his music with lines from "The Housatonic at Strockbridge" by the American poet, Robert Underwood Johnson (1853–1937), starting with the couplet:

Contented river! in thy dreamy realm—
The cloudy willow and the plumy elm . . .

The murmuring strings, which continue through most of the movement, recall the river mists of Ives's recollection, in his score. A wonderfully peaceful phrase of the solo horn is heard at intervals throughout the walk:

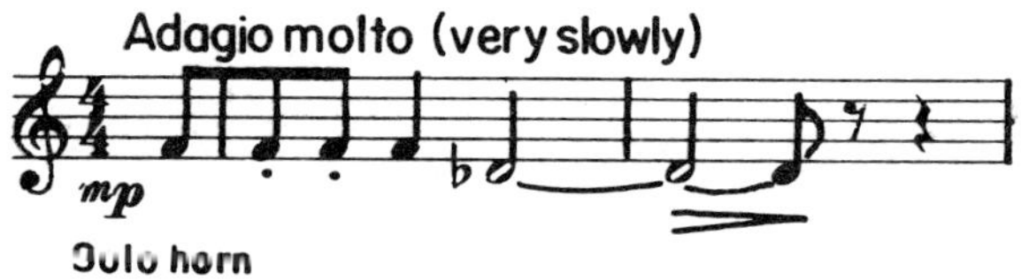

The horn phrase, a brief climax of lyric passion, and the sudden hush of the close are among the most poetic moments of a marvelously imaginative work.

Three Places in New England is scored for flute, oboe, English horn, clarinet, bassoon, 4 horns, 2 trumpets, 3 trombones, tuba, kettledrums, snare drum (with snare muffled), bass drum, cymbal, piano, pipe organ (16 foot, 32 foot, Pedal) ad lib, and the traditional string choir.

THE UNANSWERED QUESTION

Charles Ives's *The Unanswered Question*, to which he gave the subtitle, "A Cosmic Landscape," is one of the most famous works of a famous experimenter. Long before Stravinsky and other Europeans tried out the clashing keys technically referred to as "bi-tonality" or "polytonality," this independent Yankee businessman and artist had discovered these things for himself. Indeed he was so bold, so radical in his experiments, that he could find almost no one to take his music seriously until long after Stravinsky, Bartok, Hindemith, and other Europeans had made such sound fashionable and even popular.

Ives decided early in life that he never wanted to be plagued as an artist by the need to tickle the ears of the big conservative audience of average music lovers—or to tickle any one's ears except his own. He knew in advance that he must never be dependent on making money from his music. In order to achieve the independence he demanded, he went into business and became one of the most successful insurance men this country has known. He amassed a modest fortune and composed as he pleased.

The Unanswered Question still seems a highly imaginative piece, but it is no longer difficult to understand. The world today makes us so aware of unanswered questions that the basic idea of the piece is easy to grasp. The basic device of the music which once seemed so strange that it was hard to take it seriously, seems simple to us. Ives divides his chamber orchestra into two parts. The strings, which play very softly with mutes and very slowly throughout, contrast with the questioning solo trumpet and its related woodwind instruments. The fact that Ives did not even require any precise rhythmic coordination between these two halves of the orchestra, relates this piece to much experimental avant-garde music in the fourth quarter of our century.

This is the way Ives himself describes, in part, his own intentions:

> The strings play *ppp* throughout with no change in tempo. They are to represent "The Silences of the Druids—Who Know, See, and Hear Nothing." The trumpet intones "The Perennial Question of Existence," and states it in the same tone of voice each time:

> But the hunt for "The Invisible Answer" undertaken by the flutes and other human beings, becomes gradually more active, faster and louder through an *animando* to a *con fuoco*. This part need not be played in the exact time position indicated. It is played in somewhat of an impromptu way; if there be no conductor, one of the flute players may direct their playing. "The Fighting Answerers," as the time goes on, and after a "secret conference," seem to realize a futility, and begin to mock "The Question"—the strife is over for the moment. After they disappear, "The Question" is asked for the last time, and "The Silences" are heard beyond in "Undisturbed solitude."

The Unanswered Question is scored for 4 flutes, trumpet and string quartet, or string orchestra. But Ives was very flexible in his instrumental requirements for this work. He indicates that if necessary an oboe and a clarinet may replace the third and fourth flutes. The trumpet solo may be replaced by the English horn, or oboe or clarinet (if the two latter are not playing with the flutes). If a large string orchestra is used, the conductor may at his discretion use "the full treble woodwind choir." But in any case, only one trumpet plays. The trumpet should use a mute unless playing in a very large room, or with a large string orchestra.

Ives envisaged the coordination of the orchestral groups somewhat casually. "The flutes," he writes in the foreword of the score, "will end their part approximately near the position indicated in the string score; but in any case, 'The Last Question' should not be played by the trumpet until 'The Silences' of the strings in the distance have been heard for a measure or two. The strings will continue their last chord for two measures or so after the trumpet stops. If the strings shall have reached their last chord before the trumpet plays 'The Last Question,' they will hold it through and continue after, as suggested above."

Leoš Janáček

Born July 3, 1854, Hochwald, Moravia (now Hukvaldy, part of Czechoslovakia) —died August 12, 1928, Moravska Ostrava, Czechoslovakia

SINFONIETTA

Composed when Janáček was seventy-two, at the height of his international fame, the *Sinfonietta* is a simple, unpretentious work in the folk vein that characterized many of his earlier scores.

Like his Czech nationalist forbears, Dvŏrák and Smetana, Janáček was fascinated by the folk melodies of his native land and was very active in the investigation of the popular musical traditions of Czechoslovakia. However he almost never used actual folk tunes in his composition, preferring instead to build his own personal style on rhythmic, melodic, and modal traits of the Czech folk music found in the area where he was born, near the Polish border.

The son of a provincial schoolmaster and organist, Janáček was trained as a choirboy at a monastery in Brno. He continued his musical training at the Conservatories of Prague, Leipzig and Vienna, but returned to Brno, where he was active in many musical capacities for most of the rest of his career. He was conductor of the Czech Philharmonic, director of the Brno Organ School, and professor of composition at the Brno Conservatory, where he attracted many young Czech composers.

Not until he was past fifty years old did Janáček become prominent as a national composer. His best known opera *Jenufa,* passed almost unnoticed when it was first produced at the Brno Opera in 1904. It did not reach the Prague Opera until 1916, but then it was widely acclaimed. *Jenufa* was given many productions outside Czechoslovakia and became the foundation of Janáček's international reputation. It reached the Metropolitan Opera with Maria Jeritza in the title role on December 6, 1924.

The *Sinfonietta* is composed in five short movements and is closer to a serenade or divertimento than it is to symphonic style or form.

I. *Allegretto—Allegro—Maestoso.* The brief opening movement is scored for eleven trumpets, two tubas and kettledrums. It consists of a series of very short sections, many of them repeated. Most of the movement is derived from the following figure, or its variants:

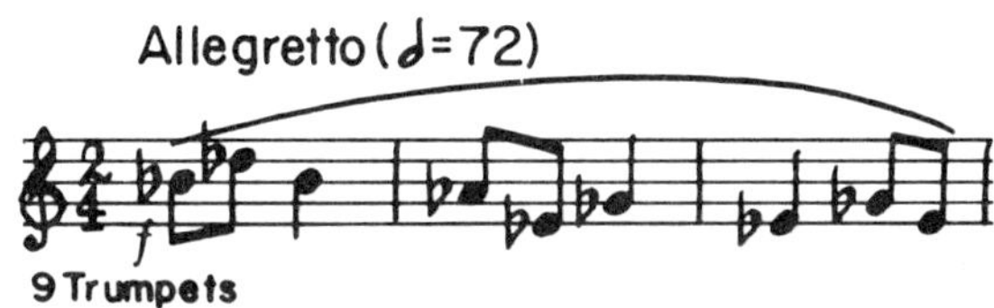

II. *Andante—Allegretto—Maestoso.* This is a longer and more elaborate movement with more varied orchestral color, but Janáček maintains the same, primitive-seeming structural principal of short, repetitious sections, each built on a persistent rhythmic figure.

III. *Moderato—Con moto—Prestissimo.* Muted strings present a flowing melody, which is taken up by woodwinds and finally by brass as the movement builds toward its *prestissimo* climax.

IV. *Allegretto—Adagio—Presto—Andante.* Light, dance-like rhythms and shifting *tempi* lend this movement its individual character.

V. *Andante con moto—Maestoso—Allegretto—Allegro.* Three flutes introduce the chief new theme of this finale. As the theme passes to other instruments, the strings maintain a murmuring accompaniment. The finale concludes with a repetition of the entire first movement in which woodwind and string instruments are added to the original trumpet and tuba color.

The *Sinfonietta* is scored for 4 flutes, piccolo, 2 oboes, English horn, 2 B-flat clarinets, E-flat clarinet, bass clarinet, 2 bassoons, 4 horns, 9 trumpets in C, 3 trumpets in F, 2 bass trumpets in B flat, 4 trombones, 2 tenor tubas, tuba, kettledrums, cymbals, bells, harp, and the customary complement of strings.

Dmitri Kabalevsky

Born December 30, 1904, St. Petersburg

OVERTURE TO COLAS BREUGNON

When Romain Rolland was asked permission for Kabalevsky to make an opera of his novel, *Colas Breugnon,* Rolland made only one stipulation: "Don't make Colas too serious. Colas without laughter won't be Colas. For the rest—*carte blanche.* Fly with your own wings." Kabalevsky's librettist V. Bragin did indeed fly with his own wings—and quite a distance.

Rolland's book, which reportedly had run through 120 Russian editions before Kabalevsky chose it, consists of the thoughts and comments of a fictional Burgundian master craftsman, Colas Breugnon, of the Age of Rabelais. Colas's observations and reflections follow no connected plot. But it was not too difficult for Kabalevsky's librettist to string selected incidents together and by taking very considerable liberties, to construct an opera plot which would find favor with Soviet authorities.

In his introduction to *Colas Breugnon,* Rolland had described the book as being "nonpolitical, nonmetaphysical, a book *à la bonne française,* which laughs at life because it finds life good. . . ." Ignoring this basic remark, Bragin took as his point of departure a comment of Colas in Chapter 2: "But who can say why these animals, these aristocrats, these politicians, these great lords were put on earth, these men who bleed our France, and, always singing her glory, empty her pockets, who, not satisfied with gnawing at our last pennies, try to devour the granaries of our neighbors, menace Germany, covet Italy, and stick their noses even into the harem of the grand Turk, . . . ah, peace, my friend! Do not let it stir your bile! Everything is as it is . . . and will be, until the day when we do things better (this will be as soon as possible)."

Such sentiments of course were made to order for a Soviet librettist. Against this background he developed some of the more exciting scenes of Rolland's book, including a peasant riot, or insurrection. The insurrection music serves as a handy climax for the Overture.

The full title of the opera is *Colas Breugnon, the Master of Clamecy.* The Overture opens with a brilliant flourish, a sort of symphonic motto, closely related to the main theme which follows immediately in *presto* tempo: a whirling dance-like figure easily associated with the *joie de vivre,* which was one of the main attributes of Colas himself. We hear it first played very softly by flutes and clarinets over the lightest of string accompaniment:

Almost immediately this mercurial theme is repeated with the choirs of the orchestra reversed: now the violins play the theme *pianissimo* against a glittering woodwind accompaniment.

The principal contrasting idea is a vigorous assertive figure announced in unison by trombone, cellos, and bassoon. A middle section of the Overture introduces a broadly flowing melody for woodwinds and violins. A brief recapitulation of the opening is interrupted by the music of the insurrection scene, which begins with a thumping solo for the kettledrums. As this dies away, we hear, as if in the far distance, a melody for clarinet followed by muted horns. The clarinet and horn themes develop slowly with mounting intensity to a climax of drive and brilliance.

The first performance of *Colas Breugnon* was given on February 22, 1938, at the Little Opera House of Leningrad. The score for the Overture enlists piccolo, 2 flutes, 3 oboes, English horn, 3 clarinets, 3 bassoons, contrabassoon, 4 horns, 3 trumpets, 3 trombones, tuba, kettledrums, snare drum, triangle, tambourine, cymbals, bass drum, xylophone, tam-tam, harp, and the customary string choir.

Leon Kirchner

Born January 24, 1919, Brooklyn, N.Y.

MUSIC FOR ORCHESTRA

Leon Kirchner composed Music for Orchestra for the New York Philharmonic as part of the Orchestra's celebration of its one hundred and twenty-fifth anniversary season (1967–1968). However, Kirchner was one of several composers commissioned who were unable to complete their scores in time for the anniversary season. He completed his score on October 7, 1969, and conducted the world premiere nine days later in Philharmonic Hall with repeats on October 17, 18, and 20, 1969. At the time of the premiere, Mr. Kirchner understandably did not have time to write a program note on his work. Moreover, Kirchner is known to feel that detailed descriptions or analyses of new works tend to be useless or misleading to the listener.

In deference to his feelings, I have not attempted any description or analysis of his score (even though it was repeated three seasons later by the New York Philharmonic and therefore could not be called "new" in the literal sense to Philharmonic audiences). Instead, I quote Kirchner's own paragraphs with which he responded to a request for a program note when Music for Orchestra was first performed by the Los Angeles Symphony Orchestra.

"Howling and stamping at the piano he had been working without food or rest for twenty-four hours. Page after page the staves were massed with symbols having something to do with life or the expression of it. The sensual experience was the pivot of all his being and thinking. Not once had he contemplated the logic, the efficiency, the impeccability of design: they were subterranean, subservient, a by-product of the passion of his mind. . . ."

An imaginary and unlikely contemporary narrative, it is, in fact, a slightly altered description of the scene Schindler and his friend Horsalka came upon when they visited Beethoven "howling and stamping . . . filthy and without food for 24 hours" in the "terrible disarray" of his studio as he worked on the "Credo" of the *Missa solemnis* in the summer of 1819.

Historical events since have cooled the artist's ambiance somewhat; the pendulum had swung; a contrasting and faintly antique theme appeared. The precise, objective language of this "new-old" theme implied spectacular developments when, as in the "sciences," the artist dealt exclusively with the "substantive" and exorcised the "unverifiable."

While in the public mind Schoenberg was the composer most associated with the origin of "substantive information" in the arts—in the guise of the twelve-tone technique—later serial composers found his materials redundant, aesthetically outmoded. But Schoenberg's contribution was not so much in the invention of the twelve-tone technique as in the results of the heroic protagonism between devastatingly abstract methodology and the enormous musical reservoir at his command: an intuitive reflection of the fierce technological versus biological encounters which had begun to produce warning tremors in our civilization.

The problematic and ungainly vertical combinations forced upon his ear by the selection of numbered notes were still "heard." Their harmonic and structural obligations, which in Schoenberg led to fascinating and intricately balanced gestalts, led, in the works of his apostles once removed, to their displacement by "ingenious" if sterile combinations of the row. It was soon clear that this new music was regressive and resulted in lifeless gesture. The "howling and stamping" of Beethoven was at lowest ebb.

The new "serialism," in "liberating the eye" from ear-bound passions, had surprising backlash consequences. The transition brought us Pollock-like constellations of sound. Graphics, games and theatrics evolved an amusing and catalytic compost. Whatever its lasting value, it reintroduced a joy in sound-making activity reminiscent and more human in scale. The orchestral apparatus invigorated by imaginative electronic onslaughts demonstrated its superior vitality and immense soniferous landscape.

The approach may be exclusively sensual and musicians may take perverse delight in the extravagant use of these innovations, yet it is clear, a new and hopefully more creative balance is being wrought between our sensual and intellectual resources, one in which it may be possible to achieve such fancies and grand architectonics as to make us feel deeply our human worth. Enough, perhaps, to "stamp and howl" at the piano once again.

Music for Orchestra is scored for 3 flutes, piccolo, 2 oboes, English horn, 3 clarinets, bass clarinet, 2 bassoons, contrabassoon, 4 horns, 3 trumpets, 3 trombones, tuba, celesta, glockenspiel, piano, chimes, wind chimes (glass), tubular bells, timpani sticks on lower strings of piano, high tom-tom, xylophone, suspended cymbal, antique cymbals, metal block, metal on tam-tam, temple blocks, wood blocks, vibraphone, bongos, kettledrums, snare drum, tenor drum, bass drum, and strings.

Mr. Kirchner was born in Brooklyn, New York, on January 24, 1919, but his family moved to California when he was nine years old. He was educated there and attended both the University of California at Los Angeles and the University of California at Berkeley. In composition his principal teachers were Arnold Schoenberg (1936–1938 and 1940–1941) and Ernest Bloch (1941–1942). He studied for an additional year with Roger Sessions in New York before serving in the U.S. Army from 1943 to 1946. After his army service he returned to Berkeley for further graduate work. There he was awarded a lectureship and also assisted Roger Sessions and Ernest Bloch. He also taught at the University of Southern California, Mills College, the University of Buffalo and the Berkshire Music Center.

In 1961 he succeeded Walter Piston as a professor of music at Harvard University, where he was subsequently appointed Walter Bigelow Rosen Professor of Music. He has received many awards: the George Ladd Traveling Fellowship (the highest musical honor conferred by the University of California at Berkeley), two Guggenheim Fellowships, a grant from the National Institute of Arts and Letters, the Naumburg Award and two New York Music Critics Circle Awards for the First and Second String Quartets. His Third String Quartet won a Pulitzer Prize in 1967. In 1962 he was elected to the National Institute of Arts and Letters and to the Academy of Arts and Sciences.

In recent seasons he has been increasingly prominent as a performer. Among the orchestras with which he has appeared as conductor or soloist are the New York Philharmonic, the Orchestra of the West German Radio at Baden-Baden, the Zürich Tonhalle, the Minnesota Orchestra, the Buffalo Philharmonic, the San Francisco Symphony, and the chamber orchestra of the Marlboro Music Festival (both at its home in Marlboro and on a European tour sponsored by the State Department). In 1969 he became the principal conductor of the Boston Philharmonia. In 1971 he was appointed a member of the Board of Overseers of the Boston Symphony.

Edouard Lalo

Born January 27, 1823, Lille—died April 22, 1892, Paris

SYMPHONIE ESPAGNOLE, FOR VIOLIN AND ORCHESTRA, OPUS 21

Like a magician's wand, the bow of the virtuoso violinist cast its spell not only over audiences but on composers throughout the Romantic period. Most of the great Romantic violin concertos were written with specific virtuosos and their personal styles in mind. Beethoven composed his single Violin Concerto with his superb but eccentric Franz Clement before him; Mendelssohn, with his Classically oriented Ferdinand David; and Brahms, with David's pupil Joachim in mind. If this is true of the peaks of the violin literature, how much greater must have been the contribution of virtuoso magic to those works of the second plane in which charm and popular appeal, verve and brilliance, played an even greater role. Lalo's *Symphonie espagnole,* despite its suitelike accumulation of five movements, is in fact a full-fledged violin concerto and Lalo was a friend of the great Spanish virtuoso Pablo de Sarasate.

Although born in Spain, Sarasate was trained in France, which became his adopted country. Lalo, although born in France, came of pure Spanish ancestry on both sides. He, too, was trained in France and his music, despite touches of Iberian exoticism, is part of the mainstream of French music. Paul Dukas put the case well when he wrote:

> Lalo seems to us above all an artist of Mediterranean sensibility whose music, in its wonderfully spontaneous outpouring, naturally takes on the aspect of an ideal dance. In this connection, great emphasis has been put on his Spanish origins. But if this fact is overemphasized one would be finally forced to find Iberian hues in the Overture to *Le Roi d'Ys* [composed on a Breton legend], in his *Russian Concerto,* or in his *Norwegian Rhapsody* . . . which would be to exaggerate. . . .
>
> The fact that Lalo composed a *Symphonie espagnole* can be explained just as well by the simple fact that he was an intimate friend of Sarasate, quite aside from his Spanish ancestry.

Lalo had had a long uphill climb to recognition, partly because of the frivolous state of French musical taste during the Second Empire. He was fifty before he achieved fame through the triumphant premiere of his Violin Concerto, Opus 20, dedicated to and first performed by Sarasate. His *Symphonie espagnole,* Opus 21, also dedicated to Sarasate, was given its first performance by the Spanish virtuoso at a Colonne Concert in Paris on February 7, 1875. It was an instant triumph and it is the only one of Lalo's works which has remained popular to the present day.

Sarasate's style, which seemed sensationally new and modern around 1860 when he first became famous, differed greatly from the more rhetorical, often passionate and fiery style of earlier Romantic violin virtuosos. His tone was not especially big, but remarkably pure, sweet and bright, of an almost uncanny purity and accuracy of intonation. His astonishingly flexible technique was of a hitherto unheard lightness. And everyone who heard him agreed that his delivery had a peculiar, quite personal rhythmic charm, particularly in Spanish music.

The *Symphonie espagnole* is in five movements, of which the third is usually omitted.

I. *Allegro non troppo.* The first movement, the most highly developed of the five, opens with a bold, motto-like fragment of the principal theme, proclaimed by the full orchestra and echoed by the solo violin. After a slight pause, the soloist anticipates the languorous *malagueña* which supplies an important episode in the finale. A longer *tutti* interruption and brilliant flourishes for the solo violin lead to the complete statement of the principal theme by the soloist, as follows:

A yearning, almost sentimental second theme in a contrasting major tonality is marked *dolce espressivo.* The structure of the movement follows traditional symphonic sonata form, including a free development of both principal themes and their recapitulation. It is characteristic of the virtuoso style of this movement and of many later passages that the solo violin is constantly plunging from its highest, most brilliant range to the lowest, most sonorous, soaring and plunging again.

II. *Scherzando; Allegro molto.* The lively second movement is based on the Spanish *seguidilla* rhythm, most obvious in the opening measures for *pizzicato* strings, which echo the traditional castanet refrain of the *seguidilla.* After a more sentimental middle section the *seguidilla* rhythms return, growing lighter and airier and diminishing to an almost Mendelssohnian delicacy.

III. *Intermezzo: Allegretto non troppo.* The third movement, which is frequently omitted, is a lighthearted interlude based on a piquant rhythm, said to be Spanish-Moorish in origin: a two-beat measure with three notes (a triplet) to the first beat and only two (even eighths) to the second. After some thirty bars of brilliant orchestral introduction, the movement is taken over by the solo violin.

IV. *Andante.* A sombre introduction dominated by the sound of low brass instruments leads to a melancholy solo, again in folk-style, which some commentators confidently diagnose as Spanish, while others have found it closer to a Scandinavian idiom! After a contrasting middle section with considerable virtuoso embellishment, the original solo melody returns, accompanied now by softly throbbing kettledrums.

V. *Rondo: Allegro.* A bouncing rhythmic phrase is obstinately repeated by one orchestral group after another to form an introduction, and later an accompaniment to the principal Rondo melody, a joyous refrain proclaimed by the solo violin:

Among the contrasting episodes of this Rondo is the languorous *malagueña* anticipated in the introduction to the first movement. For all of the brilliance of its closing pages the Rondo retains an almost diaphanous delicacy, with light *staccato* arpeggios and high trills for the soloist up to the electric final measures.

The *Symphonie espagnole* is scored for piccolo, 2 flutes, 2 oboes, 2 clarinets, 2 bassoons, 4 horns, 2 trumpets, 3 trombones, triangle, harp, bass drum, kettledrums, and the traditional string choir.

György Ligeti

Born May 28, 1923, Dicsözentmárton (Siebenbürgen), Hungary

ATMOSPHÈRES

Commissioned by the adventurous Southwest German Radio in Baden-Baden, György Ligeti's *Atmosphères* is dedicated to the memory of his compatriot, the composer Mátyás Seiber, who was killed in an automobile accident in Johannesburg on September 25, 1960. The highly complex score was completed the following year and was first performed on October 22, 1961, at Donaueschingen under the direction of Hans Rosbaud.

Mr. Ligeti explains his musical aims in *Atmosphères* as follows:

> My most basic aim as a composer is the revivification of the sonorous aspect of musical form. Those factors of contemporary composition which do not manifest themselves directly as acoustical experience seem to me of only secondary importance. However, this emphatically does not mean that I intend to limit myself to the invention of new tone colors or other sound-phenomena. It is much more important to me to discover new musical forms and a new manner of expression. My personal development began with serial music, but today I have passed beyond serialism. In *Atmosphères,* I have attempted to supersede the "structural" approach to music which once, in turn, superseded the motive-thematic approach, and to establish a new textural concept of music. In this kind of music, there are no "events," but only

"states," no contours or forms, but instead, an uninhabited, imaginary musical space. Tone color, usually a vehicle of musical form, is liberated from form to become an independent musical entity.

This so-to-speak "informal" music is embodied in a new type of orchestral sound: the sonorous texture is so dense that the individual interwoven instrumental voices are absorbed into the general texture and completely lose their individuality. This new, unaccustomed orchestral sound results from the fact that the sound of each individual instrument (consisting of a number of "partial" tones) is itself a "partial" or a still more complex acoustical structure. The "interwoven" treatment of the orchestra is the reason for the omission of all percussion and for the unusual format of the orchestral score which is noted on eighty-seven staves, since the string instruments are written completely divisi, that is, with an individual part for each player.

Atmosphères presumably occupies an extreme position, which possibly may be interpreted as a dead end. But often, it is the apparent dead end which conceals a gateway opening into fresh fields.

György Ligeti studied composition at the Klausenburg Conservatory from 1941–1943 and at the Franz Liszt Conservatory in Budapest from 1945–1949. Upon conclusion of these studies, he devoted himself to research in the field of Romanian folk music. In 1950 he was appointed professor of music theory and form at the Liszt Conservatory. After the Hungarian uprising of 1956, he fled from Hungary. For the next two years, he worked in the Electronic Music Studio of the West German Radio in Cologne. Since 1959 he has taught composition in such centers of avant-garde music as Darmstadt and Bilthoven. His works include a number of piano compositions, lieder, orchestral scores, and chorus works, as well as electronic music.

Atmosphères requires a large orchestra, each instrument of which has its own independent part, and calls for 4 piccolos, 4 flutes, 4 B-flat clarinets, 4 E-flat clarinets, 3 bassoons, contrabassoon, 6 horns, 4 trumpets, 4 trombones, tuba, piano (with two players—not pianists, but percussionists), 14 first violins, 14 second violins, 10 violas, 10 cellos, and 8 basses, three of which have a fifth string.

Franz Liszt

Born October 22, 1811, Raiding near Oedenburg (now Sopron), Hungary, (Raiding is now in Austria)—died July 31, 1886, Bayreuth

CONCERTO NO. 1 FOR PIANO AND ORCHESTRA, E-FLAT MAJOR

When the daemon stirred Liszt, and apparently it almost always did, he was the despair of all other pianists. When Clara Schumann first heard him in 1838 she was overwhelmed. She wept. "I sobbed aloud," she wrote, "it overcame me so. Beside Liszt, other virtuosos appear so small, even Thalberg." It is of course impossible to preserve the quality, the style of an artist's performance in words. But since Liszt's personality is the key to his music, the reactions of some of the great musicians who heard him play may bring us closer to the core of such a fascinating work as Liszt's E-flat Concerto. One of Liszt's qualities especially strong in this Concerto and in his performances is described by the famous German-born pianist and conductor Sir Charles Hallé. "His daring was as extraordinary as his talent. At an orchestral concert given by him and conducted by Berlioz, the 'Marche au supplice,' from the latter's *Symphonie fantastique,* that most gorgeously orchestrated piece, was performed, at the conclusion of which Liszt sat down and played his own arrangement for the piano alone of the same movement, with an effect even surpassing that of the full orchestra, and creating an indescribable *furore.*"

That poet among composers, Robert Schumann, who detested all cheap external effects, trickery, false glitter and bombast, wrote of a Liszt recital in 1840: ". . . Now the daemon began to stir in him; first he played with the public as if to try it, then gave it something more profound, until he had enmeshed every member of the audience with his art and did with them as he willed. . . . Within a few seconds tenderness, boldness, exquisiteness, wildness succeed one another; the instrument glows and flashes under the master's hands. . . . But I would sacrifice all the astonishing audacious *bravura* that he displayed here for the sake of the magical tenderness that he expressed in the following étude. With the sole exception of Chopin, as I have already said, I know of no one who could equal it."

It is well to remember the evidence of two such sensitive and inward-turned artists as Clara and Robert Schumann when we read extravagant accounts by persons more impressed by the Liszt showmanship, as in the following words of an Englishman (Henry Reeves) who heard Liszt play in Paris:

"I saw Liszt's countenance assume that agony of expression, mingled with radiant smiles of joy, which I never saw on any other human face except in the paintings of Our Saviour by some of the early masters; his hands rushed over the keys, the floor on which I sat shook like a wire, and the whole audience was wrapped in sound, when the hand and frame of the artist gave way. He fainted in the arms of the friend who was turning pages for him, and we bore him out in a fit of hysterics. The effect of this scene was really dreadful. The whole room sat breathless with fear, till Hiller came forward and announced that Liszt was already restored to consciousness and was comparatively well again. As I handed Madame de Circourt to her carriage, we both trembled like poplar leaves, and I tremble scarcely less as I write this."

There is a legend—or it could even be the sober truth, for Liszt did have a sardonic side to him—that he put words to the principal theme of his E-flat major Concerto:

The words which Liszt allegedly sang not entirely inaudibly to himself were: *"Das versteht ihr alle nicht!"* (literally: "None of you understand this," or more freely: "None of the rest of you know how to do this!"). We may safely assume that nobody else *did* equal Liszt in the grandeur and *bravura* with which he played such a work.

Liszt seems to have made his first sketches for the E-flat Piano Concerto very soon after the concert described above by Robert Schumann, that is to say in the early 1840's. According to one of Liszt's pupils, the pianist and conductor Hans von Bülow, the Concerto was completed in June 1849. Liszt revised it in 1853 and the score was published in 1857. Liszt himself was the soloist at the first performance which he played on February 17, 1855, in the hall of the palace of the Grand Duke of Weimar.

Instead of being divided into the traditional, Classical three movements, the Concerto is performed in one continuous whole which unites the elements of several movements, much as Liszt and his Romantic contemporaries tended to unify both the sonata cycle and the separate movements of the Classical symphony into a single, all-embracing, one-movement form.

I. *Allegro maestoso, tempo giusto.* The first movement begins with a proclamation by the entire string choir, in decisive octaves, of the themes quoted above. This is not only the principal theme of the first movement, but may be taken as a kind of motto for the entire Concerto. The piano enters almost at once in a series of *bravura* octave passages leading into several more cadenza-like outbursts of solo brilliance.

II. *Quasi adagio.* Hardly has the first movement faded into silence when the nocturne-like slow movement begins in the muted strings:

The dreamlike tranquility of this theme, which is almost immediately taken up by the piano solo, scarcely prepares one for the brilliant form in which it will return in the *finale.* The scherzo movement follows without pause.

III. *Allegretto vivace.* The delicate triangle rhythm which pervades this *scherzo* movement once earned the Concerto the derisive nickname of "the triangle concerto." For modern listeners the movement has an almost Mendelssohnian lightness and charm. At the end of the *scherzo* a piano cadenza takes up the opening motto theme of the work in a transition passage leading without pause into the finale.

IV. *Allegro marziale animato.* The melody of the slow movement is transformed into a gallant, marchlike theme. It is developed with increasing brilliance until the motto theme of the Concerto returns to conclude the work in a headlong, flashing *presto.*

The E-flat Concerto is scored for piccolo, 2 flutes, 2 oboes, 2 clarinets, 2 bassoons, 2 horns, 2 trumpets, 2 trombones, bass trombone, kettledrum, triangle, cymbals, and the traditional strings.

CONCERTO NO. 2 FOR PIANO AND ORCHESTRA, A MAJOR

Like his tone poems, Liszt's piano works are inconceivable without the extraordinary personality of the man himself and the period of which he was such a vivid part. Since Liszt composed in large part with his own conducting or pianism in mind, one road to an understanding of his highly individual musical style is an awareness of his style as a performer.

In 1836 and the years immediately following, when Liszt began work on this Concerto, the German-born pianist and conductor Sir Charles Hallé had many occasions to hear him perform in public and private and to compare him with Chopin and other leading pianists of the day. Of Liszt he wrote: "Such marvels of executive skill and power I could never have imagined. He was a giant, and [Anton] Rubinstein spoke the truth when, at a time when his own triumphs were greatest, he said that in comparison with Liszt all other pianists were children. Chopin carried you with him into a dreamland, in which you would have liked to dwell forever; Liszt was all sunshine and dazzling splendour, subjugating his hearers with a power that none could withstand. For him, there were no difficulties of execution, the most incredible seeming child's play under his fingers. One of the transcendant merits of his playing was the crystal-like clearness which never failed for a moment even in the most complicated and, to anybody else, impossible passages; it was as if he had photographed them in the minutest detail upon the ear of his listener. The power he drew from his instrument was such as I have never heard since, but never harsh, never suggesting 'thumping.' "

Although power was perhaps the most obvious attribute of Liszt's playing, it was by no means his chief virtue. In March 1840, the year after Liszt completed the earliest extant sketch of the A-major Concerto, Robert Schumann heard him play in Dresden. Schumann, whose delicate sensibility made him a fanatical enemy of all portentous bombast and false glitter, wrote of Liszt:

"Liszt's most amazing performance was yet to come—Weber's *Konzertstück* which he played at his second concert. As virtuoso and audience seemed to be in the most animated mood possible on that evening, the enthusiasm during and after his playing exceeded everything hitherto known here. Beginning the piece with a force and grandeur of expression that made one think of an attack on a battlefield, he carried this on with continually increasing power up to the passage where the player, as it were, places himself at the head of the orchestra, leading it forward in triumph."

Liszt completed, orchestrated, and sent his A-major Concerto to the copyist at the latest by 1849. But it was revised at least thrice, for the last time in 1861. The first performance on record took place on January 7, 1857 during

Liszt's tenure as conductor in Weimar. The soloist was Liszt's pupil, Hans von Bronsart, and Liszt conducted.

The Concerto is in one continuous movement, though with many fluctuations of tempo. It is further unified by one basic theme which runs through the entire work in many transformations. This is a dreamy, sensuous melody announced immediately in the opening bars by the clarinets, supported by typically Lisztian chromatic harmonies in the other woodwinds:

This is first developed at a languorous tempo with a piano cadenza. A vigorously contrasting theme in dotted rhythm leads to an *Allegro agitato assai* and a second thematic contrast.

The main theme returns in a nostalgic cello solo with graceful *arpeggio* piano embellishments. Another piano cadenza leads to a brilliant *Allegro deciso,* culminating in a striking, martial version of the main theme. There are further, ethereal transformations of the theme and the closing section is a flashing, vertiginous *stretto.*

The Concerto is scored for piccolo, 3 flutes, 2 oboes, 2 clarinets, 2 bassoons, 2 horns, 2 trumpets, 3 trombones, tuba, kettledrums, cymbals, and the traditional strings.

A FAUST SYMPHONY IN THREE CHARACTER PICTURES (AFTER GOETHE) FOR LARGE ORCHESTRA, TENOR AND MALE CHORUS

"Our Dr. Faust," wrote Heine with more than a touch of malice, "is such a true and deep character, thirsting for the innermost nature of things, and even in sensual matters so scholarly that he could only have been a German. There can be no doubt about his existence."

Heine was right about the existence of an actual, historical Faust. His first name seems to have been George. But the mixture of fascination, contempt, and dread his contemporaries felt for him, and the lure that his legend has exerted on generations of poets, painters, composers, playwrights, critics and philosophers are based on headier stuff than a thirst for knowledge. For one thing, he was believed to have summoned Helen of Troy back from the mists of antiquity and made her his paramour. This was an exploit worth any man's envy. It was also the stuff of poetry and drama. Christopher Marlowe's Faustus exclaims, as Helen materializes before him:

> Was this the face that launch'd a thousand ships
> And burnt the topless towers of Ilium?
> Sweet Helen, make me immortal with a kiss!
> Her lips suck forth my soul: see where it flies!

In the Second Part of Goethe's *Faust* drama, the union of Faust and Helen is the fulfillment of one of Goethe's own dreams: the marriage of Romantic and Classical art.

Most of Faust's exploits smacked of dream fulfillment, even those which were coarse or merely naughty knavery, like the pranks of Till Eulenspiegel, another rebellious folk hero of the sixteenth century. Till's popularity sprang from the insolent leer with which he regarded respectable society and his flamboyant rebellion against its shams, conventions and canons. Faust's rebellion was a more awesome one against God himself. This may have been the root of his sensational appeal to the imagination of Faust's own age, the late Renaissance. It was an age of rebellion of human (that is, secular, scientific) knowledge against what some held to be divine (theological or revealed) truth, and the even more sensational religious rebellion of Protestantism against the rule of Rome.

The central theme of the Faust story, that of a man selling himself to an evil spirit in exchange for superhuman power or knowledge, is older than Christianity itself. It is allied to the idea that some knowledge, if not evil in itself, can be acquired only through sin. In the Garden of Eden the fall of man is identified as the acquisition of knowledge forbidden by God.

With the Age of Enlightenment, however, attitudes toward knowledge changed. Goethe reversed Faust's quest from a sin into a virtue. Indeed, he went further and made Faust a symbol of the unappeasable longing of Romantic man himself, his longing for infinite knowledge, infinite experience. The Late-Romantic philosopher Oswald Spengler went further yet. In his *Decline of the West* he pictured Faust's longing for infinity as a basic trait of Western civilization, which he called simply the "Faustian" culture. Had Spengler lived to see our first explorations of outer space, he would have regarded them as a logical outcome of a basic spiritual drive of Faustian culture.

Who was this man, whose name has come to mean so much to us? Today the tiny German town of Knittlingen claims the honor of being his birthplace and has opened a museum of Faustian lore in its new Town Hall. Faust is said to have been born there in 1480, the illegitimate son of a sturdy, well-to-do citizen noted for his rigid religiosity. Faust did not inherit the family name of Gerlach. But he is believed to have learned Latin in his native town, to have taken a theologian's degree at the age of eighteen, medical degree at twenty and a doctorate of philosophy at the University of Heidelberg in 1509.

How far can one trust the reports of his contemporaries? Two years before Faust took his Heidelberg degree (reportedly at the top of his class), an Abbott Tritheim of Würzburg wrote to a mathematician-astrologer friend at Heidelberg warning him against Faust as "a vagabond, an empty babbler and a knave, worthy to be whipped, that he might no longer profess publicly abominable matters that are opposed to the Holy Church." The Abbott accused Faust of having adopted the title: *Magister Georgius Sabellicus Faustus junior,* fountain of necromancers, astrologer, *magus secundus,* chiromancer, aëromancer, pyromancer, second in hydromancy," and he follows with a bill of particulars concerning Faust's impostures. Two further documents of the time mention a fortune-teller, Georgius (or Jörg) Faustus, chiromancer, "a mere braggart and fool," who was expelled from the town of Ingolstadt on the Wednesday after St. Vitus's Day, 1528.

With the passage of the years, the reports grew more lurid. Soon Faust was reported to have studied magic at the University of Cracow; it was said that he boasted of being on cozy terms with the devil, and from that to the rumor that Faust had bartered his soul for supernatural knowledge was a small step. Melancthon appears to have denounced him as "a disgraceful beast and a sewer of many devils." Faust himself may have been a willing coarchitect of his spooky reputation. Such a reputation was of course dangerous, but it could be profitable, too, as we see from the account book of the Bishop of Bamberg which records that the Bishop paid 10 gulden, a large sum of money, to "Doctor Faustus, *philosophus*," for having cast his *indicium*, or horoscope, on February 12, 1520.

Faust's legendary exploits fill volumes, many of them published within a few years of his death. He is said to have been throttled by the Devil in 1540. Before the century was out the Faust story had been published not only in German, but in Danish, French, Dutch, Flemish, Czech and in English as "The History of the Damnable Life and the Deserved Death of Dr. John Faustus." The first to raise the legend to the realm of literature was the Elizabethan Marlowe, and one of the more recent was Thomas Mann.

When Goethe was asked who could write a Faust opera, he is said to have replied that, since the death of Mozart, the only composer who might do justice to the theme was Meyerbeer. Goethe was not noted for his musical perceptions. But his drama has been the basis of most Faust music and most of its composers have been Romantics: Spohr, Schumann, Berlioz, Wagner, Liszt, Gounod, Boïto.

Liszt first made the acquaintance of Goethe's *Faust* in the French translation of Gérard de Nerval in 1830, just before the premiere of Berlioz' *Symphonie fantastique*, and it was Berlioz who called it to his attention. At first he does not seem to have been impressed or anywhere near as interested as he was by Byron's hero Manfred. "Let me whisper quite confidentially," he wrote to a friend years later, "despite its tremendous poetic prestige . . . his character seemed to me basically bourgeois. For that reason he becomes truer, more complete, richer and more communicative (than Manfred). Faust's personality scatters and dissipates itself. He does not take action, he lets himself be driven, hesitates, experiments, loses his way, considers, bargains and is interested only in his own little happiness."

The last remark could hardly have been made by anyone who had read and could recall the tremendously moving, culminating scene of Faust's death in the Second Part of the tragedy. This makes it impossible to subscribe to the widespread notion that Liszt came closest of all the Faust-composers to grasping the vast scope of Goethe's work. Liszt's personality was far removed from that of Olympian elderly Goethe of the Second Part of *Faust*. What Liszt did was to present, at least in part, a portrait of himself, both in the first "Faust" movement and in the mocking, ironical "Mephistopheles" movement. The middle movement, the portrait of Gretchen, surely portrays much of Liszt's feeling about women, which is further developed in the ecstatic *Chorus mysticus,* which concludes the last movement.

I. *Faust: Lento assai; Allegro impetuoso; Allegro agitato ed appassionato; Affettuoso poco andante; Grandioso, poco meno mosso; Andante mesto; Allegro con fuoco; Andante maestoso assai.* The first movement opens with a striking, pensive theme which, if it had been written by a twentieth-century composer, might have been called a free "tone row," since it uses all twelve tones of the chromatic scale:

This is followed immediately by a second Faust theme, a doleful phrase in the oboe, representing the more emotional side of Faust's nature. This is a theme which will return in many transformations throughout the Symphony:

A third Faust theme, representing the more heroic side of his nature, is proclaimed by the brass with true Lisztian swagger, marked *grandioso:*

These and other themes reflecting various facets of the hero are developed in free symphonic sonata form.

II. *Gretchen: Andante soave; Etwas bewegter; Tempo primo.* The "Gretchen" movement, after a brief introduction in the cool tones of the woodwinds, presents the main Gretchen theme in the solo oboe:

It is accompanied in a most original color combination by a single solo viola. This is the theme which will be sung at the very end of the Symphony, rhythmically altered and in a great lyric expansion by the solo tenor voice, to the words: *"Das Ewig-Weibliche zieht uns hinan."* The middle part of the "Gretchen" movement brings in, logically enough, several of the Faust themes in ardently lyric versions. The movement closes with a return of the opening material.

III. *Mephistopheles: Allegro vivace, ironico; Andante; Allegro vivace; Andante mistico.* The portrait of Mephistopheles which constitutes most of the final movement is a masterpiece of picturesque *diablerie,* both in the flash and glitter of the orchestration and in its mocking transformations of the serious themes used earlier to portray Faust. This is entirely in keeping with a modern interpretation of the character of Mephistopheles, which sees in him not merely "the spirit that denies," but also the negative, cynically intellectual, self-mocking side of Faust's own nature. The following, for example, is only one of the many transformations of the second Faust theme quoted above:

But at last all the commotion and mocking die away. A mood of solemnity spreads through the orchestra which is augmented by the organ, and a male chorus with solo tenor conclude the work with the final words of the Second Part of *Faust,* the scene of Faust's redemption.

Alles Vergängliche
Ist nur ein Gleichnis;
Das Unzulängliche
Hier wird's Ereignis;
Das Unbeschreibliche
Hier ist's getan;
Das Ewig-Weibliche
Zieht uns hinan.

These lines have been put into literal English prose: "All transitory things are but a simile; the unattainable here is fulfilled; the indescribable here is achieved; the eternal feminine draws us onward."

The score for the "Faust" Symphony calls for piccolo, 3 flutes, 2 oboes, 2 clarinets, 2 bassoons, 4 horns, 3 trumpets, 3 trombones, tuba, kettledrum, cymbals, triangle, organ, harp, and the usual string choir.

MAZEPPA

Mazeppa sometimes seems one of Liszt's most wildly pictorial works. Yet in its original form it was a piece of perfectly innocent abstract music: a piano etude designed only to develop and display the performer's technique of playing in thirds. Liszt was about fifteen years old when he published it as one of his Piano Etudes, Opus 1. A dozen years later he revised this set. In the process he added the principal *Mazeppa* theme, as we know it, to the Etude in thirds. In 1840 Liszt published this Etude separately under the title *Mazeppa* and changed the end slightly to make it parallel the dramatic conclusion of a swashbuckling poem by Victor Hugo.

Ivan Stepanovich Mazeppa, the hero (or villain) of poems by Hugo and Byron and a play by Pushkin, was an historical personage: a Polish nobleman, who became a Cossack chieftain or hetman in the Ukraine, and sided with King Charles XII of Sweden against the Russian Czar Peter I in an attempt to win Ukranian independence from Russia. While still in Poland as a young page at the court of King Casimir, Mazeppa is said to have had an affair with the wife of an older courtier, who had Mazeppa seized and tied naked to a wild horse, which was then driven into the Ukraine. After a long and violent ride which almost cost Mazeppa's life, he was rescued by Cossacks and eventually became their hetman.

Hugo's poem and Liszt's revised Etude both center on Mazeppa's wild ride and rescue. But it is worth remembering that Liszt, the inventor of the storytelling tone poem, composed the music first and added the story later. In a fourth incarnation, again under the title of *Mazeppa,* Liszt included the piece in his 1851 collection of "Transcendental" Etudes. In the same year he transformed the *Mazeppa* Etude into an orchestral tone poem.

Since Liszt did not yet feel secure in his technique of orchestration, he had his Swiss composer-friend Joseph Joachim Raff work out the details of instrumentation for him. But as a result of Liszt's conducting activity at the Court of Weimar his mastery of instrumentation grew fast. Thus when it came to rehearsing *Mazeppa,* he was able to revise details of Raff's orchestration himself, sharpening fine points of balance and color. Liszt conducted the premiere at Weimar on April 16, 1854.

Mazeppa begins with a sharp chord of the orchestra: perhaps a cry of pain or the snap of the whip which sends the wild horse careening toward the Ukraine. Wild rushing scales of the strings are reinforced by chromatically rising figures for the woodwinds, building higher and higher tension, at the climax of which the trombones burst forth with the principal *Mazeppa* theme:

The orchestra gathers momentum, reaching an even higher peak of intensity as the principal theme reappears in trumpets, horns, and the entire woodwind choir.

The mood shifts, perhaps reflecting Hugo's stanzas describing nightfall, and we hear a lyric transformation of the principal theme in the woodwinds *espressivo dolente:*

A return of the principal theme leads to a catastrophic climax, suggesting the collapse of the exhausted horse as described by Hugo. Still tied to the body of the horse, the helpless Mazeppa languishes: a short *andante* in free recitative-like rhythm suggests his sighs and groans as his strength and hope ebb.

A sudden *tremolo* of excitement runs through the string section. As if from a great distance we hear a trumpet fanfare heralding the approach of the liberating Cossacks. An *allegro marciale* suggests not only Mazeppa's rescue but the triumphs which he later achieved as hetman of the Cossacks. The swift denouement of the symphonic poem parallels the headlong pace of Hugo's concluding lines: "He runs, he flies, he falls,/And rises again a king!" *("Il court, il vole, il tombe,/Et se relève roi!")*

The score of *Mazeppa* calls for piccolo, 2 flutes, 2 oboes, English horn, clarinets (1 in D, 1 in A), bass clarinet in C, 3 bassoons, 4 horns, 3 trumpets, 3 trombones, tuba, kettledrums, cymbals, triangle, bass drum, and the traditional string choir.

LES PRELUDES

Probably the most popular symphonic poem ever written, Franz Liszt's *"Les Préludes"* is something of a portrait of the composer himself. Not that it was so intended, but Liszt's swashbuckling, brilliant personality spilled over into almost everything that he wrote. As for the subject matter of this dazzling tone poem, we need not take that too literally, for Liszt himself changed it at least once, completely. How far back the original sketches for the work may date, we do not know. But in 1844 and 1845, in Paris, Liszt composed a choral work entitled *"The Four Elements" (The Earth, The Winds, the Oceans, the Stars).* It had piano accompaniments which were later orchestrated by a friend of Liszt's. In 1848 Liszt, who meanwhile had been studying orchestration, himself wrote an introduction to the entire work using themes from the four movements. It was this orchestral introduction which, after various revisions, finally became *Les Préludes.* The first performance was given under Liszt's own direction at Weimar on February 28, 1854.

The present title of the work does not refer to the fact that it was originally a prelude to a choral work. The reference is to a poem, "Les Préludes," the fifteenth in a collection entitled *Nouvelles méditations poétiques* by the popular French Romantic poet, Lamartine. Liszt prefaced his score with the following paragraph of his own. This had so little to do with the poem of Lamartine that we may safely forget the poem and concentrate on Liszt's words which, after all, are his own explanation of his own music:

"What else is life but a series of preludes to that unknown hymn, the first and solemn note of which is intoned by Death? Love is the enchanted dawn of all existence; but what fate is there whose first delights of happiness are not interrupted by some storm, whose fine illusions are not dissipated by some mortal blast, consuming its altar as though by a stroke of lightning? And what cruelly wounded soul, issuing from one of these tempests, does not endeavour to solace its memories in the calm serenity of rural life? Nevertheless, man does not resign himself for long to the enjoyment of that beneficent warmth which he first enjoyed in Nature's bosom, and when "the trumpet sounds the alarm" he takes up his perilous post, no matter what struggle calls him to its ranks, that he may recover in combat the full consciousness of himself and the entire possession of his powers."

The fact that the above words are not Liszt's first explanation of what his music meant does not necessarily disqualify them. For Liszt has written elsewhere that his music is an expression of states of emotion, and that he saw no reason why a program, if not too detailed, should not guide the listener in the *general* direction of the composer's feelings.

Like most symphonic poems, *Les Préludes* is in one movement and centers around one principal theme:

In formal structure the tone poem strongly resembles a symphonic sonata form with slow introduction, but the poetic content was undoubtedly more important to Liszt than the form. It is scored for 3 flutes, 2 oboes, 2 clarinets, 2 bassoons, 4 horns, 2 trumpets, 3 trombones, tuba, kettledrums, bass drum, military drum, cymbals, harp, and the standard string choir.

TASSO: LAMENTO E TRIONFO

During the autumn of his romance with the Countess d'Agoult when she and Liszt visited Venice together, and again in the following year (1839) when Liszt passed through the city alone, he had an experience that haunted him the rest of his life. Like most visitors before and since, he heard the gondoliers sing as they punted their graceful craft through the labyrinthine canals of the city and across the broad lagoons. And he was dumbfounded to recognize in the songs of these apparently simple men stanzas from one of the greatest epic poems of Italian literature, the *Gerusalemme liberata (Jerusalem Delivered)* by Torquato Tasso.

The melody, too, caught his imagination, and he wrote it down. He used it as the principal theme in the first of four piano pieces originally published (about 1840) under the title *Venezia e Napoli,* and again in his Overture to Goethe's drama *Tasso* (1849), which finally, after many revisions, became his tone poem *Tasso,* first performed under his own direction at a Court Concert in Weimar on April 19, 1954.

Torquato Tasso (1544–1595), the erratic sixteenth-century genius who cast a spell over the imaginations of early nineteenth-century poets and musicians, had become an almost legendary figure. His greatest works, including *Gerusalemme liberata,* were produced when he was very young. His hypersensitivity eventually led to emotional disturbances and he was confined for some years to an asylum in Ferrara, where he had been befriended by the family of the ruling duke, and where he had composed much of his greatest work. His detention in the asylum grew into a legend of his persecution for having dared to love above his rank in Ferrara. After his release, despite his declining poetic powers, he was widely honored at many Italian courts and was finally invited to Rome to be crowned poet laureate by the pope. But his health had dwindled to the point where he fell ill and died the day before the scheduled coronation. He was buried with tremendous pomp and lived on in the minds of his countrymen, admired and loved almost as much for his martyrdom as for his poetic gifts.

During his lonely visit to Venice in the fall of 1839, one of the gondoliers Liszt hired responded to his request that he sing some Tasso, although he had only a raucous, broken voice. "The tune," wrote Liszt to Mme. d'Agoult, "is very similar to the one I had already transcribed."

"This song," Liszt recalled many years later, "once made a profound impression upon me. The motive itself was a slow plaintive cadence of monotonous mourning; the gondoliers, however, by drawling certain notes, give it a particular coloring, and the mournfully drawn-out tones, heard at a distance, produce an effect not dissimilar to the reflection of long stripes of fading light upon a mirror of water." Inseparable from the mournful appeal of the melody was Liszt's strong feeling that the tragedy of the poet's life and death were compensated by his posthumous glory and the fact that Tasso was in a sense still alive two-and-one-half centuries later in the affections of the simplest of his countrymen.

In 1849, when all Germany was celebrating the one-hundredth anniversary of Goethe's birth, Liszt was stationed at the Court of Weimar where Goethe himself had spent so many fruitful years of his career. On Goethe's birthday, August 28, the Weimar Court Theater, which had long been a focus of Goethe's Weimar activities, planned to honor the poet with a performance of one of his greatest Classical dramas, *Torquato Tasso.* Liszt was invited, on extremely short notice, to compose an overture for the occasion. His earliest sketches for the Overture are dated August 1, less than four weeks before the performance. Liszt's mind returned to where he had read the poetry of Tasso together with Mme. d'Agoult and where he had heard the vitality of Tasso's art confirmed by the gondoliers. His feelings about Tasso were also colored by the poem *The Lament of Tasso* by Byron, whom Liszt admired so greatly that in many cases he preferred Byron to Goethe. Byron's Tasso voices the words of a nineteenth-century Romantic rebel, unjustly imprisoned by a tyrannical duke:

> . . . I stoop not to despair;
> For I have battled with mine agony,
> And made me wings wherewith to overfly
> The narrow circus of my dungeon wall,
> And freed the Holy Sepulchre from thrall;
> And revell'd among men and things divine,
> And pour'd my spirit over Palestine. . . .

The striking fact about Liszt's overture which, after many revisions, was to become his tone poem *Torquato Tasso,* is that it originally contained no reference whatsoever to Goethe's drama. Goethe's *Tasso* plays entirely in Ferrara, is sternly Classical in its form and diction; and in its polish and restraint is far from the Romantic passions which preoccupied Liszt.

In Liszt's preface to the published final version of his tone poem, he explains the expanded score in part as follows:

> . . . I must admit that in 1849, when I was charged with the composition of an overture to Goethe's drama, I was inspired more by Byron's deep compassion for the great man whose ghost he evoked than I was by the work of the German poet. However, in letting us hear the suffering voice of Tasso in his prison, Byron lost the opportunity to contrast the memory of this suffering, so nobly, so eloquently expressed in his *Lamentation,* with the dazzling *Triumph* which a belated justice held in store for the gallant author of *Jerusalem Delivered.* I wished to emphasize this contrast in my title, and hoped in my work to express this grand antithesis of the genius humiliated in life, yet radiant after death with a glory that annihilated his persecutors. Tasso loved and suffered in Ferrara, he was vindicated in Rome and his glory still lives in the popular songs of Venice. These three concepts are inseparable from his immortal fame. To depict them in music, we first summoned our hero's great shade as it haunts the lagoons of Venice even today; then we glimpsed his proud and melancholy countenance passing amid the festivities of Ferrara, where his masterworks were born; and finally we followed him to Rome, to the Eternal City, which by crowning him with the laurel wreath glorified in him both the martyr and the poet.
>
> FRANZ LISZT

The evolution of Liszt's *Tasso* from the original piano sketches orchestrated by Liszt's friend Conradi to the score we hear today, orchestrated with the virtuoso command which Liszt had acquired during five years of intense study and experience as a conductor, is an illuminating chapter of Liszt's artistic development. The final version is a highly integrated work, based entirely upon the gondoliers' song, which is presaged in the opening bars:

In fact, Liszt once pointed out to a friend that the entire score of *Tasso* is based on the little repeated triplet figure in the second bar of the above excerpt.

The first complete statement of the gondoliers' melody is labeled *Adagio mesto* and is heard in the dark voice of a bass clarinet, a somewhat unusual instrument to have picked for a prominent solo in orchestral music of the mid-nineteenth century, but possibly suggested by the circumstances under which Liszt first heard the song. Its opening bars are written in the score as follows:

The actual sound of the instrument is in the baritone range a major ninth below. The best guide to the music itself is Liszt's introduction, which clearly was written after the music was composed, not before.

The score of *Tasso* calls for piccolo, 2 flutes, 2 oboes, 2 clarinets, bass clarinet, 2 bassoons, 4 horns, 4 trumpets, 3 trombones, tuba, kettledrums, triangle, military drum, cymbals, bass drums, harp, and the traditional string choir.

Witold Lutoslawski

Born January 25, 1913, Warsaw

CONCERTO FOR ORCHESTRA

Witold Lutoslawski, who is widely regarded as one of the greatest contemporary Polish composers, was born in Warsaw on January 25, 1913, of a highly cultivated family. His mother was a medical doctor and his uncle, Wincenty Lutoslawski, was a leading Polish philosopher. At the age of eleven he studied piano with J. Smidowicz. In 1927 he took up the violin and wrote a Sonata for Violin and Piano, which was lost during World War I. At the Warsaw Conservatory he continued his piano studies with the prominent Polish composer and accompanist Jerzy Lefeld, and studied composition with Witold Maliszewski, a pupil of Rimsky-Korsakoff.

For two years during his Conservatory studies Lutoslawski also studied higher mathematics at the University of Warsaw. In 1936 and 1937 he took the

Conservatory diplomas in piano and composition respectively. The following year he completed his Symphonic Variations, a work said to be reminiscent of the early Stravinsky.

During the war, like many young Polish artists, he lived in constant fear of deportation. He supported himself with odd jobs and composed chamber music, piano works and started his First Symphony, which he completed in 1947. From 1945 on, for a whole decade Lutoslawski's compositions, including his Concerto for Orchestra of 1954, were strongly influenced by folk music. Rather than use this folk material in the picturesque, coloristic manner of Late-Romantic composers and contemporary Soviet practice, Lutoslawski transformed folk motives rather radically, in a style reminiscent of Bartók. He described his new style as follows:

> This mainly involved blending simple diatonic motifs with chromatic atonal counterpoint, and with nonfunctional, multicolored, capricious harmonies. The rhythmic transformation of these motifs, and the polymetrical texture resulting from them together with the accompanying elements are a part of the characteristic style which I have mentioned. In doing all this, I thought at the time that this marginal style would not be entirely fruitless and that despite its having come into being while I was writing typical "functional" music, I could possibly make use of it in writing something more serious. A suitable opportunity for putting this into practise soon turned up. This was 1950. The director of the Warsaw Philharmonic Orchestra, Witold Rowicki, asked me to write something especially for his new ensemble. This was to be something not difficult, but which could, however, give the young orchestra an opportunity to show its qualities. I started to work on the new score not realizing that I was to spend nearly four years on it. Folk music and all that follows with it—of which I have already spoken—was to be used in my new work. Folk music has in this work, however, been merely a raw material used to build a large musical form of several movements which does not in the least originate either from folk songs or from folk dances. A work came into being, which I could not help including among my most important works, as a result of my episodic symbiosis with folk music and in a way that was for me somewhat unexpected. This work is the "Concerto for Orchestra."

The Concerto was written 1950 to 1954 and first performed in Warsaw on November 26, 1954, under the direction of Witold Rowicki, to whom it is dedicated. The United States premiere was given by the Cleveland Orchestra on December 4, 1958, under the direction of Stanislaw Skrowaczewski. The first New York performances were presented by the New York Philharmonic on December 29, and 30, 1960. It is cast in three movements.

I. *Intrada. Allegro maestoso.* The opening section is built over a gigantic pedalpoint on F sharp, sustained at the bottom of the orchestra by the double basses and bassoons with rhythmic reinforcements in the harps and kettledrums. There is a gradual *crescendo* with a heavily accented rhythmic figure passing from one group of the string choir to another. The whole movement is in seven roughly symmetrical sections, closing with the material of the opening, which dies away on a sustained dissonant chord over the F-sharp pedal.

II. *Capriccio notturno e arioso. Vivace.* A scurrying, whispering figure in the violins characterizes the *Capriccio* which opens and closes this movement. In the central *arioso* section, a melody of rather angular, primitive cast is sustained by four trumpets alternating with four French horns, against *staccato* rhythms of strings, wind and percussion, including the piano.

III. *Passacaglia, toccata e corale.* This is the most elaborate movement and climax of the whole. The Passacaglia section is based on an eight-measure theme presented ten times by the double basses, first in skeleton form, then complete, as follows:

As the *Passacaglia* grows in complexity and volume of sound, the theme is taken up by one choir after another until all the strings and finally the brass as well proclaim it. There is a sudden shift upward to the dominant, and the *Passacaglia* theme is carried in the top of the orchestra by the high brass, winds and piano in brilliant octaves. After a big climax, the *Passacaglia* dies away almost to silence.

The *toccata* section begins very softly, *Allegro giusto,* with a rapid eighth-note figure. This too builds to a big climax and dies away. The more sedate, even-rhythmed chords of the chorale begin softly in the winds and heavy brass. An elaborately developed peroration concludes with a *presto* climax of the utmost brilliance.

FUNERAL MUSIC, FOR STRING ORCHESTRA

"This is my first word spoken in a language new to me," wrote Witold Lutoslawski in 1958 when his *Funeral Music* was first performed, "but it is certainly not my last."

There would have been nothing remarkable about a West European or American composer making such a statement in 1958. The *Funeral Music* involved nothing more subversive than a freely personal adaptation of twelve-tone serial techniques. But in Poland the statement and its date were both highly significant. Lutoslawski's *Funeral Music* was composed in the years 1956–1958. Thus it was begun in the year when the Polish "revolution" won a degree of cultural and political freedom that is extremely rare among the East European countries. In 1956 Poland was suddenly able to join the rest of the world of contemporary artistic and musical trends.

His *Funeral Music,* or *Murzyka zalobna,* for string orchestra is dedicated to the memory of Bartók. Little remains of the once strong folk influences in this score, which is laconic in style, economical in means, and concentrated in expression. Serial devices are freely used in ways that often produce tonal results.

The world premiere of the new score was presented by the Polish Radio Symphony Orchestra under the direction of Jan Krenz, in the Radio Concert Hall of the City of Katowice on March 26, 1958. One year later, the *Funeral Music* was offered to American listeners for the first time by the Contemporary Music Society of Houston, Texas, on April 3, 1959. Later that year the score made a strong impression at the Venice Festival and at the "Warsaw Autumn," where Western observers greeted it as the most impressive work of that festival.

The score is in four sections which are played without pause: *Prologue, Metamorphoses, Apogee* and *Epilogue.* The pensive *Prologue* begins with a tone row in the form of a flowing melody composed entirely of tritones and half-tones. This is sung first by the solo cello.

It is joined almost immediately, at a lag of only one beat, by a second solo cello carrying the same melody in canon. The solo cellos are joined successively by two solo violas, four groups of violins, then cello, and finally string bass groups, some in simple canon, some in upside-down or mirror canon. The orchestral voices accumulate until at the climax as many as fifteen may be heard at once.

Metamorphoses, which is longer than all the other three sections put together, opens in sparse, pointillistic style, almost *a la* Webern, with isolated pizzicatos dabs of soft tremolo *sul ponticello.* A series of episodes in changing styles, as in a theme and variations, grow more and more agitated, leading to a brief, dissonant climax in the *Apogee.* The *Epilogue* resumes the melodic arrangement of the row from the *Prologue.* The texture thins down gradually to the single solo cello with which the work began.

Edward MacDowell

Born December 18, 1861, New York City—died January 23, 1908, New York City

CONCERTO NO. 2 FOR PIANO AND ORCHESTRA, D MINOR, OPUS 23

It was Franz Liszt who, after hearing MacDowell play his First Piano Concerto and examining other MacDowell compositions, persuaded the American to devote himself full time to composing. It was through Liszt's support that MacDowell's works began to be performed in Germany, and his First and Second Piano Concertos were both published by the German firm of Breitkopf & Härtel. It was Liszt's death in 1886 which made the heartbroken MacDowell decide to return to the United States and make his permanent home here.

MacDowell's music, the first by a serious American composer to command wide respect outside the United States, was an outgrowth of the Late-Victorian age. MacDowell belonged to the same generation as Edith Wharton, and his music has points of resemblance to *House of Mirth* and *Ethan Frome*. Like Mrs. Wharton, MacDowell was oriented toward Europe; but where she could build on an established tradition of American letters, particularly on the work of her compatriot Henry James, MacDowell was forced to pioneer. Some of his works do have a certain American color and subject matter, yet MacDowell was firm in his refusal to seek recognition as a primarily American composer. Like Mrs. Wharton's prose, MacDowell's music always retained a certain Victorian gentility—once a factor in its success, later a cause of its fading popularity, and today a source of period appeal, which may yet restore it, along with so many other products of the Late-Victorian age, to popular acclaim.

While MacDowell is remembered for such graceful salon miniatures as "To a Wild Rose" and "To a Waterlily" and for the more individual orchestral miniatures of his *Indian Suite,* his most brilliant large-scale work is the Second Piano Concerto in D minor. This was composed, symptomatically enough, in Germany, where MacDowell spent an entire decade from his seventeenth to his twenty-seventh year. In 1884 MacDowell returned to the United States just long enough to be married to a young lady he had taught in Germany: Marian Nevins, who was to become the organizer and administrator of the famous MacDowell Colony at Peterboro, New Hampshire. The couple returned to Germany in 1884, settling first in Frankfurt, where MacDowell began his Second Piano Concerto.

MacDowell was his own soloist in the first performance of his Second Concerto in Chickering Hall, New York City, on March 5, 1899, under the direction of Theodore Thomas. The following month MacDowell played his new Piano Concerto with the Boston Symphony. Two years later the Concerto was given its first European performance by Teresa Carreño, who had already helped establish MacDowell's reputation by playing his works on her recital programs.

The Concerto is in three movements:

I. *Larghetto calmato; Poco più mosso con passione.* The stormy first movement is illuminated by lightning flashes of virtuoso brilliance, and punctuated by three thunderous cadenzas. Its quieter moments are pervaded by a melancholy lyricism embodied in the principal theme:

This melody is given out in octaves by the piano solo, clothed in an elaborate pianistic filigree which sometimes swells to great swashes of Lisztian *bravura.*

II. *Presto giocoso.* The central movement, a scherzo, is cast in rondo form with a glittering refrain announced by the soloist.

III. *Largo; Molto allegro.* The slow introduction recalls themes from the first movement. The lively, principal theme is given out first very softly by a clarinet and other winds over the faint rumble of a trill in the bass of the piano:

This theme echos from one instrument to another as the soloist climbs to the piano's high bright range and finally takes over the theme itself, to dominate the finale with exuberant virtuosity.

The Concerto in D minor is scored for 2 flutes, 2 oboes, 2 clarinets, 2 bassoons, 4 horns, 2 trumpets, 3 trombones, kettledrums, and string choir.

Gustav Mahler

Born July 7, 1860, Kališt, Bohemia—died May 18, 1911, Vienna

DAS LIED VON DER ERDE (THE SONG OF THE EARTH)

Mahler did not live to hear this work, one of his greatest, performed. He composed it during the summer of 1908 with more than a premonition of the doom that hung over him. This was the summer when his doctors told him that, unless he gave up the violent exertions of conducting, he had not long to live. Every fiber of his being revolted against such warnings: "I have accustomed myself for many years to steady, energetic activity [he wrote, from his Austrian country retreat at Toblach to Bruno Walter]—to wander about in the mountains and woods and carry away with me, like captured booty, the sketches I had made by the way. I went to my desk only as the farmer to the barn—to prepare what I had already gathered. Spiritual indisposition was a mere cloud to be dispelled by a brisk march up the mountainside. And now they tell me I must avoid every exertion. I must constantly take stock of my condition—walk but little. At the same time in this solitude my thoughts naturally become more subjective, and the sadness of my condition seems intensified."

Far from heeding his doctors' warnings, Mahler, who had just completed his first season of conducting the Metropolitan Opera, resumed his duties at the Metropolitan and before the end of the season 1908–1909 accepted in addition the full time position of conductor of the New York Philharmonic with the understanding that he would reorganize that orchestra. He did so during a season when he conducted forty-six Philharmonic concerts in addition to the first American production of Tchaikovsky's *Pique Dame* at the Metropolitan. In retrospect there seems something suicidal about such intensified activity.

Yet Mahler feared death. Because of his superstition that no man would be allowed to exceed Beethoven's total of nine symphonies, he avoided calling *Das Lied von der Erde* his ninth symphony. He gave it the subtitle of "A Symphony for Tenor, Contralto (or Baritone) and Orchestra," but no number.

Mahler was deeply drawn to the tragic mood of leave-taking he found in the German poet Hans Bethge's paraphrase of eighth-century Chinese verses published under the title of *Die chinesische Flöte* ("The Chinese Flute"). He adapted Bethge's adaptations still further, to accentuate the twilight, autumnal, nostalgic, world-weary mood in which even visions of youth, love, and spring serve only to sharpen the pain of eternal farewell. The symphonic cycle concludes with a sevenfold echo of the word, "forever . . ." (*ewig . . .*) and the opening movement is dominated by the refrain: "Dark is life, is death" *(Dunkel ist das Leben, ist der Tod):*

DAS TRINKLIED VON JAMMER DER ERDE	*THE DRINKING SONG OF EARTHLY WOE*
Schon winkt der Wein im gold'nen Pokale,	Wine in the golden goblet is beckoning,
Doch trinkt noch nicht, erst sing' ich euch ein Lied!	But drink not yet, first I will sing you a song!
Das Trinklied von Kummer soll auflachend in die Seele euch klingen.	The song of sorrow, let its mockery laugh itself into your soul.
Wenn der Kummer naht,	When sorrow approaches,
Liegen wüst die Gärten der Seele,	The soul's gardens lie desolate,
Welkt hin und stirbt die Freude, der Gesang.	Joy and song wither and die.
Dunkel ist das Leben, ist der Tod.	Dark is life, is death.
Herr dieses Hauses! Dein Keller birgt die Fülle des goldenen Weins!	Lord of this house! Thy cellar holds the fullness of golden wine!
Hier diese Laute nenn' ich mein!	Here, this lute I call mine own!
Die Laute schlagen und die Gläser leeren,	To play upon the lute, to empty glasses,
Das sind die Dinge, die zusammen passen,	These are the things that fit each other,
Ein voller Becher Weins zur rechten Zeit	At the right time a goblet full of wine
Ist mehr wert, als alle Reiche dieser Erde!	Is worth more than all the kingdoms of this earth!
Dunkel ist das Leben, ist der Tod!	Dark is life, is death!
Das Firmament blaut ewig, und die Erde	The firmament in its eternal blue and the earth,
Wird lange fest steh'n und aufblüh'n im Lenz.	These will long endure, will blossom in the springtime.
Du, aber, Mensch, wie lang lebst denn du?	But thou, O man, what is the span of thy life?
Nicht hundert Jahre darfst du dich ergötzen	Not a hundred years are you permitted to enjoy
An all dem morschen Tande dieser Erde!	The idle vanities of this earth!
Seht dort hinab! Im Mondschein auf den Gräbern	Look there below! In the moonlight upon the graves

Hockt eine wild gespenstiche Gestalt.	There crouches a wild, ghostly figure—
Ein Aff' ist's! Hört ihr, wie sein Heulen	An ape it is! Hark how his howling
Hinausgellt in den süssen Duft des Lebens!	Shrills out into the sweet airs of our life!
Jetzt nehmt den Wein! Jetzt ist es Zeit, Genossen!	Bring on the wine! The time has come, my comrades!
Leert eure gold'nen Becher zu Grund!	Drain your golden goblets to the dregs!
Dunkel ist das Leben, ist der Tod!	Dark is Life, is death!
DER EINSAME IM HERBST	THE LONELY ONE IN AUTUMN
Herbstnebel wallen bläulich überm See;	The mists of autumn build their blue wall over the sea;
Vom Reif bezogen stehen alle Gräser;	With hoarfrost covered, stands the grass;
Man meint, ein Künstler habe Staub von Jade	It seems as if an artist had strewn the dust of jade
Ueber die feinen Blüten ausgestreut.	Over delicate blossoms.
Der süsse Duft der Blumen ist verflogen;	The flowers' fragrance has spent itself;
Ein kalter Wind beugt ihre Stengel nieder.	A cold wind blows them to earth.
Bald werden die verwelkten, gold'nen Blätter	Soon the withered, golden leaves
Der Lotusblüten auf dem Wasser zieh'n.	Of lotus flowers will be scattered upon the waters.
Mein Herz ist müde. Meine kleine Lampe	My heart is weary. My little lamp
Erlosch mit Knistern, es gemahnt mich an den Schlaf.	Has gone out, sputtering, minding me of need for sleep.
Ich komm' zu dir, traute Ruhestätte!	I come to you, blest resting-place!
Ja, gib mir Ruh, ich hab' Erquickung Not!	Yea, give me rest: for I need refreshment!
Ich weine viel in meinen Einsamkeiten,	I weep and weep in all my solitude,
Der Herbst in meinem Herzen währt zu lange.	Autumn in my heart too long has lasted.
Sonne der Liebe, willst du nie mehr scheinen,	O Sun of Love, never again wilt thou shine,
Um meine bittern Tränen mild aufzutrocknen?	Gently to dry my bitter tears?

VON DER JUGEND	OF YOUTH
Mitten in dem kleinen Teiche	Midway in a little pool
Steht ein Pavillon aus grünem	Stands a pavilion of green
Und aus weissem Porzellan,	And of white porcelain,
Wie der Rücken eines Tigers	Like the back of a tiger
Wölbt die Brücke sich aus Jade	The bridge of jade arches
Zu dem Pavillon hinüber.	Across to the pavilion.
In dem Häuschen, sitzen Freunde,	In the little house, friends are seated,
Schön gekleidet, trinken, plaudern.	Gayly gowned, drinking, chatting.
Manche schreiben Verse nieder.	Some are writing verses,
Ihre seidnen Aermel gleiten	Their silken sleeves glide
Rückwärts, ihre seidnen Mützen	Backwards, their silken caps
Hocken lustig tief im Nacken.	Hang from the back of their necks.
Auf des kleinen Teiches stiller	On the smooth surface of the quiet pool
Wasserfläche zeigt sich alles	All is mirrored wondrously.
Wunderlich im Spiegelbilde.	All stands upon its head
Alles auf dem Kopfe stehend	In the pavilion of green
In dem Pavillon aus grünem	And of white porcelain;
Und aus weissen Porzellan;	Like a half-moon stands the bridge,
Wie ein Halbmond steht die Brücke,	Reversed is its bow. Friends
Umgekehrt der Bogen. Freunde,	Gayly gowned, are drinking, chatting.
Schön gekleidet, trinken, plaudern.	
VON DER SCHOENHEIT	OF BEAUTY
Junge Mädchen pflücken Blumen	Youthful maidens are plucking flowers,
Pflücken Lotsblumen an dem Uferrande.	Plucking lotus flowers at the edge of the shore.
Zwischen Büschen und Blättern sitzen sie,	Among bushes and leaves they sit,
Sammeln Blüten in den Schoss und rufen	Gathering blossoms in their laps and calling
Sich einander Neckereien zu.	To each other in jest.
Gold'ne Sonne webt um die Gestalten,	The golden sun plays about their forms,
Spiegelt sich im blanken Wasser wieder,	Reflected in the quiet water,
Sonne spiegelt ihre schlanken Glieder,	The sun mirrors their slender limbs,
Ihre Süssen Augen wieder,	Their sweet eyes,
Und der Zephir hebt mit Schmeichelkosen das Gewebe	And a zephyr with gentlest caress raises the fabric
Ihrer Aermel auf, führt den Zauber	Of their sleeves, wafts the magic
Ihrer Wohlgerüche durch die Luft.	Of their perfume through the air,
O sieh, was tummeln sich für schöne Knaben	O see, beautiful youths at play

Dort an dem Uferrand auf mut'gen Rossen.	On fiery horses, over there at the edge of the shore.
Weit hin glänzend wie die Sonnenstrahlen;	Glistening from afar like rays of the sun;
Schon zwischen dem Geäst der grünen Weiden	Between the green branches of the willows
Trabt das jungfrische Volk einher!	Fresh youth is making its way!
Das Ross des einen wiehert fröhlich auf	The steed of one whinnies for joy
Und scheut und saust dahin,	And shies and rushes past,
Ueber Blumen, Gräser wanken hin die Hufe,	Over flowers, grasses, gallop his hoofs,
Sie zerstampfen jäh im Sturm die hingesunkenen Blüten.	Whose stormy stamping crushes the fallen blossoms.
Hei! Wie flattern im Taumel seine Mähnen,	Heigh! How his mane flies in the breeze,
Dampfen heiss die Nüstern!	How his nostrils dilate!
Gold'ne Sonne webt um die Gestalten,	The golden sun plays about the forms,
Spiegelt sie im blanken Wasser wider.	Reflecting them in the quiet water.
Und die Schönste von den Jungfrau'n sendet	And the loveliest of the maidens
Lange Blicke ihm der Sehnsucht nach,	Sends the rider glances of yearning.
Ihre stolze Haltung ist nur Verstellung.	Her haughty bearing is no more than feigned.
In dem Funkeln ihrer grossen Augen,	In the sparkle of her wide eyes,
In dem Dunkel ihres heissen Blicks	In the darkening of the eager glance
Schwingt klagend noch die Erregung ihres Herzens nach.	Dies the plaint of her eager heart.

DER TRUNKENE IM FRUEHLING	THE DRUNKEN ONE IN SPRINGTIME
Wenn nur ein Traum das Leben ist,	If life is no more than a dream,
Warum denn Müh' und Plag'?	Why the fuss and bother?
Ich trinke, bis ich nicht mehr kann,	I'll drink, till drink no more I can,
Den ganzen, lieben Tag!	The whole livelong day!
Und wenn ich nicht mehr trinken kann,	And when no longer I can drink,
Weil Kehl' und Seele voll,	For throat and soul are full,
So tauml' ich bis zu meiner Tür	I'll stumble to my door,
Und schlafe wundervoll!	And sleep, and sleep and sleep.
Was hör ich beim Erwachen? Horch!	What hear I, awakening? List!
Ein Vogel singt im Baum.	A bird sings in a tree.
Ich frag' ihn, ob schon Frühling sei,	I ask him whether spring has come,
Mir ist als wie im Traum.	I feel as in a dream.
Der Vogel zwitschert: Ja!	The bird twitters: Yes!
Der Lenz ist da, sei kommen über Nacht!	The Spring overnight has come!

Aus tiefstem Schauen lauscht' ich auf
Der Vogel singt und lacht!
Ich fülle mir den Becher neu
Und leer' ihn bis zum Grund
Und singe, bis der Mond erglänzt

Am schwarzen Firmament!
Und wenn ich nicht mehr singen kann,
So schlaf' ich wieder ein.
Was geht mich denn der Frühling an?
Lasst mich betrunken sein!

While pondering, I harkened
The bird sings and laughs!
Anew I fill my goblet
And drain it to the dregs
And sing until the moon shines bright
In the dark'ning firmament!
And when no longer I can sing,
Again to sleep I'll go.
For what matters Spring to me?
Drunk only let me be!

DER ABSCHIED

Die Sonne scheidet hinter dem Gebirge.
In alle Täler steigt der Abend nieder
Mit seinen Schatten, die voll Kühlung sind.
O sieh! Wie eine Silkerbarke schwebt
Der Mond am blauen Himmelssee herauf.
Ich spüre eines feinen Windes Weh'n
Hinter den dunklen Fichten!
Der Bach singt voller Wohllaut durch das Dunkel.
Die Blumen blassen im Dämmerschein.
Die Erde atmet voll von Ruh' und Schlaf.
Alle Sehnsucht will nun träumen,
Die müden Menschen geh'n heimwärts,

Um im Schlaf vergess' nes Glück
Und Jugend neu zu lernen!
Die Vögel hocken still in ihren Zweigen.

Die Welt schläft ein!
Es wehet kühl im Schatten meiner Fichten.
Ich stehe hier und harre meines Freundes;
Ich harre sein zum letzten Lebewohl.
Ich sehne mich, O Freund, an deiner Seite
Die Schönheit dieses Abends zu geniessen.
Wo bleibst du? Du lässt mich lang allein!

THE FAREWELL

The sun is sinking 'neath the hills.
Evening descends into the vales
With its cool, quiet shadows.

Behold! As a bark of silver
The moon rises into the blue heaven.
I feel the motion of a gentle wind
Behind the dark pines.
The brook sings its music through the dark.
The flowers grow pale in the twilight.
The earth breathes the quiet of rest and sleep.
All longing goes a-dreaming,
Weary humanity is homeward bound,
To seek anew in sleep
Forgotten fortune, youth.
Birds are perched upon their branches.
The world falls into sleep.
The cool wind is in the shadow of my pines.
I stand here and await my friend,

For a last farewell.
I long, O friend, at thy side

To drink in the beauty of this evening.
Where are you? You leave me long in solitude!

Ich wandle auf und nieder mit meiner Laute	I wander to and fro with my lute
Auf Wegen die von weichem Grase schwellen.	On paths thick with soft grass.
O Schönheit! O ewigen Liebens-Lebens-trunk'ne Welt!	O Beauty! O World, forever drunk with love and life!
(Orchestral Interlude)	
Er stieg vom Pferd und reichte ihm den Trunk	He climbed from his horse and gave his friend a farewell cup;
Des Abschieds dar. Er fragte ihn, wohin	Asked him wither he was going,
Er führe und auch warum es müsste sein.	And why it needs must be.
Er sprach, seine Stimme war umflort: Du mein Freund,	He spoke, his voice choking: O my friend,
Mir war auf dieser Welt das Glück nicht hold!	Fate in this world has not been kind to me!
Wohin ich geh'? Ich geh', ich wand're in die Berge.	Wither am I bound? I go, I wander into the mountains.
Ich suche Ruhe für mein einsam Herz.	I seek rest for my lonely heart.
Ich wandle nach der Heimat, meiner Stätte.	I am wand'ring toward my native place, my home.
Ich werde niemals in die Ferne schweifen.	I shall never roam in foreign lands.
Still ist mein Herz und harret seiner Stunde!	My heart is at rest and waits its hour!
Die liebe Erde allüberall blüht auf im Lenz und grünt	The dear Earth blossoms in the Spring and buds anew.
Aufs neu! Allüberall und ewig blauen licht die Fernen!	Everywhere and forever the luminous blue of distant space!
Ewig . . . ewig . . .	Forever . . . forever . . .

(English version based on that of A. H. Meyer)

The score of *Das Lied von der Erde* calls for piccolo, 3 flutes, 3 oboes, English horn, 3 clarinets in B flat, clarinet in E flat, bass clarinet, 3 bassoons, contrabassoon, 4 horns, 3 trumpets, 3 trombones, bass tuba, 2 harps, kettledrums, celeste, mandolin, glockenspiel, triangle, cymbals, tam-tam, tambourine, bass drum, and the customary strings. It was first performed six months after Mahler's death; Bruno Walter conducted the world premiere in Munich on November 20, 1911.

SYMPHONY NO. 1, D MAJOR

To his contemporaries the new world of Mahler's symphonies was often as frightening as the upheaval of the Storm and Stress had seemed to the *ancien régime* of Mozart and Haydn. Even Mahler was overwhelmed by some of his own inspirations. Panic terror is a recurrent theme: sometimes explicit, as in the programs of his Second and Fourth Symphonies, more often implicit in the music or his conversations and letters about it. Such inspirations seemed to come from outside of himself, as if he were only a lightning rod for the emotional thunderbolts that struck him.

Not only were these feelings and this music new; they contained the seeds of a musical future which no one, including Mahler, could have conceived—a future which might have appalled him if it had not been for the tragic illness which cut short his career in 1911.

Yet this very music, which so frightened well-meaning conservatives, was born of reverence and affection for the past: reverence so intense that on more than one occasion it threatened to paralyze his creative powers, and an affection so deep that Mahler killed himself in the service of the masterpieces he adored.

It was typical of Mahler's whole approach to the symphonic world that he did not originally call his First Symphony a symphony at all but a symphonic poem. He was twenty-nine years old, just beginning his second season as director of the Budapest Opera, when the members of the Budapest Philharmonic invited him to conduct a new symphonic work of his own for their 1889–1890 season. Mahler responded with a gigantic symphonic poem in two parts (divided into five movements) which he had completed only eighteen months earlier and which was destined, after considerable revision (and the deletion of one movement) to become his Symphony No. 1.

He had begun this Symphonic Poem several years earlier, perhaps as early as 1876, the approximate date assigned by the Mahler authority Henry-Louis de La Grange to an autograph fragment for piano duet of the third movement, originally entitled simply *Scherzo*. This would put the beginnings of the Symphonic Poem back to Mahler's sixteenth or seventeenth year. He was eighteen when he began his cantata *Das Klagende Lied (The Sorrowing Song)* which seems to have supplied thematic fragments for at least one movement (the *Funeral* movement) of the Symphonic Poem. Indeed one of the most arresting traits of Mahler's new symphonic world is that so much of it has its origin in song. All four of the movements which eventually became the First Symphony draw on at least one vocal work.

The invitation of the Budapest Philharmonic was flattering for the twenty-nine-year-old composer and it was a milestone in his career, for this was to be the first public performance of a Mahler symphonic work. The program of the second subscription concert on November 20, 1889, gave no explanation or programmatic description of the music. It listed only:

Symphonic Poem in Two Parts
Part I: Introduction and Allegro Comodo
Andante
Scherzo
Part II: A la pompes funèbres (In the style of a Funeral Ceremony)
Molto appassionato

Mahler conducted and was delighted with the devotion and enthusiasm of the players in rehearsal, but the public reception was disappointing. The lively and sentimental parts of the first half were well enough received, but the second half, particularly the "funeral" movement puzzled the audience and left it cold. All but one of the Budapest critics were hostile, one of them blaming Mahler for not having furnished the audience with an explanation or programmatic guide to the music.

In January 1893 Mahler revised the entire score and gave programmatic names to the five movements. When he conducted his Symphonic Poem for the second time the following October in Hamburg, he renamed the work and added explanations to some of the titles of the movements as follows:

TITAN, a Tone Poem in Form of a Symphony

PART I

"From the Days of Youth," Flower, Fruit, and Thorn Pieces

1. "Spring Without End," (Introduction and *Allegro comodo*) (The Introduction depicts the awakening of nature from its long winter sleep.)
2. "A Collection of Flowers"
3. "Under Full Sail"

PART II

"Commedia Umana" ["Human Comedy"]

1. "Stranded!" (A funeral march in Callot's style). * The following may serve as an explanation of this movement. The external stimulus for this piece came to the composer from the satirical picture, "The Hunter's Funeral Procession," well known to all children in Austria from an old book of children's fairy tales. The forest animals accompany the dead hunter's coffin to the grave; hares carry the little banner, before them march a band of Bohemian musicians, accompanied by singing cats, toads, crows, etc., and stags, deer, foxes, and other four-legged and feathered forest animals accompany the funeral procession in farcical poses. This music is intended to express alternating moods of ironical gaiety and uncanny gloom, which is followed immediately by:
2. "Dall'Inferno" ["From the Inferno"] *Allegro furioso,* which expresses the sudden, despairing outcry of a deeply wounded heart.

Yet between these early performances and the publication of the score, Mahler had a revulsion against all symphonic programs which, he now believed, tended to distract audiences from the music itself and lead the naïve to search the music for each detail of the printed description. Mahler grew vehement in his detestation of the very kind of verbal "program" which he had once hoped would help his music to a wider public understanding. Yet he

---

* It is not clear just what Mahler meant by the style of Callot (apparently Jacques Callot [1592/3–1635], the great Baroque graphic artist famous especially for his drawings of figures from the *commedia dell 'arte*). The "pictorial parody" to which Mahler refers is by the German Romantic artist Moritz von Schwind, published also under the title "How the Animals Bury the Hunter" in Schwind's *Münchner Bilderbogen* (1848–1854).

THE EXTERNAL STIMULUS.

Mahler's initial inspiration for the funeral march movement: "How the Animals Bury the Hunter" from Moritz von Schwind's *Munich Picture Book* for children. (*Courtesy, New York Public Library*)

remained ambivalent on the subject. As late as 1896 he wrote to friendly Berlin critic-composer Max Marschalk, after a performance of the First Symphony:

> There is some justification for the title *Titan* and for the program. That is, at one time my friends persuaded me to provide a kind of program for the D-major Symphony in order to make it easier to understand; therefore, I had thought up this title and explanatory material after the actual composition. The reason I left them out this time is not only that I find them completely inadequate (and not even quite accurate) but that I have learned through past experience how the public has been misled by them. But that is the way with every program! . . .
>
> In the third movement (*marcia funebre*) it is true that I received the immediate inspiration from the well-known children's picture, "The Hunter's Funeral Procession." But in this situation what is represented is irrelevant: the important thing is the *mood* which should be expressed, and from which the fourth movement then springs suddenly, like lightning from a dark cloud. It is simply the cry of a deeply wounded heart, preceded by the spooky, ironically brooding oppressiveness of the funeral march.

I. *Langsam, schleppend; sehr gemächlich; belebtes Zeitmass.* In its final version Mahler's score is entitled simply Symphony No. 1 in Four Movements for Large Orchestra. There are no explanations or descriptions beyond the traditional tempo marks over each movement. Mahler's affection for the Romantic past, especially his Austro-German musical past, shows in the theme on which his entire first movement and moments of his finale are based. It is a simple phrase, conceived in a folk-song vein to words by Mahler himself in which he imitates the folk poetry he had known and loved since early childhood in the Romantic anthology: *Des Knaben Wunderhorn.* Both words and melody come from the second song of Mahler's *Lieder eines fahrenden Gesellen (Songs of a Wandering Journeyman): "Ging heut' Morgen übers Feld"* ("I Crossed the Meadow at Morn").

This many-faceted tune is the heart and soul of the Symphony. Out of it grow the vigorous scherzo theme and heroic theme of the finale. Even "Werner's Trumpet Song" of the second movement and the "Frère Jacques" theme of the fourth movement sound as if both had been composed to fit this context.

Almost from the very first measures of the introduction, a fragment of this theme (the falling fourth of the first two notes) permeates Mahler's eerie mood picture. The introduction includes another, quite different sound as of a far distant trumpet call: a theme which returns transformed at the climax of this rich and complex movement.

II. *Andante allegretto.* This adorable slow movement is one of the simplest and most naïve that Mahler ever wrote. He took his inspiration from a youthful work composed for a series of *tableaux vivants* illustrating one of the most popular German poems of the nineteenth century, "Der Trompeter von Säckingen," by Joseph V. von Scheffel. (The poem itself was so popular that it ran through 140 editions and furnished the basis of one of the most beloved Romantic operas of the age, Nessler's opera of the same title.) Mahler's original music for the *tableaux vivants,* performed on June 23, 1884, in Kassel, has long since disappeared. However, the scene from which this music is taken made such a strong impression on Mahler's friend Max Steinizer that he was able to write down the melody from memory a third of a century later for publication in a magazine article.

Steinizer described the original "Werner's Trumpet Song" as a serenade "wafted across the moonlit Rhine toward the castle where Margareta lives." According to Steinizer, Mahler later decided this serenade was "too sentimental."

Sentimental it certainly is, but in the best sense. The moonlit atmosphere is evoked very simply with string tremolos and a single soft note of a French horn. We hear the trumpeter's serenade *pianissimo,* as if from a great distance, in a solo which makes the trumpet sound like the most lyric, most intimate instrument imaginable. Once heard the melody is hard to forget. It is also so brief that it makes a superb symphonic subject. (Aside from its modest development in this movement, it appears extensively again in both scherzo and finale. It fits so beautifully and organically into the Symphony as a whole that its restoration, for this listener at least, greatly strengthens Mahler's masterpiece.)

Fragments of the melody are taken up, still *pianissimo,* by woodwinds, by a pair of horns and, finally, in an arc of rising warmth by the entire violin section. Muted dynamics mark even the mildly contrasting middle section, in which new phrases spring up, graceful offspring of the trumpeter's tune. There is not space to detail the felicities of Mahler's orchestration, the exquisite poetry with which he introduces the glint of a harp *arpeggio,* a violin solo of four notes only and even briefer touches of other instrumental color. Some of these, like the almost inaudible role of a kettledrum, are so subtle that they easily escape one's conscious notice.

Without actually repeating his opening section, Mahler brings back enough to create the impression of a balanced A-B-A form. At the very end the violins seem to fade and vanish upward into an evening sky.

III. *Kräftig bewegt, doch nicht zu schnell.* The scherzo takes the rhythmic character of the Bavarian Austrian folk dance known as the *Ländler.* The relation of the principal theme to that of the first movement is clear, although it is transformed by the near-waltz rhythm and tempo of the scherzo. The more relaxed central (trio) section brings us even closer to the waltz and further (though not unrecognizably far) from the Symphony's central theme. The movement is rounded off with a drastically condensed recall of the opening *Ländler* section.

IV. *Feierlich und gemessen, ohne zu schleppen.* A funeral march rhythm is set by two alternating kettledrum tones: the falling and rising fourth with which the Symphony's opening theme begins. By an almost spooky artistic sleight-of-hand, the ensuing melody (in the ghostly voice of a single, muted contrabass) seems at first to be continuation of the Symphony's opening theme, but turns out instead to be a minor-mode version of the nursery tune, *"Frère Jacques"* (known in English as "Are you sleeping, Brother John?"):

(sometimes known in German-speaking countries as *"Bruder Martin"*), which could be the animals mocking the dead huntsman in the picture; it could be a more macabre comment on the sleep of death. Bruno Walter, who knew Mahler well, believed that the composer was haunted in this movement "by the daemonic figure of Roquairol in Jean Paul's *Titan.* In him [Mahler] found the terrible inert dissonances, the scorn and the despair, the vacillation between heavenly and hellish impulses which for some time may have invaded also his wounded heart. . . ." The grotesque funeral march is interrupted twice: first by a purposely banal tune (which was Mahler's characteristic way of intensifying a tragic or sardonic mood) and second, by a long quotation of the end of the despairing final song from Mahler's *Lieder eines fahrenden Gesellen (Songs of a Wayfarer).* This movement dies away with softer and softer reiterations of the now-familiar falling fourth. The finale follows without pause.

V. *Stürmisch bewegt.* The harsh crash of a cymbal launches the stormy introduction in the course of which we hear fragments of the rather complex and lengthy theme of this movement. When the theme materializes in its full form, trumpeted forth by brass and woodwind choirs, it begins as follows:

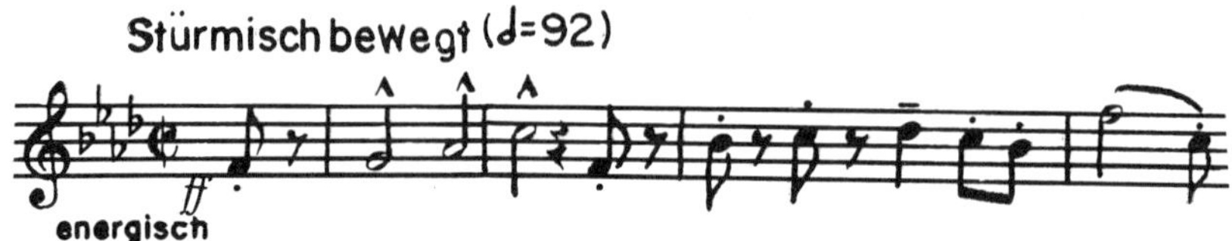

and continues with a rising figure related to themes of three preceding movements.

In the course of this movement's progress from hell to heaven (suggested by the original, discarded title) we hear a serenely songful passage for violins; distorted reminiscences of the second discarded movement, of "Frère Jacques," the falling fourth of the introduction to the first movement; a more explicit recall of the Symphony's central theme in its first-movement form, as well as a varied return of the *Finale's* principal theme. All these with several tempo fluctuations build finally to a coda of heroic sonorities in D major, which harks back once more to the Symphony's opening pages.

Mahler's score calls for an orchestra of Wagnerian *Ring* proportions: 2 piccolos, 4 flutes, 4 oboes, English horn, 4 clarinets, E-flat clarinet, bass clarinet, 3 bassoons, contrabassoon, 7 horns, 5 trumpets, 4 trombones, tuba, kettledrums, bass drum, tam-tam, cymbals, triangle, harp, and the traditional string choir.

SYMPHONY NO. 2, C MINOR, RESURRECTION

The idea for the triumphant conclusion of the Second Symphony, generally known as the "Resurrection" Symphony, came to Mahler in a flash of inspiration, "like a thunderbolt," as he himself described it. The circumstance was curious and dramatic. It was a memorial service for his benefactor and predecessor as conductor of the Hamburg Philharmonic, Hans von Bülow.

Three years earlier, when Mahler had come to be first conductor of the Hamburg Opera, he attracted the attention of Bülow, who was then nearing the end of an illustrious career, one of the most influential musicians in Europe. Bülow acclaimed the thirty-year-old Mahler as one of the greatest living conductors, took every opportunity to honor him in public, and designated Mahler to be his successor as conductor of the Hamburg Philharmonic.

Since Bülow was also famous as a crusader for new and difficult music, Mahler was disappointed to find that Bülow did not care for his compositions. Since Mahler cared infinitely more about his composing than his conducting, Bülow's attitude was a blow. The fact that Mahler worshipped Bülow as an artist only made the master's verdict more painful. But Mahler did not give up.

A work close to Mahler's heart but as yet unperformed was his tone-poem *Totenfeier (Funeral Rite).* He had conceived it in 1887 when he was working on his First Symphony and at a time when he was plagued by waking visions—almost hallucinations—of himself lying on a bier surrounded by funeral wreaths. The title of the tone-poem was almost certainly suggested to Mahler by the translation, named *Totenfeier,* of the Polish epic *Dziady* by the celebrated Romantic poet Adam Mickiewicz. As the Mahler authority La Grange has pointed out, the translation, made by Mahler's close friend Siegfried Lipiner, was published exactly at the time Mahler was beginning to work on his own *Totenfeier.* He completed it in August 1888 but it was still unperformed when he was called to Hamburg in 1891. Encouraged by Bülow's admiration of his conducting, Mahler asked him to look over the score of *Totenfeier.* The result was a painful experience which Mahler described soon after to his friend, the composer-critic Josef Förster:

> When Bülow saw how complicated the score was, he urged me to play it to him instead, [saying] "At least I will hear it in an authentic concept. . . ."
>
> I played. It occurred to me to glance at Bülow, and I see that he is holding both hands over his ears. I stop playing. Bülow who is standing at the window notices at once and urges me to continue.
>
> I play. After a little while I turn around again. Bülow is sitting at the table holding his ears. The whole scene is repeated: I stop playing, again he urges me to continue. I go ahead, and all kinds of thoughts pass through my mind: perhaps Bülow, who is a piano virtuoso, does not like my playing style or my touch, perhaps my *forte* is too passionate or too heavy handed. I remember that Bülow is extremely nervous and often complains of headaches. But I play on without interruption, without paying attention to anything else; I may even have forgotten that Bülow was present.
>
> When I had finished I awaited the verdict silently. But my only listener remained long at the table silent and motionless. Suddenly he made a energetic gesture of rejection and said: "If that is still music then I do not understand a single thing about music."
>
> We parted from each other in complete friendship, I, however, with the conviction that Bülow considers me an able conductor but absolutely hopeless as a composer.

The "complete friendship," however, had developed a fatal flaw. Mahler was not only deeply wounded, he was angered by Bülow's drastic rejection of a work that meant so much to him. Yet his intense admiration for Bülow and gratitude for Bülow's extraordinary kindnesses were too great for Mahler to allow himself any explosion of anger. Despite his explosive nature, Mahler seems to have thrust the painful feelings into the back of his mind. There they festered, creating pressures that interfered with his composing and finally brought him to a complete standstill.

Mahler was able to defy Bülow's judgment to the extent of making *Totenfeier* the foundation and first movement of a gigantic symphony. He completed the second and third movements *(Andante* and *Scherzo)* in June and July, 1893. For his fourth movement (planned as an introduction to a grand choral finale) Mahler adapted a song he had composed some years earlier to a naïve folk poem, *"O Röschen rot"* ("O little rose red") from his favorite collection of folk poetry *Des Knaben Wunderhorn (The Boy's Magic Horn).*

But the finale which was to crown the work: the answer to the first-movement *Funeral Rite,* to the question of the meaning of death and hence of life itself, refused to take shape in his mind. During the summer of 1893 Mahler sought, he struggled, he agonized and worked himself into such a state of nerves over the finale to his Second Symhony that his sisters, who kept house for him, worried about his health and almost wished he would stop composing.

Mahler himself attributed his trouble with the finale to the difficulty of finding an appropriate text for the voices he planned to include, after the model of Beethoven's Ninth Symphony. But the difficulties ran deeper. They involved both his highly charged feelings about Bülow, and a fear of competing with Beethoven (a similar fear had paralyzed Brahms's symphonic efforts for half his career), and other factors. For a masterly example of psychological detective work on this crisis in Mahler's career, the reader is referred to Theodore Reik's book, *The Haunting Melody.* Dr. Reik's wealth of evidence marshalled over twenty-five years of research and his illuminating conclusions, which have been only touched on here, make a most rewarding study.

Mahler himself described his moment of liberation in a letter:

> When I conceive a great musical picture, I always arrive at a point where I must employ the "word" as the bearer of my musical idea. . . . My experience with the last movement of my Second Symphony was such that I literally ransacked world literature even including the Bible to find the redeeming word—and finally felt forced to express my feelings and thoughts in my own words. . . . Just then Bülow died, and I attended the memorial service for him here. The mood in which I sat there and thought of the departed one was exactly that of the work which, at that time, occupied me constantly—at that moment the chorus near the organ intoned the Klopstock chorale, *"Aufersteh'n!"* It struck me like a thunderbolt and everything stood clear and vivid before my soul. The creator waits for this lightning flash, this is his 'holy annunciation.' What I then experienced, I had now to shape into tones. And yet, if I had not carried the idea with me, how could I have experienced it? There were a thousand people with me in the church at that moment

It is significant that, although the Klopstock ode struck Mahler as the liberating word, his "holy annunciation," he found it only partly satisfactory, for it refers only to the resurrection of the physical body. Mahler replaced the last part of the ode with words of his own, answering the question of the first movement and giving additional meaning to the idea of resurrection: "With wings I have won for myself I shall soar . . . aloft . . . I shall die to live again!" In prosaic words, the music he has struggled to create, will bear him to immortality after his own death. Thus this ecstatic finale is more than a momentary victory over a creative deadlock. It is more even than a triumph over the dire verdict of the dead Bülow, it embodies an intimation of that immortality for which most human beings seem to yearn, a feeling which some artists achieve at great peaks of their creative power, and which Horace put into words two thousand years ago in his famous ode: "I have built a monument more enduring than brass . . . I shall not wholly die. . . . *Non omnis moriar.*"

The day of the memorial service was March 28, 1894. As Mahler rushed to his desk, words and music were pouring into his mind. In three months, almost to the day, on June 29, the symphony was finished. Richard Strauss led the Berlin Philharmonic in the first performance of the first three movements on March 4, 1895 and on the following December 13, Mahler himself conducted the Berlin Philharmonic in the premiere of the entire work. It is scored for a characteristically large Late-Romantic orchestra: 4 flutes, 4 piccolos, 4 oboes, 2 English horns, 5 clarinets, bass clarinet, 4 bassoons, 2 contrabassoons, 10 horns, 8 trumpets, 4 trombones, tuba, kettledrums, bass drum, military drum, triangle, cymbals, high tam-tam, low tam-tam, rute, glockenspiel, 3 low bells of indeterminate pitch, 2 harps, organ, the usual strings, soprano solo, alto solo, and chorus.

I. *Allegro maestoso. Mit durchaus ernstem und feierlichem Ausdruck.* "I have called the first movement, 'Funeral Rite,'" wrote Mahler to his friend, the composer-critic Max Marschalk, "and if you wish to know, it is the hero of my First Symphony whom I bear to the grave, and whose whole life I can see reflected in a pure mirror, as it were, from an elevated viewpoint. At the same time it poses the great question: *To what purpose have you lived?* To what purpose have you suffered? Has it all been only a huge, frightful joke? We *must* all somehow answer these questions, if we are to continue living, yes, if we are to go on to die. Anyone who has heard this question must answer, and this answer I give in the last movement."

This gigantic *Allegro maestoso* starts with string tremolos, reminiscent of Beethoven's Ninth Symphony. After a succession of thematic fragments, we hear a solemn, fanfare-like theme in the woodwinds. With a sudden modulation into the distant key of E major, there appears a soaring, lyric theme for violins:

One of the most important themes in this first movement, this anticipates from afar the final choral theme of resurrection, sung in the last movement to Mahler's own words: *"Mit Flügeln die ich mir errungen."* There is a rich array of complex, interrelated themes, which develop to a cataclysmic climax. The concluding coda, with its ominous, repetitive, descending figure in the basses, again recalls Beethoven's Ninth.

II. *Andante moderato. Sehr gemächlich.* The second and third movements Mahler described as interludes, memories and fantasies following the funeral rites: "You must have had the experience of attending the funeral of a person dear to you and then, perhaps, on the way back suddenly the picture of a happy hour long, long past, arises in your mind like a ray of sun undimmed by anything—and you can almost forget what has just happened. That is the second movement."

The mood is set by a tender waltz melody, a melody so simple that it might almost be thought a peasant *Ländler,* if it were not for the delicacy and sophistication of its instrumental garb:

The melody serves as the refrain of a free rondo. At its first return the refrain is carried by muted violins against a broadly flowing song for the cello. The second return is for softly plucked *pizzicato* strings.

III. *In ruhig fliessender Bewegung.* This *scherzo* incorporates large stretches of Mahler's satirical song "Saint Anthony of Padua's Sermon to the Fishes" in which the fishes, like many a human congregation, praise the sermon to the skies as they return to their self-indulgent, fleshly lives. But Mahler uses the song only as a taking-off point. The gentle humor of the beginning grows more and more grotesque, the melody and harmony more and more distorted, until we arrive at an atmosphere of savage, almost terrifying caricature.

"When you awaken from the nostalgic daydream [of the preceding movement]," wrote Mahler, "and you must return to the confusion of real life, it can easily happen that the ceaseless motion, the restless, senseless bustle of daily activity may strike you with *horror,* as if you were watching a whirling crowd of dancers in a brightly lighted ballroom—watching them from the darkness outside and from such a great distance that you *cannot* hear the *music.* Then life can seem meaningless, a gruesome, ghostly spectacle, from which you may recoil with a cry of disgust! That is the third movement!"

IV. *"Urlicht" ("Primal Light"). Sehr feierlich aber schlicht.* This short slow movement serves as an introduction to the *finale.* The alto solo, is set to a German folk poem from the famous Romantic collection, *Des Knaben Wunderhorn* ("The Boy's Magic Horn"):

O Röschen rot,	O rosebud red,
Der Mensch liegt in grösster Not!	Mankind lies in greatest need!
Der Mensch liegt in grösster Pein!	Mankind lies in greatest woe!
Lieber möcht' ich im Himmel sein.	I would fain to Heaven go.
Da kam ich auf einem breiten Weg	I came upon a broad fair way
Da kam ein Engelein und wollt' mich abweisen.	There came an angel and would have turned me back.
Ach nein! Ich liess mich nicht abweisen.	But no! I did not let him turn me back.
Ich bin von Gott und will wieder zu Gott.	I am from God and wish to return to God.
Der liebe Gott wird mir ein Lichtchen geben,	The dear Lord will lend me a little light,
Wird leuchten mir bis in das ewig seelig Leben!	He will light my way to eternal, blissful life.

V. *Im Tempo des Scherzos. Wild herausfahrend.* The finale begins with a wild outburst of the full orchestra, which Mahler intended to recall the cry of horror and disgust in the third-movement *scherzo.* The tumult dies away to silence. Then from a great distance (the score asks for "as many horns as possible" placed very far away, to play very loudly) we hear a solemn fanfare.

> It is "the voice of him that crieth in the wilderness," [wrote Mahler in a program note, referring to Isaiah, XL, 3]. The end of all living things has come. The Last Judgement is announced and the ultimate terror of this Day of Days has arrived.
>
> The earth quakes, the graves burst open, the dead rise and stride hither in endless procession. The great and the humble of this earth: kings and beggars, the just and the unjust—all are coming—and their cry for mercy, for grace, sounds terror-stricken on our ears. Our senses fail us and all consciousness fades away at the approach of the eternal Spirit. The
>
> "Great Summons"
>
> resounds: the trumpets of the apocalypse call. Amid the ghastly silence we seem to hear a distant, distant nightingale, like a last trembling echo of earthly life. Softly there sounds a choir of saints and heavenly creatures: "Rise again, yes, thou shalt rise again." And the glory of God appears. A miraculously mild light penetrates us to the heart—all is still and blissful. And behold: there is no judgment; there are no sinners, no righteous ones, no great and no humble—there is no punishment and no reward!
>
> An almighty love shines through us with blessed knowing and being.

In the merest whisper, without orchestral accompaniment, the chorus begins the Klopstock Ode, the overwhelming message or "holy annunciation," as Mahler called it, which he received at Bülow's memorial service. The first two of Klopstock's three stanzas are used with only very slight changes of individual words, as follows:

Aufersteh'n, ja aufersteh'n wirst du,	Thou shalt rise again, yes again,
mein Staub, nach kurzer Ruh!	my dust, after a short rest!
Unsterblich Leben!	Immortal life!
wird der dich rief dir geben.	will He grant who called thee.
Wieder aufzublühn wirst du gesät!	Thou shalt be sowed like seed to flower again.
Der Herr der Ernte geht	The Lord of harvests goes forth
und sammelt Garben	to gather sheaves,
Uns ein, die starben.	Sheaves of those who died.

Thus far Mahler follows the Klopstock verses. In an ethereal transition passage the orchestra links the soaring, lyric E-major theme of the first movement to the coming resurrection melody: "With wings I have won for myself." But first come Mahler's own reassuring words for alto, soprano and, at last, for chorus:

O glaube, mein Herz	Believe, my heart,
es geht dir nichts verloren!	naught shall be lost to thee!
Dein ist, dein, ja dein, was du ersehnst!	Thine, yes thine is what thou hast longed for!
Dein was du geliebt, was du gestritten!	Thine is what thou hast loved, what thou hast striven for!
O glaube: du wardst nicht umsonst geboren!	O believe: thou wast not born in vain!
Hast nicht umsonst gelebt, gelitten!	Thou hast not lived and suffered in vain!
Was entstanden ist, das muss vergehen!	All that has arisen must pass!
Was vergangen, aufersteh'n!	All that has passed, must rise again!
Hör auf zu beben!	Now cease to tremble!
Bereite dich zu leben!	Prepare thyself to live!
O Schmerz, du Alldurchdringer!	O ever-present suffering,
Dir bin ich entrungen.	Thee I have escaped.
O Tod, du Allbezwinger!	Oh, all-conquering Death,
Nun bist du bezwungen!	Now art thou conquered!

The closing pages of the Symphony are dominated by the rising line of the resurrection melody sung first by the basses, then taken up by the other sections of the chorus, the soloists and the orchestra in a paean of triumph:

Mit Flügeln die ich mir errungen,	With wings I have won for myself,
In Liebesstreben werd' ich entschweben	I shall soar in fervent love aloft
Zum Licht zu dem kein Aug' gedrungen!	To the Light no eye has yet beheld!
Sterben werd' ich um zu leben!	I shall die to live again!
Aufersteh'n, ja aufersteh'n wirst du mein Herz in einem Nu!	Thou shalt rise again, yes again, my heart, in a single moment!
Was du geschlagen	Thy battle's brave heartbeat
Zu Gott wird es dich tragen!	Will bear thee up to God!

SYMPHONY NO. 3, D MINOR

With his own characteristic mixture of sarcasm and affection, Mahler once called his Symphony No. 3 his "monster." And a monster it must have seemed to some—monstrous in its dimensions (with a first movement lasting longer than Beethoven's entire Fifth Symphony) and monstrous in the crass contrasts of its emotional extremes.

> I expect [wrote Mahler to his friend and disciple, Bruno Walter] that the reviewing gentry, partisan and non-partisan, will again suffer attacks of the staggers, while those who can enjoy a good joke will find much to be amused by in the little promenades I am preparing for them. Unfortunately, the whole thing is infected by my notorious sense of humor "and offers many an opportunity to indulge my taste for raucous noise." Sometimes the musicians play "without the faintest consideration for each other and on these occasions my devastatingly brutal nature shows itself quite naked." It is well known that I can do nothing without indulging in trivialities. This time, however, I breach all permissible restraints. "Sometimes one has the feeling of being in some low bar or in a barnyard stall."
>
> But do come to visit us very soon and see that you are well armed when you come! Your taste, which has perhaps been somewhat purified in Berlin, will be quite ruined again.

Mahler composed his beloved "monster" during the summers of 1895 and 1896 at Steinbach on the Attersee, some thirty miles east of Salzburg. Before the end of the first summer, Mahler was convinced that his new Symphony was turning into "probably the ripest and most individual work I have yet composed." By the second summer, he felt possessed by the growth of the Symphony, which seemed to have taken on a life of its own. In a letter of July 18, 1896, to his close friend and colleague, the Wagnerian soprano, Anna Bahr-Mildenburg, he declared:

> I must have written you that I am working on a large composition. Don't you understand that this demands one's whole personality, and that one is often so deeply immersed in it, that it is as if one were dead to the outside world? Now, imagine a work of such scope that the whole world actually is reflected in it—one becomes, so to speak, only an instrument upon which the universe plays. . . . My Symphony will be something that the world has never heard before! In this score, all nature speaks and tells such deep secrets as one may

> intuit in a dream! I tell you, at certain places in the score, a quite uncanny feeling takes possession of me, and I feel as if I had not created this myself. If only I can complete the whole as I envisage it!

Some days before August 6, 1896, the score was "done to a turn" and Mahler mailed to his friend, Max Marschalk, the critic of the Berlin *Vossische Zeitung*, the following titles for the new Symphony and its six movements:

A Summer Noon's Dream

First Section:

I. Introduction: The awakening of Pan; Summer marches in (procession of Bacchus).

Second Section:

II. What the flowers of the meadow tell me.
III. What the animals in the forest tell me.
IV. What man tells me.
V. What the angels tell me.
VI. What love tells me.

Mahler was of two minds concerning explanatory titles and other verbal aids for the listener. Initially he wrote his own titles and programs. Then, finding that his words were misinterpreted, he fulminated against all "programs." And having fulminated, he would again resort to words to explain the unexplainable.

On the occasion of the world premiere of Mahler's Symphony No. 3, which he himself conducted in the small Ruhr city of Krefeld, on June 9, 1902, he had the above titles printed in the program, and then promptly regretted it. Before the end of the year 1902 he explained to another conductor:

> Those titles I originally intended for non-musicians as a point of reference and a guide to the thought, or rather, mood-content of individual movements, of movement to movement and to the whole. That I did not succeed, as indeed one never can succeed, in this intent, and only opened the way to misinterpretations of the worst kind, soon became all too clear to me. This is simply a repetition of the unpleasantness which has already happened to me on similar occasions, and I now have given up for good any further commentating, analyzing, or providing any listener's aid whatever! These titles . . . will certainly tell you something *after* you have become acquainted with the score. From them, you can gain some suggestion of how I imagined the constantly increasing articulation of feeling, from the brooding, elementary forces of nature, to the tender creations of the human heart, which in turn reach out beyond themselves, pointing the way to God.
>
> Please express this in your language, without quoting the highly inadequate titles, and then you will have acted according to my lights. I am *very* thankful to you that you have asked me about this. For the sake of the future of my existing compositions and of my future creative activity, the manner in which these are introduced to the world cannot possibly be unimportant to me.

With or without programs or titles, the Third Symphony was slow to make its way. It took twelve years to reach the United States for its first presentation on May 9, 1914, at the Cincinnati May Festival, when it was conducted by Ernst Kunwald. The New York Philharmonic first performed the Symphony on February 28, 1922, under the direction of Willem Mengelberg.

I. *Kräftig. Entschieden.* This is one of the most gigantic opening movements of symphonic literature. Its dimensions startled even Mahler himself as he was writing it. He described the experience to his friend, Natalie Bauer Lechner:

> It is terrible, the way this movement keeps growing and expanding so far beyond anything I have ever composed before—so far that my Second [Symphony] seems to me a baby by comparison. It is so much, much bigger than life-size that by comparison everything human seems to shrink to pigmy size. I am seized with horror when I realize where all this is leading, when I see the path marked out for the art of music and when I realize that the fearful responsibility of accomplishing this gigantic mission falls to me—Today I feel as one sometimes does when a bit of subconscious knowledge suddenly flashes, like a thunderbolt, into the foreground of one's awareness, like Christ in Gethsemane when he was obliged—nay, wanted—to drain the cup to the dregs. The man for whom this cup is destined cannot refuse, does not wish to refuse. Yet there must be moments when he foresees what lies ahead, and is filled with a deathly fear. This is the kind of feeling I have in contemplating this movement and what I shall have to suffer for it, without any prospect of ever seeing it recognized and appreciated.

The movement opens with a powerful theme somewhat reminiscent of Brahms's First Symphony and proclaimed *fortissimo* by eight horns in unison:

The theme is punctuated by outbursts of the full orchestra, which, however, quickly die away to silence. There follows a melancholy figure for the woodwinds like the rise and fall of a sigh. This in turn is cut through by a stabbing little fanfare of a muted trumpet.

Both this sigh figure and the dissonant trumpet fanfare are characteristically Mahlerian. All this material is developed richly until we reach a point at which one of the developments takes on the status of an independent theme, a bold and assertive trumpet figure:

After a long pause, there begins a section which we may think of as the free fantasia section of a grand-scale sonata-form movement. The recapitulation of the opening material with which the movement concludes is very free, but its architectural sense seems clear.

II. *Tempo di menuetto. Sehr mässig.* This movement, half-minuet, half-scherzo in character, opens with a simple, dance-like figure related to the opening theme of the first movement.

We hear it first in an oboe solo accompanied by *pizzicato* strings. It is taken up by violins and a clarinet solo, and touches of other woodwind color are added, but with the utmost delicacy. The effect is of chamber music.

III. *Commodo. Scherzando. Ohne Hast.* This movement is notable for several extended solos for an instrument designated as a "post horn," a ("natural" or "valveless") ancestor of our present-day French horn. This instrument has an especially bright and gleaming tone. Toward the end of the movement, one of the most poetic passages for this solo post horn is accompanied very softly by four of the normal symphonic French horns, with unforgettable effect.

IV. *Sehr langsam. ·Misterioso.* This movement includes an alto solo, using text from Nietzsche's *Thus Spake Zarathustra.* A background of murmuring strings, and two French horns playing in thirds suggest the mood of a sensuous nocturne rather than the austere Nietzschean rhapsody:

O Mensch! Gib Acht!	O man! Give heed!
Was spricht die tiefe Mitternacht?	What does the deep midnight say?
Ich schlief!	I slept!
Aus tiefem Traum bin ich erwacht!	From deepest dream I have awakened!
Die Welt ist tief!	The world is deep!
Und tiefer, als der Tag gedacht!	And deeper than the day had thought!

Tief, tief, tief ist ihr Weh!	Deep, deep, deep is its woe!
Lust tiefer noch als Herze Leid!	Ecstasy, deeper still than grief!
Weh spricht, Vergeh!	Woe cries: pass on!
Doch alle Lust will Ewigkeit!	But all ecstasy seeks eternity!
Will tiefe, tiefe Ewigkeit!	Seeks deep, deep eternity!

The next movement follows without pause.

V. *Lustig im Tempo und keck im Ausdruck.* The choral text for this movement is taken from the famous German collection of traditional poetry called *Des Knaben Wunderhorn,* source of inspiration for several generations of Romantic composers. The movement opens with a boys' choir imitating the ding-dong of joyful bells. The naïve text is sung by a women's chorus:

Bimm, bamm, bimm, bamm.	Ding, dong, ding, dong.
Es sungen drei Engel einen süssen Gesang;	Three angels sang a sweet song;
Mit Freuden es selig in dem Himmel klang,	Joyfully it sounded through Heaven,
Sie jauchzten fröhlich auch dabei,	They shouted joyfully the while
Dass Petrus sei von Sünden frei,	That St. Peter was free of sin,
Und als der Herr Jesus zu Tische sass,	And when the Lord Jesus sat at the board,
Mit seinen zwölf Jungern das Abendmahl ass:	For the last supper with his twelve disciples,
Da sprach der Herr Jesus, Was stehst du denn hier?	The Lord Jesus spoke: what doest thou here?
Wenn ich dich anseh, so weinest du mir!	As I behold thee, thou weepest!
Und sollt' ich nicht weinen, du gütiger Gott?	And should I not weep, thou merciful God?
Ich hab' übertreten die zehn Gebot.	I have broke the Ten Commandments.
Ich gehe und weine ja bitterlich.	I go my way with bitter tears.
Du sollst ja nicht weinen!	Thou shalt not weep!
Ach komm' und erbarme dich über mich!	Ah, come, and have mercy on me!
Hast du denn übertreten die zehen Gebot,	If thou hast broken the Ten Commandments
So fall' auf die Knie und bete zu Gott!	Fall on thy knees and pray to God!
Liebe nur Gott in alle Zeit!	Love only God in eternity!
So wirst du erlangen die himmlische Freud',	So shalt thou know heavenly joys,
Die selige Stadt war Petro bereit't	The heavenly city was made ready for Peter
Durch Jesum und Allen zur Seligkeit.	Through Jesus and for the salvation of all.
Bimm, bamm, bimm, bamm, bimm.	Ding, dong, ding, dong.

This movement in turn is connected to the finale without pause.

VI. *Langsam. Ruhevoll. Empfunden.* One of the most lyric of all symphonic movements, this presents Mahler at his most serene. The movement is rich in subtle color effects, though color is never used merely for its own sake. The long, melodic line rises slowly from an opening *pianissimo* to a succession of climaxes, each more glowing than its predecessor. The close is powerful, but not crass or brassy. In the final measures the composer asks for "a noble tone."

Mahler's Third Symphony is scored for 2 piccolos, 4 flutes, 4 oboes, English horn, 3 B-flat clarinets, 2 E-flat clarinets, bass clarinet, 4 bassoons, contrabassoon, 8 horns, 4 trumpets, 4 trombones, tuba, kettledrum, bass drum, snare drum, tambourine, triangle, tam-tam, bells, cymbals, 2 harps, the traditional strings, solo alto, women's chorus, and boys' choir.

SYMPHONY NO. 4, G MAJOR, FOR ORCHESTRA AND SOPRANO SOLO

The origins of Mahler's Fourth—the most modest and in some ways most beguiling of his symphonies—reach back some twenty years before Mahler's death to the time when his most potent source of inspiration was the traditional poetry of the Early-Romantic anthology *Des Knaben Wunderhorn (The Boy's Magic Horn).* Like most German Romantic artists, Mahler felt a love for folk art amounting almost to worship. In part this may have been the nostalgia of the complex, intellectual city-dweller for an Eden of lost innocence, of freshness, of naïveté, approximated in our commercial-industrial age by the seeming simplicity of peasant life and art.

However that may be, Mahler was inspired by one of the *Wunderhorn* poems called "Der Himmel hängt voll Geigen" ("Heaven Is Stock Full of Fiddles") to compose one of his happiest songs, which he named after the first line of the poem, "Wir geniessen die himmlischen Freuden" ("All Heavenly Joys Are Ours"). Mahler did not attempt here, as some composers have done, to ape the innocence of folk music. He was content to reflect in his own sophisticated language his idealization of a childlike naïveté. The manuscript piano-vocal score of this song (complete with notes for orchestration) is dated February 10, 1892; the full score, March 12 of the same year.

At one time Mahler planned to use this song for the finale of his Third Symphony. There it was to have had the title "What the Child Tells Me," with the implication that children have a simpler and deeper wisdom than the warped adult world. But his final decision was to make it the philosophical and musical basis of his much simpler Symphony No. 4. During the summer of 1899 at the resort town of Aussee, Mahler began work on the first three movements, which were to anticipate themes of the song finale and to constitute a preparation for it. By January 5, 1901 (the only date in the manuscript), he completed the second movement. The first performance of the Symphony took place in Munich on November 25, 1902. It was introduced to the United States by the New York Symphony Society under its enterprising conductor, Walter Damrosch, on November 6, 1904. Six seasons later, after many revisions (four of which have been published), Mahler himself conducted the New York Philharmonic in the world premiere of the fourth and final version of this masterpiece. The date was January 17, 1911. There was a repetition on the nineteenth. One month later Mahler conducted his last concert (February 21, 1911). He collapsed from the physical and nervous strain of which his doctors more than once had warned, and died three months later.

Mahler set great store by this final version of his Fourth Symphony. In a letter to his publishers dated July 15, 1910, he asks to have a stipulation entered in his contract that the planned new edition of his Fourth Symphony shall *not* be published until he has sent in the revisions he is making for the forthcoming performance under his own direction. But in the confusion following Mahler's death, it was some time before his widow turned over the score with Mahler's final revisions to the publishers. They issued instead the previous set of revisions sent to them by Mahler in July of 1910. For more than fifty years this remained the most authentic printed version of the Fourth Symphony. The final version lay apparently forgotten in the archive of the Universal Edition in Vienna. After World War I the scholar-critic Erwin Stein discovered the score in the vault of Universal and described it in the March-April issue of *Pult und Takstock.* But the article passed almost unnoticed. Not until 1963 was the score finally published by the International Mahler Society.

"In the three first movements," said Mahler, according to Willi Reich, "there reigns the serenity of a higher realm, a realm strange to us, oddly frightening, even terrifying. In the finale ("The Heavenly Life") the child, which in its previous existence already belonged to this higher realm, tells us what it all means. . . ."

I. *Bedächtig, nicht eilen; Recht gemächlich (Haupttempo).* Mahler attached such importance to the thematic connections between the early movements and the finale that we can hardly do better than point out the striking introductory bars (a sort of chirping rhythm of flutes and sleigh bells) which are prominent in both first and last movements, where they are used to mark off major sections of the form:

The chirping figure leads directly to a lilting, dipping melody for first violins:

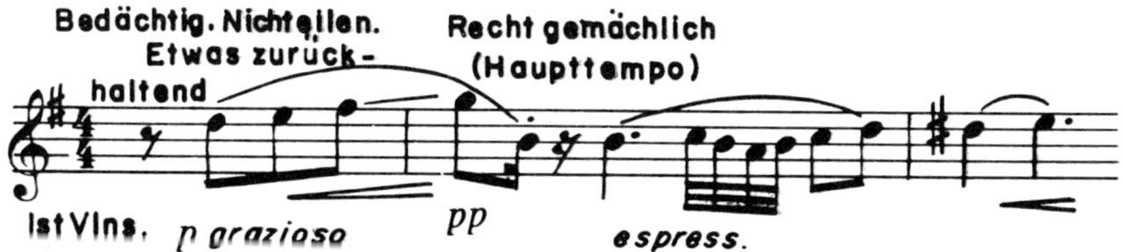

This turns out to be the principal subject of a more traditional first-movement form than Mahler used in most of his symphonies. The melody is taken up by French horns, woodwinds and lower strings, leading at last to a melody of almost Mozartean warmth sung by cellos in unison. This lyric exposition is rounded off by a little duet for oboe and bassoon, echoed by other instruments.

For a moment the return of the introductory chirping measures suggest that we are going back to the principal theme for an old-fashioned repetition of the entire exposition. But instead the chirping measures now serve to introduce the central or development section of the movement. Here Mahler not only develops themes which we have already heard, but also presents us with a striking new theme, a simple line floated far above the staff by four flutes in unison, while in a deep tonal valley below, cellos, double basses and bass clarinets sound a dark accompaniment. The maelstrom of development dies away for a return of all the principal opening themes.

Finally the familiar chirping sonorities introduce a coda, almost as elaborate as a second development section.

II. *In gemächlicher Bewegung. Ohne Hast.* In the leisurely scherzo, an amalgam of rondo and variation, a comfortable, folksy Ländler tune is developed in a spooky, almost macabre mood which Mahler once characterized with the words *"Freund Hein spielt auf,"* which can be roughly interpreted as "Death leads the music." In his prominent solo violin passages the concertmaster is directed to play two violins alternately; one of them tuned a whole tone higher than normal, giving it a rather strident sound. This is his principal theme which he is directed to play aggressively "like a fiddle" (a coarse sort of country violin):

After a merrier contrasting trio section, the opening material returns in varied form, then the trio, also varied, and a final reminder of the opening.

"The scherzo," said Mahler, "is so uncanny, almost sinister, that your hair may stand on end.—Yet in the following *Adagio,* where all complications are dissolved, you will feel that it was not really all that sinister. . . ."

III. *Ruhevoll: (Poco adagio).* Bruno Walter once asked Mahler what lay behind the "profound quiet and clear beauty" of his slow movement. Mahler explained that it had been inspired by a vision of a church sepulcher, with the reclining stone figures of the dead, "their arms closed in eternal peace." His vision is embodied in a set of free variations on two different themes. Just as Mahler's vision seems about to evaporate into nothingness, a peal of golden orchestral sonorities (French horns and trumpets) anticipates the principal theme of the finale.

IV. *Sehr behaglich.* As he finished the Fourth Symphony, Mahler is reported (by Willi Reich) to have said to friends: "What I envisioned for the last movement was very difficult. Try, if you will, to imagine a heaven of undifferentiated blue, which is much harder to suggest than changing, contrasting hues. This is the fundamental mood. But it darkens sometimes, grows spooky, even terrifying. It is not that heaven itself really dims: on the contrary it shines on and on in its eternal blue. It is only that we sometimes react to it with sudden terror, just as on the most beautiful day, when the woods are drenched in sunlight, one is often suddenly gripped by a panic fear."

The serene blue of the heavenly landscape is suggested by the innocent phrase of a solo clarinet, anticipating the opening vocal phrase of the movement:

The eight stanzas of folk poetry are punctuated after stanzas two, four, and seven by the chirping refrain familiar to us from the first movement.

Wir geniessen die himmlischen Freuden,	All heavenly joys are ours,
D'rum tun wir das Irdische meiden.	Pleasures of earth we disdain.
Kein weltlich' Getümmel	No worldly strife
Hört man nicht in Himmel	Mars our heavenly life.
Lebt alles in sanftester Ruh!	We live here in sweetest peace.
Wir führen ein englisches Leben!	We lead an angelic life,
Sind dennoch ganz lustig daneben!	Yet are merry as can be.
Wir tanzen und springen,	We dance and spring,
Wir hüpfen und singen,	We jump and sing
Sanct Peter im Himmel sieht zu!	While St. Peter in Heaven looks on.

(Orchestral refrain)

Johannes das Lämmelein auslasset	The lamb we have from St. John.
Der Metzger Herodes drauf passet.	Herod, the butcher will be.
Wir führen ein geduldig's,	We lead the meek
Unschuldig's, geduldig's,	And innocent
Ein liebliches Lämmelein zu Tod!	Little lamb to the death.
Sanct Lukas den Ochsen tat schlachten	St. Luke slaughters the oxen
Ohn' einig's Bedenken und Achten.	Without any worry or heed.
Der Wein kost' kein Heller	The wine costs us naught
Im himmlischen Keller.	From our heavenly draught
Die Englein, die backen das Brot,	And the angels bake us our bread.

(Orchestral refrain)

Gut Kräuter von allerhand Arten	Fine vegetables grow
Die wachsen im himmlischen Garten!	In the garden of Heaven.
Gut Spargel, Fisolen,	Good asparagus, good beans,
Und was wir nur wollen.	Whatever we please.
Ganze Schüsseln voll sind uns bereit!	Whole plates of them wait to be eaten.
Gut' Aepfel, gut' Birn' und gut Trauben!	Good apples, good pears, good grapes!
Die Gärtner, die Alles erlauben	The gardeners give what we wish.
Willst Rehbock, willst Haasen	And roebucks and hares
Auf offener Strassen	Run into our arms
Sie laufen herbei!	Here in the open streets!
Sollt ein Fasttag etwa kommen	And when there is a fast day
Alle Fische gleich mit Freuden angeschwommen.	The fish come swarming in.
Dort lauft schon Sanct Peter	St. Peter he runs
Mit Netz und mit Köder	With his net and bait
Zum himmlischen Weiher hinein.	To fish in the heavenly pond.
Sanct Martha die Köchin muss sein.	St. Martha must cook the catch.

(Orchestral refrain)

Kein Musik is ja nicht auf Erden,	On earth there is no music
Die uns'rer verglichen kann werden,	To be compared with ours
Elf tausend Jungfrauen	The eleven thousand virgins
Zu tanzen sich trauen!	Make bold to dance.
Sanct Ursula selbst dazu lacht!	And St. Ursula smiles on the scene.
Cäcilia mit ihren Verwandten	Cecilia, her kith and her kin
Sind treffliche Hofmusikanten!	Play like a royal band.
Die englischen Stimmen	And choirs of angels
Ermuntern die Sinnen	Lift up our spirits
Dass alles für Freuden erwacht.	To the highest of heavenly joys.

In its final version the Fourth Symphony is scored for 4 flutes, 2 piccolos, 3 oboes, English horn, 4 clarinets in B flat, A, C, and E flat, bass clarinet, 3 bassoons, contrabassoon, 4 horns, 3 trumpets, kettledrums, bass drum, triangle, sleigh bells, glockenspiel, cymbals, tam-tam, harp, and the traditional string choir.

SYMPHONY NO. 5

When Gustav Mahler conducted the first performance of his Fifth Symphony at a Gürzenich concert in Cologne in 1904, it was described as "the giant Symphony." It is characteristic of Mahler in many ways. Its fundamental adherence to the traditional four-movement pattern of Classical symphonic form is as typical of Mahler as are his radical amplifications of certain sections and telescoping of others. Characteristic, too, is Mahler's fastidious use of a gigantic orchestra for subtle, chamber music effects. Finally, his Fifth Symphony is an extreme example of his perfectionism in orchestration, which led to endless revision. Mahler's wife, Alma Maria, who was herself a gifted composer, describes, in her book about Mahler, the first tryout rehearsals of the Fifth in Vienna, months before the world premiere in Cologne:

> Early in the year there had been a reading rehearsal with the [Vienna] Philharmonic, to which I listened unseen from the gallery. I had heard each theme in my head while copying the score, but now I could not hear them at all! Mahler had overscored the percussion instruments and kettledrums so madly and persistently that little beyond the rhythm was recognized. I hurried home sobbing aloud. He followed. For a long time I refused to speak. At last I said between my sobs: "You've written it for percussion and nothing else!" He laughed and then produced the score. He crossed out all the kettledrums in red chalk and half the percussion instruments, too. He had felt the same thing himself, but my passionate protest turned the scale.

Although Mahler had completed the Fifth Symphony in the summer of 1902, at his villa in Maiernigg on Lake Wörth, the revisions described by Alma Maria were succeeded by revisions of revisions up to the year of Mahler's death. Our authority for the statement that the Fifth was reorchestrated for almost every performance under Mahler's direction is Mme Mahler herself. Finally, in one of his last letters, Mahler told his friend, Georg Göhler, "The Fifth is finished. I have been forced to reorchestrate it completely. I fail to comprehend how at that time [1902] I could have blundered so like a greenhorn. Obviously the routine I had acquired in my first four symphonies completely deserted me. It is as if my totally new musical message demanded a new technique."

Much, if not all, of Mahler's symphonic music was program music in the sense that it was inspired by extramusical thoughts or feelings or at least suggested such extramusical ideas to Mahler after he had composed it. The Fifth Symphony is related thematically to more than one of Mahler's songs. Yet Mahler had extremely mixed feelings about publishing programmatic descriptions of the content of his scores. His vehement outburst, "Perish all programs!" became famous, and the Fifth Symphony, however much it may suggest emotional cataclysm and triumph, is one of the works in which he kept to his resolve to let the music speak for itself.

One of the particular fascinations of this masterly score is the subtle web of thematic interrelationships which unifies the entire work in a way dear to the hearts of Romantic composers.

It is written in three parts, but with the first and last parts divided into two sections each. Thus, one may think of the entire work as being in five movements. However, the two movements of Part I are so intimately related through common thematic material that it is logical to think of the opening "Trauermarsch," or "Funeral March," as merely a vast expansion of the slow introductions which had been familiar since Haydn's day. It is equally possible to think of the *Adagietto,* which leads without pause to the *Rondo Finale,* as another slow introduction rather than a traditional slow movement.

PART I

I. *Trauermarsch: In gemessenem Schritt.* A solitary trumpet announces the first and most important theme of this "Funeral March." It begins like a solemn summons from afar: *

The entire orchestra takes up this shuddering triplet rhythm, building to a strong climax, which quickly makes way for a lyric second theme: a mournful, wraithlike melody. The alternation of these two themes makes up the body of the movement. But there is a contrasting middle section, which Lawrence Gilman, the late Philharmonic program annotator, admired above any part of the Symphony:

> . . . It is that passage [he wrote] in B-flat minor in which the music, grown suddenly and passionately vehement, breaks in upon the measured tread of the "Funeral Music" like an uncontrollable outburst of shattering, maniacal, wild-visaged grief. Above an *ostinato* of the double basses and bassoons, a trumpet shrieks its heaven-storming woe, against the chromatic wailing of the strings. The plangent, tumultuous despair of this passage is like nothing else in music that one can recall. Tchaikovsky's is restrained and decorous beside it. Mahler has here imagined an elemental and universal human emotion with sensibility and with justice and has turned it into direct and vivid and irresistible musical speech . . . . The artist, to be sure, is in no need of personal verification of universal themes; but it is easy to believe that this music is an intimate declaration, a personal souvenir of exceptional authenticity.

As the final paroxysm of this section subsides, we hear again very softly the triplets of the fanfare-like opening theme and thematic material of the entire opening section returns. As the music dies, the triplet fanfare lingers in the fading color of a single muted trumpet, with a final disembodied echo, *pianississimo* for solo flute.

II. *Stürmisch bewegt. Mit grösster Vehemenz.* This storm movement (to which one might well regard the preceding as one long introduction) is based freely on traditional first-movement (sonata-allegro) form. Its principal theme, launched by the woodwinds after introductory rumblings in the depths of the orchestra, is a frantic outburst related to the middle section of the opening movement:

---

* *This and the following musical examples from this composition are copyright 1964 by C. F. Peters Corporation. Reprinted by permission.*

For his second, lyric theme (which seems related to the second theme of the opening movement) Mahler specifically calls for a return to the tempo of the "Funeral March," thus emphasizing yet another link to that introductory movement.

In the development and free recapitulation that follow there are repeated references to the principal themes of both movements. Like its predecessor, this movement ends with dying echoes of its principal theme.

PART II

III. *Scherzo: Kräftig, nicht zu schnell.* The waltz-like middle movement is a *Scherzo* as rich in thematic variety and development as it is complex in form. One of its most striking traits is the prominence given to an *obbligato* horn. The horn theme appears in various guises, but most characteristically as follows:

PART III

IV. *Adagietto: Sehr langsam.* The yearning principal melody, rich in romantic *appoggiatura* effects, is directed to be played "expressively" and "soulfully":

This movement, which is scored for harp plus the usual strings, leads without pause into the *Finale* proper.

V. *Rondo Finale: Allegro giocoso. Frisch.* Far from the tragic conclusions of many other Mahler works, the Fifth Symphony proceeds from sorrow (in the opening "Funeral March") to jubilation in the *Rondo Finale.* There is a curiously pastoral mood in the opening measures, where solo woodwinds anticipate three important themes. The *Rondo* refrain, which follows, is an elaboration of the following simple, vigorous figure:

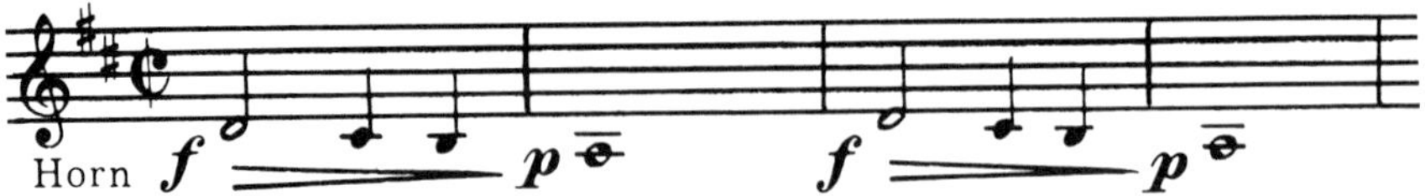

A lively cello figure is taken up by violins, violas and basses successively in *fugato* style and combined with a third theme, one of those anticipated in the opening measures:

This develops into one of the most important themes of the movement and is transformed in its final pages into a stately hymn of triumph.

The *Rondo* refrain returns. In the episodes that follow, the principal themes of the movement are developed in a richly symphonic style. There are no more simple, literal returns of the *Rondo* refrain. On the surface the music grows more complex as the interrelationships of the themes increase. In essence it becomes simpler because of their growing unity as we approach the exultant coda.

The score of the Fifth Symphony calls for 4 flutes, 3 piccolos, 3 oboes, English horn, 3 clarinets, 1 bass clarinet, 2 bassoons, contrabassoon, 6 horns (including solo *obbligato* horn), 4 trumpets, 3 trombones, bass tuba, kettledrums, bass drum, snare drum, cymbals, triangle, glockenspiel, gong, harp, and the customary strings.

SYMPHONY NO. 6, A MINOR

This is one of the most emotional works of a composer who was by nature hyperemotional, and somewhat inclined to be autobiographical in his symphonic works. It was the belief of Mahler's wife Alma Maria that his Sixth Symphony came more directly from his heart than any other of his works. On the occasion when he first played through the score of his new Symphony for her on the piano, long before the orchestral performance, she recalled: "We both wept." The preparations and rehearsals for the world premiere under Mahler's direction were especially tense emotionally. "We came to the last rehearsals [she continued], to the dress rehearsal—to the last movement, with its three great blows of fate. When it was over, Mahler walked up and down the artist's room, sobbing, wringing his hands, unable to control himself. . . .

On the day of the concert [May 27, 1906, in Essen] Mahler was so afraid that agitation might get the better of him, that out of shame and anxiety he did not conduct the Symphony well. He hesitated to bring out the dark omen behind this terrible movement."

Many persons close to Mahler believed he had strong extra-musical associations in mind when he composed the Sixth. But Mahler himself had grown chary of explanations. Early in his career, when the newness of his music had baffled many listeners, he tried to help them with descriptive titles and even detailed explanations of what the music meant. Soon he came to feel that such verbal elucidations did more harm than good. Yet Mahler believed profoundly in the extra-musical content of the music of his age. "Beginning with Beethoven," he wrote to the critic and scholar Max Kalbeck, "there exists no modern music which hasn't its inner program. Yet no music is worth anything when the listener has to be told what experience it embodies—in other words, what he is expected to experience himself. . . . A bit of mystery always remains—even for the creator!"

Soon after the premiere of the Sixth Symphony, Mahler's friend and disciple Bruno Walter wrote a letter attacking the whole idea of program music, including one of Wagner's statements on the subject. Mahler, full of the exaltation of successful creation, replied:

> The words of Wagner, which you quote, seem quite logical to me. . . . It certainly is undeniable that our music does involve the "purely human"; and everything appertaining to it, that is, including the intellectual part. . . .
>
> If a man wants to create music, he should not try to paint, poetize or describe. But what man composes is surely the whole man, his feelings, thoughts, his breathing, his suffering. There should be nothing against programs (even if they are not exactly the highest rung of the ladder), but it must be a musician who expresses himself, not an author, a philosopher or painter, all of whom are contained in the musician. . . . All the worrying of this problem reminds me of the man who begets a child, but afterwards, tortures himself with philosophical problems such as: whether it is a real child, whether he begot it with good intentions, etc., etc., etc. He loved and he was able. *Basta!* If a man does not love, and cannot, there is no child. Again, *basta!* And as one is and achieves, so is the child. Once more, *basta!*
>
> My Sixth is finished. I believe I was able. A thousand times *basta!*

Although the Sixth took Mahler less than two years (1904–06) to compose, it was many times revised and re-revised. At the first performances, Mahler had the word "Tragic" added to the title. Later he deleted the word. At one time he changed the original sequence of the movements so that in his second version, the *Andante* became the second movement. Soon thereafter, Mahler felt that this destroyed the basic idea of the Symphony and so restored the original sequence: *Allegro, Scherzo, Andante, Finale.* Mahler also made extensive changes in his orchestration—tending chiefly to clarify the rich texture of his work.

The Symphony remained a problematic work for many years: although the European premiere took place in 1906, the Sixth did not reach the United States until December 11, 1947, when the New York Philharmonic presented it under the direction of Dimitri Mitropoulos.

I. *Allegro energico, ma non troppo: Heftig, aber markig.* Against a rasping drum rhythm the violins launch a grim sort of march melody, the principal theme of the first movement: *

As the brief development of this theme dies away, an ominous, six-note rhythm is announced by two kettledrums. This is the Fate motive which plays a prominent role in the Finale as well. (Mahler himself referred to this motive by various names, including "rhythm of catastrophe."):

A brief transition in the woodwinds leads to a lyric transformation of the opening march melody. According to Alma, Mahler told her personally of this transformation: "I've tried to capture [i.e., to portray] you in a theme. I don't know whether I've succeeded . . . You'll have to take it as it is." It is one of the more passionate phrases of the Symphony:

The development is tense and dramatic. At its climax it suddenly subsides and we hear, as if from a great distance, the faint sound of cowbells. In a footnote Mahler asks to have the cowbells played very discreetly, in a realistic imitation of the sound of distant individual bells, from high and low pastures. Yet he emphasizes that this "technical direction" has no programmatic meaning whatever. In the reprise of the basic thematic material the "Alma" theme is at first omitted, only to be brought back in triumph in the closing pages.

II. *Scherzo: Wuchtig.* The principal theme of the parodistic Scherzo is derived directly from the opening rhythm and the opening theme of the first

* *This and the following musical examples from this composition are copyright 1963 of C. F. Kahnt, Lindau. Used by permission of C. F. Peters Corporation, sole agent for the U.S.*

movement. The Scherzo is rich in original orchestral color combinations, although individually many of the effects have long been standard orchestral devices. For example, strings play *col legno,* that is, with the wooden backs of their bows. Prominent xylophone sound has been interpreted as a rattling of bones. The final pages of this strange movement grow darker and darker. The last measures are scored only for bass clarinet, double bass, bassoon, three low trombones, string basses and kettledrums.

III. *Andante moderato.* The songful slow movement opens with the following melody:

This movement is linked to the first by the recurrence of the pastoral mood associated with the cowbells. The harp and celesta join in a passage of great delicacy and serenity. The movement gathers intensity as it approaches a broad and powerful climax. The final pages, of the utmost delicacy, fade away to silence.

IV. *Finale: Allegro moderato.* The immense Finale opens with a broadly declamatory phrase for the first violins followed by the Fate motive. This purely rhythmic figure, given out by two timpanists in unison, punctuates and concludes the Finale with obviously programmatic significance. "In the last movement," according to Alma Mahler, "[Mahler] describes himself and his downfall or, as he later said, that of his hero, 'the hero, who undergoes three strokes of destiny, the third of which fells him, like a tree.' These were Mahler's words." At each of the three points referred to by Alma Maria we hear the motive of Fate, or "rhythm of catastrophe" as Mahler also called it. The first two of these climactic moments are accompanied by a single blow of a heavy percussive nature which Mahler indicated should sound like the stroke of an ax. The third ax-stroke, however, was finally omitted in his last revision of the Symphony.

As the conclusion of the "Tragic" Symphony fades and the darkest instruments of the orchestra sink deeper and deeper into blackness, there is one sudden last *fortissimo* outcry of the *tutti,* and the two kettledrums reiterate, for the last time, the fateful rhythm of catastrophe.

The "Tragic" Symphony is scored for 3 piccolos, 4 flutes, 4 oboes, 2 English horns, clarinets in D and E flat, 3 clarinets in A and B flat, bass clarinet, 4 bassoons, contrabassoon, 8 horns, 6 trumpets, 3 trombones, bass trombone, bass tuba, kettledrums, glockenspiel, cowbells, low-pitched bells, bass drum, triangle, snare drum, cymbals, woodblocks, tam-tam, rute, tambourine, hammer, xylophone, 2 harps, celesta, and strings.

SYMPHONY NO.7

A great heritage can be a great burden. Many a nineteenth-century composer was haunted by the ghost of Beethoven. Brahms was a middle-aged man before he finished his first symphony, and the main reason for this hesitation seems to have been that he was made self-conscious by hearing the "tramp of a giant" like Beethoven behind him. For Mahler, the problem was still greater, because of the greater accumulated heritage, and it was complicated by the constant struggle between his desire to compose and the necessity to earn a living as a conductor.

With astonishing speed, Mahler worked his way up from provincial opera houses to become the musical director of the Vienna Court Opera, and, for a time, of the Vienna Philharmonic Orchestra. During his decade as the head of the Vienna Opera, he made it the greatest operatic institution in the world. Then he was called to conduct at The Metropolitan Opera in New York, where he was soon joined by Arturo Toscanini. It was a golden moment for opera in this country. But in his frantic desire to put away enough money to give himself up solely to composing, Mahler also undertook the direction of The New York Philharmonic, which position he held from 1909 to 1911. His friends expressed amazement, but Mahler wrote to Guido Adler: "I need a practical outlet for my musical capabilities as an essential counterbalance to the incredible inner stresses of creation; and the direction of a concert orchestra has been a lifelong wish. I am glad to have this pleasure for once in my life (quite aside from the fact that I am learning, for the technique of an opera orchestra is a quite different one, and I am convinced that a number of my weaknesses in instrumentation hitherto have sprung from this fact)."

Mahler's doctors in Vienna warned him that his many activities had already undermined his health and he must reduce them sharply. This he was temperamentally unable to do. Before the end of his fourth season in New York he collapsed and was taken back to Vienna to die.

The Seventh Symphony is one of a trio of symphonic scores, the Fifth, Sixth and Seventh, written during Mahler's tenure at the Vienna Opera. All three are purely instrumental, that is, they use neither chorus nor vocal solos. They even have certain thematic links as well as common moods. Finally, Mahler seems to have experienced an agony of uncertainty over details of each of the three scores.

The Seventh Symphony was written during the summers of 1904 and 1905, minor revisions and a fair copy being completed during the following winters.

Mahler himself conducted the first performance in Prague in 1908. His widow, Alma Maria Mahler, described the feverish preparations for the premiere (in her *Gustav Mahler: Memories and Letters*): "There were many of Mahler's friends in Prague: [Albert] Neiser, [Arnold] Berliner, [Ossip] Gabrilowitsch, and also several youthful musicians, Alban Berg, [Artur] Bodanzky, [Gerhard von] Keussler, [Otto] Klemperer. They all helped him revise the orchestration and to copy the parts. Even at the final rehearsal, he was aware of lack of balance and never ceased making alterations in the proofs as long as any possibility of doing so remained. On all the various occasions when his symphonies were performed for the first time, younger musicians gathered around to give him their help, as they did now."

Alma Maria Mahler arrived in time for the last rehearsals: "I found him in bed; he was nervous and unwell. His room was littered with orchestral parts, for his alterations were incessant in those days, not of course in the composition, but in the instrumentation. From the *Fifth* onwards, he found it impossible to satisfy himself. . . . It was a phase. His self-assurance returned with the *Eighth*, and although *Das Lied von der Erde* is posthumous, I cannot imagine his altering a note in a work so economical in its means of expression. . . . But now he was torn by doubts. He avoided the society of his fellow musicians, which as a rule he eagerly sought, and went to bed immediately after dinner to save his energy for the rehearsals . . . [yet] Mahler's health and spirits improved as the rehearsals went on, and his self-confidence rose."

The performance was only mildly successful. "The Seventh was scarcely understood by the public," wrote his wife, "it had a *succès d'estime*."

The symphony is composed in five, instead of the traditional four, movements, the central Scherzo being flanked by two nocturnes or *Nachtmusiken*.

I. *Langsam—Allegro con fuoco*. The first movement has an introduction in a gloomy, almost funereal mood. Against a shuddering rhythm of winds and strings, a tenor horn intones a jagged phrase related to the principal theme of the first movement proper, the *Allegro con fuoco*:*

There are lyric, passages for contrast as in traditional first movement form, but the structure itself is extremely elaborate and original with Mahler.

II. *Nachtmusik: Allegro moderato*. Despite the *allegro* marking, the mood and color of this movement recall the *Scène aux champs* of the third movement in Berlioz' *Fantastic Symphony*. Here the country atmosphere is emphasized by flute passages marked to be played "like bird voices" and by the use of cowbells which for Mahler had an almost mystical significance. On more than one occasion he spoke of cow-bells as being the last terrestrial sound one hears before reaching the peak of the mountain.

III. *Schattenhaft: Fliessend, aber nicht schnell*. The shadowy mood of this movement suggests spooks rather than mere shade. In function, the movement is a *scherzo*, with four contrasting "trio" sections. Its grotesque character is reflected in many details, including the passage where cellos and double-

* *This and the following musical example from this composition are copyright 1960 by Bote & Bock. Used by permission of Associated Music Publishers, Inc.*

basses are directed to play *fffff pizzicati* so violent that the string snaps back against the finger-board.

IV. *Nachtmusik: Andante amoroso.* In this movement, Mahler achieves special effects by using a mandolin and a guitar. The delicate ensemble is in chamber music style, contrapuntal in texture and fascinating in its subtle shades of instrumental color.

V. *Rondo-Finale: Allegro ordinario.* The Finale opens with a bravura solo for kettledrums and brilliant fanfares for horns and winds which introduce the principle theme:

The family relation of this theme to the first movement theme seems obvious. But Mahler went further in his characteristically Romantic linking of movements by bringing back the symphony's opening theme in the coda of his finale. The Rondo form of the Finale is very free, and the closing pages, with their combination of fanfares and earlier themes build to a tremendous rhetorical climax.

Despite the brave show of the conclusion, the Symphony has many brooding, foreboding passages, often with a suggestion of hopelessness, in which imaginative listeners have heard a premonition of the catastrophies which were to sweep away the almost oppressive richness of Mahler's cultural inheritance. But in spite of his premonitions, Mahler had a redeeming sense of humor, sometimes sardonic, which also sounds in his music. He knew that the end of Romanticism was not really the end of music but only of an epoch.

One day, Mahler was climbing the banks of a mountain stream with another musician. His friend, in a lugubrious mood, lamented that no more great music was being written. After Beethoven, Wagner, Brucker and Mahler, nothing new of importance could be expected. Suddenly, Mahler stood rooted to the ground in an attitude of mock alarm. He gestured in consternation to the stream and cried, "Great God, look there!"

What is it?" asked his anxious friend.

"The last wave," was Mahler's reply.

The Seventh Symphony is scored for 2 piccolos, 3 oboes, English horn, E-flat clarinet, 3 clarinets in A and B flat, bass clarinet, 3 bassoons, contrabassoon, tenor horn in B flat, 4 horns, 3 trumpets, 3 trombones, tuba, kettledrums, bass drum, glockenspiel, cowbells, triangle, cymbals, gong, 2 harps, guitar, mandoli, and the traditional strings.

SYMPHONY NO. 8. E-FLAT MAJOR (SYMPHONY OF A THOUSAND)
"I have just finished my Eighth!" wrote Mahler on August 18, 1906, to his friend, Willem Mengelberg, in a letter that radiates self confidence and fulfillment. "It is the biggest thing I have done so far. And so individual in content and form that I cannot describe it in words. Imagine that the whole universe begins to vibrate and resound. These are no longer human voices, but planets and suns revolving." The texts Mahler chose for his voices show his exalted aim. The first half of the Symphony is based on the ancient Latin Hymn *"Veni creator spiritus."* The second half, the answer to the invocation of the hymn, uses the mystical concluding scene of Goethe's *Faust*.

Never before had Mahler composed so swiftly, so wholly at the command of his impulse, with such assurance and with such exaltation at the conclusion of a work. This was the more remarkable because Mahler habitually had been plagued by self-doubt. His three preceding symphonies had cost him agonies of uncertainty and revisions of revisions of revisions. "From the Fifth onwards," according to his widow Alma Maria Mahler, "he found it impossible to satisfy himself; the Fifth was differently orchestrated for practically every performance; the Sixth and Seventh were continually in process of revision. It was a phase. His self-assurance returned with the Eighth. . . ."

A painful part of Mahler's self-doubt had been his fear of failing inspiration; lack of the creative spirit. Psychological blocks had immobilized him as early in his career as his Second, or "Resurrection," Symphony. Under the circumstances there can be little doubt that the "creator spiritus" invoked in the Latin hymn was (for Mahler) not only God or the Holy Ghost, but also the spark of inspiration in the creative artist. Mahler thought of this hymn as "a song of yearning, of rapturous devotion in invocation of the creative spirit, the love that moves the worlds." Was that last a conscious reference to Dante's radiant vision of God as *l'amor che move il sole e l'altre stelle* ("the love that moves the sun and the other stars") in the final line of his *Divine Comedy?* If not, then the coincidence is all the more remarkable.

The hymn text which could support so many simultaneous meanings is half a millennium older than the *Divine Comedy*. Written by an illustrious church father, Hrabanus ("the raven") Maurus, in the ninth century, it was incorporated into the Roman Catholic liturgy for Pentecost: the feast of the invisible descent of the Holy Spirit on the apostles and the gift of tongues.

As if the prayer to the creative spirit had been answered, Mahler composed his Eighth with incredible speed. The entire composition (not counting orchestration) took him only eight weeks.

Preliminary rehearsals for the world premiere in Munich were led by Mahler's devoted apostle, Bruno Walter. The final rehearsals and the premiere of December 12, 1910, were conducted by Mahler himself. The Munich management publicized the premiere with such circus-like ballyhoo that Mahler later referred to this as the Barnum and Bailey performance. Among the manager's promotional gimmicks was the nickname "Symphony of a Thousand," referring to the gigantic forces enlisted. They totalled slightly over a thousand:

7 solo singers, a boys' choir, two large choruses and an unusually large orchestra comprising 4 flutes and piccolo, 4 oboes and English horn, 4 clarinets and bass clarinet, 4 bassoons and contrabassoon, 8 French horns, 4 trumpets, 4 trombones, a large battery of percussion, organ and the usual string instruments considerably enlarged in number.

I. *Allegro impetuoso: "Veni, creator spiritus."* Despite its giant vocal apparatus and its unusual length, the first movement is based on traditional (sonata-allegro) form. The opening line of the invocation, a confident shout by the two massed choirs, *"Veni, creator spiritus,"* is the principal theme:

The cry is echoed by trombones and trumpets and in slightly changed form, back and forth between the two choruses. The contrasting second theme is sung *dolce, expressivo* by the soprano solo to the third and fourth lines of text: "Fill with overflowing grace" (*"Imple superna . . ."*).

The vast development section begins softly with an orchestral interlude in which we hear the tolling of a bell. In the course of the development, the Symphony's first theme, *"Veni creator spiritus,"* evolves into a new form which is so striking that it must be called a new theme in its own right. It appears as a powerful cry of chorus and soloists to the words: "Kindle the light of our understanding" (*"Accende lumen sensibus"*):

The development culminates in a double fugue based on the *"Veni creator spiritus"* theme.

Veni, Creator Spiritus,	*Come, O Spirit of creation,*
Mentes tuorum visita:	*Enter in the minds you made:*
Imple superna gratia	*Fill with overflowing grace*
Quae tu creasti pectora.	*The hearts Thou hast created.*
Qui Paraclitus diceris,	*Thou whom we call the Comforter*
Donum Dei altissimi,	*Thou gift to us from God on high,*
Fons vivus, ignis, caritas,	*Thou living source, thou fire, thou love,*
Et spiritalis unctio.	*Thou benediction of the Spirit.*

Infirma nostri corporis	*To our bodies, weak and frail,*
Firmans virtute perpeti.	*Give eternal strength and courage*
Accende lumen sensibus,	*Kindle the light of our understanding*
Infunde amorem cordibus.	*And pour love into our hearts.*
Hostem repellas longius,	*Drive the arch-foe farther from us*
Pacemque dones protinus:	*Grant us peace henceforth forever:*
Ductore sic te praevio,	*And through Thee, our foremost leader*
Vitemus omne pessimum.	*Let us avoid all evil.*
Tu septiformis munere	*Thou the gift, the sevenfold finger*
Destrae Paternae digitus.	*Of the right hand of God the Father,*
Per te sciamus da Patrem,	*Through Thee let us know the Father,*
Noscamus atque Filium,	*Let us also know the Son.*
Te utriusque Spiritum	*In them and in the Holy Ghost*
Credamus omni tempore.	*Let us believe forever more.*
Da gratiarum munera,	*Grant us the gift of Thy graces*
Da gaudiorum praemia.	*Grant us the anticipation of joys*
Dissolve litis vincula,	*Free us from the chains of strife*
Adstringe pacis foedera.	*And bind us in the bonds of peace.*
Gloria Patri Domino	*Glory be to God the Father;*
Natoque, qui a mortuis	*And to the Son, who from the dead*
Surrexit, ac Paraclito	*Is risen; and to the Holy Ghost*
In saeculorum saecula.	*Forever and forever more.*

II. *Poco Adagio: Allegro appassionato; Sehr langsam; Allegro, Langsam.* The second movement is a setting of the end of Goethe's *Faust, Part II.* This scene, the mystical fulfillment of all the striving of both halves of Goethe's *Faust,* seemed to Mahler the ideal fulfillment of the prayer, *"Veni creator spiritus."* Musically the second movement is dominated by the theme *"Accende lumen"* which was proclaimed in the first movement and which, in turn, derives from the opening invocation of the entire work: *"Veni creator spiritus."*

FAUST, PART II Act V, Scene 7
(Mountain gorges, forest, rocks, desert. Holy anchorites scattered up the mountainside, dwelling among the clefts.)

CHORUS AND ECHO:

Waldung, sie schwankt heran,	Forests are swaying here,
Felsen, sie lasten dran,	Rocks weight them downward sheer,
Wurzeln, sie klammern an,	Roots clutching rocks appear,

Stamm dicht an Stamm hinan.
Woge nach Woge spritzt,
Höhle, die tiefste schützt.
Löwen, sie schleichen stumm
Freundlich um uns herum,
Ehren geweihten Ort,
Heilgen Liebeshort.

Trunk close by trunk is near.
Wave dashes after wave,
Shelter hath deepest cave.
Lions, soft-footed, dumb,
Friendly around us come,
Honoring the sacred place,
Refuge of love and grace.

PATER ECSTATICUS
(hovering up and down):

Ewiger Wonnebrand,
Glühendes Liebeband,
Siedender Schmerz der Brust,
Schäumende Gotteslust.
Pfeile, durchdringet mich,
Lanzen, bezwinget mich,
Keulen, zerschmettert mich,
Blitze, durchwetteret mich;
Dass ja das Nichtige
Alles verflüchtige,
Glänze der Dauerstern,
Ewiger Liebe Kern.

Endless ecstatic fire,
Glow of pure love's desire,
Pangs of the yearning breast,
Rapture in God to rest.
Arrows, pierce through me here,
Lances, subdue me here,
Bludgeons, come, batter me,
Lightnings, come, shatter me,
That my mortality
Flee from reality,
Endless star shine above,
Core of eternal love.

PATER PROFUNDUS
(Lower Region):

Wie Felsenabgrund mir zu Füssen
Auf tiefem Abgrund lastend ruht,
Wie tausend Bäche stahlend fliessen
Zum grausen Sturz des Schaums der Flut,
Wie strak, mit eignem, kräftigen Triebe,
Der Stamm sich in die Lüfte trägt,
So ist es die allmächtige Liebe
Die alles bildet, alles hegt.
Ist um mich her ein wildes Brausen,
Als wagte Wald und Felsengrund!
Und doch stürzt, liebevoll im Sausen,
Die Wasserfülle sich zum Schlund,
Berufen gleich das Tal zu wässern;
Der Blitz, der flammend niederschlug,

As chasms at my feet descending
Burden the chasms more profound,
As a thousand radiant streams are wending
To foaming cataracts' awesome bound,
As, by its own strong impulse driven,
The tree mounts upward, straight and tall,
So to Almighty Love 'tis Given
To fashion all, to cherish all.
All round me is a savage roaring
As if swayed wood and rocky steep;
Yet plunges, lovely in its pouring,
The wealth of water to the deep,
Summoned below, the vale to brighten,
The bolt that fell with sudden flare,

Die Atmosphäre zu verbessern,	The atmosphere to cleanse and lighten
Die Gift und Dunst im Busen trug:	Which in its bosom poison bare,
Sind Liebesboten! sie verkünden	Heralds of love are they, proclaiming
Was ewig schaffend uns umwallt.	Creative powers that us enfold.
Mein Inn'res mög' es auch entzünden	May they, my inner self inflaming,
Wo sich der Geist, verworren, kalt,	Quicken my soul confused and cold,
Verquält in dumpfer Sinne Schranken,	Its blunted senses galled unceasing.
Scharf angeschloss'nem Kettenschmerz.	Bound fast in chains that cramp and smart.
O Gott! beschwichtige die Gedanken,	O God! these thoughts of mine appeasing,
Erleuchte mein bedürftig Herz.	Illumine Thou my needy heart!

CHORUS OF ANGELS:
(Soaring in the higher atmosphere, bearing the immortal part of Faust).

Gerettet ist das edle Glied	Lo! rescued is this noble one
Der Geisterwelt vom Bösen:	From evil machination;
Wer immer strebend sich bemüht	Who e'er aspiring, struggles on,
Den können wir erlösen.	For him there is salvation.
Und hat an ihm die Liebe gar	And if to him Celestial Love
Von oben teilgenommen,	Its favouring grace has given,
Begegnet ihm die selige Schar	The Blessed Host comes from Above
Mit herzlichem Willkommen.	And welcomes him to Heaven.

CHOIR OF BLESSED BOYS:
[*Together with the Chorus of Angels*]

Hände verschlinget	Hand in hand clinging,
Freudig zum Ringverein,	In a glad ring unite,
Regt euch und singet	Soaring and singing,
Heil'ge Gefühle drein:	Feeling a pure delight.
Göttlich belehret	Godlike the yearning,
Dürft ihr vertreun,	Confident be;
Den ihr verehret	For whom ye're yearning,
Werdet ihr schaun.	Him shall ye see.

CHORUS OF YOUNGER ANGELS:

Jene Rosen, aus den Händen	Roses sainted women spended,
Liebend-heiliger Büsserinnen,	Penitent through mercy glorious,
Halfen uns den Sieg gewinnen,	Helped to make the fight victorious,
Und das hohe Werk vollenden,	That the lofty work be ended,

Diesen Seelenschatz erbeuten.
Böse wichen, als wir streuten,
Teufel flohen als wir trafen
Statt gewohnter Höllenstrafen
Fühlten Liebesqual die Geister;
Selbst der alte Satans-Meister
War von spitzer Pein durchdrungen
Jauchzet auf! Es ist gelungen.

That be won this spirit-treasure.
Demons shrank in sore displeasure,
Devils fled the roses' flinging.
Not with wonted hell-pangs stinging,
Love-pangs brought them to disaster.
Even the old Satan-Master
By sharp pain was penetrated.
Shout with joy! It's consummated!

THE MORE PERFECT ANGELS:

Uns bleibt ein Erdenrest
Zu tragen peinlich,
Un wär' er von Asbest
Er ist nicht reinlich.
Wenn starke Geisteskraft
Die Elemente
An sich herangerafft,
Kein Engel trennte
Geeinte Zwienatur
Der innigen Beiden:
Die ewige Liebe nur
Vermag's zu scheiden.

Still earthly rests remain
Which have oppressed us;
They'd not be pure of stain,
Though of asbestos.
When every element
Strong spirit-forces
Have borne away and blent,
No angel divorces
The natures two in one,
So close they weave them;
Eternal Love alone
Can ever cleave them.

THE YOUNGER ANGELS:

Nebelnd um Felsenhöh'
Spür' ich soeben,
Regend sich in der näh',
Ein Geisterleben.
Die Wölkchen werden klar:
Ich seh' bewegte Schar
Seliger Knaben,
Los von der Erde Druck,
Im Kreis gesellt,
Die sicherlaben
Am neuen Lenz und Schmuck
Der obern Welt.
Sei er zum Anbeginn,
Steigendem Vollgewinn
Diesen gesellt!

Mist-like round yonder height,
I'm just discovering
Where in approaching flight
Spirit-life's hovering.
The clouds are growing clear,
I see a host draw near
Of Blessed Boys,
Freed from the stress of earth,
Circling, united!
They taste the joys
Of spring in their new birth,
Therein delighted.
Let him at once begin
Perfected joy to win,
With these united!

THE BLESSED BOYS:

Freudig empfangen wir
Diesen im Puppenstand;
Also erlangen wir
Englisches Unterpfand.
Löset die Flocken los
Die ihn umgeben!
Schon ist er schön und gross
Von heiligem Leben.

Glad we're receiving now
Him as a chrysalis,
Thereby achieving now
Pledge of angelic bliss.
Loosen all earthly flakes
That cling around him;
Fair and great now he wakes,
Divine life has crowned him.

DOCTOR MARIANUS:
(in the highest, cleanest cell)

Hier ist die Aussicht frei,
Der Geist erhoben.
Dort ziehen Frau'n vorbei,
Schwebend nach oben.
Die Herrliche mitteninn',
Im Sternenkranze,
Die Himmelskönigin,
Ich seh's am Glanze.
Höchste Herrscherin der Welt
Lasse mich im blauen
Ausgespannten Himmelszelt
Dein Geheimnis schauen!
Billige, was des Mannes Brust
Ernst und zart beweget
Und mit heiliger Liebeslust
Dir entgegen träget.

Here is the outlook free,
The soul uplifting.
Women I yonder see,
Heavenward drifting,
And glorious, midway seen,
Star-crowned, yet tender,
Heaven's own lofty Queen!
It is Her splendor.
Highest mistress of the world,
Let me, of Thy pleasure,
See Thy mystery unfurled
In the vaulted azure.
Look with grace on what doth move
Human hearts to greet Thee
And with holy bliss of love
Bears them up to meet Thee.

Unbezwinglich unser Mut,
Wenn du hehr gebietest;
Plötzlich mildert sich die Glut,
Wie du uns befriedest.
Jungfrau, rein im schönsten Sinn,
Mutter, Ehren würdig,
Uns erwählte Königin,
Göttern ebenbürtig.

All invincible we feel
When supreme Thou willest,
Swiftly tempered is our zeal
When its glow Thou stillest.
Virgin, pure in fairest sense,
Mother sweet, supernal,
Chosen Queen of our defense,
Peer of gods eternal!

CHORUS:

Dir, der Unberührbaren,
Ist es nicht benommen,
Dass die leicht Verführbaren
Traulich zu dir kommen.

O Thou of immaculate ray,
From Thee 'tis not taken
That those lightly led astray
Come with trust unshaken.

In die Schwachheit hingerafft	Rapt away, to weakness prone,
Sind sie schwer zu retten;	It is hard to save them.
Wer zerreisst aus eigner Kraft	Who by their own strength alone
Der Gelüste Ketten?	Rend the lusts that slave them?
Wie entgleitet schnell der Fuss	Whose foot does not slip awhile
Schiefem, glattem Boden!	On steep, slippery places?

CHORUS OF PENITENT WOMEN:

Du schwebst zu Höhen	To heights art soaring
Der ewigen Reiche,	Of realms eternal,
Vernimm das Flehen,	Hear our imploring,
Du Ohnegleiche,	Matchless, Maternal,
Du Gnadenreiche!	Of grace supernal!

MAGNA PECCATRIX:
(Mary Magdalen) [ST. LUKE VII:36]

Bei der Liebe, die den Füssen	By the love that ever glowing
Deines gottverklärten Sohnes	For Thy Son, the Heaven-born,
Tränen liess zum Balsam fliessen,	Shed warm tears to balsam flowing
Trotz des Pharisäer-Hohnes;	Spite of Pharisaic scorn;
Beim Gefässe, das so reichlich	By the box whose ointment precious
Tropfte Wohlgeruch hernieder,	Dropped its perfume rare and sweet;
Bei den Locken, die so weichlich	By the locks whose gentle meshes
Trockneten die heilgen Glieder	Dried the Savior's holy feet

MULIER SAMARITANA:
(Samaritan Woman)

Bei dem Bronn zu dem schon weiland	By the well to which were driven
Abram liess die Herde führen,	Abram's herds in days of yore;
Bei dem Eimer, der dem Heiland	By the pitcher once 'twas given
Kühl die Lippe durft' berühren;	Our dear Savior to restore;
Bei der reinen reichen Quelle,	By the spring, rich and supernal,
Die nun dorther sich ergiesset,	Whence flow waters far and wide,
Ueberflussig, ewig helle,	Overflowing, bright, eternal,
Rings durch alle Welten fliesset—	Pouring through the worlds their tide

MARIA AEGYPTIACA:
(Mary of Egypt)

Bei dem hochgeweihten Orte	By the sacred place where mortals
Wo den Herrn man niederliess,	Our dear Master's body laid;
Bei dem Arm der von der Pforte	By the arm which at the portals

Warnend mich zurücke stiess;	Warningly my entrance stayed;
Bei der vierzigjährigen Busse	By the forty years' repentance
Der ich treu in Wüsten blieb;	Truly passed in desert-land;
Bei dem seligen Scheidegrusse	By the blessed farewell sentence
Den im Sand ich niederschrieb	That I wrote upon the sand

ALL THREE:

Die du grossen Sünderinnen	Thou who women greatly sinning
Deine Nähe nicht verweigerst	Grantest to come nigh to Thee,
Und ein büssendes Gewinnin	By sincere repentance winning
In die Ewigkeiten steigerst,	Bliss through all eternity,
Gönn' auch dieser guten Seele,	Grant to this good soul Thy blessing,
Die sich einmal nur vergessen,	Who but once herself forgot,
Die nicht ahnte, dass sie fehle	Who knew not she was transgressing,
Dein Verzeihen angemessen!	Pardon meet refuse Thou not!

UNA POENITENTIUM:
(formerly named Gretchen, drawing closer)

Neige, neige,	Bend, oh bend now,
Du Ohnegleiche,	Matchless, attend Thou,
Du Strahlenreiche,	Thy radiance spend now,
Dein Antlitz gnädig meinem Glück!	Look on my bliss in charity.
Der früh Geliebte,	My early lover,
Nicht mehr Getrübte	His troubles over,
Er kommt zurück.	Comes back to me.

THE BLESSED BOYS:

Er überwächst uns schon	Mighty of Limb, he towers
An mächtigen Gliedern,	Already above us;
Wird treuer Pflege Lohn	Soon for this care of ours
Reichlich erwidern.	Richly he'll love us.
Wir wurden früh entfernt	Early were we removed,
Von Lebechören;	Life did not reach us,
Doch dieser hat gelernt,	But he has learned and loved
Er wird uns lehren.	And he will teach us.

UNA POENITENTIUM:
(formerly named Gretchen)

Vom edlen Geisterchor umgeben,	Girt by the noble choir of Heaven,
Wird sich der Neue kaum gewahr,	Himself the new-come scarcely knows,
Er ahnet kaum das frische Leben,	Scarce feels the fresh life newly given
So gleicht er schon der heiligen Schar.	Ere like the holy throng he grows;
Sieh, wie er jedem Erdenbande	See! how each earthly bond he's riven,
Der alten Hülle sich entrafft,	From that old vesture freed at length,
Und aus ätherischem Gewande	Now in ethereal garb of Heaven

Hervortritt erste Jugendkraft.	Appears his pristine, youthful strength,
Vergönne mir ihn zu belehren,	Oh, grant that I may now instruct him,
Noch blendet ihn der neue Tag!	Since blinds him still the newborn day.

MATER GLORIOSA:

Komm! Hebe dich zu höhern Sphären!	Come, rise to higher spheres! Conduct him!
Wenn er dich ahnet, folgt er nach.	If he feels thee, he'll go thy way.

DOCTOR MARIANUS:

Blicket auf zum Retterblick,	Penitents, look up, elate,
Alle reuig Zarten,	Where ye see salvation;
Euch zu seligem Geschik	Grateful, to your blessed fate
Dankend umzuarten!	Grow through re-creation.
Werde jeder bess're Sinn	May each better sense be keen
Dir zum Dienst erbötig;	In Thy service precious;
Jungfrau, Mutter, Königin,	O Thou Virgin, Mother, Queen,
Göttin, bleibe gnädig!	Goddess, be Thou gracious!

CHORUS MYSTICUS:

Alles Vergängliche	All earth comprises
Ist nur ein Gleichnis;	Is symbol alone;
Das Unzulängliche,	What there ne'er suffices
Hier wird's Ereignis;	As fact here is known;
Das Unbeschreibliche	All past the humanly
Hier ist's getan;	Wrought here in love;
Das Ewig-Weibliche	The Eternal-Womanly
Zieht uns hinan.	Draws us above.**

SYMPHONY NO. 9, D MAJOR

Mahler composed his Ninth Symphony during his first season as conductor of the New York Philharmonic. The last symphony he was to complete, it reflects the complex emotions of an artist who was morbidly aware that he had little time to live, that he was, probably, killing himself with work.

In 1907, after Mahler's resignation as General Music Director of the Vienna Opera, his physician diagnosed a serious heart ailment. The diagnosis was confirmed by a second specialist. Both men warned Mahler that he would have to change his entire strenuous style of life, avoiding all strain, even the

---

** *English translation of excerpt from Goethe's* Faust *by George Madison Priest. Copyright 1941 by Alfred A. Knopf, New York. Reprinted by permission.*

long country walks he loved. But Mahler was temperamentally unable to follow such counsel. He accepted an invitation to be principal conductor of the Metropolitan Opera for the following season; in the fall of 1909 he added to the Metropolitan the direction of the New York Philharmonic and worked simultaneously on his gigantic Ninth, which he completed on April 1, 1910. As he had been told, the strain was too great. Before the end of his second Philharmonic season Mahler collapsed. He conducted his last concert on February 21, 1911, and was taken back to Vienna to die.

The works of Mahler's New York years: *Das Lied von der Erde,* The Ninth Symphony, and the unfinished Tenth, are obsessed with the mood of farewell, not only in the music but in the words that abound in the sketches. Long before Mahler's final illness, such a sensitive friend as Alban Berg felt the power of this mood in the Ninth Symphony. Six months before Mahler was stricken, Berg was permitted to study the score of the first movement. He was overwhelmed. He wrote to his future wife: "Once again I have played through the score of Mahler's Ninth Symphony: The first movement is the most heavenly thing Mahler ever wrote. It is the expression of an exceptional fondness for this earth, the longing to live in peace on it, to enjoy nature to its depths—before death comes. For he comes irresistibly. The whole movement is permeated by premonitions of death. Again and again it crops up, all the elements of terrestrial dreaming culminate in it . . . most potently of course in the colossal passage where this premonition becomes certainty, where in the midst of the *höcheste Kraft* ["utmost intensity"] of almost painful joy in life [at the climax of the movement, about two thirds of the way through]. Death itself is announced *mit höchster Gewalt* ["with the utmost violence"] . . . ."

Bruno Walter, the devoted friend and disciple of Mahler, wrote (in his book, *Gustav Mahler*): "*Der Abschied* ("The Farewell") might have been used as the title of the Ninth Symphony. Born of the same mood, but without musical connection with *Das Lied von der Erde* . . . the first movement grew to be a tragically moving and noble epitome of the farewell feeling. A unique soaring between farewell sadness and a vision of Heavenly Light . . . lifts the movement into an atmosphere of celestial bliss."

But the Ninth Symphony is more. Its poignance is compounded by Mahler's awareness of his *historical* position at the end of a great line of Romantic composers. He speaks the tortured, introspective, sensitive, oversubtle language of a man who is perhaps too conscious of the great tradition he must carry on but which he knows is dying. His mood is related to that of his friend and contemporary, Pfitzner, in the latter's opera *Palestrina.* The composer feels that the entire tradition, the works of the past he has loved, the values by which he has lived, even the sensitivity to perceive these things—all are sliding with him irretrievably into oblivion. It is a Romantic obsession with dissolution and Death as strong in its way as in Wagner's *Tristan.*

Like the old German woodcuts and engravings called *Totentänze,* or, "Dances of Death," with a grinning skeleton in a hundred friendly and unfriendly guises, the four movements of this Symphony might easily be interpreted as a vast fourfold *Totentanz.* Death as a liberator, Death as fiddler for the dance, Death as the opponent in battle and finally, Death, as the consoling friend.

The movements are not traditional in either form, tempo or key relations. The first and last movements are slow, with two quick movements between. Each movement is in a different key: D major, C major, A minor and the *finale* in the remote key of D flat.

I. *Andante comodo.* The first movement begins very softly with a syncopated three note rhythm in the bottom of the orchestra (cellos and horn), a rhythm to which Mahler attached special importance, since he brings it back *fff* "with the utmost violence" at the climax of the movement, the passage which Berg called "Death itself."

After a delay of six measures the principal melody makes its first timid appearance in the second violins:

This melody appears and reappears in a dozen different guises. Soon its first two descending notes are extended to three and developed in a way to recall the central musical thought of Beethoven's "*Lebewohl*" ("Farewell") Sonata for Piano, Opus 81a:

Alone, three descending notes might recall nothing more mystical than "Three Blind Mice." But Mahler's treatment of them in the following passage:

which clashes dissonantly with another fragment of the same figure, is so close to Beethoven's similarly dissonant treatment that it can hardly have been accidental. The melancholy associations of Mahler's principal theme are further borne out by the orchestral sketch, where the return of the melody in almost its original form is taken very tenderly by a solo horn. At this point the sketch is labeled: "O vanished days of youth, O scattered love . . ." Finally the movement dies away with ever slower and softer reiterations of the melody's first two notes.

II. *Im Tempo eines gemächlichen Ländlers. Etwas täppisch und sehr derb.* The principal theme announced by clarinets and bassoon has the character of a peasant *Ländler.* But it is, of course, the "Farewell" *("Lebewohl")* theme of the first movement in a rhythmic transformation to make it sound like a dance:

The middle of the movement brings a melody for the horn which also derives from the principal melody of the first movement. There is a return to the opening material, but the dance mood palls. "A tragic undertone sounds in the joy," wrote Bruno Walter, "and one feels that 'the dance is over.' "

III. *Rondo. Burleske: Allegro assai. Sehr trotzig.* Mahler's sketch for this movement bears the title *Meinen Brüdern in Apoll* ("To My Brothers in Apollo"). It is a wild, defiant, grotesque movement, often bitterly humorous. Toward the end it becomes a contrapuntal maelstrom of many themes and there is a frenzied, *presto* coda.

IV. *Molto adagio.* In the last movement, as Bruno Walter heard it, Mahler "peacefully bids farewell to the world." It opens with a broadly flowing melody in which the violins are soon joined by the remaining strings. The Italianate melodic "turn" plays an important part in this melody and its development, which is the thematic basis of the whole movement. The poignant conclusion, with its increasingly diaphonous fragments of the melody, fades to an almost inaudible quadruple *pppp* marked *ersterbend* ("dying away"), "like the melting of a cloud into the etheral blue," as Walter had it.

The Symphony was first performed thirteen months after Mahler's death. Bruno Walter conducted. The score calls for piccolo, 4 flutes, 4 oboes, English horn, E-flat clarinet, 3 clarinets in A or B flat, bass clarinet, 4 bassoons, contrabassoon, 4 horns, 3 trumpets, 3 trombones, bass tuba, kettledrums, bass drum, snare drum, glockenspiel, triangle, cymbals, 2 harps, and the usual strings.

SYMPHONY NO. 10, F-SHARP MAJOR

A special aura has always surrounded the last, unfinished works of great artists. Whether we see the rough marble of Michelangelo's ghostly last *Pietà*, chipped and chiseled up to six days before his death, or we read the wisps of unfinished dialogue in Büchner's lacerating *Woyzeck* tragedy; whether we hear the *Missa pro defunctis* that Mozart strove so desperately to complete on his deathbed, or we are shaken by the sudden silence at the culmination of Bach's monumental *Kunst der Fuge,* where the master put down his pen—these fragments have something powerful in common. It is as if the proximity of death conferred on each artist a special intensity, a special vitality of expression. In a way, the unpolished marble, the interrupted words, the melody arrested in mid-flight—all seem more alive than if the artist had lived to complete his task.

Mahler's Tenth Symphony is such an unfinished work. As early as 1907, following Mahler's resignation as General Music Director of the Vienna Opera, his Viennese physician had diagnosed a serious heart ailment, which was confirmed by a second specialist.

During the summer of 1910 he undertook his Tenth Symphony in full knowledge that he did not have long to live. His emotions overwhelmed him. Like a true Romantic, Mahler had always been drawn to sorrow, to the mood of leavetaking, to the symbol of death that lurks behind farewells. Now, as his own death drew near it became almost impossible to distinguish between the anguish of leavetaking from his art and from his beloved wife, from the beauties of nature and from life itself.

The sketches for the Tenth Symphony are strewn with agonized marginal exclamations and exhortations. "Have mercy! Oh, Lord! Why hast thou forsaken me? Thy will be done . . ." In these pages he often addressed his wife as "my lyre." The outline of the finale ends with the words: "Almschi, to live for you, to die for you. . . ."

As his doctors had foretold, Mahler was not equal to the continued strain. Before the end of his second season with the New York Philharmonic he collapsed during a rehearsal. It was February 11, 1911. He insisted, nevertheless, on conducting the concert. By the time he took medical counsel it was too late. None of the doctors consulted in New York, Paris, and finally in Vienna, was able to help. On May 18, six days after his arrival in Vienna, he died.

After Mahler's death it was long assumed that only the first movement of the Tenth was anywhere near complete. Even that was clearly not complete in all details. During the ensuing half-century additional sketches came to light. Many musicians have tried their hands at completing sections of the score. At least four versions of the Symphony have been published, including a facsimile of the principal autograph source. The printed editions range from the "completion" by Deryck Cook of all five projected movements, to the 1964 edition of the first movement alone, by Erwin Ratz, within the framework of the scholarly complete edition issued by the Internationale Gustav Mahler Gesellschaft of Vienna printed by Universal Edition.

The Ratz edition embodies as precisely as possible only what Mahler actually put on paper. It conscientiously avoids any additional interpretive details, leaving these performance essentials to individual conductors and students.

I. *Andante; Adagio.* The first movement opens with a long, somber solo for the viola section unaccompanied. This introductory melody serves as a unifying "motto" theme for the entire Symphony. It returns in Mahler's sketches for his *Finale* but also at key points in the first movement. This leads directly to the soaring principal theme in which the first violins span a range of two full octaves:*

This and the following musical examples from this composition are copyright 1966 by Associated Music Publishers, Inc. Used by permission.

The somber motto melody returns briefly before the orchestra develops the principal theme quoted above.

There is a broad climax with a majestic, hymnlike passage for brass embellished with great splashes of harp and string-section arpeggios. The peak is a piercingly dissonant chord for the entire orchestra hurled, so to speak, against a sustained high note of the trumpet. The coda subsides to an almost lyric calm with fragments of the principal melodies dying away to silence.

The Ratz edition of this first movement calls for piccolo, 3 flutes, 3 oboes, 3 clarinets, 3 bassoons, 4 horns, 4 trumpets, 3 trombones, tuba, harp, and the traditional string choir.

During the half century following Mahler's death copious additional sketches for the Tenth Symphony were discovered. Finally, with the blessing of Mahler's widow Alma, who contributed materials from her own collection, Deryck Cooke undertook a reconstruction of the entire five-movement Symphony. Mr. Cooke has described his source materials as follows:

> When Mahler died, in 1911, he left behind a manuscript labeled "Tenth Symphony." This does not consist, as many assume, of fragmentary sketches; there are some preparatory sketch-pages, but the significant bulk is a comprehensive full-length draft of a five-movement symphony. As far as it has come to light—a few pages may still be in private hands—it consists of the following:
>
> (1) Adagio: full score (31 pages); short score and sketches (22 pages).
> (2) Scherzo: full score (39 pages); short score and sketches (23 pages).
> (3) 'Purgatorio': short score (3 pages); one sketch-page; 2 pages of full score.
> (4) (Untitled movement): short score (12 pages); sketches (12 pages); no full score.
> (5) Finale: short score (10 pages); sketches (5 pages); no full score. [. . .]
>
> The first movement's opening theme for unison violas acts as a "motto" for the whole work; and this, together with the same movement's extraordinarily violent climax, returns dramatically at the climax of the finale, in the traditional "cyclic" way. Finally, the symphony's proportions are symmetrical, as in the Seventh: the two outer movements last about twice as long as the two scherzos which they enclose, and these last about twice as long as the brief central movement. Thus to alter the sequence would destroy the work's tonal perspective, thematic argument, and structural symmetry.

I. *Andante; Adagio.* This opening movement is Mahler's own completed full score, with only tiny retouchings of instrumentation where Mr. Cooke felt it "clearly necessary."

II. *Scherzo I: Schnelle Vierteln. Gemächliches Ländlertempo.* This Scherzo recalls in gentler guise the grotesque humor of many an earlier Mahler scherzo. The first "trio" section is based on a dance-like transformation of the principal theme of the preceding movement:

III. *Allegretto moderato.* In Mahler's manuscript the title of this movement is *Purgatorio.* Mr. Cooke thinks it likely that Mahler would have eventually eliminated this, as he did some earlier works' programmatic titles. This is the shortest movement of the Symphony. For the most part it is gentle, its basic mood being set by the ghostly timbre of muted strings. Over its one outbreak of passion Mahler wrote, "Oh, Lord, why hast thou forsaken me?"

IV. *Scherzo II: Allegro pesante; Tempo di valse.* On the title page of this movement Mahler wrote: "The Devil dances it with me." The music quotes the outbreak from the preceding movement and a phrase from *Das Lied von der Erde* referring to the vanity of human hopes. It was at the end of this movement that Mahler appended his "Farewell, my lyre."

V. *Finale: Lento non troppo; Allegro moderato; Tempo primo.* The blackest orchestral color: the heavy tones of tuba and the muffled thud of a bass drum dominate the opening pages of this *Finale,* which works its way through a development section of struggle to a conclusion of peace and transfiguration. Some of the most prominent thematic material is taken from the pessimistic *Purgatorio.* There is a tremendous climax recalling the dissonant peak of the first movement. The opening motto melody of the violas is brought back. At the end of the serene closing pages Mahler once again addressed his wife: "Almschi, to live for you, to die for you."

The world premiere of Deryck Cooke's performing version of the Mahler Tenth was presented, with the approval of Alma Maria Mahler, by the London Symphony Orchestra at a London Promenade Concert of August 13, 1964, under the direction of Berthold Goldschmidt, who had also advised Mr. Cooke in preparing the score. The first performance in the United States was given by the Philadelphia Orchestra under Eugene Ormandy on November 5, 1965.

Felix Mendelssohn

Born February 3, 1809, Hamburg—died November 4, 1847, Leipzig

CONCERTO FOR PIANO AND ORCHESTRA, NO. 1, G MINOR, OPUS 25

On his way to Italy in June 1830, the twenty-one-year-old Mendelssohn stopped off in Munich. He was warmly welcomed in high social and musical circles. It was here that he met Delphine von Schauroth. Delphine was not only an unusually gifted pianist, she was attractive, beautiful, and came from a wealthy family. Felix was drawn to her and it was for her that he composed the G-minor Concerto.

He sketched the Concerto the following November in Rome and completed it in October of the following year, upon his return to Munich. It was first performed with the composer as soloist at a big benefit for the poor of Munich on October 17, 1831, in the old Odeon concert hall, which still stood in Munich up to World War II. Felix had been obliged to postpone his concert one week because the original date had conflicted with the Munich *Oktoberfest,* which he described in great detail and with relish in a letter to his father.

The day after the concert Felix wrote home that it had turned out to be

> more brilliant and more fun than I had expected. The whole thing was very animated and everything worked. The orchestra played wonderfully and the poor must have received a good whopping sum.
>
> In the evening [of the concert] when I arrived and heard the noise of all the carriages I began to take pleasure in the whole business. At half-past six the court arrived; I took my little English baton and conducted my Symphony [No. 1 in C minor]. The orchestra played superbly, with love and with fire, such as I have never heard any orchestra play under my direction: the fortes were all like a thunder clap and the *Scherzo* was very delicate and light. The audience was very pleased and the King [Ludwig] led the applause. [There followed an aria from Weber's *Euryanthe,* which was encored.] Then I came to my Concerto and was applauded long and loud. The orchestra accompanied well and the work itself was really mad: the audience really liked it. They applauded to make me come out and take a bow, which is the custom here, but I was too modest and didn't. During the intermission the King caught me by the arm, praised me highly and inquired about everything under the sun, and whether I was related to Bartholdy whom he often visits in Rome, since Bartholdy's house there was the cradle of modern art, etc.

The King seems also to have taken a more intimate interest in Mendelssohn, as we discover from a "suppressed" letter from Felix to his father, quoted by Eric Werner, his biographer:

> The main thing that the King said to me, though, was that I should marry Fräulein von Schauroth; that would be an excellent match, and why didn't I

> want to do it? That, from a king, annoyed me, and somewhat piqued, I was going to answer him, when he, not even waiting for my answer, jumped to a different subject and then to a third. . . .

The flirtation with Delphine had by now developed into a much-discussed romance; but Felix probably had not seriously considered marriage, his family was opposed, and the romance dwindled.

The G-minor Piano Concerto is in three movements which are performed without interruption.

I. *Molto allegro, con fuoco.* Mendelssohn omits the traditional orchestral exposition of the principal themes. Instead, a swift orchestral *crescendo* introduces the soloist with a burst of *bravura*: double octaves, crashing chords, and swirling scales constitute the fiery first-theme group. A tranquil, lyric second theme is also given to the pianist. The brief development and reprise of the basic themes are linked to the following movement by a bridge passage for horns and trumpets.

II. *Andante.* Cellos sing the chief melody of the songful middle movement:

The pianist then takes up the melody to embellish it with airy arpeggios, scales, and sighing appoggiaturas. Brass fanfares derived from the link between the first and second movements lead without pause into the finale.

III. *Presto; Molto allegro e vivace.* The *presto* introduction is a piece of glittering virtuosity. The principal refrain, introduced by the piano, consists of a wavelike downward swoop followed by an equally exciting climb to the crest of the next phrase:

The G-minor Concerto is scored for Mendelssohn's standard orchestra of 2 flutes, 2 oboes, 2 clarinets, 2 bassoons, 2 horns, 2 trumpets, kettledrums and strings.

CONCERTO FOR VIOLIN AND ORCHESTRA, E MINOR, OPUS 64

"I would like to write you a violin concerto for next winter," wrote Mendelssohn to his old friend Ferdinand David in July 1838. "One in E minor keeps running through my head, and the opening gives me no peace."

Like many another great composer, Mendelssohn had a specific performer in mind when he wrote his Concerto, and he consulted him frequently. Mendelssohn and David had felt immediate respect and liking for each other from their very first encounter, when David was a fifteen-year-old touring virtuoso and Mendelssohn, one year his senior. One of the leading violin virtuosos of the day, Ferdinand David was much admired by other musicians including Mendelssohn's friend Robert Schumann. David seems to have combined the serious, relatively Classical restraint of Ludwig Spohr, his teacher, with the elegance of French tradition, and a technical brilliance which had been introduced by the demonic Paganini. David's eclectic style, coupled with musical idealism and a certain pedagogical turn of mind, paralleled Mendelssohn's own attitude toward music.

In 1835 Mendelssohn was appointed director of the Gewandhaus concerts in Leipzig; he saw to it that David was engaged as concertmaster. Later Mendelssohn was instrumental in having David appointed head of the violin department at the Leipzig Conservatory. Among the many fruits of their long and happy collaboration was the Violin Concerto.

The same letter of July 1838 in which Mendelssohn first mentions the violin concerto-to-be shows clearly how he felt about his soloist and concertmaster:

> . . . I realized that there are really not many musicians who pursue such a broad, straight road in art as undeviatingly as you do, or in whose active course I could feel the same intense delight that I do in yours. Such things are seldom said face to face, so let me write today how much your rapid and gratifying development during the last few years has surprised and rejoiced me. It is sometimes discouraging to see so many with the noblest aspirations but inferior talents, and others with great talents yet low tendencies; so that to see real talent with right determination is doubly cheering. . . . As I said, therefore, the very thought of your character rejoices me, and may heaven permit us to succeed more and more in expressing our wishes and our inmost thoughts, and in holding fast all that is dear and sacred in art, so that it shall not perish! . . .

A year passed. Evidently David prodded the composer. During his 1839 summer absence from Leipzig, Mendelssohn replied:

> It is nice of you to press me for a violin concerto! I have the liveliest desire to write one for you, and if I have a few propitious days, I'll bring you something. But the task is not an easy one. You ask that it should be brilliant, and how can anyone like me do this? The whole of the first solo is to be for the E string.

As soon as David saw the partially completed score, he declared, "This is going to be something great!"

"Do you think so?" parried Mendelssohn.

"I'm sure of it," was David's reply. "There is plenty of music for violin and orchestra, but there has been only one big, truly great concerto [meaning the Beethoven Violin Concerto] and now there will be two."

Mendelssohn objected. "No, no! If I finish this concerto it will certainly not be with any thought of competing with Beethoven." And Mendelssohn was as good as his word. The Concerto which was completed seven years after his first reference to it, copied neither spirit nor form of Beethoven's masterpiece.

We know that Mendelssohn continued to show the score to David, who gave advice freely. The composer took much time and pains revising and polishing, a fact which might be borne in mind by people who repeat the old cliché of Mendelssohn's effortless elegance. Even after the score was sent to the publisher in December 1844, still more changes followed. The relatively simple but enormously effective cadenza seems largely to have been David's responsibility. Often Mendelssohn has been thought a merely eclectic composer who accepted the Classical forms handed down to him, filling them with music of facility and charm. In the Violin Concerto he not only departed from many traditional features of the Classical concerto, but did so with such success that he influenced a whole century of composers in his wake.

David was, of course, the soloist at the first performance at the Gewandhaus on March 13, 1845. Mendelssohn was ill and unable to be present for the performance, which was conducted by the Danish composer Niels W. Gade.

I. *Allegro molto appassionato.* The very beginning was unconventional for its day. Instead of the Classical preamble for the orchestra, presenting the principal themes, the solo violin proclaims the passionate melody on which the first movement is built: a soaring line which, although it begins softly, makes an impression of great intensity:

It recalls both David's request for brilliance and Mendelssohn's remark that the entire first solo would be for the E string (the highest and most brilliant of the instrument). However, the solo continues with a sweep and melodic range which make it necessary to call on the deepest capacities of the violin.

A delightfully reticent yet effective touch is the introduction of the second theme. The solo violin seems to float downward from extreme height to the lowest note of which the instrument is capable. It sustains this note, while above it soft flutes and clarinets introduce a drooping little melodic figure with a touch of melancholy.

The solo cadenza, instead of coming as it traditionally had, at the close of the movement, is very effectively placed just before the reprise of the main theme. In fact, the violin is still spinning out the rapid arpeggios of its cadenza when the orchestra enters with the theme, so that we have the impression that the violin is accompanying the orchestra instead of the other way around.

II. *Andante.* The slow movement follows without pause. A single, quiet bassoon tone, held over from the final chord of the first movement, is joined by other instruments in half a dozen measures of transition leading to the violin solo, which in its simplicity and depth of feeling has an almost religious character. There is a more agitated middle section, after which the principal melody returns in the solo violin but with a different accompaniment.

III. *Allegretto non troppo; Allegro molto vivace.* The *finale,* which is also designed to follow without pause, has a short introduction recalling the middle theme of the preceding movement. Then the tempo quickens and after a fanfare-like rhythm for the winds and preliminary flourishes for the soloist, the violin launches into a delicate, dancing figure, which recalls the mood of the *Scherzo* from Mendelssohn's incidental music for *A Midsummer Night's Dream:*

Despite a vigorous interruption by the orchestra (which corresponds to the second theme of a sonata-allegro form) the dancing figure of the solo violin dominates the finale. In the central development section the soloist does introduce a more flowing, yearning melody, which later combines with and is swept away by the airy opening theme. The closing measures have irresistible melodic verve and rhythmic drive.

The Concerto is scored for 2 flutes, 2 oboes, 2 clarinets, 2 bassoons, 2 horns, 2 trumpets, kettledrums, and the traditional strings.

INCIDENTAL MUSIC FOR A MIDSUMMER NIGHT'S DREAM

I. OVERTURE
II. SCHERZO
III. INTERMEZZO
IV. NOCTURNE
V. WEDDING MARCH

Youthful miracles are seldom repeated. Mendelssohn was only seventeen when he composed his Overture to *A Midsummer Night's Dream* with miraculous deftness and delicacy, elfin imagination and humor. Yet near the end of his life Mendelssohn did match that miracle. He was invited to compose incidental music for a Berlin production of *Ein Sommernachtstraum,* and his youthful enthusiasm for Shakespeare surged back. With the most felicitous ease, he wove the early themes into new pieces, and new ideas flowed with the Romantic freshness, grace, and imagination of old.

The Overture was composed at the time when young Felix and his beloved sister Fanny were making their first acquaintance with Shakespeare in the famous Romantic German translations of Tieck and Schlegel, which are among the poetic masterpieces of German literature. In his enthusiasm Mendelssohn himself began to dream of composing music to companion Shakespeare's immortal comedy.

In a letter written from the family home in Berlin early in July 1826, and addressed to Fanny, Mendelssohn writes: "I have grown accustomed to composing in our garden; there I completed two piano pieces in A major and E minor. Today or tomorrow I am going to dream there the *A Midsummer Night's Dream.* This is, however, an enormous audacity. . . ." A few days later—on July 18—Felix wrote his sister an enthusiastic report of the first Berlin performance of Weber's *Oberon* Overture, and ended his letter with the words: "Ever since you left, my love for you goes in E minor"—a reference to the opening *Allegro* of *A Midsummer Night's Dream* Overture, which is in E minor.

Years later, when Mendelssohn was asked by the publishers Breitkopf and Härtel to recall the ideas that had suggested the thematic sequence of the Overture and had so fired his imagination, Mendelssohn wrote: ". . . It is impossible for me to outline for the [concert] program the sequence of ideas that gave rise to the composition, for just this sequence of ideas is my Overture. It follows the play closely, however, so that it may perhaps be very proper to indicate the outstanding situations of the drama in order that the audience may have Shakespeare in mind or form an idea of the piece. I think it should be enough to point out that the fairy rulers, Oberon and Titania, appear throughout the play with all their people. . . . At the end, after everything has been satisfactorily settled and the principal players have joyfully left the stage, the elves follow them, bless the house and disappear with the dawn. So the play ends, and my Overture too."

Mendelssohn's teacher, Adolph Bernhard Marx, has left us a rather detailed account of the growth of the Overture score, with understandable emphasis on the importance of the advice which Marx gave to the young genius and which Felix, after some initial pique, accepted enthusiastically. In any case, the entire composition of the Overture, including whatever revisions were made at Marx's instigation, took less than a month. According to Felix's letter to Fanny, he cannot have begun actual work on the score before July 7 and the original score, now in the Berlin State Library, bears August 6 as the date of completion.

A popular story, passed down to us by Mendelssohn's friend Ferdinand Hiller, according to which Mendelssohn told Hiller that he worked on the Overture for a whole year during his spare time between lectures at the university, cannot possibly be true, since Mendelssohn did not enter the university before Easter of 1827. By that time, as the Mendelssohn authority Eric Werner points out, the Overture was not only completed but had already been performed at least twice in public. The first public performance of the Overture was at a concert at Stettin, conducted by Carl Loewe, on February 20, 1827.

Mendelssohn was exactly twice seventeen when the King of Prussia invited him to compose incidental music for a Berlin production of *Ein Sommernachtstraum.* The man responsible for the royal command, the director of the new production, was Ludwig Tieck, co-translator of the Shakespeare text, and one of the most musical of German poets.

The first performance of the incidental music was part of the new dramatic production at the Neues Palais in Potsdam on October 14, 1843. Only the court and invited guests were admitted. And only after the success of the production was established beyond question, was it offered to the public-at-large in the Royal Theater in Berlin, usually with sold-out houses.

Although Shakespeare asked for copious use of music in his play, Mendelssohn and Tieck in their collaboration went much further. Not only did they supply music for Shakespeare's songs, Mendelssohn composed substantial entr'actes and long stretches of background music to Shakespeare's dialogue as well as dances, marches, fanfares, sometimes just a single note to lend atmosphere to a word or an action on the stage. In concert, however, one rarely hears more than the five standard numbers: Overture, Intermezzo, Nocturne, Scherzo, Wedding March.

I. *Overture.* Long before Mendelssohn dreamed of composing the other incidental music for the play, his Overture suggested many specific references to the action of the play.

Four gleaming chords of the woodwinds summon, in imagination, the fantastic creatures of Shakespeare's comedy. First we hear the fairy music whispered by the high violins alone. As the Overture develops, there are more references to the play including the bray of Bottom, who has been endowed with an ass's head, and a heavy stamping passage associated with the Bergomask danced by Bottom and the other rustics in the final scene:

The central development section is given over to fanciful evolution of the fairy music, which is also brought back with subtle changes in the concluding section. The four woodwind chords of the beginning round off the final page.

II. *Scherzo: Allegro Vivace.* This bit of orchestral magic, with its shimmering strings, its whispering, laughing woodwinds, and its echo of Bottom's bray taken over from the Overture, introduces the opening scene of Act II, a woodland dialogue between Puck and a fairy. The opening refrain of the *Scherzo* is pure quicksilver:

It returns, rondolike, throughout the *Scherzo* and at the rise of the curtain it dances in the background of Puck's opening words: "How now, spirit! wither wander you?" To which the fairy replies:

Over hill, over dale
    Thorough bush, thorough briar,
Over park, over pale
    Thorough flood, thorough fire,
I do wander everywhere
Swifter than the moon's sphere.

The famous flight of the solo flute at the end of the *Scherzo* is one of Mendelssohn's loveliest inspirations.

III. *Intermezzo: Allegro appassionato.* The *Intermezzo* follows the end of Act II in "A Wood in Athens," where two pairs of lovers are lost at night and on the verge of desperation because Puck has caused one of the men to fall in love with the wrong lady. As Hermia calls out to her lover: "Either death, or you, I'll find immediately," the orchestra plays the agitated music of the *Intermezzo.*

IV. *Nocturne: Con moto tranquillo.* At the close of Act III Puck has lulled the four distraught lovers into a magic sleep in the forest and the scene closes with Puck's incantation:

On the ground
Sleep sound: . . .
When thou wakest
Thou takest
True delight
In the sight
Of thy former lady's eye:
. . . and all shall be well.

The *Nocturne,* with the dreaming solo horn, evokes the magic slumbers of the lovers in the forest.

V. *Wedding March: Allegro vivace.* The gorgeous *Wedding March* introduces the wedding celebration of Theseus, duke of Athens and Hippolyta, queen of the Amazons, at the beginning of Act V. Its much-repeated theme is based on a feeling of joy and excitement that need no explanation:

Familiar as it is in church and concert hall, its regal splendor is particularly effective in the theater.

Mendelssohn's orchestra for *A Midsummer Night's Dream* calls for 2 flutes, 2 oboes, 2 clarinets, 2 bassoons, 2 horns, 3 trumpets, ophicleide, 3 trombones, kettledrums, triangle, cymbals and the traditional strings.

OVERTURE, THE HEBRIDES (FINGAL'S CAVE), OPUS 26

Mendelssohn's music was nourished by the widening scope of his travel impressions from Berlin to Naples, to Vienna, to Paris, to London, and north to the Hebrides. He was an illustrious young man of twenty when his trip to the Hebrides inspired this beautiful Overture.

Fingal's Cave, named for a hero of Scotch and Irish legend, is one of several spectacular caverns on the tiny island of Staffa, one of the Hebrides Islands off the west coast of Scotland. The name Staffa, an old Norse word for a staff or column, comes from a whole series of caves which have such striking natural colonnades of basalt that they seem man-made, albeit perhaps by some race of giants. The most famous of them, Fingal's Cave, is two hundred twenty-seven feet long, lined on one side by basalt pillars of warm red, maroon and brown, richly decorated with green and gold seaweeds and lichens, flecked here and there with a pure snow-white of lime that has filtered through the walls. From the roof of the cave hang yellow, crimson and white stalactites. When the sea is smooth, visitors can be rowed directly into the cave, where there is a constant murmuring sound of the waves, which has given it another Gallic name, meaning "the cave of music."

The poet Carl Klingemann, who made the expedition to the cave with Mendelssohn, recalled the experience two days later: "We were put out in boats, and climbed—the hissing sea close beside us—over the pillar stumps to the celebrated Fingal's Cave. A greener roar of waters surely never rushed into a stranger cavern—comparable on account of the many pillars, to the inside of an immense organ, black and resounding, lying there absolutely purposeless in the utter loneliness, the wide gray sea within and without."

Music immediately crystallized in Mendelssohn's imagination. On the day of his visit to the cave, August 7, 1829, he wrote his sister, Fanny: "In

HEBRIDES: ENTRANCE TO FINGAL'S CAVE.

A nineteenth-century Romantic view of scenes that influenced Mendelssohn's "Hebrides" Overture. (*Photo, R.P. Leitsch; courtesy, New York Public Library*)

order to have you understand how extraordinarily the Hebrides affected me, the following came to my mind there." And Mendelssohn quotes what became the opening of the Overture:

Mendelssohn took this theme and the wild Romantic impression all the way to Rome, where he finished the first version of the Overture in December 1830. But over a year later, he was still dissatisfied with his score. He wrote to his family from Paris on January 21, 1832: "I cannot present 'The Hebrides' here, because I do not consider it . . . ready. The D-major middle section is very silly. The whole so-called development tastes more of counterpoint than of whale-oil and seagulls and cod-liver oil, and it ought to be the other way around."

In the following weeks, he revised the score to his satisfaction, and its first performance was given from manuscript at a concert of the London Philharmonic Society in Covent Garden, May 14, 1832. Thomas Attwood conducted. Mendelssohn wrote: "It went splendidly, and sounded so droll amongst all the Rossini things." Yet he continued to revise the Overture. In an unpublished letter to his mother dated November 28, 1833 (quoted by Eric Werner in his biography of Mendelssohn), he says: "In the last days I have made the score of 'The Hebrides' ready for publication. The Overture became much better through *threefold revisions*. . . ." Later Mendelssohn presented the London Philharmonic Society with the manuscript. At the first performance it was called "The Isles of Fingal." In his letters, Mendelssohn refers to it both as "The Hebrides," and as "The Solitary Isle." The first published score was titled "Fingal's Cave," but the orchestral parts were entitled "The Hebrides." It has become customary to use both these last designations.

Mendelssohn's seascape opens with the theme quoted above, repeated many times, suggesting the murmuring of the waves within the cave. Other related figures grow out of this rhythm, until a second, longer melody makes its appearance in the cellos and bassoons, completing the foundation for a traditional sonata-allegro structure. It is in the development, which Mendelssohn revised, that the more agitated part of the seascape contains at least the hint of a storm. The seagulls of Mendelssohn's letter are easily imagined. There are two sharp climaxes, one just before the recapitulation of the opening themes, and the other just before the end. The closing measures themselves come as a surprise, with the sudden dying away to a *pianissimo* on the opening theme.

The Overture is scored for 2 flutes, 2 oboes, 2 clarinets, 2 bassoons, 2 horns, 2 trumpets, kettledrums and the traditional string choir.

OVERTURE TO RUY BLAS, OPUS 95

Victor Hugo's drama *Ruy Blas* was only one year old when the Leipzig Theatrical Pension Fund begged Mendelssohn to write an overture and song for a benefit production. Mendelssohn read the play, found it "beneath contempt," and declared he had no time to compose an overture. When the committee came to thank him for the song he had written, they regretted politely that he had not written an overture, but added that they were quite aware that time was necessary for such a work.

This, says Mendelssohn in a letter to his mother on March 18, 1839, put him on his mettle: "I reflected on the matter the same evening. On Wednesday there was a concert rehearsal, which occupied the whole forenoon; Thursday, the concert itself; yet the Overture was in the hands of the copyist early on Friday; played three times on Monday in the concert room, tried over once in the theater and given in the evening as an introduction to the odious play. Few of my works have caused me more amusing excitement."

Thus in about one full day's working time he tossed off the little masterpiece which he never thought much of, which was not published until after his death and which he jokingly said should be called the Overture "not to *Ruy Blas,* but to the Theatrical Pension Fund."

In Hugo's stirring but somewhat improbable plot, a Spanish grandee tries to disgrace the Queen of Spain by involving her in a love affair with his valet, Ruy Blas. Disguised as a Spanish nobleman, Ruy Blas does in fact become her lover and prime minister as well. But when his master tries to blackmail the Queen into abdicating, Ruy Blas kills his master, takes poison himself, confesses his guilt to the Queen and dies with her forgiveness. To French admirers the dramatic intensity and lyricism of Hugo's verse make *Ruy Blas* one of the greatest masterpieces of the Romantic theater. Swinburne said of it: "In command and in expression of passion and pathos, of noble and of evil nature, it equals any other work of this great dramatic poet; in the lifelike fusion of high comedy with deep tragedy it excells them all."

Why Mendelssohn detested it so is not clear. Perhaps he read a poor translation. In any case he composed as if he loved it. Perhaps the challenge lent wings to his fancy. There are a sweep and spontaneity in the melodic flow, an urgency in the march of the simple harmonies, a freshness and brilliance in his orchestration, which have made this one of his most popular works.

It opens with portentous chords for brass and winds suggestive of impending tragedy. Little wisps of string tone anticipate the principal theme which, when it arrives, seems wonderfully suited to the emotional turmoil of Romantic melodrama at its most melodramatic:

There are contrasting themes of a more optimistic, even brilliant nature, a stormy development, and conclusion on a note of affirmation, almost of triumph.

The Overture to *Ruy Blas* is scored for 2 flutes, 2 oboes, 2 clarinets, 2 bassoons, 4 horns, 2 trumpets, 3 trombones, kettledrums, and the standard strings.

SYMPHONY NO. 3, A MINOR, OPUS 56, THE SCOTCH

> We went, in the deep twilight, to the palace [of Holyrood] where Queen Mary lived and loved [wrote Mendelssohn from Edinburg on July 30, 1829]. There is a little room to be seen there, with a winding staircase leading up to it. That is where they went up and found Rizzio in the little room, dragged him out, and three chambers away is a dark corner where they killed him. The adjoining chapel is now roofless; grass and ivy grow abundantly in it; and before the ruined altar Mary was crowned Queen of Scotland. Everything around is broken and moldering, and the bright sky shines in. I believe I found the beginning of my Scotch Symphony there today.

That very day Mendelssohn jotted down the opening bars of the "Scotch" Symphony:

Mendelssohn worked on the Symphony during his Italian trip the following year. But it was not until January 20, 1842 that he finished the score in Berlin. He himself conducted the premiere performance from manuscript exactly six weeks later in the Leipzig Gewandhaus. It should be pointed out that the title "Scotch" is not official and did not appear on the first edition of the score, although Mendelssohn did repeatedly refer to it in his correspondence as his "Scotch" Symphony. It is cast in the traditional four movements, but Mendelssohn specifically directed that it should be performed continuously without pauses for applause.

I. *Andante con moto—Allegro un poco agitato.* The pensive introduction begins with the phrase that flashed into Mendelssohn's mind in the ruined chapel where Mary Queen of Scots was crowned. The first appearance of the phrase is a bleak A minor, with the melancholy color of violas and oboes. Later it is sung with more warmth by the cellos in major tonalities.

As we reach the agitated main section of the first movement, the first inspiration is transformed into a more agile and extended figure, allotted chiefly to the first violins. Even when we reach the new key of E minor where, in the fairly traditional form Mendelssohn follows, we might expect a contrasting theme, we hear instead another variant of his basic inspiration. In fact, the

The Chapel of Holyrood Palace.

"I believe I found the beginning of my Scotch Symphony there today," wrote Mendelssohn (July 30, 1829). The chapel shortly before Mendelssohn's visit, painted by Louis Daguerre. (*Courtesy, Walker Art Gallery, Liverpool*)

entire first movement is virtually dominated by this central theme and its derivatives. There is a stormy coda which momentarily recalls Wagner's *Flying Dutchman.* But since both works were being composed at the same time, neither composer can have copied the other and presumably such Romantic storm music was in the air. A brief recall of the Symphony's opening page supplies the link to the second movement that follows without pause.

II. *Vivace non troppo.* The *scherzo* has a vivacious principal theme clearly related to the basic thought of the first movement as quoted above but said to be derived from an old (pentatonic) bagpipe melody. It is announced by a solo clarinet over a whispering *tremolo* of violins and violas:

Like the first movement, the *scherzo* is cast in free yet clearly traditional sonata-allegro form.

III. *Adagio.* The slow movement is built around two principal ideas: the broadly flowing melody proclaimed at the outset by the first violins, and the more somber, foreboding chords of the winds in a persistent dotted rhythm.

IV. *Allegro vivacissimo.* The wild flourish of the violins with its cascading dotted rhythms which opens the *finale* suggests to many a listener, including this one, something Scotch. But we must beware. For Robert Schumann heard in it something Italian, possibly because he knew Mendelssohn was no friend of national idioms in music. Perhaps it sounds Scotch to us only because we know Mendelssohn called it "Scotch." There is a contrasting second theme which, like the theme of the *scherzo,* seems to be derived from the initial idea of the entire Symphony. It is presented here by a trio of solo clarinet and two oboes:

The Symphony is rounded off by a vigorous but majestic *coda* based on yet another transformation of Mendelssohn's central melodic thought.

The "Scotch" Symphony is scored for 2 flutes, 2 oboes, 2 clarinets, 2 bassoons, 4 horns, 2 trumpets, kettledrums, and the usual strings.

SYMPHONY NO. 4, A MAJOR, OPUS 90, ITALIAN

Posterity has never quite forgiven Felix Mendelssohn for being happy. His offense was compounded by his being rich—rich in funds, rich in friends, rich in family affection, rich in admirers. Worse yet, he left behind him the impression of having succeeded in everything without really trying. Even in his sentimental life he suffered none of the agonies or the flaming passions of Berlioz, Chopin, Liszt or Wagner; on the contrary, he was a model of bourgeois propriety. "What might he not have accomplished if he had been poor and less respectable?" lamented the late Philip Hale.

Let us not worry about Mendelssohn's accomplishment. The man who achieved such masterpieces as his Octet at sixteen, the Overture to *A Midsummer Night's Dream* at seventeen and the "Italian" Symphony at twenty-four, has made us rich too. Perhaps the time has even come to forgive him for being happy.

Felix was twenty-one when he set out for the land which inspired his Symphony No. 4. On his way south through Germany he hobnobbed with the great and the wealthy. In Weimar he had the privilege of spending two weeks in happy talks with the unapproachable grandee of German literature, Goethe. The poet was past eighty and was slowly putting the finishing touches on Part Two of his colossal *Faust.* He was revered as one of the towering figures of his country, almost more feared than loved. Yet he unbent to this twenty-one-year-old musician whom he had admired when Felix was a child prodigy. The two spent long, happy hours together, Mendelssohn playing and explaining music, and the older man perhaps recalling the Italy that he had known on his own famous trip so many years before.

In Munich, a friend wrote that it was "worth standing by, and watching how he is the darling of every house, the center of every circle. From early in the morning, everything concentrates on him." And so it went: from Munich to Vienna and over the mountains to Venice.

"This is Italy," he exulted in a letter of October 10, 1830. "What I have been looking forward to all my life as the greatest happiness is now begun, and I am basking in it." Later he recalled: "The whole country had such a festive air that I felt as if I were a young prince making his entry."

I. *Allegro vivace.* The brilliant woodwinds in the background of the opening phrase are like the sparkle of the Italian sunshine. Over everything we hear the exultant cry of the violins, like a call to adventure:

It seems to reflect the confidence and excitement of a young man on his way, on his own, to a promised land of new beauty. His own words, "I felt like a young prince," are the real key to this movement, which unfolds with a rush of enchanting detail as the Italian landscape unfolded before him. The movement is in traditional sonata-allegro form with a contrasting second theme: a gently rocking figure for a pair of clarinets in parallel thirds.

After four months in Rome, Mendelssohn wrote home to his sisters (on February 22, 1831): "The 'Italian' Symphony is making great progress. It will be the jolliest piece I have ever done, especially the last movement. For the slow movement I have not yet found anything, and I think I will keep that for Naples."

II. *Andante con moto.* The mock dolefulness of the woodwind chant and the plodding pizzicatos of the cellos and basses in this movement may have been suggested by a religious procession which we know Mendelssohn saw in the streets of Naples. Yet, Eric Werner has pointed out that the theme of this movement bears a striking similarity to a setting of the ballad *"Es war ein König in Thule"* by Carl Zelter, with whom Mendelssohn had studied composition in Berlin.

III. *Con moto moderato.* The graceful third movement is closer to the eighteenth-century symphonic *menuetto* than the *scherzo* type established by Beethoven. The charming trio section in the middle, with its delicate woodwind effects, recalls Mendelssohn's own music for *A Midsummer Night's Dream.*

IV. *Saltarello: Presto.* The *finale* is a *saltarello,* an old Italian dance form, with a skipping figure in triple time, which reflects the hectic fun of the Roman carnival as Mendelssohn experienced it.

> I arrived at the Corso, [he wrote] and was thinking of nothing, when suddenly I was assailed by a shower of sugar candies. I looked up and saw some ladies whom I had seen occasionally at balls, but scarcely knew, and when in my embarrassment, I took off my hat to bow to them, the pelting began in right earnest. Their carriage drove on, and in the next was Miss T——, a delicate, beautiful Englishwoman. I tried to bow to her but she pelted me too; so I grew desperate, and clutching the sugar comfits, I flung them back bravely. There were swarms of my acquaintances and my blue coat was soon as white as that of a miller. The B——family were standing on a balcony, flinging comfits like hail at my head. And thus what with all the pelting and being pelted, amid a thousand jests and the most extravagant masquerade costumes, the day ended with horse races.

Toward the end of the finale, the merrymakers seem to be dispersing into the distance, but the close brings another brilliant carnival surprise.

One would scarcely guess that this Symphony cost Mendelssohn some of the bitterest moments of his life. That was what he himself said, but the bitterness came from his own hypercritical attitude toward his music. The first version of the "Italian" Symphony, begun during his trip to Italy, was finished in Berlin in 1833 and first performed by the London Philharmonic Society, under Mendelssohn's direction, on May 13 of the same year. Within a year after this first performance, he was revising the score, rewriting whole sections. Mendelssohn would not allow it to be published during his lifetime, and he died without having accomplished his purpose of still further improving the masterpiece. The German premiere did not take place until after his death.

The printed version of the Symphony is scored for 2 flutes, 2 oboes, 2 clarinets, 2 bassoons, 2 horns, 2 trumpets, kettledrums and the customary strings.

SYMPHONY NO. 5, D MINOR, OPUS 107, REFORMATION

Mendelssohn's "Reformation" Symphony was composed to celebrate the 300th anniversary of the "Augsburg Confession," that basic statement of the tenets of the Protestant faith drawn up by Melanchthon and approved by Luther. At first glance it may seem startling to find a twenty-year-old composer of Jewish descent embarked on such a celebration; however, it should be recalled that Felix Mendelssohn had been baptized a Christian at birth and was far from the first Christian in his family. Second, although he was only twenty, he was already a composer of high standing and vast experience. The official "No. 5" given to his "Reformation" Symphony is somewhat misleading. Actually he had composed twelve symphonies before he decided to dignify any work in this form by publishing it and giving it an official number, namely "No. 1." If he had continued to number his symphonies in the order in which he completed them, his "Reformation" Symphony would have been called "No. 2." The reason it is labeled "No. 5" is, very simply, that it was the fifth (and last) to be published.

Mendelssohn's precocity and facility as a composer are well known. Less widely known is the fact that, like Mozart, he habitually shaped entire works in his head before writing them down. That is to say, the complete structure and sound of the work measure for measure was a clear mental picture before it was committed to paper. This, however, did not include all the tiny and sometimes almost mechanical details of orchestral scoring.

In composing the "Reformation" Symphony Mendelssohn indulged in a rather spectacular test of his own powers: he determined to work out every detail of the instrumentation in his head before writing it down. His close friend, Eduard Devrient, the great German theater historian, who witnessed the process, was so astonished that he has described it for us: "Felix undertook to write down the entire score, the whole of the instrumentation, bar by bar. It is true that he never wrote out a composition until it was quite completed in his head, and he had played it over to those nearest to him; but nevertheless this was a gigantic effort of memory, to fit in each detail, each doubling of parts, each solo effect barwise, like an immense mosaic. It was wonderful to watch the black column slowly advance upon the blank music paper. Felix said it was so great an effort that he would never do it again; he discontinued the process after the first movement of the Symphony: It has proved his power, however, mentally to elaborate a work in its minutest details."

The composition, begun in the fall of 1829, was completed in April 1830. Mendelssohn was undecided what title to give the Symphony, yet he felt it should have a title since the music clearly refers to religious matters. One title he considered and discarded was "Confession" Symphony. The program of the first performance, however, listed it as Symphony for the Commemoration of the Church Revolution *(Symphonie zur Feier der Kirchen-Revolution).* Since the Symphony was not published until after Mendelssohn's death, we cannot be certain that the title, "Reformation" Symphony, would have been his final choice.

The actual celebrations for which the Symphony was intended never took place after all. The revolutions of 1830, which culminated in the so-called "July Revolution" in Paris and in scattered revolutions among the small independent German states were already brewing, and apparently few persons in a position of authority felt like celebrating anything.

Mendelssohn seems to have been more relieved than otherwise at the cancellation of the celebrations, for in June, 1830, he wrote to his friend, Dorn: "Perhaps it is as well for some reasons that the performance has been postponed, for it occurred to me afterwards that the chorale part and the other Catholicisms would have a strange appearance in a theater, and that the Reformation song would not sound very well at Whitsuntide."

The first performance of Mendelssohn's new Symphony was deferred until November 15, 1832, when he himself conducted the premiere at the Singakademie in Berlin.

I. *Andante—Allegro con fuoco.* The first movement opens with a slow introduction in the course of which Mendelssohn introduces the so-called "Dresden Amen," which was also used by Wagner in slightly different form in his *Parsifal.* Both composers of course were familiar with this musical phrase from their own period of residence in Dresden. Mendelssohn's quotation of the phrase is as follows:

The main body of the movement, the *Allegro con fuoco,* is a richly worked out sonata-allegro form, with themes derived from the introduction—especially the opening theme—with its emphasis on the rising fifth:

II. *Allegro vivace.* The second movement is, in form and character, a *scherzo* although Mendelssohn did not call it such—to the relief of persons who wished to find an ecclesiastical meaning in each of the movements. (The literal meaning of the Italian word *scherzo,* of course, is "joke.")

III. *Andante.* The brief slow movement is really more of an introduction to the fourth movement than an independent movement in itself. In character, it resembles a recitative of opera or oratorio, with the first violins taking the part of a solo singer. The accompaniment is allotted to the remaining string choir and consists largely of simple repeated chords. Between the "vocal" phrases we hear an occasional brief interlude of woodwinds. This movement leads without pause into the finale.

IV. *Chorale: "A Mighty Fortress is our God!" Andante con moto; Allegro vivace; Allegro maestoso.* The *finale* which follows without pause is based on the famous Lutheran chorale, *"Ein feste Burg ist unser Gott!"* ("A Mighty Fortress is our God!").

This chorale, said to have been composed by Luther himself, has always held an important place in the hearts and minds of Protestants, especially Lutherans. Its melody is announced at once by one flute alone. Gradually other woodwinds, then the brass and strings of the orchestra join in. Thereupon the tempo increases to an *Allegro vivace,* which in turn leads to the main body of the movement, *Allegro maestoso.* This is built around various phrases from the chorale and returns at the conclusion to a triumphant proclamation of the chorale's opening phrase.

The Symphony is scored for 2 flutes, 2 oboes, 2 clarinets, 2 bassoons and contrabassoon, 2 horns, 2 trumpets, 3 trombones, kettledrums, and the usual strings. The *finale* calls for a serpent, an ancient instrument named for its serpentine form. Nowadays the serpent is usually replaced by a tuba.

Peter Mennin

Born May 17, 1923, Erie, Pennsylvania

SYMPHONY NO. 3

The last bar of Peter Mennin's Symphony No. 3 was completed on the composer's twenty-third birthday. For a work of such expressive maturity and technical assurance, this seems a remarkably early date. The Symphony was given its premiere performance by the New York Philharmonic the following winter (February 27, 1947) under the direction of Walter Hendl and was repeated by the same orchestra in January 1954 and February 1962.

Mennin is of Italian-American descent (the family name was Mennini). Born in Erie, Pennsylvania, he studied at the Oberlin Conservatory before entering the Army Air Force. After World War II he resumed his study at the Eastman School of Music with Howard Hanson and Bernard Rogers and took his Ph.D. in 1947. He studied conducting with Serge Koussevitzky at the Berkshire Music Center and taught at the Juilliard School of Music from 1947 until 1958, when he was appointed director of the Peabody Conservatory in Baltimore. In 1962 Mennin accepted the post of president of the Juilliard School in New York City.

I. *Allegro robusto.* The Symphony opens with a massive syncopated figure of five notes—a sort of motto theme—to which most of the melodic material of this very melodic Symphony seems related. The initial, thunderous proclamation is followed immediately by a ten-measure melodic expansion for the entire string section, starting as follows:

A closely related melody for four horns in unison is further expanded, leading to a third, even longer melody for the entire violin section. After eighteen measures, this melody begins to combine with itself: the low strings take up the melody before the violins have finished. This third subject is also accompanied by a shorter, repetitive (*ostinato*) figure derived from the motto.

The movement grows to a powerful climax, using various devices of *ostinato* and canon, which are older than the Classical symphony by half a millennium, and which emphasize the unity of the movement. The conclusion is pensive and quiet.

II. *Andante moderato.* The songful second movement opens without harmonic background. Two related subjects of considerable length are presented by solo woodwinds. A murmuring accompaniment figure starts in the muted strings, and the texture eventually grows as contrapuntal as part of the first movement. This movement, too, rises to a passionate climax, concluding with a sudden hush of muted strings.

III. *Allegro assai.* A delicate, dancing, *ostinato* figure presented by the two halves of the viola section in canon with each other, sets the pace for this scherzo-like *finale*:

But this *ostinato* and the long melodies which arch above it in the woodwinds seem related to the Symphony's opening motto and to the melodies of both the first and second movements. Once again unity and intensification of a basic mood prove to be basic principles of organization.

Mennin's Third Symphony is scored for 3 flutes, piccolo, 2 oboes, 2 clarinets, 2 bassoons, 4 horns, 3 trumpets, 3 trombones, tuba, kettledrums, snare drum, bass drum, cymbals, and the usual strings.

Gian Carlo Menotti

Born July 7, 1911, Cadegliano, Italy

APOCALYPSE

Gian Carlo Menotti's instrumental works have tended to be overshadowed by the popularity of his works for the stage. His operas, in particular *The Medium, The Telephone, The Consul, Amahl and the Night Visitors,* and *The Saint of Bleecker Street,* are among the most successful of the mid-twentieth century. One of the symphonic scores thus overshadowed is Menotti's three-movement *Apocalypse,* composed in 1951, the same year as *Amahl and the Night Visitors.* Like *Amahl* and *The Saint of Bleecker Street,* Menotti's *Apocalypse* has a religious theme. The composer emphasizes that his score is not descriptive music and cannot be considered a tone poem. It follows none of the apocalyptic narratives, but is rather a series of poetic impressions inspired by many apocalyptic scriptures.

Jewish and Christian apocalyptic writings alone form a vast body of traditional books originating over several centuries, many of them attributed to great prophets of an earlier period, but actually of uncertain authorship. Highly emotional, rhapsodic in tone, and symbolic in language, in figures of speech, and in narrative content, much apocalyptic writing is concerned with future, overwhelming catastrophes, to be followed by the coming of the Messiah, or by the establishment of the rule of God on earth, or sometimes by the end of the world altogether.

In certain apocalyptic writings ascribed to Baruch, the Messianic kingdom is to be brought about by an aggressive Messiah, sword in hand. The kingdom is clearly of this world, and its glories are described in richly sensuous language and hyperbole: the earth is to be so fruitful that a single vine will bear ten thousand branches, each branch ten thousand twigs, each twig ten thousand shoots, each shoot ten thousand clusters, each cluster ten thousand grapes, each grape a *cor* (variously described as being 120 or 225 gallons) of wine!

In other apocalyptic revelations the New Jerusalem, the Celestial City, or the City of God is a completely other-worldly realm, described in mystical, supersensuous terms.

"Most people," Menotti has written, "know only the *Apocalypse* of St. John the Divine in the last book of the New Testament. I have read many different accounts of the *Apocalypse,* most of which are in the form of poetry; so that this composition is a sort of synthesis or general impression of all the literature on this subject, the best known of which, aside from the writings of St. John, are the versions of Baruch and Enoch.

"Whereas most of us think of the *Apocalypse* as a description, of a future catastrophe, I found inspiration in the more lyrical, ecstatic and mystical pages of the writings."

Menotti's *Apocalypse* is divided into three movements: *Improperia, The Celestial City,* and *The Militant Angels.*

I. *Improperia: Adagio, solenne.* The *Improperia* of the Roman Catholic Church are liturgical chants sung on Good Friday during the Adoration of the Cross. The word itself is traditionally, and somewhat inaccurately, translated as "Reproaches." Actually the chants are a confrontation of the benefactions of Jesus and the suffering inflicted upon him by mankind. The most famous settings of the *Improperia* are by Palestrina, who composed the texts in the simplest possible hymn style.

Menotti's movement opens with a fanfarelike trumpet passage which returns frequently in the course of the movement with many changes of tempo. One of the most important themes of the movement is a yearning melody announced very softly by the low strings and bass clarinet:

Although the composer has emphasized that his music does not tell a story in the sense of a plot, the series of contrasting slow and fast *tempi* in this movement might have been suggested by the contrasts in the text of the *Improperia* chants.

II. *The Celestial City: Andante sereno.* Three important motives supply much of the basic material of the entire movement:

The opening of this movement with its muted strings, woodwinds and celesta, has a gentle glow which grows more and more intense. The texture becomes more polyphonic and the orchestral sonorities more incandescent, recalling an apocalyptic description of the new Jerusalem: "for Jerusalem shall be builded with sapphires and emeralds and precious stones; thy walls and towers and battlements with pure gold. And thy streets, Jerusalem, shall be paved with beryl and carbuncle and stones of Ophir."

III. *The Militant Angels: Allegro ma non troppo.* Starting as a *scherzo* of gossamer lightness, the militant angels seem to grow more and more material as the orchestral texture thickens, heavier brass instruments join the fray, and the orchestra reaches its first resplendent climax. Quieter interludes recall momentarily the mood of *The Celestial City.* There is another, even grander climax of marchlike militancy and the score concludes with a dazzling recall of the fanfare theme with which the *Apocalypse* began.

The *Apocalypse* is scored for piccolo, 2 flutes, 2 oboes, English horn, 2 clarinets, bass clarinet, 2 bassoons, contrabassoon, 6 horns, 4 trumpets, 3 trombones, tuba, kettledrums, bass drum, snare drum, cymbals, triangle, glockenspiel, xylophone, bells, gong, celesta, piano, harp, and the traditional strings. The first performance of the first two movements was given by the Pittsburgh Symphony Orchestra under the direction of Victor de Sabata on October 19, 1951. After this premiere, the third movement was added to the score, and the first complete performance was given under the direction of Victor de Sabata in Philadelphia on January 18, 1952. The first New York performance was given four days later by the Philadelphia Orchestra, again under the direction of Sabata.

Olivier Messiaen

Born December 10, 1908, Avignon

LES OFFRANDES OUBLIÉES, MÉDITATION SYMPHONIQUE (FORGOTTEN OFFERINGS, SYMPHONIC MEDITATION)

Many of Olivier Messiaen's admirers consider him to be the most original French composer since Debussy. This could be a difficult point to prove in a country which counts 51,000,000 passionate individualists. But among the most prominent successors to Debussy, Messiaen does stand out for the often flamboyant individuality of his musical thought as well as the physical sound of his music. His growing passion for the use of bird songs is only one of his more striking traits.

As his name suggests, Messiaen is part Flemish in origin, but was born in the ancient southern French city of Avignon. His father, a teacher specializing in English literature, was the author of a notable French translation of Shakespeare. His mother was the Provençal poetess Cécile Sauvage. Young Olivier was as precocious in the world of words as in music. By the time he was eight he reportedly had read all of Shakespeare aloud! His first piano lessons were given him by his mother, and he soon chose music for his career. At the age of ten he was mature enough to be bowled over by the gift (from his harmony teacher) of Debussy's *Pélleas and Mélisande.* Nearly forty years later, Messiaen declared, "This present had such an influence on me that even now . . . I can analyze the whole score from memory for my pupils."

Debussy's most fruitful influence was in sensitizing Messiaen to unfamiliar worlds of music, particularly to the melodies and rhythms of Far Eastern cultures and Western music of the Middle Ages and Renaissance. Once these doors were opened to him, Messiaen continued his explorations on his own. From his study of ancient and exotic melodic modes, he went on to invent modern modes of his own. From studying Indian rhythmic theories and the rhythm of Gregorian chant as revived by the monks of Solesmes, Messiaen developed the flexibility of his own rhythmic style. He was also drawn increasingly to what he had called "the sovereign freedom of bird song." Through all this variety and innovation, a powerful unifying factor has been Messiaen's religious faith. Like a medieval artist, Messiaen has declared that the best subjects for music are theological, for theology embraces all subjects.

Messiaen's first major orchestral work was *Les Offrandes oubliées* or "The Forgotten Offerings" (*offering* being used here in the sense of a religious sacrifice). He was only twenty-one when it was first performed in the series of Concerts Straram at the Théâtre des Champs-Elysées in Paris. The date was February 19, 1931. On that first program the composer gave subtitles to the three sections of his one-movement work: *La Croix* ("The Cross"), *Le Péché* ("Sin") and *L'Eucharist*e ("The Eucharist"). The printed score omits the original subtitles but includes the composer's description of the thought and feeling behind each of the three sections:

I. [*La Croix*]. "With arms extended on the tree of the Cross, sad unto death, you pour forth your blood. You love us, gentle Jesus; we had forgot."

Très lent, douloureux, profondément triste. The slowly arching melody of the opening bars seems almost to weep with intensity of emotion. This intensity is emphasized by a simple device: the use of mutes by the string choir. This not only gives a veiled quality to the string tone, but obliges the players to make an extra physical effort to achieve the dynamic intensity prescribed by the composer:*

As the melody slows down to its most deliberate pace, we hear a closing phrase (echoed in the depths of the orchestra), which is to return during the second section (in the strident voice of a solo trumpet) and again in the third, where it becomes the chief subject of the melodic discourse.

---

* *Musical example copyright 1931 by Durand et Cie. Used by permission of the publisher. Elkan-Vogel, Inc., sole representative, U.S.*

II. [*Le Péché*]. "Driven by folly and by the sting of the serpent, we were in a breathless, frenzied, ceaseless descent into sin, as into a tomb."

Vif, féroce, désespéré, haletant. A sudden eruption of barking, snarling brass ushers in the central section: the description of frenzied humanity on its way to spiritual death. It is easy to imagine wails and shrieks of despair in the downward swoop of *glissando* strings and high, trilling woodwinds. A solo trumpet repeats, as if obsessed, its own frantic version of the meditative phrase which concluded the first section. This description of human agony breaks off suddenly at its peak. The meditative phrase returns to introduce the concluding section.

III. [*L'Eucharistе*]. "Here is the pure altar, the source of charity, the banquet of the poor; here adorable Pity offers the bread of Life and of Love. You love us, gentle Jesus; we had forgot."

Extrêmement lent. The theme which linked the three sections of this *Symphonic Meditation* becomes the principal melodic subject of "The Eucharist." It is carried by the entire first violin section which is directed to play "with a great pity and a great love." The background consists entirely of solo instruments; 4 second violins and 5 violas, all muted. As the ensemble rises in pitch, it grows softer until it dissolves into silence.

Les Offrandes oubliées is scored for 3 flutes, 2 oboes, English horn, 2 clarinets, bass clarinet, 3 bassoons, 4 horns, 3 trumpets, 3 trombones, tuba, kettledrums, bass drums, cymbals, triangle, and the traditional string choir.

Darius Milhaud

Born September 4, 1892, Aix-en-Provence—died June 22, 1974, Geneva

SUITE PROVENÇALE

What fun Milhaud must have had when he put together this saucy masterpiece! His dancing rhythms, the lilt of his tunes, the spark in his bright orchestral colors, the bite of his (occasionally bitonal) harmonies, all betray his enthusiasm for his subject matter. And no wonder, since the subject was his beloved Provence: the countryside, the cultural traditions, the language, the music, even the sunny climate of the environment in which he grew up.

Milhaud's informal autobiography, *Notes without Music*, begins with the words: "I am a Frenchman of Provence, an Israelite by religion." For centuries Milhaud's family had lived in and around Aix-en-Provence, near Marseilles. Like most educated Provencaux, he was acutely aware that his native land had been the cradle of the great literary, musical, and social culture of the age of chivalry, until the horrors of the Albigensian Crusade destroyed that civilization and Provence was overrun, annexed by the cruder French forces from the north.

The Romantic nineteenth-century revival of Provençal language and literature rekindled a fierce pride in Provençal history and traditions. But this militancy had mellowed and even acquired a benign sense of humor in Alfonse Daudet's tales of *Tartarin de Tarascon* and his autobiographical *Le Petit Chose.*

In Milhaud the feeling seems to have been an all-embracing affection for things Provençal. Although he moved to Paris while still a young man, he was often involved in cultural affairs in Provence, including several dramatic productions at the Roman theater in Orange, near Avignon. He contributed incidental music to a play about one of the most famous Provençal troubadors, *Bertran de Born,* at the Theater of Orange in 1936. From this incidental music, from his music for another play *Le Trompeur de Séville,* from Provençal folk tunes, and from melodies by the famous Baroque opera composer André Campra (1660–1744) who was also born in Aix-en-Provence, Milhaud drew the lively materials for his *Suite provençale.* The Suite is cast in eight short, tuneful movements, orchestrated with breathtaking brilliance and originality. A modern streamlined version of the old Baroque dance suite, the *Suite provençale* has striking vitality; its rhythms are pointed and strong, its accents shift, colors flash, the orchestra chuckles or roars with laughter and the story is told.

I. *Animé.* This is a dazzling quickstep march based on the following tune:

II. *Très modéré; Vif.* This movement opens at a more modern tempo with many jerky dotted rhythms, somewhat reminiscent of the opening movement of Baroque French overtures. The lively second section is over almost before it begins.

III. *Modéré.* This marchlike movement of moderate tempo has a touch of eighteenth-century formal dignity. The soft glitter of the orchestration comes largely from the use of two piccolos at the top of the orchestra and glockenspiel in the middle range.

IV. *Vif.* The sharp, insistent triple beat of the opening gives way quickly to a scurrying melodic line with considerable brilliance in the woodwinds.

V. *Modéré.* After a half-dozen bars of introduction, three trumpets take over with a square-cut little tune that recalls some of the oldest rhythmic patterns of the Middle Ages.

VI. *Vif.* This brief movement is full of surprising shifts of color from a vigorous *tutti* to delicate *staccato* strings and woodwinds, to muted brasses, back and forth in kaleidoscopic variation, and with a dazzling conclusion.

VII. *Lent.* The only slow movement of the Suite begins with dotted rhythms recalling once more the Baroque French overture, followed by an almost languishing, sentimental melody for a solo trombone:

VIII. *Vif.* The exhilarating *Finale* is based on a fife-and-drum piece, known in the eighteenth century as a *tambourin.* The effect is achieved principally by the use of two piccolos in a very high range (suggesting fifes) with the drum beat allotted to low *pizzicato* strings plus a large drum (specifically labeled *tambour provençal*). The fifelike tune which leads off the *Finale* is alloted to the first piccolo:

Milhaud's *Suite provençal* is scored for 2 piccolos, 2 flutes, 2 oboes, English horn, clarinet, small clarinet in E, 2 bassoons, 4 horns, 3 trumpets, 3 trombones, tuba, kettledrum, large drum *(tambour provençal)*, snare drum, tenor drum without snares, bass drum, cymbals, and strings.

Modest Moussorgsky

Born March 21, 1839, Karevo, district of Pskov—died March 28, 1881, St. Petersburg

A NIGHT ON BALD MOUNTAIN

Moussorgsky was proud of his symphonic poem *A Night on Bald Mountain,* proud of its originality and its Russian character as opposed to established German symphonic style. Oddly enough, Moussorgsky's work is almost never heard in its original form, but in a revision by his friend and sometime mentor Rimsky-Korsakoff. Moussorgsky had finished his *Night on Bald Mountain.* There was no need—as there had been in the case of his opera *Khovanshchina* —for someone to complete an incomplete score.

Moussorgsky completed his *Night* more than once, and in various forms. Yet he seems to have been dissatisfied with some of them, and he was under continual pressure from his friends, including Mili Balakirev, to whom the score was dedicated, to revise and "improve" his work.

Moussorgsky was only twenty-one when he wrote his composer-friend Balakirev describing a project, a commission in fact, to compose *A Night on Bald Mountain.* It is conceivable that he had imagined such a work even earlier, for we hear of a lost version for orchestra and piano. In any case, on January 7, 1861, he wrote Balakirev: "I have received an extremely interesting commission, which I must prepare for next summer. It is this: a whole act to take place on Bald Mountain . . . a witches' sabbath, separate episodes of sorcerers, a solemn march for all this nastiness, a finale—the glorification of the sabbath in which Mengden [the author] introduces the commander of the whole festival on Bald Mountain. The libretto is very good. I already have some material for it; it may turn out to be a very good thing."

The Bald Mountain, to which Moussorgsky referred—Mount Triglav near Kiev—is well known in Russian legend. The legendary witches' sabbath is held there every year on St. John's Night, June 23–24, the night before the Feast of St. John the Baptist. The black god Chernobog—or possibly Satan himself, in the form of a black goat—presides over the revelry of other devils, witches, sorcerers, and assorted evil spirits. Similar legends of the witches' sabbath are common to most European countries, except that the locale is varied. One of Goya's most famous pictures depicts the great black goat surrounded by a crowd of evil-looking harridans.

But Moussorgsky was a procrastinator. It is six years before we find a second mention of his project in another letter to Balakirev: "I've begun to sketch the witches—am stuck at the devils—the procession of Satan doesn't satisfy me yet."

This time he seems to have taken hold, for by July 12, 1867 he wrote Rimsky-Korsakoff:

> My dear and kind Korsinka,
>
> On the twenty-third of June, on the Eve of St. John's day [i.e., Midsummer Day] I finished, with God's help, *St. John's Night on Bald Mountain*—a tone picture with the following program: (1) assembly of the witches, their chatter and hubbub; (2) cortege of Satan; (3) unholy glorification of Satan; and (4) witches' sabbath. I wrote the score just like that, without any preliminary rough draft—I began on the tenth day of June, and by the twenty-third there was joy and triumph. The composition is dedicated to Mili [Balakirev], according to his own orders and, needless to say, with my personal pleasure. You must imagine, my dear, the situation—doing one clean score without sketches of any kind, and my trepidation at forwarding the score to the binder. In my picture your favorite bits came out quite well in the scoring. Besides this I have added many new things; in the *unholy glorification,* for example, there is a bit for which César [Cui] will sentence me to the conservatory [also a passage] in B minor—the witches glorifying Satan—as you can see, stark naked, barbarous and filthy. In the sabbath there is a rather original call, the strings and piccolo trilling on B-flat. . . . [For such things] they would fire me from that same conservatory in which César imprisoned me for the witches' glorification.
>
> The plan and form of the composition is rather original. The introduction is in two sections (the assembling of the witches); then a D-minor theme with a bit of development (the chatter) is linked with the cortege of Satan in B-flat major (I cunningly avoided the Hungarian March clichés; the cortege

> theme without development but followed by a response in E-flat minor (this ribald character in E-flat minor is very amusing) is concluded with a *chemical gamma* [i.e., chromatic scale] on a full movement *in moto contrario* in D major. —After this, B minor (the glorification) in Russian style with development, variations, and a semi-ecclesiastical quasi-trio; a transition to the sabbath and finally the sabbath (first theme in D minor) also in Russian style with variations.—At the close of the sabbath the chemical gamma and the figures from the introduction reappear, which is quite effective.—You can have hardly any idea of the sabbath—it has turned out very compact and, to my way of thinking, fiery. The form, variations interspersed with calls, is, I think, the most suitable for such a commotion.—The general character of the thing is hot; it doesn't drag, everything firmly linked, but without any German transitions, which is remarkably refreshing.—However, God grant that you will hear it for yourself.
>
> In my opinion, *St. John's Night* is something new and is bound to impress a thoughtful musician. I regret *that distance divides us,* for I should like us to examine the newborn score together.—Let it be understood, however, that I'm not going to start altering it; with whatever shortcomings it was born, it will have to live, if it does live. Nevertheless, by working together, we might clear up many things.—If this picture is played at a concert, Korsh's paper will surely carry a column of delicately paternal dressing down from César [Cui] to Modinka. [This is a reference to the composer-critic César Cui of Korsh's newspaper *Peterburgsky Vedomosti.* Modinka was one of the many nicknames for Modest Moussorgsky.]

In an unusually frank letter one week later to his friend, professor Vladimir Nikolsky, Moussorgsky touched on the sexual character of the sabbath:

> When he felt sufficiently stimulated by [the witches'] praise, he gave the signal for the sabbath to begin, selecting for himself those witches who had taken his fancy. Well, that's how I've done the thing! (1) The assembling, the jabber and pranks; (2) Satan's train; (3) the obscene glorification; and (4) the sabbath. If the work is performed, I wish this program to appear on the bills for the enlightenment of the audience. My music is Russian and independent in form and character, fiery and disorderly in tone. In fact, the sabbath begins with the entry of the minor devils: in the old narratives the glorification was part of the sabbath. I have labeled the episode separately in order to define the musical form (which is new) more clearly.

Moussorgsky further explained that he had divided his orchestra into separate groups, believing that listeners would appreciate the sharp contrast between the timbres of wind and strings. He added that he felt this suited the actual character of the sabbath: "a scattered but continuous cross-fire of calls, until the whole rabble unite in the final embrace." As if embarrassed at his loquacity, Moussorgsky concluded: "I am talking a lot about my *Night,* but probably for the reason that I see in this wicked prank of mine a really Russian and original achievement, quite free from German profundity and routine, born . . . on Russian soil and nurtured on Russian corn."

Proud as he was of his achievement, he was docile when Balakirev advised him to overhaul the score, which Balakirev considered to be confused. Moussorgsky did, in fact, revise it in 1880, but not in the way Balakirev suggested. At one time Moussorgsky planned to incorporate his *Night on Bald Mountain* as an intermezzo in an opera, *The Fair at Sorochinsk,* where he intended to give it the title "Dream of The Young Peasant Lad." At another time he planned to incorporate *A Night on Bald Mountain* into another opera, a collaborative effort by several composers, to be called *Mlada*. In the end none of these versions was published. Even the current scholarly edition of the works of Moussorgsky, being published in the Soviet Union, moves slowly. And we still do not know Moussorgsky's original version of his orchestral poem as he completed it on St. John's Eve of 1867.

Instead, *A Night on Bald Mountain* has been published and republished and has become a popular staple of the concert repertory in the revision by Rimsky-Korsakoff. Rimsky has told us that he based his edition on materials from the (now lost) earliest version for piano and orchestra and the two choral versions arranged for *Mlada* and *The Fair at Sorochinsk.* Moussorgsky's orchestral version of 1867 apparently was not available to Rimsky, or he may even have been ignorant of its survival, although it was actually in Balakirev's hands.

Rimsky headed his version of the score with the following brief outline:

> Subterranean sounds of supernatural voices—Appearance of the spirits of darkness, followed by that of Satan himself—Glorification of Satan and celebration of the Black Mass—The Sabbath Revels—At the height of the orgies the bell of the village church, sounding in the distance, disperses the spirits of darkness—Daybreak.

The Rimsky-Moussorgsky score begins with wild, whirring figures in the high violins. A powerful octave figure in the trombones stalks through the orchestra. We hear fast, chattering woodwinds, which recall Moussorgsky's description, alternating with shrieks and whines, also in the woodwinds. The following theme which permeates the score could suggest the prancing and cavorting of the witches:

After the climax of the sabbath orgy the orchestra falls almost silent, and we hear the bell that heralds the dawn: a peaceful phrase for solo clarinet, flute, and angelic arpeggios for the harp.

Rimsky-Korsakoff's instrumentation of *A Night on Bald Mountain* calls for piccolo, 2 flutes, 2 oboes, 2 clarinets, 2 bassoons, 4 horns, 2 trumpets, 3 trombones, tuba, kettledrums, a bell in D, cymbals, bass drum, tam-tam, harp, and the traditional string choir.

PICTURES AT AN EXHIBITION
(Orchestrated by Maurice Ravel)

The gorgeous colors in Ravel's orchestral arrangement of Moussorgsky's *Pictures at an Exhibition* has made it a showpiece for virtuoso conductors and for virtuoso orchestras. It was Serge Koussevitzky, the late conductor of the Boston Symphony Orchestra, who was responsible for Ravel's orchestration of the piano suite which Moussorgsky composed in 1874. Koussevitzky commissioned the arrangement in 1922, and it was an immediate success on May 3, 1923, at the fashionable Concerts Koussevitzky, a yearly feature of the Paris season.

Moussorgsky had been a close friend of the Russian architect and painter Victor Hartmann, who died in 1873 at the age of thirty-nine. Shortly after his death, the great Russian critic Vladimir Stassov, who had been a friend of both Hartmann and Moussorgsky, helped to arrange an exhibition of Hartmann's watercolors and drawings at the St. Petersburg Academy of Arts. Moussorgsky visited the exhibition and, deeply moved, decided to take ten of the pictures as subjects of a suite for piano, to be a memorial tribute to his friend.

Moussorgsky poured out his feelings about his friend's death in a letter to Stassov, who shared the Russian nationalist tendencies of Hartmann and Moussorgsky and had brought the two men together in the first place:

> My dear friend, what a terrible blow! "Why should a dog, a horse, a rat have life"—and creatures like Hartmann must die! . . . This is how the wise usually console us blockheads, in such cases: "He is no more, but what he has done lives and will live!" True—but how many men have the luck to be remembered? That is just another way of serving up our complacency (with a dash of onion, to bring out the tears). Away with such wisdom! When "he" has not lived in vain, but has created—one must be a rascal to revel in the thought that "he" can create no more. No, one cannot and must not be comforted, there can be and must be no consolation—it is a rotten mortality! If Nature is only coquetting with men, I shall have the honor of treating her like a coquette—that is, trusting her as little as possible, keeping all my sense about me, when she tries to cheat me into taking the sky for a fiddlestick—or ought one, rather like a brave soldier, to charge into the thick of life, have one's fling, and go under? What does it all mean? In any case, the dull old earth is no coquette, but takes every "King of Nature" straight into her loathsome embrace, whoever he is—like an old worn-out hag, for anyone is good enough, since she has no choice.
>
> There again—what a fool I am! Why be angry when you cannot change anything! Enough then—the rest is silence. . . .

Moussorgsky's piano suite, which was not published until after his death, is dedicated to Stassov. It includes the following sections [Russian titles are given here in English; other titles are given in their original languages]:

Promenade: Allegro guisto nel modo russico; senza allegrezza ma poco sostenuto. [Stassov, with whom Moussorgsky had discussed the suite as he composed it, explained in the first edition of the *Pictures at an Exhibition:* "The composer here portrays himself walking now right, now left, now as an idle person, now urged to go near a picture; at times his joyous appearance is dampened, he thinks in sadness of his dead friend. . . ."] Ravel gives the opening theme to a solo trumpet:*

Gnomus (The Gnome): Vivo. In his introduction to his first edition, Stassov tells us that Hartmann's picture was "a drawing representing a little gnome awkwardly walking on deformed legs." But elsewhere (as we are informed by Alfred Frankenstein in his detailed investigation of this topic), Stassov says that Hartmann's was a design for a carved wooden nutcracker apparently in the form of a gnome.

Promenade: Moderato comodo e con delicatezza. The original *Promenade* theme is varied here to suggest Moussorgsky's strolling through the Hartmann exhibition.

Il vecchio castello (The Old Castle). The title suggests that the old castle, before which a troubadour sings, was in Italy.

Promenande: Moderato non tanto, pesante.

Tuileries: Allegretto non troppo, capriccioso. Moussorgsky gave a subtitle for this number: "Dispute of the Children after Play." Hartmann's pictures show the famous park in Paris, peopled by children and nursemaids.

Bydlo: Sempre moderato pesante. Bydlo is a Polish word meaning "cattle." Hartmann's watercolor, which he had executed during a trip through Poland, showed a typical Polish peasant wagon with enormous wooden wheels, drawn by oxen.

Promenande: Tranquillo. Ballet of the Chicks in Their Shells: Scherzino, Vivo leggiero. The exhibition included Hartmann's costume sketch for children dancers in a ballet entitled *Trilby.* One of the costume sketches showed a child with arms and legs and head only protruding through a large chicken shell.

Samuel Goldenberg and Schmuyle. This title was invented by Stassov. Moussorgsky's title for the movement was "Two Jews; one rich, the other poor." Moussorgsky was inspired to compose this movement by two Hartmann pictures which had been presented to him by the artist. Moussorgsky loaned

---

* *Musical example copyright 1929 by Edition Russe de Musique. Renewed 1956. Copyright and renewal assigned to Boosey & Hawkes, Inc. Reprinted by permission.*

them to the Hartmann memorial exhibit and Mr. Frankenstein informs us that they were listed in the catalog of the exhibit but have since disappeared.

The Marketplace at Limoges: Allegro vivo, sempre scherzando. Hartmann's picture done on the spot at Limoges, shows a group of market women in lively conversation by their pushcarts. Moussorgsky scribbled in the margin of his score an imaginary conversation between the women which he crossed out to make place for a second conversational sketch: "Great news! M. de Puissangeout has just recovered his cow, The Fugitive. But the good crones of Limoges are not entirely agreed about this, because Mme. de Remboursac just acquired a beautiful new set of teeth, whereas M. de Panta-Pantaleon's nose, which is in the way, remains the color of a peony."

Catacombae, Sepulchrum Romanum (Catacombs, Roman Tombs): Largo. The drawing showed Hartmann himself with a fellow architect Kenel in the Paris catacombs and a guide holding a lamp.

Cum mortuis in lingua mortua: Andante non troppo, con lamento. In a footnote to his title, Moussorgsky wrote: "A Latin text: 'With the Dead in a Dead Language.' Well may it be in Latin! The creative spirit of the departed Hartmann leads me to the skulls, calls out to them, and the skulls begin to glow dimly from within."

The Hut on Fowls' Legs: Allegro con brio, feroce. Hartmann's drawing showed a clock in the form of a hut of Baba-Yaga, the Russian witch who eats human bones ground in a paste in a mortar and pestle. Since Baba-Yaga also used her mortar to ride through the sky, Moussorgsky added the suggestion of her wild flight. The *coda* to her flight leads directly into the final number of Moussorgsky's Suite.

The Great Gate of Kiev: Allegro alla breve; Maestoso; Con grandezza. Hartmann's design was his entry into a competition for a gateway to be erected at Kiev to commemorate Czar Alexander II's miraculous escape from assassination on April 4, 1866, at St. Petersburg. Hartmann's design, which inspired the climax and conclusion of Moussorgsky's Suite, is reproduced here. Capped by a cupola in the shape of an ancient Russian helmet, this is a fantasy gate in purely imaginary style. Perhaps the prancing horse and the figures silhouetted under the gate gave Moussorgsky the idea of a procession, which is suggested by a majestic development of the *Promenade* theme which opens the Suite.

Ravel's orchestration of Moussorgsky's *Pictures at an Exhibition* calls for piccolo, 3 flutes, 3 oboes, English horn, 2 clarinets, bass clarinet, 2 bassoons, contrabassoon, E-flat alto saxophone, 4 horns, 3 trumpets, 3 trombones, tuba, rattle, side drum, bass drum, cymbals, whip, triangle, xylophone, glockenspiel, bells, celesta, tam-tam, kettledrums, 2 harps, piano, and the traditional string choir.

THE GREAT GATE OF KIEV.

Alexander Hartmann's "Project for a City Gate" was designed to suggest a picturesque structure of great antiquity, its two central columns buried almost up to their capitals. The inscription on the central arch in old church Slavonic reads: "Blessed he that cometh in the name of the Lord." (*Leningrad Institute of Literature, Stassov Collection; photo courtesy, Alfred Frankenstein*)

PRELUDE TO KHOVANSHCHINA

When Moussorgsky died of chronic alcoholism at the age of forty-three, he left unfinished one of his most cherished projects: his opera *Khovanshchina.*

In *Khovanshchina,* Moussorgsky hoped to delve far deeper into the soul of the Russian people than he had even in *Boris Godunov.* For while the opera shows the attempted military revolt of the princes Khovansky against the modernization and Westernization of Russia, and the fanatical resistance of Russian Old Believers against seventeenth-century reforms of the Russian church, Moussorgsky made it clear that the focus of his thought and affection was the Russian people. Even before he had completed his revision of *Boris Godunov* he started (in the spring of 1872) to prepare himself for *Khovanshchina.* With enormous enthusiasm he launched into a vast program of reading and research in Russian history.

Tragically enough, it was about this time that Moussorgsky's friends noticed that he had begun to drink obsessively. They were profoundly concerned and did everything they could think of to rescue him from his addiction, from the ill health, poverty, and humiliation it brought. From time to time Moussorgsky would try to reassure his friends by telling them what progress he was making with *Khovanshchina.* One of the earliest of these reassurances was a letter dated Petrograd, July 23, 1873: "The Introduction to *Khovanshchina* (dawn over the Moscow River, matins at cock crow, the patrol, and the taking down of the chains) and the opening moments of the action are ready, but not written down." Two days later he wrote his friend and champion, the critic Vladimir Stassov: "The introduction to *Khovanshchina* is almost ready, the growing light of the rising sun is beautiful. . . ." But the manuscript sketch for this introduction, the first part of the opera he wrote down, is dated over two years later (September 2, 1874). When he died, vast stretches of the score had never been committed to paper.

After Moussorgsky's death, the first concern of admirers was the mass of his unpublished manuscripts. Rimsky-Korsakov undertook to prepare them for publication. The first score he rescued was *Khovanshchina.*

The introduction to *Khovanshchina* begins delicately with little wisps of *arpeggio,* which Rimsky-Korsakov gives to violas and flutes. The principal melody is announced (in the Rimsky version) by second violins and oboes against a shimmering background of muted first violins:

With slight melodic and harmonic variations the melody is taken up by one instrumental combination after another. As the oboe intones the melody against rising scales of the violins, the curtain rises slowly. It is dawn. The scene is not the Moscow River, as Moussorgsky originally planned, but Red

Square. As the music grows more animated, "the church cupolas are illuminated by the rising sun. The bells sound for early mass."

The church bells die away, and the opening melody with its background of shimmering strings seems to evaporate like morning mist. In Rimsky's version this whole final passage is transposed from Moussorgsky's F-sharp major to the key of D flat, presumably in order to mitigate Moussorgsky's "wanton" modulations. For the tonal center of the opening pages had been C-sharp, and Rimsky thus manages to bring the music back (at least enharmonically) to home base.

Rimsky-Korsakoff's orchestration for the Prelude to *Khovanshchina* is 2 flutes, 2 oboes, 2 clarinets, 2 bassoons, 4 horns, harp, kettledrums, tam-tam, and the standard string section.

Wolfgang Amadeus Mozart

Born January 27, 1756, Salzburg—died December 5, 1791, Vienna

CONCERTO FOR CLARINET AND ORCHESTRA, A MAJOR, K. 622

Mozart's love of the clarinet is a key to one important side of his musical nature. He was a boy of seven, a touring prodigy, when he first heard clarinets in the famous Mannheim orchestra, then in London and in Paris, then again on later visits to Mannheim. He was bewitched by the clarinet's sensuous sound, its sensitive dynamic shadings, the rainbow span of tone color from the almost trumpetlike brilliance of its top to the dark rich tones of its lowest (so-called *chalumeau*) range. In Vienna, during the last years of his tragically short career, Mozart's friendship with virtuoso Anton Stadler, a member of the imperial court orchestra and fellow Freemason, expanded Mozart's already remarkable mastery of the clarinet.

Stadler profited even more from his friendship with Mozart. Not only did Mozart compose two of the greatest works of the entire clarinet literature (his A-major Clarinet Quintet, K. 581 and the Clarinet Concerto) for Stadler, he allowed Stadler to exploit the free hospitality of the Mozart household. He loaned Stadler money when he could ill afford it, and when he had no money to lend, he loaned Stadler two gold watches to pawn. When Mozart died in December 1791 and was buried in an unmarked grave, the "assets" of his estate, according to the official accounting, included 500 florins of bad debts accumulated by Stadler—well over $3,000.

The Clarinet Concerto was the next-to-last work Mozart completed. Only his "Masonic" Cantata, K. 623, bears a later date. He must have begun the Concerto almost immediately after the premiere of his opera, *The Magic Flute* (September 30, 1791). A week later Mozart wrote his wife, who had gone to take the waters at nearby Baden, that he orchestrated most of Stadler's *Rondo* on October 7. Presumably he finished the score within a day or two. While we do not know the date of the first performance, it was probably soon after, as it was Mozart's habit to complete a work barely in time for a planned performance.

His manuscript has disappeared. But he is known to have composed this Concerto for Stadler's own special clarinet: an instrument which could play four semi-tones lower than the standard. Unfortunately the earliest printed editions all date from ten years or more after Mozart's death, and in all of them the solo clarinet part is "revised" to fit the range of the standard clarinet in A. Only recently has musicological sleuthing rediscovered the extent and nature of the revisions. Some thirty passages in the solo part, varying from individual, extra-low notes, to sections nine measures long, were changed—most by simply moving them up an octave, thus depriving the Concerto of substantial color resources and altering its melodic line. Those early editors had little choice if Mozart's masterpiece was to be played on a standard clarinet. But in recent years an A clarinet with the extended range of Stadler's instrument has been constructed, thus making it possible for performers to play all the notes Mozart wrote, rather than the mildly emasculated version we know and still love.

I. *Allegro.* The orchestral introduction opens with a gently caressing principal theme for the string choir:

It is characteristic of this Concerto that the clarinet-solo sections all begin on a dynamic and pitch level which brings out the almost velvety, sensuous tone of the instrument. When the solo clarinet takes up the theme, the effect is even gentler than the opening of the movement. The intimate chamber-music texture is achieved by limiting the accompaniment at first to violins alone. Violas are then added, and when the lowest strings are finally admitted, it is only to supply light touches of harmonic support. Rippling scales and arpeggios for the solo clarinet conclude the statement of the principal theme. Almost at once we hear a second contrasting melody for the solo instrument in the melancholy minor mode. Such touches of melancholy are never far away even in the sunniest moments of the lively first and third movements.

II. *Adagio.* The slow movement opens with a melody which must be one of the most beautiful ever written. It is sung by the solo clarinet, without any orchestral introduction. It is hard to believe that this seraphic melodic line is based on one of the most popular clichés of eighteenth-century Classicism—a phrase used dozens, perhaps even hundreds of times, by Mozart's contemporaries, but never with this unexplainable magic:

The more the solo part embellishes, expands, seeming to sprout leaves and tendrils, the more organically the melody seems to grow out of the clarinet tone.

III. *Rondo: Allegro.* For all its rhythmic vitality, its lively twists and turns, the refrain of this *rondo finale* begins as softly and gently in the solo instrument as did the preceding movements. Between returns of the *rondo* refrain, we hear increasingly exuberant episodes, with decorative scales and arpeggios plunging down to the lowest notes of the clarinet and racing upward ever higher. Mozart exploits the extremes of the clarinet range with masterly simplicity, as for example in the following preparation for a return of the *Rondo* refrain:

Yet for all the brilliance and gaiety there is not a superficial moment. Even this last movement has its moments of sadness. We do not need to read any deeper meaning into Mozart's music: no premonitions of his impending death, no expression of even unconscious leave-taking. But the Clarinet Concerto gives many listeners the irresistible impression that moments of unusually intense beauty carry with them an inevitable feeling of sadness, as of something too perfect to last—something by its nature so evanescent that one would like to cry out to the moment with Faust: *"Verweile doch du bist so schön"* ("Ah, tarry, thou art so fair!"). It was Mozart's next to last completed work.

The Clarinet Concerto is scored for 2 flutes, 2 bassoons, 2 horns, and the traditional string choir.

CONCERTO FOR FLUTE AND ORCHESTRA, G MAJOR, K. 313

Like most of Mozart's works, his G-major Flute Concerto was composed for a specific practical purpose. In this case the purpose was frankly to make some direly needed money for the long and expensive professional trip from Salzburg to Paris. By the end of October 1777, Mozart and his mother had gotten as far as Mannheim, with its celebrated orchestra and opera house. The Mannheim court was not especially interested in the twenty-one-year-old genius, but at last an amateur flutist De Jean, a Dutch visitor to Mannheim, came forward with a commission for a group of easy flute concertos and flute quartets.

Mozart disliked the flute as a solo instrument, so despite his financial need, he procrastinated. When the Dutchman left town in February 1778, the commission was far from finished and Mozart's fee was reduced by half. But despite his distaste for the instrument, Mozart seemed incapable of composing an indifferent work for it. The Dutch patron received a G-major Concerto far beyond the amateur's scope he had bargained for, an artistic delight for flutists and their audiences for two centuries to come.

I. *Allegro maestoso.* Before we hear the solo flute, an orchestral exposition presents the principal themes, starting with the most important of them all. Clearly this must be the theme Mozart had in mind when he chose the word "majestic" *(maestoso)* to describe the tempo. For despite the airy elegance of this Concerto as a whole, its opening theme does have a certain Rococo majesty.

When the solo flute takes over, it is not content merely to echo the orchestral themes with the conventional changes of key. In a characteristically Mozartean detour (through the region of the relative, E minor) the soloist enriches the movement with a plaintive, sighing phrase which remains the exclusive thematic property of the flute.

The exposition ends with a bouncy little cadence figure which seems to have no importance whatsoever—until Mozart's imagination seizes upon it and transforms it into a long development section of dazzling variety and brilliance. The reprise of the basic themes is shared by soloist and orchestra up to the moment for the cadenza, which Mozart left free for the soloist to display his art.

II. *Adagio ma non troppo.* The crown of the work is this songful slow movement, tinged with Romantic melancholy and colored with the nocturnal timbre of muted strings. A solemn motto-like figure in bare octaves introduces the principal melody, sung first by an oboe, then by the solo flute over murmuring violins:

A contrasting second theme, a yearning, upward-reaching melody, recalls the mood of the celebrated flute solo in the Elysian Fields scene of Gluck's Parisian *Orpheus and Eurydice.* The movement is richly developed in symphonic sonata form with a free cadenza just before the end.

III. *Rondeau: Tempo di Menuetto.* The deliciously Rococo finale is cast in the form of a French *rondeau,* with a refrain first announced by the soloist.

There are three returns of this refrain, each one slightly embellished. The intervening episodes, brilliant and virtuosic to start with, grow progressively richer in their musical content. The central episode, following French custom, is largely in the minor mode. The last episode concludes with a free cadenza leading to the final return of the *Rondeau* refrain with softly caressing final bars.

The orchestra for the G-major Flute Concerto is a small one: 2 oboes, 2 horns, and the traditional string choir. The custom of the day would also have included a harpsichord to fill out the improvised *continuo* part.

CONCERTO FOR FLUTE AND ORCHESTRA, D MAJOR, K. 314

This charming bit of fluff, touched with poetry in its middle movement and full of sparkle in its third, seems perfectly suited to the flute. Yet we know, thanks to recent Mozart research, that it was originally for oboe. Mozart composed it when he was twenty-one years old, for an Italian oboist, Giuseppe Ferlendi, who had entered the service of the archbishop of Salzburg in April 1777. We do not know exactly when Mozart completed the score but it was obviously some time before his departure for Paris in the fall of the same year.

Mozart took the oboe concerto with him. One of his most important stops on the way to the French capital was Mannheim. The famous Mannheim orchestra was one of the most skilled and most influential orchestras of the day. Its ranks included renowned *virtuosi,* some of whom were also influential composers. The first oboist of the Mannheim orchestra Friedrich Ramm played Mozart's Concerto several times with great success.

Another of Mozart's friends among the musicians of the Mannheim orchestra was the flutist Wendling. Through Wendling, Mozart obtained a lucrative commission from a Dutch amateur flutist De Jean. Mozart delivered two concertos and three flute quartets, for which he received ninety-six gulden. The first of the two flute concertos (K. 313) was an original work. But for the second Mozart adapted the Ferlendi oboe concerto, which he had composed in C major, transposing it to D major for the flute. It is in three movements.

I. *Allegro aperto.* The opening movement must have sounded especially chic in its day, for it is full to overflowing with the sharply profiled little figures, the perky rhythms, and the exuberant light spirits of the Italian *opera buffa,* which had been so influential in the formation of Classical style. The syncopated principal theme is given out by the orchestra in the opening measures and is followed immediately by a more songful contrasting melody in the first violins. The solo flute makes a brilliant entrance with a swiftly rising scale and a long, sustained high note under which the orchestra once more proclaims the principal theme of the movement. The flute continues with brilliant passage work leading into the songful second theme.

The central "development section," which was to become so important in Mozart's later works, is here little more than an adroit transition connecting the two halves of the movement. The reprise of the basic thematic materials is perfectly regular and is rounded off by a cadenza and concluding flourishes for the orchestral tutti.

II. *Andante ma non troppo.* The slow movement exploits the flute's ability to sing, particularly to sustain long notes over orchestral countermelody. A touch of poetic melancholy is added to the song by Mozart's discreet use of the familiar *appoggiatura,* as in the opening of the solo part:

III. *Allegro.* The *finale* is a light-footed *rondo.* It is based on a theme which the lovers of Mozart opera will recognize as the source of one of Mozart's sunniest inspirations in his *Abduction from the Seraglio.* This is Blonde's exuberant song, *"Welche Wonne, welche Lust,"* in which she anticipates her rescue from the seraglio by her beloved Pedrillo:

Announced in the airy tones of the flute, this refrain is immediately taken up *forte* by the orchestra.

The first episode of the solo flute begins as if it were to be a reprise of the opening refrain, but quickly branches off in other directions with arpeggios and scales. The orchestra joins in at intervals, but long before the flute has reached its climactic cadenza the orchestra has become its docile, happy slave, keeping willingly in the background, and chiming in chiefly to echo the sentiments of the beguiling solo part.

The orchestra, which Mozart has scored with great delicacy, consists only of 2 oboes, 2 horns, and the traditional string choir.

CONCERTO FOR HORN AND ORCHESTRA, E-FLAT MAJOR, K. 417

A surprising number of Mozart's works were composed out of friendship. Ignatz Joseph Leutgeb, a French horn virtuoso and former member of the Archepiscopal Court Orchestra of Salzburg, was an old friend of the Mozart family. Like Mozart, Leutgeb had gone on tours (which took him to Paris to perform his own Horn Concerto at the famous Concerts Spirituels) before he settled in Vienna. In Vienna, Leutgeb found he could not make a living from his music. So with the help of a loan from Mozart's father Leopold, Leutgeb became a cheesemonger. He bought a tiny shop, which Leopold described as "the size of a snail shell." With cheese he earned enough to continue his concert appearances, but not enough to pay back the loan on time. Mozart helped by urging his father to ease Leutgeb's repayment of the loan. But more urged his father to ease Leutgeb's repayment of the loan. But more importantly, he helped by composing four horn concertos for Leutgeb's personal use.

Normally Mozart composed concertos only for himself as soloist or on however, there can have been no fat commission nor, probably, any slim one either. In lieu of a dedication to a wealthy patron, the manuscript of the E-flat Concerto, K. 417, is inscribed in Mozart's hand with the kind of jocular insults that can be exchanged only by two men who are sure of each other's respect and affection. The heading reads: "Wolfgang Amadé* Mozart took pity on Leitgeb [sic] the ass, the ox, the clown, in Vienna on May 27, 1783." And in the upper left-hand corner of the page: "Ass Leitgeb." (Leitgeb was the Austrian dialect pronunciation and hence spelling of Leutgeb's name.)

A year earlier Mozart had peppered the manuscript score of his D-major Concerto for Leutgeb with repeated volleys of mock insults. The entrance of the solo horn is marked: "Take it easy!—for you, Signor Ass, now get moving —presto—come on!—good for you!—Courage—get it over with—animal—oh, how flat you play—ouch—oh dear—good for you, you poor thing!—oh, *seccatura di coglioni!*—ah, you make me laugh—help!—catch your breath!—get going, get going!—now this is a little better—will you never get through?—[and at the end:] what a bleating sheep's trill—finished? thank heaven! enough, enough!"

The music of the E-flat Concerto suggests that Leutgeb was a superb performer, with a gorgeous tone, a dazzling technique and perhaps not much musical sophistication. Even today, after almost two-hundred years of mechanical improvements in the French horn, the Concerto presents some tricky technical problems for the soloist. Musically the score is a triumphant demonstration of Mozart's ability to use the established clichés of his day with miraculous freshness and spontaneity.

I. *Allegro maestoso.* The opening movement is charmingly lyric in a style which used to be called a "singing allegro." That is to say, the melodic line gives the impression of vocal music, although it may move as fast as a coloratura singer. The principal themes are introduced briefly by the first violins

* Amadé is the form of his middle name habitually used by Mozart.

with tiny woodwind echoes. The solo horn makes its entrance with a slight variant of the opening theme:

Mozart uses the expected concerto version of sonata-allegro form with grace and no surprises, except possibly for a striking excursion into the minor mode in his development.

II. *Andante.* This melodious, unpretentious movement is songful in a quite different sense. The sustained arches of the solo part are, in addition to their intrinsic beauty, ideal for the display of the mellow tones of the French horn.

III. *Rondo.* Like the finales of Mozart's other horn concertos, this one is built on a simple fanfare-like theme, an imitation of the traditional hunting signals played upon the hunting horn, which was the ancestor of the orchestral horn:

This theme heard first in the solo horn is a *rondo* refrain which keeps returning throughout the movement with little contrasting episodes intervening. The whole *finale* is as fresh and exuberant as if such hunting-call rondo-finales had not been written by the dozen for dozens of years by scores of other composers. After the last return of the hunting-call refrain (at a slightly increased tempo), one is left with the wish that there were still many more returns to come. Mozart's modest orchestra consists of 2 oboes, 2 orchestral horns (in addition to the solo horn), and the traditional string choir (to which the standard practice of Mozart's day would have added a harpsichord and a bassoon).

CONCERTO FOR PIANO AND ORCHESTRA, E-FLAT MAJOR, K. 271

Mozart composed this Concerto during the month of his twenty-first birthday. At that age his feelings about the beautiful city where he was born were a mixture of love and hate. His earliest years there seem to have been happy. But during the two decades from his sixth to his twenty-sixth year, Mozart spent more than half his time away from Salzburg, on repeated trips—ten in all—to the great courts and music centers of Versailles, Paris, London, Milan, Florence, Rome, Naples, Munich, Mannheim, and Vienna.

Each time he left Salzburg, it was with a more urgent hope of finding a position at some other, more generous, enlightened, and appreciative court.

Each time he returned, Salzburg seemed smaller, more provincial, more backward, more narrow in mind and spirit; his master, the Archbishop of Salzburg, more niggardly, prejudiced, and stupid. Mozart came to refer to his native city as "a beggarly town" and his employment there as "slavery."

His longest return to Salzburg lasted almost two and a half years, from March 1775, to September 1777. In January 1777 the Salzburg visit of a famous French pianist, Mlle. Jeunehomme, must have seemed a breath of fresh air from the larger world for which Mozart yearned. To judge by the Concerto he wrote for her (K. 271 in E-flat major) Mlle. Jeunehomme must have been a sensitive musician and a brilliant *virtuosa.*

We do not know either the precise day when Mozart completed his score or the occasion of the first performance. But we do know that he favored this Concerto for his personal use on several later occasions.

And no wonder. This was not only the greatest concerto he had written, but the boldest he was ever to write. It is also the earliest Mozart piano concerto to be a standard part of our twentieth-century concert repertory.

I. *Allegro.* The very opening brings a surprise unique in all Mozart. Contrary to well-established Classical tradition, which gives the initial exposition to the orchestra alone, Mozart has the piano interrupt, as it were, to complete the phrase begun by the orchestral *tutti:*

The orchestra reasserts its opening phrase and again the soloist interrupts. After this bold beginning, however, the soloist defers to the orchestra.

At the traditional point for the entrance of the solo, instead of making its reappearance with a conventional recapitulation of the opening theme, Mozart's piano slips in with a quiet trill while the orchestra is completing its formal opening. Unlike many first movements which are content with one principal theme and one for contrast, this movement brings four important contrasting themes and several lesser ones.

For the first time in Mozart's piano concertos, the central development section, instead of bringing fresh episodes of new themes, is based entirely on themes presented in the exposition. The reprise of the opening themes is filled with harmonic surprises. Near the end of the movement comes the traditional place for a cadenza. Mozart has left us two versions of his own cadenza for this movement. After the cadenza the piano makes an unconventional reappearance, entering on a soft trill, as it did at the beginning of the movement, but concluding now with flashing arpeggios.

II. *Andantino.* A sharper contrast to the exuberant first movement can hardly be imagined. This is the first tragic movement in the long series of Mozart's piano concertos, and it is the first written in a minor key. The violins are muted throughout, except for four emphatic measures at the very end. Again and again throughout the movement, Mozart incorporates traits of dramatic recitative, the speaking eloquence of Italian opera, to intensify the personal emotion of this tragic "scene."

The Concerto opens with intertwining voices of first and second violins in a throbbing melodic figure:

Later this throbbing passage serves as accompaniment to the opening strain of the piano solo:

Suddenly, almost without warning, we are back in the serene mood of E-flat major for a long solo of melting melodic appeal. But its serenity is not unclouded. And when the minor key returns, its triumph is complete. Even the mellow song of the E-flat-major episode is transformed, with double poignant effect, into a C-minor lament. For this movement, too, Mozart has left us his eloquent cadenza.

III. *Rondo: Presto.* The refrain of this joyous *Rondo* is announced by the soloist alone, then echoed by the orchestra. There are three ingénious contrasting episodes, the most astonishing of them a tiny minuet on the following theme:

It is one of Mozart's more fanciful minuets, each phrase-repetition being embellished with entrancingly graceful and imaginative *fioriture.* A virtuoso cadenza at the end of the minuet serves as a retransition to the exuberant *Rondo* refrain. The entire *finale* is a whirlwind of originality, daring and brilliance, the firm frame of the *Rondo* being sustained by the continual returns of the catchy refrain. Mozart's modest orchestra calls only for 2 oboes, 2 horns, and the customary strings.

CONCERTO FOR PIANO AND ORCHESTRA, B-FLAT MAJOR, K. 450

This radiant Concerto reflects some of the happiest, most unclouded days of Mozart's career. It was completed on March 15, 1784 in Vienna at the peak of Mozart's popularity as a piano virtuoso and composer. He composed it for himself as soloist in the subscription concerts of the Lenten concert season.

Originally he had planned to give six concerts during Lent for his own benefit. But he agreed to appear three times at the concerts of another piano virtuoso, G. F. Richter, for the Viennese aristocracy had indicated they would not enjoy Richter's concerts unless Mozart were to take part in them. Thereupon Mozart scheduled only three public concerts for himself on the last three Wednesdays of Lent: March 17, 24, and 31. Mozart proudly sent his father in Salzburg a list of the subscribers, including many of the most distinguished aristocrats and music patrons of the capital. There were 174 of them at 6 florins each—30 more than had subscribed to the concerts of Richter and another rival series combined.

The subscription public for which Mozart wrote his concertos was not drawn from many different social and economic groups, as audiences are today, but only from the top: the aristocracy and the most cultivated and ambitious of the bourgeoisie, who vied with the aristocrats in their patronage of music. Thus the audience, so influential in forming Mozart's concertos, was far from representative of the great mass of music lovers. Its taste had been extraordinarily sensitized and sophisticated by an old aristocratic culture, but it was restricted within very definite limits. It preferred gaiety, grace, wit, nuance and charm to tragic or stormy emotions. It preferred, in the words of the great eighteenth-century music critic Charles Burney, music that expressed with "clearness and propriety whatever is graceful, elegant and tender" rather than "complicated misery and the tempestuous fury of unbridled passions."

Both types of expression were deeply rooted in Mozart's nature. But for the time being, as the conquering hero of this aristocracy, he exulted in the response which this one side of his nature evoked.

I. *Allegro.* The jaunty main theme is announced by the woodwinds (oboes and bassoons):

It is continued by the strings in a colorful alternation with the woodwinds. The solo piano makes its entrance with a cadenza-like passage of great splashing scales and arpeggios, before taking up the main theme. Other, more lyric themes follow, interspersed with virtuoso passage work, which also dominates the very free development. The recapitulation of the basic themes is also free and is capped by a cadenza for the solo instrument.

II. *Andante.* The slow movement is a theme and variations. The songful theme is divided in two, each half being played first by the orchestral strings and then embellished by the solo piano. The first variation is enriched by piano arpeggios. The second variation starts in the piano alone and the movement is rounded off with a brief *coda.*

III. *Allegro.* This finale is a *rondo* with a fanfare-like refrain, a lilting figure suggesting a hunting signal or the post-horn so beloved by eighteenth-century composers:

This refrain appears four times. The three intervening episodes are related to the refrain, but have their own themes, which are stated, developed, and restated roughly in the manner of first movement sonata form. There is a final cadenza for the pianist just before the return of the last refrain.

Mozart works his magic with one of his smallest concerto orchestras, consisting of flute (in finale only), 2 oboes, 2 bassoons, 2 horns, and the customary string choir.

CONCERTO FOR PIANO AND ORCHESTRA, G MAJOR, K. 453

The story of Mozart's starling, a pet bird that learned to sing (or whistle) the theme of the finale from his G-major Concerto, is so beguiling that some commentators have been tempted to improve on history by asserting that Mozart learned his theme from the starling, instead of the other way around. But the facts are charming enough in themselves. Fortunately, or unfortunately, no amount of interpretation can change Mozart's own records. His manuscript score of the G-major piano Concerto is dated April 12, 1784, and his account book tells us that he bought the starling (for 34 *kreuzer*) some six weeks later, on May 27.

The bird must have been gifted. For Mozart, opposite the date and the sum paid for the starling, noted the theme of the finale correct all except for one note which the bird evidently sang sharp! And below the theme Mozart wrote: "That was beautiful!" Thus it appears that the starling learned the theme on the very day that Mozart acquired it—unless we are to assume that a previous owner of the starling had *already* taught it the Mozart theme, which would certainly have enchanted the composer! In any case, Mozart became very attached to the starling. When it died three years later, he buried it in the garden of his house on the Vienna Landstrasse. For the marker over the grave Mozart wrote some heartfelt doggerel verses, which, like some of his most characteristic music, were a mixture of laughter and tears. They began: "Here lies a beloved clown. . . . "

A theme that could be sung by a starling—even a very clever starling—suggests a certain simplicity. In fact, the theme of the finale is written in a simple, semi-folk style, which recalls the character of Papageno in Mozart's opera *The Magic Flute.* Papageno, it will be remembered, also had a certain connection with the world of birds.

The G-major Concerto reflects some of the happiest days of Mozart's career: the time of his greatest popularity in Vienna. He composed it for one of his favorite pupils, Barbara Ployer, the daughter of the Viennese agent of Mozart's former employer, the Archbishop of Salzburg. Fräulein Ployer must have been extremely talented. We know from Mozart's letters that he thought highly of her. But we could guess this from the music alone. The G-major Concerto has the outward simplicity and grace to make it extremely popular with the Viennese public of the 1780s. But it has many shades of feeling, many subtleties, intended for an extremely sensitive performer.

I. *Allegro.* The first movement opens with a lengthy orchestral introduction, the principal theme sung softly by the first violins:

This gentle beginning is followed by a more conventionally assertive theme for the entire orchestra, and an astounding wealth of orchestral contrasts, including another gentle theme which seems to be important not only in this opening movement but in the slow middle movement as well:

Suddenly the orchestra falls silent. The reticent principal theme which we heard at the beginning of the movement is now taken up and elaborated by the soloist. This solo presentation of the basic thematic material is rounded off by a short passage of mildly virtuosic display: chiefly decorative arpeggios.

The central development section is far from a symphonic development, but rather a fantasia-like roaming through fresh key areas in an almost improvisatory style. The recapitulation of the opening material follows a more familiar path, leading to the traditional pause for a solo cadenza and the festive closing bars.

II. *Andante.* This irresistably appealing slow movement is the most unconventional, most original and most seductive of the three. Its form has been called variously a sonata-allegro form, a *rondo,* a theme and variations and a totally free, untrammeled form. Untrammeled it certainly is, yet the well-planned returns and variants of the opening theme give a strong, organic coherence to the movement. It is hard to resist the impression that this theme, announced so quietly by the strings, is related to the second theme quoted above:

Words cannot describe or even properly analyze this subtle movement with its amazing variety of moods.

III. *Allegretto.* The perky little tune of the *finale*, with its balanced and repeated phrases, serves as a theme for a set of crystalline variations. Each variation seems gayer and more brilliant than the last, until Mozart reaches his complex final variation: a lengthy *presto* which recalls the pell-mell comic finales of the *opera buffa* which were so popular in Mozart's day. It is amazing to realize that Mozart could accomplish so much with such a modest orchestra. He uses no clarinets, no trumpets, no kettledrums. The orchestration calls for flute, 2 oboes, 2 bassoons, 2 horns, and the traditional strings.

CONCERTO FOR PIANO AND ORCHESTRA, F MAJOR, K. 459

Perhaps the most imposing of all the many miracles that made up Mozart's career were the towering range of masterpieces he created for pianoforte with orchestra. Even today, after nearly two hundred years, Mozart is still the undisputed king of the piano concerto. In the world of opera, the symphony, the string quartet, the piano sonata, Mozart is not without rivals. But no one has approached him in the breathtaking variety and sheer number of masterpieces he has written for piano with orchestra, of which this F-major Concerto is one.

There are rare moments in history when the inclinations of artists—sometimes of a single great artist—seem perfectly in tune with the taste of an eager, appreciative public. Mozart experienced such a moment—several months in fact, from about his twenty-eighth to his thirtieth year. We are still living from the riches he poured forth during those brief months of dynamic equilibrium.

At the peak of his popularity as performer-composer he produced (aside from a flood of other masterworks) an average of four great concertos per season, most of them intended for himself as soloist at concerts of his own works. During the year 1784 alone he composed six such concertos, including this F-major Concerto. Many manuscripts are dated with the exact day of completion of each concerto. And because of the copious Mozart family correspondence, we know the day of many of their first performances.

The most intensive concert season in Vienna was during Lent, and the majority of Mozart's great concertos were composed for his own Lenten concerts. But the F-major Concerto, K. 459, was completed on December 11, 1784. No Mozart letters have survived from that time. We know only that Mozart rarely completed a concerto more than a day or two before its performance, and that this Concerto was completed three days before an important event in Mozart's life: his admission to the Masonic Lodge *"zur Wohltätigkeit."*

Mozart attached an almost religious importance to the high ideals and the bonds of friendship which characterized the Freemasons. Some of his closest friends and patrons were Masons, and he was very highly regarded among them. We know, too, that he composed music specifically for the Masons, some of it among the finest he ever wrote.

While Mozart never wrote autobiography in tones (as so many nineteenth-century Romantic composers did), it is perhaps no accident that this F-major Concerto radiates a joyous confidence and a mastery of convention which enables him to be totally unconventional without seeming so. The Concerto even has a certain playful quality throughout, but it is the playfulness of a sovereign master.

I. *Allegro.* The entire first movement is permeated by a catchy rhythm (the opening bar of the opening theme), which is one of the earmarks of Mozart's style. On occasion this rhythm can sound marchlike. But here it launches the movement ever so gently, in the characteristic Mozartean sonority of violins with a single flute:

The orchestral introduction includes a profusion of lesser themes, none of which turns out to be a true second theme in the traditional sense.

The piano solo enters as gently as did the orchestra, and with the same theme. The second theme is a mere passing episode, playful rather than lyric. The central fascination of this opening movement is its amazing variety within the overall unity due to the domination of one principal theme. This is a kind of thematic unity which Mozart may have learned from his beloved elder friend Joseph Haydn, but which Mozart was now able to achieve in his own highly personal way.

The cadenza towards the close of the movement is by the composer, and the concluding bars are lilting, dancelike figures, which recall the laughter of *opera buffa.*

II. *Allegretto.* Playfulness does not exclude such exquisite grace as we find throughout this middle movement. Nor does it exclude pensive moments. These tend to be beguiling rather than profound, despite one brief excursion into the key of C minor. In other contexts, C minor might suggest tragedy, but in this case it reverts simply and happily to the tonic C major. This seductive music recalls Mozart's own words to his father describing the true nature of concertos:

> Concertos are really a sort of halfway house between what is too difficult and too simple—they are very brilliant—attractive to the ear—natural, without ever being superficial—here and there occur passages where *only connoisseurs* are given complete satisfaction—but in such a way that the less learned listener must be pleased, without knowing why.

III. *Allegro assai.* Each movement of this Concerto seems to be an improvement over its predecessor, and the *finale* appears as the true crown of the work. It is based on a rather frisky refrain which not only recurs at intervals throughout the *finale*, but also contributes little humorous touches to some of the more serious episodes. It is introduced by the piano solo:

Almost immediately a serious note is heard: the exposition of a fugue, or *fugato,* but there is a quick return to the mercurial rhythmic pattern of the opening.

In its simplest terms, this *finale* is a *rondo*, but a *rondo* with a difference, with a close relation to Haydn's invention: the combined rondo-sonata form. But Mozart at twenty-eight was already as dexterous as the older master in juggling the traditional forms in a way which delights "the less learned listener" and dazzles the connoisseur. Nothing could be freer, nothing more exhilarating than Mozart's combination of his humorous refrain with the return of the fugal episode from the opening.

The finale includes two original Mozart cadenzas, the latter and the longer of them a characteristic masterpiece of sudden shifts of mood, wayward, lightning leaps of the imagination and as brief as the soul of wit requires.

The Concerto is scored for flute, 2 oboes, 2 bassoons, 2 horns, and the traditional string choir.

CONCERTO FOR PIANO AND ORCHESTRA, D MINOR, K. 466

This stormy Concerto is one of Mozart's most Romantic works. We do not ordinarily think of Mozart as a Romantic composer; yet, as our view of the grand sweep of history broadens and our understanding of Mozart grows, we sense the powerful trends that link Mozart to the Romantic future. And conversely, we realize how deeply the roots of Romanticism reach into the Classical past. Classicism cannot be separated from Romanticism, nor can Mozart from either of those two movements which are really one.

The D-minor Concerto is more than a Romantic *and* Classical work: it is an amazingly personal document illuminating a side of Mozart's nature which he did not often reveal. Of his twenty-three piano concertos, only two are composed in the minor mode. D minor had a particular significance in Mozart's day and to Mozart himself: he used it only on rare occasions, as a key of deepest pessimism, struggle and tragedy. His unfinished Requiem Mass—unfinished because Mozart died during its composition—is in D minor. In *Don Giovanni,* the cataclysmic appearance of the avenging stone guest, the Commendatore, is in D minor. In Mozart's *Idomeneo* the populace of Crete flees before the ravages of the sea monster in the panic-stricken D minor chorus *"Corriamo, fuggiamo."*

We cannot even imagine how this Concerto sounded in its first performance. Mozart finished the composition on February 10, 1785. On February 11 he was to be his own soloist in his own concert at the fashionable Mehlgrube (a Baroque masterpiece by J. B. Fischer von Erlach) on the New Market Place. On the very day of the concert, Mozart's father Leopold arrived from Salzburg for a visit. His letter (of February 16 to his daughter in Salzburg) is testimony both to Wolfgang's popularity and the incredible speed with which he composed and prepared a performance.

There was no time for *any* rehearsal! When father Mozart and Wolfgang arrived at the concert hall, the copyist had not yet finished writing out the orchestral parts. "Your brother did not even have time to play through the rondo [i.e., the finale] because he had to supervise the copying." Yet Leopold, a sophisticated musician, seemed far from disturbed. "The concert was incomparable," he wrote, "the orchestra excellent."

Such a Romantic work must have startled that first audience. Yet it seems to have been well received, for Mozart repeated it only four days later at another concert in Vienna. The Concerto is in the traditional three movements.

I. *Allegro.* The first bars of the D-minor Concerto open a world new to Mozart's contemporaries, new even to Mozart. Instead of a cleanly outlined principal theme, there is an agitated, syncopated D-minor tonality. Even today the mood seems threatening. How much more so must it have seemed to the elegant subscription audience at that premiere! Throbbing violins and violas are driven onward by the surge of upthrusting basses and cellos:

The atmosphere of threat is emphasized by the repressed dynamic level, kept almost to a whisper until the tension explodes into an orchestral *tutti.*

The piano solo makes its entrance with a plaintive little lyric figure, which remains the property of the soloist throughout. The orchestra retorts with the

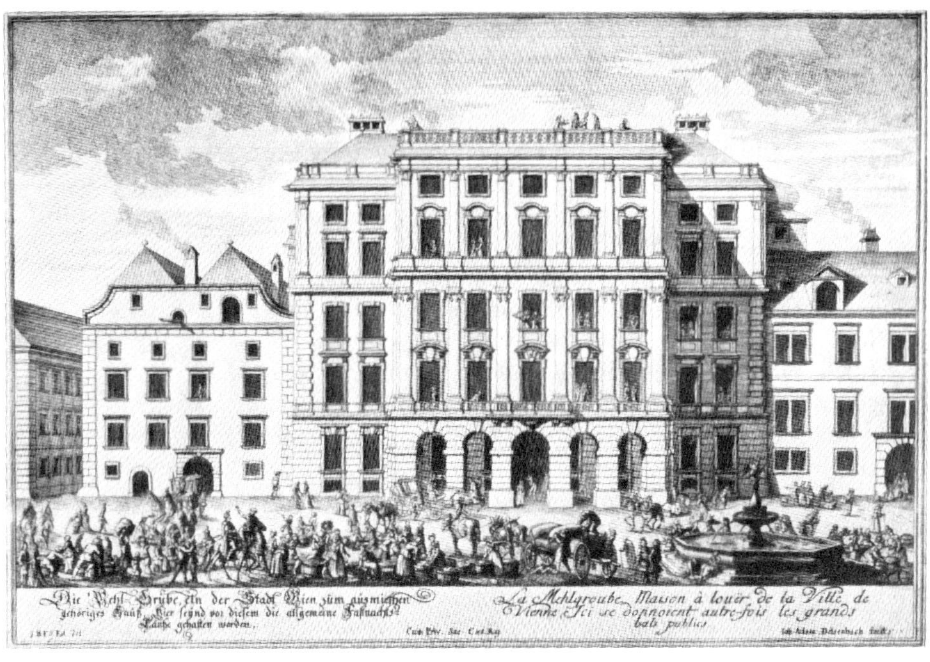

MOZART CONCERTO PREMIERES.

At the height of Mozart's popularity in Vienna, he gave many concerts in the "Casino," a fashionable ballroom and concert hall of the Mehlgrube Inn (**above**). This is where he played the premieres of his Piano Concertos in D minor, K. 466, and C major, K. 503.
Left: Mozart's concert piano, which was moved from his apartment to the Mehlgrube for these concerts. **Below:** The only surviving ticket to a Mozart concert. (*Courtesy, Mozart-Gedenkstätte Augsburg; Mozarteum, Salzburg*)

EINLASS - KARTE
ZUM
CONCERT
von
W. A. Mozart.

menacing, agitated bars of the beginning. Throughout this movement the clash of contrasting themes and the struggle between soloist and orchestra are heightened by fierce harmonic and dynamic tensions. One of the qualities of the movement which appealed so mightily to the Romantics of a later age is that of unresolved tension. At the end the conflict dies away, unresolved, but with insistent, whispered references to the menace of the opening bars.

II. *Romance.* What serenity there is in the lovely lyric strain that opens the slow movement! Coming after the storm and stress of the *Allegro,* it recalls the abrupt transition in Gluck's *Orfeo* from the furies of the underworld to the sunlit Elysian Fields. Mozart's melody is one of his most beguiling inspirations:

Yet he does not hesitate to interrupt it brutally halfway through the movement with a stormy, almost frantic G-minor episode, in which the pianist plunges from one end of the keyboard to the other. Gradually peace is restored, the lyric strain returns, and the *Romance,* like the first movement, ends in a whisper.

III. *Allegro assai.* The *finale* is one of Mozart's few rondos in the minor mode. Its fiery refrain is far from the dainty charm we associate with so many Classical rondos:

This *rondo* incorporates much of the dramatic spirit as well as the development techniques of the symphony, and it revives the power and the strife of the first movement. Then, after the soloist's cadenza, the concluding pages take a sudden turn to a joyous D major and a *coda* of irresistible charm. It is hard to know why such a sudden, happy end does not sound forced or false. But it does not.

Mozart's D-minor Concerto is scored for 1 flute, 2 oboes, 2 bassoons, 2 horns, 2 trumpets, kettledrums, and string choir. The piano on which Mozart performed the solo part in this and other concertos of this season, was an unusual one. It was longer and heavier than the usual piano of the day, and it was supplemented by a separate, specially constructed pedal keyboard. This enabled him to play certain passages which, as written in his manuscript, would be unplayable on a normal piano of Mozart's day or ours. These passages are brief, and the chief purpose of the pedal notes appears to have been to supply a grander sonority to the harmony. Thus it seems conceivable that

Mozart, contrary to widespread belief, might have been delighted rather than dismayed, by the heavier bass sonority of our modern concert grand.

CONCERTO FOR PIANO AND ORCHESTRA, C MAJOR, K. 467

On the crest of his greatest triumphs as a composer and performer, at the peak of his most prosperous season in imperial Vienna, Mozart composed this imperial Concerto as a vehicle for his own exuberant virtuosity. The headlong pace of his activity is reflected in the dates: March 9, 1785, completion of the manuscript score; March 10, premiere, with Mozart as his own soloist at a concert for his own benefit, in the Royal Imperial National Court Theater of Vienna. His father Leopold, who was visiting in Vienna, reported proudly to Mozart's sister, his beloved "Nannerl": "Your brother made 559 florins with his concert, which we had not expected since he is [also] giving a series of six subscription concerts at [the Casino in] the Mehlgrube, to which more than 150 people have subscribed—each person paying a sovereign for the six concerts. Beside that he has played very often at other people's concerts out of pure friendliness. . . . We never get to bed at night before one o'clock, we never get up before nine o'clock, and go to lunch at two or half past. Dreadful weather! Every day a concert, always studying, music, writing, et cetera. . . . If only all the concerts were over! It is impossible to describe all the rumpus and confusion: your brother's grand piano has been moved, in the time I have been here, at least twelve times from the house to the theater or to other houses."

If Mozart had written biographical music, we could hardly fail to hear echoes of his expanding triumphs in this masterpiece. But happily Mozart's creative scope was not confined to musical autobiography—at least not in any literal, limited sense. Like Beethoven, he often worked simultaneously, or in quick succession, on two deeply contrasting works. The contrasting companion piece to this C-major Concerto, K. 467, is the D-minor, K. 466, which was composed and performed only four weeks earlier. The D-minor is Mozart's stormiest, most tragic concerto.

Its C-major successor is too assertive to be called serene, except perhaps in the ravishing slow movement.

I. *Allegro.* A thousand times more dramatic than any opening blast of the trumpets is the restrained whisper, the repressed excitement with which the strings announce the principal theme:

A delicate marchlike phrase for the woodwinds alternates with the strings before the full, golden resonance of the *tutti,* including horns, trumpets and drums bursts out with an extended statement of the principal theme.

Mozart always finds new and original ways to introduce his solo instrument. The orchestral introduction comes to a strong close followed by gentle woodwind phrases, which seem to invite the soloist, as though the piano needed coaxing, to join the ensemble. When the piano finally does join, it is not with the principal theme (which in this movement is reserved almost entirely to the orchestra) but with a little fluttering figure, which grows into more brilliant figuration, working upward to a short cadenza (or *Eingang*). Underneath the concluding trill, the orchestra repeats the principal theme in its original whispering tone. Graceful piano runs and arabesques lead to a second theme carried by the soloist without accompaniment: a rather startling figure in an unexpected dominant-minor harmony. It is a moment of sharp emotional and harmonic stress, reminiscent in more than one way of the opening of Mozart's great G-minor Symphony. But the stress is soon relaxed and further flowing runs lead to one of Mozart's simplest and most beguiling inspirations, a figure given out first by the solo piano, then taken up by the woodwinds and brought back again lovingly at the end of the movement:

A passage of vigorous virtuosity leads to the highly imaginative development section, built on thematic fragments from the foregoing, with another great *crescendo* of virtuosity.

The return of the opening thematic material begins as did the introduction with a whispered statement of the principal theme. All the basic themes are now recapitulated with the exception of the tense G-minor episode, but the recapitulation is far from literal, all of the material growing and expanding with Mozart's endlessly fertile imagination. The close, surprisingly enough for a movement of such power and grandeur, is a last whispered recall of the opening theme.

II. *Andante.* The slow movement has a twofold nature. On the one hand it is like an elaborate, instrumental version of an operatic aria. On the other hand it seems an anticipation of the most Romantic of nineteenth-century nocturnes. The strings are muted throughout. Over a murmuring accompaniment of second violins and violas, the first violins sing a long and broadly arched melody:

The leisurely poetic song of the violins is taken up by the piano solo and developed. The movement does not observe any strict, traditional pattern.

When the opening strain returns to round off the movement, it comes not in the tonic key of F major, as one might expect, but in the Romantically third-related key of A-flat major. But there is nothing ostentatious about Mozart's divergences from traditional forms or procedures. The music slips back into the home key in the most natural possible fashion, and the movement concludes as peacefully as it began.

III. *Allegro vivace assai.* The finale is a rollicking *rondo,* built around a dancelike refrain stated first by the orchestra. The soloist enters with a brief little cadenza (or *Eingang*) of its own before launching into the *rondo* refrain. The lightness, the simple, bubbling humor of this *finale* are close to the spirit of the *opera buffa.* The melodies of the intervening episodes are short with piquant rhythms. There is more opportunity for solo display in another *Eingang* and a more substantial solo cadenza before the final return of the refrain and the closing measures with their brilliant sweeping scales for the soloist.

The Concerto is scored for flute, 2 oboes, 2 bassoons, 2 horns, 2 trumpets, kettledrums, and the traditional string choir.

CONCERTO FOR PIANO AND ORCHESTRA, E-FLAT MAJOR, K. 482

How obvious it may have been to others we cannot know, but to Mozart it must have been clear enough as he approached the end of his thirtieth year that something was wrong. True, he was at the very pinnacle of success: what higher honor could he covet than to hear Joseph Haydn declare, as he had in February 1785, to Mozart's father: "I tell you before God and as an honorable man, that your son is the greatest composer I know either personally or by reputation." What more powerful patron than the Austrian Emperor could have honored him with a command to compose an *opera buffa (The Marriage of Figaro)* for the Imperial Viennese Theater? From late October, 1785, Mozart worked feverishly on what was to be one of his greatest operatic masterpieces. Meanwhile, no piano virtuoso was in such demand as Mozart for the subscription concerts patronized by the moneyed music lovers of Vienna.

Yet something was seriously wrong. Perhaps in the flush of success and confidence in his own amazing powers Mozart had indulged too far in the luxury of composing to please himself rather than the simpler-minded patrons and public. To them, Mozart's works, embodying the stressful, passionate, tragic side of his nature, seemed merely too learned or eccentric. Such a great work as the stormy G-minor Quartet for Piano and Strings, completed a few days before he began *The Marriage of Figaro,* was a failure—from the publisher Hoffmeister's point of view. This was to have been the first of a series. But when it found no customers, Mozart gallantly released the publisher from his contract.

These portents could be multiplied. Worse still, Mozart was already in dire financial need. By November 20, 1785, we hear the first of those cries of distress, which foretell the abyss of debt, humiliation, and ill health into which Mozart was slowly, inexorably being drawn. We hear it in a letter to the publisher of the Quartet, begging Hoffmeister to come to his assistance "just with a little money, for," says Mozart frankly, "I need it very badly just now."

Four weeks later he had finished the E-flat Concerto and performed the premiere, probably on December 16 or 17. This is a work in which Mozart tried to turn the tide of popularity, and for the moment he was brilliantly successful. Once more he summoned all the sensuous grace, the almost physical charm with which he could make his music glow. It is among the greatest of a long line of seductive scores in E-flat. "Of all his concertos," writes C. M. Girdlestone in his penetrating volume, "this one is the queenliest. Combining grace and majesty, the music unfolds like a sovereign in progress, the queen of the twenty-three concertos."

I. *Allegro.* Majesty speaks in the opening phrase, the principal theme:

In the little phrases that follow we hear the delicate voice of a solo flute, a duet of velvet-toned clarinets echoed by a pair of bassoons and by two horns. Such beguiling touches of woodwind color give the character of a serenade. The piano solo part, too, gleams and sparkles with wreaths and garlands of scales, arpeggios and other graceful decorations.

II. *Andante.* The melancholy *Andante* in C minor is the crown of the Concerto and its most imaginative movement. A combination of *rondo* and variations, it is built on a world-weary tune carried by muted violins:

The transparent chamber music texture of the opening is made even more diaphanous by muting the violins. Except for a brief tragic climax toward the end, the chamber music effect is preserved throughout. Interestingly enough, it was this movement which the audience singled out to encore when Mozart played the Concerto on December 23, 1785, at a concert of the Viennese Tonkünstler-Societät.

III. *Allegro.* The *Rondo* finale has a rollicking, horn-call type of refrain.

Its most striking episode is a slow *Andantino cantabile* in gentle minuet style. The score calls for 1 flute, 2 clarinets, 2 bassoons, 2 horns, 2 trumpets, kettledrums, and strings.

The date of Mozart's autographed score is December 16, 1785. The date of the first performance is unknown, but it probably fell between the 16th and the performance of December 23rd mentioned above.

CONCERTO FOR PIANO AND ORCHESTRA, A MAJOR, K. 488

At the peak of his popularity, while working at top speed on his most successful comedy, *The Marriage of Figaro, or The Madcap Day,* Mozart incredibly found time to toss off a whole series of minor and even some major masterpieces on the side: his *Masonic Funeral Music,* a one-act comic opera, *Der Schauspieldirektor,* a violin sonata, miscellaneous chamber, choral, and solo vocal works, and three of his greatest piano concertos: those in E-flat major, K. 482; A major, K. 488; and in C minor, K. 491. And, if Mozart followed his usual practice in these years, he must have found time to prepare and appear as soloist at the premieres of all three piano concertos, within a few days after completion of the respective scores. Since the A-major concerto was completed on March 2, 1786, in Vienna, it most likely was performed during the following week, probably with the composer as soloist. However, since all the records of the premiere have been lost, we cannot be certain.

The A major is one of the most beloved and frequently performed of Mozart's concertos, its only rival being the D-minor Piano Concerto, K. 466. But unlike the stormy D minor, the A-major Concerto is one of Mozart's ingratiating works. This does not mean that it is lacking in depth, but its emotional intensity is masked beneath a smiling exterior in the first movement, and a captivating lyricism in the second. The distinguished French poet and critic, Adolphe Boschot, observed of this typically Mozartean ambiguity: "His luminous genius has so often sung the beauty of life and so often replied to his daily trials with songs of love and hope, that one does not discover at once the sadness which is veiled behind his geniality; in his soul and his music, even the shadows are shot through with light and the reflection of the sky makes them diaphanous."

I. *Allegro.* The graceful melody of the principal theme, announced by the orchestral strings, is touched with sadness:

This is echoed in the gleaming tones of the woodwinds, whereupon a brief *tutti* interruption leads us to a second lyric theme announced by the strings alone, with a touch of almost tearful melancholy in its drooping chromatic line.

The two principal themes having been established by the orchestra, the piano soloist now takes them up with only slight variation. After a brief passage of purling virtuosity for the soloist, the piano is silent for a moment as the strings round off this exposition very softly with the following close:

This apparently last-minute melodic thought now becomes the basis of the entire development section, a passage of great brevity and intensity, culminating in the first outbreak of tragic emotion in this concerto. But this passes quickly and the piano takes over in a short cadenza-like passage, leading to a recapitulation of the opening themes. The longer and more formal cadenza at the conclusion of the movement is written out by Mozart himself in the autograph manuscript, an unusual procedure in an age when most cadenzas were left to the discretion of the soloist.

II. *Adagio.* The slow movement is in the relative key of F-sharp minor, a key so rare in Mozart's work that his choice of it here portends something special: a melancholy so deep and so resigned that it borders on despair. Yet the melody is of such ravishing beauty and sensuous charm that it almost conceals the intensity of emotion. Its appeal is enhanced by a langorous, lilting rhythm known as a *siciliano:*

Notice how beautifully the piano sings, how Mozart seems always to have in mind the human voice, that most personal of all instruments. Listen, too, for the wonderful silvery coloring of the orchestra: how the flutes and clarinets mingle with the tone of the piano. This is one of Mozart's most beautiful slow movements—and one of his most profound.

It is interesting to realize, however, that much as the simplicity of the piano melody appeals to us, this was not what Mozart expected his listeners to hear when the melody was repeated. We know that Mozart improvised and embellished much of the piano part when he performed his own concertos. Indeed, in slow movements it was standard practice for the written notes to be ornamented, often very profusely, by the performer, exactly as arias were intended for embellishment by their singers. Although such variants were rarely preserved, one manuscript has survived to us giving an embellished version of this slow movement, not by Mozart himself, but apparently by a friend or student, who did his work so well that Mozart appears to have preserved this manuscript among his own papers. The ornamentations are extremely florid, and might shock those purists among us, who believe that Mozart was more "Classically" restrained than he may have been in actual fact.

III. *Allegro assai.* After the melancholy of the slow movement, the high spirits of the *finale* are like a sudden release from prison. The opening *rondo* refrain leaps upward a full octave, cascading downward in a florid run, only to leap upward once more:

Between the recurrences of this exuberant refrain Mozart has enclosed an enchanting little symphonic sonata with two contrasting themes: a dainty, playful one announced by the soloist alone, and a plaintive melody given first to the woodwinds and later elaborated by the piano. The final return of the *rondo* refrain is another burst of high spirits, which do not deny the melancholy which has gone before, but balance it and, in a sense, heal it, within the higher unity of the Classical style.

The modest orchestration of the A-major Concerto omits oboes, trumpet, and drums. The score calls for flute, 2 clarinets, 2 bassoons, 2 horns, the standard string choir, and the solo piano, which, in Mozart's day, was not expected to be merely a solo, but to join discreetly during orchestral tuttis as a member of the orchestral ensemble, taking over the traditional role of the keyboard *continuo,* without which no orchestral group was considered complete.

CONCERTO FOR PIANO AND ORCHESTRA, C MINOR, K. 491

"Concertos," Mozart explained to his father in a letter of December 28, 1782, "are a happy medium between what is too hard and too easy—they are very brilliant—pleasing to the ear—natural, without turning vapid.—Here and there—are passages which *only connoisseurs* can appreciate—yet so written—that non-connoisseurs cannot fail to enjoy them, though without knowing why."

This was a prescription sure to please the canny, practical elder Mozart. Old Leopold had brought up his son to have precisely this attitude not only toward concertos, but toward music in general. And he largely succeeded—not because he succeeded in imposing his will, but because Mozart naturally loved to entertain, to please. He loved especially the subtle and infinitely difficult art of giving pleasure to both connoisseur and nonconnoisseur at the same time. If he had always followed his own words, he might have had a more prosperous career and he might have lived longer. Also he would never have written two of his greatest piano concertos: the D minor of 1785, and the C minor, K. 491, of the following year.

During his prosperous years in Vienna, one of Mozart's top sources of income was his annual series of Lenten subscription concerts featuring his own works and usually capped by his own appearance as piano virtuoso in the premiere of a concerto written for himself and for the occasion. At its peak, Mozart's list of subscribers read like a *Who's Who* of wealthy Viennese music lovers, including the cream of Viennese aristocracy and, on occasion, the Emperor himself.

But for all his love of applause, all his joy in being understood, Mozart could be no mere follower of his public's taste, no matter how exalted or fashionable that public might be. Even during his teens, wilder, darker, emotions, a deep-lying, often hidden part of his nature, had erupted in such works as the defiant "Little" G-minor Symphony and in his opera *Lucio Silla,* composed for Milan, when he was sixteen. It is significant that despite Mozart's first jubilant reception in Italy, he was never again during his entire career invited to write another opera for that country. As he matured, such outbursts remained rare, but they grew in power and depth.

There is no simple, biographical explanation of these explosions. They were not caused by the financial miseries, the professional disappointments, or failing health of his last years. The D-minor and C-minor Concertos may well have *contributed* to the decline of his popularity, for tragedy was not popular in Mozart's day. But they cannot have been *caused* by his misfortunes for the simple reason that they were written earlier, at the peak of his worldly success.

The C-minor Concerto was completed on March 24, 1786, and first played by Mozart at his own subscription Concert of April 7 in the Vienna Hoftheater, barely three weeks before the completion of what was to be his most popular comedy, *The Marriage of Figaro.*

I. *Allegro.* The ominous opening theme, with its stern octave texture, its jagged leaps and its tremendous harmonic tensions, is a portent of struggle:

It begins in an undertone but expands suddenly to the stormy majesty of a full orchestral *tutti,* the fullest orchestra Mozart had ever used in a concerto, including clarinets and trumpets in addition to the more usual flutes, oboes, horns, and kettledrums. Plaintive little phrases come and go in the woodwinds, but the stage is not fully set for the entrance of the piano solo until the orchestra rounds off this introduction with a return of the powerful opening figure.

The entrance of the solo is a dramatic understatement. The piano sings a melancholy lyric phrase distantly related to the principal orchestral theme:

In the dialogue that ensues, the piano becomes more and more urgent, both in its lyricism and in its harmonic expansion of the traditionally decorative section of scales and arpeggios. The musical development grows more and more symphonic, and the sense of struggle is sustained even in the tragic quiet of the closing pages.

II. *Larghetto.* The serene opening of this slow movement is deceptive. Its beautiful E-flat major theme announced by the piano alone is deeply melancholy. In melody, harmony, mood and tempo it is related to the heartbreaking grace of the Countess's E-flat aria *"Porgi amor"* in *The Marriage of Figaro:*

In the episodes between recurrences of this melody the music reverts to the darker keys of C minor, A-flat, and F-minor.

III. *Allegretto.* Even in his *finale*, Mozart finds little release from the tensions of his opening movement. The variation form, so popular and so handy for the expression of lighter feelings, is used here to suggest an inescapable pattern, to emphasize a constant return to the inexorable tonic minor and to the structure of the opening theme:

In a way most unusual for Mozart, the very handwriting of his manuscript shows agitation, struggle and even indecision: passages are revised, re-revised and sometimes left unclear as to which is meant to be the final version.

The Concerto is scored for flute, 2 oboes, 2 clarinets, 2 bassoons, 2 horns, 2 trombones, kettledrums and the traditional strings.

CONCERTO FOR PIANO AND ORCHESTRA, C MAJOR, K. 503

Sandwiched in between his two most popular operatic masterpieces, *The Marriage of Figaro* (1786) and *Don Giovanni* (1787), and simultaneously with one of his greatest symphonic masterpieces (his "Prague" Symphony in D major), Mozart composed this Olympian C-major Piano Concerto, Köchel No. 503.

(The Concerto and the Symphony were completed in Vienna on December 4 and 6 respectively, 1786.) When one recalls the string of chamber works also completed in the preceding weeks, one score more beautiful than the next, the achievement seems almost supernatural. The year 1786 was a peak of Mozart's career.

Mozart remains today the greatest composer of piano concertos we know. No other composer has ever approached him in the number of acknowledged masterpieces for this difficult combination of piano solo and symphony orchestra. Even Beethoven wrote only three piano concertos that rank with his own greatest symphonies; Brahms only two; Schumann and Tchaikovsky one each. Chopin and Liszt, the fabulous pianists of the Romantic age, wrote their greatest music for piano solo. Only Mozart has left us such a gigantic range of piano concertos, surpassing even his own finest symphonies in brilliance, depth, variety of expression and individuality of form.

Mozart composed most of his great piano concertos for himself as performer. We do not know precisely when he first performed this C-major Concerto. We do know that he composed it for one of the four concerts he gave during the 1786 Advent concert season (the weeks immediately preceding Christmas). Since Mozart habitually finished his works two or three days before the scheduled performance, this Concerto was probably performed soon after December 4, 1786, the date of completion recorded by Mozart himself. It is in the traditional three movements:

I. *Allegro maestoso.* The movement opens with a grandeur and a spaciousness unrivaled in Mozart's works. The entire orchestra joins in a series of majestic chords of the simplest, most basic harmony, descending and then rising again in the following general pattern:

Softly echoing phrases of bassoons and oboes give an intimate touch to the opening page, and with a turn from the tonic major to the minor a cloud seems to pass over the landscape. A new, more agitated rhythmic pattern echoes back and forth from one instrumental group to another. Swiftly rising scales of the violins spread through the orchestra, enriching the texture of the music. A delicate little marchlike tune fluctuates between major and minor and still further thematic riches are introduced before the solo piano makes its (somewhat timid) first appearance.

The orchestra resumes its majestic opening chords, but now with the piano embellishing the softer answering phrases. Far from following the thematic pattern of the orchestral exposition, the solo exposition grows more and more virtuosic, with broken octaves, arpeggios, chromatic runs, and a long concluding trill marking the end of the section. The development that follows is ingeniously and, for Mozart, rather strictly built entirely of themes and fragments already introduced in the expositions.

II. *Andante.* The graceful opening phrase of the flute, doubled at the lower octaves by violins and bassoons, sets the tone for the slow movement:

The florid embellishments of the movement are lavished for the most part by the solo piano.

III. *Allegretto.* The rondo-form *finale* starts with a lilting tune of almost folk-dance simplicity:

Without ever laying aside its *rondo* character, this movement develops into one of Mozart's more serious finales. This last of Mozart's C-major concertos calls for flute, 2 oboes, 2 bassoons, 2 horns, 2 trumpets, kettledrums, and the standard string choir.

CONCERTO FOR PIANO AND ORCHESTRA (CORONATION), D MAJOR, K. 537

With this graceful score of 1788, Mozart apparently hoped to charm his way back into the favor of the fickle Viennese. It seems incredible that he should have failed, but he did. Up to his thirtieth year, Mozart had known intoxicating triumphs as a piano virtuoso. In the three years 1784–1786 he had composed *twelve* piano concertos, the crowning glory of his orchestral works, on a par with his last three, greatest symphonies, and far overshadowing them in volume, variety, and scope. He celebrated the last of these triumphs in December 1786, when he appeared for the last time in one of his own public subscription concerts. With it the great outpouring of concerto masterworks came to a sudden halt. During the five remaining years of his life there were only two stragglers: the "Coronation" Concerto and the B-flat major Concerto, K. 595 of 1791.

It may have been the triumph of *Don Giovanni* in Prague in October 1787 which encouraged Mozart to attempt to regain the prominent position he had so recently held in Viennese musical life. "The "Coronation" Concerto was apparently composed in the hope of such a comeback, probably during the Lent concert season of 1788. The concert never materialized, however, nor did his hopes for a concert the following June. His last three symphonies composed that spring and summer, the E-flat major, G minor, and the "Jupiter" in C major, also were probably written for a similar concert or concert series which never took place. Mozart made no further attempt to reestablish his position.

The first performance of the "Coronation" Concerto took place almost by accident in Dresden on April 14, 1789, during Mozart's trip to Berlin: ". . . during dinner [Mozart wrote to his wife] word came that I was to play the next day, Tuesday, the 14th, at half past five at Court.—That is something extraordinary here; for it is usually very hard to get a hearing; and you know that I had no thought of anything in Dresden.— . . . the following day I played the new Concerto in D at Court; next morning, Wednesday the 15th, I received a very beautiful [snuff] box . . . ."

The name "Coronation" Concerto is based on the tradition, reinforced by the statement of the title page of the first edition of the score, that this was one of the two concertos which Mozart performed in his concert in the Frankfurt Stadttheater on September 23, 1790, during the festivities for the coronation of Leopold II as Emperor of the Holy Roman Empire.

When Leopold made the trip from Vienna to be crowned in Frankfurt, Mozart was not among the musicians of his court whom he took with him. But Mozart decided that, with so many powerful and influential persons assembled for the coronation, it would be worth his while professionally to make the trip on his own. The "Coronation" Concerto was an apt choice for the occasion, for it contains not a note of the emotional depths or the storm and stress which Mozart knew often upset conservative listeners.

Present-day listeners, on the other hand, should avoid the pitfall of measuring the "Coronation" Concerto by the great piano concertos with the emotional urgency of the D minor, K. 466, for example, or the C major, K. 503. The whole texture of the "Coronation" Concerto can scarcely be called symphonic by mature Mozartean standards. It is much closer to the graceful allure of a *divertimento* or serenade and if approached with this exception, it proves a most engaging work.

It is scored for the usual strings plus flute, 2 oboes, 2 bassoons, 2 horns, 2 trumpets and kettledrums *ad libitum*. The "*ad libitum*," which apparently applies to all the winds, bass and kettledrums, is striking, for it occurs in only one other of the concertos included in Mozart's autograph list of his own works. Its purpose apparently was to make the concerto which he hoped to play publicly in Vienna easy to perform. Mozart has handled the winds and brass reticently, chiefly for doubling or the reinforcement of the *tutti*. Omission of the winds and brass would scarcely affect the structure of the score, although it would diminish its brilliance.

I. *Allegro*. The movement begins softly with a bit of musical small talk, a succession of familiar phrases that succeed each other in familiar fashion, yet with grace and charm which, taken on their own terms, are not merely entertaining, but quite irresistible. When the solo piano enters the conversation, it has little to add except the expected modulation into the dominant key, accompanied by garlands of purling scales and the repetitious cadential bows which punctuated all polite conversation in the *style galant* of the age. Of symphonic development or any real clash of ideas or emotions there is none, and indeed it would have seemed out of place in this gently festive atmosphere.

II. *Larghetto*. The songful slow movement is the most intimately Mozartean part of this Concerto. Its main theme is announced by the soloist in an eight-bar strain of which Mozart himself wrote down only the right-hand melody.

Here, as in the first entrance of the solo in the first movement and in numerous other places, Mozart did not bother to write in the left-hand part. Since he was his own soloist, he himself needed no more than a reminder of the simpler parts of the music he carried in his head. Sensitive Mozart scholars have occasionally scolded the composer for pedestrian, unimaginative left-hand passages which are not by Mozart at all and, as far as can now be told, were added by the Concerto's first publisher, Johann André.

Since the unaccompanied entrance of the piano automatically sets the pace of this movement, Mozart did not write down any tempo mark either. The word *Larghetto* was added in the manuscript by another unidentified hand.

III. *Allegretto*. Here, too, the tempo mark is entered in Mozart's manuscript by another hand. As in the middle movement, the piano leads off without orchestral assistance, in a simple statement of the principal theme.

In this case it is a *rondo* refrain which is to alternate and combine with the sections of a sonata-rondo form, a combination beloved by Haydn. Two of the most poetic passages in this movement are the gentle interplays of woodwinds, strings and piano solo leading into the two principal returns of the *rondo* refrain.

Mozart's Piano Concerto in D major, K. 537, calls for an orchestra consisting of flute, 2 oboes, 2 bassoons, 2 horns, 2 clarinets, kettledrums, and the traditional strings.

CONCERTO FOR PIANO AND ORCHESTRA, B-FLAT MAJOR, K. 595

The piano was Mozart's instrument. The piano concerto was his form: the form in which he achieved his most brilliant success, both as performer and as composer; the form on which he lavished the largest number of supreme masterpieces, far outnumbering his greatest symphonies and solo piano works. He was the first great master of this form, and no other composer has yet rivaled the riches with which he endowed it.

During the last year of his life, Mozart was no longer popular. The musical public no longer flocked to the concerts or "academies," as they were called, at which he conducted his own works and starred himself as soloist in piano concertos written expressly for the occasion. Pupils dropped away. His financial problems grew desperate. His fading fortunes in Vienna were not compensated by a corresponding demand for his services elsewhere.

His last piano concerto, that in B-flat, K. 595, reflects the most intimate moods of his last year. It had neither the Olympian splendor of the two great C-major Concertos, the sociable brilliance of the earlier concertos, nor the tragic drama of the popular D-minor and C-minor Concertos. A mood of gentle, almost philosophical resignation permeates much of this Concerto. It has no trace of bitterness, but rather an almost exalted tone, as if he rose above the crude material cares and strains that used up his body. Completed between *Così fan tutte* and *The Magic Flute*, it combines the sensuous grace of the former with the spirituality of the latter.

Mozart dated his score January 5, 1791. Since he could no longer drum up subscribers enough for an academy of his own, he performed his B-flat Concerto on a program presented by a prominent clarinettist Joseph Bähr (or Beer), on March 4, 1791.

I. *Allegro.* The opening theme, a singing *Allegro,* seems little more than a graceful embellishment of the tonic B-flat chord:

On the surface this resembles the mood of Mozart's early concertos, where sheer sensuous beauty, grace, charm, and gallant entertainment were the main concerns. But here the sensuous lure has become infinitely more sophisticated. And as the movement progresses, it takes on the ambiguous beauty (the double and triple levels of meaning, so to speak) we find in the most ravishing scenes of *Così fan tutte.*

The graceful melodic arch of the second principal theme sweeps downward over a two-octave span, recalling Donna Elvira's lament: *"Mi tradì quel alma ingrata"* from *Don Giovanni.* Almost at once the phrase is echoed with a minor inflection:

More emphatically still, this recalls the major-minor fluctuations of anger, sorrow, and love in Elvira's aria. This momentary darkening of the harmonic landscape, as it were, is characteristic of the B-flat Concerto.

Another striking example occurs early in the ensuing development, where the Concerto's opening theme is suddenly transported into the distant realm of B minor. In many ways this development section is among the subtlest and most original in Mozart, with the piano weaving garlands of arpeggios and scales as a background for tiny thematic fragments tossed back and forth from one orchestral group to another.

II. *Larghetto.* The slow movement seems serenity itself; balm, even for a soul that has suffered as much as Mozart. It is in Mozart's beloved key of E-flat major and it breathes the tenderness, the noble resignation of the Countess's great E-flat aria *"Porgi amor"* in *The Marriage of Figaro.* But the refrain which opens this slow *rondo* is, as C. M. Girdlestone has penetratingly observed, like a farewell. It sings of an irrevocable parting. Mozart had no conscious inkling that he would not live to the end of the year, or that this was to be his last concerto. Yet, who knows what intuitions shaped his music?

III. *Allegro.* The refrain of the concluding *rondo* recalls the "hunting horn" themes of many an earlier, carefree finale:

It is a happy theme—and more. What more the melody meant to Mozart is suggested by the song he composed only a few days after completing the concerto: "Yearning for Spring" *("Sehnsucht nach dem Frühling").* "Come sweet May, and make the trees grow green again," are the words he set to the melody of his *rondo* refrain. The key word is "yearning."

The *finale* has three ingenious episodes, partly contrasting, partly derived from the "hunting horn" refrain which returns to complete the Concerto. This typically ambiguous blend of yearning and joy was Mozart's last word in the form which he had made forever his own.

The B-flat Concerto is scored for flute, 2 oboes, 2 bassoons, 2 horns, and the standard string choir.

CONCERTO FOR TWO PIANOS AND ORCHESTRA, E-FLAT MAJOR, K. 365

Among the most warmhearted, exuberant outpourings of Mozart's perennially astounding genius are the twenty-odd minutes of magic we know as his Concerto for Two Pianos in E-flat, Köchel Catalogue listing number 365. Mozart seems to have composed the Concerto for himself and his dearly loved sister Nannerl, to perform together on an occasion close to his twenty-third birthday, which is to say, soon after his return to the bosom of his affectionate family in Salzburg after an eighteen-month-long absence in Munich, Augsburg, Mannheim, Paris, Strasbourg and lesser towns on the way. The temptation to read biographical meaning into the Concerto is almost irresistible. This music seems to tell us that all is (or was then) well with the world, with the composer, with his performing partner and with his fortunate listeners.

The sad truth is that Mozart's feelings as he returned to Salzburg must have verged on despair. He had left the city eighteen months earlier with high expectations of escaping its narrow, provincial atmosphere and the petty tyranny of his employer and master, the Archbishop of Salzburg. At the courts of Munich and Mannheim he was much admired, he made warm friendships among the famous musicians there, but no appointment was forthcoming. In Mannheim he fell in love with the beautiful, sensitive, gifted soprano Aloysia Weber. In Paris he won a certain renown, but he was neither aggressive enough, man of the world enough, bootlicker or politician enough to make his way to the centers of power and influence. Mozart's mother, who accompanied him on the trip, was far from the master wire-puller that his father had been on earlier trips.

Three months after their arrival in Paris, Frau Mozart died. After another three months of growing depression and discouragement, it became obvious that Mozart had failed in the object of his long, expensive trip. With a heavy heart he started home. On the way back he learned that Aloysia had been unfaithful to him. In a life that was to be rich in bitter experiences, Mozart had already drunk deep of disappointment and failure. The only gain which he brought back to his "Salzburg slavery," as he called it, was maturity.

The warmth of his E-flat Concerto is no pose. Its gaiety is no smiling mask, no paradoxical denial of his personal feelings. Indeed it is quite possible that Mozart's feelings for his sister, the overflowing affection, the joyous *entente cordiale* reflected in the dialogue of the two pianos, were actually intensified by his tragic trip and his grim professional discouragement. Nineteenth-century Romantics were not the only ones for whom music could be a consolation, even an escape.

We know neither the exact date nor the circumstances of the composition; only that it must have been soon after January 15 or 16, 1779, the date of Mozart's return. We know that he liked this Concerto because he performed it on at least two later occasions in Vienna, with great success, his collaborator at the second piano being his gifted, but ugly pupil, Fräulein Auernhammer. For these occasions Mozart expanded the orchestration of his Concerto,

MOZART AND NANNERL AT THE PIANO.

Mozart composed his E-flat Concerto for his sister "Nannerl" and himself, shown at the piano in this family portrait. The mother is symbolically restored to the family through her portrait on the wall beside father Leopold. (*Oil painting, Johann della Croce; courtesy, Mozarteum, Salzburg*)

adding a pair of clarinets, a pair of trumpets and kettledrums. Unfortunately this revised score was lost, and we therefore hear the Concerto nowadays in the original version with an orchestra consisting of 2 oboes, 2 bassoons, 2 horns, and the standard string choir.

I. *Allegro.* The Concerto begins rather grandly. A lordly opening phrase for the orchestral *tutti* is followed immediately by a gentler, softer reply from the strings:

After the orchestra has concluded its introduction, the two pianos enter together with a sonorous variant of the above theme. A profusion of short, graceful pharases bridges the way to an irresistibly lilting second theme given out by the second piano:

There are enough attractive themes to furnish half a dozen concertos, but Mozart keeps pouring them forth with reckless generosity. It would take longer than the Concerto lasts even to list all the beguiling turns of phrases, the delicious details exchanged between the two soloists. Totally unconventional is the so-called recapitulation, or reprise of the opening theme, which suddenly veers off into the minor mode. But the lilting second theme given out, as before, by the second piano, restores the gaiety of the beginning.

II. *Andante.* The songful slow movement is like an operatic *da capo* aria or duet, delicately embellished. Sometimes the two pianos carry the main melodic lines, sometimes it is the violins, sometimes two clarinets, sometimes a pair of oboes with the pianos supplying lightly arpeggiated backgrounds.

III. *Rondo: Allegro.* The *Rondo* refrain, which returns again and again in the course of the *finale* is announced softly at first by the strings alone:

The intervening episodes include a dramatic passage in minor modes, a symphonic style development of the refrain itself and an elaborate cadenza.

FIVE CONCERTOS FOR VIOLIN AND ORCHESTRA
NO. 1, B-FLAT MAJOR, K. 207
NO. 2, D MAJOR, K. 211
NO. 3, G MAJOR, K. 216
NO. 4, D MAJOR, K. 218
NO. 5, A MAJOR, K. 219

Mozart was never taught to play the violin; he just seemed to know how. During one of his tours as a child prodigy, someone in Vienna made him a present of a half-size violin. Back home in Salzburg the seven-year-old Wolfgang soon surprised his father by asking to join a sight-reading session at which six new string trios by a family friend were being tried out. When Father Mozart dismissed the idea as ridiculous, since his son had never had a violin lesson, Wolfgang pleaded that lessons weren't really necessary to know how to play *second* violin. When his father told him to go away and stop bothering the grown-ups, the boy began to cry and stumbled off with his little violin. But one of the players, Andreas Schachtner, who told the story years later to Mozart's sister Nannerl, asked that the child be allowed to stay and to play Schachtner's part (second violin) together with him:

> At last Papa Mozart said, "Play your fiddle along with Herr Schachtner, but you must play so softly we can't hear you, or else you will have to go away."
>
> It was done, and Wolfgang fiddled along with me. To my astonishment, I soon noticed that I was quite superfluous. I laid aside my violin quietly and glanced at your father: tears of admiration and happiness were streaming down his face. And so Wolfgang played through all six trios. When we were through, our praise made him so bold that then he claimed he could even play the first violin part. So for the fun of it, we tried him out, and we nearly died laughing when, in spite of a whole mess of mistakes and irregularities, he actually did play the [first violin] part and got through it without once breaking down.

Later that year, when the Mozart family again went on tour, Wolfgang already began to make appearances, not only in his former role of harpsichordist or pianist, but as a violin soloist. Everywhere they went Wolfgang listened and learned. In Italy he expanded his violin technique, in France he added brilliance of style, and in Vienna he heard the Austrian melodies that echo through all five of these violin concertos, composed when he was nineteen. As he grew older Mozart lost interest in the violin, possibly because one of his official jobs was to play violin in the orchestra of the Archbishop of Salzburg, whom he increasingly detested. His father suspected that the slackening of Wolfgang's interest was due to a lack of confidence in his own astounding flair for the instrument. "You don't realize yourself," he once wrote his son, "how well you play the violin when you are on your mettle and perform with confidence, spirit, and fire."

In 1775, at home in Salzburg between tours, Mozart composed his only five violin concertos that we know to be completely his own. (Two more of doubtful authenticity survive: K. 271a in D major, and K. 268 in E-flat major, both apparently based on sketches of Mozart completed by a later hand. K. 271a may even be a considerably later adaptation and "improvement" of a completed, but lost Mozart original.) The five authentic concertos were very likely composed for Mozart's personal use, but we are not certain, since we do not know exactly when or by whom they were first performed. We do know that Mozart performed them after 1775 and that they are neither Austrian nor German nor French nor Italian in style, but a highly personal amalgam of all the styles he had absorbed during his travels. They are a musical reflection of early Classical and Rococo Europe: aristocratic, graceful, humorous, and marvelously melodious. They are not the greatest music Mozart ever produced, but these youthful outpourings have irresistible appeal. One is tempted to believe that they will be heard as long as there are violinists to play them.

CONCERTO FOR VIOLIN AND ORCHESTRA, NO. 1, B-FLAT MAJOR, K.207

For reasons unfathomable to a Mozart-lover this is sometimes considered an easy concerto. Easy to listen to? Certainly. Even at first hearing this is inviting music, as was intended; though with any luck the listener will find each repetition brings the music closer to his heart.

But easy to play? Hardly. Mozart is one of the cruelest tests of any performer's art. This is especially true when he seems simplest: when, as in this Concerto, there are no hidden depths, when his aim is merely to entertain us for a few moments with the profusion of his musical invention, to beguile us with the grace of a short instrumental *cantilena,* or perhaps to dazzle us for fleeting seconds with the sparkle, with turns and scales that were a dime a dozen in his day—except that Mozart turns them into diamonds.

This is the first of the set of five which Mozart composed when he was nineteen, the first and most innocently spendthrift of ideas enough for two or three concertos. He completed it at home in Salzburg on April 14, 1775, just over a month after his return from Munich, where he had composed and staged his triumphantly successful carnival comic opera *La finta giardiniera* for the court opera house known today as the Altes Residenztheater, or Cuvilliées-Theater.

I. *Allegro moderato.* After the briefest of orchestral introductions, the solo violin enters with the principal theme, over a feather-light accompaniment of violins and violas only:

The tiny development section ventures briefly into minor keys, but more for a change of color than of mood. A touch of virtuosity leads to the customary pause for a solo cadenza before the close.

II. *Adagio.* The songful slow movement is written in one of Mozart's favorite keys for the expression of sensuous warmth: E-flat major. Here the warmth is enhanced by the velvet sonority of sustained French horns. Its principal theme is an eighteenth-century type which Mozart later transfigured in his Countess's aria *"Porgi amor"* that opens Act Two of his *Marriage of Figaro.* But in this movement the theme is all decorative grace:

III. *Presto.* The delicate *bravura* of the solo part and the deliciously light scoring of this *finale* tend to disguise its rich symphonic development, and recall instead some of Mozart's most charming serenade music. The modest orchestra for this B-flat Concerto consists of 2 oboes, 2 French horns, and the traditional string choir which, in Mozart's day, would have been supplemented by a harpsichord or piano as a thorough-bass instrument.

CONCERTO FOR VIOLIN AND ORCHESTA, NO. 2, D MAJOR, K. 211

Although composed in the very Austrian surroundings of Mozart's native Salzburg (and completed there on June 14, 1775), this is the most strikingly French of the five violin concertos. It is also the most worldy, the most fashionable, the most *galant,* to use the complimentary term of that day. It is scored for 2 oboes, 2 horns, and the traditional string choir, which would have been supplemented in Mozart's day by a keyboard instrument: either harpsichord or piano.

I. *Allegro moderato.* The Rococo elegance, strongest in the first movement, is perhaps most pointed in the very opening bar, like a stiffly formal bow, the *révérence* of a polished courtier. The little flutterings that follow in the violins offer an effective contrast, but are about as casual as Marie Antoinette playing at being a shepherdess.

The solo violin enters with the same formal bow, but the flutterings, ever more intricate, dominate the solo and tuttis alike, maintaining a mood of exquisite artifice through the movement's final bars.

II. *Andante.* A touch of sentiment suffices for the slow movement, which follows French models with its uninterrupted song for solo violin against the simplest possible accompaniment. The orchestra does little more than introduce the opening theme with the aforementioned touch of sentiment:

III. *Rondeau: Allegro.* The frolicsome *finale* is French in more ways than Mozart's spelling of *rondeau* (instead of the standard Italian *rondo*). Mozart follows French concerto models in dispensing with an orchestral introduction and giving his opening refrain to the soloist:

French, too, is the tradition of the minor-key episode midway through the *Rondeau*—a minor that is purposely more playful than profound. For in the *galanterie,* which Mozart mastered with such effortless ease, profundity and passion alike were taboo.

Although he was not primarily a *galant* composer, Mozart was possibly the most versatile who ever lived. He had absorbed French influences from age seven, when he visited the Versailles of Louis XV, was received by the royal family (included Madame de Pompadour), by music lovers among the highest French aristocracy, and by French musicians. At nineteen he was a veteran to whom it was child's play to don the mask of the most fashionable French composers of the day and absorb what suited him on his voyage of self-discovery toward a paradox: the most international, yet the most deeply personal style of his age.

CONCERTO FOR VIOLIN AND ORCHESTRA, NO. 3, G MAJOR, K. 216

Completed in Salzburg on September 12, 1775, this is the third of the five violin concertos Mozart composed that year. It follows the established three-movement form of the day.

I. *Allegro.* The spirited chief theme of the movement is presented at once by the full orchestra:

The broad orchestral introduction presents several lesser musical ideas before the solo violin makes its first appearance with its own lightly embellished version of the theme quoted above. Each time the soloist appears, it is with an important thematic contribution. A telling touch is the conclusion of the central development section for the soloist, with a few bars of recitative imitated directly after the vocal style of contemporary Italian opera.

II. *Adagio.* Muted first violins spin out an initial phrase of such ravishing beauty that one can only bow one's head and be thankful for the provincial teen-age musician whose musical thoughts nearly two hundred years ago in Salzburg can move us so strongly today:

The use of flutes to replace the oboes and the crystalline little sonata form probably contribute to the magic of this movement.

III. *Rondeau: Allegro.* The *finale* starts innocuously enough as a light-hearted *Rondeau* with an extra-simple refrain. The movement is filled with echoes of German or Austrian folk song—until we come to a sudden shadow when the G major of the Concerto darkens to a G minor and the tempo slows momentarily to an *andante.* But the threat is brief and is followed by a quick return to the innocent-sounding G major, and a last recall of the lilting *Rondeau* refrain. The quiet "finished-before-you-know-it" close, is the best Mozartean sleight-of-hand.

The score calls for 2 oboes, 2 flutes, 2 horns, and the customary strings which, in Mozart's day, would have been supplemented by a harpsichord or piano as a thorough-bass instrument.

CONCERTO FOR VIOLIN AND ORCHESTRA, NO. 4, D MAJOR, K. 218

Mozart's manuscript of this D-major Concerto is dated simply: "Salzburg, October, 1775."

I. *Allegro.* The orchestral introduction leads off with the principal theme of the movement: a stock figure which Mozart borrowed from contemporary Neapolitan opera, a fanfarelike figure, a call to attention, so to speak, followed by this coquettishly graceful phrase:

But though he begins with a conventional theme, the richness and variety he draws from it when the solo violin makes its entrance are surprisingly original. A more flowing lyric phrase is also introduced by the orchestra:

Other themes are reserved for the soloist, who departs just enough from standard operational procedure to show Mozart's mastery of convention as well as his imaginative genius in departing from it.

II. *Andante cantabile.* The broadly flowing theme of the slow movement has an almost Handelian repose:

As in an operatic *cavatina,* the orchestra formally introduces the soloist who, once he appears on the scene, dominates it from start to finish. But while this movement is more serious in content than its predecessor, it is no less witty in detail.

III. *Rondeau: Andante grazioso.* The *finale* is a *rondo* with a double refrain announced at once by the solo violin:

A dancelike phrase, as delicately poised as any ballerina, passes quickly to a wistful, questioning, unfinished phrase, which in turn is answered by a sudden outburst of gaiety in a semi-jig rhythm. The entire finale sustains this impression of capricious improvisation. The quicksilver refrain alternates with episodes which are by turns skittish, grave and masterful.

Yet masterful alone is the word for the formal structure which turns out, on closer examination, to be an incredibly resourceful combination of *rondo* form and sonata-allegro, a combination with which Haydn was also experimenting at this time. Mozart's coolly calculated structure never obtrudes on the listener's attention, but serves only an expressive purpose. It is an astounding achievement for a nineteen-year-old, even a nineteen-year-old genius.

The manuscript of this D-major Concerto calls for an orchestra of 2 oboes, 2 horns, and the traditional string choir.

CONCERTO FOR VIOLIN AND ORCHESTRA, NO. 5, A MAJOR, K. 219

The A-major Concerto is the last of the five Mozart composed in 1775 and the last of his violin concertos which survives in its original state unaltered by the editors or adaptors. It is also the ripest of the five in emotional content and the most fascinating in form.

I. *Allegro aperto.* The opening movement is in the traditional sonata form as adapted to the concerto, and yet it has individual touches which make it unique. For example, the airy opening orchestral phrase is not, as established tradition would have it, the Concerto's principal theme. Or rather, it is only part of the principal theme. For when the solo violin makes its entrance, it soon turns out that the opening orchestral phrase is merely the *accompaniment* of the soloist's principal theme.

The opening of the violin solo itself is a dramatic and typically Mozartean surprise. The spirited tempo of the orchestra halts. There is a pause and the violin enters, almost absentmindedly, as it were, at a dreamy *adagio* pace, with a rhapsodic melody which seems unrelated to what had gone before. Only after this pensive passage and another dramatic pause does the solo violin seem to remember the main business of the day and belatedly launch into the vigorous principal theme:

The exposition is rich in melodies and the development, although brief, is striking for its succession of minor tonalities which probably struck Mozart's contemporaries with a stormier intensity than they do most of us today.

II. *Adagio.* The slow middle movement is in E major, a key which Mozart loved for melodies of particular sensuous appeal. It is built almost entirely around the melody of the opening bars. But Mozart does not confine this movement (or any of the others) to sensuous appeal alone. Halfway through, the music begins to modulate into a series of melancholy minor harmonies as it did in the first movement and will do even more strikingly in the finale.

III. *Rondeau: Tempo di menuetto.* If there is anything more graceful than the refrain which opens this *Rondeau* (which never seems to return often enough), it is possibly the intervening episodes. Their melodies, not quite so courtly and minuetlike, take a more ecstatic flight. One of them, conforming to the tradition of the French *rondeau,* is in the minor mode—but what a minor! This is the piquant, exotic, swirling, driving sort of music which Mozart's contemporaries thought of as Turkish (*alla turca*) or Hungarian (*all 'ongarese*) and which the nineteenth century would have called "gypsy." Mozart seems to have enjoyed this episode as much as we do, for he extended it until it was almost as long as the whole first part of the movement and included a crashing orchestral *tutti* borrowed from himself, from the finale of a ballet written for the Milan production of his opera *Lucio Silla* (1773). The title of the ballet, *Harem Jealousies* (*Le Gelosie del seraglio,* Anh. 109) suggests that Mozart really did think of this as Turkish music:

There is a special grace in the final return of the minuet refrain, and the utter simplicity of its final phrase comes closer to perfection than is given to most mortal works. The modest orchestral score calls for only 2 oboes, 2 horns, and the traditional strings, which in Mozart's day, would have been supplemented by a harpsichord or piano as a thorough-bass instrument.

The mastery and inspiration of the whole are amazing in a nineteen-year-old boy, even in a nineteen-year-old genius. Two years later Mozart left Salzburg for the long trip to Paris. While he was away his father wrote him: "Always on my way home a feeling of melancholy steals over me. And as I come near our house I seem to hear you still—playing the violin."

MASONIC FUNERAL MUSIC, K. 477

When Mozart became a Freemason we do not know with any precision. It must have been early in the 1780s, soon after he settled in Vienna, but before his father's 1785 visit to the imperial city. For it was in March of the latter year that father Leopold was admitted to the Vienna lodge of which Wolfgang was already a member. We do know that for Mozart, as for many of the leading spirits of his age, including many intellectuals, artists, writers, rulers, and musicians of the eminence of the two Mozarts and Joseph Haydn, Freemasonry filled profound social, intellectual, and emotional needs. Among its greatest attractions for Mozart was certainly its idealization of friendship, of the brotherhood of man, of something we should call a democratic feeling, of a very concrete practice of brotherhood and mutual help between rich and poor, great and humble. Mozart's *Magic Flute* was to be the ultimate glorification of these ideals.

It was undoubtedly the degree of personal fulfillment Mozart enjoyed in his associations at the lodge, *Zur neugekrönten Hoffnung,* which enabled him to write such a surprisingly personal piece of music for the relatively formal funeral ceremony for two recently deceased "brothers," one of them the late grand master of the lodge. In his list of his own works, Mozart entered the title *Masonic Funeral Music on the death of Brothers Mecklenburg and Esterházy.* "Brother Mecklenburg" was the Imperial-Royal Major General Count Georg August von Mecklenburg-Strelitz; "Brother Esterházy" was the Court Chancellor of Hungarian Siebenbürgen Count Franz Esterházy von Galanta, of the fabulous princely family who were Haydn's patrons. Count Esterházy, who had been the grand master of Mozart's lodge, died on November 7, 1785, the Duke of Mecklenburg the day before. The funeral ceremony of the lodge, for which Mozart's music was written, took place on November 17.

This brief score is unique in Mozart's life work, yet it is profoundly characteristic of him as an artist and as a man. Far from fearing death, Mozart seems, in a way that almost anticipates the nineteenth-century Romantics, to have looked upon death as a friend. He regarded dying simply as a transition to a better world. His pity, his grief, which could be lacerating, were for the loss of those who remained behind.

The eloquent score begins with four heavy sighs of the wind instruments. As they die away, a restless, melancholy first-violin figure threads its way through the orchestra. Marchlike rhythms materialize in the orchestral basses and the approach of a processional is heralded by blasts of the wind instruments.

The processional melody itself is a stern liturgical strain, a *cantus firmus* apparently adapted from local church tradition, possibly associated with the tones of the penitential psalms which Mozart had studied in preparation for composing this music. Against restless weavings of the violins, the marchlike *cantus firmus* is carried at first by oboes and clarinets, soon joined by the entire woodwind band. With this climax, the grief which hitherto has been subdued, seems to break through all restraints.

The procession seems to pass. Phrases from the opening page return, and the whole is rounded off with a typically Mozartean coda, in which the gentle, penetrating melancholy of chromatic woodwind lines is combined with sob-like broken rhythms for the violins. There is no feeling of struggle, of battling an implacable enemy, but only a deep grief. And to this grief Mozart gives himself with his whole heart.

Mozart seems to have completed his score about November 10, 1785, in Vienna. In its first version the score called for clarinet, basset horn, 2 oboes, 2 French horns, 2 violins, 2 violas and bass. To these Mozart added as an afterthought 2 more basset horns and a *gran fagotto* (which was probably a contrabassoon, although we cannot be absolutely sure).

EIN MUSIKALISCHER SPASS (A MUSICAL JOKE), K. 522

Seldom has so much wit been lavished to produce an impression of witlessness—of helpless, bumbling incompetence. This delectable trifle, a masterpiece of satirical art, was tossed off in Vienna while Mozart's mind must have been occupied with the vaster project of his *Don Giovanni*. June 14, 1787, is the completion date inscribed on Mozart's autograph (which has been missing from the Prussian State Library in Berlin since the end of World War II).

For what occasion this featherweight score was composed, or who its fortunate first listeners were, we may never know. But since Mozart rarely composed anything without an immediate performance in view, the occasion probably followed completion of the score within a matter of days.

Mozart's *Musical Joke* had an ancient and honorable lineage. Parodies of bumbling performers had been cultivated by his father and by generations of composers before him. But Mozart's *Joke* differed from most of its predecessors in satirizing primarily the bumbling composer and only secondarily his unhappy performers. Thus the well-known alternative titles conferred on the score after Mozart's death: *Bauernsinfonie (Peasant Symphony)* and *Dorfmusikanten (Village Musicians)* completely obscure the point of the piece. The butt of Mozart's wit is the would-be composer who lacks both technique and imagination. (Possibly an aristocratic amateur or a desperately unfit pupil? Mozart had known plenty of both.)

Mozart did not classify his *Musical Joke.* But to label it a *divertimento,* as is often done, is misleading. For the imagined composer of this score is attempting nothing so modest as a *divertimento;* his object all sublime is a symphony.

I. *Allegro.* Our master knows, approximately, how a symphony goes. But even his first and most important theme struggles in vain to get off the ground:

Tradition tells him that his second principal theme should begin in the dominant key (C major). But how to get there? His first attempt at a transition or bridge is frustrated by the orchestra, which obstinately keeps reverting to the home key of F major. Since his bridge does not work, he simply jumps with both feet, as it were, into the key of C major. Somehow our hero manages to reach the end of his exposition, where he salutes his achievement with a vigorous fanfare. The graver problems of the so-called development section are met after a fashion, by making it short.

II. *Minuetto: Maestoso.* The minuet, normally far simpler than first-movement form, also presents its comic hurdles. The most obvious of these occurs in a passage for two horns marked "softly" *(dolce).* But with the modest talents of his horns players, what was to have been a poetic interlude turns out in this excruciating form:

III. *Adagio cantabile.* In the traditionally songful slow movement our composer clearly has in mind the standard graces of eighteenth-century *style gallant.* In imitating the clichés of his betters he is awkward, but with a difference. He is an awkward composer being *portrayed* for us by one of the supreme masters of all time. The result is a paradox: an awkwardness with a certain grace, or at least charm. It is as if Don Giovanni were masquerading as Leporello. And we can not take it amiss when an ambitious cadenza leads the unhappy first violin into a desperate, stratospheric flight that sounds more and more like a twentieth-century whole-tone scale.

IV. *Presto.* But the best is yet to come. The *rondo finale* is full of pitfalls; even the opening refrain presents monstrous problems. The effort to force this basic recurrent refrain to end in the proper key (tonic F major) involves our master in a harmonic wrench that is almost Chaplinesque.

In the ensuing episode our master does battle with the problem of *fugato.* It is an unequal struggle which will be especially relished by any earnest novice who has tried to write a fugue. This entire *finale* is so rich in humor on every level from the subtleties of late-eighteenth-century *rondo* style to the slapstick final cadence, that there is almost too much to grasp in just one hearing.

The outwardly simple score calls for only 2 horns and strings. Scholars are not entirely agreed as to whether Mozart intended the score for 6 solo players or for horns and string orchestra, but the weight of opinion strongly favors the symphonic group.

THE ABDUCTION FROM THE SERAGLIO OVERTURE, K. 384

Mozart's first great public triumph in Vienna was his comic opera, or *Singspiel, Die Entführung aus dem Serail* ("The Abduction from the Seraglio"), first produced at the Vienna Hof-und National-Theater on July 16, 1782. Mozart was twenty-six. He had just left what he called his "slavery" to an arrogant Archbishop of Salzburg. He was a free-lance now and a success in the musical capital of the world. Finally, he was in love with the girl who was to become his wife one month after the premiere of this opera.

No wonder the *Entführung* is filled with youthful exultation. Carl Maria von Weber called it a picture of "what every man's joyous, youthful years are to him, years the bloom of which he will never recapture. . . . I venture to say that in the *Seraglio* Mozart had attained the peak of his artistic experience, to which only the experience of the world had to be added later. Mankind was entitled to expect from him several more operas like *Figaro* and *Don Giovanni,* but with the best will in the world he could never have written another *Seraglio.*"

The story of the opera is a Spanish nobleman's attempted rescue of his fiancée from Turkish captivity. Turkish plots were popular in eighteenth-century plays, operas, and novels, and Turkish music had a special vogue in Vienna in Mozart's time. The Viennese populace loved to watch public appearances of the Turkish ambassador, who on state occasions was accompanied through the streets by so-called Janizary music. What struck the Viennese about this Turkish military music were the big drums, cymbals, and triangles. These characteristic percussion instruments were incorporated into a great deal of Viennese Classical music for special exotic passages of "Turkish" music, of which Mozart, Haydn, and Beethoven all composed famous examples.

Mozart wrote his father that the Overture to his *Entführung* was very short and kept alternating loud and soft with the Turkish music in the loud parts. "It modulates on and on, from key to key so that I don't believe anyone could fall asleep, even if he hadn't slept at all the whole night before." Here is the principal theme of this Turkish music:

In addition to its "Turkish" music, Mozart's Overture has a tiny, slow middle section, where we hear a plaintive minor variant of the hero's opening aria, *"Hier soll ich dich denn sehen,"* which the hero sings as he waits in the pasha's garden in the hope of finding his captive fiancée. In the opera, the Overture has no formal conclusion, but leads directly into the first act. A brief concert ending is usually supplied for orchestral programs.

The Overture to the *Entführung* is scored for piccolo, 2 oboes, 2 clarinets, 2 bassoons, 2 horns, 2 trumpets, kettledrums, triangle, cymbals, bass drum, and the traditional strings.

DON GIOVANNI OVERTURE, K. 527

The composition of the Overture to *Don Giovanni* has always seemed a miracle, from the very day (or rather the very night) it was set on paper. In itself the music is, of course, a major miracle. But what really astounded Mozart's contemporaries was the speed with which he wrote it. For Mozart this was a mere nothing. As usual, he had long since composed the music in his head. But he was something of a procrastinator, and did not look forward to the mechanical work of committing music to paper. There are many stories, current in his own time, of the pleasure he took in having company, even noisy and conversational company, while he wrote out the actual notes of one masterpiece or another.

In the case of *Don Giovanni*, which had its world premiere on October 29, 1787, in Prague, Mozart put off writing out the Overture until the evening before the dress rehearsal (some accounts even say the eve of the premiere, which seems unlikely)! The most reliable account is presumably what his wife Constanze later told her second husband, Georg von Nissen, whose biography of the composer is one of our most precious sources: ". . . In the evening he told his wife that he wanted to write the Overture that night, and asked her to make him some punch and stay up with him to keep him merry. She did so, told him fairy tales of *Aladdin's Lamp* . . . and so on, which made him laugh until the tears came to his eyes. But the punch made him sleepy, so that he nodded whenever she paused, and worked only while she was talking. But since this exertion, his sleepiness, his frequent nodding and catching himself made the work terribly hard, his wife made him lie down on the couch promising to wake him up in an hour. But he slept so soundly that she did not have the heart to do so, and only wakened him after two hours had passed. This was at five o'clock. The copyist had been ordered for seven o'clock; at seven o'clock the Overture was finished."

At the rehearsal the orchestra showed themselves to be the superb musicians that Mozart knew. The composer is reported to have said at the conclusion of the Overture: "A few notes did fall under the desks, but it was a fine performance."

The Overture is no piece of program music, no synopsis of the opera plot, but purely and simply a musical confrontation between the avenging power of the stone guest (in the slow introduction) and the irresistible temperament and vitality of the dissolute Don. It is only in the opera itself that the conflict is played out.

The legend is, of course, the ancient one in which the immoral and irresistible lover of many women is finally dragged down to hell by the stone statue from the funeral monument to the father of one of the Don's female victims. A climactic scene in most versions of the legend, as well as in Mozart's opera, shows the Don mocking the monument by inviting the statue to dinner. The ultimate climax is the unexpected appearance of the stone guest at Don Juan's feast and the Don's descent to hell.

It is the music of this terrifying climax of the opera which the composer condenses into the thirty measures of his slow introduction. The crashing D-minor chords suggest the statue itself; the tonality of D minor had long been associated in Mozart's and his contemporaries' minds with conflict, tragedy and doom. The uncanny whisperings and murmurings of the violins that follow, punctuated by further blasts of the orchestral *tutti*, are followed by a bare four measures of the spooky rising and falling scales derived from the final scene of the Don's undoing. Each lover of *Don Giovanni* will have his own favorite telling details in this introduction alone, to say nothing of the fiery *Allegro* that follows.

Although it uses no theme from the opera, the *Allegro* seems clearly a portrayal of the almost superhuman, restless drive of Don Giovanni. It is cast in traditional sonata-allegro form, resembling a miniature first movement of a symphony with several energetic themes which grow, expand, do battle with each other in a brief, climactic development and then are restated in their home tonality. Home tonality for the Don is D major, as opposed to the otherworldly D minor of the introduction. As the Overture approaches its close, Mozart allows the music to glide smoothly and without interruption into the opening scene of the opera. But since a concert performance of the Overture must not leave the listener hanging in mid-air harmonically or otherwise, Mozart composed a concert ending of thirteen measures to round it off. There also exists a somewhat more elaborate concert conclusion to the Overture composed by Mozart's contemporary, Johann André.

The Overture to *Don Giovanni* is composed for 2 flutes, 2 oboes, 2 clarinets, 2 bassoons, 2 horns, 2 trumpets, kettledrums, and the traditional string choir.

OVERTURE TO THE MAGIC FLUTE, K. 620

On September 28, 1791, Mozart completed the last music he wrote for the stage: the Overture to *The Magic Flute* and the second-act introduction, the sublimely melancholy "March of the Priests." Two days later he conducted the premiere at Emanuel Schickaneder's suburban theater, the Theater auf der Wieden.

Two months later, Mozart lay on his deathbed. Unable to witness the triumph of his opera in the theater, Mozart was very much present in spirit. He would follow performances, watch in hand. "Now the first act is ending," he would say, and "Now comes the place, *'Dir, grosse Königin der Nacht.'* " The opera was close to Mozart's heart, not merely because its growing success was the one ray of cheer in his last tragic weeks, but because he had put so much of himself into it, including his highest ethical ideals.

Of Mozart's entire operatic output, *The Magic Flute* came nearest to embracing all the many facets, the seeming contradictions of his incredibly many-sided nature. Schickaneder's libretto invited variety, from slapstick clowning to the most exalted idealism. Yet the range of the libretto seems almost small compared to the scope of the music, which reaches from the naïve simplicity of Austrian folk-song style to the coloratura brilliance and passion of Italian *opera seria;* from the sternly contrapuntal style of the Protestant chorale prelude to the magic warmth and richness of the Viennese symphonic style. All of these usually disparate worlds are embraced in Mozart's light and simple-sounding score.

New to Mozart's operatic style was the ethical symbolism with which *The Magic Flute* abounds. Three solemn chords, which return during the opera as part of the ritual of Sarastro's Temple of Wisdom, open the slow introduction to the Overture. The number three was an important symbol in the idealistic order of the Freemasons, to which both Mozart and Schickaneder belonged, and the teachings of Sarastro and his priests were closely related to the humanitarian doctrine of the Freemasons. To emphasize the point further, the action of *The Magic Flute* was presented in settings suggesting ancient Egypt, where Freemasonry was believed to have originated.

The quiet measures and the shifting harmonies that follow those solemn opening chords are like a slow damming up of energies which, in the fast *Allegro* section of the Overture, burst into a stream of glittering, dancing counterpoint. This counterpoint, too, has its symbolic implication—it recalls the only contrapuntal scene of the entire opera, the dramatic climax where Tamino and Pamina are prepared for their trial by fire and water, before being admitted to the mysteries of Isis and Osiris. This beautiful contrapuntal fabric of the Overture is woven principally out of the following theme:

Starting in the second violins, the theme spreads in fugal fashion from one string section to another and then, much like a famous passage in the finale of the "Jupiter" Symphony, it deserts the fugue to follow the course of classical sonata allegro form. As if to emphasize his symbolic intent, Mozart repeats the three solemn chords at a crucial point halfway through the Overture—this time in precisely the rhythm used to greet new members into a Masonic lodge.

The great Mozart scholar, Alfred Einstein, once wrote that Mozart compressed into this Overture the struggle and victory of all mankind. But with all its impressive symbolism and its lofty spiritual content, the Overture preserves a delicate fairy-tale atmosphere. There is quicksilver in the learned counterpoint. And the whole is invested with Mozart's unfailing charm, like an outward sign of inward grace.

The Overture to *The Magic Flute* is scored for 2 flutes, 2 oboes, 2 clarinets, 2 bassoons, 2 horns, 2 trumpets, 3 trombones, kettledrums, and the traditional string choir.

THE MARRIAGE OF FIGARO OVERTURE, K. 492

Is there any music in all the world as fresh as the Overture to *The Marriage of Figaro?* It is so fresh that no one ever thinks of calling it "young for its age" roughly two centuries, (*Figaro* being the oldest opera in the standard repertory and older than the oldest standard symphony). It is as fresh as Mozart's little pageboy Cherubino, when he jumps out of the Countess's boudoir window, bouncing off the ground below and away so fast that no one sees his face. In the slang sense, too, it is fresh. Beaumarchais's *Marriage de Figaro* was a very fresh French play in 1782, when private readings horrified Louis XVI and titillated the French aristocracy. *"Cela est détestable,"* said Louis, *"cela ne sera jamais joué."* But it *was* played: first in private, with Louis's queen, Marie Antoinette, as Susanna, and finally in public to sensational acclaim. Today the play is a classic which no longer titillates. But Mozart's Overture is still fresh.

It starts in a breathless whisper. The whisper becomes a wisp of a theme, so swift that it is gone before you know it. Now you hear it, now you don't:

Suddenly the full force of the *tutti* hits us with festive trumpets and drums. The quick contrasts continue with giggling violins, rippling flutes and oboes. The kaleidoscopic shifts of mood might reflect the subtitle of Beaumarchais's play: *The Madcap Day* or *La folle journée.*

Halfway through, at the climax, Mozart composed a slow middle section, *Andante con moto,* with a sentimental 6/8 tune for a solo oboe. But after the score was finished he thought better of it, ripped out the sheet with the slow movement, and wrote in a cut, which now leads us from the brief climax of the Overture straight into the reprise of the opening whisper, so that the madcap mood continues, its swirling humor uninterrupted from start to finish. It all ends with ebullient, rushing scales and a brilliant fanfare for the full orchestra.

Mozart's *Marriage of Figaro (Le nozze di Figaro)* and the Overture to it were first performed in the Vienna Burgtheater on May 1, 1786. Mozart himself conducted. The Overture is scored for 2 flutes, 2 oboes, 2 clarinets, 2 bassoons, 2 horns, 2 trumpets, 2 kettledrums, and the traditional strings.

EINE KLEINE NACHTMUSIK, K.525

It is a measure of Mozart's scope that he could turn, in the middle of the second act of his almost Shakespearean tragicomedy, *Don Giovanni,* to one of the lightest, most beguiling and most popular of all his scores, *Eine kleine Nachtmusik.*

Mozart's autograph, now alas incomplete, for it lacks one of the original five movements, is dated August 10, 1787. We know that Mozart was in Vienna but nothing more of the circumstances of composition. It had been a long time since he had written any serenades of the kind he once lavished on the court and aristocracy of Salzburg.

Nachtmusik is, of course, simply a German translation of the word "serenade." But there is more than the German title of the *Little Serenade* to distinguish it from Mozart's earlier serenades and *divertimenti* which may have served equally well as dinner music for the Archbishop of Salzburg, or as open-air entertainment. Indeed, the weight of evidence in Mozart's autograph and his own catalog of his works suggests that *Eine kleine Nachtmusik* was intended for a quintet of solo strings. With eighteenth-century performance practice having been as elastic as it was, however, there is no reason why the score might not have been performed by a tiny chamber orchestra. Originally it had five movements, including two minuets. The minuet which originally came in second place, between the *Allegro* and *Romanze,* seems to have disappeared sometime before the year 1800.

I. *Allegro.* The graceful opening theme, which is also the principal theme in the movement, could hardly be simpler or more transparent in its Classical harmonic balance. Yet is has an impetus which carries us forward:

As so often, Mozart uses the familiar melodic turns, the harmonic commonplaces of his day, with inimitable freshness. An especially telling example is the closing theme of this tiny exposition, a whispering phrase with repeated notes and trills for the first violin, which might almost have been written by half a dozen late-eighteenth-century composers—yet not quite. Indeed, it is this whispering, chuckling fragment which serves Mozart for some of the most delicate surprises in his brief development section. The reprise of the basic themes is as "regular" as any textbook writer could wish. Yet somehow it always seems new.

II. *Romanze: Andante.* The mood is more tender in the lyric slow movement. The title *Romanze* usually referred to a short song of sentimental character, but was occasionally used by Mozart and Beethoven for instrumental movements of special delicacy. Here, the form is rather like a very free set of variations on the opening two-part strain.

III. *Menuetto: Allegretto.* The charm of the surviving Minuet lies in part in its brevity and simplicity. The trio section, marked *sotto voce,* has a flowing line of a grace remarkable even for Mozart.

IV. *Rondo: Allegro.* The skipping refrain of the *Rondo* is a tune which, once heard, is hard to forget:

It was Mozart's older friend, Haydn, who first developed the ingenious combination of rondo and sonata forms which so enriched his and Mozart's instrumental music. Here Mozart fuses the two forms with a seeming simplicity, which was one of his special gifts and which has endeared this *Little Serenade* to generations of admirers.

SERENADE, D MAJOR, K.320 (POSTHORN)

It is always amazing to be reminded (as we constantly are by Mozart research) how shifting and flexible the boundaries were in his day between orchestral and chamber music: among the symphony, *sinfonia concertante,* serenade, cassation, *divertimento, Finalmusik,* octet, string quintet, quartet, etc.

A perfect example of this is Mozart's "Posthorn" Serenade. The nickname "Posthorn," by the way, does not stem from Mozart, but from a brief detail of his orchestration and from audiences' love (then as now) for nicknames. One of the trios in the sixth-movement *Minuet* of this Serenade has a short solo for posthorn, an instrument used by the mail coaches or post chaises for buglelike signals, a close relative of the ancient hunting horn and the more recent orchestral horn or French horn.

The elaborate development of this "Posthorn" Serenade has long led musicians to suspect that Mozart had composed it for some especially important event, hitherto unidentified. It was also known that the Mozart family occasionally referred to this particular Serenade (and certain others) as a *Finalmusik* (or *final musique,* as Mozart often wrote it in his correspondence). By delving into local archives and into personal diaries of contemporaries of the Mozart family, it was discovered that such *Finalmusiken* were a local Salzburg tradition. Upon the completion of their final examinations, it was the custom for graduate students of the University of Salzburg to offer a serenade to their professors and to the Archbishop of Salzburg. These final examinations normally took place early in August. The *Finalmusiken* offered by the happy students were, of course, always especially commissioned for the specific occasion. Mozart was commissioned on more than one occasion to compose the students' *Finalmusik.* The work we know as the "Posthorn" Serenade, and which the Mozart family correspondence mentions as his "most recent *final musique*," is dated August 3, 1779.

Aside from encore performances on the date of the festivities, repetitions of such *Finalmusiken* in their entirety were rare. This must have seemed a sinful waste of great music, so it is hardly surprising that excerpts from such *Finalmusiken* (as well as other serenades) have been found in many manuscripts, and even in printed editions cut down to four—or even three—movement "symphonies." But only during the last decade or so has the *enormous* popularity of these excerpted "symphonies" been documented by *dozens* of manuscript copies and printed editions found in important music collections and distributed especially in areas now known as Southern Bavaria, Czechoslovakia, Austria, and northern Italy.

Not until the early 1970s was a copyist's manuscript of the Symphony drawn from the "Posthorn" Serenade discovered in the Library of the Conservatory of Graz in central Austria, with corrections entered in Mozart's own handwriting—clear evidence that if Mozart did not make these particular excerpts himself, he did not disapprove of them. We now know that the three-movement Symphony (consisting of movements I, V, and VII of the "Posthorn" Serenade) was so popular in the eighteenth century that it spread quickly from city to city—first in manuscripts sold by professional copyists, then in printed editions the first of which was published in 1792 as Mozart's "Opus 22"! Five additional printed editions (including a two-hand clavier arrangement and another for harpsichord, cello, and violin) and as yet uncounted manuscript copies continuing into the nineteenth century, attest the popularity of this three-movement "symphony." Mozart himself used the three movements in one of his own most famous concerts of his own music in Vienna on March 23, 1783, in the presence of the Emperor. And he also used the third and fourth movements of the "Posthorn" Serenade (the *Concertante* and the *Rondo*) to which he gave the independent title of *Sinfonia concertante* on the program of at least one other Viennese concert.

In its original form of August 3, 1779, the *"Posthorn"* Serenade consisted of seven movements.

I. *Adagio maestoso; Allegro con spirito.* After six introductory measures of pomp and circumstance, the main body of the first movement opens in a rush of joyous excitement, agitated syncopations and fragments of marchlike rhythms. When at last we come to a clear theme, it seems to be a humorous one. It alternates between a gruffly aggressive one-measure figure for all the strings in octaves, and gently melodious, almost pleading phrases for the first violins:

The great Mozart authority Alfred Einstein was firmly convinced that this was Mozart's humorous depiction of his own repeated appeals to be allowed to leave Salzburg on artistic tours, and the obstinate refusals of his hated employer, the Archbishop. But any student who has ever suffered through an oral examination will hardly need the suggestion that the same passage could easily be taken as a high-spirited caricature of a dialogue between a sternly sadistic examining professor and the gentler replies of a hopeful student. With or without anecdotage, the movement ends in a mood of rejoicing.

II. *Menuetto:* The first *Minuet* is a rather elaborately developed one, which alternates festive tuttis with whispering replies of the upper string instruments. A charming trio-section, kept on the most intimate chamber level, is a *sotto-voce* conversation among solo flute, solo bassoon, and strings.

III. *Concertante: Andante grazioso.* This movement in G major is a tiny chamber concerto for three pairs of solo woodwinds—flutes, oboes and bassoons—with a discreet background of strings and horns. Each soloist has a chance to display his grace and wit. There is even a written-out group cadenza: a humorously garrulous moment in which each soloist tries to interrupt the others until all are chattering together in an exuberant conversational free-for-all.

IV. *Rondeau: Allegro ma non troppo.* A companion piece to the preceding movements, this *Rondeau,* also in G major, continues the *concertante* style of group conversation, but in even lighter, wittier and more dexterous form.

V. *Andantino.* The deep seriousness of this slow movement is emphasized by the tonality of D minor. There is no need to seek any external anecdotal explanation for the intensity of emotion which borders on the tragic. The movement begins very softly with its upward reaching principal theme in the first violins:

VI. *Menuetto.* This Minuet movement is remembered especially for its second trio section with a solo for posthorn, which has given the Serenade its nickname:

The posthorn, which was rarely used in the eighteenth century without programmatic meaning, may have been intended as a reference to the impending departure from Salzburg of many a graduate student.

VII. *Finale: Presto.* The exuberant *Finale* is as rich thematically as many of Mozart's most mature symphonies. It includes an unusually elaborate symphonic development section and a final coda, emphasizing once more the mood of celebration for which the score was commissioned.

To suit the festive occasion, the "Posthorn" Serenade (or *final musique*) employed a rather large orchestra consisting of piccolo, 2 flutes, 2 oboes, 2 bassoons, 2 horns, solo posthorn, 2 trumpets, kettledrums, and the traditional string choir to which a keyboard instrument (harpsichord or piano) would have been added if the Serenade were performed indoors, though not, of course, for open-air performances.

SERENADE NO. 10, B-FLAT MAJOR, K. 361

Mozart's choice of music for his own wedding celebration (or *Hochzeitsfestin,* as he called it) was, understandably, one of his greatest scores: the masterpiece we know as his Serenade No. 10 in B-flat major, K. 361. At least this is the work to which all the evidence assembled by Mozart's greatest biographer, Herman Abert, points.

Mozart had begun the composition of the Serenade early in 1781 at the time when he was supervising the production of his opera *Idomeneo* at the Bavarian Court Theater in Munich. The score may well have been intended for the highly skilled players of the Munich Orchestra (formerly the famous Mannheim Orchestra, which had moved to Munich with the Mannheim court at the time the Elector Palatine inherited the dukedom of Bavaria). Very likely, too, it was written in the hope of winning an appointment to the Bavarian court, which never materialized. It was completed in Vienna in the summer of 1781, during the height of Mozart's struggle to escape from what he felt to be the "slavery" of his service to the Archbishop of Salzburg.

The mixed moods of this Serenade seem ideally suited to a wedding celebration, from the heart-piercing beauty of the *Adagio* to the infectious abandon of the concluding Rondo. Mozart wrote his father that both he and his bride, Constanze, wept at the ceremony in St. Stephen's Cathedral, Vienna, on August 4, 1782. The witnesses and even the priest were so moved that they, too, wept. Afterwards they were merry at the wedding breakfast (or rather *souper,* as Mozart called it) given them by friendly Baroness von Waldstädten. Her hospitality, according to Mozart was "more princely than baronial."

The Serenade, which is in seven movements, bears no title in Mozart's hand. A later hand gave the manuscript a title: *Gran partita,* one of the many eighteenth-century designations for this general type of work. Nowadays it is customarily grouped with Mozart's serenades.

I. *Largo; Allegro molto.* The first movement begins traditionally enough with an almost pompous introduction of repeated chords. But the subjective Mozartean touch is heard at once in the delicate little phrases for clarinet between the big chords. The remainder of the slow introduction continues in this characteristically thoughtful Mozartean strain in which a pair of clarinets is played off against a pair of oboes.

The fast main section of this first movement is far from the marchlike mood of many a serenade opening movement. It begins almost in a whisper. Occasional *forte* interjections seem outnumbered by the more delicate, lyric, even whimsical passages. Another Mozartean trait is the series of excursions, both here and in later movements of the Serenade, into the melancholy realm of G minor.

II. *Menuetto.* The first *Minuet* is ceremonious but not heavy and its texture is occasionally lightened by diaphanous solo sections, featuring Mozart's beloved clarinet sound. Being a *Minuet* on a large scale, this one has two trios. The first, especially beguiling, is written for 4 clarinets: 2 B-flat clarinets of standard orchestral usage, and 2 of the less familiar basset horns *(corni di bassetto),* which are not horns at all but alto clarinets. The second trio is as striking as the first, but in a totally different way. It is in the relatively rare key of G minor, which when used by Mozart was often a key of pessimism or even tragedy. A restless triplet motion runs through almost the entire trio, from bassoon to oboe to basset horn. The only interruption of this triplet motion is a striking, repeated phrase for the French horn, echoed by the upper woodwinds. This is one of Mozart's most varied and fascinating minuets.

III. *Adagio.* Another of the many miracles of this score is the *Adagio* in E-flat major, one of Mozart's favorite keys—a key which we associate with the gentle melancholy of the Countess's "Porgi amor" in *The Marriage of Figaro* and with certain of the more exalted moments of *The Magic Flute.* Over a murmuring accompaniment we hear a duet between solo oboe and solo clarinet. The oboe leads with a long-held, softly swelling tone followed by graceful Rococo curlicues. The clarinet follows with, if possible, an even more ravishingly sensuous answer. The dialogue gives an impression of a felicity so sharp that it is sometimes close to pain, perhaps to tears. It is one of Mozart's most profound movements, yet one which Alfred Einstein could rightly call "a Notturno . . . a scene from *Romeo* under starry skies, a scene in which longing, grief and love are wrung like a distillation from the beating hearts of the lovers."

IV. *Menuetto: Allegretto.* The brief second *Minuet* has two tiny trios, both full of gentle wit and subtle surprises.

V. *Romanze: Adagio; Allegretto.* Only the brief opening and closing sections of this movement are in the slow tempo traditional for a *Romanze.* The longer central section is a lively C minor, with scurrying bassoon figures lending a special color to the orchestral sound.

VI. *Theme and Variations* [*Andante*]. Mozart's rather playful theme is presented by the clarinet, with echoes of the woodwind ensemble. It is followed by six fairly simple variations, including a melting *adagio*.

VII. *Rondo: Allegro molto*. The irrepressible gaiety of this *finale* reminds us of Haydn in his lighter moods. The folklike simplicity of the refrain is in a style both composers loved:

The quieter episodes are inimitably Mozartean in the sensuous appeal of his clarinet melodies and the curious chromaticisms of the passage leading into the exuberant return of the *Rondo* refrain.

This work is scored for 2 oboes, 2 clarinets, 2 basset horns (this seems to be Mozart's first use of the basset horn), 4 French horns, 2 bassoons, and one string bass. Mozart's manuscript, now in the Library of Congress, definitely specifies *contra basso*, that is, string bass, and does *not* offer the option of replacing the string bass by a contrabassoon which is erroneously offered in many modern editions. However, since the contrabassoon of Mozart's day was relatively primitive and today's contrabassoon is a more sophisticated instrument, many conductors are convinced that the contrabassoon is in fact better adapted to the sound they are convinced Mozart would have preferred. Thus they believe they are fulfilling his ideal by changing his orchestration to a contrabassoon.

SINFONIA CONCERTANTE, E-FLAT MAJOR, K. 297b

It is hard to imagine that this enchanting work may not be by Mozart. Yet the version which has come down to us (for solo flute, oboe, bassoon and horn) can hardly be as Mozart composed it. This score, which turned up in the late nineteenth century, seems to be a rather slipshod copy or even an adaptation of a lost Mozart original. But even this has been questioned. All we know for certain from Mozart's correspondence, is that he did compose a *Sinfonia concertante* for a similar (but not identical) group of winds in Paris when he was twenty-two years old, and that this score disappeared.

On April 5, 1778, Mozart wrote from Paris to his father that he was about to compose a *sinfonia concertante* for three virtuosos from the famous Mannheim orchestra: Johann Baptist Wendling, flutist; Friedrich Ramm, oboist; Georg Wenzel Ritter, bassoonist; plus the itinerant horn virtuoso Jan Vaclav Stich, better known by his Italian name of Giovanni Punto. The new work was to be performed at the fashionable Concerts Spirituels, but nothing came of it.

On May 1, Mozart wrote his father that the performance of the *Sinfonia concertante* had hit a snag, or "hanky-panky" (*Hickl-hackl,* he called it). Evidently he suspected an intrigue for, he wrote:

> I have enemies here too. Where have I not had them?— But that is a good sign. I had to compose the *Sinfonia concertante* in greatest haste, and went to great pains, and the four soloists were, and still are, completely in love with it. Le Gros [director of the Concerts Spirituels] had the score for four days for copying. But I still found it lying in the same place. Finally the day before [the concert] I didn't see it, but searched in a pile of music and found it hidden. I pretended not to notice this, and asked Le Gros: "A propos, have you sent the *Sinfonia concertante* to be copied yet?"—"No, I forgot it." Since I naturally can't order him to have it copied or performed, I said nothing. Two days later, when it should have been performed, I went to the concert. Ramm and Punto came to me in great heat and asked why my *Sinfonia concertante* was not being performed. "I don't know, (I replied) this is the first I've heard of this, I know nothing at all." Ramm fell into a great rage and denounced Le Gros right there in the green room—in French—saying it was ugly of him, and so on. What annoyed me most of all about the whole business is that Le Gros didn't say a word about it to me and I was the only one not to be told. If he had only made some excuse that the time had been too short or something of the kind, but nothing . . .

What was worse, the score was lost. Unfortunately Mozart had kept no copy of the work. And although he later told his father that he intended to write down the *Sinfonia concertante* again from memory as soon as he got back home in Salzburg, Mozart authorities are agreed that he would certainly not have replaced a flute by a clarinet for Salzburg.

The autographed score has never been recovered. Some seventy years after Mozart's death, a manuscript copy of the *Sinfonia concertante,* as we know it today, turned up among the papers of the famous Mozart biographer, Otto Jahn. Jahn left no information as to the source of the manuscript, which, in its highly Romantic interpretive phrasing and dynamics, was clearly far from authentic.

Despite the questionable form in which it has survived, most Mozart scholars believe it to be basically authentic, indeed one of the finest works of his early maturity.

As the title *Sinfonia concertante* suggests, it occupies the sort of middle ground between symphony and concerto. And with its four soloists pitted against the orchestra, it recalls the interplay of *concertino* and *ripieno* in the Baroque *concerto grosso* of Bach's and Handel's day. It is in three movements.

I. *Allegro.* The opening movement is the richest of the three in sheer abundance of ideas and thematic development. As in the Classical solo concerto, the principal themes are presented first by the orchestra alone. The rather grand gesture of the opening theme leads to a series of more intimate, caressing phrases, one of the more graceful of which is offered at once by the first violins:

After the four soloists make their joint appearance the oboe is first to take up this theme, which is developed by all the soloists, one after the other. Another of the most beguiling thoughts of the first movement is given out first by the violins and later by the solo oboe in the dominant key:

There is a development section, then the return of the principal themes is rounded off by a long coda-like cadenza for the four soloists.

II. *Adagio.* After a brief but gravely ceremonious orchestral opening, the second movement is dominated by the sustained song of the solo instruments. Each virtuoso contributes his characteristic sensuous color, one of the most striking passages being the typically Mozartean minor-key entrance of the bassoon midway through the movement, in a brief development section. The clarinet contributes a tender variant of the first theme quoted above. The resemblance is most obvious in the thematic reprise which brings the movement to an end:

III. *Andantino con variazoni.* A lighthearted melody, which might have been taken from a Parisian *opéra-comique,* is the theme on which Mozart spins out ten graceful variations:

The ten variations are playful and decorative rather than deep, and the soloists have ample chance to shine. Toward the end an unexpected moment of melancholy serves chiefly to emphasize the rollicking gaiety of a giguelike *coda.*

In the only form which has come down to us, the *Sinfonia concertante* is scored for an orchestra of 2 oboes, 2 horns, and strings, plus solo oboe, clarinet, horn, and bassoon.

SINFONIA CONCERTANTE FOR VIOLIN, VIOLA, AND ORCHESTRA, E-FLAT MAJOR, K. 364

One of the most ravishingly beautiful works of Mozart's maturity, his E-flat *Sinfonia concertante* has been surprisingly neglected by many major orchestras —at least in this country. Our New York Philharmonic, according to its historian, Professor Howard Shanet of Columbia University, seems to have waited until its seventy-seventh season to perform the work on January 3, 1919. By that time Mozart's masterpiece was 140 years old. If we can believe the great conductor-impresario Theodore Thomas (one of the most potent forces in the development in our orchestral life), it was not until April 8, 1865, that he himself conducted the American premiere at one of the concerts by his own orchestra in this city.

Yet this *Sinfonia concertante* is held in deep affection by great numbers of contemporary Mozart lovers, as is attested by its numerous recordings and by its frequent performances among smaller ensembles.

A certain mystery surrounds the genesis of the music. Its whole style, including dozens of technical details and personal idiosyncrasies (which in Mozart's case often changed from month to month), tells us with almost 99 percent certainty that the score must have been written during the last months of Mozart's "Salzburg slavery," as he himself called it: that is, during his last sojourn in his native city in the service of the irascible Archbishop of Salzburg.

Mozart had just returned from his heartbreaking tour of 1777–1779 to Mannheim and Paris and other important musical centers where he had hoped to find a position worthy of his fabulous talents. The failure of his professional ambitions, the death of his mother in Paris and the return to provincial Salzburg were bitter blows. Yet he had grown in adversity.

In all likelihood the *Sinfonia concertante* for Violin, Viola and Orchestra was composed during the latter half of 1779. Like most of his contemporaries, Mozart rarely wrote a major work except for a specific occasion, for a specific patron and with specific performers in mind. But since he was living at home, the copious family correspondence, which is such a mine of information about so many Mozart works, tells us nothing; and no other relevant documents seem to have survived. The music itself was not published until ten years after Mozart's death, and thereafter the manuscript, with all the many clues it might have supplied, was lost. We do not even know the names of the skilled violinist and violist for whom the *Sinfonia concertante* could have been designed at that time in Salzburg—unless, of course, Mozart had himself in mind as the violist. For, to his father's deep disappointment, Mozart was tending more and more to prefer the viola to the violin when he performed ensemble music. On the other hand, Father Leopold himself enjoyed considerable fame as a violinist. So it is conceivable that this happy score was shaped, in part, by the unique father-son relationship which, in the nature of things, was coming to an end at the very moment that Mozart entered the last and greatest era of his creative life.

The popular *sinfonia concertante* form was a kind of cross between a symphony and a concerto, except that the soloists were normally two or more in number. It was a form which Mozart had encountered especially in Mannheim and Paris. The difficulty and prominence of the solo parts varied from composer to composer, as did the richness of the orchestral part. In this specific work the opening movement is of a breadth and richness equal to any of Mozart's greatest symphonies. Indeed the work as a whole ranks not as a transition to his last and greatest masterpieces but as a full-fledged member of that group.

I. *Allegro maestoso.* Although this magnificent movement could have been written by no other composer than Mozart, it shows clearly the influences that he had absorbed during his recent trip. The opening theme itself (as has been pointed out by H.C.R. Landon) echoes, note for note, the opening rhythm of an F-major symphony by the famous Mannheim composer Carl Stamitz. It is followed by a profusion of themes, each more endearing than the last, including an especially Mozartean phrase for a pair of horns echoed by a pair of oboes:

This in turn is succeeded by a lengthy orchestral crescendo, during which a tiny trilling violin figure rises to a dynamic climax in a style made popular by the Mannheim orchestra.

Only at this point, as the orchestral climax ebbs, do the two soloists make their joint entrance, unobtrusively at first, on a long-held high E-flat, then descending in a graceful curve and with a sonority of almost piercing sweetness produced in part by the *tessitura* and by the octave duplication of the two instruments:

Having entered as equals, the two soloists continue in roles of artistic parity, one picking up the thread of conversation from the other, producing an effect of unity in endless variety. A perfect example is the melody, which in conventional analysis might be called the subordinate theme or "side group," in the dominant key of B-flat, given out first by the solo violin, then picked up by the viola:

The orchestral development is as fertile thematically as it is rich in sonority. Part of this richness is due to the fact that Mozart uses two sections of dark-hued orchestral violas. In order, on the other hand, to have the solo viola stand out from the orchestral violas, Mozart wrote the solo viola part in the key of D major. This meant that the solo violist was obliged to tune his instrument a half tone higher than normal, with the result that the solo viola produced a more brilliant tone than the violas of the orchestra. (This requirement often produces considerable difficulty for viola soloists, since there is an ever-present danger that the tuning pegs of his instrument may tend to slip back to their normal position, thus throwing the whole instrument out of tune and interrupting the performance, with all the psychological tensions that such a danger imposes on the soloist. For this reason many modern performers bypass Mozart's directions for the specialized tuning or *scordatura,* keep the normal tuning and play the part as if it were written in E-flat like the rest of the composition.)

Although this *Sinfonia concertante* is at least as much a concerto as it is a symphony, Mozart avoids the usual concerto form, which allots one exposition of the thematic material to the orchestra alone, and a second exposition to the soloist(s). Despite this omission and the highly condensed reprise of principal themes with which the movement concludes, the total surpasses in length any first movement of Mozart's last and greatest symphonies. Its inexhaustible inventiveness makes the movement seem brief.

It is interesting to remember that Mozart himself composed the cadenza for the two soloists which occurs just before the conclusion, a cadenza which in its brevity and variety could well serve as a model for soloists who must supply their own cadenzas in works where Mozart followed the more usual custom of allowing the soloists complete liberty at this important moment.

II. *Andante.* The slow movement, traditionally songful, is one of the most intensely emotional that Mozart had yet composed. It is in the key of C minor, in itself a rarity for that day, although Mozart had used it only a few months earlier for the slow movement of his so-called "Jeunehomme" Piano Concerto. Remarkable as that Piano Concerto is, particularly in its slow movement, it cannot rival the intensity, indeed the near-tragedy of the mood with which this *Andante* begins and ends. Its principal theme, based on a familiar cliché of the period, is nevertheless unforgettably individual:

The central section returns to the basic key of E-flat major, but an E-flat major which in this context seems unutterably poignant. The second half of the movement reverses the key scheme and concludes with a brief cadenza and a final reminiscence of the opening theme.

III. *Presto.* The *finale,* Mozart at his most joyous, is a *rondo,* but a *rondo* with a difference. It opens with this dancing refrain:

There are three returns of the *Rondo* refrain, with three intervening episodes, all of them cunningly interrelated, and including a quartet passage for two horns and two oboes recalling the episode for the same combination of instruments in the first movement. This is no literal quotation from the first movement, but the connection is obvious: charming if it was intentional and all the more remarkable if it was not consciously planned.

In addition to the two solo instruments, the score calls for 2 oboes, 2 horns, first and second violins, first and second violas, cellos, and double basses which, contrary to the conventional usage of Mozart's day, occasionally have their own part independent of the cellos. The custom of Mozart's day would also have called for a *continuo* harpsichord and bassoon to round out the ensemble, although they are not specified in the score and are often omitted in modern performances by large orchestras.

SYMPHONY IN G MINOR, (NO. 25) K. 183

Mozart's "Little" G-minor Symphony (so called to distinguish it from the "Great" G-minor, Mozart's next to last symphony) is brief, but packed with explosive power. Mozart was seventeen and had just returned to his home in Salzburg from his final Italian tour, during which he had produced his opera *Lucio Silla* in Milan. In *Lucio Silla* he had dared to reflect some of the Storm and Stress which was agitating composers and dramatists throughout Europe and which found a strong echo in Mozart's adolescent heart.

But tragic emotions did not endear him to Milanese opera buffs and Mozart was not invited back. Nor was the Storm and Stress popular with the conservative musical establishment in Salzburg, Vienna or Esterháza, despite the emotion-charged scores which both Gluck and Haydn had contributed there.

We do not know for what occasion Mozart composed his "Little" G-minor Symphony. Indeed it is only since World War II that modern light-filter techniques and special photographic devices have made it possible to decipher the date of Mozart's manuscript which, for unknown reasons, had been virtually obliterated. But we do know that out of Mozart's entire production of forty-odd symphonies, only two are in minor keys, both of these in G minor. And we know that G minor had a very special significance to Mozart. In his *Magic Flute,* G minor is the key of Pamina's aria, "Ach, ich fühl's," the key of utter despair and the wish to die. Whenever Mozart even approaches G minor in a vocal work, it is to express the utmost intensity of suffering. The purely instrumental works in that key: the "Little" G-minor Symphony, and the G-minor String Quintet with two violas, and the late G-minor Symphony, K. 550, all seem to share a common emotional climate. The "Little" G-minor Symphony is dated October 5, 1773.

I. *Allegro con brio.* In comparison with the larger, greater G-minor Symphony of Mozart's later years, the "Little" G-minor is wilder and perhaps more despairing. The spirit of revolt, which is so often implied in works of the musical Storm and Stress, seems more furious here, more unrestrained, with an adolescent emotion which has not yet been tamed by an adverse world. Even the trembling syncopations of the four opening measures presage what is to come in the almost physical outburst of the principal theme:

This first outburst seems to subside quietly enough, only to burst forth again in the major key, its energy now being emphasized by the insistent rhythm of four horns (an expansion beyond the normal pair of French horns customary in most symphonies of the period). Not until the last part of the exposition do we reach momentarily the more polite and contained manner, the daintier style of standard early Classicism. The central development section of the movement is one of struggle, not, of course, in the manner of Beethoven, but in a much more personal, Mozartean manner quite astounding for so young a composer.

II. *Andante.* Although E-flat major, the key of the slow movement, is often Mozart's vehicle for the sunniest or most warmly sensuous feelings, this movement is remarkably subdued. The muted violins here are, of course, nothing new, yet the veiled quality of their tone, together with the sighlike, broken melodic line and the subtle harmonic twists give this movement a quality all its own:

The laconic close is characteristic of Mozart.

III. *Menuetto.* If one remembers the courtly grace, the aristocratic polish and the traditional associations with Versailles which were part of the heritage of the minuet, this movement sounds stark indeed. It opens with bare octaves of the entire orchestra (including horns!) in a theme which is closer to a peasants' stamp than the aristocratic tread of tradition:

The middle section, given over entirely to the winds, brings us the Symphony's only moment of almost dreamlike beauty and serenity.

IV. *Allegro.* The final movement, although closely related to the first with its bare octaves and agitated syncopations, is even more extraordinary in its emotional intensity, its sharpened sense of inner struggle and its stark, stormy contrasts.

Mozart was no revolutionist, either in art or politics. He heartily detested most of the ideas of the intellectual left of his day, as far as he was aware of them at all. Yet, all intellectual consideration aside, one cannot help feeling that in this Symphony the artist gave voice to feelings which in the decade of the 1780s were to explode with repercussions we still feel today. It was later than anyone, including Mozart, realized.

The "Little" G-minor Symphony is scored for 2 oboes, 2 bassoons, 4 horns, and the traditional strings.

SYMPHONY NO. 29, A MAJOR, K. 201

Paradoxically, it has taken a growing sophistication in concert audiences and professional musicians to appreciate some of Mozart's simplest inspirations. Or perhaps we should say "apparently simple," since none of Mozart's mature inspirations is as simple as it seems. Mozart completed this enthralling A-major Symphony in Salzburg when he was only eighteen. It was one of a group which included another early masterpiece, the "Little" G-minor Symphony, K. 183. They were written after the trip to Vienna in the winter of 1773–74, when the Mozarts, father and son, had visited their friend Anton Mesmer (the inventor of mesmerism) and Father Leopold apparently sought in vain a position for his son at the Imperial Court. The influence of the Vienna visit shows in many ways. For one thing, Mozart returns to the four-movement symphonic form, with a minuet in third place, as was the custom in Vienna. For another, this Symphony shows an increased seriousness, in addition to the Italianate grace and charm of its predecessors.

I. *Allegro moderato.* The first movement begins softly, but with a striking theme somewhat reminiscent of the theme of Mozart's "Linz" Symphony. It is easy to recognize this theme as it recurs by its characteristic skip of an octave:

Horns and oboes join the strings for a *tutti* repetition of the main theme, which is rounded off by repeated emphatic cadences of the full orchestra and a pause before presentation of the second theme.

The separate sections of this movement are so clearly marked in the Classical spirit that the form is exceptionally easy to follow. The second theme, announced softly by the first violins with the lightest of string accompaniments, is a graceful, lilting figure with a recurrent trill:

A brief closing section with more emphatic cadences for full orchestra rounds off this little exposition. A tiny development section spins out two phrases in fetching sequences and leads back quickly to a restatement of the Symphony's opening themes.

II. *Andante.* The slow movement, although cast in the same form as the first, is entirely different in character: almost a serenade in spirit, with its song of muted violins, its enchanting Rococo ornamentation and its delicate texture, which seems closer to a string quartet than a symphony. It is full of eighteenth-century clichés and turns that were used a hundred times before and after by other composers, but here they are so spontaneous and lovely that each phrase bears repeating and repeating. And still the movement seems too short.

III. *Menuetto.* This is no longer the courtly dance of periwigged cavaliers and ladies with stately *panniers.* There is a vigor to the dotted rhythms of this movement and a near violence in the sudden fortissimos that anticipate the spirit of Beethoven. The lyric contrast of the middle trio section throws the vigor of the *Menuetto* proper into even stronger relief.

IV. *Allegro con spirito.* The *finale* is gay and energetic, with a zestful main theme that may call to mind the first-movement theme quoted above, because of the octave jumps they share:

But the resemblance goes beyond the octave jump to an indefinable kind of family resemblance which shows another side of Mozart's maturing symphonic art. This movement also has the richest and most dramatic development section of any that Mozart had written so far. The first two measures of this main theme are spun out in sequences of increasing harmonic richness and tossed from top to bottom of the orchestra, with growing exuberance, until an upward rush of the violins and a dramatic pause usher in the return to the original thematic material. Despite the true symphonic richness of this movement, it has a verve and a lightness, almost a dancelike quality, which recall the little Rococo rondos with which the contemporary Italian symphony was wont to conclude.

The A-major Symphony is scored simply for 2 oboes, 2 horns, and the traditional string choir.

SYMPHONY NO. 31, D MAJOR, PARIS K. 297

As a child prodigy on tour, Mozart had been petted and pampered by monarchs and musicians from London to Naples, and from Paris to Vienna. As he matured, he grew frantic to escape permanently from the petty, provincial atmosphere of Salzburg, the city where he was born. He longed for the sort of important position he should have held in one of the great European music centers, but never achieved.

When he revisited Paris in his twenty-second year, he was scarcely noticed. For Mozart had neither the aggressiveness nor the gift for bootlicking that made the fortunes of dozens of lesser talents in the French capital. Besides, the Parisians were far too excited by an operatic battle between the supporters of Gluck and those of Piccinni to notice a provincial Austrian who had been a beguiling infant prodigy but was now merely a young genius.

Mozart returned the lack of regard with interest; he despised Parisian musical life. But when Le Gros invited him to compose a symphony for the famous *Concerts Spirtuels,* he adapted himself somewhat to Parisian taste. The success this earned him was one of the few rays of light in an otherwise gloomy visit. His vivid letters home kept his father posted. The new symphony was scheduled to open the *Concert Spirituel* on Corpus Christi Day (June 18, 1778). Mozart himself rather fancied his new symphony, but he was in doubt whether the Parisians would like it or not.

> And to tell the truth [he wrote], I don't much care. . . . The *few* intelligent Frenchmen who are there will like it; I'll guarantee that. As for the stupid ones, I can't see that there is any great misfortune not to please them. Still I have hopes that even the asses may find something in it to give them pleasure. Besides, I was careful not to forget the *premier coup d'archet!*—and that's enough! [The Parisians seem to have been especially proud of the ability of their orchestra to all start together with the first bow-stroke, or *coup d'archet.*] What a fuss these donkeys here make over it!—What the devil! I don't see any difference—they begin together—as they do in other places. It's ridiculous.

By Mozart's standards, the orchestra was poor. It was overworked, and the rehearsals were so bad that he was frightened to think what the performance would be like.

> I have never heard anything worse in all my life [he wrote]. You can't imagine how they bumbled and scratched through the Symphony twice—I was really worried—I would have liked to rehearse it once more, but they had so many things to rehearse there was no time left, so I had to go home and to bed worried, dissatisfied, and angry. I decided that I simply would not go to the concert the next day. But by evening the weather was good, and I finally decided to go, but with the resolution that, if the performance went as badly as the rehearsal, I would go up and take the violin out of the hands of M. Lahousé, the concert master, and conduct it myself. I prayed *God* to make it go well, since everything was for his highest honor and glory, and so the Symphony began, . . .
>
> Right in the middle of the first *Allegro,* there was a place I was sure they would like. All the listeners were electrified and there was tremendous applause. And since I knew, when I was writing it, what an effect it would make, I repeated the passage toward the end, and they began applauding all over again.
>
> They liked the *Andante* too, and the final *Allegro* even more. Since I had heard that all the final allegros here begin just like the first one—with all the instruments at once and usually in unison—I began with only the first and second violins, playing very softly for just eight measures and a loud forte immediately afterwards. Just as I had expected, when they heard the soft beginning, the audience went: "Sh-h-h . . ." Then came the *forte.* . . . For them, hearing the *forte* and clapping their hands were practically the same thing. So after the Symphony, out of pure joy, I went right to the Palais Royal, ate a nice ice, said the rosary I had promised, and went home.

For the second performance of the Symphony, Le Gros asked Mozart to write a new slow movement.

> Le Gros is so pleased with the Symphony that he calls it the best one he has. But [Mozart confessed] the *Andante* did not have the good fortune to please him. He says there are too many modulations in it—and it's too long. But the reason for that was that in the slow movement the audience forgot to make such a long and loud noise with their clapping as they did in the first and last movements. For the *Andante* is what most pleased me, all the connoisseurs, amateurs, and most of the audience. It is just the *contraire* of what Le Gros says. It is very natural—and short. But still, on order to please him and (as he claims) many others, I have written a new *Andante.* Each one is good in its own way, for each has a different character. But I like the second one more. . . . The Symphony will be performed for the second time with the new *Andante* on the fifteenth of August, the Feast of the Assumption of the Virgin.

This was the first time Mozart had written for such a large orchestra: 2 flutes, 2 oboes, 2 clarinets (which he had never before used in a symphony),

2 bassoons, 2 horns, 2 trumpets, kettledrums, and the traditional string choir. Composed in late May and early June, 1778, the Symphony is in three movements.

I. *Allegro assai.* The famous *premier coup d'archet* of which the Parisians were so proud, is called into play for the first chord of the pompous opening theme with its upward sweeping strings:

The basic material of the whole movement consists of alternations of such pompous *tutti* passages with graceful, often dainty filigree work for strings alone, or for strings with transparent background of woodwinds. Mozart betrays his opinion of his French auditors by his anxious avoidance of depth and emotional intensity. Yet the movement has brilliance, power and sometimes grandeur.

II. *Andante.* Although the original version of this movement was published in Paris during Mozart's day, he himself preferred the second version, which is performed nowadays. This is decorative music, of a grace and elegance we find in the fanciful Rococo architecture of Mozart's youth.

III. *Allegro.* Eight bars of whispering violins lead to the brilliant *tutti* which unleashed the storm of applause during the music! The fanfare-like *tutti* theme recalls the opening of the first movement:

The device is effective and Mozart promptly repeats it. In this exuberant finale, he gives his imagination and temperament freer rein. In some of the soft passages, there is a charmingly delicate interplay of contrapuntal lines among the strings and solo woodwinds. The grander *tutti* passages, without ever becoming disturbingly passionate, have an energy and drive that must have swept receptive listeners off their feet. No wonder this Symphony was a success.

SYMPHONY NO. 34, C MAJOR, K. 338; WITH MINUET, K. 409

The miracle of this little C-major Symphony, which originally had only three movements, is not so much its effortless elegance, its irresistible, sensuous appeal, the beguiling lilt of its finale, or even the Romantic melancholy with which the opening movement is so strongly tinged. These were all qualities which had come naturally to Mozart in other works at an incomprehensibly early age. The miracle of this Symphony is the maturity and subtlety with which the twenty-four-year-old master reconciles and combines apparently contradictory moods in a convincing psychological unity.

The Symphony was written during the last months of Mozart's service to the hated Archbishop of Salzburg: Hieronymus von Colloredo. These were decisive months in Mozart's career. He had returned to Salzburg in January 1779 from the tragic trip to Paris, where his mother had died and he himself had met humiliating professional disappointment. On the last lap of his homeward trip he discovered that he had been jilted by his first serious love, the soprano Aloysia Weber. Whether misfortune matured him, or the temporary separation from his dominating father, or growing confidence in his own artistic powers is hard to say.

The Symphony was completed on August 29, 1780. Its limitation to three movements was a concession to the conservative Salzburg taste, for Mozart, under the progressive influences of Vienna and Mannheim, had long been accustomed to the four-movement form. In content the Symphony is astonishingly forward-looking and Romantic, especially in its first movement.

I. *Allegro vivace.* Festive fanfares of horns, trumpets and timpani open with all the traditional pomp of the *opera seria* overture, the ancestor of the Classical symphony. The fanfare is answered by an echo in minor, which at first seems no more than a melancholy afterthought. But hardly have the gleaming tones of trumpets and horns restored the bright major mode, when the music veers again toward the darker regions of G minor, E minor, F minor and A-flat major. At the end of the exposition, a garrulous little cadential figure expands without warning into ominous octaves of the entire string section, probing deeper and deeper toward a tragic C minor:

This threat never quite materializes, but it is followed by repeated ambiguous shifts from major to minor, from sunlight to shadow, from confidence to timid sighs and agitated whispers. The C-major tonic of this Symphony proves a richly ambiguous key.

II. *Menuetto (K. 409).* The autograph of this Symphony includes the beginning of a minuet, which is crossed out. The *Minuet* which belongs to this Symphony was composed almost two years later in Vienna probably for a concert in the Viennese Augarten on May 26, 1782. This is one of the richest and most beautiful minuets Mozart ever wrote. In addition to the strings, horns, trumpets, kettledrums, bassoons and oboes of the other movements this one is scored for flutes. At the time Mozart added this *Minuet,* he also added flute parts to the first and last movements of the Symphony and perhaps to the *Andante di molto* as well.

III. *Andante di molto.* This is a tender, lyric movement for five-part string orchestra (the violas divided into two parts) with bassoons. The string parts are all marked *sotto voce.* The movement has an almost Rococo grace and delicacy that recall the *Andante* of Mozart's popular serenade, *Eine kleine Nachtmusik.*

IV. *Allegro vivace.* This is one of the most exhilarating finales in all Mozart. Its rushing scales and lilting 6/8 rhythm make the most sluggish listener want to kick up his heels or perhaps fly through the air like the daring young man on the flying trapeze:

This Symphony is probably the one about which Mozart wrote his father from Vienna, April 11, 1781: "I forgot to write you in my last letter that the Symphony went *magnifique* and had all possible *succés* [sic]—40 violins played—the wind instruments were all doubled—10 violas—10 double basses, 8 violoncelli, and 6 bassoons." Mozart's delight in the large body of sound should make us cautious in demanding that our modern orchestras always be cut down to chamber size for Mozart. But it is significant that when Mozart did use as many strings as a modern orchestra, he doubled the winds and brass and used *six* bassoons.

SYMPHONY NO. 35, D MAJOR (HAFFNER) K. 385

"The new Haffner Symphony was a complete surprise to me," wrote Mozart to his father on February 15, 1783. "I had completely forgotten what it was like—this should really make a good effect."

How could a composer forget his own symphony? Mozart was twenty-six and had just achieved his first big popular success in Vienna with the triumphant premiere of his opera *The Abduction from the Seraglio* when his father wrote him from Salzburg with a pressing request. Mayor Sigmund Haffner had been elevated to the nobility. This was an important event, and for the festivities at the mayor's mansion, a new work was wanted from Salzburg's most famous son: a serenade.

"Serenade" (*serenata* or *Nachtmusique*) was a broad term for a group of chamber orchestra pieces, usually five or more movements, rather lighter than were customary for a symphony—entertainment music to be played perhaps during dinner or for some important social gathering.

Father Mozart's request was not well timed. Wolfgang was frantically busy, conducting his new opera, arranging excerpts from it, fulfilling pressing commissions, and he was planning to be married in two weeks. He replied to his father (July 20, 1782):

> By Sunday week my opera has to be completely arranged for wind instruments, or someone else will get ahead of me, and reap the profits: and now I am supposed to write a new symphony [i.e., serenade] too! How will it be possible? . . . Oh well, I will have to give up my nights to it, for it cannot be done any other way; and to you, my dear father, they shall be devoted. You shall certainly receive something every post-day and I will work as fast as possible, short of sacrificing good composition to haste.

But a week later, he wrote his father:

> You will make a face when you see that you are receiving only the first *Allegro* but there's no help for it. I had to compose another serenade [*"Nachtmusique"*] at top speed, but for wind instruments only, otherwise I could have used the same one for you. On Wednesday the 31st, I will also send the two *Minuets,* the *Andante,* and the final piece; and if I can, I'll also send a march. . . .

Yet even Mozart's facility had its limits. On the promised day, he wrote his father:

> You see, my intentions are good, but what one can't do, simply cannot be done! I just will not smear any old notes down on the paper—so I can't send you the rest of the score until next post-day.

It was a week later, August 7, when Mozart, now a bridegroom of three days, sent the last installment, a short march. "I hope it will arrive in good time and that you will find it to your taste," he wrote. "The first *Allegro* must be done with great fire, and the last should go just as fast as possible." The performance of this music in its original serenade form took place early in August.

Six months later, Mozart needed a new symphony in a hurry for a series of concerts he was about to give of his own works. Recalling last summer's serenade, he wrote his father (February 5, 1783) asking him to return the score. By the simple process of discarding two of the six movements (the march and one of the minuets), and augmenting the orchestra with flutes and clarinets, Mozart intended to transform his serenade into a symphony.

On Sunday, March 23, 1783, Mozart's concert at the National Theatre (Burgtheater) roused such storms of enthusiasm that Cramer's *Magazin der Musik* declared "No one here can remember" any example of such tremendous acclaim from both the Emperor and the general public. The magazine estimated Mozart's receipts at 1,600 Gulden.

It did indeed make the "good effect" Mozart expected. Six days after the concert, Mozart wrote to his father:

> The theater could not possibly have been more crowded and all the boxes were taken. . . . But what pleased me most was that His Majesty the Emperor was there too, and that he was so pleased, and what loud applause he gave

> me. . . . It is his custom to send the money to the box office before he comes to the theater, otherwise I might really have expected more from him, for his satisfaction was boundless. . . . He sent twenty-five ducats.

I. *Allegro con spirito.* The dignity of Mayer Haffner's new rank is reflected in the *grandezza* of the opening theme with its lordly octaves for the entire orchestra, with the added pomp of kettledrums:

The first movement is dominated by this striking theme. Mozart follows Haydn's practice of adapting his principal theme with only the slightest change, where a contrasting second theme might be expected. But the development section is richer and bolder than was customary in light entertainment music, and this may explain why Mozart was so ready to convert the erstwhile serenade into a symphony.

II. *Andante.* Mozart reverts to the simpler graces of traditional serenade style in the slow movement. Its seductive melodic line, confided mostly to the violins, is embellished by all manner of trills and turns and apoggiaturas, and the texture is miraculously transparent throughout.

III. *Menuetto.* The *Minuet* movement again recalls Haydn. It is a vigorous, almost athletic piece, like certain Haydn minuets of peasant-dance inspiration, rather than the courtly, aristocratic dance of tradition. The central trio section emphasizes graceful lilting phrases for the woodwinds.

IV. *Presto.* This *finale,* which Mozart asked to have performed "as fast as possible," is airy and witty. One almost suspects that the principal theme, which echoes the buffo triumph of the harem-keeper Osmin, ("Ha! Wie will ich triumphieren!") from Mozart's own triumph, *The Abduction from the Seraglio:*

may have carried a delicate message to the bigwigs of Mozart's native Salzburg from which he was so happy to have escaped.

The "Haffner" Symphony is scored for 2 flutes, 2 oboes, 2 clarinets, 2 bassoons, 2 horns, 2 trumpets, kettledrums, and the traditional string choir.

SYMPHONY No. 36, C MAJOR, (LINZ) K. 425

The "Linz" Symphony, like so many others of Mozart's works, was written for a special occasion and at breakneck speed.

"When we arrived at the gates of Linz," wrote Mozart to his father on October 31, 1783, "a servant was waiting there to conduct us to the old Count Thun's where we are still living. I can't tell you how they overwhelm us with kindness in this house. On Thursday, November 4th, I am going to give a concert in the theater, and since I haven't a single symphony with me, I am up to my ears writing away at a new one which must be finished by then."

Mozart had taken his bride Constanze to visit with his father and sister in Salzburg. He had hoped old Leopold might be reconciled to the marriage when he had an opportunity to become acquainted with Constanze. But that hope never quite materialized, and both Mozart and his young wife were deeply disappointed when they started back to Vienna three months later. On the way back they passed through Linz. In Linz there lived a Count Thun, the father-in-law of a distinguished pupil of Mozart's in Vienna. He asked the young couple to his palace and entertained them royally. He also asked Mozart to write a new symphony for a private concert he had planned for the fifth day after their arrival.

The Symphony was finished the day before the concert. Such speed would be unbelievable if we didn't know that Mozart thought out a great deal of his music in his head—often an entire work—before putting a single note on paper. Once Mozart had such a composition in his mind, writing it out was a fast mechanical process. It was said that he could sit down in a room full of dancing, playing, chattering people and, with a glass of punch handy, enjoy their fun while his pen flew across the page.

In spite of the gay and sociable atmosphere in which it was written, the "Linz" Symphony is more than merely playful or sentimental society music of the kind that had been traditional in symphonies up to then. New emotions of manly fire and thoughtful melancholy break through the polite restraints, and they seemed disturbing to the conservatives of Mozart's day.

I. *Adagio; Allegro spiritoso.* The opening of the first movement is majestic, almost portentous. This is the earliest symphony in which Mozart introduces his first movement with a slow passage of the kind Haydn had used for many years. Then there is a sudden transition to a reflective, almost pessimistic mood, with sliding, chromatic scales that lead into the mettlesome *Allegro* of the first movement proper. Yet even here the principal theme has a pensive cast.

II. *Poco adagio.* The second movement is unusually somber. It is dangerous to try to read Mozart's personal experiences into his works, but it is possible that the disappointment of his visit to Salzburg contributed to the melancholy with which he sings in this movement.

III. *Minuetto.* In this joyous *Minuet* with its boldly swinging tempo and rhythms it has been customary to see the influence of Haydn writ large. The truth is that the strongest influence in this movement is Mozart. And for all of Mozart's adoration and love of Haydn, the time had nearly arrived when the influence ran in the reverse direction—from Mozart to Haydn.

IV. *Presto.* The *Finale* begins in a festive mood:

There are joyous outbursts of the full orchestra, brilliant rushing figures in the violins, bright contrasts and catchy rhythms. But for all the gaiety with which the movement begins and ends, it touches in the middle on the pessimism of the slow movement, like the memory of a hurt that cannot quite be banished. Toward the end, festivity returns, and the Symphony closes on a note of affirmation.

The Symphony is scored for 2 oboes, 2 bassoons, 2 horns, 2 trumpets, kettledrums, and the customary strings.

SYMPHONY NO. 38, D MAJOR, (PRAGUE) K. 504

The "Prague" Symphony, with its echos of *The Marriage of Figaro* and its anticipation of *The Magic Flute,* belongs to the last and greatest years of Mozart's career. When he completed his score on December 6, 1786, he had five years to live. Although his fame as one of the greatest composers of the age never dimmed, he had passed the peak of his popularity in Vienna.

But in Prague the feeling was different. There *Figaro* was an enormous, continuous success. The public and even the Prague newspaper gloried in it, claiming that the Prague production was better than the Viennese, partly because the Prague orchestra was so much better than the Viennese, particularly in the wind section which had so much to do in *Figaro.* The newspaper suggested and Mozart's friends suggested that he come to Prague to hear the superb production.

On January 8 Mozart set out for Prague, taking with him a new Symphony in D major. For while the demand for his concerts had dropped off in Vienna, it seemed likely there would be occasion for one in Prague. The music season was at its height in the Bohemian capital; all the Bohemian nobility were in residence in their town palaces and Mozart and his wife were soon housed as the guests of Count Johann Joseph Thun, one of the most influential music patrons of Prague.

They arrived around noon of January 11 and by six o'clock were already plunged into a festive social whirl. "At six o'clock [wrote Mozart to a friend] I drove with Count [Joseph Emanuel] Canal to the so-called Bretfeld Ball, where the cream of the beauties of Prague are wont to assemble. That would have been something for you, my friend. . . . As for me, I didn't dance and I didn't flirt. The first because I was too tired, the second because of my native bashfulness. But with the greatest joy, I watched all the people hopping around to their heart's content to the music of my *Figaro* turned into *Contratänze* and *Teutsche.* For here they talk about nothing but *Figaro;* they play nothing, sing nothing, whistle nothing but *Figaro;* they go to no opera but *Figaro* and forever *Figaro.* Truly this is a great honor for me."

A few days later Mozart went to a performance of *Figaro.* Before the Overture was finished, the news of his presence had spread through the house, and before the curtain rose he was overwhelmed with welcoming applause. On January 22 he himself conducted the performance of *Figaro,* which was an even greater triumph. And in between the two opera performances he gave, for his own benefit, the concert he had had in mind. He roused great enthusiasm with his free improvisations at the piano, one of them a series of variations on Figaro's aria, "Non più andrai." His new Symphony, which later became known as the "Prague" Symphony, also included a theme from *Figaro.* This was neither the first nor the last time, incidentally, that Mozart used one of his own comic opera tunes as a symphonic theme.

I. *Adagio—Allegro.* A slow introduction full of dramatic tension leads to the principal theme of the *Allegro,* an agitated syncopated figure, concluding with a lively phrase strikingly similar to the famous theme of the Overture to *The Magic Flute.*

Despite the thematic riches of this exposition, with half a dozen distinct and contrasting themes, it never becomes confused. Alfred Einstein called the development that follows "one of the greatest, most serious, most aggressive in all Mozart's works."

II. *Andante.* The slow movement is far more than the traditional lyric interlude of earlier symphonies. It has all the sensuous melodic appeal one could wish, but also a depth and a seriousness bordering on pessimism.

III. *Presto.* A wave of delighted recognition must have run through that first audience as they heard the opening theme of the *finale:*

The fans of *The Marriage of Figaro* must have recognized it as the orchestral figure which accompanies the hilarious little duet of Susanna and Cherubino, "Aprite presto," in that opera:

The whole *finale* is dominated by the hectic merriment of that duet. But in addition, it has a more powerful drive and a hint of the greater depth which Mozart infused even into his comic operas.

Finally, one can almost feel the pleasure and pride the listeners as well as the performers must have taken in the striking prominence and beauty of the parts Mozart gave the famous Bohemian wind section to play. The melodies dance, the instrumentation sparks and glows and the whole laughing, hectic world of eighteenth-century comic opera comes to life for us again in this memento of some of the happiest days of Mozart's life.

The *Prague* Symphony is scored for 2 flutes, 2 oboes, 2 bassoons, 2 horns, 2 trumpets, kettledrums, and the traditional string choir.

SYMPHONY NO. 39, E-FLAT MAJOR, K. 543

The incredible riches of Mozart—the warmth and serenity he could bestow on mankind in the midst of his own nagging poverty—are nowhere more dramatically demonstrated than in this glowing Symphony in E-flat major, No. 39. At the very time the composer wrote a heartbreaking series of begging letters to his well-to-do merchant friend, Puchberg—letters which show him sinking deeper and deeper into a morass of debt and misery—Mozart produced one of the greatest miracles of his amazing career. In the space of some two months, he wrote, aside from other works, his three last and greatest symphonies: the E-flat major, the G-minor and the "Jupiter" in C major.

On June 17, 1788, apparently in the midst of composing the E-flat Symphony, he moved out of Vienna to cheaper lodgings in the suburbs. His old landlord would not let him go until he had paid up all the back rent—which meant more struggles and more begging letters for loans from the faithful Puchberg.

Nine days after Mozart and his ailing wife moved into their cheap suburban quarters, he set his signature to the finished E-flat Symphony: a flood of golden melody, one of the most cheerful and heartwarming symphonies ever penned.

I. *Adagio; Allegro.* The long introduction establishes a mood of wonderful, quiet dignity, a spiritual harmony and serenity, which show how high Mozart's spirit could rise above the care and suffering so soon to destroy his body. The main part of the first movement is a graceful "singing *allegro*" that is the essence of Mozartean charm. Its opening theme seems simple enough:

But for all its simplicity, it is richly developed. There are brilliant passages for full *tutti,* a lively second theme and endless variety and imagination in this movement—a perfect example of Classical symphonic form. One source of its perfection is that it seems to grow spontaneously without a hint of coaxing or goading from the composer's pen.

II. *Andante con moto.* The songful second movement is pensive and restrained. It is richly colored in its middle section and in the repeat of the opening thematic material. In the middle it becomes momentarily more passionate as it delves into the almost portentous keys of F minor and E-flat minor.

III. *Menuetto: Allegretto.* The thumping vigor of the *Minuet* recalls the festive joyousness of the opening movement. It is cast in strictly symmetrical three-part dance form; the middle part, a trio for woodwinds, is an enchanting musical idyll with a graceful, rocking phrase in the clarinets, echoed by the flutes.

IV. *Finale: Allegro.* The *Finale* has a decidedly Haydnish tinge, with the soft start and sudden loud *tutti* repetition of its mercurial opening theme:

The movement is full of witty quips, energetic humor and high spirits—convincing evidence that at the moment he conceived this music Mozart was one of the happiest men. The sensitive, wounded pride, the humiliation and the momentary despair seemed to have dissolved into thin air. The Symphony is self-confident, even exultant in its final page.

Mozart's Symphony No. 39 calls for an orchestra of one flute, 2 clarinets, 2 bassoons, 2 horns, 2 trumpets, kettledrums, and the traditional string choir.

SYMPHONY NO. 40, G MINOR, K. 550

Mozart wrote his last three and greatest symphonies, the E-flat major (K. 543), the G minor and the C major, or "Jupiter" (K. 551), in the incredibly short space of two months.

The E-flat major is a warmly lyric, sunny work, and the "Jupiter", for all the delicacy of certain passages, seems proud, triumphant music. But lest anyone think that Mozart was the sort of perpetually smiling cherub he was once considered to be, the tragic G-minor Symphony separates the other two. The contrast is important.

Today it is hard for many of us to realize how rare the use of *any* minor key was in Mozart's time. Especially tragic emotions were associated with the key of G minor, not only by Mozart but by his contemporaries. In Mozart's *Magic Flute,* G minor is the key of Pamina's despairing aria, "Ach, ich fühl's." Whenever Mozart even approaches G minor in his vocal works, it is to express the utmost intensity of suffering. The purely instrumental works in that key: the wild, defiant, "Little" G-minor Symphony, the G-minor String Quintet with two violas, and of course the late G-minor Symphony, K. 550, all seem to share a common emotional climate.

I. *Molto allegro.* Over an agitated accompaniment figure of the violas, the violins have the throbbing principal theme, which is repeated after sharp cadential chords of the full orchestra.

After a pause the graceful second theme weaves downward through the orchestra in a major key. Out of these two the whole movement is built. The development section begins with a violent harmonic wrench into a distant and foreign tonality. Here the main theme is developed first into melodic sequences, then into more intense, contrapuntal style, and finally the theme is chopped up into little pieces, tossed back and forth from one part of the orchestra to another, and repeated, now in a shout, now in a whisper. As the excitement dies down, the first part of the movement returns, but with a difference. This time the second theme, too, sings in the minor key, with unforgettable poignancy.

II. *Andante.* The slow second movement has the Rococo frills we associate with the eighteenth century, usually with music of a lighter sort. But what a different language they speak here! All through this section of the Symphony there is a restless, pulsing undertone, which rises, even in the *Andante,* to a sharp, agonized climax.

III. *Minuet: Allegretto.* Although this movement is called a minuet, it is far from the courtly grace and polite charm traditional in that dance. This is an aggressive, straightforward, square-toed piece, with a hearty thumping rhythm. The pretty little trio in the middle brings the only glimpse of sunshine we have in the entire Symphony.

IV. *Allegro assai.* This fast *finale* is full of grim, hectic humor, which is next door to tragedy. A theme of the type that was compared to a skyrocket in Mozart's day bounds upward through the orchestra:

It bounds lightly enough at first, but soon there are wild, rushing figures in the violins, and the rest of the instruments join the fray. Not even the singing second theme can hold up the dynamic drive of this *finale*, sharp harmonies clash and for a moment chaos seems loose. There is a quick, tragic climax like the one in the first movement. Then order is restored. The themes return in clearer form, and the work closes with insistent, almost despairing reiterations of the dark, fundamental G minor.

The original version of the G-minor Symphony, completed on July 25, 1788, in Vienna, was scored for flute, 2 oboes, 2 bassoons, 2 horns, and the customary strings. The second version, adds 2 clarinets to the above list and also makes some alterations in the oboe parts. Mozart's manuscript of the additions and alterations for the second version of the Symphony is undated.

SYMPHONY NO. 41, C MAJOR, (JUPITER) K. 551

We may never know whether Mozart himself ever heard this last and, perhaps, greatest of his symphonies. No record of its performance during his lifetime has ever been found. Yet it was unlike Mozart to compose a large work without knowing beforehand where, when and by whom it would be performed. Each work was normally geared to the character of its intended audience as well as the ability of the performers. The nineteenth-century Romantic practice of composing first and only afterward looking for a performer and audience, was virtually unknown.

But, who can say? Mozart was a special case. He had never fitted comfortably into the eighteenth-century pattern where the composer found his security in the role of a liveried servant. For the last ten years of his career he was essentially what we would call a free-lance. This was a precarious life. He did very well at the peak of his popularity as a composer and piano virtuoso (1784–1786). But soon, as he began to write somewhat more for his own taste, and less for the light taste of the Viennese, his affairs took a catastrophic turn. Neither his great fame nor the popularity in Prague of his operas *The Marriage of Figaro* (1786) and *Don Giovanni* (1787) paid enough to keep him out of debt.

By June 1788, one month after the Viennese production of *Don Giovanni*, Mozart was in grim financial need. This was the time when he wrote a series of humiliated letters to his faithful friend and fellow Freemason, Michael Puchberg, a well-to-do merchant, begging for one loan after another. Mozart's pitiful explanations of why he couldn't pay back Puchberg's last loan and why, if he would only lend him a little more, he could really straighten out his affairs this time and produce enough music to pay it all back—these seem to have moved Puchberg as much as they do the reader today. Many of the letters bear Puchberg's notation that he sent so-and-so much immediately, although he was apparently too hardheaded to share Mozart's rosy dreams of repayment.

Mozart's distracted letters to Puchberg start at the time of his three last and greatest symphonies: No. 39 in E-flat major, No. 40 in G minor, and No.

41 in C major, the "Jupiter." This last is dated August 10, 1788. If we could judge from this music, Mozart would have been the happiest, most successful man in the world when he wrote it. The E-flat major Symphony is likewise a radiant work. Of the three, only the G minor could be imagined to express Mozart's desperate situation. But the storm and stress of the G minor have to do with deeper things than Mozart's financial anguish. Nor did the brilliance and power of the "Jupiter" mean that Puchberg had paid the bills.

It is hard to know when Mozart expected to perform these three masterpieces, unless it was at a subscription concert series he had originally planned for June of that year. But the series was postponed again and again, through the summer and into the fall, and in the end probably never took place at all.

I. *Allegro vivace.* The very opening bars establish the two basic moods of the Symphony. A heroic figure for full orchestra alternates with a serene, reflective phrase for strings alone:

The amazing thematic richness of this exposition concludes with a lilting, dancing phrase, a self-quotation of a comic aria Mozart had composed earlier that year for insertion into somebody else's *opera buffa.* This gaily mocking melody was originally sung to the words:

Voi siete un pò tondo	You've but sluggish wit,
Mio caro Pompeo!	Dear Signor Pompeo!
L'usanze del mondo	Go and learn a bit
Andante a studiar.	Of the ways of the world.

What at first seems a charming bit of melodic fluff, becomes the most important theme in the dramatic development that follows. It reminds us once again of the close links between Italian *opera buffa* and the classical Viennese symphony.

II. *Andante cantabile.* The slow movement begins with an almost conventional melodic formula. But soon a characteristic Mozartean undercurrent of suppressed agitation begins to stir below the charming surface. The muted violins create a special mood of intimacy.

III. *Menuetto: Allegretto.* This *Minuet* suggests the playful serenity of the first movement. The droll woodwind phrases of the trio recall Haydn.

IV. *Molto allegro.* The opening theme of the *finale*:

was one of Mozart's favorites; he had already used it in two of his masses and in his B-flat Symphony, K. 319. A few measures later he gives the theme to five string sections in succession, as in the beginning of a fugue or *fugato,* which gave rise to the misleading designation of the "Jupiter" as the "Symphony with the Fugue Finale." But the *finale* quickly abandons fugal style for a richly symphonic working out, in which Mozart's dazzling contrapuntal sleight-of-hand (including a famous passage of quintuple counterpoint!) serves only to emphasize the joyful play of forces that characterize the rest of the Symphony, and to fuse them to an incandescent climax.

The "Jupiter" Symphony (which did not acquire its nickname until some time after Mozart's death) is scored for one flute, 2 oboes, 2 bassoons, 2 horns, 2 trumpets, timpani, and the usual strings.

Otto Nicolai

Born June 9, 1810, Königsberg—died May 11, 1849, Berlin

OVERTURE TO THE MERRY WIVES OF WINDSOR

One of the most popular of all overtures, this little masterpiece, like Nicolai's comic opera itself, overflows with melodies, sentiment, and wit. The opera is based on Shakespeare's comedy of the same name and was first produced on March 9, 1849, at the Royal Opera in Berlin, when Nicolai was thirty-eight years old.

The Overture begins with the music of the opera's final scene: moonrise over Windsor Forest, with shimmering high violins and a sentimental melody that seems to rise from the shadowy depths of the orchestra, climbing, until we hear it in the high gleaming tones of the flute. The lively *Allegro* principal part of the Overture follows with the prank, in which a swarm of neighbors' children disguised as forest fairies and fanciful forest insects punish the fat knight Falstaff for his attempted sins. They tease him, pinch and tweak and poke and pummel and sting him until he begs for mercy and is forgiven.

The most infectiously lilting theme of the Overture, however, never occurs in the opera itself, which seems a pity since it has almost irresistible grace and charm:

The melody is so beautiful that Wagner was not ashamed to appropriate it for one of the most ingratiating episodes in the third act of his *Meistersinger.* The rest of Nicolai's Overture is mostly a potpourri of the fantastic refrains of the pretended forest fairies and the gales of musical laughter with which the opera ends.

The Overture to Nicolai's opera is scored for piccolo, 2 flutes, 2 oboes, 2 clarinets, 2 bassoons, 4 horns, 2 trumpets, 3 trombones, kettledrums, bass drum, cymbals, and the usual string choir.

Carl Nielsen

Born June 9, 1865, Nörre-Lyndelse—died October 2, 1931, Copenhagen

SYMPHONY NO. 5, OPUS 50

Carl Nielsen, like his countryman Hans Christian Andersen, was born a peasant on the little Danish island of Fyn. And like Andersen before him, Nielsen lived to become a national hero at home and a cultural symbol of his country abroad. In the latter role Nielsen has often been compared with Sibelius. Both men were born in the same year. Both were late leaders of the Romantic Nationalism which swept European arts during the nineteenth century and which included both Grieg in Norway and Nielsen's teacher, Niels Gade, in Denmark.

Nielsen shared Sibelius's strong affinity for orchestral music, Nielsen's six symphonies (composed 1894–1925) and Sibelius's seven (composed 1899–1924) are generally considered their greatest and most characteristic works. Closely related to the symphonies are Sibelius's Violin Concerto and Nielsen's three concertos for violin, flute, and clarinet, respectively.

The strongest stylistic parallel between the two masters was their evolution from their broadly emotional, richly colored early works to the more laconic, occasionally ascetic style of their maturity. But there the resemblance ends.

While Sibelius came of a sophisticated, fairly well-to-do middle-class family, Nielsen's forbears were villagers and peasants. In the little town of

Nörre-Lyndelse where Nielsen was born, his father was a house painter and a fiddler for country dances. Since the family was poor and there were many children, young Carl became a shepherd boy when he was still very young. Fortunately he was still young when his musical gifts were discovered, and he was given the opportunity to take violin lessons from the village schoolmaster. He was also quick to learn to play a brass instrument, with the result that at the age of fourteen he joined a military band at Odense, the capitol city of Fyn. It soon became clear that young Nielsen deserved and could profit from a far more professional training. A group of friends got together and raised enough money to send Nielsen to the Royal Conservatory at Copenhagen when he was nineteen years old. There it was that Nielsen studied with Niels Gade. Another factor which surely went far to separate the styles of Nielsen and Sibelius, is the fact that whereas Sibelius completed his musical training with studies in Germany and Austria, Nielsen, on completing the Copenhagen conservatory course, was awarded a year's fellowship for study in France and Italy. It was in Paris that he met his compatriot, the sculptress Anne Marie Brodersen, whom he soon married.

Before he had developed the strongly personal note of his more modern and mature works, Nielsen won early recognition and strong encouragement with his Opus 1, a Suite for Strings first performed in 1888. But as he became less traditional and more individual the puzzled public grew cooler. For many years he was forced to earn his living as a violinist in the orchestra of the Copenhagen Royal Opera, where in 1908 he was appointed conductor. Nielsen had to wait until he was fifty years old before public honors, wide artistic influence, and broad popular acclaim were his.

His Second Symphony, *The Four Temperaments* completed in 1902, showed leanings toward polytonality. His opera *Saul and David,* produced in 1902, established him as a mature, modern composer, with an independent mind. Most of his symphonies have programmatic titles: *The Four Temperaments* (No. 2), *Sinfonia Espansiva* (No. 3), *The Inextinguishable* (No. 4), *Sinfonia Semplice* (No. 6).

The Fifth Symphony, begun in 1920 and finished on January 15, 1922, is identified simply as Opus 50. It was performed later in the same year by the Danish State Radio Orchestra under the direction of Mogens Woeldike. The United States premiere was given by the National Symphony of Washington, D.C., under the direction of Erik Tuxen on January 3, 1951.

I. *Tempo giusto—Adagio non troppo.* Although this Symphony has no subtitle, the atmospheric opening suggests a descriptive purpose: conceivably a melancholy landscape or a seascape. Against a murmuring minor third in the violas, a pair of bassoons suggests distorted horn-calls. Muted cellos add a freely repetitive bass over which the violins sing a yearning modal melody.

As this dies away, a softly obstinate rasping rhythm of the snare drum suggests the approach of a rather sinister march. The movement accelerates to a climax with other simple *ostinato* figures and developments of the horn-call:

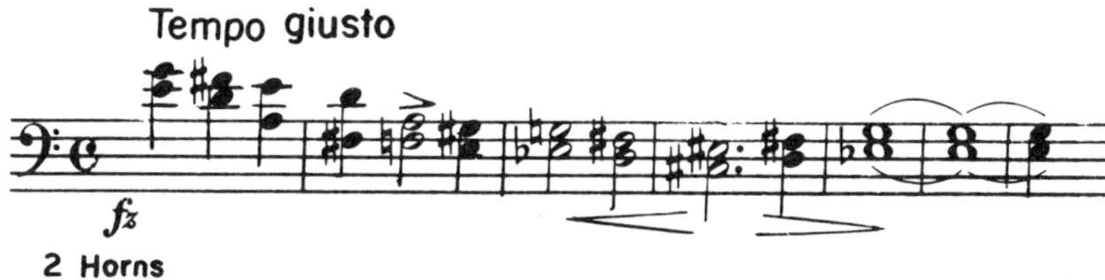

As the orchestra slows to *Adagio non troppo,* a new theme grows out of the horn-calls. This develops, with increasing polyphonic complexity, to two sharp climaxes. The movement dies away with a free cadenza for a distant-sounding clarinet against the fading rhythms of the side drum.

II. *Allegro—Presto—Andante un poco tranquillo—Allegro.* The principal theme of the *finale* is announced at the start by full orchestra:

The *finale* is in four sections, all thematically interrelated and all reminiscent of the horn-call figures of the first movement. The *Presto* section starts in an excited whisper with a simple, insistent theme, heard first in the violins alone, then developed in fugal style. The following *Andante* transforms the opening theme of the movement, also in fugal style. The concluding *Allegro* brings back the opening material and builds to a climax of massive impact.

Nielsen's Fifth Symphony is scored for piccolo, 2 flutes, 2 oboes, 2 clarinets, 2 bassoons, contrabassoon, 4 horns, 3 trumpets, 3 trombones, tuba, kettledrums, snaredrum, cymbals, triangle, tambourines, celesta and the conventional strings.

Niccolò Paganini

Born October 27, 1782, Genoa—died May 27, 1840, Nice

CONCERTO FOR VIOLIN AND ORCHESTRA, NO. 1, OPUS 6

To call this fire-breathing warhorse on which Paganini charged to victory across the length and breadth of Europe, to call *this* virtuoso vehicle a mere D-major concerto not only maligns the work, it is downright inaccurate. For Paganini composed this burst of genius in E-flat. And he performed it in E-flat—to the utter bedazzlement, bewilderment, and mystification of musicians—even of violin virtuosos—who could not figure out (for many years) how it was physically possible to play such music in the key of E-flat. And the joke remains that few of the greatest violinists of our century have cared or dared to perform it in E-flat.

But technical magic was only half the tale. The other half of the story was Paganini's enormous emotional power and his great creative fantasy. (The latter faculty is amply demonstrated by the number of later composers who based entire compositions on material borrowed from Paganini's celebrated *Capricci.*) Finally, he was a composer-performer who could wring the hearts of his listeners. When the illustrious Berlin critic Ludwig Rellstab first heard Paganini, he was duly impressed by the Italian's fabulous fireworks and said so. But it was Paganini's musical emotion which bowled him over, particularly in the slow movement of the concerto (possibly this Concerto): "The *Adagio* of his Concerto is so simple that a student could play it without difficulty—it is a simple, melancholy air. . . . Never in my life have I heard such weeping. It was as if the lacerated heart of this suffering Mortal had been turned over in his breast and were pouring out its agonies to us. . . . I had never known that there existed such tones in music. He spoke, he wept, he sang, and all the virtuosity is nothing in comparison with this *Adagio.*"

And Schubert declared, "In Paganini's *Adagio* I heard an angel sing."

The widespread rumors that Paganini had bartered his soul in exchange for supernatural musical powers did nothing to hurt him at the box office, although they were ridiculed by the composer and his more serious admirers. But the whiff of sulfur and the shadow of Old Nick pursued Paganini to his grave. Upon his death he was refused burial in consecrated ground. For three years and three months ecclesiastical authorities fought a bitter battle with Paganini's heirs until a special Vatican council decreed that he should be allowed a Christian burial.

During his lifetime Paganini's uncanny appearance did little to dispel such rumors. Even the skeptical Heinrich Heine was reminded of them:

> At length a dark form appeared on the stage [wrote Heine], looking as if it had risen from the underworld. This was Paganini in his black gala clothes: his black coat and vest of a terrible cut, such as is probably dictated by the hellish etiquette of Proserpine's court; his black trousers flapping disconsolately against his bony legs. His long arms seemed lengthened by the violin he carried in one hand and the bow in the other—both perpendicular and almost touching the ground, as he trotted out his ungainly acknowledgements before the public. In the angular contortions of his body there was a wooden horror, and at the same time, something stupidly animalistic that involuntarily called forth our laughter; but his face which, in the garish illumination of the orchestra, seemed still more corpselike in its pallor, contained an expression so pleading, so idiotically humble, that a horrible sympathy crushed the desire to laugh it out of existence. Did he learn these obeisances from an automaton or from a dog? Is this pleading glance that of a being stricken with a fatal disease, or hides there behind it the scorn of a cunning miser? Is this a living being who wishes to delight his audience at the moment of his dissolution in the art-arena with his last quivering gasp, like a dying gladiator? Or is it a corpse that has risen from the grave—a

PAGANINI BY DELACROIX (1832).

The aura of magic, the dark demonic side of Paganini's art, are what Delacroix tried to catch on this canvas, rather than a character-probing portrait like those of his friends Chopin and George Sand. (*Courtesy, The Phillips Collection, Washington, D.C.*)

> vampyr with a violin, who would suck, if not the blood from our hearts, at least the money from our pockets?
>
> Such questions crossed our minds while Paganini went through his interminable bending and bowing. But all such thoughts had perforce to vanish instantly, at the moment in which the marvelous master placed his violin under his chin and began to play. . . .

Paganini's playing was far, far harder to describe. New and infinitely more flexible bowing techniques, a profusion of "natural harmonics" and "artificial harmonics," played at fabulous speeds and with hitherto-unknown accuracy of intonation, whole sequences of harmonics produced in pairs ("double-stops") were among his more complex developments, although many were based on long-known and partly forgotten phenomena. But some of Paganini's devices ("tricks," they were often called) were extremely simple —like the tuning of his violin, (mis-tuning or *scordatura* would be a more accurate word) so that all of the strings of the instrument sounded a half-tone higher than the standard tuning. This enabled Paganini to write and to *play* the solo part of his E-flat Concerto as if it were in D. D being the easiest of all keys for a violinist, this made possible the fingering of certain passages that would have been unimaginably difficult in the key of E flat. This simple trick went long undetected, for Paganini was always careful to tune his violin in private and jealously guarded his manuscripts. There was another important result of this trick, which was eventually described during Paganini's own lifetime by Karl Guhr, the concertmaster and conducter of theater orchestras in both Frankfurt and Paris: "In certain works, such as the Concerto in E flat . . . the tone of the soloist flashes into sudden brilliance, contrasting with the subdued sounds of the orchestra, like a dragon-fly glittering in the rain. This effect is produced by a simple dodge. The maestro raises the pitch of his instrument by a semitone. Thus he plays in the key of D, while the open strings are tuned a semitone higher than the orchestral instruments. This contrast greatly heightens the effect of his brilliant arabesques."

Nowadays this Concerto is almost invariably played in D major, and for many excellent reasons. Today, many of our top-flight artists are trained to have absolute pitch, which means that to read or play a part written in D major is to hear D major in the mind's ear. If the violin is tuned to make all the pitches come out a half-tone higher, the result for the performer with absolute pitch is a continuous half-tone clash, dissonance that amounts to almost unbearable torture. In addition there is the ever-present possibility that the strings tuned higher than normal will stretch or slip in the middle of the performance, which can be nerve-wracking.

In our own day of big violin techniques, now that Paganini's technical "secrets" have become the common knowledge of all highly trained violinists, artists tend to emphasize the expressive qualities of Paganini's music—the qualities which won the hearts of such great contemporary composers and critics as Berlioz, Schumann, Chopin, and Schubert.

I. *Allegro maestoso.* A substantial orchestral introduction presents the principal theme of the movement, a lightly descending *staccato* figure and the contrasting lyric theme. At its very entrance the solo instrument transforms the principal theme with great melodic skips, sweeping arpeggios and triple-stops. The lyric contrast is even greater when it comes in the solo part, arching above the staff in a graceful phrase marked simply "sweetly" *(dolce):*

This soaring figure is heard against a minimal background of soft strings and a single sustained tone of a clarinet. In general, however, brilliance carries the day in this opening movement with its sweeping scales, arpeggios, double-stops in parallel thirds, sixths, octaves and tenths, *staccato* and *legato,* often employing the high harmonics, both natural and artificial, for which Paganini was so famous.

II. *Adagio.* The slow movement, like the one apostrophized by Rellstab, is simple. It is in the key of the relative minor, B minor, and may easily have been intended as a lament, or even as the depiction of a tragic scene. Paganini, describing the origin of one slow movement (it has never been entirely clear whether he meant this movement or the slow movement of his Second Concerto), declared that it had been inspired by a tragic prison scene he had witnessed in which one of the greatest Italian actors of his time, Giuseppe de Marini, played the part of a prisoner weeping and praying to heaven for succor.

III. *Rondo: Allegro spiritoso.* The spell of the melancholy slow movement is broken by the lightly skipping *Rondo* theme designed not only for sensuous charm but to exhibit the featherweight bowing agility of the soloist:

The slightly modernized orchestra used in most twentieth-century performances consists of 2 flutes, 2 oboes, 2 clarinets, bassoon, contrabassoon, 2 horns, 2 trumpets, 3 trombones, kettledrums, bass drum, cymbals, and the traditional string choir.

Walter Piston

Born January 20, 1894, Rockland, Maine

SYMPHONY NO. 4

Perhaps because he has favored symphonies, chamber music, and the more abstract forms, Walter Piston's music is often labeled Neo-Classical. But if Piston must be labeled "neo-" something, Neo-Baroque would be fully as appropriate, for his fascination with the Baroque age and the virtuoso craft of Johann Sebastian Bach is one of Piston's abiding strengths. A rare combination of sobriety and grace, of warmth and intellect, of strong feeling and faintly mocking humor—to name these attributes is only to graze some surface qualities of Piston's art.

Some of the apparent paradoxes of Piston's music are paralleled by his mixed heritage and training. Born a "down east" Yankee of Rockland, Maine, Piston is descended from an Italian grandfather, Antonio Pistone, who emigrated to Rockland. Although composers are romantically supposed to be creatures of inspiration rather than intellect, Piston graduated from Harvard College *summa cum laude,* which clearly was not accomplished on inspiration alone. Then having completed his general education at the intellectual citadel of New England, Piston promptly took off for France and the (by all accounts) electrifying tutelage of Nadia Boulanger, who lived to congratulate her former pupil on his seventieth birthday with words of affection and admiration.

In the intervening years Piston had retired from Harvard University where he taught for over one-third of this century—from 1924 to 1960. The brilliance and depth of his teaching are suggested by the fact that in the year when this writer was privileged to take part in Piston's class in fugue, there were several composers taking the course for the third successive time because of the fresh technical and artistic insights they gained from each repetition.

Piston's command of the craft of music is the admiration and envy of his colleagues. Less often do we hear about the character of his craftsmanship. Virtuosity can be a mere juggling for effect, manipulation of contrapuntal devices, of orchestral or harmonic color, for the sake of dazzling the listener. Piston's virtuosity, however, shies away from facile tricks. It seems rather to stem from his zest and skill in molding the raw materials of music. He has such relish for a rhythm that sits just right, for an imaginative combination of instrumental color, for the magic of counterpoint, that his own pleasure is somehow communicated to the unanalytical listener.

But for all his love of the musician's craft, Piston seems to love melody more. The Fourth Symphony is a strongly melodic work, and at the time it was written Piston said in an interview, "My music is becoming more relaxed, I think; more flowing, less angular and nervous. I feel a greater sense of ease in the Fourth Symphony than I have ever felt before." And speaking of the initial theme of his Symphony he said, "About that first long melody . . . I felt most strongly that I was following it wherever it was going, instead of pushing it along!"

I. *Piacevole.* Piston describes this as "an easygoing, moderately fast movement in large two-part form. There are two principal themes, both melodic. The first is stated at the outset by the first violins:*

The second [theme], somewhat quieter, is first played by the clarinet, supported by other woodwinds." When the themes are recapitulated in the second half of the movement, the clarinet melody returns in the more plaintive tones of the oboe.

II. *Ballando.* "A dancing movement," is Piston's description, "in rondo form A-B-A-C-A-B-A. The principal theme, A, is characterized by free rhythms and irregular meter. The B section is a waltz, and the middle section, C, is reminiscent of country fiddling."

III. *Contemplative.* "A continous *adagio* movement," writes Piston, "growing by means of new aspects of the melodic phrase played at the opening by the clarinet alone":

The clarinet phrase is then heard "in varied form by violas and English horn. The climax is marked by a statement of this theme in chordal form by the brass."

IV. *Energico.* The *finale* is a traditional sonata-allegro form. Piston describes the first theme as "rugged and rhythmic, the second being by contrast more songful in character, and easily identified when first played by the oboe. There is a short development and a recapitulation building to a climax at the end."

The Symphony is scored for piccolo, 2 flutes, 2 oboes, English horn, 2 clarinets, bass clarinet, 2 bassoons, contrabassoon, 4 horns, 3 trumpets, 3 trombones, tuba, kettledrums, triangle, woodblock, snare drum, cymbals, bass drum, 2 harps, and the standard string choir.

---

* *This and the following musical example from this composition are copyright 1953 by Associated Music Publishers, Inc. Used by permission.*

Francis Poulenc

Born January 7, 1899, Paris—died January 30, 1963, Paris.

CONCERTO FOR TWO PIANOS AND ORCHESTRA, D MINOR

Francis Poulenc was an astonishing bundle of contradictions unified by a highly personal approach to music. His religious works, important as they are, reflect only one side of his nature. Much of his music, and his character too, was skeptical, worldly, witty, with more than a touch of malice. He was demonstratively antisentimental, yet he had a lifelong affection for the *Lieder* of Franz Schubert. His song cycle, *Tel jour, telle nuit* of 1937, was greeted by Roland Manuel as the "perhaps unique example of a cycle of French *mélodies* which belong naturally in the tradition of the *Lied* and may well take their place next to [Schubert's] *Winterreise,* and [Schumann's] *Dichterliebe.*"

When he was released from military service at the end of World War I, Poulenc gravitated quite naturally to a group of five other young Parisian composers, all admirers of Erik Satie and Jean Cocteau. Beside Poulenc they included Georges Auric, Louis Durey, Arthur Honegger, Darius Milhaud, and Germaine Tailleferre. Drawn together by a common rebellion against the mysticism of César Franck, the vagueness of Debussy and his impressionist imitators, against the grandiloquence and superrefinement of an outmoded Romanticism, the group was attracted to jazz, to French music-hall style, and to the traditional French virtues of economy and clarity. They called themselves the *Nouveaux Jeunes.* But in 1920 an article in the newspaper *Comoedia* by Henri Collet gave the group a new name, *The Six,* which stuck, even long after the group had parted ways.

"We used to meet regularly at my home over a period of two years [writes Milhaud, in his *Notes Without Music*]. Paul Morand would make cocktails and then we went off to a little restaurant at the top of the rue Blanche. . . . After dinner we used to roam through the Montmartre fairground, delighted with the old-fashioned roundabouts, the strange shops, quaint attractions such as the Daughter of Mars, the rifle ranges and lotteries, the menageries and the din from the barrel-organs with their perforated rolls that seemed to blare out simultaneously every tune and ditty to be heard at that time at the Paris music-halls and revues. . . . Eventually we returned to my home. The poets read their verse and we played our latest works. . . . Many fruitful artistic collaborations may be traced back to these gatherings, and also certain works illustrating to what amounted to the new music-hall aesthetic."

The unity of *The Six,* however, did not last for long. Their one and only collaboration (and even this did not include Durey) was the ballet, *Les Mariés de la Tour Eiffel,* produced in 1921, by the Swedish Ballet in Paris. Two years later, Poulenc composed his own ballet, *Les Biches,* for Diaghilev's *Ballets Russes,* which was an overwhelming public and critical success. This was the basis of Poulenc's worldwide reputation and was decisive for his career. The theater was to claim much of his attention with three more ballets, a quantity of incidental music for the spoken drama, music for three films and an *opéra bouffe, Les Mamelles de Tirésias* of 1944, to a libretto by Guillaume Apollinaire. He has also written many song cycles and considerable chamber music.

In 1932 the famous patroness of music, Princess Edmond de Polignac commissioned Poulenc to write a two-piano concerto. Poulenc was delighted by the unusual undertaking and set to work with such zest that the score was completed in less than three months. It was first performed on September 5 of the same year at Venice in the International Music Festival with Poulenc himself and his childhood friend, Jacques Février, as soloists. Désiré Defauw conducted the orchestra of La Scala from Milan. It is in three brief movements:

I. *Allegro ma non troppo.* Although it opens with brilliant, driving passage work for both solo pianos, the first movement gets its saucy humor from sparkling fragments of Parisian popular tunes: couplets and *chansonettes* from the stage and *café-concerts* of several years back. There is a slower middle section with a languishing, almost sentimental melody recalling Poulenc's declared love of *"l'adorable manuvaise musique."*

II. *Larghetto.* The tender slow movement opens in a spirit of true Neoclassicism (that is, in the manner of the Haydn-Mozart era) with the following theme announced by the first piano:

After a romantically tinged, more agitated middle section, the opening theme is recalled.

III. *Allegro molto.* The *finale* returns to the mood of the opening movement, but with even greater verve and brilliance. Here again the glittering kaleidescope of melodic fragments is interrupted by a soft, almost sentimental interlude.

The orchestra for this Concerto for Two Pianos consists of piccolo, 2 flutes, 2 oboes, English horn, 2 clarinets, 2 bassoons, 2 horns, 2 trumpets, 2 trombones, tuba, small side drum without snare, military drum without snare, military drum with snare, bass drum, tambourine, triangle, 8 first violins, 2 second violins, 4 violas, 4 cellos, and 4 contrabasses.

Sergei Prokofieff

Born April 23, 1891, Sontsovka, Ekaterinoslav—died March 4, 1953, Moscow

CONCERTO FOR PIANO AND ORCHESTRA, NO. 2, G MINOR, OPUS 16

Prokofieff was still a conservatory student when he composed his Second Piano Concerto during the winter of 1912–1913. He was only twenty-one, yet he was already known in St. Petersburg and Moscow as a brilliant young pianist-composer. He had made his solo debut four years earlier playing his own works at one of the St. Petersburg Evenings of Modern Music. His first appearance with orchestra followed during the summer of 1912 when he played the first performances of his own First Piano Concerto in both St. Petersburg and Moscow. For his final examination at the conservatory in the spring of 1914 he was to have the satisfaction of playing his own First Concerto before a jury of twenty examiners, each of whom had before him a printed copy of the Concerto which had just been published by the Moscow firm of Jurgenson.

Prokofieff had begun to compose and to play the piano before he was six—almost as young as Mozart. By the time he was nine he had written an opera. Two years later he began lessons in composition with Reinhold Glière, and at thirteen he enrolled at the St. Petersburg Conservatory, where his teachers included Rimsky-Korsakoff, Liadoff, Tcherepnine and the famous pianist Annette Essipova.

Early in April, 1913, Prokofieff's former teacher, the composer and critic Nicolas Miaskoffsky, informed a friend in Moscow: "Sergei Prokofieff is finishing his Second Piano Concerto in four movements. It is very fresh and interesting, and in a more intimate vein than the First, but also more difficult. He played some of it for me—there are wonderful bits, quite novel and most intriguing." And on July 15, Miaskoffsky reported: "He has just begun to memorize his astounding Concerto."

The premiere of the Second Concerto, with Prokofieff as soloist, took place on September 5, 1913 at Pavlovsk, a resort town 17 miles south of St. Petersburg, where many well-to-do St. Petersburg families had summer homes. The occasion aroused great curiosity in the Russian capital and a considerable crowd of music lovers seems to have made the trip to Pavlovsk. The performance of the "piano Cubist and Futurist," according to one St. Petersburg newspaper, aroused such interest that on the train to Pavlovsk before the concert one heard on every side: "Prokofieff, Prokofieff."

In a detailed report of the concert, the *Petersburg Gazette* described the composer as "a youth with the face of a *Peterschule* student," who struck the keyboard "with a dry, sharp touch." Most of the audience was startled, annoyed or scandalized. Some left, some stayed and hissed. Prokofieff seems to have preserved his composure, bowing ironically to the hisses and defying the irate by playing an encore.

The style of Prokofieff's music obviously was related to the style of his playing. Everyone who heard Prokofieff seemed to agree that he was overpoweringly brilliant. Six years later, when he made his New York debut at Aeolian Hall, Richard Aldrich wrote in *The New York Times:*

> He is an individual virtuoso with a technique all his own. He can create big sonorities, sometimes mellow to richness, more often brittle and raucous. His fingers are steel, his wrists, steel, his biceps and triceps, steel, and scapula steel. He is a tonal steel trust. He has speed, surely, but a narrow gamut of dynamics, all crash or whisperings; no tonal gradations, with a special aptitude in the performance of double notes, octaves and chords taken at a dizzy tempo, again orchestral, all this. It is for Prokofieff the mere breaking of a butterfly on a wheel to play other men's music. But the gracious butterfly of Scriabin was metamorphosed into a gigantic, prehistoric pterodactyl with horrid snout and crocodile wings which ominously whirred as they flew over the pianist. Ah! a Jabberwock it was, not a butterfly.

Unfortunately we probably can never know how the Second Concerto sounded at its first performance, for the original score was lost. The present version was "reconstructed" by the composer ten years later, and first performed with Prokofieff as soloist at the Concerts Koussevitzky in Paris in 1924. As we hear the work today, its occasional harmonic harshnesses are so few and far between that, barring the possibility that Prokofieff toned down the Concerto in his reconstruction, it is almost impossible to imagine that it once sounded wild and chaotic.

I. *Andantino; Allegretto; Andantino.* The first movement opens with a long lyric piano solo in a vein that seems to us today very romantic and close to Rachmaninoff, for example. The first measures present the principal theme, marked *narrante* and suggesting a leisurely bardic style:*

After the solo presentation of this material, the woodwinds take up the melody and pursue it in dialogue with the piano. There is a momentary contrast with a livelier rhythm and a drier, more astringent thematic line which, however, is related to the principal theme. The latter soon returns and in fact dominates the whole first movement. About halfway through, the pianist

* *This and the following musical example from this composition are copyright by Breitkopf & Härtel (A. Gutheil). Copyright assigned to Boosey & Hawkes, Inc. Reprinted by permission.*

launches into a long cadenzalike passage which is extended to include a development section and recapitulation. The orchestra is kept discreetly in the background until the very end of the movement.

II. *Scherzo: Vivace.* The tiny second movement is all glittering scales and mechanical figurations for the piano. It has strong driving power and comes to a swift, surprising end.

III. *Intermezzo: Allegro moderato.* This movement opens with a heavy *ostinato* figure:

Pitted against raucous, sustained tones of the brass, this produces a touch of what may have been considered "primitivism" by shocked members of the Concerto's early audience. Midway through the movement, there are passages of more tranquil melody and reminiscences of the first movement.

IV. *Allegro tempestoso.* The *finale* is a *bravura* piece with brilliant octave passages and giant skips which became characteristic of Prokofieff's more vigorous piano style. There is a contrasting section with a long piano solo in a gentle rocking rhythm. The orchestra joins the piano in this characteristic motion which is then built to a big climax followed by a cadenza and a return to the *Allegro tempestoso* of the opening.

The G-minor Concerto is scored for 2 flutes, 2 oboes, 2 clarinets, 2 bassoons, 2 trumpets, 4 horns, 3 trombones, tuba, kettledrums, bass drum, tambourine, snare drum, cymbals and the traditional strings.

CONCERTO FOR PIANO AND ORCHESTRA, NO. 3, C MAJOR, OPUS 26

Prokofieff completed his Third Piano Concerto during the summer of 1921 in the small town of St. Brevin on the coast of Brittany. As early as 1911 he had planned to write a large virtuoso concerto, but, as he says in his memoirs, he made very little progress at the time, and only one passage of "parallel ascending triads" was preserved. "This I now inserted," writes Prokofieff, "at the end of the first movement of the Third Concerto. In 1913 I had composed a theme for variations, which I kept for a long time for subsequent use. In 1916-17 I had tried several times to return to the Third Concerto. I wrote a beginning for it (two themes) and two variations on the theme of the second movement."

At about the same time, Prokofieff was considering composing what he called a "white" quartet, that is to say, a string quartet which should be so completely diatonic that it would contain no accidentals at all (the kind of music, he explains, that could be played on the white keys of the piano alone). Some of his "white" themes were composed in St. Petersburg, some on the

Pacific Ocean and others in the United States. However, Prokofieff confesses, he found the task too difficult aesthetically: "I was afraid it would prove too monotonous and now in 1921 I decided to split up the material: The subordinate theme became the theme of Renata in *The Flaming Angel;* the principal theme I used for the monastery; the first and second themes of the finale went into the finale of the Third Concerto. Thus, when I began working on the latter, I already had the entire thematic material with the exception of the subordinate theme of the first movement and the third theme of the finale."

The following winter Prokofieff played the first performance of his Third Concerto with the Chicago Symphony on December 16 and 17, with Frederick Stock conducting. In New York he appeared as soloist in the Concerto on January 26 and 27 under the direction of Alfred Coates.

The composer has analyzed his score as follows:

I. *Andante; Allegro.* "The first movement opens quietly with a short introduction. The theme is announced by an unaccompanied clarinet:

and is continued by the violins for a few bars. Soon the tempo changes to *Allegro,* the strings having a passage in sixteenths, which leads to the statement of the principal subject by the piano. Discussion of this theme is carried on in a lively manner, both the piano and the orchestra having a good deal to say on the matter. A passage in chords for the piano alone leads to the more expressive second subject, heard in the oboe with a *pizzicato* accompaniment. This is taken up by the piano and developed at some length, eventually giving way to a bravura passage in triplets. At the climax of this section, the tempo reverts to *Andante,* and the orchestra gives out the first theme *ff.* The piano joins in, and the theme is subjected to an impressively broad treatment. In resuming the *Allegro,* the chief theme and the second subject are developed with increased brilliance, and the movement ends with an exciting *crescendo.*"

II. *Theme and Variations.* "The second movement consists of a theme with five variations. The theme is announced by the orchestra alone, *andantino:*

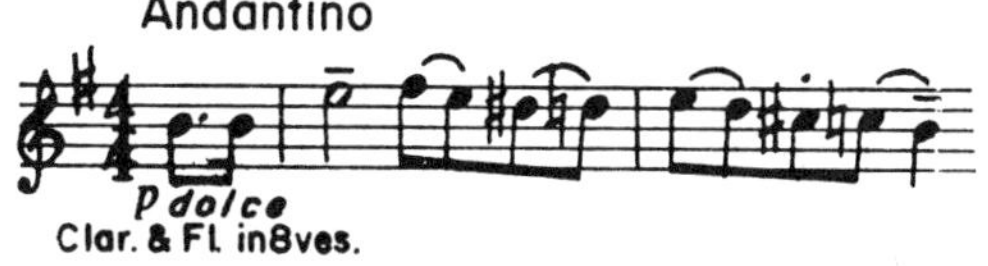

"In the first variation, the piano treats the opening of the theme in quasi-sentimental fashion and resolves into a chain of trills, as the orchestra repeats the closing phrase. The tempo changes to *allegro* for the second and the third variations, and the piano has brilliant figures, while snatches of the theme are introduced here and there in the orchestra. In Variation Four, the tempo is once again *andante,* and the piano and orchestra discourse on the theme in a quiet and meditative fashion. Variation Five is energetic *(allegro giusto)*. It leads without pause into a restatement of the theme by the orchestra, with delicate chordal embroidery in the piano."

III. *Allegro ma non troppo.* "The *finale* begins with a *staccato* theme for bassoons and *pizzicato* strings:

which is interrupted by the blustering entry of the piano. The orchestra holds its own with the opening theme, however, and there is a good deal of argument, with frequent differences of opinion as regards key. Eventually, the piano takes up the first theme and develops it to a climax.

"With a reduction of tone and slackening of tempo, an alternative theme is introduced in the woodwinds. The piano replies with a theme that is more in keeping with the caustic humor of the work. This is developed, and there is a brilliant *coda*."

The Concerto is scored for piccolo, 2 flutes (one interchangeable with piccolo), 2 oboes, 2 clarinets, 2 bassoons, 4 horns, 2 trumpets, 3 trombones, kettledrums, cymbals, castanets, tambourine, bass drum, and the standard string choir.

CONCERTO FOR VIOLIN AND ORCHESTRA, NO. 1, D MAJOR, OPUS 19

In his salad days Prokofieff's musical experiments must have seemed almost as unpredictable as his country's politics. When World War I broke out he was only twenty-three and so innocent of politics that the hostilities took him wholly by surprise. He had just graduated from the St. Petersburg Conservatory, and as a graduation present his mother had given him a trip abroad. He went to London to meet Diaghileff, whose Russian opera and ballet company was on a triumphant tour. Although the political tensions in London must have been almost unbearable, Prokofieff felt only the artistic excitements: Stravinsky's *Firebird* and *Petrouchka*, Ravel's *Daphnis and Chloé*, the singing of Chaliapin, the conducting of Richard Strauss. "Everything in London was so interesting," he wrote later, "that I was hardly aware of the approaching European war and it was by sheer chance that I returned to St. Petersburg a few days before it broke out."

At home he was safe from the draft. As the only son of a widow, he was exempt from service. For the time being he was free to concentrate on his many styles of music, his chameleon capacity for quick change which made his music so unpredictable to some and so irritating to others. Even Diaghileff reproached him with a fondness for too many kinds of music. "In art you must know how to hate," was Diaghileff's advice, as Prokofieff recalled, "otherwise your music will lose all individuality." "But surely that would lead to narrowness," Prokofieff objected. "The cannon shoots far because it doesn't scatter its fire," was Diaghileff's retort.

Prokofieff remained unconvinced. He seems rather to have treasured the four separate styles or, "basic lines along which my work had developed up to this point [1914]." The first of these, which he called his Classical or Neo-classical line, is most familiar from his First Symphony, which he himself named "Classical" Symphony. The second, which he called his "modern trend," first took the form of "a search for my own harmonic language, developing later into a search for a language in which to express powerful emotions." It was a harsh harmonic language associated, in such a spectacular work as the *Scythian Suite,* with considerable violence.

Prokofieff relished the scandals, the outrage and imprecations caused by his more aggressive works. At the premiere of the *Scythian Suite,* he recalled, "The kettledrummer banged right through his drum, and [Alexander] Siloti [the conductor] promised to send me the torn parchment as a keepsake."

The third style Prokofieff called his "*toccata,* or . . . 'motor' line . . . perhaps the least important." His fourth, which was of growing importance to him, was lyric. As an early example of this style Prokofieff specifically mentioned the opening theme of his First Violin Concerto:*

This gentle melody first came to Prokofieff in 1915 as the principal subject for a *concertino.* During the following two years the *concertino* gradually grew into a full-fledged violin concerto, which Prokofieff completed during the agitated summer of 1917.

Again one marvels at Prokofieff's ability to detach himself from even the most crucial political developments. He had dodged bullets in St. Petersburg in February, 1917. In March the Csar abdicated and a provisional government took over. By mid-July the Bolsheviks, under the leadership of Trotsky and Lenin, made their unsuccessful attempt to seize power from the provisional government in St. Petersburg. And Prokofieff?

"I spent the summer of 1917 in the country near St. Petersburg all alone," he writes in his autobiography, "reading Kant and working a great deal." The summer was devoted largely to the graces of the "Classical" Symphony and the more complex, but equally ingratiating, First Violin Concerto. For advice on bow markings and other technical matters, Prokofieff consulted the well-known Polish violinist, Paul Kochanski, who was scheduled to play the first performance of the Concerto in November 1917, at the Siloti concerts in St. Petersburg. But fate, in the form of the final, successful Bolshevik bid for

* *This and the following musical examples from this composition are copyright by Edition Gutheil. Copyright assigned to Boosey & Hawkes, Inc. Reprinted by permission.*

power, decided otherwise. It was six years before the Violin Concerto was given its first performance by a different soloist, orchestra, and conductor in another country.

After extensive tours of Europe and the United States, Prokofieff settled in Paris in October 1923. On the eighteenth of that month Serge Koussevitzky conducted the world premiere of the Violin Concerto at one of his fashionable Concerts Koussevitzky, with his concertmaster, Marcel Darrieux, as soloist. Richard Burgin, concertmaster of the Boston Symphony, was soloist with that orchestra in the United States premiere of the Concerto on April 24, 1925.

I. *Andantino.* Against the discreet, autumnal color of violas *tremolando,* the soloist intones "dreamily" *(sognando)* the principal melody of the movement, quoted above. This theme, Prokofieff emphasized in one of his letters, "must not be dragged; it must by all means be *Andantino,* and not *Andante.*" Traditional flourishes of virtuoso passage work lead to a second theme, full of lively little skips, trills, grace notes and other embellishments. A long pause precedes the development section, where these two themes are distorted, fragmented and combined. The conclusion, which is slower than the rest of the movement (*Andante assai; assai più lento che la prima volta*), seems an ethereal *coda* rather than an academic recapitulation.

II. *Scherzo: Vivacissimo.* This puckish movement demonstrates Prokofieff's love of *scherzo* styles and the infinite possibilities they offer to a composer with a sense of humor. This glittering refrain dances upward into the stratosphere:

Twice interrupted by more vigorous episodes, it returns to round off the *Scherzo* with a sudden flash of brilliance.

III. *Moderato; Allegro moderato.* The *finale* brings a return to the gentle lyricism of the first movement. The soloist's principal phrase seems to float upward with lazy grace:

The Concerto concludes with an ingenious combination of the above principal theme and the principal theme of the first movement, embellished with delicate trills of the solo violin in its highest range.

Prokofieff's score calls for 2 flutes (one interchangeable with piccolo), 2 oboes, 2 clarinets, 2 bassoons, 4 horns, 2 trumpets, tuba, kettledrums, side drum, tambourine, harp, and the traditional strings.

CONCERTO NO. 2 FOR VIOLIN AND ORCHESTRA, G MINOR, OPUS 63

This Concerto was a turning point in Prokofieff's career. To ears irritated by the harmonic harshness of much twentieth-century music, Prokofieff's Second Violin Concerto hardly sounds modern at all. It abounds in graceful melodies, consonant harmonies, sensuous orchestral color, dexterous form and consistently inviting manners, which have won it great popularity not only in the Soviet Union but also abroad. Soviet writers are apt to attribute this happy state of affairs to the fact that this is one of the first works Prokofieff wrote after he voluntarily returned to the U.S.S.R. and settled permanently there. And they may be right. Prokofieff returned late in 1933. His G-minor Violin Concerto, begun about the time he started work on his ballet *Romeo and Juliet,* was finished in 1935.

"Soviet realism" is a phrase that springs readily to the lips of contemporary Soviet critics. An outsider may be forgiven for wondering what the phrase means as applied to instrumental music. But it is clear that to insiders "Soviet realism" is a thing, that it is a good thing and that the G-minor Violin Concerto is full of it.

An outsider hearing the same Concerto, hearing it against a possibly broader background of West European and American music, would be struck not by the Soviet character of the Concerto but rather by the way it parallels a widespread change of style which was particularly striking in the 1930s, and which affected composers geographically and spiritually as widely separated as Shostakovich and Aaron Copland, Hindemith and Bartók. The popular label for this trend, Neoclassicism, was a misnomer, for it also included neo-Baroque, neo-Renaissance, even bits of neo-Gothic and neo-Romanticism.

The last seems best suited to the Prokofieff Concerto. It might even be called neo-Mendelssohn, if that could be said without the sneer sometimes attached to Mendelssohn's name today. Whatever the label and the perspective, the Concerto is an urbane and charming work. The genesis of the score has been described by the composer in his autobiography:

> In 1935 a group of admirers of the French violinist [Robert] Soëtans asked me to write a *violin concerto* for him, giving him exclusive rights to perform it for one year. I readily agreed since I had been intending to write something for the violin at that time and had accumulated some material. As in the case of the preceding concertos, I began by searching for an original title for the piece, such as "concert sonata for violin and orchestra," but finally returned to the simplest solution: Concerto No. 2. Nevertheless, I wanted it to be altogether different from No. 1 both as to music and style.
>
> The variety of places in which that Concerto was written is a reflection of the nomadic concert-tour existence I led at that time: the principal theme of the first movement was written in Paris, the first theme of the second movement in Voronezh, the orchestration I completed in Baku, while the first performance was given in Madrid, in December 1935 [with Enrique Arbos conducting the Madrid Symphony Orchestra].

I. *Allegro moderato.* The somber first theme, an even-flowing melody, is sung by the solo violin alone and unaccompanied. The melody is picked up by other instruments leading at last to the graceful *cantilena* of the second theme, one of Prokofieff's most beguiling themes, alloted here to the soloist: *

As the movement develops, the two melodies are interwoven.

II. *Andante assai.* The middle movement opens even more songfully. Over an accompaniment of plucked strings (deftly doubled by 2 clarinets) the solo violin sings in phrases too long and drawn out for the human voice:

The mood is that of a languorous serenade, but the movement is richly developed in a semi-rondo form, the opening melody serving as the *rondo* refrain, with three contrasting episodes between. The last return of the refrain is a dreamlike reminiscence in the French horn, the soloist confining himself to a placid recall of the opening accompaniment figure.

III. *Allegro ben marcato.* The entire finale is dominated by vigorous dance rhythms. Despite contrasting episodes, the dance rhythm increases in momentum and drive up to the *tumultuoso* conclusion.

The Concerto is scored for a modest orchestra: pairs of flutes, oboes, clarinets, bassoons, horns and trumpets plus the traditional string choir. The percussion includes bass drum, snare drum, triangle, cymbals, and castanets.

LIEUTENANT KIJÉ, SYMPHONIC SUITE, OPUS 60

One of Prokofieff's most distinctive gifts was his flair for combining satire and sentiment. When Prokofieff returned to the U.S.S.R. in the early 1930s and finally decided to settle there, he was anxious to start working on Soviet subjects and to develop his own musical style in a direction suited to Soviet life. "But the musical idiom in which one could speak of Soviet life was not

---

* *This and the following musical examples from this composition are copyright by Edition Gutheil. Copyright assigned to Boosey & Hawkes, Inc. Reprinted by permission.*

yet clear to me," he wrote in his *Autobiography*. "It was clear to no one at this period, and I did not want to make a mistake.

"Hence I was much pleased when the Belgoskino Studios invited me [in 1933] to write the music for the film *Leiutenant Kijé*. This gave me a welcome opportunity to try my hand, if not at a Soviet subject, then at music for Soviet audiences, and mass audiences at that." The film seemed ideally suited to Prokofieff. It was an affectionate period portrait of early nineteenth-century Russia, combined with a satire on official bungling.

Lieutenant Kijé never existed. He was a figment of the Czar's imagination: the result of an error in reading a military report. No one dared point out a mistake by the Czar. So a fictional military man had to be invented, endowed with parents, a wife, a career, and finally a burial to get rid of him.

Prokofieff was delighted with the subject, and his film music was a tremendous success. The following year he made a symphonic suite out of his movie score. "This gave me much more trouble than the music for the film itself," Prokofieff recalled, "since I had to find the proper form, reorchestrate the whole thing, polish it up and even combine several of the themes." The Suite was performed in 1933 in Moscow and was given its United States premiere on October 14, 1937, by the Boston Symphony Orchestra under the direction of Serge Koussevitzky. It is in five movements.

I. *The Birth of Kijé*. Kijé is appropriately ushered into this world by a fanfare on a military cornet which we hear from offstage as if from a great distance. The rasp of a military drum and a jaunty piccolo introduce the satirical military march.

II. *Romance*. There are two alternative versions of this movement, one for baritone solo, to words describing the fluttering of an amorous heart. The more frequently performed version is for orchestra alone.

III. *Kijé's Wedding*. There is a purposely banal touch to the melody of this section, suggesting that part of the wedding festivities takes place in a tavern.

IV. *Troïka*. To an accompaniment suggesting the motion of the traditional Russian three-horse sleigh, complete with sleigh bells, we hear another instrumental version of a tavern song.

V. *The Burial of Kijé*. Kijé's exit from this world is merry rather than otherwise, considering how relieved his inventors must have been to get rid of him. The music resembles a summary of his life beginning with the cornet fanfare of his birth, recalling the episodes of his romance and his wedding. At the end the solo cornet fades away into silence.

The Suite is scored for piccolo, 2 flutes, 2 oboes, 2 clarinets, 2 bassoons, tenor saxophone, 4 horns, 2 trumpets, 3 trombones, tuba, cornet, harp, piano, celesta, bass drum, military drum, triangle, cymbals, tambourine, sleigh bells, and standard strings.

ROMEO AND JULIET (TWO SUITES FROM THE BALLET)

At a little supper held after the successful Leningrad premiere of Prokofieff's ballet *Romeo and Juliet* (January 11, 1940), the Juliet, Galina Ulanova, ended her toast to the composer with this bit of fractured Shakespeare:

> Never was a story of more woe
> Than this of Prokofieff's music for Romeo.

Prokofieff, she assures us, seemed to enjoy the joke more than anyone else. And well he might. The success of *Romeo and Juliet* had cost him years of irritation and humiliation, as well as plain hard work. And there was more to come—six more years and still further revision of the music—before the ballet triumphed in the Moscow Bolshoi production of December 1946, which established the ballet in the position it holds today.

Official Soviet biographers of Prokofieff are apt to gloss over the difficulties his score encountered in the U.S.S.R. and the fact that its world premiere was not given in the U.S.S.R. at all, but at Brno in Czechoslovakia (December 1938). In his autobiography Prokofieff is franker; he gives facts although he does not openly complain: "In the latter part of 1934 there was talk of the Kirov Theatre of Leningrad staging a ballet of mine. I was interested in a lyrical subject. Shakespeare's *Romeo and Juliet* was suggested. But the Kirov Theatre backed out and I signed a contract with the Moscow Bolshoi Theatre instead. In the spring of 1935 Radlov [a régisseur of the Leningrad Theatre] and I worked out a scenario, consulting with the choreographer on questions of ballet technique. The music was written in the course of the summer, but the Bolshoi Theatre declared it impossible to dance to and the contract was broken." In addition to being first taken up and then turned down by both the Kirov and Bolshoi theaters, Prokofieff had had to face a storm of unfavorable publicity over the fact that he and his co-planners had given Shakespeare's tragedy a happy ending. In the original ballet version Romeo arrived in Juliet's tomb at the right moment to find her alive and everything ended well. The reason for what Prokofieff himself later characterized as a "bit of barbarism" was, he said, purely choreographic: "Living people can dance, the dying cannot." "Curiously enough [he wrote], whereas the report that Prokofieff was writing a ballet on the theme of *Romeo and Juliet* with a happy ending was received quite calmly in London, our own Shakespeare scholars proved more papal than the pope and rushed to the defense of Shakespeare. But what really caused me to change my mind about the whole thing was a remark someone made to me about the ballet: "Strictly speaking, your music does not express any real joy at the end." That was quite true. After several conferences with the choreographers, it was found that the tragic ending could be expressed in the dance and in due time the music for that ending was written."

Having been balked of stage premieres in the two leading centers of the U.S.S.R., Prokofieff decided to salvage at least parts of the music by arranging two symphonic suites from his ballet. These were performed at Moscow in 1936 and Leningrad in 1937. Meanwhile, the ballet itself, as Prokofieff wrote with tactful understatement, was "rather unlucky."

"In 1937 [wrote Prokofieff in his autobiography] the Leningrad Ballet School signed an agreement undertaking to produce it on the occasion of its 200th anniversary, and in 1938 the Brno Opera (Czechoslovakia) agreed to stage it, too. The Ballet School violated the agreement [the third Soviet institution to have done this] and so the premiere took place in Brno in December 1938 [three and one half years after the score was completed. Two seasons later] the Kirov Theatre produced the ballet in January 1940 with all the mastery for which its dancers are famed—although with some slight divergences from the original version. One might have appreciated their skill more had the choreography adhered more closely to the music. Owing to the peculiar acoustics of the Kirov Theatre and the need to make the rhythms as clear-cut as possible for the dancers, I was obliged to alter a good deal of the orchestration. This explains why the same parts in the Suites are more translucent than in the ballet score."

In her memorial article of 1954, entitled "The Composer of My Favorite Ballets," Galina Ulanova describes with sympathetic humor some of Prokofieff's tribulations during the Leningrad rehearsals. To begin with, he disagreed with the choreographer, Leonid Lavrovsky. Ulanova says there were heated agruments. Lavrovsky declared that the score was too short for a full-length performance and Prokofieff would have to make additions. "I have written exactly as much music as is necessary," was Prokofieff's reply, "and I am not going to add a single note. The ballet is complete as it is. Take it or leave it."

Prokofieff's "unusual orchestration" and the delicate chamber quality of the music gave the dancers difficulty, as did what Ulanova calls Prokofieff's frequent change of rhythm. At one point the dancers were harried by being unable to hear the music. "I know what you want!" he shouted, "you want drums, not music!" The dancers invited him to come on stage and sit beside them through an entire scene. Ulanova recalled that Prokofieff looked very annoyed but on leaving said, "Very well, I shall rewrite the music here and add something."

It is not clear whether Prokofieff merely added to the orchestration of certain passages or actually added new music for the Leningrad production. What is clear, from the official biography by I. V. Nestyev, is that he did compose additional music for the Bolshoi production of 1946. These additions were completed in the summer of 1946, and the Bolshoi premiere took place on December 22. Nestyev calls this final version "a somewhat enriched and more dramatic version of the Leningrad production of 1940, although the choreography and decor, by Lavrovsky and Williams respectively, remained largely unchanged." Juliet was again danced by Ulanova, who became identified with that role. The staging was lavish and was widely regarded as one of the finest productions ever presented at the Bolshoi.

Prokofieff's score was used also by Frederick Ashton for a three-act ballet, somewhat shorter than the Soviet original, which he produced for the Royal Danish Ballet in Copenhagen on May 19, 1955. The Ashton ballet was produced in New York City in 1956 with great success, many years before the Bolshoi production was brought to New York. Other shorter versions using the Prokofieff music have been choreographed by Birgit Cullberg in Stockholm in 1944 and by Serge Lifar at the Paris Opéra on December 29, 1955.

The complete Prokofieff ballet, which is an evening-filling work, is rarely heard in the concert hall. But the first two Suites which Prokofieff based on his original ballet (before the orchestration was reinforced to cope with the acoustics of the Kirov Theatre in Leningrad) have enjoyed considerable popularity. Neither Suite is a simple collection of excerpts nor is the ballet sequence observed. "Some numbers were taken directly from the ballet without alteration," Prokofieff explains in his autobiography, "others incorporated diverse other material."

The First Suite was first heard in Moscow on November 24, 1936, under the direction of N. S. Golovanov. The United States premiere was presented by the Chicago Symphony Orchestra on January 21, 1937 with Prokofieff himself conducting. It consists of seven numbers:

I. *Folk Dance: Allegro giocoso.* This is part of the folk festival which opens Act II of the Ballet. Four striking chords for the full orchestra are followed by a jig, or reel-like tune, played by oboes and English horn imitating the pipes of street musicians. As the dance grows more excited, the rhythms are marked by tambourines, drums, and finally the melody is taken up by a blaring cornet answered by a saxophone, bassoons, and cellos. At the end the dancing seems to fade into the distance.

II. *Scene: Allegretto.* This tiny movement seems scarcely more than an introduction to the following *Madrigal.* Like the opening movement it is based on a folk-dance type of tune, piped by two bassoons, alternating briefly with violins, and oboe, and a light *tutti,* including piano.

III. *Madrigal: Andante tenero.* Taken from the Act II ballroom scene, this *Madrigal* seems to reflect the lovers' conversation. Tender opening phrases for violins are answered by a sprightly flute (an instrument identified earlier in the ballet with Juliet) repeating phrases from Juliet's preceding dance. The violin phrase returns more warmly, and the violin-flute dialogue culminates in a brief, soaring woodwind line, whereupon the exchange ends hurriedly with two quick, answering phrases, as if interrupted.

IV. *Minuet: Assai moderato.* An earlier part of the same ballroom scene, this describes the arrival of the guests at the Capulet mansion. The pompous opening refrain, which recurs, might characterize the welcoming hosts, while the contrasting episodes could well suggest the picturesque variety of arriving guests.

V. *Masks: Andante marciale.* This excerpt, which follows the *Minuet* in the original ballet score, depicts the arrival of Romeo, Mercutio, and Benvolio, all masked. Stealthy percussion sounds are joined by a furtive clarinet in its lowest register, and finally by staccato strings, to underscore the caution of the three Montagues as they enter the enemy house.

VI. *Romeo and Juliet: Larghetto.* The famous balcony scene opens with whispering, muted violins and harp, suggesting the stillness of the night in the garden. Romeo's melody from the dialogue of the *Madrigal* returns, again in the strings, with the utmost tenderness. It is answered by Juliet's hesitant, but gracefully arching phrase for solo flute. Aside from two brief, but passionately lyric outbursts, the orchestra is held down almost to a whisper, as if the two lovers were afraid of being overheard.

VII. *The Death of Tybalt: Precipitato; Presto; Adagio drammatico.* This finale of the First Suite is an amalgam of episodes from the end of Act II: the duel between Tybalt and Mercutio in which Mercutio is fatally wounded (but omitting Mercutio's death and Romeo's resolve to avenge him), the duel between Romeo and Tybalt, Tybalt's death, and a few bars of new music bridging over to Tybalt's funeral procession.

The Second Suite from *Romeo and Juliet* was first performed in Leningrad on April 15, 1937. It was heard soon afterward on symphony programs in Paris, Prague, London, and Boston, Massachusetts where Prokofieff himself conducted the Boston Symphony in the United States premiere on March 25, 1938. This Suite, too, is in seven movements.

I. *The Montagues and the Capulets: Andante; Allegro pesante; Moderato tranquillo.* The slow introduction to this movement, drawn from Act I of the Ballet, is the music accompanying the Duke as he forbids further fights between Montagues and Capulets on pain of death. The main body of the movement comes from the Second Act ballroom scene, dominated by the heavy-footed "Dance of the [Capulet] Knights" with their characteristic theme:

In a gently contrasting middle section, the solo flute personifies Juliet with a more graceful transformation of the theme of the Dancing Capulet Knights:

II. *Juliet, the Young Girl: Vivace; Più tranquillo.* With its quickly shifting moods, this brief episode from the second scene of Act I, characterizes the young girl (not yet fourteen) whom her nurse calls to her mother's side to be asked what she thinks of marriage, specifically of marriage to the young Count

Paris, whom she is to meet that evening at the ball. The music is by turns skittish, elegant, graceful, and pensive.

III. *Friar Laurence: Andante espressivo.* The ecclesiastical mood of this music is the background for the scene in Friar Laurence's cell. Romeo is waiting for Juliet, to whom he is to be married by the friendly Friar.

IV. *Dance of the Five Couples: Vivo.* This is another episode from the folk-festival scene which opens the Second Act. In this case five couples dance during a pause in a passing parade. The rhythmic background as of plucked guitars, mandolins, or lutes, is supplied by orchestral strings, piano, harp, and a military drum. The tunes are piped by a solo oboe alternating with a flute.

V. *Romeo and Juliet Before Parting: Lento; Andante; Adagio.* This is the scene of the lovers' farewell after their first and last night as man and wife. Against softly trembling strings, a mournful flute suggests the bleakness of approaching day. Tiny wisps of melody for muted violins, clarinet, oboe, and flute recall the lovers' conversation about the nightingale and the lark. A sudden outburst of melodic warmth in mellow horn tones suggests a last embrace, and finally the melancholy woodwind phrases and the fading orchestral color recall Juliet's lines:

> Oh, God! I have an ill-divining soul.
> Methinks I see Thee, now Thou art below,
> As one dead in the bottom of a tomb.
> Either my eyesight fails or thou look'st pale.

VI. *Dance of the Maids with the Lilies: Andante con eleganza.* This delicate tone painting almost never rises above a restrained *piano.* Subdued woodwind solos blend with muted strings and one solo violin, also muted, as if for fear of wakening the sleeping Juliet.

VII. *Romeo at Juliet's Tomb: Adagio funèbre.* This final movement of the Second Suite is taken from the concluding scene of the Ballet, including Juliet's funeral procession and Romeo's arrival at the tomb. The sound of the funeral procession begins very softly, as if at a great distance, in the very highest strings. As it draws nearer, lower instruments join in, and we hear a shuddering figure in the violins. When the opening phrase returns for the third time, it is almost shouted by trombones as if in a paroxysm of woe, as if for something greater than the mourning of Juliet's family, her friends, and even her Romeo. After the procession has faded into silence, muted orchestral strings rise to ethereal heights while from the depths of the orchestra we hear still discern a dark, intermittent throbbing.

The two *Romeo and Juliet* Suites are scored for piccolo, 2 flutes, 2 oboes, English horns, 2 clarinets, bass clarinets, 2 bassoons, contrabassoon, tenor saxophone, 4 horns, cornet, 3 trumpets, 3 trombones, tuba, kettledrums, snare drum, triangle, xylophone, celesta, maracas, bells, tambourine, cymbals, harp, piano, and the standard string choir plus a solo viola d'amore (for which a solo viola may be substituted at will).

SCYTHIAN SUITE (ALA AND LOLLI), OPUS 20

Prokofieff's *Scythian Suite* was his first work for a huge modern orchestra ("modern," that is, in 1915) and he exulted in the sound vistas it opened out for him to embody his most barbaric imaginings of the gods of a barbaric ancient people. For barbarism was all the rage. Béla Bartók's *Allegro barbaro* of 1911 and Stravinsky's *Rite of Spring* of 1913 are only two of the more famous examples of a trend which affected also the other arts. The leader of the Russian Acmeist poets, Nikolai Gumilyov, declared: "As Adamists we are to some degree beasts of the forest. In any case we will not give up the beast in us in exchange for neurasthenia." Another of the Acmeist poets was Sergei Gorodetzky, who collaborated with Prokofieff on the scenario of the *Scythian Suite*.

The proposal which eventually resulted in the *Scythian Suite* came from Serge Diaghileff, the creator of the now-legendary Ballets Russes de M. Serge de Diaghileff. In Paris the great Russian impresario listened to Prokofieff's Second Piano Concerto and immediately invited the twenty-three-year-old composer to write a ballet for him. Diaghileff even toyed with the idea of producing a ballet to the score of the Second Piano Concerto, but ended by commissioning Prokofieff to compose a ballet "on a Russian fairy tale or a prehistoric theme."

Prokofieff returned from the French capital to St. Petersburg only a few days before the outbreak of World War I and, with sublime unconcern for that conflict, got in touch with the poet Sergei Gorodetzky, whom Diaghileff had recommended, to work out the scenario of the new ballet. The sensation of Stravinsky's *Rite of Spring* ballet was fresh in Prokofieff's mind, and with Gorodetzky's Acmeist leanings, it is no great surprise that they settled on a primitive prehistoric subject rather than a fairy tale.

The subject they chose was Russian in the sense—and only in the one sense—that the primitive Scythians described by Herodotus inhabited the area north of the Black Sea stretching between the Carpathian Mountains and the River Don. It is Herodotus, too, who describes the Scythians' gruesome habits of scalping and drinking the blood of their slain enemies, and other less humane customs. But the great historian left the religious mythology of the Scythians largely a blank to be filled in by the poet and composer.

Their scenario was built upon the most primitive motives of ancient Slav mythology: the conflicts of light and darkness personified in a sun god, Veles; his daughter Ala (an idol representing the creative powers of nature); Chuzhbog, a god of darkness, destruction and evil; Chuzhbog's seven loathsome subterranean monsters: and the Scythian warrior, Lolli. Prokofieff was especially attracted by the potentialities of a frenzied orgy of the evil spirits. "It is all much too pretty," said Prokofieff one day, criticizing the work of his poet-collaborator. He kept urging Gorodetzky to concoct the most barbaric images possible, images which would stun the audience. Gorodetzky, who had imagined music in the style of Rimsky-Korsakoff, was sometimes bewildered by

Prokofieff's demonstrations at the piano. The two met almost every day for a time. After a brief interruption in the fall of 1914, their collaboration extended past the end of the year.

In February Prokofieff took the finished piano score of the ballet to show to Diaghileff, who was then in Milan. Diaghileff rejected both the plot, which he found contrived and static, and the music, which sounded to him, of all things, *"à la Tcherepnine!"* Both impresario and composer agreed that Prokofieff would try again with another ballet.

But Prokofieff thought too much of his work to discard it. Back in St. Petersburg he decided that most of his ballet was "well worth saving." So he transformed it, with slight revisions, into his four-movement *Scythian Suite,* and set about the orchestration. "By this time I had sufficient mastery of orchestration to tackle a large orchestra and try to carry out a number of ideas," Prokofieff later recalled. "The first two movements were orchestrated very easily. I spent much more time on the last two, and as a result, they are more interesting in texture. I spent almost as much time on the closing sunrise as on half of the Suite."

Prokofieff was invited to conduct the premiere of his *Scythian Suite* at Alexander Siloti's seventh subscription concert in the Maryinsky Theater in St. Petersburg on January 29, 1916. The performance "went off with a tremendous hullabaloo," he wrote to a Moscow friend. And in his autobiography he wrote:

> After the *Suite* there was an uproar similar to the one following my first appearance at the second concert at Pavlovsky, except that this time, the whole of musical Petrograd was assembled. Glazounov, whom I had looked up with the express purpose of inviting him to the concert, flew into a rage, and left the hall eight measures before the end because he could no longer listen to the "Dawn" section. . . . The timpanist tore the kettledrum head with his heavy blows, and Siloti promised that he would send me the mangled piece of leather as a keepsake. In the orchestra itself there were noticeable signs of antagonism. "Just because I have a sick wife and three children, must I be forced to suffer this hell?" grumbled the cellist, while behind him the trombones blew fearful chords right into his ears. Siloti, in fine fettle, walked up and down the hall, repeating: "Right on the nose, right on the nose!" which was as much as to say that he and Prokofieff had given the public a slap in the face. "A scandal in high society," remarked the critic in the magazine *Music* not without a certain malicious pleasure. "The first movement was received in silence," wrote another newspaper, "the last called forth both applause and stormy protests. Despite this, the composer, who had conducted his own 'barbaric' work, took a number of bows."

The four movements were given the following program:

I. *The Adoration of Veles and Ala* [*Allegro feroce*]. The music describes an invitation to the sun god Veles, worshipped by the Scythians as their highest deity. This is followed by a sacrifice to the beloved idol Ala, daughter of Veles.

II. *Chuzhbog and the Dance of the Evil Spirits* [*Allegro sostenuto*]. The evil god summons the seven pagan monsters from their subterranean realms and, surrounded by them, dances a frenzied round. [Over a pounding bass *ostinato,* one of the few identifiable themes of the score is given out in parallel fourths, fifths and octaves by six horns, woodwinds and strings]:*

III. *Night* [*Andantino*]. Chuzhbog comes to Ala in the darkness and great harm befalls her. The moon rays fall upon Ala and the moon maidens descend to bring her consolation.

IV. *The Glorious Departure of Lolli and the Procession of the Sun* [*Tempestuoso*]. The Scythian hero Lolli goes forth to save Ala. He fights Chuzhbog. In the uneven battle Lolli would have perished, but as night passes the sun god rises and smites the evil deity. With the description of that conquering sunrise the Suite comes to an end.

The *Scythian Suite* orchestra calls for piccolo, 3 flutes, alto flute, 3 oboes, English horn, 3 clarinets, E-flat clarinet, bass clarinet, 3 bassoons, contrabassoon, 3 C trumpets (4th C trumpet ad lib), small E-flat trumpet, alto trumpet in F, 8 horns, 4 trombones, tuba, kettledrums, bass drum, military drum, tambourine, triangle, tam-tam, 2 pair of cymbals, bells, xylophone, celesta, 2 harps, piano, and the usual string choir.

CLASSICAL SYMPHONY, OPUS 25

Prokofieff's witty, affectionate homage to Haydn, his *Classical Symphony,* was composed at what seems the unlikeliest of all possible times for such a lighthearted work: during the military catastrophe of World War I, the disintegration of the czarist government, and the start of the Russian Revolution. Prokofieff came close enough to violence to dodge bullets during the February (1917) Revolution in Petrograd, but the experience does not seem to have left deep scars.

The earliest sketches for the first, second and fourth movements (some of which were later discarded) date from 1916, as does his popular Gavotte in D which became the third movement of the *Classical Symphony.* Concerning his completion of the work, Prokofieff writes in his autobiography:

> I spent the summer of 1917 in the country near Petrograd all alone, reading Kant and working a great deal. I deliberately did not take my piano with me, for I wished to try composing without it. Until this time I had always composed at the piano, but I noticed that the thematic material composed away

---

* *Musical example copyright 1923 by Breitkopf and Härtel. Renewed 1950. Copyright and nenewal assigned to Boosey & Hawkes, Inc. Reprinted by permission.*

> from the piano was often better. At first it seems strange when transferred to the piano, but after one has played it a few times everything falls into place. I had been toying with the idea of writing a whole symphony without the piano. I believed that the orchestra would sound more natural. That is how the project for a symphony in the Haydn style had come into being. I had learned a great deal about Haydn's technique from Tcherepnine and hence felt myself on sufficiently familiar ground to venture forth on this difficult journey without a piano.
>
> It seemed to me that had Haydn lived in our day he would have retained his own style while accepting something of the new at the same time. That was the kind of symphony I wanted to write: a symphony in the classical style. And when I say that my idea was beginning to work, I called it the *Classical Symphony:* in the first place because it was simpler, and secondly, for the fun of it, to "tease the geese", and in the secret hope that I would prove to be right if the symphony really did turn out to be a piece of classical music.
>
> I composed the symphony in my head during my walks in the country.

On September 10, 1917, Prokofieff finished the orchestration of the *Classical Symphony.* Next month the Kerensky government was overthrown in the Bolshevist (October) Revolution.

Six months later, on April 21, Prokofieff conducted the first performance of his symphony with the former Court Orchestra in Petrograd. Among those present was the Bolshevik People's Commissar of Education, A. V. Lunacharsky. A few days later, Prokofieff had himself introduced to Lunacharsky at his office in a room of the former Imperial Winter Palace. Prokofieff asked permission to make a trip abroad. "I would like to get a breath of fresh air," he said.

"Don't you think we have enough fresh air here now?" asked the commissar.

"Yes, but I would like to breathe the physical air of seas and oceans."

After a moment's thought, Lunacharsky replied, "You are a revolutionary in music and we are revolutionaries in life. We ought to work together. But if you want to go to America, I shall not stand in your way."

Early in September, Prokofieff arrived in New York and in November his *Classical Symphony* was given its first American performance by the Russian Symphony Orchestra of New York. In this country it has remained Prokofieff's most popular work.

I. *Allegro.* The dapper little first movement is a miniature version of the first-movement form which served Haydn and Mozart so well. Prokofieff's mimicry—almost a caricature of Rococo grace—is clearest in his mincing second theme, which is to be played very softly with the tip of the violin bow, *con eleganza:* *

** Musical example copyright 1926 by Edition Russe de Musique. Copyright assigned to Boosey & Hawkes, Inc. Reprinted by permission.*

II. *Larghetto.* Over a gently rocking accompaniment of the other strings a graceful yet stately melodic line is drawn by the first violins. Soon the first violins are joined by the sparkle of a solo flute. There is a contrasting section of gently plucked string tone which swells to a brilliant *tutti,* and a return to the first graceful melody.

III. *Gavotta: non troppo allegro.* The delightful harmonic surprises of Prokofieff's cadences are one of the earmarks of his style and an attractive spice in this otherwise somewhat bland movement.

IV. *Finale: Molto vivace.* The dashing *Finale* is the most brilliant of the four brief movements, and also has the most persistent dynamic drive. The Symphony is scored for an orchestra of Classical proportions: 2 flutes, 2 oboes, 2 clarinets, 2 bassoons, 2 horns, 2 trumpets, timpani, and strings.

SYMPHONY NO. 5, B-FLAT MAJOR, OPUS 100

"I regard the Fifth Symphony as the culmination of a long period of my creative life," wrote Prokofieff in 1945. "I conceived it as a symphony of the grandeur of the human spirit." The composer also declared that this score was "very important to me, since it marked my return to the symphonic form after a long interval."

The Symphony was written during the summer of 1944, after Prokofieff had returned from a war-imposed evacuation of Moscow. The premiere took place in Moscow on January 13, 1945, as part of a concert of Prokofieff's works. Prokofieff himself conducted the new score in what later proved to have been his last appearance on the podium.

The performance took place in an atmosphere of national elation. Just before the concert began, news was received of a great Soviet victory won on the Vistula. "The opening bars of the Symphony," according to Prokofieff's official biographer, Israel V. Nestyev, "were heard against the thunderous background of an artillery salute. Prokofieff's compelling music perfectly suited the mood of the audience. The critics commented on this in their glowing reviews of the new composition. Kabalevsky, extolling the Symphony as the embodiment of man's courage, energy and spiritual grandeur, also made a special note of its profoundly national character."

It is more than likely that Prokofieff did actually intend to infuse a strong national feeling into this music. Nationalism itself as a source of inspiration for operatic and symphonic music had sprung up over a hundred years earlier in Europe. And indeed, aside from Prokofieff's relatively modern harmonic vocabulary, the first and third movements of this Symphony seem very nineteenth century in their expansive Romanticism.

I. *Andante.* Although the tempo mark might imply that this movement is merely a slow introduction, it is actually a traditional first movement sonata-allegro form just a little more broadly paced than usual. The form is traditional down to details of first and second themes, bridge and *codetta,* development, recapitulation and grand concluding *coda.*

The principal theme, which will return at the opening of the *finale,* starts with the first bar of the Symphony, a broadly arched theme, given out by flutes and bassoon in octaves:

It is echoed by the violins and by various orchestral combinations before we reach the flowing second theme sung softly by flute and oboe over delicate string accompaniment.

The development starts with the return of the opening theme played *sotto voce* in the depths of the orchestra by double basses and cellos and punctuated by low brass and woodwind chords. From this low pitch, low volume and dark instrumental color, the development rises gradually to a grand climax, the peak of which turns out to be the return or recapitulation of the opening material. The *coda* concludes the movement with a rhetorical flourish. It is only fair to add that this very section is the one which seems to have made the greatest impression upon many Soviet listeners, and Mr. Nestyev comments: "This is perhaps the most impressive episode of the entire Symphony for it embodies with the greatest clarity the work's highest purpose—glorification of the strength and beauty of the human spirit."

II. *Allegro marcato.* A light *staccato* hammering of the first violins is the accompaniment for a scampering syncopated figure for the solo clarinet:

This mercurial little theme returns almost immediately in the violins, and we are plunged into one of Prokofieff's liveliest scherzos which is full of laughter, lighthearted and sardonic by turns. Its conclusion is a strident climax.

III. *Adagio.* Over a gently pulsing string accompaniment a clarinet melody of considerable elegance arches downward. The whole movement is lyric, although there is an agitated climax midway through. The clarinet has the final word with a graceful rising *arpeggio*.

IV. *Allegro giocoso*. The opening theme of the first movement is recalled very softly by the string section before the boisterous *finale* proper begins. This is the familiar grotesque, parodistic Prokofieff: a whirlwind of energy, driving, dazzling and swept by gusts of mocking laughter.

The Fifth Symphony is scored for piccolo, 2 flutes, 2 oboes, English horn, 3 clarinets, bass clarinet, 2 bassoons, contrabassoon, 4 horns, 3 trumpets, 2 trombones, bass trombone, tuba, harp, piano, kettledrums, cymbals, triangle, tam-tam, bass drum, military drum, and the standard strings.

Sergei Rachmaninoff

Born April 1, 1873, Oneg, district of Novgorod—died March 28, 1943, Beverly Hills

CONCERTO FOR PIANO AND ORCHESTRA, NO. 2, C MINOR, OPUS 18

Although Rachmaninoff was stern and forbidding in his concert platform appearance, he had the popular touch in composing. His Prelude in C-sharp minor, No. 2, Opus 3, written at the age of nineteen, the year he graduated from the Moscow Conservatory, became one of the most celebrated pieces in the world. American audiences were so addicted to it that during the latter years of his career, they would never permit the Russian virtuoso to end his encores after a concert until he had played this Prelude. It is said that he came (understandably enough) to detest the piece.

His Second Piano Concerto, probably the most popular piano concerto written in this century, has a curious history. After graduation from the Conservatory, Rachmaninoff continued to live in Moscow, where Tchaikovsky was still the center of musical worship. The life of a certain circle of artists in Moscow seemed to reflect many of the emotions of Tchaikovsky's music—its pessimism, its sudden fluctuations from the most violent excitement to deepest depression. Moscow musicians were attached to their famous restaurants, many of which featured unusual gypsy choruses. Many of them too were pervaded by an atmosphere of dissipation, which according to some spectators sprang less from a spontaneous joy in life than an overwhelming and often bitter pessimism.

Rachmaninoff seems to have taken part in this artistic life during the brilliant beginnings of his career, but soon this manner of living began to pale for him. The abysmal failure of his First Symphony in 1897 was a laming shock. And as he lost interest in the kind of life he had been leading, he began to lose confidence in his own ability to compose. Not even a very successful trip which he made to London, nor the request of the London Philharmonic to perform a piano concerto of his was stimulus enough to pull him out of the depression into which he had fallen.

Rachmaninoff didn't consider his First Piano Concerto good enough for London, so he had promised them a new one. But when he tried to write it, he found his inspiration was failing him. His friends began to worry about him. A Princess Alexandra Lieven, who took a motherly interest in young Rachmaninoff, even managed to arrange a visit to Tolstoy. But not even the counsels of that great patriarch of Russian literature could stir him, until finally he consented to go to a certain Dr. Dahl, who was much discussed at the time for his hypnotic cures.

> My relations [said Rachmaninoff] had told Dr. Dahl that he must at all costs cure me of my apathetic condition and achieve such results that I would again begin to compose. Dahl had asked what kind of composition they desired and had received the answer, "a piano concerto," for this was what I had promised the people in London, and had given it up in despair. Consequently, I heard the same hypnotic formula repeated day after day, while I lay half-asleep in an armchair in Dahl's study. "You will begin to write your concerto . . . . You will work with great facility . . . . The concerto will be of an excellent quality . . . ." It was always the same, without interruption.
>
> Although it may sound incredible, this cure really helped me. Already at the beginning of the summer I began again to compose. The material grew in bulk, and new musical ideas began to stir within me—far more than I needed for my concerto. By the autumn I had finished two movements of the concerto: the *Andante* and the finale—and a sketch of a suite for two pianos.

And when the Concerto was finished in 1900, Rachmaninoff gratefully dedicated it to Dr. Dahl. It is in three movements.

I. *Moderato.* The first movement begins softly with the piano alone in a long series of unaccompanied chords, like the tolling of some distant, deep-throated bells. Their dark sonority is typical of Rachmaninoff; they also recall the centuries-old Russian love of enormous bells, whose pitches are low (and timbre dark) in proportion to their size. The tolling swells imperceptibly until the orchestra joins in *con passione* with a somber melody that seems at first to derive from the motion of tolling bells:*

* *This and the following musical examples from this composition are copyright by Edition Russe de Musique. Copyright assigned to Boosey & Hawkes Ltd. Reprinted by Boosey & Hawkes, Inc.*

The tolling develops into a far-flung melody. The melody is taken up by dark-voiced cellos while the piano weaves garlands of accompaniment. A sudden brilliant burst of the orchestral *tutti* answered by a somber phrase for the violas leads to the melodious second theme for piano:

Both themes are developed very lyrically. The reprise of the opening theme in the orchestra is disguised by a brilliant counterfigure for the piano solo in a majestic marchlike rhythm. The return of the yearning second melody is given to a mellow French horn over an almost inaudible trembling of the entire string section. The lyric continuation leads to a short *coda* and a sudden conclusion in a burst of rhythmic energy.

II. *Adagio sostenuto.* (This movement was called *Andante* by Rachmaninoff —a term used then for "slow movement." The actual tempo of this movement is *Adagio Sostenuto.)* This nocturnelike movement begins with muted strings. The piano solo accompanies little yearning phrases of the flute, clarinet, and oboe: tiny fragments that recall the sentimental second melody of the preceding movement. Gradually the woodwind solos are joined by the right hand of the pianist in little duet episodes while the left hand continues to furnish the accompaniment. From high woodwinds, the melodic lead passes to the dark timbre of bassoon and violas which Rachmaninoff particularly favors throughout this Concerto. For a brief moment the piano seems to explode in a burst of fireworks, a cadenza which quickly subsides into the dreamy nocturne mood of the beginning.

III. *Allegro scherzando.* The brilliant *finale* begins with rhythmic mutterings in the low range of the orchestra, answered by a sudden splashing cadenza for the piano introducing the driving rhythm of the refrain:

Despite its dynamic drive, this refrain seems to have a family resemblance to the lyric themes of the first two movements. The driving tempo subsides, giving way to what is perhaps the most familiar and irresistibly alluring melody of the entire Concerto given out first in the low, rich tones of the violas reinforced by a solo oboe:

The soloist takes up the melody in a passionate development which leads rather surprisingly to an episode of almost seraphic calm. But the *scherzo* tempo soon returns, increasing to a headlong *presto.* The return of the viola melody is given to the more brilliant violins. Another brief cadenza for the piano and a final turn of tonality from C-minor to a triumphant C major bring back the viola melody, this time taken up by all the highest instruments of the orchestra in a glittering climax as soloist and orchestra race to a whirlwind finish.

The Second Concerto is scored for 2 flutes, 2 oboes, 2 clarinets, 2 bassoons, 4 horns, 2 trumpets, 2 trombones, tuba, kettledrums, bass drum, cymbals, and the traditional string choir.

CONCERTO FOR PIANO AND ORCHESTRA, NO. 3, D MINOR, OPUS 30

Rachmaninoff completed his Third Concerto in 1909, barely in time for his first tour of the United States. He himself was the soloist in the world premiere, which took place in New York City on November 28, 1909, with the Symphony Society of New York under the direction of Walter Damrosch. The second New York performance, some two months later, was presènted by the New York Philharmonic under the direction of Gustav Mahler, again with the composer as soloist.

The rehearsal for the Philharmonic concert remained long in Rachmaninoff's memory. Years later he recalled the experience:

> At that time Mahler was the only conductor whom I considered worthy to be classed with Nikisch. He touched my composer's heart straightaway by devoting himself to my Concerto until the accompaniment, which is rather complicated, had been practiced to the point of perfection, although he had already gone through another long rehearsal. According to Mahler, every detail of the score was important—an attitude which is unfortunately rare among conductors.
>
> The rehearsal began at ten o'clock. I was to join it at eleven, and arrived in good time. But we did not begin to work until twelve, when there was only half an hour left, during which I did my utmost to play through a composition which usually lasts thirty-six minutes. We played and played . . . . Half an hour was long past, but Mahler did not pay the slightest attention to this fact. I still remember an incident which is characteristic of him. Mahler was an unusually strict disciplinarian. This I consider an essential quality for a successful conductor. We had reached a difficult violin passage in the Third Movement which involves some rather awkward bowing. Suddenly Mahler, who had conducted this passage *a tempo,* tapped his

desk: "Stop! Don't pay any attention to the difficult bowing marked in your parts . . . . Play the passage like this," and he indicated a different method of bowing. After he had made the first violins play the passage over alone three times, the man sitting next to the leader put down his violin:

"I can't play the passage with this kind of bowing."

Mahler (quite unruffled): "What kind of bowing would you like to use?"

"As it is marked in the score."

Mahler turned towards the leader with an interrogative look, and when he found the latter was of the same opinion he tapped the desk again:

"Please play it as written!"

This incident was a definite rebuff for the conductor, especially as the excellent leader of the Moscow Philharmonic Orchestra had pointed out to me this disputed method of bowing as the only possible way of playing the passage. I was curious to see how Mahler would react to this little scene. He was most dignified. Soon afterwards he wanted the double-basses to tone down their playing of a passage. He interrupted the orchestra and turned to the players:

"I would beg the gentlemen to make more of a diminuendo in this passage." Then, addressing the argumentative neighbor of the leader with a hardly perceptible smile: "I hope you don't object."

Forty-five minutes later Mahler announced: "Now we will repeat the first movement."

My heart froze within me. I expected a dreadful row, or at least a heated protest from the orchestra. This would certainly have happened in any other orchestra, but here I did not notice a single sign of displeasure. The musicians played the first movement with a keen or perhaps even closer application than the previous time. At last we had finished. I went up to the conductor's desk, and together we examined the score. The musicians in the back seats began quietly to pack up their instruments and to disappear. Mahler blew up: "What is the meaning of this?"

The leader: "It is after half-past one, Master."

"That makes no difference! As long as I am sitting, no musician has a right to get up!

After the initial performance of his Concerto in New York, Rachmaninoff played it on tour with the Boston Symphony Orchestra, not only in Boston but in Philadelphia, Baltimore, New York, Hartford, and Buffalo. The outstanding success of these appearances led the trustees of the Boston Symphony to offer him the conductorship of the orchestra. Rachmaninoff felt that such an occupation would keep him too far away and for too long a time from Moscow and from his composing, and so declined. But what stood out more vividly in his memory of his first American tour was his first encounter with Mahler at the head of the New York Philharmonic in the rehearsals for his Concerto.

The Third Concerto is cast in the three traditional movements—fast, slow, fast—the second of which merges without pause into the *finale.*

I. *Allegro ma non tanto.* After two preparatory measures of throbbing orchestral accompaniment, the pianist enters with a melancholy melody which twists and turns upon itself within a strikingly narrow range:

This theme, which returns in various transformations in all three movements, has been called characteristically Russian, possibly because of the pessimism, the almost hopeless sadness which seems to pervade it. After it has been sung at length by the solo piano, it is developed in the dark tone of violas combined with two French horns. A tiny piano cadenza introduces the quiet bridge section to the second principal theme. This is a gentle *staccato* figure for the strings, soon transformed by the pianist into a flowing lyric line. Here are two stages of that swift evolution:

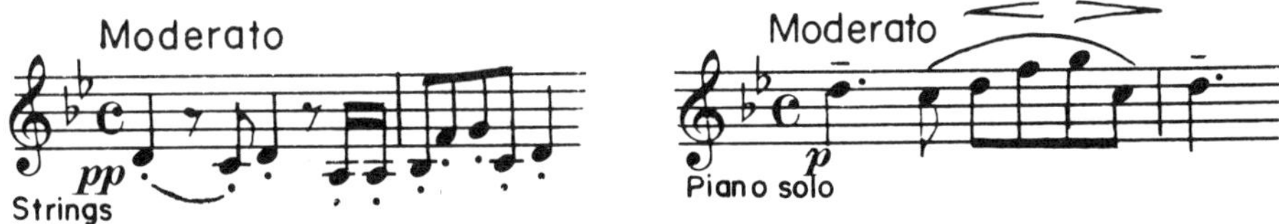

As it develops, this movement occasionally recalls the traditional sonata-allegro form, but it is too free to be pinned down to any familiar formula. Near the end of the movement there is an elaborate written-out cadenza in which the piano is joined briefly by solo winds: flute, then oboe, clarinet, and finally two French horns. The movement is rounded off with a brief coda-like recall of both principal themes.

II. *Intermezzo: Adagio.* A pensive introduction derived from the opening theme of the first movement leads into the rhapsodic body of the movement, which is dominated by the soloist. In a livelier middle section with an accompaniment of *pizzicato* strings and delicate pianist filigree, the woodwinds sing yet another transformation of the Concerto's opening theme:

The Intermezzo leads without pause into the *Finale.*

III. *Finale: Alla breve.* In the exuberant, driving rhythms of the *Finale* we hear still further transformations of the Concerto's opening. Two interruptions, a light-footed *scherzando* and a *lento* which recall both the first and second themes of the opening movement, lead back to the mood, tempo and themes of the beginning. The rhythmic excitement grows, the tempo increases to *vivace* and finally to *vivacissimo,* with a *presto* climax and conclusion of great brilliance.

The score of Rachmaninoff's Third Piano Concerto calls for 2 flutes, 2 oboes, 2 clarinets, 2 bassoons, 4 horns, 2 trumpets, 3 trombones, tuba, kettledrums, bass drums, snare drum, cymbals, and the traditional string choir.

RHAPSODY ON A THEME OF PAGANINI, FOR PIANO AND ORCHESTRA, OPUS 43

This popular score was born of the magic of virtuosity. Its basic theme is the invention of Niccolò Paganini, probably the most glamorous virtuoso of the Romantic era. And although Rachmaninoff's Rhapsody upon the theme was composed as late as 1934, this, too, belongs in the grand tradition of nineteenth-century Romantic virtuosity, with all it implies of technical wizardry in the service of a vivid, commanding personality. If the truth could be known, we might find that it was primarily personality, or let us say personal style, rather than fleet fingers, that made the great Romantic virtuosos the potent figures they were, not merely in the eyes of a hero-worshiping public, but in the eyes of such serious composer-critics as Robert Schumann and Hector Berlioz.

Niccolò Paganini, who himself wrote the first variations on this theme in the twenty-fourth of his own *Ventiquattro capricci per violino solo,* Opus 1, was the prototype of the Romantic virtuoso. Not only did he dazzle with technical feats that at the time seemed almost supernatural, he could switch suddenly to a simple, soulful style of melody that moved his listeners to tears. And through it all his bearing had a touch of the demonic, which did little to offset the popular superstition that he was in league with the devil. A trace of his musical personality seems to survive in his Twenty-four *Capricci,* which are among the most individual works ever written for violin. It is not surprising that Schumann, Liszt, and Brahms, as well as Rachmaninoff, chose to base entire new compositions on these themes.

Rachmaninoff is remembered as a towering figure of his own generation. Like Paganini, he was a composer of distinction and popularity, with a strongly individual style in his composition as well as his public performances. Like Paganini, he made a striking physical impression on stage: tall, almost gaunt, with a somber, unbending, unsmiling dignity, totally absorbed in his powerful projection of the music in hand. In another age his melancholy public manner would surely have spawned romantic legends, which could easily have been nourished by his unexplained fondness for and frequent use of the medieval Gregorian sequence, the "*Dies irae,*" a portion of the Mass for the Dead describing the terrors of the Last Judgment.

The original title of the present work was *Rhapsodie (en forme de variations) sur un thème de Paganini.* Rachmaninoff later deleted the parenthetical phrase. It consists of an introduction, the theme, and twenty-four variations, the seventh, tenth and twenty-fourth of which add, for no obvious reason, the chant of the "Dies irae."

The Paganini theme is stated, appropriately enough, by the violins, reinforced by the piano on the strong beat:

However, this theme is preceded by an introduction of eight bars and by a variation labeled *Precedente*. This interesting variation is actually a skeleton outline of the theme. It bears such a striking resemblance to the skeletonlike first variation in the finale of Beethoven's *Eroica* Symphony (which also *precedes* its theme) that Rachmaninoff must, consciously or unconsciously, have taken the idea from the older master.

The variations that follow the theme make particular use of its persistent rhythmic pattern, especially the tiny motif of four sixteenths plus an eighth. Two-thirds of the way through the Rhapsody, the tempo slows and variation 18, *Andante cantabile*, presents a lyric inversion of the motif as ingenious technically as it is persuasive in its songful melancholy:

Thereafter the vivacious opening tempo is restored and the variations grow increasingly brilliant to the climactic pages, where the *"Dies irae"* once more combines with fragments of the Paganini theme.

The Rhapsody is scored for piccolo, 2 flutes, 2 oboes, English horn, 2 clarinets, 2 bassoons, 4 horns, 2 trumpets, 3 trombones, tuba, kettledrums, bass drum, cymbals, side drum, triangle, glockenspiel, harp, and the customary string choir.

SYMPHONY NO. 2, E MINOR, OPUS 27

"I have escaped from my friends," said Rachmaninoff with a broad smile of satisfaction to a Russian acquaintance who ran into him on the sidewalks of Dresden during the winter of 1906–07. "Please don't give me away!"

Rachmaninoff's need to escape from his friends was quite real. Because of his popularity in Moscow as a pianist, conductor, composer, clubman, committeeman, colleague, and guest, he was in constant demand. Russian hospitality was lavish, and Rachmaninoff had been a sociable man. Sociability alone took its toll of time when sociability began at midnight and lasted to dawn. With serious professional demands on his time, little remained for composing. A drastic change in his pattern of life seemed necessary. So in the fall of 1906 Rachmaninoff, his wife, and daughter left Moscow on a train for Warsaw and the West.

Some years earlier Rachmaninoff had heard a performance of *Die Meistersinger* at the Dresden Royal Opera under Ernst von Schuch—a performance of such powerful inspiration and of such miraculous precision that Rachmaninoff was swept with enthusiasm. Dresden, in addition, was only two hours from Leipzig, with its illustrious Gewandhaus Orchestra lead by Nikisch, whom Rachmaninoff considered the greatest living conductor. Finally Dresden, as the capital of the Kingdom of Saxony had a dignity and repose deeply attractive to an artist of Rachmaninoff's needs at that moment. And here he settled incognito, in search of the inward and outward peace he needed for composing.

His search was rewarded. He began to compose, not only his Opus 6 collection of Russian songs and his first Piano Sonata; for the first time in over ten years—since the catastrophic failure of his First Symphony, which had plunged him into such paralyzing despondency, he began to work on purely orchestral compositions: his symphonic poem *The Isle of Death* and his Second Symphony. He began work on his Second Symphony in October 1906, almost immediately upon settling in Dresden, and finished the first draft close to New Year's Day of 1907. The orchestration took him several months more, but he was able to complete it in time for the premiere at St. Petersburg on January 26, 1908, which he himself conducted. The new score obliterated the stigma of failure of the First Symphony and soon became one of Rachmaninoff's most popular works both in Russia and the United States. It is in the traditional four movements.

I. *Largo; Allegro moderato.* The Symphony opens with a somber phrase for the cellos and string basses, a thematic germ, or motto as it were from which the first movement, and much of the entire Symphony grow. The slow introduction is dominated by a more lively figure derived from the motto and heard first in the first violins:

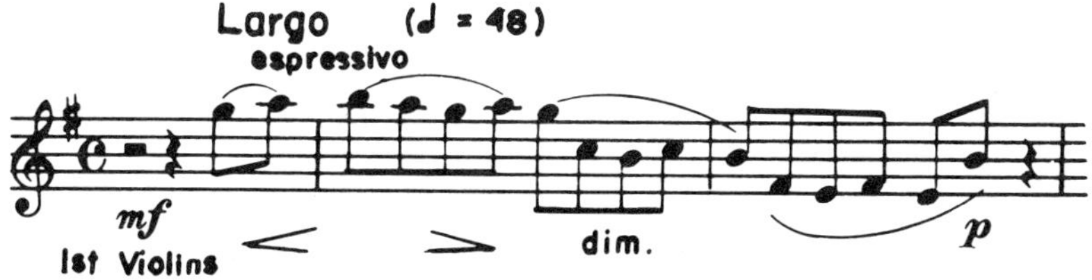

Twisting and turning upon itself in characteristic Rachmaninoff style, this variant of the initial motto builds slowly to a great climax, then subsides until only a lone English horn is left to recall the opening motto.

The principal theme of the movement, closely and clearly related to the opening motto, is given out by the first and second violins in unison:

There is a gradual increase of tempo, building to a warm climax for the entire orchestra, which then sinks back into silence. A solo clarinet leads to the lyric second theme: a gentle sighing figure for woodwinds answered by murmuring strings. The exposition is rounded off by a flowing, soaring melody for the violins in octaves. This, too, dies away almost to silence, and the development of themes begins almost in a whisper, with one solo violin rhapsodizing on the last preceding violin melody. The orchestra grows more animated as the twisting, turning, opening theme of the *Allegro* begins to permeate the instrumental fabric. This is developed to a series of climaxes, the last of which replaces the conventional reprise of the principal theme in its original form. The reprise of the second theme, with its sighing woodwinds and fluttering strings, is more traditional, as is the recall of the soaring violin melody. The movement is rounded off with a coda built on a passionate transformation of the principal *Allegro* theme.

II. *Allegro molto.* The *scherzo* is launched with its principal theme, a bold figure for four horns in unison which, once heard, is hard to forget:

The bold horn figure is taken up at once by the violins in a closely related but far sprightlier, skipping, dancing figure which dominates this movement. The *scherzo* refrain is followed by several contrasting episodes, among them a long, flowing melody sung by the violins in octaves. At the conclusion, the *scherzo* rhythm dies away in the depths of the orchestra to silence.

III. *Adagio.* This slow movement contains some of Rachmaninoff's most appealing melodic material, although it is often cut in performance. It is dominated by two melodies: first an upward-reaching phrase heard at the very start in the violins and, second, a song—or aria, one might almost call it—for solo clarinet, which follows immediately. The movement is enriched by passing references to themes from the earlier movements, particularly the first theme of the opening *Allegro*. But it is chiefly this movement's melodies: that of the violins and of the solo clarinet, which carries the burden of expression, often separately, sometimes combined in elaborate contrapuntal weavings.

IV. *Allegro vivace.* The *Finale* opens with a wild burst of energy and a rough-and-tumble rhythmic theme which irresistibly recalls the Neapolitan *tarantella.* This wild abandon is suddenly interrupted by a raucous blast for muted horns leading to a brief march episode which in turn is swept away by a resurgence of the *tarantella* theme. There is a strongly contrasting lyric, broadly flowing theme for all the violins and the violas singing in sonorous octaves in which they are joined at the climax by the orchestral cellos as well.

Again there are reminiscences from preceding movements, even a seven-measure interruption at *adagio* tempo bringing back a melody from the slow movement, combined with a theme from the first. But the *tarantella* rhythm and the vigorous theme associated with it carry the day. It is this music that brings the exuberant conclusion.

Rachmaninoff's Second Symphony is scored for piccolo, 3 flutes, 3 oboes, English horn, 2 clarinets, bass clarinet, 2 bassoons, 4 horns, 3 trumpets, 3 trombones, tuba, kettledrum, cymbals, snare drum, bass drum, glockenspiel, and the traditional string choir.

Maurice Ravel

Born March 7, 1875, Ciboure, Basses-Pyrénées—died December 28, 1937, Paris

ALBORADA DEL GRACIOSO

Ravel's love for Spanish things may stem from the fact that he himself was half Basque, his mother being of an ancient Basque family. The great Spanish composer Manuel de Falla was struck by the truly Spanish character of Ravel's "free use of rhythms, modal melodies and all the ornamental embellishments of our popular song. . . ."

In the age of courtly love, of the troubadours of Provence and northern Spain, the *alborada,* or simply *alba,* was a form of poetry with song about a lover's departure from his beloved at the early dawn. Often this took the form of a dialogue between the lover and a trusted friend who had stood guard through the night to warn of approaching dangers. Later the *alborada* became a type of dance, popular especially in the north Spanish province of Galicia, near the Basque country where Ravel was born. (The Spanish-French border cuts the Basque area in half. Ravel was born north of the border.)

Ravel seems to have had both types of *alborada* in mind when he wrote this scintillating music. It opens with a strumming of the string instruments, suggesting a serenader's guitar. A splash of harp sound introduces lively scraps of melody in the woodwinds: oboe, English horn, clarinet . . . until suddenly, all idea of a song is blotted out by a burst of brilliant orchestral dance rhythms.

There is a contrasting middle section, a sudden quiet, when a solo bassoon sings a melancholy phrase. This could be the lonely musing of the friend standing guard in the night. On the other hand, since the title of this piece suggests the song of a jester (the Spanish *gracioso* means "joker," "jester," or "fool"), this might be the voice of the proverbial sad clown.

There is a return to the wild whirl of the dance, continual, whimsical shifts of mood, and the close comes with another dazzling flourish for full orchestra, including some witty *glissando* slides for trombone. Ravel's *Alborada del gracioso* (literally: "The Jester's Morning Song") was composed in 1905 as one of a set of piano pieces entitled *Miroirs.* Ravel himself arranged his *Alborada* in 1918 for an orchestra consisting of piccolo, 2 flutes, 2 oboes, English horn, 2 clarinets, 2 bassoons, contrabassoon, 4 horns, 2 trumpets, 3 trombones, tuba, kettledrums, crotales (tiny antique cymbals), triangle, tambourine, castanets, snare drum, cymbals, bass drum, xylophone, 2 harps, and the traditional string choir.

The first performance of this orchestra arrangement was given in Paris on May 17, 1919, by the Pasdeloup Orchestra under the direction of Rhené-Baton.

BOLERO

A minor miracle, inexplicably and irresistibly exciting on first hearing, Ravel's *Bolero* remains a brilliant and effective and unquenchably popular work. Its first performance at the Paris Opéra on November 22, 1928 (as a ballet) was a sensational success. Ravel himself conducted the first concert performance with the Lamoureux Orchestra in Paris on January 11, 1930. The American premiere on November 14, 1929 in Carnegie Hall, when Arturo Toscanini conducted the New York Philharmonic was described as "a bombshell." The following year, when Ravel heard Toscanini's interpretation at a Paris concert of the New York Philharmonic, he told Toscanini, in a backstage meeting, that his tempo was ridiculously fast. Apparently undismayed, Toscanini observed that a *bolero* is not a funeral march, which seemed tantamount to telling the composer that he did not know the proper tempo for his own composition!

After the first explosions of enthusiasm and attacks, Ravel tried to make his intensions clear in a letter published in the *London Daily Telegraph* in July 1931: "I am particularly desirous that there should be no misunderstanding about this work [he wrote]. It constitutes an experiment in a very special and limited direction and should not be suspected of aiming at achieving anything other or more than it actually does. Before its first performance I issued a warning to the effect that what I had written was a piece . . . consisting wholly of 'orchestral tissue without music'—of one very long, gradual crescendo. There are no contrasts and there is practically no invention save the plan and the manner of its execution. The themes are altogether impersonal . . . folk-tunes of the usual Spanish-Arabian kind, and (whatever may have been said to the contrary) the orchestral writing is simple and straightforward throughout, without the slightest attempt at virtuosity . . . I have carried out exactly what I intended, and it is for the listeners to take it or leave it."

The entire score is built on a single melody of two 16-bar phrases, each repeated as follows: *AA, BB*. Two military drums mark the characteristic *bolero* rhythm, for four measures of introduction. Then a single flute initiates the melody as follows:*

The repetition of the phrase is carried by a solo clarinet. A solo bassoon takes the second phrase and a small clarinet its repetition. There are three repetitions of the *AA, BB* pattern while the orchestration grows in color, brilliance and volume. A final *A, B* without repeats leads, at the climax, to a sudden shift of key from C major to E major and a concluding sequence of violent dissonance.

The score for *Bolero* enlists piccolo, 2 flutes, 2 oboes, oboe d'amore, English horn, E-flat clarinet, 2 B-flat clarinets, bass clarinet, contrabassoon, 4 horns, 1 small trumpet in D, 3 C trumpets, 3 trombones, tuba, 3 saxophones (a sopranino in F, soprano in B-flat, and tenor in B-flat), harp, 3 kettledrums, cymbals, tam-tam, celesta, 2 side drums, and the standard strings.

Ravel's score was commissioned by the beautiful and wealthy Ida Rubinstein for her own ballet company. She danced the principal part in a Spanish inn scene, a locale that Goya might have painted. A woman dances alone on a trestle table surrounded by men, who follow her motions with a fixed stare. As she grows more and more animated, their excitement is fired. They beat out an accompaniment with their hands and pounding heels. Finally, at the moment of the shift of key to E major, knives are drawn and there is a violent tavern brawl.

CONCERTO FOR PIANO AND ORCHESTRA, G MAJOR

The polished paradox was one of Ravel's specialties—in speech as well as in his art. He once called his G-major Concerto "a concerto in the strict sense, written in the spirit of Mozart and Saint-Saëns." He added, less paradoxically, "I believe that a concerto can be gay and brilliant, and that there is no necessity for it to aim at profundity or big dramatic effects. It has been said that the concertos of some great classical composers were written not *for* but *against* the piano, and I think that this criticism is quite justified." (Ravel may have had in mind the famous quip of Hans von Bülow, to the effect that Brahms's Violin Concerto had been written not for, but against the violin.)

Ravel once told John Burk, the distinguished former program annotator of the Boston Symphony Orchestra, that "he felt that in this composition he had

---

* *Musical example copyright 1928, by Durand et Cie. Used by permission of the publisher. Elkan-Vogel, Inc., sole representative, U.S.*

expressed himself most completely, and that he had poured his thoughts into the exact mold that he had dreamed.'' The first dream, if we are to believe the English scholar Edward Lockspeiser, was a Basque Rhapsody for Piano and Orchestra in several movements, which Ravel intended to play during his 1927–1928 tour of the United States. It has even been maintained that the opening theme of the Concerto quoted below is based on the rhythm of an ancient dance of the Basque region of Navarre—a local variant of the *bransle* (or brawl, as it was sometimes known in England).

However that may be, Ravel did not begin systematic work on the composition until after his return to France. He composed it simultaneously with his Concerto for the Left Hand, which is a more serious work, and both concertos were completed in the fall of 1931. The first performance of the G-major Concerto was given by Marguerite Long on January 14, 1933, with Ravel conducting the Lamoureux Orchestra at the Salle Pleyel in Paris.

I. *Allegramente.* The gossamer lightness of the opening, with its sparky little tune for piccolo solo against shimmering bitonal arpeggios for the piano, soft string tremolos, pizzicatos, and a scarcely audible roll of the side drum, is an effect to remember:*

Hardly has the piccolo introduced the melody when it is taken up by a glittering trumpet solo, and it returns again to cap the climax of the brilliant first movement.

II. *Adagio assai.* The slow movement begins with a long nocturne-like solo for unaccompanied piano:

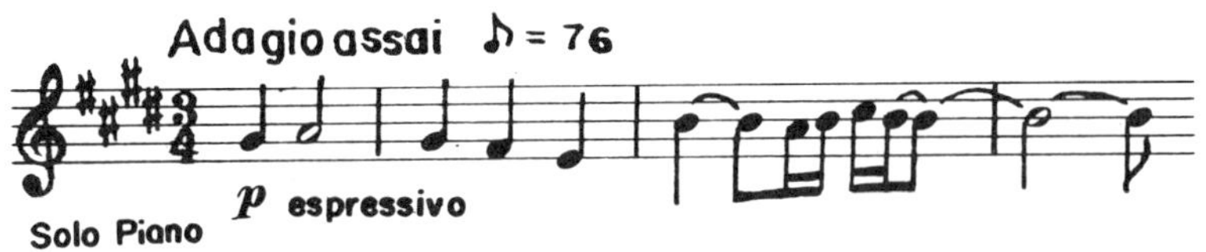

The ease with which the melody seems to flow may be misleading, for Ravel has told us that he constructed it very laboriously, two bars at a time, taking the slow movement of Mozart's Clarinet Quintet as a model.

III. *Presto.* The finale is a dazzling piece of virtuosity for the soloist with light-textured, witty orchestral accompaniment.

---

* *This and the following musical example from this composition are copyright 1932 by Durand et Cie. Used by permission of the publisher. Elkan-Vogel, Inc., sole representative, U.S.*

The many fragments of American jazz idiom are easier to hear than the alleged *rondo* form of the *finale*. In any case, the entire conclusion flies at such supersonic speed that it seems to finish before it has started.

During Ravel's career, his music was sometimes criticized as artificial. But to Ravel this hardly seemed a criticism. "How do they know that I am not by nature artificial?" he quipped. Or was it a quip? The question has also been characterized as a *cri de coeur*. Ravel's friend, critic and biographer Roland Manuel once wrote of him: "It is difficult to imagine Ravel in a suppliant posture, urging his heart to bring forth the genius within. Should his skill ever fail him, he can never plead sincerity as an excuse. Art . . . is not, in his eyes, the supreme truth, but rather the most dazzling lie—a marvelous imposture. . . . If this music pleases you, or moves you to tears, know that it is made by a man who did not go down on his knees 'before and after,' who wept no tears in writing it and who agrees with a great poet who said: 'He who wishes to write down his dream must himself be very wide awake.' "

The G-major Concerto is scored for piccolo, flute, oboe, English horn, B-flat clarinet, small E-flat clarinet, 2 bassoons, 2 horns, trumpet, trombone, harp, strings, kettledrums, bass drum, side drum, cymbals, gong, triangle, wood block, and whip.

CONCERTO FOR THE LEFT HAND FOR PIANO AND ORCHESTRA

At the Paris premiere of this Concerto on January 17, 1933, the famous French critic and historian Henry Prunières could hardly believe that it was not being played by two hands. At times, he said, he could even imagine four. Yet the soloist was the one-armed Austrian pianist Paul Wittgenstein, who had commissioned the Concerto from Ravel.

Paul Wittgenstein, born in Vienna in 1887, began a promising piano career in the early 1900s, but lost his right arm at the Russian front in World War I. Undaunted, he continued his career after the war. Since the repertory for left hand alone was small, he commissioned works from Ravel, Richard Strauss, Prokofieff, Hindemith, Britten, and others.

Ravel and Wittgenstein first met in Vienna in 1930. Ravel was already working on a piano concerto in G major for himself as soloist. But he accepted the commission for the Left Hand Concerto and, although Ravel habitually worked with the most painstaking deliberation, both concertos were completed by the autumn of 1931. Wittgenstein was able to play the first performance in Vienna on November 27.

Ravel wrote his friend, M.D. Calvocoressi:

> Planning the two piano concertos simultaneously was an interesting experience. The one in which I shall appear as the interpreter . . . is written very much in the same spirit as those of Mozart and Saint-Saëns. . . .
>
> The concerto for the left hand alone is very different. It contains many jazz effects; the writing is not so light. In a work of this kind, it is essential

> to give the impression of a texture no thinner than that of a part written for both hands. For the same reason, I resorted to a style that is much nearer to that of the more solemn kind of traditional concerto. A special feature is that after a first section in this traditional style, a sudden change occurs and the jazz music begins. Only later does it become manifest that the jazz music is built on the same theme as the opening part.

The Concerto is in one continuous movement divided into three balanced sections: the two described by Ravel plus a return to the opening material. The introduction, famous for its orchestral suggestion of darkness, begins with only cellos and double basses playing very softly in their deepest range. Against this background a contrabassoon in its low range mutters a theme which later develops into the principal melody of the Concerto. Slowly other instruments are added: horns in their low range, a bassoon, a clarinet and the scarcely audible rumble of a bass drum. Brighter instruments join in, rising to a sonorous climax.

The piano solo enters with a thunderous cadenza, which obliterates any awareness of the limitations of the left hand. The cadenza introduces the principal theme which, aside from its full sonorities, has the following melody:*

The main theme is resumed by the orchestra alone, building to a second climax of positively Wagnerian acoustics. It would be hard to imagine a greater contrast than the following piano solo with its transparent texture and the cool melancholy of its lyric line.

In the jazzy central section, the two chief musical ideas are a downward-rushing series of parallel triads, given out by trombones but often repeated by the piano soloist, and a jaunty jiglike tune which, as the composer pointed out, is distantly related to the principal melody of the beginning.

The Concerto for the Left Hand is scored for piccolo, 3 flutes, 2 oboes, English horn, E-flat clarinet, 2 clarinets in A and B flat, bass clarinet, 2 bassoons, contrabassoon, 4 horns, 3 trumpets, 3 trombones, tuba, kettledrums, triangle, side drum, cymbals, bass drum, wood block, tam-tam, harp, and the customary strings.

---

* *Musical example copyright 1931 by Durand et Cie. Used by permission of the publisher. Elkan-Vogel, Inc., sole representative, U.S.*

DAPHNIS AND CHLOE

Among the handful of musical masterpieces for which Serge Diaghilev's Russian ballet was directly responsible, Ravel's *Daphnis and Chloé* ranks high. Igor Stravinsky, a master not easily blinded by mere glamour, once called Ravel's *Daphnis* "not only Ravel's best work, but also one of the most beautiful products of all French music." On almost any level it is a seductive work. Yet, for all its intoxicating orchestral color, its sensuous harmonies and orgiastic rhythms, *Daphnis* is a patrician score. Ravel was a spiritual aristocrat who knew elemental drives and could appear to give them full rein without straining his mastery of form or his precise craftsmanship.

Daphnis and Chloé was commissioned by Serge Diaghilev and produced by his Ballets Russes at the Théâtre du Chatelet in Paris on June 8, 1912. The choreography was by Fokine, the sets by Bakst, Pierre Monteux conducted and the two title roles were mimed by the now almost legendary dancers, Nijinsky and Karsavina.

It was not easy to weld all the disparate elements of *Daphnis and Chloé* into a unified whole. Based on a pastoral romance attributed to the fourth-century Greek sophist Longus, translated by the late Renaissance French poet Jacques Amyot, and recast by the Russian Fokine, the original scenario was further substantially adjusted by Ravel for his own purpose. He seems to have begun his composition in 1909, with the purpose of creating a "great choreographic symphony . . . a vast musical fresco, less scrupulous archeologically than faithful to the Greece which was imagined and depicted by the French artists of the end of the eighteenth century." He completed his first version in piano score as early as May 1, 1910, but in 1911 a radical revision brought a complete reworking of the concluding "General Dance," which was developed to twice its original length.

As the performance date approached, tensions developed. Bakst's original scene designs made Ravel wince. Bakst quarreled with Diaghilev over the preparation of the sets. Nijinsky and Fokine quarreled, apparently over their differing interpretations of the role of Daphnis. And the entire *corps de ballet* was irritated by Ravel's intricate 5/4 rhythms in the concluding "General Dance."

As a ballet *Daphnis* never was truly popular, but as a concert work it has become a twentieth-century classic. According to the composer, it is constructed "symphonically" on a rigorous tonal pattern, with a small number of basic themes whose development reinforces the unity of the entire score. It is in one act divided into three scenes, the last two of which correspond roughly to two popular concert suites which may be performed separately or together.

As the curtain rises at the beginning of the ballet, we see a meadow at the edge of a sacred wood. To the right, a grotto, at the entrance to which stand statues of three nymphs cut out of the live rock in the style of archaic sculptures. A little toward the rear on the left a great boulder suggests vaguely the form of the god Pan. To the rear sheep are grazing. It is a bright spring afternoon. At the rise of the curtain the stage is empty.

Almost at once we hear one of Ravel's basic themes, a soft chant of three stopped horns—a theme which some commentators have called the voice of Nature: *

The chant of the horns is immediately echoed by a wordless offstage chorus, which Ravel uses from time to time throughout his score, giving almost the impression of slightly humanized orchestral instruments. (At Diaghilev's request, Ravel made an instrumental arrangement of the chorus part to reduce the expense of producing the ballet in small theaters of minor centers, but he insisted on the artistic importance of the chorus. In concert performances nowadays the chorus is more often omitted.) Above the chant appears a delicately etched melody for solo flute, which also returns in various transformations later in the score. At the conclusion of the flute melody we hear the mellow voice of a solo horn in a melody which some feel Ravel intended to be a love theme:

A group of young men and girls enter carrying baskets and offerings for the nymphs. Among the group are Daphnis and Chloé. The ceremony continues with a religious dance. Daphnis does not yet realize that he loves Chloé. Chloé suffers at seeing the maidens embrace Daphnis during the dance and Daphnis resents the young men who crowd about Chloé. The company propose a contest between the clownish shepherd Dorco and Daphnis. The prize will be a kiss from Chloé. Dorco executes a grotesque dance, Daphnis a light and graceful one. Daphnis and Chloé fall into each others arms while the crowd admires their beauty. Chloé runs off and Daphnis lapses into dreamy languor.

Shouts of alarm are heard and several girls dash past, pursued by pirates. Daphnis hurries off to protect Chloé, whose life he fears may be in danger. A moment later Chloé appears. In her anxiety she throws herself before the altar of the nymphs, but the pirates seize her and carry her off. Daphnis returns.

---

* *This and the following musical examples from this composition are copyright 1929 by Durand et Cie. Used by permission of the publisher. Elkan-Vogel, Inc., sole representative, U.S.*

Realizing she has been abducted he curses the gods and falls senseless to the ground.

The light fades and one by one the statues of the three nymphs come to life. (This is the point at which the First Suite from the ballet begins.) They descend from their pedestals and notice Daphnis. They wipe away his tears, waken him, and lead him toward the large rock where they invoke the god Pan. Little by little the god becomes visible and Daphnis prostrates himself, appealing to Pan for his aid. Suddenly the entire stage is plunged into darkness.

From behind the scenes, the wordless chorus is heard, unaccompanied. From the distance we hear fanfares of a horn, then of a trumpet. The full orchestra enters in a brilliant *crescendo* and we are in the camp of the pirates.

The scene is a jagged coastline with the sea in the background. The pirates come running in, some carrying booty, others carrying torches which fill the stage with garish light. They do a warlike dance before their chief and finally fall exhausted to the ground. Chloé is brought in, her hands tied. She implores the pity of her abductors in a dance. Twice she tries to flee but each time is brought back again. The pirate chief woos Chloé, but suddenly the atmosphere changes and strange gleams illumine the night. Pan appears in a cloud and takes Chloé from her captors. The scene seems to melt and as the first dawn appears we are back on the edge of that sacred wood. (It is at this point that the Second Suite from the ballet begins.)

The sunrise is one of the most gorgeous passages of the entire ballet. It is built around a simple rising sequence derived from the solo horn melody heard at the opening of the ballet:

The score bears detailed indications of the following action:

> No sound but the murmur of rivulets of dew trickling from the rocks. Daphnis is still lying before the grotto of the nymphs. Little by little day breaks. Bird songs are heard. In the distance a shepherd passes with his flock. Another shepherd crosses the back of the stage. Herdsmen arrive searching for Daphnis and Chloé. They find Daphnis and awaken him. In anguish he looks around for Chloé. At last she appears, surrounded by shepherdesses. They throw themselves into each other's arms. Daphnis notices Chloé's crown. His dream was a prophetic vision: the intervention of Pan is clear. The old shepherd Lammon explains that if Pan saved Chloé, it was in remembrance of the nymph Syrinx, with whom the god once fell in love.
>
> Daphnis and Chloé mime the adventure of Pan and Syrinx. Chloé impersonates the young nymph, wandering in the meadow. Daphnis appears in the role of Pan and declares his love. The nymph repulses him. The god

grows more insistent. She disappears among the reeds. In despair he plucks some stalks, fashions them into a flute [pipes of Pan] and plays a melancholy tune. Cholé returns and her dance follows the accents of the flute. The dance grows more and more animated and, in a mad whirl, Chloé falls into Daphnis's arms. On two sheep before the altar of the nymphs he swears his fidelity. A group of young girls, dressed as Bacchantes and shaking tambourines, enters. Daphnis and Chloé embrace tenderly. A group of young men invade the stage. Joyous tumult. General Dance.

The excitement of the General Dance (which seems to have had the working title of "Bacchanal" during the working out of the ballet) is expressed by still another transformation of the solo horn melody, this time cast in the 5/4 meter which caused the *corps de ballet* such agonies during the rehearsals. This final transformation of the melody has a resemblance to one of the prominent themes of Rimsky-Korsakoff's *Scheherazade,* but the resemblance seems accidental:

Ravel's orchestra calls for piccolo, 2 flutes, flute in G, 2 oboes, English horn, clarinet in E-flat, 2 clarinets in B-flat, bass clarinet, 3 bassoons, contrabassoon, 4 horns, 4 trumpets, 3 trombones, tuba, kettledrums, snare drum, castanets, crotales, cymbals, wind machine, bass drum, side drum, tambourine, tam-tam, triangle, celesta, glockenspiel, xylophone, 2 harps, and the usual string choir.

MOTHER GOOSE (MA MERE L'OYE)

Like most of Ravel's famous orchestral works, his *Mother Goose* was originally composed for piano. The origins of the Mother Goose tales, like those of the Arabian Nights, are lost in the mists of prehistory. The earliest famous printed collection on which Ravel drew was the Baroque anthology of Perrault published in 1697 under the title *Histoires ou contes du temps passé, avec des moralitez (Stories or tales of the olden times, with morals)* known familiarly today as *Ma Mère l'oye.* This was his source for "The Sleeping Beauty" and "Hop-o' my Thumb." A contemporary and imitator of Perrault, the Countess d'Aulnoy was his source for "The Ugly Little Girl, Empress of the Pagodas," and he took "Beauty and the Beast" from a *Children's Treasury of Moral Tales (Magazin des Enfants, Contes Moraux)* published by Marie Leprince de Beaumont in 1757.

Ravel composed his *Mother Goose* as a set of five piano duets for a very young and gifted sister and brother team, Mimi and Jean Godebski, children of Ravel's friends Ida and Cyprien Godebski. The first public performance of the original piano-duet version was presented on April 20, 1910 at the Paris

Salle Gaveau by two little girls: Jeanne Leleu and Geneviève Durony, age ten. The following year Ravel transformed the pieces into a ballet, adding a prelude, a new opening scene, and interludes connecting the individual numbers, which he orchestrated. The ballet was first performed at the Théâtre des Arts in Paris on January 28, 1912.

Prelude. This dreamlike introduction opens with delicately muted fanfares suggesting "the horns of Elfland faintly blowing." The orchestral strings, also muted, begin to tremble as if in anticipation of the tales to come. The episodes follow without pause.

I. *Spinning Wheel Dance and Scene.* Here we are introduced to the Sleeping Beauty, Princess Florine. In a corner of the room an old woman is spinning at her wheel. Florine stumbles, pricks her finger on the spindle, and falls into a deep sleep.

II. *Pavane of the Sleeping Beauty.* The maids of honor are unable to arouse the princess from her deep sleep. The old woman throws off her ragged garb and reveals herself as the Good Fairy. She commands two little blackamoors to guard Florine while she sleeps. For the ballet Ravel added new measures which link the familiar *Pavane* to the following scene.

III. *Conversation of Beauty and the Beast.* Beauty tells the Beast that when she realizes how kindhearted he is, he does not seem so ugly. He asks her to be his wife. At first she refuses but then takes pity on him. When she accepts, the Beast is transformed into a prince "as beautiful as the God of Love."

IV. *Hop-o' My Thumb.* At the head of this piece Ravel quotes from Perrault's fairy tale: "He believed that he would have no difficulty in finding his way by means of the breadcrumbs which he had strewn wherever he had passed; but he was greatly surprised when he could not find a single crumb; the birds had come and eaten them all."

A solo oboe seems to describe the winding path Hop-o' My Thumb followed. Halfway through there are suggestions of the chirpings and twitterings of birds. Here, too, Ravel added transitional measures leading to the following scene.

V. *The Ugly Little Girl, Empress of the Pagodas.* The Ugly Little Girl, a former princess, had been made ugly by a wicked witch. Ashamed of her looks, she hid herself in a faraway castle. Walking in the forest one day she met a huge Green Serpent who once had been a handsome prince. Together they made a sea voyage in a little boat that was wrecked on the shore of a country inhabited by Pagodas, tiny people with bodies made of jewels, crystal, and porcelain. Their mysterious king turned out to be the Green Serpent. Eventually both the Ugly Little Girl and the Green Serpent are restored to their original appearance, and the two are married.

The music describes the following episode in the story: "She undressed and went into the bath. The Pagodas and Pagodines began to sing and play on instruments; some had theorbos made of walnut shells; some had violas made of almond shells, for they were obliged to proportion the instruments to their figure." The delicacy of Ravel's orchestra, too, is proportioned to both the instruments and the figures of the Pagodas and Pagodines. A charming example is the high-pitched sparkle of the little theme allotted to the piccolo:*

VI. *The Fairy Garden.* This section describes the Sleeping Beauty's awakening by Prince Charming. There is a joyous fanfare as the other characters gather about her and the Good Fairy gives the couple her blessing.

Mother Goose is scored for 2 flutes, piccolo, 2 oboes, English horn, 2 clarinets, 2 bassoons, contrabassoon, 2 horns, celesta, harp, glockenspiel, 2 kettledrums, triangle, cymbals, bass drum, tam-tam, xylophone, and the customary string choir.

RAPSODIE ESPAGNOLE

"M. Ravel may look upon us as old fogies if he pleases but he will not with impunity make fools of us," declared the embattled French critic Émile Paladilhe. Paladilhe was a member of the jury which in 1905 rejected Ravel for the *Prix de Rome* for the fourth consecutive time.

There was a national scandal. Ravel was thirty years old, a well-known composer of *Jeux d'eau,* a masterly string quartet, and many lesser works. Only two years after the *affaire Ravel,* as the incident was called, he produced two more masterpieces: his *Rapsodie espagnole* and the opera *L'Heure espagnole.* Unfortunately, Paladilhe and men of his ilk held the keys to Rome. This gross rebuff may have been one reason for Ravel's refusal, fifteen years later, to accept the Legion of Honor, which he treated contemptuously as a badge of mediocrity.

Composed in 1907 in a space of thirty days, the *Rapsodie espagnole* is Ravel's earliest published work for full orchestra. It established him at once as a master, or more: as a virtuoso of modern orchestral color. Furthermore, it brilliantly confirmed Ravel's flair for the musical expression of Spain, which he had shown as early as 1895 in his Habañera for Two Pianos, his *Alborada del gracioso* and was to confirm again with his opera, *L'Heure espagnole.* The Spanish composer Manuel de Falla himself has testified to the authenticity of Ravel's style in the *Rapsodie:* "It surprises one by its (genuinely) Spanish character. In absolute agreement with my own intentions (and diametrically opposed to Rimsky-Korsakoff in his *Capriccio*) this 'Hispanization' is not achieved merely by drawing upon popular or 'folk' sources (except in the Jota in *Feria*) but rather through the free use of the modal rhythms and melodies

---

* *Musical example copyright 1912 by Durand et Cie. Used by permission of the publisher. Elkan-Vogel, Inc., sole representative, U.S.*

and ornamental figures of our 'popular' music, none of which has altered in any way the natural style of the composer."

I. *Prélude à la nuit: Très modéré.* Perhaps the most striking quality of this "Prelude to the Night" is its delicate dynamic range, which starts *pianissimo* and never rises above a *mezzo forte.* The entire movement is a mosaic of tiny motifs, of which the most prominent is the tiny four-note descending figure heard in the opening bars and continuing, with only slight interruptions, throughout. The odd, diaphanous sound of the opening is due in part to the unusual spacing of muted violins and muted violas two octaves apart:*

II. *Malagueña: Assez vif.* This kaleidoscopic piece opens with a repetitive little *ostinato* figure plucked out by the string basses, over which other motifs are briefly introduced. A muted trumpet accompanied by tambourine is echoed by violins. The English horn starts a rhapsodic, almost Oriental-sounding melody, but is soon overtaken by echoes of the descending four-note theme from the first movement. There is a fading close which seems suddenly to evaporate into thin air.

III. *Habañera: Assez lent et d'un rythme las.* This movement is the orchestral garb of the *Habañera* Ravel composed for two pianos in 1895, as one of the two movements of his *Sites auriculaires.* His autographs of the *Habañera* are headed with a quotation: *"Au pays parfumé que le soleil caresse"* ("In the fragrant land caressed by the sun"). Looking back on this *Habañera* in later years, Ravel felt that "this work with its *ostinato* pedal point and its chords with multiple appoggiaturas, contained "the germ of several elements which were to predominate in my later compositions."

IV. *Feria: Assez animé.* This glittering Spanish festival is a blaze of color—or rather two blazes separated by a quieter section where the mournful voice of the English horn chants an ornate melody soon taken over and embellished by a velvet-toned clarinet:

The score of the *Rapsodie* calls for a large orchestra: 2 piccolos, 2 flutes, 2 oboes, English horn, 2 clarinets, bass clarinet, 3 bassoons, sarrusophone,

* *This and the following musical example from this composition are copyright 1908 by Durand et Cie. Used by permission of the publisher. Elkan-Vogel, Inc., sole representative, U.S.*

4 horns, 3 trumpets, 3 trombones, tuba, 4 kettledrums, bass drum, cymbals, triangle, tambourine, castanets, side drum, tam-tam, xylophone, celesta, 2 harps and the customary string choir. The first performance of the *Rapsodie* was presented at a Colonne Concert in Paris during March 1908.

LE TOMBEAU DE COUPERIN

Ravel delighted in paradoxes. When a critic declared that his music was artificial, he replied: "How do they know I'm not artificial by nature?" He is said to have regarded music as primarily a *divertissement*. Yet he wrote the six movements of the original (piano solo) version of *Le Tombeau de Couperin* in memory of six friends and comrades who had fallen on the Western front. This was in 1917, when he had just received his own medical discharge, was in poor health and was, moreover, emotionally wracked by a seventh death, that of his mother.

Under the circumstances, could he possibly have composed these *in memoriam* movements as entertainment music? The answer is: he could and did. But Ravel wore many masks, and *Le Tombeau de Couperin* is also more than entertainment music.

It was conceived in 1914 as a homage to French eighteenth-century (Baroque) music. The first sketches were laid away with the outbreak of war. Completed in 1917, it was first performed in its original piano version by Marguerite Long on April 11, 1919. Before the year was out, Ravel heard that Rolf de Maré's Swedish Ballet wished to produce a dance production of *Le Tombeau*, but in an orchestral version. Delighted, he selected four of the original six movements: The Prélude, Forlane, Minuet and Rigaudon, and orchestrated them.

The premiere of the orchestral *Tombeau de Couperin* was given by the Pasdeloup Orchestra of Paris under the direction of Rhené-Baton on February 28, 1920. On November 8 of the same year the ballet premiere was presented by the Swedish Ballet at the Théâtre des Champs-Elysées, conducted by D. E. Inghelbrecht.

I. *Prélude: Vif.* A swift stream of sixteenth-notes, recalling many a Baroque keyboard *allegro,* flows gently over ambiguously shifting harmonies.

II. *Forlane: Allegretto.* The *forlane* is an ancient dance type distantly related to the French Baroque jig. The lilt of Ravel's bittersweet theme, once heard, is hard to forget:*

* *This and the following musical example from this composition are copyright 1919 by Durand et Cie. Used by permission of the publisher. Elkan-Vogel, Inc., sole representative, U.S.*

III. *Menuet: Allegro moderato.* The hushed delicacy of this movement hardly recalls either Couperin or the *grand siècle* of Louis XIV. But Ravel declared that the homage he intended in *Le Tombeau de Couperin* was "less, in reality, to Couperin himself than to eighteenth-century French music." As if to emphasize the traditional French virtues, Ravel wrote with the utmost restraint, understatement, sobriety, elegance and economy of means. His depth of emotion is revealed only obliquely.

IV. *Rigaudon: Assez vif.* The *rigaudon* (our rigadoon) was a lively seventeenth-century dance type. Ravel's brilliant Rigaudon *finale* is built around this flashing figure:

Le Tombeau de Couperin is scored for 2 flutes, 2 oboes, English horn, 2 clarinets, 2 bassoons, 2 horns, trumpet, harp, and the customary string choir.

LA VALSE (THE WALTZ), CHOREOGRAPHIC POEM FOR ORCHESTRA

The idea of composing a symphonic apotheosis of the Viennese waltz, a sort of homage to Johann Strauss, Jr., occurred to Ravel as early as 1906. The title was to be simply *Wien (Vienna).* In 1918, almost immediately after the armistice of World War I, the project again came to mind. This time the great Russian impresario Serge Diaghilev offered to produce Ravel's projected work as a ballet during the 1920 summer season of the Diaghilev Ballets Russes.

Ravel spent the winter of 1919–1920 secluded in southern France in Lapras, a tiny village in the Rhône valley some sixty miles above Avignon, to work on the score. On December 22, he wrote his friend Roland-Manuel: "I'm working again at *Wien.* It's going great guns. [*Ça gaze.*] I was able to take off at last, and in high gear." A few weeks later, he added: "I'm waltzing madly! I began to orchestrate on the thirty-first of December."

Ravel's mad waltzing was interrupted by a minor public scandal, when the French government unexpectedly awarded him the Legion of Honor and he indignantly refused it. The official decoration had been awarded him at the instigation of admirers who had not realized what Ravel's attitude would be. When he read the news in the papers of January 16, he was horrified and telegraphed Roland-Manuel to refuse for him. "What an absurd affair," he wrote. "Who could have played this trick on me? . . . And I must finish *Wien* by the end of this month."

"You can imagine the state I've been in," he wrote later. "It has had a disastrous effect on my orchestration all through the day. . . . Have you noticed that people who have got the Legion are like morphinomaniacs, who will go to any lengths to make others share their passion, perhaps in order to justify it in their own eyes?" Erik Satie could not resist a jibe at his former friend. "Ravel refuses the Legion of Honor," he wrote, "but all his music accepts it. What is essential is not so much to refuse the Legion of Honor as not to have deserved it in the first place."

Despite the delay, Ravel finished the orchestration of *Wien* before the end of March 1920. In late April or early May he returned to Paris, where he took part in a two-piano performance of *Wien* as a preliminary hearing for Diaghilev, several members of Diaghilev's staff, and Massine, Poulenc, and Stravinsky. According to Poulenc, Diaghilev pronounced the work a "masterpiece . . . but," he declared, "it's not a ballet." Ravel gathered up his manuscript, walked out, and broke with Diaghilev permanently.

The first concert performance of *La Valse* was given the following winter (December 12, 1920) by the Lamoureux Orchestra under the direction of Camille Chevillard. The prewar working title, *Wien (Vienna)*, was not considered tactful in France so soon after World War I, so it was changed to the more neutral *La Valse.* It was immediately popular in the concert hall. It was not produced as a ballet until November 20, 1928, when Ida Rubenstein staged it at the Paris Opéra. Ravel himself described the background of the work:

> After *Le Tombeau de Coupérin* [1917] the state of my health prevented me from working for some time. When I started to compose again it was only to write *La Valse,* a choreographic poem, the idea of which had come to me before I wrote the *Rapsodie espagnole.* I had intended this work to be a kind of apotheosis of the Viennese waltz, with which was associated in my imagination an impression of a fantastic and fatal sort of dervish's dance. I imagined this waltz being danced in an imperial palace about the year 1855.

The stage picture which Ravel had in mind is described in a note prefacing the score:

> From time to time, through rifts in turbulent clouds, waltzing couples can be glimpsed. The clouds gradually disperse and a huge ballroom is revealed, filled with a great crowd of whirling dancers.
>
> Gradually the stage grows lighter. The light of the chandeliers bursts out full.

The misty darkness and "turbulent clouds" of the opening are suggested by the hoarse whisper of muted double basses, playing *tremolo.* A muffed thudding beat, as of a distant dance orchestra, is marked by low notes of the harps and plucked double basses. Little by little, as the waltzing couples are glimpsed, fragments of a waltz melody begin to emerge: first in two bassoons, then in muted violas, and finally in a fragment of the second violin section muted and playing tremolo over the fingerboard: *

** This and the following musical examples from this composition are copyright 1921 by Durand et Cie. Used by permission of the publisher. Elkan-Vogel, Inc., sole representative, U.S.*

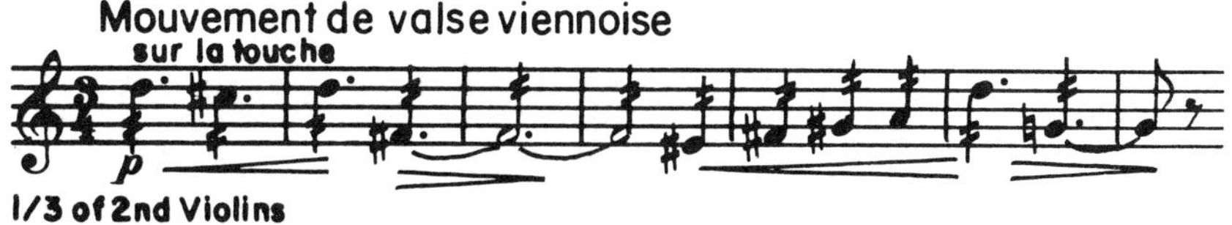

But the dark colors dominate until the melody rises into the first violin section; all the string players begin, one by one to remove their mutes, they give up bowing "over the fingerboard" and return with normal bowing to the full-bodied brilliance of traditional string tone. The volume swells, the pitch rises, rippling harp glissandos add glitter to the sound, until "the light of the chandeliers bursts out full" at this first dazzling climax for the entire orchestra:

New waltz melodies appear with greater and greater clarity as, for example, in this trumpet solo:

As the whirling couples approach more and more what Ravel described as a "fatal sort of dervishes' dance," the waltz rhythms distort and harmonies grow tense. Finally timbers clash and swirl in a seeming chaos of orchestral colors, grinding dissonance, berserk rhythms, and savage syncopations. The conclusion is one last eruption of violence.

La Valse is scored for piccolo, 3 flutes, 3 oboes, English horn, 2 clarinets, bass clarinet, 2 bassoons, contrabassoons, 4 horns, 3 trumpets, 3 trombones, tuba, 3 kettledrums, bass drum, snare drum, tambourine, cymbals, castanets, gong, glockenspiel, triangle, crotales (tiny "antique" cymbals with thick metal), 2 harps, and strings.

Max Reger

Born March 19, 1873, Brand, Germany—died May 11, 1916, Leipzig

VARIATIONS AND FUGUE FOR ORCHESTRA ON A THEME BY MOZART, OPUS 132

Max Reger once seemed a fearful iconoclast. Yet from the vantage point of the mid-twentieth century we hear him as a leading conservative of his day. Bach, Beethoven, and Mozart were his gods. His worship of the past masters of German tradition was reflected through all the copious output of his relatively brief career. A contemporary of Richard Strauss, Debussy, and the young Stravinsky, Reger played a far less sensational role than they during the years preceding World War I. Outside of Germany he has never enjoyed the professional admiration or the popular enthusiasm which have long been his in his homeland.

Yet he was a pivotal figure. During the years of radical experimentation culminating in Stravinsky's *Sacre du printemps* and Schoenberg's twelve-tone serialism, Reger was perhaps the most important link in the long chain leading from the eighteenth century (through such works as the *Brahms-Handel Variations* and the *Brahms-Haydn Variations*) to the powerful neotraditional trends of the twentieth century: the neo-Baroque and Neo-classicism.

Born in the Bavarian Upper Palatinate near Regensburg, Reger was originally destined to follow in his father's footsteps as a schoolmaster. But his father, who was also an expert organist, opened the way to a quite different career by providing young Max with a near-professional training in organ, piano, and music theory. Max started to compose at an early age, but the decisive experience came when he was fifteen, with a visit to Bayreuth festival performances of *Die Meistersinger* and *Parsifal.* Although he passed the entrance examinations to a teachers' seminary, his compositions soon won him admission to the theory and composition classes of the great musicologist, Hugo Riemann.

Reger attracted wide attention as a composer only after 1901, when he moved to Munich. His bold expansion of traditional harmonic style and modulation had already incurred the displeasure of his influential teacher, Riemann. In Munich his works met still more violent opposition and even vituperation. In 1907 he was called to the University of Leipzig as professor of composition and music director, and four years later he assumed the additional duties of conductor of the court orchestra of Meiningen. He was also active as pianist and guest conductor in other cities while maintaining a steady stream of new compositions.

Overwork and emotional tensions brought on a heart attack early in 1914, but Reger made an excellent recovery. During his swift convalescence he composed his *Mozart Variations,* the most lighthearted of his important scores. On

May 29, 1914, he announced the completion of the Variations and expressed the hope to his friends in Leipzig that the new work would be performed next season by the Leipzig Gewandhaus Orchestra. But this was not to be. The score encountered obstinate resistance from the board of directors where, as Reger bitterly complained, he was considered to be "a blood-red anarchist." The first performance finally took place in Berlin on February 5, 1915, under the direction of the composer.

Andante grazioso. The theme on which Reger based his eight variations and fugue is the melody on which Mozart himself built his own variations for the opening movement of his Piano Sonata in A major, K. 331. Each half of the theme is first presented by the woodwind choir, then repeated by the strings. Reger gives the opening phrase to the solo oboe:

Variation I: L'istesso tempo. The melody is carried by woodwind, embellished by playful arpeggios and scales of the strings. Later the roles of winds and strings are reversed, and the melody is heard in a mirror inversion.

Variation II: Poco agitato. The mirror inversion is now presented in F major and the original Mozartean harmonies are given a Regerish twist.

Variation III: Con moto. The theme is still further transformed in a chromatic A minor with smooth-flowing eighth notes.

Variation IV: Vivace. Richer harmonies and a livelier rhythmic pattern lead to a brilliant climax.

Variation V: Quasi presto. Chromatic wraiths of melody flit through the orchestra. They coalesce for a brief climax, then vanish suddenly into silence.

Variation VI: Sostenuto. The gentle mood of the beginning returns in a flowing D major.

Variation VII: Andante grazioso. The theme returns now in its original form, but transposed into F major. The mellow voice of French horn sings the opening phrase in unison with the cello section.

Variation VIII: Molto sostenuto. The final variation in free, almost symphonic style, prepares the way for the concluding fugue.

Fugue: Allegretto grazioso. The airy fugue theme enters high in the first violins and spreads downward through the orchestra, adding second violins, violas and cellos, double basses and bassoon. The puckish exposition leads to a brilliant climax. The fugue is rounded off by the return of the principal melody in gleaming trumpets and horns.

Reger's modest orchestra calls for 3 flutes, 2 oboes, 2 clarinets, 2 bassoons, 2 trumpets, 4 horns, kettledrums, harp, and the traditional strings.

Ottorino Respighi

Born July 9, 1879, Bologna—died April 18, 1936, Rome

THE FOUNTAINS OF ROME

Though composed during World War I, Respighi's *Fountains of Rome* is still in the Late-Romantic tradition of virtuoso orchestral coloration lavishly used for descriptive as well as expressive purpose. Completed in 1916, it was first performed on February 10, 1918 in Rome, under the direction of Arturo Toscanini at a concert for the benefit of artists disabled in World War I.

With his imaginative exploitation of a large, modern orchestra Respighi has tried, as he notes in the score, to express "the sentiments and visions suggested to him by four of Rome's fountains at the hour in which the character of each is most in harmony with the surrounding landscape, or in which their beauty appears most suggestive to the observer." The four are The Fountain of the Valle Giulia at dawn; the Triton fountain in the morning; the Fountain of Trevi at noon; and the Villa Medici fountain at sunset.

I. *The Fountain of Valle Giulia at Dawn.* As the music opens, murmuring muted violins and soft woodwinds sketch an almost impressionistic picture of a pastoral landscape in the soft twilight of morning. "Droves of cattle pass and disappear in the fresh, damp mists of a Roman dawn."

II. *The Triton Fountain in the Morning.* "A sudden loud and insistent blast of horns above the trills of the whole orchestra introduces the second part, the Triton Fountain. It is like a joyous call, summoning troops of naiads and tritons, who come running up, pursuing each other and mingling in a frenzied dance between the jets of water."

III. *The Fountain of Trevi at Midday.* "Next there appears a solemn theme, borne on the undulations of the orchestra. It is the Fountain of Trevi at Midday. The solemn theme, passing from the wood to the brass instruments, assumes a triumphal character:

Trumpets peal; across the radiant surface of the water there passes Neptune's chariot, drawn by sea horses and followed by a train of sirens and tritons. The procession then vanishes, while faint trumpet blasts resound in the distance."

IV. *The Villa Medici Fountain at Sunset.* "The fourth part, the Villa Medici Fountain, is announced by a sad theme [for solo flute and English horn] which rises above a subdued warbling.

THE TREVI FOUNTAIN OF ROME AT NOON.

Neptune and his cohorts almost seem to move in this eighteenth-century Baroque fantasy by Nicola Salvi which inspired the splashing, flashing colors of Respighi's twentieth-century tone poem. (*Photo, Louis Goldman; courtesy Raph Photo Researchers*)

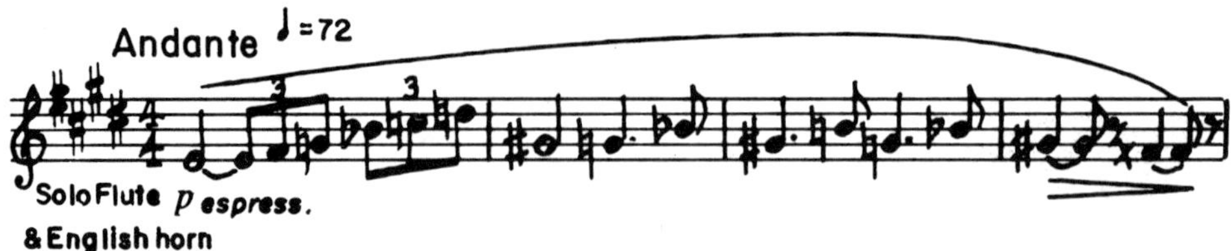

It is the nostalgic hour of sunset. The air is full of the sound of tolling bells, birds twittering, leaves rustling. Then all dies peacefully into the silence of the night".

Respighi's *The Fountains of Rome* is scored for piccolo, 2 flutes, 2 oboes, English horn, 2 clarinets, bass clarinet, 2 bassoons, 4 horns, 3 trumpets, 3 trombones, bass tuba, kettledrums, triangle, cymbals, carillon, celeste, bells, 2 harps, piano, organ (optional), and the traditional strings.

THE PINES OF ROME

After the sensational success of his *Fountains of Rome,* completed in 1917, Respighi composed two more tone poems on Roman subjects: *The Pines of Rome* and *Roman Festivals.* Each depicts in highly colored orchestral style, four contrasting aspects of a characteristically Roman sight. An Italian critic has claimed that Respighi's Rome was the decadent modern Rome of the sensualist and epicure d'Annunzio, rather than Classical Rome. However that may be, Respighi the orchestral painter commanded a palette of spectacular range and subtlety and on occasion, as in "The Pines of the Appian Way," of overwhelming power.

Respighi was a frankly eclectic artist—influenced most strongly by his teacher Rimsky-Korsakoff, with whom he worked in Russia, but also by the French impressionists, by Richard Strauss and, at least in passing, by Gregorian chant. His *Pines of Rome,* composed in 1924, was first heard at the Augusteo in Rome during the season 1924–1925 under the direction of Bernardino Molinari. It was given its American premiere by the New York Philharmonic in Carnegie Hall on January 14, 1926, under the direction of Arturo Toscanini. At that time Respighi wrote to Lawrence Gilman, the distinguished author of the Philharmonic program notes: "While in his preceding work, *The Fountains of Rome,* the composer sought to reproduce by means of tone an impression of Nature; in *The Pines of Rome,* he uses Nature as a point of departure, in order to recall memories and vision. The century-old trees which so characteristically dominate the Roman landscape become witnesses to the principal events in Roman life."

In the printed score, the four movements of *The Pines of Rome* are described as follows:

1. *"The Pines of Villa Borghese" (Allegretto vivace).* Children are at play in the pine grove of the Villa Borghese, dancing the Italian equivalent of "Ring around a Rosy"; they mimic marching soldiers and battles; they chirp with

excitement like swallows at evening; and they swarm away. Suddenly the scene changes . . .

2. *"Pines near a Catacomb" (Lento).* . . . and we see the shadows of the pines, which crown the entrance of a catacomb. From the depths rises a dolorous chant which spreads solemnly, like a hymn, and then mysteriously dies away:

3. *"The Pines of the Janiculum" (Lento).* There is a tremor in the air. The pines of Janiculum Hill are profiled in the full moon. A nightingale sings.

4. *"The Pines of the Appian Way" (Tempo di marcia).* Misty dawn on the Appian Way. Solitary pines stand guard over the tragic *campagna.* The faint, unceasing rhythm of numberless steps. A vision of ancient glories appears to the poet's fantasy: trumpets blare and a consular army erupts, in the brilliance of the newly risen sun, toward the Sacred Way, mounting to a triumph on the Capitoline Hill.

Respighi's resplendent score calls for piccolo, 3 flutes, 2 oboes, English horn, 2 clarinets, bass clarinet, 2 bassoons, contrabassoon, 4 horns, 3 trumpets, 4 trombones and 6 bucinae (the bucinae, so labeled in Respighi's score, were ancient Roman war trumpets; in discreet parentheses, the composer indicates that the parts are to be played by modern brass instruments: filicorni or Flügelhörner); also kettledrums, cymbals, small cymbals, triangle, tambourine, raganella (rattle), bass drum, tam-tam, bells, celesta, pipe organ, harp, piano and the traditional string choir. In the third movement, the voice of the nightingale is provided by a recording of a nightingale singing.

Wallingford Riegger

Born April 29, 1885, Albany, Georgia—died April 2, 1961, New York City

STUDY IN SONORITY, OPUS 7

Although Wallingford Riegger was one of the most original and fruitful experimenters on the American musical scene, he was never willing to adopt a fashionably iconoclastic style. Throughout his life he kept a refreshing scorn for the merely fashionable, for fads and cliques. The prominence that he deserved came to Riegger late in life, beginning really with the New York Music Critics' Circle Award of 1948 for his Third Symphony. His death occurred only a few days after the announcement that he had received the Brandeis University Award for 1961.

"My advent as a composer," he once wrote of himself, with his characteristic self-deprecating humor, "could hardly be described as meteoric." His Opus 1, which did not appear until he was thirty-five years old, was an eminently traditional Trio in B minor for violin, cello and piano. Far from his earliest work (Riegger had simply not dignified his preceding scores with opus numbers), it was far from unoriginal, despite its conservative late-Romantic idiom.

Not until 1924, after protracted internal debate and long consideration of Schoenberg's evolving practice of twelve-tone music, did Riegger initiate the profound changes in his own style, which led by 1927 to his *Study in Sonority for Ten Violins or Any Multiple Thereof,* to give its full title. This was the turning point in Riegger's development. It was given a modest premiere by students of the Ithaca Conservatory with the composer conducting, on August 11, 1927. Since then it has been performed many times. After half a century it remains fresh and fascinating music, and incidentally a masterly demonstration of unimagined violin sonorities and color.

The Study opens, like many of Riegger's mature works, with a unison statement of a simple theme, in this case a rising four-note figure, followed by a dissonant chord of extreme complexity. These two elements are the basic materials of the entire work. In both the melodic and harmonic developments that follow, one feels the constant recurrence of the intervals of the opening figure: the augmented fourth and minor seconds:

In addition to harmonic and melodic devices, this Study demonstrates unusual methods of tone production, such as throwing the bow with an almost whiplike motion at the upper end of the violin strings and striking the back of the violin with the wood of the bow. Other details of performance are minutely prescribed, including the seating position of the ten violins (or ten groups of violins) in relation to the conductor.

Nicolai Rimsky-Korsakoff

Born March 18, 1844, Tikhvin, near Novgorod—died June 21, 1908, Liubensk, near St. Petersburg

CAPRICCIO ESPAGNOL, OPUS 34

Rimsky-Korsakoff loved orchestral color and used it with the virtuosity of a great painter whose native gift has been strengthened and refined by years of patient analysis and study. His inborn flair was so great that when he was still in his twenties, hardly more than a student composer, César Cui, who had been Rimsky's artistic guide, offered him the job of orchestrating part of Cui's new opera, *William Ratcliffe*. Years later, when Rimsky was over thirty, he plunged into a severe, systematic, self-administered course of musical techniques which aroused the admiration of Tchaikovsky. "I do not know how to express all my respect for your artistic temperament," wrote Tchaikovsky, "I am a mere artisan in music, but you will be an artist in the fullest sense of the word." Over a decade later, Tchaikovsky was dazzled. "Your *Spanish Caprice*," he wrote to Rimsky, "is a *colossal masterpiece of instrumentation*, and you may regard yourself as the greatest master of the present day." The *Capriccio* found many admirers. But Rimsky himself, writing in his autobiography, was modest concerning his achievement:

> The opinion reached by both critics and the public, that the *Capriccio* is a *magnificently orchestrated piece*, is wrong. The *Capriccio* is a brilliant *composition for the orchestra*. The change of timbres, the felicitous choice of melodic designs and figuration patterns, exactly suiting each kind of instrument, brief virtuoso cadenzas for instruments solo, the rhythm of the percussion instruments, etc., constitute here the very *essence* of the composition and not its garb or orchestration.
>
> The Spanish themes, of dance character, furnished me with rich material for multiform orchestra effects. All in all, the *Capriccio* is undoubtedly a purely external piece, but vividly brilliant for all that. I was a little less successful in its third section (*"Alborada,"* in B-flat major), where the brasses somewhat drown the melodic designs of the woodwinds; but this is very easy to remedy, if the conductor will pay attention to it and moderate the indications of the shades of force in the brass instruments by replacing the *fortissimo* with a simple *forte*.

The melodies used in Rimsky's *Capriccio espagnol* go back to his sketches, written down in 1886, for a virtuoso violin work with orchestra on Spanish themes. The following summer Rimsky changed his mind and decided to make the work a display piece for the entire orchestra. "According to my plans," he wrote in *My Musical Life*, "the *Capriccio* was to glitter with dazzling orchestra color. . . . " During the season of 1887–1888 Rimsky conducted the five Russian symphony concerts performed by the orchestra of the Imperial Russian Opera House of St. Petersburg, in the so-called Small Theater. The success of the premiere, which took place on October 31, 1887, was presaged in rehearsal: as professionals the players took to the new score at once. "At the first rehearsal [Rimsky tells us], the first movement had hardly been finished when the whole orchestra began to applaud. Similar applause followed all the other parts wherever the pauses permitted. I asked the orchestra for the privilege of dedicating the composition to them. General delight was the answer. The *Capriccio* went without difficulties and sounded brilliant."

At the concert itself it was played with a perfection and enthusiasm the like of which it never equaled again even when led by Nikisch himself. Despite its length the composition called forth an insistent encore.

The score, published before the end of the year, bears a dedication to the artists of the Imperial Russian Opera House orchestra—all sixty-seven of them. It is in five movements, to be played without pause.

I. *Alborada. Vivo e strepitoso.* The *Alborada,* a kind of *aubade,* or morning serenade, begins with a brilliant outburst for full orchestra and concludes with a passage of ethereal delicacy.

II. *Variations. Andante con moto.* The theme is presented in the mellow splendor of French horn tone.

There are five changes of color for the five variations, and a cadenza for solo flute

III. *Alborada. Vivo e strepitoso.* Musically this is almost a repetition of the opening movement, but in a new tonality and with different orchestral color.

IV. *Scene and Gypsy Song. Allegro.* A dramatic roll of the side drum introduces a series of cadenzas for several instruments. A harp *glissando* introduces the gypsy song, which later combines with fragments from the cadenza.

V. *Fandango of the Asturias.* The *fandango* is an Andalusian dance, traditionally played with guitar and castanet accompaniment. At the close the *Alborada* of the first movement returns as a *coda.*

The *Capriccio* is scored for piccolo, 2 flutes, 2 oboes, English horn, 2 clarinets, 2 bassoons, 4 horns, 2 trumpets, 3 trombones, bass tuba, kettle drums, side drum, bass drum, cymbals, triangle, tambourine, castanets, harp, and string orchestra.

OVERTURE THE GREAT RUSSIAN EASTER, OPUS 36

"The Bright Holiday" was the Russian folk name for Easter. Rimsky-Korsakoff designed his Overture, "The Great Russian Easter," as a carefully calculated explosion of orchestral color reflecting popular Russian feelings on this highest Christian feast, when the solemn pageantry of Christian ritual mixed with ancient pagan memories celebrating the rebirth of nature.

Rimsky took his melodies from the *Obikhod*, a collection of the best-known canticles of the Greek Orthodox Church. He began his composition early in 1888 and completed it that summer while working on the score of his *Scheherazade*. That winter the Russian Symphony Concerts of St. Petersburg were put under Rimsky's direction and he included the world premiere of his "Great Russian Easter" on December 3, 1888, at the Club of Nobility.

The principal theme of the Overture is presented at the very beginning of the slow introduction in a solemn unison of all the woodwinds:

Rimsky associated this passage with Isaiah's prophecy of the resurrection of Christ. The melody is taken up majestically by trombones and finally in the dark orchestral color of the tuba. This latter passage suggested to Rimsky the Holy Sepulcher, which slowly began to glow with an ineffable light as the moment of the Resurrection approached. The orchestra swells suddenly to an almost blinding brilliance, then dims as suddenly, and is followed by the *allegro* outburst of the main section of Easter rejoicing.

> The solemn trumpet voice of the Archangel [wrote Rimsky in his autobiography] was replaced by a tonal reproduction of the joyous, almost dance-like bell-tolling, alternating now with the sexton's rapid reading and now with the conventional chant of the priests reading the glad tidings of the Evangel. The *obikhod* theme, "Christ is arisen," which forms a sort of subsidiary part of the Overture, appeared amid the trumpet-blasts and the bell-tolling, constituting also a triumphant coda. In this Overture, were thus combined reminiscences of the ancient prophecy of the Gospel narrative and also a general picture of the Easter service with its "pagan merry-making." The capering and leaping of the biblical King David before the ark, do they not give expression to a mood of the same order as the mood of the idol-worshipers' dance? Surely the Russian Orthodox chime is instrumental dance-music of the church, is it not? And do not the waving beards of the priests and sextons clad in white vestments and surplices, and intoning "Beautiful Easter" in the tempo of *Allegro vivo*, etc., transport the imagination to pagan times? And all these Easter loaves and twists and the glowing tapers—how far a cry from the philosophic and socialistic teaching of Christ! This legendary and heathen side of the holiday, this transition from the gloomy and mysterious evening of Passion Saturday to the unbridled pagan-religious merry-making on the morn of Easter Sunday, is what I was eager to reproduce in my Overture.

Rimsky felt very strongly that his orchestra, for all its vivid colors, could not in itself convey all he had in mind. In order to appreciate his Overture "even ever so slightly," he felt it was necessary for the hearer to have attended an Easter morning service "at least once" in a great Orthodox cathedral "thronged with people from every walk of life, with several priests conducting the cathedral service—something that many intellectual Russian hearers, let alone hearers of other confessions, quite lack nowadays." For this reason, Rimsky asked his friend, Count Golyenishchev-Kootoozov to write a descriptive poem. But the composer was dissatisfied with his friend's poem and so at last wrote his own words, a combination of quotations from both the Old and the New Testaments and words of his own which he had printed in early editions of his Overture:

> Let God arise, let His enemies be scattered, let them also that hate Him flee before Him.
>
> As smoke is driven away, so drive them away; as wax melteth before the fire, so let the wicked perish at the presence of God. (Psalm LXVIII. 1-2)
>
> And when the Sabbath was past, Mary Magdalene and Mary, the Mother of James, and Salome had bought sweet spices, that they might come and anoint Him. And very early in the morning the first day of the week, they came unto the sepulcher at the rising of the sun. And they said among themselves, Who shall roll us away the stone from the door of the sepulcher? And when they looked, they saw that the stone was rolled away, for it was very great.
>
> And, entering into the sepulcher, they saw a young man sitting on the right side clothed in a long white garment, and they were affrighted. And he saith unto them, Be not affrighted; ye seek Jesus of Nazareth which was crucified. He is risen. (Mark XVI. 1-6.)
>
> And the joyful tidings were spread abroad all over the world, and they who hated Him fled before Him, vanishing like smoke.
>
> "Resurrexit!' sing the chorus of angels in Heaven to the sound of the archangels' trumpets and the fluttering of the wings of the seraphim. "Resurrexit!" sing the priests in the temples, in the midst of clouds of incense, by the light of innumerable candles, to the chiming of triumphant bells.

The Overture is scored for 3 flutes (one interchangeable with piccolo), 2 oboes, 2 clarinets, 2 bassoons, 4 horns, 2 trumpets, 3 trombones, tuba, 3 kettledrums, glockenspiel, triangle, cymbals, bass drum, tam-tam, harp, and the customary strings.

SCHEHERAZADE, SYMPHONIC SUITE, OPUS 35

The Arabian Nights of our childhood, stories older than the memory of man, the ancient dreams of many races, color the fairy-tale pages of Rimsky-Korsakoff's Symphonic Suite, *Scheherazade.*

Where did these tales come from? Centuries before they were heard in Europe, the fantastic yarns were spun by poets, beggars, and professional story-tellers in the marketplaces of Egypt. A thousand years ago, they were already famous as the *Thousand Nights and a Night.* Some of the stories and their framework had been heard before in Persia. And before that, probably in India. No one knows where they began. They were revived in the eighteenth century and dazzled the European world from the first moment of publication. A virtuoso French adaptation of the tales by Antoine Galland called *Les mille et une nuits* was introduced to Europe in installments, starting in 1704 with the adventures of Sinbad the Sailor and continuing for fourteen years. One by one, by twos, by threes, by the dozen, they poured from Galland's eloquent pen: fairy tales, love stories, novellas, legends, didactic and humorous narratives, anecdotes, fables, parables—all embellished with hundreds of poems and poetic fragments.

Oriental subjects from Turkey to Egypt and China had long played a modest role in the arts of the West. But the enormous vogue of *The Thousand and One Nights* was a part of the larger wave which swept the Continent: a new fashion called *turquerie* (like *chinoiserie*), which left its imprint on architecture, painting, poetry, drama, opera, and even on politics. Idealization of distant Eastern lands was partly a disguise for attacking sacrosanct institutions of the West: the Church and divine-right monarchy. *Turquerie* not only colored the lofty social criticism of Montesquieu's *Lettres persanes,* Voltaire's philosophical *Zadig* and Samuel Johnson's *Rasselas,* but also farcical entertainments offered by the *commedia dell'arte* on the Paris fairgrounds. Even European military bands were revolutionized by *turquerie.* "Turkish" marches influenced finally even symphonic and chamber music of Haydn, Mozart, and Beethoven. The most familiar example to present-day opera lovers is Mozart's *Abduction from the Seraglio.*

The popularity of the *Arabian Nights* continued into the nineteenth century, and Rimsky-Korsakoff retold them in an orchestral language more gorgeous than any Russian before him had ever mastered. His *Scheherazade* unfolds like a rich dream-panorama of the *Arabian Nights,* sometimes a rather jumbled dream, but always a colorful adventure. Hints of the stories the composer had in mind are in the titles of the separate movements, but he was careful to warn us that they are disconnected episodes and visions. Even the recurring musical themes do not always have the same connotation.

"I meant these hints to direct but slightly the hearer's fancy on the path which my own fancy had traveled [wrote Rimsky-Korsakoff in his autobiography]. All I desired was that the hearer, if he liked my piece as *symphonic music,* should carry away the impression that it is beyond doubt an oriental narrative of some numerous and varied fairy-tale wonders, and not merely four pieces played one after the other and composed on the basis of themes common to all four movements."

The score was composed during the summer of 1888 at Nyezhgovity on the shore of Lake Cheryemenyetskoye, and first performed the following season at St. Petersburg. On the flyleaf of the score, Rimsky-Korsakoff put the following note: "The Sultan Schahriar, persuaded of the falseness and faithlessness of all women, had sworn to put to death each of his wives after the first night. But the Sultana Scheherazade saved her life by arousing his interest in tales which she told him during a thousand and one nights. Driven by curiosity, the Sultan put off his wife's execution from day to day and at last gave up his bloody plan altogether. Scheherazade told many marvelous tales to the Sultan. For her stories, she borrowed from poets their verses, from folksongs their words, and she strung together fairytales and adventures."

I. *"The Sea and Sinbad's Ship." (Largo e maestoso; Lento; Allegro non troppo.)* The first movement opens with the principal theme of the entire work: a heavy, forbidding motto proclaimed in thunderous octaves.

This might be the ferocious Sultan, except that, as Rimsky himself pointed out, it returns in later movements at points where there is no thought at all of the Sultan. This stern announcement is answered by pacifying woodwind chords and then by the voice of Scheherazade: a graceful, sinuous violin solo.

The Sultana's first narrative has three principal themes: the stern motto of the start, the theme of Scheherazade herself (which is not always confined to the solo violin), and a rocking, wave-like theme, suggesting the billows of Sinbad's sea.

II. *"The Story of the Kalendar Prince" (Lento).* The wheedling, cajoling voice of the Sultana introduces the adventure of the Kalendar Prince. One wonders which of the several Kalendar princes of the *Arabian Nights* Rimsky had in mind. There were at least three princes who disguised themselves as Kalendars, members of a mendicant order of wandering dervishes. Each of these masquerading Kalendar princes tells his own tale. Unfortunately, Rimsky does not tell us which one he had in mind. Or perhaps it is fortunate, for again our fancy is free to roam. The story begins with a jaunty bassoon solo, the melody of which grows livelier as it is taken up by the sweeter-voiced oboe, now with a harp accompaniment. The color of the melody changes like the shifting lights on the fabled Arabian Sea as the tune is taken up successively by violins, by a whole bevy of woodwinds, by a solo horn, until we come to an abrupt interruption.

The last five notes of Scheherazade's theme suddenly erupt (in an entirely new form) in the bottom of the orchestra. They are answered by a shuddering *tremolo* of the violins, against which a brassy trombone flings out a seemingly new motive:

But startling as the new theme seems, its triplet figure is derived from the languid melody of Scheherazade we have heard so often. The story takes a whole new turn with this new fanfare-like theme, echoed by a muted trumpet and ultimately by various alternations and combinations of brasses, woodwinds, and strings that glint and gleam with true Oriental splendor.

III. *"The Young Prince and the Young Princess" (Andantino quasi allegretto).* The sinuous opening song of the violins suggests that whichever prince and princess are depicted here, their story is a romantic one. The narrative is embellished by rippling scales of flutes and clarinets, and then interrupted by a softly rasping sound of a military drum. The subtle rhythms of plucked and muted strings are accentuated with a touch of tambourine and triangle tone. Soon the harp joins, and again Rimsky's orchestra displays an iridescence of tone color so rich and subtly shifting that one is reminded of the spreading of a peacock's tail. For a moment we catch the voice of Scheherazade herself, but soon it is submerged in the fascination of the tale she tells.

IV. *"Festival at Baghdad; The Sea; The Ship Goes to Pieces Against a Rock Surmounted by a Bronze Warrior" (Allegro molto; Allegro molto e frenetico; Vivo; Allegro non troppo e maestoso).* A nervous transformation of the main motto theme alternates with the voice of Scheherazade as an introduction to the *Finale,* which is like a confused dream of Oriental splendor and terror. The Festival begins with a lightly fluttering dance of the solo flute. Other instruments join as the excitement swells. The dance seems more and more frenzied until it takes on an undertone of fear. Rhythms clash and the tempo grows.

All at once the Festival seems to be on shipboard. The waves of Sinbad's majestic sea swell into overwhelming mountains, and woodwinds scream as the ship crashes on the magic rock. The storm and the sea subside, and the story is done. The voice of Scheherazade's violin fades away upward through a final, serene chord of the orchestra, like the passing of a dream.

All these marvels of orchestral color are achieved with a relatively small and traditional orchestra: piccolo, 2 flutes, 2 oboes, English horn, 2 clarinets, 2 bassoons, 4 horns, 2 trumpets, 3 trombones, bass tuba, kettledrums, snare drum, bass drum, tambourine, cymbals, triangle, tam-tam, harp, and strings.

George Rochberg

Born July 5, 1918, Paterson, New Jersey

SYMPHONY NO. 2

Even on first hearing, George Rochberg's Second Symphony communicates a sense of urgency, of poignance, of depth. It also has that elusive attribute we call style. No one expects a new work of art or a new friend to display all his qualities at first meeting but this Symphony grows with successive hearings.

The Symphony was composed chiefly in 1955 and 1956, although sketches for it date back to 1952. The world premiere was given in Cleveland by George Szell and the Cleveland Orchestra on February 26, 1959. The same forces brought the work to New York in February 1960. The Symphony was first performed by the New York Philharmonic in Carnegie Hall December 30, 1961, with Werner Torkanowsky conducting.

Rochberg's First Symphony was given its first hearings in March 1958 by the Philadelphia Orchestra under Eugene Ormandy in Philadelphia and soon after in New York. George Rochberg was born 1818 in Paterson, New Jersey and brought up in nearby Passaic, where he had his first music lessons. He studied at the Mannes School (now the Mannes College of Music) in New York. After serving in the army, Rochberg resumed his studies at the Curtis Institute in Philadelphia, where he was a pupil of Gian Carlo Menotti. On Menotti's recommendation he was made a member of the Curtis faculty in 1948.

In 1950 Rochberg went to Italy on a Fulbright fellowship. On his return to the United States he became music editor of the Theodore Presser Company in Philadelphia, while continuing to teach at the Curtis Institute. He has received several other awards including a Guggenheim Fellowship. In 1960 he became chairman of the music department of the University of Pennsylvania.

The *Second Symphony* is in four connected movements, which are played without pause, and are all based on a single twelve-tone row. However, Mr. Rochberg's use of serial techniques is a personal one. He does not hesitate to use themes and fragments of themes for symphonic development in the Viennese Classical tradition, and the writing, to this listener at least, is often strongly tonal.

I. *Declamando.* The first movement is in traditional sonata-allegro form, with a vigorous main theme declaimed in thunderous octaves by the brass, wind, and percussion:*

---

* *Musical example © 1958, Theodore Presser Company. Used by permission.*

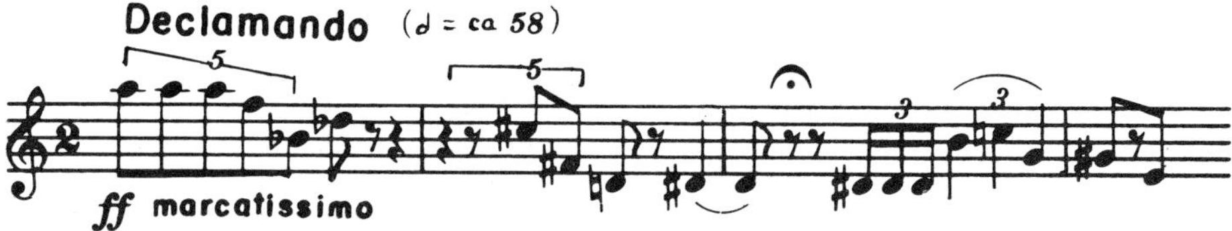

This theme, which contains the basic tone-row, breaks down into three phrases, used later as individual symphonic motives. Particularly the six-note motive of the opening and the triplet rhythm, which starts the last phrase, are to return prominently.

There are two contrasting lyric themes and a stormy development in which the rhythmic motives play a big part. The return of the opening themes is not a literal repetition, but a contrapuntal combination. After the final climax a tiny bridge of seven measures leads, without pause, to a *scherzo.*

II. *Allegro scherzando.* The second movement is like a Classical *scherzo,* both in its exuberant spirit and its familiar A-B-A form. Again there is a very quiet bridge (*Adagio*) to the following movement.

III. *Molto tranquillo.* The slow movement is mostly intimate and delicate in chamber-music style. There are frequent recalls of the more agitated first and second movements, interrupting the basic chamber style.

IV. *Finale: Tempo primo ma incalzando.* The heavy brass proclaim the symphony's opening theme against wild, rushing figures in the winds and strings. The rest of the movement consists chiefly of a slow buildup of two slow-moving melodic lines moving in counterpoint against each other and punctuated by sharp outbursts of the quintuplet rhythm from the symphony's opening measure. The melodic and rhythmic tensions grow to a powerful climax. The conclusion is a dark, almost tragic *coda,* with slow, static chords dying away into silence.

Rochberg's Second Symphony is scored for piccolo, 2 flutes, 2 oboes, English horn, 2 clarinets, bass clarinet, 2 bassoons, contrabassoon, 4 horns, 3 trumpets, 3 trombones, tuba, kettledrums, snare drum, tenor drum, bass drum, xylophone, triangle, tambourine, cymbal, gong, harp, and the usual strings.

Gioacchino Rossini

Born February 29, 1792, Pesaro—died November 13, 1868, Paris

OVERTURE TO THE BARBER OF SEVILLE

The reign of Napoleon I collapsed just as that of Gioacchino Rossini was starting. The whole European continent seemed to heave a sigh of relief, just as Napoleon had predicted. People turned away from the horror and grandeur of the Napoleonic era and tried, with Rossini's help, to remember what it was like to laugh again.

Rossini's early music, like the Overture to his *Barber of Seville,* is typical of that reaction: the reaction which comes after wars (in this case, nearly a whole generation of wars) when people are exhausted by suffering and heroism and hope to be amused as easily and painlessly as possible. That is what helped make Rossini the man of the hour, of the year, the decade, and enabled him to overshadow Beethoven for a while, even in Beethoven's Vienna.

Rossini was a famous cook and a famous wit, and you can hear this in his music. He could dish up an opera—even a masterpiece like *The Barber of Seville*—as easily and spicily as he made an omelet. He wrote it down as fast as he could make the pen go. (The *Barber* is said to have taken him less than three weeks.) What if he did repeat himself sometimes? It was good enough to hear twice. His listeners nicknamed him Monsieur Crescendo because he made a habit of those long, exhilarating crescendos, beginning in a whisper and rising to a flashing, glittering tempest. He did it everywhere: in arias like the famous "Calumny" aria in *The Barber of Seville* and in his operatic overtures. It was a trick, but it was a good one, and it still works. And if the tempest was sometimes more like a tempest in a teapot, that was the only kind of storm people were in a mood to hear for many years. Napoleon had given them enough military and political lightning and thunder to last for a long time.

The Overture which has introduced Rossini's *The Barber of Seville* for over 150 years originally had nothing to do with *The Barber.* It was composed for Rossini's serious opera, *Aureliano in Palmira,* and first performed the day after Christmas, 1813, at La Scala of Milan. Rossini knew a good thing when he wrote it and so, two seasons later at the San Carlo in Naples, he adapted the Overture to *Aureliano* to introduce his new serious opera, *Elisabetta, Regina d'Inghilterra.* A few weeks after *Elisabetta,* he composed two operas for Rome, the second of which, *Almaviva, or The Useless Precaution,* was produced at the Teatro Argentina on February 20, 1816. This was the *Barber of Seville,* which was not given its present title until August 10 in Bologna. Somewhere between February and August, between Rome and Bologna, the original Overture to *The Barber* was lost. So for the Bologna premiere Rossini used his *Aureliano* Overture for the third time. This time the Overture stuck. And it became so identified with the lighthearted *Barber of Seville* that fanciful commentators have written lengthy explanations of just which episodes of the hilarious plot it depicts.

The Overture begins with a bit of operatic pomp and circumstances, *Andante maestoso,* and comes to a majestic stop before launching into the main part of the Overture, the *Allegro vivace,* which seems to us superbly right for laughter. If we did not know positively the serious nature of *Aureliano,* one would to tempted to say that Rossini's mercurial theme has a particularly witty sparkle:

There is a wonderful lilt to a second principal theme as well, and Rossini uses it to build up a characteristic avalanche of excitement of the kind that won him his nickname.

In its 1816 version, the Overture to Rossini's *Barber of Seville* calls for 2 flutes, 2 oboes, 2 clarinets, 2 bassoons, 2 trumpets, 2 horns, kettledrums, bass drum, and the traditional strings.

OVERTURE TO LA GAZZA LADRA

We are so used to thinking of Rossini as the prince of comedians, the king of operatic jesters, with a *bon mot,* a quip, a crack for everything, including himself, that we are apt to forget that he was also king of serious opera. We are also apt to forget, if indeed we ever knew, that many of his exhilirating overtures, which to us seem to flash with wit from start to finish, were in fact perfectly serious.

Thus it is with *La gazza ladra,* which overwhelmed the impressionable audience of La Scala in Milan on May 31, 1817. The title, *The Thieving Magpie,* suggests a comic work. Actually the opera was based on a harrowing melodrama, *La Pie voleuse,* by two French playwrights, J. M. T. Baudouin d'Aubigny and L. C. Ciagniez. The plot was founded on a supposedly true tragedy of an innocent servant girl executed for stealing a silver spoon which had, in fact, been stolen by a magpie. In the French village where this took place, the townsmen having discovered too late the innocence of the girl, are said to have instituted a yearly mass for her soul, which was known for many years as the "Magpie" Mass.

For an Italian opera of 1817, the story had to have a happy end. This was easily accomplished, but not until the audience had been moved to floods of tears—especially during the second-act prison scene, from which the *Allegro* of the Overture is taken.

It is our good fortune that Stendahl, whose enthusiasm for Rossini transports us back to that happy age, witnessed the premiere of *La gazza ladra.* "I was myself in the audience for that first performance," he writes with pride, "and it was one of the most glittering, the most single-minded triumphs I have ever witnessed." Stendahl knew as well as we do that the Overture was a little masterpiece. In the opening *Maestoso marziale* of the Overture, with its marchlike rhythms and its stirring rasp of the military drum, he believed he heard the hero, "the young conscript, covered with medals and glory, returning to the bosom of his rustic family, . . ."

In the *Allegro,* Stendahl points out, "the overture takes on a note of sadness, but even this sadness is shot through and through with fire and *vivacity,* for it is the melancholy of youth, not of age; and in fact, all the chief actors of the opera are young." The passage to which Stendahl refers is note for note the orchestral accompaniment to the agitated *cabaletta* of the prison-scene duet, as the heroine, Ninetta, declares: "Ah! In my name pray give this ring to my Gianetto! . . . Tell him," she continues, "that up to my last breath I live and breathe for him alone. But do not tell him of my anguish, how my heart, ah! I am delirious! I shall see my beloved never more." Here is the orchestral theme which accompanies her lugubrious words:

This serves as the principal theme in a sonata-allegro form of tremendous fire and *brio.*

The audience was swept away. "Before the end of the first *presto,*" says Stendahl, "The theater was a tempest of delight; and the public *en masse* was encouraging the orchestra with extempore accompaniments! From this point onward, the opera went from triumph to triumph, and the performance was one long scene of delirium." At the end of the overture, Stendahl assures us: "The pit, having clapped and cheered to the echo, having shouted for five whole minutes on end, having in fact created such an uproar and pandemonium that no conceivable stretch of the imagination can visualize it, found itself in the end utterly exhausted, too weak to cheer a moment longer; and then it was that I observed each man turn to his neighbor and start talking—a phenomenon which is totally foreign to the suspicious temperament of the average Italian. Meanwhile, in the boxes, the crabbedest the oldest, the most cantankerous of spectators were gasping and squeaking: *"O bello! O bello!"*

The overture to *La gazza ladra* is scored for piccolo, flute, 2 oboes, 2 clarinets, 2 bassoons, 4 horns, 2 trumpets, trombone, kettledrums, triangle, bass drum, side drum, and the customary string choir.

OVERTURE TO L'ITALIANA IN ALGERI (THE ITALIAN WOMAN IN ALGIERS)

Whether it was an opera, an omelet, or a *bon mot* (often at his own expense), Rossini seems to have tossed them all off with equal ease. He whipped up his first great comic opera, *L'Italiana in Algeri,* in a mere twenty-seven days, according to a Venetian newspaper report two days after the premiere, which Rossini himself conducted at the Teatro San Benedetto of Venice on May 22, 1813. But the Venice correspondent of Leipzig's *Allgemeine musikalische Zeitung* declared that Rossini had told him *personally* that the entire *Italiana* had taken him only *eighteen* days. After the premiere, which was a resounding success, Rossini is alleged to have remarked: "I thought that after hearing my opera, the Venetians would treat me as a crazy man. They have showed themselves to be crazier than I am."

Stendhal, who held *L'Italiana* in special affection, felt that it was written in the flower of Rossini's genius and his youth. He pointed out that Rossini "was living in that aimiable Venetian country, the gayest in Italy and perhaps in the world. The result of the Venetian character [continued Stendhal] is that the people want above all in music agreeable songs, light rather than passionate. They were served to their hearts' desire in *L'Italiana;* never has a public enjoyed a spectacle more harmonious with its character, and of all the operas that have ever existed this is the one destined to please the Venetians most."

Stendhal adds that as he was traveling through Venetian territory in 1817 he found *L'Italiana* being produced at the same time in Brescia, Verona, Venice, Vicenza, and Treviso. The opera reached the United States on November 17, 1832, when it was first performed by the Montresor Company in the Richmond Hill Theatre at the corner of Varick and Charlton Streets in New York City. The Metropolitan Opera Company presented *L'Italiana* for four performances during the 1919–1920 season and revived it again during the 1973–1974 season. It is still performed fairly frequently in Europe.

The brief Overture opens with a slow introduction which contrasts softly plucked string color with the elegant cantilena of a solo oboe. The main theme is a delicately sparkling *Allegro* for high woodwinds, echoed almost immediately in the softer tones of the string choir. A carefully stylized storm, perhaps more of a tempest in a teacup, leads to the contrasting lyric theme, a song for solo oboe:

This is answered by a fluttering flute, leading to a characteristically brilliant Rossinian *crescendo.*

A tiny bridge passage, too brief to be called a development, leads to a reprise of all the principal themes, concluding with an even more dynamic *crescendo.*

The Overture to *L'Italiana in Algeri* calls for flute, 2 oboes, 2 clarinets, 2 bassoons, 2 horns, 2 trumpets, kettledrums, and the classical string choir.

OVERTURE TO LA SCALA DI SETA (THE STEPS OF SILK)

The Overture to *La scala di seta* begins with a graceful, slow introduction. Then the lively *staccato* notes of the principal theme scamper upward through the orchestra like the bubbles through a glass of champagne:

The idea couldn't be simpler, but it is so engaging that Rossini repeats it immediately four times over, the last two times in the wind instruments alone. The second theme starts with a lovely lyric arch, but soon the woodwind instruments burst into Rossinian giggles. The hilarity and excitement mount in a familiar *crescendo,* and our exposition is ended. The listener needs no guide through Rossini's beguiling development or the recapitulation which is given an added touch of brilliance by the inclusion of the piccolo-flute and an even more exciting *crescendo* for the close.

The Overture to *La scala di seta* is scored for piccolo, flute, pairs of oboes, clarinets, bassoons, and horns, plus the traditional string choir.

OVERTURE TO SEMIRAMIDE

Rossini's *Semiramide* was a serious opera. In its day (the premiere was February 3, 1823, in the fabled *La Fenice* of Venice) it was considered almost unbearably dramatic. Nowadays it is occasionally revived as a vehicle for agile singers. But the Overture seems to have inextinguishable vitality, a verve and brilliance that still dazzle us.

What is it that gives such exhilaration to the Rossini overtures? May it not be, in part at least, that they were written so fast? Rossini's contract gave him forty days to write *Semiramide,* but he only took thirty-three. Overtures he seems to have composed in a matter of hours.

The Babylonian Queen Semiramis in her operatic incarnation (based on Voltaire's tragedy) has connived with her lover at the murder of her husband, King Ninus. The lover hopes to marry her and ascend the throne, but she falls in love with a handsome young general Arsace (who, although neither of them knows this, is in reality her son, Prince Ninia). King Ninus's tomb opens and his ghost emerges to prophesy that his successor on the throne will be Arsace. The high priest informs Arsace of his true identity and bids him avenge his father's murder. Arsace obeys, but the dagger thrust intended for the lover strikes the guilty Semiramis instead. The lover is condemned, and Arsace is proclaimed king.

The Overture is cast in traditional sonata-allegro form with a long introduction in which four French horns chant a hymnlike passage from Act I: a great ensemble oath of fealty to the queen. The main part of the Overture begins with a theme taken from the orchestral introduction to the final scene of the opera in the subterranean mausoleum of King Ninus. It seems incredible that this lighthearted phrase could ever have sounded spooky:

One catchy theme follows another, culminating in one of the best of the famous Rossini crescendos. After a brief development section the same sequence of themes leads to another grand *crescendo* and the swift, incisive close.

Rossini's orchestra here calls for piccolo, flute, 2 oboes, 2 clarinets, 2 bassoons, 4 horns, 2 trumpets, 3 trombones, kettledrum, bass drum, and the customary strings.

OVERTURE TO WILLIAM TELL

The story of William Tell, the tyrant-killer, leader of his country's revolution against a hated foreign rule, and the famous trial of marksmanship when he was forced to shoot an apple placed on his son's head, seemed made to order for a Romantic grand opera. It became, in fact, the last and grandest opera of Rossini's career. Produced at the Paris Opéra on August 3, 1829, it was enthusiastically acclaimed, by public and critics alike, as Rossini's masterpiece. And the Overture became what is quite probably the most popular operatic overture ever written.

It is in four sections. The first three seem to describe Swiss mountain scenes, which form the background of the opera. The serene opening, famous for its five solo cellos, suggests a mountain sunrise; the second, an Alpine storm; and the third is a *Ranz des vaches,* a Swiss cattlemen's call to the flocks, played here on the English horn. The final section of the Overture begins with fiery trumpet fanfare, like a call to revolt, merging into a revolutionary march for the Swiss patriots:

Rossini had written this march seven years earlier as a quickstep for a military band in Venice. He liked it well enough to incorporate it into the revolutionary *finale* of the second act of *William Tell.* Later he removed the March from Act Two, and so we know it today only as the climax of the brilliant Overture.

The Overture to *William Tell* is scored for piccolo, flute, 2 oboes, 2 clarinets, 2 bassoons, 4 horns, 2 trumpets, 3 trombones, kettledrums, triangle, and the customary string choir.

Albert Roussel

Born April 5, 1869, Tourcoing—died August 23, 1937, Royan

BACCHUS ET ARIANE, SUITE NO. 2

One of the least glamorous and least publicized French masters of our century, Albert Roussel scarcely fits the conventional pictures of a French artist. But since his death in 1937 his stature has continued to grow, while many a composer once considered more engagingly Gallic has faded.

Good taste, graceful form, clarity, logic, balance, restraint, simplicity, elegance: these are the types of labels usually attached to the French spirit. But happily for the rest of the world, the French spirit is far too self-contradictory to be contained in any such simple formulas. Balance and restraint will hardly do to describe the explosive passions of Berlioz's music, the canvases of Géricault and Delacroix or the intoxicating rhetoric of Victor Hugo. Good taste is not a primary concern of Rabelais or the Rabelaisian *chansons* of his day. Neither the Gothic cathedrals nor the music composed to be performed in them could possibly be considered simple or restrained. And who would think of attributing graceful form to the sprawling grandeur of Balzac's *Comédie humaine?*

Roussel's finest and most characteristic works, particularly his Third and Fourth symphonies and his ballets, have sturdy, stamping rhythms recalling country dances rather than the glamour of the ballroom. They have a melodic tensile strength which never allows their long lines to sag. And their harmonies, conservative for their time and firmly based on tradition, have an originality and bite that continue to yield fresh surprises.

Roussel's two-act ballet, *Bacchus and Ariadne,* was given its world premiere on May 22, 1931, at the Paris Opéra, with choreography by Serge Lifar, who also danced the role of Bacchus. The conductor was Philippe Gaubert.

The scenario of the ballet by Abel Hermant is based on the ancient myths of Theseus, Ariadne, and Bacchus, which had been used by dramatic composers from Monteverdi to Richard Strauss. On his way home to Greece, Theseus, with Ariadne and the Greek youths and maidens whom he has rescued from the Minotaur, lands on the desert island of Naxos. They celebrate their deliverance with dances, in the course of which a sinister figure in a black cloak appears and casts a spell upon Ariadne, who loses consciousness. Theseus and the young men attack the intruder, but are terrified when he reveals himself as the god Bacchus. He orders Theseus and his companions to leave the island, and after their departure, performs a passionate dance around the sleeping Ariadne. In her dream Ariadne rises and joins in Bacchus's dance, at the end of which he puts her to rest on the ground again and disappears.

Suite No. 2 from the ballet includes the entire Second Act. Ariadne's slumber is suggested by murmuring muted strings of the introduction. Ariadne wakens as the peaceful introduction fades into silence. Sudden, startled figures of the clarinet suggest her astonishment and anxiety as she looks about her. She rises, rushes hither and thither searching for Theseus and his companions. Her growing despair, as she realizes that she has been deserted, is reflected in a plunging chromatic motive for the violins. Ariadne climbs with great difficulty to the peak of a rock and is about to throw herself into the ocean below, but falls instead (with a spectacular *glissando*) straight into the arms of Bacchus, who appears suddenly from behind the rock. The orchestra resumes the music of Ariadne's dream dance with Theseus in Act One. Then he dances alone for Ariadne to the increasingly vigorous gigue-like rhythms, building to a great *crescendo* of excitement. At the climax the music fades suddenly to silence as Bacchus takes Ariadne into his arms and kisses her. A long melody associated with the magic of Bacchus's kiss begins softly in the warm middle range of the string section reinforced by the orchestral horns:*

The magic of the kiss brings the entire island to life: vine-wreathed fauns and maenads, followers of Bacchus, appear from among the rocks, bursting in an almost crudely vigorous dance *(con ruvidezza)*. Two of them present Ariadne with a golden goblet filled with wine. Ariadne dances alone, dreamily, tenderly, to the intimate sound of a solo violin. Her long and inexhaustibly inventive melody begins with this recurrent phrase:

As Ariadne's dance grows more fervent, she is joined by Bacchus in a powerfully rhythmic dance based on the unusual metric pattern of ten-eighths. The duet grows into a brilliant bacchanal. This reaches its climax with an expansive orchestral version of the theme of Bacchus's kiss as the god leads

* *This and the following musical example from this composition are copyright 1931 by Durand et Cie. Used by permission of the publisher, Elkan-Vogel, Inc., sole representative, U.S.*

Ariadne to the highest pinnacle of the rock and crowns her with a diadem of stars plucked from the heavens.

The Second Suite from Roussel's *Bacchus and Ariadne* is scored for piccolo, 2 flutes, 2 oboes, English horn, 2 clarinets, bass clarinet, 2 bassoons, contrabassoon, 4 horns, 4 trumpets, 3 trombones, tuba, kettledrums, cymbals, triangle, side drum, tambourine, tam-tam, bass drum, celesta, 2 harps, and the traditional body of strings.

SYMPHONY NO. 3, G MINOR, OPUS 42

Roussel's career was as sober as his music. Although he studied music as a young man and showed great aptitude, he did not, for a long time, pursue it professionally. Instead he became (like Rimsky-Korsakoff) a naval officer and remained in that career until he was twenty-five. But musical friends pressed him to follow his manifest gift and by 1894 professional advice set his last doubts at rest. Two years later he became one of D'Indy's first pupils at the newly founded Schola Cantorum in Paris. He absorbed influences as far apart as César Franck and Stravinsky, slowly forging himself a strongly individual style. Even more slowly he came to be recognized as one of the leading composers of his day.

Maturity came with his ballet pantomime *Le festin de L'araignée* of 1913, perhaps his most famous work, and his opera-ballet *Padmavati,* composed in 1914–1918. Roussel's Third Symphony was commissioned by Serge Koussevitzky for the Boston Symphony and was first performed in Boston in 1930.

I. *Allegro vivo.* The brief, vigorous, almost pugnacious first movement presents us at the very start with two very characteristic phrases. The first is an aggressive, swinging rhythm that presently turns into an accompaniment figure:

Above this figure the violins and woodwinds fling out an exultant, expansive melodic line which, in its very different way, has as much impetus as its accompaniment:

After a slight relaxation of the driving tempo, a solo flute sings a quieter, even more lyric theme of wonderful, flowing grace. There is swift, brilliant climax, and the movement ends with a restatement of the opening thematic materials.

II. *Adagio.* Solo woodwinds introduce the long, flowing melody carried by strings over a gentle rocking accompaniment. The contained warmth of this melody rises to two big climaxes, each dying away quickly. The close is given to a solo violin which starts tenderly with the main melody, climbing slowly to the highest reach of the orchestra where it fades to silence.

III. *Vivace.* The dancelike theme of this movement borders on the boisterous. It starts in a carefree, popular vein, but its development is considerably more sophisticated.

IV. *Allegro con spirito.* Mercurial, sparkling little woodwind figures chase each other through the opening bars. Their rhythms are soon underlined by triangles, trumpets and horns. With a flash of brilliance, including a harp *glissando,* the strings all join the fray. Even with the full orchestral *tutti,* this finale sounds transparent: all light and incandescence right up to its final, flashing cadence.

The G-minor Symphony is scored for piccolo, 2 flutes, 2 oboes, English horn, 2 clarinets, bass clarinet, 2 bassoons, contrabassoon, 4 horns, 4 trumpets, 3 trombones, tuba, kettledrums, bass drum, side drum, tambourine, triangle, cymbals, tam-tam, celesta, 2 harps, and the usual strings.

Carl Ruggles

Born March 11, 1876, Marion, Massachusetts—died October 24, 1971, Bennington, Vermont

MEN AND MOUNTAINS

Carl Ruggles, who at his death had passed the patriarchal age of ninety-five, is one of the most uncompromisingly idealistic composers this country has produced. Never during the quarter-century of his most active composing career—roughly 1920 to 1945—never does he seem to have been swayed by fads or fashions, to have imitated the successes of other composers, or to have swerved from total honesty of expression or the most exacting standards of craftsmanship.

One result of the demands Ruggles made of himself and his art is that the total list of his works is small. He composed slowly and was given to extensive revision. He apparently destroyed or disavowed everything he composed before his forty-second year! This included an opera, *The Sunken Bell,* based on Gerhart Hauptmann's fairy-tale drama, *Die versunkene Glocke,* an allegory of an artist destroyed by his own superhuman aspirations! (Hauptmann's artist-hero is Heinrich, a bell-founder whose masterwork, a bell of great beauty, is lost in the depths of a lake while being transported to the church for which it was created. Thereafter Heinrich tries obsessively to replace the lost masterwork with a bell of such perfection that it will silence all other bells. The effort is foredoomed, and Heinrich finally embraces death as surcease from the torture of his self-set, unachievable goal.) But Ruggles was made of tougher fiber than his discarded operatic hero.

The earliest work he allowed to survive is a song, "Toys," composed when he was forty-three or forty-four! His *Angels,* for six muted trumpets, dates from 1921; *Portals,* from 1926 in its original version for thirteen solo strings (its revised version for string orchestra is dated 1929). His four *Evocations* for solo piano were composed over the decade 1934–1943. There are also four orchestral scores: *Men and Mountains* of 1926, *Sun-Treader* (1932), *Organum* (1945), and the straggler *Affirmations* of 1957.

Men and Mountains began as a three-movement work called *Men and Angels.* Each of the three movements of that finished composition was later revised to become a separate composition: *Sun-Treader, Angels,* and *Men and Mountains,* which in turn evolved into three movements entitled "Men," "Lilacs," and "Marching Mountains." The initial version of the new work was given its first performance on December 7, 1924, at a concert of the International Composers' Guild at Aeolian Hall in New York; Eugene Goossens conducted members of the State Symphony Orchestra. The score, published in *New Music,* October 1927, enlisted single woodwinds (piccolo, oboe, English horn, clarinet, bassoon), 2 horns, 2 trumpets, trombone, piano, cymbals and the traditional strings.

But there were other versions: one for chamber orchestra of 21 instruments and a revision for large orchestra involving not merely reinstrumentation, but large changes in the music itself. The latter revision had its first performance in New York on March 19, 1936. The score bears a quotation from William Blake: "Great things are done when men and mountains meet."

The day after the premiere, Lawrence Gilman (who was also the program annotator of the New York Philharmonic) wrote: "Mr. Ruggles is well fitted to set Blake to music. He is a natural mystic, a rhapsodist, a composer who sees visions and dreams, fantastic dreams. The wild, gigantic, tortured symbols of Blake's imagination, his riotous and untrammeled excursions in the world behind the heavens, are all of a piece with Mr. Ruggles' thinking. There is a touch of the apocalyptic, the fabulous, about his fantasies. He is the first unicorn to enter American music. He is the master of a strange, torrential and perturbing discourse."

I. *Men: Rhapsodic Proclamation for Horns and Orchestra.* Despite its brevity, this is a powerfully assertive movement with clearly sculpted polyphonic lines, clashing harmonies, syncopated rhythms and shifting meters.

II. *Lilacs.* The slow movement, although dissonant, has a grace in its profusion of melodic lines and individual clustering phrases which seems to fit the title. More important than the grace is the composer's deep feeling.

III. *Marching Mountains.* A powerful flourish sets the stage for a majestic march rhythm. Like more traditional marches, this one has a contrasting middle section in a gentler mood, after which the march stalks forth again. The sharply climactic conclusion could be a hint of the great happenings "when men and mountains meet."

In 1951 Ruggles again revised *Men and Mountains* for an orchestra consisting of piccolo, 2 flutes, 2 oboes, English horn, 2 clarinets, 2 bassoons, contrabassoon, 4 horns, 3 trumpets, 3 trombones, tuba, piano, kettledrums, cymbals, tenor drum, bass drum, and strings.

PORTALS

Charles Ruggles was a fierce perfectionist. He polished, honed, finished, refinished, corrected, revised, and re-revised his works with relentless, obsessive determination. As a result his considerable fame is based on a tiny list of works, a half dozen of them dating from twenty-five years of his most intense productivity.

His self-criticism was balanced by an Olympian self-confidence and leavened by a robust, often earthy sense of humor. One of the most printable of Ruggles anecdotes was told by his friend, the distinguished composer Henry Cowell, who visited him at the converted schoolhouse in Arlington, Vermont, where Ruggles spent the latter years of his life. One morning, when Cowell arrived, he found Ruggles "sitting at the old piano, singing a single tone at the top of his raucous composer's voice, and banging a single chord at intervals over and over. He refused to be interrupted in this pursuit, and after an hour or so, I insisted on knowing what the idea was. 'I'm trying over this damned chord,' said he, 'to see whether it still sounds superb after so many hearings.' 'Oh,' I said tritely, 'time will tell whether the chord has lasting value.' 'The hell with time!' Carl replied. 'I'll give this chord the test of time right now. If I still find I like it after trying it over several thousand times, it'll stand the test of time all right!' "

"One wonders," wrote Gilbert Chase, "which chord that was: perhaps the tremendous chord that concludes the coda of *Portals*—rising majestically and mysteriously as if in answer to the quotation from Walt Whitman [which Ruggles prefixed to his score], 'What are those of the known but to ascend and enter the unknown?' "

The characteristic opening phrase of *Portals* has a different kind of majesty, a more energetic striving, in its great jagged arch, which peaks over a range of two and a half octaves:*

* *This and the following musical example are copyright 1930 by Carl Ruggles, assigned to American Music Edition, New York, N.Y. © 1957 American Music Edition, New York, N.Y. International copyright secured. All rights reserved. Carl Fischer, Inc., sole selling agents. Used by permission of the publisher*

There follows instant, drastic contrast: a quiet, intimate, more gently expressive phrase for two violas alone. These two phrases are the two poles of the score.

Like most of Ruggles's surviving compositions, *Portals* is short: some four to five minutes. Both themes are developed and recapitulated in a form of two roughly corresponding halves. The opening phrase, for example, makes its return in the following intensified and expanded shape, vaulting this time over a more than three-octave range:

The violent contrasts of *Portals* are rounded off by a six-measure *coda* marked "Slow and Serene," a conclusion which Charles Seeger has called "one of the most exquisite pages in all modern music."

Camille Saint-Saëns

Born October 9, 1835, Paris—died December 16, 1921, Algiers

CONCERTO FOR CELLO AND ORCHESTRA, A MINOR, OPUS 33

A *Parisien de Paris*, as Parisian as you can be, Camille Saint-Saëns was born in the middle of that Latin Quarter, which had been a center of French wit and learning for seven centuries before he appeared on the scene. To his native tradition Saint-Saëns was to make generous contributions of his own as creator, catalyst, critic, organizer, protector, pedagogue, and finally as feared conservative.

French music is often praised for its "Classical" virtues of clarity, restraint, balance and elegance. Fortunately there is more to French tradition than these overpublicized traits. Indeed, Saint-Saëns was a leader in rescuing French instrumental music from its mid-century doldrums of elegance, balance, restraint and clarity, and in steering it back into the turbulent mainstream of European development.

The situation he set out to reform was odd. During his youth, roughly the middle third of the century, France had no living symphonic tradition. Berlioz's symphonic revolution in his *Fantastic Symphony, Harold in Italy*, etc., was never continued, not even by Berlioz himself. More and more the great Parisian public of the Second Empire was bored by serious music. To call a man a symphonist became almost an insult. Opera reigned supreme, and the great mid-century masterpiece was Gounod's *Faust*.

Saint-Saëns, with his restless intellect, looked beyond the borders of France, and his pride as a Frenchman was hurt. Aware of his country's glorious past and of his own astounding gifts, he felt a growing challenge. The turning point came with the military defeat of France at the hands of the upstart Prussia. The collapse of the Second Empire not only shocked the pride of the country, but acted as a spur to French artists and intellectual leaders. It seemed a summons for a rebirth of French culture.

Only a few months after the humiliating armistice, Saint-Saëns, with the backing of a surprisingly large group of people anxious to support a renewal of serious French music, founded the National Music Society. Over the next half-century, particularly during the years of Saint-Saëns's leadership, this became one of the most influential institutions in French musical life, encouraging the composition and sponsoring the performance of new works by César Franck, Chausson, Chabrier, d'Indy, Lalo, Lekeu, Duparc, Debussy and Ravel, as well as Saint-Saëns himself. Not only was French musical culture rejuvenated within France: the works of Saint-Saëns and his colleagues were increasingly admired and performed in other countries—so much so that by the beginning of the twentieth century France appeared to have taken over the leadership of the musical avant-garde, which for the past hundred years had been held by central Europeans.

One of Saint-Saëns's earliest contributions to the cause was his A-Minor Cello Concerto completed in 1872 and first performed on January 19, 1873, by the Paris Conservatory Orchestra with its distinguished first cellist, August Tolbecque, as soloist. Dedicated to Tolbecque, the Concerto is a modest work: engagingly unpretentious, yet far from frivolous and equally far from being academic.

From the very start, Saint-Saëns shows that he has solved the problem which has beset virtually every composer of cello concertos: the problem of making his low-pitched solo instrument easily audible against the sonorous background of an entire symphony orchestra. The Concerto is cast in three continuous movements so tightly knit that they sound almost like one.

I. *Allegro non troppo.* There is no orchestral introduction. Saint-Saëns begins in a more modern style: one sharp chord of the orchestra introduces the solo instrument in the downward sweeping, two-octave theme which is to dominate the score:

Gracefully and effectively conceived for the sonorities of the cello, this theme is repeated, not only in its original form, but with greater and greater variation, until sometimes all we can recognize of the original theme is its rolling triplet rhythm or the half-note rise and fall of its tailpiece. Gradually the rhythmic drive relaxes and we pass imperceptibly into the second movement.

II. *Allegretto con moto.* This movement is a delicate interlude based on a dancelike theme heard as if from a great distance, in the veiled tones of muted strings. Once the dance rhythm has been established, the solo cello enters alone, singing very softly, as if to itself:

Under the last, floating tone of this cello phrase, the orchestra resumes its delicate dance. There is a suggestion of a waltz, leading to a free cadenza for the cello alone and concluding with a series of rising trills for the solo instrument. As the movement subsides the solo instrument forms the connecting link to the *finale.*

III. *Allegro non troppo; Un peu moins vite.* The *finale* picks up the development of the Concerto's principal theme, culminating in vigorous echoes of its concluding half-tone rise and fall. The orchestral echoes are followed by a fourfold echo of the cello alone:

Notice how subtly this dying rise and fall prepares us for the rise-and-fall motive of the following melody:

Equally subtly and unobtrusively this motive is related to the rise and fall of the cello melody in the second movement! As the orchestra takes up this new melody, the soloist, for the first time in this modest Concerto, begins to develop more and more virtuoso brilliance, including swift scales, octaves, *arpeggio* passages and a dizzy ascent into the tonal stratosphere with precarious high harmonics. The tempo increases with the excitement of the music and the recall of other themes from the opening movement.

Saint-Saëns's A-minor Concerto is scored for 2 flutes, 2 oboes, 2 clarinets, 2 bassoons, 2 horns, 2 trumpets, kettledrums, and the traditional string choir.

CONCERTO FOR PIANO AND ORCHESTRA, NO. 2, G MINOR, OPUS 22

The idealistic Saint-Saëns, the crusading leader in the great rebirth of French music in the late nineteenth century, could also be a frivolous wit, as noted for his rapier repartee as for his slapstick clowning at convivial gatherings of music lovers. He was a distinguished man of the world, equally at home in the highest Parisian society, and in the most bohemian artistic circles. He was a brilliant, versatile composer with a many-faceted mind: he was a playwright, critic and essayist. And in addition to composing, he was a respected conductor and a polished pianist, who performed the solo parts in all five of his piano concertos at their premieres. His pianism seems to have mirrored his qualities as a composer (or vice versa). It was remarkable for its effortless technique, its clarity, elegance, infectious rhythm, and sparkling tone, but rarely attempted to overwhelm listeners with passionate emotion.

Saint-Saëns composed this Second Concerto in seventeen days during the spring of 1868, in response to the great pianist Anton Rubinstein, who wished to appear before the Parisian public in a new role as conductor. Saint-Saëns promised to compose a concerto for the occasion, with the result that Rubinstein conducted the premiere on May 13, 1868, at the Salle Pleyel, with Saint-Saëns as soloist. It is in the customary three movements.

I. *Andante sostenuto.* the first movement opens with an impressive cadenza, displaying the solo instrument alone with great splashing arpeggios and thundering chords before the orchestra enters. Almost immediately the soloist takes over again with the leisurely melodic opening theme. The solo part grows more and more brilliant as the themes are developed and recapitulated, leading to another cadenza for the soloist alone before the emphatic chords which round off the movement.

II. *Allegro scherzando.* This puckish dancelike *rondo* begins with a catchy refrain for the soloist, which is instantly imitated by the upper strings:

After each contrasting episode, the refrain reappears with an airy grace that grows more beguiling at each return.

III. *Presto.* The *finale* is pure quicksilver. Rhythmically it is a *tarantella,* so light and fast that one can hardly imagine it danced by human feet. It glitters, it sparkles, and if the soloist occasionally plunges down into the thundering depths of the instrument it is only to shoot upwards again with rocket-like *bravura.*

This Concerto calls for an orchestra consisting of 2 flutes, 2 oboes, 2 clarinets, 2 bassoons, 2 horns, 2 trumpets, harp, kettledrums, and the standard string choir.

CONCERTO FOR PIANO AND ORCHESTRA, NO. 4, C MINOR, OPUS 44

"In our nervous and tormented contemporary art, this music [of Saint-Saëns] stands out for its calm, its tranquil harmonies, its smooth modulations, its crystalline purity, its fluid style without jolts, and a certain Atticism. Even its Classical coldness feels good as a sort of reaction against the exaggerations, even the sincere exaggerations, of our new art. There are moments when one feels transported back to Mendelssohn, or even to Spontini and the school of Gluck." So wrote even the romantically minded Romain Rolland, the admirer of Richard Strauss, over half a century ago, praising the Gallic virtues of his countryman, Camille Saint-Saëns.

Saint-Saëns was an accomplished pianist and he played the solo parts of the premieres of all his five piano concertos. His playing seems to have mirrored his qualities as a composer: it was remarkable for its technical ease, its clarity, repose, elegance, and brilliance, but rarely attempted to project any overwhelming emotion.

The Fourth Piano Concerto in C minor was written in 1875, between two of Saint-Saëns's tone poems, *Danse macabre* and *La Jeunesse d'Hercule*. It is cast in two movements instead of the traditional three; each movement is subdivided into what is really two movements, so that the total effect is four.

I. *Allegro moderato, Andante.* Although it is not so marked, the opening section is a theme and three variations. The theme (which is also used in the *Allegro vivace* of the second movement) begins in the orchestra:

The first half of this theme (eight measures) is immediately repeated by the piano solo. The answering half of the theme is then played by the orchestra and likewise repeated by the soloist. The variations follow the same general pattern except that the concluding variations are a little freer in structure.

The *Andante* follows without pause, but has the character and form of an independent second movement in a slow A-flat major. Its most characteristic theme is a hymnlike passage in ethereal high woodwind color, with this leading phrase:

A more contrasting theme for the piano solo leads to a more pompous return of the hymnlike episode.

II. *Allegro vivace, Andante, Allegro.* The fast first section of this movement (really a scherzo section) is based on the opening theme of the first movement. The brief *Andante,* which serves as a bridge between the two fast sections of this movement, uses material from the *Andante* of the first movement. The final *Allegro* is a brilliant *rondo* in C major based on the following variant of the first *Andante:*

The episodes of this rondo-finale recall themes from earlier parts of the Concerto, which combine with fragments of the *Rondo* refrain in a contrapuntal climax to this strongly integrated work.

Saint-Saëns scored his Fourth Piano Concerto for 2 flutes, 2 oboes, 2 clarinets, 2 bassoons, 2 horns, 2 trumpets, 3 trombones, kettledrums, and the usual string choir.

INTRODUCTION AND RONDO CAPRICCIOSO FOR VIOLIN AND ORCHESTRA, OPUS 28

Saint-Saëns's *Introduction and Rondo Capriccioso* is perhaps the most famous of his lighter compositions. Composed in 1870, for Pablo Sarasate, then a young virtuoso near the beginning of his career, it was given its first performance by Sarasate in Paris. It is an immediately appealing work in which brilliance alternates with melancholy and both are continuously elegant. In the slow introduction, marked *Andante (malinconico),* the rhapsodic violin solo is given an accompaniment of pizzicato strings, suggesting a guitar. The lively rondo opens with the principal refrain:

This lilting refrain alternates with brilliant episodes designed to display the virtuosity of the soloist. The score concludes in a still livelier coda with flashing scales and arpeggios for the solo violin.

The modest accompanying orchestra calls for 2 flutes, 2 oboes, 2 clarinets, 2 bassoons, 2 horns, 2 trumpets, kettledrums, and the customary strings.

LE ROUET D'OMPHALE (OMPHALE'S SPINNING WHEEL)

The prodigious M. Saint-Saëns, who was an infant prodigy more precocious than Mozart and who remained active far into his eighties, was one of the driving forces in the rejuvenation of French music after the disaster of the Franco-Prussian War. His versatility as a performer, composer and organizer was dazzling, and he was in touch with all the current trends of music, although he did not sympathize with them all.

He did not disapprove of the new trend toward descriptive, program music. He commented quite logically: "Is the music in itself good or bad? That's the whole question. Aside from that it will be neither better nor worse for being music with a program. . . . Descriptive music is interesting whether one knows the subject or not, but its charm is greater when to the purely musical pleasure is added the pleasure of the imagination following, *without hesitation,* a predetermined path . . . all the faculties of the mind are brought into play at the same point."

It would have been surprising, therefore, if Saint-Saëns had not tried his hand at the recent musical invention of the symphonic poem or tone poem. *Le Rouet d'Omphale,* his first symphonic poem, had originally been a descriptive piano piece, composed in 1871. Revised and orchestrated, it was first performed in Paris on April 14, 1872.

Omphale was a Lydian queen to whom Zeus sent Hercules as a slave to expiate a murder he had committed. There are various versions of this story, both Greek and Roman. The score bears the following introductory sentences: "The subject of this symphonic poem is feminine seduction, the triumphant battle of weakness against strength. The spinning wheel is only a pretext, chosen only because of its rhythm and the general character of the piece.

"People who may be interested in searching out details may find at the letter 'J' Hercules groaning in the bondage from which he is unable to free himself [a heavy phrase given to double basses, cellos, violas in octaves with contrabassoon, bassoons and trombone]:

and at the letter 'L,' Omphale mocking the vain efforts of the hero [a lighthearted phrase for solo oboe, accompanied only by two soft clarinets]":

One may be permitted to wonder whether Omphale gives up her mocking in the end as the spinning wheel slows down to silence.

Le rouet d'Omphale is scored for piccolo, 2 flutes, 2 oboes, 2 clarinets, 2 bassoons, contrabassoon, 4 horns, 2 trumpets, 3 trombones, kettledrums, cymbal, triangle, bass drum, harp, and the traditional strings.

SYMPHONY NO. 3, C MINOR, OPUS 78

We often praise Saint-Saëns for his "Classical" virtues of clarity, restraint, balance, elegance—all traditionally associated with France. But fortunately there is more to the art of Camille Saint-Saëns. Indeed, it was primarily Saint-Saëns who initiated the rescue of French instrumental music from its Second Empire fetish of elegance, from its fear of originality (which had relegated Berlioz to the role of a musical eccentric), its fear of strong emotion as a bottomless pit. Saint-Saëns helped lead French instrumental music back from the musical backwaters into the mainstream of European development.

This mainstream was basically a Romantic one, so it is no accident that Saint-Saëns's Third Symphony, his most popular and probably his greatest work, was dedicated "to the memory of Franz Liszt," a Romantic firebrand, one of the most revolutionary spirits of the century, who became (partly through Saint-Saëns) a liberating and fertilizing influence on French music. Before the end of the century, not only had French musical life been rejuvenated, but the works of Saint-Saëns and his colleagues were increasingly admired in other countries—so that by 1900 France had taken over the international leadership of the musical *avant garde*.

Saint-Saëns Third Symphony was commissioned by the London Philharmonic Society and was first performed by that orchestra on May 19, 1886 with Saint-Saëns conducting. For all its traditionally French and supposedly Classical or Neo-Classical qualities, this is a Romantic work: Romantic specifically in its formal integration of the traditional four movements into two, in its thematic interconnections from movement to movement, in its technique of thematic transformation, in its colorful orchestration, in the yearning tensions of its melodies and harmony, and in stylistic details which recall Schubert, Liszt, and even Wagner.

Saint-Saëns himself pointed out that the Symphony "embraces in principle the four traditional movements, but the first, halted in its development, serves as the introduction to the *Adagio*, and the *Scherzo* is left by the same process to lead to the finale."

I. *Adagio, Allegro moderato, Poco adagio.* The slow introduction, with a woodwind theme to be developed in the *Allegro moderato*, suggests the mournful tensions of the introduction to Act III of Wagner's *Tristan and Isolde*. The *Allegro moderato* begins with whispering strings which recall the opening of Schubert's "Unfinished" Symphony. But the resemblance is not uncomfortably close. This theme returns in many transformations throughout the Symphony:

Over this figure we soon hear a quicker version of the woodwind theme from the Introduction.

"After a short development, in which the two themes are presented simultaneously," wrote Saint-Saëns in a note for the London premiere "the [first] theme reappears in a characteristic form, for full orchestra, but only for a short time. A second transformation of the initial theme includes now and then the plaintive notes of the Introduction. Varied episodes bring gradual calm and thus prepare the *Adagio* in B-flat. The extremely peaceful and contemplative theme is given to the violins, violas, and violoncellos, which are supported by organ chords:

This first movement ends in a Coda of mystical character, in which we hear alternately the chords of D flat and E minor."

II. *Allegro moderato; Presto; Maestoso.* The second movement opens with an aggressive refrain for strings and kettledrums. This is followed by still another rhythmic transformation of the first theme of the first movement. Into this, says the composer, "there enters a fantastic spirit that is frankly disclosed in the *Presto.* Here arpeggios and scales, swift as lighting, on the piano, are accompanied by the syncopated rhythm of the orchestra, and each time they are in a different tonality (F, E, E flat, G). The repetition of the *Allegro moderato* is followed by a second *Presto;* but scarcely has it begun before a new theme is heard, grave, austere (trombone, tuba, [cellos], and double basses), strongly contrasted with the fantastic music:

There is a struggle for the mastery, and this struggle ends in the defeat of the restless, diabolical element. The new phrase rises to orchestral heights, and rests there as in the blue of a clear sky.

"After a vague reminiscence of the initial theme of the first movement, a *Maestoso* in C major announces the approaching triumph of the calm and lofty thought. The initial theme of the first movement, wholly transformed, is now presented by divided strings and the pianoforte (four hands), and repeated by the organ with the full strength of the orchestra. A brilliant Coda, in which the initial theme by a last transformation, takes the form of a violin figure, ends the work."

Saint-Saëns's Third Symphony is scored for piccolo, 3 flutes, 2 oboes, English horn, 2 clarinets, bass clarinet, 2 bassoons, contrabassoon, 4 horns, 3 trumpets, 3 trombones, tuba, triangle, cymbals, bass drum, kettledrums, organ, piano (4 hands), and the customary string choir.

Arnold Schoenberg

Born September 13, 1874, Vienna—died July 13, 1951, Los Angeles

CONCERTO FOR PIANO AND ORCHESTRA, OPUS 42

Is it possible that this most controversial musician of our century was at heart a conservative? There were and are many admirers who believe Schoenberg was just that. And Schoenberg himself in one of his own essays, "*On revient toujours*" ("One always returns [to one's first loves]") has confessed to a lasting nostalgia for his early Romantic style and to having indulged this nostalgia from time to time even in his mature years. "For me," he added, "these stylistic differences are of no great importance. I do not know which of my compositions are better; I like them all, for I liked them when I was writing them."

Such deviations from the straight-and-narrow twelve-tone path seemed to certain disciples who were more orthodox than the master himself, a betrayal of his revolutionary ideals. They decided that the master had succumbed to the fleshpots of America. (Schoenberg had emigrated to the United States in 1933.)

But the fleshpots really are too simple an explanation. Schoenberg was not that simple a man. Even the sunny climate of California, where he finally settled, cannot fully account for a certain mellowing of Schoenberg's style in this Concerto.

Whatever the reasons (presumably they were many) and whatever the special cases, Schoenberg did compose, soon after his arrival in this country, works which admitted traditional tonality and works, like the Piano Concerto, in which some critics believed they found clear traces of tonality. (It is only fair to add that Schoenberg himself wrote, almost indignantly, to René Leibowitz in 1947: "I do not know where in the Piano Concerto a tonality is expressed.")

Nevertheless, for Schoenberg this Piano Concerto has an oddly Brahmsian sound. Which means, among other things, that it is easier for the average music-lover to grasp, more familiar in its melodic, its rhythmic and even in its harmonic style than the works of his middle years. The Piano Concerto belongs to the last decade of his iconoclastic career and for Schoenberg it is not merely conservative—it is positively archaic.

We know, of course, that such archaic trends are a striking feature of the late styles of many great masters. Mozart, Haydn, and Brahms among them. *"Torniamo a l'antico,"* exclaimed Verdi in his late years, *"sarà un progresso."* And he ended his operatic career with a fugue (the *"Tutto nel mondo"* finale of his *Falstaff*). None of this is surprising in Mozart, Haydn, Beethoven, Brahms or Verdi. But in Schoenberg? In this fearsome revolutionary, this high priest of chaos (otherwise known as "atonality"), in this subversive *diabolus in musica:* this supposed inventor of the "twelve-tone system"?

The traces of Brahms in Schoenberg's Piano Concerto are less surprising when we recall that Schoenberg grew up in a Vienna where Brahms was worshiped, that Schoenberg himself was among the worshipers, and where Brahms was still alive and active until Schoenberg's twenty-third year. Most of us tend to think of Schoenberg as belonging to the Wagnerian camp, and it is true that the Brahms and Wagner camps were mortal enemies. But again, Schoenberg was not that simple a man.

The immediate stimulus for the composition of Schoenberg's Piano Concerto appears to have come from an improbable source: his onetime pupil Oscar Levant. In his *Memoirs of an Amnesiac,* Levant wrote that he asked Schoenberg for "a slight piano piece." Levant apparently made a down payment and reported that Schoenberg was extremely pleased: "When I returned to New York [continued Levant] there was correspondence, and suddenly this small piano piece burned feverishly in Schoenberg's mind and he decided to write a piano concerto. He sent me some early sketches and it is possible that in the main row of tones my name or initials were involved. However, I wasn't prepared for a piano concerto and in the meantime Hans (sic) Eisler assumed the role of negotiator for Schoenberg. Among other things, the fee grew to a vast sum for which, as the dedicatee, I was promised immortality."

For a variety of reasons Levant eventually withdrew from the agreement. He mentioned meeting with Schoenberg several years afterward when, "in a spasm of goodwill [Levant] said, 'I owe you some money.' [Schoenberg] nodded in agreement and I gave him a check. He was very cheerful about the whole thing. I didn't really owe him any money—it was just an excuse to ameliorate the whole situation."

According to Schoenberg's own notes on his sketches, he began work on the Concerto on July 5, 1942. The completed full score is dated December 26, 1942. The world premiere was presented on a broadcast of the NBC Symphony Orchestra conducted by Leopold Stokowski with Eduard Steuermann as soloist.

The Concerto is in four movements which are played continuously. In a letter to Oscar Levant, Schoenberg gave a capsule characterization of the movements as follows:

Life was so easy
suddenly hatred broke out (*Presto* ♩ = 72)
a grave situation was created *(Adagio)*
But life goes on *(Rondo)*

Like most Schoenberg works composed since 1923, the Piano Concerto is based on a row (or "set" or "series") comprising all twelve notes of the chromatic scale arranged in a special sequence. Such a row is often difficult to identify by ear—even for a professional musician. This Piano Concerto, however, is an exception in that Schoenberg uses his basic tone row as a theme, i.e., as an identifiable melody. We hear it at the very beginning of the first movement: a melody which returns frequently in the course of the Concerto, often altered, sometimes fragmented and sometimes in its original form.

I. *Andante.* The basic melody, which opens the work, is played first by the piano without orchestral accompaniment:

This basic melody or theme includes a complete twelve-tone row or set. Schoenberg does not number the tones in his score, but the numbers are supplied here to show how Schoenberg has incorporated the row in his melody. Certain of the notes are given no number: these are notes which are repeated. The repetition of the notes between numbers eleven and twelve is particularly "unorthodox" in terms of strict twelve-tone theory, but Schoenberg was following his artistic impulse rather than rigid rules. The basic melody continues, still in the right-hand part of the piano soloist, in three successive transformations: first backwards and upside-down, then backwards and, finally, in its simple upside-down form.

After the presentation of the row in these four basic forms by the pianist, it is taken over by the first violins, once more in all four basic versions, but now with the piano supplying a secondary counter-melody.

Thus far the accent has been on melody, but now the melody is broken up into smaller fragments starting with the piano and continuing in various choirs of the orchestra. As this development continues, the opening melody as printed above is brought back by the first violins playing very softly with mutes. The movement concludes with a sharp climax of trilling French horn, piano, cymbals and woodwinds. The *scherzo* continues at once without pause.

II. *Molto allegro.* The second movement has all the characteristics of a traditional *scherzo,* although Schoenberg does not call it a *scherzo.* The main theme is an upward leaping figure heard first in the double basses, and answered by a curious descending figure in the unusual orchestral color of violas and cellos played with the wooden back of the bow (*col legno*) and combined with snare drum, xylophone and muted French horn.

There is a contrasting middle section *Poco tranquillo,* after which the original *scherzo* material returns. Like the first movement, the *scherzo* concludes with a loud climax and a sudden cutoff, leading without pause into the following movement.

III. *Adagio.* The slow movement restores the emphasis on melody, but contrapuntal melody, that is to say, several lyric strands being woven together simultaneously. This contrapuntal section explodes suddenly into a piano cadenza, which is so carefully organized that it constitutes almost an entire contrasting middle section, after which the principal theme of the *Adagio* returns. This movement, like its predecessors, concludes with a loud climax and sudden cutoff. But this time there is a bridge to the following movement in the form of a cadenza-like piano solo. The finale follows without pause.

IV. *Giocoso (moderato).* The final movement is a lively *rondo* in the tradition of Mozart and Haydn—as far as the form is concerned. That is to say, a refrain is announced at once by the piano soloist as follows:

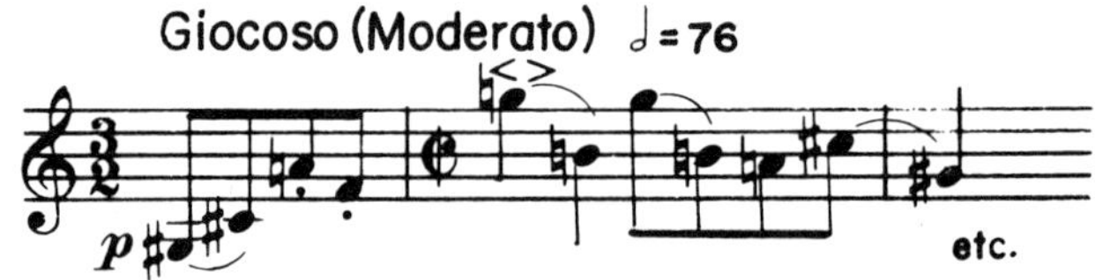

After a brief contrasting episode, consisting of various fragments of the tone row, the rondo-refrain returns, this time in the first violins. A second and rather longer contrasting episode recalls the themes from both the slow movement and the opening movement of the Concerto. This leads to one more segment of the rondo-refrain, this time in the low range of the piano solo. The Concerto is rounded off by a return to the opening melody of the first movement presented as it was there in all four basic forms, but orchestrated now in a style of triumphant majesty. After this emphasis on the melodic unity of the entire score, there is a brilliant closing *stretto,* recalling fragments from the finale and concluding with a motto-like quotation of the first five tones of the rondo-refrain.

The Schoenberg Piano Concerto is scored for piccolo, 2 flutes, 2 oboes, 2 clarinets, 2 bassoons, 4 horns, 2 trumpets, 3 trombones, tuba, kettledrums, bells, gong, cymbal, xylophone, piano, bass drum, snare drum and the traditional string choir.

FIVE PIECES FOR ORCHESTRA, OPUS 16

The strange new world of beauty opened up to us in the first decade of our century by Arnold Schoenberg's *Five Pieces for Orchestra* no longer seems quite so strange. But it does seem more beautiful. And in addition to their beauty, we now know, these *Five Pieces* were possibly the most influential turning point in the orchestral music of the first half of our century—more influential in the long run than even such a work of genius as Stravinsky's *Sacre du printemps.* For the *Sacre,* with all its elemental drive, its intoxication, and brilliance, was in many ways the end of an evolution, rather than a beginning.

Schoenberg's influence on the other hand, seemed more like a buried, undetonated bomb. Musicians all knew the bomb was there and it caused much agitated controversy. But as the years rolled past, many concluded that it was not, after all, a force to be taken too seriously by anyone except Schoenberg's disciples.

Then suddenly, after World War II, the bomb did explode. Suddenly there seemed to be hardly a serious young composer this side of the Iron Curtain who escaped or wanted to escape the repercussions of Schoenberg's style and techniques. Schoenberg and his two chief disciples, Anton Webern and Alban Berg, displayed an unsuspected fascination for a whole new generation of audiences and professional musicians—even those *east* of the curtain. Once more, as in the 1920s, Berg's *Wozzeck* began the rounds of European opera houses, reaching Paris, London, and finally the venerable Metropolitan Opera in a production which (to everyone's surprise) proved extremely popular. As to Webern, the conductor-critic Robert Craft could claim with justification that a majority of the youngest Western European composers at midcentury considered their time to be "the age of Webern."

It is not recorded that Hindemith felt any belated longing to become a disciple of Schoenberg or Webern. But the elderly Igor Stravinsky, long considered the opposite musical pole to Schoenberg, incorporated a number of characteristic devices of Schoenberg and Webern into his own style and went out of his way to pay glowing public tribute to the genius of both composers.

This belated triumph of Schoenberg's influence paralleled the post-World War II resurgence of Expressionism—a movement had first taken shape in the visual and literary arts at the very time when Schoenberg was shaping his revolutionary musical style.

What wild and fruitful years those were! In 1905 the "Wild Men" or Fauves held their first big exhibit in Paris. In 1906 the painters of *Die Brücke* held their first exhibit in the showroom of a Dresden lamp factory. In 1907 Picasso painted his savage masterpiece *Les Demoiselles d'Avignon,* to which the whole cubist movement is sometimes traced. In 1908 Schoenberg broke away from traditional tonality with his *Three Pieces for Piano,* Opus 11, and his orchestral *Five Pieces.* The following year, 1909, Webern composed his *Six Pieces for Orchestra* in Vienna, Stravinsky's *Petrouchka* was given its premiere in Paris by Diaghilev's Russian Ballets, and in Munich a New Artist Association was founded, out of which was to grow the famous *Blauer Reiter* group. Schoenberg was so taken by the *Blauer Reiter* painters that he joined them and exhibited his own paintings at their first show in 1911, along with such men as Wassily Kandinsky, Franz Marc, and Henri Rousseau. The following year,

1912, Schoenberg's *Five Pieces* were given their world premiere by Sir Henry Wood at a London Promenade Concert.

Today it is amazing how Romantic these *Five Pieces* sound in the subtle blends of orchestral color, which Schoenberg handled with such consummate, loving skill. And they are palpably mood music, in the best nineteenth-century Romantic tradition. At the world premiere in London, in 1912, the individual movements had no title. But for the repetition there in 1914, the program annotator, Mrs. Rosa Newmarch, convinced Schoenberg, who had come to London to conduct the 1914 performance himself to name the movements. He christened them *"Vorgefühle," "Vergangenes," "Der wechselnde Akkord," "Peripetie,"* and *"Das obligate Rezitativ,"* (which have been translated as "Premonitions," "Yesteryears," "The Changing Chord," "Peripetia," and "The Obligatory Recitative.") Subsequently he altered "The Changing Chord" to the more suggestive title "Summer Morning by a Lake (Colors)."

How difficult this music still seemed despite the new subtitles may be gauged by Ernest Newman's friendly review in *The Musical Times* confessing he had not the foggiest understanding of the music, although it is obvious from the way he wrote that he had studied the score in advance. Indeed, Newman suspected that the composer was at that time "perhaps the only man in the world who knows what the music is intended to suggest." The impression of the work on Mr. Newman's sympathetic ears "was rather like the experience we sometimes have with the telephone, with an odd minute or two of lucid conversation coming out of a blur of irrelevant noise, as a train runs into the murk and reek of a tunnel and out into the sunlight again."

Telephone conversations tend to be clearer nowadays, and so does much of the music that once seemed so chaotic. In 1949 Schoenberg revised the orchestration of the *Five Pieces* for what he called a "normal-sized orchestra."

I. *Premonitions* is based on the following theme played immediately at the start by muted cellos and then by the clarinet:*

There is scarcely a measure of the movement which is not derived in some way from this basic theme. In broad form the movement consists of an introduction developing the basic theme in free rhapsodic fashion, followed by an elaborate contrapuntal development starting in free fugal style and culminating in some of the most learned devices of *stretto,* augmentation and so on, all used to heighten the expressive tension of the climax.

II. *Yesteryears.* This pensive, lyric movement is based on a motto-like theme of only five notes, announced at the very start by a single muted cello.

* *Musical example copyright 1952 by C. F. Peters Corporation. Reprinted by permission.*

As in the first movement, the new listener will do well not to try to follow the contrapuntal complexities, but listen instead for the often quite exquisite combinations of tone color, the simpler melodic lines and their rich harmonic underpinnings.

III. *Summer Morning by a Lake (Colors).* This movement is almost entirely mood evoked by slowly shifting harmonic and instrumental color. There are virtually no themes, melodies, or counterpoint in the traditional sense.

IV. *Peripetia.* It is not absolutely clear whether Schoenberg used the word here in its classical Greek meaning of a reversal of fortune, or in the more casual German usage of *Peripetie* meaning simply denouement (of a plot). In any case, the music is highly dramatic with sudden fluctuations of tempo, texture and mood, rising to a sharp final climax.

V. *The Obligatory Recitative.* What Schoenberg hoped to suggest by this title is not clear since the movement seems to bear no relation at all to any familiar style of recitative. However, in a purely subjective sense, the music does seem to have a wonderfully "speaking" quality of expressiveness, and this may be what the composer had in mind. The closing measures are of a particularly affecting intimacy in a delicate chamber-music style. Nowadays the *Five Pieces* are often heard in Schoenberg's reduced 1949 version "for normal-sized orchestra" of 2 piccolos, 3 flutes, 2 oboes, English horn, E-flat clarinet, 2 clarinets in A, bass clarinet, 2 bassoons, contrabassoon, 4 horns, 3 trumpets, 3 trombones, tuba, kettledrums, xylophone, gong, cymbals (one of which has to be played with a cello bow *tremolando* across the rim), bass drum, triangle, harp, celesta, and the traditional strings.

PELLEAS AND MELISANDE, SYMPHONIC POEM, OPUS 5

Schoenberg was twenty-eight when he composed this passionate, sensuous music. Although he was born and trained (largely self-trained) in Vienna, his *Pelleas and Melisande* was composed in Berlin. The reason for Schoenberg's brief move to Berlin was simple: he had difficulty earning a living in conservative Vienna. Berlin seemed the livelier and professionally more promising of the two cities, especially since Schoenberg's first published work, his Romantic string sextet *Verklärte Nacht,* Opus 4, had been issued by a Berlin publisher. When Schoenberg was offered the position of conductor for the Berlin Ueberbrettl (founded in 1900 in the Buntes Theater by Ernst von Wolzogen), he accepted.

In December 1901 he moved to Berlin. Wolzogen's Ueberbrettl was a new departure, an attempt to launch what we might call a pop-art musical theater, in which the song texts were provided by leading avant-garde poets and playwrights such as Richard Dehmel, Frank Wedekind and Wolzogen himself. The music was largely by composers whose fame has not lasted. But Schoenberg also composed the scores of seven *Brettllieder* (which he never published). He also arranged other men's music in addition to conducting. But the Ueberbrettl productions were too slight to satisfy Schoenberg's artistic aspirations and too unremunerative to provide an adequate living.

Fortunately Richard Strauss, who had taken an intense interest in the music of his younger colleague, was able to help practically as well as artistically. Financially he helped by recommending Schoenberg for the position of composition teacher at one of Berlin's leading music schools, the Stern Conservatory, and by arranging to have a substantial stipend of the Liszt Fellowship (administered by the Allgemeine Deutsche Musikverein) awarded to Schoenberg in 1902. Artistically Strauss provided stimulus by pointing out Maeterlinck's drama *Pelléas et Mélisande* as a potential subject for an opera. Schoenberg gave long and serious thought to the opera project, but in the end decided to make it a symphonic poem instead.

It seems incredible, but when Schoenberg began his symphonic poem in July 1902, he was unaware that in the meantime (April 30, 1902) Debussy had *already* produced his revolutionary opera *Pelléas et Mélisande* at the Opéra-Comique in Paris. (Fauré's incidental music to the Maeterlinck drama had been performed four years earlier; that of Sibelius was to come in 1905.) Schoenberg composed his large and complex score in a mere six months, completing it by February 28, 1903.

"I had first planned to convert *Pelleas and Melisande* into an opera," wrote Schoenberg many years later in a foreword to a broadcast recording of the tone poem, "but I gave up this plan, though I did not know that Debussy was working on his opera at the same time. I still regret that I did not carry out my initial intention. It would have differed from Debussy's. I might have missed the wonderful perfume of the poem; but I might have made my characters more singing.

"On the other hand, the symphonic poem helped me, in that it taught me to express moods and characters in precisely formulated units, a technique which an opera would perhaps not have promoted so well. Thus my fate evidently guided me with great foresight."

In July 1903 Schoenberg returned to Vienna, where he conducted the first performance of his *Pelleas and Melisande* on January 26, 1905. The reception was mixed. What Schoenberg remembered in later years was the passion his score aroused. "The first performance . . . under my own direction, provoked great riots among the audience and even the critics. Reviews were unusually violent and one of the critics suggested putting me in an asylum and keeping music paper out of my reach. Only six years later, under Oscar Fried's direction, it became a great success, and since that time has not caused the anger of the audience." The first performance in the United States was presented by the New York Philharmonic under the direction of Josef Stransky on November 18, 1915.

Pelleas and Melisande is Schoenberg's only symphonic poem. In form it resembles a four-movement symphony, the movements being performed without interruption. It is an astounding achievement in that Schoenberg was able to reconcile Maeterlinck's dramatic form with the traditional symphonic cycle. "I tried to mirror every detail of [the drama], with only a few omissions and slight changes of the order of the scenes. Perhaps, as frequently happens in music, there is more space devoted to the love scenes." The atmosphere is redolent of the starlit garden where Wagner's Tristan and Isolde hold their tryst.

It is clear that what attracted Schoenberg in Maeterlinck's tragedy was its parallel to *Tristan and Isolde* with its central theme of death-bringing love. The fact that Schoenberg's motive of fate or doom plays as large a role in his music as Wagner's death motives do in *Tristan and Isolde* bears this out. Admirers of Wagner will hear many other reminiscences of his *Tristan and Isolde,* though they are almost never mere imitations. One striking aspect of Schoenberg's score is the great melodic warmth of the music associated with Melisande's jealous husband Golaud.

The four movements of Schoenberg's tone poem correspond to: I. the exposition of the drama (Golaud's discovery of Melisande in the forest, her first meeting with Pelleas and her growing love for him); II. the growth of their mutual passion and Golaud's suspicions (the scenes at the well, the castle tower and the subterranean vaults); III. the farewell and love scene of Pelleas and Melisande; IV. the death of Melisande.

I. Schoenberg's exposition begins with a slow introduction, corresponding to Maeterlinck's opening scene in the forest where Prince Golaud discovers Melisande weeping by the side of a pool. Almost at once we hear (in the dark color of the bass clarinet) the brief Fate motive which will recur in many guises throughout the score:*

Against the shadowy background of forest music the plaintive motive of Melisande is outlined by a solo oboe:

Schoenberg makes sure that we shall remember the Melisande motive by repeating and developing it immediately in a richly imitative passage where almost every instrument of the orchestra seems to take up the theme. Before Melisande's theme has died away we hear a hint of the more elaborate motive that will characterize Golaud.

The full-fledged Golaud theme makes its first appearance at the beginning

* *This and the following musical examples from this composition are copyright 1912 by Universal Edition. Renewed 1939. Used by permission of Belmont Music Publishers.*

of the first movement proper. It is a warmly developed complex theme in which the melody of Golaud is extended by a melodic fragment associated with the wedding ring, suggesting, perhaps, the personification of Golaud as a loving husband:

The idea of the marriage is further suggested by combining the Melisande theme in the violins and the Golaud melody in the cello. The combined melodies are interrupted abruptly by a roll of the kettledrums and an ugly eruption of the Fate motive in the heavy brass leading to a sharp climax in which the Wedding Ring motive is blared forth by six horns while the highest woodwinds seem to shriek the theme of Fate.

A sudden change of mood introduces the theme of Pelleas, which Schoenberg describes as "youthful and knightly" in character. It begins in the muted brilliance of a trumpet solo:

The Pelleas theme, which is as long and complex as the Golaud theme, concludes with a vaulting, yearning melody sung by almost the entire string section. The principal themes of this exposition are rounded out by an ecstatically rising melody heard first in a solo clarinet and continued far up over the treble staff by a solo violin; this is the motive of the Awakening of Melisande's Love:

II. The action of the drama is carried forward in a second movement corresponding roughly to the *scherzo* of a symphony. It begins with the scene between Pelleas and Melisande by the well, where Melisande is playing with her wedding ring, throwing it up over the water and catching it in her hand. Lightly fluttering flutes and other high woodwinds suggest the glitter of the water and the bright sunlight of the scene. The motive of the Wedding Ring plays an important part here as does the motive of Pelleas. Schoenberg adds a note to the scene which Maeterlinck was obliged to depict in two successive scenes. The wedding ring slips through Melisande's fingers and falls into the well. At the exact same moment (we learn in the following scene of the drama) Golaud, who was riding through the forest, was thrown from his horse as it shied at some unknown terror. As a composer, Schoenberg is able to combine the two ideas of the ride through the forest and Melisande's dangerous game with her wedding ring. The two come to a simultaneous climax as a heavy distorted version of the Golaud theme tumbles downward in the trombones and tuba, punctuated by savage blows of the kettledrums.

The musical scene changes to a description of the evening when Melisande sits at the window of her tower combing her long golden hair as Pelleas passes. Several simultaneous transformations of the Melisande motive combine with the theme of Pelleas (in a solo cello) and the theme of the Awakening of Melisande's Love in a solo clarinet. The glamour of the moment is further suggested by great splashes of harp tone and tremolos of the high strings. The scene comes to an abrupt end with a motive associated with Golaud's jealousy.

The second movement concludes with the visit of Golaud and Pelleas to the dank vaults beneath the castle. In Schoenberg's words: "When Golaud leads Pelleas to the frightening subterranean tombs, a musical sound is produced which is remarkable in many respects; especially, because here, for the first time in musical literature, is used a hitherto unknown effect: a *glissando* of the trombones." A short transition leads into the third movement which follows without pause.

III. The entire third movement, corresponding to the slow movement of a symphony, is taken up with the night scene in the park. The farewell of Pelleas soon develops into a love duet and concludes with Golaud's murder of Pelleas and wounding of Melisande. The long melody given to muted first violins depicting the first open confession of love between Pelleas and Melisande is new, yet it seems mysteriously related to the theme of Golaud. It is one of the paradoxes of this fascinating work that the beautiful theme of Golaud is not only the most prominent melody in the score but it seems to permeate the entire love scene of Pelleas and Melisande. The love music which of course also includes the motives of Pelleas and Melisande comes to its tragic conclusion with another violent explosion of the Fate motive combined with a broken fragment of the Wedding Ring theme. As the music dies away, we hear a symbolically broken version of the Pelleas theme.

IV. The conclusion of the symphonic poem corresponds to the finale of a four-movement symphony and the final act of Maeterlinck's drama. The scene of Melisande's death is based on a long pedal point in the lowest instruments of the orchestra over which long descending lines of the woodwinds grow softer and softer. At last the theme of the Awakening of Melisande's Love rises slowly upward in the ethereal tones of a solo violin and seems to melt into thin air. A lamenting epilogue brings back the theme of Melisande, but it is the warm melody of Golaud which dominates the final pages and permeates even the sad final cadence.

Schoenberg's score calls for a large and varied orchestra: 2 piccolos, 3 flutes, 3 oboes, 2 English horns, E-flat clarinet, 3 clarinets in A and B flat, 2 bass clarinets, 3 bassoons, contrabassoon, 8 horns, 4 trumpets, 5 trombones, tuba, 2 harps, kettledrums, bass drum, large snare drum, gong, cymbals, triangle, glockenspiel, 16 first and 16 second violins, 12 violas, 12 cellos, and 8 string basses.

A SURVIVOR FROM WARSAW, OPUS 46

Schoenberg's *A Survivor From Warsaw* is based in part on personal experiences described to him by survivors of the Nazi battle of extermination in the ghetto of Warsaw. Schoenberg himself wrote the text in English (except for the few German lines of the Nazi sergeant, and the Hebrew hymn *"Sh'má Yisroel,"* with which the work concludes). The music is based on a twelve-tone row, which also serves as a symbol—as an old-fashioned theme—emphasizing the increasingly religious side of Schoenberg's nature and of his art.

Composed in fulfillment of a commission from the Koussevitzky Music Foundation, *A Survivor from Warsaw* was completed on September 23, 1947. The world premiere was presented by the Albuquerque, New Mexico, Civic Symphony Orchestra under the direction of Kurt Frederick, on November 4, 1948.

As in that rare form of theme and variations, in which the variations are heard first and the theme on which they are based is revealed only in conclusion, Schoenberg reveals the basic form of his row only at the last, where it supplies the opening melody of the Hebrew hymn. Virtually everything that precedes this, is derived in one way or another from the basic philosophical-musical concept of the hymn. Like the subtle interrelations of assonance, rhyme, and metaphor in poetry, the often hidden connections among the several segments of Schoenberg's score undoubtedly contribute (at least on an unconscious level) to the powerful effect it can have on the receptive listener.

The opening trumpet figure, like four notes of a distorted fanfare, and its mirror-echo in the second trumpet, are both derived from the first four notes of the basic row, which are also the first four pitches of the Hebrew hymn:*

* *This and the following musical examples from this composition are copyright 1949 by Boelke-Bomart, Inc. Used by permission of Associated Music Publishers, Inc.*

These could be taken to suggest the evil reveille with which the drama begins. Of other thematic connections it must suffice here to mention two. During the first segment of text, when the narrator mentions "the old prayer they had neglected for so many years—the forgotten creed," the French horn intones very softly an anticipation of the final hymn:

In the fourth segment of the text at the words: " . . . hard, so hard that I could not help falling down," the cellos outline softly the mirror, or upside-down version, of the hymn's opening phrase:

Schoenberg's basic tone row, which also serves as his principal theme in the more traditional sense, is the basis of the concluding hymn sung by the chorus (and reinforced by trombone):

The most important guide to the music is the text iself, most of which is to be delivered in a sort of stylized speech, or *Sprechstimme,* the rhythm and inflections of which are set by a variety of musical notation.

> I cannot remember ev'rything, I must have been unconscious most of the time; I remember only the grandiose moment when they all started to sing, as if prearranged, the old prayer they had neglected for so many years—the forgotten creed!
>
> But I have no recollection how I got underground to live in the sewers of Warsaw so long a time.
>
> The day began as usual. Reveille when it still was dark—get out whether you slept or whether worries kept you awake the whole night: you had been

separated from your children, from your wife, from your parents, you don't know what happened to them; how could you sleep?

They shouted again: "Get out! The sergeant will be furious!" They came out; some very slow, the old ones, the sick men, some with nervous agility. They fear the sergeant. They hurry as much as they can. In vain! Much too much noise, much too much commotion and not fast enough!

The Feldwebel [Sergeant] shouts: *"Achtung! Still gestanden! Na wird's mal, oder soll ich mit dem Gewehrkolben nach-helfen? Na jut; wenn ihr's durchaus haben wollt!"*

The sergeant and his subordinates hit everyone: Young or old, strong or sick, guilty or innocent—It was painful to hear the groaning and moaning.

I heard it though I had been hit very hard, so hard that I could not help falling down. We all on the ground who could not stand up were then beaten over the head.

I must have been unconscious. The next thing I knew was a soldier saying, "They are all dead!" Whereupon the sergeant ordered to do away with us.

There I lay aside half-conscious. It had become very still—fear and pain— Then I heard the sergeant shouting: *"Abzählen!"*

They started slowly, and irregularly: One, two, three, four, *"Achtung."* The sergeant shouted again: *"Rascher! Nochmals von vorn anfangen! In einer Minute will ich wissen wieviele ich zur Gaskammer abliefere! Abzählen!"*

They began again, first slow: one, two, three, four, became faster and faster, so fast that it finally sounded like a stampede of wild horses, and all of a sudden, in the middle of it, they began singing the *Sh'má Yisroel.*

[CHORUS]

Sh'má Yisroel Adonai elohēnu Adonai eḫod. V'ohavto es Adonai elōhėkho b'khol l'vov'kho uv'khol nafsh'kho uv'khol m'odekho. V'hoyu ha-d'vorim hoeleh asher onohi m'tzav'kho V'hoyu hayyōm al l'vovaykho, V'shinantom l'vonaykho v'dibbarto bom b'shivt'kho b'veyssayho uv'lekht'kho badderekh uv'shokh'h'kho uv'kumaykho.

[Hear o Israel, the Lord is our God, the Lord is One. And Thou shalt love the Lord, thy God, with all thine heart and with all thy soul and with all thy might. And these words, which I command you this day, shall be upon thine heart. Thou shalt teach them diligently unto thy children and shalt talk of them when thou sittest in thy house, and when thou walkest by the way, and when thou liest down, and when thou risest up.]

In addition to spoken narration and men's chorus, *A Survivor from Warsaw* is scored for piccolo, 2 flutes, 2 oboes, 2 clarinets, 2 bassoons, 4 horns, 3 trumpets, 3 trombones, tuba, an extensive percussion section including xylophone, bells, chimes, military drum, bass drum, kettledrums, cymbals, triangle, tambourine, tam-tam, castanets, harp, and the traditional string choir.

VARIATIONS FOR ORCHESTRA, OPUS 31

These Variations for Orchestra, Opus 31, constituted a landmark in the evolution of Schoenberg's art. This was Schoenberg's first work for full orchestra constructed according to his own new method of "composition with twelve tones." Because of his enormous influence on so many other prominent composers, a landmark in Schoenberg's development proved to be also a landmark in the evolution of twentieth-century symphonic music.

As Schoenberg and other twelve-tone composers have emphasized again and again, it is totally unnecessary for the listener to have any technical grasp whatsoever of the twelve-tone method in order to enjoy the music. It is enlightening, however, to realize that this method evolved first in chamber music. This fact was brought out in an interview with Schoenberg by his former student, Erwin Stein, barely two weeks after completion of the Variations. Stein opened the interview (which was published in the periodical *Pult und Takstock* in October 1928) by asking why it had been so many years since Schoenberg had composed an orchestral work:

Schoenberg: To tell the truth, my most recent work using orchestra is the Lieder for Orchestra, Opus 22 [composed 1913–1916]; *Jacob's Ladder,* which is half finished, is also [intended] for orchestra, although I have not yet written out the orchestral score. This interruption in my production for orchestra can be explained above all by the fact that, as you know, I have been occupied since the summer of 1921 with my composition with twelve tones, the laws of which I first had to explore with an ensemble of restricted size because, for the moment at least, octave doublings [i.e., reinforcing one instrumental part by a second instrument or a group of instruments an octave above or below] seems to me inadmissible.

Stein: Have you been able to avoid octave doublings completely [in the Variations]?

Schoenberg: With the exception of an occasional carelessness on my part or a slip of the pen, there are only a few, rare passages where octaves are doubled in passing. I am sometimes a little more tolerant in handling percussion instruments. . . . You know that for some time my goal had been to devise orchestral structures in which sonorous intensity and balance are achieved by means of relatively few voices. More and more I have been avoiding the creation of orchestral sonority by mere multiplying of instruments and have relied instead on the natural result of the movement and interrelationship of the individual voices. . . .

Stein: I am amazed that your new work should be written for a practically normal orchestra.

Schoenberg: If it were not for America, we in Europe would be composing only for reduced orchestras, chamber orchestras. . . . In radio broadcasting, a small number of sonic entities are enough to express all artistic thoughts. The phonograph and various mechanical instruments are evolving such clear sonorities that eventually we shall be able to write much less heavily instrumented compositions for them. Even the iconoclasts of the musical world hardly ever attempt to yell their ideas anymore, and true artists never at all. The public is beginning to understand without our needing to resort to shouting into their ears. . . .

Stein: Why is it that in recent years you have so often written in so-called traditional forms?

Schoenberg: I am grateful to you for saying "so-called" traditional forms. I hope that in time people will realize that the form of these Variations represents something new and I will be happy if I am still around when it *is* realized. The only old thing about traditional forms is their names, and these names are convenient, because we no longer incline to invent poetic titles. . . .

Stein: Why did you interrupt your work on the Variations for such a long time?

Schoenberg: . . . I began these Variations in May 1926, and after a few weeks made such progress that I expected to be finished in a few weeks more. Then a trip interrupted my work. Several weeks later when I tried to resume work, I was unable to rediscover the basic principles of the variation on which I had been working . . . of which I had only that sketchy outline. After searching in vain for a long time, I abandoned the composition. Still, I kept returning to it in the hope of finding what had eluded me, and last summer I made up my mind to finish it, no matter what the cost. I spent a week in the same fruitless search. . . . I took up the task once more, and after still another effort and another defeat, I decided to give it up and to adopt another principal for my variation. At the very moment when I set to work on this, I found a sheet of paper which I had seen a hundred times without paying any attention to it, and on it was the solution I had sought so long—a solution that agreed perfectly with the one I had just invented anew!

Even before he had finished his score, Schoenberg received a request from one of the greatest conductors of the day, Wilhelm Furtwängler, for the privilege of conducting the world premiere. Schoenberg gladly agreed. He completed the Variations on September 21, 1928 (according to his letter of that date to Furtwängler), and on the following December 2, Furtwängler conducted the Berlin Philharmonic in the premiere performance. The Berlin audience reacted with some hissing and catcalls as well as applause. Schoenberg was indignant. "Frankly," he wrote to Furtwängler, "I expected that you would repeat the work at the next concert, to show this rabble that *you do only what you consider right!*"

The American premiere of the Variations followed on October 18, 1929, in Philadelphia, with Leopold Stokowski conducting.

The Variations consist of an Introduction, Theme, nine Variations and a substantial Finale. In addition to his twenty-four-measure theme, Schoenberg introduced as an afterthought, but with considerable satisfaction, a well-known four-note motive, which spells out the name BACH (in German notation: B-flat, A, C, B natural). The purpose of this addition was a homage to Johann Sebastian Bach.

Introduction: Mässig, ruhig. Out of an almost impressionistic mist of tone, fragments of the theme emerge more and more clearly. Near the end of the Introduction the BACH motive is heard very softly in the solo trombone: *

Theme: Molto moderato. The twenty-four-measure principal theme is announced quietly by the cellos with a minimum of accompaniment. It begins with the following set of twelve pitches:

The remainder of the theme, including the final measures in which the violins take over from the cellos, is derived entirely from these opening measures.

Variation I: Moderato. The First Variation presents the theme in the bass instruments of the orchestra, melodically unchanged, but rhythmically disguised.

Variation II: Langsam. The Second Variation is a congeries of canons. The most important canon is carried by the solo violin and oboe. The violin has the theme upside down (or in mirror form); each violin phrase is followed, at a slight lag, by the solo oboe in free imitation:

Variation III: Mässig. Here the theme appears transformed in the horns, except for the final phrases which are taken over by the solo trumpet.

Variation IV: Waltz Tempo. Still further transformed, the theme appears here as a delicate accompaniment figure in the harp, celesta and mandolin.

Variation V: Bewegt. The theme is back in the bottom of the orchestra, punched out by the contrabassoon, trombone and string basses in the opening measures. But soon it is engulfed and transformed in the growing complexity of this Variation, one of the richest and most colorful of the entire set.

---

* *This and the following musical examples from this composition are copyright 1929 by Universal Edition. Renewed by Gertrude Schoenberg. Used by permission of Belmont Music Publishers.*

Variation VI: Andante. In contrast to the preceding Variation, this one has the transparent texture of chamber music. The theme is disguised in an inner voice carried by the solo cello.

Variation VII: Langsam. Softly glinting tones of the glockenspiel, celesta, piccolo, and solo violin high above the staff transform the theme still further.

Variation VIII: Sehr rasch. Against a background of vigorously strumming strings, the transformed theme is tossed about from oboes to bassoons to flutes, clarinets and first violins.

Variation IX: L'istesso tempo, aber etwas langsamer. The last is also one of the most complex Variations with its constantly shifting tempo.

Finale. Beginning with the delicate texture of the Introduction, this Finale is a climactic summary of the moods, tempos, colors and thematic transformations of the entire score. It is also punctuated and almost dominated by the BACH motive.

The subtle instrumental coloration of the Variations calls for a large orchestra: 2 piccolos, 4 flutes, 4 oboes, English horn, E-flat clarinet, 4 clarinets, bass clarinet, 4 bassoons, contrabassoon, 4 horns, 3 trumpets, 4 trombones, tuba, harp, kettledrums, bass drum, side drum, tambourine, celesta, glockenspiel, xylophone, triangle, flexatone (a flat piece of steel struck by wooden clappers), gong, mandolin, and the traditional strings.

VERKLÄRTE NACHT (TRANSFIGURED NIGHT), OPUS 4

This impassioned Romantic music was composed by a twenty-five-year-old student. Actually Schoenberg was only twenty-four in the summer of 1899, when (according to his teacher Alexander von Zemlinsky) he began his *Verklärte Nacht* in a little mountain village of Payerbach, just south of Vienna. One often repeated story insists that he completed the entire score during a three-week September holiday. That would have been jig time, even for a Rossini. But Schoenberg's complex manuscript, with its many alterations, its lengthy cuts and insertions, tells a different story. The date of conclusion is recorded on it in Schoenberg's own handwriting: December 1, 1899.

The proud teacher used his influence to urge the prestigious Tonkünstlerverein of Vienna to produce the new masterpiece. "But I had no luck," Zemlinsky recalled in his memoirs. "The piece was 'tested' and the result absolutely negative. One member of the jury gave his judgment in these words: 'Why, that sounds as if someone had taken the score of *Tristan* with the ink still wet and smudged it over!' " Yet despite this setback, it was the Tonkünstlerverein that finally did present the world premiere of *Verklärte Nacht* in 1903 in its original version as a string sextet, performed by the augmented Rosé Quartet. For many years it was (and statistics might reveal that it *still* is) Schoenberg's most popular work—chiefly, one suspects, because it shares the comfortably familiar idiom of late Romanticism and the warm emotional climate of Wagner, Brahms, and Tchaikovsky. It is perhaps closest of all to the erotic chromaticism of Wagner's *Tristan.*

But it is also Schoenberg. To the end of his life, he carried something of *Verklärte Nacht* within him. In 1917 he arranged *Verklärte Nacht* for string orchestra, changing nothing, merely multiplying the body of strings and adding double basses at certain points to reinforce the low cello line. Again in 1943 he revised the string orchestra version, this time thinning out the texture slightly and toning down, or omitting altogether, some of the more expansively Romantic expression marks.

Only two years before his death Schoenberg declared (in a famous essay, *On Revient toujours [a ses premiers amours]*): "It was not given to me to continue writing in the style of *Verklärte Nacht* . . . Fate led me along a harder path. But the wish to return to the earlier style remained constantly within me, and from time to time I have given in to this desire." And while he never overlooked the predominant influences of Brahms and Wagner in *Verklärte Nacht*, he insisted:

"Nevertheless I do believe that a little bit of Schoenberg may also be found in it, particularly in the breadth of the melodies, in contrapuntal and motivic developments, and in the quasi-contrapuntal movement of harmonies and harmonic basses against the melody. Finally, there are even passages (measures 137–139 for example) of indeterminate tonality, which doubtless may be seen as portents for the future."

The inspiration for *Verklärte Nacht* came from one of the most distinguished poets of the day, Richard Dehmel, who bridged the sensuous Impressionism of an earlier generation and the intense spirituality of the coming Expressionism. *Verklärte Nacht* was the opening poem in Dehmel's 1896 collection of lyrics entitled *Weib und Welt* ("Woman and World").

The poem falls into five sections of unequal length, corresponding to five main sections of the music and of the following prose summary:

> Two mortals walk through bare, cold woods. The moon above sails with them and they gaze into its light. The moon sails above lofty oaks. Black jagged peaks reach up into the cloudless heaven. A woman's voice speaks:
>
> I bear a child, and not from you. I walk in sin beside you. I have wronged myself profoundly. I had lost faith in happiness and yet felt such longing for meaning in life, for the joys and the tasks of motherhood, that I brazenly, shudderingly gave myself to a stranger's embrace, and thought myself blest. Now life has taken revenge, for now I have met you. I have met you.
>
> With ungainly gait she stares aloft; the moon sails with them. Her dark glance drowns in moonlight. A man's voice speaks:
>
> The child you have conceived must be no burden to your soul. See: how brightly all creation shimmers in the moonlight, as if embraced in one aureole. You and I are adrift together upon a cold ocean, but a special warmth reaches from you to me, from me to you. That warmth will transfigure the child. You will bear the child to me—from me. You have brought glory into my soul, you have made me a child again.
>
> He embraces her sturdy hips. Their breaths kiss in the air. Two mortals walk through the exalted brightness of the night.

Over a repeated plodding bass tone, the first section begins with a falling phrase which is recalled many times, most notably perhaps at the very end of the music where the closing line of the poem recalls the opening line. There is a brief suggestion in the high violins of the moonlight.

The second section begins with an agitated rhythm, perhaps intended to suggest the guilt in the woman's words. We come quickly to a nostalgic phrase for the cellos, answered by a solo violin and viola. This phrase was associated by Schoenberg's friend and earlier biographer Egon Wellesz with the woman's longing for the joys of motherhood:

We need not seek any extensive literal equivalents between the musical and poetic phrases. But some of the tenderer feelings of the woman's speech are probably reflected in this yearning phrase for the first violins:

The third section, introduced by a declamatory solo for first violins, is dominated by the opening theme of the work associated with the lovers' walk.

The fourth section, the reply of the man, is made up largely of themes from the speech of the woman in section two. The difference is that in place of the anguish and agitation of the woman's words, we meet here a great tenderness and lyric expansion building to a passionate climax.

The concluding section, which one might think of musically as a coda, begins with a pause of the entire orchestra, then picks up on the same impassioned level with which the man's speech concluded. As the stress of emotion dies away, we hear once more the opening motive of the lovers' walk and, finally the infinitely delicate, high string sonorities suggesting "the exalted brightness of the night."

Franz Schubert

Born January 31, 1797, Lichtenthal (now a part of Vienna)—
died November 19, 1828, Vienna

ROSAMUNDE OVERTURE AND BALLET MUSIC

When Schubert was inspired, music took shape in his mind faster than his pen could move across paper. And in his incidental music to the Romantic drama *Rosamunde, Princess of Cypress* he was often inspired. He began composing on November 30, 1823, and finished on December 18, 1823, two days before the premiere. Not much time was left to rehearse either the music or the two ballets, and no time at all to compose an overture. In fact Schubert never did compose an overture to *Rosamunde.* Instead he used an overture already composed for an earlier work.

One of Schubert's close friends, the famous Romantic painter Moritz von Schwind, describing the *Rosamunde* premiere to a mutual friend, wrote that the Overture was taken from Schubert's opera *Alfonso and Estrella.* But Schwind's comments on the music do not fit the Overture to *Alfonso and Estrella.* On the other hand, they do fit Schubert's Overture to an earlier "magic play" *(Zauberstück)* called *The Magic Harp (Die Zauberharfe).* Add to this the fact that the *Zauberharfe* Overture was published (in a four-hand piano version) shortly before Schubert's death as the Overture to *Rosamunde,* and the conclusion seems almost inescapable. It is the *Zauberharfe* Overture that must have been used to introduce *Rosamunde,* the same that is customarily performed today under the title of Overture to *Rosamunde.*

The drama, *Rosamunde, Princess of Cypress,* survived for exactly two performances. Even though Schubert's music had been singled out by the Viennese press for high praise, it fell into obscurity along with the play and was not brought to light again in its entirety until 1867, when Sir George Grove of dictionary fame and his friend Arthur Sullivan made a joint expedition to Vienna for the purpose of unearthing Schubert's still-neglected manuscripts. The two men were successful beyond their wildest dreams: in the booty they brought back to London were parts of Schubert's *Rosamunde* music, performed in London for the first time since the Viennese production of the drama.

Overture. Andante; Allegro vivace. The form of the Overture (as originally composed for *Die Zauberharfe*) is the standard one consisting of a slow introduction followed by a lively sonata-form movement. The principal theme, announced almost in a whisper by the first violins, has a familiar Schubertian lilt:

Ballet I. Allegro moderato; Andante un poco assai. It is not really necessary to know the wildly improbable plot of *Rosamunde, Princess of Cypress* to enjoy Schubert's music. The opening *Allegro* may well have served for the grand procession introducing a series of festivities. Its development is rich and imaginative enough to justify Alfred Einstein's suggestion that it could easily serve as a finale to Schubert's "Unfinished" Symphony, which, like this excerpt, is in the key of B minor.

The following *Andante* in G major is a gentle, lyric episode, perhaps intended for a dance of young girls.

Ballet II. Andantino. Equally gentle is the final ballet movement from the last act of *Rosamunde.* The simple melody has a characteristic Schubertian charm that seems to grow with the years. The caressing principal theme never seems to lose its freshness:

The orchestra for the *Rosamunde (Zauberharfe)* Overture and ballet excerpts calls for 2 flutes, 2 oboes, 2 clarinets, 2 bassoons, 4 horns, 2 trumpets, 3 trombones, kettledrums, and the standard choir of strings.

SYMPHONY NO. 4, C MINOR, (TRAGIC)

It is possible that this Symphony may have been given one private performance during Schubert's lifetime. But Schubert never heard it performed publicly, any more than he did his "Unfinished," or the greatest of them all: the colossal C major. The public premiere took place in Leipzig on November 19, 1849, twenty-one years after Schubert's death. August Ferdinand Riccius conducted the Euterpe Society.

At the time he wrote this Fourth Symphony, Schubert was nineteen and beginning to tire of his position as a teacher in the school headed by his father. During the very month of April when he completed his score, he applied for a better position as musical director in the newly founded music department of the German Normal School Institute in Laibach. His modest application read as follows:

> 1. Applicant has been educated at the *Konvikt* [i.e., Imperial and Royal Seminary] and was a Court Chorister and composition pupil of [Antonio] Salieri, first Court Conductor, on whose kind recommendations he applies for this post.
>
> 2. He has gained such thorough knowledge and experience in every type of composition for organ, violin, and the voice that, as the enclosed refer-

ences testify, he is considered in every way the most capable among all competitors for the post.

3. He promises the best possible application of his abilities to the carrying out of his duties should he be graciously considered a fitting applicant to fill the post.

FRANZ SCHUBERT

(Presently assistant schoolmaster on the staff of his father's school in Vienna, Himmelpfortgrund, No. 12.)

The title "Tragic" was Schubert's own, although it seems to have been an afterthought. It has long been customary—even among Schubert specialists—to point out that the Symphony is not "really" tragic at all. The late respected Dr. Percy Goetschius assured us that the title is "inaccurate, pompous and a bit pretentious. For no youth of nineteen summers really knows what tragedy signifies—at least Schubert did not; he bases his conception of it upon what he has heard or read, not upon what he has *felt* and known."

The learned doctor's adjectives apply better to him than to Schubert. Schubert would not be the first "youth of nineteen summers" to have known tragedy. (Mozart was only seventeen when he composed his "little" G-minor Symphony. Yet, for nearly a hundred years Mozart was widely thought to be the smiling cherub of music, the composer of serene and cloudless joys.) What if Schubert's concept of tragedy did not correspond precisely to ours or to that of Dr. Goetschius? Obviously, it would be our loss if we allowed anybody's definition of the word "tragic" (even Schubert's) to lessen our enjoyment of this small miracle by one of the greatest composers who ever lived.

I. *Adagio molto; Allegro vivace.* A powerful melancholy, bordering on Romantic gloom, pervades the slow introduction. The stormy *Allegro vivace* is based on the following carefully balanced, yet somehow explosive theme:

Schubert scholars, who find the shadow of Beethoven throughout the "Tragic" Symphony, compare this theme to the Bonn master's C-minor String Quartet, Opus 18, and his *Coriolanus* Overture in the same key.

As a matter of objective fact, the theme is a variant of a standard eighteenth-century thematic cliché. In both mood and formal detail it is far closer to Eurydice's anguished aria, "*Che fiero momento,*" in Gluck's *Orfeo* than to Beethoven. And we know that Schubert heard and loved Gluck. But the working out is characteristically and magnificently Schubertian in its harmonic stride and its structural idiosyncrasies, which anticipate, if only from afar, the grandeur of his last Symphony, the C-major.

II. *Andante.* This beautiful flow of melody speaks for itself:

The theme comes close to the unforgettable melody of the Schubert A-flat Impromptu, Opus 142, No. 2. The customary criticism of this movement as structurally weak, too drawn out, *too* lyric(!), and the great musicologist Einstein's dismissal of its *dolcezza* as "a piece of affectation" seem scarcely credible when one listens to the music.

An agitated contrasting section is related to the main theme of the first movement. At the end, as the movement fades into silence, fragments of both sections are united.

III. *Menuetto: Allegro vivace.* The robust rhythms of the Minuet proper contrast with a lyric trio section, which recalls, once more, the theme of the first movement.

IV. *Allegro.* It can hardly be accidental that the finale is related to the first movement in its main theme, in its stormy development and in the resplendent C major of its conclusion. The "Tragic" Symphony is scored for flutes, oboes, clarinets and bassoons in pairs, with four horns, two trumpets, kettledrums, and the traditional string choir.

SYMPHONY NO. 5, B-FLAT MAJOR

When he composed this enchanting little Symphony, sometimes referred to as "The Symphony without Trumpets and Drums," Schubert was only nineteen. He wrote it for an orchestra so small that we today would call it a chamber orchestra: a private ensemble, an outgrowth of the string quartet which used to meet in Schubert's home. When the quartet expanded into a small orchestra, it was conducted by Otto Hatwig, composer and a violinist of the Vienna Burgtheater. The first performance of Schubert's B-flat Symphony was given at Hatwig's house, in the Schottenhof, Vienna, in the autumn of 1816. This was the only performance of his Symphony Schubert ever heard.

At the time he composed it, Schubert had just gone through an artistic crisis. His immediately preceding symphony, to which he gave the title "Tragic," was written under the influence of Beethoven's stormy symphonic masterworks. But a guiding intuition told the nineteen-year-old that he was not yet ready to digest the entire Beethoven heritage as it then existed, and he had a momentary revulsion against it. There is an illuminating passage in Schubert's diary for June 1816 (that is, between the completion of his "Tragic" and the start of his Fifth Symphony) describing Beethoven's influence as "that eccentricity which joins and confuses the tragic with the comic, the agreeable with the repulsive, heroism with howlings and the holiest with harlequinades, without distinction, so as to goad people to madness instead of dissolving them in love, to incite them to laughter instead of lifting them to God."

Schubert returned later to his adoration of Beethoven, but only after having firmly established and reconfirmed his own strong personality.

After Schubert's death, the manuscript of the B-flat Symphony was lost. It was nearly forty years before the orchestral parts were rediscovered in Vienna, and by an odd irony, it took two Englishmen to do it: Sir George Grove of dictionary fame and Sir Arthur Sullivan, who had come to Vienna to hunt for lost Schubert manuscripts. The first public performance of this Symphony took place fifty-seven years after it was composed, in the London Crystal Palace on February 1, 1873, under the direction of August Manns.

I. *Allegro.* Four *pianissimo* bars of introduction lead directly into the graceful main theme of the first movement:

Although the nineteen-year-old Schubert was already completely master of this form, it is not his structural mastery that holds us so much as the grace of the first theme, the second theme, the whole movement, indeed, the entire Symphony from start to finish. We hear this quality in the dialogue between string choir and the woodwinds, as thematic fragments are tossed back and forth, and even in the vigorous development where the dotted rhythm of the opening theme is used to build an imposing climax.

II. *Andante con moto.* This slow movement has a warmly Mozartean appeal, but it reminds each Mozart lover of a different Mozart work. In fact, Schubert's opening phrase is a simple variation of a well-worn eighteenth-century formula, familiar from the opening of Handel's so-called "Largo" (actually a "larghetto" aria "*Ombra mai fu*"), from the Minuet finale of Mozart's F major Violin Sonata, K. 377, and from the last piece Mozart composed in his last opera: the "March of the Priests" from *The Magic Flute.* Yet despite its many ancestors, Schubert's child walks on its own graceful feet. In fact, it seems almost a dance—in Schubertian slow motion.

III. *Menuetto: Allegro molto.* The *Minuet,* in G major, starts in an assertive mood, which recalls the *Minuet* of Mozart's great G-minor Symphony. But Schubert quickly branches out on his own and, without making any effort to be original, is so ingratiating in his own very personal vein that he recalls Mozart only in the effortless flow of melodic inspiration. This movement is in the traditional minuet form with a contrasting trio section and a return to the minuet proper.

IV. *Allegro vivace.* The mecurial opening theme of this movement recalls the spirit of many a Haydn rondo finale.

But again the reminiscence is momentary; the Schubertian grace, with which the theme is developed, wings far above anything that even Haydn wrote in this particular vein. The movement is a masterpiece so natural in its growth, so easy in its technical command, that one forgets to be impressed; one forgets even the portentous word "masterpiece" and surrenders to the spontaneous joy which Schubert obviously felt himself and communicated to the little circle of friends for whom the Symphony was written.

Schubert's Fifth Symphony calls for 1 flute, 2 oboes, 2 bassoons, 2 horns, and the traditional string choir.

SYMPHONY NO. 6, C MAJOR, OPUS 140 (THE LITTLE C MAJOR)

When he finished this delicious Symphony, often called the "Little" C-major to distinguish it from his last and greatest symphony in the same key, Schubert was only twenty-one. He composed the Symphony for an ensemble so small that we would be inclined to call it a chamber orchestra. It had, in fact, grown out of a string quartet which used to meet in Schubert's home. When the quartet was expanded into an orchestra, it was conducted by the violinist, Otto Hatwig, who in 1818 gave the premiere of the Sixth at his apartment in the famous Schottenhof (one of the oldest building complexes in Vienna, more or less continually rebuilt since the Middle Ages, when the original Schottenkirche monastery, and land itself were owned by the Irish—popularly known as "Scottish"—Benedictine monks). The public premiere did not take place until the month after Schubert's death, at a concert at the Gesellschaft der Musikfreunde, on December 14, 1828, in the Vienna Redoutensaal, under the direction of Johann Baptist Schmiedel.

While Schubert's Sixth was influenced to some extent by Beethoven's First Symphony, it is closer to the spirit of Haydn and even of Rossini who was then tremendously popular in Vienna. It is in the traditional four movements.

I. *Adagio; Allegro vivace.* Aside from the grand gesture of the opening bars, the slow introduction is delicate and sensitive, dying away at the end to a Romantic *pianissimo.* The main theme is a lilting, almost dancelike figure:

It is delicately scored for woodwinds alone, then repeated by a vigorous *tutti.* The second principal theme, a gently syncopated figure, is likewise announced first by the woodwinds. The entire movement is kept light throughout. There is none of the tragic introspection of the *Unfinished* Symphony nor the grandeur of the late C-major Symphony. All is cheerfulness and youthful exuberance through the coda, which ends with a brilliant speeded-up development of the principal theme.

II. *Andante.* The simple songfulness of the basic opening strain is not far from the spirit of the Austrian folk music, which also inspired so many of Schubert's *Ländler* and waltzes. We hear it first almost in a whisper from the first violins:

It is taken up very softly by the woodwinds. As the movement develops, it grows more sensuous and Italianate. But the folk-song strain returns more than once, and rounds off the final bars in the ethereal tones of a high flute echoed by a velvet-voiced clarinet.

III. *Scherzo: Presto.* In the violent fluctuations of volume from whispering strings to a resplendent full *tutti,* Schubert's Scherzo shows its derivation from the Beethoven First Symphony. Yet it is also inimitably Schubert, particularly in the more relaxed trio section, where it recalls the peasant *Ländler.*

IV. *Allegro moderato.* Like the principal themes of all three preceding movements, this one is announced very softly:

Its rondo-like lilt could recall some of Haydn's early finales. But Schubert's two-part form is simpler than a rondo. And in the lightness and unforced gaiety of his finale, Schubert is delightfully and spontaneously himself. Again and again we hear echoes of the dance, although in this movement the spirit is perhaps closer to ballet divertissement than to any peasant tread.

The Sixth Symphony is scored for 2 flutes, 2 oboes, 2 clarinets, 2 bassoons, 2 horns, 2 trumpets, kettledrums, and the standard string choir.

SYMPHONY NO. 8, B MINOR, UNFINISHED

We shall probably never know why Schubert left his B-minor Symphony incomplete. He began it on October 30, 1822, finished the first two movements and almost completed the sketch for his *scherzo*. He even orchestrated the first nine measures of the *scherzo* and then laid the work aside. Since the first two movements are among the greatest and most compact in symphonic literature, it is tantalizing to speculate why Schubert never finished his work. But a century and a half of speculation have brought us hardly any closer to understanding. The Schubert scholar Martin Chusid has pointed out that Schubert began and interrupted the "Unfinished" Symphony toward the end of a period of artistic struggles when he left a far higher proportion of unfinished works than at any other time in his career. More specifically, Chusid believes that Schubert may have recognized so many points of resemblance between his unfinished score and Beethoven's Second Symphony (one of Schubert's prime favorites) that he feared he could be accused of plagiarism and therefore made a conscious decision not to complete the score. Even so perceptive a scholar as Alfred Einstein declared that Schubert never *could* have finished the work, for nothing to approach the originality, power, and skill of the two first movements could ever have been made from the material of Schubert's sketch for the *scherzo*. But let us not set the limits to Schubert's creative power. The mere fact that *we* cannot imagine how he would have finished the score does not mean that he would have been unable to do it, had he wished, or had he not been distracted.

Schubert seems to have presented the unfinished score to his friend Anselm Hüttenbrenner out of gratitude for a Diploma of Honorary Membership in the Music Society of Graz forwarded to him by Hüttenbrenner. Over thirty years after Schubert's death, Anselm's brother Joseph Hüttenbrenner wrote Johann Herbeck, the conductor of the Gesellschaft der Musikfreunde. He urged Herbeck to look over the symphonies, overtures, songs, quartets, and choruses of Anselm. Toward the end of his letter he added that Anselm had "a treasure in Schubert's B-minor Symphony, which we put on a level with the great Symphony in C, his instrumental swan song, and any one of the symphonies by Beethoven."

It took Herbeck five years to act on this sensational news, although he was in Graz several times, close to Anselm's home. Finally, in May 1865, Herbeck went to a humble inn where the old and tired Anselm was in the habit of breakfasting. They met. After a few words, Herbeck said, "I am here to ask permission to produce one of your works in Vienna." Anselm, visibly cheered, invited Herbeck home. His workroom was crammed with a confusion of dusty, yellowing papers. Anselm showed his manuscripts from which Herbeck chose an overture for performance. "It is my purpose," he declared, "to bring forward three contemporaries: Schubert, Hüttenbrenner, and Lachner, in one concert before the Viennese public." And he added as casually as he could: "It would naturally be very appropriate to represent Schubert by a new work."

"Oh," replied Anselm, "I still have a lot of things by Schubert." And he pulled a bundle of papers from a chest. Herbeck's eye lighted on a manuscript labelled in Schubert's hand: *Symphonie in H moll.* He looked through the manuscript and endeavored not to sound excited as he said: "This would do. Will you let me have it copied immediately at my cost?"

"There's no hurry," replied Anselm. "Take it with you."

On December 17, 1865, after Schubert had been dead for thirty-seven years, the premiere of the "Unfinished" Symphony was given under Herbeck's direction at a concert of the Gesellschaft der Musikfreunde in Vienna.

I. *Allegro moderato.* A mysterious introductory phrase for cellos and double basses seems the very embodiment of Romantic yearning. Yet it is reticent compared to the emotional tension it will be called upon to express halfway through the movement. Its very first appearance is as follows:

A murmuring figure for violins supplies the accompaniment for a song of unforgettable melancholy in which the oboe and clarinet join.

After a typically sudden Schubertian transition we hear one of the best remembered of all symphonic themes. This too is a song, sung in the warmer tones of the cello section. With its gentle, almost waltzlike lilt, it could have been written, as Alfred Einstein said, "by Schubert only in Vienna":

A return of the mysterious introductory phrase now builds to an almost Tchaikovskian explosion of emotion. After a brief development section the themes return in their original shape and the movement closes with a *coda* which once more recalls the opening bars.

II. *Andante con moto.* After the emotional stresses of the first movement the seraphic opening of the *Andante* seems to promise peace:

But melancholy and yearning return at the shift to a plaintive clarinet melody with its softly throbbing accompaniment, and a stormy evolution follows. Even the serenity of the final page is tinged with sadness.

The two movements are scored for 2 flutes, 2 oboes, 2 clarinets, 2 bassoons, 2 horns, 2 trumpets, 3 trombones, 2 kettledrums, and the traditional string choir.

SYMPHONY NO. 9, C MAJOR

If ever a city had a right to consider itself the capital of the musical world, it would have been Vienna in the era which embraced Schubert's lifetime: the late-eighteenth and early-nineteenth centuries. Yet one wonders how deep or widespread the famous Viennese musicality really was. Mozart's neglect in Vienna was well known. His last three and greatest symphonies do not seem to have been performed at all during his lifetime. Nor did Schubert ever hear either of his two C-major Symphonies performed. There is a tradition that Schubert offered the "Great" C major (sometimes listed as No. 7, more often as No. 9) to the Vienna Gesellschaft der Musikfreunde in the last spring before his death and that the society turned it down as being too long and too difficult to perform. The same illustrious society did refuse the work twice again on these grounds: once, a month after Schubert's death, and again in 1839—after it had *already* been performed on March 21, 1839 by the Gewandhaus Orchestra in Leipzig!

Not until eleven years after Schubert's death, when Schumann "discovered" the manuscript of the Schubert Ninth (in the possession of the composer's brother Ferdinand) and persuaded Mendelssohn to perform it at the Gewandhaus concerts in Leipzig, was a Viennese orchestra found to follow the Leipzig example. "Who knows how long it would have lain neglected there in dust and darkness [wrote Schumann] had I not immediately arranged with Ferdinand Schubert to send it to the management of the Gewandhaus concerts in Leipzig, or rather to the conducting artist himself [Mendelssohn]. . . . The Symphony reached Leipzig, where it was performed, its greatness recognized, performed again and received with delighted and almost universal admiration."

Mendelssohn did more. He tried immediately, though in vain, to persuade the London Philharmonic to perform the Symphony. In 1844, when he went to London himself as guest conductor of the London Philharmonic, he wanted to put it on his own program. But in rehearsal, the players were laughingly and openly contemptuous of the music, and so once more Schubert's masterpiece was shelved. Parisian musicians were not much better. Two years earlier in Paris, Habeneck's orchestra of the Concerts du Conservatoire had refused, in rehearsal, to go beyond the first movement of the Ninth Symphony. However, the still-young New York Philharmonic did perform the work on January 11, 1851. Ten months later, when it was first heard in Paris Berlioz wrote: "The Symphony . . . is, to my thinking, worthy of a place among the loftiest productions of our art." But it was nearly fifty years (1897) before it was heard again in France. Londoners first heard it in 1856.

The Symphony *is* long, yet its inspiration never flags, from the foursquare theme that opens the first movement to the overwhelming *coda* of the *Finale.* When Schumann coined his famous phrase of the "heavenly lengths" of the Symphony, his accent was on the first word. And he added: "How refreshing is this feeling of overflowing wealth!"

I. *Andante; Allegro ma non troppo.* What a powerful melodic arch spans the opening page of this Symphony, like a gateway to the entire work! It serves also as a structural framework since the first movement, opens and closes with the same broad arch. It also becomes a foundation, for it is the thematic basis from which the most important themes of this first movement are derived.

With what cunning our supposedly naïve composer has contrived his arch! It is put together of a very few tiny rhythmic patterns—those short, sharp rhythms which lend themselves so perfectly to symphonic development —yet the overall effect is of breadth and power. Part of its fascination comes from Schubert's avoidance of the traditional melodic structure of four measures plus four, for an eight-measure phrase. If you listen carefully or glance at the melody below, you will see that Schubert has used a more surprising sequence of three, plus three, plus two. This gives a touch of Romantic ambiguity to the simple seeming theme. It is presented first in the bare tones of two unaccompanied horns:

Quietly the rest of the orchestra takes up the theme, harmonizes, embroiders upon it, and extracts the rhythmic fragment of its second measure. As the introduction draws to a close and the tempo quickens, that bold dotted rhythm sets the whole orchestra rocking with exuberance and power until the main theme of the *Allegro* has crystallized into its definitive form:

The orchestra expands upon this principal theme, but the energetic drive dies down rather unexpectedly, giving way to a second, gentler, deliciously rocking figure in the woodwinds. And now, instead of proceeding at once to the traditional development of this theme, Schubert in a wonderfully imaginative passage has the trombones take up very softly a fragment based on the second measure of the introductory theme. The trombone was a relative newcomer to the symphony orchestra. It had been introduced in symphonies during Schubert's own lifetime by Beethoven, who had used it chiefly for loud passages of *tutti* reinforcement. But the trombone playing *pianissimo* in a melodic role was an original (and extremely poetic) effect. This trombone theme grows and swells, takes hold of the whole orchestra and mounts to a blazing climax.

The development section, which brings still bolder fragmentations and recombinations of all the above themes, is on a heroic scale, as are the return of the basic themes and the exhilarating coda, with its triumphant recall of the Symphony's opening measures.

II. *Andante con moto.* After the half-dozen bars of soft *staccato* string introduction, which establish a subdued march rhythm, a melancholy, almost pathetic little tune is piped by a solo oboe. This is the principal melody of the movement, from which several others derive. But there are consolatory phrases for the strings and just before the oboe's melody returns, a hush falls over the orchestra, leading to a passage where, as Schumann wrote: "a horn-call sounds from a distance, as if it were descended from another world. And every other instrument seems to listen, as if some heavenly messenger were hovering through the orchestra."

III. *Scherzo: Allegro vivace.* The third movement begins in a burly, robust mood, recalling some of Beethoven's scherzos. A graceful contrasting theme follows. But almost at once this melody begins to develop and expand in a way as simple as it is powerful and characteristic of this Symphony.

IV. *Finale: Allegro vivace.* Like the first movement, this *Finale* is built on a vast scale and with concentrated might; it is an apotheosis of the power of rhythm. A triplet figure, which is part of the principal opening theme, plays an important role through most of the movement. Its rhythm accompanies even the grandly swinging second theme:

This was the passage at which the players of the London Philharmonic began to giggle while they were rehearsing under Mendelssohn's direction in 1844, showing such scorn for the music that Mendelssohn withdrew the work from his program. Today this theme and its lengthy development seem among Schubert's greatest inspirations. In the *coda,* its four repeated notes reach such threatening intensity that more than one listener has been reminded of the approach of the stone statue in the supper scene of *Don Giovanni.* But the threat is brief. Schubert goes on to show us that Beethoven was not the only one who could laugh and exult with the elements. The final page of Schubert's manuscript, with its swift, impatient hand, reflects this triumph and exultation.

Schubert's Ninth Symphony is composed for 2 flutes, 2 oboes, 2 clarinets, 2 bassoons, 2 horns, 2 trumpets, 3 trombones, kettledrums, and string choir.

William Schuman

Born August 4, 1910, New York City

AMERICAN FESTIVAL OVERTURE

When William Schuman composed his "American Festival" Overture for Serge Koussevitzky and the Boston Symphony Orchestra, he was one of the youngest generation of prominent American composers. Although he was far from a novice (his Second Symphony had already been performed in New York and Boston and broadcast over the CBS radio network), it was this "American Festival" Overture that first introduced him to many new admirers, including this writer. The eminence to which he has since risen, especially as a composer of symphonic works, has more than fulfilled the promise of this exhilarating early work. Koussevitzky conducted the first performance of the Overture on October 6, 1939, to open the second of two pre-season concerts "in honor of the American composer." It proved a rousing critical and public success and was soon taken into the repertory of other orchestras. Not entirely satisfied with his final page after hearing the Boston Symphony performances, Schuman revised it before publication.

The Overture is based on the simplest of themes: a motto-like descending and rising minor third, with which the work begins.

This theme, the composer tells us, was chosen before he himself realized its origin. Only in the course of composing did he remember that this was a "call to play" that had been part of his boyhood experience growing up in New York City. The Overture is definitely not program music. Yet knowing the origin of the theme, we may hear in it some of the ebullience of LaGuardia's New York. But if so, one must add that there is at least an echo of Bach's Leipzig as well. For the score has a dash of vigorous fugal writing surely suggested by Schuman's love of Bach. In any case, the theme is superb symphonic material to be tossed back and forth among the orchestral choirs and the whole has an energy and spontaneity which one likes to think typically American. It is scored for 2 flutes, piccolo, 2 oboes, English horn, 2 clarinets, bass clarinet, 4 horns, 2 trumpets, 3 trombones, tuba, kettledrums, bass drum, cymbals, snare drum, xylophone, and strings.

For the occasion of the first performance of the Overture Schuman supplied the following notes:

> The first three notes of this piece will be recognized by some listeners as the "call to play" of boyhood days. In New York City it is yelled on the syllables "Wee-Awk-Eee" to get the gang together for a game or a festive occasion of some sort. This call very naturally suggested itself for a piece of music being composed for a very festive occasion. From this it should not be inferred that the Overture is program music. In fact, the idea for the music came to my mind before the origin of the theme was recalled. The development of this bit of "folk material," then, is along purely musical lines.
>
> The first section of the work is concerned with the material discussed above and the ideas growing out of it. This music leads to a transition section and the subsequent announcement by the violas of a fugue subject. The entire middle section is given over to this fugue. The orchestration is at first for strings alone, later for woodwind alone and, finally, as the fugue is brought to fruition, by the strings and woodwinds in combination. This climax leads to the final section of the work, which consists of the opening materials paraphrased and the introduction of new subsidiary ideas. The tempo of the work is fast.
>
> WILLIAM SCHUMAN

FANTASY FOR CELLO AND ORCHESTRA: A SONG OF ORPHEUS

William Schuman's Fantasy for Cello and Orchestra: *A Song of Orpheus* was commissioned by the Ford Foundation for Leonard Rose as part of the Foundation's program of inviting outstanding performers to choose composers to write music expressly for their use. The Fantasy was begun on September 28, 1960, and completed on the following Fourth of July. It was first performed with Mr. Rose as the soloist and the Indianapolis Symphony Orchestra under the direction of Izler Solomon on February 17, 1962. On the occasion of that première Mr. Schuman provided the following background to his score:

> The song "Orpheus With His Lute," upon which the Fantasy is based, was composed in 1944 for a production of *Henry VIII*. Some years ago my friend Vincent Persichetti, the composer, suggested that the song would make an excellent theme for a set of variations. His suggestions came to mind when I was searching for an idea for the work I had agreed to compose for Leonard Rose. Although the composition is not in the form of a set of variations, all the music grows out of the melodic line of the song which is stated at the very beginning of the composition. The words of the song are written in the

cello part in order to enable the soloist to perform the melody with the clarity of a singer's projection. Knowing that the words should enhance listening pleasure, the composer requests that William Shakespeare's text be printed in the concert program books, or, if this is not possible, recited before the work is performed.

WILLIAM SCHUMAN

Orpheus with his lute made trees,
And the mountain tops that freeze,
  Bow themselves, when he did sing:
To his music plants and flowers
Ever sprung; as sun and showers
  There had made a lasting spring.

Everything that heard him play,
Even the billows of the sea,
  Hung their heads, and then lay by.

In sweet music is such art,
Killing care and grief of heart,
  Fall asleep, or hearing, die.
    ——William Shakespeare *Henry VIII*

The opening line of the solo cello is as follows:*

As the graceful lyricism of this cello solo unfolds, the instruments of the orchestra creep in with unobtrusive support. After the solo cello has completed the song, the oboe in turn takes up the melody in a duet with the solo cello. When the oboe reaches the last, long-held note of the song, the cello has a solo cadenza which forms a bridge to the scherzo-like middle section of the Fantasy.

Here it is that the composer gives freest reign to the symphonic imagination for the development of characteristic turns and fragments of the song.

Another long cadenza-like passage for the cello, with occasional orchestral support, leads back to the opening tempo and to the mood of the original song. The muted, dying close is like a final distillate of the song on which the score is based. The orchestra of the Fantasy calls for 3 flutes, piccolo, 2 oboes, English horn, clarinets, bass clarinet, 2 bassoons, 4 horns, harp, and the customary strings.

---

* *Musical example © 1963, Merion Music, Inc. Used by permission.*

NEW ENGLAND TRIPTYCH: THREE PIECES FOR ORCHESTRA AFTER WILLIAM BILLINGS

What is American music? To answer that much-mooted question in terms of character or style is as impossible as it is to describe that mythical person, the typical American. There is no such person. And perhaps no such music either.

Yet no one would have the slightest difficulty in naming some obviously American piece of music. Around the world jazz is recognized as being characteristically, unmistakably American—and specifically American of the United States. Or, to go to the other end of our history, the music of William Billings is fast coming to stand for an age—the birth of a nation—and for a character we like to think fundamentally American.

William Schuman has written that he is not alone among American composers to feel an identity with Billings. But it would be hard to think of another composer whose music seems closer in spirit to Billings. This is not to claim that Schuman is more "American" than some other distinguished contemporaries, but to mention what appears to be a strong and fruitful affinity, an attraction which has drawn Schuman to this early American composer on more than one occasion.

Schuman's *New England Tryptich* based on three pieces by Billings, was composed in 1956 and was commissioned by Andre Kostelanetz. It is scored for 3 flutes, 3 oboes, 4 clarinets, 2 bassoons, 4 horns, 3 trumpets, 3 trombones, tuba, kettledrums, percussion, and the usual string choir.

The following information is furnished by the composer:

> William Billings (1764–1800) is a major figure in the history of American music. The works of this dynamic composer capture the spirit of sinewy ruggedness, deep religiosity and patriotic fervor that we associate with the Revolutionary period. Despite the undeniable crudities and technical shortcomings of his music, its appeal, even today, is forceful and moving. I am not alone among American composers who feel an identity with Billings and it is this sense of identity which accounts for my use of his music as a point of departure. These pieces do not constitute a "fantasy" on themes of Billings, nor "variations" on his themes, but rather a fusion of styles and musical language.
>
> I. *"Be Glad Then, America."* Billings' text for this anthem includes the following lines:
>
> Yea, the Lord will answer
> And say unto his people—behold!
> I will send you corn and wine and oil.
> And ye shall be satisfied therewith.
> Be glad then, America.
> Shout and rejoice.
> Be glad and rejoice.
> Fear not O land,
> Hallelujah!

A timpani solo begins the short introduction which is developed predominantly in the strings. This music is suggestive of the "Hallelujah" heard at the end of the piece. Trombones and trumpets begin the main section, a free and varied setting of the words "Be Glad Then America, Shout and Rejoice." The timpani, again solo, leads to a middle fugal section stemming from the words "And Ye Shall Be Satisfied." The music gains momentum, and combined themes lead to a climax. There follows a free adaptation of the "Hallelujah" music with which Billings concludes his original choral piece and a final reference to the "Shout and Rejoice" music.

II. *"When Jesus Wept."*
When Jesus wept the falling tear
In mercy flowed beyond all bound;
When Jesus groaned, a trembling fear
Seized all the guilty world around.

The setting of the above text is in the form of a round. Here, Billings's music is used in its original form, as well as in the new settings with contrapuntal embellishments and melodic extensions.

III. *"Chester."* This music, composed as a church hymn, was subsequently adopted by the Continental Army as a marching song. The original words, with one of the verses especially written for its use by the Continental Army, follow:

Let tyrants shake their iron rods,
And slavery clank her galling chains,
We fear them not, we trust in God,
New England's God forever reigns.
The foe comes on with haughty stride,
Our troops advance with martial noise
Their vet'rans flee before our youth,
And gen'rals yield to beardless boys.

SYMPHONY NO. 3

It is hard to believe that this fresh and vital symphony was composed way back in 1940–1941, the earliest of the symphonies Schuman acknowledges and still allows to be performed. (His First and Second symphonies have been withdrawn for revision.) This first major orchestral work of Schuman's maturity was a turning point of his career in more ways than one and established him as a major figure on the American musical scene.

In 1939, after the successful launching of Schuman's "American Festival" Overture by the Boston Symphony Orchestra, Serge Koussevitzky reportedly said to Schuman: "Now you must hate Roy Harris!" Not that Koussevitzky had anything against Harris, but he felt strongly that Schuman had so far matured and mastered his craft that he should liberate himself from any influence, including that of Roy Harris, who had been one of his teachers and whom both Schuman and Koussevitzky admired.

Schuman's next orchestral work, his Third Symphony, was completed on January 11, 1941, and dedicated to Serge Koussevitzky, who conducted the first performance the following October 17. Koussevitzky was so enthusiastic about the score that he included it on the next New York program of the Boston Symphony on November 22. In New York it won the first award of the Music Critics' Circle as the best new American orchestral work of the season. In addition, it so impressed Carl Engel, president of the music publishing firm of G. Schirmer, that he persuaded his board of directors to pay Schuman a monthly stipend so that he could devote less time to teaching and more to composing. In turn, Schirmer became Schuman's publishers.

Perhaps one reason this Symphony sounds so fresh today is that our ears have caught up with Schuman. Dissonances which could sound harsh back in 1941 no longer do. On the contrary, they have turned into a sensuous pleasure especially those fine crunchy polychords and polytonal combinations, which Schuman loved so much even then! The form is unconventional but strongly effective. It is in two parts, each containing two connected movements. All four movements are based on the Symphony's opening theme.

PART I: *Passacaglia and Fugue.*

Passacaglia. A strikingly lyric phrase for violas is the firm foundation for the *Passacaglia* (and, in various transformations, for the entire Symphony). It is introduced quietly, but the melody is angular, with striking intervals (notably falling fourths) which generate strong tensions as the work develops:

The exposition of the theme is not finished with this first hearing in the violas alone. The next layer of the foundation is laid with entrance of the second violins repeating the theme, but starting at the next higher pitch. Five more entrances follow (cellos, first violins, low winds, horns, high winds).

With the theme firmly impressed on our ears, the composer leads us on to the variations which are the traditional essence of a *passacaglia.* There are four in all:

1. In the first variation the melody is carried by trumpets and trombones against a background of faster moving strings.

2. The second variation is brief. Its character comes chiefly from the rather aggressive polychord, a combination of C major and A major reiterated with savage insistence by the low instruments, while above this there moves a rapid little woodwind figure derived from the *Passacaglia* theme.

3. The third variation is a more smoothly flowing melody for violins against rushing figures in the lower strings.

4. Variation number four is carried chiefly by a quartet of trombones moving in slow melodic motion against a background of quicker dotted figures derived from the *Passacaglia* theme. This variation continues without break to the first note of the *Fugue*.

The *Fugue* follows without pause. Its theme, much briefer than the *Passacaglia* theme, is derived from it in that it uses the same striking intervals, but scrambled in sequence and rhythms. It makes a powerful, dramatic entrance, proclaimed by four horns reinforced by low *pizzicato* strings:

Rather than follow the traditional pattern of Baroque fugues, each entrance of this *Fugue* subject begins a half-tone higher than its predecessor. As in the *Passacaglia,* there are seven entrances of the subject. The elaborate exposition is followed by three variations on the *Fugue* theme and a *coda* with references to both the *Passacaglia* and *Fugue*.

PART II: *Chorale—Toccata.*

A quiet introduction for dark-voiced cellos and violas ushers in the chorale melody, a poetic trumpet solo. A flute takes over from the trumpet, and then finally the quartet of strings. The entire orchestra brings the climax in a massive contrapuntal statement of the theme, then dies away slowly to a low bassoon B-flat.

Over this B-flat pedalpoint, a snare drum softly rasps out the rhythm of the long *Toccata* theme. The melodic form of the theme is announced by the bass clarinet:

As with the earlier themes of the symphony, the *Toccata* theme is taken up in imitation by other instruments of the orchestra. This toccata-finale develops into a brilliant display piece dominated by the driving rhythm of the principal theme. It concludes with the recall of themes from earlier movements.

The Schuman Symphony No. 3 is scored for 2 flutes and piccolo, 2 oboes, English horn, E-flat clarinet, 2 B-flat clarinets, bass clarinet, 2 bassoons, 4 horns, 4 trumpets, 4 trombones, tuba, timpani, snare drum, bass drum, cymbals, xylophone and strings. The composer recommends as "most desirable" the addition of a third flute or second piccolo, third oboe, third clarinet, third bassoon, contrabassoon, a second quartet of horns, and a piano.

SYMPHONY FOR STRINGS (SYMPHONY NO. 5)

Many of the composers who make up our present-day concert repertory have been distinguished executants: conductors, pianists, organists, violinists; the list is almost inexhaustible. Many have been distinguished teachers. Some have been musicologists. But very few have combined such a variety of careers with such distinction as William Schuman. To name only the four most important of his noncomposing activities, Mr. Schuman was for many years a faculty member of Sarah Lawrence College. While continuing to teach and compose, he gained experience in the business-artistic world as director of publications for G. Schirmer, Inc. From 1945 to 1962 he held the key position of president of the Juilliard School of Music in New York City. And in 1962 he became president of Lincoln Center for the Performing Arts. Yet despite the importance of his contributions in these roles, most of us continue to think of him primarily as a composer. And one suspects that Mr. Schuman does too, for he continues to set aside a major portion of his time for creative activity.

High among his creative achievements, perhaps highest of all, ranks the increasingly powerful series of his symphonies. Of these, one of the most accessible bears no official number, but is simply called Symphony for Strings. In actual order of composition this is Mr. Schuman's fifth, falling between his Symphony No. 4 of 1941 and his Sixth Symphony of 1948. Completed on July 31, 1943, at New Rochelle and first performed on November 12 of the same year by the Boston Symphony Orchestra under the direction of Serge Koussevitzky, the Symphony for Strings was commissioned by the Koussevitzky Foundation as a memorial for Natalie Koussevitzky. The work was an immediate success, promptly published and recorded, widely performed and broadcast in the United States and abroad, and for many years acclaimed as his finest work. It is cast in three movements.

I. *Molto agitato ed energico.* The symphony opens with its principal melody: a complex arch of twelve measures set forth in a brilliantly powerful unison of first and second violins, unaccompanied, on the G string. It begins as follows:

The melody is immediately repeated with a discreet accompaniment of the low strings. A second theme, related to the first, is proclaimed *fff vigoroso* by the violas and developed canonically, appearing successively in the first and second violins, cellos and double basses. This develops to a resounding polychordal climax. The traditional first-movement sonata-allegro form, if it was present in Schuman's mind, is very freely treated. There is a development section based on the first theme, both themes are then brought back in altered form, and the movement concludes with another great *crescendo* climax.

II. *Larghissimo.* One of the striking features of this symphony is the subtle interrelationship of its principal themes, most of which seem to be derived from one facet or another of the symphony's opening unison melody.

The second movement is introduced by a powerful series of polytonal chords, which are related to the polytonal climax of the first movement and to a scalar fragment of the symphony's opening melody. The main body of the second movement is built on another broadly arching melody related to both the opening of this movement, and through it, to the opening of the first movement. This transformation is announced "tenderly" by the first violins, which are joined successively by second violins, and finally by violas each one chanting the identical melody. A further, climactic development of the melody leads back to the powerful chords of the opening, after which the music dies away to a conclusion of almost angelic serenity and consonance.

III. *Presto.* The finale of the Symphony for Strings suggests a free rondo form with a sprightly refrain derived from a fragment of the symphony's opening melody:

The first of the contrasting episodes exploits the versatility of the string body in plucked (*pizzicato*) sonorities and colors combined and contrasted with the sustained sonorities of bowed notes. The second episode of contrasts is related to the main melody of the preceding movement, with the violas alone taking the melodic lead followed by cellos and, at a longer interval, by first and then second violins. There is a strong suggestion of a final return of the rondo refrain building to a climactic *coda*-like conclusion.

Robert Schumann

Born June 8, 1810, Zwickau—died July 29, 1856, Endenich

CONCERTO FOR CELLO AND ORCHESTRA, A MINOR, OPUS 129

Schumann hated empty show, virtuosity for virtuosity's sake. "I cannot write a concerto for the virtuosos," he declared early in his career. "I must try for something else." Schumann was at his finest when most intimate, when his sensitive, wayward imagination was least fettered.

His Cello Concerto reflects this appealing side of his nature. Beyond a frolicsome moment or two in the *Finale,* it offers no opportunity for conventional virtuosity. Schumann's inspiration seems to have flowed with the same spontaneous grace we hear from start to finish of this endearing music; he composed it in the incredibly short space of fifteen days, from October 10 to 24, 1850. Yet, he was dissatisfied with certain details and as late as 1854 he was still making minor changes.

Barely a month before composing the Cello Concerto, Schumann and his wife Clara had moved from Dresden to Düsseldorf. They were both overjoyed by their new surroundings. One fruit of this joy was Schumann's "Rhenish" Symphony; another was the Cello Concerto. As always, Clara was not only a tender wife, but a perceptive, appreciative co-artist. "Last month," she wrote on November 16 in her diary, "he composed a concerto for violoncello that pleased me very much. It appears to be written in the true violoncello style." And almost a year later (October 11, 1851) she added: "I have played Robert's Violoncello Concerto again and thus procured for myself a truly musical and happy hour. The romantic quality, the flight, the freshness and the humor, and also the highly interesting interweaving of cello and orchestra are, indeed, wholly ravishing, and what euphony and what deep sentiment are in all the melodic passages!"

The Concerto is characteristic not only of Schumann but of the Romantic movement in a broader sense. The linking of the three movements of the Concerto into a continuous whole was part of a Romantic search for unity. The recall of the main theme of the first movement in a working-out section of the *finale* also was a Romantic device for the integration of larger cyclic forms. Finally the cello itself, which Schumann had loved since childhood, was a favorite instrument of the Romantics.

I. *Nicht zu schnell.* Three soft, sustained woodwind chords introduce the principal theme. Over murmuring strings the solo cello sings the following lyric phrase, the first half of the principal theme:

The *tutti* interruption is brief. By and large the orchestra remains a discreet background throughout the Concerto. The solo cello takes over again to sing a notably melodic second theme, close in character to the first. Livelier passagework concludes this exposition and leads us to the brief development section, where the principal themes evolve in a continually flowing, lyric vein. A short transitional passage for the solo cello anticipates the main theme of the middle movement, which follows without pause.

II. *Langsam.* The principal melody is chanted at the opening by the soloist:

A beautifully imaginative touch is the prominence Schumann gives to the first cellist of the orchestra in a style which at moments suggests a duet with the soloist. The overall shape of the movement is a simple A-B-A. At the conclusion the tempo accelerates. Over a string tremolo, the cello recalls fragments of the past melody, then plunges into a cascade of notes leading without pause into the *finale.*

III. *Sehr lebhaft.* The *Finale* is a combination of rondo and symphonic sonata form. While the solo cello is still primarily melodic, it is also lighter and more playful, and more given to catchy rhythms. Its brighter solo passages are fiery and effective, without ever indulging in display for its own sake, even in the final cadenza composed by Schumann himself.

The Cello Concerto is scored for a modest orchestra of 2 flutes, 2 oboes, 2 clarinets, 2 bassoons, 2 horns, 2 trumpets, kettledrums, and the traditional strings. The first performance took place after Schumann's death. Ludwig Ebert was the soloist at the Leipzig Conservatory on June 9, 1860.

CONCERTO FOR PIANO AND ORCHESTRA, A MINOR, OPUS 54

Schumann's Piano Concerto reflects in many ways his relation to his adored wife Clara. Nearly two years before they were married he had planned a piano concerto, probably even then with Clara in mind. He wrote her (from Vienna): "My concerto is a compromise between a symphony, a concerto and a huge sonata. I see I cannot write a concerto for the virtuosos—I must plan something else." For the moment, nothing came of it.

The day after their wedding (which took place on September 12, 1840) Schumann opened the joint diary that he and Clara were to keep throughout their life together, with the following tender solemnity:

> My most beloved young wife! Let me greet you with a tender kiss on this special day, the first of your womanhood, the first of your twenty-first year. The little book which I open herewith has a very particular, intimate meaning; it is to record everything that affects us together in our household and married life, our wishes, our hopes . . . your fair hopes and mine—may heaven bless them; your anxieties and mine . . . in short, all our joys and sorrows. . . .

A document of almost heartbreaking tenderness, it tells, in the early years, of soaring confidence and joys as Schumann's genius grew, nurtured and strengthened by their mutual love. Only a few weeks after the wedding Schumann sketched his "Spring" Symphony in a single burst of inspiration. Then late in March, 1841, he wrote in the diary: "My next symphony will be called 'Clara' and in it I will paint her portrait with flutes, oboes, and harps."

He never wrote his "Clara" Symphony. But in the ensuing weeks he did compose a one-movement symphonic piece, in which oboes and flutes played dominant roles and, instead of harps, the instrument most personally identified with Clara, the pianoforte, took the lead. It is impossible to imagine that Robert did not have Clara in mind as he composed this Fantasy for Piano and Orchestra, which eventually became the first movement of his Piano Concerto and was forever after closely identified with Clara as performer. It was she who was the soloist at a reading of the Fantasy with the Leipzig Gewandhaus Orchestra on August 13, when the "Spring" Symphony was rehearsed.

Pictures of Robert and Clara Schumann together are rare. Photography was still in its experimental stage. But a charming little daguerrotype (preserved in the Schumann Museum of his birthplace, Zwickau) showing Clara seated demurely at the piano with Robert looking on, does give a hint of the relationship, so gentle yet so strong, which was the mainstay of both their lives (see illustration).

It seems strange that this gentle A-minor Fantasie was once considered difficult to understand. Schumann made several attempts to have it published under various titles, including an *Allegro affettuoso,* then as a *Concert Allegro,* Opus 48. Nobody wanted it. Four years later he added an intermezzo and finale, so that, as Clara wrote in the diary: "It has now become a concerto which I mean to play next winter. I am very glad about it for I have always wanted a great bravura piece by him." And a month later, on July 31, 1845: "Robert has finished his concerto and handed it over to the copyist. I am happy as a king at the thought of playing it with orchestra."

Clara, of course, was the soloist at the premiere of the Concerto, which took place at one of her own concerts in the auditorium of the Hôtel du Saxe in Dresden, on December 4, 1845. On this occasion the three movements were

Clara and Robert Schumann.

A small daguerrotype preserved in the Schumann House in Zwickau, East Germany, suggests something of the tender personal and professional relation of the two great artists. (*Courtesy, Robert Schumann-Haus, Zwickau*)

called: *Allegro affettuoso, Andantino* and *Rondo.* She played it again that winter in Leipzig with their friend Mendelssohn conducting and the next year in Vienna with her husband on the conductor's stand. In the following years they joined hands many times again in this Concerto, and during the tragic years after Schumann's death Clara continued to spread the gospel of her husband's "difficult" music. The public had listened to her before they had to him, but as a revered elderly artist she had the joy of knowing that in part, through her efforts, Schumann was respected and loved everywhere as she herself had loved him, and that this Concerto, so intimately identified with them both, had played a major role in bringing this about.

I. *Allegro affettuoso.* The only introduction is a furious cascade of chords for the piano soloist. The principal, plaintive melody for oboe is taken up by the piano and recurs in tender dialogue between the piano and orchestra:

It forms the basis of the entire first movement, returning in various impulsive melodic transformations, and in a brilliant marchlike version at the close. As a matter of fact, this same theme, or fragments of it subtly transformed, serves as the thematic kernel of all three movements.

II. *Intermezzo: Andantino grazioso.* This playfully lyric interlude has the sensitive, intimate quality of many of Schumann's most delicate miniatures for piano solo. It is a beguiling little three-part (A-B-A) form, with its opening theme based on a four-note rhythm derived from the theme of the first movement—the four rising notes in the middle of the theme. At the end of this movement the opening notes of the first-movement theme return to link the *Intermezzo* to the *Finale* and prepare for the *Finale's* opening theme.

III. *Allegro vivace.* The main theme of this last movement derives very clearly from the first-movement theme, thus establishing a thematic unity which became dear to the hearts of Romantic composers:

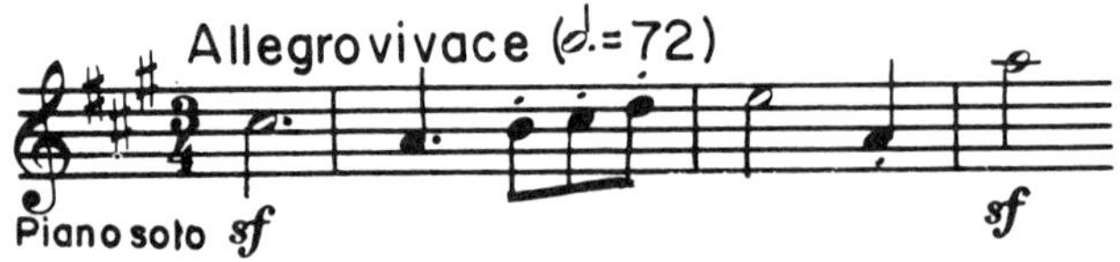

Like the first movement, the *Finale* is in a free sonata form, with a light-footed, delightfully syncopated contrasting theme and a *coda* of infectious rhythmic drive and brilliance. The Concerto is scored for pairs of flutes, oboes, clarinets, bassoons, horns, trumpets, kettledrums and the customary strings.

OVERTURE TO MANFRED, OPUS 115

The enigmatic figure of Manfred created by George Gordon, Lord Byron, seems almost predestined to capture the introspective, tortured imagination of Robert Schumann. Yet the affinity was more than personal.

On most of the European continent, Byron has always been more appreciated than in England. But in Germany he was idolized. "The English may think what they please of Byron," wrote Goethe, "but this much is certain: they have no [present-day] poet to compare to him." *Manfred* was Byron's first great poem of revolt. In addition, he personified Romantic melancholy, that all-pervasive *mal du siècle.* His melancholy, guilt-ridden hero grew so popular that *Manfred* was translated literally dozens of times into French, Spanish, Italian, German, Dutch, Danish, Russian, Polish, Czech, Hungarian, Romanian, and Romaic.

Byron himself described his dramatic poem to his publishers as being "of a very wild, metaphysical, and inexplicable kind. Almost all of the persons—but two or three—are spirits of the earth and air, or the waters; the scene is in the Alps; the hero is a kind of magician, who is dominated by a species of remorse, the cause of which is left half-explained. He wanders about, invoking these spirits, which appear to him and are of no use; at last he goes to the very abode of the Evil Principle, in *propria persona,* to evoke a ghost, which appears and gives him an ambiguous and disagreeable answer; and in the third act he is found by an attendant, dying in a tower, where he has studied his art."

The supernatural apparatus of Byron's poetic drama has lost much of its appeal. But the poem's burden of guilt is as modern as the alienation and despair of many a twentieth-century society. Surveying humanity and creation from the lofty Alpine peak of the Jungfrau, Manfred might be commenting on today's headlines:

> . . . we,
> Half dust, half deity, alike unfit
> To sink or soar, with our mix'd essence make
> A conflict of its elements, and breathe
> The breath of degradation and of pride,
> Contending with low wants and lofty will
> Till our mortality predominates,
> And all men are—what they name not to themselves
> And trust not to each other.

Schumann was deeply stirred. He liked to read the poem aloud in an intimate circle. On at least one occasion, when reading it to two friends from Düsseldorf, according to his early biographer Wasielewski, "his voice suddenly faltered, he burst into tears and was so overcome that he could read no further."

Schumann's first sketch for his *Manfred* music was penned in a burst of enthusiasm on April 5, 1848, the very day after he had completed his opera *Genoveva.* He finished his *Manfred* score (although he made some later revisions) on November 22, 1848. Schumann himself conducted the first concert performance of the Overture at a Leipzig Gewandhaus "Schumann Evening" on March 14, 1852. The American premiere of the Overture was presented by the New York Philharmonic six seasons later, on November 21, 1857, under the direction of Theodore Eisfeld.

"I have come to the conclusion [wrote Schumann to Liszt on December 25, 1851] that all the spirit apparitions must appear corporeally. I intend to send Herr Genast [the Weimar *régisseur*] details for the staging. Of the musical numbers, dear friend, I commend especially the Overture to your heart. If I may say so to you, I feel it is one of the strongest of my artistic children, and I hope that you may agree with me."

The slow introduction to the Overture begins with three abrupt chords answered by a melancholy oboe figure rising in slow half-steps, then falling back in a long chromatic descent. The rest of the introduction anticipates several other themes from the fast section of the Overture, all characterized by the chromatic half-steps typical of the style and development of the Overture. The introduction gathers speed and merges directly into the "passionate tempo" of the principal theme:

A whole group of contrasting lyric themes add to the yearning intensity of the music, which then explodes in an agitated development section. In form the music is a traditional sonata-allegro (first-movement symphonic form) with a long and poetic *coda.* As the initial excitement of the *coda* dies down, the slow oboe theme of the introduction returns, and the music fades to silence, recalling the death of Manfred at the end of Byron's poem.

The *Manfred* Overture is scored for 2 flutes, 2 oboes, 2 clarinets, 2 bassoons, 4 French horns (2 with valves and 2 natural horns), 3 trumpets, 3 trombones, and the traditional strings.

SYMPHONY NO. 1, B-FLAT MAJOR, OPUS 38 (SPRING)

"Within the last few days," wrote Schumann to his old friend Ernst Wenzel early in 1841, "I have completed, at least in outline, a labor which has kept me in a state of bliss, but also exhausted me. Think of it! A whole Symphony—moreover, a Spring Symphony! I can hardly believe, myself, that it is finished."

Like many a Romantic composer, Schumann was deeply immersed in literature. The concluding couplet of a poem by another friend, Adoph Böttger, seems to have been Schumann's point of departure for his Symphony. A year after finishing his Symphony, he sent a portrait of himself to Böttger, with the opening notes of his "Spring" Symphony and the words: "Beginning of a symphony inspired by a poem of Adoph Böttger. To the poet in remembrance of Robert Schumann." Böttger later identified the poem. Its two concluding lines evoke the rhythm of the Symphony's opening theme:

O wende, wende deinen Lauf,	(O turn, o turn aside thy course,
—Im Tale blüht der Frühling auf!	For the valley blooms with spring.)

> I wrote the Symphony toward the end of the winter of 1841, [wrote Schumann on November 23 of the following year to the composer Spohr] and if I may say so, in that flush of spring which carries a man away, even in his old age, and surprises him again each year. I did not intend to describe or paint, but I firmly believe that the time when it came into being influenced its character and form, and made it what it is.

The "flush of spring" which moved the thirty-year-old composer existed in his imagination. The "Spring" Symphony was actually begun in December, 1840, and completed during the first two snowy months of 1841. But since these were the early months of married life with his beloved Clara, they were, to Schumann, spring. On January 25, 1841 Clara noted in their joint diary: "Today, Monday, Robert has nearly finished his symphony. It was composed chiefly at night—for some nights my poor Robert has not slept on account of it. He calls it "Spring" Symphony. . . . A spring poem gave him the first impulse toward composing." The next day Clara recorded triumphantly that the final composition sketch of the entire four-movement structure had taken shape in a final burst of inspiration "begun and finished in four days . . ." The Symphony was Robert's first orchestral venture in this large form.

The orchestration itself took longer, of course, and after completing it on February 20, Robert wrote in the diary: "The Symphony has given me many happy hours. But now, after sleepless nights, comes exhaustion. I am like a young wife after a confinement—so light, so happy, and yet so ill and weak. My Clara understands this and treats me with double consideration—a kindness which I will repay. But I would never come to the end, if I were to tell all the love Clara has shown me during this time. I might have sought through millions without finding anyone who would treat me with such thoughtfulness and understanding."

Schumann did not exaggerate. There can be no question that it was Clara, with her delicate artistic intuitions and the emotional security she brought him, who unleashed the pent-up energies of Schumann's frail genius. He took strength from his love returned. The agonies and uncertainties of their long-drawn-out engagement, the humiliating battles they had fought against

Clara's father, who was determined to prevent their marriage, had hampered Robert's inspiration and prevented him from producing anything larger than exquisite miniatures. Now his confident spirit soared. This was not only the springtime of his married life, but the spring of his creative career.

Clara was delighted and after hearing Robert play it over to her on the piano, she wrote timidly in their diary that she would like to say a little about the Symphony, too; "but I should never finish talking about the buds, the scent of violets, the fresh green leaves, the birds in the air—all of which one hears living and stirring through it in youthful strength. Don't laugh at me, dear husband," she said. "If I can't express myself poetically, still the poetic spirit of this work has reached my inmost heart."

Less than six weeks after he finished it, Schumann's Symphony was performed at a pension-fund concert for the members of the illustrious Gewandhaus Orchestra of Leipzig. Clara, already a popular soloist, played piano works of her husband, of the young Chopin, Mendelssohn, Domenico Scarlatti, and Thalberg. And Felix Mendelssohn, who had helped Robert with orchestration problems during the rehearsals of the Symphony, now conducted it "with the greatest love and care" as "pleasure shone from his eyes." The Symphony was enthusiastically applauded by the normally conservative Leipzig audience and Schumann's symphonic career was launched as auspiciously as could be imagined.

I. *Andante un poco maestoso—Allegro molto vivace.* The slow introduction to the Symphony begins with a fanfare-like motive in the horns and trumpets, which Schumann wanted to sound "as if from on high, like a call to awaken":

The call is echoed by the full orchestra. "In what follows of the introduction," continued Schumann, "there might be a suggestion of the growing green of everything, of a butterfly taking wing, and in the *allegro* of the gradual assembly of all that belongs to spring. But these are fantastic thoughts that came to me *after* I had finished the work."

The main theme of the first movement proper is a quick transformation of the opening trumpet-call:

There is another gentle rocking figure in the woodwinds, and the oboe plays a new melody. All these are developed elaborately, and in the return of the opening themes Schumann took slight Romantic liberties with the Classical symphonic form.

II. *Larghetto.* The intimate *Larghetto* is one of the loveliest movements in all Schumann. Its graceful, far-flung melodic arch, is heard first in the violins:

This melody returns toward the end in the rich tone of a solo horn and oboe, and finally, in a slightly changed version, becomes the subject of the third movement, the *Scherzo,* which follows without any break. This transition is pure magic. Toward the end of the slow movement the orchestral color begins to change; the trombones enter softly transforming the melody so subtly you hardly realize it, until with an abrupt change of tempo, we are in the *scherzo.*

III. *Molto vivace—Molto più vivace.* The principal theme of the *scherzo* is the lovely *Larghetto* melody of the second movement transformed into the following vigorous, stamping figure in the new key of D minor. This *scherzo,* with its two contrasting trio sections, is full-blooded and masculine—the perfect counterpart to the feminine charm of the *Larghetto.*

IV. *Allegro animato e grazioso.* The *finale* begins with a majestic flourish of the full orchestra, and then comes an enchanting lightfooted, tripping figure in the violins. So delicate is this theme that Schumann cautioned a conductor who was to lead the work: "I like to think of it as the farewell of spring, and so I shouldn't want it to be played too frivolously."

A few measures further on (in the transition between the two principal themes of his *finale*) Schumann quotes himself, and surely not by accident. He quotes the principal theme from the *finale* of one of his favorite (and most interesting) works for piano solo, *Kreisleriana,* only slightly altered in rhythm to fit its new context, as follows:

Schumann was somewhat given to riddles and unacknowledged quotations from his own (and occasionally from Clara's) compositions. The literary, psychological and symbolic associations of Schumann's *Kreisleriana* (and its inspiration in the works of E.T.A. Hoffmann) are too complex to describe here, except to mention that the *Kreisleriana* seems to have been, in part, a self-portrait of Schumann. The part of the *Kreisleriana* quoted here was composed as an afterthought. Schumann noted in his diary of May 5, 1838, two days after he thought he had finished the work: "Kreisler piece in G minor, 6/8, with D-minor trio, composed in fire." Elsewhere he speaks of having composed the Symphony, too, "in fire." But we may never know what the connection was.

The "Spring" Symphony is scored for 2 flutes, 2 oboes, 2 clarinets, 2 bassoons, 4 horns, 2 trumpets, 3 trombones, kettledrums, triangle, and strings.

SYMPHONY NO. 2, C MAJOR, OPUS 61

"Drums and trumpets (*trombe* in C) have been sounding in my mind for quite a while now," wrote Schumann late in September 1845, to his friend, Felix Mendelssohn. "I have no idea what will come of it." What did come of it—three months later—was Schumann's C-major Symphony, which begins, ends, and is punctuated with a striking motto-fanfare for trumpets in C.

In a curious way the composition of this C-major Symphony was tied up with Schumann's recovery from a serious illness. Schumann's emotional constitution seems to have been so sensitive, so delicate, that he suffered from shocks an ordinary person might have taken in his stride. His ecstatically happy marriage to Clara Wieck, in 1840, gave him immense new reserves of physical and emotional stamina. But after their joint tour to Russia in 1844, Schumann began to be troubled by growing nervousness, depression, and even occasional loss of memory. Late that year he had a serious breakdown, which obliged him temporarily to give up all work: his composing and the editorship of the crusading *Neue Zeitschrift für Musik*, which he had founded, as well as his less congenial teaching at the Leipzig Conservatory. On his doctor's advice, the Schumanns moved to the quieter atmosphere of Dresden, where they had lived before and where he gradually recovered.

Toward the end of his convalescence Schumann began work on his Second Symphony, apparently in the conviction that he could rout the lingering traces of his illness by an heroic struggle as a composer. The sketch for the Symphony is said to have been accomplished with tremendous speed in just one week's time: from the twelfth through the eighteenth of December 1845. Perhaps as a result of Schumann's conscious struggle, this Symphony has a certain heroic quality that to some listeners recalls Beethoven. Yet Schumann remained true to his own nature and produced in the heartfelt, intimate *Adagio* some of the most characteristic and most moving pages he ever penned.

The completion of the Symphony took much longer. There were days when work on the Symphony seemed to exhaust the composer, to revive past agonies. But there were weeks when progress on the score raised his spirits and his high spirits in turn nourished the growing score. Then Clara would rejoice: "What a joyful sensation it must be [she wrote] when an abundant imagination like his bears one to higher and higher spheres. . . . I am often quite carried away with astonishment at my Robert! Whence does he get all his fire, his imagination, his freshness, his originality? One asks that again and again, and one cannot but say that he is one of the elect, to be gifted with such creative power." The score was completed in October 1846. Between the world premiere by the Leipzig Gewandhaus Orchestra under Mendelssohn's direction on November 5, 1846, and the repetition of the Symphony by the same forces eleven days later, Schumann made substantial changes in the orchestration, including the addition of three trombones.

I. *Sostenuto assai—Allegro ma non troppo.* The mysterious, slow introduction opens very softly with the trumpet motto which recurs from time to time through the Symphony:

Simultaneously we hear an ominous creeping figure in the strings, which also develops considerable importance. The motto theme repeats, the tempo increases gradually, we hear hints of the chief *Allegro* theme to come, and a little cadenza-like outburst of the violins leads directly into the main, fast part of the movement. Its principal theme has a jagged, driving rhythm, recalling Schumann's own characterization of this movement as "moody and refractory." Schumann uses the traditional first-movement (sonata-allegro) form, with an extended *coda.* This climax and conclusion of the movement is capped by the return of the motto theme.

II. *Scherzo: Allegro vivace.* The agitated *Scherzo* seems to lash out with a whiplike figure derived from the slow motion of the introduction to the Symphony. There are two contrasting trio sections and a last return of the fiery opening material, which combines with the fanfare from the start of the Symphony.

III. *Adagio espressivo.* The third movement is built on a nostalgic melody sung first by the violins:

It is taken up by the oboe, which then combines with a bassoon melody, a melancholy strain, which Schumann confessed having introduced at that point with particular pleasure. The yearning and passion grow to an ecstatic climax in the woodwind instruments against poignant trills of the violins. There is a short passage of counterpoint for contrast, and the song returns to close in the sweeter major mode. When Schumann completed this movement, the crown of the Symphony and one of its most beautiful pages, he had fallen into such nervous misery that the Symphony had to be put temporarily aside.

IV. *Allegro molto vivace.* "In the finale," wrote Schumann, "I first began to feel like myself again; and indeed, I was much better after I had completed the work." The movement is brilliant and vigorous. It is related to the memorable *Adagio* by a transformation of that movement's principal melody, which appears here as the lyric subordinate theme:

The Symphony is further unified by the recall (near the close) of the trumpet motto theme. It sounds at first softly, as at the opening of the Symphony, but it grows, perhaps symbolically in Schumann's mind, to a more assertive tone and to an exultant, victorious conclusion.

The score of the C-major Symphony calls for 2 flutes, 2 oboes, 2 clarinets, 2 bassoons, 2 horns, 2 trumpets, 3 trombones, bass trombone, kettledrums, and strings.

SYMPHONY NO. 3, E-FLAT MAJOR, OPUS 97, (RHENISH)

More than any other of Robert Schumann's four symphonies, his Third, or "Rhenish" Symphony, is frankly descriptive music. Written soon after the Schumanns went to live in the Rhenish city of Düsseldorf, the Symphony is a glorification of the life, the landscape and the most famous building of the Rhineland: the Cathedral of Cologne.

It was September 2, 1850, when Robert, his beloved Clara and their children arrived in Düsseldorf. Schumann had been appointed conductor of the local chorus and orchestra, a position to which he looked forward because of the opportunity it would give him to get the intimate feel of orchestral music under his own hands. Before the end of the month he and Clara had visited Cologne, where they were especially impressed by the Cathedral. Before the year was out, Robert had visited the Cathedral again and witnessed a solemn ceremony elevating the Archbishop of Cologne to the rank of cardinal. The ceremony made a deep impression on him and he recalled the picture in the fourth movement of his "Rhenish" Symphony, which was finished before the end of the year.

The first performance of the "Rhenish" Symphony was in Geisler Hall, Düsseldorf, on February 6, 1851, at the sixth concert of the Allgemeine Musikverein. Schumann conducted from manuscript.

I. *Lebhaft.* The exultant opening may reflect Schumann's confidence and joy in his new surroundings. The first movement contains some of the most brightly colored music Schmann has given us. What vitality there is in the buoyant syncopations of the principal theme, which is proclaimed at once by the full orchestra without the formality of an introduction!

II. *Scherzo: Sehr mässig.* The second movement, an easy going *Scherzo,* seems originally to have had the subtitle "Morning on the Rhine." It resembles a peasant dance, the *Ländler,* from which the waltz is descended.

III. *Nicht schnell.* The third movement is a graceful, lyric interlude, corresponding to the traditional, songful, slow movement of the Classical symphony. It is based on two melodies: the first a duet for clarinets and the second a graceful chain of thirds for the darker-colored violas.

IV. *Feierlich.* Over the fourth movement Schumann originally wrote: "In the character of the accompaniment to a solemn ceremony." But later he struck out this explanation, remarking: "One should not show his heart to the people, for the general impression of a work of art is more effective. Then the listener will at least not set up any absurd connections in his mind." Yet we do know that this impressive music was inspired by what Schumann saw and felt in the Cathedral.

To enhance the religious solemnity of the fourth movement, Schumann added three trombones to his orchestra. It is these trombones that announce, very softly, the principal theme of the movement, which is taken up later and developed in various forms by other instruments:

What did the Cathedral mean to Schumann? He was twenty when he first saw it. We who know it today only as a rather academically finished structure can have little idea of the awesome impression it made on the traveller of Schumann's day, when it was still an unfinished ruin. An anonymous print of 1824 shows the Cathedral much as Schumann must have seen it at his first visit in September, 1830, with lesser buildings still huddled, medieval-style against its walls.

The medieval builders had completed the eastern choir of the cathedral. On the western façade the south tower had progressed no further than its second story. The gap between choir and tower, the full length of the gigantic nave, had been waiting for five hundred years to be filled. Left behind by Gothic engineers, a great crane stood motionless on the stump of the south tower, a familiar, beloved silhouette on the skyline of Cologne. By 1816 the crane, decayed, bent, and in danger of collapse, had to be torn down. But the

THE CATHEDRAL OF COLOGNE IN 1824.

The unfinished Cathedral cast a strong spell on Romantic poets, painters, architects, and musicians from Goethe to Robert Schumann. The stirring process of its completion inspired two movements of Schumann's "Rhenish" Symphony. (*Photo Rauch; courtesy, Bavaria Verlag*)

inhabitants of Cologne were so attached to it that a subscription was raised and the ancient crane was ceremoniously restored on September 11, 1819.

Romantics saw the ruin as a mute call to action, a pathetic appeal to fulfill a medieval dream and the naive faith it embodied. They visited the inside of the choir and were overwhelmed by its majesty, the mystery of its Gothic shadows. It was a Romantic visitor to the choir of Cologne whose imagination first saw "lofty, slender Gothic pillars grouped like trees in an ancient forest," their highest branches crossing and intertwining in a dim vault of pointed arches, where the eye could scarcely follow.

By the time the Schumanns visited Cologne again in 1850, the whole nation was astir with the grandiose project of completing the Cathedral. The elevation of the Archbishop of Cologne to the rank of the Cardinal was part of a project charged with emotion. No wonder Schumann remembered the ceremony.

V. *Lebhaft.* The final movement of the "Rhenish" Symphony opens in the mood of a brilliant folk-festival scene and ends with a triumphal return of the Cathedral music.

The Symphony is scored for 2 flutes, 2 oboes, 2 clarinets, 2 bassoons, 4 horns, 2 trumpets, 3 trombones (for the 4th and 5th movements only), kettledrums, and the usual strings.

SYMPHONY NO. 4, D MINOR, OPUS 120

Schumann composed his D-minor Symphony during the first ecstatically happy year of his marriage to Clara Wieck. During his long courtship Schumann had suffered agonies from the opposition of Clara's father, who had put every conceivable legal, moral and emotional obstacle in the lovers' way. After their wedding, the tranquillity, warmth and understanding that Clara brought into Schumann's life gave him a tremendous creative impetus.

In the diary which they kept jointly, Clara wrote late in the spring of 1841 that Robert had begun another symphony, "which is to be in one movement, but with an *adagio* and a finale. As yet I have heard nothing of it," [she continued] "but from seeing Robert's bustling and hearing the chord of D minor sound wildly in the distance, I know in advance that another work is being wrought in the depths of his soul. Heaven is kindly disposed toward us: Robert cannot be happier in the composition than I am when he shows me such a work." A few days later she added, "Robert is composing steadily. He has already completed three movements and I hope the symphony will be ready by his birthday."

It was not finished for Schumann's birthday (June 8), but Clara's (September 13), which also turned out to be, the day on which they christened their first child Marie. "One thing makes me happy," wrote Schumann in their diary, as he presented Clara with the new score, "the consciousness of being still far from my goal, of being obliged to keep doing better, and with this the feeling that I have the strength to reach it."

Despite his original intention of composing in one continuous movement, only the *Scherzo* and *finale* were linked to each other in the first version. When this was given its first performance at a Leipzig Gewandhaus concert on December 6, 1841, it was not very successful, and Schumann himself seemed dissatisfied. He put it aside for ten years, and after publishing two more symphonies (to which he gave the numbers Two and Three) he revised the D-minor and published it as his Symphony No. 4.

In the revised version, first performed at the Spring Festival of the Lower Rhine in Düsseldorf on March 3, 1853, Schumann's changes were considerable. He altered the orchestration, changed the thematic development, pruning elaborate contrapuntal work, especially in the *finale*, in order to gain a broader, simpler line, and changed the opening of the *finale* to give it a stronger thematic link to the opening movement. He emphasized the unity of the score by linking all four movements in one uninterrupted stream of music, as he had originally intended.

I. *Ziemlich langsam; Lebhaft.* The slow introduction begins with a pensive melody which unifies the Symphony, returning again and again in various rhythmic and melodic transformations throughout the score:

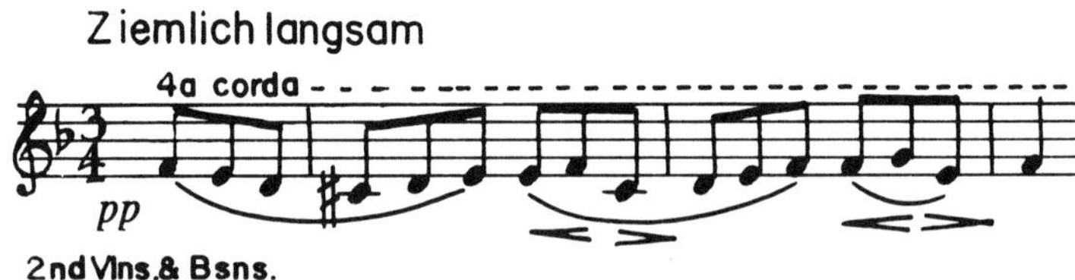

Gradually the music gains momentum as it nears the principal *Lebhaft* section; a rushing, whirling figure derived from the preceding melody takes shape:

This figure dominates the movement, which is a free fantasia in symphonic style but not in traditional symphonic form. As it develops, a striking new figure emerges: three vigorous chords, harmonic hammer blows as it were, which return in the opening themes of both the *Scherzo* and *finale*.

II. *Romanze: Ziemlich langsam.* In the second movement, which follows without pause, a mournful tune sung by oboe and cellos alternates with the languorous melody of the introduction to the first movement. In a contrasting middle section this same melody of the introduction sounds in the sunnier major mode, extended and embroidered by a graceful solo violin.

III. *Scherzo: Lebhaft.* The *Scherzo* bursts out with the hammer-blow rhythm of the first movement, marking the strong beats of a vigorous three-measure phrase derived from the melody of the introduction:

The more serene middle section recalls the embroidered version of the same melody from the middle of the preceding movement.

IV. *Langsam; Lebhaft.* The bridge to the finale is a pensive transition recalling memories of the first movement (the hammer-blow rhythm and the swirling figure) which are now recombined to form the opening of the exultant finale:

Two gracefully contrasted singing themes spread through the orchestra. After a traditional development, a partial reprise recalls the two singing themes only. The richly melodious *coda* ends in a headlong *presto.*

The D-minor Symphony is scored for 2 flutes, 2 oboes, 2 clarinets, 2 bassoons, 4 horns, 2 trumpets, 3 trombones, kettledrums, and the traditional strings.

Alexander Scriabin

Born January 6, 1872, Moscow—died April 27, 1915, Moscow

POEM OF ECSTASY, OPUS 54

"To be regarded merely as a musician would be the worst fate that could befall me," Scriabin is said to have declared to his friend Leonid Sabaniev. "It would be terrible to remain nothing more than a composer of sonatas and symphonies."

Scriabin's *Poem of Ecstasy* is the second of a group of three symphonic poems with mystical overtones. The first of the three is the *Divine Poem,* Opus 43, the second the *Poem of Ecstasy* and the third *Prometheus, the Poem of Fire,* Opus 60. The *Divine Poem* depicts "the struggle between Man enslaved to a personal God and Man who is himself God but lacking the will to proclaim his divinity. Thus frustrated, he immerses himself in the pleasures of sense, depicted in the second section of the work. But internal divine powers assist him toward liberation, and in the third and last section of the tone poem he gives himself up to the joys of 'untrammeled existence'."

For his *Poem of Ecstasy* Scriabin wrote a long explanatory poem, the meaning of which is difficult to condense into prose. The opening lines, which recur like a refrain, have been translated as follows:

The Spirit
Winged by the thirst for life,
Takes flight
On the heights of negation.
There in the rays of his dream
Arises a magic world
Of marvelous images and feelings.
  The Spirit playing.
  The Spirit longing.
The Spirit with fancy creating all,
Surrenders himself to the bliss of love.

The English musicologist Gerald Abraham tells us, on the authority of Scriabin's friends Y.D. Engel and Leonid Sabaniev, that Scriabin began the composition of his *Poem of Ecstasy* in a little villa at Bogliasco, near Genoa, where he rusticated for ten months starting in June 1905, with Tatiana Schlözer, his muse and love, for whom he had left his wife. The consequent scandal created many enemies for Scriabin in his native Moscow and throughout the world. But he heard of a conductor in New York, Modest Altschuler, who was interested in contemporary Russian music. Scriabin wrote Altschuler and received in reply an urgent invitation to visit America, to appear there as soloist in his own Piano Concerto and to give solo recitals. Scriabin went; but when Tatiana joined him here in January 1907, Vassily Safonov, the conductor of the New York Philharmonic, barred Scriabin's works from this Orchestra's programs. (Safonov was a friend of the deserted Mme. Scriabin.) Scriabin and Tatiana finally left the United States under something of a cloud and in some haste, according to friends who castigated the "social hypocrisy of the Americans."

In the spring of 1907 Scriabin wrote from Paris that he had finished his *Poem of Ecstasy*. During the summer he revised the instrumentation with the help of Modest Altschuler who visited him for two weeks in Switzerland. Altschuler later recalled: "Scriabin is neither an atheist nor a theosophist, yet his creed includes ideas somewhat related to each of these schools of thought. There are three divisions in his poem: (1) His soul in the orgy of love; (2) The realization of a fantastical dream; (3) The glory of his own art."

The *Poem of Ecstasy* had its world premiere in St. Petersburg under the direction of Hugo Wahrlich near the end of 1908. The first American performance followed shortly after on December 10, 1908, when Modest Altschuler conducted the Russian Symphony Society in New York City.

The *Poem of Ecstasy* is composed in one continuous whole, with fluctuating tempos and several themes which recur throughout. The first of these is heard at the very beginning of the opening section, *Andante, languido,* in the voice of a solo flute, echoed by solo violin and piccolo. The most prominent of the recurrent themes is introduced by two trumpets "with a noble and gentle majesty":

This is the theme which returns during the final ecstatic climax, proclaimed in a blaze of glory, by 8 horns, trumpet, pipe organ (with accompanying bells) and harp, with brilliant, trilling figurations of high strings and winds.

The *Poem of Ecstasy* is scored for piccolo, 3 flutes, 3 oboes, English horn, 3 clarinets, bass clarinet, 3 bassoons, contrabassoon, 8 horns, 5 trumpets, 3 trombones, tuba, kettledrums, bass drum, cymbals, tam-tam, triangle, small bells, large bell, celesta, 2 harps, pipe organ, and the traditional strings.

PROMETHEUS, THE POEM OF FIRE, OPUS 60

Prometheus, the Poem of Fire is the last of Scriabin's completed orchestral works and is widely considered to be his greatest. It is the third "poem" of a trilogy that was to have been a tetralogy. The first, *The Divine Poem,* completed in 1905, was Scriabin's Symphony No. 3. *The Poem of Ecstasy,* completed in 1908, was given no symphonic title, although its style was symphonic. *Prometheus, the Poem of Fire,* completed in 1911, was to have been followed by a final *Mysterium,* a climactic magnum opus, which was envisaged as integrating all of the arts, including an art of perfume. Scriabin expected the premiere of this apocalyptic work, which was to take place in India, to transform not only the composer and performers but all of humanity.

The Prometheus of Scriabin's musical imagination was only distantly related to the Prometheus of Greek mythology. Since fire was Prometheus's stolen gift to mankind, Scriabin felt he could be identified with Lucifer, "the Light Bringer," and even with Satan, who was also a disobedient rebel.

A program note by Leonid Sabaniev, which Scriabin authorized for the world premiere of *The Poem of Fire,* observes that "Prometheus, Satan and Lucifer all meet in ancient myth. They represent the active energy of the universe, its creative principle. The fire is light, life, struggle, increase, abundance and thought. At first this powerful force manifests itself wearily, as languid thirsting for life. Within this lassitude, then, appears the primordial polarity between soul and matter. The creative upsurge or gust of feeling registers a protest against this torpor. Later it does battle and conquers matter —of which it itself is a mere atom—and returns to the quiet and tranquillity . . . thus completing the cycle."

Scriabin began work on his *Prometheus* early in 1909 before leaving for Brussels, where he arrived with his companion, Tatiana, on April 1, 1909. Before he christened the new score *Prometheus,* Scriabin apparently had his *Mysterium* in mind. The chorus, which plays only a minor part toward the end of *Prometheus,* was to have a much greater role in the *Mysterium.* It was to be clad in solid white and the audience for the *Mysterium* was to be similarly garbed. At what point it became clear to Scriabin that he was composing not his final *Mysterium* but a work which would precede it, we do not know. But by November at the latest his correspondence gives the title as *Prometheus, the Poem of Fire* and on December 5, 1909, he writes: "I am working like a madman on *Prometheus*—successfully these past days, although I am right tired . . . have not left the house in more than two weeks."

Scriabin had formed a friendship with Serge Koussevitzky, who was just beginning his conductorial career in Russia and greatly admired Scriabin's works. It was agreed that Koussevitzky would conduct the first performance of *Prometheus,* which was originally planned for 1910. The score was not finished in time for 1910, but this did not prevent Scriabin from joining Koussevitzky on his famous Volga River tour, in the course of which Koussevitzky's orchestra gave nineteen concerts in eleven Volga cities, some of which had never had an orchestral concert before.

Koussevitzky prepared the premiere with the utmost care, taking nine rehearsals for the complex score. His orchestra was essentially that of the Bolshoi Theater. At the first performance, which took place in Moscow on March 15, 1911, Scriabin (who was a celebrated piano virtuoso) himself played the important piano part. The public reception of the new work was favorable, but not as enthusiastic as it had been for *The Poem of Ecstasy* and other earlier Scriabin works.

There was, from Scriabin's point of view, one important defect in this world premiere. He had conceived *Prometheus* as a work for orchestra and colored light. The score includes a part for color organ, a keyboard which was to project colors on a screen. Scriabin had worked out an exact table of color correspondences for each of the twelve tones of the chromatic (tempered) scale. At the premiere the color organ did not function. Indeed, Scriabin was never to see a performance of *The Poem of Fire* with his colored lights. (The first performance to realize this part of Scriabin's score was the American premiere presented in Carnegie Hall by the Russian Symphony Orchestra, Modest Altschuler conducting, on March 20, 1915. The effect, however, was far from successful; the consensus of opinion being that the rather crude light effects merely distracted the listeners' attention from the music.) There have been few attempts to cope with this part of the score and Scriabin himself authorized performances without the light organ and without the brief choral participation in the final pages. In a letter of October 1912 to Alexander Siloti, Scriabin declared that the omission of the chorus "is tolerable, provided there is STILL THE ORGAN PART."

Even aside from the color organ and chorus, the musical apparatus for *Prometheus* is on the grandiose side: piccolo, 3 flutes, 3 oboes, English horn, 3 clarinets, bass clarinet, 3 bassoons, contrabassoon, 8 horns, 5 trumpets, 3 trombones, tuba, kettledrums, bass drum, gong, large bells (especially devised by Koussevitzky for the premiere), campanelli, celesta, triangle, 2 harps, pipe organ and a piano part so prominent as almost to suggest at moments a concerto. In the complex symbolisms of visual color and tone color, the piano solo with its imperious entry (it is so marked in the score) symbolizes Man.

Harmonically, the entire score of *Prometheus,* with its lush sonorities and enormous variety of harmonic color, is derived from one single chord, which Scriabin called the "mystical chord," and which he juggled in various ways to produce different chords and themes. As he demonstrated the derivations to his friend, Sabaniev, he declared: "There is no difference between melody and harmony. They are one and the same. I have followed this principle strictly in *Prometheus.* There is not a wasted note, not a wedge where a mosquito could get in and bite!"

The mystical chord consists of a rising sequence of fourths, the first augmented, the second diminished, the third augmented and the last two, perfect fourths (A, D sharp, G, C sharp, F sharp, B). It is this combination of tones (rearranged, so that the lowest tone is G) which opens the score with misty tremolos of the strings, bowing high over the fingerboard. This, according to Faubion Bowers in his biography of Scriabin, represents "the Cosmos as it was before Karma, before lives had been lived and deeds accumulated predestination. Out of this long sustained chord dimly rises the melody of the Creative Principle. Then, a muted trumpet sends up the Will theme. . . ." Bowers relays in considerable detail the increasingly mystical symbolism of the score until emotion takes over and at the end: "The music becomes delirious. The *coda* is lost in vertigo."

One would have to be a theosophist (as Scriabin was) and a student of Scriabin's extraordinary mind to follow all the significances which he apparently heard (and saw) in this astounding score. But one should beware of thinking it only a period piece. In ways that few people realized at the time, and few since have taken the trouble to discover, the score points toward the future and to some of the most rigorous and fruitful devices of later twentieth-century music. As well-versed an authority as George Perle has called Scriabin "the first to exploit serial procedures systematically as a means of compensating for the loss of traditional tonal functions."

Roger Sessions

Born December 28, 1896, Brooklyn, New York

SYMPHONY NO. 8

It is impossible for any one work, even so rich a work as this Eighth Symphony to give an idea of the astoundingly varied, fruitful, and much honored career of Roger Sessions—whose music is nevertheless far too little known to the average American concertgoer. A man of wide-ranging interests in literature, the visual arts, history and politics, and an accomplished linguist, Sessions was educated at Harvard and Yale. In composition his teachers were Horatio Parker and Ernest Bloch. Sessions himself has taught at Smith College, the Cleveland Institute of Music, the University of California at Berkeley, and at Princeton University. Through his many prominent pupils, his organization of the Copland-Sessions Concerts of modern music in New York, and through his own compositions, he has been a major influence on contemporary American music.

Sessions's Eighth Symphony was commissioned by the New York Philharmonic Symphony in connection with the celebration of its 125th anniversary season. It was first performed by the Philharmonic on May 2, 3, and 6, 1968, under the direction of William Steinberg. For these premiere performances Sessions kindly penned the following notes:

> My Eighth Symphony was composed during the fall and winter of 1967–1968. It thus follows hard on the composition of my Sixth and Seventh Symphonies, which were completed respectively in 1966 and 1967.
>
> Probably this is the shortest of my symphonies. As in the case of No. 5, composed in 1963–64, the work is played without pause. Whereas my Fifth Symphony consists of three relatively short movements, the eighth is in two somewhat longer ones: a very slow first movement followed by a fast and more elaborate one.
>
> The Symphony was commissioned by, and written in homage to, the New York Philharmonic Society on the occasion of its hundred and twenty-

fifth anniversary. There is also a personal dedication to my daughter, Elizabeth.

The term "symphony" implies for me a work of large design, generally characterized by contrasts between sections of extended duration. It does not necessarily imply adherence to so-called "standard" forms, which were in any case never so "standard" as they are often reputed to be. I have never been able to interest myself in such categories as "*the* Symphony," "*the* Sonata," and the like, which I regard as, at best, devices which enable one to file away works by such composers as, say, Webern, Mahler, or Liszt by squeezing them into the same folder with Haydn or even Corelli and Handel; at worst I feel they are academic devices which inhibit more understanding than they promote.

The present work is scored for a moderately large orchestra; flutes and oboes in threes, including piccolo, alto flute (in the first movement only), and English horn; clarinets and bassoons in four, including E-flat clarinet, bass clarinet, and contrabassoon; four horns, three trumpets, four trombones, and tuba; tympani and a large percussion section; piano, harp, xylophone, marimba, vibraphone, and glockenspiel—the latter four instruments, in my orchestral conception, seem to me to belong with the piano and the harp rather than with the drums and bells; finally, of course, the strings.

In this work there are no literal repetitions, though there are many very clear associative elements, both thematic and otherwise. This is generally, though not invariably, the case with most of my music of the last thirty-five years or more. It is not the result of any theoretical or dogmatic commitment on my part, nor is it the result of "chance," but because of the demands of the music in each particular instance. I mention this in connection with the following descriptive summary, which is intended simply to help the attentive listener who hears the work for the first time.

I. The Symphony opens with a descending melodic line played by the first violins and flutes in unison; the flutes are replaced by the English horn as the melody approaches the lower middle register. This passage is recalled twice in the course of the work. In modified and fragmented form it recurs just before the final episode of the first movement; and, once more in modified though continuous form, it brings the whole symphony to its close in the very last measures.

After these opening measures, the first movement, *Adagio e mesto,* develops in three distinct episodes. In the first of these, a phrase characterized by reiterated melodic intervals of a second is twice interrupted by muted violins and violas which carry the melodic line downward to the cadence. At that point the meter breaks up into irregular groups, as woodwinds and violins carry on a kind of dialogue, which leads back to the dark sonorities with which this episode began.

The second episode is characterized by a melody of the oboe which, by its successive entrances, divides the episode into three sections. The second of these sections introduces, first, in the high violins, reminiscences of the first part of the movement; the third leads directly to an outburst of the full orchestra, forming the climax of the movement. As this subsides, the high violins, over the rustling maracas, are heard again, as at the opening of the movement, and lead to the final episode, which is shorter than the others, and brings reminiscences of the first episode, in the form of melodic fragments. These expand into the final passage of the violins, which bring the movement to a quiet close.

II. The second movement, *Allegro con brio,* is introduced by a short motif (on the woodwinds and xylophone, answered by the strings) which does not reappear till near the close of the movement. The two fast sections which form the main body of the movement are characterized by the frequent recurrence of a three-note figure, which occurs twice in the opening phrase of the violins and clarinet, and which takes many forms and generates many varied phrases as the movement proceeds. The first of these two fast sections leads to a quieter episode, in which the solo violin—introduced by passages on the harp—plays a leading role. The music grows more restless and leads to a climax, after which the harp passages return, and lead to a resumption of the fast movement, which becomes more elaborate, and introduces more varied and contrasting material. After the second of two large climaxes, the music subsides once more; the solo violin returns briefly. Both melody and harmony are different than before. A very brief passage in the strings alone leads directly to a final resumption of the fast movement, which, however, quickly dissolves, leaving only the first violins and their descending line, once more over the soft rustle of the maracas. The line passes to the violoncelli, which are joined by oboe, English horn, and a muted horn in what may be called the final gesture of the work.

May I note once more that the above is an *ex post facto* description of externals, and is designed simply to aid the listener hearing the work for the first time, to orient himself. I have purposely avoided matters of technique, including the dodecaphonic principle which underlies the vocabulary and the structure of this work. The dodecaphonic principle has been now in existence for forty years, and its basic principles are available for those who are curious about it. Some composers, of which I am one, find it helpful in gaining the musical results that they want. But it can never be strongly enough emphasized that it is the musical result, and not the technical means by which it is accomplished, that matters, and which is the composer's article of faith. This is why I feel that matters of technique are irrelevant in a context like the present one.

ROGER SESSIONS

Dmitri Shostakovich

Born September 25, 1906, St. Petersburg—died August 9, 1975, Moscow

SYMPHONY NO. 1, OPUS 10

This fresh and surprisingly masterful score was Shostakovich's graduation piece at Leningrad Conservatory. He was eighteen years old when he wrote it and nineteen when it was first performed (May 12, 1926) in Leningrad under the direction of Nicolai Malko. The graduation piece was quick to make its way outside Russia. In November 1927 Bruno Walter conducted it in Berlin, and twelve months later Leopold Stokowski introduced it to the United States at a concert of the Philadelphia Orchestra. Arturo Toscanini conducted the first New York Philharmonic performance on April 8, 1931.

The Soviets were quick to realize that Shostakovich was the most gifted of their younger composers, and he became a sort of unofficial composer laureate. He composed music of more depth and more power after this engaging work, and his Seventh Symphony, composed during the German siege of Leningrad in World War II, was given far wider publicity on the wave of emotion its subject inspired during the war. But this First Symphony, still his most popular, has a spontaneity that makes it particularly appealing.

I. *Allegretto—Allegro non troppo.* An angular, grotesque figure—one of the principal themes—for solo trumpet, muted, opens the introduction. The main body of the movement, *Allegro non troppo,* opens with a jaunty idea which scampers along in the clarinet, like a cross between a quick march tune and a bit of old-fashioned ragtime:

This theme is particularly interesting because it returns as a theme of the third movement, transformed and in a much slower tempo, and again in another transformation in the finale. A lovely lyric theme for solo flute follows and the themes are worked out pretty much in the Classical tradition, except that in the final restatement the themes are brought back in reverse order: this time, the flute is heard first and the clarinet theme printed above comes second.

II. *Allegro.* This is a perky little *scherzo,* with a theme full of quicksilver and mocking laughter. It has a slow middle section that might have been labeled *religioso* if it hadn't been composed in Soviet Russia.

III. *Lento.* The lyric slow movement opens with a melancholy, chromatically tinged melody which is related to the clarinet theme of the first movement quoted above. In this movement it is sung first by a solo oboe:

Then it is taken up by the strings and finally developed to an impassioned climax. A dramatic roll of the snare drum leads without pause into the *finale.*

IV. *Allegro molto—Lento—Allegro molto.* The *finale* is fast, with agitated, whirling figures building towards the climax with its famous passage for the kettledrum alone:

There are interesting transformations of various themes, including the principal *Allegro* theme of the first movement, and the closing measures are brilliant and frantic with a great fanfare of the brass instruments.

The Symphony is scored for 2 piccolos, 3 flutes, 2 oboes, 2 B-flat clarinets, 2 bassoons, 4 horns, 2 trumpets, alto trumpet in F, 3 trombones, tuba, 3 timpani, triangle, snare drum, cymbals, bass drum, gong, bells, piano, and the traditional strings.

SYMPHONY NO. 5, OPUS 47

What would one give to be able to read the mind of Dmitri Shostakovich as he composed his Fifth Symphony, the score which was to rescue him from the outer darkness, the bleak Siberia of official Soviet disfavor, and restore him to his former sunny eminence as uncrowned composer laureate of the U.S.S.R.!

Having begun so brilliantly at the age of nineteen with a First Symphony that immediately made the rounds of the music capitals of the world and remains a popular work, having gone from success to success in his native land, Shostakovich must have staggered when the ax fell. It fell first on his opera, *Lady Macbeth of the Mtsensk District,* which was denounced by *Pravda* as un-Soviet, unwholesome, cheap, eccentric, tuneless, "a leftist [sic] monstrosity" with action that was "coarse, primitive, vulgar." This was January 28, 1936. Nine days later, *Pravda* returned to attack Shostakovich's ballet, *The Clear Stream.* This time Shostakovich was accused of having depicted in his music not the real peasants of a Soviet collective farm, as he had intended, "but tinsel *paysans* from a pre-Revolutionary chocolate box . . ."

Despite their crippling rebuke, Soviet authorities were well aware of Shostakovich's talents, and of his national value. Other Soviet composers and musicians expressed their confidence in his ultimate rehabilitation and he was encouraged to continue his creative work. Soviet commentators, and Shostakovich himself, later declared that this had been a time of severe soul-searching. There is no reason to doubt their statements. But one may be permitted to wonder just what kind of soul-searching. Shostakovich completed his Fourth Symphony on which he was working, and it was put into rehearsal by the Leningrad Philharmonic in December, 1936, but he found the members of the orchestra unenthusiastic and withdrew his score.

Did he experience a true change of heart? Did he really agree with the authorities that he, as a Soviet artist, should compose music that would have greater appeal for the Soviet masses: music that was simpler, more tuneful, more monumental, optimistic, heroic? Conceivably he did. For this was a decade in which great artists of other countries (Aaron Copland and Paul

Hindemith, to name only two prominent examples) turned momentarily away from the tense harmonies of rather complex styles, to simpler, more melodious manners designed consciously to woo a larger audience. Whatever his motives, Shostakovich succeeded. His Fifth Symphony, composed on a heroic scale with an expansively, emotionally slow movement, catchy *scherzo* rhythms, and an opening perhaps deliberately designed to recall Beethoven, was a smashing success. According to the authoritative periodical, *Sovietskaya Muzica* of March 1938, Shostakovich himself described his Fifth Symphony as "a Soviet artist's practical, creative reply to just criticism."

Elsewhere, Shostakovich declared: "The theme of my Symphony is the stabilization of a personality. In the center of this composition—conceived lyrically from beginning to end—I saw a man with all his experiences. The Finale resolves the tragically tense impulses of the earlier movements into optimism and joy of living." The first performance of the Symphony took place on November 21, 1937, in Leningrad, under the direction of Eugene Mravinsky, as part of the festival of the twentieth anniversary of the Soviet Republic. Typical of the Soviet critical reactions was the comment of the prominent author, Alexei Tolstoy, who wrote in *Izvestia:* "The powerful, rousing sounds of the *Finale* stirred the audience. All rose to their feet, infused with joy and happiness streaming from the orchestra like a spring breeze. We cannot but trust the Soviet listener. His reaction to music is a just verdict. Our listener is organically unreceptive to decadent, gloomy, pessimistic art, but he responds enthusiastically to good art that is clear, bright, joyful, optimistic, viable."

The Fifth Symphony was enthusiastically received at its United States premiere, a broadcast by the NBC Symphony under the direction of Arthur Rodzinski on April 9, 1938. It was quickly recorded, taken into the repertories of other American symphony orchestras, and became a popular work. It is in the traditional four movements.

I. *Moderato.* The first movement opens with a boldly jagged theme reminiscent of the subject of Beethoven's "Great Fugue," Opus 113. Initiated by cellos and double basses in octaves, it is immediately imitated by all the violins in powerful octave sonorities.

The jagged rhythm subsides to a gently rocking accompaniment figure, over which the first violins introduce a second theme, a gently lyric phrase derived, although rather distantly, from the opening theme. The exposition is rounded off by yet another version, a soaring, lyric version of the opening jagged theme, accompanied now by gentle pulsations of the lower strings.

The heart of the movement lies in a central development section of clashing harmonies and rhythms, beginning with a pounding *ostinato* rhythm in the depths of the piano with double basses and cellos. The gentle, lyric phrase of the symphony's opening page is transformed by French horns, then by trombones and shrill woodwinds into a combative, dynamic phrase. The climax of excitement merges into a reprise of the opening thematic material, now greatly enhanced in intensity, volume, and color. The movement is rounded off by a peaceful *coda.*

II. *Allegretto.* The second movement is in traditional *scherzo* form, with a heavily frolicsome *scherzo* proper, and a more delicate central trio section introduced by a rather coquettish melody for solo violin.

III. *Largo.* The slow movement is perhaps the most stirring of all four, the most original, the most deeply felt. Shostakovich showed his greatest strength where so many of his contemporaries seemed weakest: in melody. This great melodic arch could scarcely have been put together by a mere technician, however skilled, or by a mere suppliant for official favor, however sleek. It grows simply and naturally from the subdued lyricism of the first bars:

rising to the more rhythmic motive introduced by first violins:

and culminating in a climax of tremendous intensity before subsiding into the deep calm of the beginning.

IV. *Allegro non troppo.* The finale is built around a thunderous rondo refrain proclaimed by trumpets, trombones and tuba over crashing kettledrums. Ideas come so fast to Shostakovich that it can hardly be called mere fertility—it is a volcanic eruption of ideas. But like many volcanoes, this one sends up along with the fire of inspiration a certain amount of slag and ashes. Alongside passages of imposing grandeur and power, there are bits of brassy bombast, dramatic in intent and intensely theatrical in effect. There are moments when a listener feels swept along by sheer temperament.

The score of Shostakovich's Fifth Symphony calls for piccolo, 2 flutes, 2 oboes, clarinet in E-flat, 2 clarinets in A, 2 clarinets in B-flat, 2 bassoons, contrabassoon, 4 horns, 3 trumpets, 3 trombones, tuba, kettledrums, snare drum, triangle, cymbals, bass drum, gong, 2 harps, small bells, xylophone, celesta, piano, and the traditional string choir.

SYMPHONY NO. 6, OPUS 53

After the triumph of his Fifth Symphony with which Shostakovich restored himself to the good graces of Soviet authorities, there seems to have been widespread expectation that his Sixth Symphony would be cast in a similarly heroic "positive" vein. This was suggested in the many letters he was said to have received from various parts of the Soviet Union, congratulating him on the Fifth Symphony and spurring him on to fresh efforts in that direction. Shostakovich himself seems to have had something of the sort in mind for he announced that his next symphony would be on the subject of Lenin.

But somewhere between the announcement and the execution the original project perished or was sidetracked. When the Sixth Symphony materialized, it not only did not bear the name of Lenin, it was obviously not a political work, nor even a very positive one. On the contrary, it was dominated by the romantic melancholy of its slow opening movement.

So it is not surprising that the first performance on December 3, 1939, in Moscow found little echo in the Soviet press. Shostakovich was not rebuked as he had been after his opera *Lady Macbeth of Mtsensk,* but the general attitude was one of disappointed expectations. Even postwar Soviet apologists for Shostakovich still have found it necessary to explain away the supposedly "negative" character of this first movement. For example, his biographer Ivan Martinov explains its mood of "defeat" as a reflection of the people's dreary lot under the Tsarist regime. In this interpretation, the merry third movement becomes a reflection of post-revolutionary joy in life.

However that may be, the first movement is the most substantial of the three, if only because it takes up more than half the length of the symphony. It is also, to this listener, some of the finest music Shostakovich has given us; one of his most thoughtful, least self-conscious, least rhetorical and most spontaneous symphonic movements. Since Shostakovich can hardly be suspected of writing it with any political advantage in mind, we can assume, that in this movement, he composed as closely as he dared to his heart's desire.

I. *Largo.* The unhurried principal melody springs from a simple thematic germ: the rise and fall of a minor third which permeates the whole movement.

This is followed almost at once by the second most important theme incorporating not only the minor third but the striking drop of a diminished seventh, thus recalling many a famous fugue of Bach, Handel and other Baroque composers. The trill at the bottom of this melodic leap also plays a crucial part in the development to come:

As they develop together, the two themes are sometimes linked in one continuous melodic phrase, sometimes chopped into small mosaic fragments.

Often the large orchestra is reduced to a delicate chamber ensemble as when the small, thin voice of the piccolo flute carries the melody against a spare background of second violins and harp. Or again, a single normal flute is accompanied by two clarinets alone.

The first big climax reaches its peak in a fierce orchestral tremor derived from the trill of the second theme. Gradually the tremor subsides in volume and pitch, descending half-step by half-step through an entire octave, finally fading into the background where it continues as a murmur of the violas. Against this, the English horn launches a series of deeply melancholy woodwind solos. After several other colorful developments, the movement dies away with fragments of the opening theme against the faint trill of the violas.

II. *Allegro.* This *scherzo* goes as fast as the wind and as weightlessly. Like the other two movements, it has the vivid orchestral colors of the Glinka tradition. Its grotesque humor is part of another old Russian tradition.

III. *Presto.* The rondo-like finale is a gleeful, zestful, superficial, and, withal, irresistible burst of high spirits. Its rhythms set the feet tingling. One leaps upward in an *arpeggio* covering almost two octaves, much like the glittering "Mannheim rocket" themes of Mozart and Haydn's day:

The music constantly skims along the edge of the banal, but never falls in, even when the "Mannheim rocket" is turned upside-down and the theme takes a dizzy plunge. Even the final march tune refuses to plod but flies ahead, as if on wings, concluding its trajectory with sharply exploding timpani and a shower of orchestral sparks.

The Sixth Symphony score calls for piccolo, 2 flutes, 2 oboes, English horn, E-flat clarinet, 2 clarinets, bass clarinet, 3 bassoons, contrabassoon, 4 horns, 3 trumpets, 3 trombones, tuba, kettledrums, tambourine, snare drum, triangle, cymbals, bass drum, gong, xylophone, celeste, harp, and the traditional strings.

SYMPHONY NO. 9, OPUS 70

"It is a merry little piece," said Shostakovich of his Ninth Symphony. "Musicians will love to play it, and critics will delight in blasting it." Shostakovich had just finished playing a piano preview of his Ninth to members of the Soviet and foreign press. If he expected them to blast it, he had himself, in part, to blame. For his earlier announcement had led listeners to expect a heroic work in the vein of his own two preceding symphonies. In his Seventh Symphony, Shostakovich had portrayed the 1941 Nazi onslaught on the Soviet Union. His Eighth, composed during the summer of 1943, described the suffering and destruction of the war, the turn of the tide after the German debacle at Stalingrad, and the westward sweep of Soviet armies as they drove the Germans from their soil. Shostakovich had let it be known that these Symphonies were the first two of a trio. The last was to be a celebration of victory.

But the merry Ninth was no such epic affair. Begun in the interval between the end of the war in Europe and the Allied victory in Asia, it was composed, as befitted a lighthearted piece, in the short space of six weeks at the Soviet Composers' Rest Home near Ivanovo, some one hundred and fifty miles northeast of Moscow. It was completed on August 30, 1945. The first performance was played by the Leningrad Philharmonic under the direction of Eugene Mravinsky in Leningrad on November 3 of the same year. Serge Koussevitzky conducted the first United States performance the following summer, at the opening concert of the Berkshire Festival at Tanglewood, on July 25, 1946.

Whereas Shostakovich's Seventh and Eighth symphonies had lasted over an hour each and called for gigantic orchestral forces, the Ninth is scaled down to less than half an hour's time and a small orchestra of almost Classical limits: indeed, there are moments when Shostakovich's Ninth recalls the "Classical" Symphony of Prokofieff. It is cast in five movements, the last three to be played continuously.

I. *Allegro.* A mannerly little theme which almost, but not quite, recalls Haydn, skips lightly down the tonic chord and ends with an emphatic trill. This is the principal theme of the movement:

Immediately the theme is turned upside-down, bounced up in the flute, down again in the first violins, and continued by a mocking oboe.

Suddenly, without bridge or transition, as fast as a blast on the trombone and a thumping "oompah" accompaniment can be established, a jaunty, contrasting theme is squeaked out by a piccolo flute at the top of the orchestra. A pair of clarinets try to start a sentimental duet in parallel thirds of an almost Bellinian cast, but are soon swallowed up in the general merriment. There are moments in the following development section when it sounds as if things were getting serious, as one thematic fragment bombards another in the contrapuntal meleé. But the danger soon passes. Before we know it we are back in the reprise of the basic themes and the movement ends in an exuberant *coda*.

II. *Moderato.* The slow movement is spun out of a graceful phrase for solo clarinet:

The solo develops into a duet, then with the addition of a flute into a trio, and finally into a woodwind ensemble. Muted strings usher in a contrasting section which leads back to a reprise of the opening melody now sung by a solo flute. The muted strings reappear briefly and the movement is rounded off by dying echoes of the opening melodic arch.

III. *Presto.* The mercurial *scherzo* opens with a refrain for woodwinds, immediately succeeded by breathless whisperings for the strings alone and then by a wild free-for-all of the entire orchestra. The rondo refrain returns twice more, and then is linked to the following *Largo.*

IV. *Largo.* Despite its portentous octaves for heavy brass, alternating with a pensive recitative for the solo bassoon, this *Largo* scarcely seems an independent movement. It is more a moment of contrast between the *scherzo* and the scherzo-like *finale,* which follows without pause.

V. *Allegretto.* A leisurely romp for the bassoon, the traditional jokester of the orchestra, opens the *finale.*

A lilting violin melody supplies the traditional lyric foil in what turns out to be a familiar sonata-allegro form. A swift development leads to a big climax which marks the return of the original playful bassoon tune, now thundered out by the full orchestra with emphasis on the heavy brass. The *coda* starts with whirlwind speed and seems to get even faster as it races to the brilliant final measures.

Shostakovich's Ninth Symphony is scored for piccolo, 2 flutes, 2 oboes, 2 clarinets, 2 bassoons, 4 horns, 2 trumpets, 3 trombones, tuba, kettledrums, triangle, tambourine, snare drum, cymbals, bass drum, and the traditional strings.

Jean Sibelius

Born December 8, 1865, Tavastehus, Finland; died September 20, 1957, Järvenpää, Finland

CONCERTO FOR VIOLIN AND ORCHESTRA, D MINOR, OPUS 47

So far as we know, there is no Finnish mythology in this Concerto, no tone-painting of the Finnish landscape, as there is in so much of Sibelius's music. But who can say? The language Sibelius speaks in his Violin Concerto is the same as that of his symphonic poems. He uses the same vocabulary, and his melody has the same characteristic turns which, for him, recalled the ancient Finnish runes.

Sibelius was thirty-eight when he completed the first version of his Violin Concerto. He had already written *En Saga,* the four Lemminkäinen tone poems, and his first two symphonies. But he had not yet achieved the original mastery of symphonic form and idiom that were soon to be his. This may be one reason why he was dissatisfied with the first version completed in 1903 and performed on February 8, 1904 in Helsinki. The version we hear today is a thorough revision completed and first performed in 1905 in Berlin under the direction of Richard Strauss with Carl Halir as soloist. The first performance in America was given on November 30, 1906, by the violinist Maud Powell with the New York Philharmonic in Carnegie Hall.

The Concerto is in three movements:

I. *Allegro moderato.* Over the murmur of muted violins, a melancholy, rhapsodic theme is sung by the solo violin:

This is the principal melody of the first movement. It is soon echoed and developed by the darker woodwind instruments. A second, more forceful, plodding theme painted in the dark colors of cellos and bassoons, ends with the characteristic drop of a fifth. These themes begin to grow and sprout new phrases and themes, as simply and logically as a tree thrusts out new branches, providing plenty of opportunity for virtuoso display of the solo violin. But the solo part never seems ostentatious passage-work or cadenzas; it remains an organic part of the growth of the music.

II. *Adagio di molto.* The second movement begins with a poignant little phrase in thirds for the woodwinds, like the rise and fall of a sigh. It is echoed bleakly by other wind instruments, and then the violin takes up a deep-throated song of almost Tchaikovskian melancholy. The movement works up to a great climax of interweaving orchestral voices built around this theme, and then suddenly breaks off and dies away with a few nostalgic phrases.

III. *Allegro ma non tanto.* The *finale* is a wild, dance movement, with a savage, lumbering main theme which the eminent English conductor and program annotator Donald Tovey called a polonaise for polar bears. This is announced at once by the solo violin:

In order to make the solo violin clearly audible in the dark, low range, Sibelius cuts the orchestral accompaniment down to even lower pitch and to chamber-music size: 2 violas, 2 cellos, a single string bass, and a kettledrum—all playing extremely softly. But always and again the solo part shoots up like a rocket into the night sky, sputtering sparks as it soars aloft, to do its own infinitely more agile version of the same dance. There are incredibly difficult passages of thirds, arpeggios, harmonics, double-stops, and the whole battery of violinistic fireworks, without there being a single bar of display for mere display's sake. The dance gathers momentum as it passes from one climax to another, and the end comes with a series of brilliant skyward sweeps of the violin, punctuated by sharp, decisive chords of the full orchestra.

The Violin Concerto is scored for 2 flutes, 2 oboes, 2 clarinets, 2 bassoons, 4 horns, 3 trumpets, 3 trombones, kettledrum, and the standard string choir.

THE SWAN OF TUONELA, OPUS 22, NO. 3

Sibelius's *The Swan of Tuonela* is not only one of his most popular works, it is among his earliest and most characteristic masterpieces. Composed in 1893, it was first intended as the prelude to a projected opera based on the Finnish folk epic, the *Kalevala. The Swan of Tuonela* does not describe any specific episode but rather creates a mood. The early editions of Sibelius's score carried this explanatory note: "Tuonela, the kingdom of Death, the Hades of Finnish mythology, is surrounded by a broad river of black water and swift current. On it, in majestic course, floats and sings the Swan of Tuonela."

Sibelius's score was twice revised: in 1897 and again in 1900. Sibelius himself conducted the world premiere of the original version on April 13, 1896, at Helsinki. The American premiere was presented by the Chicago Symphony Orchestra in Chicago on December 6, 1901.

On first hearing, this wonderfully subjective music can give the impression of a rhapsodic, almost improvised, tone picture. But this well-calculated Romantic effect is achieved by a cunningly devised musical structure, based on the ancient "bar" form, which can be traced back to the medieval troubadours.

Another part of Sibelius's magic comes from his orchestration. The stage is set, so to speak, in four opening measures by the string choir alone, subdivided into *seventeen* separate parts, all muted (except the double basses). The song of the Swan of Tuonela is sung by the English horn. Its very first phrase is the principal theme of the entire work:

An answering figure, rising from a solo viola, is a secondary thought. The emotional climax comes in the final section, where the string choir takes the melodic lead. But this moment of passion quickly dies away and the Swan resumes its melancholy song.

The Swan of Tuonela is scored for oboe, English horn, bass clarinet, 2 bassoons, 4 horns, 3 trombones, kettledrums, bass drum, harp, and full string choir.

SYMPHONY NO. 1, E MINOR, OPUS 39

Sibelius's First Symphony, in E minor, which was completed in 1899, was first performed on April 26 of that year in Helsinki under the composer's direction. Despite certain superficial resemblances to Russian composers (Borodin in the first movement, Tchaikovsky in the second and third), the thirty-two-year-old Finnish symphonist had already a powerful individuality. We meet at once melodic and rhythmic characteristics which remain typical of him through all seven of his symphonies and major tone poems—traits which he shares with no one else. The harmony, although conservative for 1899, has his personal stamp. The orchestration, including the characteristically cold sound of high woodwinds, is original and imaginative.

I. *Andante, ma non troppo; Allegro energico.* The striking introduction consists of one long melody for a single clarinet accompanied only by soft muttering of the kettledrum during its first half and bleakly unaccompanied for the remainder. In itself this already reflects one of Sibelius's most personal characteristics: his love of loneliness.

With its long-held opening note and its vigorous downward plunge at the end of the first phrase, the principal theme of the first movement also is unmistakably Sibelius:

Another striking and almost equally important theme of this first movement, a yearning melody for the first violins, is repeated with rising fervor and leads back to a grandiose proclamation of the principal theme by the entire orchestra. A rich array of themes is developed briefly. The reprise of the basic themes begins not with the first theme quoted above but with the yearning melody of the violins. The last climax of the movement dies away suddenly with a dramatic roll of the timpani and concludes with two quiet *pizzicato* chords, which also will return to round off the *Finale*.

II. *Andante (ma non troppo lento).* The slow movement resembles an extremely free three-part, A-B-A form. Against a mournfully persistent repetition of low harp tones, muted violins in octaves with muted cellos sing another characteristically melancholy theme, which bears a family resemblance to the yearning melody of the first movement. Like its predecessor, this one is characterized by a passionate, insistent wavering back and forth on two neighboring notes:

The movement grows more vigorous, even fiery, then suddenly breaks off for a series of brief, but very colorful episodes. Fragments of the yearning violin melody now lament and sigh in the voice of the solo cello. This is followed by a warmly romantic quartet of horns accompanied by harp arpeggios. A stormy mood is built up in swirling woodwind figures, then rushing violins and finally sharp, barking brass. The melancholy mood, color and melody of the opening dominate the closing pages.

III. *Scherzo: Allegro.* Against a pounding *pizzicato* rhythm of the low strings, the kettledrums announce the sharply rhythmic main theme of the *Scherzo.* This is immediately taken up by the violins, echoed by the woodwinds and further fragmented and tossed back and forth from one group of instruments to the other. There is a contrasting, slow middle section and a return to the vigorous opening material.

IV. *Finale (Quasi una fantasia): Andante; Allegro molto.* The *Finale* begins with a passionate proclamation by all the strings (except the double basses) of the lonely clarinet melody which had introduced the first movement. Fragments of the melody are echoed and developed first by a pair of flutes, then oboes, then woodwinds as a group before we arrive at the main body of the *Finale*. This consists of two different thematic groups: the first an almost scherzo-like passage, which might have been inspired by memories of folk dances; the second a powerfully sustained melody announced on the G string of all the violins playing in unison:

The dancelike themes are brought back for an extended, stormy development followed by the return of the slow melody which builds to a rhapsodic climax. As in the first movement, the final climax is followed by a dramatically diminishing drumroll and two soft *pizzicato* chords.

The First Symphony is scored for 2 flutes, 2 oboes, 2 clarinets, 2 bassoons, 4 horns, 3 trumpets, 3 trombones, tuba, kettledrum, bass drum, cymbals, triangle, harp, and strings.

SYMPHONY NO. 2, D MAJOR, OPUS 43

At the end of the last century, when Sibelius was young, Finland was a part of Russia—a very restless and unhappy part. The domination of the Russian czars was relatively recent, but for more than eight hundred years before that, Finns had been under the political domination of Sweden. Yet the Finns had never lost their longing for independence. Somehow they had preserved a measure of spiritual and cultural independence. And now, following a series of czarist decrees curbing Finnish liberties: free speech, the right of assembly and the minimum of political representation they had enjoyed, the old aspirations for national identity burst into flame.

Whether the Romantic interest in the distant, legendary past of all nations stimulated a new national consciousness, or whether the resurgence of national consciousness strengthened their awareness of Finnish cultural traditions would be hard to say. Probably it worked both ways. At any rate, in the closing years of the nineteenth century, when Sibelius returned from studies in Western Europe to his native land, Finnish art, folk music, the Finnish legends of the *Kalevala* and the Finnish language itself were experiencing a great renaissance. Sibelius was caught up in an enthusiastic group of patriotic young writers, painters, poets, musicians, men of the theater, students and critics, who had rediscovered their Finnish heritage. And for many years his music showed their influence.

One reason the Finnish people adore Sibelius is that they associate him with the winning of their independence. But if politics were the only reason they feel the way they do about him, he might have been forgotten in the maelstrom of World War II and postwar developments. There are deeper reasons. For example, Sibelius's musical intuition led him to write melodies so much like Finnish folk music that some commentators simply assumed they were folk songs. Yet we have Sibelius's own word for it that he never used a folk tune in any of his big orchestral works. Actually, it was not until after he was an established figure in the field of European music that Sibelius first heard, during a visit to Karelia, the ancient Finnish melodies which were still sung to the runes of the national epic, the *Kalevala*. It was only then that he realized with astonishment and delight how near his own music came to the thousand-year-old musical speech of his countrymen.

Sibelius's Second Symphony belongs to the same period as his patriotic *Finlandia*. It was begun in Italy in the spring of 1901, and completed that year in Finland. The first performance took place on March 3, 1902, at Helsinki under the composer's direction. Two years later, on January 2, the Symphony was introduced to the United States by the Chicago Symphony Orchestra under the direction of Theodore Thomas. Although Sibelius never ascribed any specific program to his Second Symphony, he was convinced in his youth that all true music had a conscious or unconscious program. Furthermore, Georg Schnéevoigt, a close friend of Sibelius and one of his most famous interpreters at home and abroad, said definitely that the first movement depicts the quiet pastoral life of the Finns undisturbed by thoughts of oppression. The second movement is charged with patriotic feeling, but the thought of brutal rule over the people brings with it timidity of the soul. The third, in the nature of a *scherzo*, portrays the awakening of national feeling, the desire to organize in defense of their rights, while in the *finale* hope enters their breasts and there is comfort in the anticipated coming of a deliverer.

As recently as 1946 the leading Finnish musicologist Professor Ilmari Kronn declared that in his Second Symphony Sibelius wished to depict "Finland's struggle for political liberty."

I. *Allegretto*. Over quietly pulsing, repeated chords in the strings, oboes and clarinets announce a simple tune of almost folk-song simplicity:

echoed first by a French horn and finally by a clarinet. A melancholy, pastoral mood pervades the movement, which avoids any passion or high drama.

II. *Tempo andante, ma rubato.* Soft pizzicatos in the dark, low tones of the cellos and double basses set the pace for the first theme, a lament for two bassoons marked *lugubre:*

We hear next a characteristic Sibelius device of swelling brass chords cut off at their peak with a sort of barking effect. This figure is taken up by the orchestral *tutti,* developed and recalled on the impressive closing page.

III. *Vivacissimo.* The *Scherzo,* like a bleak, snow-scurried landscape, is said to portray the awakening of Finnish nationalism. The brief trio section, *Lento e suave,* has an intensely nostalgic theme which begins with eight repetitions of the same note. This theme returns once more at the end of the *scherzo* and merges into a mounting sequence built on the first three notes of the first *finale* theme quoted below. The long *crescendo* of this rising sequence leads without pause into the *finale.*

IV. *Allegro moderato.* This is a mighty chant of triumph: the dream, it may be, of the fatherland that will have burst its shackles. This is the climax of the Symphony: bold, spacious music of monumental simplicity. The first theme:

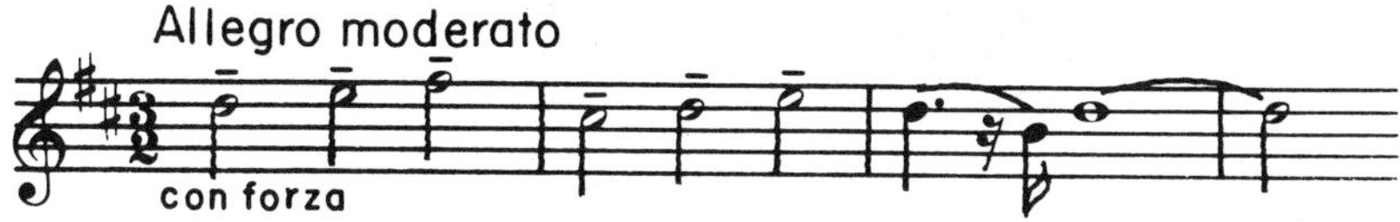

appears first in simple shape, and is later extended far beyond the form quoted above. The powerful march of the second theme:

is heightened by a rushing *ostinato* figure in the lower strings. At the end of a dramatic development section the simple, elemental three-note fragment of the first theme climbs slowly and inexorably from the bottom of the orchestra to a climax of staggering power.

The Second Symphony is scored for 2 flutes, 2 oboes, 2 clarinets, 2 bassoons, 4 horns, 3 trumpets, 3 trombones, tuba, kettledrums, and the traditional string choir.

SYMPHONY NO. 3, C MAJOR, OPUS 52

Sibelius's Third Symphony marked a turning point in his career, in his personal life, in his artistic development, and anticipated a broad trend in the development of the twentieth-century symphony. It marked, most significantly of all, a rejection of the late nineteenth-century style of expansive emotionalism, of epic sweep, of folkloristic color, of the almost Tchaikovskian piling of climax upon climax, which had so greatly enhanced the popular appeal of his First and Second symphonies. In the Third Symphony, which Sibelius composed during the four year span 1904 to 1907, ten years before Neoclassicism became a strong trend among the *avant garde* of a younger generation, Sibelius launched his own trend toward a more laconic style of disciplined power.

This shift of artistic direction coincided with a shift in Sibelius's personal life. He felt a need for greater concentration in his work: "It was necessary for me to get away from Helsinki [he later told his biographer, Karl Ekman]. My art demanded another environment. In Helsinki, all melody died within me. Besides, I was too sociable to be able to refuse invitations that interfered with my work. I found it very difficult to say no. I had to get away."

Sibelius had always loved the Finnish forest. Now he and his wife, Aino, were attracted to Lake Tuusula northeast of Helsinki, where some of their artist and writer friends had already built homes. Waterfront property was expensive, so they acquired a woodland tract close to the lake and to the village of Järvenpää (Lake's End). By the fall of 1904 the spacious log house in the woods was ready and Sibelius, with his wife and three daughters, moved to the domain which was to be his for over half a century, until his death at the age of ninety-one.

As soon as Sibelius had settled at Järvenpää, according to Ekman, he began work on the Third Symphony. The world premiere was scheduled for March, 1907, at a concert of the Royal Philharmonic Society in London under Sibelius's direction. But the score was not ready in time, so the premiere took place on September 26 at a concert which Sibelius conducted at Helsinki. Two months later he conducted it at St. Petersburg, and in February 1908 he conducted the postponed English premiere.

The change in Sibelius's style was immediately pointed out by the famous Finnish critic, the "conscience" and champion of Sibelius, Karl Teodor Flodin. "Sibelius stands without doubt at the height of his art," wrote Flodin in the *Nya Pressen.* "He has cast all mannerisms aside and, whereas he used to repeat himself, he now reaches down into a new reservoir."

The Symphony is in three movements, of which the third combines aspects of both *scherzo* and *finale:*

I. *Allegro moderato.* The first movement is dominated by the nervous intensity of its opening page. There is no slow introduction, and the principal theme group develops out of the powerful seven-note rhythmic pattern with which the Symphony begins:

Sibelius leads to his songful second theme not by a gradual modulation but, as Schubert loved to do, by a sudden shift of key, in this case to the key of B minor. Against a rocking staccato figure of violas and violins, the cellos sing a nostalgic melody, circling in almost archaic fashion within the narrow range of a fourth:

The development of these themes begins in a delicate, chamber music style, building to a climax which overlaps with a reprise of the opening material. Here the opening themes are brought back with such skill and imagination that one has the feeling that everything up to now has been simply preparation for this powerful conclusion.

II. *Andantino con moto, quasi allegretto.* The melancholy woodwind duets of the middle movement pass from pairs of flutes, to clarinets, to oboes, to mixed and muted strings.

III. *Moderato; Allegro (ma non tanto).* The *finale* falls into two distinct parts. A scherzo-like series of brief passages is built from tiny thematic fragments, often held together by long pedal points.

The *finale* proper evolves from one simple marchlike theme recalling the archaic, narrow range and repetitive rhythmic patterns, which played such a strong role in the opening movement. It begins here in the cello section:

The Third Symphony is scored for 2 flutes, 2 oboes, 2 clarinets, 2 bassoons, 4 horns, 2 trumpets, 3 trombones, kettledrums, and the traditional string choir.

SYMPHONY NO. 4, A MINOR, OPUS 63

Can Sibelius have frightened himself by the path on which he strikes out so boldly in his Fourth Symphony? Did he fear he had plumbed too great a depth of gloom, of Dostoevskian dark, that he had betrayed too frank a disdain of sensuous appeal, of "mere" beauty? Whatever his reason, Sibelius was never again to write anything so radical, so profoundly personal, as this score, which he began in the spring of 1910 and finished in February 1911. Today many of Sibelius's admirers consider this his greatest symphony.

Certain biographers have sought an explanation of the Fourth Symphony in a passing fear and depression. During a visit to England in 1908 a painful throat condition, which had bothered Sibelius for some time, became so acute that he interrupted his tour to return to Finland, where he submitted to an exploratory operation. The operation was unsuccessful and Sibelius, fearing that he had cancer of the throat, made a trip to Germany to consult a specialist there. The trouble was diagnosed as a malignant tumor; however, it was successfully removed. The possibility, which Sibelius had had to face, of a slow and painful death, and of leaving his wife and children without support, would have tried the emotional stamina and balance of a much less sensitive person. Yet this seems too simple an explanation of a masterpiece.

Possibly Sibelius was stimulated by neither depression nor fright, but simply, like Richard Strauss before him, decided that he had gone as far as he cared to in exploring what must then have seemed the outer limits of traditional tonality, of dissonance, of polytonality and of phantasmagoric orchestral colors. Just as Richard Strauss suddenly turned his back on the dramatic, emotional and harmonic extremes of his own *Elektra,* to compose in a conservative style for *Der Rosenkavalier,* so Sibelius turned away from the acrid harmonies and the laconic speech of his Fourth Symphony, to compose his last three symphonies in a more expansive, accessible style.

Paradoxically enough, although the Fourth is unique among Sibelius's symphonies, it is now widely regarded as his most characteristic. But it did not seem so when it was new. When Sibelius conducted the premiere on April 3, 1911, in Helsinki, on a program of his own works, its reception was very mixed. When it was introduced to Sweden, the Symphony was hissed; a Danish audience, according to Sibelius, "did nothing"; in England and the United States critics were generally bewildered.

When Walter Damrosch introduced Sibelius's Fourth Symphony to the United States in a performance by the New York Symphony Society on March 2, 1913, even so eminent a critic as William Henderson remarked that Sibelius had "parted company with himself and joined the futurists." When the Symphony was introduced to Boston the following October, my father, Olin Downes, a crusader for Sibelius, wrote that the music was "uncompromising, powerful and imaginative." Sibelius, he observed, "juxtaposes not only instruments but harmonies, not only harmonies but keys, with a mastery and audacity which according to at least the majority will be ridiculous, and perhaps to a small minority sublime." To prepare listeners for a first hearing of the new work, he published in the pages of the *Boston Post* an analysis, which Philip Hale reprinted in his program notes for the first Boston Symphony performance. Lawrence Gilman on a later occasion reprinted the analysis in his distinguished program notes for the New York Philharmonic:

> I. *Tempo molto moderato, quasi adagio.* Of the four movements of this Symphony, the first is freest in its form. There is a somber, lowering introduction. Bold, harsh progressions for the brass lead from an opening that has hovered about from E minor through various minor keys to the key of F-sharp major. This place might be called the opening of the movement proper. The mood is gentle and melancholy. The passage leads in turn to a very curious shifting background in counterpoint for the strings against which various woodwind instruments call strangely. Later there is a return to the gentle mood of the F-sharp major section, and this brief movement, the first movement of a symphony described as in "A minor," comes to an end in the lovely and pastoral key of A major.
>
> II. *Allegro molto vivace.* The scherzo is not less singular, although its form is clear enough. It is wild and restless. The extraordinary juxtapositions of certain instruments and tonalities remain to be heard before the effect can be described. After a curious climax, built chiefly on two notes of one of the themes, a motive shouted repeatedly by many instruments, this movement ends softly and suddenly.
>
> III. *Il tempo largo.* The slow movement has more sheer beauty than any of the others. It commences with dialogue of the wind instruments and the free preluding of various choirs. Then under a shimmering accompaniment of the upper strings, the cellos intone the real theme of the movement, a broad and noble song, almost Bruckner-like in these qualities, which, with some episodic interruptions, is repeatedly proclaimed by the orchestra and always more impressively. The movement ends mysteriously, a C sharp held by violas and muted horns, with wood and stringed instruments echoing fragments from an earlier passage.
>
> IV. *Allegro.* But of the four movements, the last is, perhaps, the most brusque and fantastical. The first phrase of the theme, at once given out by the violins, is scarcely heard again, but the second half of the theme is employed in variation, and a brief motive taken from it is the predominant thought of the movement. This motive consists, first of four notes composed of a triplet and a quarter, followed by a sort of rejoinder of three quarter notes, often sounded on the bells or stopped horns. Then there is the passage where the strings, tremolo, ascend gradually over a vibrating bass, and the flutes and oboes, practically in another key, call eerily. After the clashings of reiterated successive chords of the dominant-seventh and tonic of A flat, a curious chant in three-part harmony and in marchlike rhythm is developed by the woodwind.
>
> Very curious and interesting should this effect be, although not more so than many other passages of the Symphony. . . . Farther on occurs a passage where the horns and woodwind instruments sustain the chord of C major in its second position, while strings whirr up and down the scale, the bells ring exultantly, and a trumpet, swelling the initial tone of its figure from *ppp* to *fff*, throws out the fragment of the opening theme previously mentioned. The

marchlike theme is resumed and developed. The string passage with the off-key cries of the woodwind recurs, rondo fashion, and finally this remarkable movement comes to an end in a most gray and arid manner: a complaint of the oboe (the skip of a seventh), and soft despondent chords from the strings —always softer, always more gray—in the key of A minor.

OLIN DOWNES

The score of Sibelius's Fourth Symphony calls for 2 flutes, 2 oboes, 2 clarinets, 2 bassoons, 4 horns, 2 trumpets, 3 trombones, kettledrums, bells, and the traditional string choir. (Although the score specifically calls for bells, listed in German as *Glocken,* a tradition which Finnish conductors claim to have from Sibelius himself, calls for the lighter tone of glockenspiel instead of the heavier bells.)

SYMPHONY NO. 5, E-FLAT MAJOR, OPUS 82

The original version of Sibelius's Fifth Symphony followed a creative period rich in descriptive program music. But when Sibelius was asked whether his Fifth Symphony had a program, he replied emphatically that it was absolutely symphonic. The Symphony is a much-revised score; it exists in three different versions, the first of which was completed in 1915, when, perhaps because of the development of World War I, Sibelius felt deeply pessimistic. An entry in his diary for September 1915, reads: "In a deep dell again. But I already begin dimly to see the mountain I shall surely ascend. . . . God opens his door for a moment and his orchestra plays the Fifth Symphony."

The first performance of the original version was conducted by Sibelius himself at a concert celebrating his fiftieth birthday at Helsinki in December 1915. The second version was performed almost immediately after its completion in 1916, but Sibelius was still dissatisfied. In the spring of 1918 he wrote in a letter: "I am working daily at the Fifth Symphony in a new form, practically composed anew. The first movement is reminiscent of the old, the third reminiscent of the end of the old first movement. The fourth movement has the old themes, but stronger in revision. The whole, if I may say so, a vital climax to the end. Triumphal." This version was completed in 1919. The first performance appears to have been that conducted by Sibelius himself in London with the Queen's Hall Orchestra early in 1921.

During the research for his Sibelius biography, Harold E. Johnson examined a set of orchestral parts for the Fifth Symphony in the possession of the Helsinki City Orchestra said to consist of the second version of the Fifth Symphony, plus the alterations to make it conform to the final version. These parts, Mr. Johnson tells us, show that despite Sibelius's letter quoted above, the only important differences between the second and third versions consist of a reorchestration of the slow movement and the addition of the magnificent peroration to the *finale.* Is it possible that the Sibelius letter tells the truth, that the second revision *was* as far reaching as he describes it, and that the parts Mr. Johnson saw represent yet another, third revision?

There has been considerable discussion and disagreement among Sibelius critics as to whether the Fifth Symphony is in three or four movements. In the score the movements are not numbered. Since Sibelius's letter quoted above mentions four movements, it seems likely that this is what he intended, although the letter was written before he completed the final revision.

I. *Molto moderato.* The Symphony opens with a melancholy fanfare-like theme for French horn, which reappears throughout the Symphony.

This theme, particularly its first four notes, is developed and carried forward by various woodwinds. While contrasting themes do occur, particularly in the woodwinds, the spirit of this movement broods deeper and deeper into blackest melancholy. The second movement follows without pause.

II. *Allegro moderato—Presto.* Although the second movement follows the first without break and even uses some of the same thematic material, this is a *scherzo* in spirit. The atmosphere is more agitated and the movement ends with great waves of string arpeggios surging upward against long-drawn-out chords of the brass.

III. *Andante mosso, quasi allegretto.* The third, slow movement is calmer and considerably simpler. It consists of a set of variations on an innocuous-seeming theme. In two of the variations the theme quoted below from the *finale* is anticipated in the double basses of the orchestra.

IV. *Allegro molto.* The *finale* begins with a rush of fantastic whispering in the strings. Presently, underneath these eerie whirrings, we hear a strong *ostinato* motive in the horns, rising and falling like the massive cadence of the sea:

This recurrent figure dominates the finale: sometimes in its bold original form, sometimes like a shivering echo, high up among the strings. Toward the end and in the great coda-peroration, the horns again take up the theme, piling climax upon climax with ever more clashing dissonances. The music broadens with tremendous majesty to the series of sharp, emphatic closing chords.

The orchestra for the Fifth Symphony consists of 2 flutes, 2 oboes, 2 clarinets, 2 bassoons, 4 horns, 3 trumpets, 3 trombones, kettledrums, and the customary strings.

SYMPHONY NO. 6, OPUS 104

The lyricism of this little-known Symphony, its cool, almost aristocratic grace, its transparent textures, come as a surprise to those who know Sibelius only as the stormy master of his strongly Tchaikovskian first two symphonies and his overpowering Fifth and Seventh. It is curious that the composer's own original concept for the Sixth Symphony was in the more familiar Sibelian vein. It was to be "wild and impassioned in character," he wrote in 1918, "somber, with pastoral contrasts. Probably in four movements, with the end rising to a somber roaring of the orchestra in which the main theme is drowned."

Five years later, when the Symphony was completed, it did not roar at all, and the end dwindled Romantically into silence. Nor did the score have much that seemed "wild and impassioned" in comparison with the heroic Fifth. In fact, the relation of Sibelius's Sixth Symphony to its predecessor is so like the relation of Beethoven's Sixth to his Fifth, that one is tempted to call the Sibelius "pastoral."

It was first performed by the Helsinki City Orchestra on February 19, 1923, under the direction of the composer, who on this occasion made one of his last appearances as conductor. It is in four movements.

I. *Allegro molto moderato.* The Symphony opens with a serene flow of transparent string melodies interweaving, undulating, parting and combining, without definite thematic profile. The principal theme enters after almost thirty bars of this serene preluding. The solo oboe sings a typically melancholy, Sibelian phrase: a slow climb of five notes to a long-held A, swelling and diminishing.

This is answered by a pair of flutes gracefully dipping and rising again, likewise concluding on a long-held A, swelling and diminishing. The harmonies remain almost demonstratively simple, archaic, with a modal flavor, until the break between the first theme group and the second. At this psychological point, the string choir, swelling on the first complex harmony we have heard, suddenly clashes with a different key: a solemn C major in the brass. The effect is not harsh, for the volume is kept low, but after the limpid flow of the opening section, the richness of this clash of keys and colors is dramatic.

Now we return to the harmonic simplicity of the opening: a pair of flutes warbling in thirds are echoed in the way Sibelius so loved, by a second pair of woodwinds in thirds, this time, oboes. The dialogue of the instruments leads to a broadly flowing melody for the violins, with a strong family resemblance to the Symphony's opening oboe theme. There is a short development, in which fragments, chiefly from the earlier part of the movement, are tossed about from first violins to second violins to violas, from one pair of woodwinds to another. These orchestral exchanges die down almost to a whisper when the slow-moving principal theme begins to climb upward from the bass regions of the orchestra. This, in turn, brings us to a triumphant restatement of the original thematic material, embellished now with exuberant splashes of woodwind color. A mysterious *coda,* a sort of dreamlike distortion of what has gone before, brings the movement to a tranquil close.

II. *Allegretto moderato.* Instead of a solemn slow movement, Sibelius gives us, after a dozen or so bars of introduction, a gracefully lilting melody which is divided between first and second violins and later shared by the winds. The form of the movement is rather like a theme with free variations, the principal melody returning always in the violins. It is rounded off by another enigmatic coda which suggests here and there wraithlike fragments of the principal melody.

III. *Poco vivace.* Although the third movement is a *scherzo,* it is cast in rondo rather than traditional *scherzo* form with its conventional trio section. Although it is pervaded by a sort of galloping rhythm, it is such an airy gallop that the mood is closer to Mendelssohn's *Midsummer Night's Dream* than to some of the thunderous jocosities of more monumental late Romantic symphonies.

IV. *Allegro molto.* If the form of the *finale* is untraditional, it is far from confusing. Its principal theme is a joyous four-measure phrase, an outburst of all the brighter instruments of the orchestra:

This bright outburst meets a mellow response from the lower strings. The pattern is repeated once, twice, thrice, with slight variations each time before we launch into a more complex central section which takes up fragments of the opening outburst and reminiscences of the opening movement. These are combined with fresh lyric ideas and an ever-broadening melodic flow until we arrive at the last *coda* of all, the final recall of earlier melodic ideas, once more dying away into silence with just the faintest suggestion of the Symphony's opening oboe song, now descending to rest.

In keeping with its spirit of restraint, Sibelius's Sixth Symphony uses modest orchestral forces: 2 flutes, 2 oboes, 2 clarinets, bass clarinet, 2 bassoons, 4 horns, 3 trumpets, 3 trombones, kettledrums, harp, and the traditional string choir, which, however, is often subdivided into 6 or 8 separate melodic parts.

SYMPHONY NO. 7, C MAJOR, OPUS 105

There is something about the last symphony of a great composer, his final answer to the challenge of a great tradition, which holds a special fascination for us. Whether by an accident of fate or by force of our imagination, Beethoven's Ninth, Mozart's "Jupiter," Schubert's great C major Symphony, and Tchaikovsky's *"Pathétique"*—to name only some of the most striking examples—seem set apart from other symphonies by the same masters. And each seems unique among the great chain of masterpieces we know as the symphonic tradition.

The Seventh and last Symphony of Sibelius is in one movement. In its terseness and expressive concentration it is unique among his symphonies. It has a curious history. Sibelius himself was at first uncertain whether to call it a symphony or a symphonic fantasy. And this uncertainty illumines a whole complex of problems facing any composer who builds today on stylistic and formal foundations reaching back into the century of Haydn and Mozart.

The first mention of the Seventh Symphony occurs in a well-known letter of 1918, in which Sibelius after discussing plans for his Fifth and Sixth symphonies, continues: "The VIIth symphony. Joy of life and vitality, with appassionato passages. In 3 movements—the last a 'Hellenic rondo'. . . . It looks as if I were to come out with all three symphonies at the same time. . . . With regard to VI and VII, the plans may be altered according to the development of the musical ideas. As usual, I am a slave to my themes and submit to their demands."

The demands of the themes and their development in the Seventh Symphony were so radical that the 1918 plans are unrecognizable in the finished score of 1924. Whether Sibelius threw his first plans overboard and started afresh, or whether the final product was a long and painful process of evolution, we may never know. Not only did the Symphony shrink from three movements to one, but its highly original form and thematic interrelationships were such that Sibelius hesitated to call it a symphony at all.

"On March 2, 1924, at night, as I entered in my diary," Sibelius told his biographer, Karl Ekman, "I completed *Fantasia sinfonica*—that is what I first thought of calling my seventh symphony in one movement." Not only did Sibelius consider calling it *Fantasia sinfonica,* he conducted the premiere under that title in Stockholm later that month: March 24, 1924. Later that year, when he signed a contract for its publication, it was still called *Fantasia sinfonica,* Opus 105. But when it was published in 1925, Opus 105 had once again become a symphony.

The Romantic ideal of "organic" unity, as expressed in the growth of one theme out of another (until all musical ideas of a composition were related to a single thematic seed or germ), favored the one-movement form. So did the Romantic love of concealing the subdivisions of large forms with subtle transitions. So it is no surprise that the one-movement symphony, like the one-movement sonata, had had a special attraction for composers of the Romantic age. These trends reach a climax in Sibelius's Seventh Symphony.

Even the most casual listener will recognize the one point on which all professional analysts seem agreed: that the style of the work is symphonic, that it includes lengthy passages in the character of a dramatic first movement, a *scherzo,* and a climactic *finale.* Commentators who question whether the Seventh is a "true" symphony and, if so, where its internal boundaries divide its "movements" from each other, are really paying a compliment to Sibelius as a Late Romantic symphonist.

It is possible to derive all the themes of this Symphony from a thematic germ of two adjacent notes: one above and one below a central note. But it may be more rewarding at the start to follow two or three full-fledged themes with striking individual profiles. The first of these is heard after only half a dozen introductory bars: it is a typically Sibelian figure of weaving woodwinds, flutes, and bassoons, echoed by clarinets:

The second, related to the first yet powerfully contrasted, is announced by a solo trombone which caps the first big climax of the exposition:

The central section of the symphony, flanked by two *scherzo* sections, is an *Allegro molto moderato* dominated by this vigorous fanfare-like theme:

The conclusion, too brief for a traditional reprise, recalls the trombone theme of the opening, and comes to rest with a powerful statement of the thematic germ, the falling whole-step and the rising half-step, out of which the whole symphony may be said to have grown.

The Seventh Symphony is scored for 2 flutes, 2 oboes, 2 clarinets, 2 bassoons, 4 horns, 3 trumpets, 3 trombones, kettledrums, and the traditional string choir.

Bedrich Smetana

Born March 2, 1824, Leitomischl, Bohemia (now Litomysl, Czechoslovakia)—died May 12, 1884, Prague

THE MOLDAU

The Moldau (or *Vltava,* to use its proper Czech name) must be one of the most seductive pieces of musical nationalism ever written—seductive in a good sense, that is. It was the product of a special moment in the history of an enormously gifted people and the personal genius of the man who is commonly known as the "father of Czech music." It was composed on the crest of the great wave of revolutionary nationalism which swept Europe in the nineteenth century, and which came to the Czech people as an artistically and intellectually liberating force.

Although Smetana was indeed the father of modern Czech music, he was far from the first great Czech musician. It is often pointed out that a whole wave of Czech composers at the end of the eighteenth century were probably stimulated by the Prague triumphs of Mozart. This is quite true as far as it goes but the special genius of the Czech people for music reaches as far back as we have any records.

A glory and a tragedy of the Czech people ever since the Middle Ages has been the long line of Czech artists (or Bohemians as they were often called) who left their homeland, sometimes permanently, to enrich the musical life of other peoples, near and far. As early as the fourteenth century Bohemian wandering minstrels, Bohemian fiddlers (*Behemer fedeler*) and flautists (*flauteurs de Behaigne*) were famous throughout the areas that were later to become Germany and France. While the oldest Czech music that survives is vocal (the famous *Hospodine, pomiluj ny,* sung at the coronation of Bohemian kings, has an attested pedigree of a thousand years), the Czechs seem always to have excelled in instrumental music. How highly Mozart valued their skill is shown in the orchestral parts he wrote for their woodwind virtuosos in his *Prague* Symphony and of course in his *Don Giovanni* which he composed specifically for Prague.

Mozart's triumphs in Prague had been prepared by generations of Czech composers at home and abroad. Only since the middle of the twentieth century have Czech musical scholars and performing musicians formed an effective team to bring the incredible riches of their own musical past to the attention of the world.

Thus Smetana could build on traditions dating back at least half a millennium. He was only twenty-four years old when the domino-like series of revolutions of 1848-1849 swept Europe, stirring Czech politicians, scholars, and artists to (temporarily) unsuccessful revolts of their own.

Smetana was closely identified with the liberal-democratic revolutionaries of that time and composed patriotic songs which are said to have been sung on the barricades in Prague. After the collapse of the revolutions, Smetana's professional beginnings were enormously difficult, despite the enthusiastic praise and practical assistance offered him by no less a personality than Franz Liszt. Therefore when the Philharmonic Society of Göteborg, Sweden offered him the musical directorship of its orchestra, he accepted, although with a heavy heart, because it meant temporary exile from his beloved homeland. Smetana's letters to his friends sound homesick even before he left the country.

Then in 1860 when the Hapsburg regime in Vienna at last granted the province of Bohemia a certain degree of cultural and even political autonomy, a strong movement developed in Bohemia for the foundation of a "national" opera house in Prague. Smetana decided that, come what may, his place was now in Prague. He resigned his Göteborg conductorship and was back in Prague by 1861, and soon won widespread recognition as a leader of the patriotic movement in the Bohemian arts.

Between 1863 and 1866 Smetana worked on his opera *The Bartered Bride* which became, first to the Bohemian people and later to the Czechoslovak nation, a modern symbol of their ancient cultural identity and traditions. From 1874 through early 1875 he composed in rapid succession the first three tone poems of a cycle *My Fatherland* (*Má Vlast*) which was the climax of his symphonic career. The score of *The Moldau* was completed in Prague on November 18, 1874. It was first performed in Prague on April 4, 1876 with Adolf Czech conducting the Auxiliary Society of the Choral and Orchestral Personnel of the Royal Bohemian Provincial Theater.

It was a triumphant success, which meant all the more to Smetana who had been afflicted by a growing deafness and who had become totally deaf by the time he embarked on this score which enshrined him in the hearts of his countrymen. Like Beethoven at the premiere of his Ninth Symphony, Smetana was present but never heard a note of his music.

The Moldau is one long poem to the beauties of the Czech countryside. When he sent the score to his publishers, Smetana wrote the following skeleton outline of what he had in mind:

> Two springs pour forth their streams in the shade of the Bohemian forest, the one warm and gushing, the other cold and tranquil. Their waves, joyfully flowing over rocky beds, unite and sparkle in the rays of the morning sun. The forest brook, rushing on, becomes the River Vltava (Moldau). Coursing through Bohemia's valleys, it grows into a mighty stream. It flows through dense woods from which come joyous hunting sounds, and the notes of the hunter's horn drawing ever nearer and nearer.
>
> It flows through emerald meadows and lowlands, where a wedding feast is being celebrated with songs and dancing. By night, in its glittering waves, wood and water nymphs hold their revels. And these waters reflect many a fortress and castle—witnesses of a bygone age of knightly splendor, and the

martial glory of days that are no more. At the Rapids of St. John the stream speeds on, winding its way through cataracts and hewing a path for its foaming waters through the rocky chasm into the broad riverbed, in which it flows on in majestic calm toward Prague, welcomed by time-honored Vyšehrad, to disappear in far distance from the poet's gaze.

For the guidance of conductors and music lovers who consult his score, Smetana has indicated very precisely the subjects of the eight sections of his tone poem. The first describing the sources of the Vltava begins with an unaccompanied flute melody. This is the cold brook. The cold flute sound is soon joined by a warmer clarinet moving in little wavelets, depicting, of course, the warm brook which is the other source of the Vltava. This is but one of a thousand details which would be fruitless to list here but show the affectionate skill of Smetana's pen. Next we hear the unforgettable flowing melody of the river Moldau itself:

The Czech people understandably have taken this Moldau melody to their hearts; it has even become a Czech folksong, sung nowadays to an old Czech rhyme, *"Kočka leze dìrou"* (roughly translated: "The cat crawls through the hole, and the dog through the window"). Yet oddly enough, this beautiful melody, the focus of such strong Czech emotion, comes from a Swedish folksong *"Ack, Värmeland du sköna"* praising the beauties of the Swedish province of Värmland, just north of Göteborg. (Taken from a Swedish folksong collection of 1816, this was the most popular number in a folk play presented in 1846 by the Swedish dramatist F. A. Dahlgren of Göteborg, whom Smetana knew during his residence there from 1856 to 1861. Smetana's adaptation of the Swedish melody, whether conscious or [more probably] unconscious, in no way detracts from the beauty or significance of his masterpiece. But it may warn us against attaching too mystical a significance to the folk origins of national styles in music.) Next the Moldau passes through a forest where we hear vigorous horn calls and trumpet fanfares traditionally associated with hunting scenes.

As the echos of the hunt die away we hear a lively folk dance which Smetana intended to suggest a peasant wedding celebration. These festive rhythms in turn fade into the distance, night falls, a mysterious quiet surrounds the river, and the diaphanous tones of high muted strings suggest the shimmer of moonlight. Weaving strains of flutes and clarinets punctuated by an occasional splash of the harp evoke in Smetana's words a "dance of water nymphs."

The Moldau now broadens as its melody is carried forward with increasing volume by the full orchestra. All at once the orchestral stream is churned up by more jagged rhythms as we come to the "Rapids of St. John." At these rapids, which were familiar to Smetana, the broad river is forced between narrow, rocky banks, and the melody of the Moldau itself grows more turbulent with shorter, chopped-up phrases and momentarily tenser harmonies. The river broadens out triumphantly after passing through the narrows and approaches the city of Prague where the mountain fortress Vyšehrad, rich in heroic legend, looks down. The orchestra recalls a theme from the preceding symphonic poem of Smetana's cycle suggesting the heroic deeds of Czech history. From here the river sweeps on past the great city and disappears from the poet's view.

The Moldau is scored for piccolo, 2 flutes, 2 oboes, 2 clarinets, 2 bassoons, 4 horns, 2 trumpets, 3 trombones, tuba, harp, kettledrums, bass drum, cymbals, triangle, and the traditional strings.

OVERTURE TO THE BARTERED BRIDE (PRODANA NEVESTA)

The great wave of revolutionary nationalism which swept Europe in the nineteenth and early twentieth centuries came to the Czech people as an immensely fertilizing and liberating force. Among its many artistic fruits were Smetana's patriotic tone poems (the most popular being *The Moldau*) and his nine operas, including *The Bartered Bride.*

Smetana is often considered the father of Czech musical nationalism. He was only twenty-four when the liberal-patriotic revolutions of 1848–1849 swept Europe like a prairie fire, stirring Czech patriots to an unsuccessful revolution of their own, and launching Smetana on his career as a nationalist composer. From 1863 to 1866 he worked on his second opera, *The Bartered Bride,* a simple comedy of Czech peasant life in a style strongly influenced by Czech folk music. The English title, though traditional, is not particularly accurate. The Czech title *Prodaná nevěsta* means literally "the fiancée [who was] sold."

To Czech listeners *The Bartered Bride* is much more than an opera. It has become almost a symbol of the Czech people themselves. Happily *The Bartered Bride* captivates even non-Czech listeners with its melodic invention, its orchestral brilliance and its temperamental brio.

The music of the Overture is taken largely from the lively *finale* of Act II, when the townspeople witness the signing of a contract in which the hero deliberately gives the (false) impression that he is selling his claim to his own fiancée. The Overture opens with a brilliant flourish for full orchestra, followed by a lively scherzo-like figure spun out very delicately by the second violins alone. Presently they are joined by the first violins and finally by the lower strings, building up to a climax of excitement on the crest of which a syncopated dance figure, another chief theme of the Overture, is heard. There is considerable development of both the dance theme and the scherzo-like figure. The whole is punctuated and concluded by reappearances of the Overture's opening flourish.

The Overture to *The Bartered Bride* is scored for an orchestra of piccolo, 2 flutes, 2 oboes, 2 clarinets, 2 bassoons, 4 horns, 2 trumpets, 3 trombones, kettledrums, and the traditional strings.

Karlheinz Stockhausen

Born August 22, 1929, Mödrath, near Cologne

HYMNEN

One of the most controversial composers of the second half of the twentieth century, Karlheinz Stockhausen, has also been one of the most influential, especially in Central Europe. His meteoric career, particularly since his first tour of the United States and Canada in 1958, has made him as charismatic a figure in Tokyo as he is in Warsaw, London, or New York. During these same years Stockhausen has also been one of the principal sources and propagators of new ideas in European music. His almost messianic faith in the central importance of technical procedures (from post-Webern total serialism to the most complex electronic manipulations of music, speech, and noise) seems counterbalanced by an equally mystical faith in the ethical and sociopolitical powers of music for the regeneration of mankind.

The original version of Stockhausen's *Hymnen* (the title of which means "anthems" in the sense of national anthems) was commissioned by the West German Radio of Cologne and first performed there on November 30, 1967, with Aloys Kontarsky, pianist; Johannes Fritsch, violist; Rolf Gehlhaar and David Johnson, percussionists; Harald Bojé operating the electronium; the composer directing and monitoring, with the technical assistance of David Johnson and Werner Scholz. When the New York Philharmonic subsequently commissioned a new work from Stockhausen, the composer responded with an orchestral version of the Third Region of *Hymnen* (the complete work consists of four "Regions"). On February 25, 1971, Stockhausen directed and monitored the first United States performance of *Hymnen*, including the world premiere of the Third Region with the orchestra of the Philharmonic. For this occasion Stockhausen supplied the following notes:

> I am an artist who, as the phrase goes, has "arrived." It is said that I belong to the Establishment and my position, therefore, is on the *right*. How stupid! Does it mean nothing that when I was so young that I could hardly talk, my mother was taken away from our home and later murdered on government order because she was a superfluous consumer of food in wartime? That my father, after six years in the army, died the so-called "hero's death"? That as a child I was beaten by all kinds of strangers, that as a sixteen-year-old in a front-line field hospital I was a daily witness of inhuman cruelties, of the miserable deaths of thousands with ghastly wounds, with phosphorus burns,

with broken bodies? That I saw boys of my own age, old men, civilians and so-called deserters strung up on telephone wires? That for years I cowered in bomb shelters, inhaling the stink of thirty, forty, fifty thousand corpses in civilian cities that had been flattened to the ground? That for five years more I was a common laborer, a factory worker, a potato thief, a coal-filcher, and thereafter worked nightly as a bar pianist for black marketeers and occupation troops? That since the "great" war I have watched the revolting reconstruction and greed of the "economic miracle," the great forgetting, the fear of the atom bomb, the expulsions, the tortures, the oppression in the lesser wars of other countires—and that I am impotent against all this? Arrived? Established? *Where?*

The other day I read reports of torturing in Vietnam. Should I go to America and make music for the Americans? What good will it do if I cancel?

My composition *Hymnen,* another project for the integration of all races, all religions, all nations: will it be shoved aside as a stupid, naïve utopia, as many German newspapers have scornfully written?

Does anyone really think I am a cynic, that I have given up the world and am having my "little joke" when in the new orchestral version of the Third Region, for example, I combine the American national anthem with the anthems of all other nations in an effort to achieve something more than a primitive *collage,* to evoke a unity in which hate is abolished as a result of mediation among all mutually hostile forces? What more can a composer do than create musical worlds which do not merely mirror the human world as it is today but which offer visions, intimations of better worlds, in which projects in the realms of sound, of fragments, of *objets trouvés* become mutually compatible and grow together to realize the divine mission of ONE united world? If even a hint could be caught, could be understood of the cause to which I give myself in *Hymnen,* this work would have a meaning. I have no illusions that the wars with all their sufferings are going to stop tomorrow. On the contrary: I see terrible trials ahead of us. I understand the infinite slowness of growth from the subconscious to the conscious human being, from the lethargic animal in us to the enlightened being that really knows why it is alive and what kind of future it wants.

But I want it to be known that my music is directly involved with this development. It is intended to serve as a means of purification. Let each person think over what he might be able to do better, or more clearly than I have. Let each decide for himself whether he too seeks the unity of "Anthems"—which are the musical symbols of the various nations, whether he shares supranational, universal concepts, and whether he can help realize them.

America—land of refugees, of exiles, of the melting pot: this music is made to measure for you. You could become a model for the whole world, if you would live as this music prophesies—if you would set a good example . . . !

Several years ago I conceived a plan for the composition of a large work comprising electronic, vocal and instrumental music, using the national anthems of all countries. I began the composition in the electronic music studio of the Cologne Radio (Westdeutsche Rundfunk) in 1966. In December, 1967, four "Regions," lasting about 113 minutes, were completed.

I. Each "Region" uses certain anthems as *centers,* to which many other national anthems, with their characteristic initial phrases, have been related. The First Region has two centers: the "Internationale" and the "Marseillaise." Emerging from an international gibberish of short-wave broadcasts, its form becomes rigorous and strongly directional.

II. The First Region merges into the Second. The bridge is the sharp "flood-sound" which at the beginning of the "Marseillaise" hissed upwards from a low, distorted tone and subsequently hovered over the whole First Region. Now it stands isolated for a long time, and then, after being sliced by nine sound columns (with which the Second Region begins), it will plunge downwards and become recognizable as the clamor and shouting of people, which then transform themselves into bird shrieks—the "boo-at boo-at" of swamp ducks—then to yelling, and finally to a deep, dark reminiscence of the "Marseillaise" in an eightfold slower pace.

The Second Region has four further centers: the anthem of the Federal Republic of Germany and a *Personal* center (a reflection on a second "anthem" from Germany's past) which suddenly interrupts, revealing the process involved in the making of the entire piece; this interruption is a spontaneous recording of a moment of speech during the studio work, in which the present perfect, past and pluperfect become simultaneous (last sentence: "We could go even one dimension deeper. . . . ").

III. From the middle of the Second Region through the end of the Third, I have composed, on commission from the New York Philharmonic, a version combining orchestra and electronic music, which I call the *Third Region of Hymnen with Orchestra.* (Thus, I hope, this work will also be played and listened to by people who meet at so-called "symphony concerts.")

This *Third Region of Hymnen with Orchestra* begins after the studio talk of the Second Region with a group of African anthems, mixed together and alternating with the beginning of the Russian anthem. Between the Second and the Third Region I have composed a Russian Bridge for orchestra alone.

The Third Region has three centers. It begins with the slow continuation of the Russian anthem, now alone, the only one made exclusively from electronic sounds and embodying the greatest harmonic and rhythmic extension that I have composed to date. The American anthem follows as the second center, and, through fleeting collage and pluralistic mixture, has the most colorful relationships to all the other anthems. The last shortwave sound pipes "in a few seconds across the ocean" and flows into the exalted center of the Spanish anthem. The Third Region lasts approximately twenty-four minutes.

IV. The Fourth Region has a double center: the Swiss anthem and an anthem belonging to the utopian realm of Hymunion in Harmondie ruled by Pluramon, which is the longest and most penetrating of all; it is formed from the closing chord of the Swiss anthem made into a quietly pulsating bass *ostinato* above which are concentrated gigantic blocks, planes and pathways, in whose clefts resound the echoes of shouted names. The Fourth Region lasts approximately thirty-two and one-half minutes.

Hymnen (for radio, television, opera, ballet, record, concert hall, church, outdoors) is so composed that various scripts of librettos for films, operas or ballets may be prepared for it. The ordering of the characteristic parts and the total duration are variable. Depending upon the dramatic requirements, [individual] "Regions" may be lengthened, added or left out. There is also a concert version of the work for tape and 6 soloists.

National anthems are the most widely known music imaginable. Everyone knows the anthem of his own country, and perhaps those of several others, or at least their beginnings.

When one integrates in a composition known music with unknown, new music, one can hear especially well *how* it was integrated: untransformed, more or less transformed, more or less transposed, modulated, etc. The more self-evident the *what*, the more attentive the listener becomes to the *how*.

Naturally, national anthems are more than national anthems: they are "loaded" with time, with history—with past, present and future. They accentuate the subjectivity of peoples in a time when uniformity is all too often mistaken for universality. One must also make a clear distinction between subjectivity and influences among subjective musical objects on the one hand and individualistic isolation and separation on the other. The composition *Hymnen* is *not* collage.

Many-faceted interrelationships have been established among various anthems as well as among these anthems and new abstract sound shapes, for which we have no names.

Numerous compositional processes of intermodulation were applied in *Hymnen*. For example, the rhythm of one anthem is modulated with the harmony of another; this result is modulated with the dynamic envelope of a third anthem; this result in turn is modulated with the timbral constellation and melodic contour of chosen electronic sounds; finally, this result is given a specific spatial motion. Sometimes parts of anthems are allowed to enter the environment of electronic sounds in raw, almost unmodulated form; sometimes modulations lead almost to the point of unrecognizability. There are many degrees in between, many levels of recognizability.

In addition to the national anthems, other "found objects" have been used: scraps of speech, sounds of crowds, recorded conversations, sounds from shortwave radio receivers, recordings of public events, demonstrations, a christening of a ship, a Chinese store, a diplomatic reception and so on.

The large dimensions of time, dynamics, harmony, timbre, spatial motion, total duration and openness of the composition arose in the course of the work out of the universal character of the material and the breadth and openness which I myself experienced in my encounter with this project—the unification and integration of seemingly unrelated old and new phenomena.

KARLHEINZ STOCKHAUSEN

KONTRA-PUNKTE

Stockhausen's *Kontra-Punkte (Counter-Points)* is the earliest work the composer has called representative of his mature musical thinking. It was completed in 1952 and scored for a chamber orchestra of ten instruments (violin, cello, flute, clarinet, bass clarinet, bassoon, trumpets, trombone, harp, piano). It was first performed by members of the Cologne Radio Symphony Orchestra under the direction of Hermann Scherchen at the Cologne Festival of New Music on May 26, 1953.

For a 1956 broadcast of *Kontra-Punkte*, Stockhausen wrote the following general introduction: "Concerning My Music."*

> The constant goal of my searches and efforts: the power of transformation—its operation in time: in music. Hence a refusal of repetition, of variation, of development, of contrast. Of all, in fact, that requires "shapes"—themes, motives, objects, to be repeated, varied, developed, contrasted; to be dismembered, rearranged, augmented, diminished, displayed in modulation, transposition, inversion or retrograde. All this I renounced when I first began to work with "pointillism." Our own world—our own language—our own grammar: nothing neo- . . . ! But then what? For me there followed *Kontra-Punkte:* a series of metamorphoses and renewals both deeply hidden and extremely apparent—tending to no visible end. Never is the same thing heard twice. Yet one has the clear feeling that an immutable and extremely homogeneous continuity is never abandoned. There is a hidden power of cohesion, a relatedness among the proportions: a structure. Not similar shapes in a changing light. Rather this: different shapes in a constant, all-permeating light.

The "hidden power of cohesion" refers to the composer's carefully calculated technical structure. This almost "total serialization" is described elsewhere by the composer in the following more concrete terms:

> My *Kontra-Punkte* sprang from the idea that in a world of multiple sounds, the conflicts among individual sounds and time relations, should be solved in such a way as to create a situation in which only things homogeneous and immutable are perceived. The work is in only one movement. Six different "tone-color" groups are used: flute and bassoon, clarinet and bass clarinet, trumpet and trombone, piano, harp, violin, and cello (three pairs of wind instruments blown differently and three kinds of string instruments struck, plucked and bowed, respectively). These different tone colors merge into a single one: the struck strings of the piano. The other instruments drop out in this order: trumpet, trombone, bassoon, violin, bass clarinet, harp, clarinet, cello, and flute. There are six different degrees of dynamic intensity (from *ppp* to *sfz*), and one after the other they diminish to a *pp*. Large differences between very long and very short notes are avoided; only closely related, medium-length notes remain (16th notes, 16th-note triplets, dotted-16th notes, 16th-note quintuplets, and so forth). Through the opposition of vertical and horizontal sound relations a homogeneous two-part counterpart is obtained. These external countersigns are clearly audible. By following these clues, and guided by his musical taste, the listener can decide whether I have discovered the right relations and the necessary degree of sensitivity for the profound structural material which lies at the basis of this construction.

For the New York Philharmonic performances of *Kontra-Punkte* in December 1972 and January 1973, the composer supplied the following basic information on his education and career:

---

* *Karl H. Wörner,* Stockhauser *(translated by Bill Hopkins), (Berkeley & Los Angeles: University of California Press, 1973).*

From 1947 to 1951 Stockhausen studied simultaneously at the Staatliche Hochschule für Musik at Cologne and the University of Cologne (German literature and philology, philosophy, musicology). In 1952 he studied rhythm and aesthetics with Olivier Messiaen in Paris. At the same time he became a member of the "Musique concrète" group of the French [National] Radio in Paris, where he was enabled to experiment and achieve what he terms the first synthesis of "sound spectra" with electronically produced sine waves.

Beginning in 1953 he was a regular member of the Electronic Music Studio of the West German Radio Station at Cologne. From 1963 on he was chief of that Studio. During the years 1954 through 1956 he also carried on studies in phonetics and communications research with Professor Werner Meier-Eppler of the University of Bonn. In 1958 he made his first tour of the United States and Canada, including thirty concert-lectures. From that year on he made annual tours as conductor, interpreter and lecturer (usually in conjunction with small groups of selected soloists) in many countries. In 1965 he was guest professor of composition at the University of Pennsylvania in Philadelphia. In 1966-67 he was guest professor for composition at the University of California in Davis. Meanwhile, from 1953 on, he had been a regular professor of the International Holiday Courses in New Music in Darmstadt. At the 1970 World's Fair at Osaka, he supervised 183 daily performances of his own works for a total of approximately 1,000,000 listeners in the Spherical Auditorium of the German Pavilion.

Richard Strauss

Born June 11, 1864, Munich—died September 8, 1949, Garmisch-Partenkirchen

DON JUAN, TONE POEM AFTER NICOLAUS LENAU, OPUS 20

Strauss was only twenty-four years old when he began and twenty-five when he finished this explosive score under the stimulus of his enthusiasm for Wagner's *Tristan und Isolde*.

Many another composer beguiled by Wagner turned into a grandiloquent, magniloquent epigone. Strauss was beguiled and turned into—himself. *Don Juan* is the first work that shows him complete master, not of Wagnerism, but of a new musical sensibility of his own: a more nervous pattern of feeling and thinking in correspondingly sudden harmonic shifts, in extravagantly leaping melodies, in sensuous techniques of orchestration and a hundred dazzling devices undreamed of, even by the old magician of Bayreuth. In the matter of form, too, Strauss emerges here as the greatest master of the one-movement "tone-poem," that distinctive creation of the Romantic movement.

The speed of Strauss's growth, and his natural affinity for fame were a source of anxiety to his friends and envy to others. He was only twenty when audiences in faraway New York heard their Philharmonic play his F-minor

Symphony under so august a director as Theodore Thomas (December 13, 1884). The great turning point in Strauss's career came only ten months later, when he received his first important position as assistant conductor of Hans von Bülow's orchestra in Meiningen. Among the violinists of Bülow's orchestra was the German poet, composer and author, Alexander von Ritter. It was Ritter who taught Strauss the revolutionary "modern" music from which he had been protected by his conservative father. Ritter's influence, Strauss later recalled, was like "a storm wind. He pushed me into developing the expressive, poetic side of music, following the examples of Berlioz, Liszt, and Wagner."

It was *Tristan* (in an Italian production at Bologna, May, 1888) that completed the twenty-four-year-old's conversion to Wagner. The following year he applied for a position as coach at the Festspielhaus in Bayreuth, where *Tristan* was being prepared. Between *Tristan* productions, *Don Juan* was born.

The legendary Don Juan appears (like Faust) to have been a creation of sixteenth-century folk imagination. The theme of a man irresistible to all women has always fascinated his potential victims as well as men who could fancy themselves heroes of the tale. Moral proprieties were preserved by the avenging stone guest: the statue who came to dinner and dragged Don Juan down to hell.

But Strauss's *Don Juan* is based on a nineteenth-century Romantic variant of the legend: *Don Juan, A Dramatic Poem* (1844) by the Austrian Nicolaus Lenau. Lenau's hero is no mere aristocratic rake. His catalog of conquests represents his search for the ideal woman, who will be womanhood incarnate, his longing, "to enjoy in one woman all women, since he cannot possess them as individuals." This Don is a dreamer and philosopher as well as one driven by the storm of youthful desire, and his desertions of one victim after another represent his successive disappointments in his restless, compulsive search for the ideal.

In a series of loosely connected episodes, more epic than dramatic, Lenau depicts Don Juan's conquests: Maria, Clara, Anna, Isabella. None resists him. Yet each possession proves empty; instead of fulfillment he finds only satiety. With the years, disillusion, boredom, contempt, and finally loathing fill his heart. It is these, rather than the stone guest and hellfire, that are his undoing. "This loathing," said Lenau, "is the devil that fetches him." But the Don has no regrets:

> The storm was fair that drove me on and on.
> It has raged and passed and now is still.
> And all wishes and all hopes now seem dead.
> Perhaps a lightning bolt from heights I scorned
> Has killed my power to love and made my world
> Into a desert ringed about by night;
> Or perhaps not; the fuel has burned out,
> And the hearth is cold and dark.

In his final duel Don Juan has the upper hand; victory is in his grasp. Yet he purposely lowers his guard, exposes himself to the fatal thrust because victory and even life itself have lost their lure. Excerpts from the long Lenau poem are printed at the head of Strauss's score.

The structure of the tone poem closely resembles the traditional first-movement sonata-allegro form. After a preliminary flourish, the first important theme of the tone poem shows us the Don on his impetuous way to adventure:

This is a theme that we will hear again and again, each recurrence seeming to represent the start of a new episode. There follow several passages of love music, each describing the character of the woman in whom Don Juan hopes to find the ideal.

Among them we hear the tender, ecstatic voice of a solo violin, sweet, confiding, with a certain aristocratic reticence which gradually gives way to growing warmth as the violins soar to a great lyric climax.

But the new ecstasy is short-lived. Already the Don is off and we hear his first theme again as the search is renewed. Is this the goal? Over gently murmuring strings and horns the oboe sings a song of forgetfulness and bliss. But once again the orchestra rouses itself and the dream disperses. Then through a brilliant *tremolo* of the high strings there flashes a theme of such knightly pride and magnificence as has hardly been equalled in music. More than any other, this new theme, proclaimed at first by all four horns in unison, portrays the essential nobility of Strauss's Don Juan:

There is even a touch of scorn in the theme, as though for a moment the Don stood above his own compulsions and his doom.

But this does not prevent the same theme from being reduced to tiny mocking phrases, in the glittering tone of the glockenspiel, for example. There are moments of frivolity too. At one of these, Richard Strauss stopped a rehearsal of the Boston Symphony Orchestra, which he conducted in 1904, during a tour of the United States, and said to the players, "Gentlemen, I must confess, I did not intend this passage to be *so* beautiful; that [woman] was just a common tramp [*ein gemeines Mensch*]!"

Once again the Don is off on adventure. The orchestra approaches a tremendous climax and then stops dead in its tracks. There is a terrible pause. The music fades suddenly as a dissonant trumpet note cuts through—the rapier-thrust of death. There is no lamenting peroration, only stoical acceptance of the end of all man's searching—and silence.

Strauss himself conducted the enormously successful first performance of *Don Juan* with the Court Orchestra in the Grand Ducal Theater of Weimar on November 11, 1889. The first American performance appears to have been that of the Boston Symphony on October 30, 1891, under the direction of Arthur Nikisch.

The opulent-sounding orchestra calls for the relatively modest list of 3 flutes, piccolo, 2 oboes, English horn, 2 clarinets, 2 bassoons, contrabassoon, 4 horns, 3 trumpets, 3 trombones, tuba, 3 kettledrums, bells, cymbals, triangle, harp, and the usual strings.

DON QUIXOTE (INTRODUCTION, THEME WITH VARIATIONS AND FINALE), FANTASTIC VARIATIONS ON A THEME OF KNIGHTLY CHARACTER, OPUS 35

That preposterous, yet somehow winning person, Don Quixote de la Mancha, seems always to have had a real existence of his own, independent of his first author. We know, as a matter of historical fact, that the Don was launched on his improbable career early in the year 1605 by Miguel de Cervantes Saavedra. He so endeared himself to his readers that it was only a matter of weeks before three pirated editions had appeared, and in less than six months the Knight of the Rueful Countenance had become a figure of proverb. He has continued to grow with each generation of readers and creative artists, whose imaginations he has stirred.

Cervantes presented his Don Quixote first of all as a figure of satire, occasionally even of farce, an old-fashioned impoverished gentleman of La Mancha, who spent all his time reading books on chivalry, such as were still popular in Cervantes's day, and meditating on the adventures of bold knights, villainous giants, evil magicians and enchanted princesses, until at last "through his little sleep and much reading, he dried up his brains in such sort, as he wholly lost his judgment." Thereupon, "He fell into one of the strangest conceits that a madman ever stumbled on in this world . . . that he himself should become a knight errant, and go throughout the world with his horse and armour to seek adventures and practice in person all he had read was used by knights of yore. . . ." It is not until considerably later in the tale that Cervantes's Don inspires pity and affection.

Today we see the Don not only as Cervantes created him, but also through the nineteenth-century eyes of Honoré Daumier and Gustave Doré. For many the Don is the voice of the solo cello in Richard Strauss's tone poem. Strauss composed his score in his native city of Munich in 1897, the year after his *Also sprach Zarathustra*. It was first performed at the Gürzenich Concerts in Cologne under the direction of Franz Wüllner on March 8, 1898.

By 1897 Strauss had developed an orchestral style of unparalleled virtuosity, flexibility and vividness of description, a style which alternately shocked and dazzled his listeners. But his startling orchestral colors were obtained from largely traditional pigments: 2 flutes, piccolo, 2 oboes, English horn, 2 B-flat clarinets, E-flat clarinet, bass clarinet, 3 bassoons, contrabassoon, 6 horns, 3 trumpets, 3 trombones, tenor tuba, bass tuba, strings, harp, kettledrums, bass drum, military drum, tambourine, cymbals, triangle, small bell, and wind machine (for Variation VII).

Introduction: A gallant, prancing theme associated with the books of chivalry which snared our hero's imagination opens the score:

As the Don's mind weakens, the theme begins to wander and the harmonies go awry. Thereupon, over a glamorous harp accompaniment a solo oboe sings a rather timid but noble melody—Don Quixote's ideal vision of womanly beauty and virtue, the fair Dulcinea. At once his excitement boils. He imagines her threatened. His theme sounds heroically in the brass, only to degenerate into a series of dotty discords, indicating clearly enough his state of mind.

Theme: Don Quixote now sees himself as the personification of chivalry, so the theme of knight errantry quoted above turns into his own:

It is played by the instrument which will be associated with him through the Variations, a solo cello.

He is followed down the road by the lumbering theme of Sancho Panza in the bass clarinet and tenor tuba. Later in Sancho's more garrulous moments he will be personified by the solo viola.

I. The first variation describes the adventure of the windmills. In spite of Sancho's frantic warnings, the Don sees the windmills as giants. Lance set, he charges their vast, waving arms as they creak and groan in the wind. He is whirled up to the heavens and smashed back to earth with a terrifying thump.

II. The second variation brings another threat: a fabulous army of all the nations of the earth led by the great Emperor Alifanfaron. The army approaches slowly in a vast cloud of dust, accompanied by a distinct sound of baa-ing in the muted brass. Sancho warns again that it is only a flock of sheep, but already the Don has charged. A bold military fanfare clashes with the panic-stricken bleating of the enemy and our hero would have surveyed the field in triumph except for the shepherds, who "began to salute his pate with stones as great as one's fist."

III. Our Knight and Sancho discuss the ways of chivalry. The garrulous viola doubts the point of such a life. His master rebukes him for his earthbound mind and describes the ideal with waxing enthusiasm. The knightly theme repeats the point. With the last repetition, the theme ends on a note one half-tone higher than normal and we are magically lifted into the land of Don Quixote's quixotic dreams:

The instruments shimmer, a glow spreads through the orchestra. The melody of the ideal soars and sings with a nobility which tells you better than any words that this is the true reality—a thousand times more real than fat, querulous Sancho Panza and the world of sheep. The radiance grows and the transfigured voice of the Don mounts to a rapturous climax. The clod Sancho attempts a realistic reminder, but the orchestra, in a burst of temper, silences him.

IV. A distant, doleful ecclesiastical chant announces the approach of penitent pilgrims. For Don Quixote, they are threatening desperadoes. He attacks bravely; they knock him senseless and go their prayerful way.

V. Sancho sleeps, but the Don keeps vigil beside his weapons. A vision of Dulcinea appears, clothed in fantastic glissandos of the harp.

VI. In the cold daylight three coarse country wenches approach. One has a tambourine, and Sancho identifies her to his master as Dulcinea. The melody of ideal womanhood is transformed into a banal, witless ditty. The Knight understands that a magician has transformed his princess and vows vengeance.

VII. The Don and his servant are blindfolded and persuaded to mount a wooden horse which is to carry them through the air. The breathless speed of their course, the dizzy heights, the winds that whistle through outer space, are evoked by high woodwind instruments and harp glissandos. But the low D sustained throughout in the bottom of the orchestra suggests that the pair have never left ground.

VIII. The Don spies an empty boat lying oarless on the river bank. He understands at once that this has been sent to their aid by some kindly spirit. The Knight's theme is transformed into a barcarole as they careen downstream. They capsize and manage to scramble ashore. They offer brief thanksgivings for their miraculous escape and go on to the next adventure.

IX. Two bassoons in whining counterpoint represent two Benedictine monks in whom Don Quixote sees evil magicians. This time the Knight knows victory. The two monks take to their heels, terrified by his warlike cries.

X. In order to save Don Quixote from his own follies, a kindly neighbor from La Mancha masquerades as a rival knight and challenges the Don to single combat, on condition that if our hero loses he shall retire to his home for a full year. His defeat is swift and crushing. The homeward march begins over a desolate throbbing pedalpoint of the kettledrum, like the tread of the broken hero. It rises to a mighty dirge for defeated ideals and shattered illusions. Don Quixote tries to console himself with prospects of the idyllic life of a shepherd: Pastoral phrases echo in the woodwinds. But gradually his mind clears.

The *Finale* is Don Quixote's farewell to his dreams and to life. Sanity returns, his theme leaves off its cavorting and melts into warm diatonic melody, tinged with greatness:

But the Don's strength ebbs. The voice of the cello grows fainter as wisps of the original theme flit through the orchestra. Then it falters and is silent. The serene final cadence is like a smile of understanding.

EIN HELDENLEBEN (A HERO'S LIFE), TONE POEM FOR LARGE ORCHESTRA, OPUS 40

Monstrous conceit is only one of the crimes for which Strauss was indicted when it was discovered that he had made himself the hero of his latest tone poem, none too modestly entitled *A Hero's Life.* But Strauss, who had more than his share of urbanity, did not always take either his heroism or his *Heldenleben* as seriously as did his embattled critics. The latter gave him considerable malicious amusement, when they thought they recognized musical portraits of themselves in the section of the tone poem entitled "The Hero's Adversaries," with their grotesque, chattering noises and the ponderous pedantry of the low brass references to forbidden parallel fifths.

Among Strauss's earliest references to the new score, which took shape during 1898, is a letter dated July 25 from the tiny mountain resort of Marquartstein, where he was vacationing in the interval between the conclusion of his final season as conductor of the Bavarian Court Opera in Munich and his first season as conductor of the Prussian Royal Opera in Berlin: "Since Beethoven's *Eroica* is so extremely unpopular with our conductors and hence rarely performed, I am filling a desperate need by composing a tone poem of substantial length entitled *Hero's Life,* which has no funeral march to be sure, but is yet in E-flat major with lots of horn sound, since horns are, after all, the thing for heroism. Thanks to the healthy country air, my sketch has progressed so well here that, if no special delay develops, I can hope to finish the work by New Year's."

Apparently the sketch was virtually complete when the letter was written. Eight days later, in Munich, he began to write out the full score of *Ein Heldenleben,* and he completed it in Berlin on December 27. The premiere followed almost immediately under Strauss's own direction. The orchestra was that of the well-known Museumsgesellschaft of Frankfurt-am-Main, and the date of the concert was March 3, 1899. Almost exactly one year later *Heldenleben* was introduced to the United States by the Chicago Symphony under the direction of Theodore Thomas at a concert on March 10, 1900, in Chicago. The New York Philharmonic introduced *Ein Heldenleben* to this city on the following December 8 under the direction of Emil Paur.

Strauss himself published no program or plot for his latest tone poem. Indeed, he said to his admirer, Romain Rolland, "There is no need for a program. It is enough to know that a hero is battling his enemies." Nevertheless, when Strauss toured the United States during the 1921-22 season and saw the descriptive analysis of *Ein Heldenleben* by the late distinguished author of the New York Philharmonic program notes, Lawrence Gilman, Strauss told Gilman that his program note conveyed faithfully the significance of the music. We reprint here Mr. Gilman's note with two musical examples added:

1. *The Hero.* We hear first the chief theme of the Hero, the valorous opening subject for the low strings and horns, joined later by the violins.

There are subsidiary themes, picturing different aspects of the Hero's nature —his pride, depth of feeling, inflexibility, sensitiveness, imagination. This section comes to a defiant, heaven-storming close, *fff,* with a hold on the dominant-seventh chord of E flat.

2. *The Hero's Adversaries.* Herein are pictured the Hero's opponents and detractors—an envious and malicious crew, filled with all uncharitableness. Flute, oboes, piccolo, English horn, clarinets utter shrill and snarling phrases. There is also a malignly ponderous phrase, in fifths, for tenor and bass tubas, intended to picture the malevolence of the dull-witted among the foe. The theme of the Hero appears in sad and meditative guise. But his dauntless courage soon reasserts itself, and the mocking horde are put to rout.

3. *The Hero's Courtship.* A solo violin introduces the Hero's beloved. She reveals herself at the start as capricious, an inconsequent trifler, an elaborate coquette. The directions printed above the violin part in the score—"flippantly," "playfully," "insolently," "sedately," "soothingly," "angrily," "scoldingly," et cetera—suggest the changing aspects of the emotional scene. But a grave and earnest phrase—heard at first in the cellos, double basses, trombones and horns—recurs again and again, with the effect of an increasingly

fervent appeal, in the dialogue of the two protagonists. And then the orchestra breaks into a love song of heroic sweep and passion.

There are rapturous phrases for the strings, gorgeously adorned with *glissandi* in the harps; the oboe sings an ardently tender song. As the ecstasy subsides, the mocking voices of the foe are heard remotely, like the distant croaking of night birds through an enchanted dream.

4. *The Hero's Battlefield.* But suddenly the call to arms is heard, and it may not be ignored. Distant fanfares (trumpets behind the scenes) summon the Hero to the conflict. The orchestra becomes a battlefield; the music "evokes the picture of countless and waging hosts, of forests of waving spears and clashing blades," wrote Huneker of this section. Through the dust and uproar we are reminded of the inspiration of the Beloved, which sustains and heartens the champion, whose theme contests for supremacy with that of his adversaries. A triumphant orchestral outburst proclaims at last his victory. Yet he exults alone—the world regards his conquest with cold and cynical indifference.

5. *The Hero's Works of Peace.* Now begins a celebration of the Hero's victories of peace, suggesting his spiritual evolution and achievements. We hear quotations of themes from Strauss's earlier works: reminiscences of *Tod und Verklärung, Don Quixote, Don Juan, Till Eulenspiegel, Macbeth, Also sprach Zarathustra,* the music-drama *Guntram* and the exquisite song, *"Traum durch die Dämmerung."* It may be doubted if Strauss has ever written more persuasively than in this example of polyphonic ingenuity, in which an uncanny contrapuntal skill is made to yield subduingly lovely music. Note, for example, the exceeding beauty of that G-flat-major passage in which the tenor tuba, violas and bass clarinet sing the melody of *"Traum durch die Dämmerung"* against a theme from *Don Quixote* on the cellos, horn and *cor anglais.*

6. *The Hero's Retreat from the World, and Fulfillment.* The tubas mutter the uncouth and sinister phrase which voices the dull contempt of the benighted adversaries. Even the glorious achievements of the Hero's brain, his spiritual conquests, have won him only envy and derision. Furiously he rebels, and the orchestra rages. But his anger subsides. Over a persistent tapping of the kettledrum, the *cor anglais* sings a gentler version of his theme. An agitating memory of storm and strife again disturbs his mood. But the solo violin reminds him of the consoling presence of the beloved one. Peace descends upon the spirit of the Hero. There are pages of tender and exalted beauty, with an intimate dialogue between horn and violin—music of which Philip Hale once dared to say that it was "worthy of Beethoven in his supreme moments of rapt meditation." In the trumpets, the chief theme, immensely broadened, rises in solemn majesty to a climax of memorable splendor—a great chord of E-flat major that fills the orchestral heavens with dazzling

> light. The finale, majestic and serene, recalls the words of the luminous Shankara: "For the circling world is like a dream, crowded with desires and hates; in its own time it shines as real, but on awakening it becomes unreal."

Ein Heldenleben is scored for piccolo, 3 flutes, 4 oboes, English horn, E-flat clarinet, 2 B-flat clarinets, bass clarinet, 3 bassoons, contrabassoon, 8 horns, 5 trumpets, 3 trombones, B-flat tenor tuba, bass tuba, kettledrums, bass drum, small military drum, big snare drum, cymbals, gong, triangle, 16 first violins, 16 second violins, 12 violas, 12 cellos, 8 double basses, and 2 harps.

METAMORPHOSES

Was there ever a gentler, more civilized reaction to violence and destruction? Strauss's supremely lyric *Metamorphoses* was written during the final and most violent phase of World War II, a holocaust unequaled in the history of the world. Looking back from the safety of decades later we can remember (or read in a history book) that this was the end of World War II. But to individuals living through that daily hell the future was as terrifying as the present.

Hitler had taught the world to take his threats seriously. And had he not promised, if defeated, to bring European civilization down to utter ruin with him, in a fiery finale *à la Götterdämmerung?* By the winter of 1944–1945 it was clear that he was failing—had failed—and that his fanatical, bitter-end resistance was bringing with it the apocalyptic kind of destruction he had foretold. "Is Paris burning?" came the repeated maniacal cables from the headquarters of the Führer who had ordered the French capital destroyed by land mines and fire when he realized he could not hold it against the allies.

For Strauss a very personal emotion was attached to the symbols of that German culture, which Hitler had already done so much to destroy, and which was now disappearing even physically: the Goethe House in Frankfurt, the opera houses and concert halls where Strauss and his father before him had spent their lives contributing the best of which they were capable.

As the pace of destruction grew, the eighty-year-old master, his movements already restricted by the Nazi regime, withdrew more and more into himself. A particular shock was the destruction of his beloved Munich, including two opera houses: the tiny Residenz-Theater, where Mozart had conducted his own works, and the National-Theater where Wagner had supervised the premieres of *Tristan and Isolde* and *Die Meistersinger,* where Strauss's father had been the brilliant first-horn player of the orchestra, and where the younger Strauss had so often conducted his now-fabled productions of Mozart, of Wagner, and his own once-controversial scores. With the opera houses went large areas of Munich, including the family house where Strauss was born. "Mourning for Munich" *("Trauer um München")* is one of the marginal notes we find in the manuscript sketches for *Metamorphoses.*

The external stimulus for the composition of Strauss's last major score came in July 1944. Paul Sacher, conductor of the Collegium Musicum, Zürich, asked whether Strauss would consider composing a work for string orchestra to be given its world premiere by the Zürich Collegium. Strauss accepted. The sketches, which he seems to have begun by September 1944, are fascinating for many reasons, chief among them the growth and transformation—the metamorphosis—of many themes which allude to Strauss's own works, to Wagner and, most obvious of all, to Beethoven. It is as if Strauss, at the very end of his life (and, for all he knew, the end of the civilization to which he belonged) were looking back in love, gratitude and a sadness bordering on despair to the great men and the great traditions which had nourished him.

As the work progressed so did the isolation of Strauss and the ring of destruction which was closing about him. One letter, to his sister Hanna Rauchberger, is dated: "Garmisch, immediately after the destruction of the Hoftheater. Dear Hanna," it reads, "many thanks for the kind letter. I cannot write any more today. I am beside myself. Affectionate greetings, Richard."

Yet the work evolved, the themes branched and grew into new themes. One theme in particular, which haunted Strauss from beginning to end, finally revealed itself to be an unconscious recall of the "Funeral March" from Beethoven's "Eroica" Symphony.

During the night of February 13–14 came the Allied air attack which destroyed most of Dresden, including the opera house which had first produced all of Strauss's greatest operas. In answer to a letter from his librettist Joseph Gregor in Vienna, Strauss replied: ". . . I too am in despair! The Goethe House, the holiest house in the world, destroyed! My beautiful Dresden—Weimar—Munich—gone, all of them!"

The composition sketch was completed early in March. The full score is dated: "Begun 13 March 1945" and at the end "Garmisch, 12 April 1945." The first performance, supervised by Strauss and conducted by Paul Sacher, was presented by the Collegium Musicum in the Small Tonhallesaal of Zürich on January 25, 1946.

The score calls for twenty-three strings (10 violins, 5 violas, 5 cellos, 3 double basses), each of which has its individual part, although there are many moments when for the sake of special emphasis Strauss doubles two or more instruments on a single melodic line.

The music opens in a dark mood. The entire body of cellos reinforced by one double bass pronounces four heavy chords, a striking, Straussian progression which punctuates this work at crucial moments: *

* *This and the following musical examples from this composition are copyright 1946 by Boosey & Hawkes Ltd. Renewed 1973. Reprinted by permission of Boosey & Hawkes, Inc.*

A varied repetition of these harmonies leads to the second and most important theme of the score. It consists of four repeated notes followed by a syncopated descending line:

This is the theme which haunted Strauss throughout the sketching and composing of his score and which, according to the composer's own testimony, he himself did not recognize in its full identity until late in the process of composing.

A third and even more lyric theme, beginning like the above with four repeated notes, follows immediately. The melancholy turn of this phrase will remind many listeners of King Mark's lament from *Tristan and Isolde,* particularly his words "*Wozu die Dienste ohne Zahl. . . .*" ("To what avail thy countless deeds of faithful service. . . ."):

Gradually the tempo begins to flow. More and more themes are introduced, virtually all of them hinting, or alluding in passing, to a familiar work, the references often tantalizing the memory and ear. In many cases the references must have been only half conscious on the part of the composer himself. Some themes may never have revealed their identity as clearly as did the Beethoven "Funeral March." For all its amazing contrapuntal skill and psychological complexity, the score seems simple, its musical message deeply emotional rather than intellectual.

The tide of development and associations reaches full flood, dominated more and more by the Beethoven reminiscence. There is a sudden suspension of motion. We return to the *Adagio ma non troppo* of the beginning and an expanded statement of the heavy-hearted opening chords. In the following epilogue, as the fervor of the music dies away, we hear, ten bars before the end, Beethoven's own version of his "Funeral March" theme in the double basses, and above it, played by six violins, Strauss's own metamorphosis. Under Beethoven's theme Strauss wrote "IN MEMORIAM!"

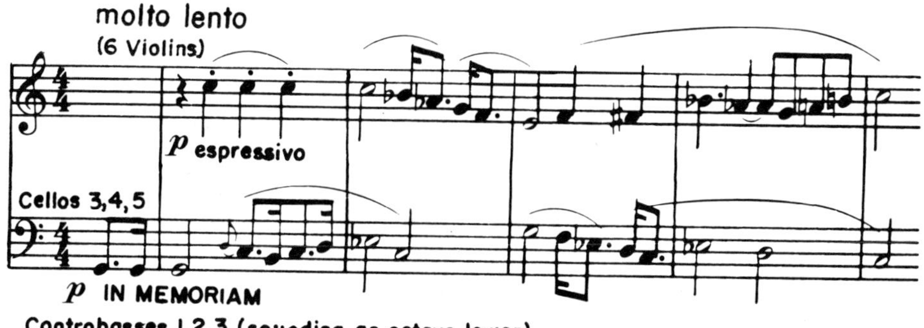

"DANCE OF THE SEVEN VEILS" FROM *SALOME*

Richard Strauss's opera *Salome* is founded on the biblical tale of the daughter of Herodias, who danced before Herod and received as her reward the head of the Baptist on a charger. In St. Mark's account it is Salome's mother, Herodias, who advises Salome to ask for the head. In Oscar Wilde's play, which furnished the text for the opera, Wilde substituted the motive of Salome's love for Jochanaan.

The action takes place on a moonlit terrace of the palace of Herod. From his prison well, we hear the voice of Jochanaan (John the Baptist) denouncing Salome's mother, the sinful Herodias. Salome comes hurriedly from the banquet hall to breathe the fresh air and avoid the lustful gaze of her stepfather, Herod. Hearing the prophet, she desires to see him; and seeing him she desires to kiss his mouth. But Jochanaan has eyes and lips only for his God and he curses Salome as he returns to his prison well. By a cruelly simple logic, Salome's desire to kiss his mouth becomes a desire for his death. This in turn becomes a fanatical determination. There is a musical phrase associated with her determination and her repeated demands, later in the opera: "I demand the head of Jochanaan" (*"Ich fordre den Kopf des Jochanaan!"*):*

Herod, Herodias and their banquet guests come out onto the terrace. The infatuated Herod asks Salome to dance for him, promising her in return anything she asks, up to half his kingdom. Salome grasps the chance to fulfill her will. The stage musicians strike up a wild dance, but Salome gestures imperiously to them to change the character of the dance. The music accompanying

* *This and the following musical examples from this composition are copyright 1905 by Adolph Furstner. Renewed 1933. Copyright and renewal assigned to Boosey & Hawkes, Inc. Reprinted by permission.*

her gesture tells us what the dance is about: trumpets and trombones snarl the motive, "the head of Jochanaan!" (*den Kopf des Jochanaan!*) Immediately the rhythm of the dance slows down to a gently rocking figure. The whining woodwind melody has a langorous Oriental allure. But the gently rocking accompaniment figure keeps reminding us, now in a whisper, of the real subject of the dance: *"den Kopf des Jochanaan"*:

Two other themes dominate the "Dance of the Seven Veils," both of them associated with the earlier scene in which Salome wooed Jochanaan in vain. One is the motive of Salome herself:

The other is the sweeping melody with which she poured out her unappeasable longing, as she does again in her final scene: "Nothing in the world was so white as thy body" (*"Nichts in der Welt war so weiss wie dein Leib"*):

At the climax of her dance she hovers for a moment over the prison well of the doomed prophet before throwing herslf at Herod's feet to ask her ghoulish reward.

The "Dance of the Seven Veils" calls for an orchestra of 1 piccolo, 3 flutes, 2 oboes, English horn, Heckelphone, 1 E-flat clarinet, 2 clarinets in A, 2 clarinets in B flat, bass clarinet, 3 bassoons, contrabassoon, 5 horns, 4 trumpets, 4 trombones, tuba, 4 kettledrums, 1 small kettledrum, gong, cymbals, bass drum, snare drum, tambourine, triangle, xylophone, castanets, glockenspiel, celesta, 2 harps, 16 first violins, 16 second violins, 10 to 12 violas, 10 cellos, and 8 double basses.

TILL EULENSPIEGEL'S MERRY PRANKS, AFTER OLD-TIME ROGUISH FASHION, IN RONDEAU FORM, OPUS 28

Who was Till Eulenspiegel, that Richard Strauss should have written a tone-poem about him? Like other rebels and pranksters dear to the imagination of the Renaissance, Till Eulenspiegel may have been a real historical person. But if he was, he had become a legend by the time the earliest surviving account of his exploits was printed in 1515.

The anonymous book, *Ein kurtzweilig lesen von Dyl Eulenspiegel geboren uss dem land zu Brunsswick,* was republished in 1519 and quickly translated into Dutch, Danish, Latin, Swedish, Czech, French, and English. Such was his popularity that twenty editions of Till's story had been published in French alone by the beginning of the eighteenth century. And his French surname, Ulenspiègle, was metamorphosed into a new French word for a rogue: *espiègle.* A nineteenth-century version of the story, the Belgian writer Charles de Coster's *Légende de Thyl Uylenspiegel et de Lamme Goedzak,* which transformed Till into a sixteenth-century Flemish hero, may have sparked Strauss's imagination.

Strauss, something of a rebel and prankster himself (he jokingly identified himself with Till), could hardly help being drawn to him. De Coster's *Légende* was republished in a popular edition in 1893 and by June of that year Strauss was sketching his own libretto for an Eulenspiegel opera. But the failure in May, 1894 of Strauss's first opera *Guntram* may have discouraged his operatic ambitions for Till. By the winter of 1894–1895 Strauss was at work on his symphonic poem, which he finished on May 6, 1895.

Whether Strauss ever had a connected narrative in mind for his tone-poem, we may never know. It is clear that he associated his music with pictures or episodes of Till's adventures. But when Franz Wüllner, the conductor, wanted a concrete story to help his audience understand Strauss's revolutionary score on the occasion of its world premiere (Cologne, November 5, 1895), Strauss replied:

> It is impossible for me to provide a program for *Eulenspiegel:* if I were to put into words the thoughts which the various incidents suggested to me, they would often make a quite strange impression and might even give arise to offense. Let us leave it therefore to our hearers to crack the nut which the rogue presents to them. By way of helping them to a better understanding it seems enough to point out the two Eulenspiegel motives:*

* *Listeners familiar with* Till Eulenspiegel *may notice that the first of the two themes does not occur anywhere in the score in the form Strauss notes here. The omission of the C sharp after the C natural probably was an oversight on Strauss's part, but one cannot be sure, particularly in view of Strauss's habitual, meticulous attention to detail. See "Richard Strauss und Franz Wüllner im Briefwechsel," ed. Dietrich Kämper,* Beiträge zur Rheinischen Musikgeschichte, *Bd. 51 (Cologne: Arno Volk, 1963).*

which, in the most manifold disguises, moods and situations, pervade the whole up to the catastrophe when Till is strung up to the gibbet after the motive:

has been pronounced upon him. For the rest, let the merry citizens of Cologne guess at the musical prank which a rogue has played on them.

The tone-poem opens with a lyric expansion of the first Eulenspiegel motive. Over these opening measures Strauss wrote in the score of a friend, Wilhelm Mauke: "Once upon a time there was a clowning rogue." The second Eulenspiegel motive is extended and developed into one of the boldest and most celebrated French horn themes ever penned, over which Strauss wrote: " . . . whose name was Till Eulenspiegel."

The horn repeats the full flourish against a shimmering *tremolo* of violins. It is echoed by two oboes, then by clarinets, and by other instruments, leading to a short, sharp climax, and the introduction is over.

Till's adventures follow fast. We need not worry much about the rondeau in the title, for this is a free, Straussian rondeau, which has only a bowing acquaintance with the traditional form. Both Eulenspiegel themes return often, in marvelously ingenious transformations. We seem to hear Till spread chaos in the marketplace as he charges through on horseback. After each prank he mocks his pursuers and saunters off, thumbing his nose as he scampers out of reach. He is pursued again, caught and condemned to death with grotesque ferocity. He squeaks a last jest and is strung up. In Coster's tale, the final unbearable prank that Till played on his enemies was that after he was buried he refused to lie quiet in his grave, as a dead person should. The end of Strauss's music is an impudent, roistering, nose-thumbing version of the first Eulenspiegel theme, suggesting that Till defies annihilation and that his irrepressible spirit lives on.

The tone poem is scored for piccolo, 3 flutes, 3 oboes, English horn, clarinet in D, 2 clarinets in B flat, bass clarinet, 3 bassoons, contrabassoon, 4 horns in F, 4 horns in D *ad libitum,* 3 trumpets in F, 3 trumpets in D *ad libitum,* 3 trombones, tuba, kettledrums, bass drum, military drum, cymbals, triangle, 16 first violins, 16 second violins, 12 violas, 12 cellos, and 8 string basses.

THUS SPAKE ZARATHUSTRA (ALSO SPRACH ZARATHUSTRA) TONE POEM (FREELY AFTER FRIEDRICH NIETZSCHE) FOR LARGE ORCHESTRA, OPUS 30

Strauss's flamboyant tone poem *Thus Spake Zarathustra* was inspired by a book so extraordinary that it might almost have been called a tone-poem in its own right. "Where does this *Zarathustra* really belong?" asked Friedrich Nietzsche as he labored in 1883 at his unfinished masterpiece. "Almost, I think, among the symphonies." It was a prophetic insight.

A professional philosopher, poet, philologist, and critic, Nietzsche had also trained as a composer and he knew whereof he spoke. Yet when it became known that Richard Strauss was composing a tone poem on Nietzsche's *Thus Spake Zarathustra,* hoots of derision were mixed with roars of indignation. Set philosophy to music? What next?

But Nietzsche's *Zarathustra* was never intended to be philosophy in any systematic sense. On the contrary, today's reader is apt to be struck first by the emotional high voltage of this torrential prose poem: its nervous virtuosity, the glitter of its verbal fireworks, its lethal epigrams which once passed as profound insights, the fierce fervor of its militant atheism—the numberless outward signs of an inward fever.

Strauss was drawn to Nietzsche by deeper bonds of temperament and artistic sensibility than by any system of logic. From the eighty-odd chapter heads of *Also sprach Zarathustra* Strauss chose eight which he found suggestive and reshuffled them to suit his purpose. It is not clear whether he did this before or after writing the music. He composed the score between February 4 and August 24, 1896. This was the year of Strauss's promotion from second to first conductor of the Royal Bavarian Opera in Munich. But despite the high regard in which Strauss was held as a conductor, conservative Munich was not anxious to have the honor of his premieres. The first performance of *Zarathustra* was given by the Museums-Orchester of Frankfurt-am-Main on November 27, 1896, under Strauss's own direction.

It is difficult to guess what program, if any, Strauss had in mind as he composed the music—beyond the titles of Nietzsche's masterpiece! Whatever he had in mind, Strauss seems to have been content to authorize or at least to countenance a series of conflicting (and in part contradictory) programs. In view of Nietzsche's scorn for religion, and particularly for the Christian religion, the program published just before the Frankfurt premiere of *Zarathustra* is puzzling:

> First movement: Sunrise, Man feels the power of God. *Andante religioso.* But man still longs. He plunges into passion (second movement) and finds no peace. He turns toward science, and tries in vain to solve life's problem in a fugue (third movement). Then agreeable dance tunes sound and he becomes an individual, and his soul soars upward while the world sinks far below him.

Puzzling, too, is the fact that the section of the music which Strauss eventually labeled *"Von den Hinternweltlern"* ("Of the Otherworldsmen"—

Nietzsche's contemptuous name for those religiously inclined) originally bore the title "Of the Divine." Strauss wrote a third explanation of his *Zarathustra* for his friend Otto Florscheim at the time of the Berlin premiere: "I did not intend to write philosophical music or to portray in music Nietzsche's great work. I meant to convey by means of music an idea of the development of the human race from its origin, through the various phases of its development, religious and scientific, up to Nietzsche's idea of the superman. The whole symphonic poem is intended as my homage to Nietzsche's genius, which found its greatest exemplification in his book *Thus Spake Zarathustra.*"

Finally, when *Zarathustra* was published, the printed score bore as introduction the opening paragraphs of Nietzsche's work:

> When Zarathustra was thirty years old, he left his homeland and the lake of his homeland and went into the mountains. There he enjoyed his spirit and his solitude, and for ten years did not weary of it. But at last his heart changed—and rising one morning with the rosy dawn, he went before the sun, and spake unto it:
>
> "Thou great star! What would be thy happiness if thou hadst not those for whom thou shinest.
>
> "For ten years hast thou climbed unto my cave: thou wouldst have wearied of thy light and of the journey, had it not been for me, mine eagle and my serpent.
>
> "But we awaited thee every morning, took from thee thine overflow, and blessed thee for it.
>
> "Lo! I am weary of my wisdom, like the bee that hath gathered too much honey; I need hands outstretched to take it.
>
> "I would fain bestow and distribute until the wise of mankind have once more become joyous in their folly, and the poor happy in their riches.
>
> "For this must I descend into the deep; as thou doest in the evenings, when thou goest behind the sea, and givest light also to the nether-world, thou exuberant star!
>
> "Like thee must I go down, as men say, to whom I shall descend.
>
> "Bless men then, thou tranquil eye, that canst behold even the greatest happiness without envy!
>
> "Bless the cup that is about to overflow, that the water may flow golden out of it, and carry everywhere the reflection of thy bliss!
>
> "Lo! This cup is going to empty itself, and Zarathustra is again going to be a man."
>
> —Thus began Zarathustra's descent.

Strauss's score opens with an introductory depiction of dawn, which today, almost a century after it was composed, still has startling grandeur. The basic theme given out by four trumpets could scarcely be simpler:

The climax of the sunrise calls on the full strength of Strauss's large orchestra plus the pipe organ which makes its grandest effect when the orchestra is suddenly cut off and we hear, for half a measure, the pipe organ alone.

Although the music is continuous throughout, the remainder is divided into eight sections, each bearing a chapter title from Nietzsche's *Thus Spake Zarathustra:*

1. "Of the Otherworldsmen" (*"Von den Hinterweltlern"*). We hear a fragment of Christian creed labeled (in the horn parts): *Credo in unum Deum* ("I believe in one God"). The warmly lyric outpouring that follows in the string choir is to be performed "reverently" (*"mit Andacht"*) and sounds more compatible with Strauss's original title, "Of the Divine" than with the Nietzschean title it now bears.

2. "Of the Great Yearning" (*"Von der grossen Sehnsucht"*). Zarathustra's yearning is suggested by the first of many transformations of the basic theme quoted above. That slowly rising three-note figure turns into a vaulting melody, which we hear very softly at first:

3. "Of Joys and Passions" (*"Von den Freuden und Leidenschaften"*). Two agitated, swirling themes dominate this section: the first twists and turns upon itself. The second leaps upward into the orchestral stratosphere and cascades down almost to its starting point.

4. "The Dirge" (*"Das Grablied"*). Both the preceding themes are now combined with the theme of Zarathustra's great yearning.

5. "Of Learning" (*"Von der Wissenschaft"*). Here Strauss extends his basic three-note theme into a complex fugue subject using all twelve degrees of the chromatic scale:

Since the fugue is traditionally considered a "learned" composition, its relation to the title is obvious. But it bears no relation at all to the corresponding chapter of Nietzsche's book. Nietzsche's chapter deals with the evil art of an "old magician" whom he denounces in terms of his denunciations of Richard Wagner as this "old magician, this Klingsor of Klingsors."

6. "The Convalescent" (*"Der Genesende"*). This section begins with various versions of the fugue subject piling up and combining (as in the *stretto*

of an academic fugue). Suddenly the academic complexities fade away and a transformation of the yearning theme skips upward in a dancelike cadence for solo cello.

7. "The Dance Song" (*"Das Tanzlied"*). The dance rhythms of convalescent Zarathustra turn into a Viennese waltz! This proves a somewhat startling idiom for Nietzsche's fierce prophet. Some of Strauss's commentators have attempted to depict the vitality of the waltz rhythms as a symbol of the Life Force. Others have accused Strauss of one more lapse of good taste. But the explanation may be much simpler. Strauss adored the music of the Viennese "waltz king" Johann Strauss, Jr., which he imitated in several of his own works with considerable success. Moreover Strauss had a strong streak of Till Eulenspiegel in him, an irreverent, often self-mocking humor. And the picture of Nietzsche's prophet of the superman waltzing to the sentimental thirds and sixths of gypsy violins (in a Viennese turn-of-the-century café-concert?) does have a certain mischievous appeal. The climax of the waltz leads without pause into the final section of the tone-poem.

8. "Somnambulist's Song" (*"Nachtwandler Lied"*). Nietzsche's original title is often translated as "Night Wanderer's Song," but the primary meaning of *Nachtwandler* is "sleepwalker." In his final version of the book Nietzsche changed this to *"Das trunkene Lied,"* "The Song of Rapture" or more literally "The Drunken Song." Strauss preferred the original title, perhaps because of the hushed conclusion his music demanded. It begins with a bell tolling the twelve strokes of midnight. The close is peaceful and mysterious, leaving an unresolved harmonic progression, like an unanswered question: high, ethereal woodwinds repeat, ever more softly, a simple B-major chord, while at the bottom of the orchestra the string basses quietly, obstinately reiterate the low C with which the work began.

In 1896 this unresolved end was so disturbing to some and puzzling to all that it was widely taken to represent the World Riddle, a riddle which, as Philip Hale remarked, remained "unsolved by Nietzsche, by Strauss and even by Strauss's commentators."

Strauss's tone-poem is scored for 2 piccolos, 3 flutes, 3 oboes, English horn, E-flat clarinet, 2 B-flat clarinets, bass clarinet, 3 bassoons, contrabassoon, 6 horns, 4 trumpets, 3 trombones, 2 bass tubas, 4 kettledrums, bass drum, cymbals, triangle, glockenspiel, 1 low bell in E, 2 harps, organ, 16 first violins, 16 second violins, 12 violas, 12 cellos, and 8 contrabasses.

TOD UND VERKLÄRUNG (DEATH AND TRANSFIGURATION), TONE POEM, OPUS 24

It is hard to believe that when Strauss completed this apocalyptic score (on November 18, 1889) he was not yet twenty-six years old. This young firebrand —for so he seemed to his dazzled and often indignant contemporaries—was inspired by Wagner's *Tristan und Isolde.* He had been bowled over by an

Italian performance (the *first* Italian production) of the opera at Bologna in June, 1888. The immediate result was a revolution in Strauss's musical style and the composition of his first great tone-poem *Don Juan.* The second result was that Strauss, although he was already a famous conductor, sought the relatively humble position of rehearsal coach at the Wagner Festival Theater in Bayreuth where *Tristan* was being prepared for the summer festival of 1889. The third result was Strauss's dazzling tone-poem *Tod und Verklärung.*

Not only the music, the very title of *Tod und Verklärung* obviously was inspired by Wagner's masterpiece. The two concert excerpts we know today as the Prelude and *"Liebestod"* from *Tristan und Isolde* were conducted by Wagner under the title *"Liebestod und Verklärung."*

Perhaps the most obvious musical influence of *Tristan* on Strauss's new score shows on its opening page, which suggests the faint, irregular breathing of a dying man. In Act III the sick Tristan lies on a pallet in the courtyard of his castle. As he lingers on the border between life and death, he is sustained only by his hope that Isolde is on her way to join him. Exhausted by his frenzied visions and hallucinations, he has collapsed, motionless. His attendant Kurwenal bends over the body to listen for the sound of breathing or of a heartbeat. The scarcely audible, syncopated string sounds from the first measures of *Tod und Verklärung* are a direct echo of Wagner's orchestra at the corresponding point of *Tristan und Isolde.*

In a letter to his friend Friedrich von Hausegger in 1894 Strauss explained the idea behind his *Tod und Verklärung:*

> It was six years ago [i.e., 1888, the year of his "discovery" of *Tristan und Isolde*] when the idea came to me to write a tone poem describing the last hours of a man who had striven for the highest ideals, presumably an artist. The sick man lies in bed breathing heavily and irregularly in his sleep. Friendly dreams bring a smile to the face of the sufferer; his sleep grows lighter; he awakens. Fearful pains once more begin to torture him, fever shakes his body. When the attack is over and the pain recedes, he recalls his past life; his childhood passes before his eyes; his youth with its striving and passions and then, while the pains return, there appears to him the goal of his life's journey, the idea, the ideal which he attempted to embody in his art, but which he was unable to perfect because such perfection could be achieved by no man. The fatal hour arrives. The soul leaves his body, to discover in the eternal cosmos the magnificent realization of the ideal which could not be fulfilled here below.

After the music was finished, Strauss's close friend and professional associate, Alexander von Ritter, wrote, in consultation with Strauss, a short explanatory poem, which was printed in the program of the premiere. For the published score Ritter wrote a longer and more explicit poem which, we must assume, Strauss preferred to the shorter one. It has long been fashionable to claim that music expresses nothing but music. Strauss considered the conventional division of music into "pure" and "program" music to be pretentious nonsense. Be that as it may, it is obvious that Ritter's poem is (at the very least) an authorized description of what Strauss wished his public to have in mind in listening to *Tod und Verklärung.* The poem is divided into four sections, corresponding to the four main divisions of the music (which are played without pause). It may be paraphrased as follows:

I. *Largo.* "In a small bare room, dimly lit by a candle stump, a sick man lies on his pallet. Exhausted by a violent struggle with death, he lies asleep. In the ghastly stillness of the room, like a portent of impending death, only the quiet ticking of a clock is heard. A melancholy smile lights the invalid's pale face: does he dream of golden childhood as he lingers on the border of life?"

II. *Allegro molto agitato.* "But death grants him little sleep or time for dreams. He shakes his prey brutally to begin the battle afresh. The drive to live, the might of death! What a terrifying contest! [At the climax of the orchestral battle we hear briefly the theme of the Ideal or of Transfiguration, which returns to dominate the fourth and final section of the tone-poem:]

Neither wins the victory and once more silence reigns."

III. *Meno mosso, ma sempre alla breve.* "Exhausted from the battle, sleepless, as in a delirium, the sick man now sees his life pass before him, step by step, scene by scene. First the rosy dawn of childhood, radiant, innocent; then the boy's aggressive games, testing, building his strength—and so maturing for the battles of manhood, to strive with burning passion for the highest goals of life: to transfigure all that seems to him most noble, giving it still more exalted form—this alone has been the high aim of his whole existence. Coldly, scornfully, the world set obstacle upon obstacle in his way. When he believed himself near his goal, a thunderous voice cried: 'Hold!' But a voice within him still urged him on, crying: 'Make each hindrance a new rung in your upward climb.' Undaunted he followed the exalted quest. Still in his death agony he seeks the unreached goal of his ceaseless striving, seeks it, but alas, still in vain. Though it grows closer, clearer, grander, it never can be grasped entire or perfected in his soul. The final iron hammer-blow of death rings out, breaks his earthly frame, covers his eyes with eternal night."

IV. *Moderato.* "But from the endless realms of heavenly space a mighty resonance returns to him bearing what he longed for here below and sought in vain: redemption, transfiguration." [In the climax of the final pages the theme of Transfiguration, itself transformed, climbs higher and higher, with blinding brilliance, to the highest reaches of the brass, woodwinds and strings:]

Death and Transfiguration is scored for 3 flutes, 2 oboes, English horn, 2 clarinets, bass clarinet, 2 bassoons, contra-bassoon, 4 horns, 3 trumpets, 3 trombones, bass tuba, kettledrums, tam-tam, 2 harps, and strings.

Igor Stravinsky

Born June 17, 1882, Oranienbaum—died April 6, 1971, New York City

AGON, A BALLET FOR TWELVE DANCERS

In 1953, when he began the composition of *Agon,* it had been ten years since Stravinsky had composed any ballet music. Many of his admirers assumed that his return to ballet meant a return to a Neoclassical style. And Stravinsky did begin the score of *Agon* in a familiar harmonic style of dissonant modality. But before he had completed half of his score, he interrupted himself to compose a threnody, *In Memoriam Dylan Thomas* (1955), and his *Canticum sacrum* in honor of Venice, its cathedral, and its patron Saint Mark; during the course of writing these two works Stravinsky evolved into a full-fledged twelve-tone composer.

When he resumed the score of *Agon* in the spring of 1956, he realized that his style had changed so far that he no longer felt at home with the first part of his ballet. But rather than recompose the completed movements, he revised them so subtly that he was able to link them to the latter movements of *Agon* without giving up his desire to finish the score in serial style. Nevertheless, on the closing page of *Agon* Stravinsky returned to a strong diatonic tonality. Thus the score opens and closes in an emphatic C major. The final bar is dated April 27, 1957.

Agon was commissioned by Lincoln Kirstein and George Balanchine through a grant of the Rockefeller Foundation to the New York City Ballet in 1954. The first concert performance of the score was given in Los Angeles at a seventy-fifth birthday concert for Stravinsky on June 17, 1957, by the Los Angeles Festival Orchestra with Robert Craft conducting. The first stage performance was given by the New York City Ballet at the New York City Center on December 1st of the same year. The principal dancers were Diana Adams, Melissa Hayden, Todd Bolender, and Arthur Mitchell.

Conceived with Balanchine as the choreographer, *Agon* was planned as an abstract ballet having no story or subject matter. Even the title, a Greek word for contest, was not intended to be taken seriously but rather in a "decorative" sense. Stravinsky took ideas for many of the dance numbers, particularly in the middle sections (Sarabande, Gaillarde and Bransles) from seventeenth-century French court dances described in F. de Lauze's *Apologie de la danse* and Marin Mersenne's *Harmonie universelle.*

Stravinsky's expression had become much more concentrated and epigrammatic than in his earlier works. "My past and present time world cannot be the same," said Stravinsky in his *Conversations.** "I know that portions of *Agon* contain three times as much music for the same clock length as some other pieces of mine. Naturally, a new demand for greater in-depth listening changes time perspective."

Balanchine's choreography, worked out in collaboration with Stravinsky, was totally abstract. Balanchine himself compared it to "an IBM electrical computer," adding, "It is a machine, but a machine that thinks." John Martin in his New York Times review of the premiere declared that Balanchine was wrong, "for not even the IBM has attempted a machine that deals in high wit. *Agon* certainly does. Not that it is funny; when you find yourself smiling it is simply with the pleasure of seeing the choreographer deliberately tie himself into compositional knots and resolve them with ease and a touch of bravado right on the final beat."

The formality, the intellectuality, the abstraction of the ballet led even the most enthusiastic admirers of Stravinsky and Balanchine to expect that it would appeal only to a select few. In actual fact it proved a big box office success. This was probably due to the close collaboration of a composer and a choreographer whose mutual understanding had been developed over a period of more than three decades. Their joint production of *Agon* achieved a degree of integration rare in ballet since the legendary days of Diaghilev.

The ballet is designed in four strongly symmetrical groups of three dances apiece. The four groups are linked by a *Prelude* and two *Interludes* as follows:

1. *Pas-de-Quatre* (Four Male Dancers)
2. *Double Pas-de-Quatre* (Eight Female Dancers)
3. *Triple Pas-de-Quatre* (Eight Female, Four Male Dancers)

Prelude

1. *Sarabande-Step* (Solo Male Dance)
2. *Gailliarde* (Two Female Dancers)
3. *Coda* (One Male, Two Female Dancers)

Interlude

1. *Bransle Simple* (Two Male Dancers)
2. *Bransle Gay* (One Female Dancer)
3. *Bransle de Poitou* (Two Male, One Female Dancer)

---

* Conversations with Igor Stravinsky *by Stravinsky and Robert Craft, Doubleday and Co., Inc., Garden City, N.Y. Copyright 1958, 1959 by Igor Stravinsky.*

STRAVINSKY AND BALANCHINE.

From the first Stravinsky-Balanchine collaboration on *Apollo* (Paris, 1928) to their joint New York production of *Agon* in 1958, composer and choreographer spurred each other's imagination. (*Courtesy, Culver Pictures*)

Interlude

1. *Pas-de-Deux* (One Male, one Female Dancer)
2. *Four Duos* (Male and Female)
3. *Four Trios* (Male and Two Female)

The only specific choreographic directions in the score are at the opening: "As the curtain rises, four male dancers are aligned across the rear of the stage with their backs to the audience," and the corresponding direction before the final curtain: "The female dancers leave the stage. The male dancers take their position as at the beginning—back to the audience."

The opening *Pas-de-quatre* is a fanfare-like piece with nervous *staccato* rhythms for trumpets and horns. The rhythmic high voltage continues in the second piece, the *Double Pas-de-quatre,* with an *ostinato* pattern for first violins recalling the driving rhythms of some late Baroque concertos raised to a higher power:*

The Prelude is divided into two strongly contrasting halves, the first fanfare-like, the second almost mystical with strange, veiled sonorities which usually startle and puzzle listeners at a first hearing. These sonorities are produced by a novel combination of double basses playing high harmonics, with harp, kettledrum and two flutes. These same sonorities return in both Interludes.

Invariably the colors are striking and the rhythms ingenious. The dominant color of the *Bransle Gay,* for example, is a combination of two flutes, two bassoons and castanets. The intricate rhythms of the woodwinds contrast with the rigid rhythmic *ostinato* of the castanet:

The ballet concludes with a recall of the opening movement and a return to the choreographic grouping at the rise of the curtain.

The score of *Agon* calls for a large and varied orchestra, including 3 flutes (one interchangeable with piccolo), 2 oboes, English horn, 2 B-flat clarinets, bass clarinet, 2 bassoons, contrabassoon, 4 horns, 4 trumpets, 2 tenor trombones, bass trombone and the traditional string choir, plus harp, mandolin,

---

* *This and the following musical example from this composition are copyright 1957 by Boosey & Hawkes, Inc. Reprinted by permission.*

piano, xylophone, castanets, three tom-toms or high kettledrums in E flat, G flat and B flat in addition to normal kettledrums. The bigness of the orchestra is paradoxical because the texture of the music is, for the most part, extremely transparent. Stravinsky never uses the full ensemble; much of the time he writes in chamber style.

CAPRICCIO, FOR PIANO AND ORCHESTRA

When Stravinsky migrated to the United States in 1939, he surprised some of his more naïve admirers (of whom this writer was one) by announcing that he did not consider himself a Russian composer. He was, he declared, a composer in the Latin tradition.

This should not have been a surprise. For Stravinsky had long since become a French citizen and his residence in France totaled nearly a quarter of a century. But more important: he had absorbed so much French thought and feeling that Frenchmen came increasingly to think of him as one of themselves.

Just what proportion of Gallic spirit makes Stravinsky's *Capriccio* the dazzling, ironical, graceful confection that it is, would be hard to say. Stravinsky himself pointed out Weber's *Konzertstück* as his chief model. But Weber, for all his brilliance and charm, never had this kind of wit. Others hear echoes of Mendelssohn and Tchaikovsky. But there is a nonsentimentality in Stravinsky's score and dryness that seem characteristically French and—Stravinskyan.

The *Capriccio* was composed in France in 1928 and 1929, partly to fulfill Stravinsky's need for another piano concerto of his own. The first performance took place on December 6, 1929, in the Salle Pleyel in Paris, with Stravinsky himself as soloist and Ernest Ansermet conducting the Paris Symphony Orchestra. It is in three movements, played without pause.

I. *Presto; Doppio movimento.* The first movement is framed by a brief introduction and *coda,* which share the same two contrasting themes: loud, slashing scales of the orchestra, alternating with a soft, pensive passage for solo string instruments. The main body of the movement is also built around two contrasting themes: a heavy, rumbling, syncopated figure in the piano's low range, and a chic little wisp of a melody, *leggiero scherzando,* announced by the piano solo and immediately taken up by a solo flute:*

* *This and the following musical example from this composition (Revised Edition) are copyright 1952 by Boosey & Hawkes, Inc. Reprinted by permission.*

II. *Andante rapsodico.* The slow movement follows without pause. It is in simple A-B-A form with an elaborately embellished melodic line and a brief cadenza for the piano just before the closing measures, which lead directly into the *finale.*

III. *Allegro capriccioso ma tempo giusto.* Like the first movement, this brilliant *finale* has a brief introduction and a heavily syncopated theme announced by the piano. The parallel even extends to a graceful contrasting theme, *scherzando grazioso:*

which is tossed back and forth with marvelous dexterity and thematic sleight-of-hand from solo to orchestra and back again. The close is of breathtaking brilliance.

Capriccio is scored for piccolo, 2 flutes, 2 oboes, English horn, 2 clarinets, bass clarinet, 2 bassoons, 4 horns, 2 trumpets, 3 trombones, tuba, kettledrums, piano solo, and strings.

CARD GAME (JEU DE CARTES) A BALLET IN THREE ACTS

Stravinsky's *Jeu de cartes* abounds in tunes easy to whistle on the way home—carefree, humorous, sometimes outright satirical tunes, many of them adapted from earlier masters of melody, but all transmuted by Stravinsky's characteristic alchemy into a strongly personal expression. Despite the ominous time in which it was written (1936), despite Stravinsky's growing awareness of the threat of Nazi Germany, *Jeu de cartes* is one of his gayest, most inviting scores.

If this frisky ballet score should seem, in retrospect, like music for dancing on a volcano, Stravinsky could point out that the original concept had been in his mind for more than a decade, which would date it from the pre-depression twenties, the jauntiest years between World Wars I and II. The idea was a ballet in which "dancers, dressed as playing cards, would perform against a gaming-table backdrop of green baize." Poker was Stravinsky's favorite relaxation while composing *Jeu de cartes,* and indeed he had always been interested in card games. But he believes that the attraction was older than his knowledge of cards. Most probably, he has written, the attraction sprang from his childhood holidays at German spas.

> . . . My first impression of a German casino . . . is still a vivid memory. I remember now, too, and remembered when I composed the music, the "trombone" voice with which the master of ceremonies at one of these spas would announce a new game. *"Ein neues Spiel, ein neues Glück,"* he would say, and

> the rhythm and instrumentation of the theme with which each of the three "Deals" of my ballet begins are an echo or imitation of the tempo, timbre, and indeed the whole character of that invitation.

If he had chosen to identify the period and the setting of *Jeu de cartes,* Stravinsky declared, it would have been "a Baden-Baden of the Romantic Age, and it is as part of that picture that the tunes by Rossini, Messager, Johann Strauss, and from number [66] in the first movement of my own Symphony in E-flat, are to be imagined floating in from the Municipal Opera or from the concert by the Kursaal Band."

The score of *Jeu de cartes* was almost finished when Lincoln Kirstein and Edward Warburg gave Stravinsky the commission for a ballet. This was during Stravinsky's visit to the United States in 1935 and 1936. The choice of subject was left to Stravinsky, who worked out the action in collaboration with a friend of his son Theodore M. Malaieff.

In its final form as published in the original score of *Jeu de cartes* the scenario was as follows:

> The characters in this ballet are the chief cards in a game of Poker, disputed between several players on the green cloth of a card-room. At each deal the situation is complicated by the endless guiles of the perfidious Joker, who believes himself invincible because of his ability to become any desired card.
>
> During the first deal, one of the players is beaten, but the other two remain with even "straights," although one of them holds the Joker.
>
> In the second deal, the hand that holds the Joker is victorious, thanks to four Aces who easily beat four Queens.
>
> Now comes the third deal. The action becomes more and more acute. This time it is a struggle between three "flushes." Although at first victorious over one adversary, the Joker, strutting at the head of a sequence of Spades, is beaten by a "Royal Flush" in Hearts. This puts an end to his malice and knavery. As La Fontaine once said:
>
> We must wage continual war against the wicked.
> Peace in itself is a fine thing,
> I agree; but what use can it be
> With enemies who do not keep their word?

Stravinsky did not give even this much scenario to Balanchine, for he felt that the action was inherent in the music and he trusted Balanchine's understanding and imagination. He rehearsed *tempi* briefly with Balanchine in New York early in 1937, left on a concert tour and did not return until rehearsals were far advanced. At this point, he took very active part in the preparation, appearing punctually at rehearsals and staying habitually for six hours. Kirstein recalled that Stravinsky had about him "the slightly disconcerting concentration of a research professor or a newspaper editor, the serious preoccupation of a man who has so many interrelated activities to keep straight and in smooth-running order that he finds it necessary to employ a laconic, if fatherly and final politeness . . . During successive run-throughs of the ballet he would slap his knee like a metronome for the dancers, then suddenly interrupt everything, rise and, gesticulating rapidly to emphasize his points, suggest a change." Kirstein emphasizes that Stravinsky's changes were never mere whim but always based on considered technical authority and always helpful and cooperative in spirit. On one occasion, Kirstein recalled, Stravinsky composed some additional music to allow for a further development in the choreography.

The first performance of *Jeu de cartes* was given by the newly formed American Ballet with Stravinsky conducting at the Metropolitan Opera House on April 27, 1937. The part of the Joker was danced by William Dollar. The full title of the work translates as *Card Game, a Ballet in Three Deals,* but it is usually known in this country by the more idiomatic title of *The Card Party.*

I. *First Deal.* Each of the ballet's three deals opens with the theme of the "master of ceremonies" mentioned above: a festive, formal invitation. The first deal itself is organized in a free three-part (A-B-A) form. The opening A is based on a graceful little phrase for solo flute, which develops into a chatty dialogue with the solo bassoon. The middle (B) section is a sudden outburst of great brilliance and driving rhythms, after which the opening phrases are briefly recalled.

II. *Second Deal.* The master of ceremonies' invitation leads this time to a little march, followed by five variations (variations in the musical as well as the choreographic sense). The first of these, given to muted strings, uses a skittish little phrase with a distant resemblance to the jocular *Allegretto scherzando* of Beethoven's Eighth Symphony:

Variation II offers a gentle contrast, but Variation III resumes the Beethoven-like phrase of I. In a sudden change of mood, Variation IV offers one of the most graceful tunes from Johann Strauss's *Fledermaus,* sung here by the first violins, which soon transform it into pure Stravinsky. Variation V builds to a rhythmic climax leading directly into a recall of the march and a capricious closing section.

IV. *Third Deal.* This time the master of ceremonies' theme leads to an extended waltz rich in reminiscences of Johann Strauss, Tchaikovsky, and Ravel's *La Valse.* This is succeeded by a mercurial *Presto* growing out of one of Rossini's catchiest tunes, the principal theme of the Overture to *The Barber of Seville:*

With dazzling sleight of hand, Stravinsky shifts his rhythms and textures to a point which has led some commentators to claim that he has also parodied the principal theme of Beethoven's Fifth Symphony. For the most part, the ballet has been spun out in a delicate, almost chamber-music style. But in the final pages Stravinsky uses the full heft and tonal splendor of his large orchestra.

The score calls for 2 flutes, piccolo, 2 oboes, English horn, 2 clarinets, 2 bassoons, 4 horns, 2 trumpets, 3 trombones, tuba, kettledrums, bass drum, 12 first violins, 10 second violins, 8 violas, 6 cellos, and 6 double basses.

CONCERTO FOR VIOLIN AND ORCHESTRA, D MAJOR

Neoclassical is the label commonly given to this Concerto, written in 1931, and to many other Stravinsky works of this and the neighboring decades. Yet in this Concerto Stravinsky seems to have had Bach or the Italian Baroque composers in mind more often than he did Haydn or Mozart. And in the final analysis, to call this music Neoclassical, Neo-Baroque, or neo-anything, does a gross injustice to a work so thoroughly Stravinskian, so strongly individual, and so nonderivative of any model whatsoever. It is true that Stravinsky has a very healthy respect, almost a reverence, for tradition. But this does not make him an epigone. He is eclectic, as Mozart was eclectic, and with just as little danger of losing his individuality.

This Concerto was instigated by Willy Strecker, co-owner and director of the firm of Schott, which published the score. Strecker introduced the American violinist, Samuel Dushkin, to Stravinsky and suggested that Stravinsky compose something for him. Stravinsky resisted the idea, both because he felt he was not intimate enough with the technique of the violin to compose idiomatically for it, and because he feared that Dushkin would be the usual type of virtuoso, with little musicianship, interested chiefly in brilliant display.

Hindemith, however, suggested to Stravinsky that his very unfamiliarity with the violin might be a blessing in disguise, in that he would have no tendency to compose simply what would be "suggested by the familiar movement of the fingers." A closer acquaintance with Dushkin, who gave him considerable help on technical aspects of the violin part, reassured him on the second point.

Stravinsky composed the Concerto in 1931, the first two movements at Nice, which had been his home for seven years. But Nice had become too distracting a spot, too sociable, or at least too much of a magnet for the sociable. In search of solitude Stravinsky chose a small town by the name of

Voreppe near Grenoble and rented a villa called *La Vironnière.* "The pure air of the Isère Valley," wrote Stravinsky in his autobiography, "the peacefulness of the country, a very beautiful garden, and a large comfortable house, induced us to settle there for good, and there we stayed for three years."

Stravinsky could not wait to return to the composition of the Violin Concerto. "I finished my latest composition," he wrote, "among half-unpacked trunks and boxes and the coming and going of movers, upholsterers, electricians, and plumbers. My faithful friend Dushkin, who was near Grenoble, not far from us, used to come to see me every day." And the composer adds that his work "was made particularly pleasant by the enthusiasm and understanding with which Dushkin followed my progress."

Dushkin was the soloist in the first performance of the Concerto, which Stravinsky conducted with the Berlin Radio Orchestra at Berlin on October 23, 1931. Although Stravinsky had studied a number of the standard violin concertos before launching on his own composition, his score finally took the unfamiliar four-movement form of *Toccata, Aria I, Aria II,* and *Capriccio.*

I. *Toccata.* The first movement opens with four sharp chords of the solo violin and strings, a sort of motto theme, which returns in more or less recognizable form at the beginning of each movement and, in some cases, to mark off the major subdivisions of a movement:

In Stravinsky's words, this motto serves as "a passport to the music." Immediately after the motto, two trumpets present the main theme of the *Toccata,* which is almost more a rhythmic fragment than a theme in the usual sense:

There is a contrasting theme in the traditionally contrasting key of the dominant (A major) but this has no important role to play. A mildly contrapuntal section may recall the traditional development section and the movement concludes with recalls of the main theme.

II. *Aria I.* After the opening motto, the violin solo takes a dominating melodic role. The movement is freely in three-part A-B-A form, with a contrasting, rhythmically urgent middle section.

III. *Aria II.* Here too we have an A-B-A form with a new and highly embellished form of the motto introducing each of the three sections of the movement.

IV. *Capriccio.* The *finale* is a dazzling showpiece for the soloist, and a delectable experience for the listener. The motto is still further modified. The rhythmic variety and imagination of the movement are amazing. The French horn *dolce cantabile* introduces a new melody. At the end there is a *presto coda* with syncopation and rhythmic cross patterns that prove brilliant and exciting.

Stravinsky's score for the Violin Concerto calls for piccolo, 2 flutes, 2 oboes, English horn, small clarinet in E flat, 2 clarinets, 3 bassoons, contrabassoon, 4 horns, 3 trumpets, 3 trombones, bass trombone, tuba, kettledrums, and the standard string choir.

THE FIREBIRD

"Mark him well," said Diaghileff to his prima ballerina Tamara Karsavina during a rehearsal of *The Firebird* at the Paris Opéra in June 1910. He pointed to Stravinsky: "He is a man on the eve of celebrity."

He was indeed. Twenty-eight years old, unknown outside Russia, Igor Fyodorovich Stravinsky was scarcely known even at home in St. Petersburg save as a brilliant pupil of Rimsky-Korsakoff. But he had had the good luck to have two brief orchestral pieces, *Fantastic* Scherzo and *Fireworks,* conducted by Alexander Siloti at the latter's famous orchestral concerts in St. Petersburg during the winter of 1909. In the audience was Serge Diaghileff, who was immersed in plans for a new ballet company. This was to bring together dancers, choreographers, writers, painters and composers, of the highest rank and the boldest, innovative imaginations. Diaghileff needed a composer-collaborator. His appraising ear told him that the man who had imagined *Fireworks* showed the kind of promise he needed. As a tentative first step, he commissioned Stravinsky to orchestrate some small pieces for the opening season of his Ballets Russes in Paris. The pieces were two Chopin numbers (the opening Nocturne and final Waltz) for Fokine's ballet *Les Sylphides* and a Grieg piano piece for the ballet *Le Festin.*

Stravinsky's luck held. For the second Paris season of the Ballets Russes in Paris, Diaghileff had commissioned Liadov to write the music for a ballet on a subject of Russian legend, the Firebird. But Liadov proved so dilatory that Diaghileff was alarmed. By common consent the commission was transferred to Stravinsky, who received Diaghileff's telegram of invitation at the end of the summer of 1909. Stravinsky seems to have been afraid that he might not complete the score in time for the 1910 spring season, but he was flattered to be the collaborator of Fokine and other famous men. He accepted, and began work early in November, even before Diaghileff's commission was officially confirmed. He completed his skeleton score the following March and by mid-April he mailed the full orchestration to Diaghileff in Paris. The final retouches of the score, which is dedicated to his teacher Rimsky-Korsakoff, are dated May 18, 1910.

The premiere of *The Firebird* on June 25, 1910, at the Paris Opéra, was conducted by Gabriel Pierné. The choreography was by Michel Fokine. The legendary cast was headed by Karsavina as the Firebird. Fokine himself danced the part of Ivan Tzarevich and Fokina was the Thirteenth Princess. The production not only made ballet history, it placed Stravinsky overnight, as Diaghileff had predicted, in the front rank of contemporary composers.

For the rest of Stravsinky's long life, this remained his most popular work. The music could hardly be more Romantic in the folk song and dance style of its striking melodies and rhythms, its lush harmonies, and gorgeous orchestral colors. Stravinsky even outdid his teacher, Rimsky-Korsakoff in the virtuosity, the subtlety, and originality of his instrumentation. After his *Firebird,* Stravinsky's taste and style changed fast: *Petrushka* and *The Rite of Spring* followed in swift succession. In later years Stravinsky was sometimes annoyed at admirers who wished he would go back to the lush style of *The Firebird,* and in moments of extreme irritation he would refer to the beautiful score as "that great audience lollipop."

The story of the Firebird is based on the many Russian legends about the young Czarevich Ivan; the beneficent fairy, the Firebird; and the green-taloned monster Kashchei. In the end, with the Firebird's help, Ivan liberates the Princess from the green-taloned monster, and they are married.

As the Czarevich is wandering through a forest at night, he sees in a glow of light the Firebird plucking golden fruit from a silver tree. The Firebird tries to hide, but Ivan seizes her. She pleads to be released and offers one of her fiery plumes as a pledge to come to Ivan's aid if ever he should need it. Ivan is moved to pity and lets the pretty creature fly away. In the first light of dawn the Czarevich finds himself in the park of an ancient castle, the castle of Kashchei. Twelve beautiful damsels come out of the castle to play with the golden apples. By their beauty and the modesty of their bearing, Ivan guesses them at once to be princesses. A thirteenth princess in particular holds his eye. Unable to keep his hiding place Ivan appears from the shadows and the princesses dance their beautiful *Khorovod,* or round dance. As it grows lighter, the princesses hasten back to their captivity in Kashchei's castle.

For a moment the Czarevich is disconsolate, but with a sudden resolve, he wrenches open the gates of the castle. Great bells sound a fiendish carillon and a grotesque throng emerges: the slaves, freaks, courtiers, two-headed monsters, the Kikimoras and Bolibochkis, the fearsome entourage of Kashchei and, finally, the ogre himself. Ivan is taken prisoner and Kashchei attempts to turn him to stone like all other knights that have ventured into his territory.

But Ivan remembers the Firebird's magic plume which he waves. True to her promise, the Firebird appears and her magic throws the ugly denizens of the castle into a wild dance. The monsters try to defend themselves and with a loud crash of the orchestra, beginning a second, *Infernal Dance,* they appear momentarily to regain control. However, at the conclusion of the dance, they collapse from exhaustion and the Firebird lulls them into a magic sleep with her beautiful *Berceuse.* Meanwhile, she guides Ivan to a buried casket wherein he finds a huge egg enclosing Kashchei's evil soul which he smashes on the ground.

Kashchei dies, his palace and retinue disappear in darkness, and when the light returns, the Princesses are released and the captive stone knights come to life. There is general rejoicing and Ivan receives the thirteenth princess as his bride.

Stravinsky extracted three concert suites from *The Firebird.* The first, published in 1911, uses the enormous orchestra and the lush instrumental colors of the original score. The Second Suite, reorchestrated for a much smaller, conventional ensemble, was published in 1919. This is the version most frequently performed on concert programs today. The Third Suite, published in 1946, uses the same reduced orchestra as the 1919 version, but includes additional selections from the ballet.

Firebird Suite No. 1 (1911)

I. *Introduction; Kashchei's Enchanted Garden; Dance of the Firebird.* The introduction to the ballet begins in the darkest colors of the low stringed instruments, muted, suggesting an eerie, legendary night and the nearness of the monster's castle. As the curtain rises the Czarevich Ivan, wandering through the forest at night, sees a glow of light. A glint of celesta suggests the approach of the Firebird, and a sudden trembling, which spreads through the entire string section, announces her presence. Her solo variation or *pas seul* is orchestrated with extravagant fantasy, with shimmering strings and splashes of high, brilliant woodwind sounds, like the fluttering of wings and the exuberant dips and curves of the Firebird's flight. (The Suite omits the episode in which Ivan captures the Firebird.)

II. *The Supplication of the Firebird.* Once captured, the Firebird becomes a gentle, tender, pleading creature, depicted in beautiful, sustained melodic lines for the violas and woodwinds. Part of the crux of the ballet story, as Stravinsky envisaged it, is the fact that Ivan is moved to pity by the pleading of the Firebird. She gives him one of her fiery plumes as a pledge to come to Ivan's aid if ever he should need it. Ivan lets the pretty creature fly away. (In the next episode, omitted from the Suite, the Czarevich finds himself in the park of a forbidding fortress, the castle of Kashchei. Twelve beautiful princesses come out of the castle but a thirteenth Princess catches his eye.)

III. *The Princesses' Game with the Golden Apples (Scherzo).* The airy grace of the Princesses and their innocent game is suggested by the quicksilver darting and dashing of high woodwinds and delicate *spiccato* strings. This bubbling phrase returns almost like a refrain. (In a few measures, omitted from the Suite, Ivan, unable to keep to his hiding place, appears from the shadows. But the Princesses remain to dance their beautiful *Khorovod* or rounddance.)

IV. *The Princesses' Khorovod.* The dance of the Princesses is tender and lyrical, using melodies in the vein of Russian folk songs. A piccolo and two flutes anticipate a theme which will be transformed with glittering pomp for the final scene of the ballet. They are answered by a gentle dialogue of solo oboe and flute, still in a folk vein. The refrain of the Princesses' dance appears first in soft tones of the first violins:

The background is muted strings. There is a tender question in the clarinet and a plaintive answer from the oboe. At the end the music fades into silence like a dream. (The Suite omits the break of day, the approach of Kashchei's monsters, the capture of Ivan, Kashchei's attempt to turn him to stone, the arrival of the Firebird and the first frenzied dance of the monsters.)

V. *Infernal Dance of King Kashchei.* An ugly crash of the entire orchestra launches Kashchei and his demons into their final evil gyrations. Syncopated rhythms like the following:

and clashing harmonies course through the orchestra with a violence and drive that seem at moments to forecast *The Rite of Spring.*

The orchestration for the 1911 version of *The Firebird* Suite calls for 2 piccolos, 3 flutes, 3 oboes, English horn, 3 clarinets in A, clarinet in D, bass clarinet, 3 bassoons, 2 contrabassoons, 4 horns, 3 trumpets, 3 trombones, tuba, 3 harps, piano, triangle, tambourine, bass drum, campanelli, xylophone, celesta, gong, kettledrum, cymbals, and the traditional strings. To sum up, the orchestra for this First *Firebird* Suite (identical with the ballet score) is far more sumptuous in color and almost half as large again as that for the Second Suite. Stravinsky decided between the 1911 and the 1919 Suites that the orchestra for the First had been "wastefully large."

Firebird Suite No. 2 (1919)

In contrast to the First *Firebird* Suite, the orchestra for the Second Suite is drastically reduced. It consists of only piccolo, 2 flutes, 2 oboes, English horn, 2 clarinets, 2 bassoons, 4 horns, 2 trumpets, 3 trombones, tuba, kettledrums, bass drum, tambourine, triangle, cymbals, xylophone, piano, harp, and the traditional string choir.

I. *Introduction; The Firebird and Her Dance; Variation of the Firebird.* This first movement corresponds to the first movement of the First Suite described above (except for the omission here of the brief orchestral description of Kashchei's enchanted garden and the first appearance of the Firebird).

II. *The Princesses' Round: Khorovod.* This movement is identical with number IV of the First Suite, despite the slight difference in title.

III. *Dance of King Kashchei.* (Identical with number V of the First Suite.)

IV. *Berceuse and Finale.* The *Berceuse* with which the Firebird lulls the monsters to sleep is the most beguiling orchestral magic. The nostalgic bassoon phrases at the beginning are like the "Once upon a time" of a fairy tale. At the close a whispering *tremolo* of the strings floats down through the orchestra. (The brief episode of the destruction of Kashchei's soul is omitted and the Second Suite continues without interruption into the Finale.) A solo horn sings an echo of the flute melody we heard in the scene of the princesses:

There is a rippling *glissando* of the harp and the strings chant the same melody with growing fervor. Finally the whole orchestra is exulting in the song of deliverance and, with a mighty procession of brass chords, against a shimmering pedal point of strings, the fairy tale ends in a burst of fantastic brilliance.

Firebird Suite No. 3 (1949)

The Third *Firebird* Suite, also called Ballet Suite, includes more of the original ballet numbers than either the First or Second Suite—enough, in fact, to serve as a score for abbreviated stage productions of the ballet. It is scored for substantially the same reduced orchestra as Suite No. 2, except for the addition of a snare drum.

I. *Introduction; Prelude and Dance of the Firebird; Variations (Firebird).* This movement corresponds substantially to number I of the Second Suite.

II. *Pantomime I.* This is a brief depiction of Ivan's capture of the Firebird.

III. *Pas de deux: Firebird and Ivan Czarevich.* This corresponds to number II of the First Suite.

IV. *Pantomime II.* This is a brief orchestral passage depicting the entrance of the thirteen enchanted princesses.

V. *Scherzo: Dance of the Princesses.* This corresponds to number III of the First Suite.

VI. *Pantomime III.* Orchestral music describing the sudden appearance of Ivan to the thirteen princesses.

VII. *Rondo (Khorovod).* This is number II of the Second Suite.

VIII. *Infernal Dance.* This is number III of the Second Suite: the Dance of Kashchei.

IX. *Lullaby (Firebird).* This corresponds to the *Berceuse* of the Second Suite.

X. *Final Hymn.* This includes the finale of the Second Suite and of the ballet.

CONCERT SUITE FROM L'HISTOIRE DU SOLDAT

"If every good piece of music is marked by its own characteristic sound," said Stravinsky in his *Expositions and Developments*, "then the characteristic sounds of *Histoire* are the scrape of the violin and the punctuation of the drums. The violin is the soldier's soul, and the drums are the diablerie."

Stravinsky specializes in characteristic sound. That of the *The Story of the Soldier* has interesting origins in Stravinsky's own nature and in the world of 1917–1918. It was a turning point in Stravinsky's art and that of the Western World.

> My choice of instruments [Stravinsky later explained] was influenced by a very important event in my life at that time, the discovery of American jazz. . . . The *Histoire* ensemble resembles the jazz band in that each instrumental category—strings, woodwinds, brass, percussion—is represented by both treble and bass components. The instruments themselves are jazz legitimates, too, except the bassoon, which is my substitution for the saxophone. (The saxophone is more turbid and penetrating than the bassoon, and I therefore prefer it in orchestral combinations, as it is used in Berg's Violin Concerto, for instance, and, especially the bass saxophone, in [Hindemith's] *Von Heute auf Morgen.*) The percussion part must also be considered as manifestation of my enthusiasm for jazz. I purchased the instruments from a music shop in Lausanne, learning to play them myself as I composed. . . . My knowledge of jazz was derived exclusively from copies of sheet music, and as I had never actually heard any of the music performed, I borrowed its rhythmic style not as played, but as written. I *could* imagine jazz sound, however, or so I liked to think. Jazz meant, in any case, a wholly new sound in my music, and *Histoire* marks my final break with the Russian orchestral school in which I had been fostered.

This passion for percussion, which gives *The Story of the Soldier* so much of its character, is something Stravinsky calls "another of my biological facts. To bang a gong, bash a cymbal, clout a woodblock (or critic) has always given me the keenest satisfaction. . . ." The lean sound of this pivotal work is also due, in part, to the lean days in which it was written. Early in 1918, when *L'Histoire du soldat* began to take shape, both Stravinsky and his novelist-poet-librettist friend, Charles Ferdinand Ramuz, were feeling the economic pinch of the closing months of World War I. Stravinsky was completely cut off from all former sources of family income in Russia. He was cut off from all royalty income from his publishers, the Edition Russe du Musique, for that firm had its headquarters in Berlin.

Casting about for an artistically interesting solution to their difficulties, the two friends, who had collaborated before, decided to attempt a theatrical work of a drastically practical nature, a work which could be taken on tour of Switzerland (the country in which both men were then domiciled) even under wartime conditions. They envisaged a small group of instrumentalists and even smaller company of players easy to recruit and inexpensive to support.

The work, they felt, should require no large stage; it should be presentable in almost any type of hall or auditorium, or even in the open air. Instead of an opera or traditional drama with incidental music, Ramuz suggested a flexible dramatic form using a narrator.

The subject was suggested by Stravinsky, who had recently read a collection of folk tales once current among Russian military draftees—tales in which the Devil played prominent and colorful roles. Stravinsky was particularly drawn to one of the stories in which, he reported, "the Soldier tricks the Devil into drinking too much vodka. He then gives the Devil a handful of shot to eat, assuring him it is caviar, and the Devil greedily swallows it and dies." Stravinsky outlined for Ramuz other episodes from the same collection concerning "the Soldier who deserts and the Devil who always comes to claim his soul." Although the tales were originally Russian, the two friends agreed that their own work should have a broadly human appeal as well as a timely one. For their own production, the soldier would be dressed in a former Swiss army uniform, and the text would have touches of Swiss dialect. (Later, when the work was performed outside Switzerland, text and costumes were adjusted to preserve the work's topical character.)

For his orchestra Stravinsky chose seven: one percussionist plus two for each instrumental family. Strings were represented by violin and double bass; woodwinds by clarinet and bassoon; brass by cornet and trombone; and the percussion by a large battery, all to be played by one musician. The cast was limited to three: the Soldier, the Devil and the Princess. There was to be a minimum of scenery. The seven-man orchestra plus conductor were to be clearly visible on one side of the stage. On the other side the Narrator was to be seated on a stool (or barrel) before a small table with a glass and a carafe of white wine.

The original production of *The Story of the Soldier,* presented on September 28, 1918, at the Municipal Theater of Lausanne, was under the musical direction of Ernest Ansermet. The whole undertaking (which was more expensive than the two creators had expected) was made possible by the generosity of Werner Reinhart of Winterthur, who paid for "everybody and everything," as Stravinsky recalled, "and finally even commissioned my music." The original cast included three relatively inexperienced university students plus the famous theatrical couple, Georges Pitoëff (as *régisseur*) and Ludmila Pitoëff, who danced the role of the Princess. The Narrator was Elie Gagnebin, the Soldier was Gabriel Rosset and the Devil was Jean Villard-Gilles.

The role of the Devil, who had to speak, act, mime and dance, presented difficulties. It was decided to divide the role into two parts. Early in September Stravinsky and Ramuz came to a decision which, alas, was never carried out. On September 5, 1918, Ramuz wrote to a friend: "Last night Stravinsky told me of his intention to dance the last scene. That will be perfect. Please encourage him to do so." And in a letter to Stravinsky undated but possibly written on the same day Ramuz writes: "And then please dance the final scene yourself. You will do it with rhythmic vitality and save the day." This plan, temporary though it was, throws a sharp light on the atmosphere which must have prevailed at that first production. Obviously professional slickness was not a primary aim. Finally, the dancing portion of the Devil's role was taken by Georges Pitoëff.

The exhilarating atmosphere of the rehearsals was described by Villard-Gilles:

> Stravinsky and Ramuz were in charge of daily rehearsals—the former always in a frenzy of enthusiasm, inventiveness, joy, indignation, headache; leaping on the piano as if it were a dangerous foe that had to be subdued by a bout of fisticuffs, then bounding onto the stage, swallowing glasses of kirsch whose after-effects had to be combated with the aid of aspirin: the latter, calm, attentive, friendly, rather bashful when giving advice, seeing things from our point of view, trying (like us) to find the right answers, showing an indomitable patience, and following with malicious enjoyment the genial capers of his collaborator. In the presence of these two artists with their complementary temperaments, we felt ourselves imbued with vital intensity and could think of nothing but our work.

The Concert Suite from *The Story of the Soldier* includes the eight most important numbers:

I. *"The Soldier's March: Marching Tunes."* Before the curtain rises, distorted fragments of marching tunes describe the weary homeward trek of a soldier on a fortnight's leave. "He was tramped from morn to eve," the Narrator tells us.

[The Soldier sits down by the bank of a stream, opens his haversack, takes out his old brown fiddle and plays.]

II. *"The Soldiers Violin."* While the soldier is absorbed in his tunes, the Devil enters disguised as a little old man carrying a butterfly net. He stops to listen to the music, hides, finally comes out of his concealment and approaches the Soldier, who jumps up in alarm.

[The Devil persuades the Soldier to exchange his violin for a magic book which will bring him wealth. He invites the Soldier to spend three days with him, during which the Soldier is to teach him how to play the violin, while the Devil teaches the Soldier the use of the magic book. But when the Soldier returns to his native village, his friends and even his mother are startled and frightened, and he finds his fiancée married with two children! He realizes that the three days with the Devil were really three years. He tries to console himself with the immense wealth that the magic book brings. But the book and the wealth bring no happiness, so he tears up the book and goes back to his life of adventure. Coming to a new land, he learns that the King's daughter is ill and the man who cures her can have her hand in marriage. He resolves to try his luck and sets off for the palace.]

III. *"Royal March."* During the March the curtain rises briefly to reveal a room in the palace where the Devil, dressed as a virtuoso violinist, holds the Soldier's violin.

[The Soldier arrives at the palace, only to find that the Devil is ahead of him. Following the advice of the Narrator, the Soldier invites the Devil to a game of cards. He purposely loses all his worldly wealth to the Devil, thus depriving the Evil One of his power. The Soldier seizes his violin, and standing beside the Devil, begins to play.]

IV. *"Little Concert."* The Devil collapses and the curtain falls as the Soldier makes his way in triumph to the Princess's room.

V. *"Three Dances: Tango, Waltz, Ragtime."* The Princess is lying on her bed. As the Soldier begins to play the Tango, she rises slowly and begins to dance. The rhythmic progression from Tango to Ragtime cures the Princess.

[As the Soldier and the Princess fall into each other's arms, the Devil enters in his proper Devil's costume. He tries to take back the violin. The Soldier defends himself until, with a sudden inspiration, he begins to play.]

VI. *"The Devil's Dance."* At the first sound of the Dance the Devil begins to twitch. He tries to hold his legs still but is unable to resist the magic of the violin. He dances, more and more frenetically, until he falls to the ground exhausted. At a sign from the Soldier, the Princess takes the Devil by one paw and between them they drag the fiend off into the wings.

[The Soldier and the Princess return and fall into each others arms. During their embrace the Devil swears vengeance if the Soldier should ever fall into his power again.]

VII. *"Chorale."* During the Chorale the Narrator warns the Soldier not to seek to add to his present happiness the other happiness he had long ago. The Princess asks him about his past and the Soldier begins to reminisce.

[The Princess proposes that they visit the land of his happy childhood. He reminds her that this is forbidden. But she pleads until he gives in, thinking that perhaps this time his mother will know him, perhaps she will come and live with them—"Then I would really have it all." But as he crosses the frontier, the Devil reappears. He has the violin again and begins to play.]

VIII. *"The Devil's Triumphal March."* The Soldier hangs his head. Then very slowly, but without resisting, he follows the Devil. From offstage a voice calls. The Soldier hesitates, but the Devil waves him on. They disappear. The voice calls for the last time. The notes of the violin fade away. The curtain falls slowly as the percussion goes on alone to the sinister end.

PETRUSHKA

"Petrushka" was the second of the three great ballet scores Stravinsky composed in rapid succession for Serge Diaghilev's Russian Ballet on the eve of World War I. If anything could be as arresting as the music itself, it was the speed with which Stravinsky's style developed from one score to the next.

In *The Firebird* of 1910, Stravinsky's orchestra glows with a Romantic tenderness and gleams iridescent colors we associate with his teacher Rimsky-Korsakoff. In the *Petrushka* of 1911, the colors are harsh, often strident, and what tenderness there is, is masked. Grotesque action is paralleled by grotesque sounds.

Even the inspiration was sometimes grotesque. Stravinsky has written that the famous "Petrushka chord," a bi-tonal combination of C major and F-sharp major, was conceived as an insult—Petrushka's insult to the audience—which the spirit of the puppet repeats at the end of the ballet.

In his autobiography, Stravinsky describes the genesis of *Petrushka:*

> Before tackling *The Rite of Spring,* which would be a long and difficult task, I wanted to refresh myself by composing an orchestral piece in which the piano would play the most important part—a sort of *Konzertstück.* In composing the music, I had in my mind a distinct picture of a puppet, suddenly endowed with life, exasperating the patience of the orchestra with diabolical cascades of arpeggios. The orchestra in turn retaliates with menacing trumpet blasts. The outcome is a terrific noise which reaches its climax and ends in the sorrowful and querulous collapse of the poor puppet. Having finished this bizarre piece, I struggled for hours, while walking beside the Lake of Geneva, to find a title which would express in a word the character of my music and, consequently, the personality of this creature.
>
> One day I leaped for joy, I had indeed found my title—*Petrushka,* the immortal and unhappy hero of every fair in all countries. Soon afterwards, Diaghilev came to visit me at Clarens, where I was staying. He was much astonished when, instead of sketches of the *Sacre,* I played him the piece I had just composed and which later became the second scene of *Petrushka.* He was so much pleased with it that he would not leave it alone and began persuading me to develop the theme of the puppet's sufferings and make it into a whole ballet. While he remained in Switzerland, we worked out together the general lines of the subject and the plot in accordance with ideas which I suggested. We settled the scene of action: the fair, with its crowd, its booths, the little traditional theater, the character of the magician, with all his tricks; and the coming to life of the dolls—Petrushka, his rival and the dancer—and their love tragedy, which ends with Petrushka's death. I began at once to compose the first scene of the ballet, which I finished at Beaulieu, where I spent the winter (1910–1911) with my family.

As Stravinsky's collaborator on the stage action and scenario of the ballet Diaghilev chose Alexandre Benois, his former associate from whom he was momentarily estranged. Benois had designed the stage sets and costumes and had devised the scenario for Diaghilev's famous production of *Scheherazade.* Diaghilev, however, had credited Léon Bakst with the authorship of the scenario in the printed programs, and Benois had resigned from the company in a huff. Diaghilev's sure instinct told him that Benois was precisely the man needed for *Petrushka* and therefore used all his personal charm and wiles to win back Benois. Benois, for his part, found the proposal irresistible. In his *Reminiscences of the Russian Ballet* he explained the lure he felt:

> Petrushka, the Russian Guignol or Punch, no less than Harlequin, had been my friend since my earliest childhood. Whenever I heard the loud, nasal cries of the traveling Punch and Judy showman: "Here's Petrushka! Come, good people, and see the Show!" I would get into a kind of frenzy to see the

enchanting performance, which consisted . . . in the endless tricks of an idle loafer, who ends up by being captured by a hairy devil and dragged off to Hell.

As to Petrushka himself, I immediately had the feeling that it was a duty I owed to my old friend to immortalize him on the real stage. I was still more tempted by the idea of depicting the Butter Week Fair [Butter Week, the last week of Carnival which was traditionally celebrated by feasting on all manner of luxuries including butter-made pastries]. . . . Besides the duty I felt to Petrushka and my wish to immortalize the St. Petersburg Carnival, I had yet another reason for accepting [Diaghilev's] offer—I suddenly *saw* how this ballet ought to be presented. . . .

The dolls should come to life at the command of a magician, and their coming to life should be somehow accompanied by suffering. The greater the contrast between the real, live people and the automatons who had just been given life, the sharper the interest of the action would be. It would be necessary to allot a considerable part of the stage to the mass of real people—the "public" at the fair—while there would only be two dolls, the hero of the play, Petrushka, and his lady.

Soon I decided that there should be a third character—the Blackamoor. In the street performances of Petrushka there was invariably a separate intermezzo, inserted between the acts: two Blackamoors, dressed in velvet and gold, would appear and start unmercifully hitting each other's wooden heads with sticks. I included a similar Blackamoor among my "chief characters." If Petrushka were to be taken as the personification of the spiritual and suffering side of humanity—or shall we call it the poetical principle?—his lady Columbine would be the incarnation of the eternal feminine; then the gorgeous Blackamoor would serve as the embodiment of everything senselessly attractive, powerfully masculine and undeservedly triumphant.

During December 1910 Stravinsky visited St. Petersburg both to see his mother and to work with Benois who, fortunately, was enchanted with all of the Petrushka music Stravinsky had composed so far. "The 'Russian Dance' proved to be really magic music," Benois recalled. "As for 'Petrushka's Cry' [Stravinsky's original title for Scene 2 in Petrushka's Cell], having listened to it about three times I began to discern in it grief, and rage, and love, as well as the helpless despair that dominated it."

Early in the spring of 1911 Stravinsky and Benois joined the Diaghilev company, which was playing at the Constanzi Theater in Rome. Stravinsky continued working on the score in close collaboration with Benois and Michel Fokine, the great choreographer of Diaghilev's Ballets Russes. The impression of the final production of *Petrushka*, which was repeatedly described by critics in city after city, as a work of art so unified that it appeared to be the invention of one genius, a composer-poet-painter-choreographer-conductor-producer—this impression was closer to fact than fiction. The rehearsals were held in a not-very-clean basement restaurant amid the unbearable heat of the Roman spring with Stravinsky at the piano hammering out the measures of his not-quite-completed manuscript while Fokine (often critical of certain details) drilled the dancers, who in turn were intimidated, confused, frustrated, by the complex rhythms of Stravinsky's music. Yet, as the unified product took shape, there was a growing exhilaration, confidence, and pride in this communal effort which would be a milestone in the history of ballet.

When the troupe moved to Paris for the spring season, the scenario of *Petrushka* had been worked out in full detail, and rehearsals were continued on the stage of the Paris Opéra. In his *Memoirs of a Ballet Master*, Fokine recalls at length the enormous difficulties which remained to be solved for the dancers, even in this final phase. Every time Fokine believed the dancers had learned Stravinsky's rapid changes of the beat, he would discover that they had forgotten again. Matters were further complicated by the complex scenery, which the dancers complained left them too little space to move. Stravinsky added to the dancers' difficulty by insisting on placing four large drums barely out of sight in the wings, although his score specifically calls for only two.

The leading roles were taken by a cast which has an aura of legend about it: the ballerina was Tamara Karsavina, Enrico Cecchetti (the illustrious character dancer of the Russian Imperial Ballet) was the Old Magician, the Blackamoor was danced by Alexander Orlov, and the title role was taken by Vaslav Nijinsky, the most famous male dancer of the twentieth century. Nijinsky in particular made a contribution to the ballet, which seems to have surprised his greatest admirers.

A shy, rather moody person, Nijinsky often gave the impression of a great athlete, a tumbler of almost supernatural strength and grace, but of severely limited mind. His schooling had been entirely in traditional ballet, and his most publicized achievements were his soaring, gravity-defying leaps. Yet as the new *Petrushka* took shape among those collaborators of genius, Nijinsky penetrated the complex character of the title role with a poignance that astonished professional actors. A portrait photograph of Nijinsky as Petrushka suggests how deeply he grasped Benois's concept of the role and how sharply he was able to communicate by facial expression alone. His miming of the puppet was so affecting that Sarah Bernhardt, after seeing him in that role, reportedly said: "I am afraid, I am afraid—because I have just seen the greatest actor in the world!"

The first performance of *Petrushka* was presented at the Théâtre du Chatelet in Paris on June 13, 1911. Pierre Monteux conducted and the production was an overwhelming success. Yet such was the daring of the production as a whole that Diaghilev was afraid to take *Petrushka* on tour. For the time being he felt that only a sophisticated Parisian audience would stand for so much innovation.

The first performance outside of France—the Viennese premiere in January 1913—seemed to confirm Diaghilev's fears. At the first rehearsal with the Vienna Philharmonic in the Staatsoper in Stravinsky's presence, the musicians reportedly branded the music as "dirty" and refused to play it, adding that such a work should not be performed within the sacred halls of the

PETROUCHKA.

Left: Vaslav Nijinsky in the title role of the first *Petrouchka* production in 1911. (*Courtesy, New York Public Library*) **Above:** Stage design for the first and last scenes (1911) by Alexandre Benois. (*Courtesy, New York Public Library*) **Below:** Costume design for the first *Petrouchka* by Alexandre Benois. (*Courtesy, A.A. Bakhrushin Central Theatrical Museum, Moscow*)

Vienna Opera. The orchestra was eventually persuaded to play after all, the premiere took place at the Opera, but the incident was immediately reported all over the city and did the Diaghilev troupe no good. There were only two Viennese performances of *Petrushka,* and it was reported that the performance of some members of the orchestra verged on sabotage. By contrast, the reception of *Petrushka* in London the following month was enthusiastic and the first United States performance at the Century Theater, New York City, on January 24, 1916, was a triumph.

The original score of *Petrushka,* like that of the *Firebird,* calls for a very large orchestra consisting of 2 piccolos, 4 flutes, 4 oboes, English horn, 4 clarinets, bass clarinet, 4 bassoons, contrabassoon, 4 horns, 3 trumpets (including a small trumpet in D), 3 trombones, 2 cornets, tuba, 2 harps, piano, celesta, xylophone, glockenspiel, cymbals, kettledrum, bass drum, 2 snare drums (one of them on stage in the wings), 1 long drum (*tambourin,* also in the wings), tambourine, triangle, gong, and the traditional body of strings.

I. The first scene is set in Admiralty Square of old St. Petersburg during the last three days of carnival in 1830. The music opens with a bright bustle of a fair day. The curtains part and we see the surging crowds, the thousand and one glittering distractions of the fair are reflected separately and all together in the kaleidoscopic rhythms and harmonies of the orchestra: first an organ grinder and a dancing girl, then a group of revelers reel across the scene, finally the organ grinder begins to blow a trumpet and on the opposite side of the stage a music box and another dancing girl add their part to the joyous confusion. The crowd grows thicker and more exuberant.

Two drummers appear outside a little puppet theater and their drums hush the crowd into an expectant silence. The showman, the old wizard, appears. The impression his hocus-pocus makes on the gullible populace is reflected in the mysterious mutterings and whirrings of the orchestra. Then the showman plays a foolish little tune on the flute and the charm is complete. The curtain of the puppet theater rises and behold: three animated puppets, Petrushka, the Blackamoor and the Ballerina. They do a wild Russian dance to music as garish, frantic and angular as themselves:*

Then the curtain falls, the drums rasp again and there is a change of scene.

II. We see Petrushka's bare, small, prisonlike room. There is a crash; a door opens and Petrushka is kicked through it, falling flat on the floor. But

* *This and the following musical example from this composition are copyright by Edition Russe de Musique. Copyright 1947 assigned to Boosey & Hawkes, Inc. Revised version copyright 1948. Renewed 1974. Reprinted by permission.*

now we find that, sawdust as he is physically, Petrushka has a pathetic glimmering of a human soul. Petrushka struggles hopelessly in his prison and paws the walls to escape:

We hear his frantic gropings in the grotesque arpeggios of the piano. Finally trumpets, cornets, and trombones scream out in rage and frustration.

Suddenly the door opens and in trips the tinselly little Ballerina. Petrushka loves her, and the orchestra endows her with all the glamor of his imagination. But she will have none of him.

III. The third scene is the luxurious room of the Blackamoor. The Ballerina enters and finds the handsome, brutal Blackamoor very romantic. He makes love to her. The empty-headed banality of the music and of their mutual enchantment make the tragedy of Petrushka all the more heartrending. Suddenly the door opens and Petrushka himself appears. But he is chased away by the jealous Blackamoor.

IV. The scene returns to the festive crowd outside the tent. At the climax of the gaiety, there is a wild thrashing behind the curtain of the puppet theater and out dashes Petrushka, pursued by the infuriated Blackamoor. The Blackamoor draws his scimitar and deals Petrushka a vicious blow. With a final grotesque spasm the puppet dies. There is consternation among the onlookers. A policeman arrives, but the old wizard demonstrates to everyone that after all Petrushka was only made of sawdust. The merrymakers disperse in the dusk. Suddenly, as the old wizard is dragging off the sawdust doll, Petrushka's spirit appears above the theater, menacing him, thumbing his nose as his own dissonant, "insulting" theme sounds in the orchestra. The wizard drops the sawdust doll in terror and disappears into the darkness. The light dims, the orchestra fades to a whisper, ending on an unresolved melodic dissonance: the two root notes of the "Petrushka chord"—C natural followed by a low F sharp.

The story goes that Diaghilev tried to persuade Stravinsky to change the end. "You end your ballet on a question?" he protested. "Well," Stravinsky used to comment in later years, "at least he understood that much!"

When Stravinsky revised his *Petrushka* in 1947, he provided an optional concert ending which eliminated the quiet close that had disturbed Diaghilev and ends with a brilliant *fortissimo*. The new version uses a reduced orchestra consisting of 1 piccolo, 3 flutes, 2 oboes, English horn, 3 clarinets, bass clarinet, 2 bassoons, contrabassoon, 4 horns, 3 trumpets, 3 trombones, tuba, kettledrum, bass drum, side drum, tambourine, triangle, cymbals, gong, xylophone, celesta, harp, piano, and the traditional string choir. There are also some musical changes: the rhythmic notation has been simplified and in many places the orchestral accompaniments to prominent melodies have been rewritten in a more contrapuntal style.

PULCINELLA SUITE

On a spring afternoon of 1919 while Stravinsky and Diaghilev were walking together in the Place de la Concorde, Diaghilev suggested Stravinsky look at "some delightful eighteenth-century music with the idea of orchestrating it for a ballet." When he added that the composer was Pergolesi, Stravinsky felt that Diaghilev must be out of his mind. At that time the only Pergolesi works Stravinsky knew were the *Stabat mater* and *La Serva padrona* and he could not have been less interested. But he promised to look at the music and give his opinion.

"I looked," Stravinsky recalled, "and I fell in love."

Stravinsky's long love affair with the eighteenth century lasted over thirty years. What started almost casually with Diaghilev's invitation to dress up some Pergolesi melodies for a new production of the Ballets Russes de Diaghilev blossomed into the ballet of *Pulcinella*. That beguiling work led to further exploration of the eighteenth century, a long voyage of discovery that was also self-discovery.

"*Pulcinella,*" Stravinsky recalled [in *Dialogues and a Diary*] "was my discovery of the past, the epiphany through which the whole of my late works became possible. It was a backward look, of course—the first of many love affairs in that direction—but it was a look in the mirror, too. No critic understood this at the time and I was therefore attacked for being a *pasticheur*, chided for composing 'simple' music, blamed for deserting 'modernism', accused of renouncing my 'true Russian heritage'."

But by 1919 Stravinsky had reached a point at which the Romantic tradition of Russian nationalism, in which he had composed *The Firebird, Petrushka* and *The Rite of Spring*, began to seem a constraining, narrowing, indeed a provincial influence. Was this due to his isolation from Russia enforced by war and the Bolshevist Revolution? Was it his more intense participation in Western musical life? Whatever the reasons, Stravinsky felt a growing desire to absorb, and be absorbed into, the mainstream of Western European tradition.

A cry did go up that Stravinsky had sold his Russian birthright for a mess of Neoclassical pottage. It was hard, even for many of Stravinsky's greatest admirers, in the early 1920s, to see that his new direction meant growth, not renunciation. One wonders if Stravinsky himself realized at the time how important a turning point this was to be.

Pulcinella was only a beginning. Stravinsky was no man to be content with mere orchestrating of early masters. The more powerfully he felt drawn to the eighteenth-century master, the greater was his dilemma:

"Should my line of action be dominated by my love or by my respect for Pergolesi's music" (he asked himself)? "Is it love or respect that urges us to possess a woman? Is it not by love alone that we succeed in penetrating to the very essence of a being? But, then, does love diminish respect? Respect alone remains barren and can never serve as a productive or creative factor. In order to create, there must be a dynamic force, and what force is more potent than love? To me it seems that to ask the question is to answer it."

Stravinsky chose twenty excerpts attributed (many inaccurately) to Pergolesi: trio sonatas, harpsichord sonatas, the popular canzona *"Se tu m'ami"* and half a dozen arias from the operas *Il Flaminio, Lo Frate 'nnammorato* and *Adriano in Siria*. Stravinsky arranged these for chamber orchestra of thirty-three players: flutes, oboes, bassoons and horns in pairs, 1 trumpet, 1 trombone and strings divided into a solo string quintet (or *concertino*) and a *tutti* (or *ripieno*). The operatic numbers Stravinsky arranged for soprano, tenor and bass arias, trios, and duet. The three singers sit in the orchestra and are not identified with any of the characters on stage.

According to a note prefixed to the score of *Pulcinella*, the scenario was based on a Neapolitan manuscript dating from 1700 and said to contain a number of comedies centering around Pulcinella, the traditional sly hero of Neapolitan *commedia dell'arte.* The episode chosen as the basis for the libretto of the ballet and entitled *The Four Similar Pulcinellas,* is outlined as follows:

"All the local girls are in love with Pulcinella; but the young men to whom they are betrothed are mad with jealousy and plot to kill him. The minute they think they have succeeded, they borrow costumes resembling Pulcinella's to present themselves to their sweethearts in disguise. But Pulcinella—cunning fellow!—had changed places with a double, who pretended to succumb to their blows. The real Pulcinella, disguised as a magician, now resuscitates his double. At the very moment when the four young men, thinking they are rid of their rival, come to claim their sweethearts, Pulcinella appears and arranges all the marriages. He himself weds Pimpinella, receiving the blessing of his double (Fourbo), who in his turn has assumed the magician's mantle."

Composed between 1919 and April 20, 1920, at Morges, Switzerland, *Pulcinella* was first performed by the Diaghilev Russian Ballet at the Paris Opéra on May 15, 1920, under the direction of Ernest Ansermet. The sets were by Picasso and the choreography by Massine, who himself danced the title role. Karsavina took the part of Pimpinella, and the company's famous balletmaster, Cecchetti, danced the minor role of the Doctor.

From the twenty numbers of his ballet, Stravinsky arranged eleven for a *Pulcinella Suite* of eight movements as follows:

I. *Sinfonia (Overture)*
II. *Serenata*
III. (a) *Scherzino*
(b) *Allegro*
(c) *Andantino*
IV. *Tarantella*
V. *Toccata*
VI. *Gavotta con due variazioni*
VII. *Duetto*
VIII. (a) *Minuetto*
(b) *Finale*

The *Suite* is arranged for the same small orchestra as the ballet, except that the vocal parts in number II (tenor aria, "*Mentre l'erbetta*") and number VIII (a) (originally a solo *canzona* "*Pupilette fiammette*," transformed in the ballet into a vocal trio for soprano, tenor, and bass) are replaced by instruments. The first version of the *Pulcinella Suite*, arranged about 1922, was given its world premiere by the Boston Symphony Orchestra on December 22, 1922, under the direction of Pierre Monteux. In 1974 Stravinsky revised the Suite, making only minute changes, chiefly of metronome markings, and altering the title of number VII *Duetto*, to *Vivo*.

THE RITE OF SPRING (LE SACRE DU PRINTEMPS), PICTURES OF PAGAN RUSSIA

Music has never been the same since May 29, 1913, when Stravinsky's ballet *The Rite of Spring** exploded on the stage of the Paris Théâtre des Champs-Elysées. It caused a riot in the audience: there were whistles, catcalls, arguments, insults, people punched each other, and for years after one young composer treasured the ripped collar of his shirt as a precious relic of that battle.

Behind the scenes Vaslav Nijinsky, the leading star of the Diaghilev Ballets Russes, who had designed the choreography, became very pale when he heard the noise and wanted to jump out onto the stage and lead a counter-riot against the demonstrators, but Stravinsky held him back. "It was war over art for the rest of the evening," wrote the American poet and critic Carl Van Vechten, "and the orchestra played on unheard, except occasionally when a slight lull occurred." A young man who had stood up behind Van Vechten in order to see better, got so excited he beat his fists rhythmically on the writer's head. "My emotion was so great," Van Vechten recalled, "that I didn't feel the blows for some time. They were perfectly synchronized with the music. When I did, I turned around. His apology was sincere. We had both been carried beyond ourselves."

If *The Rite of Spring* caused a riot in the audience, its effect among musicians was more like an earthquake. This fiercely dissonant music, with its clashing chords, clashing keys, clashing rhythms, and overpowering orchestral sonorities, could neither be fought nor ignored, any more than one can ignore a thunderstorm or an express train at a crossing. Composers were hypnotized by its primitive power. Some of them tried to imitate it. Prokofieff echoed it in his barbaric *Scythian Suite*. Honegger even named a work after an express train: *Pacific 231*. Others reacted violently against *The Rite* and veered off in the opposite direction. One of those who went farthest in the opposite (Neoclassical) direction was Stravinsky himself; but that is another story.

---

* *Neither of the established English or French titles is an accurate translation of the Russian original. Stravinsky has explained that* The Coronation of Spring *is nearer his original meaning than* The Rite of Spring. *A literal translation of the Russian could be either* Sacred Spring *or* Holy Spring, *according to Stravinsky's biographer, Eric Walter White. The traditional French title,* Le Sacre du printemps, *was devised by Léon Bakst.*

The first idea for the *Sacre* flashed into Stravinsky's mind in 1910, while he was finishing his popular ballet *The Firebird*. In his imagination, he saw, "a solemn pagan rite: wise elders, seated in a circle, watching a young girl dance herself to death. They were sacrificing her to propitiate the god of spring." Despite this vision, Stravinsky first conceived the work as a symphony.

It was the great impresario of the Russian Ballet, Serge Diaghilev, who persuaded Stravinsky to make it a ballet. Stravinsky agreed to work out a scenario in collaboration with the Russian artist Nicholas C. Roerich. Roerich was not only a painter of high reputation who had already designed stage sets for Diaghilev, he was also an archaeologist and an authority on the ancient Slavs. He was reported to be deeply stirred by the links he believed he found connecting mythology, geology, and the "seismic and cosmic forces of nature." Together the painter-archaeologist and composer examined ancient Slavic art, artifacts and costumes, some of the latter serving as models for the first production of the *Rite of Spring*.

After their initial collaboration Roerich sent Diaghilev a skeleton outline of the action:

> In the ballet of *The Rite of Spring* as conceived by myself and Stravinsky, my object is to present a number of scenes of earthly joy and celestial triumph as understood by the Slavs . . . My intention is that the first set should transport us to the foot of a sacred hill, in a lush plain, where Slavonic tribes are gathered together to celebrate the spring rites. In this scene there is an old witch, who predicts the future, a marriage by capture, round dances. Then comes the most solemn moment. The wise elder is brought from the village to imprint his sacred kiss on the new-flowering earth. During this rite the crowd is seized with a mystic terror . . . After this uprush of terrestrial joy, the second scene sets a celestial mystery before us. Young virgins dance in circles on the sacred hill amid enchanted rocks; then they choose the victim they intend to honor. In a moment she will dance her last dance before the ancients clad in bearskins to show that the bear was man's ancestor. Then the graybeards dedicate the victim to the god Yarilo.

Some twenty years after the completion of *The Rite of Spring*, Stravinsky wrote in his *Autobiography* a suggestion that his revolutionary score was "music, first and last." He appears to have forgotten the importance of the visual inspiration both in the initial idea which occurred first to him spontaneously and in the strong stimulus of Roerich's suggestions as shown in a letter Stravinsky wrote to Roerich on September 26, 1911:

> I have already begun to compose, and, in a state of passion and excitement, have sketched the Introduction for "*dudki*" [reedpipes] as well as the "Divination with Twigs." The music is coming out very fresh and new. The picture of the old woman in squirrel furs sticks in my mind, and she is constantly before my eyes as I compose the "Divination with Twigs." I see her running in front of the group, sometimes stopping them and interrupting the rhythmic flow.

Stravinsky finished the score on March 29, 1913 with a dedication to Roerich. The style shows an intuitive affinity for primitive music far beyond any knowledge which one would expect a sophisticated composer to have had at that early date. The most characteristic themes in *The Rite of Spring* (all but one of which are original Stravinsky) are built of narrow-gauge melodies, seldom extending beyond a compass of four or five notes. The accompaniments consist overwhelmingly of tiny, repetitive (*ostinato*) figures. Finally, although the harmonies are highly sophisticated and often sharply dissonant, they are often sustained, unchanged over broad stretches in a way that recalls the static harmonies of very ancient folk music such as the drone of bagpipes.

The Ballet is in two halves, the first of which is titled "The Adoration of the Earth."

PART I: THE ADORATION OF THE EARTH

1. *Introduction: Lento, tempo rubato.* Melancholy phrases of a Lithuanian folk tune, the only borrowed melody in the score, set the mood, designed to evoke the mystery of the physical world in the spring.

2. *Harbingers of Spring; Dance of the Adolescents: Tempo giusto.* A heavy stamping rhythm with violent off-beat accents on an unchanging, percussive harmony initiates this section. This single, savage dissonance, which Stravinsky prefered to call a chord of the 13th, is heard by some as a bitonal combination of an E major triad with a seventh chord on E flat.*

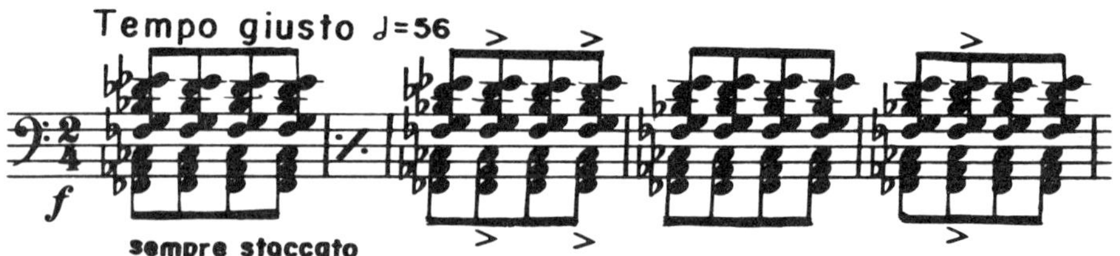

This is followed immediately by an *ostinato* figure:

Such static harmony is a familiar technique of primitive music (for instance in the drone of bagpipes) as is the device of the *ostinato* (an "obstinately" repeating figure). Several such ostinatos are used separately and in combination with other ostinatos or static harmonies, or as accompaniments to melodies throughout the *Sacre*.

3. *Game of the Abduction: Presto.* A breathless, frantic section, punctuated by sharp chords of the full orchestra at irregular intervals.

---

* *This and the following musical examples from this composition are copyright 1921 by Edition Russe de Musique. Copyright assigned 1947 to Boosey & Hawkes, Inc. Reprinted by permission.*

4. *Spring Rounds: Tranquillo—Sostenuto e pesante—Vivo—Tranquillo.* Another characteristic of much primitive music is a narrow melodic range, often restricted to four notes or even less. The following melody is given out in a stream of dissonant parallel chords, over a heavy, dragging *ostinato* figure:

5. *Games of the Rival Cities: Molto allegro.* Another four-note melody is heard between explosive outbursts of the full orchestra.

6. *Entrance of the Celebrant:* [same tempo]. A stark new theme played by four horns in octaves announces the arrival of the Wise Man.

7. *Adoration of the Earth (The Wise Man); Lento.* Four very soft bars of mystical, dissonant harmonies.

8. *Dance to the Earth: Prestissimo.* Over clashing kettledrums and bass drum rhythms of four-against-three, this concluding section of Part I rises to a frenetic pitch of excitement, with tiny fanfare-like figures in the horns, wild swirling violins, and heavy syncopated chords of brass and winds.

PART II: THE SACRIFICE

9. *Introduction: Largo.* Stravinsky gave this introduction the subtitle "The Pagan Night," although this does not appear in the score.

10. *Mysterious Circles of the Adolescents: Andante con moto.* The string choir is divided into thirteen parts for some of the delicate effects of this section. A melancholy folk-like melody is passed from violins to horns to oboes. A rapid increase of tempo and repeated heavy chords lead into the following section.

11. *Glorification of the Chosen One: Vivo.* This section with its changing metres: 5/8, 9/8, 7/8, 4/8 etc., seems almost pure rhythm. There are moments when the whole orchestra seems to be one enormous percussion instrument.

12. *Evocation of the Ancestors:* [same tempo]. Sudden, dramatic crescendos on the timpani and bass drum together alternate with simple fanfare-like chords for winds and brass.

13. *Ritual of the Ancestors: Lento.* From a gently pulsing accompaniment rhythm, this section rises to a great *tutti* climax with a broadly swaggering theme for four horns, and then subsides to almost nothing.

14. *Ritual Dance of the Chosen One.* This sacrificial dance in which the chosen victim dances herself to death was the germ of the entire concept of the *Sacre*. Rhythmically it is the most complex, and perhaps the most violent (yet far from the loudest) section of the entire work. Like the music of many peoples whom we lightly call savages, it is sophisticated, subtle, strong, and it sustains an amazing pitch of high tension.

The *Rite of Spring* is scored for a very large orchestra: 2 piccolos, 3 flutes, alto flute, 4 oboes, 2 English horns, small E-flat clarinet, 3 B-flat clarinets, 2 bass clarinets, 4 bassoons, 2 contrabassoons, 8 horns, small trumpet in D, 4 trumpets in C, 3 trombones, 4 tubas, 5 kettledrums, bass drum, tambourine, gong, triangle, antique cymbals, scratcher, and the usual string choir.

Shortly after the score was published in 1921, Stravinsky made a few minor revisions, apparently as a result of his impressions of the revival of the ballet in the 1920–21 season. In 1943 he undertook to rescore the final "Ritual Dance of the Chosen One" both to facilitate its performance and to clarify the sound. "The instrumentation has been changed too," Stravinsky wrote, "improved, I think—in many ways. The music of the second horn group, for example, is considerably amended—I never was satisfied with the horn parts. . . ." He also radically rescored the string parts. But the changes were confined to the final episode of the ballet.

THE SONG OF THE NIGHTINGALE

For Stravinsky's first opera, he chose the subject of Hans Christian Andersen's fairy tale "The Nightingale," a parable of the power of music to vanquish death. The opera in turn furnished the material for his symphonic poem which he called *The Song of the Nightingale*. His choice of a fairy-tale subject may well have been influenced by his admiration and affection for his teacher Rimsky-Korsakoff, for Rimsky had written several successful fairy-tale operas, the last of which, *The Golden Cockerel*, was completed in 1907. In 1908 Stravinsky drafted the libretto for his *Nightingale* in collaboration with his friend Stepan Mitoussov. "This work was greatly encouraged by my master," wrote Stravinsky in his autobiography, "and to this day I remember with pleasure his approval of the preliminary sketches. . . . It grieves me much that he was never to hear them in their finished form, for I think he would have liked them." The death of Rimsky-Korsakoff interrupted Stravinsky's work as did also an important commission to orchestrate two Chopin piano pieces for the opening and closing of the ballet *Les Sylphides*, which Diaghilev presented in Paris in the spring of 1909.

In the summer of 1909 Stravinsky resumed work on *The Nightingale* and completed the orchestration of the first act. At this point he was interrupted by another Diaghilev commission which proved decisive for Stravinsky's future. This was the invitation to compose an entire ballet, *The Firebird*, for the following spring season of the Diaghilev ballet at the Paris Opéra. The sensational success of *The Firebird* placed Stravinsky in the front rank of contemporary composers. In quick succession he composed for Diaghilev two more ballets: *Petrushka* and *The Rite of Spring.* After the premiere of *The Rite of Spring* in 1913, a newly founded Free Theater of Moscow invited Stravinsky to complete his opera *The Nightingale*. At first Stravinsky hesitated. In the interval of the four years that had elapsed since he completed the first act of *The Nightingale*, his musical style had changed almost beyond recognition. He wrote in his autobiography: "I feared that in view of my new manner the subsequent scenes would clash with [Act I]. I informed the directors of the Théâtre Libre of my misgivings, and suggested that they should be content with [Act I] alone, presenting it as an independent little lyrical scene. But they insisted upon the entire opera in three acts, and ended by persuading me."

Through the fall and winter of 1913–14 Stravinsky worked on the second and third acts, but even before he had finished the score the news reached him that the Moscow Free Theater had gone bankrupt. Diaghilev immediately decided to produce *The Nightingale* the following season at the Paris Opéra. The premiere took place on May 26, 1914, with Pierre Monteux conducting. The United States premiere took place at the Metropolitan Opera House on March 6, 1926, with Marion Talley in the title role.

Early in 1917, Diaghilev proposed that he produce *The Nightingale* as a ballet, with the singers seated in the orchestra. Stravinsky made a counter-proposal: "I had been thinking of making a symphonic poem for the orchestra by combining the music of the second and third acts of *Le Rossignol,* which were homogeneous, and I told Diaghilev that I would place that at his disposal if he cared to make a ballet of it. He warmly welcomed the suggestion, and I adapted a scenario from Andersen's fairy story to serve the purpose. I at once set myself to the arrangement of this poem. . . ."

Stravinsky completed the score of the symphonic poem, *The Song of the Nightingale*, at Morges, Switzerland, in 1917. The first concert performance was given on December 6, 1919, at Geneva by the Orchestre de la Suisse Romande, under the direction of Ernest Ansermet. The first ballet production was presented by Diaghilev's company at the Paris Opéra on February 2, 1920. Scenery and costumes were designed by Henri Matisse, choreography was by Leonide Massine, and Tamara Karsavina danced the title role.

The symphonic poem, which is reorchestrated in a more transparent, almost chamber orchestra style, omits the first act of the opera and substantial portions of Acts II and III. The poem begins in the porcelain palace of the Emperor of China, where the nightingale is expected momentarily. The scene was suggested by the following pasage from the fairy tale: "The palace was festively adorned. The walls and the flooring, which were of porcelain, gleamed in the rays of thousands of golden lamps. The most glorious flowers, which could ring clearly, had been placed in the passages. There was a running to and from and a through draft, so that all the bells rang loudly." Here and in two ceremonial procession scenes Stravinsky used an ancient (Pentatonic) five-note scale to suggest the exotic Chinese world.

During a "Chinese March" the court dignitaries make their solemn entrance. The Emperor is carried in on his canopied chair. The nightingale, represented first by a solo flute and later by a solo violin, begins its song with an elaborate cadenza. Its song is so beautiful that tears come to the Emperor's eyes. (For reasons of symphonic balance, a major portion of the opening music of the symphonic poem is brought back at this point.)

A mechanical nightingale is brought to the Chinese Emperor as a gift of the Emperor of Japan. When it is made to sing (with the voice of a solo oboe) the real nightingale is so offended that it flies away. [At the conclusion of the mechanical nightingale's song, the Emperor notices that the real nightingale has disappeared. He orders the mechanical nightingale to be carried in procession to the imperial bedroom.] In the symphonic poem the song of the mechanical nightingale is followed immediately by the procession.

The opening of the third act of the opera (which follows immediately in the symphonic poem) shows a room in the imperial palace at night. There is moonlight. The Emperor lies sick in bed. Seated at the bedside, Death wears his Imperial crown and holds the Imperial sword and Imperial standard. The symphonic poem omits the chorus of ghosts and their dialogue with the terrified Emperor, picking up the music with the return of the nightingale. The renewed song of the nightingale beguiles not only the Emperor but Death itself. Death begs the nightingale to continue its song but the bird does so only on condition that Death return to the Emperor first the crown, then the precious sword and the standard. Death returns them all and finally disappears altogether. [The symphonic poem omits the brief passage in which the Emperor thanks his beloved nightingale, and the nightingale promises to return every night to sing to the Emperor.]

The music continues with the procession of the courtiers who, believing that the Emperor is dead, approach his bedchamber in solemn ceremony. At the last moment the curtains hiding the bedchamber from them part, and the Emperor is seen standing in full regalia in the center of the room, now flooded with sunlight. The courtiers prostrate themselves as the Emperor exclaims "Good morning to everybody!" While the curtain falls slowly, we hear the offstage voice of a fisherman (played in the symphonic poem by a soft trumpet) singing:

> The Night is dispersed by the new sun
> Gay birds sing, day has begun.
> Listen well, and in their voice
> Hear that of heaven, and rejoice.

The symphonic poem *The Song of the Nightingale* is scored for 2 flutes, 2 oboes, 2 clarinets, 2 bassoons, 4 horns, 3 trumpets, 3 trombones, tuba, kettledrums, triangle, bass drum, cymbals, tambourine, gong, snare drum, celesta, piano, 2 harps, and the traditional string choir.

SYMPHONY IN C

In celebration of the fiftieth anniversary of the Chicago Symphony, Stravinsky was invited to compose a symphony—which turned out to be the Symphony in C. Stravinsky accepted the commission during a tour of this country and completed the first two movements after his return to Paris in the winter and spring of 1939. The third movement was composed during his stay at Cambridge, Massachusetts, during the academic year 1939–1940, when he occupied the Charles Eliot Norton Chair of poetics at Harvard University. In the summer of 1940 Stravinsky moved to Hollywood, where he completed the Symphony in August. The first performance was given by the Chicago Symphony under Stravinsky's direction on November 7, 1940. It caused a sensation because of Stravinsky's return to Classical symphonic forms, techniques, and even to the lighter, ingenuous character of much early Classicism. It is cast in the traditional four movements.

I. *Moderato alla breve.* The brief introduction presents two very decided musical ideas. One is a four-note rhythm, so similar to the main theme of Beethoven's Fifth Symphony that the resemblance can hardly have been accidental. The other is an even briefer melodic figure: B-C-G presented in a variety of rhythmical guises.

The other main theme of the movement is a long and graceful melody spun out by a solo oboe over a dainty staccato tick-tock accompaniment of violins and violas. The oboe melody starts with, and keeps returning to, the B-C-G figure familiar from the introduction:

There are a number of graceful subordinate themes, and the oboe melody dominates even in the central development section.

II. *Larghetto.* It is again the delicate sound of the oboe which carries the principal melody until it is joined, first by a flute, then clarinet, and finally violins. The texture of the movement is light and transparent even in its more agitated middle section. The reprise of the opening melodies is clothed in even more sensuous orchestral colors and leads into the third movement.

III. *Allegretto.* The shifting, complex rhythms of this cherzo-like movement do have a dance quality, though they seem far removed from the traditional minuet or the more ancient *passepied* often mentioned in this connection. It concludes with a very imaginative and somewhat free fugue based on variants of this theme:

IV. *Largo; Tempo giusto, alla breve.* The *finale* begins with, and is punctuated in the middle, by a lethargic *Largo* painted in the blackest tones of low bassoons. There is a brief hint of the Symphony's opening motto, which returns more brightly, clearly and with almost jazzy syncopations in the fast body of the *finale.* At the conclusion the motto goes through slower and slower transformations in soft, hymnlike woodwinds echoed at the very end by a hushed chord of muted strings.

The modest orchestra of the Symphony in C calls for piccolo, 2 flutes, 2 oboes, 2 clarinets, 2 bassoons, 4 horns in F, 2 trumpets in C, 3 trombones, tuba, kettledrums, and the customary strings.

SYMPHONY IN THREE MOVEMENTS

Stravinsky's Symphony in Three Movements was commissioned by the New York Philharmonic and was given its world premiere by this Orchestra under the composer's direction on January 24, 1946. On that occasion Stravinsky wrote for the program notes:

> My Symphony in Three Movements is dedicated to the Philharmonic-Symphony Society of New York as an homage and appreciation of my twenty years' association with that eminent musical institution.
>
> This Symphony has no program, nor is it a specific expression of any given occasion; it would be futile to seek these in my work. But during the process of creation in this, our arduous time of sharp and shifting events, of despair and hope, of continual torments, of tension and, at last, cessation and relief, it may be that all those repercussions have left traces in this Symphony. It is not I to judge.

The Symphony in Three Movements is, in many ways, a paradoxical work. It combines some of the violence of *The Rite of Spring* with a so-called Neoclassicism usually thought to be at the opposite pole from the revolutionary *Rite*. It avoids traditional symphonic form and procedures, yet it is given the title of Symphony. It is far from being program music, yet much of it was associated in Stravinsky's mind with specific visual impressions, personal experiences, and strong emotional reactions to the events of World War II.

Many years later, in *Dialogues and a Diary*, Stravinsky recalled some of the connections between this Symphony and the harrowing events of the time:

> I will not say that it expresses my feelings about them, but only that, without the participation of what I think of as my will, they excited my musical imagination. And the impressions that activated me were not general, or ideological, but specific: each episode in the Symphony is linked in my imagination with a specific cinematographic impression of the war. . . .
>
> The formal substance of the Symphony—Three Symphonic Movements would be a more exact title—exploits the idea of counterplay between several types of contrasting elements. One such contrast, the most obvious, is that of harp and piano, the principal instrumental protagonists. Each has a large

> obbligato role and a whole movement to itself and only at the turning-point fugue, the Nazi *queue de poisson,* are the two heard together and alone.
>
> But enough of this. In spite of what I have said, the Symphony is not programmatic. Composers combine notes. That is all. How and in what form the things of this world are impressed upon their music is not for them to say.*

I. The first movement bears no tempo name, only the metronome marking: 160 quarter notes to the minute. According to Stravinsky's conversations with Robert Craft (in *Dialogues and a Diary*), it was "inspired by a war film, this time of scorched-earth tactics in China." The musical substance, according to two of Stravinsky's friends, Alexander Tansman and Roman Vlad, was first envisaged as a symphonic work with solo piano which would explain the prominent role of the piano in the first movement.

The introduction opens with a boldly aggressive figure compounded of slashing scales and bare, heavy octaves. In the closing measures of the introduction, two horns play softly, but distinctly, a motto-like theme.

This theme permeates the first movement in a dozen transformations and combinations, prominent and obscure. The middle section of this movement, according to Stravinsky,

> . . . was conceived as a series of instrumental conversations to accompany a series of cinematographic scenes showing the Chinese people scratching and digging in their fields. The music for clarinet, piano and strings that mounts in intensity and volume until the explosion of the three chords at number 69, and then begins all over again, was all associated in my mind with this Chinese documentary.**

A reprise of the principal themes is very condensed and the concluding *coda* is marked by the aggressive figure which opened the introduction.

II. *Andante.* The more delicate slow movement shows no such close connection to the events or impressions of the war years. Quite to the contrary, its opening and most important theme seems to echo the mock gravity, the

---

* *These paragraphs are quoted by permission from* Dialogues and a Diary, *by Igor Stravinsky and Robert Craft, published by Doubleday & Co.,* © *1962, 1963 by Igor Stravinsky.*

deliciously unctuous humor of Count Almaviva as he greets Dr. Bartolo in the second act of Rossini's *The Barber of Seville* with the words: *"Pace e gioia sia con voi!"*

But we must guard against any conclusion that Stravinsky meant to recall either Rossini or Mozart, although some listeners are also reminded here of Dr. Bartolo's first aria from *The Marriage of Figaro.* The fact is, according to Eric Walter White's book on Stravinsky,* that the movement was composed for a scene of the apparition of the Virgin in a film adaptation of Franz Werfel's *The Song of Bernadette.* Stravinsky never completed the film score, but used this material for the slow movement of his new Symphony. There is a livelier middle section, after which the Rossinian theme returns. An interlude of seven measures links the slow movement to the *finale,* which follows without pause.

III. *Con moto.* The heavy stride and bold, vaulting figures with which the *Finale* begins, recall the motto-like theme of the first movement. The climax is a fugue which moves within such narrow confines that it seems, by comparison, almost immobile. Anticipated by a solo trombone alone, the fugue subject is announced by the piano and echoed by the harp.

Only after completing this movement did Stravinsky realize that it embodied impressions of the end of the war:

> The beginning of the movement is partly and in some inexplicable way a reaction to the newsreels and documentaries I had seen of goose-stepping soldiers. The square march beat, the brass band instrumentation, the grotesque *crescendo* in the tuba, these are all related to those abhorrent pictures. . . .
>
> But to return to the plot of the movement, in spite of contrasting episodes, such as the canon for bassoons, the march music predominates until the fugue, which is the stasis and the turning point. The immobility at the beginning of this fugue is comic, I think—and so, to me, was the overturned arrogance of the Germans when their machine failed. The exposition of the fugue and the end of the Symphony are associated in my plot with the rise of the Allies, and the final, rather too commercial, D-flat sixth chord—instead of the expected C—in some way tokens my extra exuberance in the Allied triumph. . . .**

---

* *Eric Walter White,* Stravinsky the Composer and His Works *(Berkeley and Los Angeles: University of California Press, 1966.)*

** Dialogues and a Diary, *by Igor Stravinsky and Robert Craft, published by Doubleday & Co. © 1962, 1963 by Igor Stravinsky.*

The Symphony in Three Movements is scored for piccolo, 2 flutes, 2 oboes, 3 clarinets, bass clarinet, 2 bassoons, contrabassoons, 4 horns in F, 3 trumpets in C, 3 trombones, tuba, kettledrums, bass drum, piano, harp and strings.

SYMPHONY OF PSALMS

The *Symphony of Psalms* mirrors religious feelings that were important to Stravinsky for most of his life. The immediate occasion for the composition was a commission to celebrate the fiftieth anniversary of the Boston Symphony Orchestra in 1930. But as Stravinsky tells in his *Chronicle of My Life,* the commission coincided with a long-standing inclination.

> The idea of composing a symphonic work of considerable scope had occupied me for a long time. I therefore willingly accepted a proposition which coincided entirely with my inclinations. I was given full liberty in the form of the piece, as well as the forces that I might require for its performance. . . . My work on the *Symphony of Psalms* began in the first part of the year [1930], and was frequently interrupted by a number of concerts in Europe, in which I took part at times as conductor, at times as pianist. My most recent work, the *Capriccio* was having a considerable success in different cities. . . . At the beginning of the summer, I could at last give my whole time to my symphony, of which I had then completed only one part. As for the two others, I wrote them entirely—at first at Nice, then at Charavines, through which I was passing, at the edge of the little Lake Paladru [between Grenoble and Lyon]. On the 15th of August I put the last touches on the draft of the score and then was able to work at ease on the orchestration, which I had already begun at Nice.

When it was completed in the early fall the score was inscribed (in French): "This Symphony, composed to the glory of GOD, is dedicated to the 'Boston Symphony Orchestra' on the occasion of the fiftieth anniversary of its existence."

Because of an unexpected postponement of the first Boston Symphony performance, the world premiere was given by the Brussels Philharmonic Society in Brussels under the direction of Ernest Ansermet on December 13, 1930. The Boston Symphony performance under the direction of Serge Koussevitzky followed six days later.

Following strict ecclesiastical tradition (and perhaps also his own sense of the rather stern, impersonal beauty of this music), Stravinsky asks for mixed chorus, with soprano and alto parts sung by boys. However, the score expressly provides that women's voices may be substituted, and in actual practice this has been done by most conductors, including the composer himself.

The color of the orchestra, too, is striking. Here, as in his later Mass, Stravinsky omits the high strings altogether as well as the sensuous sound of the clarinets. The score calls for 4 flutes and piccolo, 4 oboes and English horn, 3 bassoons and contrabassoon, 4 horns, 5 trumpets (including one in D), 3 trombones and tuba, harp, 2 pianos, kettledrums, bass drum, cellos, and string basses.

The form of the *Symphony of Psalms* has little, if anything, to do with Classical symphonic form. Stravinsky uses the word in a much more ancient and simple meaning of "sound-combinations." The three movements, which are performed without pause, embody prayer, thanksgiving and a hymn of praise. The text, specifically required to be sung in Latin, is taken from the Psalter of the Vulgate.

I. There is no tempo marking for this movement in words but rather a metronome marking of 92 quarter notes per minute. The text is the Vulgate Psalm 38, verses 13 and 14, corresponding to Psalm 39, verses 12 and 13 of the King James Version. The short introduction, punctuated by sharp, percussive chords of E minor, establishes a stiffly hieratical mood. The opening *Exaudi* of the altos moves like a lament or a wail, back and forth, almost obsessively, over the single half step, E to F.

Exaudi orationem meam, Domine, et deprecationem meam;	Hear my prayer, O Lord, and give ear unto my cry;
Auribus percipe lacrimas meas.	Hold not Thy peace at my tears.
Ne sileas, quoniam advena ego sum apud te, et peregrinus sicut omnes patres mei.	For I am a stranger with Thee, and a sojourner as all my fathers were.
Remitte mihi, ut refrigerer prius quam abeam, et amplius non ero.	O spare me, that I may recover strength before I go hence, and be no more.

The second movement follows without pause.

II. This movement bears no tempo marking in words but only the metronome indication of 60 eighth notes per minute. Musically speaking this movement is a double fugue.

The exposition of the first subject is the orchestral introduction. The subject is announced by a solitary oboe: *

The vocal fugue subject is initiated by sopranos while the orchestra continues its own fugal development of its own subject.

* *This and the following musical examples from this composition are copyright 1931 by Edition Russe de Musique. Renewed 1958. Copyright and renewal assigned to Boosey & Hawkes, Inc. Revised edition copyright 1948 by Boosey & Hawkes, Inc. Reprinted by permission.*

The vocal fugue is set to Vulgate Psalm 39, verses 2, 3, and 4 (corresponding to the King James Version Psalm 40, verses 1, 2, and 3).

Expectans expectavi, Dominum, et intendit mihi.	I waited patiently for the Lord: and he inclined to me.
Et exaudivit preces meas et eduxit me de lacu miseriae, et de luto faecis.	And he heard my cry, and brought me up also out of an horrible pit, out of the miry clay.
Et statuit super petram pedes meos, et direxit gressus meos.	And he set my foot upon a rock, and established my goings.
Et immisit in os meum canticum novum, carmen Deo nostro.	He hath put a new song in my mouth, even praise unto our God.
Videbunt multi et timebunt; et sperabunt in Domino.	And many shall see it and fear: and shall trust in the Lord.

The third movement follows without pause.

III. The metronome indication for the tempo in this movement is given as 48 quarter notes per minute.

Psalm 150 has the same number in both the Vulgate and the King James Version. (Although the score indicates that the entire Psalm text is used, the sixth line is in fact omitted as indicated below). This final hymn of praise is a more restrained, more mystical movement than one might expect from the familiar text. The serene *"Alleluia"* of the opening and closing pages, leads in both cases to a solemn, three-note, motto-like phrase on the repeated word, *"Laudate, laudate. . . ."*

The faster middle section revolves around the almost mechanical rhythm of a sharply articulated *"Laudate Dominum."* The slow concluding section builds to a great climax and leads with a sudden hush, to the eloquent *coda* with its refrain-like melody:

This melody seems to grow with repetition, its poignance enhanced by the four-note *ostinato* accompaniment figure:

The final page brings a last recall of the peaceful *"Laudate, laudate, . . . Dominum."*

Alleluia.	Alleluia.
Laudate Dominum in sanctis Ejus:	Praise God in His sanctuary:
Laudate Eum in firmamento virtutis Ejus.	Praise Him in the firmament of His power.
Laudate Eum in virtutibus Ejus.	Praise Him for His mighty acts.
Laudate Eum secundum multitudinem magnitudinis Ejus.	Praise Him according to his excellent greatness.
Laudate Eum in sono tubae.	Praise Him with the sound of the trumpet.
[*Laudate Eum in psalterio et cithara.*]*	[Praise Him with the psaltery and the harp.]
Laudate Eum in tympano et choro.	Praise Him with the timbrel and dance.
Laudate Eum in cordis et organo.	Praise Him with stringed instruments and organs.
Laudate Eum in cymbalis benesonantibus;	Praise Him upon the loud cymbals;
Laudate Eum in cymbalis jubilationibus.	Praise Him on the high sounding cymbals.
Omnis spiritus laudet Dominium.	Let everything that hath breath praise the Lord.
Omnis spiritus laudet Eum.	Let everything that hath breath praise Him.
Alleluia.	Alleluia.
Laudate Dominium.	Praise the Lord.

Peter Ilyitch Tchaikovsky

Born May 7, 1840, Votinsk, District of Viatka—died November 6, 1893, St. Petersburg

CAPRICCIO ITALIEN (ITALIAN CAPRICCIO), OPUS 45

The Roman carnival of 1880 was in full swing and Tchaikovsky was in Rome. But a worm gnawed at his heart. Or so he wrote on February 17 to his "beloved friend" Nadeja von Meck. "I do not understand why I cannot sleep," he added. "*Dieu,* what an incomprehensible and complicated mechanism the human organism is!"

The "wild folly" of the carnival season bothered him, yet he could not shut his ears to its melodic and rhythmic appeal. "I have been working,"

* *This line is ommited in Stravinsky's score.*

Tchaikovsky confessed, "and during the last few days I have sketched the rough draft of an *Italian Capriccio* based on popular melodies. I think it has a bright future; it will be effective because of the wonderful melodies I happened to pick up, partly from published collections and partly out in the streets with my own ears." Although Tchaikovsky seems to have sketched his first draft at top speed (within a single week, starting January 27), the full score was not completed until after his return to Russia in the spring.

The slow introduction of the *Capriccio* starts with a brass fanfare: a bugle call Tchaikovsky heard daily from his Roman headquarters in the Hotel Costanzi, next door to the barracks of the Royal Italian Cuirasseurs. The fanfare is answered by the string choir which chants a languorous, melancholy strain punctuated by shuddering brass rhythms.

As the tempo quickens, one catchy melody chases the other through Tchaikovsky's many-colored orchestra. The *Capriccio* ends with a vertiginous *tarantella* and a burst of brilliance which tell us that no matter how melancholy he was or how sharply the worm may have gnawed at his heart, he could not wholly close his ears to the spirit of carnival in the Eternal City.

Tchaikovsky's score calls for an orchestra of piccolo, 3 flutes, 2 oboes, 2 clarinets, English horn, 2 bassoons, 4 horns, 2 cornets in A, 2 trumpets in E, 2 tenor trombones, bass trombone, tuba, kettledrums, glockenspiel, triangle, tambourine, bass drum, cymbals, harp, and the usual strings.

CONCERTO FOR PIANO AND ORCHESTRA, NO. 1, B-FLAT MINOR, OPUS 23

"Think what healthy appetities these Americans must have" wrote Tchaikovsky when he heard of the enthusiastic reception of his B-flat minor Concerto, given its world premiere by Hans von Bülow in Boston on October 25, 1875. The triumph was repeated in other cities of Bülow's American tour and Tchaikovsky observed: "Each time Bülow was obliged to repeat the whole finale of my concerto! Nothing like that happens in our country."

In Boston the appetite for music—or at least for Bülow-cum-Tchaikovsky—was positively voracious. Seven concerts in thirteen days (October 18 through 30), topped off by a farewell repetition of the Tchaikovsky Concerto, were hardly enough for the Athens of America—as Bostonians, only half-jokingly, called their city. They welcomed Bülow so enthusiastically that his letters home described the New Englanders as "a vastly improved edition of the old—much warmer, more sympathetic, and even more cultivated (*gesitteter*) than the old-English—and [says Bülow, in English] they have more 'ginger' in them."

He was also delighted with the Bostonian (Chickering) pianos he had contracted to use on his American tour. To his old school friend Jessie Laussot, Bulöw wrote (in English): "Very glad that I began in 'Athens' and not in Yankeepolis [sic]—ditto that I play on Chickerings who [sic] are the best ones in both worlds. Yes, Ma'am. So it is."

Bülow was even delighted with the skill of his small pick-up orchestra ("largely German, industrious, their intelligence not yet drowned in lager beer") but he was far from pleased with his conductor. Carl Bergmann was permanent conductor of the New York Philharmonic and the authoritative *Dwight's Journal of Music* called him "the best conductor in America." But Bülow privately called him a beer bum (*Bierlümmel*) and got rid of him before the concert introducing the Tchaikovsky Concerto. In Bergmann's place he persuaded the well-known Boston pianist Benjamin Johnson Lang (like Bülow, a pupil of Liszt) to direct the orchestra. "The performance under the American Lang, whom I improvised as a conductor and made famous on the spot," Bülow declared, "was very decent; and yesterday [October 30], when we repeated it, really fiery."

Dwight's Journal reported after the repetition of the Tchaikovsky Concerto:

> Mr. B.J. LANG, who had been called to succeed Mr. BERGMANN, . . . being himself a pianist and an enthusiastic admirer of Von Bülow, was in better sympathy and understanding with him for the rendering of the extremely difficult, strange, wild, ultra-modern Russian Concerto. It is the composition of a young professor at the Conservatory of Moscow, a pupil of Rubinstein (indeed the work contained not a few suggestions of the master) and is dedicated to Bülow, who complimented Boston with its very first performance. A compliment well meant, and warmly responded to by the applauding audience—twice—for this program was repeated for the seventh concert.
>
> It opens richly and the first Allegro is full of striking passages and brilliant, but sometimes bizarre, effects of instrumentation. One peculiarity is the frequent indulgence of the pianoforte in rhapsodical, cadenza-like flights of startling execution, while the orchestra waits, as it were, outside. This lends quite a bravura character to a movement which seemed also melodramatic rather than in the Classical concerto spirit. . . .
>
> In the finale we had the wild Cossack fire and impetus without stint—extremely brilliant and exciting, but could we ever learn to love such music? How wonderfully Von Bülow rendered it, there is no need of telling: all that a hearty sympathy, a masterly conception, and an infallible technique could do for it, it had in the fullest degree; and the young author well knew that his work could not suffer in such hands.

In New York the appetite for the art of Bülow and "the young author" was even greater. Fourteen concerts squeezed into nineteen days (November 15 through December 3) must have tried the stamina of a Hercules. But Bülow declared: "Never, anywhere, have I felt so well, I might say so happy." And he wrote his friend Klindworth (another Liszt pupil): "Whereas before I often played like a pig, I now, on occasion, play like a god. Chickerings' gorgeous pianos, undeniably the best in both worlds, have turned me into a top-flight pianist."

Chickering shared a well-planned part of the glory. Chickering Concert Hall, just completed on the northwest corner of Fifth Avenue and Fifteenth Street, with the obvious purpose of rivaling Steinway Hall, was inaugurated by Bülow's widely heralded New York debut on Monday, November 15, 1875. The orchestra was directed by Leopold Damrosch. The beauties of the new hall,

CHICKERING HALL INAUGURATION.

On November 15, 1875, Hans von Bülow's New York debut inaugurated the new hall, with Leopold Damrosch conducting. The New York premiere of Tchaikovsky's Piano Concerto was offered one week later by the same forces in the same hall. (*Frank Leslie's Illustrated Weekly; courtesy, Culver Pictures*)

its arcaded facade, its elegant interior were rapturously detailed by many publications, and the spectacle of that inaugural concert was preserved by Frank Leslie's popular *Illustrated Weekly* of December 4, 1875. The very night of his debut Bülow wrote home:

> I have just come from the extremely brilliant and most magnificently inaugurated concert hall. My eighteenth American concert, which was also my first in New York, was, *tout simplement,* the most colossal success of my entire career as a virtuoso and, as my excellent manager tells me, the greatest triumph he has witnessed here in thirty years. . . . My old friend Damrosch [from Breslau, Germany] vindicated his reputation and conducted admirably.

One week later the Tchaikovsky Concerto was presented by the same forces in the same hall. To his friend Klindworth at the Moscow Conservatory, Bülow was more specific:

> The concerto went much better here under Damrosch than in Boston. It was a distinct success and is to be repeated next Saturday. In fact Tchaikovsky has become popular in the New World; and if Jürgenson [Tchaikovsky's Russian publisher] were not such a damned jackass but would send over a reasonable quantity of Tchaikovsky's music, he could do a lot of business. [Bülow included a batch of reviews of the concert.] Concerning Tchaikovsky. I would like you to give him a little pleasure by showing him the enclosed reviews. You know, it was through you that I first knew him and learned to appreciate him, so it is a case of *les amis de nos amis. . .*

Tchaikovsky, dazzled and bemused by the clippings longed to hear Bülow play his Concerto—all the more, because he had just heard the Concerto in St. Petersburg, but in a wretched performance, "miserably distorted, thanks chiefly to a conductor who did everything to produce an accompaniment that was an atrocious cacophony instead of music. The pianist K. interpreted it conscientiously, but in a flat style devoid of taste or charm. The piece had no success."

> It is not strange [reflected Tchaikovsky in a second letter to Bülow] that between the two most celebrated artists of our epoch, it is you, who have known me only briefly, rather than Anton Rubinstein who, after all, was my teacher, who are giving my music such necessary and beneficent support? That Olympian God has never shown anything but sovereign disdain for my works and I can confess privately to you that I have always felt deeply wounded by this. . . . If I tell you these things, dear sir, it is to make you understand the immense gratitude I owe you, to you, who have not been my teacher and are not even a compatriot. . . .
>
> Your devoted admirer and grateful
> P. TCHAIKOVSKY

What Tchaikovsky did not tell Bülow was the even greater humiliation he had suffered from Anton Rubinstein's celebrated brother Nicholas. Tchaikovsky had composed his score at high speed, chiefly during November and December 1874. Being no professional pianist himself, and almost morbidly self-critical, he wanted to have a professional performer's opinion on his new work. He made the mistake, as it turned out, of asking his affectionate, if rather domineering friend, Nicholas Rubinstein, head of the Moscow Conservatory where Tchaikovsky himself was a faculty member. Before a Christmas Eve party to which both men were invited, Rubinstein suggested that Tchaikovsky play over his new work in one of the Conservatory classrooms. Later Tchaikovsky described the painful experience in a letter to his friend and patron, Mme. von Meck. When he finished playing the first movement, Rubinstein said nothing whatever.

> If you only knew how uncomfortably foolish you feel [wrote Tchaikovsky] if you invite a friend to share a dish you have prepared with your own hands, and he eats and is silent. At least say something! If you like, find fault, in a friendly way, but for heaven's sake speak—say something, no matter what! But Rubinstein said nothing. He was preparing his thunder. . . . As a matter of fact I did not require any opinion on the artistic form of my work; it was purely the technical side which was in question. . . . I took patience and played the concerto to the end. Again silence.
>
> "Well?" said I, as I arose. Then there burst from Rubinstein's mouth a mighty torrent of words. He spoke quietly at first, then he waxed hot, and finally he resembled Zeus hurling thunderbolts. It seems that my concerto was utterly worthless, absolutely unplayable. Certain passages were so commonplace and awkward they could not be improved, and the piece as a whole was bad, trivial, vulgar. I had stolen this from somebody and that from somebody else, so that only two or three pages were good for anything and all the rest should be wiped out or radically rewritten. . . .
>
> An unbiased spectator could only have thought that I was a stupid, ignorant spoiler of music paper, who had had the impertinence to show his rubbish to a celebrated man. . . .
>
> I left the room without a word and went upstairs. I was so excited and angry I could not speak. Soon afterward Rubinstein came up to me and seeing how upset I was called me into another room. There he repeated that my concerto was impossible and pointed to several places that required a complete revision, adding that if I would suit the concerto to his requirements, he would bring it out at his concert. "I shall not alter a single note," I replied. "I shall have the concerto printed exactly as it stands." That is, in fact, what I have done.

Tchaikovsky did more. He erased the intended dedication to Nicholas Rubinstein and inscribed it instead to Hans von Bülow, who he had been told was a great admirer of his works. Flattered by the dedication and delighted with the concerto, Bülow wrote Tchaikovsky a warm letter, praising the originality, nobility and power of the piano concerto:

> The ideas are so original, so noble, so powerful, the details are so interesting, and though there are many of them, they do not impair the clarity and the unity of the work. The form is so mature, ripe, distinguished in style, intention and labor being everywhere concealed. I would weary you if I were to

> enumerate all the characteristics of your work, characteristics which compel me to congratulate equally the composer and those who are destined to enjoy it.

Bülow was about to leave on his tour of North America. Having heard that audiences in the larger cities were abreast of current European composition, he was proud to be able to take with him an as yet unperformed masterpiece by a genius of the most brilliant promise. Thus it happened that the Concerto had its premiere in Boston. And it became the ultramodern sensation of Bülow's staggering tour, on which it is recorded that, he performed 139 out of 172 scheduled concerts.

I. *Allegro non troppo e molto maestoso: Allegro con spirito.* In a vigorous four-bar preamble the French horns anticipate the theme to follow. Then against the piano's crashing D-flat major chords, the orchestra flings forth a grandly arched melody which is immediately taken up by the soloist:

Thus far, all has been introduction. The main section of the movement, *Allegro con spirito,* has as its main theme a curiously jerky, vivacious figure, a melody Tchaikovsky heard sung at a fair at Kamenko by a blind beggar:

"It is curious," he wrote to Mme. von Meck, "that in Little Russia every blind beggar sings exactly the same tune with the same refrain. I have used part of this refrain in my pianoforte concerto."

II. *Andantino semplice; Prestissimo.* Over an accompaniment of muted strings, a solo flute sings the pensive melody, which is taken up by the piano. There is a scherzo-like middle section of almost chamber music delicacy, and the movement is rounded-off with a brief return of the opening melody.

II. *Allegro con fuoco.* The finale is a rondo with a wild, dance-like refrain announced by the piano solo. A magnificently lyric contrasting theme is announced by the violins in octaves, and echoed in the piano:

It is this theme which Tchaikovsky uses to build a final climax of a breadth and grandeur which rivals the introduction to the first movement. The Concerto is scored for 2 flutes, 2 oboes, 2 clarinets, 2 bassoons, 4 horns, 2 trumpets, 2 trombones, bass trombone, kettledrums, and the customary strings.

CONCERTO FOR VIOLIN AND ORCHESTRA, D MAJOR, OPUS 35

With the possible exception of the Mendelssohn Violin Concerto, to which it is related in many ways, Tchaikovsky's Opus 35 seems to have become the most popular violin concerto ever written. But this was not always so. The Concerto had a difficult path, starting with the composer. After completing the score in 1878, Tchaikovsky was dissatisfied with his slow movement. He discarded the slow movement (which he later published as a violin-pianoforte piece, *Souvenir d'un lieu cher,* Opus 42, No. 3), and composed an entirely new *Andante* for the Concerto.

He sent the final version to his patroness Mme von Meck. But although this "beloved friend" was his almost fanatical admirer, she found fault with the Violin Concerto and said so in detail. Tchaikovsky, however, knew better and defended his Concerto:

> Your frank judgment on my Violin Concerto pleased me very much. It would have been very disagreeable to me if you, from any fear of wounding the petty pride of a composer, had kept back your opinion. However, I must defend a little the first movement of the Concerto.
>
> Of course, it houses, as does every piece that serves virtuoso purposes, much that appeals chiefly to the mind; nevertheless, the themes are not painfully evolved; the plan of this movement sprang suddenly in my head and quickly ran into its mold. I shall not give up the hope that in time the piece will give you greater pleasure.

Tchaikovsky intended to dedicate his Concerto to Leopold Auer, the teacher of Heifetz, Elman and many other illustrious violinists, and a celebrated virtuoso in his own right. But Auer, after looking over the new Concerto, declared it to be "unplayable." Finally, another violinist, Adolf Brodsky, who worked two years off and on at the Concerto, performed it for the first time at a Vienna Philharmonic concert on December 4, 1881, under the direction of Hans Richter. But of ten Viennese critics only the two least important approved of the new Concerto. Here, in part, is what Eduard Hanslick, the dean of Central European critics wrote:

> For a while the Concerto has proportion, is musical, and is not without genius, but soon savagery gains the upper hand and lords it to the end of the first movement. The violin is no longer played: it is yanked about, it is torn asunder, it is beaten black and blue. I do not know whether it is possible for anyone to conquer these hair-raising difficulties, but I do know that Mr. Brodsky martyrized his hearers as well as himself. The *adagio,* with its tender

> national melody, almost conciliates, almost wins us. But it breaks off abruptly to make way for a *finale* that puts us in the midst of the brutal and wretched jollity of a Russian *kermess.* We see wild and vulgar faces, we hear curses, we smell bad brandy. Friedrich Fischer once asserted in reference to lascivious paintings that there are pictures which "stink in the eye." Tchaikovsky's Violin Concerto brings to us for the first time the horrid idea that there may be music that stinks in the ear.

Tchaikovsky is said to have carried Hanslick's virulent review around for many months, and it was a source of pain to him for the rest of his life. Presumably, Hanslick never changed his petty mind. But Leopold Auer did. He lived to play Tchaikovsky's Concerto with brilliant success; he taught it to his finest pupils and contributed greatly to establishing it in its present eminence.

I. *Allegro moderato.* In keeping with the predominantly lyric tone of the Concerto, the first movement starts quietly, simply and melodiously in the first violins alone. There is a very brief introduction, anticipating the main theme of the movement, but no extended symphonic exposition. The songful first theme is given out softly by the soloist over the simplest of accompaniments:

The pace quickens slightly as the soloist, with all manner of virtuoso flourishes, approaches the second principal theme, an equally songful one, *con molto espressione:*

The two themes provide almost none of the traditional contrast of the Classical concerto form. But each is so seductive and so admirably suited to the lyric character of the violin itself that only a pedant would quarrel with the composer. The opening theme returns with a more vigorous rhythmic accompaniment and leads into a development section full of violinistic acrobatics and fireworks, culminating in an extremely effective and difficult cadenza.

As in the first movement of the Mendelssohn Violin Concerto, the soloist is still playing his cadenza when the orchestra enters very softly in the background with the traditional return or recapitulation of the Concerto's basic themes.

II. *Canzonetta: Andante.* Tchaikovsky's new slow movement turned out to be one of his most sensitive and ingratiating inspirations. The simple elegiac mood is set by a discreet woodwind ensemble. The muted solo violin almost seems to whisper the melancholy chief theme over an accompaniment of muted violins, violas and French horn. Later there is another brighter, but equally graceful melody for the soloist. The movement is very short. It seems about to fade into silence, but leads instead without interruption into the *Finale*.

III. *Finale: Allegro vivacissimo.* A fiery orchestral introduction leads directly to a cadenza anticipating the main theme. The theme itself is a dance-like, light-footed rondo tune, wonderfully suited to symphonic development. Throughout the *Finale* Tchaikovsky exploits the violin's capacity for brilliance and agility, using the sustained melody of the episodes chiefly as a foil for the dazzling scales and the dizzy leaps of the soloist.

The Concerto is scored for 2 flutes, 2 oboes, 2 clarinets, 2 bassoons, 4 horns, 2 trumpets, kettledrums, and the usual strings.

FRANCESCA DA RIMINI,OPUS 32

The tragedy of Francesca da Rimini is the most famous episode in Dante's *Divine Comedy*. It is based on a historical event which was well known in Dante's day. Francesca was sought in marriage by an elderly nobleman of Rimini, Gianciotto Malatesta. But Gianciotto wooed her by proxy through his handsome younger brother, Paolo. Francesca, believing Paolo to be her future husband, fell in love with him. When she came to Rimini and found herself married to Gianciotto, it was too late; she and Paolo were unable to restrain their love. One day Gianciotto surprised them together and murdered them.

Tchaikovsky had originally planned to compose an opera on Francesca da Rimini, but gave up the project because of disagreement with his librettist. He began the Orchestral Fantasy during a visit to Paris in 1876. By October 26 he announced to his brother Modest that he had finished everything except the orchestration:

"I have worked at it with love, and the love, I think, has been quite successful. Regarding the whirlwind, perhaps it could correspond better to Doré's picture: it has not turned out exactly as I wished. However, an accurate estimate of the work is impossible as long as it has been neither orchestrated nor performed."

The masterly orchestration was completed in November. The score calls for piccolo, 3 flutes, 2 oboes, English horn, 2 clarinets, 2 bassoons, 4 horns, 2 cornets, 2 trumpets, 2 tenor trombones, bass trombone, tuba, kettledrums, cymbals, bass drum, gong, harp, and the usual string choir. It was first performed at a concert of the Russian Musical Society in Moscow on March 9, 1877 and repeated with even greater success at St. Petersburg on March 11 of the following year.

Tchaikovsky follows Dante's description of his meeting with the souls of Paolo and Francesca. He was also stirred by Gustave Doré's grandiose illustrations of this episode in the Second Circle of the *Inferno*. Here, according to the medieval concept of hell, punishment is meted out for sins of the flesh. Here the souls of famous adulterers—Helen of Troy, Paris, Cleopatra, Tristan, Isolde —find their appropriate punishment. Just as in life they were driven by storms

INSPIRATION FOR TCHAIKOVSKY'S "FRANCESCA."

Tchaikovsky was inspired not only by the tragedy of Francesca da Rimini, as told by Francesca herself in Dante's *Inferno,* but by Gustave Doré's vision of the eternal tempest, which is the punishment of the guilty lovers. (*Wood engraving for Dante's Commedia, Inferno, Canto V, Gustave Doré; courtesy, Metropolitan Museum of Art, Harris Brisbane Dick Fund, 1917.*)

of passion, so now they are tossed forever on the winds of an infernal tempest which fills the second circle of Hell. As the ghosts of Paolo and Francesca approach, Dante calls out to them and begs them to pause and tell the story of how they first lost their hearts to each other.

Francesca tells the story briefly, with the utmost simplicity. She begins with the famous words: "There is no greater pain than happiness remembered in time of misery." Her companion weeps at the tale. She and Paolo were reading together one day, quite innocently, the story of the loves of Lancelot, when their eyes met over the book. They came to a moment where Lancelot kissed his love. "And then," says Francesca:

> He who never will be separate from me,
> Kissed me on the mouth, trembling all over.
> The book and writer both were love's purveyors.
> We read no more in it that day.

The music opens with a stern *Andante lugubre,* intended to recall the inscription over the gateway to Hell: "Leave all hope behind, ye who enter here." An *Allegro vivo* suggests the winds which harry the sinners through the second circle. A soft-voiced clarinet begins Francesca's tragic story. After the climax the winds start softly once again and build up to a screaming tempest, as the souls of the lovers are swept away on the storm, each the eternal torment and the eternal consolation of the other.

THE NUTCRACKER, OPUS 71

Although Tchaikovsky was one of the greatest ballet composers who ever lived and *The Nutcracker* is one of his most popular works, he himself felt, almost before he had started composing, that it was poor music. To begin with he could not warm to the subject: a fantastic children's fairy tale by E.T.A. Hoffmann called *The Nutcracker and the Mouse King.* The actual ballet scenario assigned to Tchaikovsky by the Maryinski Theater of St. Petersburg was based not on the original tale by Hoffmann, but on a French version translated by Alexandre Dumas, the elder, and published as Dumas's own work, *The Story of a Nutcracker (Histoire d'un casse-noisette).* This is the reason that for many years the ballet was known in Russia and even in English-speaking countries as *Casse-Noisette.*

Tchaikovsky was also irritated by the demands of his illustrious collaborator, the choreographer of the Russian Imperial Ballet Marius Petipa, who attempted to dictate in preposterous detail exactly how many measures of what kind of music Tchaikovsky should compose for each minute episode. A sample of his instructions runs: "Sweet music: sixty-four measures. Eight measures of sparkling music. Twenty-four measures of noisy, joyous music. . . . Sixteen measures of rococo music (minuet tempo)." Tchaikovsky did not keep to the letter of Petipa's demands, but they did not help his depressed mood.

The ballet had been commissioned early in 1891. By July 7 Tchaikovsky wrote to his favorite nephew Vladimir Davidov:

> In accordance with my promise, I write to inform you that I finished the sketches of the ballet yesterday. You will remember that I bragged to you when you were here that I could finish the ballet in five days. But I have scarcely finished it in a fortnight. No, the old man is breaking up. Not only does his hair drop out, or turn as white as snow, not only does he lose his teeth, which refuse their service, not only do his eyes weaken and tire easily, not only do his feet walk badly, or rather drag themselves along, but he loses bit by bit the capacity to do anything at all. The ballet is infinitely worse than *The Sleeping Beauty*—so much is certain; let's see how the opera [*Iolanthe*] will turn out. If I arrive at the conclusion that I can no longer furnish my musical table with anything but warmed-up fare, I will give up composing altogether.

One ray of light, however, was Tchaikovsky's discovery during a visit to Paris of a newly invented orchestral instrument, the celesta, which Tchaikovsky described to his publisher as "something between a piano and a glockenspiel." In fact, the sound of the celesta is far closer to the glockenspiel, the resemblance to the piano being chiefly that it has a keyboard. Tchaikovsky informed his publisher that it had a "divinely beautiful" tone and, since he planned to use it in his new ballet, the publishers should secure a celesta immediately. "Have it sent direct to St. Petersburg," Tchaikovsky begged, "but no one there must know about it. I am afraid that Rimsky-Korsakoff and Glazounoff might hear of it and use it before I do. I expect it will make a tremendous impression." Tchaikovsky finished the instrumentation of his ballet in February 1892.

Even before the full ballet could be produced by the Maryinsky Theater, Tchaikovsky himself conducted a suite of excerpts in the spring of 1892 with the Russian Musical Society in St. Petersburg. Five numbers of the suite had to be encored, but still Tchaikovsky was not reassured. Before the Maryinsky production was completed Petipa fell ill and his choreography was completed by Lev Ivanoff. The premiere finally took place on December 17, 1892. Alas for Tchaikovsky's self-confidence, the premiere itself was only mildly successful. With repetitions and improvements in the cast, however, the ballet soon took hold.

The ballet scenario was originally set in early nineteenth-century Germany (in the period of E.T.A. Hoffmann) but is now usually transported to nineteenth-century St. Petersburg. At a Christmas party "the President" and his wife are entertaining a party of their children's friends with their parents. Before the Christmas presents are distributed there is a miniature march for the children. Soon a magician Drosselmeyer brings strange Christmas presents: clockwork toys, a Harlequin and a Columbine which dance for the children to their fascinated delight. Finally Clara, the daughter of the house, is presented with a grotesque Nutcracker for which she immediately conceives a great affection. Her brother Fritz is jealous, they quarrel, and the Nutcracker is thrown aside. After the guests leave and the children are put to bed, Clara worries about her beloved Nutcracker and cannot go to sleep. She sneaks downstairs into the room with the Christmas tree and presents which is now strangely transformed. The Christmas tree has grown vastly and the toys come to life. The room is invaded by an army of mice seeking the gingerbread man. The toy soldiers rise to the defense, led by the gallant Nutcracker. At the crisis of the battle, when the mice seem about to win, Clara throws her slipper at the mouse king, putting the mice to rout and the Nutcracker is transformed into a handsome prince. The Prince invites Clara to go with him on a visit to the Kingdom of Sweets.

On their way they pass (Scene 2) through a snowy forest. The dance of the snowflakes apparently was one of the most spectacular moments of the original ballet production, with fifty-nine figures, all in white, carrying wands of sparkling snowflakes. In many recent versions of the ballet the snowflakes dance in homage to Clara and her Prince.

At the palace of the Sugar-Plum Fairy (Act II) a great festival has been prepared for Clara's entertainment. This consists of a whole series of "character" dances and a grand duet or *pas de deux* in classical-ballet style for the Sugar-Plum Fairy and the Prince, which is the climax and conclusion of the ballet.

The Suite which Tchaikovsky extracted from his ballet score consists of eight numbers, including most of the best music. Aside from the opening Overture and the children's March from the first Act, the excerpts do not follow the plot of the ballet but are arranged in the most effective musical sequence, all drawn from the entertainment at the castle of the Sugar-Plum Fairy and concluding with the Waltz of the Flowers.

1. *Miniature Overture: Allegro giusto.* The enchanting lightness of this *Overture* is due partly to the fact that Tchaikovsky omits the low stringed instruments from the orchestra and keeps to the brighter violins, violas and woodwind instruments, with special emphasis on the high, sparkling tone of three piccolos.

2. *March.* Much the same playful mood and bright color return in this *March,* with its perky rhythms emphasized by cymbals and by rhythmic pluckings of the cellos and double-basses.

3. *Dance of the Sugar-Plum Fairy.* The Sugar-Plum Fairy is personified by the celesta, the tone of which so entranced Tchaikovsky and which he, as far as we know, was the first composer to use, in this specific piece. The celesta is a delicate instrument with soft, gleaming bell-like tones, and looks somewhat like a small upright piano.

4. *Russian Dance: Trepak.* This is the only national Russian note in the whole scene, a wildly energetic folk dance that rises to a *prestissimo* climax of excitement.

5. *Arab Dance.* Muted violas and cellos supply the gently rocking rhythm for a languorous dance melody, which is shared by soft woodwind instruments and muted violins.

6. *Chinese Dance.* The exotic mood of this *Dance* is set at the very opening by two bassoons which play the same harmony all the way through. In the very highest part of the orchestra, flutes and piccolos have the shrill, capricious melody, decked out with trills and other flourishes.

7. *Dance of the "Mirlitons."* The dancing *mirlitons* of this ballet are a special kind of crunchy pastry filled with whipped cream, a delicious accompaniment to either tea, coffee, or chocolate. But since *mirliton* is also the French word for a special kind of children's instrument often called a kazoo, (a kind of toy wind instrument) the title of this dance is often (quite incorrectly) translated as the "Dance of the Reed Pipes." Tchaikovsky keeps to the basic thought of a woodwind instrument and writes this graceful dance for a trio of orchestral flutes.

8. *Waltz of the Flowers.* Like many other serious composers, Tchaikovsky felt enormous admiration for the Viennese "waltz king" Johann Strauss, Jr. to whom he pays his respects in the graceful waltz which concludes the Suite.

The Suite is scored for 3 piccolos, 3 flutes, 2 oboes, English horn, 2 clarinets, bass clarinet, 4 bassoons, 4 horns, 2 trumpets, 3 trombones, tuba, harp, kettledrums, cymbals, triangle, tambourine, glockenspiel, celesta, and the standard strings.

ROMEO AND JULIET FANTASY OVERTURE

The composers who have been inspired, or who thought they were inspired by Shakespeare, make an endless list. And in that list, Tchaikovsky is one of the very few whose music speaks with the elemental passion and strife that grip us as do the words of Shakespeare. Yet incredible as it may seem, *Romeo and Juliet* was only the fourth of Tchaikovsky's published orchestral works. He composed it when he was twenty-nine. And it stands out among his works—a sudden blaze of inspiration, revealing a unique genius which, though it seldom burned with a steady flame, reached peaks of intensity equalled by few.

No amount of biography, history, analysis, or even speculation seem able to explain this masterpiece. It cannot be explained by his rather mild "love affair," as Tchaikovsky liked to call it, with the great singer, Désirée Artôt, who came to Moscow during the winter of 1868–1869 with an Italian opera company. Tchaikovsky admired Artôt intensely, wrote to his brother, Modest, enthusing about her "exquisite gesture, her grace of movement, her artistic poise!" and even considered marrying her, much against the advice of his friends. Artôt, for her part, cannot have taken his passion seriously, for within a month she married a popular baritone in Warsaw, where she had gone to sing. Tchaikovsky wept the next time he saw her on the stage a year later, but hardly suffered a broken heart.

A more concrete influence was Balakirev, whom Tchaikovsky admired, and to whom he had dedicated his symphonic poem, *Fate.* Balakirev not only suggested the Shakespearean subject for Tchaikovsky's next work, but actually wrote out a detailed program for the *Romeo* and a corresponding outline of the musical form, including the series of keys he thought would be appropriate. Balakirev had much to criticize in the original version of Tchaikovsky's *Romeo and Juliet,* which was completed in 1869. He objected especially to the original introduction, as lacking in beauty and power and not even sketching the character of Friar Laurence. "You need something here," Balakirev continued, "on the line of Liszt's chorales . . . with an ancient Catholic character, . . . whereas your scene . . . bears quite a different character—the character of Haydn's quartet themes, the genius of petty bourgeois music, awakening a strong thirst for beer." Tchaikovsky duly wrote a new introduction in his revision of 1870, to Balakirev's complete satisfaction, and made several corresponding changes where the music of the introduction reoccurs in the score. In 1880 Tchaikovsky revised his score for the last time, but his chief changes, according to Gerald Abraham, were the addition of dynamic markings.

For the analytically inclined it is fascinating to see how beautifully and eloquently the dramatic thread of the Romeo and Juliet story dovetails with Tchaikovsky's romantic version of traditional sonata-allegro form. But while this and other avenues of technical analysis might bring us closer to understanding, the core of the matter still eludes us. Can Tchaikovsky's youth have played a role in the quality of the music? When he completed his first version of the score, he was almost the same age Shakespeare was when he finished writing *Romeo and Juliet.*

The slow, hymnlike introduction recalls the peace of Friar Laurence's cell. The kindly friar himself is suggested by a prayerful, organlike passage for woodwinds. But the peace is soon broken. In a fiery *Allegro,* the ancient feud of the Montagues and Capulets rages through the orchestra.

Then, after a long hesitation, the love music of Romeo and Juliet begins in the soft, caressing voice of a solo clarinet:

At first its mood and even certain turns of phrase are reminiscent of Tchaikovsky's song *"Nur wer die Sehnsucht kennt,"* better known under the title of "None But the Lonely Heart." In Tchaikovsky's sketches for a duo from *Romeo and Juliet,* found in his papers after his death (and later orchestrated by his friend, Tanieviev), this marvelous, soaring melody builds the climax, a phrase on which Romeo sings: "Oh, tarry, night of ecstasy! Oh, night of love, stretch thy dark veil over us."

As the plot develops (in the "development" section of the music) the tender communion of the lovers is interrupted by the fury of the street brawls. The love music and the brawls clash and combine with the theme of Friar

Laurence. All these opposing forces rise to a great outburst of orchestral fury which is overwhelmed by the love music, only to die away in broken, sorrowing phrases. Finally the love music is transformed into a despairing lament, and the end comes with sharp, tragic chords of the orchestra.

The first performance of *Romeo and Juliet* was conducted by Nicholas Rubinstein at a concert of the Musical Society in Moscow on March 16, 1870. The score calls for piccolo, 2 flutes, 2 oboes, 2 clarinets, English horn, 2 bassoons, 4 horns, 2 trumpets, 3 trombones, bass tuba, kettledrums, cymbals, bass drum, harp, and the customary strings.

SERENADE IN C MAJOR, FOR STRING ORCHESTRA, OPUS 48

"You can imagine, beloved friend," Tchaikovsky wrote in October 1880, to his patron Nadeja von Meck, "that my muse has been benevolent of late, when I tell you that I have written two long works very rapidly: the festival overture [this was the *1812 Overture*] and a Serenade in four movements for string orchestra. The overture will be very noisy. I wrote it without much warmth or enthusiasm; and therefore it has no great artistic value. The Serenade, on the contrary, I wrote from an inward impulse: I felt it; and I venture to hope that this work is not without artistic qualities."

Tchaikovsky confided to the publisher Jurgenson that this work took the form of a serenade by accident. When he made the preliminary sketches he had envisioned it as something between a symphony and a string quartet. Its final form was an inspiration that delights all his admirers, the most sophisticated as well as the most undemanding. The first performance of the Serenade was given at the Moscow Conservatory late in 1880. The first public concert performance was also in Moscow on January 16, 1882. It was warmly welcomed.

Despite his usual tendency to underestimate even his best works, Tchaikovsky seems to have had a special fondness for this score. "I wish with all my heart that you could hear my Serenade properly performed," he wrote to Mme. von Meck in 1881. "It loses so much when played on the piano. I think that the middle movements, as played by the strings, would win your sympathy. . . . The first movement is my homage to Mozart: It is intended to be an imitation of his style, and I should be delighted if I thought I had in any way approached my model."

I. *Piece in Form of a Sonatina: Andante non troppo; Allegro moderato.* The slow introduction is based on a chorale-like theme which returns toward the end of this movement and again at the end of the *Finale:*

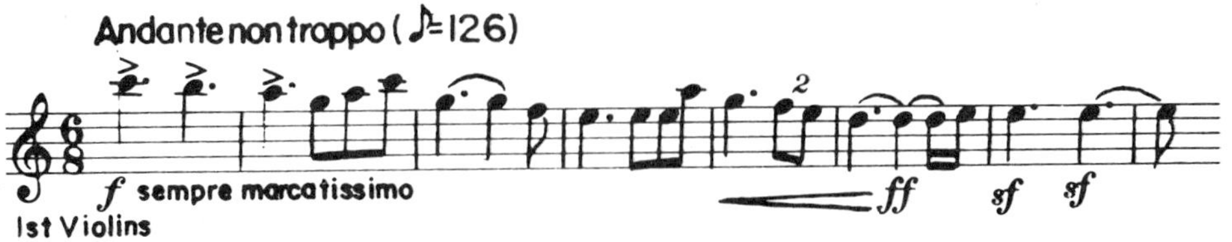

The main body of the Piece in Form of a Sonatina is lively and energetic with a strongly rhythmic first theme and a lightly skipping second theme for contrast.

II. *Waltz: Moderato, tempo di valse.* The graceful, lilting melody of this *Waltz* is one of the most popular and most charming in all of Tchaikovsky:

He had an especial flair and so loved the Viennese waltz style that his melody is hard to forget.

III. *Elegy: Larghetto elegiaco.* The wistful mood of the opening contrasts with a livelier middle section. For the return of the opening music the entire orchestra plays with mutes, producing a delicately veiled tone.

IV. *Finale: Andante; Allegro con spirito.* The slow introduction is based on a Russian folk tune, a Volga "hauling song." There is a bustling main theme:

This is related to the slow introduction to the first movement, which also returns toward the end in its original form. The conclusion comes with another brilliant outburst of the bustling main theme.

SYMPHONY NO. 2, C MINOR, OPUS 17, (LITTLE RUSSIAN)

The Second Symphony is unique among Tchaikovsky's six, for its strongly nationalistic flavor, specifically in its copious use of Little Russian folk music. Little Russia, the large area of southern Russia around Kharkov and Kiev, down to the Black Sea and the Sea of Azov, is better known as the Ukraine. It was not Tchaikovsky who first called his Second Symphony "Little Russian," but Tchaikovsky's friend, the eminent Russian music critic and professor at the Moscow Conservatory, Nicholas Kashkin. Early in the summer of 1872 Tchaikovsky visited his beloved sister, Alexandra, and her husband, Leo Davidov, on their estate in Kamenka in the Kiev Government. The songs he heard from the inhabitants of the little Ukranian town gave Tchaikovsky the idea to compose a new symphony. He began it at Kamenka, continued it while visiting a friend at Ussovo and completed it in Moscow. By November it was almost finished. Tchaikovsky apologized to his brother Modest for his long silence caused by the Symphony: "Modi, my conscience pricks me. That is my punishment for not having written to you for so long. But what can I do when the symphony, which is nearing completion, occupies me so entirely that I can think of nothing else? . . . It will be performed as soon as I can get the parts copied. It seems to me my best work, at least so far as correctness of form is concerned, a quality for which I have not so far distinguished myself."

During the Christmas holidays Tchaikovsky went to St. Petersburg, where he showed the manuscript of his new Symphony to Rimsky-Korsakoff and the other members of the Russian nationalist group known as the "Mighty Five": Moussorgsky, Borodin, Balakireff and Cui. They were enthusiastic, perhaps because they thought that Tchaikovsky's extensive use of folk melodies meant that he was veering towards their course.

The first performance of the new Symphony was given by the Imperial Music Society under the direction of Nicholas Rubinstein in Moscow on February 7, 1873. "My Symphony had great success," wrote Tchaikovsky to his friend, the great critic Vladimir Stassov in St. Petersburg. "So great, in fact, that N. Rubinstein is repeating it at the tenth concert by 'general request'." Yet Tchaikovsky was dissatisfied, especially with the first two movements.

Six years later, when he was about to revise his Second Symphony, he wrote from Paris to his "beloved friend," Madame von Meck, that "only the last movement can be left intact." On December 30, 1879 (this time from Rome), he wrote her: "Today I set out to remodel my Second Symphony. It went so well that before lunch I had made a rough draft of nearly half of the first movement [this is the only movement that Tchaikovsky appears to have completely recomposed]. How I thank the fate that made Bessel fail in his contract and never print this score! How much seven years can mean when a man is striving for progress in his work! Is it possible that seven years hence I shall look upon what I write today as I look now at my music written in 1872? I know it is possible because perfection—the ideal—is boundless, and in seven years I shall not yet be old."

The revised version was first performed by the Musical Society of St. Petersburg under the direction of K. Sike on February 2, 1881. Tchaikovsky's Second Symphony, in the final version as we know it today, was brought to the United States by the New York Symphony Society on December 8, 1883, only two years after it had been presented in Moscow. The founder-conductor of the Symphony Society, Leopold Damrosch, prided himself on keeping his New York audiences abreast of the European musical scene. Although Leopold Damrosch and his son Walter are remembered today particularly for their battle to establish the late Wagner works both in opera and in New York concert life, they pioneered for many other contemporary composers, notably Tchaikovsky. It was Walter Damrosch, his father's successor as the conductor of the Symphony Society, who was responsible for bringing Tchaikovsky to North America to take part in the festival performance inaugurating New York's Music Hall, later known as Carnegie Hall.

I. *Andante sostenuto; Allegro vivo.* The slow introduction begins with a melancholy solo for French horn, a melody taken from the Ukrainian variant of the folk song, "Down by Mother Volga." The fast main section begins with a theme which might easily be another Russian folk tune:

A contrasting lyric theme sung by the oboe has a gracefully rising chromatic line. Both themes are developed to a brilliant climax, followed by a reprise of the basic theme. A return of the slow opening tempo, with horn solo and muffled echo in the bassoon, rounds off the movement.

II. *Andantino marziale, quasi moderato.* The slow movement begins and ends with a soft two-note *ostinato* for the timpani, providing a sort of seesaw accompaniment to a march theme. This is the tragic wedding march from the last act of Tchaikovsky's opera *Undine,* composed in 1869 and later destroyed, except for certain excerpts which Tchaikovsky used in other works.

III. *Scherzo: Allegro molto vivace.* The agitated *Scherzo* has superb rhythmic drive which is interrupted only for a whimsical trio emphasizing the woodwinds.

IV. *Finale: Moderato assai.* Here, in the movement Tchaikovsky himself liked best of the four, he rings ingenious changes—harmonic, contrapuntal and instrumental—on the Little Russian folk tune, "The Crane":

A second more elaborate theme appears, is combined with "The Crane" and then swept aside again in the final exuberant climax of the *presto coda.*

The Symphony is scored for 2 flutes, piccolo, 2 oboes, 2 clarinets, 2 bassoons, 4 horns, 2 trumpets, 3 trombones, tuba, kettledrums, cymbals, bass drum, gong, and the customary string choir.

SYMPHONY NO. 4, F MINOR, OPUS 36

The idea of Fate played a tremendous role in Tchaikovsky's feelings about himself, about his Fourth Symphony, and about the two women who played crucial roles in his life at the time the Fourth Symphony was written.

"Fate, the mocker," he wrote in 1875, "has arranged that for the past ten years all whom I most love in the world are far from me. I am extremely lonely in Moscow. . . . Perhaps this is partly my own fault. I do not make friends easily. . . . Nearly all winter I was constantly unhappy, sometimes on the verge of despair. I longed for death. With the coming of spring these attacks have ceased, but I know that with every winter they will return stronger than ever."

The first of the two women was Nadeja von Meck, the "beloved friend," whom he never met, but who supported him, or partly supported him with her own money for many years. Mme. von Meck, who belonged to a completely different world both socially and financially, had fallen under the spell of Tchaikovsky's music. She began tactfully by giving him several commissions, which finally grew into a yearly stipend, relieving him of most material worries. But at the same time she had the intuitive good sense to specify that they should never meet. For years Tchaikovsky poured out his soul to her in long, long letters of self-analysis, analysis of his music, passionate letters of confidence and confession. For a man who lived in a world of private dreams and nightmares, even more than many artists do—for a man of Tchaikovsky's emotional instability, to whom existence was a cruel, incomprehensible tragedy—this shadowy, abstract intimacy with his "beloved friend" was a wonderful boon. Their friendship was shadowy, however, only in the sense that it involved Tchaikovsky in none of the difficulties of a direct human relationship. Her money was concrete enough.

The second of the two women was Antonina Ivanova Milyukova, a young student at the Conservatory where Tchaikovsky taught. She, too, had fallen under the spell of his music and wrote him frantic, adoring letters. These turned into ardent love letters, which first amused Tchaikovsky, then alarmed him, and finally flooded him with feelings of guilt. He was in the midst of composing his opera, *Eugen Onegin*, and had just finished the famous letter scene in whith Tatiana pours out her maidenly love for the hero, a love which is met with kindly but painful rejection. Although Tchaikovsky was not attracted to women, he finally consented to meet Antonina, but instead of helping matters this only made them worse. She threatened to commit suicide if he would not see her again, until at last it was a question of marriage. Tchaikovsky made it plain that he did not love her; all he could offer was friendship and solicitude. But she persisted and so, partly because he felt guilty of encouraging her, partly out of pity, partly because he hoped that marriage would cure him of his abnormality, and partly, as he had put it some months earlier, "to shut the mouths of all despicable gossips," he gave in and they were married.

It ended, as anyone who knew either Tchaikovsky or his wife could have predicted, in an explosion. Within a month, Tchaikovsky, in the most frightful agitation, rushed out of their Moscow home and spent the summer away from his wife. In the fall, he made one more attempt to take up their life together, and this time his mistaken chivalry brought him to the verge of madness.

He fled to St. Petersburg, had a complete nervous breakdown on the way, was taken to the hotel nearest the station there, where he lay unconscious for two days and then passed into a high fever. His doctors ordered him to go to Switzerland, and, gradually, in a quiet village on Lake Geneva, he won back his peace of mind and strength. And then, with the help of Mme. von Meck, he went back to his interrupted Fourth Symphony.

For a man of Tchaikovsky's artistic leanings, it would seem inevitable that some of his personal suffering found its way into the music he was writing at this time. His completion of the sketch for the Fourth Symphony coincides with his engagement to Antonina in May 1877. He orchestrated the first movement during August and September, the comparatively calm period between his two flights from his wife. The other three movements were completed during his convalescence in the Swiss Alps. Additional evidence connecting Tchaikovsky's talk of Fate, the Fate music in his Fourth Symphony and the tragedy of his marriage, is contained in a letter to Mme. von Meck, where he writes: "We cannot escape our fate, and there was something fatalistic about my meeting with this girl."

Tchaikovsky frankly admitted that his Symphony had a extramusical meaning, but declared it was impossible to put his meaning into words. Fortunately, he contradicted himself in a long, confidential letter to Mme. von Meck:

> Our Symphony has a program. That is to say it is possible to express the content in words, and I will tell you—and you alone—the meaning of the entire work and its separate movements. Naturally I can only do so as regards its general features.
>
> [I. *Andante sostenuto. Moderato con anima.*] The Introduction is the kernel, the quintessence, the chief thought of the whole Symphony. [Here Tchaikowsky quotes his opening theme.]

> This is Fate, the fatal power which hinders one in the pursuit of happiness from gaining the goal, which jealously provides that peace and comfort do not prevail, that the sky is not free from clouds—a might that swings, like the sword of Damocles, constantly over the head, that poisons continually the soul. This might is overpowering and invincible. There is nothing to do but submit and vainly to complain.

> The feeling of depression and loneliness grows stronger and stronger. Would it not be better to turn away from reality and lull one's self in dreams?

Oh joy! a sweet and tender dream enfolds me. A serene and radiant presence leads me on:

Deeper and deeper the soul is sunk in dreams. All that was dark and joyless is forgotten. . . .

No—these are but dreams: roughly we are awakened by Fate. Thus we see that life is only an everlasting alternation of somber reality and fugitive dreams of happiness. Something like this is the program of the first movement.

[II. *Andantino in modo di canzona.*] The second movement shows another phase of sadness. Here is that melancholy feeling which enwraps one when he sits at night alone in the house exhausted by work; the book which he had taken to read has slipped from his hand; a swarm of reminiscences has arisen. How sad it is that so much has already *been* and *gone!* And yet it is a pleasure to think of the early years. One mourns the past and has neither the courage nor the will to begin a new life. One is rather tired of life. One would fain rest awhile, recalling happy hours when young blood pulsed warm through our veins and life brought satisfaction. We remember irreparable loss. But these things are far away. It is sad, yet sweet, to lose one's self in the past.

[III. *Scherzo, Pizzicato ostinato: allegro.*] There is no determined feeling, no exact expression in the third movement. Here are capricious arabesques, vague figures which slip into the imagination when one has taken wine and is slightly intoxicated. The mood is now gay, now mournful. One thinks about nothing; one gives the fancy loose rein, which humors itself in evolving the most singular patterns. Suddenly there rush into the imagination the picture of a drunken peasant and a gutter song. Military music is heard passing by in the distance. These are disconnected pictures which come and go in the brain of the sleeper. They have nothing to do with reality; they are unintelligible, bizarre, out at the elbows.

[IV. *Finale: Allegro con fuoco.*] If you find no pleasure in yourself, look about you. Go to the people. See how they can enjoy life and give themselves up entirely to festivity. The picture of a folk holiday. Hardly have we had time to forget ourselves in the happiness of others when indefatigable Fate reminds us once more of its presence. The other children of men are not concerned with us. They do not spare us a glance nor stop to observe that we are lonely and sad. How merry and glad they all are. All their feelings are so inconsequential, so simple. And do you still say that all the world is immersed in sorrow? There still *is* happiness, simple, naïve happiness. Rejoice in the happiness of others—and you can still live.

I can tell you no more, dear friend, about the Symphony.

The Fourth Symphony is scored for 2 flutes, 2 oboes, 2 clarinets, 2 bassoons, 4 horns, 2 trumpets, 3 trombones, bass tuba, kettledrums, and the traditional strings.

SYMPHONY NO. 5, E MINOR, OPUS 64

Among the paradoxes of his personality was this: Tchaikovsky was a man so honest that he doubted his own honesty. While composing the Fifth Symphony, he wrote in his diary that he felt he was never entirely sincere in his letters. "Regardless to whom or why I write, I always worry about what impression the letter will produce not only on the correspondent but even on some casual reader. Therefore, I am posing. Sometimes, I *try* to make the tone of the letter simple and sincere, i.e., make it *seem* so. But, except for letters written in a moment of emotion, I am never myself in a letter." He seems to have had much the same qualms about the Fifth Symphony when it was new. To his "beloved friend" Nadeja von Meck he wrote: "Having played my Symphony twice in Petersburg and once in Prague, I have come to the conclusion that it is a failure. There is something repellent in it, some overexaggerated color, some insincerity of fabrication which the public instinctively recognizes. It was clear to me that the applause and ovations referred not to this but to other works of mine, and that the Symphony itself will never please the public. All this causes a deep dissatisfaction with myself."

Tchaikovsky's first mention of his Fifth Symphony appears to be in a letter of May 27, 1888, to his brother, Modest, to whom he confessed his fears that his imagination had "dried up." He was haunted by the fear that he was "written out," that he had no more music in him. Yet he did not give in easily to his fears. "I am hoping to collect, little by little, material for a symphony," he writes in the same letter. And the following month, he declared to Mme. von Meck: "Now I shall work my hardest. I am exceedingly anxious to prove to myself, as to others, that I am not played out as a composer. . . . Have I told you that I intend to write a symphony? The beginning was difficult; but now inspiration seems to have come. However, we shall see."

By August 6 he could write to Mme. von Meck that he had been working "with good results. I have orchestrated half of the Symphony." And three weeks later: "I am so glad that I have finished the Symphony that I forget my physical troubles. . . . In November I shall conduct a whole series of my works in St. Petersburg, at the Philharmonic, and the new Symphony will be one of them."

The first performances of the Symphony, both under Tchaikovsky's direction, took place on November 17 and 24, 1888, at St. Petersburg. The audiences were enthusiastic, but the critics almost unanimously lamented it as unworthy of Tchaikovsky. Modest believed that the reason the Fifth Symphony was slow to make its way among critics was his brother's lack of self-confidence as a conductor. It appears that if, during rehearsals, any orchestral musicians seemed to react negatively to a new score, Tchaikovsky would feel that he was wasting their time. He would rush apologetically through the remainder of the rehearsal, and conduct the performance without conviction, so that the initial impression of the work was weak. Only after a later performance of the Fifth Symphony in Hamburg, where the musicians were delighted and enthusiastic, did Tchaikovsky pick up courage. After the concert he wrote to his nephew, Vladimir Davidov: "The Fifth Symphony was magnificently played and I like it far better now, after having held a bad opinion of it for some time."

Was there any program or poetic concept behind the new Symphony? We know that the Fourth Symphony had such a program; Tchaikovsky himself described it at length. The Sixth also had a program, which Tchaikovsky never divulged. "Let him guess it who can," he wrote to his nephew. Although Tchaikovsky apparently never mentioned any program for his Fifth Symphony, it is unified by a striking theme which reappears so dramatically in all four movements that a "plot" of some sort is strongly suggested.

I. *Andante; Allegro con anima.* The core of the Fifth Symphony is the foreboding theme which begins the slow introduction:

Announced by two clarinets in their low, hollow-sounding *chalumeau* range, the melody is hard to forget. Many commentators interpret it as a menacing theme of Fate. Since we cannot read Tchaikovsky's mind, let us be content to call it the central theme, or motto of the Symphony.

The dark color of the introduction seems to linger on into the fiery *Allegro* of the first movement proper. Although its first theme has an infectious lilt, we hear it initially in the odd sonority of a clarinet and bassoon playing an octave apart. As the color grows brighter, the theme is fragmented and built up to a steep climax before the orchestra subsides for the contrasting lyric theme. This is one of Tchaikovsky's most yearning melodies:

The development section is a battlefield of rhythms and sonorities, the chief contenders being the brass choir versus the massed orchestral *tutti*.

II. *Andante cantabile, con alcuna licenza.* After a brief introduction in the deeper strings, a solo French horn sings the principal melody, which is, if possible, even more nostalgic than the songful theme above. How Tchaikovsky could ever have considered such an inspiration "fabricated" or "insincere" is difficult to understand:

The emotional intensity swells as the horn solo grows into a horn duet, followed by a solo oboe with a new melody, and, in the middle section, a solo clarinet in yet another strain of characteristically Tchaikovskian melancholy.

Suddenly this lyricism is interrupted by the motto theme in a *fortissimo* trumpet blast. There is a pause. Then, as if in protest, the opening melodies return and again the longing swells to a passionate outpouring. Once again, there is a terrifying eruption of the motto, this time in heavier trombone tones. The nostalgic mood is shattered, and the movement dies away with pleading, broken phrases.

III. *Valse: Allegro moderato.* On the surface, the third movement may seem merely a charming waltz. But there is an undertone of melancholy which never completely disappears. The melody is developed from an Italian street song which Tchaikovsky had heard ten years earlier and described in a homesick letter to Mme. von Meck: "Do you remember I wrote you from Florence about the boy I heard one evening on the street, whose beautiful voice so affected me? Three days ago, to my great joy I found the boy again, he sang for me again. . . . I don't remember when a simple popular song has had such effect on me. This time he introduced me to a new Florentine song, so charming that I want to find him again and make him sing it several times, so that I can write down the words and music." Just before the end of this wistful movement, the motto theme stirs in the depths of the orchestra, like an unhappy memory.

IV. *Andante maestoso; Allegro vivace.* In the opening *Andante* the memory of gloom, defeat, Fate, or whatever it may be—in short, the motto theme—is transformed into a song of triumph, first merely by shifting the key from E minor to E major, second by entrusting the melody to the warm tones of the strings. Then, as the melody marches on to the woodwind choir, the strings weave a background of flowing triplet rhythm, a traditional symbol of rejoicing.

A roll of the kettledrums leads to the final *Allegro vivace.* A whole bevy of rapid, joyous woodwind figures courses through the orchestra. The motto theme returns in ever more glowing colors. There is an extraordinarily compact and concentrated, polyphonic development section and the Symphony rushes on to an exultant close. In the concluding bars the motto theme is still further transformed into trumpet fanfares irresistibly suggestive of victory.

The Fifth Symphony is scored for piccolo, 3 flutes, 2 oboes, 2 clarinets, 2 bassoons, 4 horns, 2 trumpets, 3 trombones, tuba, kettledrums, and the traditional strings.

SYMPHONY NO. 6, B MINOR, OPUS 74 (PATHÉTIQUE)

This Symphony has always posed a problem. Tchaikovsky admitted to his nephew, Vladimir Davidoff, to whom the Sixth Symphony is dedicated, that it had a program. But he refused to tell what it was. "Let him guess it who can," he wrote.

There was no lack of guessers until, between World Wars I and II, there turned up among Tchaikovsky's sketches a sheet of music paper with the following penciled notes:

> The ultimate essence of the plan of the Symphony is *LIFE*. First part—all impulsive passion, confidence, thirst for activity. Must be short. (Finale *DEATH*—result of collapse.)
>
> Second part love; third disappointments; fourth ends dying away (also short).

This was found among papers and drafts which led Gerald Abraham and other authorities on Tchaikovsky and Russian music to believe it belongs to the year 1892. In May 1892 Tchaikovsky began a symphony in E flat, which he soon set aside as "an empty pattern of sounds." But this seems to have had no relation to the life-and-death subject outlined above. The conclusion seems almost inescapable that the gloomy little sketch did represent an early program for the Sixth Symphony.

"I am now wholly occupied with the new work [the Sixth Symphony]," he wrote his brother Anatole on February 22, 1893, "and it is hard for me to tear myself away from it. I believe it is being born as the best of my works. I must finish it as soon as possible, for I have many affairs to wind up, and I must also go to London soon. I told you that I had completed a symphony which suddenly displeased me, and I tore it up. Now, I have composed a new symphony, *which I certainly shall not tear up*." On his return from London, Tchaikovsky wrote his older brother, Modest, that he was head-over-heels in his Symphony: "The orchestration gets more difficult, the farther I go. Twenty years ago, I let myself write easily without much thought, and it was all right. Now I have become cowardly and uncertain. I have sat all day over two pages. What I wished for has constantly come to nothing. In spite of this I do make progress."

On August 24, 1893, he wrote his publisher, Jürgenson, that he had finished the orchestration: "I give you my word of honor that never in my life have I been so contented, so proud, so happy, in the knowledge that I have written a good piece." To another friend, he wrote, "I myself consider it the best and especially the most open-hearted of my works. I love it as I have never loved any of my other musical creations."

The world has agreed with him. In spite of the brilliance and excitement of his Fourth and Fifth Symphonies, it is clear that the *"Pathétique"* is the work of a man at last complete master of symphonic form and idiom and, most important of all, master of his own wild emotions. The sable splendor of this music is no masquerade. His deviations from the Classical norm all ring true. There is no traditional slow movement, for example, but instead an uneasy dance in five-four meter. And the *finale,* instead of being light, witty, militant or triumphant, is a song of farewell and despair.

I. *Adagio; Allegro non troppo.* In the slow introduction, the dark voice of a solo bassoon introduces what will later become the main theme of the first movement: a figure that turns and twists and grovels at the bottom of the orchestra:

When the tempo quickens, this theme is fragmented and tossed about from instrument to instrument with rising agitation. Then the excitement dies down to prepare for the famous melody of the second theme, which is like a recollection of happiness in time of pain. The development opens with a crash. It is tortuous and intricate, its nervous pace sometimes approaching the pitch of hysteria. Finally it rises to another powerful climax. The traditional recapitulation of the opening themes is condensed, and the movement closes on a solemn cadence for the brasses with the resigned falling scale of *pizzicato* strings.

II. *Allegro con grazia.* There is no traditional slow movement, but instead an oddly graceful dance in five-four meter, like a waltz with a mysterious limp.

III. *Allegro molto vivace.* The third movement begins softly, in almost impressionistic confusion. Indistinct whirling figures appear and vanish. Then, we hear a hint of a distant march:

It seems to approach, grows louder, defiant, almost arrogant. It seems to sweep everything before it; but for all its swagger and defiance, there is terror behind this power. There is a furious climax, which nevertheless seems far from any triumph; it could equally well be a crash to destruction.

IV. *Adagio lamentoso; Andante.* The lamenting *finale* could almost be called a requiem, except that this music envisions no eternal rest or, apparently, anything at all beyond the grave. The opening phrase of the strings is like a pathetic sigh for the blackness and nothingness of the end. Even the wonderfully melodious second theme, a simple flowing line for the violins, has more the color of an affectionate, lingering farewell than a consoling thought:

The climax to which this movement builds is not one of affirmation or of defiance in the face of tragedy, but almost a savoring of the depths of despair. It fades away to the tolling of a gong (tam-tam). When the melodious second theme returns, it is transformed into the gloomy tonic minor mode, and its falling line seems almost symbolic as it descends in pitch, grows darker in color and finally dies away on a long *diminuendo* to an almost inaudible *pppp*.

The score calls for 3 flutes, piccolo, 2 oboes, 2 clarinets, 2 bassoons, 4 horns, 2 trumpets, 3 trombones, tuba, tam-tam, kettledrums, bass drum, cymbals, and strings.

The first performance of the Sixth Symphony was conducted by Tchaikovsky himself on October 28, 1893, at St. Petersburg. It was only moderately successful, and the critics were decidedly cool.

Georg Philipp Telemann

Born March 14, 1681, Magdeburg—died June 25, 1767, Hamburg

SUITE, A MINOR, FOR FLUTE AND STRING ORCHESTRA

Few composers are blessed with the effortless grace that Telemann shows in this beguiling Suite. Fewer still combine his spontaneous charm with such sturdy musical substance. And no major composer we know has equaled him in sheer productivity. We are impressed by Bach's total of over 300 cantatas, but Telemann produced over 1,700! Bach has left us four orchestral suites (called overtures in his day). Telemann composed over *two hundred.* And this was no mere fluff! Telemann was a serious musician with a stupendous technique. Handel reportedly said of him that Telemann composed a cantata as easily as another man would write a letter.

None of Telemann's works (as far as they have been rescued from oblivion) equals the power of a Handel *Messiah* or the stupendous organ chorales of J.S. Bach. But power and profundity were not his primary aims. These had come to seem old-fashioned virtues. Telemann appealed to laymen and professionals alike—largely because his music seemed newer, lighter, simpler and hence, more "natural," to use the newly popular term associated with Jean-Jacques Rousseau.

We do not know when Telemann composed this A-minor Suite. The undated manuscript was discovered in the 1930s in the Darmstadt Library by the Telemann authority Horst Büttner. Like the Bach suites and many others of Telemann's day, this one begins with a traditional French overture followed by a number of lighter movements, mostly dance types.

I. *Ouverture.* The introductory section, a majestic *grave* or *lento* with vigorous "dotted" rhythms, was in a tradition of representational pomp that dated back to Lully, the court composer of Louis XIV.

The main body of the *Overture* is a lively fugue, led off by the first violins with each string section joining in with its own version of the theme. So far everything has been quite grand and Baroque in spirit. Suddenly the texture lightens and the solo flute takes over, accompanied only by violins, in a sparkling, capricious spinning out of the fugue theme. All at once we have the impression that we are listening to a very "modern" concerto for solo flute—a charming effect and a perfect symbol of a work which crosses and recrosses the dividing line between Baroque and Rococo. The majestic closing section reflects the mood, texture and tempo of the introduction.

II. *Les plaisirs.* This is a playful, dancelike movement, first for orchestra alone, then for flute solo accompanied only by the harpsichord, and finally a return to the opening music.

III. *Air à l'italien.* This "Aria in Italian Style" is a deliberate instrumental imitation of *the* operatic form of the day, the so-called *da capo* aria. A brief orchestral introduction leads to the solo (with the flute taking over the role of the human voice). Solo and orchestral accompaniment are kept clearly distinct from each other. The lively middle section of the *Aria* is followed by a reprise of the opening.

IV. *Menuet.* The opening section, light and piquant in its rhythms, is for string orchestra alone. The middle section is a solo for the flute with the orchestra confined to discreet accompaniment. The movement is rounded off by a reprise of the opening section.

V. *Passepied.* Another popular dance type, this lively *Passepied* follows the same form as the *Menuet.* A first section for strings contrasts with a central flute solo (accompanied only by *continuo* with harpsichord), and is followed by a reprise of the opening section.

VI. *Polonaise.* Although it is far from the rousing polonaise rhythms familiar to us from Chopin's piano works, this Polish national dance type was already popular in its more sedate Rococo version.

VII. *Réjouissance: Viste.* The "Rejoicing" of the title is easy to hear in the agile, fluttering phrases of the solo flute and its echo in the orchestra. This is a brilliant, virtuoso display for the soloist.

Virgil Thomson

Born November 25, 1896, Kansas City, Missouri

THE SEINE AT NIGHT

Soon after Virgil Thomson had completed *The Seine at Night* in 1947, this score and his earlier *Symphony on a Hymn Tune* were played over for a group of friends. According to Henry Cowell, one of the listeners asked "How does it happen, Mr. Thomson, that you have two such widely different styles? The *Symphony* is so stark and plain and the new tone-poems so delicately impressionistic in color."

"Oh," replied Thomson blandly, "the *Symphony on a Hymn Tune* was written to present Kansas City to the Parisians, and *The Seine at Night* is intended to describe Paris to people from Kansas City."

Thomson was well qualified to present Kansas City to Paris and vice versa, for he was raised in Kansas City and worked as an organist and choir master there until he was drafted into the army for World War I at the age of twenty-one. After the war and some further study at Harvard, Thomson went to Paris to study with Nadia Boulanger. There he made friends with Gertrude Stein, Eric Satie and the group of young French composers known as The Six, who were in revolt against Impressionism. From 1925 until the outbreak of World War II Thomson made his home in Paris. In 1940 he returned and became music critic of the *New York Herald Tribune*, remaining until 1954, when he resigned to devote himself entirely to composing and conducting.

The Seine at Night is dedicated to the Kansas City Philharmonic Orchestra. It is not really as different from Thomson's other works up to this time as many listeners first thought it was. Habitually he had always tended to avoid lush romantic harmonies in favor of simple triads which sometimes made for radically simple sounds, and sometimes, when the triads clashed, for very sharp dissonance. *The Seine at Night*, too, is strongly triadic, and the impressionistic effect of some of its harmonies are due to the mild dissonances between the triads and melodies like the following, which opens the score:

The modal sound of this principal theme is characteristic of *The Seine at Night* and so is the extremely simple, triadic background. However, this little tone-poem is anything but simple in its artistic essence, which is precise, fastidious, and achieves a maximum of harmonic and instrumental color with minimum means. The violins, occasionally reinforced by the woodwinds, continue the melodic flow, which rises in successive waves, higher and higher, until a brilliant orchestral climax brings in the heavy brass. This subsides quickly leaving the first theme floating in the upper regions of the orchestral winds, with slowly rising harp glissandos in the background. Now it is the woodwinds that continue the gentle melodic flow, against a background chiefly of simple string triads.

This whole delicate tone picture seems already to fade away, when a succession of wavelike figures on the strings brings a passing brilliance. Once more, just before the end, the gentle motion of the beginning is resumed, it rises to one more climax of glowing color, and then evaporates into silence.

Thomson's *The Seine at Night* is scored for an orchestra of 3 flutes, 3 oboes, 3 clarinets, 3 bassoons, 4 horns, 3 trumpets, 3 trombones, tuba, kettledrums, percussion, harp, celesta, and the regular strings.

Edgard Varèse

Born December 22, 1883, Paris—died November 6, 1965, New York City

ARCANA

When Varèse finished the first version of his *Arcana* in 1927, it was one of the boldest scores of its day and one of the most irritating to people of conservative taste. Today, by comparison, it seems positively tame: a far from arcane extension of attitudes and techniques which Stravinsky had brought to a preliminary climax in his 1913 *Rite of Spring* and then abandoned.

Although Varèse considered himself an American composer and was domiciled in New York City during all of his mature life, he was born in France and did not come to the United States until 1915, when he was thirty-two years old. Like several twentieth-century composers, he had studied mathematics and science before music. By the time he became one of the most brilliant pupils of D'Indy, Roussel and Busoni, he was already a rebel, ready to defend his own ideas and even to disregard, on occasion, the orders of his illustrious teachers.

Among Varèse's earliest and most prophetic convictions was that modern science should make possible the new acoustical effects which he was constantly imagining and which could be only approximated on the conventional instruments then available. He became "obsessed," as he himself said, with the concept of space in music. He once told me that this obsession came to him, neither from the Berlioz *Requiem* (of which he conducted a memorable performance soon after his arrival in New York) nor from the Venetian polychoral style of the sixteenth century (with which he was very familiar), but from claustrophobia, which had plagued him when he was a child.

Most music sounded to him terribly "corseted." "When you project a tone in an enclosed space," he said, "it is like an object attached to the end of an elastic. Before you know it, it comes back and hits you in the face. I like music that explodes into space. I like a nice rich sound." From the age of twenty he felt sure "that somehow I would someday realize a new kind of music that would be spatial—from then on I thought only of music as spatial. . . ."

Today, as we listen to such relatively early works of Varèse as *Arcana*, there is a temptation to hear them as preliminaries, as first steps toward his late electronic works—especially since we know that Varèse later went through a period of more than ten years of experimentation and searching for new sounds—a decade during which he completed no new works, but at the end of which he did find what he was searching for, namely the newly invented means of producing electronic music. He had imagined the sounds before he was able to produce them. The liberation that this proved to be for Varèse's creative faculties, and the renewed productivity of his last years could easily trap us into viewing everything that went before as a preparation for his electronic works. But to listen with such hindsight would be to falsify so richly inventive and self-sufficient a score as *Arcana*.

Varèse began *Arcana* in 1925, the year when he bought the house on Sullivan Street in New York City which was his home for the rest of his life. The title, *Arcana*, or its original French form, *Arcanes*, was an afterthought. It came to him while composing, when his wife showed him a copy of Paracelsus' *The Hermetic Philosophy*. This suggested the title for the work that was taking shape. In addition he prefaced the score with the following quotation from Paracelsus: "One star exists higher than all the rest. This is the apocalyptic star. The second star is that of the ascendant. The third is that of the elements—of these there are four, so that six stars are established. Besides there is still another star, imagination, which begets a new star and a new heaven."

In order to avoid misunderstanding, Varèse later said of the above quotation: "This extract is equivalent to a dedication; it makes of my symphonic poem a kind of tribute to the author of those words; but they did not inspire it, and the work is not a commentary upon them."

Much of Varèse's work on *Arcana* was done during the summer and fall of 1925 in Paris. Since Mrs. Varèse had shouldered the responsibility for remodeling and furnishing their Sullivan Street house, she could not accompany him. So Varèse's numerous letters kept her posted on the progress of *Arcana*. One of the most interesting, dated Friday, October 9 [1935] enclosed several bars of fanfares, with the description of a dream in which he heard them. On the reverse of the scrap of music paper with the fanfares he wrote:

> The two Fanfares I dreamed—I was on a boat that was turning around and around—in the middle of the ocean—spinning around in great circles. In the distance I could see a light house, very high—and on the top an angel—and the angel was you—a trumpet in each hand. Alternating projectors of different colors: red, green, yellow, blue—and you were playing Fanfare no. 1, trumpet in right hand. Then suddenly the sky became incandescent—blinding—you raised your left hand to your mouth and the Fanfare 2 blared. And the boat kept turning and spinning—and the alternation of projectors and incandescence became more frequent—intensified—and the fanfares more nervous—impatient . . . and then—*merde*—I woke up. But anyway they will be in *Arcanes*.*

On a subsequent postcard he jotted: "*Arcanes*—Never have I written music as solid, as joyous—as full of force, of life, of sun. *Arcanes* is developing in a new phase—"

---

* *Translation by Louise Varèse, from her* Varèse, a Looking-Glass Diary, *Vol. I: 1883–1928 (New York: W.W. Norton and Co.) p. 238.*

VARÈSE: "THE FANFARES I DREAMED . . ."

The fanfares for *Arcana,* which Varèse dreamed, were so vivid that he noted them down in a letter to his wife. His two-line comment translates:

here are the whistlings or rather the Fanfares of Pinto –2– or rather, the 2nd a variant of the 1st. They are noted at real pitch, that is they sound as written. Show to no one except Carlos** whom you must hug for me. (On the piano this sounds con, but it will really fart in the orchestra.)*

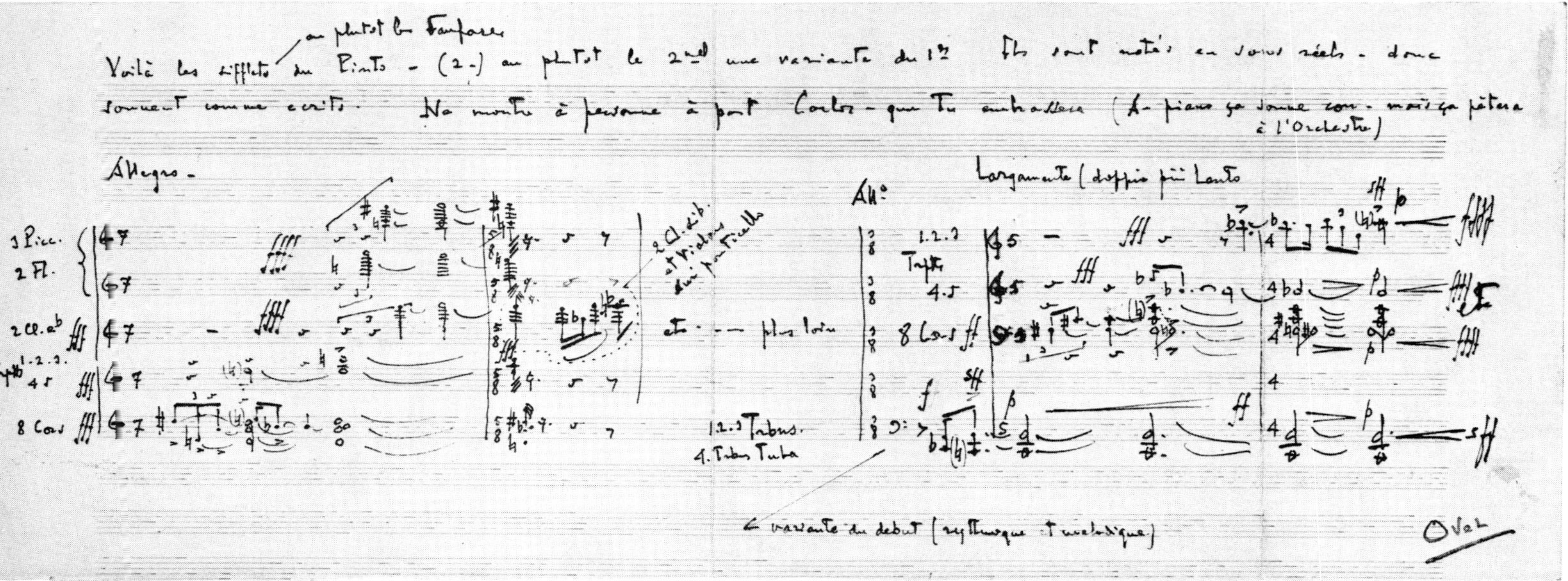

(Courtesy, Louise Varèse)

*Pinto: a pet name for Varèse's wife, Louise, who wore bangs that reminded him of a Pinto pony.

**Carlos Salzedo, the famous harpist, who was a co-crusader with Varèse for contemporary music.

Then, on October 29, Varèse wrote that he had destroyed everything he had written and was beginning all over again. But the dream-fanfares persisted intact. The curious listener can hear fanfare number 1 at the very beginning (measures three and four of the printed score) precisely as recorded from Varèse's dream, while the second bursts from the brass and woodwind in measures nineteen through twenty-two: literally a dream come true!

The very foundation of the work is a single idea, which Varèse called an *idée fixe* (a term he borrowed from Berlioz), rather than a conventionally symphonic theme. This "obsessive idea" consists of three notes: an ascending minor third repeated in a syncopated rhythm. It is given out at once in the first measure, almost like a motto, by the dark combination of Heckelphone, bassoons, tuba, cellos, and kettledrums.

The structure of the score has been compared with the repetitive pattern of the Baroque passacaglia. The *idée fixe* returns in a hundred guises, from jazzy syncopations to jaunty Gallic marching tunes, to moments when, as Stravinsky himself observed, "perhaps some of *me* peaks through . . . too. . . ." Many listeners would agree with Stravinsky that there are fleeting echoes of his *Rite of Spring*, *Petrushka*, and *The Firebird*. But the totality of *Arcana* does not sound derivative. Varèse's originality, especially his imagination in the new world of sonority he created, dominates from start to finish.

The first performance of Arcana was presented at the Philadelphia Academy of Music on April 8, 1927, by the Philadelphia Orchestra, under the direction of Leopold Stokowski. The New York premiere followed four days later. Berlin and Paris both waited five years before they heard the revolutionary score of Varèse, who already loomed as a major figure on the international scene. Varèse revised his score in 1930 and again in 1960, deleting certain bits which he may have felt referred too obviously to American jazz idiom, and altering a conclusion of the score, which may have seemed too obvious in another sense.

The orchestra required for *Arcana* is enormous: some 120 instruments with especial emphasis on percussion, which almost balances the strings and winds in importance. Specifically the score calls for 3 piccolos, 2 flutes, 3 oboes, English horn, Heckelphone, 2 high clarinets in E flat, 2 B-flat clarinets, contrabass clarinet, 3 bassoons, 2 contrabassoons, 8 horns, 5 trumpets, 2 tenor trombones, 1 baritone trombone, 1 bass trombone, tuba, contrabass tuba, 6 kettledrums, 2 bass drums, side drum, snare drum, string drum, 3 tambourines, medium gong, high tam-tam, low tam-tam, 2 pairs of cymbals, suspended cymbal (with drumstricks), Chinese cymbal, 4 triangles, slap-stick, 3 Chinese blocks (both high and low, with drumsticks and metal sticks), 2 coconuts, 2 guiros, rattle, xylophone, glockenspiel, bells, 16 first violins, 16 second violins, 14 violas, 12 cellos, and 10 basses tuned to low C.

ECUATORIAL

Although he hated to be called an experimental composer ("All my experimenting is done *before* I compose"), one would do Edgard Varèse no injustice to call him a prophet and a pioneer—one of the boldest and loneliest (in his early years) and one of the most lionized after "modern" music appeared at last to have caught up with him. Fortunately Varèse had immense self-confidence. He *knew* the general belief that an artist can be "ahead of his time" is lazy-minded nonsense. "An artist is never *ahead* of his time," Varèse often declared, "but most people are *behind* their own time."

The first work in which Varèse incorporated an electronic instrument was *Ecuatorial.* He pursuaded Leon Theremin, the inventor of the first electronic musical instrument, the "thereminvox," to construct two instruments according to the composer's specifications.

But it would be misleading to imply that Varèse's musical imagination was stimulated only by spatial concepts and dreams of new sonorities. His intellectual curiosity was enormous and the inspiration for his *Ecuatorial* was an ancient Mayan prayer from a sacred book, the *Popol Vuh* of the Maya Quiches, a tribe associated with the area of present-day Guatemala.

The prayer, translated into Spanish by Father Jimines, was incorporated into the *Léyendas de Guatémala,* published in 1930 by the Guatemalan poet and student of Mayan civilization Miguel Angel Asturias. Asturias, who knew and admired Varèse, sent him a copy of his book, and Varèse was at once taken by a prayer which Asturias described as "the invocation of the tribes lost in the mountains after abandoning the City of Abundance."

Varèse was extremely susceptible to, and sometimes inspired by, beautiful singing. According to Louise Varèse's memoir of her husband, *Varèse, A Looking-Glass Diary,** he composed *Ecuatorial* with the great Russian bass, Feodor Chaliapin, in mind:

> Soon after he began the score [writes Mrs. Varèse], one evening at a party, we were sitting with Chaliapin drinking champagne, his favorite drink (how many times the waiter refilled his glass I failed to count), when Varèse in his eager way began describing his work and dramatically recited part of the text, an invocation from the Maya's sacred book. . .
>
> "What nobility!" Varèse exclaimed. "But I simply must have a bass voice with a baritone—a lyric quality (an oratorio bass would kill it) and absolutely a singer who is an actor with imagination." Then he laughed and said to Chaliapin, "You see what I mean!"
>
> At which Chaliapin, matching Varèse's enthusiasm with true Russian responsiveness cried: "I'll do it! I must be the first to sing your work. Waiter, champagne!" And we drank to the coming collaboration.

But this was not to be. The first performance of *Ecuatorial* took place in Town Hall, New York on April 15, 1934, with Chase Baromeo, bass, and

---

* *New York: W.W. Norton and Co., 1972.*

Nicolas Slonimsky conducting, under the auspices of the Pan-American Association for Composers. The performance was a failure—partly because of faulty balances among the (amplified) bass voice, the thereminvox oscillators and the orchestra, which consisted of 4 trumpets, 4 trombones, piano, pipe organ, kettledrum, 2 snare drums, 2 tenor drums, 3 bass drums, 2 tam-tams, cymbals, suspended cymbal, temple blocks, tambourine plus two thereminvox oscillators.

It was twenty-seven years before there was a second performance. For this occasion, which the writer remembers very vividly, Varèse revised his score to the extent of substituting a small male chorus for the bass solo, and two *ondes Martenots* (reaching up to approximately 12,000 cycles per second) for the primitive early thereminvox. The all-Varèse program, under the direction of Robert Craft, in Town Hall on May 1, 1961, was a tribute to the seventy-eight-year-old composer and a triumph which must have warmed his heart.

According to Varèse's preface to *Ecuatorial,* his title was intended merely to suggest the regions where pre-Colombian art flourished. "I can see the music as having something of the same elemental rude intensity of those strange, primitive works. The execution should be dramatic and incantatory, guided by the imploring fervor of the text, and should follow the dynamic indications of the score."

Here is the official English translation of the Spanish text [which in turn is a translation of the Mayan *Popol Vuh*]:

> O Builders, O Moulders! You see, You hear. Do not abandon us, Spirit of the Sky, Spirit of the Earth. Give us our descendants, our posterity as long as there are days, as long as there are dawns. May greens roads be many, the green paths you give us. Peaceful, very peaceful may the tribes be. Perfect, very perfect may life be, the existence you give us. O Master Giant, Path of the Lightning, Falcon! Master-magi, Powers of the Sky, Procreators, Begetters! Ancient Mystery, Ancient Sorceress, Ancestress of the Day, Ancestress of the Dawn! Let there be germination, let there be Dawn. Hail Beauties of the Day, Givers of Yellow, of Green! Givers of Daughters, of Sons! Give life, existence to my children, to my descendants. Let not your power, let not your sorcery be their evil and their misfortune. May it be happy, the life of your upholders, your providers before your mouths, before your faces, Spirit of the Sky, Spirit of the Earth. Give Life, Give Life! Give Life, O All-Enveloping Force in the Sky, on the earth, at the four corners, at the four extremities, as long as dawn exists, as long as the tribe exists!

INTEGRALES

Begun in a Parisian studio (rue Notre-Dame-des-Champs) in the summer of 1924 and completed early 1925 in New York, *Intégrales* was one of the first scores to show with uncompromising clarity and force, the direction in which Varèse was heading. When it was first performed in the spring of 1926 in New York by the Philadelphia Orchestra under the direction of Leopold Stokowski for the International Composers Guild, there were those who pulled a long face, but the applause, according to Lawrence Gilman, writing in the *New York Herald-Tribune*, "was so insistent that Mr. Stokowski repeated the work to an audience plainly reluctant to call it a day."

The score is in one movement of three sections. In the first, the basic idea (indeed, one might almost call it a "theme") is announced by a shrill-voiced E-flat clarinet. It consists of one repeated tone preceded by two grace notes in a swift upward leap of an augmented fourth:

Immediately the idea is repeated, the repetitions of the single tone growing more insistent. As the idea is taken up by a muted trumpet, an oboe, a trumpet without mute and a solo horn, it grows and flowers, so to speak, the repeated tone reaching out to its neighbors, but without ever losing its striking identity:

The second section begins (after a strong climax of the brass and a sudden silence) with the softly dissonant whistle of high piccolos. The basic idea is developed, particularly the rhythmic aspect of its repeated tone.

The concluding section (which also begins after a strong, dissonant climax) starts with barely audible percussion. An oboe seems to develop the idea of a sustained or repeated note reaching out to its neighbors, but this time in a chromatic, almost Oriental-sounding style. There are other developments of the basic idea heard at the beginning of the score and the conclusion is reached with another powerfully dissonant climax.

Intégrales is scored for 2 piccolos, oboe, E-flat clarinet, B-flat clarinet, horn, 2 trumpets, 3 trombones (including contrabass trombone) and a large percussion battery including suspended cymbal, snare drum, tenor drum, string drum ("lion" or "bull roar"), castanets, pair of cymbals. Chinese blocks, sleigh bells, chains, tambourine, low gong, low tam-tam, triangle, wire brush (to be played on the shell of the bass drum), bass drum and slap stick (or whip).

IONISATION

From the time that he ran away from home at the age of eighteen to become a composer, Edgard Varèse was a rebel. From his earliest youth, he dreamed of a "music made of sound set free." As a young boy he was fascinated by experiments which the German scientist Helmholz had made with sirens. "I made some modest experiments of my own with sirens," Varèse told this writer, "and I found I could obtain beautiful parabolic and hyperbolic curves equivalent for me to the parabolas and hyperbolas in the visual domain. From then on I knew that somehow I would someday realize a new kind of music that would be spatial."

So strong was Varèse's need to create new musical sounds that for a ten-year period starting in 1937 he completed no new works. Was he frustrated by the limitations of conventional instruments? With the post-World War II development of electronic instruments, Varèse found tools to realize some of his early dreams.

Meanwhile, one of the boldest and most imaginative works of Varèse's maturity, composed in 1931 and 1932 in Paris, was his *Ionisation.* Hardly had he begun his new score (entirely for percussion) than he discovered a new eloquent musical instrument: the feet of the now legendary Spanish flamenco dancer Vincente Escudero. Fanatically devoted to the sternest traditions of his ancient art, Escudero seemed endowed with almost superhuman rhythmic vitality, which may have been one of his attractions for Varèse. Dispensing with any orchestral accompaniment, even with his traditional Spanish castanets, Escudero could orchestrate his own dances with the subtle shades of color, dynamics, rhythm, and counterpoint of his footwork. According to whether he struck the floor with the toe, the heel, or the sole of his boot, with what force, what tempo, *accelerando* or *ritardando, crescendo* or *diminuendo,* or *subito piano,* he had a thousand nuances and surprises at his command. It is hard for anyone who has not watched and *listened* to consummate flamenco dancing to begin to imagine the *sound* of the greatest of them all.

Varèse was almost hypnotized. For weeks he worked at *Ionisation* with the thought of Escudero as a collaborator. He even began to refer to *Ionisation* as his Escudero piece. But as *Ionisation* took on a life and a will of its own, Varèse reluctantly realized that he could not confine it closely enough to the strict traditions of Escudero's great art. *Ionisation* could not be tied down, and in the end Varèse could have written of it (and many another piece), as he had earlier apropos of his *Intégrales*: "The music is not a story, is not a picture, is not a psychological nor a philosophical abstraction. It is quite simply my music. It has definite form, which may be apprehended more justly by listening to the music than by rationalizing about it. I repeat what I have before written, analysis is sterile. To explain by means of it is to decompose, to mutilate the spirit of the work. As to the title of a score, it is of no importance. It serves as a convenient means of cataloguing the work. I admit that I get much amusement out of choosing my titles—a sort of parental pastime, like christening a newborn child, very different from the more intense business of begetting. I find no fun in family names. I often borrow from higher mathematics or astronomy, only because these sciences stimulate my imagination and give me the impression of movement, of rhythm. For me there is more musical fertility in the contemplation of the stars—preferably through a telescope—and the high poetry of certain mathematical expositions than in the most sublime gossip of human passions. However there are no planets or theorems to be looked for in my music. Music, being a special form of thought, can, I believe, express nothing but itself."

Ionisation was first performed at a Carnegie Hall concert of the Pan American Association of Composers on March 6, 1933, with Nicolas Slonimsky conducting. It was received with enormous enthusiasm by one part of the audience and with horror-struck puzzlement by the other.

The impact of the new work seemed all the greater for its brevity: it lasts barely six minutes. The score calls for percussion instruments—37 of them to be played by 13 musicians: two sirens (one high, one low in pitch), 2 tam-tams (one high, one low), gong, cymbals, 3 bass drums of different sizes, bongos, snare drums, gourd (to be scratched with a wooden stick), slapsticks, 3 Chinese blocks of different pitches, Cuban claves, triangle, Maracas (Cuban rattle-gourds with grape shot inside), sleigh bells, castanets, tambourine, anvils of two different pitches, chimes, celesta, and piano.

Out of these 37 percussion instruments only 3 have exact pitches, that is, are able to play specific notes of the scale, instead of merely high or low. These three are cannily reserved for the climax and peroration of the work. Lesser contrasts of instrumental timbre are used throughout with rhythmic contrasts to give the brief score its firm structure.

Ralph Vaughan Williams

Born October 12, 1872, Down Ampney, Gloucestershire—died August 26, 1958, London

FANTASIA ON A THEME BY THOMAS TALLIS

It is no accident that Vaughan Williams, one of the most profoundly English composers of our century, should have been enthralled by a melody of Thomas Tallis, one of the greatest composers of the English Renaissance. In fact it was this brief melody which inspired the earliest of Vaughan Williams's major orchestral works and one of the finest he ever wrote.

Vaughan Williams and his contemporaries were acutely aware of the long era of sterility in English music—virtually two hundred years from the death of Purcell to the end of the nineteenth century. This was the age when English composers appeared to be so overwhelmed by the genius of their adopted countryman Handel, and later by the "invasions" of brilliant foreigners with Mendelssohn in the lead, that they could think only of trying to imitate them. Whether this is the complete explanation or not, England, which for centuries had been one of the most fertile musical countries in the world, produced little that lasted in their own affections or in the esteem of other countries. By the end of the nineteenth century England began to respond to the great wave of Romantic nationalism which had proved so productive in other countries. There was a passionate desire among English musicians to cast off the fetters of imitation and to reestablish the glorious traditions of English composition, which reached far back into the Middle Ages. In England as elsewhere, folk song was one of the strongest sources of tradition; religious music was another. For Vaughan Williams the two sources were happily united when he decided, quite reluctantly at first, to take on the responsibility of editing a new edition of the *English Hymnal.* He was afraid of undertaking such a time-consuming responsibility because, as he wrote:

> ". . . this meant two years with no 'original' work except a few hymn tunes. I wondered then if I was wasting my time. But I know now that two years of close association with some of the best (as well as some of the worst) tunes in the world was a better musical education than any amount of sonatas and fugues."

In choosing new melodies to add to the *Hymnal,* Vaughan Williams searched not only through folk-song collections but through the most promising church collections known to him, especially, of course, English sources. It was thus that he came upon the nine melodies which Thomas Tallis contributed to the 1567 *English Psalter* published by Archbishop Mathew Parker. Tallis, who was as doughty a musical force as he seems to have been pliable in his religious professions, contributed both Catholic and Protestant music to his country's heritage. Protestantism was relatively new as an established faith (dating only from Henry VIII's break with Rome in 1534). It had been followed by a brief return to Catholicism in 1555, an official reestablishment of Protestantism with the accession of Elizabeth I, and the completion of the official Thirty-nine Articles of Faith in 1563. Archbishop Parker's *Psalter* was published four years later and suppressed shortly thereafter, but the tunes were fortunately preserved for posterity.

Vaughan Williams was attracted by all nine of the melodies which Tallis had contributed, but one in particular fascinated him irresistibly. It was the third Tallis melody, in the Phrygian church mode, set to the archbishop's metrical translation: "Why fumeth in sight: the Gentiles spite, In fury raging stout?" This was the Archbishop's version of the question better known to us as: "Why do the heathen rage and the people imagine a vain thing?" Whether Tallis's melody as sung in his day suggested any form of militancy, of raging, or fuming, may be questioned. However that may be, the notes emerge far more peacefully in Vaughan Williams transcription for the 1910 *English Hymnal* where he set it to verses beginning "When, rising from the bed of death." The beautiful melody has been given various texts in the course of the years. The 1940 *Hymnal of the Protestant Episcopal Church in the United States of America* replaces the Anglican text with the mid-nineteenth-century verses of

Horatius Bonar beginning "I heard the voice of Jesus say, 'Come to me and rest; Lay down, Thou weary one, lay down Thy Head upon my breast.' " Vaughan Williams finds in the Tallis melody a beauty far surpassing any of the hymn *texts* we have discovered from Tallis's day to ours. It may even be that he discovered a special kind of beauty which Tallis himself never imagined. It is perhaps a Romantic vision of Tallis's era and faith, which has its own validity, quite apart from any question of historical accuracy.

Vaughan Williams completed his orchestral Fantasia in June 1910, and it was first performed on September 6 of the same year in Gloucester Cathedral by the London Symphony Orchestra under the direction of Vaughan Williams himself. The Gloucester premiere was part of the famous Three Choirs Festival, one of the most ancient musical festivals we know, dating back to the early eighteenth century. The three choirs referred to in the title are the cathedral choirs of Gloucester, Worcester, and Hereford. The festival is held annually at each cathedral city in rotation, early in September. The programs, extending over a week, are traditionally devoted in large part to church music, much of it performed in the respective cathedrals. But secular programs are also performed. Vaughan Williams's Fantasia was performed in Gloucester Cathedral itself, and is clearly conceived for the acoustical surroundings of such a large and resonant edifice.

The orchestra, composed entirely of strings, is divided into three groups: a quartet of solo strings, a first orchestra of massed strings, and a second orchestra consisting of nine players. The score directs that the two orchestras should be placed apart from each other if possible. Clearly what Vaughan Williams had in mind was the Renaissance practice of separating two, three, or even four choirs and placing them in the large spaces of the cathedral so that they could alternate, echo each other, and join in various acoustical groupings.

The Fantasia opens with a quiet introduction in which a first fragment of the Tallis melody is introduced by the lower strings of all three groups. This fragment is immediately followed by an original phrase of Vaughan Williams, a phrase wavering up and down over adjacent half-tones, with a particularly poignant effect which is developed in the course of the Fantasia, almost more extensively than the Tallis tune itself. The original Tallis melody is introduced by cellos, violas, and second violins all playing in unison, beginning as follows:*

* *Musical example copyright J. Curwen & Sons Ltd., London. Copyright 1943 in U.S.A. by Hawkes & Son (London) Ltd. Reprinted by permission of Boosey & Hawkes, Inc.*

This first statement of the Tallis melody is followed immediately by a more impassioned version, now carried into the upper range of the orchestra, dominated by the warmer tone color of the violins. A brief interlude in which the separate orchestras answer each other back and forth, is followed by a middle section lead off by a solo viola in a variant of the Tallis melody.

A solo violin takes up the embellished tune and is soon joined by the other members of the string quartet in succession. Now all three groups—the solo quartet, the large orchestra, and the small orchestra—take up variants of the melody, alternating, then combining in music of increasing fervor, building to a passionate climax. The brief concluding section recalls the melodic fragments of the introduction and dies away on a peaceful simple G-major triad to the merest whisper, and then silence.

Vaughan Williams twice revised his score, in 1913 and 1919, the chief alteration being the elimination of one entire repetition of the original Tallis melody in the opening pages. The Fantasia remains probably Vaughan Williams's most popular orchestral work in the concert hall. However, it seems clear that it loses an essential dimension in these formal surroundings. The eminent English critic J. A. Fuller Maitland described the effect of this music in the surroundings for which it was intended in his review of its first performance. After describing the score in detail, he added:

> The work is wonderful because it seems to lift one into some unknown region of musical thought and feeling. Throughout its course one is never quite sure whether one is listening to something very old or very new. . . . The voices of the old church musicians . . . are around one, and yet there is more besides, for their music is enriched with all that modern art has done since. Debussy, too, is somewhere in the picture and it is hard to tell how much of the complete freedom of tonality comes from the new French school and how much from the old English one. But that is just what makes this Fantasia so delightful to listen to; it cannot be assigned to a time or a school, but it is full of visions which have haunted the seers of all times. We can recall no piece of pure instrumental music produced at a Three Choirs Festival which has seemed to belong to its surroundings so entirely as does this Fantasia.

SYMPHONY NO. 2, G MAJOR (A LONDON SYMPHONY)

One of England's greatest composers, Ralph Vaughan Williams was an avowed Romantic and, particularly before 1915, a Nationalist in his music. Considering how unfashionable both Romanticism and Nationalism have become in the mid-twentieth century, it is a tribute to his genius that his "London" Symphony holds us and moves us as it does today. As a matter of fact, the "London" Symphony was probably the peak of his musical Nationalism which waned noticeably in the years after World War I.

Out of a combination of English folk-song idiom, the Tudor composers of the sixteenth century and Purcell of the late seventeenth, he compounded his own intensely personal, intensely English style. He was perfectly aware of what he was doing and wrote a touchingly modest and reasonable *apologia* for his artistic practice:

> Every composer cannot expect to have a worldwide message, but he may reasonably expect to have a special message for his own people, and many young composers make the mistake of imagining that they can be universal without at first having been local. Is it not reasonable to suppose that those who share our life, our history, our customs, our climate, even our food, should have some secret to impart to us which a foreign composer, though he be perhaps more imaginative, more powerful, more technically equipped, is not able to give us? This is the secret of the national composer. . . . But is he prepared with his secret? Must he not limit himself to a certain extent so as to give his message its full force? . . . What a composer has to do is to find out the real message he has to convey to the community and say it directly and without equivocation. . . . If the roots of your art are firmly planted in your own soil and that soil has anything individual to give you, you may still gain the whole world and not lose your own souls.

We do not know precisely when Vaughan Williams began to sketch the ideas which eventually turned into the "London" Symphony. At first he considered making them into a symphonic poem. By 1912, during a visit to friends in Cambridge, he hauled out of his bag the sketch for the first two movements of a "London" Symphony which he demonstrated on an upright piano. The full score was completed in time for a premiere at Queens Hall, London, on March 27, 1914, under the direction of Geoffrey Toye.

The Symphony was a resounding success. In fact the audience and Vaughan Williams's friends were far more delighted with the work than he himself was. For over the years there followed an endless series of major and minor revisions. The original manuscript full score sent to Fritz Busch in Germany in July 1914 was lost. It was reconstructed from the instrumental parts and performed in 1915 and again in 1918. Immediately thereafter, Vaughan Williams began making cuts in the score condensing certain sections, rewriting others. Even before the first edition of the score was published in 1920, the work was twice revised. Further revisions were incorporated in a score published in or about 1936—the publishers Stainer and Bell are not absolutely sure of the year.

Vaughan Williams himself commented briefly on his Symphony for the program of the Liverpool Philharmonic Society concert of December 1, 1925:

"It has been suggested that this symphony has been misnamed, it should rather be called 'Symphony by a Londoner.' That is to say it is in no sense descriptive, and though the introduction of the 'Westminster Chimes' in the first movement, the slight reminiscence of the 'Lavender Cry' in the slow movement, and the very faint suggestion of mouth organs and mechanical pianos in the Scherzo give it a tinge of 'local colour,' yet it is intended to be listened to as 'absolute' music. Hearers may, if they like, localize the various themes and movements, but it is hoped that this is not a necessary part of the music. There are four movements":

I. *Lento; Allegro risoluto.* "The first," continues Vaughan Williams, "begins with a slow prelude; this leads to a vigorous allegro—which may perhaps suggest the noise and hurry of London, with its always underlying calm." This vastly evocative canvas of the first movement opens almost inaudibly with the lowest strings of the orchestra muted in a characteristic Vaughan Williams motive of rising fourths. There is an impression as of mists gradually clearing as the rising fourths merge into flowing melodic lines until suddenly the fourths become a brilliant brass fanfare leading us to the *Allegro risoluto.*

"Noise and scurry" were two words that Vaughan Williams himself often used to his close associate, Michael Kennedy, to describe the basic mood of this movement. That feeling is embodied in the principal theme of the movement flung out here by high strings and woodwinds in unison:

The movement follows freely the traditional first movement form of sonata-allegro. There is a vigorous second theme given out by brass and winds, followed at once by a lightly sparkling dance tune. After a rich development the basic themes return considerably transformed, and the movement culminates in a burst of sunny brilliance.

II. *Lento.* "The second (slow) movement," says Vaughan Williams, "has been called 'Bloomsbury Square on a November afternoon.' This may serve as a clue to the music, but it is not a necessary 'explanation' of it." The mood is set at once, as in the opening movement, with a background of low, muted strings, over which a solitary English horn intones the melancholy subject:

III. *Scherzo (Nocturne) Allegro vivace.* "If the hearer will imagine himself standing on Westminster Embankment at night, surrounded by the distant sounds of the Strand, with its great hotels on one side, and the 'New Cut' on the other, with its crowded streets and flaring lights, it may serve as a mood in which to listen to this movement."

IV. *Andante con moto: Maestoso alla marcia (quasi lento); Allegro; Andante sostenuto.* "The last movement consists of an agitated theme in triple-time alternating with a march movement at first solemn and, later on, energetic. [A note said to have been written with the composer's agreement by Albert Coates in 1920 speaks of a hunger-march at this point.] At the end of the *finale* comes a suggestion of the noise and fever of the first movement—this time much subdued—then the 'Westminster Chimes' are heard once more: on this follows an 'Epilogue' in which the slow prelude [i.e., to the first movement] is developed into a movement of some length."

This poetic close is perhaps even more poignant today than when it was new. It had a specific association in the composer's mind. In a letter of September 30, 1957, to Michael Kennedy, Vaughan Williams wrote: "For actual coda [i.e., the conclusion of this Symphony] see end of Wells's *Tono-Bungay*." This is Wells's chapter called "Night and the Open Sea" in which the narrator, passing down the Thames in a destroyer, seems "to be passing all England in review."

> To run down the Thames is to run one's hand over the pages in the book of England from end to end. . . . There come first squalid stretches of mean homes right and left and then the dingy industrialism of the South side, and on the North bank the polite long front of nice houses, artistic, literary, administrative people's residences, that stretches from Cheyne Walk [close to Vaughan Williams's home] nearly to Westminster and hides a wilderness of slums. . . . We tear into the great spaces of the future and the turbines fall to talking in unfamiliar tongues. Out to the open we go, to windy freedom and trackless ways. Light after light goes down. England and the Kingdom, Britain and the Empire, the old prides and the old devotions, glide abeam, astern, sink down upon the horizon, pass—pass. The river passes—London passes—England passes. . . .

The "London" Symphony is scored for 3 flutes (one alternating with piccolo), 2 oboes, English horn, 2 clarinets, bass clarinet, 2 bassoons, contrabassoon, 4 horns, 2 trumpets, 2 cornets, 3 trombones, tuba, kettledrums, side drum, triangle, bass drum, cymbals, glockenspiel, harp, and the traditional strings.

SYMPHONY NO. 4, F MINOR

Vaughan Williams's most famous comment on his most controversial Fourth Symphony is said to have been made during a rehearsal for the premiere at Queen's Hall, London, on April 10, 1935: "I don't know whether I like it—but it's what I meant."

The words were characteristic of the man: humorously self-deprecating on the surface, firm as a rock underneath. When an admirer, baffled by the style of the new Symphony, suggested that Vaughan Williams had not intended to make it beautiful, perhaps because he had been inspired by ugly events (this was the time of rampant Nazism and threats of war), the composer took earnest issue with him:

> I agree with you [he wrote] that all music must have *beauty*—the problem being what *is* beauty—so when you say you do not think my F mi. symph. beautiful, my answer *must* be that I *do* think it beautiful—*not* that I did not *mean* it to be beautiful because it reflects unbeautiful times. . . . We know that beauty can come from unbeautiful things (King Lear, Rembrandt's School of Anatomy, Wagner's Niebelungs etc.) . . .I wrote it not as a definite picture of anything external—e.g. the state of Europe—but simply because it occurred to me like this—I can't explain why . . .

It seems incredible that this melodious symphony should have been considered "harsh" or "grim." But this was 1935, when so important a critic as Eric Blom could declare in the *Birmingham Post:*

> His [Vaughan Williams's] latest work is as harshly and grimly uncompromising in its clashing, dissonant polyphony as anything the youngest adventurer would dare to fling down on music paper. That the symphony is a tremendously strong, convincing and wonderfully devised work cannot be questioned.

Edwin Evans called it "a vigorous, uncompromising work, with no superfluous matter about, only downright assertions." Harsh or not, the audience adored it. One newspaper described the ovations for Vaughan Williams as "almost without parallel at Queen's Hall." The "vociferous applause," according to another, grew "almost hysterical when the composer took his bow."

Part of the triumph, of course, must have been a tribute to the sixty-year-old Vaughan Williams, who was firmly entrenched in his countrymen's hearts as the greatest English composer of his time.

Yet for all his triumph, Vaughan Williams himself was not entirely satisfied. He knew what he "meant," but he made his meaning clearer in a series of revisions over the years, some very small. The tiniest of all (the last note of the flute solo at the end of the slow movement) was one of the most important. "The note was originally F," he wrote, "but I have always felt it was wrong, and I have taken twenty years trying to find the right note, and in the new parts and the large scores it is altered to E, . . . "

Vaughn Williams sketched the score in late 1931 and early 1932 and completed the original version in 1934. The Symphony is in four movements, the third of which leads without pause into the *Finale*. It is unified by two themes—two striking four-note figures which permeate the score. The more important of these, the central theme of the entire Symphony, consists of the final bracketed notes in the first musical example.

I. *Allegro.* The Symphony opens with an incisive melody etched in cutting minor seconds plus an octave drop. In its last four (bracketed) notes it incorporates the central theme of the Symphony:*

---

* *This and the following musical examples from this composition are copyright in the U.S.A. and all countries, 1935, by the Oxford University Press, London. Reprinted by permission.*

This entire phrase is launched with a dissonance of tremendous propelling power, which Vaughan Williams liked to say he had "cribbed" from the famous dissonance in the *finale* in Beethoven's Ninth Symphony. This is followed closely by the other four-note figure, which remains important throughout the score. This is a boldly climbing figure proclaimed by trumpets, *fortissimo:*

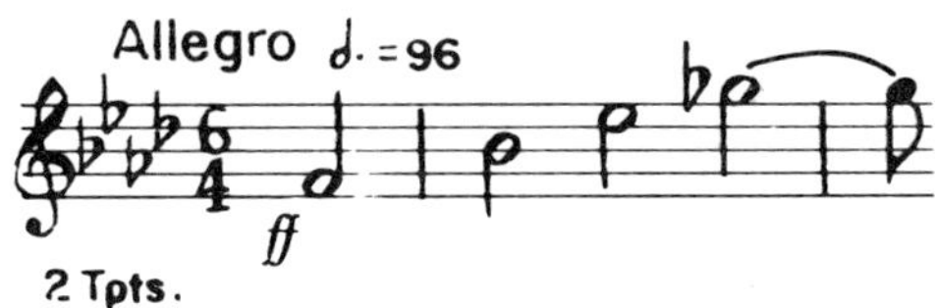

After the vigorous opening section the strings sing a warmly contrasting *cantilena*, the start of which recalls the opening of the Symphony. The tempo relaxes for an equally emotional string melody, this one in D major with many repeated notes. All through the development which follows, the central four-note theme stands out in varied rhythmic and harmonic guises.

> There is no complete recapitulation of the first subjects [writes Vaughan Williams] but after a few notes suggestive of the opening, the *cantilena* passage follows immediately, this time in the bass, with a counter-melody in the treble. This works up to a *fortissimo*. The music then dies away, and ends with a soft and slow repetition of the D major theme, this time in D flat.

II. *Andante moderato.* The introductory phrase entoned by muted brass is derived from the climbing four-note figure in the first movement. The *Andante*'s principal subject is a long melody sung by the first violins over a *pizzicato* accompaniment. Halfway through, the movement is divided by a soft, descending phrase of the solo flute. This returns in extended form at the conclusion, while muted brass recalls the Symphony's principal theme.

III. *Scherzo; Allegro molto.* The *Scherzo* theme, based on the climbing figure of the opening movement, bounds up over three and a half octaves:

It is interrupted by barking trumpets and trombones proclaiming the central four-note theme.

The middle (trio section) of the *Scherzo* is a *fugato* on another leaping theme announced by the solo tuba. The *Scherzo* leads without pause into the fourth movement.

IV. *Finale con epilogo fugato (Allegro molto).* The opening theme of the *Finale* is, according to the composer, "a more energetic version of the [flute] cadence figure from the second movement." There is a lyric, contrasting theme related to the Symphony's opening bar. A traditional sonata-allegro structure ends with a *coda* in the form of a fugal epilogue. The subject of the fugal epilogue, the composer tells us, is the central four-note theme "played first on the trombones and then heard both in its original form and inverted, combined with other subjects of the finale. The work ends with a reference to the opening bars of the first movement."

The F-minor Symphony is scored for 3 flutes, piccolo, 3 oboes, English horn, 2 clarinets, bass clarinet, 2 bassoons, contrabassoon, 4 horns, tuba, kettledrums, side drums, bass drum, triangle, cymbals, and the customary string choir.

Antonio Vivaldi

Born March 4, 1678 in Venice—died probably July 26 or 27, 1741

THE FOUR SEASONS (LE QUATTRO STAGIONI), OPUS 8, CONCERTOS NOS. 1-4

Antonio Vivaldi was a violin virtuoso of such brilliance and such renown that he was listed as a tourist attraction in his native city of Venice. A 1713 travelers' guide to Venice declares that "among the best to play the violin are Gian-Battista Vivaldi and his priest-son [Antonio]." Because of his flaming red hair he was known as the "red priest" *(prete rosso)* of Venice.

Fiery hair and fiery temperaments seem to have been a Vivaldi family trait. Antonio was not the only member of the clan to be called *rosso* or *rossi*. His music, too, had an Italian fire, which endeared him to his countrymen and attracted the most serious foreigners—for example Johann Sebastian Bach, who enriched his own style by studying and transcribing Vivaldi's works.

In an enormously prolific age, Vivaldi was one of the most prolific and influential composers: discounting whatever may have been lost, he left us over four *hundred* concertos, 221 of them for violin alone. His forty-odd operas, were composed mostly for Venice, the flourishing operatic center of the day.

Vivaldi's compositions and his services as a violin virtuoso were in demand all over Europe, but he chose, understandably, to center his activities in Venice. For nearly forty years he was the Music Director *(Maestro de'concerti)* of the *Pio Ospedale della Pietà,* one of the four most famous Venetian conservatories for girls, whose weekly orchestral concerts attracted visitors from all Europe.

Goethe and Jean-Jacques Rousseau were only among the most famous visitors who wrote enthusiastically about the Venetian conservatory concerts. Many of Vivaldi's concertos must have been performed for the first time at the *Pietà* with Vivaldi himself as conductor and soloist. In August 1739 a famous French traveler, the Président Charles de Brosses, described these conservatory concerts:

> The most marvelous music is that of the *ospedali.* There are four of them, all composed of bastard girls, or orphans, or of girls whose parents cannot afford the expense of bringing them up. They are reared at the expense of the State and trained only to excel in music. And indeed they sing like angels and play the violin, the flute, the organ, the oboe, the violoncello, the bassoon; in short, there is no instrument big enough to scare them. They are cloistered like nuns. They are the only executants, and at each concert about forty of them perform. I swear to you there is nothing so pleasant as to see a young and pretty nun* robed in white, with a garland of pomegranate flowers in her hair, conducting the orchestra and beating time with all imaginable grace and precision.

For special occasions, all four of the top *ospedali* would collaborate, each contributing the cream of their best players to form an elite orchestra for a festive program in the Venetian Philharmonic Hall *(Sala dei Filarmonici)* on the Piazza San Marco. The peculiar magic of many such occasions was caught on canvas by the virtuoso brush of the Venetian Francesco Guardi. A small canvas (today in the Alte Pinakothek of Munich) painted in 1782 to celebrate the visit to Venice of the "Counts of the North," the Russian Grand Duke Paul Petrovitch and the Grand Duchess Maria Feodorovna, suggests the elegance and glamor of such an occasion forty years after Vivaldi's death.

The concert rooms of the *ospedali* can hardly have been as glamorous as Guardi's *Sala dei Filarmonici.* But the arrangement of this hall is almost identical with descriptions of the conservatory concerts. The seating of the orchestra strikes the modern concert-goer as odd. Presumably this was a Venetian specialty.

Three balconies run the length of the hall. In the top balcony we can distinguish thirteen singers; in the second, ten violinists or violists; in the lowest row, two doublebasses, cello, and violone flanked by eight more violinists—for a total of twenty instruments. The total of thirty-three performers (plus two or three who did not get into the picture) is close to the total of forty described by the Président de Brosses and other music-loving travelers. Guardi shows us no continuo instrument (such as harpsichord or organ) nor does this performance seem to have included any wind instruments.

---

* *De Brosses uses the term "nun" loosely. The girls were wards of the state who wore nunlike habits.*

VENETIAN PHILHARMONIC HALL, 1780, BY GUARDI.

On the Piazza San Marco of Venice, the Sala dei Filarmonici, where Vivaldi's music must often have been performed in the earlier eighteenth century. *(Original in Alte Pinakothek, Munich; photo Bruckmann; courtesy, Art Reference Bureau)*

Vivaldi's *Seasons* are composed only for strings. The usage of the time would have required at least one, probably two, keyboard instruments. Guardi's picture clearly omits some players on the far left and these may well have included the continuo group.

In all likelihood Vivaldi's *Four Seasons* were performed several times at concerts of the *ospedali* and probably at gala affairs in the *Sala dei Filarmonici. The Seasons,* first published in Amsterdam, bore a fulsome dedication to one of Vivaldi's foreign patrons: to the Hungarian Count Morzin (or Marzin as Vivaldi spelled it) a member of the same affluent family who were soon to list Joseph Haydn among their employees.

The Four Seasons (I quattro stagioni) were only the first of a set of twelve concertos which Vivaldi published in 1725 under the collective title of *Il cimento dell'armonia e dell'inventione (The Trial of Harmony and Invention),* Opus 8. Within a matter of weeks a Parisian publisher issued his own pirated edition of Vivaldi's *Cimento*—eloquent testimony to Vivaldi's wide reputation.

On the title page Vivaldi describes himself as *maestro* "in Italy" of Count Venceslav Morzin and of Prince Philip, Landgrave of Hesse-Darmstadt. In the dedication Vivaldi mentions that Morzin had long since graciously acknowledged the pleasure he took in *The Fours Seasons* (from which one can assume that they were composed considerably earlier than 1725). Nevertheless, Vivaldi expresses the hope that the concertos may seem almost new not only for the reason he is prefacing each concerto with a sonnet explaining the music, but also because much of the musical depiction itself has been expanded.

While the sonnets (possibly written by Vivaldi himself) are not thrilling poetry, it is obvious that the music really was designed, detail for humble detail, to portray what the sonnets spell out in words. We may question how serious Vivaldi was, or how serious he expected us to be in listening to the details of his "program" music, as we should call it today. But there can be no question of the gusto with which he composed the descriptive details. And to avoid any possible misunderstanding, Vivaldi has each line of the sonnets printed again over the precise passage of the music it explains; and he even prints further clarifying words.

Vivaldi poured the descriptive details he so obviously relished in *The Seasons* into the form of the Late-Baroque concerto form he himself was bringing to its highest peak of brilliance.

This usually consisted of three movements (fast, slow, fast), the two fast movements being cast in *ritornello* form. This latter form takes its name from the refrain, or *ritornello,* stated at the beginning of the movement, recalled briefly at intervals throughout, and restated at the conclusion. Between returns of the *ritornello,* a lighter, smaller group of instruments, or even a solo, played episodes which originally contrasted with the *ritornello.*

To sample Vivaldi's use of descriptive poems, we reprint his Spring and Fall sonnets from the set of four.

The Spring" ("La primavera"),
E major, Opus 8, No.1

(Notice the capital letters with which Vivaldi marked the sections of his sonnet which describe the similarly lettered sections of his music.)

Giunt' è la Primavera e festosetti	A	*Spring has returned and festively*
La salutan gl' Augei con lieto canto,	B	*Is greeted by the birds in happy song;*
E i fonti allo spirar de' Zeffiretti	C	*And fountains fanned by little Zephyrs*
Con dolce mormorio scorrono intanto.		*Murmur sweetly in the constant flow*
Vengon' coprendo l'aer di nero anamto	D	*When skies are mantled all in black*
E lampi, e tuoni ad annuntiarla eletti		*Lighteningflash and thunder roar;*
Indi tacendo questi, gl'Augelletti	E	*When these have done the little birds*
Tornan' di nuovo al lor canoro incanto:		*Return to carol their enchanting song.*
E quindi sul fiorito ameno prato	F	*While upon the flowering meadow*
Al caro mormorio de fronde e piante		*Amid the murmuring leaves and boughs*
Dorme 'l Caprar col fido can' à lato.		*Sleep goatherd and his trusty dog.*
Di pastoral Zampogna al Suon festante	G	*To country bagpipes' festive sound*
Danzan Ninfe e Pastor nel tetto amato		*Dance nymphs and shepherds underneath*
Di primavera all' apparir brillante.		*Beloved springtime's brilliant skies.*

I. *Allegro.* The opening *ritornello* setting the mood of this entire movement is labeled: "*A. Spring has returned.*" The jaunty tune might almost have been suggested by the rhythm of the original Italian words, or vice versa:

The first contrasting solo for violin solo with accompaniment of two other violin solos from the orchestra is labeled the "Song of the Birds" and consists of soft trilling and delicate solo runs. Halfway through the episode the label from the sonnet continues: "is greeted by the birds with happy song." After a quick recall of the opening *ritornello,* a second episode (corresponding to letter C of the sonnet) consists of softly murmuring violins anticipating the murmuring of Wagner's forest in *Siegfried* a century and a half later. A second recall of the *ritornello* is followed by (letter D) the "lightning flash and thunder" depicted by swift scales for the violins followed by low tremolos for the entire string body.

II. *Largo e pianissimo sempre.* The slow movement begins at letter F with an orchestral description of the goatherd's slumber (depicted by a slow flowing melody of the solo violin) plus an extra descriptive dividend which evidently could not be fitted into the sonnet. The goatherd's "trusty dog" far from sleeping is obviously keeping watch, for the violas are directed to imitate his bark with repeated notes played "very loudly and abruptly"! The listener can feel the pleasure this innocent detail must have given Vivaldi, for the dog continues to bark throughout the entire movement.

III. *Allegro: Rustic Dance.* The opening strain (letter G of the sonnet) suggests the rustic bagpipes, both in the lilting tune of the violins and in the sustained notes of the lower strings, imitating the bagpipe drone.

"The Summer" (*"L'estate"*), G minor, Opus 8, No. 2

I. *Allegro non molto.* "Under the heat of the summer sun," Vivaldi's poem tells us, "man and beast droop." The opening phrases of the concerto droop in sympathy. A more lively passage for solo violin depicts the cuckoo call, the turtledove and the goldfinch. The gentle whispering of Zephyrs (violins and violas) is interrupted by "impetuous winds" and the sudden buffeting of Boreas depicted by rushing scales of the violins and a sudden burst of vigor in the entire ensemble. A plaintive violin solo paints the weeping of a shepherd who fears an approaching storm. More buffetings of Boreas close the first movement.

II *Adagio: Presto.* The shepherd's repose slow solo violin phrase is disturbed by his fright at distant thunder (*Presto:* heavy tremolo for the full string orchestra). He tries to sleep again *(Adagio)* but flies and gnats torment him.

III. *Presto: Impetuous summer storm.* The opening *ritornello* is labeled with words from the sonnet: "Ah, his fears were all too justified." Lightning crisscrosses through the orchestra in darting scales of first and second violins in rapid succession:

The thunder roars in string basses and cellos.

"The Fall" (*"L'autunno"*), F major, Opus 8, No. 3

Celebra il Vilanel con balli e Canti	A	Peasants celebrate with dance and song
Del felice raccolto il bel piacere		The joys of a succesful harvest.
E del liquor di Bacco accesi tanti	B	Many, fired by Bacchus' glowing draught,
Finiscono col Sonno il lor godere.	C	End their celebration with a slumber.
Fà ch' ogn' uno tralasci e balli e canti	D	Many leave the songs and dances
L'aria che temprata dà piacere,		To seek the pleasures of cool air.
E la Staggion ch' invita tanti e tanti		Now is the time that summons all
D'un dolcissimo Sonno al bel godere.		To savor full the joy of gentle sleep.
L'cacciator alla nov' alba à caccia.	E	Huntsmen at the break of day depart
Con corni, Schioppi, e canni escono fuore	F	With horns and hounds and guns, they go.
Fugge la belva, e Sequono la traccia;		The quarry flees, while they pursue.
Già Sbigottita, e lassa al gran rumore	G	Bewildered and exhausted by the noise
De' Schioppi e canni, ferita minaccia		Of guns and hounds, the wounded prey
Languida di fuggir, mà oppressa muore.	H	Almost escapes, but then succumbs and dies.

I. *Dancing and Singing of the Peasants: Allegro.* The first movement corresponds to the first quatrain of the sonnet (A-B-C). The vigorous opening *ritornello* is labeled with the first two lines (letter A). The second two lines (B and C) start an episode which bears the additional title "The Drunkard." The exuberance of the drinker, the growing befuzzlement of his mind, his faltering steps, and his lurches are allotted to the virtuoso violin soloist (surely Vivaldi himself at the first performances). The songs of the more sober celebrants keep returning in a form of the *ritornello* as the gyrations of the drunkard grow wilder:

At last the drunkards collapse into sweet slumber for which Vivaldi, in a surprising departure from the normal swift tempo of the first movement, slows suddenly to a *Larghetto.*

II. *The Sleeping Drunkards: Adagio.* The slow second movement which grows softer and softer with deepening slumber, corresponds to the second quatrain of the sonnet (letter D).

III. *The Hunt: Allegro.* Hunting horns have delighted musicians as far back as we have any record, but the *ritornello* of this movement in which violins imitate a primitive hunting call must be one of the earliest examples of a great composer basing an entire orchestral movement on such a theme.

The episodes, again given over chiefly to the solo violinist, illustrate the flight of the quarry and its languishing death.

"The Winter" *("L'inverno"),* F minor, Opus 8, No. 4

I. *Allegro non molto.* The first movement opens with a description of the shivers caused by winter cold. The shivers are graphically indicated by trills of the violins. (It will be recalled that the older British term for the trill is "shake" and the connotation of trembling apparently was current in most European countries.) Swift arpeggios and scales for the solo violin depict the severity of the "horrid wind," and a series of vigorous chords suggest fast running and stamping of feet. This activity is apparently of little avail, however, for the first movement closes with rapid tremolos depicting chattering teeth.

II. *Largo.* The traditionally slow and songful middle movement is not only deliciously descriptive in its use of violin pizzicatos to suggest the drops of rain which "drench hundreds" outdoors, but warmly suggestive in the flowing melody of the violin solo, which expresses the tranquil contentment of more fortunate souls who sit indoors by the open fire.

III. *Allegro.* The finale opens with a long sequence of slithery, sliding phrases intended to depict the perils of walking on ice. The *tutti* joins in with a slower rhythm indicating "slow steps" and the fear of falling. Great swooping scales, however, and more jerky, broken figures show that the precautions were useless and one falls. Even worse perils lie ahead. The following drastic figure:

is the ice, breaking into separate chunks. Another plunging scale of the soloist suggests (although this last point is not specified in words) that someone falls in. A moment later, however, we are safe indoors, listening to the "warring winds," Sirocco and Borea, outside. Vivaldi's closing words over the last seven measures of the concerto are "This is winter, but such that it brings joy."

Richard Wagner

Born May 22, 1813, Leipzig—died February 13, 1883, Venice

OVERTURE TO THE FLYING DUTCHMAN

As an unknown twenty-six-year-old, Richard Wagner set out to make his fortune in Paris. On the way he took a small Norwegian ship across the North Sea. In mid-voyage the tiny sailing-vessel was caught in a terrifying storm. The superstitious sailors told of an ancient legend, which they half-believed, of a phantom ship that rode the storm and could not be sunk. The only live man aboard was the master, a Dutchman.

Once this Dutchman had tried to round the Cape of Good Hope in a gale. In his rage at the opposing elements he had sworn he would prevail against Hell itself. Then, said the tale, Lucifer was heard in a loud laugh from the deep, and the blasphemous Dutchman was doomed to fight the gale until the sound of the last trumpet. His crew had long since become ghosts, but the Dutchman lived on, unable to find peace or rest, unable to find death at any man's hand, even his own, always driven and driving through the storm.

This was not the first time Wagner had heard the legend of the Flying Dutchman, but this time the terrors of the northern sea and the half-belief of the Norwegian sailors took hold of his imagination, and the Dutchman became the hero of an opera which Wagner completed in 1841, after his arrival in Paris. To the original legend he added an important twist, which he had from the story as told by Heinrich Heine. Every seven years the Dutchman was allowed to go ashore and search for a woman who would be true to him unto death. Such a woman, if ever he succeeded in finding her, would release him from the curse. The opera is the story of his salvation.

The Overture is built around the figure of the tormented Dutchman:

Throughout most of the Overture, his motive is surrounded by the howling wind, which we hear in the eerie open fifths of the stringed instruments, or it is tossed about on wild, wavelike figures. The other chief motive of the Overture is the prayerful melody of Senta, who accomplishes his salvation.

In May, 1853, Wagner conducted several orchestra concerts at Zurich, and included on the program the Overture to his *Flying Dutchman*. For that occasion he wrote the following description of the emotional content of his music:

> The fearful ship of the Flying Dutchman rides the tempest. It nears the coast and puts to land, where its captain once was promised he would find redemption. We hear the compassionate strains of the promise of salvation, like a combined lament and prayer. Hopelessly, the condemned man listens. Weary and longing for death, he comes ashore, while his crew, listless and tired of life, silently bring the ship to rest.
>
> How often the unhappy man has gone through the same motions! How often has he steered his ship from the sea to the shores of man, where once in every seven years he is permitted to land; how often has he dreamt that he had reached the end of his trials and ah! how often, frightfully disillusioned, has he set sail again upon his wild voyage! To force his own death, he has roused the sea and storm against himself. Into the yawning whirlpool he has plunged his ship, but the whirlpool did not swallow it; against the surfbound cliffs he urged it—but the rocks have never wrecked it. All the fearsome dangers of the deep, at which he had laughed in a wild lust of adventure, they now laugh at him—they do not harm him; he is curst and doomed to all eternity to hunt the watery waste for treasure that gives him no satisfaction, never finding the only thing that could redeem him!
>
> A stately ship sweeps by; he hears the familiar songs of men rejoicing at the approach of home. Enraged by this glad sound, he rushes forward through the storm, affrights and silences the singers, and puts the joyous crew to flight. Then from the depth of his misery he cries out for salvation; in the barren world of men, where he has his existence, only a woman can bring him release! Where, in what distant land does his rescuer live? Where does there beat a compassionate heart for sufferings so great as his? Where is she who will not flee in horror from him, like these cowards who shudder and cross themselves at his approach?
>
> A ray of light penetrates the gloom. Like a lightning flash it pierces his tortured soul. It fades, and leaps to life once more: the seaman keeps the lodestar firmly in view, and steers boldly through waves and billows toward it. What draws him on so powerfully? It is a woman's glance, which, full of noble sorrow and divine compassion, shines through to him! A womanly heart has opened its depths to the doomed man's infinite sorrows, to sacrifice itself for him, to end his sorrows and her life together. At this divine deed the unhappy man at last can die; his ship breaks to pieces and is engulfed by the ocean. Yet he rises from the waves, redeemed and whole, led by his redemptress's hand to the dawn of an exalted love.

Wagner's orchestra consists of piccolo, 2 flutes, 2 oboes, English horn, 2 clarinets, 2 bassoons, 4 horns, 2 trumpets, 3 trombones, tuba, kettledrums, harp, and the customary string choir.

GÖTTERDÄMMERUNG (TWILIGHT OF THE GODS): SIEGFRIED'S FUNERAL MUSIC

"Siegfried's Funeral Music" (sometimes known as "Siegfried's Funeral March") is the symphonic interlude which links the two scenes of Act Three in Wagner's *Twilight of the Gods.* On a hunting trip by the banks of the Rhine, Siegfried has been murdered—stabbed in the back by Hagen, the leader of the forces of darkness. Hagen, has tricked Siegfried into apparent betrayal of Brünnhilde, and then duped Brünnhilde into abetting his murder.

Siegfried's first appearance in the Prologue of *Götterdämmerung* came with the sunrise on Brünnhilde's mountain peak. The sun sets as he dies in the valley of the Rhine, breathing Brünnhilde's name. The questioning motive of fate in the trombones is answered by the kettledrums' spectral rhythm of Death. Siegfried's body is raised onto his own shield. A mist steals up from the Rhine and gradually fills the stage as he is borne off through the deepening shadows. The theme of Siegfried's Volsung forebears, recalled by somber brasses, is interrupted by the angry crash of the full Death motive:

The moon breaks through the mist for a moment and illumines Siegfried's upturned face as the orchestra unleashes a flood of memories. It weaves together the poignant themes of Siegfried's parents, Sigmund and Sieglinde: the melodies of their tragic love and of the whole unhappy Volsung race. Higher and higher over them all swirls the triumphant Death motive, until a solo trumpet cuts through the orchestra, with the theme of Siegfried's Sword, that symbolic sword which had been his and his father's before him, and which once had meant hope of salvation from the powers of darkness:

Like a persistent rondo refrain, the Death motive returns as the orchestral lament approaches its climax on two Siegfried motives, the first given to the trumpet family as follows:

The second Siegfried motive based on the hero's horn-call (which played such a large role in "Siegfried's Rhine Journey") is proclaimed by a resplendent orchestral *tutti*.

The poignance of this interlude is partly due to the Wagner's skill in suggesting many levels of musical, dramatic, and philosophical meaning, a skill which has been eloquently described by Thomas Mann in his famous essay, "Suffering and Greatness of Richard Wagner:"

> . . . The overpowering accents of the music that bears away Siegfried's corpse no longer refer to the woodland youth who set forth in order to learn fear; they instruct our feeling in what is really passing there behind falling veils of mist. The sun-hero himself lies on his bier, struck down by blind darkness, and the word comes to the aid of our emotions: "the fury of a wild boar," it says, and "his is the accursed boar," says Gunther, pointing to Hagen, "who mangled the flesh of this noble youth." A perspective opens out into the first and furthest of our human picture-dreamings. Tammuz, Adonis whom the boar slew, Osiris, Dionysius, the dismembered ones, who are to return as the Crucified whose side a Roman spear must pierce that men may know him—all that was and ever is, the whole world of slain and martyred loveliness this mystic gaze encompasses; and so let no one say that he who created Siegfried was in Parsifal untrue to himself.

One last blaze of light in the orchestra (the Siegfried motive) is followed by another return of the Death motive, a melancholy transformation of Brünnhilde's melody, a pale minor-mode echo of Siegfried, and the tale is told.

Wagner's score for the "Funeral Music" calls for piccolo, 3 flutes, 2 oboes, English horn, 3 clarinets, bass clarinet, 3 bassoons, contrabassoon, 4 horns, 3 trumpets, bass trumpet, 4 Wagner tubas, bass tuba, 4 trombones, 6 harps, kettledrums, triangle, cymbals, tenor drum, and the traditional body of strings.

GÖTTERDÄMMERUNG (TWILIGHT OF THE GODS): SIEGFRIED'S RHINE JOURNEY

"Siegfried's Rhine Journey" is a symphonic interlude which links the Prologue to the First Act of the *Twilight of the Gods.* This final opera of the four-part *Nibelung's Ring*, was composed during the last flood tide of Wagner's creative powers. His sketch of the Prologue and Act I, including the "Rhine Journey," is dated June 5, 1870. The entire opera was completed in November 1874 and first performed on August 17, 1876 at Bayreuth. A many-faceted work, it can be enjoyed on many different levels of meaning simultaneously.

The "Rhine Journey" interlude is first of all eloquent music. Secondly, although the curtain is lowered during most of the interlude, it is vividly descriptive, partly by virtue of its familiar musical themes: motives of Siegfried, of Brünnhilde, of the fire that surrounds her rock, of the Rhine, the Rhinedaughters, the Rhinegold, and the curse-laden ring.

Among musical journeys this must be one of the boldest in scope and execution. It transports Siegfried from the mythical mountain peak of Brünnhilde's rock to a more realistic realm: the sordid world of power politics which is his undoing. It takes him from the sunlit peak of his own highest achievement (the winning of Brünnhilde) down into the valley of the shadow of death, where there is neither rod nor staff of any god to comfort him, much less protect him from evil, from betrayal by villains and weaklings and, at the bitter end, by his own wife.

But despite the accents of doom with which the concert excerpt begins and ends, most of the "Journey" is fraught with irresistible orchestral splendor. It begins with sunrise on the Valkyries' Rock. Starting at the darkest moment before dawn, deep trombones sound the questioning motive of Fate. A long, sinuous line of the cellos winds upward as the first light climbs over the horizon. The Siegfried motive stirs sleepily in the horns, first in fragmentary form, then more complete, as if the hero were waking to consciousness:

Siegfried's theme is answered by a tender, lyric phrase for clarinet, depicting Brünnhilde:

As the light increases, the orchestral texture brightens, the pitch rises, Brünnhilde's melody is taken up by the more sensuous violins and carried to a climax, where it merges into the Siegfried motive now proclaimed with all the weight and brilliance of combined trumpets and horns. The rapturous duet is now elided to the moment of parting.

As Brünnhilde's eyes follow Siegfried down the moutainside, the orchestral melody, too, descends, its color and spirit fading as he is lost to sight. Then, all at once, from the valley we hear his horn-call:

As Brünnhilde catches sight of him in the distance with an ecstatic gesture of greeting, the curtain falls, and the orchestra takes up the theme of the horn-call. This call, like Siegfried himself, passes through the flickering motive of the magic fire surrounding Brünnhilde's mountain. The orchestral flames are overwhelmed by the forward peace of the Siegfried motive and the broadly sweeping theme of the River Rhine:

The cry of the Rhinedaughters for their lost gold bursts from the orchestra, combining with fragments of the Siegfried theme. As the Rhinedaughters' song continues, it merges into melodies associated with the Rhinegold and the motive of the cursed ring itself. The pace of the "Journey" subsides and the musical landscape darkens as if in premonition of the tragedy that lies ahead. Since the interlude merges without pause into the next scene of the opera, a brief concert ending is usually appended.

"Siegfried's Rhine Journey" is scored for Wagner's large *Ring* orchestra including piccolo, 3 flutes, 3 oboes, English horn, 3 clarinets, bass clarinet, 8 horns, 3 trumpets, bass trumpet, 4 trombones, tuba, kettledrums, cymbals, glockenspiel, and the traditional strings.

PRELUDE TO LOHENGRIN

It would be hard to imagine more visual music than the Prelude to *Lohengrin*. Some of the most luminous tone painting in the entire realm of Early Romantic music, these nine minutes of subtle sound are a climax in the art of orchestration. Yet this dazzling vision is also a symbol with intense emotional meaning. More important than any analysis of its form or orchestration is the content which Wagner himself attempted to pin down in words for the program notes of concerts he conducted at Zurich in May 1853. Although Wagner's fervid Romantic literary style does not translate easily, it is unsurpassed as a guide to his musical thought:

> From a hate- and strife-filled world love seemed to have vanished. In no single human community did love remain the clear basis of law. From the sterile preoccupation with profit and ownership, which governed worldly affairs, the human heart, in its unquenchable longing for love, began to crave the satisfaction of a need which, the more imperious and powerful it grew under the pressure of reality, the less it could be satisfied in this same reality. Hence mankind's ecstatic imagination placed both the source and the goal of this incomprehensible longing for love beyond the confines of the real world. And in the desire for a reassuringly material symbol of this immaterial, spiritual thing, imagination gave it a miraculous form, which soon was conceived as actually existing, although unapproachably far away, and was believed in, longed for, and sought for, under the name of the Holy Grail. This was the precious vessel out of which our Savior drank at the last supper with His disciples; in which His blood was caught when, for love of His

brethren, He suffered upon the cross; and which has been presevd to this day in devoted warmth as the source of undying love. Once, when this sacred chalice had been taken away from unworthy mankind, it was brought back from heavenly heights by a band of angels, and entrusted to a band of fervent, solitary men, miraculously strengthening and inspiring them by its presence, purifying and consecrating them as earthly crusaders for eternal love.

This miraculous descent of the Holy Grail, accompanied by an angelic host, and its consignment to the custody of exalted men, was selected by the composer of *Lohengrin* (a knight of the Grail) as the subject for musical portrayal in the prelude to his drama and which he now takes the liberty of presenting in visual terms to the reader's imagination.

To the ecstatic seeker of divine love a barely perceptible, yet magically attractive vision, seems to condense out of the pure blue ether of the sky. The infinitely delicate outline of a miraculous band of angels takes shape, floating imperceptibly down from Heaven and bearing the sacred vessel. As the apparition grows more distinctly visible to those on earth, it pours out exquisite odors, like streams of gold, enchanting the senses of the beholder, penetrating the most intimate recesses of his trembling heart with sacred emotions.

Ecstasies of pain and of pleasure alternate in the bosom of the beholder, where the apparition's life-giving magic awakens the repressed impulses of love to miraculous growth. But no matter how generously the bosom may swell, it is strained to bursting with a mighty longing, a desire for self-surrender, for self-dissolution, such as the human heart has never known before. Yet at the same time the close approach of the divine apparition to the transfigured senses brings joys indescribable. And when at last the holy vessel itself is displayed, and the sight of its naked reality is offered to those worthy, when the divine contents of the Grail radiates beams of ideal love, like the light of heavenly flames, making all hearts tremble in the fiery brilliance of this eternal glow, then the beholder sinks to his knees, lost in reverent self-abnegation. Now the Grail pours out its blessing on him who is swallowed up in the ecstasy of love, consecrating him a Knight of the Grail. The fiery brilliance subsides to a milder glow, spreading over the earth in a breath of unspeakable joy and tenderness, filling the supplicant's breast with unsuspected bliss. The angel band, still smiling down, float in chaste joy back to the heights, having returned to earth the source of love, which had ceased to flow on earth. They have left the Grail in the custody of pure men into whose hearts its contents pour in blessing, and the seraphic hosts disappear into the bright light of the celestial blue from which they first emerged.

Like the "bright light of the celestial blue" with which the vision begins and ends, a delicate, long drawn out chord of violins alone begins and ends the Prelude. Out of this high sustained harmony there crystallize, very softly at first, the outlines of the Holy Grail:

As the vision descends earthward new instruments are added, the theme descends in pitch and reaches its climax in a brief blaze of orchestral glory with full brass and woodwind sustained by a roll of the kettledrums and embellished by the metallic crash of the cymbals. The withdrawal of the heavenly hosts upward into the ethereal blue is swifter than was their approach. The orchestra, too, seems to float heavenward, growing lighter and more transparent as it rises and concluding with the disembodied sound of four solo violins *pianissimo*.

The Prelude is scored for 3 flutes, 2 oboes, English horn, 2 clarinets, bass clarinet, 3 bassoons, 4 horns, 3 trumpets, 3 trombones, tuba, timpani, cymbals, and strings. Wagner completed the score of his *Lohengrin* in April 1848, and the first performance was presented in Weimar on August 28, 1856, under the direction of Franz Liszt.

PRELUDE TO THE MASTERSINGERS OF NUREMBERG (DIE MEISTERSINGER VON NÜRNBERG)

Most ordinary mortals would have been crushed by the load of misfortune and discouragement with which Wagner had to cope at the time he began one of the greatest of operatic comedies. *Die Meistersinger* had first taken shape in Wagner's mind in 1845 as a sort of parody or rather satyr play to follow his *Tannhäuser,* on which he was working at the time.

Seventeen years later, after the completion of his death- and passion-fraught *Tristan and Isolde,* after the fiasco of *Tannhäuser* in Paris, after the accumulation of mountainous debts, after a long series of lesser discouragements and perhaps as a reaction to all of these, Wagner began actual composition of his warmhearted comedy. He began oddly enough with the Overture or Prelude as he later renamed it. It was late in March 1862. He had just taken new quarters in the town of Biebrich outside Mainz. In his autobiography Wagner describes the moment of inspiration or crystallization of his concept.

> One evening from the balcony of my house as I watched a fine sunset light up in glory the splendid view of "golden" Mainz and the majestically flowing Rhine, the Prelude to my *Meistersinger* suddenly sprang up clearly in my mind as I had once before beheld it in a troubled mood, as if it had been a distant mirage, and I proceeded to draft the Prelude precisely as it appears today in the score, that is, setting forth very definitely the main motives of the whole drama. Then I went on at once to work at the text, composing the scenes in due sequence.

The Prelude opens with the sturdy, ceremonious C-major theme of the Mastersingers themselves.

The Prelude is dominated by this and two other equally straightforward C-major themes associated with the Mastersingers' Guild. One of these, the March of the Mastersingers, is an authentic Mastersinger melody of the sixteenth century:

These themes contrast with those associated with young Walther von Stolzing, his love for Eva, and his attempts to win her as his bride. Since the Mastersingers stand for tradition and establishment, while Walther represents youth, inspiration, innovation, and rebellion, the contrasting groups of themes embody the basic conflict of the opera, in which Walther is almost frustrated. In the final scene, however, young love and the Mastersingers, inspiration and "the rules," are reconciled—which is exactly what Wagner does, symbolically, at the exultant climax of his Prelude, by combining one of Walther's melodies (a phrase later incorporated into Walther's victorious "Prize Song"):

with the theme of the Mastersingers, with the Mastersingers' March, and with a fourth, scherzo-like theme associated with the malevolent Beckmesser, all interwoven in one passage of breathtaking contrapuntal virtuosity and dramatic power.

The score of Wagner's *Meistersinger* calls for piccolo, 2 flutes, 2 oboes, 2 clarinets, 2 bassoons, 4 horns, 3 trumpets, 3 trombones, tuba, kettledrums, bass drum, trianglė, cymbals, glockenspiel, and harp.

PRELUDE AND GOOD FRIDAY MUSIC FROM PARSIFAL

From Wagner's first impulse to write a Parsifal opera to the actual production of *Parsifal* at the Festspielhaus of Bayreuth on July 22, 1882, lie nearly forty years of artistic maturing. Only a composer who had mastered the tortured longings of *Tristan und Isolde* on the one hand and the sunlit serenity of *Die Meistersinger* on the other could have encompassed the emotional extremes of *Parsifal*.

The first impulse came to Wagner in 1845 just after finishing the composition of *Tannhäuser*. He went to Bohemia for a holiday cure, taking with him the poems of the medieval mystic Wolfram von Eschenbach. "With the book under my arm, I hid myself in the neighboring woods," writes Wagner in his autobiography, "and seated by a brook, feasted myself on Titurel and Parzival in Wolfram's strange, yet touchingly attractive, poem." Immediately he was seized with a burning desire to mould this material into musico-dramatic form, but desisted because his doctor had ordered him to avoid excitement.

The questing figure of Parsifal passed often through Wagner's mind in the ensuing years, particularly in connection with the Third Act of *Tristan,* where Parsifal originally was to have played a significant role. Yet it was a Good Friday which first crystallized the dramatic outline of a Parsifal opera in his mind. This happened in April 1857. After a cold, rainy spring, the garden of a villa near Zurich was flooded with warm sunshine. "The garden was breaking into leaf, the birds were singing," Wagner later recalled, "and I could rejoice in the fruitful quiet I had so long thirsted for. Suddenly it came to me that this was Good Friday, and I remembered the great message it had once brought to me as I was reading Wolfram's *Parzival.* . . . Its essence now became clear to me in overwhelming significance, and on the basis of the Good Friday idea I quickly conceived an entire drama of which I made brief and hasty sketch in three acts."

Thus the Parsifal subject was tied up in Wagner's mind with the symbolism of Good Friday, especially the springtime symbol of physical rebirth, of spiritual rebirth through the sacrifice on the cross, and the birth of wisdom through compassion. *Parsifal* is not a religious opera, although it does use many of the symbols of Christian ritual and myth.

From the musical ritual of the Dresden Church, Wagner took the rising sixths of an ancient Amen-formula and incorporated them into his motive of the Holy Grail:

The Grail is the cup from which Christ drank at the Last Supper and which received His blood as he suffered upon the cross. Together with the spear which pierced his side, the Grail was preserved in the Temple of Montsalvat and guarded by a band of knights pure in heart and strong in faith.

Klingsor, a knight who was refused membership in the services of the Grail, seeks revenge by tempting the pure knights to a magic garden where the delights of the flesh await them in the embraces of devilishly beautiful flower maidens and, most dangerous of all, the wiles of Kundry. One of Wagner's most striking creations, Kundry is a nature divided against herself. In one incarnation she is the most dangerous of all temptresses, who has seduced even Amfortas, the King of the Knights of the Grail. In her other incarnation, she escapes the power of Klingsor and serves the knights as a tortured penitent, an ugly, coarse-robed woman, whose nature the knights cannot fathom.

During Amfortas's ecstasy in Kundry's embrace, Klingsor stole the sacred spear and wounded Amfortas with it. Amfortas escaped with his life, but the wound will not heal until the spear is won back from Klingsor. A divine prophecy has declared that the spear will be won back only by a guileless fool, made wise through compassion. The story of the opera is the fulfillment of the prophecy.

The Prelude was explained for King Ludwig II by Wagner, who headed his interpretation: "Love [Charity]*—Faith—Hope?" Wagner designated the long opening melody of the Prelude as "Love" and quoted the words to which it is sung in the Act I Grail scene, recalling the ceremony of communion: *"Nehmet hin meinen Leib, nehmet hin mein Blut, um unsrer Liebe Willen!"* ("Take ye my body, take my blood, in token of our love!")

Wagner designated the second theme as Faith:

There follows, wrote Wagner, a promise of redemption through faith.

> Firmly and stoutly Faith declares itself, exalted, unshakeable even in suffering.—The promise is repeated and answered by Faith from the remote heights —hovering downwards, as it were on the pinions of the white dove—taking more and more complete possession of the breast, the heart of man, filling all nature with the mightiest force, then looking aloft again to heaven's vault in sweet tranquillity.
>
> But once more, from out the awe of solitude, there throbs the lament of loving compassion: [a dark tremolo on the double basses and soft kettledrum roll introduce fragments of the opening theme of Love] fear, dismay, the holy sweat of the Mount of Olives, the divine death-throes of Golgotha,—the body pales, the blood wells forth and glows with heavenly blessing in the Chalice, pouring out the grace of redemption on all that lives and suffers. We are made ready for Amfortas, the sinning keeper of the holy relic, who,

* *The biblical* "caritas" *is translated in the King James version as* "charity," *but in the German Bible as* "Liebe" or "love."

> racked with repentance, quails before the divine chastisement which the sight of the glowing Grail brings with it; will the gnawing anguish of his soul find redemption?—Once more we hear the promise, and—*we hope!*

(In the First Act, when Parsifal finds his way to the domain of the Grail, he is not recognized and is dismissed as only a fool. However, his education through compassion has already begun. It reaches its climax in the Second Act, when he finds his way to Klingsor's magic garden. The unexpected result of Kundry's kiss is that Parsifal understands the anguish of Amfortas's guilt. Armed with his newfound compassion, he is proof against Kundry's wiles and Klingsor's attack. Instead of being wounded by the spear Klingsor hurls, Parsifal seizes the holy spear in midair, destroying Klingsor's evil magic with the sign of the cross. After years of search Parsifal finds his way back to the domain of the Grail, bringing the sacred spear and with it, salvation for Amfortas and his knights. It is Good Friday.)

The concert excerpt known as the "Good Friday Music" begins with Parsifal's own motive:

as the old knight, Gurnemanz hails the fulfillment of the prophecy, blesses Parsifal, and greets him as the new King of the Knights of the Grail and successor to Amfortas. Parsifal's first deed as King is to baptize Kundry, who at last is able to weep tears of repentance and joy. The noonday sun floods the woods and fields. As Parsifal views the miracle of spring, a new melody wells up in the orchestra: over murmuring strings a solo oboe sings the Good Friday melody, which blossoms as gently as a flower of the Good Friday meadow:

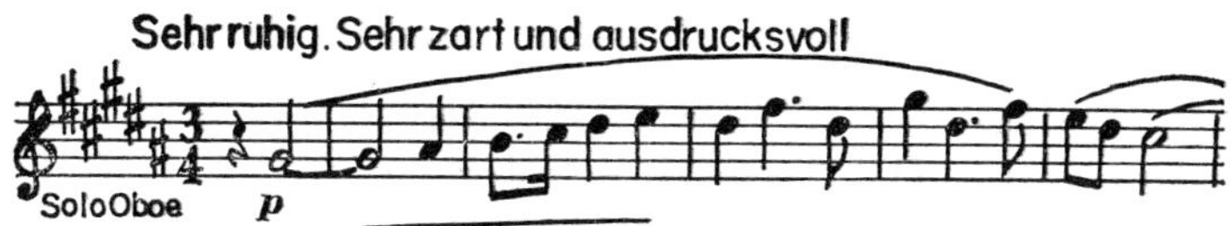

Parsifal expresses his wonder and Gurnemanz explains that this is the magic of Good Friday. But on the day of the Savior's suffering, cries Parsifal, he would expect all nature to mourn. The Good Friday melody gives answer in an outpouring of beatific tenderness. Gurnemanz explains that nature cannot grasp God's pain.

> His wasted body on the cross it cannot see
> and so it looks aloft to man redeemed,
> free from sin and all its weight of terror,
> by God's love-sacrifice made clean and pure.
> Today each blade, each meadow flower that blooms

knows well no foot of man will tread it down,
but as God unmurm'ring died for him,
in love and pity the cross endured,—
so man in tender, holy mood
treads softly on the earth today.
Thus all creation gratefully sings,
all that doth bloom and fade again,
well knowing nature's pardon won,
earth's heart today made pure and free of stain.

The Prelude and "Good Friday Music" are scored for 3 flutes, 3 oboes, English horn, 3 clarinets, bass clarinet, 3 bassoons, contrabasson, 4 horns, 3 trumpets, 2 tenor trombones, bass trombone, tuba, kettledrums, and strings.

A SIEGFRIED IDYLL

It is hard to believe that the composer who once felt love as a wild, destroying passion, as the love-death of *Tristan and Isolde,* could ever have known domestic bliss. But years later, Wagner did enjoy a period of relative peace and domestic fulfillment. In November 1870, his heart overflowing with gratitude, he composed (as a birthday present for his wife Cosima) the blissfully contented music we know as *A Siegfried Idyll.* Here, love did not mean any Tristanish night, death, and dreams. On the contrary, it meant dawn, birth, and reality. The music referred to their baby son "Fidi" (Siegfried), but also to more intimate secrets in Richard's and Cosima's past.

Cosima's birthday fell on December 25. In the Wagner household, this combined birthday and Christmas present was familiarly called *Die Treppenmusick* (The Staircase Music) because its first performance was played on the staircase of Villa Triebschen,* their home on Lake Lucerne. Wagner took the greatest precautions to be sure that the work and its first performance were a complete surprise. Early on Christmas morning, 1870, fifteen players from Lucerne, whom Wagner had secretly rehearsed, assembled silently on the little winding stairs of the Villa, with Wagner, who was conducting, at the top. Cosima was overwhelmed:

> I can give you no idea, my children, about this day, [wrote Cosima in her diary] nor about my feelings. I shall only tell you quite barely what hap-

* *This spelling (*Triebschen, *instead of the older* Tribschen *or* Tripschen*) was Wagner's invention. Always fascinated by word origins, Wagner deduced his own (imaginary) etymology, and from it his "corrected" spelling. Tribschen, the old name for the site (a small peninsula jutting into Lake Lucerne on which the villa was built) is the spelling used today by careful German writers. Strict scholarship would call for the use here of* both *spellings: the historically correct one* and *Wagner's usual spelling. (Yet Wagner himself was inconsistent and occasionally lapsed into the older, correct spelling.) In order to avoid the distractions and potential confusions of such painstaking exactitude, Wagner's usual spelling is used here.*

> pened: As I awoke, my ear caught a sound, which swelled fuller and fuller; no longer could I imagine myself to be dreaming: music was sounding, and such music! When it died away, Richard came into my room with the children and offered me the score of the symphonic birthday poem. I was in tears, but so was all the rest of the household. Richard had arranged his orchestra on the staircase, and thus our *Triebschen* was consecrated forever. . . . After lunch the orchestra came into the house downstairs, and now the *Idyll* was heard once again, to the profound emotion of us all.

The *Idyll* was a private and personal document, never intended for the ears of the outside world. Only years later, under grim financial pressure and to the distress of both Wagner and Cosima, was this music published—under the official title of *A Siegfried Idyll.* Its original, more meaningful title was *Tribschener Idyll.* The manuscript title page included the nickname of Wagner's baby son, Siegfried, and recalled the color of the sunrise on the morning of his birth in the spring of 1869. It read in full: *Tribschener Idyll, with Fidi's Birdsong and Orange Sunrise, as a Symphonic Birthday Greeting from Richard to Cosima.* The music recalled other personal memories, the most intimate of which were not unraveled until after Cosima's death sixty years later.

Wagner's unconventional family life had been of a complexity we need not try to describe here. It is enough to recall that Cosima, while still legally married to Hans von Bülow, left him in 1866 and went to live at Villa Triebschen as the protectress and muse of Richard Wagner. She had already born Wagner a daughter, Isolde. Their second daughter, Eva, was born at Triebschen in 1868 and their son Siegfried in 1869.

It was long supposed that all the themes of the *Idyll,* except for an old German lullaby, were taken from Wagner's opera *Siegfried.* The *Idyll*'s first and principal theme is a beatific melody that precedes Brünnhilde's words in the last act: *"Ewig war ich"* ("Immortal was I"):

But this melody did not *originate* in the opera. It was first conceived for a string quartet intended as a present to Cosima, six years earlier when they were first in love. So this reference to their first intimacy, in the work celebrating their domestic felicity, had a meaning for both Wagner and Cosima beyond the beauty of the music itself, a meaning kept carefully secret.

A soft, caressing continuation from the opening theme leads to the old German cradlesong, *"Schlaf', Kindchen, schlafe"* ("Sleep, Little Child, Sleep"), piped very simply by the oboe.

But the allusions of these innocent-seeming themes are anything but simple. Ernest Newman, the English Wagner scholar who untangled the sources of the *Idyll,* pointed out that this lullaby was jotted down in Wagner's diary long before Siegfried's birth and that it referred not to Siegfried but to the baby Eva. We may never know the full extent of the private allusions in the *Idyll.* Is it only a coincidence, for example, that the lullaby consists of the notes of the *Idyll*'s first theme, but reversed? Or should we say that the opening theme could be derived from the lullaby? The lullaby theme is presented here in the same key as the opening theme to make the relationship clear:

The opening theme returns, the strings put on mutes, and the music shifts dreamily into a distant key where, the woodwinds introduce the melody, *"O Siegfried, herrlicher! Hort der Welt!"* ("O Siegfried, thou glorious hope of the world!") which Brünnhilde sings in their last-act duet. This melody, too, originated in the string quartet sketches of 1864.

These melodies work up to a brief climax which is suddenly cut off as a solo horn introduces the energetic theme associated in the opera with Siegfried as a young man. The song of the forest bird from the Act II forest murmurs, and other themes from the opera, fashion another brief climax. Finally the lullaby returns, clothed in even more glowing poetry. The close of the *Idyll* suggests the approach of peaceful sleep.

The staircase at Triebschen is short and narrow. Any players that could be squeezed onto it—even standing—would necessarily have been a tiny chamber ensemble. The score for the *Idyll* calls for flute, oboe, 2 clarinets, trumpet, 2 horns, bassoon, 1st and 2nd violins, viola, cello, and double bass.

OVERTURE TO TANNHAUSER

Wagner's Romantic opera, *Tannhauser and the Contest of Song on the Wartburg,* based on medieval legends of the conflict between sacred and profane love, was produced in Dresden under the composer's direction in 1845. The Overture to the opera soon became a popular concert excerpt, and Wagner wrote a description of the ideas it embodied. His own program note written for a famous series of concerts he conducted at Zurich in May, 1873, is still the best guide to the feelings and visions he wished his music to suggest:

> At first the orchestra introduces us to the "Pilgrims' Chorus" alone. It approaches, swells to a mighty outpouring and finally passes into the distance. —Twilight: dying echoes of the chorus.—As night falls, magic visions show themselves. A rosy mist swirls upward, sensuously exultant sounds reach our ears, and the blurred motions of a fearsomely voluptuous dance are revealed. [At this moment the feverish *Allegro* of the Overture begins; the harmonics turn chromatic; and we hear the first of many bacchanalian themes associated with the unholy revels in the legendary Venusberg:]

This is the seductive magic of the Venusberg, which appears by night to those whose souls are fired by bold, sensuous longings. Lured by the tempting visions, the slender figure of a man draws near: it is Tannhäuser, the minstrel of love. Proudly he sings his jubilant chant of love, exultantly and challengingly, as if to force the voluptuous magic to come to him.—He is answered by wild shouts. The rosy clouds envelop him more closely. Intoxicating fragrances surround him. In a tempting half-light his clairvoyant eyes now behold an indescribably attractive woman's figure. He hears a voice call him with the trembling sweetness of a Siren's song, promising the fulfillment of the bold man's wildest dreams. It is Venus herself who has appeared to him.

His heart and senses glow, the blood in his veins takes fire, an irresistible attraction draws him nearer and he steps before the goddess with his exultant chant of love, which he now sings in ecstatic praise of Venus. As if in response to his magic summons the wonders of the Venusberg are now revealed to him. Impetuous shouts and cries of ecstasy are heard on every side. In drunken joy the Bacchantes rush upon him and draw him into their wild dance, further and further into the glowing arms of the goddess herself, who embraces him with fiery passion and sweeps him in drunken ecstacy into the farthest realms of ceasing to be. [. . .] The storm subsides. Only a soft, sensuous moan lingers on the air over the spot where late the unholy ecstacy held sway, and where night now reigns supreme.—Yet already the morning dawns: from the far distance the pilgrim's chorus is heard again. As it draws ever nearer and day repulses night, those lingering moans, which had seemed like laments of the damned, are transfigured into a murmur of joy so that at last, when the sun rises in splendor, and the joyous pilgrims' chorus proclaims salvation to all the world and to all living things, the joyous murmur grows and swells to mightiest, noblest rejoicing. Redeemed from the curse of ungodly shame, the Venusberg itself joins its exultant voice to the godly chant. Thus each pulse of life leaps and throbs to the song of salvation, and those dissevered elements, soul and senses, God and Nature, are united in the sacred kiss of love.

The Overture to *Tannhäuser* is scored for piccolo, 3 flutes, 2 oboes, 2 clarinets, 2 bassoons, 2 valve horns, 2 natural horns, 3 trumpets, 3 trombones, tuba, kettledrums, triangle, cymbals, tambourine and the traditional string choir.

PRELUDE AND LOVE-DEATH FROM TRISTAN AND ISOLDE

In its earliest surviving versions the greatest love-tragedy of the Western world, the legend of Tristan and Isolde, is already touched with the love of death. Paradoxically enough, this may be the chief source of the power with which the legend has gripped our imagination through eight centuries.

In a brilliantly penetrating book *Love in the Western World (L'Amour et l'occident)* Denis de Rougement argues that the seeming glorification of the Tristan legend is a mask for the frightening truth, that the lovers' true search is for passion in its original meaning of suffering, and their ultimate goal: death. Deep insight into the human heart can be a frightening experience, and few composers have had as penetrating a glance as Wagner. As his uncanny intuition probed closer and closer to the core of the Tristan legend, he was appalled. "This *Tristan* is turning into something *terrifying!*" he wrote to Mathilde Wesendonck, with whom he was in love while composing it. "I'm afraid the opera will be forbidden—unless it is turned into a parody by bad performances. Only mediocre performances can save me!"

Wagner's opera, completed on August 6, 1859, is a tragedy of two lovers who can never belong to each other in this life, who find the complications, the conventions and ethical obligations of life to be only obstacles to the fulfillment of their love and who therefore seek the consummation of their love in death. As Wagner presents the story, Tristan and Isolde have been in love long before the opera begins. Already in the first Act they seek death by drinking what they both believe to be a death potion. It is only the belief that they are about to die which enables them to admit their guilty love for each other. The fact that they have actually drunk a love potion changes nothing, psychologically speaking. It merely frustrates and momentarily postpones their search for death.

The Prelude opens with a prolonged sigh of unfulfillable passion:

This phrase which dominates the opera and concludes its final page, was not named by Wagner though it has been given various labels associated with grief, longing and desire. As the phrase echoes, and the music swells to its anguished climax, notice how the harmonies never once are resolved in a single satisfying tonic cadence. This avoidance of harmonic rest is Wagner's way of symbolizing a passion which, by its nature, cannot be consummated.

In a program note for a performance of the Prelude which he conducted in Paris in 1860, Wagner wrote:

> The world, power, fame, splendor, honor, chivalry, friendship, all are dissipated like an empty dream. One thing only remains: longing, longing, insatiable longing, forever springing up anew, pining and thirsting. Death, which means passing away, perishing, never awakening, their only deliverance. . . . In one long succession of linked phrases [the composer has] let that

insatiable longing swell from the first, timid avowal. . . . through anxious sighs, hopes and fears, laments and desires, bliss and torment, to the mightiest striving the most powerful effort to break through. . . . into the sea of lover's endless delight. In vain! The exhausted heart sinks back to pine away in a longing that can never attain its end . . . till in final exhaustion the dimming sight glimpses the highest bliss—the bliss of dying, of ceasing to be, of final release into that wondrous realm from which we only stray the further the more we struggle to enter it by force. Shall we call this realm Death? Or is it not rather the wonder-world of Night, from which, as legend tells, the ivy and the vine grew from the graves of Tristan and Isolde to entwine in inseparable embrace? ["Love-Death" was Wagner's original concert title for this Prelude.]

"Transfiguration" was his original title for the finale of the opera. Tristan has expired in the arms of Isolde. King Mark, who has been told the story of the love potion, arrives to forgive and unite the lovers. But it is too late. Isolde no longer sees or hears the people about her, in her trance, as she looks down at Tristan's body. A light shines from his face and a song wells up which she alone can hear: the melody of their second-act love duet. Her voice joins in the great sweeping arch of the orchestral melody built on sequences of the Love–Death theme. "Is it I alone who hear this wondrous melody?" she sings (*"Höre ich nur diese Weise"*):

As the music rises higher and higher and floods on to its magnificent climax, Isolde is swept on the crest of the song, past the sorrowing onlookers, to join Tristan in the vast wave of the breath of the world (*"in des Welt Athems wehen dem all"*). Night and Death and Love are one.

The Prelude and "Liebestod" (or "Love-Death" and "Transfiguration," to repeat Wagner's originial titles) are scored for 2 flutes, 2 oboes, English horn, 2 clarinets, bass clarinet, 3 bassoons, 4 horns, 3 trumpets, 3 trombones, bass tuba, kettledrums, harp, and the traditional strings.

William Walton

Born March 29, 1902, Oldham, Lancashire

SYMPHONY NO. 1

Sir William Walton's Symphony No. 1, composed in the years 1933 through 1935, has an unusual background. Up to the time of this symphony, Sir William had been known principally for colorful program music or music associated with a text. He first became widely known through his witty *Facade* of 1922, a jazzy, allusive chamber work, designed to accompany the reading of poems by his friend Edith Sitwell. His Overture, *"Portsmouth Point,"* was inspired by a Rowlandson drawing of the same name which was reprinted in the score. *Belshazzar's Feast,* a large-scale work on a biblical text, for baritone solo and two brass bands, was a resounding success in 1931, despite its allegedly worldly character which precluded its performance in cathedral, as was planned for the Three Choirs Festival.

Walton's only abstractly symphonic works up to this point had been his *Sinfonia concertante* of 1927 and Viola Concerto of 1929. The success of these led many of his admirers to hope for a symphony.

Sir William agreed to a performance date. The writing of the symphony was not accomplished without struggle. Work proceeded more slowly than he expected, and the premiere was postponed. By the fall of 1934, the fourth movement being still incomplete, Walton took the unusual step of allowing Sir Hamilton Harty to perform the first three movements alone with the London Symphony Orchestra. The *finale* was completed the following summer, and the first performance of the full four movements was presented at a concert of the BBC in London on November 6, 1935, again under the direction of Sir Hamilton Harty. Sir William made a further slight alteration in the score during the subsequent recording of the symphony by Sir Hamilton and the London Symphony Orchestra.

Sixteen years after he had completed the score, as distinguished an authority as Mosco Carner was to write that Walton's First Symphony was "an essential landmark in English symphonic thinking and by now has become almost a classic."

The Symphony is often spoken of as being in B-flat minor and indeed the first movement is clearly centered about that key. But it is worth noting that the composer assigns it no official key in his title. Furthermore, while the first and last movements are firmly anchored to a tonality, this is not achieved by traditional eighteenth and nineteenth century processes of "functional" harmony. Like many twentieth-century composers, Sir William reaches back to the archaic, not to say primitive, device of long-held, repeatedly emphasized bass notes, to establish a feeling of tonal stability.

I. *Allegro assai.* In the mysterious opening bars, the central tonality is immediately established and emphasized by the following strikingly rhythmic figure in the second violins: *

Over this figure, which persists for many bars, a solo oboe intones a melancholy phrase of a somewhat Sibelian tinge, centering about a sustained, repeated D flat. This plaintive phrase dominates the first movement.

As in traditional symphonic form, there is a second section in a contrasting tonality. Whereas the opening centered around B flat, the contrasting section centers around C, the new tonality being established by a massive insistence on sustained low C's for the double basses, cellos, bassoons, tuba, and rolling kettledrum. The screaming dissonances of high woodwinds and strings, far from obscuring the basic C, seem only to reinforce it. There are other formal traits in which Sir William follows Classical and Romantic precedent. We need mention only that there is a middle section of thematic development, a highly condensed reprise of the opening and a climactic *coda.*

II. *Presto, con malizia.* The *scherzo,* which comes second, is directed to be played "with malice." A sharply rhythmic introduction breaks off with a crash. Under whispering violins and violas, the lowest strings (double basses with cellos) and woodwinds (bassoons) hop about in the bottom of the orchestra in an oddly syncopated rhythm. The syncopation grows wilder with changing time signatures and the theme is taken up by one orchestral group after another. As we reach the first climax of the movement, all the strings in octaves hammer out a theme which is a rhythmic transformation of the main theme of the preceding movement.

III. *Andante con malinconia.* The slow movement, primarily melodic, begins, like the first, with a softly sustained tonality which is to be the "key" center. Above it, a solo flute chants, *doloroso molto espressivo,* a long arching melody:

---

* *This and the following musical example from this composition are copyright 1936 by the Oxford University Press, London. Reprinted by permission.*

The entire movement seems to grow from this central melodic arch which appears to branch and flower into many related and interrelated phrases. Much of the character of the movement is due to the fact that most of this melodic growth takes place chiefly in the woodwind choir.

IV. *Maestoso; Brioso ed ardamente; Vivacissimo; Maestoso.* The *finale* falls into four main sections. The vigorous opening theme of the *Maestoso* is derived from the first movement. The second section, which is to culminate in a grand fugue, begins with boldly slashing figures for the highest woodwinds and strings. The fugue itself opens with a bare unaccompanied subject, marked to be performed "with fire." The *Vivacissimo* section of the *finale* also culminates in a fugal section. And the concluding *Maestoso,* developed from the opening, surpasses all preceding climaxes in power and brilliance.

The symphony is scored for 2 flutes, piccolo, 2 oboes, 2 clarinets, 2 bassoons, 4 horns, 3 trumpets, 3 trombones, tuba, kettledrums, military drum, gong, cymbals, and strings. It is dedicated to the Baroness Ima Doernberg.

The first performance in the United States was presented by the Chicago Symphony Orchestra on January 23, 1936, under the direction of Sir Hamilton Harty.

Ben Weber

Born July 23, 1916, St. Louis, Missouri

CONCERTO FOR PIANO AND ORCHESTRA, OPUS 52

One of the most modest—indeed, retiring—figures among major American composers of our time, Ben Weber speaks a strongly individual language. While he is not among the faddish, far-out experimenters, he has, like any genuinely creative artist, developed new paths for himself which are an extension of musical tradition. At first hearing, one may be primarily attracted by Weber's communicative gift which is of an intensity granted to few. On closer acquaintance, his melodic imagination, his subtle sense of instrumental color, and other less obvious attractions seem to grow. The following factual notes on the composer and his work were supplied by Mr. Weber for the premiere performances of his Concerto by the New York Philharmonic with William Masselos as soloist under the direction of Leonard Bernstein on March 24, 25, 26, and 27, 1961.

> On July 23, 1916, Ben Weber was born in St. Louis, Missouri. He became no prodigy, there is no history of music in his family, and in fact during his student days he was under constant pressure to turn to the study of medicine, which he did for about a year. He turned from this to music, which was a lifelong attraction, and took his musical training at De Paul University in Chicago. He studied there, musical theory, piano, and voice. He resented the authoritarian attitude of the one teacher of composition he came in contact

with, and proceeded to teach himself by analysis of scores and by listening to as much music as possible. He hated Mozart, now one of his greatest loves. No one listening to his Piano Concerto will believe this.

Within a few years after coming to New York in 1945, to live permanently, Ben Weber began to attract serious attention from his colleagues and critics alike. He has been the recipient of many awards and fellowships: two Guggenheims, an Award and Citation from the National Institute of Arts and Letters in 1950, two awards from the Paul Fromm Foundation (including commissions for works), four residence grants from Yaddo Colony. He was one of two Americans chosen to compose works for the Convegno Musicale in Rome, 1954, for which he wrote his Concerto for Violin and Orchestra, which proved a success there. It received its American premiere in Atlanta, Georgia in 1974. Weber was also commissioned by the Louisville Orchestra to compose a work for its series—(Prelude and Passacaglia), performed by the New York Philharmonic Orchestra under Dimitri Mitropoulos in 1954. For many years he was an active member of the Board of the International Society for Contemporary Music, and has been a board member and president of the American Composers Alliance.

The Concerto for Piano and Orchestra, Opus 52, is one of the works commissioned by the Ford Foundation "Program in the Humanities and the Arts." It was written specifically for Mr. Masselos and at his request, under the conditions of the grant. The orchestration of the Piano Concerto was completed in early February of 1961, only a few weeks before its Philharmonic premiere the following month.

I. *Deciso, non tanto allegro.* This movement has a *tutti* of some 40 bars before the entrance of the soloist. It is of a rather marchlike character. At the very beginning of the movement is a melodic fragment developed out of the series (of 12 tones) used as a basis for the musical organization of the first movement.

This same melodic formation recurs towards the close of this movement as a kind of "reprise," elaborated simultaneously in the solo instruments, as a closing *tutti,* and ending with the same notes and chord that are used for the first entrance of the piano. Many ramifications of the material occur during the body of the movement—the whole serving as a *fantasia,* and not as a movement in sonata-form, in spite of the reprise. The character of the whole movement is vigorous and somewhat unrelenting.

II. *Andantino, con rubato.* The slow movement uses a variant of the tone-series, and the first appearance is in the solo piano, as though improvising a simple melody:

This is then taken up in a delicate orchestration and continued in free-style, always clearly melodic in utterance, and simple in expressivity. The middle section is a *passacaglia* of five variations, the compositional novelty being that the passacaglia-theme (drawn from the tone series), in all but the last variation, drops a whole tone in each variation section, the very last variation is based over the theme at its original pitch. The *coda* is a dissolution of the whole atmosphere of the movement, and points towards the last movement.

III. *Allegro.* The final movement utilizes still a third variant of the tone series, finally producing scale-like forms which are used as some of the accompanying material, some time after the movement gets under way. The form is basically that of a rondo, with emphasized rhythmic structures rather than melodic ones for the most part. There is more "development" of specific sections in this movement than in any of the others. The piano is a driving force again as it was in the first movement. The piano's final comment is a simple one, melodic, dissolving into the low register, accompanied by muted lines in strings, and random percussion comments.

This Concerto for Piano and Orchestra is scored for piccolo, 2 flutes, 2 oboes, English horn, 2 clarinets, bass clarinet, 2 bassoons, contrabassoon, 4 horns, 2 trumpets, 2 tenor trombones, bass drum, high gong, low gong, triangle, cymbals, and the usual strings.

Carl Maria von Weber

Born November 18, 1786, Eutin—died June 5, 1826, London

KONZERTSTÜCK (CONCERT PIECE FOR PIANO AND ORCHESTRA), OPUS 79

The composer of *Der Freischütz* was always at his best, whether writing an opera or a piano concerto, when he had a dramatic plot for his music. His charming old-fashioned *Konzertstück* is really a Romantic piano concerto in one movement and, as you might guess from the music alone, it has a plot: a very simple plot, but enough to fire Weber's imagination. He composed the *Konzertstück* at the time his most famous opera *Der Freischütz,* was being prepared for its premiere at the Berlin Opera House in 1821. In fact he put the finishing touches on the *Konzertstück* during the morning of the opera's premiere. He played it over immediately to one of his pupils, Julius Benedict and his wife, and, apparently in very good humor, he explained in some detail the dramatic plot he had in mind.

A lady, a *châtelaine,* sits alone in her tower, gazing away into the distance. Her knight has gone on a crusade to the Holy Land. Years have passed and battles been fought. She wonders whether he is still alive and whether she will ever see him again. In her excited imagination she sees a vision of her knight lying wounded and forsaken on the battlefield. If only she could fly to his side and die with him! She falls back unconscious. Then, from the distance there is a sound of a trumpet, there is a flashing and fluttering in the forest coming nearer and nearer. We hear the hint of a march:

> It is the crusaders, knights, and squires, with banners waving and people shouting. And he is among them. She sinks into his arms. Love is triumphant. The woods and waves sing of their love, and a thousand voices proclaim his victory.

This is hardly a story which would overwhelm a modern audience, but all that matters is that it excited Weber. And since he was able to communicate his excitement in music instead of words, it remains as stirring today as it was over a century ago. The freshness and simplicity of the music are irresistible. The naïve pomp and chivalry of the march, the frantic rejoicing of the *finale* make us forget for a moment the sophistication of modern music and exult with Weber over the rescue of his imaginary *châtelaine*.

The orchestration for Weber's *Konzertstück* calls for 2 flutes, 2 oboes, 2 clarinets, 2 bassoons, 2 horns, 2 trumpets, bass trombone, kettledrums, and the customary string choir.

OVERTURE TO EURYANTHE

"My reception when I appeared in the orchestra to conduct the premiere of *Euryanthe* was the most enthusiastic and brilliant that one could imagine," wrote Weber to his wife the day after the premiere on October 25, 1823. "There was no end to it. At last I gave the signal for beginning. Stillness of death. The Overture was applauded madly, and there was a demand for a repetition; but I went ahead so that the performance might not be too long or drawn out."

It was the epochal success of his *Der Freischütz* in Berlin that had earned Weber a commission for the Kärntnertor Court Opera in Vienna. Weber began his *Euryanthe* in 1821 and worked at it, with interruptions, for nearly two years. He composed the Overture between September 1 and October 19, 1823. The premiere of the opera six days later was extremely successful. Despite the opposition of the Italian faction, which dominated the Viennese Court Opera, there were twenty performances in the first season. But after the first season, *Euryanthe* was handicapped by its foolish libretto. Yet the brilliance, spontaneity, and imaginativeness of the music have aroused enthusiasm whenever the opera has been revived. Schumann was enchanted by it. "This music is too little known and appreciated," he wrote in 1847. "It is heart's blood, the noblest he had, and this opera certainly cost him a part of his life; but he is also immortal. It is a chain of sparkling jewels from beginning to end—all brilliant and flawless. How splendid the characterization of certain figures such as Eglantine and Euryanthe—and how the instruments sound! They speak to us from the innermost depths."

Euryanthe took long to cross the ocean. The first clearly documented performance in the United States was at the Metropolitan Opera House on December 23, 1887, under the direction of Anton Seidl. Lilli Lehmann sang the title role in a distinguished cast including Max Alvary, Marianne Brandt, and Emil Fischer.

The Overture has always been popular in the concert hall. It opens with a brilliant flourish for full orchestra: *Allegro marcato, con molto fuoco.* The brass and woodwinds proclaim a gallant phrase with which the hero affirms his reliance on God and his beloved Euryanthe: *"Ich bau' auf Gott und meine Euryanth."* A tender, contrasting phrase sung by the first violins is taken from the hero's second-act aria and is sung to the words: *"O Seligkeit, dich fass' ich Kaum"* ("O bliss which I scarce can grasp"):

The development section is introduced by a famous passage of Romantic ghost music. It is taken from a first-act narrative in which Euryanthe describes the funeral vault of the unfortunate Emma, who had taken poison when her beloved was killed in battle. The appearance of Emma's ghost is depicted by the disembodied sound of eight muted solo violins. Halfway through this brief passage the eight violins are joined by the viola section playing the merest whisper of a tremolo. The ghost music is followed by an impetuous development of the Overture's opening themes and a return of the lyric melody, *"O Seligkeit, dich fass' ich Kaum,"* leading to a triumphant orchestral peroration.

The Overture is scored for 2 flutes, 2 oboes, 2 clarinets, 2 bassoons, 4 horns, 2 trumpets, 3 trombones, timpani, and the usual strings.

OVERTURE TO DER FREISCHÜTZ

How wonderfully fresh *Der Freischütz* is! After more than a century and a half, almost every bar of that youthful opera is as fresh as the forest air after a storm. Its Overture could be an overture to one of Grimm's fairy tales. As a matter of fact, *Der Freischütz is* a fairy tale opera sprung from the early nineteenth-century epoch and atmosphere in which the Grimm brothers assembled their great collection of German folklore. It is a typical *Märchen*, as the Germans call these tales, set in a forest with ghosts, evil spirits, seven charmed bullets (with which the devil tempts huntsmen's souls), a loving couple, a friendly hermit, and a happy ending.

The Overture reflects the shifting moods of the forest. What could be more Romantic than those serene sunlit bars of the opening, with the tranquil weavings of the strings and the golden chant of the horns? Suddenly a shadow passes through the forest. A shuddering *tremolo* of the strings and the mysterious plucked basses represent Samiel, the tempter who buys men's souls with seven charmed bullets:

Then comes pandemonium: the wild midnight storm in the Wolf's Glen, where the bullets are cast, ghosts and goblins appear, and, finally, Samiel himself, the Wild Huntsman. Was the Wild Huntsman Wotan or the Devil? Probably he was a little of both. For when Christianity came to Germany, it turned the old gods into demons. Their key is C minor, their instrumental color dark (i.e., low in pitch).

The forces of good are personified by the hermit and the heroine, Agathe. They are represented musically by the climax of Agathe's great aria *"Leise, leise,"* thanking Heaven for the safe return of her betrothed, Max. Her melody furnishes the contrasting second theme of Weber's Overture:

Good and evil clash in a symphonic development. Evil seems about to triumph with the brief reprise of the storm music, but this dies away with the shuddering diminished sevenths of Samiel. There is a dramatic silence. Then, as if it were a sudden burst of sunlight, Agathe's jubilant air returns in a blazing C major. The forest is cleansed of evil spirits and the joyous impetuosity of the music says, as only music can: "They lived happily ever after."

The triumphant first performance of the entire opera *Der Freischütz* was given in Berlin on June 18, 1821, under the direction of Weber. But the Overture to the opera had an earlier premiere on October 8, 1820, in Copenhagen, also under Weber's direction. This, too, was a triumph, and the Overture has remained one of the most popular ever written.

The Overture to *Der Freischütz* is scored for 2 flutes, 2 oboes, 2 clarinets, 2 bassoons, 4 horns, 2 trumpets, 3 trombones, kettledrums, and the usual strings.

OVERTURE TO OBERON

The horn call that opens this Overture is sheer magic.

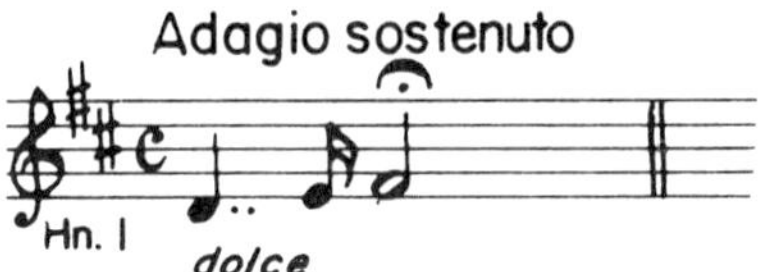

In the action of Weber's opera, these three notes are a magic summons to the Elf-King Oberon to rescue the hero, Sir Huon. Huon, like Tamino in Mozart's *Magic Flute,* has been sent on a perilous rescue mission with his chief protection a magic musical instrument. Huon's adventure recalls other legendary horn-calls. Roland, like Huon, was a knight of Charlemagne and like him, called with his horn for help against Saracen foes in the battle of Roncevaux.

For listeners, the horn-call has additional kinds of magic, among them sheer sensuous sound. It is difficult to separate this sound from traditional associations of the horn. Since the orchestral horn was descended from the old hunting horn, and its German name, *Waldhorn,* means forest horn, it has often been used to suggest the poetry of the deep woods. Weber was among the most imaginative pioneers in the whole evolution of orchestral color which characterized the Romantic age. In his *Oberon* we sense how he savored the soft glow of the French horn, the velvet caress of the clarinet, the freshness of violin sound, and dozens of subtle combinations.

In the Overture, the solo horn-call is answered by muted strings, irridescent flutes, and clarinets—all sounds associated with Oberon's elfin world. A scarcely audible fanfare, as of mysterious, distant trumpets, is marked to be played "as softly as possible." To English-speaking listeners, this passage irresistibly recalls "the horns of Elfland faintly blowing."

A *tutti* crash introduces the fiery *Allegro* on themes of Huon's adventures. Rushing violin figures forecast the triumphant escape of the lovers, Huon and his Princess Reiza, as they board the ship which is to carry them to safety from her father, the tyrannical Haroun al Raschid. The horn-call and elf music return briefly, suggesting Oberon's intervention. A clarinet sings a love melody from Huon's first-act aria. Soon the violins take up Reiza's exultant passage from her famous aria, "Ocean, thou mighty Monster," the melody to which she sings, "My husband, my Huon, we are saved, we are saved":

More quotations from the opera, including a lusty, stamping rhythm associated with the two elves, Puck and Droll, enrich the development. The peroration, with the return of Reiza's melody, is irresistibly exciting.

Weber was a sick man when he embarked on the commission for his opera, *Oberon*, to an English libretto by James Robinson Planché. When he arrived in London, he was already in an advanced stage of consumption. Yet, he himself conducted the enormously successful premiere at the Royal Covent Garden Opera on April 12, 1826. It was his last triumph. He died on June 5. He was only thirty-nine.

The Overture is scored for pairs of flutes, oboes, clarinets, and bassoons, 4 horns, 2 trumpets, 3 trombones, kettledrums, and the usual strings.

Anton Webern

Born December 3, 1883, Vienna—died September 15, 1945, Mittersill, Austria

FIVE MOVEMENTS, OPUS 5, VERSION FOR STRING ORCHESTRA

Today, decades after his death, Anton Webern still seems a paradoxical figure. Largely ignored by the musical world during his lifetime, this shy, gentle, unaggressive man was transformed soon after his death into one of the most potent forces in mid-twentieth-century music. His tiny life work (barely three hours of music, mostly exquisite miniatures) fascinated a whole generation of composers and, for a time, surpassed the influence of even such a giant as Stravinsky. After his death, one of the composers most attracted to Webern was Stravinsky himself.

It seems a paradox that Webern's highly emotional music is usually "explained" in terms of theory, of abstruse technical procedures, of formal ingenuities and intellectual complexity. But this is putting the cart before the horse. Certainly Webern's music *can* be enormously rewarding to analyze. It *is* intellectual, of course, but so is the music of Bach, Wagner, Josquin Desprez and dozens of others. All of them can be fascinating to analyze—*after* one has come to enjoy the music, as music. But it is probably safe to say that not one of these composers ever dreamt that the first, best road to enjoyment of his music lay through technical dissection.

Another seeming paradox is that Webern's music, for all its modernity, is deeply Romantic. The slow movements of this Opus 5 are only two among many obvious examples. Both movements are (among other things) "mood" music in the best tradition of nineteenth-century Romanticism.

The only "warning" that might be useful to a listener who has never heard any Webern before is that his music tends to be very short. To take an extreme example, the middle movement of Opus 5 lasts approximately forty seconds. Webern makes his point swiftly and with the utmost economy of notes. Often he recalls the fastidious art of the Japanese poets of *haiku,* in which an entire poem is limited to a total of seventeen syllables distributed over three lines. Yet within these self-imposed limits, Webern, like the Japanese poets, manages to evoke powerful images and emotions.

In 1909 when he composed the original (string quartet) version of Opus 5, Webern was still studying with Schoenberg. But he was such an advanced student that he was already influencing his teacher as much as he was learning from him. Twenty years later Webern rescored the Five Movements for string orchestra. The original quartet version was filled with wonderful expressive subtleties, little details which are a joy to mull over at one's leisure. The orchestral version is by comparison a whole magic garden of exotic and delicate musical colors. Although the composer uses only a traditional string orchestra, he often subdivides the traditional sections, and frequently selects a soloist from the individual sections, so that one may hear, for example, two independent groups of cellos plus a solo cellist. Often a single phrase, which may have been originally the property of one instrument, will be broken up and redistributed, so that it is begun by a violin, continued by a viola and completed by a cello. This is one of a dozen ways in which Webern varies the color of a melodic line within a tiny space, and does it so skillfully that the listener may never be aware of the device.

I. *Heftig bewegt.* Into the space of approximately two-and-a-half minutes, Webern concentrates a variety of shifting moods, contrasting themes, a scope of color and dynamics such as one might expect to find in a leisurely opening movement of a Romantic sonata. In fact, this movement has often been analyzed as a sonata-allegro form. But the connection is tenuous at best. The sheer variety of physical sound (from the plucked *pizzicato* to the most shimmering *tremolo*) is what strikes the listener first. A close second is the kaleidoscopic variety of emotional change.

II. *Sehr langsam.* This dark, brooding movement is played almost entirely with the instruments muted. It is lyric, introspective music, dying away into silence in a typically Romantic conclusion.

III. *Sehr lebhaft.* The middle movement might be called a *scherzo.* Jocular or not, it is mercurial, swift and, as mentioned above, some forty seconds long.

IV. *Sehr langsam.* This is another Romantic mood piece, again strongly lyrical, with recognizable themes that alternate and recur, with tiny touches of delicate color in the highest range of the violins.

V. *In zarter Bewegung.* The melodic tensions of this moderately paced *finale* may recall the tensions of Beethoven's late string quartets (especially his "Great" Fugue). This is the longest of Webern's Five Movements—almost three-and-a-half minutes. But the savoring of its rich content can last a lifetime.

FIVE PIECES FOR ORCHESTRA, OPUS 10

If he were not a pivotal figure in the history of music—if his influence on the following generation and on so great a contemporary as Igor Stravinsky had not been so profound—Anton Webern might be called merely a late Late-Romantic, for he was deeply linked to the Romantic past. This showed not only in his music, but in his character and even, in a sense, in his tragic fate.

Among the Romantic traits of Webern's character was the fanatical idealism with which he followed an unpopular, largely scorned and ridiculed musical path to the bitter end. Like so many of his nineteenth-century predecessors, Webern found himself almost automatically at odds with the broad public and with the majority of his uncomprehending colleagues. This in turn may have driven his sensitive nature to still further withdrawal from the hurly-burly of the musical marketplace.

If the financial results of Webern's artistic isolation weighed heavily upon him, the political consequences were devastating. Denounced by the Nazis as a *Kulturbolschewist,* he knew well enough what to expect when the Nazis took over his native Austria. But while his teacher, Schoenberg, and many other artists emigrated to Western Europe or the United States, Webern felt unable to leave. The Nazis immediately relieved him of all public functions. For a long time he was confined to private teaching, but the number of his students dwindled. Finally he was saved from complete financial disaster by the publishers of Universal Edition, who had the courage to engage him as a free-lance lector and proofreader. At the close of the war, when a rich professional life and official honors seemed to be coming his way, Webern was accidentally —or through some misunderstanding which has never been entirely explained —shot by an American occupation soldier.

The Five Pieces for Orchestra were composed in 1911 and 1913 while Webern was an operatic conductor and coach in Danzig and Stettin. These years belong to the pre-twelve-tone era of Webern's career. So even the most intellectual listeners cannot be tempted to follow any intricate, abstract, "mathematical" pattern. Listeners unfamiliar with this music may find the most rewarding approach to be the completely unanalytical one of simply surrendering to the fascination of the delicately shifting colors and moods in these carefully wrought miniatures.

Webern carries the Romantic love of miniature form to an extreme. Only one of the movements takes more than a minute; the shortest last fourteen seconds. The scope of the sound too is miniature: the most usual level is a whisper from *pianissimo* down to "scarcely audible." There is one single loud climax: in the last measure of the second piece. This climax uses a grand total of eight instruments! Otherwise the texture is so thin that harmony as such almost ceases to exist. We hear, instead, individual wisps of melody with subtle touches of added color here and there. The orchestra consists entirely of solo instruments: flute (interchangeable with piccolo), oboe, B-flat clarinet (interchangeable with B-flat bass clarinet), E-flat clarinet, horn, trumpet, trombone, harmonium, celesta, mandolin, guitar, harp, glockenspiel, xylophone, percussion and 4 solo strings.

For the Viennese premiere of the Five Pieces for Orchestra, the program gave descriptive headings for each of the five movements. Although Webern did not reproduce these titles in the published score, we list them below, repeating the composer's caution that they were intended as suggestions of the moods in which the movements were composed—not as indications of "subject matter" or as titles. The printed score has only the tempo marks:

I. *Urbild ("Primal Image, or Concept"); Sehr ruhig und zart.*
II. *Verwandlung ("Metamorphosis"): Lebhaft und zart bewegt.*
III. *Rückkehr ("Return"): Sehr langsam und äusserst ruhig.*
IV. *Erinnerung ("Memory"): Fliessend, äusserst zart.*
V. *Seele ("Soul"): Sehr fliessend.*

SIX PIECES FOR ORCHESTRA, OPUS 6

Webern dedicated his Six Pieces for Orchestra: "To Arnold Schoenberg, my teacher and friend in greatest love." Webern always emphasized his indebtedness to Schoenberg. Yet Webern's radically pioneering works appear in turn to have influenced his master.

The Six Pieces are characteristically Webern in their abandonment of traditional thematic developments and their avoidance of recurring themes used for the sake of formal structure. A logical result of this new style was the radical brevity of the pieces: all six of them total about ten minutes playing time. Also characteristic of Webern is the condensed, aphoristic style and the delicate, solo writing.

For his gossamer chamber effects, Webern used an enormous apparatus, which he reduced quite drastically nearly twenty years later. But even the reduced orchestra of 1928 still suggests a Strauss tone-poem or a Mahler symphony rather than the fragile texture of Webern. To compare the 1909 version with that of 1928, the 1909 figures are listed first; 1928 figures follow in parentheses: 2 (1) piccolos, 4 (2) flutes, 1 (0) alto flute, 4 (2) oboes, 3 (2) B-flat clarinets, 1 (0) E-flat clarinet, 2 (1) bass clarinets, 3 (2) bassoons, 1 (1) contrabassoon, 6 (4) horns, 6 (4) trumpets, 6 (4) trombones, 1 (1) tuba, kettledrums, 1 (0) celesta, 1 (1) glockenspiel, 1 (1) cymbals, 1 (1) triangle, 1 (1) sidedrum, 1 (1) bass drum, 1 (1) gong, 1 (1) set of low bells of no definite pitch, 1 (0) switch (*Rute*), 2 (1) harps, and strings.

The first performance of the Six Pieces in their original version of 1909 took place in the Grosser Musikvereinsaal of Vienna on March 31, 1913 under Schoenberg's direction.

I. *Langsam.* Even at a moderate tempo, the quick changes of pure instrumental color, often favoring a gleaming high register, produce an effect of aural irridescence. This movement, for example, begins with four low notes of a solo flute, followed by a single note of a muted trumpet, two chords on the celesta, three more flute notes, one soft note from a French horn, with three soft chords from muted violas and cellos.

II. *Bewegt.* This is a tense, agitated movement, with often jerky rhythms and percussive *staccato* chords for the strings. The climax and conclusion come with shrill, dissonant chords for the woodwinds and brass, the harshness of which is accentuated by trills for trumpets and clarinets.

III. *Mässig.* With only eleven measures, this is the shortest of the movements. Its chamber-music style of orchestration is especially characteristic.

IV. *Sehr mässig.* This funeral march movement starts with seven measures of very soft percussion alone. Gradually woodwinds and muted brass are added, including tubas and trombones, which provide a striking, slow *ostinato.* At the climax the woodwinds and brass are suddenly silent, leaving only the percussion group, which swells to a second, furious *fortissimo.*

V. *Sehr langsam.* The unearthly, hoarse whisper of muted low strings playing tremolos near the bridge in their very lowest range makes an unforgettable opening, in stark contrast to the closing measures with their delicate, high harmonics of the same instruments.

VI. *Langsam.* The music grows more and more delicate to the end. Against a background of "scarcely audible" deep bells, the soft chords of the celesta and the low tones of the harp die away to silence.

SYMPHONY, OPUS 21

The eight minutes of Anton Webern's only symphony encompass such emotional and intellectual high tension, that each note seems like a highly charged electric particle moving in a powerful magnetic field. Specialists in Webern's style have declared that his Symphony, Opus 21, completed when he was forty-five years old, is the first work in which his originality stands fully revealed. During the next seventeen years of his life, Webern composed only ten more works, none of them longer than the Symphony.

One cause for such minute production was Webern's poverty, which forced him to spend much of his time teaching and even in musical hackwork to make ends meet. Another cause, from 1937 on, was the heavy hand of Nazi rule which classed Webern with "cultural Bolshevists," and forced his complete withdrawal from public life. Yet, the most cogent reason for the small number of Webern's works was probably the very nature of the man and of his music.

During his lifetime Webern's music attracted little public attention, most of it unfavorable, and even today his music does not bulk large on our concert programs. Nevertheless, the Symphony and the ten works written between the Symphony and Webern's tragic death in 1945 had a tremendous effect on the post-World War II generation of composers. Not even his teacher, Arnold Schoenberg, not even their mutual friend, Alban Berg, who has been much more popular with concert and opera audiences, have so strongly influenced the development of music since the war.

Completed in 1928, Webern's Symphony was given its first performance by the League of Composers in New York City on December 18, 1929. In July 1931 it was performed in London at the Festival of the International Society for Contemporary Music. It employs a small ensemble (string orchestra plus solo clarinet, bass clarinet, 2 horns, and harp) and is cast in only two movements:

I. *Ruhig schreitend.* The entire first movement is composed of a variety of canons on the following tone row:

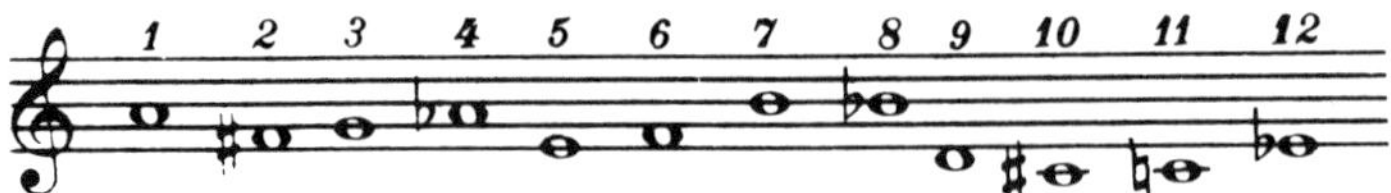

It opens with a double mirror canon, that is, four voices, one pair of which follows the other pair in upside-down imitation. The opening section (exposition) is repeated, as was customary in the Classical symphony. The latter part too (corresponding to development and recapitulation) is repeated, as it used to be in the early evolution of Classical first-movement form.

II. *Variations.* The second movement consists of a theme, seven variations and a brief *coda.* The theme is a mirror inversion of the original tone row:

In a lecture delivered at a private house in Vienna on March 2, 1932, Webern discussed this movement as an example of his constant striving for greater and greater unity in his works, through closer and closer interrelationships of all the parts. He explained that his theme for this variation movement has the same peculiarity as the row of the first movement, namely that

> . . . its second half reflects the first half in reverse order [cancrizans]. This constitutes a particularly intimate relationship. Thus there are only twenty-four possible forms of the row, for half [of the forty-eight normal variants of any given row] are identical with the other half. . . . The accompaniment of the theme at the beginning is made up of its crab [cancrizans] version. The melody of the first variation is a transposition of the row starting on C. The accompaniment is a double canon. . . . More interrelationship is not possible. Not even the [Renaissance] Netherlands composers succeeded in going so far. . . . In the fourth variation there are a number of mirror melodies. This variation itself is the midpoint of the entire movement, and from here on everything moves backwards. Thus the whole movement itself is composed of a double crab canon! . . . What you find here . . . crabs, canons, mirrors, et cetera . . . is always [different forms of] the same thing . . . it is not to be taken as virtuoso artifice . . . that would be preposterous! The aim is to create as many interrelationships as possible, and you must admit that there are many interrelationships!
>
> In conclusion I must point out that this [i.e., such interrelationships] is to be found not only in music. We find analogies in language. I was delighted to find that such interrelationships also often occur in Shakespeare, in alliteration and assonance. He even turns phrases backward. Karl Kraus's handling of language is also based on this; unity also has to be created there, since it enhances comprehensibility.

And I leave you with an old Latin saying:

SATOR
AREPO
TENET
OPERA
ROTAS

[These fine words may be translated as: "The Sower Arepo Keeps the Work Circling." Webern's arrangement of the Latin words was intended to illustrate some of the basic devices of twelve-tone technique: the readings in forward direction, backward, upside-down, and upside-down backward.]

VARIATIONS, OPUS 30

"Dazzling, dazzling" was Stravinsky's admiring phrase for the late works of Anton Webern. Webern had begun his career in a style of ripe Romanticism of strongly emotional music with lush harmonies and voluptuous orchestral color. But the dominant trend of Webern's development was a stripping down to essentials, a relentless search for inner truth. The emotional intensity remained, but it was shorn of rhetoric, and grew more and more concentrated, precise, epigrammatic.

Webern's Variations, Opus 30 was his next-to-last work. When he completed the score in the winter of 1940–41, he believed he had produced a basically simple work—simple, first of all because it was so sparse, so sparing of notes. Webern was a little apprehensive.

> When people see the score [he asked his friend Willi Reich], won't their first reactions be: "Why, there's nothing there?" They will miss the swarms of notes they're used to seeing in R. Strauss, for example. Of course! Indeed, this brings up the most important point: this is fundamentally a question of a different *style*.
>
> Very well, but what kind of style? This doesn't look like a pre-Wagner score, or Beethoven, for instance, nor does it look like Bach. Do we have to go back still further? Yes, but—way back, so far that there were no such things as *orchestral* scores. Still, it ought to be possible to discover some similarity with the Netherlands School—something archaic—like Josquin Desprez orchestrated? The answer to that would still have to be an emphatic "no!" Well then, what kind of *style*? I believe, as I said before, a new one.

In addition to sparseness of texture; Webern sought the utmost concentration of form:

> I had suspected it would be difficult [he wrote] but I never dreamed it would take so long. I sat at it for weeks and weeks. And now, I do think, something very simple and perhaps even inevitable [*selbstverständlich*] has come of it.
>
> The piece lasts about a quarter of an hour, almost all of it in very fast tempo, but partly with a *sostenuto* effect. My broad aim, to which I held, was to give the overall impression of a sort of overture form based on a theme and variations.

By "sort of overture form" Webern meant something recognizably close to traditional sonata-allegro form. The basic structure, he explained, was a theme and six variations. The first twenty measures served both as the theme for the variations and as the introduction to the sonata-allegro. The first variation corresponded to the first theme of the sonata-allegro; the second variation served as the bridge (from the first to the second theme group of the sonata allegro). The third variation corresponded to the second thematic group of the sonata-allegro, the fourth variation served as a recapitulation in development-section style, the fifth variation served as another bridge, and the final variation corresponded to the *coda* of the sonata-allegro. The combination of forms limped a little, but Webern was delighted by the synthesis and by the multiplication of interrelationships among the sections of his musical structure.

A further simplification and concentration was served by Webern's highly sophisticated manipulations of his basic thematic material. The entire work was derived from a single set, or row, comprising all twelve notes of the chromatic scale.

The row itself is so arranged that its last six tones repeat (in reverse) the intervals of the first six tones:

Thus the entire work is based on the first six tones of the score (performed by double bass and oboe). More recent commentators have pointed out that the first six tones (and hence the entire row) consist basically of only two intervals: a minor second and a minor third. This means that ultimately the entire composition is generated by the first three notes of the solo double bass which are the first three notes of the score. The jagged rhythms and the jagged leaps in this opening statement of the basic twelve-tone series create tremendous tensions characteristic of Webern's late style:

The Variations, Opus 30, are scored for flute, oboe, clarinet, bass clarinet, horn, trumpet, trombone, bass tuba, kettledrums, celesta, harp, and the traditional string choir. Webern exaggerated when he estimated the performance time at a quarter of a hour; it is closer to nine or at most ten minutes. Since Webern's music was banned in Germany and Austria during World War II, the first performance of the Variations was given at Winterthur, Switzerland under the direction of Hermann Scherchen on March 3, 1943. Webern was permitted to make the trip to the premiere. It was then five years since he had heard any public performance of a work of his. He never heard another.

Bernd Alois Zimmermann

Born March 20, 1918, Bliesheim, near Cologne—died August 10, 1970, Königsdorf

PHOTOPTÓSIS, PRELUDE FOR LARGE ORCHESTRA

The tragic death of Bernd Alois Zimmermann at the age of fifty-two cut short a career which had seemed on the verge of well-earned international celebrity. In central Europe, where even small opera houses can afford the luxury of keeping up with the twentieth century, Zimmermann was probably best known for the sensational success of his opera *The Soldiers (Die Soldaten).* First produced at Cologne in February 1965, his radical opera made its way to a number of other stages causing widespread enthusiasm and, even among conservative critics, a certain grudging admiration.

Unlike a number of contemporary composers who have been stimulated by their studies of mathematics, Zimmermann's interests and education suggested to him musical devices associated with collage and montage in the visual arts and with literary techniques of James Joyce and Ezra Pound. One of Zimmermann's characteristic traits was a special feeling about time—namely, that past, present, and future are really all simultaneous. This feeling showed in *Die Soldaten* in Zimmermann's simultaneous stage presentation of three separated events.

In his purely instrumental music a similar device consists of quoting fragments from other composers—sometimes several of them, simultaneously. Among the better-known compositions in which he uses this technique is *Photoptósis.*

Photoptósis was commissioned to celebrate the hundredth anniversary of the City Savings Bank of Gelsenkirchen, a small but artistically progressive city in the Ruhr, where it was first performed on February 14, 1969 by the Gelsenkirchen Civic Orchestra under the direction of Ljubomir Romansky. The United States premiere was presented at the Kennedy Center in Washington, D.C. when Michael Gielen conducting the National Symphony Orchestra on August 30, 1972.

A brief one-movement work, *Photoptósis* is basically nonthematic, except for one central section of musical collage, or montage. The score opens with an almost inaudible whisper from all choirs of the orchestra. One symptom of the extreme sublety with which this work is "engineered" is an indication that the fourth flute is to execute a *crescendo* and *decrescendo* by repeatedly depressing the D key of his instrument, but without blowing into the flute. There is a very gradual buildup of orchestral sonorities, using long sustained tones on some instruments and feather-light reiterations of mechanical figurations on others. Eventually the orchestra reaches several climaxes in which the instruments are directed to play literally "with all their power."

The central section of the *Photoptósis* begins with a raucous outburst, which we soon recognize, however, as a dramatic moment from the *Finale* of Beethoven's Ninth Symphony. Before the clamor of the Ninth has died away, the pipe organ is directed to begin the ancient hymn *"Veni creator spiritus."* Scriabin's *Poem of Ecstasy* is alluded to by a solo flute and violin. The *Scherzo* of the Beethoven Ninth appears and disappears briefly, followed by weaving arpeggios from Wagner's *Parsifal,* which in turn is capped by a combination of Bach's First Brandenburg Concerto with Tchaikovsky's "Sugar-Plum Fairy."

The section of collages is followed by a resumption of the climactic sonorities which preceded it. The final page is marked by a particularly massive tone cluster which the pianist executes with both forearms and elbows.

The large orchestra for *Photoptósis* includes 2 piccolos, 4 flutes, 3 oboes, 2 *oboe d'amore,* English horn, 4 clarinets, 2 basset horns, bass clarinet, 3 bassoons, contrabassoon, 5 horns, tuba, 4 trumpets, bass trumpet, 4 trombones, contrabass trombone, full organ, harp, piano, celesta, kettledrums, antique cymbals, suspended cymbals, normal cymbals, 3 triangles of different sizes, 2 gongs, large gong, side drum, tenor drum, bass drum, 3 tom-toms, maracas, plus the full complement of strings.

INDEX

Abel, Carl Friedrich, 7
Abert, Hermann, 663
Abraham, Gerald, 846, 965, 976
Adler, Guido, 552
Agoult, Countess d', 507, 508
Albéniz, Isaac, 337
Altschuler, Modest, 846, 847, 849
Andersen, Hans Christian, 691, 940–41
André, Anton, 384
Andrews, Edward D., 265
Anne, Queen of England, 375
Ansermet, Ernest, 913, 925, 935, 941, 947
Argentina (dancer), 334
Ashton, Frederick, 714
Asturias, Miguel Angel, 985
Attwood, Thomas, 581
Auden, W. H., 160, 204
Auer, Leopold, 957, 958
Auernhammer (pianist), 641
Aulnoy, Countess d', 742
Auric, Georges, 700

Bach, Carl Philipp Emanuel, 1–4
  Symphony for Orchestra with Twelve Obbligato Instruments, 1–4
Bach, Johann Christian, 4–7
  Symphony in D Major, 6–7
  Symphony in G Minor, 4–6
  Temistocle, 6, 7
Bach, Johann Sebastian, 1, 4, 7–28
  "Brandenburg" Concertos, 7–17, 20, 367
  Concerto for Two Violins and Orchestra, 16, 19–21
  Concerto for Violin, Oboe, and Orchestra, 21–22
  Concertos for Violin and Orchestra, 17–19
  Kunst der Fuge, 567
  Orchestral Suites, 23–28
Bahr-Mildenburg, Anna, 535
Bakst, Léon, 739, 928, 936*n*
Balakirev, Mili Alekseyevich, 598–99, 601, 964–66, 968
Balanchine, George, 909–10, 915
Ballets Russe de Monte Carlo, 458
Ballets Russes de Diaghilev, 339, 717, 739, 747, 791, 919, 927, 929, 934–37, 940, 941
Barber, Samuel, 28–34
  Adagio for Strings, 33
  Capricorn Concerto, 30
  Concerto for Piano and Orchestra, 28–29
  Concerto for Violin and Orchestra, 30–31
  First Essay for Orchestra, 30, 32–33
  Medea, 30
  School for Scandal, Overture to, 30, 33–34
  Second Essay for Orchestra, 33
  Second Symphony, 30
Barbirolli, John, 52, 166, 208
Barrère (flutist), 308
Bartered Bride, The Overture to, 881–82
Bartók, Béla, 35–54, 717
  Allegro barbaro, 38, 46, 717
  Bluebeard's Castle, 46, 50
  Concerto for Orchestra, 35–37
  Concerto for Violin and Orchestra, 43–46
  Dance Suite, 46
  Danube, The, 38

Divertimento for Strings, 48–50
First Piano Concerto, 37–39
Miraculous Mandarin, The, 46, 50–52
Music for Strings, Percussion, and Celesta, 52–54
Second Piano Concerto, 39–41
Sixth String Quartet, 49, 50
Third Piano Concerto, 41–43
Wooden Prince, The, 50
Barzun, Jacques, 131, 136, 147, 249
Baudelaire, Charles, 304, 310
Beaumarchais, Pierre de, 658
Beethoven, Ludwig van, 54–112
"Appassionata" Sonata, 96, 97
Christus am Oelberg, 58, 86–89
Concerto for Violin and Orchestra, 64–67, 96, 99, 493, 574
Consecration of the House Overture, 69, 74–75
Coriolanus, Overture to, 75–76, 809
Creatures of Prometheus, Overture to, 77–78, 91
Egmont, Overture to, 78–80
"Eroica" Piano Variations, 91
"Eroica" Symphony, No. 3, 77, 84, 91–95, 730, 893, 897
Fantasy in C minor for Piano, Chorus and Orchestra, 99
Fidelio, 66, 80–86, 96
Overture to, 80–81, 83
"Great" Fugue, 1034
Kontretänze, 91
"Lebewohl" [*"Farewell"*] Sonata, 566
"Leonore" Overtures, 78, 80–86
Mass in C major, 99
Missa solemnis, 67–74, 491
"Pathétique" Sonata, 58
First Piano Concerto, 54–56
Second Piano Concerto, 56–58
Third Piano Concerto, 58–60
Fourth Piano Concerto, 60–62, 96, 99
Fifth Piano Concerto "Emperor", 62–64
"Razumovsky" String Quartets, 96
Ruins of Athens, Overture to, 81
SYMPHONIES:
First Symphony, 58, 812
Second Symphony, 58, 88–91, 189, 814
Third Symphony, 77, 84, 91–95
Fourth Symphony, 95–99
Fifth Symphony, 91, 96, 98–101, 535, 874, 917
Sixth Symphony "Pastoral", 99, 102–4, 874
Seventh Symphony, 104–6
Eighth Symphony, 106–8, 916
Ninth Symphony, 67, 69, 108–12, 193, 194, 225, 237–38, 242, 530–32, 876, 879, 997, 1042
Wellington's Victory, or the Battle at Victoria, 106
Benois, Alexandre, 928–30
Berg, Alban, 113–27, 552, 565, 791, 924, 1037
Concerto for Violin and Orchestra, 113–15, 924
Lulu, 113, 115–19
Lyric Suite, 119–20
Three Orchestral Pieces, 120–23
Wozzeck, 123–27, 791
Berliner, Arnold, 552
Berlioz, Hector, 127–58, 497, 816
Beatrice and Benedict, Overture to, 133
Benvenuto Cellini, 138
Overture to, 134–35
Corsair Overture, 135–36
Damnation of Faust, 127–30
Fantastic Symphony, 128, 130, 137, 145, 147–55, 497, 778
Harold in Italy, 130–32, 778
Herminie, 152, 153
King Lear, Overture to, 136–38
Lélio, 137
Requiem, 981
"Roman Carnival" Overture, 138–40
Romeo and Juliet, 130, 140–44
Royal Hunt and Storm, 145–47
Symphonie Funèbre et Triomphale, 156–58
Trojans, The, 145–47
Bernhardt, Sarah, 930
Bernstein, Leonard, 158–65, 205, 268–70, 341, 358, 379–80, 469, 1026
Age of Anxiety, The, 158–62
Fancy Free, 158, 164
"Jeremiah" Symphony, 158
On the Town, 158, 164
Serenade, 162–64
Waterfront Suite, 164
West Side Story, 164–65
Wonderful Town, 164
Besseler, Heinrich, 9, 16, 25
Bethge, Hans, 516
Billings, William, 287, 822
Billroth, Theodor, 177, 195, 197
Bizet, Georges, 165–67
Symphony in C Major, 165–67
Blacher, Boris, 291
Blake, William, 776
Blauer Reiter group, 791
Bloch, Ernest, 167–68, 492, 850

Schelomo, Hebrew Rhapsody, 167–68
Blom, Eric, 996
Blume, Friedrich, 224
Bodanzky, Artur, 552
Boepple, Paul, 314
Bolender, Todd, 909
Bolshoi Ballet, 712–13
Bonney, William, 266
Borodin, Alexander, 968
Boschot, Adolphe, 630
Boulanger, Nadia, 248, 249, 314, 380, 698, 980
Boulez, Pierre, 168–74, 269, 291, 310
"Improvisations on Mallarmé", 170
Pli selon pli, 168–74
Bowers, Faubion, 849
Brahms, Johannes, 174–204, 320, 322–23
"Academic Festival" Overture, 184–85
Concerto for Violin and Orchestra, 179–81, 215, 493, 735
Concerto for Violin, Violoncello, and Orchestra, 181–84
First Piano Concerto, 174–76
German Requiem, A, 175, 193
"Immer leiser wird mein Schlummer", 179
Second Piano Concerto, 177–79
Serenades, 187–92
SYMPHONIES:
First Symphony, 192–94, 537
Second Symphony, 195–96
Third Symphony, 196–99, 324
Fourth Symphony, 199–202
"Tragic" Overture, 186
Variations on a Theme by Haydn, 202–4
Brandt, Marianne, 1030
Braunstein, Joseph, 82, 470
Bridge, Frank, 209
Three Idylls, 209
Britten, Benjamin, 204–11
Ballad of Heroes, 207
First String Quartet, 204, 207
Illuminations, Les, 204, 207
Passacaglia, 204–7
Paul Bunyan, 204
Peter Grimes, 204–7
Sea Interludes, 204–7
Seven Sonnets of Michelangelo, 204, 207
Sinfonia da Requiem, 204, 207–9
Variations on a Theme by Frank Bridge, 209–11
Violin Concerto, 204, 207
Brodsky, Adolf, 957
Brosses, Charles de, 999
Brown, Earle, 211–13, 245
Available Forms II, 211–13
Folio, 211
Twenty-five Pages, 211
Bruch, Max, 214–16, 323
Concerto for Violin and Orchestra, 214–15
Kol Nidre, 214, 215
Scottish Fantasy, 214–16
Bruckner, Anton, 216–43
Mass F minor, 220, 222
Mass in D minor, 217
SYMPHONIES:
First Symphony, 216–20, 240
Second Symphony, 220–22
Third Symphony, 222–27, 240
Fourth Symphony "Romantic", 227–30
Fifth Symphony, 225, 230–33
Sixth Symphony, 233–35
Seventh Symphony, 235–38, 243
Eighth Symphony, 225, 238–41, 243
Ninth Symphony, 241–43
Büchner, Georg, 124, 567
Buhlig, Richard, 245
Bülow, Hans von, 177, 199, 216, 322, 325, 498, 528–30, 735, 888, 951–56, 1019
Burgin, Richard, 708
Burk, John, 735
Burleigh, Henry T., 328
Burlington, Lord, 376
Burney, Charles, 2–3, 285, 370, 399, 428, 617
Busch, Fritz, 993
Büsch, Johann Georg, 3
Busoni, Ferruccio Benvenuto, 981
Byron, Lord, 135–36, 502, 505, 509, 833

Cage, John M., 244–46
Atlas Eclipticalis, 244–46
Music of Changes, 244
Variations IV, 245
Winter Music, 244–46
Cairns, David, 131
Calder, Alexander, 211
Calvocoressi, M. D., 737
Campos, Ruben M., 277
Campra, André, 597
Canal, Count Joseph Emanuel, 684
Caplet, André, 299
Carner, Mosco, 1024
Carreño, Teresa, 514
Carter, Elliott, 246–51
Concerto for Orchestra, 246–48
Defense of Corinth, The, 248, 249
Holiday Overture, 248–49
Piano Concerto, 247
Piano Sonata, 247
Variations for Orchestra, 250–51

Casella, Alfredo, 252–53
Giara, La, 252–53
Caston, Saul, 289
Cecchetti, Enrico, 930, 935
Cervantes Saavedra, Miguel de, 890
Chabrier, Emmanuel, 254–55, 277
España, 254–55, 277
Chaliapin, Feodor, 985
Chapman, George, 311
Chase, Gilbert, 777
Chausson, Ernest, 255–57
Poème, 255–56
Symphony in B-flat Major, 256–57
Chávez, Carlos, 279
Chevillard, Camille, 302
Chirico, Giorgio de, 252
Chopin, Frédéric, 257–61, 919, 940, 979
First Piano Concerto, 257–60
Second Piano Concerto, 260–61
Christian Ludwig, Margrave of Brandenburg, 7–9
Christina, Queen of Sweden, 284
Churchill, Mary Senior, 279
Chusid, Martin, 814
Claudel, Paul, 306
Clement, Franz, 64, 493
Clementi, Muzio, 470
Coates, Alfred, 705
Cocteau, Jean, 700
Collet, Henri, 700
Collin, Heinrich Joseph von, 75, 76
Colloredo, Hieronymus von, 678
Concerts Spirituels, 613, 675
Cooke, Deryck, 568–70
Coolidge, Elizabeth Sprague, 262, 263
Cooper, James Fenimore, 136
Copland, Aaron, 262–83, 314
Appalachian Spring, 262–66, 275, 281
Billy the Kid, 266–68, 275, 281
Clarinet Concerto, 281
Connotations for Orchestra, 268–71
"Fanfare for the Common Man", 283
Lincoln Portrait, 271–75, 281
Music for the Theatre, 274–75
Orchestral Variations, 269, 270
Piano Fantasy, 269
Piano Quartet, 269, 281
Piano Variations, 262, 269, 278, 279
Salón Mexico, El, 266, 275–77, 281
"Short" Symphony, 278–81
Statements for Orchestra, 278–79
Symphonic Ode, 269
Tender Land, The, 269
Third Symphony, 269, 281–83
Vitebsk, 278, 279
Copland-Sessions Concerts, 850
Corelli, Arcangelo, 284–86, 369
"Christmas" Concerto, 284–86
Coster, Charles de, 901
Cowell, Henry, 245, 287–88, 290, 469, 475, 480, 777, 979
Fifth String Quartet, 288
Hymn and Fuguing Tune, 287–88
Symphonies, 287–88
Violin Sonata, 288
Cowell, Mrs. Henry, 287
Crabbe, George, 204
Craft, Robert, 248, 791, 909, 945, 986
Crane, Hart, 263
Creston, Paul, 289–90
First Symphony, 290
Janus, 289–90
Seven Theses for Piano, 290
Crumb, George, 291–94
Ancient Voices of Children, 291–94
Cui, César, 599, 757, 968
William Ratcliffe, 757
Cunningham, Merce, 245, 246, 263
Czech, Adolf, 879
Czerny, Carl, 63, 65

Dahlgren, F. A., 880
Dalcroze Institute, 314
Dallapiccola, Annalibera, 295
Dallapiccola, Luigi, 295–98
Musical Notebook of Annalibera, 295, 296
Prisoner, The (Il Prigioniero), 295
Songs of Imprisonment, 295
Songs of Liberation, 295, 296
Variations for Orchestra, 295–98
Damrosch, Leopold, 952, 954, 968
Damrosch, Walter, 200, 346, 348, 350, 352, 540, 726, 870, 968
Dante Alighieri, 959
Darrieux, Marcel, 708
Dash, Michael, 291
Daudet, Alfonse, 597
Daumier, Honoré, 890
David, Ferdinand, 493, 573–74
David, Jacques-Louis, 362
Davidov, Alexandra, 967
Davidov, Leo, 967
Davidov, Vladimir, 962, 974, 975
Davison, Archibald T., 247, 249
Debussy, Claude, 255, 298–310, 339
"Afternoon of a Faun," Prelude to, 305–10
Images (Gigues, Ibéria, Rondes de printemps), 298–302, 337

Mer, La, 302–4
Nocturnes (Nuages, Fêtes, Sirènes), 304–5
Pelléas et Mélisande, 124, 302, 595, 794
Defauw, Désiré, 701
Degas, Edgar, 304
Dehmel, Richard, 793, 805
Dello Joio, Norman, 310–13
Variations, Chaconne, and Finale, 310–13
Demuth, Norman, 343
Denby, Eric, 263
DeQuincy, Thomas, 150
Dessoff, Otto, 190, 220
Devrient, Eduard, 588
Diaghilev, Serge, 262, 339, 458, 700, 706–7, 717–18, 739, 747, 791, 919–20, 928–30, 932–34, 936–37, 940–41
Diamond, David, 314–15
Ame de Debussy, L', 314
Eighth Symphony, 314–15
Elegy, 314
Homage to Erik Satie, 314
Diémer, Louis, 343
Dithyramb , 262
Dohnányi, Ernst von, 46
Dollar, William, 916
Donne, John, 311
Doré, Gustave, 307, 890
Downes, E. Olin, 308, 354, 870–72
Druckman, Jacob, 316–17
Synapse, 316
Windows, 316–17
Duboeuf, Estelle, 152–53
Duhalde, Jean Baptiste, 461
Dujardin, Édouard, 306
Dukas, Paul, 304, 306, 317–19, 339, 493
Sorcerer's Apprentice, The, 317–19
Dumas, Alexandre, the elder, 961
Dunn, Thomas, 382
Durand, Jacques, 298, 299, 302
Durey, Louis, 700
Durony, Geneviève, 743
Dushkin, Samuel, 917–18
Dvořák, Antonin, 319–30
"Carnival" Overture, 319–20
Concerto for Cello and Orchestra, 320–22
Concerto for Violin and Orchestra, 322–24
Eighth Symphony, 326–27
"In Nature's Realm" Overture, 319
"Nature, Life and Love", 319
Ninth Symphony "New World", 324, 327–30
"Othello" Overture, 319
Slavonic Dances, 322, 323, 326
Seventh Symphony, 324–26
Einstein, Alfred, 658, 662, 664, 814–15
Eisfeld, Theodore, 834
Eisler, Hans, 788
Ekman, Karl, 868, 876
Elgar, Edward, 330–33
Cockaigne (In London Town), 330–31
"Enigma" Variations, 331–33
Pomp and Circumstance March, 330
Elizabeth Sprague Coolidge Foundation, 291
Elman, Mischa, 352, 957
Emmanuel, Maurice, 343
Engel, Carl, 824
Erlach, J. B. Fischer von, 623
Eschenbach, Wolfram von, 1014
Escudero, Vincente, 988
Essipova, Annette, 702
Esterházy family, 382, 396, 400, 404, 447
Esterházy, Prince Anton, 392
Esterházy, Prince Nikolaus, 383, 398–400, 420, 427
Evans, Edwin, 996

Falla, Manuel de, 275, 300, 333–40, 733, 744
Amor Brujo, El (Love, the Magician), 333–37
Nights in the Gardens of Spain, 337–39
Three-Cornered Hat, The, 252, 339–40
Vida breve, La, 333
Feldman, Morton, 245
Fénélon, Félix, 306
Feodorovna, Grand Duchess Maria, 999
Ferrand, Humbert, 129, 148
Festin, Le (ballet), 919
Fétis, François-Joseph, 150–52
Février, Jacques, 701
Finney, Ross Lee, 291
Fischer, Emil, 1030
Fischer, Friedrich, 958
Fischer, Ludwig, 439
Flodin, Karl Teodor, 868
Fokine, Michel (choreographer), 739, 919–20, 930, 940
Forster, E. M., 204
Forster, G. Baqueiro, 275
Foss, Lukas, 340–42
Cello Concerto, 341
Phorion, 341
Time Cycle, 341
Variations, 340–42
Foster, Stephen, 272
Franck, César, 255, 343–46, 392
Symphonic Variations, 343–44
Symphony in D minor, 344–46, 392
Frankenstein, Alfred, 603, 604
Franz Joseph I, Emperor, 225

Frederick, Kurt, 798
Fried, Oscar, 794
Friedrich Wilhelm I, King of Prussia, 7
Furtwängler, Wilhelm, 38, 455, 802

Gabrilowitsch, Ossip, 552
Gade, Niels, 574, 691, 692
Gagnebin, Elie, 925
Gainsborough, Thomas, 4
Galitzin, Prince Nicholas, 69
Galland, Antoine, 761
Galli, Rosina, 252
García Lorca, Federico, 291–92
Gaubert, Philippe, 772
Gauguin, Paul, 306
Gehlhaar, Rolf, 882
Geiringer, Karl, 193, 200, 401
Genzinger, Marianne von, 437
George I, King of England, 375–76
George III, King of England, 446, 447
Georg, Stefan, 306
Gericke, Wilhelm, 200
Gershwin, George, 346–56
  American in Paris, An, 346–50
  Concerto in F, 350–52
  Lady Be Good, 351
  La La Lucille, 351
  Oh, Kay!, 347, 351
  Rhapsody in Blue, 346, 347, 350, 352–56
Gide, André, 306
Gielen, Michael, 1041
Gilman, Lawrence, 546, 754, 776, 871, 894–96, 987
Ginastera, Alberto, 356–60
  Beatrix Cenci, 356
  Bomarzo, 356
  Concerto for Piano and Orchestra, 356–59
  Concerto for Violin and Orchestra, 359–60
  Don Rodrigo, 356
Girard, Narcisse, 137
Girdlestone, C. M., 640
Gladkowska, Constantia, 261
Glinka, Mikhail, 360–61
  Russlan and Ludmilla, Overture to, 360–61
Gluck, Christoph Willibald, 362–64, 399–400, 625, 809
  Alceste, Overture to, 362–63
  Iphigénia in Aulis, Overture to, 362
  Orfeo ed Euridice, 362, 400, 625, 809
Göbl, Alois, 324
Godebski, Cyprien, 742
Godebski, Ida, 742
Godebski, Jean, 742
Godebski, Mimi, 742
Goethe, Johann Wolfgang von, 26, 78–80, 127–28, 150, 317–18, 394, 501–2, 508–9, 555, 557, 586, 833, 999
Göhler, Georg, 545
Goldman, Richard Franko, 248–49
Göllerich, August, 234
Golovanov, N. S., 714
Golyenishchev-Kootoozov, Count, 760
Goossens, Eugene, 283, 776
Gorman, Ross, 354, 355
Gorodetzky, Sergei, 717
Gossec, François Joseph, 414
Gounod, Charles, 165, 345, 778
  Faust, 345, 778
  First Symphony, 166
  Sappho, 166
Goya, Francisco, 599
Gozzi, Carlo, 461
Graham, Martha, 30, 262–63
  Appalachian Spring, 262–66
  Hérodiade, 262
  Imagined Wing, 262
  Serpent Heart, The, 30
Grieg, Edvard, 364–65, 691, 919
  Concerto for Piano and Orchestra, 364–65
Grierson, Francis, 307
Griesinger, Georg August, 423, 427, 447
Grimm, Julius, 175
Grofé, Ferde, 351, 356
Gropius, Manon, 113, 114
Grove, George, 109, 330, 807, 811
Grünewald, Matthias, 455
Guardi, Francesco, 999
Guhr, Karl, 696
Gyrowetz, Adalbert, 416

Haas, Otto, 243
Haas, Robert, 221, 227, 231, 234, 236, 240
Habeneck, François Antoine, 138–39, 816
Haffner, Sigmund, 679, 681
Hahn, Reynaldo, 166
Hale, Philip, 167, 586, 871, 906
Halir, Carl, 861
Hallé, Charles, 497, 499
Handel, George Frideric, 366–79, 978
  Concerto grosso, Op. 3, No. 1, 342, 366–67
  Grand Concertos, Op. 6, 366–72
  Messiah, 388, 978
  Ode to St. Cecilia's Day, 368
  Royal Fireworks Music, 372–75
  Water Music, 375–79
Hanslick, Eduard, 190–91, 220, 230, 238, 322, 957–58
Hanson, Howard, 591

Harris, Roy, 379–81, 823
  Third Symphony, 379–81
Harrison, Lou, 245
Hartmann, Victor, 602–4
Harty, Hamilton, 1024, 1026
Hatwig, Otto, 810, 812
Hauptmann, Gerhart, 775
Hausegger, Friedrich von, 907
Hausegger, Siegmund von, 243
Hausmann, Robert, 182
Hawkins, Erick, 263
Hayden, Melissa, 909
Haydn, Joseph, 1, 4, 6, 381–452, 621, 628, 660
  Concerto for Cello and Orchestra, C major, 381
  Concerto for Cello and Orchestra, D major, 383
  Concerto for Clavier and Orchestra, 385–88
  Concerto for Trumpet and Orchestra, 388–89
  Feldpartita, 202
  Sinfonia concertante, 389–92
  SYMPHONIES:
    Symphony No. 22 "Philosopher", 345, 392–93
    Symphony No. 26 "Lamentatione", 394–96, 407
    Symphony No. 31 "Hornsignal", 396–98
    Symphony No. 45 "Farewell", 398–400
    Symphony No. 48 "Maria Theresia", 400–4, 431
    Symphony No. 60 "Il Distratto", 404–7
    Symphony No. 82 "L'Ours", 407
    Symphony No. 83 "La Poule" (The Hen), 408–11
    Symphony No. 84, E-flat major, 411–13
    Symphony No. 85 "Queen of France", (La Reine), 407, 409, 413–14
    Symphony No. 86, D major, 414–16
    Symphony No. 88, G major, 416–18
    Symphony No. 92 "Oxford", 418–20
    Symphony No. 93, D major, 420–23
    Symphony No. 94 "Surprise", 423–25
    Symphony No. 95, C minor, 42527
    Symphony No. 96 "The Miracle", 427
    Symphony No. 97, C major, 431–33
    Symphony No. 98, D-flat major, 434–36
    Symphony No. 99, E-flat major, 436
    Symphony No. 100 "Military", 438–41
    Symphony, No.101 "Clock", 441–44
    Symphony No. 102, B-flat major, 444–46
    Symphony No. 103 "Drum Roll", 447–50
    Symphony No. 104, D major, 450–52
Heifetz, Jascha, 352, 957
Heine, Heinrich, 500, 694, 1006
Heinse, J. J. W., 364
Helmholz, Hermann von, 988
Henderson, William, 870
Hendl, Walter, 590
Herbeck, Johann, 220, 221, 814–15
Herbert, Victor, 320
  Second Cello Concerto, 320
Herzogenberg, Elisabeth von, 177, 195, 199
Hess, Willy, 66
Hill, Edward Burlingame, 247
Hill, Urelli Corelli, 104
Hiller, Ferdinand, 576
Hindemith, Paul, 310–12, 452–61, 791, 917, 924
  Concert Music for Strings and Brass, 452–53
  Concerto for Violin and Orchestra, 453–55
  Hérodiade, 262
  Marienleben, Das, 458
  Mathis der Maler Symphony, 455–57
  Nobilissima visione, 457–60
  Symphonic Metamorphoses of Themes by Weber, 460–61
  Von Heute auf Morgen, 924
Hitler, Adolf, 896
Hoffmann, E. T. A., 100, 837, 961–62
Holst, Gustav, 247, 249
Honegger, Arthur, 462–65, 700, 936
  Pacific 231, 462–63, 936
  Second Symphony, 463–65
Horenstein, Jascha, 120
Horst, Louis, 263
Hovhaness, Alan, 245
Hugo, Victor, 147, 150, 505, 582
Hurst, Fannie, 354
Hüttenbrenner, Anselm, 814–15
Hüttenbrenner, Joseph, 814

Ichiyanagi, Toshi, 246
Imperio, Pastora, 333
Indy, Vincent d', 343, 345, 466–68, 774, 981
  Symphony on a French Mountain Air, 466–67
Inter-American Music Festival, 357
International Society for Contemporary Music, 38, 115, 170, 275
Ives, Charles, 248, 250, 468–87
  Celestial Railroad, 475
  Central Park in the Dark, 468–69
  Children's Day Parade, 473
  First String Quartet, 473, 476
  SYMPHONIES:
    Second Symphony, 468, 470–74
    Third Symphony "Camp Meeting", 472–74

Fourth Symphony, 474–78
"Holidays" Symphony, 478–83
Three Outdoor Scenes, 469
Three Places in New England, 483–86
Unanswered Question, The, 486–87

Jahn, Otto, 666
James, Henry, 514
Janáček, Leoš, 487–88
Jenufa, 488
Sinfonietta, 487–88
Jeritza, Maria, 488
Joachim, Joseph, 179–82, 184, 187–88, 190, 192, 214, 323, 493
Johns, Jasper, 246
Johnson, Samuel, 761
Joyce, James, 296, 1041
Julliard School, 250, 317, 591, 826

Kabalevsky, Dmitri, 489–90
Colas Breugnon, Overture to, 489–90
Kahn, Gustave, 306
Kaiser, Fritz, 66
Kalbeck, Max, 184, 193, 203, 549
Kandinsky, Wassily, 791
Karsavina, Tamara, 339, 739, 919–20, 930, 935, 941
Kashkin, Nicholas, 967
Kaunic, Josephina, 321
Kazan, Elia, 164
Kennedy, Michael, 995
Kern, Jerome, 271
Portrait of Mark Twain, 271
Kilmansegge, Baron, 376
Kirchner, Leon, 490–92
Music for Orchestra, 490–92
Kirkpatrick, John, 475, 476, 478
Kirov Ballet, 712–13
Kirstein, Lincoln, 267, 909, 915, 916
Klausenberg Conservatory, 496
Kleiber, Erich, 119, 120, 124
Klemperer, Otto, 552
Klingemann, Carl, 579
Klopstock, Friedrich, 3–4, 530, 533–34
Kochanski, Paul, 707
Kodály (composer), 46
Königslöw, Otto von, 214
Kostelanetz, Andre, 271, 274, 822
Kotzebue, August Friedrich von, 75
Koussevitzky Foundation, 35, 164, 205, 281, 316, 357, 826
Koussevitzky, Natalie, 162, 826
Koussevitzky, Serge, 35, 36, 160, 162, 205, 269, 274, 379–80, 453, 591, 602, 708, 711, 774, 819, 823–24, 848–49, 859, 947

Kraft, Anton, 383, 384
Krasner, Louis, 113
Kreisler, Fritz, 352
Kuffner, Christoff, 91

Labroca, Mario, 252
Laforgue, Jules, 306
La Grange, Henry-Louis de, 523, 529
Lalo, Edouard, 493–95
Norwegian Rhapsody, 493
Roi d'Ys, Overture to, 493
Russian Concerto, 493
Symphonie espagnole, 493–95
Lamartine, Alphonse de, 506, 507
Landon, H. C. Robbins, 202, 394, 403, 413, 416, 419–20, 424, 429, 434, 436, 438, 442, 669
Laussot, Jessie, 951
Lauze, F. de, 910
Lavrovsky, Leonid, 713
League of Composers, 274, 278, 1037
Lehmann, Lilli, 1030
Leibowitz, René, 787
Leinsdorf, Erich, 28
Leipzig Conservatory, 838
Leleu, Jeanne, 743
Lenau, Nicolaus, 888
Lenin, V. I., 707
Leo, Leonardo, 370
Léonore, ou l'amour conjugale, (Gaveaux),83
Leopold, Prince of Anhalt-Köthen, 9, 12, 16, 20
Leopold II, Emperor of Holy Roman Empire, 637
Leslie, Frank, 954
Lessing, Gotthold Ephraim, 2, 3
Leutgeb, Ignatz Joseph, 613
Levant, Oscar, 788,
Levi, Hermann, 192, 219, 240
Liadov, Anatol Constantinovich, 702, 919
Lichnowsky, Prince Karl, 58, 70, 81, 86, 96–97
Liechtenstein, Prince, 221
Liechtenstein, Princess Maria Josepha Hermengild, 384
Lieven, Princess Alexandra, 724
Lifar, Serge, 714
Ligeti, György, 495–96
Atmosphères, 495–96
Lippold, Richard, 246
Liszt, Franz, 152, 261, 365, 496–510, 514, 834, 878, 952
Faust Symphony in Three Character Pictures, A, 500–4
First Piano Concerto, E-flat major 231, 496–99

"Four Elements, The", 506
Mazeppa, 504–6
Préludes, Les, 345, 506–7
Second Piano Concerto, A major, 499–500
Tasso, 507–10
Lobkowitz, Prince, 60
Lockspeiser, Edward, 736
Loewe, Carl, 577
Long, Marguerite, 736
Longfellow, Henry Wadsworth, 328
Loring, Eugene, 267
Louis-Philippe, King of France, 147, 156
Louis XIV, King of France, 23, 286, 978
Louis XV, King of France, 647
Louis XVI, King of France, 658
Loüys, Pierre, 306
Löwe, Ferdinand, 233, 243
Lully, Jean-Baptiste, 75, 286, 978
Lutoslawski, Witold, 510–13
Concerto for Orchestra, 510–12
First Symphony, 511
Funeral Music, 512–13
Sonata for Violin and Piano, 510

MacDowell, Edward, 514–15
First Piano Concerto, 514
Indian Suite, 514
Second Piano Concerto, 514–15
Mackerras, Charles, 382
Maderna, Bruno, 212, 316
Maeterlinck, Maurice, 306, 794, 797
Mahler, Alma Maria, 113, 545, 548, 551, 552, 555, 569, 570
Mahler, Gustav, 225, 234, 269, 299, 473, 516–70, 726–27
Klagende Lied, Das [*Sorrowing Song, The*], 523
Lieder eines fahrenden Gesellen [*Songs of a Wandering Journeyman*], 526
Lied von der Erde, Das [*Song of the Earth, The*], 516–22, 565, 570
Song of the Earth, The, 516–22, 565, 570
SYMPHONIES:
First Symphony, 522–28
Second Symphony "Resurrection", 523, 528–35
Third Symphony, 535–40
Fourth Symphony, 523, 540–44
Fifth Symphony, 544–48
Sixth Symphony, 123, 548–51
Seventh Symphony, 552–54
Eighth Symphony "of a Thousand", 555–64
Ninth Symphony, 123, 564–67
Tenth Symphony, 565, 567–70
Totenfeier [*Funeral Rite*], 529–30
Maitland, J. A. Fuller, 992
Malaieff, Theodore M., 915
Malko, Nicolai, 852
Mallarmé, Stéphane, 170–72, 262, 304–9, 311
Mandyczewski, Eusebius, 408, 426, 444
Manet, Édouard, 306
Manns, August, 811
Mann, Thomas, 502, 1009
Manuel, Roland, 700, 737
Marc, Franz, 791
Maria Theresia, Empress of Austria, 401, 403
Marie-Antoinette, Queen of France, 363, 407–9, 413, 414, 658
Marini, Giuseppe de, 697
Marlowe, Christopher, 500, 502
Marschalk, Max, 525, 531, 536
Martin, John, 910
Martinez Sierra, Gregorio, 333–34
Mason, Lowell, 475
Mason, William, 189
Masselos, William, 1026, 1027
Massenet, Jules Émile Frédéric, 255
Massine, Leonide, 339, 458, 748, 935, 941
Matisse, Henri, 941
Mattheson, Johann, 371
Mauclair, Camille, 255–56, 304, 306
Maurus, Hrabanus, 555
May, Florence, 201
Mecklenburg-Strelitz, Count Georg August von, 651
Meck, Nadeja von, 950, 955–57, 966, 968–71, 973, 975
Meisl, Carl, 75
Mendelssohn, Fanny, 576, 579
Mendelssohn, Felix, 26, 571–90, 816, 818, 832, 836, 838, 839
Concerto for Piano and Orchestra, 571–72
Concerto for Violin and Orchestra, 573–75, 957–58
Fourth Symphony "Italian", 585–88
Fifth Symphony "Reformation", 588–90
"Hebrides" Overture, "Fingal's Cave", 579–81
Midsummer Night's Dream, A, 196, 575–79, 586
Ruy Blas, Overture to, 582–83
Third Symphony "Scotch", 583–85
Mengelberg, Willem, 44, 252, 354, 537, 555
Mennin, Peter, 590–92
Third Symphony, 590–92
Menotti, Gian Carlo, 32, 592–94, 764
Amahl and the Night Visitors, 592

Apocalypse, 592–94
Consul, The, 592
Medium, The, 592
Saint of Bleecker Street, The, 592
Telephone, The, 592
Merrill, Stuart, 306
Mersenne, Marin, 910
Mesmer, Anton, 673
Messiaen, Olivier, 594–96, 887
Offrandes oubliées, Les [Forgotten Offerings], 594–96
Michelangelo Buonarotti, 567
Mickiewicz, Adam, 529
Milhaud, Darius, 347, 596, 700
Suite Provençale, 596–98
Milyukova, Antonina Ivanova, 970–71
Mitchell, Arthur, 909
Mitchell, Howard, 357
Mitropoulos, Dimitri, 158, 269, 549, 1027
Monet, Claude, 304, 306
Montesquieu, Baron de, 761
Monteux, Pierre, 739, 930, 936, 941
Morand, Paul, 700
Morzin, Count Venceslav, 1001
Mottl, Felix, 236, 237
Moussorgsky, Modest, 598–607, 968
Boris Godunov, 606
Khovanshchina, 598, 606–7
Night on Bald Mountain, A, 598–602
Pictures at an Exhibition, 602–4
Mozart, Constanze, 655, 663, 682
Mozart, Leopold, 396, 613, 623, 626, 632, 651, 668, 673
Mozart, Nannerl, 641
Mozart, Wolfgang Amadeus, 1, 4, 6, 364, 421, 607–90
Abduction from the Seraglio, 439, 612, 654, 679, 761
Abduction from the Seraglio, Overture to, 654–55
Clarinet Quintet, 736
Clemenza di Tito, 54
Concerto for Clarinet and Orchestra, 607–9
Concerto for Flute and Orchestra, G major, 609
Concerto for Flute and Orchestra, D major, 611
Concerto for Horn and Orchestra, 613–14
CONCERTOS FOR PIANO AND ORCHESTRA:
Concerto for Piano and Orchestra, E-flat major, 614
Concerto for Piano and Orchestra, B-flat major, 617
Concerto for Piano and Orchestra, G major, 618
Concerto for Piano and Orchestra, F major, 620
Concerto for Piano and Orchestra, D minor, 622
Concerto for Piano and Orchestra, C major, 626
Concerto for Piano and Orchestra, E-flat major, 628
Concerto for Piano and Orchestra, A major, 630
Concerto for Piano and Orchestra, C minor, 632
Concerto for Piano and Orchestra, C major, 634
Concerto for Piano and Orchestra, D major, 636
Concerto for Piano and Orchestra, B-flat major, 639
Concerto for Two Pianos and Orchestra, 641–43
CONCERTOS FOR VIOLIN AND ORCHESTRA:
First Violin Concerto, 645–46
Second Violin Concerto, 646–47
Third Violin Concerto, 647–48
Fourth Violin Concerto, 648–49
Fifth Violin Concerto, 649–51
Cosi fan tutte, 639
Don Giovanni, 623, 634, 636, 638, 652, 654, 659, 688, 818, 878
Don Giovanni, Overture to, 655–56
Eine kleine Nachtmusik, 659–60
Entfuhrüng aus dem Serail, Die *see* Abduction
Finta giardiniera, La, 645
Harem Jealousies, 650
Idomeneo, 623, 663
Lucio Silla, 633, 650, 671
Magic Flute, The, 5, 607, 618, 639, 651, 664, 672, 683, 687, 811, 1032
Magic Flute, The Overture to, 657–58
Marriage of Figaro, The, 417, 628, 630, 633, 634, 640, 646, 654, 664, 683–85, 688, 946
Marriage of Figaro, The, Overture to, 358–59
Masonic Funeral Music, 630, 651–52
Missa pro defunctis, 567
Musical Joke, A, Ein Musikalischer Spass 652–54
Requiem Mass, 23, 399, 567, 623
Schauspieldirektor, Der, 630
Serenade, "Posthorn", 660
Serenade "Gran partita", 663
Serenade "Eine kleine Nachtmusik",659–60
Sinfonia concertante K.297b, 665–67

Sinfonia concertante K.364, 668–70
Symphonies:
Symphony No. 25 "Little" G minor, 633, 671–73, 687, 809
Symphony No. 29, A major, 673–75
Symphony No. 31,"Paris", 675–77
Symphony No. 34, C major, 677–79
Symphony No. 35 "Haffner", 679–81
Symphony No. 36 "Linz", 673, 682–83
Symphony No. 38 "Prague", 634, 683–85, 878
Symphony No. 39, E-flat major, 685
Symphony No. 40, G minor 671, 686–88
Symphony No. 41 "Jupiter", 637, 658, 686, 688–90, 876
Zauberflöte, Die, *see Magic Flute*
Muffat, Gottlieb, 268, 369
Componimenti musicali, 368

Napoleon I, Emperor of the French, 766
Neel, Boyd, 209, 210
Neiser, Albert, 552
Nerval, Gérard de, 127, 502
Nestyev, Israel V., 713, 721
Newman, Ernest, 792, 1019
Newmarch, Rosa, 792
New School for Social Research, 290
Nicolai, Otto, 690–91
Merry Wives of Windsor, The, Overture to, 690–91
Nielsen, Carl, 691–93
Fifth Symphony, 691–93
Saul and David, 692
Niemecz, Primitivus, 442
Nietzsche, Friedrich, 903–6
Nijinsky, Vaslav, 739, 930, 936
Nikisch, Arthur, 220–21, 236, 256, 726, 731, 758, 890
Nikolsky, Vladimir, 600
Nissen, Georg von, 655
Noguchi, Isamu, 263
Nowak, Leopold, 221, 228, 232, 234, 240, 243, 383

Oettingen-Wallerstein, Prince, 419
Ondřicek, Frantisek, 323
Oppersdorf, Count Franz von, 96, 97
Orel, Alfred, 243
Orlov, Alexander, 930
Ormandy, Eugene, 31, 42, 279, 570, 764
Ottoboni, Pietro, 284, 285
Ozawa, Seiji, 340
Paganini, Niccolò, 130–31, 141, 360, 573, 693–97, 729
Capriccios, 360
Concerto for Violin and Orchestra, 693–97
Paladilhe, Émile, 744
Palestrina, Giovanni da, 593
Paracelsus, Philippus, 982
Parker, Horatio, 475, 478, 479, 850
Parker, Mathew, 990
Pásztory, Ditta, 42
Payne, John, 306
Pedrell, Felipe, 339
Pergolesi, Giovanni Battista, 934
Perle, George, 850
Perrault, Charles, 742
Perse, St. John, 246
Petipa, Marius, 961, 962
Petrovitch, Grand Duke Paul, 999
Pfitzner Hans, 565
Palestrina, 565
Philip, Prince, Landgrave of Hesse-Darmstadt, 1001
Picasso, Pablo, 791, 935
Pierluigi, Giovanni, 470
Pierné, Gabriel, 300, 919
Pirandello, Luigi, 252
Piston, Walter, 247, 249, 492, 698–99
Fourth Symphony, 698–99
Pitoëff, Georges, 925, 926
Pitoëff, Ludmila, 925
Planché, James Robinson, 1033
Pleyel, Ignatz, 135, 423, 424
Ployer, Barbara, 619
Plutarch, 76
Pohl, Karl Ferdinand, 202
Polignac, Princess Edmond de, 701
Pollock, Jackson, 211
Polzelli, Luigia, 428
Pompadour, Madame de, 647
Poulenc, Francis, 347, 700–1, 748
Biches, Les, 700
Concerto for Two Pianos and Orchestra, 700–1
Mamelles de Tirésias, Les, 701
Tel jour, telle nuit, 700
Pound, Ezra, 1041
Powell, Maud, 861
Prix de Rome, 306, 744
Prokofieff, Sergei, 347, 702–23, 859, 936
Concertos for Piano and Orchestra:
First Piano Concerto, 702
Second Piano Concerto, 702–4
Third Piano Concerto, 704–6
First Symphony "Classical", 707, 719–21, 859
Fifth Symphony, 721–23
First Violin Concerto, 706–8

Flaming Angel, The, 705
Lieutenant Kijé, 710–11
Romeo and Juliet, 712–16
Scythian Suite, 717–19, 936
Second Violin Concerto, 709–10
Proust, Marcel, 296
Prunières, Henry, 737
Puchberg, Michael, 685, 688–89
Punto, Giovanni, 665, 666
Purcell, Henry, 989
Pushkin, Alexander, 360, 505

Rachmaninoff, Sergei, 352, 723–33
First Symphony, 723
Isle of Death, The, 731
Prelude in C-sharp minor, 723
Rhapsody on a Theme of Paganini, 729–30
Second Piano Concerto, 723–26
Second Symphony, 730–33
Third Piano Concerto, 726–29
Raff, Joseph Joachim, 505
Ramm, Friedrich, 611, 665, 666
Ramuz, Charles Ferdinand, 924–25
Ratz, Erwin, 568
Rauchberger, Hanna, 897
Rauschenberg, Robert, 246
Ravel, Maurice, 339, 347, 602–4, 733–49
Alborada del gracioso, 733–34, 744
Bolero, 734–35
Concerto for Piano and Orchestra, 735–37
Concerto for the Left Hand, 737–38
Daphnis and Chloé, 706, 739–42
Habanera for Two Pianos, 744
Heure espagnole, L', 744
Jeux d'eau, 744
Ma Mère l'oye (Mother Goose), 742–44
Rapsodie espagnole, 337, 744–46, 748
Tombeau de Couperin, Le, 746–47
Valse, La, 747–49, 916
Redlich, Hans, F., 376
Reed, W. H., 331
Reeves, Henry, 497
Reger, Max, 750–51
Variations and Fugue on a Theme by Mozart, 750–51
Régnard, Jean-François, 404, 405
Régnier, Henri de, 307
Reichardt, J. F., 60
Reich, Willi, 113, 541, 543
Reik, Theodore, 530
Reinecke, Carl, 186
Reiner, Fritz, 35
Reinhardt, Max, 75
Reinhart, Werner, 925
Rellstab, Ludwig, 694
Renoir, Auguste, 306
Respighi, Ottorino, 252, 752–55
Fountains of Rome, The, 752–54
Pines of Rome, The, 252, 754–55
Roman Festivals, 754
Riccius, August Ferdinand, 808
Richter, G. F., 617
Richter, Hans, 186, 195, 199, 225, 228, 236, 241, 322, 325, 332, 957
Riegger, Wallingford, 754
Study in Sonority, 755–56
Third Symphony, 755
Riemann, Hugo, 750
Ries, Ferdinand, 58
Rimsky-Korsakoff, Nikolai, 510, 598, 599, 601–2, 606–7, 702, 754, 757–63, 919–20, 927, 940, 968
Capriccio espagnol, 757–58
Golden Cockerel, The, 940
"Great Russian Easter" Overture, 759–60
Scheherazade, 742, 760–63
Ritter, Alexander von, 888, 907–8
Ritter, Georg Wenzel, 665
Rochberg, George, 764–65
First Symphony, 764
Second Symphony, 764
Rodin, Auguste, 306
Rodzinski, Artur, 32, 44, 262, 274, 460, 855
Roerich, Nicholas C., 937–38
Rogers, Bernard, 314, 591
Rolland, Romain, 489, 782
Romansky, Ljubomir, 1041
Rosbaud, Hans, 39, 495
Rose, Leonard, 820
Rosenthal, Moritz, 352
Rosset, Gabriel, 925
Rossini, Gioacchino, 766–72, 916, 946
Aureliano in Palmira, 766
Barber of Seville, The, 916, 946
Barber of Seville, Overture to, 766–67
Gazza ladra, La, Overture to, 767–68
Italiana in Algeri, L', Overture to, 769–70
Scala di Seta, La, Overture to, 770
Semiramide, Overture to, 770–71
William Tell, Overture to, 771–72
Rougement, Denis de, 1022
Rousseau, Henri, 791
Rousseau, Jean-Jacques, 394, 461, 978, 999
Roussel, Albert, 772–75, 981
Bacchus et Ariane, 772–74
Festin de L'araignée, Le, 774
Fourth Symphony, 772
Padmavati, 774
Third Symphony, 772, 774–75
Rowicki, Witold, 511

Rowlandson, Thomas, 1024
Rubinstein, Anton, 217, 499, 781, 954
Rubinstein, Ida, 735, 748
Rubinstein, Nicholas, 954–55, 966, 968
Rudolph, Archduke, 67, 68
Ruggles, Carl, 775–78
  Men and Mountains, 775–77
  Portals, 776–78
Rus, Antonin, 324

Sabaniev, Leonid, 846, 848, 849
Sabata, Victor de, 594
Sacher, Paul, 48–49, 52, 464, 896
Sádlo, Miloš, 382
Safonov, Vassily, 847
Saint-Saëns, Camille, 778–87
  Concerto for Cello and Orchestra, 778–80
  Danse macabre, 782
  Fourth Piano Concerto, 782–83
  Introduction and Rondo Capriccio, 783
  Rouet d'Omphale, Le, (Omphale's Spinning Wheel), 784–85
  Second Piano Concerto, 781
  Third Symphony, 785–87
Salomon, Johann Peter, 389–91, 408, 420–22, 424, 426–28, 432, 438, 444
Sándor, György, 42
Sarasate, Pablo de, 215, 493, 783
Satie, Erik, 245, 252, 700, 748, 980
  Parade, 314
Sauvage, Cécile, 594
Scalero, Rosario, 34
Scarlatti, Alessandro, 342
Scarlatti, Domenico, 369
Schalk, Franz, 225, 231, 233
Schauroth, Delphine von, 571, 572
Scherchen, Hermann, 124, 1041
Schickaneder, Emanuel, 657
Schiller, Friedrich von, 108, 110–11, 394, 461
Schillinger, Joseph, 213
Schindler, Anton, 68, 75, 81, 82, 100
Schlegel, August Wilhelm von, 576
Schlözer, Tatiana, 846–48
Schmidt, Johann Philipp Samuel, 364
Schmiedel, Johann Baptist, 812
Schnéevoigt, Georg, 866
Schneider, Friedrich, 62
Schoenberg, Arnold, 119–21, 245, 341, 468, 492, 787–806, 1034, 1036–37
  Concerto for Piano and Orchestra, 787–90
  Five Pieces for Orchestra, 790–93
  Pelleas and Melisande, 793–98
  Survivor from Warsaw, A, 798–800
  Three Pieces for Piano, 791
  Variations for Orchestra, 801–4
  Verklärte Nacht (Transfigured Night), 793, 804–6
Scholz, Bernhard, 184
Scholz, Werner, 882
Schtnberg, Harold, 474–75
Schreiber, Johann Ludwig, 10
Schroeder, Alwin, 320
Schubert, Ferdinand, 816
Schubert, Franz, 694, 807–19
  Alfonso and Estrella, 807
  Rosamunde Overture and Ballet Music, 807–8
  Symphony No. 4 "Tragic," 808–10
  Symphony No. 5, B-flat, 810–12
  Symphony No. 6 "Little" C-major, 812–13
  Symphony No. 8 "Unfinished", 814–16
  Symphony No. 9, 816–19, 876
  Winterreise, Die, 700
  Zauberharfe, Die (The Magic Harp), 807
Schuch, Ernst von, 731
Schulz, Johann Philipp Christian, 62
Schuman, William, 819–27
  "American Festival" Overture, 819, 823
  Fantasy for Cello and Orchestra: *A Song of Orpheus*, 820
  Fifth Symphony (Symphony for String) 826
  New England Triptych, 822
  Symphony for Strings, 826
  Second Symphony, 819, 823
  Third Symphony, 823–26
Schumann, Clara (Wieck, Clara), 174–77, 180, 187–88, 190, 193, 201, 496–97, 828–30, 832, 835, 838, 840, 843
Schumann, Robert, 152, 174–77, 180, 187, 190, 192, 193, 202, 497, 499, 573, 816, 828–45
  Concerto for Cello and Orchestra, 828–29
  Concerto for Piano and Orchestra, 829–32
  Dichterliebe, 700
  Kreisleriana, 837–38
  Manfred, Overture to, 833–34
  SYMPHONIES:
    Symphony No. 1 "Spring", 834–38
    Symphony No. 2 C major, 838–40
    Symphony No. 3 "Rhenish", 840–43
    Symphony No. 4 D minor, 843–45
Schwind, Moritz von, 807
Scott, Walter, 152
Scriabin, Alexander, 846–50, 1042
  Divine Poem, 846
  Poem of Ecstasy, 846–48, 1042
  Prometheus, the Poem of Fire, 847–50
Seeger, Charles, 778
Seiber, Mátyás, 495

Seidl, Anton, 228, 327, 329, 1030
Serafin, Tullio, 252
Servandoni, Giovanni Niccolò, 372, 374
Sessions, Roger, 314, 492, 850–52
  Eighth Symphony, 850–52
Seyfried, Ignatz von, 58
Shakespeare, William, 75–76, 127, 133, 576–77, 712, 821, 964
Shanet, Howard, 668
Shaw, George Bernard, 314, 330
Shostakovich, Dmitri, 852–61
  Clear Stream, The, 854
  Fifth Symphony, 854–57
  First Symphony, 852–54
  Lady Macbeth of the Mtsensk District, 854, 857
  Ninth Symphony, 859–61
  Seventh Symphony, 37, 853, 859
  Sixth Symphony, 857–59
Shumsky, Oscar, 31
Sibelius, Aino, 868
Sibelius, Jean, 691, 692, 861–77
  Concerto for Violin and Orchestra, 861–62
  En Saga,, 861
  Swan of Tuonela, The, 862–63
  SYMPHONIES:
    First Symphony, 863–65
    Second Symphony, 865–67
    Third Symphony, 868–69
    Fourth Symphony, 870–72
    Fifth Symphony, 872–73
    Sixth Symphony, 874–75
    Seventh Symphony, 876–77
Siloti, Alexander, 718, 849, 919
Sitwell, Edith, 1024
Skrowaczewski, Stanislaw, 511
Slonimsky, Nicolas, 480, 483, 986, 989
Smaliens, Alexander, 34
Smetana, Bedřich, 878–82
  Bartered Bride, The (Prodaná nevěsta), 879, 881
  Má Vlast (My Fatherland), 879
  Moldau, The (Vltava), 878
Smithson, Henrietta, 133, 147, 148
Société Nationale de Musique, 256, 307, 319
Solomon, Izler, 820
Sourek, Otakar, 319, 322, 324
Sousa, John Philip, 354
Spalding, Albert, 31
Spender, Stephen, 293
Spengler, Oswald, 501
Spiess, Hermine, 197
Spivakovsky, Tossy, 44
Spohr, Ludwig, 573, 835
Stadler, Anton, 607–8
Stamitz, Carl, 669
Starker, Janos, 382
Stassov, Vladimir, 602, 603, 606, 968
Steinberg, William, 850
Stein, Erwin, 541, 801
Stein, Gertrude, 980
Steinizer, Max, 526
Stendhal, 768, 769
Stephanie, Stephan, the Elder, 405
Stern Conservatory, 794
Stern, Isaac, 164
Stern, Leo, 321
Sterne, Lawrence, 2
Steuermann, Eduard, 788
Stevens, Halsey, 39
Stich, Jan Vaclav, 665–66
Stock, Frederick, 705
Stockhausen, Karlheinz, 244, 882–87
  Hymnen, 882–85
  Kontra-Punkte (Counter-Points), 885–87
Stokowski, Leopold, 269, 280, 347, 352, 474, 852, 984, 986–87
Storm, Theodor, 119
Strauss, Johann, Jr., 747, 906, 916, 964
Strauss, Richard, 531, 894, 861, 887–909
  Also sprach Zarathustra, 890, 903–6
  Death and Transfiguration, 123, 906–9
  Don Juan, 887–90, 907
  Don Quixote, 890–93
  Elektra, 870
  Heldenleben, Ein (A Hero's Life), 893–96
  Metamorphoses, 896–98
  Rosenkavalier, Der, 870
  Salome ("Dance of the Seven Veils"), 50, 899–900
  Thus Spake Zarathustra, 890, 903–6
  Till Eulenspiegel's Merry Pranks, 901–2
  Tod und Verklärung, 123, 906–9
Stravinsky, Igor, 248, 347, 354, 360, 739, 748, 791, 909–50, 1039
  Agon, 909–13
  Canticum sacrum, 909
  Capriccio, for Piano and Orchestra, 913–14
  Card Game, 914–17
  Concerto for Violin and Orchestra, 917–19
  Fantastic Scherzo, 919
  Firebird, The, 706, 919–23, 927, 932, 934, 937, 940, 984
  Fireworks, 919
  Histoire du Soldat, L', 924–27
  In Memoriam Dylan Thomas, 909
  Jeu de Cartes, 914–17
  Oiseau de feu, see Firebird

Petrushka, 40, 706, 791, 920, 927–34, 941, 984
Pulcinella, 934–36
Rite of Spring, The, 99, 717, 750, 791, 920, 922, 928, 934, 936–41, 944, 981, 984
Sacre du printemps, see Rite of Spring
Story of the Soldier, The, 924–27
Symphony in C, 943–44
Symphony in Three Movements, 944–47
Symphony of Psalms, 947–50
Strecker, Willy, 917
Sullivan, Arthur, 807, 811
Swedish Ballet, 252, 700, 746
Swieten, Baron van, 87
Swinburne, Algernon, 582
Székely, Zoltán, 44
Szell, George, 764
Szigeti, Joseph, 35

Tailleferre, Germaine, 700
Tallis, Thomas, 989–92
Tansman, Alexander, 347, 945
Tasso, Torquato, 507–9
Taylor, Deems, 348
Tchaikovsky, Anatole, 976
Tchaikovsky, Modest, 959, 967, 973, 976
Tchaikovsky, Peter Ilyitch, 757, 950–78
Capriccio Italien, 950–51
Concerto for Violin and Orchestra, 957–59
Concerto for Piano and Orchestra No. 1, 951–57
Eugene Onegin, 970
Francesca da Rimini, 959–61
Nutcracker, The, 961–64, 1042
Overture 1812, 966
"Pathétique" Symphony, 876, 975–78
Pique Dame, 516
Romeo and Juliet Fantasy Overture, 964
Serenade in C major, 966–67
Souvenir d'un lieu cher, 957
SYMPHONIES:
Symphony No. 2 "Little Russian", 967–69
Symphony No. 4, F minor, 969–72
Symphony No. 5, E minor, 973–75
Symphony No. 6 "Pathetique", 876, 975–78
Telemann, Georg Philipp, 978–79
Suite, A minor, for Flute and Orchestra, 978–79
Thayer, Alexander Wheelock, 87
Theremin, Leon, 985
Thomas, Theodore, 236, 320, 514, 668, 867, 888, 894
Thomson, Virgil, 245, 271, 287, 979–81
Mayor LaGuardia Waltzes, The, 271
Seine at Night, The, 979–81
Symphony on a Hymn Tune, 979
Thun, Count Johann Joseph, 682, 683
Tieck, Ludwig, 576, 577
Tiersot, Julien, 466
Tolbecque, August, 779
Tolstoy, Alexei, 855
Tolstoy, Leo, 724
Tomášek, Vaclav, 54–56
Torkanowsky, Werner, 764
Toscanini, Arturo, 32, 552, 734, 752, 853
Tost, Johann Peter, 416
Tovey, Donald Francis, 137, 147, 862
Toye, Geoffrey, 993
Trotsky, Leon, 707
Tudor, David, 244, 245
Tyson, Alan, 65

Ueberbrettl, 793
Ulanova, Galina, 712, 713

Valéry, Paul, 306, 311
Vallas, Léon, 343
Van Vechten, Carl, 354, 936
Varèse, Edgard, 981–89
Arcana, 981–84
Ecuatorial, 985–86
Intégrales, 986–88
Ionisation, 988–89
Varèse, Louise, 982, 985
Vaughan Williams, Ralph, 989–98
Fantasia on a Theme by Thomas Tallis, 989–92
Symphony No. 2 "London", 992
Symphony No. 4, F minor, 995–98
Verdi, Giuseppe, 788
Verlaine, Paul, 299, 304, 306
Vigano, Salvatore, 77
Viotti, Giovanni Battista, 439
Vivaldi, Antonio, 998–1006
Four Seasons, The (Le quattro stagioni), 998–1006

Wagner, Cosima, 224, 1018–19
Wagner, Richard, 222, 224, 225, 235–36, 364, 1006–23
Flying Dutchman, The, 204, 585
Flying Dutchman, The Overture to, 1006–7
Götterdämmerung, 1008–11, 127
Siegfried's Funeral Music, 1008
Siegfried's Rhine Journey, 1009
Lohengrin, Prelude to, 1011–13
Meistersinger, Die, 330, 691, 731, 750, 896

Meistersinger, Die Prelude to, 231, 1013–14
Parsifal, 750, 1014–18, 1042
Prelude And Good Friday Music, 1014
Ring of the Nibelung, 225, 231, 236, 345, 1009
Siegfried Idyll, A, 1018–20
Tannhäuser, 217–18, 1013
Tannhäuser Overture to, 1020–21
Tristan und Isolde, 120, 123, 152, 217, 224–25, 239, 565, 804, 887–88, 896, 898, 906–7, 1013–14, 1021–23
Prelude And Love Death, 1021
Wagner, Siegfried, 1018–20
Wahrlich, Hugo, 847
Waldstädten, Baroness von, 663
Walpole, Horace, 394
Walter, Bruno, 33, 158, 516, 522, 527, 535, 542, 549, 555, 565, 567, 852
Walton, William, 1024–26
First Symphony, 1024–26
Viola Concerto, 1024
Warburg, Edward, 915
Weber, Aloysia, 641, 678
Weber, Ben, 1026–28
Concerto for Piano and Orchestra, 1026–28
Weber, Carl Maria von, 460–61, 654, 1028–33
Euryanthe, 571
Euryanthe, Overture to, 1029–30
Freischütz, Der, 1028, 1029
Freischütz, Der, Overture to, 1030–31
Konzertstück, 499, 913, 928, 1028–29
Oberon, Overture to, 576, 1032–33
Webern, Anton, 113, 119, 245, 791, 1033–41
Five Movements, 1033–34
Five Pieces for Orchestra, 1035–36
Six Pieces for Orchestra, 791, 1036–37
Symphony, 1037–39
Variations, 1039–41
Wedekind, Frank, 115–16, 793
Weidinger, Anton, 388–89
Weigl, Joseph Franz, 382
Weingartner, Felix von, 166, 363
Weisberg, Arthur, 291
Weiss, Adolph, 245
Wellesz, Egon, 806
Wendling, Johann Baptist, 611, 665
Wenzel, Ernst, 834
Werfel, Franz, 946
Werner, Eric, 571, 577, 581, 587
Wesendonck, Mathilde, 1022
Wharton, Edith, 514
Whistler, James McNeill, 306
White, Eric Walter, 936*n*, 946
Whiteman, Paul, 350, 352, 354
Whitman, Walt, 271, 307, 777
Wieck, Clara, *see* Schumann, Clara
Whitney, Robert, 250
Willis, Thomas, 316
Wittgenstein, Paul, 737
Wolff, Christian, 245
Wolzogen, Ernst von, 793
Wood, Henry, 792
Wüllner, Franz, 890, 901

Xenakis, Yannis, 244

Yoshida, Hidekazu, 245
Young, La Monte, 246
Ysaÿe, Eugène, 255

Zelter, Carl, 587
Zemlinsky, Alexander von, 804
Zhukovsky, Vasily, 360
Zimmermann, Bernd Alois, 1041–42
Photoptósis, 1041–42
Soldaten, Die [Soldiers, The], 1041